Marketing
An Introduction

Full-Circle Learning

MyLab™: Learning Full Circle for Marketing, Management, Business Communication, and Intro to Business

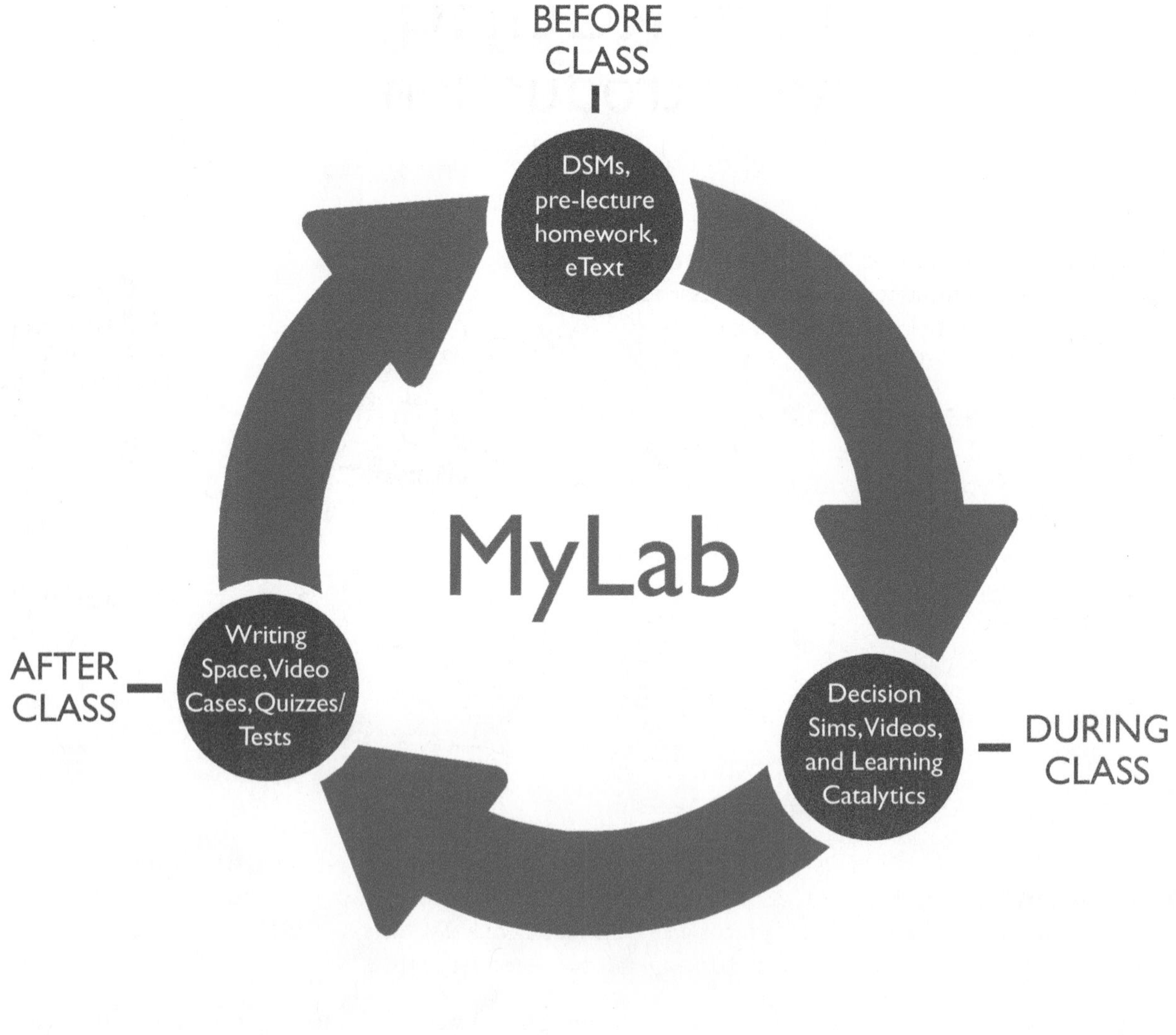

MyMarketingLab Improves Student Engagement Before, During, and After Class

MINI VIDEO LIBRARY – Robust video library with over 100 new book-specific videos that include ... assign assessments, the ability for instructors to add YouTube ... the ability for ... and the ability for ...

... for students ... in the ... make ... evaluation of ... and ... the ... of ...

... with new exercises, engaging ... learning ... concepts covered ...

* **Interactive Content** ... assessment ... students ...

* **... (DMS)** – ... with ... questions ... through ... learning ... personalized ... and ... mobile ...

* **Writing Space** ... with new commenting tabs, new prompts, and a new tool for students called Pearson Writer ... single location to develop and assess concept mastery and critical thinking, the Writing Space offers ... create your own writing assignments ... with students ... and easily.

Writing Space ... students ... work ... by comparing it against ... comparison database available ... TII ...

* **Additional Features** – Included with the MyLab are a powerful homework and test manager, robust ... and shareable content.

PEARSON ALWAYS LEARNING

Gary Armstrong • Philip Kotler

Marketing
An Introduction

A Custom Edition for
Fayetteville Technical Community College

Taken from:
Marketing: An Introduction, Thirteenth Edition
by Gary Armstrong and Philip Kotler

Cover photographs courtesy of Fayetteville Technical Community College.

Taken/Excerpts taken from:

Marketing: An Introduction, Thirteenth Edition
by Gary Armstrong and Philip Kotler

New York, NY 10013

Pearson Custom Edition.

Pearson Education, Inc., 330 Hudson Street, New York, New York 10013
A Pearson Education Company
www.pearsoned.com

Printed in the United States of America

1 16

000200010272038979

EF

PEARSON

ISBN 10: 1-323-42554-3
ISBN 13: 978-1-323-42554-1

Chapter Four Group Assignment

Design a Plan for a Research Project

(Exercise developed by Sharon Seaford at FTCC)

Step 1) Assemble into groups of 3 to 5 students. In each group, decide on an imaginary research project concerning a product (goods and/or services). The product you choose can be a new or an existing product. First define your problem. Then design a research plan that includes each of these:

- Exploratory Research
- Descriptive Research
- Causal Research (if it applies)

Step 2) Design a survey with five questions (at least one open-ended and one closed-ended question).

Step 3) Answer the following questions:

- Who will you sample?
- What is your unit size?
- What is your procedure and contact method? ie. telephone, personal, mail, and/or online.

Be creative and have fun!

Packaging and Labeling Questionnaire for Presentation
Chapter Seven-Product, Services, and Brands: Building Customer Value

Instructions: Please read pages 204-205 in your textbook before attempting this project. The following provides you with a guideline for your presentation/demonstration to the class. For traditional/face-to-face classes, you must bring your package to class for the presentation/demonstration. For on-line classes, please attach a photograph of your package as an attachment to the Discussion Forum on Blackboard. Thank you.

Sharon Seaford- FTCC

1. Name of Product______________________________________.

2. Explain how the packaging/labeling protects the product.

3. What message does the packaging/labeling communicate to customers?

4. Could the packaging be improved to make it more convenient to use? Explain.

5. Is the packaging one that is convenient to retailer? Explain.

6. Is the packaging environmentally friendly?

7. Does the packaging contain product codes? Where are they located?

8. Does the packaging/labeling offer any protection against misuse for consumer safety? Explain.

9. How does the packaging meet the needs of the consumer as well as the distributor? Explain.

10. How would you improve the packaging/labeling? Explain.

To Kathy, Betty, Mandy, Matt, KC, Keri,
Delaney, Molly, Macy, and Ben; Nancy, Amy, Melissa, and Jessica

About the Authors

As a team, Gary Armstrong and Philip Kotler provide a blend of skills uniquely suited to writing an introductory marketing text. Professor Armstrong is an award-winning teacher of undergraduate business students. Professor Kotler is one of the world's leading authorities on marketing. Together they make the complex world of marketing practical, approachable, and enjoyable.

GARY ARMSTRONG is Crist W. Blackwell Distinguished Professor Emeritus of Undergraduate Education in the Kenan-Flagler Business School at the University of North Carolina at Chapel Hill. He holds undergraduate and master's degrees in business from Wayne State University in Detroit, and he received his Ph.D. in marketing from Northwestern University. Dr. Armstrong has contributed numerous articles to leading business journals. As a consultant and researcher, he has worked with many companies on marketing research, sales management, and marketing strategy.

But Professor Armstrong's first love has always been teaching. His long-held Blackwell Distinguished Professorship is the only permanent endowed professorship for distinguished undergraduate teaching at the University of North Carolina at Chapel Hill. He has been very active in the teaching and administration of Kenan-Flagler's undergraduate program. His administrative posts have included Chair of Marketing, Associate Director of the Undergraduate Business Program, Director of the Business Honors Program, and many others. Through the years, he has worked closely with business student groups and has received several UNC campuswide and Business School teaching awards. He is the only repeat recipient of the school's highly regarded Award for Excellence in Undergraduate Teaching, which he received three times. Most recently, Professor Armstrong received the UNC Board of Governors Award for Excellence in Teaching, the highest teaching honor bestowed by the 16-campus University of North Carolina system.

PHILIP KOTLER is S. C. Johnson & Son Distinguished Professor of International Marketing at the Kellogg School of Management, Northwestern University. He received his master's degree at the University of Chicago and his Ph.D. at M.I.T., both in economics. Dr. Kotler is author of *Marketing Management* (Pearson), now in its 15th edition and the most widely used marketing textbook in graduate schools of business worldwide. He has authored dozens of other successful books and has written more than 50 books and 150 articles in leading journals. He is the only three-time winner of the coveted Alpha Kappa Psi award for the best annual article in the *Journal of Marketing*.

Professor Kotler was named the first recipient of four major awards: the *Distinguished Marketing Educator of the Year Award* and the *William L. Wilkie "Marketing for a Better World" Award*, both given by the American Marketing Association; the *Philip Kotler Award for Excellence in Health Care Marketing* presented by the Academy for Health Care Services Marketing; and the *Sheth Foundation Medal for Exceptional Contribution to Marketing Scholarship and Practice*. He is a charter member of the Marketing Hall of Fame, was voted the first Leader in Marketing Thought by the American Marketing Association, and was named the Founder of Modern Marketing Management in the Handbook of Management Thinking. His numerous other major honors include the Sales and Marketing Executives International *Marketing Educator of the Year Award;* the European Association of Marketing Consultants and Trainers *Marketing Excellence Award;* the *Charles Coolidge Parlin Marketing Research Award;* and the *Paul D. Converse Award,* given by the American Marketing Association to honor "outstanding contributions to science in marketing." A recent *Forbes* survey ranks Professor Kotler in the top 10 of the world's most influential business thinkers. And in a recent *Financial Times* poll of 1,000 senior executives across the world, Professor Kotler was ranked as the fourth "most influential business writer/guru" of the twenty-first century.

Dr. Kotler has served as chairman of the College of Marketing of the Institute of Management Sciences, a director of the American Marketing Association, and a trustee of the Marketing Science Institute. He has consulted with many major U.S. and international companies in the areas of marketing strategy and planning, marketing organization, and international marketing. He has traveled and lectured extensively throughout Europe, Asia, and South America, advising companies and governments about global marketing practices and opportunities.

Brief Contents

Contents

Preface

The Thirteenth Edition of *Marketing: An Introduction!*

Fresh. Proven. Practical. Engaging.

These are exciting times in marketing. Recent surges in digital technologies have created a new, more engaging, more connected marketing world. Beyond traditional tried-and-true marketing concepts and practices, today's marketers have added a host of new-age tools for engaging consumers, building brands, and creating customer value and relationships. In these digital times, sweeping advances in "the Internet of Things"—from social and mobile media, connected digital devices, and the new consumer empowerment to "big data" and new marketing analytics—have profoundly affected both marketers and the consumers they serve.

More than ever, the 13th edition of *Marketing: An Introduction* introduces the exciting and fast-changing world of marketing in a fresh yet proven, practical, and engaging way.

Marketing: Creating Customer Value and Engagement in the Digital and Social Age

Top marketers share a common goal: putting the consumer at the heart of marketing. Today's marketing is all about creating customer value and engagement in a fast-changing, increasingly digital and social marketplace.

Marketing starts with understanding consumer needs and wants, determining which target markets the organization can serve best, and developing a compelling value proposition by which the organization can attract and grow valued customers. Then, more than just making a sale, today's marketers want to *engage* customers and build deep customer relationships that make their brands a meaningful part of consumers' conversations and lives.

In this digital age, to go along with proven traditional marketing methods, marketers have a dazzling set of new online, mobile, and social media tools for engaging customers anytime, anyplace to jointly shape brand conversations, experiences, and community. If marketers do these things well, they will reap the rewards in terms of market share, profits, and customer equity. In the 13th edition of *Marketing: An Introduction,* you'll learn how *customer value* and *customer engagement* drive every good marketing strategy.

Marketing: An Introduction makes learning and teaching marketing more productive and enjoyable than ever. The 13th edition's streamlined approach strikes an effective balance between depth of coverage and ease of learning. The 13th edition builds on proven content developed over 12 previous editions, yet it has been thoroughly revised to provide the freshest insights into current marketing concepts and practices.

The 13th edition remains highly approachable, with an organization, writing style, and design well suited to beginning marketing students. Its learning design—with integrative features at the start and end of each chapter plus insightful author comments throughout—helps students to learn, link, and apply important concepts. The text presents the practical side of marketing, with engaging examples and illustrations throughout that help to bring marketing to life. And when combined with MyMarketingLab, our online homework and personalized study tool, *Marketing: An Introduction* ensures that students will come to class well prepared and leave class with a richer understanding of basic marketing concepts, strategies, and practices.

What's New in the 13th Edition?

Once again, we've thoroughly revised *Marketing: An Introduction* to provide the freshest coverage of the latest trends and forces that affect marketing. We've poured over every page, table, figure, fact, and example in order to keep this the best text from which to learn about and teach marketing. The new edition provides substantial new content, expanded coverage, and fresh examples throughout each chapter.

- The 13th edition adds fresh coverage in both traditional marketing areas and on fast-changing and trending topics such as customer engagement marketing, mobile and social media, big data and the new marketing analytics, omni-channel marketing and retailing, customer co-creation and empowerment, real-time customer listening and marketing, building brand community, marketing content creation and native advertising, B-to-B social media and social selling, tiered and dynamic pricing, consumer privacy, sustainability, global marketing, and much more.
- This new edition continues to build on its *customer engagement* framework—creating direct and continuous customer involvement in shaping brands, brand conversations, brand experiences, and brand community. New coverage and fresh examples throughout the text address the latest customer engagement tools, practices, and developments. See especially Chapter 1 (refreshed sections on *Customer Engagement and Today's Digital and Social Media* and *Consumer-Generated Marketing*); Chapter 4 (big data and real-time research to gain deeper customer insights); Chapter 5 (creating social influence and customer community through digital and social media marketing); Chapter 8 (customer co-creation and customer-driven new-product development); Chapter 11 (omni-channel retailing); Chapter 12 (marketing content curation and native advertising); Chapter 13 (salesforce social selling); and Chapter 14 (direct digital, online, social media, and mobile marketing).
- No area of marketing is changing faster than *online, mobile, social media, and other digital marketing technologies.* Keeping up with digital concepts, technologies, and practices has become a top priority and major challenge for today's marketers. The 13th edition of *Marketing: An Introduction* provides thoroughly refreshed, up-to-date coverage of these explosive developments in every chapter—from online, mobile, and social media engagement technologies discussed in Chapters 1, 5, 12, and 14 to "real-time listening" and "big data" research tools in Chapter 4, real-time dynamic pricing in Chapter 9, digitizing the in-store retail shopping experience in Chapter 11, and social selling in Chapter 13. A Chapter 1 section on *The Digital Age: Online, Mobile, and Social Media Marketing* introduces the exciting new developments in digital and social media marketing. Then a Chapter 14 section on *Direct, Online, Social Media, and Mobile Marketing* digs more deeply into digital marketing tools such as online sites, social media, mobile ads and apps, online video, email, blogs, and other digital platforms that engage consumers anywhere, anytime via their computers, smartphones, tablets, Internet-ready TVs, and other digital devices.
- The 13th edition continues to track fast-changing developments in *marketing communications* and the creation of *marketing content.* Marketers are no longer simply creating integrated marketing communications programs; they are joining with customers and media to curate customer-driven marketing content in paid, owned, earned, and shared media. You won't find fresher coverage of these important topics in any other marketing text.
- The 13th edition of *Marketing: An Introduction* continues to improve on its *innovative learning design.* The text's active and integrative presentation includes learning enhancements such as annotated chapter-opening stories, a chapter-opening objective outline, explanatory author comments on major chapter sections and figures, and Marketing at Work highlights that provide in-depth examples of marketing concepts and practices at

work. The chapter-opening layout helps to preview and position the chapter and its key concepts. Figures annotated with author comments help students to simplify and organize chapter material. New and substantially revised end-of-chapter features help to summarize important chapter concepts and highlight important themes, such as *marketing ethics, financial marketing analysis,* and *online, mobile, and social media marketing*. This innovative learning design facilitates student understanding and eases learning.
- The 13th edition provides 16 new end-of-chapter company cases by which students can apply what they learn to actual company situations. It also features 16 brand-new video cases, with brief end-of-chapter summaries and discussion questions. Finally, all of the chapter-opening stories, Marketing at Work highlights, and end-of-chapter features in the 13th edition are either new or substantially revised.

Five Major Customer Value and Engagement Themes

The 13th edition of *Marketing: An Introduction* builds on five major customer value and engagement themes:

1. ***Creating value* for *customers in order to capture value* from *customers in return.*** Today's marketers must be good at *creating customer value, engaging customers,* and *managing customer relationships*. Outstanding marketing companies understand the marketplace and customer needs, design value-creating marketing strategies, develop integrated marketing programs that engage customers and deliver value and satisfaction, and build strong customer relationships and brand community. In return, they capture value from customers in the form of sales, profits, and customer equity.

   This innovative *customer value and engagement framework* is introduced at the start of Chapter 1 in a five-step marketing process model, which details how marketing *creates* customer value and *captures* value in return. The framework is carefully developed in the first two chapters and then fully integrated throughout the remainder of the text.
2. ***Customer engagement and today's digital and social media***. New digital and social media have taken today's marketing by storm, dramatically changing how companies and brands engage consumers and how consumers connect and influence each other's brand behaviors. The 13th edition thoroughly explores the contemporary concept of *customer engagement marketing* and the exciting new digital and social media technologies that help brands to engage customers more deeply and interactively. It starts with two major Chapter 1 sections: *Customer Engagement and Today's Digital and Social Media* and *The Digital Age: Online, Mobile, and Social Media Marketing.* A refreshed Chapter 14 on *Direct, Online, Social Media, and Mobile Marketing* summarizes the latest developments in digital engagement and relationship-building tools. Everywhere in between, you'll find revised and expanded coverage of the exploding use of digital and social tools to create customer engagement and build brand community.
3. ***Building and managing strong, value-creating brands***. Well-positioned brands with strong brand equity provide the basis upon which to build customer value and profitable customer relationships. Today's marketers must position their brands powerfully and manage them well to create valued brand experiences. The 13th edition provides a deep focus on brands, anchored by a Chapter 7 section on *Branding Strategy: Building Strong Brands*.
4. ***Measuring and managing return on marketing***. Especially in uneven economic times, marketing managers must ensure that their marketing dollars are being well spent. In the past, many marketers spent freely on big, expensive marketing programs, often without thinking carefully about the financial returns on their spending. But all that has changed rapidly. "Marketing accountability"—measuring and managing marketing return on investment—has now become an important part of strategic marketing decision making. This emphasis on marketing accountability is addressed in Chapter 2,

Appendix 3: *Marketing by the Numbers,* and end-of-chapter Marketing by the Numbers features and throughout the 13th edition.

5. ***Sustainable marketing around the globe***. As technological developments make the world an increasingly smaller and more fragile place, marketers must be good at marketing their brands globally and in sustainable ways. New material throughout the 13th edition emphasizes the concepts of global marketing and sustainable marketing—meeting the present needs of consumers and businesses while also preserving or enhancing the ability of future generations to meet their needs. The 13th edition integrates global marketing and sustainability topics throughout the text. It then provides focused coverage on each topic in Chapter 15.

An Emphasis on Real Marketing and Bringing Marketing to Life

Marketing: An Introduction, 13th edition, takes a practical marketing management approach, providing countless in-depth, real-life examples and stories that engage students with marketing concepts and bring modern marketing to life. In the 13th edition, every chapter has an engaging *First Stop* opening story plus *Marketing at Work* highlights that provide fresh insights into real marketing practices. Learn how:

- Netflix uses "big data" to personalize each customer's viewing experience. While Netflix subscribers are busy watching videos, Netflix is busy watching *them*—very, very closely.
- Wildly innovative Google has become an incredibly successful new product "moonshot factory," unleashing a seemingly unending flurry of diverse products, most of which are market leaders in their categories.
- Nike—by far the world's largest sports apparel company—does much more than just make and sell sports gear. The iconic brand creates customer value by building deep engagement and a sense of community with and between the Nike brand and its customers.
- Toy market leader LEGO uses innovative marketing research—lots and lots of it—to dig out fresh customer insights, then uses the insights to create irresistible play experiences for children around the world.
- Mighty Kellogg, the world's largest cereal maker, may be losing its snap, crackle, and pop as shifts in the marketing environment change how people today eat breakfast.
- Harley-Davidson's market dominance comes from a deep understanding of the emotions and motivations that underlie consumer behavior. Harley doesn't just sell motorcycles; it sells freedom, independence, power, and authenticity.
- Ultra low-price Spirit Airlines is thriving despite industry-low customer experience ratings. You don't get much when you fly Spirit. Then again, you don't pay for what you don't get.
- Marketers are now using real-time online, mobile, and social media marketing to engage customers in the moment, linking brands to trending topics, events, causes, personal occasions, or other happenings in their lives.
- Amazon has become the poster child for direct and digital marketing. Its passion for creating superb online customer experiences has made it one of the most powerful names on the Internet.
- Direct marketing insurance giant GEICO has gone from bit player to behemoth thanks to a big-budget advertising campaign featuring a smooth-talking gecko and an enduring "15 minutes could save you 15 percent" tagline.
- Outdoor apparel and gear maker Patagonia's "Conscious Consumption" mission takes sustainability to new extremes by telling consumers to buy *less* of its products.
- Cosmetics maker L'Oréal has become the "United Nations of Beauty" by achieving a global-local balance that adapts and differentiates brands in local markets while optimizing their impact across global markets.

Beyond such features, each chapter is packed with countless real, engaging, and timely examples that reinforce key concepts. No other text brings marketing to life like the 13th edition of *Marketing: An Introduction*.

Learning Aids That Create Value and Engagement

A wealth of chapter-opening, within-chapter, and end-of-chapter learning devices help students to learn, link, and apply major concepts:

- ***Integrated Chapter-Opening Road Maps.*** The active and integrative chapter-opening spread in each chapter features an *Objective Outline* that outlines chapter contents and learning objectives, a brief *Previewing the Concepts* section that introduces chapter concepts, and a *First Stop* opening vignette—an engaging, deeply developed, illustrated, and annotated marketing story that introduces the chapter material and sparks student interest.
- ***Marketing at Work highlights.*** Each chapter contains two carefully developed highlight features that provide an in-depth look at real marketing practices of large and small companies.
- ***Author comments and figure annotations.*** Throughout each chapter, author comments ease and enhance student learning by introducing and explaining major chapter sections and figures.
- ***Reviewing and Extending the Concepts.*** Sections at the end of each chapter summarize key chapter concepts and provide questions, exercises, and cases by which students can review and apply what they've learned. The *Chapter Review and Critical Thinking* section reviews major chapter concepts and links them to chapter objectives. It provides a helpful listing of chapter key terms by order of appearance with page numbers that facilitate easy reference. Finally, it provides discussion questions and critical thinking exercises that help students to keep track of and apply what they've learned in the chapter.

  The *Minicases and Applications* section at the end of each chapter provides brief *Marketing Ethics; Online, Mobile, and Social Media Marketing;* and *Marketing by the Numbers* applications cases that facilitate discussion of current issues and company situations in areas such as mobile and social marketing, ethics, and financial marketing analysis. It also includes a *Video Case* section that contains short vignettes with discussion questions to be used with a set of short videos that accompany the 13th edition. An end-of-chapter *Company Cases* section identifies which of the company cases found in Appendix 1 are best for use with each chapter.
- ***Company Cases.*** Appendix 1 contains 16 all-new company cases that help students to apply major marketing concepts to real company and brand situations.
- ***Marketing Plan appendix.*** Appendix 2 contains a sample marketing plan that helps students to apply important marketing planning concepts.
- ***Marketing by the Numbers appendix.*** An innovative Appendix 3 provides students with a comprehensive introduction to the marketing financial analysis that helps to guide, assess, and support marketing decisions. An exercise at the end of each chapter lets students apply analytical and financial thinking to relevant chapter concepts and links the chapter to the Marketing by the Numbers appendix.
- ***Careers in Marketing.*** Appendix 4 helps students to explore marketing career paths open to them and lays out a process for landing a marketing job that best matches their special skills and interests.

More than ever before, the 13th edition of *Marketing: An Introduction* creates value and engagement for you—it gives you all you need to know about marketing in an effective and enjoyable total learning package!

A Total Teaching and Learning Package

A successful marketing course requires more than a well-written book. Today's classroom requires a dedicated teacher, well-prepared students, and a fully integrated teaching system.

A total package of teaching and learning supplements extends this edition's emphasis on creating value and engagement for both the student and instructor. The following aids support *Marketing: An Introduction,* 13th edition.

Instructor Resources

At the Instructor Resource Center, www.pearsonhighered.com/irc, instructors can easily register to gain access to a variety of instructor resources available with this text in downloadable format. If assistance is needed, our dedicated technical support team is ready to help with the media supplements that accompany this text. Visit http://247.pearsoned.com for answers to frequently asked questions and toll-free user support phone numbers.

The following supplements are available with this text:

- **Instructor's Resource Manual**
- **Test Bank**
- **TestGen® Computerized Test Bank**
- **PowerPoint Presentation**

Acknowledgments

No book is the work only of its authors. We greatly appreciate the valuable contributions of several people who helped make this new edition possible. As always, we owe extra-special thanks to Keri Jean Miksza for her dedicated and valuable contributions to *all* phases of the project and to her husband Pete and daughters Lucy and Mary for all the support they provide Keri during this very absorbing project.

We owe substantial thanks to Andy Norman of Drake University for his skillful help in developing chapter vignettes and highlights, company and video cases, and the Marketing Plan appendix. This and many previous editions have benefited greatly from Andy's assistance. We also thank Laurie Babin of the University of Louisiana at Monroe for her dedicated continued efforts in preparing end-of-chapter materials and for keeping our Marketing by the Numbers appendix fresh. Additional thanks also go to Jennifer Barr, Tony Henthorne, and Douglas Martin.

Many reviewers at other colleges and universities provided valuable comments and suggestions for this and previous editions. We are indebted to the following colleagues for their thoughtful inputs:

REVIEWERS

George Bercovitz, *York College*
Pari S. Bhagat, Ph.D., *Indiana University of Pennsylvania*
Sylvia Clark, *St. John's University*
Linda Jane Coleman, *Salem State University*
Mary Conran, *Temple University*
Datha Damron-Martinez, *Truman State University*
Lawrence K. Duke, *Drexel University*
Barbara S. Faries, MBA, *Mission College*
Ivan Filby, *Greenville College*
John Gaskins, *Longwood University*
Karen Halpern, *South Puget Sound Community College*
Jan Hardesty, *University of Arizona*
Hella-Ilona Johnson, *Olympic College*
David Koehler, *University of Illinois at Chicago*
Michelle Kunz, *Morehead State University*
Susan Mann, *University of Northwestern Ohio*
Thomas E. Marshall, M.B.E., *Owens Community College*
Nora Martin, *University of South Carolina*
Erika Matulich, *University of Tampa*
Marc Newman, *Hocking College*
John T. Nolan, *SUNY, Buffalo State*
Nikolai Ostapenko, *University of the District of Columbia*
Vic Piscatello, *University of Arizona*
Bill Rice, *California State University*
David Robinson, *University of California, Berkeley*
William M. Ryan, *University of Connecticut*
Elliot Schreiber, *Drexel University*
Lisa Simon, *Cal Poly, San Luis Obispo*
Robert Simon, *University of Nebraska, Lincoln*
Keith Starcher, *Indiana Wesleyan University*
John Talbott, *Indiana University*
Rhonda Tenenbaum, *Queens College*
Deborah Utter, *Boston University*
Tom Voigt, *Judson University*
Terry Wilson, *East Stroudsburg University*

We also owe a great deal to the people at Pearson Education who helped develop this book. Senior Acquisitions Editor Mark Gaffney provided resources and support during the revision. Senior Project Manager Jacqueline Martin and Program Manager Jennifer Collins provided valuable assistance and advice in guiding this complex revision project through development, design, and production. We'd also like to thank Stephanie Wall, Lenny Ann Kucenski, Judy Leale, Jeff Holcomb, and Eric Santucci for their able assistance along the way. We are proud to be associated with the fine professionals at Pearson. We also owe a mighty debt of gratitude to Charles Fisher and the team at Integra.

Finally, we owe many thanks to our families for all of their support and encouragement—Kathy, Betty, Mandy, Matt, KC, Keri, Delaney, Molly, Macy, and Ben from the Armstrong clan and Nancy, Amy, Melissa, and Jessica from the Kotler family. To them, we dedicate this book.

Gary Armstrong
Philip Kotler

Marketing

An Introduction

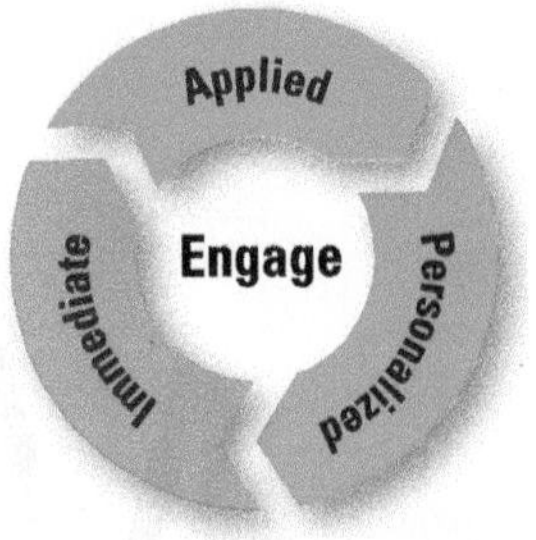

1 Marketing

Creating Customer Value and Engagement

CHAPTER ROAD MAP Objective Outline

- **OBJECTIVE 1-1** **Define marketing and outline the steps in the marketing process.** What Is Marketing? (4–5)
- **OBJECTIVE 1-2** **Explain the importance of understanding the marketplace and customers and identify the five core marketplace concepts.** Understanding the Marketplace and Customer Needs (6–8)
- **OBJECTIVE 1-3** **Identify the key elements of a customer-value driven marketing strategy and discuss the marketing management orientations that guide marketing strategy.** Designing a Customer-Driven Marketing Strategy (9–12) Preparing an Integrated Marketing Plan and Program (12–13)
- **OBJECTIVE 1-4** **Discuss customer relationship management and identify strategies for creating value *for* customers and capturing value *from* customers in return.** Engaging Customers and Managing Customer Relationships (13–20); Capturing Value from Customers (20–23)
- **OBJECTIVE 1-5** **Describe the major trends and forces that are changing the marketing landscape in this age of relationships.** The Changing Marketing Landscape (24–31)

Previewing the Concepts

This chapter introduces you to the basic concepts of marketing. We start with the question: What is marketing? Simply put, marketing is engaging customers and managing profitable customer relationships. The aim of marketing is to create value for customers in order to capture value from customers in return. Next we discuss the five steps in the marketing process—from understanding customer needs, to designing customer value-driven marketing strategies and integrated marketing programs, to building customer relationships and capturing value for the firm. Finally, we discuss the major trends and forces affecting marketing in this new age of digital, mobile, and social media. Understanding these basic concepts and forming your own ideas about what they really mean to you will provide a solid foundation for all that follows.

Let's start with a good story about marketing in action at Nike, the world's leading sports apparel company and one of the best-known brands on the planet. Nike's outstanding success results from much more than just making and selling good sports gear. It's based on a customer-focused marketing strategy by which Nike creates customer value through deep brand–customer engagement and close brand community with and among its customers.

First Stop

Nike's Customer Value-Driven Marketing: Engaging Customers and Building Brand Community

The Nike "swoosh"—it's everywhere! Just for fun, try counting the swooshes whenever you pick up the sports pages or watch a basketball game or tune into a televised soccer match. Over the past 50 years, through innovative marketing, Nike has built the ever-present swoosh into one of the world's best-known brand symbols.

Product innovation has always been a cornerstone of Nike's success. Nike makes outstanding shoes, clothing, and gear, whether for basketball, football, and baseball or golf, skateboarding, wall climbing, bicycling, and hiking. But from the start, a brash, young Nike revolutionized sports marketing. To build image and market share, the brand lavishly outspent competitors on big-name endorsements, splashy promotional events, and big-budget, in-your-face "Just Do It" ads. Whereas competitors stressed technical performance, Nike built customer engagement and relationships.

>> The Nike swoosh—it's everywhere. Nike has mastered social networking, both online and off, creating deep engagement and community with and among customers.

© Steve Hellerstein/Alamy

Beyond shoes, Nike marketed a way of life, a genuine passion for sports, a "just-do-it" attitude. Customers didn't just wear their Nikes, they *experienced* them. As the company once stated on its Web page, "Nike has always known the truth—it's not so much the shoes but where they take you." Nike's mission isn't to "make better gear," it's to "connect with and inspire athletes around the world." Few brands have become more ever-present and valued than Nike in their customers' lives and conversations.

Whether customers connect with Nike through ads, in-person events at Niketown stores, a local Nike running club, or one of the company's profusion of community Web and social media sites, more and more people are bonding closely with the Nike brand. Connecting once required simply outspending competitors on big media ads and celebrity endorsers that talk *at* customers. But in these digital times, Nike is forging a new kind of brand–customer connection—a deeper, more personal, more engaging one. Nike still invests heavily in traditional advertising. But the brand now spends a lion's share of its marketing budget on cutting-edge digital and social media marketing that interacts *with* customers to build brand engagement and community.

Nike's innovative use of online, mobile, and social media recently earned the brand the title of "top genius" in "digital IQ" among 42 sportswear companies in one digital consultancy's rankings. Nike also placed first in creating brand "tribes"—large groups of highly engaged users—with the help of social media platforms such as Facebook, Twitter, Instagram, YouTube, and Pinterest. For example, the main Nike Facebook page has more than 42 million Likes. The Nike Soccer page adds another 35 million, the Nike Basketball page 7 million more, and Nike Running another 3 million. More than just numbers, Nike's social media presence engages customers at a high level, gets them talking with each other about the brand, and weaves the brand into their daily lives.

Nike excels at cross-media campaigns that integrate digital media with traditional tools to connect with customers. An example is Nike's recent "Risk Everything" World Cup soccer campaign. The Risk Everything campaign began with captivating four- to five-minute videos embedded in Nike social media sites and its own Risk Everything Web site. The campaign—featuring Nike-sponsored soccer superstars such as Portugal's Cristiano Ronaldo, England's Wayne Rooney, Brazil's Neymar, and a dozen others—was built around an intense, provocative World Cup story line of taking risks to gain the glory of succeeding against rival teams and nations.

In one Risk Everything video—"Winner Stays"—two teams of young men faced off on a local soccer field for a pickup game, pretending to be (then turning into) the superstars. The scene transformed into a legendary bout on a global stage. As the video ended, a young boy stepped in for Ronaldo and under immense pressure scored the winning goal. According to one analyst, the Risk Everything videos were "the perfect blend of product placement, provocative storytelling, and real-time marketing." Although the videos were filled with Nike swooshes, products, and stars, highly engaged viewers hardly realized that they were consuming ad content.

Nike's outstanding success results from much more than just making good sports gear. The iconic brand delivers customer value by building deep engagement and a sense of community with and between the Nike brand and its customers.

By the end of the final World Cup match, the Risk Everything videos had produced 372 million views, 22 million engagements (Likes, comments, shares), and 650,000 uses of #riskeverything. Nike reigned as the "most-viewed brand" of the World Cup in terms of online video, trouncing rival adidas. In fact, Nike's online views accounted for an incredible one-half of all the views attributed to the event's 97 World Cup marketing campaigns—and Nike wasn't even an official sponsor. Along with the Risk Everything videos, Nike ran a full array of traditional television, print, radio, cinema, and gaming advertising. Taken as a whole, across all media, the Risk Everything campaign generated more than 6 *billion* impressions in 35 countries. Now that's customer engagement.

Nike has also created customer value and brand community through groundbreaking mobile apps and technologies. For example, its Nike+ apps have helped Nike become a part of the daily fitness routines of millions of customers around the world. The Nike+ FuelBand device, for instance, converts just about every imaginable physical movement into NikeFuel, Nike's own universal activity metric. So whether your activity is running, jumping, baseball, skating, dancing, stacking sports cups, or chasing chickens, it counts for NikeFuel points. Everyday athletes can use NikeFuel to track their personal performance, then share and compare it across sports and locations with others in the global Nike community. The Nike+ mobile app lets users watch their progress, get extra motivation on the go, and stay connected with friends. Nike+ has engaged a huge global brand community. To date, more than 5 million Nike+ users worldwide have logged 1,118,434,247 miles. That's 44,914 trips around the world or 4,682 journeys to the moon and back.

Thus, Nike delivers customer value well beyond the products it makes. It has built a deep kinship and sense of community with and between the Nike brand and its customers. Whether it's through local running clubs, a performance-tracking app, primetime TV ads, videos, and other content in any of its dozens of brand Web sites and social media pages, the Nike brand has become a valued part of customers' lives and times.

As a result, Nike remains the world's largest sports apparel company, an impressive 44 percent larger than closest rival adidas. During the past decade, even as a sometimes-shaky economy left many sports footwear and apparel rivals gasping for breath, Nike's global sales and income have sprinted ahead by more than double. "Connecting used to be, 'Here's some product, and here's some advertising. We hope you like it,'" notes Nike's CEO. "Connecting today is a dialogue." Says Nike's chief marketing officer, "The engagement levels we have received... drive huge momentum for our brand. This is just the beginning of how we will connect with and inspire athletes around the world."[1]

Today's successful companies have one thing in common: Like Nike, they are strongly customer focused and heavily committed to marketing. These companies share a passion for understanding and satisfying customer needs in well-defined target markets. They motivate everyone in the organization to help build lasting customer relationships based on creating value.

Customer relationships and value are especially important today. Facing dramatic technological advances and deep economic, social, and environmental challenges, today's customers are relating digitally with companies and each other, spending more carefully, and reassessing how they engage with brands. New digital, mobile, and social media developments have revolutionized how consumers shop and interact, in turn calling for new marketing strategies and tactics. In these fast-changing times, it's now more important than ever to build strong customer relationships based on real and enduring customer value.

We'll discuss the exciting new challenges facing both customers and marketers later in the chapter. But first, let's introduce the basics of marketing.

Author Comment
Pause here and think about how you'd answer this question before studying marketing. Then see how your answer changes as you read the chapter.

What Is Marketing?

Marketing, more than any other business function, deals with customers. Although we will soon explore more-detailed definitions of marketing, perhaps the simplest definition is this one: *Marketing is engaging customers and managing profitable customer relationships.* The twofold goal of marketing is to attract new customers by promising superior value and to keep and grow current customers by delivering satisfaction.

For example, Walmart has become the world's largest retailer—and the world's largest *company*—by delivering on its promise "Save Money. Live Better." Coca-Cola has earn a 49 percent global share of the carbonated beverage market—more than twice Pepsi's share—by fulfilling its "open happiness" motto with products that "spread smiles and open happiness every day all across the world." Facebook has attracted more than 1.4 billion active Web and mobile users worldwide by helping them to "connect and share with the people in their lives."[2]

Sound marketing is critical to the success of every organization. Large for-profit firms, such as Google, Target, Procter & Gamble, Coca-Cola, and Microsoft, use marketing. But so do not-for-profit organizations, such as colleges, hospitals, museums, symphony orchestras, and even churches.

You already know a lot about marketing—it's all around you. Marketing comes to you in the good old traditional forms: You see it in the abundance of products at your nearby shopping mall and the ads that fill your TV screen, spice up your magazines, or stuff your mailbox. But in recent years, marketers have assembled a host of new marketing approaches, everything from imaginative Web sites and smartphone apps to blogs, online videos, and social media. These new approaches do more than just blast out messages to the masses. They reach you directly, personally, and interactively. Today's marketers want to become a part of your life and enrich your experiences with their brands—to help you *live* their brands.

At home, at school, where you work, and where you play, you see marketing in almost everything you do. Yet there is much more to marketing than meets the consumer's casual eye. Behind it all is a massive network of people, technologies, and activities competing for your attention and purchases. This book will give you a complete introduction to the basic concepts and practices of today's marketing. In this chapter, we begin by defining marketing and the marketing process.

Marketing Defined

What *is* marketing? Many people think of marketing as only selling and advertising. We are bombarded every day with TV commercials, catalogs, spiels from salespeople, and online pitches. However, selling and advertising are only the tip of the marketing iceberg.

Today, marketing must be understood not in the old sense of making a sale—"telling and selling"—but in the new sense of *satisfying customer needs.* If the marketer engages consumers effectively, understands their needs, develops products that provide superior customer value, and prices, distributes, and promotes them well, these products will sell easily. In fact, according to management guru Peter Drucker, "The aim of marketing is to make selling unnecessary."[3] Selling and advertising are only part of a larger *marketing mix*—a set of marketing tools that work together to engage customers, satisfy customer needs, and build customer relationships.

Broadly defined, marketing is a social and managerial process by which individuals and organizations obtain what they need and want through creating and exchanging value with others. In a narrower business context, marketing involves building profitable, value-laden exchange relationships with customers. Hence, we define **marketing** as the process by which companies engage customers, build strong customer relationships, and create customer value in order to capture value from customers in return.[4]

Marketing
The process by which companies engage customers, build strong customer relationships, and create customer value in order to capture value from customers in return.

The Marketing Process

» Figure 1.1 presents a simple, five-step model of the marketing process for creating and capturing customer value. In the first four steps, companies work to understand consumers, create customer value, and build strong customer relationships. In the final step, companies reap the rewards of creating superior customer value. By creating value *for* consumers, they in turn capture value *from* consumers in the form of sales, profits, and long-term customer equity.

In this chapter and the next, we will examine the steps of this simple model of marketing. In this chapter, we review each step but focus more on the customer relationship steps—understanding customers, engaging and building relationships with customers, and capturing value from customers. In Chapter 2, we look more deeply into the second and third steps—designing value-creating marketing strategies and constructing marketing programs.

This important figure shows marketing in a nutshell. By creating value *for* customers, marketers capture value *from* customers in return. This five-step process forms the marketing framework for the rest of the chapter and the remainder of the text.

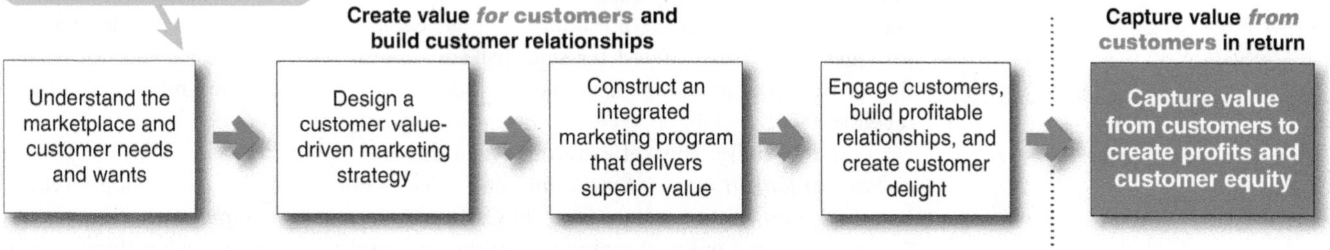

» Figure 1.1 The Marketing Process: Creating and Capturing Customer Value

Author Comment
Marketing is all about creating value for customers. So, as the first step in the marketing process, the company must fully understand consumers and the marketplace in which it operates.

Understanding the Marketplace and Customer Needs

As a first step, marketers need to understand customer needs and wants and the marketplace in which they operate. We examine five core customer and marketplace concepts: (1) *needs, wants, and demands*; (2) *market offerings (products, services, and experiences)*; (3) *value and satisfaction*; (4) *exchanges and relationships*; and (5) *markets.*

Customer Needs, Wants, and Demands

Needs
States of felt deprivation.

Wants
The form human needs take as they are shaped by culture and individual personality.

The most basic concept underlying marketing is that of human needs. Human **needs** are states of felt deprivation. They include basic *physical* needs for food, clothing, warmth, and safety; *social* needs for belonging and affection; and *individual* needs for knowledge and self-expression. Marketers did not create these needs; they are a basic part of the human makeup.

Wants are the form human needs take as they are shaped by culture and individual personality. An American *needs* food but *wants* a Big Mac, french fries, and a soft drink. A person in Papua, New Guinea, *needs* food but *wants* taro, rice, yams, and pork. Wants are shaped by one's society and are described in terms of objects that will satisfy those needs. When backed by buying power, wants become **demands**. Given their wants and resources, people demand products and services with benefits that add up to the most value and satisfaction.

Outstanding marketing companies go to great lengths to learn about and understand their customers' needs, wants, and demands. They conduct consumer research, analyze mountains of customer data, and observe customers as they shop and interact, offline and online. People at all levels of the company—including top management—stay close to customers:[5]

» **Staying close to customers: Energetic new Target CEO Brian Collins makes regular unannounced visits to Target stores, accompanied by local moms and loyal Target shoppers.**
Ackerman + Gruber

> Target's energetic new CEO, Brian Cornell, makes regular unannounced visits to Target stores, accompanied by local moms and loyal Target shoppers. » Cornell likes nosing around stores and getting a real feel for what's going on. It gives him "great, genuine feedback." Similarly, Boston Market CEO George Michel makes frequent visits to company restaurants, working in the dining room and engaging customers to learn about "the good, the bad, and the ugly." He also stays connected by reading customer messages on the Boston Market Web site and has even cold-called customers for insights. "Being close to the customer is critically important," says Michel. "I get to learn what they value, what they appreciate."

Market Offerings—Products, Services, and Experiences

Demands
Human wants that are backed by buying power.

Market offerings
Some combination of products, services, information, or experiences offered to a market to satisfy a need or want.

Consumers' needs and wants are fulfilled through **market offerings**—some combination of products, services, information, or experiences offered to a market to satisfy a need or a want. Market offerings are not limited to physical *products.* They also include *services*—activities or benefits offered for sale that are essentially intangible and do not result in the ownership of anything. Examples include banking, airline, hotel, retailing, and home repair services.

More broadly, market offerings also include other entities, such as *persons, places, organizations, information,* and *ideas.* For example, San Diego recently launched a $9 million "Happiness Is Calling" advertising campaign that invites visitors to come and enjoy the city's great weather and good times—everything from its bays and beaches to its downtown nightlife and urban scenes. And the Ad Council and

Marketing myopia
The mistake of paying more attention to the specific products a company offers than to the benefits and experiences produced by these products.

the National Highway Traffic Safety Administration created a "Stop the Texts. Stop the Wrecks." campaign that markets the idea of eliminating texting while driving. The campaign points out that a texting driver is 23 times more likely to get into a crash than a non-texting driver.[6]

Many sellers make the mistake of paying more attention to the specific products they offer than to the benefits and experiences produced by these products. These sellers suffer from **marketing myopia**. They are so taken with their products that they focus only on existing wants and lose sight of underlying customer needs.[7] They forget that a product is only a tool to solve a consumer problem. A manufacturer of quarter-inch drill bits may think that the customer needs a drill bit. But what the customer *really* needs is a quarter-inch hole. These sellers will have trouble if a new product comes along that serves the customer's need better or less expensively. The customer will have the same *need* but will *want* the new product.

Smart marketers look beyond the attributes of the products and services they sell. By orchestrating several services and products, they create *brand experiences* for consumers. For example, you don't just visit Walt Disney World Resort; you immerse yourself and your family in a world of wonder, a world where dreams come true and things still work the way they should. "Let the magic begin!" says Disney. » Similarly, Mattel's American Girl does much more than just make and sell high-end dolls. It creates special experiences between the dolls and the girls who adore them.[8]

» Marketing experiences: American Girl does more than just make and sell high-end dolls. It creates special experiences between the dolls and the girls who adore them.

> To put more smiles on the faces of the girls who love their American Girl dolls, the company operates huge American Girl experiential stores in 20 major cities around the country. Each store carries an amazing selection of dolls plus every imaginable outfit and accessory. But more than just shopping spots, American Girl stores are exciting destinations unto themselves, offering wonderfully engaging experiences for girls, mothers, grandmothers, and even dads or grandpas. There's an in-store restaurant where girls, their dolls, and grown-ups can sit down together for brunch, lunch, afternoon tea, or dinner. There's even a doll hair salon where a stylist can give a doll a new hairdo. American Girl also offers "perfect parties" to celebrate a birthday or any day, as well as a full slate of special events, from crafts and activities to excursions. Much more than a store that sells dolls, says the company, "it's the place where imaginations can soar." A visit to American Girl creates "Fun today. Memories forever."

Customer Value and Satisfaction

Consumers usually face a broad array of products and services that might satisfy a given need. How do they choose among these many market offerings? Customers form expectations about the value and satisfaction that various market offerings will deliver and buy accordingly. Satisfied customers buy again and tell others about their good experiences. Dissatisfied customers often switch to competitors and disparage the product to others.

Marketers must be careful to set the right level of expectations. If they set expectations too low, they may satisfy those who buy but fail to attract enough buyers. If they set expectations too high, buyers will be disappointed. Customer value and customer satisfaction are key building blocks for developing and managing customer relationships. We will revisit these core concepts later in the chapter.

Exchanges and Relationships

Exchange
The act of obtaining a desired object from someone by offering something in return.

Marketing occurs when people decide to satisfy their needs and wants through exchange relationships. **Exchange** is the act of obtaining a desired object from someone by offering something in return. In the broadest sense, the marketer tries to bring about a response to some market offering. The response may be more than simply buying or trading products and services. A political candidate, for instance, wants votes; a church wants membership; an orchestra wants an audience; and a social action group wants idea acceptance.

Marketing consists of actions taken to create, maintain, and grow desirable exchange *relationships* with target audiences involving a product, service, idea, or other object. Companies want to build strong relationships by consistently delivering superior customer value. We will expand on the important concept of managing customer relationships later in the chapter.

Markets

Market
The set of all actual and potential buyers of a product or service.

The concepts of exchange and relationships lead to the concept of a market. A **market** is the set of actual and potential buyers of a product or service. These buyers share a particular need or want that can be satisfied through exchange relationships.

Marketing means managing markets to bring about profitable customer relationships. However, creating these relationships takes work. Sellers must search for and engage buyers, identify their needs, design good market offerings, set prices for them, promote them, and store and deliver them. Activities such as consumer research, product development, communication, distribution, pricing, and service are core marketing activities.

Although we normally think of marketing as being carried out by sellers, buyers also carry out marketing. Consumers market when they search for products, interact with companies to obtain information, and make their purchases. In fact, today's digital technologies, from online sites and smartphone apps to the explosion of social media, have empowered consumers and made marketing a truly two-way affair. Thus, in addition to customer relationship management, today's marketers must also deal effectively with *customer-managed relationships*. Marketers are no longer asking only "How can we influence our customers?" but also "How can our customers influence us?" and even "How can our customers influence each other?"

>> **Figure 1.2** shows the main elements in a marketing system. Marketing involves serving a market of final consumers in the face of competitors. The company and competitors research the market and interact with consumers to understand their needs. Then they create and exchange market offerings, messages, and other marketing content with consumers, either directly or through marketing intermediaries. Each party in the system is affected by major environmental forces (demographic, economic, natural, technological, political, and social/cultural).

Each party in the system adds value for the next level. The arrows represent relationships that must be developed and managed. Thus, a company's success at engaging customers and building profitable relationships depends not only on its own actions but also on how well the entire system serves the needs of final consumers. Walmart cannot fulfill its promise of low prices unless its suppliers provide merchandise at low costs. And Ford cannot deliver a high-quality car-ownership experience unless its dealers provide outstanding sales and service.

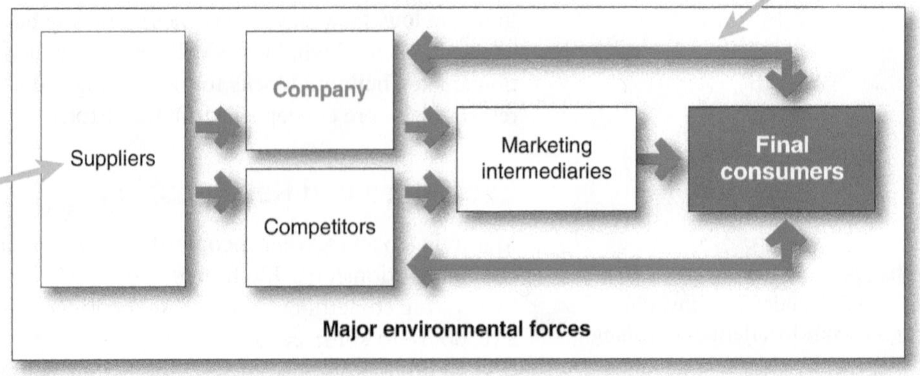

>> **Figure 1.2 A Modern Marketing System**

Author Comment
Once a company fully understands its consumers and the marketplace, it must decide which customers it will serve and how it will bring them value.

Designing a Customer Value-Driven Marketing Strategy

Once it fully understands consumers and the marketplace, marketing management can design a customer value-driven marketing strategy. We define **marketing management** as the art and science of choosing target markets and building profitable relationships with them. The marketing manager's aim is to engage, keep, and grow target customers by creating, delivering, and communicating superior customer value.

Marketing management
The art and science of choosing target markets and building profitable relationships with them.

To design a winning marketing strategy, the marketing manager must answer two important questions: *What customers will we serve (what's our target market)?* and *How can we serve these customers best (what's our value proposition)?* We will discuss these marketing strategy concepts briefly here and then look at them in more detail in Chapters 2 and 6.

Selecting Customers to Serve

The company must first decide *whom* it will serve. It does this by dividing the market into segments of customers (*market segmentation*) and selecting which segments it will go after (*target marketing*). Some people think of marketing management as finding as many customers as possible and increasing demand. But marketing managers know that they cannot serve all customers in every way. By trying to serve all customers, they may not serve any customers well. Instead, the company wants to select only customers that it can serve well and profitably. For example, Nordstrom profitably targets affluent professionals; Dollar General profitably targets families with more modest means.

Ultimately, marketing managers must decide which customers they want to target and on the level, timing, and nature of their demand. Simply put, marketing management is *customer management* and *demand management.*

Choosing a Value Proposition

The company must also decide how it will serve targeted customers—how it will *differentiate and position* itself in the marketplace. A brand's *value proposition* is the set of benefits or values it promises to deliver to consumers to satisfy their needs. JetBlue promises to put "You Above All" by bringing "humanity back to travel." By contrast, Spirit Airlines gives you "Bare Fare" pricing: "Less Money. More Go." » Facebook helps you "connect and share with the people in your life," whereas Twitter's Vine app gives you "the best way to see and share life in motion" through "short, beautiful, looping videos in a simple and fun way for your friends and family to see."[9]

» **Value propositions: Vine gives you "the best way to see and share life in motion" through "short, beautiful, looping videos in a simple and fun way for your friends and family to see."**
Twitter, Inc.

Such value propositions differentiate one brand from another. They answer the customer's question: "Why should I buy your brand rather than a competitor's?" Companies must design strong value propositions that give them the greatest advantage in their target markets.

Marketing Management Orientations

Marketing management wants to design strategies that will engage target customers and build profitable relationships with them. But what *philosophy* should guide these marketing strategies? What weight should be given to the interests of customers, the organization, and society? Very often, these interests conflict.

There are five alternative concepts under which organizations design and carry out their marketing strategies: the *production, product, selling, marketing,* and *societal marketing concepts.*

The Production Concept

Production concept
The idea that consumers will favor products that are available and highly affordable; therefore, the organization should focus on improving production and distribution efficiency.

The **production concept** holds that consumers will favor products that are available and highly affordable. Therefore, management should focus on improving production and distribution efficiency. This concept is one of the oldest orientations that guides sellers.

The production concept is still a useful philosophy in some situations. For example, both personal computer maker Lenovo and home appliance maker Haier dominate the highly competitive, price-sensitive Chinese market through low labor costs, high production efficiency, and mass distribution. However, although useful in some situations, the production concept can lead to marketing myopia. Companies adopting this orientation run a major risk of focusing too narrowly on their own operations and losing sight of the real objective—satisfying customer needs and building customer relationships.

The Product Concept

Product concept
The idea that consumers will favor products that offer the most quality, performance, and features; therefore, the organization should devote its energy to making continuous product improvements.

The **product concept** holds that consumers will favor products that offer the most in quality, performance, and innovative features. Under this concept, marketing strategy focuses on making continuous product improvements.

Product quality and improvement are important parts of most marketing strategies. However, focusing *only* on the company's products can also lead to marketing myopia. For example, some manufacturers believe that if they can "build a better mousetrap, the world will beat a path to their doors." But they are often rudely shocked. Buyers may be looking for a better solution to a mouse problem but not necessarily for a better mousetrap. The better solution might be a chemical spray, an exterminating service, a house cat, or something else that suits their needs even better than a mousetrap. Furthermore, a better mousetrap will not sell unless the manufacturer designs, packages, and prices it attractively; places it in convenient distribution channels; brings it to the attention of people who need it; and convinces buyers that it is a better product.

The Selling Concept

Selling concept
The idea that consumers will not buy enough of the firm's products unless the firm undertakes a large-scale selling and promotion effort.

Many companies follow the **selling concept**, which holds that consumers will not buy enough of the firm's products unless it undertakes a large-scale selling and promotion effort. The selling concept is typically practiced with unsought goods—those that buyers do not normally think of buying, such as life insurance or blood donations. These industries must be good at tracking down prospects and selling them on a product's benefits.

Such aggressive selling, however, carries high risks. It focuses on creating sales transactions rather than on building long-term, profitable customer relationships. The aim often is to sell what the company makes rather than to make what the market wants. It assumes that customers who are coaxed into buying the product will like it. Or, if they don't like it, they will possibly forget their disappointment and buy it again later. These are usually poor assumptions.

The Marketing Concept

Marketing concept
A philosophy in which achieving organizational goals depends on knowing the needs and wants of target markets and delivering the desired satisfactions better than competitors do.

The **marketing concept** holds that achieving organizational goals depends on knowing the needs and wants of target markets and delivering the desired satisfactions better than competitors do. Under the marketing concept, customer focus and value are the *paths* to sales and profits. Instead of a product-centered *make-and-sell* philosophy, the marketing concept is a customer-centered *sense-and-respond* philosophy. The job is not to find the right customers for your product but to find the right products for your customers.

>> **Figure 1.3** contrasts the selling concept and the marketing concept. The selling concept takes an *inside-out* perspective. It starts with the factory, focuses on the company's existing products, and calls for heavy selling and promotion to obtain profitable sales. It focuses primarily on customer conquest—getting short-term sales with little concern about who buys or why.

In contrast, the marketing concept takes an *outside-in* perspective. As Herb Kelleher, the colorful founder of Southwest Airlines, once put it, "We don't have a marketing department; we have a customer department." The marketing concept starts with a well-defined

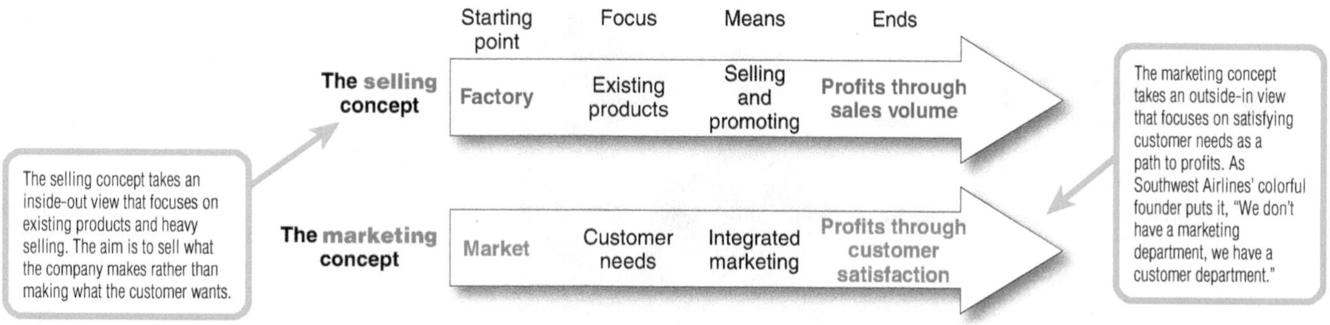

>> Figure 1.3 Selling and Marketing Concepts Contrasted

market, focuses on customer needs, and integrates all the marketing activities that affect customers. In turn, it yields profits by creating relationships with the right customers based on customer value and satisfaction.

Implementing the marketing concept often means more than simply responding to customers' stated desires and obvious needs. *Customer-driven* companies research customers deeply to learn about their desires, gather new product ideas, and test product improvements. Such customer-driven marketing usually works well when a clear need exists and when customers know what they want.

In many cases, however, customers *don't* know what they want or even what is possible. As Henry Ford once remarked, "If I'd asked people what they wanted, they would have said faster horses."[10] For example, even 20 years ago, how many consumers would have thought to ask for now-commonplace products such as tablet computers, smartphones, digital cameras, 24-hour online buying, digital video and music streaming, and GPS systems in their cars and phones? Such situations call for *customer-driving* marketing—understanding customer needs even better than customers themselves do and creating products and services that meet both existing and latent needs, now and in the future. As an executive at 3M put it, "Our goal is to lead customers where they want to go before *they* know where they want to go."

The Societal Marketing Concept

Societal marketing concept
The idea that a company's marketing decisions should consider consumers' wants, the company's requirements, consumers' long-run interests, and society's long-run interests.

The **societal marketing concept** questions whether the pure marketing concept overlooks possible conflicts between consumer *short-run wants* and consumer *long-run welfare.* Is a firm that satisfies the immediate needs and wants of target markets always doing what's best for its consumers in the long run? The societal marketing concept holds that marketing strategy should deliver value to customers in a way that maintains or improves both the consumer's *and society's* well-being. It calls for *sustainable marketing*, socially and environmentally responsible marketing that meets the present needs of consumers and businesses while also preserving or enhancing the ability of future generations to meet their needs.

Even more broadly, many leading business and marketing thinkers are now preaching the concept of *shared value,* which recognizes that societal needs, not just economic needs, define markets.[11] The concept of shared value focuses on creating economic value in a way that also creates value for society. A growing number of companies known for their hard-nosed approaches to business—such as GE, Dow, Google, IBM, Intel, Johnson & Johnson, Nestlé, Unilever, and Walmart—are rethinking the interactions between society and corporate performance. They are concerned not just with short-term economic gains but with the well-being of their customers, the depletion of natural resources vital to their businesses, the viability of key suppliers, and the economic well-being of the communities in which they operate.

One prominent marketer calls this *Marketing 3.0.* "Marketing 3.0 organizations are values-driven," he says. "I'm not talking about being value-driven. I'm talking about 'values' plural, where values amount to caring about the state of the world." Another marketer calls it *purpose-driven marketing.* "The future of profit is purpose," he says.[12]

As Figure 1.4 shows, companies should balance three considerations in setting their marketing strategies: company profits, consumer wants, *and* society's interests. British-based cosmetics retailer Lush operates this way:[13]

> Lush is known for "Fresh Handmade Cosmetics"—premium beauty products made by hand from the freshest possible natural ingredients. It sells products with evocative names such as Flying Fox shower gel, Angels on Bareskin cleanser, and Honey I Washed the Kids soap. But Lush does much more than just make and sell body care products for profit. It also dedicates itself to doing right by customers, employees, the environment, and society. Its do-good mission is spelled out in a seven-point statement titled "A Lush Life: We Believe. . . ." For example, the company believes in inventing and making its own products from fresh organic fruits and vegetables using little or no preservatives or packaging. Lush has a strict policy against animal testing and supports fair-trade and community trade efforts. Each year, the company invests heavily in sustainable initiatives and support of grassroots charities. Lush takes care of its employees—"We believe in happy people making happy soap . . ." In fact, Lush seems to wish well to everyone, everywhere—"We believe in long candlelit baths, sharing showers, massage, filling the world with perfume, and the right to make mistakes, lose everything, and start again." Only in its final belief does Lush mention profits—"We believe our products are good value, that we should make a profit, and that the customer is always right." Thanks to its societal mission, Lush is thriving like fresh flowers in springtime. It now operates stores in 50 countries, with e-commerce sites in 27 countries. Its sales have nearly doubled in just the past three years, suggesting that doing good can benefit both the planet and the company.

The societal marketing concept: Cosmetics retailer Lush does more than just make and sell premium body care products for profit. It also dedicates itself to doing right by customers, employees, the environment, and society.

Lush Fresh Handmade Cosmetics

Author Comment
The marketing strategy discussed in the previous section outlines which customers the company will serve and how. Now, the company develops marketing plans and programs—a marketing mix—that will deliver the intended customer value.

Preparing an Integrated Marketing Plan and Program

The company's marketing strategy outlines which customers it will serve and how it will create value for these customers. Next, the marketer develops an integrated marketing program that will actually deliver the intended value to target customers. The marketing program builds customer relationships by transforming the marketing strategy into action. It consists of the firm's *marketing mix*, the set of marketing tools the firm uses to implement its marketing strategy.

Figure 1.4 Three Considerations Underlying the Societal Marketing Concept

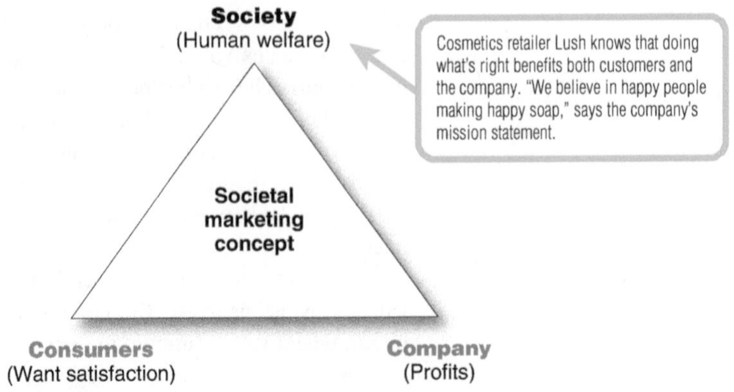

The major marketing mix tools are classified into four broad groups, called the *four Ps* of marketing: product, price, place, and promotion. To deliver on its value proposition, the firm must first create a need-satisfying market offering (product). It must then decide how much it will charge for the offering (price) and how it will make the offering available to target consumers (place). Finally, it must engage target consumers, communicate about the offering, and persuade consumers of the offer's merits (promotion). The firm must blend each marketing mix tool into a comprehensive integrated marketing program that communicates and delivers the intended value to chosen customers. We will explore marketing programs and the marketing mix in much more detail in later chapters.

LINKING THE CONCEPTS

Stop here for a moment and stretch your mind. What have you learned so far about marketing? Set aside the more formal definitions we've examined and try to develop your own understanding of marketing.

- In *your own words*, what *is* marketing? Write down *your* definition. Does your definition include such key concepts as customer value, engagement, and relationships?
- What does marketing *mean* to you? How does it affect your daily life?
- What brand of athletic shoes did you purchase last? Describe your relationship with Nike, adidas, New Balance, Asics, Reebok, Puma, Converse, or whatever brand of shoes you purchased.

Author Comment
Doing a good job with the first three steps in the marketing process sets the stage for step four, building and managing customer relationships.

Engaging Customers and Managing Customer Relationships

The first three steps in the marketing process—understanding the marketplace and customer needs, designing a customer value-driven marketing strategy, and constructing a marketing program—all lead up to the fourth and most important step: engaging customers and managing profitable customer relationships. We first discuss the basics of customer relationship management. Then we examine how companies go about engaging customers on a deeper level in this age of digital and social marketing.

Customer Relationship Management

Customer relationship management
The overall process of building and maintaining profitable customer relationships by delivering superior customer value and satisfaction.

Customer relationship management is perhaps the most important concept of modern marketing. In the broadest sense, **customer relationship management** is the overall process of building and maintaining profitable customer relationships by delivering superior customer value and satisfaction. It deals with all aspects of acquiring, engaging, and growing customers.

Relationship Building Blocks: Customer Value and Satisfaction

The key to building lasting customer relationships is to create superior customer value and satisfaction. Satisfied customers are more likely to be loyal customers and give the company a larger share of their business.

Customer-perceived value
The customer's evaluation of the difference between all the benefits and all the costs of a market offering relative to those of competing offers.

Customer Value. Attracting and retaining customers can be a difficult task. Customers often face a bewildering array of products and services from which to choose. A customer buys from the firm that offers the highest **customer-perceived value**—the customer's evaluation of the difference between all the benefits and all the costs of a market offering relative to those of competing offers. Importantly, customers often do not judge values and costs "accurately" or "objectively." They act on *perceived* value.

To some consumers, value might mean sensible products at affordable prices. To other consumers, however, value might mean paying more to get more. For example, what's a cooler worth—one of those insulated containers you take camping or haul to a picnic or tailgate party? If it's a YETI cooler, you can expect to pay from $229 to as much as $1,300 for the top-of-the-line Tundra model. However, despite their high prices and spare, boxy designs, YETI coolers have achieved an almost cult status among the field-and-stream set and on construction sites, ranches, and even military bases. The company's slogan—"YETI Coolers—Wildly Stronger. Keeps Ice Longer!"—suggests the reasons why. Devoted users will tell you that a YETI does keep things cooler—with a FatWall design (with twice the insulation of competitors) and an interlocking lid system with a gasket that keeps the cold in. And rugged YETI coolers are made to last—no more busted hinges, failed latches, or caved-in lids. They're even certified as grizzly bear resistant by the Interagency Grizzly Bear Committee. One reporter describes a YETI as "a cooler fit for the apocalypse," and the company claims it's "The cooler you've always wanted. The last cooler you'll ever need." So, is a YETI cooler worth the premium price compared with less expensive coolers made by Igloo or Rubbermaid? To many consumers, the answer is no. But to YETI's target buyers, the answer is a resounding yes.[14]

Perceived value: Is a YETI cooler worth its premium price? To devoted YETI users, the answer is a resounding "yes." The "Wildly Stronger. Keep Ice Longer!" coolers are even certified as grizzly bear proof by the Interagency Grizzly Bear Committee.

Courtesy YETI Coolers and the Interagency Grizzly Bear Committee (IGBC)

Customer satisfaction
The extent to which a product's perceived performance matches a buyer's expectations.

Customer Satisfaction. **Customer satisfaction** depends on the product's perceived performance relative to a buyer's expectations. If the product's performance falls short of expectations, the customer is dissatisfied. If performance matches expectations, the customer is satisfied. If performance exceeds expectations, the customer is highly satisfied or delighted.

Outstanding marketing companies go out of their way to keep important customers satisfied. Most studies show that higher levels of customer satisfaction lead to greater customer loyalty, which in turn results in better company performance. Companies aim to delight customers by promising only what they can deliver and then delivering more than they promise. Delighted customers not only make repeat purchases but also become willing marketing partners and "customer evangelists" who spread the word about their good experiences to others.

For companies interested in delighting customers, exceptional value and service become part of the overall company culture. For example, year after year, Ritz-Carlton ranks at or near the top of the hospitality industry in terms of customer satisfaction. Its passion for satisfying customers is summed up in the company's credo, which promises that its luxury hotels will deliver a truly memorable experience—one that "enlivens the senses, instills well-being, and fulfills even the unexpressed wishes and needs of our guests."[15]

Creating customer satisfaction: Ritz-Carlton hotels deliver a truly memorable experience, one that "enlivens the senses, instills well-being, and fulfills even the unexpressed wishes and needs of our guests."

Toronto Star via Getty Images

Check into any Ritz-Carlton hotel around the world, and you'll be amazed by the company's fervent dedication to anticipating even your slightest need. Without ever asking, they seem to know that you're allergic to peanuts and want a king-size bed, a hypoallergenic pillow, extra body gel, the blinds open when you arrive, and breakfast with decaffeinated coffee in your room. Each day, hotel staffers—from those at the front desk to those in maintenance and housekeeping—discreetly observe and record even the smallest guest preferences. Then, every morning, each hotel reviews the files of all new arrivals who have previously stayed at a Ritz-Carlton and prepares a list of suggested extra touches that might delight each guest. For example, according to one Ritz-Carlton manager, if the chain gets hold of a picture of a guest's pet, it will make a copy, have it framed, and display it in the guest's room in whatever Ritz-Carlton the guest visits.

Once they identify a special customer need, Ritz-Carlton employees go to legendary extremes to meet it. For instance, to serve the needs of a guest whose son had food allergies, a Ritz-Carlton chef in Bali located special eggs and milk in a small grocery store in another country and had them delivered to the hotel. In another case, when a businessman attending a conference at the Ritz-Carlton Orlando ordered his favorite soda during a dinner in a hotel ballroom, his banquet server told him that the hotel didn't serve that beverage but he would see what he could do. To no one's surprise, the server quickly returned with the requested beverage, and for the rest of the week he had the drink waiting for the guest. But here's the best part. A year later when the guest returned for the conference, as he sat in the ballroom waiting for dinner the first night, the same server walked up with his favorite drink in hand. As a result of such customer service heroics, an amazing 95 percent of departing guests report that their stay has been a truly memorable experience. More than 90 percent of Ritz-Carlton's delighted customers return.

Other companies that have become legendary for customer delight and their service heroics include Zappos.com, Amazon.com, Chick-Fil-A, Nordstrom department stores, and JetBlue Airways (see Marketing at Work 1.1). However, a company doesn't need to

MARKETING AT WORK 1.1

JetBlue: Delighting Customers and Bringing Humanity Back to Air Travel

There's an old adage in the airline industry: "You're not flying planes, you're flying people." These days, however, it seems that many big airlines overlook the people factor. Instead, they focus on moving their human cargo as efficiently as possible while charging as much as the traffic will bear. The American Customer Satisfaction Index rates the airline industry near the bottom among 47 industries in customer satisfaction, barely ahead of perennial cellar-dwellers subscription TV and Internet service providers.

Not so at JetBlue Airways. From the very beginning, young JetBlue (little more than 15 years old) has built a reputation for creating first-rate, customer-satisfying experiences. Its slogan—"YOU ABOVE ALL"—tells the JetBlue faithful that they are at the very heart of the company's strategy and culture. JetBlue is on a heartfelt mission to bring humanity back to air travel.

At JetBlue, customer care starts with basic amenities that exceed customer expectations, especially for a low-cost carrier. JetBlue's well-padded, leather-covered coach seats allow three inches more legroom than the average airline seat. Although the airline doesn't serve meals, it offers the best selection of free beverages and snacks to be found at 30,000 feet (including unexpected treats such as Terra Blues chips, Linden's chocolate chip cookies, and Dunkin' Donuts coffee). Every JetBlue seat has its own LCD entertainment system, complete with free 36-channel DirecTV and 100-plus channels of SiriusXM Radio. JetBlue rounds out the amenities with a recently launched industry first—Fly-Fi, an in-flight high-speed Internet service with free basic browsing on all equipped planes.

JetBlue continuously innovates to find new ways to delight customers. Its "Even More Space" seats give customers the option of going from "roomy to roomier," allow early boarding, and give early access to overhead bins. Its "Even More Speed" service provides VIP passage through airport security screening. And JetBlue's Mint service puts a new spin on first-class air travel, offering front-of-the-plane, lie-flat "sweet seats," some of them in enclosed suites with their own doors. According to JetBlue, Mint services deliver "unexpected,

» **Creating customer satisfaction: JetBlue creates first-rate, customer-satisfying experiences. Its slogan—"JetBlue: YOU ABOVE ALL"—tells customers that they are at the very heart of JetBlue's strategy and culture.**

JetBlue

individualized 'mo-mints' that revive and engage, keeping you in mint condition during your travels."

Such tangibles help keep JetBlue travelers satisfied. But former JetBlue CEO David Barger knows that the tangibles are only a small part of what really makes JetBlue special. "The hard product—airplanes, leather seats, satellite TVs—as long as you have a checkbook, . . . can be replicated," says Barger. "It's the JetBlue *culture* that can't be replicated. The *human* side of the equation is the most important part of what we're doing." It's that JetBlue culture—the near-obsessive focus on the customer flying experience—that creates not just satisfied JetBlue customers but *delighted* ones.

At JetBlue, developing a customer-centered corporate culture starts with hiring quality people whose personal values match JetBlue's values—from work-at-home part-time call center reservationists to baggage handlers to flight attendants and even pilots. By the time JetBlue employees are on board and trained, they not only *know* the company's core values—safety, integrity, caring, passion, and fun—they *live* them. It's those heartfelt values that result in outstanding customer experiences. And the outstanding customer experiences make JetBlue's customers the most satisfied and loyal in the industry.

Whereas passengers on most competing airlines regard flying as an experience just to be tolerated, many JetBlue customers actually look forward to flying. And customers themselves spread the good word about JetBlue with evangelistic zeal. Recently crowned a "social media all-star" by *Fortune* magazine, JetBlue has been a leader in using a full range of social media to engage customers and get them talking with each other about the brand. And whereas other airlines are just now discovering the power of customer dialogue, throughout its history, in ads and promotions, JetBlue has often let its customers do the talking.

For example, its "Experience JetBlue" Web site features authentic testimonials from some of the airline's most devoted fans, who were found through Twitter and Facebook. The customers give glowing first-person accounts about why they like flying JetBlue. "It's like an open bar for snacks," says one customer. "They're constantly walking around offering it, so I'm never thirsty or hungry." Another JetBlue fan, a 6'3" woman from Portland, Oregon, likes the seating: "I can stretch and sit crosslegged—no black-and-blue knees," she says. "The customer service is above and beyond," declares a third customer, a small business owner from Boston. "[Coach on] JetBlue is very similar to flying first class."

In a former advertising campaign called "Sincerely, JetBlue," actual customers gave voice to even deeper JetBlue experiences. In one ad, for example, customer Melissa confided, "Let me tell you, I wanted not to like you, if only because everyone seems to love you. I got on a flight with a pen and paper, waiting to take down every irritating detail." But, she continued, "two flights later, I was staring at the same blank piece of paper. You've done nothing wrong and everything more than right, if that's possible." After detailing all the right things the airline does, she mock-lamented, "JetBlue, I wanted not to like you but it can't be done—at all. Sincerely, Melissa, Portland, Oregon."

In other Sincerely, JetBlue ads, customers recounted specific service heroics by dedicated JetBlue employees. For example, customer Ann recounted how, when her JetBlue flight was delayed by a snowstorm, the airline eased the long wait by providing pizza and even a live band. "My [three-year-old] son was dancing. I was dancing," she remembers. "It made a horrible experience really nice." And the Steins from Darien, Connecticut, told how they arrived late at night for a family vacation in Florida with their three very tired small children only to learn that their hotel wouldn't take them in. "Out of nowhere we heard a voice from behind us, go ahead, take my room," the Steins recalled. "A superhero in a JetBlue pilot's uniform, who sacrificed his room graciously, saved our night. And we slept like babies. Thank you, JetBlue."

Delighting customers has been good for JetBlue. Last year, the airline reported record revenues of $5.8 billion, up 75 percent in just the past five years, with profits soaring more than sixfold. Even during recent hard economic times, as many competing airlines were cutting routes, retiring aircraft, laying off employees, and losing money, JetBlue was adding planes, expanding into new cities, hiring thousands of new employees, and turning profits.

Perhaps even more important to future success, customers continue to adore their JetBlue. For nine straight years, the customer-centered company has topped the J. D. Power and Associates customer satisfaction rankings among major U.S. airlines. For the past five years, JetBlue has flip-flopped with fellow customer-service champ Southwest Airlines for the airline industry's highest customer loyalty scores in the respected Satmetrix Net Promoter rankings. Every year, more than 60 percent of customers have rated JetBlue 9 or 10 on a 0-to-10-point scale indicating the likelihood that they would recommend JetBlue to others.

So, JetBlue really means it when it tells customers YOU ABOVE ALL. "Above all else," says JetBlue's Customer Bill of Rights, "JetBlue Airways is dedicated to bringing humanity back to air travel. We strive to make every part of your experience as simple and as pleasant as possible." Adds JetBlue's senior VP of marketing: "[YOU ABOVE ALL] gets us back to our DNA, to our original mission."

Sources: "Industry Sector Reports: Airlines," Satmetrix, www.satmetrix.com/expertise/benchmarks-by-industry/travel-and-hospitality/, accessed June 2015; Iris Mansour, "Best in Customer Service," *Fortune*, August 29, 2013, http://money.cnn.com/gallery/technology/2013/08/29/social-media-all-stars.fortune/2.html; March Gunther, "Nothing Blue about JetBlue," *Fortune*, September 3, 2009, http://archive.fortune.com/2009/09/03/news/companies/jetblue_airways_airline.fortune/index.htm; Kevin Randall, "Red, Hot, and Blue: The Hottest American Brand Is Not Apple," *Fast Company*, June 3, 2010, www.fastcompany.com/1656066/red-hot-and-blue-hottest-american-brand-not-apple; Rupal Parekh, "The Newest Marketing Buzzword? Human," *Advertising Age*, September 20, 2013, http://adage.com/print/244261/; "The American Customer Satisfaction Index: Benchmarks by Industry," www.theacsi.org/customer-satisfaction-benchmarks/benchmarks-by-industry, accessed September 2015; and http://experience.jetblue.com/, investor.jetblue.com; and www.jetblue.com/about/, accessed September 2015.

have over-the-top service to create customer delight. For example, no-frills grocery chain ALDI has highly satisfied customers, even though they have to bag their own groceries and can't use credit cards. ALDI's everyday very low pricing on good-quality products delights customers and keeps them coming back. Thus, customer satisfaction comes not just from service heroics but from how well a company delivers on its basic value proposition and helps customers solve their buying problems. "Most customers don't want to be 'wowed,'" says one marketing consultant. "They [just] want an effortless experience."[16]

Although a customer-centered firm seeks to deliver high customer satisfaction relative to competitors, it does not attempt to *maximize* customer satisfaction. A company can always increase customer satisfaction by lowering its prices or increasing its services. But this may result in lower profits. Thus, the purpose of marketing is to generate customer value profitably. This requires a very delicate balance: The marketer must continue to generate more customer value and satisfaction but not "give away the house."

Customer Relationship Levels and Tools

Companies can build customer relationships at many levels, depending on the nature of the target market. At one extreme, a company with many low-margin customers may seek to develop *basic relationships* with them. For example, Procter & Gamble's Tide detergent does not phone or call on all of its consumers to get to know them personally. Instead, Tide creates engagement and relationships through brand-building advertising, Web sites, and social media presence. At the other extreme, in markets with few customers and high margins, sellers want to create *full partnerships* with key customers. For example, P&G sales representatives work closely with Walmart, Kroger, and other large retailers that sell Tide. In between these two extremes, other levels of customer relationships are appropriate.

Beyond offering consistently high value and satisfaction, marketers can use specific marketing tools to develop stronger bonds with customers. For example, many companies offer *frequency marketing programs* that reward customers who buy frequently or in large amounts. Airlines offer frequent-flier programs, hotels give room upgrades to frequent guests, and supermarkets give patronage discounts to "very important customers." These days almost every brand has a loyalty rewards program. However, some innovative loyalty programs go a step beyond the usual. » Consider Walgreens:[17]

Members of Walgreens' Balance Rewards program earn points for in-store or online product purchases, redeemable for purchases in Walgreens stores or online. And members receive surprise offers and giveaways, everything from free movie passes to gift cards. But in line with the chain's mission "to keep our community happy and healthy," the unique Walgreens Balance Rewards program goes beyond just points for purchases. It also includes programs that reward customers for taking steps toward a happy, healthy, well-balanced life. The program has included giving members points for every mile they walk or run, every daily weigh-in as they track their weight, and every prescription and immunization. Walgreens even provides online and mobile tools that help members set healthy goals and track their progress, celebrating their achievements with milestone badges. Thus, the Walgreens Balance Rewards program builds stronger customer relationships and helps the brand by helping customers, befitting the chain's slogan: "Walgreens: At the corner of happy & healthy."

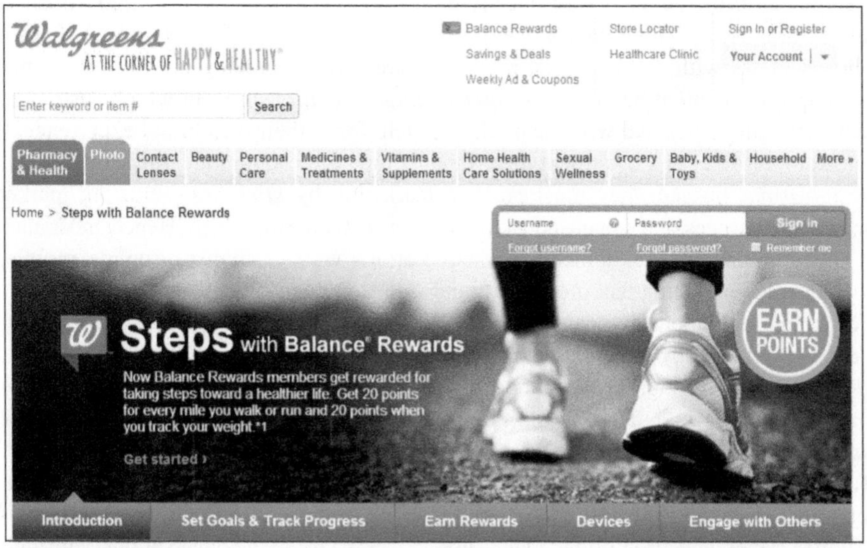

» **Relationship marketing tools: The innovative Walgreens Balance Rewards program builds stronger customer relationships and helps the brand by helping customers, befitting the chain's slogan: "Walgreens: At the corner of happy & healthy."**

Other companies sponsor *club marketing programs* that offer members special benefits and create member communities. For example, Apple encourages customers to form local Apple user groups. More than 800 registered Apple user groups worldwide offer monthly meetings, a newsletter, advice on technical issues, training classes, product discounts, and a forum for swapping ideas and stories with like-minded Apple fans. Similarly, buy a Weber grill and you can join the Weber Nation—"the site for real people who love their Weber grills." Membership gets you exclusive access to online grilling classes, an interactive recipe box, grilling tips and 24/7 telephone support, audio and video podcasts, straight-talk forums for interacting with other grilling fanatics, and even a chance to star in a Weber TV commercial. "Become a spatula-carrying member today," says Weber.[18]

Engaging Customers

Significant changes are occurring in the nature of customer–brand relationships. Today's digital technologies—the Internet and the surge in online, mobile, and social media—have profoundly changed the ways that people on the planet relate to one another. In turn, these events have had a huge impact on how companies and brands connect with customers, and how customers connect with and influence each other's brand behaviors.

Customer Engagement and Today's Digital and Social Media

The digital age has spawned a dazzling set of new customer relationship-building tools, from Web sites, online ads and videos, mobile ads and apps, and blogs to online communities and the major social media, such as Twitter, Facebook, YouTube, Instagram, and Pinterest.

Yesterday's companies focused mostly on mass marketing to broad segments of customers at arm's length. By contrast, today's companies are using online, mobile, and social media to refine their targeting and to engage customers more deeply and interactively. The *old marketing* involved marketing brands *to* consumers. The *new marketing* is **customer-engagement marketing**—fostering direct and continuous customer involvement in shaping brand conversations, brand experiences, and brand community. Customer-engagement marketing goes beyond just selling a brand to consumers. Its goal is to make the brand a meaningful part of consumers' conversations and lives.

Customer-engagement marketing
Making the brand a meaningful part of consumers' conversations and lives by fostering direct and continuous customer involvement in shaping brand conversations, experiences, and community.

The burgeoning Internet and social media have given a huge boost to customer-engagement marketing. Today's consumers are better informed, more connected, and more empowered than ever before. Newly empowered consumers have more information about brands, and they have a wealth of digital platforms for airing and sharing their brand views with others. Thus, marketers are now embracing not only customer relationship management but also *customer-managed relationships,* in which customers connect with companies and with each other to help forge their own brand experiences.

Greater consumer empowerment means that companies can no longer rely on marketing by *intrusion.* Instead, they must practice marketing by *attraction*—creating market offerings and messages that engage consumers rather than interrupt them. Hence, most marketers now combine their mass-media marketing efforts with a rich mix of online, mobile, and social media marketing that promotes brand–consumer engagement and conversation.

For example, companies post their latest ads and videos on social media sites, hoping they'll go viral. They maintain an extensive presence on Twitter, YouTube, Facebook, Google+, Pinterest, Instagram, Vine, and other social media to create brand buzz. They launch their own blogs, mobile apps, online microsites, and consumer-generated review systems, all with the aim of engaging customers on a more personal, interactive level.

Take Twitter, for example. Organizations ranging from Dell, JetBlue, and Dunkin' Donuts to the Chicago Bulls, NASCAR, and the Los Angeles Fire Department have created Twitter pages and promotions. They use "Tweets" to start conversations with and between Twitter's more than 288 million active users, address customer service issues, research customer reactions, and drive traffic to relevant articles, Web and mobile marketing sites, contests, videos, and other brand activities.

Similarly, almost every company has something going on Facebook these days. Starbucks has more than 38 million Facebook "fans"; Coca-Cola has more than 94 million.

And every major marketer has a YouTube channel where the brand and its fans post current ads and other entertaining or informative videos. Instagram, LinkedIn, Pinterest, Snapchat, Vine—all have exploded onto the marketing scene, giving brands more ways to engage and interact with customers. Skilled use of social media can get consumers involved with and talking about a brand.

The key to engagement marketing is to find ways to enter consumers' conversations with engaging and relevant brand messages. Simply posting a humorous video, creating a social media page, or hosting a blog isn't enough. Successful engagement marketing means making relevant and genuine contributions to consumers' lives and interactions. » Consider T-shirt and apparel maker Life is good:[19]

» **Engaging customers: Life is good starts with a deeply felt, engagement-worthy sense of purpose: spreading the power of optimism. Then it creates online and social media tools that let people engage and help co-author the brand's story.**

© WWPhotography/Alamy Stock Photo

For starters, Life is good has an authentic, engagement-worthy sense of purpose: spreading the power of optimism. The brand is about helping people to open up, create relationships, and connect with other people. The company's infectious philosophy is best represented by the "Life is good" slogan itself and by Jake—the familiar beret-wearing, happy-go-lucky stick figure who quickly became a pop-culture icon. Life is good backs its optimism philosophy with good deeds, donating 10 percent of its net profits each year to help kids in need.

Online and social media have become a perfect fit for sharing the Life is good message. Today, the brand fosters a thriving community of Optimists, with more than 2.5 million Facebook fans, 290,000 Twitter followers, 15,300 followers on Instagram, and an active YouTube channel. But the strongest engagement platform is the brand's own Web site, Lifeisgood.com, one of the most active customer-engagement sites found anywhere online. The site's "Live It" section gives brand fans a breath of "fresh share." It's a place where they share photos, videos, and stories showing the brand's role in their trials, triumphs, and optimism. To Life is good, true engagement is about deep meaningful relationships that go beyond the products it is selling. Says Life is good CEO Bert Jacobs: "You can't build a brand on your own; we have entered a world where customers co-author your story."

Consumer-Generated Marketing

Consumer-generated marketing
Brand exchanges created by consumers themselves—both invited and uninvited—by which consumers are playing an increasing role in shaping their own brand experiences and those of other consumers.

A growing form of customer-engagement marketing is **consumer-generated marketing**, by which consumers themselves are playing a bigger role in shaping their own brand experiences and those of others. This might happen through uninvited consumer-to-consumer exchanges in blogs, video-sharing sites, social media, and other digital forums. But increasingly, companies themselves are inviting consumers to play a more active role in shaping products and brand content.

Some companies ask consumers for new product and service ideas. For example, at its My Starbucks Idea site, Starbucks collects ideas from customers on new products, store changes, and just about anything else that might make their Starbucks experience better. "You know better than anyone else what you want from Starbucks," says the company at the Web site. "So tell us. What's your Starbucks idea? Revolutionary or simple—we want to hear it." The site invites customers to share their ideas, vote on and discuss the ideas of others, and see which ideas Starbucks has implemented.[20]

Other companies invite customers to play an active role in shaping ads. For example, for the past nine years, PepsiCo's Doritos brand has held a "Crash the Super Bowl" contest in which it invites 30-second ads from consumers and runs the best ones during the game. The consumer-generated ads have been a huge success. Last year, Doritos opened up the contest to people in all 46 countries where Doritos are sold. From more than 4,900 entries, Doritos aired two fan-produced ads during the Super Bowl. Past campaigns have produced numerous top-place finishers in *USA Today's* AdMeter rankings, earning their creators $1 million in cash prizes from PepsiCo's Frito-Lay division. In the recent campaign, the prizes were instead awarded based on fan votes at Doritos.

com. The winner, "Middle Seat"—a clever ad about a man who uses a bag of Doritos to entice a pretty woman to sit next to him on a plane flight only to find that she has a fussy baby in tow—earned its amateur creators the $1 million plus a "dream job" working at Universal Studios. The homemade commercial cost $2,000 to make and took just four hours to shoot.[21]

Despite the successes, however, harnessing consumer-generated content can be a time-consuming and costly process, and companies may find it difficult to glean even a little gold from all the garbage. Moreover, because consumers have so much control over social media content, inviting their input can sometimes backfire. For example, McDonald's famously launched a Twitter campaign using the hashtag #McDStories, hoping that it would inspire heartwarming stories about Happy Meals. Instead, the effort was hijacked by Twitter users, who turned the hashtag into a "bashtag" by posting less-than-appetizing messages about their bad experiences with the fast-food chain. McDonald's pulled the campaign within only two hours, but the hashtag was still churning weeks, even months later.[22]

As consumers become more connected and empowered, and as the boom in digital and social media technologies continues, consumer brand engagement—whether invited by marketers or not—will be an increasingly important marketing force. Through a profusion of consumer-generated videos, shared reviews, blogs, mobile apps, and Web sites, consumers are playing a growing role in shaping their own and other consumers' brand experiences. Engaged consumers are now having a say in everything from product design, usage, and packaging to brand messaging, pricing, and distribution. Brands must embrace this new consumer empowerment and master the new digital and social media relationship tools or risk being left behind.

Partner Relationship Management

When it comes to creating customer value and building strong customer relationships, today's marketers know that they can't go it alone. They must work closely with a variety of marketing partners. In addition to being good at *customer relationship management,* marketers must also be good at **partner relationship management**—working closely with others inside and outside the company to jointly engage and bring more value to customers.

Partner relationship management
Working closely with partners in other company departments and outside the company to jointly bring greater value to customers.

Traditionally, marketers have been charged with understanding customers and representing customer needs to different company departments. However, in today's more connected world, every functional area in the organization can interact with customers. The new thinking is that—no matter what your job is in a company—you must understand marketing and be customer focused. Rather than letting each department go its own way, firms must link all departments in the cause of creating customer value.

Marketers must also partner with suppliers, channel partners, and others outside the company. Marketing channels consist of distributors, retailers, and others who connect the company to its buyers. The *supply chain* describes a longer channel, stretching from raw materials to components to final products that are carried to final buyers. Through *supply chain management,* companies today are strengthening their connections with partners all along the supply chain. They know that their fortunes rest on more than just how well they perform. Success at delivering customer value rests on how well their entire supply chain performs against competitors' supply chains.

Author Comment
Look back at Figure 1.1. In the first four steps of the marketing process, the company creates value *for* target customers and builds strong relationships with them. If it does that well, it can capture value *from* customers in return, in the form of loyal customers who buy and continue to buy the company's brands.

Capturing Value from Customers

The first four steps in the marketing process outlined in Figure 1.1 involve engaging customers and building customer relationships by creating and delivering superior customer value. The final step involves capturing value in return in the form of sales, market share, and profits. By creating superior customer value, the firm creates highly satisfied customers who stay loyal and buy more. This, in turn, means greater long-run returns for the firm. Here, we discuss the outcomes of creating customer value: customer loyalty and retention, share of market and share of customer, and customer equity.

Creating Customer Loyalty and Retention

Good customer relationship management creates customer satisfaction. In turn, satisfied customers remain loyal and talk favorably to others about the company and its products. Studies show big differences in the loyalty of customers who are less satisfied, somewhat satisfied, and completely satisfied. Even a slight drop from complete satisfaction can create an enormous drop in loyalty. Thus, the aim of customer relationship management is to create not only customer satisfaction but also customer delight.

Customer lifetime value
The value of the entire stream of purchases a customer makes over a lifetime of patronage.

Keeping customers loyal makes good economic sense. Loyal customers spend more and stay around longer. Research also shows that it's five times cheaper to keep an old customer than acquire a new one. Conversely, customer defections can be costly. Losing a customer means losing more than a single sale. It means losing the entire stream of purchases that the customer would make over a lifetime of patronage. For example, here is a classic illustration of **customer lifetime value**:[23]

Customer lifetime value: To keep customers coming back, Stew Leonard's has created the "Disneyland of dairy stores." Rule #1—The customer is always right. Rule #2—If the customer is ever wrong, reread Rule #1.

Courtesy of Stew Leonard's

Stew Leonard, who operates a highly profitable four-store supermarket in Connecticut and New York, once said that he sees $50,000 flying out of his store every time he sees a sulking customer. Why? Because his average customer spends about $100 a week, shops 50 weeks a year, and remains in the area for about 10 years. If this customer has an unhappy experience and switches to another supermarket, Stew Leonard's has lost $50,000 in lifetime revenue. The loss can be much greater if the disappointed customer shares the bad experience with other customers and causes them to defect.

To keep customers coming back, Stew Leonard's has created what has been called the "Disneyland of Dairy Stores," complete with costumed characters, scheduled entertainment, a petting zoo, and animatronics throughout the store. From its humble beginnings as a small dairy store in 1969, Stew Leonard's has grown at an amazing pace. It's built 30 additions onto the original store, which now serves more than 300,000 customers each week. This legion of loyal shoppers is largely a result of the store's passionate approach to customer service. "Rule #1: The customer is always right. Rule #2: If the customer is ever wrong, reread rule #1."

Stew Leonard is not alone in assessing customer lifetime value. Lexus, for example, estimates that a single satisfied and loyal customer is worth more than $600,000 in lifetime sales, and the estimated lifetime value of a Starbucks customer is more than $14,000.[24] In fact, a company can lose money on a specific transaction but still benefit greatly from a long-term relationship. This means that companies must aim high in building customer relationships. Customer delight creates an emotional relationship with a brand, not just a rational preference. And that relationship keeps customers coming back.

Growing Share of Customer

Share of customer
The portion of the customer's purchasing that a company gets in its product categories.

Beyond simply retaining good customers to capture customer lifetime value, good customer relationship management can help marketers increase their **share of customer**—the share they get of the customer's purchasing in their product categories. Thus, banks want to increase "share of wallet." Supermarkets and restaurants want to get more "share of stomach." Car companies want to increase "share of garage," and airlines want greater "share of travel."

To increase share of customer, firms can offer greater variety to current customers. Or they can create programs to cross-sell and up-sell to market more products and services to existing customers. For example, Amazon is highly skilled at leveraging relationships with its 244 million customers to increase its share of each customer's spending budget:[25]

Once they log onto Amazon.com, customers often buy more than they intend, and Amazon does all it can to help make that happen. The online giant continues to broaden its merchandise assortment, creating an ideal spot for one-stop shopping. And based on each customer's purchase and search history, the company recommends related products that might be of interest. This recommendation system influences perhaps a third of all sales. Amazon's ingenious Amazon Prime two-day shipping program has also helped boost its share of customers' wallets. For an annual fee of $99, Prime members receive delivery of all their purchases within two days, whether it's a single paperback book or a 60-inch HDTV. According to one analyst, the ingenious Amazon Prime program "converts casual shoppers, who gorge on the gratification of having purchases reliably appear two days after the order, into Amazon addicts." As a result, Amazon's 40 million Prime customers now account for more than half of its U.S. sales. On average, a Prime customer spends 2.4 times more a non-Prime customer.

Building Customer Equity

We can now see the importance of not only acquiring customers but also keeping and growing them. The value of a company comes from the value of its current and future customers. Customer relationship management takes a long-term view. Companies want to not only create profitable customers but also "own" them for life, earn a greater share of their purchases, and capture their customer lifetime value.

What Is Customer Equity?

Customer equity
The total combined customer lifetime values of all of the company's current and potential customers.

The ultimate aim of customer relationship management is to produce high *customer equity*.[26] **Customer equity** is the total combined customer lifetime values of all of the company's current and potential customers. As such, it's a measure of the future value of the company's customer base. Clearly, the more loyal the firm's profitable customers, the higher its customer equity. Customer equity may be a better measure of a firm's performance than current sales or market share. Whereas sales and market share reflect the past, customer equity suggests the future. >> Consider Cadillac:[27]

In the 1970s and 1980s, Cadillac had some of the most loyal customers in the industry. To an entire generation of car buyers, the name *Cadillac* defined "The Standard of the World." Cadillac's share of the luxury car market reached a whopping 51 percent in 1976, and based on market share and sales, the brand's future looked rosy. However, measures of customer equity would have painted a bleaker picture. Cadillac customers were getting older (average age 60), and average customer lifetime value was falling. Many Cadillac buyers were on their last cars. Thus, although Cadillac's market share was good, its customer equity was not.

Compare this with BMW. Its more youthful and vigorous image didn't win BMW the early market share war. However, it did win BMW younger customers (average age about 40) with higher customer lifetime values. The result: In the years that followed, BMW's market share and profits soared while Cadillac's fortunes eroded badly. BMW overtook Cadillac in the 1980s. In recent years, Cadillac has struggled to make the Caddy cool again with edgier, high-performance designs that target a younger generation of consumers. More recently, the brand has billed itself as "The New Standard of the World" with marketing pitches based on "power, performance, and design," attributes that position it more effectively against the likes of BMW and Audi. Recent ads invite consumers to "Dare Greatly" and "Drive the world forward." However, for the past decade, Cadillac's share of the luxury car market has stagnated. The moral: Marketers should care not just about current sales and market share. Customer lifetime value and customer equity are the name of the game.

>> Managing customer equity: To increase customer equity, Cadillac is making the classic car cool again among younger buyers, encouraging consumers to "Dare Greatly."

General Motors

Building the Right Relationships with the Right Customers

Companies should manage customer equity carefully. They should view customers as assets that need to be managed and maximized. But not all customers, not even all loyal customers, are good investments. Surprisingly, some loyal customers can be unprofitable, and some disloyal customers can be profitable. Which customers should the company acquire and retain?

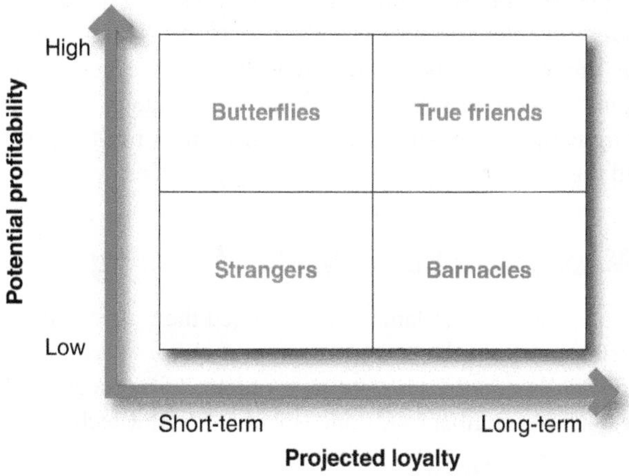

>> Figure 1.5 Customer Relationship Groups

The company can classify customers according to their potential profitability and manage its relationships with them accordingly. **>> Figure 1.5** classifies customers into one of four relationship groups, according to their profitability and projected loyalty.[28] Each group requires a different relationship management strategy. *Strangers* show low potential profitability and little projected loyalty. There is little fit between the company's offerings and their needs. The relationship management strategy for these customers is simple: Don't invest anything in them; make money on every transaction.

Butterflies are potentially profitable but not loyal. There is a good fit between the company's offerings and their needs. However, like real butterflies, we can enjoy them for only a short while and then they're gone. An example is stock market investors who trade shares often and in large amounts but who enjoy hunting out the best deals without building a regular relationship with any single brokerage company. Efforts to convert butterflies into loyal customers are rarely successful. Instead, the company should enjoy the butterflies for the moment. It should create satisfying and profitable transactions with them, capturing as much of their business as possible in the short time during which they buy from the company. Then it should move on and cease investing in them until the next time around.

True friends are both profitable and loyal. There is a strong fit between their needs and the company's offerings. The firm wants to make continuous relationship investments to delight these customers and nurture, retain, and grow them. It wants to turn true friends into *true believers*, who come back regularly and tell others about their good experiences with the company.

Barnacles are highly loyal but not very profitable. There is a limited fit between their needs and the company's offerings. An example is smaller bank customers who bank regularly but do not generate enough returns to cover the costs of maintaining their accounts. Like barnacles on the hull of a ship, they create drag. Barnacles are perhaps the most problematic customers. The company might be able to improve their profitability by selling them more, raising their fees, or reducing service to them. However, if they cannot be made profitable, they should be "fired."

The point here is an important one: Different types of customers require different engagement and relationship management strategies. The goal is to build the *right relationships* with the *right customers.*

LINKING THE CONCEPTS

We've covered a lot of ground. Again, pause for a moment and develop *your own* thoughts about marketing.

- In *your own words*, what *is* marketing and what does it seek to accomplish?
- How well does JetBlue manage its relationships with customers? What customer relationship management strategy does it use? What relationship management strategy does Walmart use?
- Think of a company for which you are a "true friend." What strategy does this company use to manage its relationship with you?

Author Comment

Marketing doesn't take place in a vacuum. Now that we've discussed the five steps in the marketing process, let's look at how the ever-changing marketplace affects both consumers and the marketers who serve them. We'll look more deeply into these and other marketing environment factors in Chapter 3.

The Changing Marketing Landscape

Every day, dramatic changes are occurring in the marketplace. Richard Love of HP observed, "The pace of change is so rapid that the ability to change has now become a competitive advantage." Yogi Berra, the legendary New York Yankees catcher and manager, summed it up more simply when he said, "The future ain't what it used to be." As the marketplace changes, so must those who serve it.

In this section, we examine the major trends and forces that are changing the marketing landscape and challenging marketing strategy. We look at five major developments: the digital age, the changing economic environment, the growth of not-for-profit marketing, rapid globalization, and the call for sustainable marketing practices.

The Digital Age: Online, Mobile, and Social Media Marketing

The explosive growth in digital technology has fundamentally changed the way we live—how we communicate, share information, access entertainment, and shop. More than 3 billion people—42 percent of the world's population—are now online; 58 percent of all American adults own smartphones. These numbers will only grow as digital technology rockets into the future.[29]

Most consumers are totally smitten with all things digital. For example, according to one study, 44 percent of Americans keep their mobile phone next to them when they sleep—they say it's the first thing they touch when they get up in the morning and the last thing they touch at night. In just the past few years, people in the United States averaged more time per day with digital media (5.25 hours) than viewing traditional TV (4.5 hours).[30]

Digital and social media marketing Using digital marketing tools such as Web sites, social media, mobile apps and ads, online video, email, and blogs to engage consumers anywhere, at any time, via their digital devices.

The consumer love affair with digital and mobile technology makes it fertile ground for marketers trying to engage customers. So it's no surprise that the Internet and rapid advances in digital and social media have taken the marketing world by storm. **Digital and social media marketing** involves using digital marketing tools such as Web sites, social media, mobile ads and apps, online video, email, blogs, and other digital platforms to engage consumers anywhere, anytime via their computers, smartphones, tablets, Internet-ready TVs, and other digital devices. These days, it seems that every company is reaching out to customers with multiple Web sites, newsy Tweets and Facebook pages, viral ads and videos posted on YouTube, rich-media emails, and mobile apps that solve consumer problems and help them shop.

At the most basic level, marketers set up company and brand Web sites that provide information and promote the company's products. Many companies also set up branded community sites, where customers can congregate and exchange brand-related interests and information. For example, Petco's Pet Talk Place site is a place where pet lovers can "connect, share, and learn" via discussions boards dedicated to dogs ("the bark"), cats ("the purr"), fish ("the splash"), birds ("the chirp"), reptiles ("the hiss"), and other types of pets. At cosmetics seller Sephora's Beauty Talk community site, like-minded members discuss, debate, and compare makeup, hair, fragrance, or skin care products to find the best match for them. And Sony's GreatnessAwaits.com site serves as a social hub for PlayStation PS4 game enthusiasts. It's a place where fans can follow social media posts about PS4, watch the latest PS4 videos, discover which PS4 games are trending on social networks, share content, and interact with other fans—all in real time. To date, GreatnessAwaits.com has earned more than 4.5 million page views, curated more than 3.3 million pieces of social content, and featured 75,000 fans.[31]

Beyond brand Web sites, most companies are also integrating social and mobile media into their marketing mixes.

Social Media Marketing

It's hard to find a brand Web site, or even a traditional media ad, that doesn't feature links to the brand's Facebook, Twitter, Google+, LinkedIn, YouTube, Instagram, Pinterest, or other social media sites. Social media provide exciting opportunities to extend customer engagement and get people talking about a brand. More than 90 percent of all U.S. companies now use social media as part of their marketing mixes, and 71 percent believe that social marketing is core to their business.[32]

Some social media are huge—Facebook has more than 1.2 billion active monthly members. Twitter has more than 232 million active users; Pinterest draws in 53 million users; and Instagram racks up an estimated 300 million active monthly visitors. Reddit, the online social news community, has nearly 174 million unique visitors each month from 185 countries. But more focused social media sites are also thriving, such as CafeMom, an online community of 20 million moms who exchange advice, entertainment, and commiseration at the community's online, Facebook, Twitter, Pinterest, YouTube, Google+, and mobile sites.

Online social media provide a digital home where people can connect and share important information and moments in their lives. As a result, they offer an ideal platform for *real-time marketing,* by which marketers can engage consumers in the moment by linking brands to important trending topics, real-world events, causes, personal occasions, or other important happenings in consumers' lives (see Marketing at Work 1.2).

Using social media might involve something as simple as a contest or promotion to garner Facebook Likes, Tweets, or YouTube postings. But more often these days, large organizations of all kinds use a wide range of carefully integrated social media. >> For example, space agency NASA uses a broad mix of social media to educate the next generation of space explorers on its mission to "boldly go where no man has gone before." In all, NASA has more than 480 social media accounts spanning various topics and digital platforms. The agency has more than 10 million Facebook fans, 9 million Twitter followers, 2.5 million Instagram followers, and 30,000 YouTube subscribers. One of NASA's largest-ever social media campaigns supported the recent test launch of the Orion spacecraft, which will eventually carry humans to deep space destinations, such as Mars or an asteroid:[33]

> The extensive campaign included a dozen or more YouTube "I'm On Board" videos starring actors from classic science-fiction TV shows, such as *Star Trek* and *The Incredible Hulk.* Even *Sesame Street*'s Elmo added his support, proudly displaying his "I'm On Board" boarding pass, chatting up astronauts, and relaying facts and launch information on the *Sesame Street* Twitter feed and other digital platforms. The campaign offered social media users a chance to put their names on a microchip aboard the space vehicle—more than a million people signed on. During the flight, NASA's social media team briefed the public through Twitter, Facebook, and Instagram posts. In all, it's a new NASA. People once followed NASA events from afar by gathering around their TV sets. Not anymore. Now, the space agency engages fans directly through interactive social media. "You can ask an astronaut a question," says NASA's social media manager. "You can...really be part of the experience in a much different way than ever before. It's not your father and grandfather's space agency anymore.

>> **NASA uses an extensive array of social media to engage and educate the next generation of space explorers. The agency invites you to "follow, share, and be a part of the conversation on popular social media sites with NASA."**
NASA

Mobile Marketing

Mobile marketing is perhaps the fastest-growing digital marketing platform. Four out of five smartphone users use their phones to shop—browsing product information through apps or the mobile Web, making in-store price comparisons, reading online product reviews, finding and redeeming coupons, and more.[34] Smartphones are ever present, always on, finely targeted, and highly personal. This makes them ideal for engaging customers anytime, anywhere as they move through the buying process. For example, Starbucks customers can use their mobile devices for everything from finding the nearest Starbucks and learning about new products to placing and paying for orders.

MARKETING AT WORK 1.2

Real-Time Marketing: Engaging Consumers in the Moment

A funny thing happened during Super Bowl XLVII in New Orleans. Early in the third quarter, the lights in the Mercedes-Benz Superdome suddenly went out. As 71,000 attendees and 106 million viewers restlessly bided their time and scratched their heads, engineers worked feverishly for a full 34 minutes to repair the power outage and bring the lights back on. But whereas the blackout was a disaster for Superdome management and CBS Sports, and an annoyance for players and fans, at least one marketer saw it as an opportunity. Shortly after the blackout began, Nabisco's Oreo brand tweeted out a simple message: "Power out? No problem. You can still dunk in the dark."

That now-famous single tweet, conceived and approved within just minutes, grabbed more attention for Oreo than the brand's extravagant first-quarter advertisement. Within an hour, the "dunk in the dark" message was retweeted nearly 16,000 times and racked up more than 20,000 Facebook likes, resulting in tens of millions of favorable exposures. In the following days, Oreo received tons of media coverage and was hailed as "The Brand That Won the Blackout Bowl." Those were pretty impressive results for a one-off joke by a cookie maker.

Oreo's successful Super Bowl one-liner triggered a surge in real-time marketing, and to this day it's hailed as the model for real-time success. Brands of all kinds are now trying to create their own "Oreo moments" by aligning marketing content with real-world events and trending topics through timely tweets, videos, blog entries, and social media posts. Done right, real-time marketing can engage consumers in the moment and make the brand more relevant.

Done poorly, however, real-time engagements can come off as little more than awkward or inappropriate intrusions. Too often, brands simply toss standalone, last-minute ads or messages into social channels, "hoping to catch lightning in a bottle." But hastily prepared or self-serving real-time messages can easily backfire, painting the brand as opportunistic or out of touch.

For example, after a video went viral showing Baltimore Ravens running back Ray Rice knocking his then-fiancée unconscious, thousands of women took to Twitter to discuss abusive relationships, referencing the hashtags #WhyIStayed and #WhyILeft. Jumping into the trending discussion, frozen pizza maker DiGiorno added three words: "#WhyIStayed You had pizza." As might be expected, the Twittersphere lit up with disgust at the insensitive pitch, leaving the number-one frozen pizza brand scrambling to explain itself. The best response it could muster was a feeble, "A million apologies. Did not read what the hashtag was about before posting."

Today, many real-time marketing efforts center on major media events, such as the Super Bowl, the Grammys, and the Academy Awards. These events let marketers engage huge, ready-made audiences. For example, when its blockbuster feature *The LEGO Movie* failed to win a nomination in the Best Animated Movie category at the recent Oscars, LEGO turned the snub into an opportunity to engage viewers in real time during the Academy Awards TV spectacular. During a performance of the movie's Oscar-nominated song—"Everything Is Awesome"—performers handed out Oscars made of golden LEGO bricks to celebrities in the audience. Simultaneously, the brand tweeted coordinated real-time images and the message "#EverythingIsAwesome at the #Oscars!" With pictures of stars such as Meryl Streep, Clint Eastwood, Oprah Winfrey, and Bradley Cooper posing with their LEGO Oscars, #LegoOscar became the number-one trending topic on Twitter.

Others companies attached real-time efforts to events in the competitive or natural environments. For example, with each new Apple iPhone model, at the very same time that Apple executives are on stage unveiling the features of the new phone, Samsung marketers are flooding social media with clever real-time "The next best thing is already here" responses. Starbucks, a social media powerhouse with nearly 36 million Facebook fans and more than 7 million Twitter followers, has long used real-time marketing to link the brand to current events important to its customers. For example, after Winter Storm Nemo hit the northeastern United States with heavy snowfall and hurricane-force winds in early 2013, Starbucks

» Real-time marketing: Oreo's spectacularly successful "You can still dunk in the dark" tweet triggered a surge in real-time marketing, as brands of all kinds are now trying to create their own "Oreo moments" by aligning marketing content with real-world events and trending topics.

© Isabella Cassini/Alamy

Twitter and Facebook promotions offered "Snow Day" free coffee to customers in affected areas. "We wanted to make a grand [and timely] gesture," said a Starbucks digital marketer.

Minute-by-minute marketing strikes rarely succeed. Instead, to be consistently successful, real-time marketing must be part of a broader, carefully conceived strategy that makes the brand itself an engaging and relevant part of consumers' lives. According to one marketing strategist, brands must "evolve their entire plan to marketing in a real-time world." Today's smartphone-wielding, social media–saturated customers "are no longer just second-screen *viewing*—they are second-screen *living*." Smart brands build agile, ongoing real-time marketing programs that listen in on the social space and respond with relevant marketing content that blends smoothly with the dynamics of customers' real-time social sharing.

For example, although the Oreo "dunk in the dark" tweet might have seemed off the cuff, it was only the latest in a long series of real-time marketing efforts designed to make Oreo a part of consumers' daily discourse. In the months preceding the Super Bowl, Oreo had successfully carried out its "Daily Twist" campaign. Each day for 100 days, the brand posted consumer-inspired Oreo cookie art tied to a relevant event. There was a Mars Rover Landing Oreo (an open-face cookie with tire tracks through its red crème filling), an Elvis Week Oreo (with an Oreo profile of The King of Rock'n' Roll), and a Shark Week Oreo (with a jagged bite taken out of it, of course). The groundbreaking Daily Twist campaign gave Oreo a fourfold increase in Facebook shares and boosted its Instagram following from 2,200 to more than 85,000.

Oreo wages an ongoing social media and mobile campaign to engage consumers in the moment, skillfully injecting the brand into consumers' lives and conversations. For example, there was the wildly popular "Twist, Lick, Dunk" mobile game app that had 4 million users dunking 4 billion virtual Oreo cookies. Then there was the catchy 90-second "Oreo Cookie Balls" rap video, tweeted and posted on YouTube and other social media, showing clever ideas for eating and serving cookie balls during the end-of-year holiday season—it quickly went viral with more than 1.6 million views on YouTube alone. And leading up to a recent Halloween season, Oreo Laboratorium, a series of brief stop-motion videos, showed different Oreo creatures and asked fans to "Name the Nomster." Such gems illustrate how Oreo keeps itself smack dab in the middle of the consumer consciousness by making real-time marketing an everyday event.

Whether connected to a social cause, a trending topic or event, a consumer's personal situation, or something else, the essential concept behind successful real-time marketing is pretty simple: Find or create ongoing connections between the brand and what's happening and important in consumers' lives, then engage consumers genuinely in the moment. One marketing executive suggests that real-time marketers should equate the practice to "meeting somebody in a social gathering—you don't accost them, instead you try to find a commonality of interest."

Sources: Georgia Christopher Heine, "Ads in Real Time, All the Time," *Adweek*, February 18, 2013, p. 9; David Griner, "DiGiorno Is Really, Really Sorry about Its Tweet Accidentally Making Light of Domestic Violence," *Adweek*, September 9, 2014, www.adweek.com/print/159998; Danielle Sacks, "The Story of Oreo: How an Old Cookie Became a Modern Marketing Personality," *Fast Company*, October 23, 2014, www.fastcocreate.com/3037068; Christopher Palmeri, "'Lego Movie' Picks Up Tweets Not Trophies at Academy Awards," *Businessweek*, February 23, 2015, www.bloomberg.com/news/articles/2015-02-23/lego-movie-picks-up-tweets-not-trophies-at-academy-awards-show; and www.360i.com/work/oreo-daily-twist/ and https://twitter.com/oreo/status/298246571718483968, accessed September 2015.

Mobile marketing: Redbox uses mobile marketing to engage its customers, personalize its service, and promote DVD rentals. Its "The 10 Days of Deals" mobile campaign generated nearly 1.5 million text messages, resulting in more than 200,000 new Redbox Text Club members.

AP Images for Redbox

Marketers use mobile channels to stimulate immediate buying, make shopping easier, enrich the brand experience, or all of these. Consider Redbox:[35]

> Redbox DVD rental kiosks are unmanned, so the company has to find innovative ways to engage customers and personalize its service—most of which it does through its Web site and mobile app, text messaging, and email. Customers can use the Redbox mobile app to locate Redbox kiosks, check availability of movies and games, and reserve rentals for quick pickup. Mobile customers can also join the Redbox Text Club to receive texts about the latest Redbox news, releases, and members-only deals. Text Club members are Redbox's most valuable customers, so the company launched a 10-day-long mobile marketing campaign to increase membership. Using large call-to-action stickers on kiosks, a blast of email, and posts on its Facebook and other social media pages, Redbox offered discounts of between 10 cents and $1.50 on the next DVD rental to customers who texted the word "DEALS" to 727272.The campaign—called "The 10 Days of Deals"—generated nearly 1.5 million text messages from some 400,000 customers, resulting in more than 200,000 new Text Club members. "Mobile is like having a kiosk in your hand," explains Redbox's chief marketer. "It's an incredibly important part of our [marketing] strategy."

Although online, social media, and mobile marketing offer huge potential, most marketers are still learning how to use them effectively. The key is to blend the new digital approaches with traditional marketing to create a smoothly integrated marketing strategy and mix. We will examine digital, mobile, and social media marketing throughout the text—they touch almost every area of marketing strategy and tactics. Then, after we've covered the marketing basics, we'll look more deeply into digital and direct marketing in Chapter 14.

The Changing Economic Environment

The Great Recession of 2008 to 2009 and its aftermath hit American consumers hard. After two decades of overspending, new economic realities forced consumers to bring their consumption back in line with their incomes and rethink their buying priorities.

In today's post-recession era, consumer incomes and spending are again on the rise. However, even as the economy has strengthened, rather than reverting to their old free-spending ways, Americans are now showing an enthusiasm for frugality not seen in decades. Sensible consumption has made a comeback, and it appears to be here to stay. The new consumer spending values emphasize simpler living and more value for the dollar. Despite their rebounding means, consumers continue to buy less, clip more coupons, swipe their credit cards less, and put more in the bank.

Many consumers are reconsidering their very definition of the good life. "People are finding happiness in old-fashioned virtues—thrift, savings, do-it-yourself projects, self-improvement, hard work, faith, and community," says one consumer behavior expert. "We are moving from mindless to mindful consumption."[36] The new, more frugal spending values don't mean that people have resigned themselves to lives of deprivation. As the economy has improved, consumers are again indulging in luxuries and bigger-ticket purchases, just more sensibly.

In response, companies in all industries—from discounters such as Target to luxury brands such as Lexus—have realigned their marketing strategies with the new economic realities. More than ever, marketers are emphasizing the *value* in their value propositions. They are focusing on value for the money, practicality, and durability in their product offerings and marketing pitches.

For example, for years discount retailer Target focused increasingly on the "Expect More" side of its "Expect More. Pay Less." value proposition. Its carefully cultivated "upscale-discounter" image successfully differentiated it from Walmart's more hard-nosed "lowest-price" position. But when the economy soured, many consumers worried that Target's trendier assortments and hip marketing also meant higher prices. So Target has shifted its balance more toward the "Pay Less" half of the slogan, making certain that its prices are in line with Walmart's and that customers know it. Although still trendy, Target's marketing now emphasizes more practical price and savings appeals. Offering "more for your money" holds a prominent place in the Target mission. "We think a lot about your budget and how to give you the best value every time you shop with us," says the company.[37]

In adjusting to the new economy, companies may be tempted to cut their marketing budgets and slash prices in an effort to coax more frugal customers into opening their wallets. However, although cutting costs and offering selected discounts can be important marketing tactics, smart marketers understand that making cuts in the wrong places can damage long-term brand images and customer relationships. The challenge is to balance the brand's value proposition with the current times while also enhancing its long-term equity. Thus, rather than slashing prices in uncertain economic times, many marketers hold the line on prices and instead explain why their brands are worth it.

The Growth of Not-for-Profit Marketing

In recent years, marketing has also become a major part of the strategies of many not-for-profit organizations, such as colleges, hospitals, museums, zoos, symphony orchestras, foundations, and even churches. The nation's not-for-profits face stiff competition for support and membership. Sound marketing can help them attract membership, funds, and support.

For example, Alex's Lemonade Stand Foundation is a not-for-profit organization with a special mission: "Fighting childhood cancer, one cup at a time." It all started with a simple lemonade stand, run by four-year-old Alexandra "Alex" Scott, who was battling cancer. Alex wanted to raise money for doctors so that they could "help other kids, like they helped me." In its first summer, little Alex's lemonade stand raised $2,000. By age 8, with the help of founding sponsor Volvo and a nationwide network of volunteer-held lemonade stands, Alex had raised $1 million for pediatric cancer research. Although Alex has passed away, Alex's Lemonade Stand Foundation (ALSF) keeps her dream alive through a comprehensive marketing effort:[38]

>> Alex's Lemonade Stand Foundation's marketing revolves around a well-designed Web site (www.AlexsLemonade.org), which details the organization, its mission, sponsored research, a logo gifts and gear store, and special events such as National Lemonade Days, the Great Chefs Event, and Alex's Million Mile—Run, Walk, Ride. The site also gives detailed instructions for holding a successful local lemonade stand, backed by a fundraising kit containing ALSF-branded banners, signs, posters, and flyers. ALSF makes good use of social media. Its blog discusses issues of childhood cancer and shares stories about ALSF "heroes and amazing supporters." And its well-curated Facebook, Instagram, Twitter, YouTube, Pinterest, and LinkedIn sites have created an active community of dedicated fans.

Finally, ALSF has assembled a network of corporate marketing partners—from Volvo, Northwestern Mutual, and Toys "R" Us to Applebee's, Rita's Italian Ice, and A&P. For example, at Applebee's, if you donate to ALSF, you get a coupon for a free kid's meal or frozen lemonade. At Rita's, you can buy a paper lemon for $1 or text to a number to donate $5. Volvo holds raffles for new cars, with all proceeds going to ALSF. Northwestern Mutual supports ALSF's Family Travel Fund, which pays for gasoline and other expenses to help families get their children to and from treatment. Thus, Alex's one lemonade stand sparked a foundation that effectively markets her cause to raise funds to fight childhood cancer. Since 2005, Alex's Lemonade Stand Foundation has raised more than $100 million and funded more than 475 medical research projects.

>> Not-for-profit marketing: Alex's Lemonade Stand Foundation (ALSF) effectively markets its mission of "Fighting childhood cancer, one cup at a time." ALSF has raised more than $100 million for pediatric cancer research.

Alex's Lemonade Stand Foundation for Childhood Cancer

Government agencies have also shown an increased interest in marketing. For example, the U.S. military has a marketing plan to attract recruits to its different services, and various government agencies are now designing social marketing campaigns to encourage energy conservation and concern for the environment or discourage smoking, illegal drug use, and obesity. Even the once-stodgy U.S. Postal Service has developed innovative marketing to sell commemorative stamps, promote its Priority Mail services, and lift its image as a contemporary and competitive organization. In all, the U.S. government is the nation's 39th largest advertiser, with an annual advertising budget of more than $980 million.[39]

Rapid Globalization

As they are redefining their customer relationships, marketers are also taking a fresh look at the ways in which they relate with the broader world around them. Today, almost every company, large or small, is touched in some way by global competition. A neighborhood florist buys its flowers from Mexican nurseries, and a large U.S. electronics manufacturer competes in its home markets with giant Korean rivals. A fledgling Internet retailer finds itself receiving orders from all over the world at the same time that an American consumer goods producer introduces new products into emerging markets abroad.

American firms have been challenged at home by the skillful marketing of European and Asian multinationals. Companies such as Toyota, Nestlé, and Samsung have often outperformed their U.S. competitors in American markets. Similarly, U.S. companies in a wide range of industries have developed truly global operations, making and selling their products worldwide. Quintessentially American McDonald's now serves 70 million customers daily in more than 36,000 local restaurants in more than 100 countries worldwide—68 percent of its corporate revenues come from outside the United States. Similarly, Nike markets in 190 countries, with non-U.S. sales accounting for 52 percent of its worldwide sales.[40] Today, companies are not just selling more of their locally produced goods in international markets; they are also sourcing more supplies and components abroad and developing new products for specific markets around the world.

Thus, managers in countries around the world are increasingly taking a global, not just local, view of the company's industry, competitors, and opportunities. They are asking: What is global marketing? How does it differ from domestic marketing? How do global competitors and forces affect our business? To what extent should we "go global"? We will discuss the global marketplace in more detail in Chapter 15.

Sustainable Marketing—The Call for More Environmental and Social Responsibility

Marketers are reexamining their relationships with social values and responsibilities and with the very Earth that sustains us. As the worldwide consumerism and environmentalism movements mature, today's marketers are being called on to develop *sustainable marketing* practices. Corporate ethics and social responsibility have become hot topics for almost every business. And few companies can ignore the renewed and very demanding environmental movement. Every company action can affect customer relationships. Today's customers expect companies to deliver value in a socially and environmentally responsible way.

The social responsibility and environmental movements will place even stricter demands on companies in the future. Some companies resist these movements, budging only when forced by legislation or organized consumer outcries. Forward-looking companies, however, readily accept their responsibilities to the world around them. They view sustainable marketing as an opportunity to do well by doing good. They seek ways to profit by serving immediate needs and the best long-run interests of their customers and communities.

Some companies, such as Patagonia, Timberland, Method, Ben & Jerry's, and others, practice *caring capitalism*, setting themselves apart by being civic minded and responsible. They build social and environmental responsibility into their company value and mission statements. »For example, Ben & Jerry's, a division of Unilever, has long prided itself on being a "values-led business," one that creates "linked prosperity" for everyone connected to the brand—from suppliers to employees to customers and communities:[41]

» Sustainable marketing: Ben & Jerry's three-part "linked prosperity" mission drives it to make fantastic ice cream (product mission), manage the company for sustainable financial growth (economic mission), and use the company "in innovative ways to make the world a better place" (social mission).

© ZUMA Press, Inc/Alamy

> Under its three-part mission, Ben & Jerry's wants to make fantastic ice cream (product mission), manage the company for sustainable financial growth (economic mission), and use the company "in innovative ways to make the world a better place" (social mission). Ben & Jerry's backs its mission with actions. For example, the company is committed to using wholesome, natural, non-GMO, fair-trade-certified ingredients and buys

from local farms. It employs business practices "that respect the earth and the environment," investing in wind energy, solar usage, travel offsets, and carbon neutrality. Its Caring Dairy program helps farmers develop more sustainable practices on the farm ("Caring Dairy means happy cows, happy farmers, and a happy planet"). The Ben & Jerry's Foundation awards nearly $2 million annually in grassroots grants to community service organizations and projects in communities across the nation. Ben & Jerry's also operates 14 PartnerShops, scoop shops that are independently owned and operated by community-based not-for-profit organizations. The company waives standard franchise fees for these shops.

Sustainable marketing presents both opportunities and challenges for marketers.

Author Comment
Remember Figure 1.1 outlining the marketing process? Now, based on everything we've discussed in this chapter, we'll expand that figure to provide a road map for learning marketing throughout the remainder of the text.

So, What Is Marketing? Pulling It All Together

At the start of this chapter, Figure 1.1 presented a simple model of the marketing process. Now that we've discussed all the steps in the process, **>> Figure 1.6** presents an expanded model that will help you pull it all together. What is marketing? Simply put, marketing is the process of engaging customers and building profitable customer relationships by creating value for customers and capturing value in return.

The first four steps of the marketing process focus on creating value for customers. The company first gains a full understanding of the marketplace by researching customer needs and managing marketing information. It then designs a customer-driven marketing strategy based on the answers to two simple questions. The first question is "What

This expanded version of Figure 1.1 at the beginning of the chapter provides a good road map for the rest of the text. The underlying concept of the entire text is that marketing creates value for customers in order to capture value from customers in return.

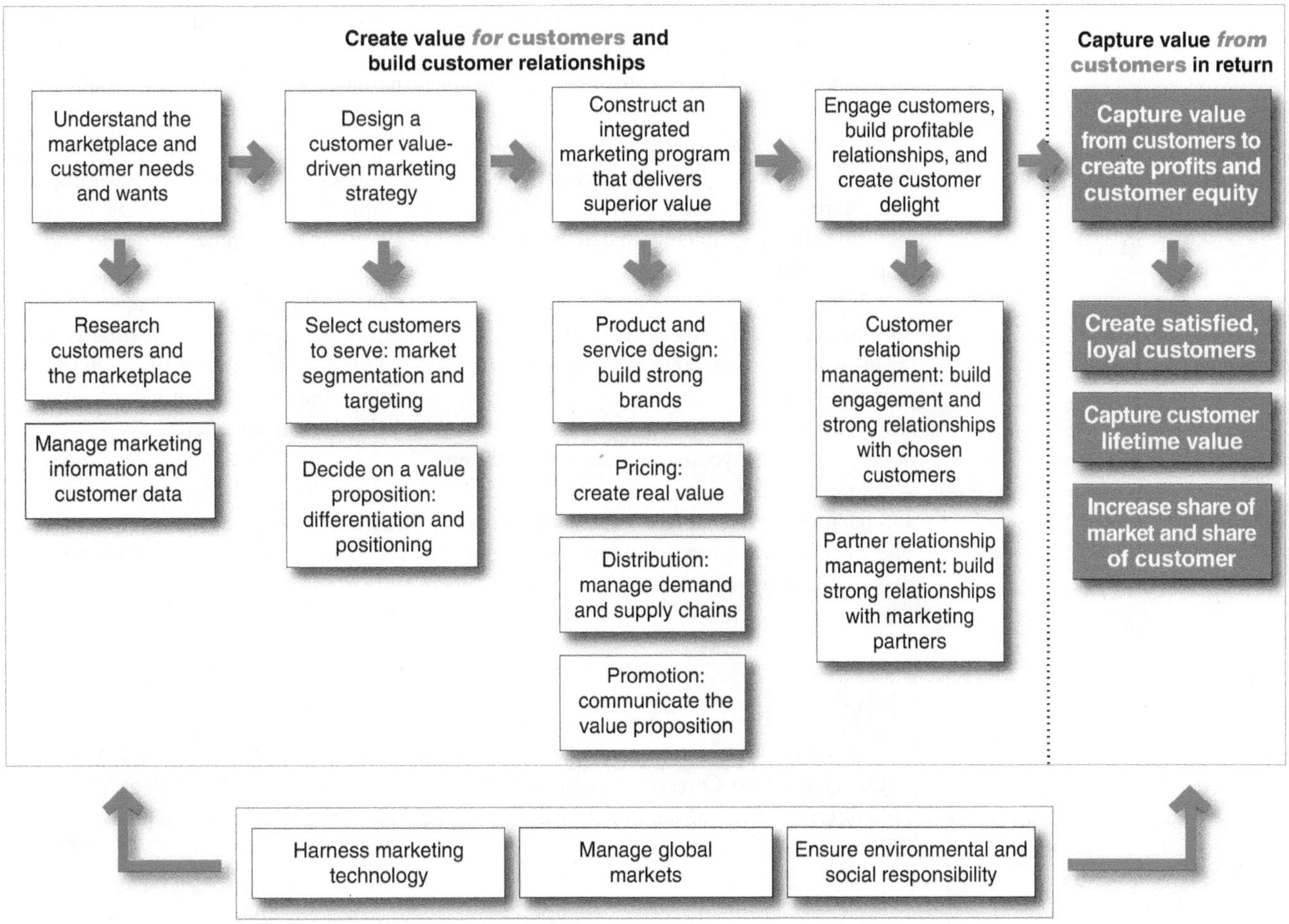

>> Figure 1.6 An Expanded Model of the Marketing Process

consumers will we serve?" (market segmentation and targeting). Good marketing companies know that they cannot serve all customers in every way. Instead, they need to focus their resources on the customers they can serve best and most profitably. The second marketing strategy question is "How can we best serve targeted customers?" (differentiation and positioning). Here, the marketer outlines a value proposition that spells out what values the company will deliver to win target customers.

With its marketing strategy chosen, the company now constructs an integrated marketing program—consisting of a blend of the four marketing mix elements, the four *P*s—that transforms the marketing strategy into real value for customers. The company develops product offers and creates strong brand identities for them. It prices these offers to create real customer value and distributes the offers to make them available to target consumers. Finally, the company designs promotion programs that engage target customers, communicate the value proposition, and persuade customers to act on the market offering.

Perhaps the most important step in the marketing process involves building value-laden, profitable relationships with target customers. Throughout the process, marketers practice customer relationship management to create customer satisfaction and delight. They engage customers in the process of creating brand conversations, experiences, and community. In creating customer value and relationships, however, the company cannot go it alone. It must work closely with marketing partners both inside the company and throughout its marketing system. Thus, beyond practicing good customer relationship management and customer-engagement marketing, firms must also practice good partner relationship management.

The first four steps in the marketing process create value *for* customers. In the final step, the company reaps the rewards of its strong customer relationships by capturing value *from* customers. Delivering superior customer value creates highly satisfied customers who will buy more and buy again. This helps the company capture customer lifetime value and greater share of customer. The result is increased long-term customer equity for the firm.

Finally, in the face of today's changing marketing landscape, companies must take into account three additional factors. In building customer and partner relationships, they must harness marketing technologies in the new digital age, take advantage of global opportunities, and ensure that they act sustainably in an environmentally and socially responsible way.

Figure 1.6 provides a good road map to future chapters of this text. Chapters 1 and 2 introduce the marketing process, with a focus on building customer relationships and capturing value from customers. Chapters 3 through 5 address the first step of the marketing process—understanding the marketing environment, managing marketing information, and understanding consumer and business buyer behavior. In Chapter 6, we look more deeply into the two major marketing strategy decisions: selecting which customers to serve (segmentation and targeting) and determining a value proposition (differentiation and positioning). Chapters 7 through 14 discuss the marketing mix variables one by one. The final two chapters examine special marketing considerations: global marketing and sustainable marketing.

MyMarketingLab

If assigned by your instructor, complete the questions marked with the ✪ from the EOC Discussion Questions section in the MyLab. To complete the Marketing by the Numbers problems found in this section, go to your Assignments in the MyLab.

REVIEWING AND EXTENDING THE CONCEPTS

CHAPTER REVIEW AND CRITICAL THINKING

Objectives Review

Today's successful companies—whether large or small, for-profit or not-for-profit, domestic or global—share a strong customer focus and a heavy commitment to marketing. The goal of marketing is to engage customers and manage profitable customer relationships.

OBJECTIVE 1-1 Define marketing and outline the steps in the marketing process. (pp 4–5)

Marketing is the process by which companies create value for customers and build strong customer relationships in order to capture value from customers in return. The marketing process involves five steps. The first four steps create value *for* customers. First, marketers need to understand the marketplace and customer needs and wants. Next, marketers design a customer-driven marketing strategy with the goal of getting, engaging, and growing target customers. In the third step, marketers construct a marketing program that actually delivers superior value. All of these steps form the basis for the fourth step: engaging customers, building profitable customer relationships, and creating customer delight. In the final step, the company reaps the rewards of strong customer relationships by capturing value *from* customers.

OBJECTIVE 1-2 Explain the importance of understanding the marketplace and customers and identify the five core marketplace concepts. (pp 6–8)

Outstanding marketing companies go to great lengths to learn about and understand their customers' *needs, wants,* and *demands.* This understanding helps them to design want-satisfying market offerings and build value-laden customer relationships by which they can capture *customer lifetime value* and greater *share of customer.* The result is increased long-term *customer equity* for the firm.

The core marketplace concepts are needs, wants, and demands; market offerings (products, services, and experiences); value and satisfaction; exchange and relationships; and markets. Companies address needs, wants, and demands by putting forth a value proposition, a set of benefits that they promise to consumers to satisfy their needs. The value proposition is fulfilled through a market offering, which delivers customer value and satisfaction, resulting in long-term exchange relationships with customers.

OBJECTIVE 1-3 Identify the key elements of a customer value-driven marketing strategy and discuss the marketing management orientations that guide marketing strategy. (pp 9–13)

To design a winning marketing strategy, the company must first decide whom it will serve. It does this by dividing the market into segments of customers (*market segmentation*) and selecting which segments it will cultivate (*target marketing*). Next, the company must decide *how* it will serve targeted customers (how it will *differentiate and position* itself in the marketplace).

Marketing management can adopt one of five competing market orientations. The *production concept* holds that management's task is to improve production efficiency and bring down prices. The *product concept* holds that consumers favor products that offer the most in quality, performance, and innovative features; thus, little promotional effort is required. The *selling concept* holds that consumers will not buy enough of an organization's products unless it undertakes a large-scale selling and promotion effort. The *marketing concept* holds that achieving organizational goals depends on determining the needs and wants of target markets and delivering the desired satisfactions more effectively and efficiently than competitors do. The *societal marketing concept* holds that generating customer satisfaction *and* long-run societal well-being through sustainable marketing strategies is key to both achieving the company's goals and fulfilling its responsibilities.

OBJECTIVE 1-4 Discuss customer relationship management and identify strategies for creating value *for* customers and capturing value *from* customers in return. (pp 13–23)

Broadly defined, *customer relationship management* is the process of engaging customers and building and maintaining profitable customer relationships by delivering superior customer value and satisfaction. *Customer-engagement marketing* aims to make a brand a meaningful part of consumers' conversations and lives through direct and continuous customer involvement in shaping brand conversations, experiences, and community. The aim of customer relationship management and customer engagement is to produce high *customer equity,* the total combined customer lifetime values of all of the company's customers. The key to building lasting relationships is the creation of superior *customer value* and *satisfaction.* In return for creating value *for* targeted customers, the company captures value *from* customers in the form of profits and customer equity.

OBJECTIVE 1-5 Describe the major trends and forces that are changing the marketing landscape in this age of relationships. (pp 24–31)

Dramatic changes are occurring in the marketing arena. The digital age has created exciting new ways to learn about and relate to individual customers. As a result, advances in digital and social media have taken the marketing world by storm. Online, mobile, and social media marketing offer exciting new opportunities to target customers more selectively and engage them more deeply. The key is to blend the new digital approaches with traditional marketing to create a smoothly integrated marketing strategy and mix.

The Great Recession caused consumers to rethink their buying priorities and bring their consumption back in line with their incomes. Even as the post-recession economy has strengthened, Americans are now showing an enthusiasm for frugality not seen in decades. The challenge is to balance a brand's value proposition with current times while also enhancing its long-term equity.

In recent years, marketing has become a major part of the strategies for many not-for-profit organizations, such as colleges, hospitals, museums, zoos, symphony orchestras, foundations, and even churches. Also, in an increasingly smaller world, many marketers are now connected *globally* with their customers, marketing partners, and competitors. Finally, today's marketers are also reexamining their ethical and societal responsibilities. Marketers are being called on to take greater responsibility for the social and environmental impacts of their actions.

Pulling it all together, as discussed throughout the chapter, the major new developments in marketing can be summed up in a single concept: *engaging customers and creating and capturing customer value*. Today, marketers of all kinds are taking advantage of new opportunities for building value-laden relationships with their customers, their marketing partners, and the world around them.

Key Terms

Objective 1-1
Marketing (p 5)

Objective 1-2
Needs (p 6)
Wants (p 6)
Demands (p 6)
Market offerings (p 6)
Marketing myopia (p 7)
Exchange (p 7)
Market (p 8)

Objective 1-3
Marketing management (p 9)
Production concept (p 10)
Product concept (p 10)
Selling concept (p 10)
Marketing concept (p 10)
Societal marketing concept (p 11)

Objective 1-4
Customer relationship management (p 13)
Customer-perceived value (p 13)
Customer satisfaction (p 14)
Customer-engagement marketing (p 18)
Consumer-generated marketing (p 19)
Partner relationship management (p 20)
Customer lifetime value (p 21)
Share of customer (p 21)
Customer equity (p 22)

Objective 1-5
Digital and social media marketing (p 24)

Discussion Questions

1-1. Define marketing and outline the steps in the marketing process. (AASCB: Communication)

1-2. Describe how the *marketing concept* differs from the other marketing management orientations. (AACSB: Communication; Reflective Thinking)

1-3. What is customer-engagement marketing and how is it related to the surge in digital and social media technologies? (AACSB: Communication; Reflective Thinking)

1-4. When implementing customer relationship management, why might a business desire fewer customers over more customers? Shouldn't the focus of marketing be to acquire as many customers as possible? (AACSB: Communication; Reflective Thinking)

1-5. Discuss how technology is affecting marketing. (AACSB: Communication)

Critical Thinking Exercises

1-6. Select three companies competing in the same product or service category. How does each differentiate and position itself, and how do they execute these strategies in their marketing mixes? Which competitor is most successful? Which element(s) of that competitor's marketing mix has contributed to its success? (AACSB Communication; Analytic Reasoning)

1-7. Go to a company, organization, or specific brand Web site that has a link to Facebook, Google+, YouTube, Twitter, and/or Pinterest. Click on the links and describe how that company is using social media to market its products or services. Evaluate its effectiveness in creating customer engagement. (AACSB: Communication; Use of IT; Reflective Thinking)

1-8. In a small group, create a presentation about careers in marketing. Search the Internet for information regarding the different career options available in marketing and the skills, education, and experience necessary to advance in the field of marketing. Then select a company and describe the marketing career opportunities available there. (AACSB: Communication; Use of IT; Reflective Thinking)

MINICASES AND APPLICATIONS

Online, Mobile, and Social Media Marketing Do Us A Flavor

Two Lay's chip flavors—Cheesy Garlic Bread and Kettle Cooked Wasabi Ginger—were created by consumers as part of Frito-Lay's wildly successful "Do Us A Flavor" marketing campaign (www.dousaflavor.com). Launched in July 2012 in a pop-up shop in New York's Times Square, the event took on new dimensions in 2015 by incorporating real-time marketing. In response to interesting Tweets during the three-month-long submission period, digital shop Deep Focus produced 20 one-minute YouTube clips featuring two potato puppets named Marvin and Duncan (also known as the Taste Spuds). Google has now developed the "Flavorcast Heat Map" showing trending ingredients for each state, and consumers can see state-versus-state contests in the Flavor Showdown Gallery on the Web site. Consumers submit their flavor's name, up to three ingredients, and a chip style. They can also vote online at the Web site or via social media, and finalists' flavors are developed and shipped to stores a few months later, where they can be purchased and then voted upon. The creator of the winning flavor receives $1 million. But Lay's is the big winner of this campaign. The first contest's goal was 1.2 million submissions, but Lay's received 3.8 million submissions, 22.5 million Facebook visits a week, and a 12 percent increase in sales.

1-9. Some have argued that real-time marketing success is luck-based, whereas responsive marketing is more strategy-based. Research these two concepts and support or refute this statement. (AACSB: Communication; Reflective Thinking)

1-10. Select a brand in a different product category and create a responsive campaign that incorporates online, mobile, and social media to create customer engagement. How would you measure the success of your campaign? (AACSB: Communication; Reflective Thinking)

Marketing Ethics Extreme Baby Monitoring

Every parent's fear when putting an infant to sleep is Sudden Infant Death Syndrome (SIDS)—the sudden unexplainable death of an otherwise healthy baby. In the United States, about 2,000 infants die each year of SIDS, the third leading cause of infant death. For $199, parents can buy monitors that track babies' vital signs, such as respiration, heart rate, skin temperature, sleeping position, and quality of sleep. The Mimo Smart Baby Monitor is a cute clip-on turtle that attaches to a special organic cotton onesie, and the Owlet Baby Monitor is a smart sock that looks like a little toeless boot. If parents don't want to attach these devices on their little ones, they can opt for the SafeToSleep Breathing Monitor sheet with a built-in monitor. All of these devices stream data to parents' smartphones. Manufacturers of these devices promote them to parents for "your baby's health" or to give "that extra assurance" to protect against SIDS. However, several government agencies such as the Food and Drug Administration, the Consumer Product Safety Commission, the Centers for Disease Control and Prevention, and the National Institutes of Health as well as the American Academy of Pediatrics all agree that these devices cannot protect a baby from SIDS. But fear sells, and most of these manufacturers cannot keep up with the demand for their products.

1-11. Is it right for marketers to play on parents' fear to sell products that experts conclude are not necessary or effective? (AACSB: Communication; Ethical Reasoning; Reflective Thinking)

1-12. Discuss other examples of marketers using emotion to sell products. Are they ethical? (AACSB: Communication; Ethical Reasoning)

Marketing by the Numbers What's a Customer Worth?

How much are you worth to a given company if you continue to purchase its brand for the rest of your life? Many marketers are grappling with that question, but it's not easy to determine how much a customer is worth to a company over his or her lifetime. Calculating customer lifetime value can be very complicated. Intuitively, however, it can be a fairly simple net present value calculation, which incorporates the concept of the time value of money. To determine a basic customer lifetime value, each stream of profit (C, the net cash flow after costs are subtracted) is discounted back to its present value (PV) and then summed. The basic equation for calculating net present value (NPV) is:

$$\text{NPV} = \sum_{t=0}^{N} \frac{C_t}{(1 + r)^t}$$

Where,

t = time of the cash flow
N = total customer lifetime
r = discount rate
C_t = net cash flow (the profit) at time t (The initial cost of acquiring a customer would be a negative net cash flow at time 0.)

NPV can be calculated easily on most financial calculators or by using one of the calculators available on the Internet, such as the one found at www.investopedia.com/calculator/NetPresentValue.aspx.

1-13. Assume that a customer shops at a local grocery store spending an average of $200 a week, resulting in a retailer profit of $10 each week from this customer. Assuming the shopper visits the store all 52 weeks of the year, calculate the customer lifetime value if this shopper remains loyal over a 10-year life span. Also assume a 5 percent annual interest rate and no initial cost to acquire the customer. (AACSB: Communication; Analytic Reasoning)

1-14. Describe ways marketers can increase the lifetime value of a customer. (AACSB: Communication; Reflective Thinking)

Video Case Eskimo Joe's

Since 1975, Eskimo Joe's has been a popular watering hole in Stillwater, Oklahoma. Through word of mouth and a popular logo spread via T-shirts, it rapidly became a favorite place to grab a beer for students at Oklahoma State. But what started as a basic beer joint has grown into something much more.

When the drinking age changed from 18 to 21 in the 1980s, Eskimo Joe's had to decide how it would move forward. That challenge helped the company to recognize that its product is much more than just a cold mug of beer. Instead, people flocked to Eskimo Joe's for the fun atmosphere and customer-friendly service. This realization led to an expansion into different businesses that have now spread the Eskimo Joe's logo all over the planet.

After viewing the video featuring Eskimo Joe's, answer the following questions:

1-15. Describe Eskimo Joe's market offering.

1-16. What is Eskimo Joe's value proposition? How does its value proposition relate to its market offering?

1-17. How does Eskimo Joe's build long-term customer relationships?

Company Cases 1 FedEx/4 Campbell's/14 Alibaba

See Appendix 1 for cases appropriate for this chapter. **Case 1, FedEx: Making Every Customer Experience Outstanding**. From the time FedEx opened for business over 40 years ago, the company strategy has been built on a foundation of obsessive customer focus. **Case 4, Campbell's: Watching What You Eat**. Through extensive marketing research, Campbell's maintains its customer focus. **Case 14, Alibaba: The World's Largest E-Tailer Is Not Amazon.** Alibaba is on track to hit $700 billion in annual revenues within two years by providing everything customers need and desire.

MyMarketingLab

If assigned by your instructor, complete these writing sections from your Assignments in the MyLab.

1-18. Compare and contrast needs, wants, and demands. Which one(s) can marketers influence? (AACSB: Communication; Reflective Thinking)

1-19. Is it fair to single out specific products for restrictions such as when New York City proposed size cap on soft drinks? Discuss this argument from all sides of this issue: government, soft drink marketers, and consumers. (AACSB: Written and Oral Communication; Reflective Thinking)

2 Company and Marketing Strategy

Partnering to Build Customer Engagement, Value, and Relationships

CHAPTER ROAD MAP Objective Outline

OBJECTIVE 2-1 **Explain company-wide strategic planning and its four steps.** Company-Wide Strategic Planning: Defining Marketing's Role (40–43)

OBJECTIVE 2-2 **Discuss how to design business portfolios and develop growth strategies.** Designing the Business Portfolio (43–48)

OBJECTIVE 2-3 **Explain marketing's role in strategic planning and how marketing works with its partners to create and deliver customer value.** Planning Marketing: Partnering to Build Customer Relationships (48–50)

OBJECTIVE 2-4 **Describe the elements of a customer value-driven marketing strategy and mix and the forces that influence it.** Marketing Strategy and the Marketing Mix (50–56)

OBJECTIVE 2-5 **List the marketing management functions, including the elements of a marketing plan, and discuss the importance of measuring and managing marketing return on investment.** Managing the Marketing Effort (56–60); Measuring and Managing Marketing Return on Investment (60–61)

Previewing the Concepts

In the first chapter, we explored the marketing process by which companies create value for customers to capture value from them in return. In this chapter, we dig deeper into steps two and three of that process: designing customer value-driven marketing strategies and constructing marketing programs. First, we look at the organization's overall strategic planning, which guides marketing strategy and planning. Next, we discuss how, guided by the strategic plan, marketers partner closely with others inside and outside the firm to engage customers and create value for them. We then examine marketing strategy and planning—how marketers choose target markets, position their market offerings, develop a marketing mix, and manage their marketing programs. Finally, we look at the important step of measuring and managing marketing return on investment (marketing ROI).

First, let's look at Starbucks, a good company and a good marketing strategy story. Starbucks met with enormous early success by focusing not just on coffee, but on the coffee-drinking experience. The company has since taken a bumpy ride from boom to bust and back to boom again. Along the way, it learned that good marketing strategy means more than just growth, sales, and profits. It means skillfully engaging customers and creating value for them. At its core, Starbucks doesn't sell just coffee, it sells "The Starbucks Experience."

First Stop

Starbucks's Customer Value-Driven Marketing Strategy: Delivering "The Starbucks Experience"

More than 30 years ago, Howard Schultz transformed the coffee industry by bringing a European-style coffeehouse to America. He believed that people needed to slow down—to "smell the coffee" and to enjoy life a little more. The result was Starbucks, founded with a whole new strategy for engaging customers and creating customer value.

Starbucks didn't sell just coffee, it sold "The Starbucks Experience"—"an uplifting experience that enriches people's lives one moment, one human being, one extraordinary cup of coffee at a time." Starbucks gave customers what it calls a "third place"—a place away from home and away from work. At Starbucks, the smells, the sound of beans grinding, watching baristas blend and brew the brand's specialty coffees—all became as much or more a part of the customer experience as the coffee itself.

More than just coffee, Starbucks sells the Starbucks Experience, one that "enriches people's lives one moment, one human being, one extraordinary cup of coffee at a time."

Associated Press

Over the next two decades, customers flocked to Starbucks cafés. By 2007, some 15,000 Starbucks stores dotted the nation and globe, and the company's sales and profits rose like steam off a mug of hot java. However, Starbucks's enormous success drew a host of competitors. It seemed that every rival—from independent coffeehouses to fast-food restaurants—was peddling its own brand of premium coffee.

To maintain its phenomenal growth in the increasingly overcaffeinated marketplace, Starbucks brewed up an ambitious growth strategy. It opened new stores at a breakneck pace, seemingly *everywhere*. For example, one three-block stretch in Chicago contained six of the trendy coffee bars. In New York City, there were two Starbucks in one Macy's store. In fact, cramming so many stores so close together caused one satirical publication to run this headline: "A New Starbucks Opens in the Restroom of Existing Starbucks." The company also blanketed the country with Starbucks kiosks and coffee stands in everything from Target stores and supermarkets to hotel lobbies, and service businesses from airlines to car dealerships proclaimed "We proudly serve Starbucks coffee."

The more Starbucks grew, however, the more it drifted away from the core mission and values that had made it so successful. The company's almost obsessive focus on growth for growth's sake began to take a toll on the prized Starbucks Experience. Far from its roots as a warm and intimate coffeehouse, Starbucks began to evolve into more of a caffeine filling station. More and more, the premium brand found itself competing with the likes of—gasp!—McDonald's for many of the same customers.

Founder Howard Schultz, who had stepped down as CEO in 2000, expressed concern. In a 2007 memo to Starbucks management, Schultz lamented that the company's push for growth had "led to the watering down of the Starbucks Experience" and that Starbucks was "losing its soul." Schultz was right that something was wrong. By early 2008, when Schultz reassumed his role as Starbucks president and CEO, the company found itself in hot water. For the first time ever, the average number of transactions per U.S. store fell off and same-store sales growth slowed. Within just the previous two years, Starbucks's stock had tumbled nearly 80 percent. According to one analyst, "The financial vultures circled. Obituaries were drafted."

Instead of presiding over the brand's demise, however, Schultz reacted quickly to restore its luster. He cooled the pace of Starbucks's growth, closed underperforming locations, and replaced most of the company's top executives. Most important, Schultz laid plans to reestablish the brand's core mission and values and to refocus the company on giving customers the authentic Starbucks Experience. "As we grew rapidly and had phenomenal success," Shultz announced, "we started to lose sight of our focus on the customer and our commitment to continually and creatively enhance the Starbucks Experience." Starbucks needed to shift its focus back to customers—to "reignite the emotional attachment with customers."

Starbucks has become America's—the world's—largest coffeehouse by skillfully engaging customers and delivering superior customer value. At its core, Starbucks doesn't sell just coffee. It sells "The Starbucks Experience."

To emphasize the point, at a cost of $30 million, Schultz transported 10,000 Starbucks store managers to a morale-building reorientation in New Orleans. A short time later, Starbucks dramatically closed all of its U.S. locations for three hours to conduct nationwide employee training on the basics of producing satisfying customer experiences.

Those early actions began a process of continual renewal by which Starbucks has reignited the Starbucks customer experience through new products, innovative store formats, and new platforms for engaging customers. Beyond improvements in its signature coffee products, Starbucks has developed new products that take the Starbucks Experience into new areas. For example, a few years ago, Starbucks successfully launched Via, an instant coffee that's as good at home as fresh-brewed is in stores. More recently, Starbucks added Fizzio to its menu—freshly carbonated and handcrafted sodas in classic flavors.

The company is also experimenting with new store formats, such as the new high-end Starbucks Reserve Roastery and Tasting Room in Seattle that's part café, part shrine, and part working roastery. Schultz describes the new interactive store as "Niketown meets Apple meets Starbucks"—think of it as the Starbucks Experience on steroids. In another big move, Starbucks purchased Teavana—a specialty tea retailer with more than 400 locations in five countries. Schultz sees the Teavana acquisition as pivotal to Starbucks's renewal and reinvention. Tea is "a $90 billion global category, ripe for innovation," he says. "We're going to do for tea what we've done for coffee."

Starbucks's renewal extends the Starbucks Experience well beyond employee relearning, new products, and innovative stores formats. Over the past decade, as much as any brand, Starbucks has built customer engagement and brand community through digital and mobile platforms. Its highly successful mobile payments app, My Starbucks Rewards loyalty program, and prepaid Starbucks Cards now give Starbucks "a direct, real-time, personalized, two-way digital relationship with its customers," says the company's chief digital officer. The Starbucks Rewards mobile payment app has 12 million active users, and digital products now account for roughly 35 percent of payments at Starbucks's North American stores.

Today, a rejuvenated Starbucks is once again fully engaged with customers and delivering the one-of-a-kind Starbucks Experience. And once again, sales and profits are really perking. Every week, Starbucks serves more than 70 million customers face to face in 20,200 stores in 64 countries. Over the past six years, revenues have increased 70 percent, profits have shot up fivefold, and Starbucks's stock price has skyrocketed by a factor of 12.

The moral of the Starbucks story: Good marketing strategy means keeping your eye squarely on delivering customer value. The objective isn't just growth or sales or profits; it's engaging customers in a meaningful way and creating value for them. If a company takes care of customer engagement and value, good performance will result. "It's not just about ringing a register and performing a task," says Schultz. "It's also about creating an emotional, enduring relationship and connection with our...customers. At our core, we celebrate the interaction between us and our customers through the coffee experience. Life happens over coffee."[1]

Author Comment
Company-wide strategic planning guides marketing strategy and planning. Like marketing strategy, the company's broader strategy must also be customer focused.

Company-Wide Strategic Planning: Defining Marketing's Role

Each company must find the game plan for long-run survival and growth that makes the most sense given its specific situation, opportunities, objectives, and resources. This is the focus of **strategic planning**—the process of developing and maintaining a strategic fit between the organization's goals and capabilities and its changing marketing opportunities.

Strategic planning
The process of developing and maintaining a strategic fit between the organization's goals and capabilities and its changing marketing opportunities.

Strategic planning sets the stage for the rest of planning in the firm. Companies usually prepare annual plans, long-range plans, and strategic plans. The annual and long-range plans deal with the company's current businesses and how to keep them going. In contrast, the strategic plan involves adapting the firm to take advantage of opportunities in its constantly changing environment.

At the corporate level, the company starts the strategic planning process by defining its overall purpose and mission (see >> **Figure 2.1**). This mission is then turned into detailed supporting objectives that guide the entire company. Next, headquarters decides what portfolio of businesses and products is best for the company and how much support to give each one. In turn, each business and product develops detailed marketing and other departmental plans that support the company-wide plan. Thus, marketing planning occurs at the business-unit, product, and market levels. It supports company strategic planning with more detailed plans for specific marketing opportunities.

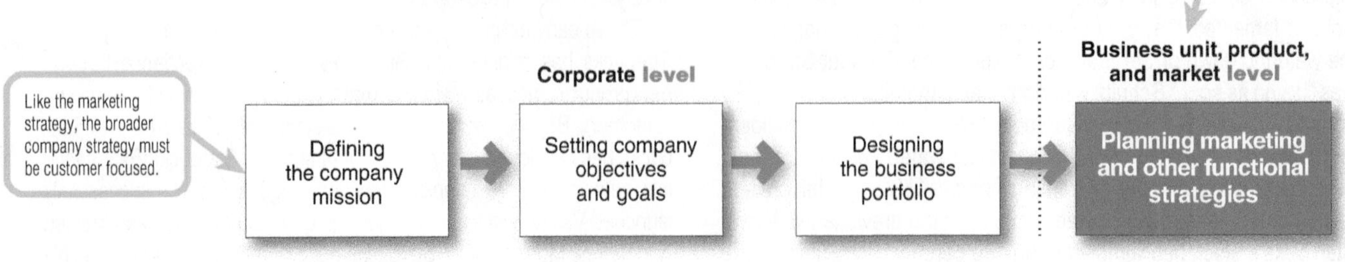

>> **Figure 2.1 Steps in Strategic Planning**

Defining a Market-Oriented Mission

An organization exists to accomplish something, and this purpose should be clearly stated. Forging a sound mission begins with the following questions: What *is* our business? Who is the customer? What do consumers value? What *should* our business be? These simple-sounding questions are among the most difficult the company will ever have to answer. Successful companies continuously raise these questions and answer them carefully and completely.

Mission statement
A statement of the organization's purpose—what it wants to accomplish in the larger environment.

Many organizations develop formal mission statements that answer these questions. A **mission statement** is a statement of the organization's purpose—what it wants to accomplish in the larger environment. A clear mission statement acts as an "invisible hand" that guides people in the organization.

Some companies define their missions myopically in product or technology terms ("We make and sell furniture" or "We are a chemical-processing firm"). But mission statements should be *market oriented* and defined in terms of satisfying basic customer needs. Products and technologies eventually become outdated, but basic market needs may last forever. For example, social scrapbooking site Pinterest doesn't define itself as just an online place to post pictures. Its mission is to give people a social media platform for collecting, organizing, and sharing things they love. And Chipotle's mission isn't to sell burritos. Instead, the restaurant promises "Food with Integrity," highlighting its commitment to the immediate and long-term welfare of customers and the environment. To back its mission, Chipotle serves only the very best natural, sustainable, local ingredients. » **Table 2.1** provides several examples of product-oriented versus market-oriented business definitions.[2]

Mission statements should be meaningful and specific yet motivating. Too often, mission statements are written for public relations purposes and lack specific, workable guidelines. Instead, they should emphasize the company's strengths and tell forcefully how it intends to win in the marketplace. For example, Google's mission isn't to be the world's best search engine. It's to give people a window into the world's information, wherever it might be found.[3]

» Table 2.1 Product- versus Market-Oriented Business Definitions

Company	Product-Oriented Definition	Market-Oriented Definition
Chipotle	We sell burritos and other Mexican food.	We give customers "Food With Integrity," served with a commitment toward the long-term welfare of customers and the environment.
Facebook	We are an online social network.	We connect people around the world and help them share important moments in their lives.
Home Depot	We sell tools and home repair and improvement items.	We empower consumers to achieve the homes of their dreams.
NASA	We explore outer space.	We reach for new heights and reveal the unknown so that what we do and learn will benefit all humankind.
Revlon	We make cosmetics.	We sell lifestyle and self-expression; success and status; memories, hopes, and dreams.
Ritz-Carlton Hotels & Resorts	We rent rooms.	We create "The Ritz-Carlton experience,"—a memorable stay that far exceeds guests' already high expectations.
Starbucks	We sell coffee and snacks.	We sell "The Starbucks Experience," one that enriches people's lives one moment, one human being, one extraordinary cup of coffee at a time.
Walmart	We run discount stores.	We deliver low prices every day and give ordinary folks the chance to buy the same things as rich people. "Save Money. Live Better."

Finally, as we discovered in the chapter-opening Starbucks story, a company's mission should not be stated as making more sales or profits; profits are only a reward for creating value for customers. Instead, the mission should focus on customers and the customer experience the firm seeks to create. >> Thus, the fast-growing Buffalo Wild Wings restaurant chain's mission isn't just to sell the most wings at a profit:[4]

>> **Customer-focused mission: The fast-growing Buffalo Wild Wings chain's mission is to provide a total eating and social environment that "fuels the sports fan experience." As a result, it creates in-store and online experiences that promote brand fan engagement.**

Reprinted with permission of Buffalo Wild Wings, Inc.

Customers do, in fact, come to Buffalo Wild Wings ("B-Dubs" to regulars) to eat wings and drink beer, but they also come to watch sports, trash talk, cheer on their sports teams, and meet old friends and make new ones—that is, a total eating and social experience. "We realize that we're not just in the business of selling wings," says the company. "We're something much bigger. We're in the business of fueling the sports fan experience. Our mission is to WOW people every day!" Each table has two types of servers, a food-order server and a "guest experience captain," whose job is to make sure that guests can see whatever game they came to watch on one of the 40 to 60 screens lining the walls, over the bar, and about everywhere else. True to that broader mission, Buffalo Wild Wings creates in-store and online promotions that inspire camaraderie. "It's about giving them tools to not just be spectators but advocates of the brand," says the chain. For example, the brand's very active Web site draws 3 million visitors per month; its Facebook page has more than 12 million fans. Pursuing a customer-focused mission has paid big dividends for Buffalo Wild Wings. The wing joint's sales and profits have both jumped 250 percent in the past four years, and the company brags that it's the number-one brand in its industry for fan engagement. The chain's "hottest wing coating available comes with a warning to B-Dubs customers: 'keep away from eyes, pets, and children.' The sauce is called Blazin'," says one analyst. "That term also happens to be a good description of the stock's performance lately."

Setting Company Objectives and Goals

The company needs to turn its broad mission into detailed supporting objectives for each level of management. Each manager should have objectives and be responsible for reaching them. For example, most Americans know CVS as a chain of retail pharmacies selling prescription and over-the-counter medicines, personal care products, and a host of convenience and other items. But CVS—recently renamed CVS Health—has a much broader mission. >> It views itself as a "pharmacy innovation company," one that is "helping people on their path to better health." The company's motto: "Health is everything."[5]

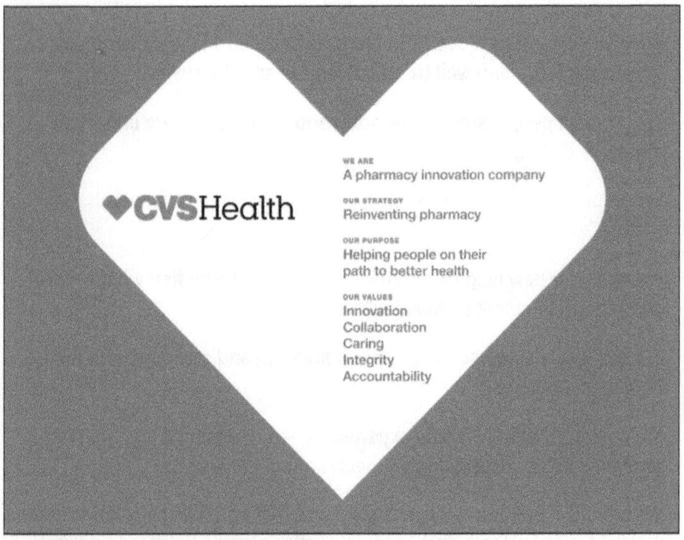

>> **CVS Health's overall mission is to be a "pharmacy innovation company" that "helps people on their way to better health." Its marketing strategies and programs must support this mission.**

CVS Caremark Corporation

CVS Health's broad mission leads to a hierarchy of objectives, including business objectives and marketing objectives. CVS Health's overall business objective is to increase access, lower costs, and improve the quality of care. It does this through the products it sells at its retail pharmacies and by taking a more active role in overall health-care management through research, consumer outreach and education, and support of health-related programs and organizations. However, such activities are expensive and must be funded through improved profits, so improving profits becomes another major objective for CVS Health. Profits can be improved by increasing sales or by reducing costs. Sales can be increased by improving customer engagement and raising the company's share of the health-care market. These goals then become the company's current marketing objectives.

Marketing strategies and programs must be developed to support these marketing objectives. To increase customer engagement, sales, and market share, CVS Health has reshaped and broadened its lines of products and services. For example, it recently stopped selling tobacco products, items not compatible with its "better health" mission. And it has placed CVS MinuteClinic locations in nearly 1,000 of its more than 7,800 stores, providing walk-in medical care in more than 23 million patient visits since 2000. CVS Health has also broadened its range of customer contact activities to include tailored advising to customers managing chronic and specialty health conditions.

These are CVS Health's broad marketing strategies. Each marketing strategy must then be defined in greater detail. For example, the company's rapidly expanding MinuteClinic services will require more advertising and promotional efforts, and such efforts will need to be spelled out carefully. In this way, CVS Health's broad mission is translated into a set of specific short-term objectives and marketing plans.

Designing the Business Portfolio

Business portfolio
The collection of businesses and products that make up the company.

Guided by the company's mission statement and objectives, management now must plan its **business portfolio**—the collection of businesses and products that make up the company. The best business portfolio is the one that best fits the company's strengths and weaknesses to opportunities in the environment.

Most large companies have complex portfolios of businesses and brands. Strategic and marketing planning for such business portfolios can be a daunting but critical task. For example, ESPN's brand portfolio consists of more than 50 business entities, ranging from multiple ESPN cable channels to ESPN Radio, ESPN.com, *ESPN The Magazine*, and even ESPN Zone sports-themed restaurants. In turn, ESPN is just one unit in the even more complex portfolio of its parent company, The Walt Disney Company. Through skillful portfolio management, however, ESPN has built a cohesive brand, unified powerfully under its mission to serve sports enthusiasts "wherever sports are watched, listened to, discussed, debated, read about, or played" (see Marketing at Work 2.1).

Similarly, GE is a giant $149 billion conglomerate operating in dozens of consumer and business markets, with a broad portfolio of products that "move, power, build, and cure the world." Most consumers know GE for its home appliance and lighting products, part of the company's GE Home & Business Solutions unit. But that's just the beginning for GE. Other company units—such as GE Transportation, GE Aviation, GE Energy Management, GE Power & Water, GE Gas & Oil, GE Healthcare, and others—offer products and services ranging from jet engines, diesel-electric locomotives, wind turbines, and off-shore drilling solutions to aerospace systems and medical imaging equipment. GE Capital offers a breadth of business financial products and services. Successfully managing such a broad portfolio takes plenty of management skill and—as GE's long-running corporate slogan suggests—lots of "Imagination at work."[6]

Business portfolio planning involves two steps. First, the company must analyze its *current* business portfolio and determine which businesses should receive more, less, or no investment. Second, it must shape the *future* portfolio by developing strategies for growth and downsizing.

Analyzing the Current Business Portfolio

Portfolio analysis
The process by which management evaluates the products and businesses that make up the company.

The major activity in strategic planning is business **portfolio analysis**, whereby management evaluates the products and businesses that make up the company. The company will want to put strong resources into its more profitable businesses and phase down or drop its weaker ones.

Management's first step is to identify the key businesses that make up the company, called *strategic business units* (SBUs). An SBU can be a company division, a product line within a division, or sometimes a single product or brand. The company next assesses the attractiveness of its various SBUs and decides how much support each deserves. When designing a business portfolio, it's a good idea to add and support products and businesses that fit closely with the firm's core philosophy and competencies.

MARKETING AT WORK 2.1

ESPN: Skillfully Managing a Complex Brand Portfolio

When you think about ESPN, you probably think of it as a cable TV network, or a magazine, or maybe a Web site. ESPN is all of those things. But over the years, ESPN has grown to become a huge and complex brand portfolio consisting of more than 50 different entities. Thanks to skillful portfolio management, however, ESPN is much more than just a haphazard collection of media entities. Instead, it's an immersive brand experience—a meaningful part of customers' lives. ESPN is synonymous with sports entertainment, inexorably linked with customers' sports memories, realities, and anticipations.

In 1979, entrepreneur Bill Rasmussen took a daring leap and founded the round-the-clock sports network ESPN (Entertainment and Sports Programming Network). Despite many early skeptics—seriously, a 24-hour sports network?—ESPN is now a multibillion-dollar sports empire and a "can't-live-without-it" part of the daily routines of hundreds of millions of people worldwide. Today, ESPN is as much recognized and revered as iconic megabrands such as Coca-Cola, Nike, Apple, and Google. No matter who you are, chances are good that ESPN has touched you in some meaningful way. And no matter what the sport or where, ESPN seems to be everywhere at once.

Here's a brief summary of the incredible variety of entities tied together as part of the ESPN portfolio:

Television: From its original groundbreaking cable network, the ESPN brand has sprouted eight additional U.S. networks—ESPN3D, ESPN2, ESPN Classic, ESPNEWS, ESPNU, ESPN Deportes (Spanish language), the Longhorn Network, and the SEC Network. With its signal now flowing into almost 115 million U.S. households at an industry-topping cost of $6 per household per month—TNT is a distant second at $1.48—ESPN is by far the most-sought cable network. Additionally, ESPN International serves fans through 26 international networks in 61 countries on all seven continents. ESPN is the home of the NBA Finals, WNBA, MLB, Monday Night Football, IndyCar, the NHRA, college football, college basketball, tennis's Grand Slam events, golf's Masters and British Open, the Little League World Series, and more. This list grows every year as ESPN continues to outbid the major broadcast networks to capture the rights to major sports events. For 14 straight years, American men have named ESPN their favorite channel.

Radio: Sports radio is thriving, and ESPN Radio is the largest sports radio network, broadcasting more than 8,500 hours of content annually to 23 million listeners through nearly 500 U.S. affiliates. Overseas, ESPN has radio and syndicated radio programs in 11 countries. ESPN Radio extends its reach even further through Sirius XM, digital distributors Slacker Radio and Tune In, and its own ESPNRadio.com.

Online: ESPN Digital Media is composed of 19 U.S. Web sites, including the flagship ESPN.com. These digital destinations capture some 75 million unique visitors and 6.8 billion minutes of usage every month. ESPN accounts for 31 percent of all online sports activity, more than the combined totals of its two closest competitors. ESPNRadio.com is the world's most-listened-to online sports destination. And ESPN's Podcasts are downloaded more than 369 million times per year.

With access to its own content from television, radio, and print, ESPN has a plentiful supply of material to feed its digital efforts. But ESPN also leads the game in the exploding mobile arena. It employs a "mobile first" strategy, in which it orients all of its Web sites around mobile, thus optimizing performance. ESPN delivers mobile sports content via all major U.S. wireless providers—including real-time scores, stats, late-breaking news, and video-on-demand. Its mobile sites and apps lead the sports category in unique visitors and average audience per minute. The digital strategy has led to ESPN3, a multi-screen live 24/7 sports network available at no cost to tens of millions of homes that receive their high-speed Internet connection from an affiliated service provider.

» ESPN is much more than just a haphazard collection of media entities. It's a skillfully managed brand portfolio that delivers an immersive sports entertainment experience, inexorably linked with customers' sports memories, realities, and anticipations.

Publishing: When ESPN first published *ESPN The Magazine* in 1998, critics gave it little chance against mighty *Sports Illustrated*. Yet, with its bold look, bright colors, and unconventional format, the ESPN publication now serves more than 15 million readers each month and is the leading publication among men ages 18 to 34. Digital-only consumption of *ESPN The Magazine* is soaring, whereas a relatively stagnate *Sports Illustrated* is struggling to make the shift to a digital world.

Even More: As if all this weren't enough, ESPN also manages events, including the X Games, the Winter X Games, the Bassmaster Classic, the Jimmy V Classic, and several football bowl games. It also develops ESPN-branded consumer products and services, including DVDs, video games, apparel, and even golf schools. If reading all this makes you hungry, you may be near an ESPN Zone, which includes a sports-themed restaurant, interactive games, and sports-related merchandise sales. You'll now find ESPN content in airports and on planes, in health clubs, and even on gas station video panels. All this translates into annual revenues of $11 billion, making ESPN more important to its parent The Walt Disney Company than the Disneyland and Disney World theme parks combined.

What ties this huge collection of ESPN entities together? The brand's customer-focused mission: It wants to serve sports enthusiasts "wherever sports are watched, listened to, discussed, debated, read about, or played." ESPN has a philosophy known as "best available screen." It knows that when fans are at home, they'll watch the big 60-inch flat-screen. But during the morning hours, smartphones light up more. During the day, desktops dominate, and in the evening, tablet activity increases. ESPN is on a crusade to know when, where, and under what conditions fans will reach for which device, and to provide the most seamless, high-quality experience for them.

It's no surprise, then, that sports fans around the world love their ESPN. To consumers everywhere, ESPN means sports. Tech savvy, creative, and often irreverent, the well-managed, ever-extending yet carefully integrated brand portfolio continues to build meaningful customer engagement and experiences. If it has to do with your life and sports—large or small—ESPN covers it for you, anywhere you are, 24/7. Perhaps the company should rename ESPN to stand for Every Sport Possible—Now.

Sources: Dorothy Pomerantz, "Are You Willing to Pay $36 per Month for ESPN?" *Forbes*, March 25, 2015, www.forbes.com/sites/dorothypomerantz/2015/03/25/are-you-willing-to-pay-36-per-month-for-espn/; Anthony Kosner, "Mobile First: How ESPN Delivers to the Best Available Screen," *Forbes*, January 30, 2012, www.forbes.com/sites/anthonykosner/2012/01/30/mobile-first-how-espn-delivers-to-the-best-available-screen/2/; Derek Thompson, "The Global Dominance of ESPN," *The Atlantic*, August 14, 2013, www.theatlantic.com/magazine/archive/2013/09/the-most-valuable-network/309433/; and information from http://espnmediazone.com/us/espn-inc-fact-sheet/ and www.espn.com, accessed September 2015.

The purpose of strategic planning is to find ways in which the company can best use its strengths to take advantage of attractive opportunities in the environment. For this reason, most standard portfolio analysis methods evaluate SBUs on two important dimensions: the attractiveness of the SBU's market or industry and the strength of the SBU's position in that market or industry. The best-known portfolio-planning method was developed by the Boston Consulting Group, a leading management consulting firm.[7]

Growth-share matrix
A portfolio-planning method that evaluates a company's SBUs in terms of market growth rate and relative market share.

The Boston Consulting Group Approach. Using the now-classic Boston Consulting Group (BCG) approach, a company classifies all its SBUs according to the **growth-share matrix**, as shown in >> **Figure 2.2**. On the vertical axis, *market growth rate* provides a measure of market attractiveness. On the horizontal axis, *relative market share* serves as a measure of company strength in the market. The growth-share matrix defines four types of SBUs:

1. ***Stars.*** Stars are high-growth, high-share businesses or products. They often need heavy investments to finance their rapid growth. Eventually their growth will slow down, and they will turn into cash cows.
2. ***Cash cows.*** Cash cows are low-growth, high-share businesses or products. These established and successful SBUs need less investment to hold their market share. Thus, they produce a lot of the cash that the company uses to pay its bills and support other SBUs that need investment.

>> Figure 2.2 The BCG Growth-Share Matrix

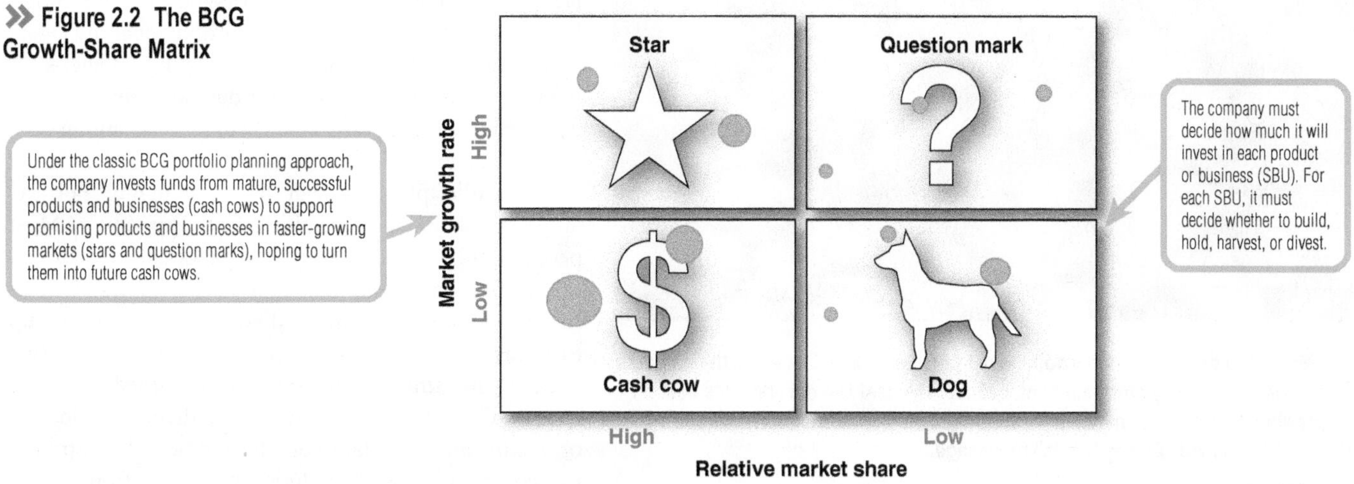

3. ***Question marks.*** Question marks are low-share business units in high-growth markets. They require a lot of cash to hold their share, let alone increase it. Management has to think hard about which question marks it should try to build into stars and which should be phased out.
4. ***Dogs.*** Dogs are low-growth, low-share businesses and products. They may generate enough cash to maintain themselves but do not promise to be large sources of cash.

The 10 circles in the growth-share matrix represent the company's 10 current SBUs. The company has two stars, two cash cows, three question marks, and three dogs. The area of each circle is proportional to the SBU's dollar sales. This company is in fair shape, although not in good shape. It wants to invest in the more promising question marks to make them stars and maintain the stars so that they will become cash cows as their markets mature. Fortunately, it has two good-sized cash cows. Income from these cash cows will help finance the company's question marks, stars, and dogs. The company should take some decisive action concerning its dogs and its question marks.

Once it has classified its SBUs, the company must determine what role each will play in the future. It can pursue one of four strategies for each SBU. It can invest more in the business unit to *build* its share. Or it can invest just enough to *hold* the SBU's share at the current level. It can *harvest* the SBU, milking its short-term cash flow regardless of the long-term effect. Finally, it can *divest* the SBU by selling it or phasing it out and using the resources elsewhere.

As time passes, SBUs change their positions in the growth-share matrix. Many SBUs start out as question marks and move into the star category if they succeed. They later become cash cows as market growth falls and then finally die off or turn into dogs toward the end of the life cycle. The company needs to add new products and units continuously so that some of them will become stars and, eventually, cash cows that will help finance other SBUs.

Problems with Matrix Approaches. The BCG and other formal methods revolutionized strategic planning. However, such centralized approaches have limitations: They can be difficult, time consuming, and costly to implement. Management may find it difficult to define SBUs and measure market share and growth. In addition, these approaches focus on classifying current businesses but provide little advice for future planning.

Because of such problems, many companies have dropped formal matrix methods in favor of more customized approaches that better suit their specific situations. Moreover, unlike former strategic planning efforts that rested mostly in the hands of senior managers at company headquarters, today's strategic planning has been decentralized. Increasingly, companies are placing responsibility for strategic planning in the hands of cross-functional teams of divisional managers who are close to their markets. In this digital age, such managers have rich and current data at their fingertips and can adapt their plans quickly to meet changing conditions and events in their markets.

Portfolio planning can be challenging. For example, think about The Walt Disney Company. »Most people think of Disney as theme parks and wholesome family entertainment. But in the mid-1980s, Disney set up a powerful, centralized strategic planning group to guide its direction and growth. Over the next two decades, the strategic planning group turned The Walt Disney Company into a huge and diverse collection of media and entertainment businesses. The sprawling company grew to include everything from theme

» **Managing the business portfolio: Most people think of Disney as theme parks and wholesome family entertainment, but over the past two decades, it's become a sprawling collection of media and entertainment businesses that requires big doses of the famed "Disney Magic" to manage.**

Martin Beddall/Alamy

resorts and film studios (Walt Disney Pictures, Touchstone Pictures, Pixar Animation, and Marvel Studios) to media networks (ABC Television plus ESPN, Disney Channel, parts of A&E and the History Channel, and a half dozen others) to consumer products (from apparel and toys to interactive games) and a cruise line.

The newly transformed company proved hard to manage and performed unevenly. To improve company performance, Disney disbanded the centralized strategic planning unit, decentralizing its functions to Disney division managers. For example, although carefully coordinated with other Disney units, in many respects ESPN runs autonomously. As a result of such decisions, The Walt Disney Company retains its position at the head of the world's media conglomerates. And even through the recently uneven economy, Disney's sound strategic management of its broad mix of businesses, plus a touch of the famed Disney magic, has helped it fare better than rival media companies.[8]

Developing Strategies for Growth and Downsizing

Beyond evaluating current businesses, designing the business portfolio involves finding businesses and products the company should consider in the future. Companies need growth if they are to compete more effectively, satisfy their stakeholders, and attract top talent. At the same time, a firm must be careful not to make growth itself an objective. The company's objective must be to manage "profitable growth."

Marketing has the main responsibility for achieving profitable growth for the company. Marketing needs to identify, evaluate, and select market opportunities and lay down strategies for capturing them. One useful device for identifying growth opportunities is the **product/market expansion grid**, shown in >> **Figure 2.3**.[9] We apply it here to performance sports apparel maker Under Armour:[10]

Product/market expansion grid
A portfolio-planning tool for identifying company growth opportunities through market penetration, market development, product development, or diversification.

> Less than 20 years ago, Under Armour introduced its innovative line of comfy, moisture-wicking performance shirts and shorts with the mission "to make all athletes better through passion, design, and the relentless pursuit of innovation." Since then, it has grown at a torrid pace. In just the past five years, Under Armour's sales have quadrupled. Its earnings have grown at a blistering rate of 20 percent in every quarter during that five-year period. Under Armour is now the nation's second-best-selling apparel brand behind Nike. Looking forward, the company must look for new ways to keep growing.

Market penetration
Company growth by increasing sales of current products to current market segments without changing the product.

First, Under Armour might consider whether the company can achieve deeper **market penetration**—making more sales in its current product lines and markets. It can spur growth through marketing mix improvements—adjustments to its product design, advertising, pricing, and distribution efforts. For example, Under Armour offers an ever-increasing range of styles and colors in its original apparel lines. And it boosted its spending on advertising and professional athlete and team endorsements last year by 35 percent over the previous year. The company has also added direct-to-consumer distribution channels, including its own retail stores and sales Web sites. Direct-to-consumer sales have tripled over the past seven years and now account for some 30 percent of total revenues.

Market development
Company growth by identifying and developing new market segments for current company products.

Second, Under Armour might consider possibilities for **market development**—identifying and developing new markets for its current products. Under Armour can review new *demographic markets*. >> For instance, the company recently stepped up its marketing to women consumers, with new products and a highly acclaimed $15 million women-focused promotion campaign called "I Will What I Want." Under Armour can also pursue

>> **Figure 2.3 The Product/Market Expansion Grid**

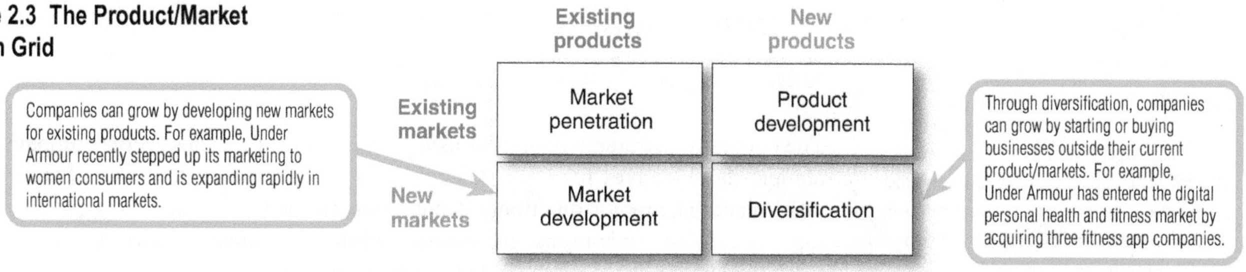

» **Strategies for growth: Under Armour has grown at a blistering rate under its multipronged growth strategy. In recent years, the brand has stepped up its marketing to women, as in its highly acclaimed "I Will" advertising campaign.**

UNDER ARMOUR, INC.

new *geographical markets*. For example, the brand is rapidly making a name for itself in international markets, including Japan, Europe, Canada, and Latin America. It recently opened its first-ever brand store in China. Although Under Armour's international sales grew 94 percent last year, they still account for only 12 percent of total sales, leaving plenty of room for international growth.

Third, Under Armour can consider **product development**—offering modified or new products to current markets. For example, the company added athletic shoes to its apparel lines in 2006, and it continues to introduce innovative new athletic-footwear products, such as the recently added Under Armour SPEEDFORM line. Sneaker sales rose 44 percent last year yet still account for only about 13 percent of total sales, again leaving plenty of growth potential.

Finally, Under Armour can consider **diversification**—starting up or buying businesses outside of its current products and markets. For example, the company recently expanded into the digital personal health and fitness tracking market by acquiring three fitness app companies—MapMyFitness, MyFitnessPal, and Endomondo. Under Armour might also consider moving into nonperformance leisurewear or begin making and marketing Under Armour fitness equipment. When diversifying, companies must be careful not to overextend their brands' positioning.

Companies must develop not only strategies for growing their business portfolios but also strategies for *downsizing* them. There are many reasons that a firm might want to abandon products or markets. A firm may have grown too fast or entered areas where it lacks experience. The market environment might change, making some products or markets less profitable. For example, in difficult economic times, many firms prune out weaker, less-profitable products and markets to focus their more limited resources on the strongest ones. Finally, some products or business units simply age and die.

Product development
Company growth by offering modified or new products to current market segments.

Diversification
Company growth through starting up or acquiring businesses outside the company's current products and markets.

When a firm finds brands or businesses that are unprofitable or that no longer fit its overall strategy, it must carefully prune, harvest, or divest them. For example, over the past several years, P&G has sold off dozens of major brands—from Crisco, Folgers, Jif, and Pringles to Duracell batteries, Right Guard deodorant, Aleve pain reliever, CoverGirl and Max Factor cosmetics, Wella and Clairol hair care products, and its Iams and other pet food brands—allowing the company to focus on household care and beauty and grooming products. And in recent years, GM has pruned several underperforming brands from its portfolio, including Oldsmobile, Pontiac, Saturn, Hummer, and Saab. Weak businesses usually require a disproportionate amount of management attention. Managers should focus on promising growth opportunities, not fritter away energy trying to salvage fading ones.

Author Comment
Marketing can't go it alone in creating customer value. Under the company-wide strategic plan, marketing must work closely with other departments to form an effective internal company value chain and with other companies in the marketing system to create an external value delivery network that jointly serves customers.

Planning Marketing: Partnering to Build Customer Relationships

The company's strategic plan establishes what kinds of businesses the company will operate and its objectives for each. Then, within each business unit, more detailed planning takes place. The major functional departments in each unit—marketing, finance, accounting, purchasing, operations, information systems, human resources, and others—must work together to accomplish strategic objectives.

Marketing plays a key role in the company's strategic planning in several ways. First, marketing provides a guiding *philosophy*—the marketing concept—that suggests the company strategy should revolve around creating customer value and building profitable relationships with important consumer groups. Second, marketing provides *inputs* to strategic planners by helping to identify attractive market opportunities and assessing the firm's potential to take advantage of them. Finally, within individual business units, marketing designs *strategies* for reaching the unit's objectives. Once the unit's objectives are set, marketing's task is to help carry them out profitably.

Customer engagement and value are the key ingredients in the marketer's formula for success. However, as noted in Chapter 1, although marketing plays a leading role, it alone cannot produce engagement and superior value for customers. It can be only a partner in attracting, engaging, and growing customers. In addition to *customer relationship management*, marketers must also practice *partner relationship management*. They must work closely with partners in other company departments to form an effective internal *value chain* that serves customers. Moreover, they must partner effectively with other companies in the marketing system to form a competitively superior external *value delivery network*. We now take a closer look at the concepts of a company value chain and a value delivery network.

Partnering with Other Company Departments

Value chain
The series of internal departments that carry out value-creating activities to design, produce, market, deliver, and support a firm's products.

Each company department can be thought of as a link in the company's internal **value chain**.[11] That is, each department carries out value-creating activities to design, produce, market, deliver, and support the firm's products. The firm's success depends not only on how well each department performs its work but also on how well the various departments coordinate their activities.

For example, True Value Hardware's goal is to create customer value and satisfaction by providing shoppers with the hardware and home improvement products they need at affordable prices along with top-notch customer service. Marketers at the retail-owned cooperative play an important role. They learn what customers need and help the 3,500 independent True Value retailers stock their store shelves with the desired products at competitive prices. They prepare advertising and merchandising programs and assist shoppers with customer service. Through these and other activities, True Value marketers help deliver value to customers.

However, True Value's marketers, both at the home office and in stores, need help from the company's other functions. True Value's ability to help you "Start Right. Start Here." depends on purchasing's skill in developing the needed suppliers and buying from them at low cost. True Value's information technology people must provide fast and accurate information about which products are selling in each store. And its operations people must provide effective, low-cost merchandise handling and delivery.

A company's value chain is only as strong as its weakest link. Success depends on how well each group performs its work of adding customer value and on how the company coordinates the activities of various functions. True Value's recent marketing campaign—"Behind Every Project Is a True Value"—recognizes the importance of having everyone in the organization—from in-store managers and employees to home-office operations

The value chain: These True Value ads recognize that everyone in the organization—from operations managers Tom Statham (left) to marketing research analyst Jeff Alvarez (right)—must contribute to helping the chain's customers handle their home improvement projects. They form the foundation for the brand's "Behind Every Project Is a True Value" positioning.

managers and marketing research analysts—understand the needs and aspirations of the chain's do-it-yourself customers and help them handle home improvement projects.

Ideally, then, a company's different functions should work in harmony to produce value for consumers. But, in practice, interdepartmental relations are full of conflicts and misunderstandings. The marketing department takes the consumer's point of view. But when marketing tries to improve customer satisfaction, it can cause other departments to do a poorer job *in their terms*. Marketing department actions can increase purchasing costs, disrupt production schedules, increase inventories, and create budget headaches. Thus, other departments may resist the marketing department's efforts.

Yet marketers must find ways to get all departments to "think consumer" and develop a smoothly functioning value chain. One marketing expert puts it this way: "True market orientation... means that the entire company obsesses over creating value for the customer and views itself as a bundle of processes that profitably define, create, communicate, and deliver value to its target customers.... Everyone must do marketing regardless of function or department." Says another, "Engaging customers today requires commitment from the entire company. We're all marketers now."[12] Thus, whether you're an accountant, an operations manager, a financial analyst, an IT specialist, or a human resources manager, you need to understand marketing and your role in creating customer value.

Partnering with Others in the Marketing System

In its quest to engage customers and create customer value, the firm needs to look beyond its own internal value chain and into the value chains of its suppliers, its distributors, and, ultimately, its customers. Consider McDonald's. People do not swarm to McDonald's only because they love the chain's hamburgers. Consumers flock to the McDonald's *system*, not only to its food products. Throughout the world, McDonald's finely tuned value delivery system delivers a high standard of QSCV—quality, service, cleanliness, and value. McDonald's is effective only to the extent that it successfully partners with its franchisees, suppliers, and others to jointly create "our customers' favorite place and way to eat."

More companies today are partnering with other members of the supply chain—suppliers, distributors, and, ultimately, customers—to improve the performance of the customer **value delivery network**. Competition no longer takes place only between individual competitors. Rather, it takes place between the entire value delivery network created by these competitors. Thus, Ford's performance against Toyota depends on the quality of Ford's overall value delivery network versus Toyota's. Even if Ford makes the best cars, it might lose in the marketplace if Toyota's dealer network provides a more customer-satisfying sales and service experience.

Value delivery network
A network composed of the company, suppliers, distributors, and, ultimately, customers who partner with each other to improve the performance of the entire system in delivering customer value.

LINKING THE CONCEPTS

Pause here for a moment to apply what you've read in the first part of this chapter.

- Why are we talking about company-wide strategic planning in a marketing text? What *does* strategic planning have to do with marketing?
- What are Starbucks's strategy and mission? What role does marketing play in helping Starbucks to accomplish its strategy and mission?
- What roles do other Starbucks departments play, and how can the company's marketers partner with these departments to maximize overall customer value? What roles do Starbucks's suppliers play?

Author Comment
Now that we've set the context in terms of company-wide strategy, it's time to discuss customer value-driven marketing strategies and programs.

Marketing Strategy and the Marketing Mix

The strategic plan defines the company's overall mission and objectives. Marketing's role is shown in **>> Figure 2.4**, which summarizes the major activities involved in managing a customer-driven marketing strategy and the marketing mix.

Figure 2.4 Managing Marketing Strategies and the Marketing Mix

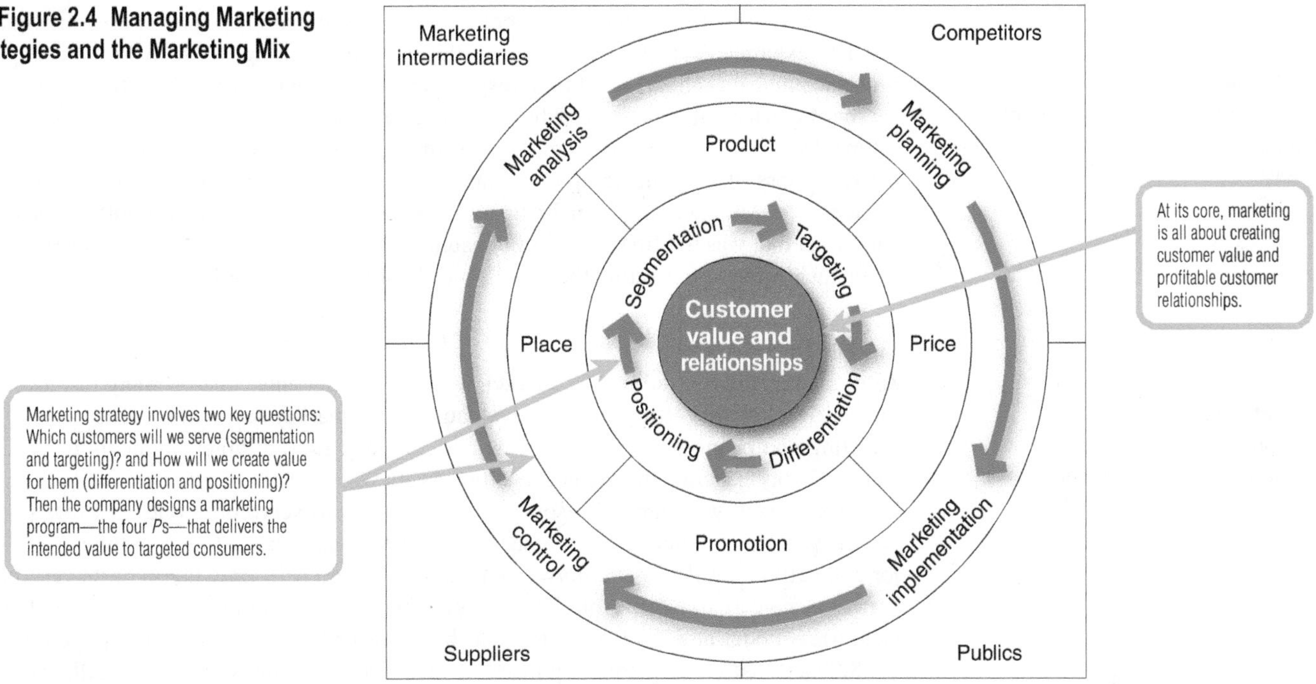

Marketing strategy
The marketing logic by which the company hopes to create customer value and achieve profitable customer relationships.

Consumers are in the center. The goal is to create value for customers and build profitable customer relationships. Next comes **marketing strategy**—the marketing logic by which the company hopes to create this customer value and achieve these profitable relationships. The company decides which customers it will serve (segmentation and targeting) and how (differentiation and positioning). It identifies the total market and then divides it into smaller segments, selects the most promising segments, and focuses on serving and satisfying the customers in these segments.

Guided by marketing strategy, the company designs an integrated *marketing mix* made up of factors under its control—product, price, place, and promotion (the four *Ps*). To find the best marketing strategy and mix, the company engages in marketing analysis, planning, implementation, and control. Through these activities, the company watches and adapts to the actors and forces in the marketing environment. We will now look briefly at each activity. In later chapters, we will discuss each one in more depth.

Customer Value-Driven Marketing Strategy

To succeed in today's competitive marketplace, companies must be customer centered. They must win customers from competitors and then engage and grow them by delivering greater value. But before it can satisfy customers, a company must first understand customer needs and wants. Thus, sound marketing requires careful customer analysis.

Companies know that they cannot profitably serve all consumers in a given market—at least not all consumers in the same way. There are too many different kinds of consumers with too many different kinds of needs. Most companies are in a position to serve some segments better than others. Thus, each company must divide up the total market, choose the best segments, and design strategies for profitably serving chosen segments. This process involves *market segmentation, market targeting, differentiation*, and *positioning*.

Market Segmentation

Market segmentation
Dividing a market into distinct groups of buyers who have different needs, characteristics, or behaviors and who might require separate marketing strategies or mixes.

The market consists of many types of consumers, products, and needs. The marketer must determine which segments offer the best opportunities. Consumers can be grouped and served in various ways based on geographic, demographic, psychographic, and behavioral factors. The process of dividing a market into distinct groups of buyers who have different needs, characteristics, or behaviors and who might require separate marketing strategies or mixes is called **market segmentation**.

Every market has segments, but not all ways of segmenting a market are equally useful. For example, Tylenol would gain little by distinguishing between low-income and high-income pain-relief users if both respond the same way to marketing efforts. A **market segment** consists of consumers who respond in a similar way to a given set of marketing efforts. In the car market, for example, consumers who want the biggest, most comfortable car regardless of price make up one market segment. Consumers who care mainly about price and operating economy make up another segment. It would be difficult to make one car model that was the first choice of consumers in both segments. Companies are wise to focus their efforts on meeting the distinct needs of individual market segments.

Market segment
A group of consumers who respond in a similar way to a given set of marketing efforts.

Market Targeting

After a company has defined its market segments, it can enter one or many of these segments. **Market targeting** involves evaluating each market segment's attractiveness and selecting one or more segments to enter. A company should target segments in which it can profitably generate the greatest customer value and sustain it over time.

Market targeting
The process of evaluating each market segment's attractiveness and selecting one or more segments to enter.

A company with limited resources might decide to serve only one or a few special segments or market niches. Such nichers specialize in serving customer segments that major competitors overlook or ignore. For example, Ferrari sells only 2,200 of its very-high-performance cars in North America each year but at very high prices—such as its Ferrari California model at $198,000 or the 740-horsepower F-12 Berlinetta at an eye-opening $318,000. Most nichers aren't quite so exotic. Profitable low-cost airline Allegiant Air avoids direct competition with larger major airline rivals by targeting smaller, neglected markets and new flyers. Nicher Allegiant "goes where they ain't." And small online-search startup DuckDuckGo thrives among privacy-minded users in the shadows of search giants Google and Microsoft's Bing (see Marketing at Work 2.2).

Alternatively, a company might choose to serve several related segments—perhaps those with different kinds of customers but with the same basic wants. Gap Inc., for example, targets different age, income, and lifestyle clothing and accessory segments with six different store and online brands: Gap, Banana Republic, Old Navy, Piperlime, Athleta, and INTERMIX. The Gap store brand breaks its segment down into even smaller niches, including Gap, GapKids, babyGap, GapMaternity, and GapBody.[13] Or a large company (for example, car companies like Honda and Ford) might decide to offer a complete range of products to serve all market segments.

Most companies enter a new market by serving a single segment; if this proves successful, they add more segments. For example, Nike started with innovative running shoes for serious runners. Large companies eventually seek full market coverage. Nike now makes and sells a broad range of sports apparel and equipment for just about anyone and everyone, in about every sport. It designs different products to meet the special needs of each segment it serves.

Market Differentiation and Positioning

After a company has decided which market segments to enter, it must determine how to differentiate its market offering for each targeted segment and what positions it wants to occupy in those segments. A product's *position* is the place it occupies relative to competitors' products in consumers' minds. Marketers want to develop unique market positions for their products. If a product is perceived to be exactly like others on the market, consumers would have no reason to buy it.

Positioning
Arranging for a product to occupy a clear, distinctive, and desirable place relative to competing products in the minds of target consumers.

Differentiation
Actually differentiating the market offering to create superior customer value.

Marketing mix
The set of tactical marketing tools—product, price, place, and promotion—that the firm blends to produce the response it wants in the target market.

Positioning is arranging for a product to occupy a clear, distinctive, and desirable place relative to competing products in the minds of target consumers. Marketers plan positions that distinguish their products from competing brands and give them the greatest advantage in their target markets.

Audi promises "Truth in Engineering"; Subaru is "Confidence in Motion." Coke is all about "open happiness"; Pepsi says "live for now." Del Monte is "Bursting with Life"; Cascadian Farm products are "Certified Organic. Guaranteed Delicious." At Panera, you can "Live Consciously, Eat Deliciously; at Wendy's, "Quality Is Our Recipe."

Such deceptively simple statements form the backbone of a product's marketing strategy. For example, from its founding, Southwest Airlines has positioned itself as "The LUV Airline," a positioning recently reinforced by the colorful heart in its new logo and plane graphics design. >> As recent Southwest advertising affirms, "Without a heart, it's just a machine." The airline has "always put Heart in everything it does."

In positioning its brand, a company first identifies possible customer value differences that provide competitive advantages on which to build the position. A company can offer greater customer value by either charging lower prices than competitors or offering more benefits to justify higher prices. But if the company *promises* greater value, it must then *deliver* that greater value. Thus, effective positioning begins with **differentiation**—actually *differentiating* the company's market offering to create superior customer value. Once the company has chosen a desired position, it must take strong steps to deliver and communicate that position to target consumers. The company's entire marketing program should support the chosen positioning strategy.

>> Positioning: Southwest's positioning as "The LUV Airline" is reinforced by the colorful heart in its new logo and plane redesign. Southwest has "always put heart in everything it does."

Southwest Airlines Co.

Developing an Integrated Marketing Mix

After determining its overall marketing strategy, the company is ready to begin planning the details of the **marketing mix**, one of the major concepts in modern marketing. The marketing mix is the set of tactical marketing tools that the firm blends to produce the response it wants in the target market. The marketing mix consists of everything the firm can do to engage consumers and deliver customer value. The many possibilities can be collected into four groups of variables—the four *P*s. >> **Figure 2.5** shows the marketing tools under each *P*.

- ***Product*** means the goods-and-services combination the company offers to the target market. Thus, a Ford Escape consists of nuts and bolts, spark plugs, pistons, headlights, and thousands of other parts. Ford offers several Escape models and dozens of optional features. The car comes fully serviced and with a comprehensive warranty that is as much a part of the product as the tailpipe.
- ***Price*** is the amount of money customers must pay to obtain the product. For example, Ford calculates suggested retail prices that its dealers might charge for each Escape. But Ford dealers rarely charge the full sticker price. Instead, they negotiate the price with each customer, offering discounts, trade-in allowances, and credit terms. These actions adjust prices for the current competitive and economic situations and bring them into line with the buyer's perception of the car's value.
- ***Place*** includes company activities that make the product available to target consumers. Ford partners with a large body of independently owned dealerships that sell the company's many different models. Ford selects its dealers carefully and strongly

>> Figure 2.5 The Four *P*s of the Marketing Mix

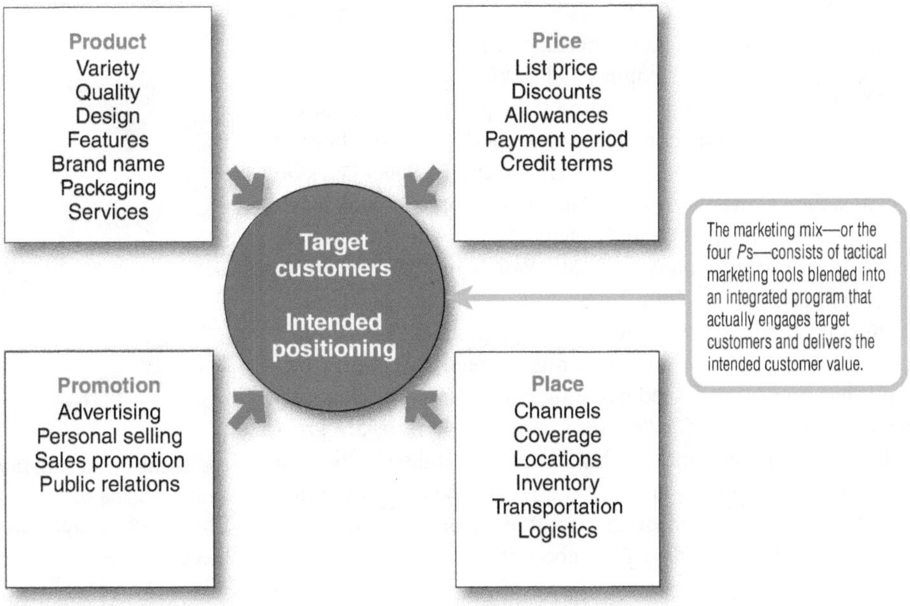

MARKETING AT WORK 2.2

DuckDuckGo: Google's Tiniest, Fiercest Competitor

Google dominates global online search with its massive 67 percent market share. Three other giants—Microsoft's Bing, Yahoo!, and China-based Baidu—combine for another 31 percent of the market. That leaves a precious 2 percent sliver of the market for dozens of other search engines trying to get a foothold. What's more, Google and the other search giants have deep pockets from their non-search businesses, letting them spend abundantly to hold and grow market share. So how does a small search engine wannabe compete against global powerhouses? The best answer: It doesn't—at least not directly. Instead, it finds a unique market niche and runs where the big dogs don't.

Enter DuckDuckGo, a plucky search engine start-up that's carving out its own special market niche. Instead of battling Google and other giants head-on, DuckDuckGo provides a customer benefit that the market leaders can't—privacy. Then it energizes its unique niche with brand personality and user community. One look at DuckDuckGo's icon—a quirky bow-tied duck—gives you the sense that, like the small locomotive in the classic children's story, this might be "the little engine that could."

DuckDuckGo isn't just surviving in its niche, it's exploding. The company is still comparatively tiny—it averages about 9 million daily searches compared with Google's nearly 6 billion. But DuckDuckGo's daily search volume has surged nearly tenfold in just the past three years, whereas Google's volume growth has lagged a bit.

When Gabriel Weinberg first launched DuckDuckGo seven years ago, most people questioned his sanity. How could a small upstart challenge the likes of mighty Google? But rather than simply mimicking Google, Weinberg went a different direction, developing a quality search engine with a key differentiating feature. DuckDuckGo now positions itself strongly on "Smarter Search. Less Clutter. Real Privacy."

DuckDuckGo focuses only on search. It offers a streamlined, clutter-free, customizable user interface with far fewer sponsored ads. As with other search engines, a DuckDuckGo query returns link-by-link search results based on third-party sources, but the results are filtered and reorganized to reduce spam. And beyond the usual search-result links, for many searches, DuckDuckGo provides direct "Instant Answers" in the form of zero-click information boxes above the search results. "When you do a search, you generally want an answer," says Weinberg. "It's our job to try to get an answer." With Instant Answers, DuckDuckGo can "help you get where you want to go in fewer clicks."

The Instant Answer feature is a good one, so good in fact that it has now been copied by Google and Bing. For example, run a Google search for "davinci" or "how long is the great wall" and along with the familiar list of blue links you'll get a white box containing a mini-biography of Leonardo Da Vinci or displaying the length of the Great Wall of China (5,500.3 miles) and other interesting facts about it.

DuckDuckGo would tell you that its Instant Answers are often better. Its answers rely not just on third-party data sources but also on the deep and diverse knowledge of its active, growing, and loyal community of users and developers. DuckDuckGo's community provides additional power behind its searches. In a Wikipedia-like fashion, DuckDuckGo users come up with ideas about what the answers should be, suggest sources, and even develop answers themselves. "DuckDuckGo is a search engine driven by community—you're on the team!" says the company. "We're not just servers and an algorithm. We're so much more."

Still, even though DuckDuckGo had Instant Answers long before Google, Google's response illustrates a typical nicher dilemma. Market leaders usually have huge resources and can quickly copy the start-up's most popular features. "At any point," notes one analyst, "the Googles or Facebooks or Apples of the world can just mimic what made you different, slam-dunking your shattered dreams into the waste bin of tech history."

Fortunately for DuckDuckGo, it has one crucial differentiator that the Googles of the world simply can't mimic. Real privacy. Google's entire model is built around personalization for customers and behaviorally targeted marketing for advertisers. That requires collecting and sharing data about users and their searches. When you search on Google, the company knows and retains in detail who you are, what you've searched for, and when you've searched. It then integrates your online identity and data with its services.

» Niche marketing: DuckDuckGo thrives in the shadows of giant search engine competitors by giving its user community something the Googles of the world can't mimic—real privacy.

Duck Duck Go, Inc.

By contrast, DuckDuckGo is specifically designed to be less invasive and less creepy than its competitors. DuckDuckGo doesn't know who you are. It doesn't log user IP addresses or use cookies to track users over time or other online locations. Users don't have accounts. In fact, DuckDuckGo doesn't even save user search histories. Perhaps most important, when users click on DuckDuckGo's search results links, the linked Web sites don't receive any information generated by the search engine. As one privacy advocate puts it, "DuckDuckGo is a solid search engine that lets you surf the Web without leaving behind a bunch of bread crumbs for Uncle Sam or anyone else to follow.... The sites you visit are being kept at arm's length."

So DuckDuckGo has become the preferred search engine for people concerned about online privacy, and that's a fast-growing group. "If you look at the logs of people's search sessions, they're the most personal thing on the Internet," Weinberg says. "Unlike Facebook, where you choose what to post, with search you're typing in medical and financial problems and all sorts of other things." Today, more and more people are thinking about the privacy implications of their search histories. "It was extreme at the time," says Weinberg of DuckDuckGo's early privacy positioning. But today, he adds, "It's become obvious why people don't want to be tracked."

How does DuckDuckGo make money? Last year, Google made almost all of its $66 billion of revenue from search-related advertising, and most of that business involved large-scale, behaviorally targeted advertising that relies on the very tracking tools that DuckDuckGo shuns. However, even without tracking users, smaller DuckDuckGo can be profitable. It simply focuses on the other part of Google's business—delivering contextual search ads based on the topic of the search itself. So when users search for "curved OLED TVs," DuckDuckGo shows ads and links for TV manufacturers and retailers who've paid for the associated key words.

Thus, in many ways, DuckDuckGo is David to Google's Goliath. But unlike David, DuckDuckGo isn't out to slay the giant. It knows that it can't compete head-on with the Googles and Bings of the world—it doesn't even try. Then again, given the depth of consumer engagement and loyalty that DuckDuckGo engenders in its own small corner of the online search market, Google and the other giants may find it difficult to compete with DuckDuckGo for privacy-minded users. DuckDuckGo is currently the nation's 11th-most-popular search engine based on unique monthly visitors. And as privacy grows in importance, so will DuckDuckGo.

That's what niche marketing is all about—a well-defined brand engaging a focused customer community with meaningful brand relationships that even large and resourceful competitors can't crack. Smart niching has made DuckDuckGo "Google's tiniest, fiercest competitor," says the analyst. "Our vision is simple," says DuckDuckGo. "To give you great search results without tracking you."

Sources: John Paul Titlow, "Inside DuckDuckGo, Google's Tiniest, Fiercest Competitor," *Fast Company*, February 20, 2014, www.fastcompany.com/3026698/inside-duckduckgo-googles-tiniest-fiercest-competitor; "DuckDuckGo Direct Queries per Day," https://duckduckgo.com/traffic.html, accessed June 2015; "Privacy, DuckDuckGo, and the Battle for Search Market Share," *Perioncodefuel,* February 13, 2015, www.codefuel.com/blog/privacy-duckduckgo-battle-search-market-share/; "Top 15 Most Popular Search Engines—April 2015," www.ebizmba.com/articles/search-engines, accessed September 2015; and https://duckduckgo.com/about and www.netmarketshare.com, accessed September 2015.

supports them. The dealers keep an inventory of Ford automobiles, demonstrate them to potential buyers, negotiate prices, close sales, and service the cars after the sale.

- ***Promotion*** refers to activities that communicate the merits of the product and persuade target customers to buy it. Ford spends nearly $2.6 billion each year on U.S. advertising to tell consumers about the company and its many products.[14] Dealership salespeople assist potential buyers and persuade them that Ford is the best car for them. Ford and its dealers offer special promotions—sales, cash rebates, and low financing rates—as added purchase incentives. And Ford's Facebook, Twitter, YouTube, Instagram, and other social media platforms engage consumers with the brand and with other brand fans.

An effective marketing program blends the marketing mix elements into an integrated marketing program designed to achieve the company's marketing objectives by engaging consumers and delivering value to them. The marketing mix constitutes the company's tactical tool kit for establishing strong positioning in target markets.

Some critics think that the four *P*s may omit or underemphasize certain important activities. For example, they ask, "Where are services? Just because they don't start with a *P* doesn't justify omitting them." The answer is that services, such as banking, airline, and retailing services, are products too. We might call them *service products*. "Where is packaging?" the critics might ask. Marketers would answer that they include packaging as one of many product decisions. All said, as Figure 2.5 suggests, many marketing activities that might appear to be left out of the marketing mix are included under one of the four *P*s. The issue is not whether there should be four, six, or ten *P*s so much as what framework is most helpful in designing integrated marketing programs.

There is another concern, however, that is valid. It holds that the four *P*s concept takes the seller's view of the market, not the buyer's view. From the buyer's viewpoint, in this age of customer value and relationships, the four *P*s might be better described as the four *A*s:[15]

Four *Ps*	Four *As*
Product	Acceptability
Price	Affordability
Place	Accessibility
Promotion	Awareness

Under this more customer-centered framework, *acceptability* is the extent to which the product exceeds customer expectations; *affordability* the extent to which customers are willing and able to pay the product's price; *accessibility* the extent to which customers can readily acquire the product; and *awareness* the extent to which customers are informed about the product's features, persuaded to try it, and reminded to repurchase. The four *A*s relate closely to the traditional four *P*s. Product design influences acceptability, price affects affordability, place affects accessibility, and promotion influences awareness. Marketers would do well to think through the four *A*s first and then build the four *P*s on that platform.

Author Comment
So far we've focused on the *marketing* in marketing management. Now, let's turn to the *management*.

Managing the Marketing Effort

In addition to being good at the *marketing* in marketing management, companies also need to pay attention to the *management*. Managing the marketing process requires the five marketing management functions shown in **Figure 2.6**—*analysis, planning, implementation, organization,* and *control.* The company first develops company-wide strategic plans and then translates them into marketing and other plans for each division, product, and brand. Through implementation and organization, the company turns the plans into actions. Control consists of measuring and evaluating the results of marketing activities and taking corrective action where needed. Finally, marketing analysis provides the information and evaluations needed for all the other marketing activities.

Marketing Analysis

SWOT analysis
An overall evaluation of the company's strengths (S), weaknesses (W), opportunities (O), and threats (T).

Managing the marketing function begins with a complete analysis of the company's situation. The marketer should conduct a **SWOT analysis** (pronounced "swat" analysis), by which it evaluates the company's overall strengths (S), weaknesses (W), opportunities (O),

Figure 2.6 Managing Marketing: Analysis, Planning, Implementation, and Control

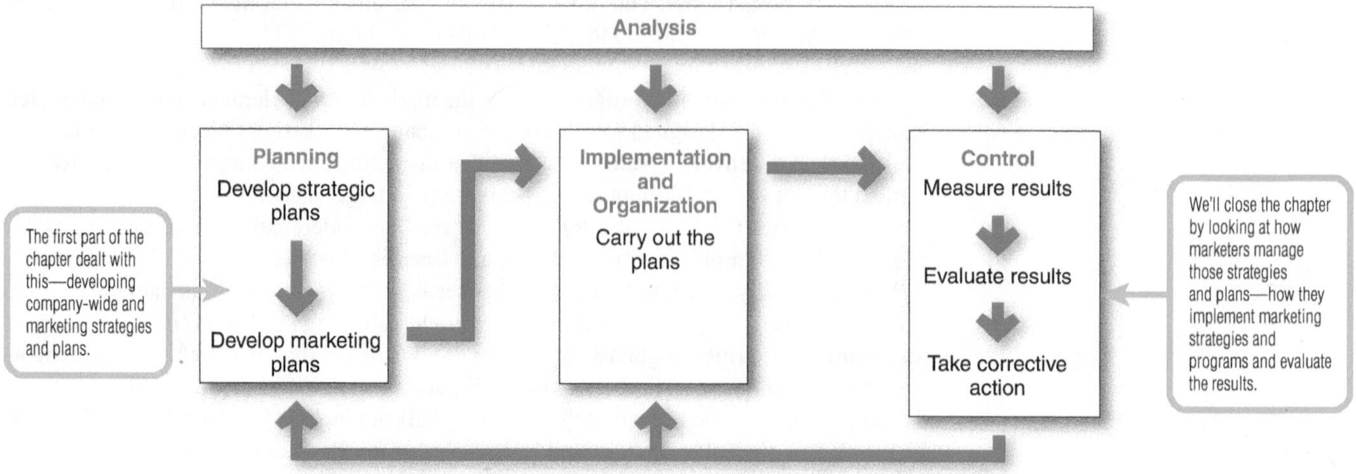

>> Figure 2.7 SWOT Analysis: Strengths (S), Weaknesses (W), Opportunities (O), and Threats (T)

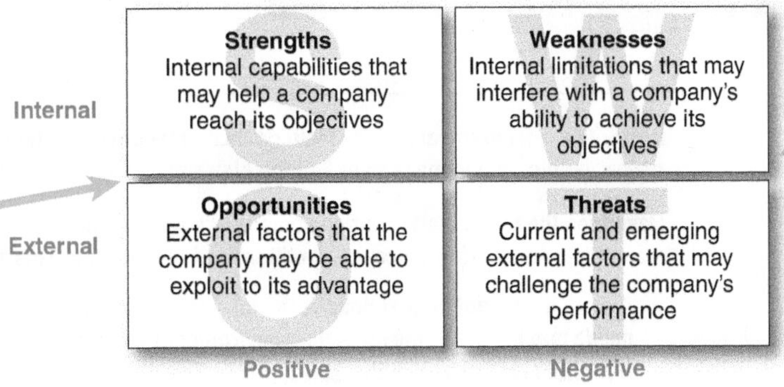

The goal of SWOT analysis is to match the company's strengths to attractive opportunities in the environment while eliminating or overcoming the weaknesses and minimizing the threats.

Hang on to this figure! SWOT analysis (pronounced "swat" analysis) is a widely used tool for conducting a situation analysis. You'll find yourself using it a lot in the future, especially when analyzing business cases.

and threats (T) (see **>> Figure 2.7**). Strengths include internal capabilities, resources, and positive situational factors that may help the company serve its customers and achieve its objectives. Weaknesses include internal limitations and negative situational factors that may interfere with the company's performance. Opportunities are favorable factors or trends in the external environment that the company may be able to exploit to its advantage. And threats are unfavorable external factors or trends that may present challenges to performance.

The company should analyze its markets and marketing environment to find attractive opportunities and identify threats. It should analyze company strengths and weaknesses as well as current and possible marketing actions to determine which opportunities it can best pursue. The goal is to match the company's strengths to attractive opportunities in the environment while simultaneously eliminating or overcoming the weaknesses and minimizing the threats. Marketing analysis provides inputs to each of the other marketing management functions. We discuss marketing analysis more fully in Chapter 3.

Marketing Planning

Through strategic planning, the company decides what it wants to do with each business unit. Marketing planning involves choosing marketing strategies that will help the company attain its overall strategic objectives. A detailed marketing plan is needed for each business, product, or brand. What does a marketing plan look like? Our discussion focuses on product or brand marketing plans.

>> Table 2.2 outlines the major sections of a typical product or brand marketing plan. (See Appendix 2 for a sample marketing plan.) The plan begins with an executive summary that quickly reviews major assessments, goals, and recommendations. The main section of the plan presents a detailed SWOT analysis of the current marketing situation as well as potential threats and opportunities. The plan next states major objectives for the brand and outlines the specifics of a marketing strategy for achieving them.

A *marketing strategy* consists of specific strategies for target markets, positioning, the marketing mix, and marketing expenditure levels. It outlines how the company intends to engage target customers and create value in order to capture value in return. In this section, the planner explains how each strategy responds to the threats, opportunities, and critical issues spelled out earlier in the plan. Additional sections of the marketing plan lay out an action program for implementing the marketing strategy along with the details of a supporting *marketing budget*. The last section outlines the controls that will be used to monitor progress, measure return on marketing investment, and take corrective action.

Marketing Implementation

Marketing implementation
Turning marketing strategies and plans into marketing actions to accomplish strategic marketing objectives.

Planning good strategies is only a start toward successful marketing. A brilliant marketing strategy counts for little if the company fails to implement it properly. **Marketing implementation** is the process that turns marketing *plans* into marketing *actions* to

» Table 2.2 Contents of a Marketing Plan

Section	Purpose
Executive summary	Presents a brief summary of the main goals and recommendations of the plan for management review, helping top management find the plan's major points quickly.
Current marketing situation	Describes the target market and the company's position in it, including information about the market, product performance, competition, and distribution. This section includes the following: • A *market description* that defines the market and major segments and then reviews customer needs and factors in the marketing environment that may affect customer purchasing. • A *product review* that shows sales, prices, and gross margins of the major products in the product line. • A review of *competition* that identifies major competitors and assesses their market positions and strategies for product quality, pricing, distribution, and promotion. • A review of *distribution* that evaluates recent sales trends and other developments in major distribution channels.
Threats and opportunities analysis	Assesses major threats and opportunities that the product might face, helping management to anticipate important positive or negative developments that might have an impact on the firm and its strategies.
Objectives and issues	States the marketing objectives that the company would like to attain during the plan's term and discusses key issues that will affect their attainment.
Marketing strategy	Outlines the broad marketing logic by which the business unit hopes to engage customers, create customer value, and build customer relationships, plus the specifics of target markets, positioning, and marketing expenditure levels. How will the company create value for customers in order to capture value from customers in return? This section also outlines specific strategies for each marketing mix element and explains how each responds to the threats, opportunities, and critical issues spelled out earlier in the plan.
Action programs	Spells out how marketing strategies will be turned into specific action programs that answer the following questions: *What* will be done? *When* will it be done? *Who* will do it? *How* much will it cost?
Budgets	Details a supporting marketing budget that is essentially a projected profit-and-loss statement. It shows expected revenues and expected costs of production, distribution, and marketing. The difference is the projected profit. The budget becomes the basis for materials buying, production scheduling, personnel planning, and marketing operations.
Controls	Outlines the controls that will be used to monitor progress, allow management to review implementation results, and spot products that are not meeting their goals. It includes measures of return on marketing investment.

accomplish strategic marketing objectives. Whereas marketing planning addresses the *what* and *why* of marketing activities, implementation addresses the *who, where, when,* and *how*.

Many managers think that "doing things right" (implementation) is as important as, or even more important than, "doing the right things" (strategy). The fact is that both are critical to success, and companies can gain competitive advantages through effective implementation. One firm can have essentially the same strategy as another yet win in the marketplace through faster or better execution. Still, implementation is difficult—it is often easier to think up good marketing strategies than it is to carry them out.

In an increasingly connected world, people at all levels of the marketing system must work together to implement marketing strategies and plans. At John Deere, for example, marketing implementation for the company's residential, commercial, agricultural, and industrial equipment requires day-to-day decisions and actions by thousands of people both inside and outside the organization. Marketing managers make decisions about target segments, branding, product development, pricing, promotion, and distribution. They talk with engineering about product design, with manufacturing about production and inventory levels, and with finance about funding and cash flows. They also connect with outside people, such as advertising agencies to plan ad campaigns and the news media to obtain publicity support. The sales force urges and supports independent John Deere dealers and large retailers like Lowe's in their efforts to convince residential, agricultural, and industrial customers that "Nothing Runs Like a Deere."

Marketing Department Organization

The company must design a marketing organization that can carry out marketing strategies and plans. If the company is very small, one person might do all the research, selling, advertising, customer service, and other marketing work. As the company expands, however, a marketing department emerges to plan and carry out marketing activities. In large companies, this department contains many specialists—product and market managers, sales managers and salespeople, market researchers, and advertising and social media experts, among others.

To head up such large marketing organizations, many companies have now created a *chief marketing officer* (or CMO) position. This person heads up the company's entire marketing operation and represents marketing on the company's top management team. The CMO position puts marketing on equal footing with other "C-level" executives, such as the chief operating officer (COO) and the chief financial officer (CFO). As a member of top management, the CMO's role is to champion the customer's cause—to be the "chief customer officer." To that end, British Airways even went so far as to rename its top marketing position as Director of Customer Experience.[16]

Modern marketing departments can be arranged in several ways. The most common form of marketing organization is the *functional organization*. Under this organization, different marketing activities are headed by a functional specialist—a sales manager, an advertising manager, a marketing research manager, a customer service manager, or a new product manager. A company that sells across the country or internationally often uses a *geographic organization*. Its sales and marketing people are assigned to specific countries, regions, and districts. Geographic organization allows salespeople to settle into a territory, get to know their customers, and work with a minimum of travel time and cost. Companies with many very different products or brands often create a *product management organization*. Using this approach, a product manager develops and implements a complete strategy and marketing program for a specific product or brand.

Marketers must continually plan their analysis, implementation, and control activities.

Kzenon/Shutterstock

For companies that sell one product line to many different types of markets and customers who have different needs and preferences, a *market* or *customer management organization* might be best. A market management organization is similar to the product management organization. Market managers are responsible for developing marketing strategies and plans for their specific markets or customers. This system's main advantage is that the company is organized around the needs of specific customer segments. Many companies develop special organizations to manage their relationships with large customers. For example, companies such as P&G and Stanley Black & Decker have created large teams, or even whole divisions, to serve large customers, such as Walmart, Target, Kroger, or Home Depot.

Large companies that produce many different products flowing into many different geographic and customer markets usually employ some *combination* of the functional, geographic, product, and market organization forms.

Marketing organization has become an increasingly important issue in recent years. More and more, companies are shifting their brand management focus toward *customer management*—moving away from managing only product or brand profitability and toward managing customer profitability and customer equity. They think of themselves not as managing portfolios of brands but as managing portfolios of customers. And rather than managing the fortunes of a brand, they see themselves as managing customer-brand engagement, experiences, and relationships.

Marketing Control

Marketing control
Measuring and evaluating the results of marketing strategies and plans and taking corrective action to ensure that the objectives are achieved.

Because many surprises occur during the implementation of marketing strategies and plans, marketers must practice constant **marketing control**—measuring and evaluating results and taking corrective action to ensure that the objectives are attained. Marketing control involves four steps. Management first sets specific marketing goals. It then measures its performance in the marketplace and evaluates the causes of any differences between expected and actual performance. Finally, management takes corrective action to close the gaps between goals and performance. This may require changing the action programs or even changing the goals.

Operating control involves checking ongoing performance against the annual plan and taking corrective action when necessary. Its purpose is to ensure that the company achieves the sales, profits, and other goals set out in its annual plan. It also involves determining the profitability of different products, territories, markets, and channels. *Strategic control* involves looking at whether the company's basic strategies are well matched to its opportunities. Marketing strategies and programs can quickly become outdated, and each company should periodically reassess its overall approach to the marketplace.

Author Comment
Measuring marketing return on investment has become a major emphasis. But it can be difficult. For example, a Super Bowl ad reaches more than 100 million consumers but may cost more than $4 million for 30 seconds of airtime. How do you measure the return on such an investment in terms of sales, profits, and building customer engagement and relationships? We'll look at this question again in Chapter 12.

Measuring and Managing Marketing Return on Investment

Marketing return on investment (or marketing ROI)
The net return from a marketing investment divided by the costs of the marketing investment.

Marketing managers must ensure that their marketing dollars are being well spent. In the past, many marketers spent freely on big, expensive marketing programs and flashy advertising campaigns, often without thinking carefully about the financial returns on their spending. Their goal was often a general one—to "build brands and consumer preference." They believed that marketing produces intangible creative outcomes, which do not lend themselves readily to measures of productivity or return.

In today's tighter economic times, however, all that has changed. The free-spending days have been replaced by a new era of marketing measurement and accountability. More than ever, today's marketers are being held accountable for linking their strategies and tactics to measurable marketing performance outcomes. One important marketing performance measure is **marketing return on investment** (or **marketing ROI**). *Marketing ROI* is the net return from a marketing investment divided by the costs of the marketing investment. It measures the profits generated by investments in marketing activities.

In one recent survey, 64 percent of senior marketers rated accountability as a top three concern, well ahead of the 50 percent rating the hot topic of integrated marketing communications as a top concern. However, another survey found that only about 36 percent of chief marketing officers felt able to quantitatively prove the short-term impact of marketing spending on their business; only about 29 percent felt able to prove long-term impact. Another CMO survey showed that a startling 57 percent of CMOs don't take ROI measures into account when setting their marketing budgets, and an even more startling 28 percent said they base their marketing budgets on "gut instinct." Clearly, marketers must think more strategically about the marketing performance returns of their marketing spending.[17]

>> Figure 2.8
Marketing Return on Investment

Source: Adapted from Roland T. Rust, Katherine N. Lemon, and Valerie A. Zeithaml, "Return on Marketing: Using Consumer Equity to Focus Marketing Strategy," *Journal of Marketing*, January 2004, p. 112. Used with permission.

Beyond measuring marketing return on investment in terms of standard performance measures such as sales or market share, many companies are using customer relationship measures, such as customer satisfaction, engagement, retention, and equity. These are more difficult to measure but capture both current and future performance.

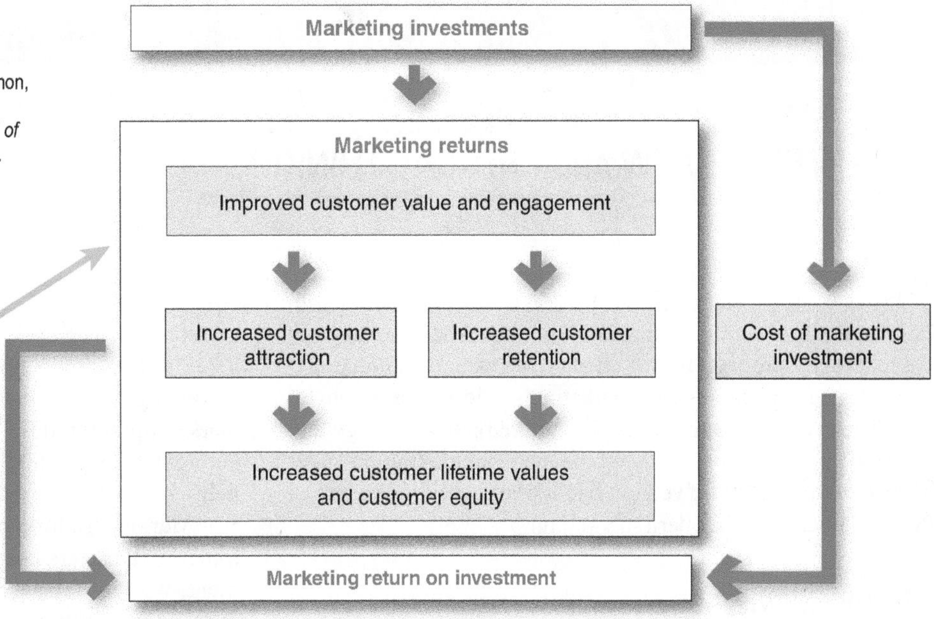

Marketing ROI can be difficult to measure. In measuring financial ROI, both the *R* and the *I* are uniformly measured in dollars. For example, when buying a piece of equipment, the productivity gains resulting from the purchase are fairly straightforward. As of yet, however, there is no consistent definition of marketing ROI. For instance, returns such as engagement, advertising, and brand-building impact aren't easily put into dollar returns.

A company can assess marketing ROI in terms of standard marketing performance measures, such as brand awareness, sales, or market share. Many companies are assembling such measures into *marketing dashboards*—meaningful sets of marketing performance measures in a single display used to monitor strategic marketing performance. Just as automobile dashboards present drivers with details on how their cars are performing, the marketing dashboard gives marketers the detailed measures they need to assess and adjust their marketing strategies. For example, VF Corporation uses a marketing dashboard to track the performance of its more than 30 lifestyle apparel brands—including Wrangler, Lee, The North Face, Vans, Nautica, 7 For All Mankind, Timberland, and others. VF's marketing dashboard tracks brand equity and trends, share of voice, market share, online sentiment, and marketing ROI in key markets worldwide, not only for VF brands but also for competing brands.[18]

Increasingly, however, beyond standard performance measures, marketers are using customer-centered measures of marketing impact, such as customer acquisition, customer engagement, customer retention, customer lifetime value, and customer equity. These measures capture not only current marketing performance but also future performance resulting from stronger customer relationships. **>> Figure 2.8** views marketing expenditures as investments that produce returns in the form of more profitable customer relationships.[19] Marketing investments result in improved customer value, engagement, and satisfaction, which in turn increase customer attraction and retention. This increases individual customer lifetime values and the firm's overall customer equity. Increased customer equity, in relation to the cost of the marketing investments, determines return on marketing investment.

Regardless of how it's defined or measured, the marketing ROI concept is here to stay. In good times or bad, marketers will be increasingly accountable for the performance outcomes of their activities.

MyMarketingLab

If assigned by your instructor, complete the questions marked with the ✪ from the EOC Discussion Questions section in the MyLab. To complete the Marketing by the Numbers problems found in this section, go to your Assignments in the MyLab.

REVIEWING AND EXTENDING THE CONCEPTS

CHAPTER REVIEW AND CRITICAL THINKING

Objectives Review

In Chapter 1, we defined marketing and outlined the steps in the marketing process. In this chapter, we examined company-wide strategic planning and marketing's role in the organization. Then we looked more deeply into marketing strategy and the marketing mix and reviewed the major marketing management functions. So you've now had a pretty good overview of the fundamentals of modern marketing.

OBJECTIVE 2-1 Explain company-wide strategic planning and its four steps. (pp 40–43)

Strategic planning sets the stage for the rest of the company's planning. Marketing contributes to strategic planning, and the overall plan defines marketing's role in the company.

Strategic planning involves developing a strategy for long-run survival and growth. It consists of four steps: (1) defining the company's mission, (2) setting objectives and goals, (3) designing a business portfolio, and (4) developing functional plans. The company's mission should be market oriented, realistic, specific, motivating, and consistent with the market environment. The mission is then transformed into detailed supporting goals and objectives, which in turn guide decisions about the business portfolio. Then each business and product unit must develop detailed marketing plans in line with the company-wide plan.

OBJECTIVE 2-2 Discuss how to design business portfolios and develop growth strategies. (pp 43–48)

Guided by the company's mission statement and objectives, management plans its business portfolio, or the collection of businesses and products that make up the company. The firm wants to produce a business portfolio that best fits its strengths and weaknesses to opportunities in the environment. To do this, it must analyze and adjust its current business portfolio and develop growth and downsizing strategies for adjusting the future portfolio. The company might use a formal portfolio-planning method. But many companies are now designing more-customized portfolio-planning approaches that better suit their unique situations.

OBJECTIVE 2-3 Explain marketing's role in strategic planning and how marketing works with its partners to create and deliver customer value. (pp 48–50)

Under the strategic plan, the major functional departments—marketing, finance, accounting, purchasing, operations, information systems, human resources, and others—must work together to accomplish strategic objectives. Marketing plays a key role in the company's strategic planning by providing a marketing concept philosophy and inputs regarding attractive market opportunities. Within individual business units, marketing designs strategies for reaching the unit's objectives and helps to carry them out profitably.

Marketers alone cannot produce superior value for customers. Marketers must practice partner relationship management, working closely with partners in other departments to form an effective *value chain* that serves the customer. And they must also partner effectively with other companies in the marketing system to form a competitively superior value delivery network.

OBJECTIVE 2-4 Describe the elements of a customer value-driven marketing strategy and mix and the forces that influence it. (pp 50–56)

Customer engagement, value, and relationships are at the center of marketing strategy and programs. Through market segmentation, targeting, differentiation, and positioning, the company divides the total market into smaller segments, selects segments it can best serve, and decides how it wants to bring value to target consumers in the selected segments. It then designs an integrated marketing mix to produce the response it wants in the target market. The marketing mix consists of product, price, place, and promotion decisions (the four *P*s).

OBJECTIVE 2-5 List the marketing management functions, including the elements of a marketing plan, and discuss the importance of measuring and managing marketing return on investment. (pp 56–61)

To find the best strategy and mix and to put them into action, the company engages in marketing analysis, planning, implementation, and control. The main components of a marketing plan are the executive summary, the current marketing situation, threats and opportunities, objectives and issues, marketing strategies, action programs, budgets, and controls. Planning good strategies is often easier than carrying them out. To be successful, companies must also be effective at implementation—turning marketing strategies into marketing actions.

Marketing departments can be organized in one way or a combination of ways: functional marketing organization, geographic organization, product management organization, or market management organization. In this age of customer relationships, more and more companies are now changing their organizational focus from product or territory management to customer relationship management. Marketing organizations carry out marketing control, both operating control and strategic control.

More than ever, marketing accountability is the top marketing concern. Marketing managers must ensure that their marketing dollars are being well spent. In a tighter economy, today's marketers face growing pressures to show that they are adding value in line with their costs. In response, marketers are developing better measures of marketing return on investment. Increasingly, they are using customer-centered measures of marketing impact as a key input into their strategic decision making.

Key Terms

Objective 2-1
Strategic planning (p 40)
Mission statement (p 41)

Objective 2-2
Business portfolio (p 43)
Portfolio analysis (p 43)
Growth-share matrix (p 45)
Product/market expansion grid (p 47)
Market penetration (p 47)
Market development (p 47)
Product development (p 48)
Diversification (p 48)

Objective 2-3
Value chain (p 49)
Value delivery network (p 50)

Objective 2-4
Marketing strategy (p 51)
Market segmentation (p 51)
Market segment (p 52)
Market targeting (p 52)
Positioning (p 52)
Differentiation (p 53)
Marketing mix (p 53)

Objective 2-5
SWOT analysis (p 56)
Marketing implementation (p 57)
Marketing control (p 60)
Marketing return on investment (marketing ROI) (p 60)

Discussion Questions

2-1. Define *strategic planning* and briefly describe the four steps that lead managers and the firm through the strategic planning process. Discuss the role marketing plays in this process. (AASCB: Communication)

2-2. Name and define the four product/market growth strategies. (AACSB: Communications; Reflective Thinking)

2-3. Define each of the four *P*s. What insights might a firm gain by considering the four *A*s rather than the four *P*s? (AACSB: Communication; Reflective Thinking)

2-4. How are marketing departments organized? Which organization is best? (AACSB: Communication, Reflective Thinking)

2-5. Why must marketers practice marketing control, and how is it done? (AACSB: Communication)

Critical Thinking Exercises

2-6. Form a small group and conduct a SWOT analysis for your school, a group that you are a member of, a publicly traded company, a local business, or a nonprofit organization. Based on your analysis, suggest a strategy from the product/market expansion grid and an appropriate marketing mix to implement that strategy. (AACSB: Communication; Reflective Thinking)

2-7. The Boston Consulting Group (BCG) Matrix is a useful strategic tool. Another classic portfolio planning method useful to marketers is the GE/McKinsey Matrix (see www.quickmba.com/strategy/matrix/ge-mckinsey/). How is the GE/McKinsey Matrix similar to and different from the BCG matrix? (AACSB: Communication; Reflective Thinking)

2-8. Create a mission statement for a nonprofit organization you would be interested in starting. Have another student evaluate your mission statement while you evaluate the other student's statement, suggesting areas of improvement. (AACSB: Communication; Reflective Thinking)

MINICASES AND APPLICATIONS

Online, Mobile, and Social Media Marketing Google's Mission

Founded in 1998 as an Internet search engine, Google's mission statement remains the same to this day: to "organize the world's information and make it universally accessible and useful." Google is certainly successful, with revenues growing from $3.2 billion in 2002 to $66 billion in 2014, 90 percent of which comes from advertisers. Google is expanding rapidly into other areas well beyond its search engine, such as self-driving cars, smart contact lenses that measure a person's blood sugar levels, Internet-bearing balloons to create Internet hotspots anywhere on earth, and even magnetic nanoparticles to search for disease within the human bloodstream. Google has been on a buying frenzy recently, purchasing security, biotech, and robotic companies in a quest to capitalize on the Internet of Things (IoT) phenomenon. Experts predict there will be 25 million connected devices in our homes and workplaces by 2020. Google recently announced its new IoT operating system, dubbed Brillo (after the Brillo scrubbing pad because it is a scrubbed-down version of its Android operating system), targeted to developers of smart products connected to the Internet, such as ovens, thermostats, and even toothbrushes. It has also developed Weave, the corresponding IoT language that will allow smart products to speak to each other. Perhaps one day you will be sitting in your Google self-driving car, streaming the news, checking your blood sugar, and cooling your home by turning down your thermostat on the way home from work.

2-9. Conduct research on Google to learn more about its products and services. Some say the time has come for Google to create a new mission statement. Do you agree? Explain. (AACSB: Communication; Reflective Thinking)

2-10. Create a new mission statement for Google that will take it through the rest of this century. (AACSB: Communication; Reflective Thinking)

Marketing Ethics Family Feud

Otsuka Kagu, a well-known furniture store in Japan, made news recently because of an ugly family feud between the founding father and his daughter. Mr. Otsuka started the store in 1969 and built it into one of Japan's leading furniture retailers, now a publicly traded company. Mr. Otsuka's business model focused on high-end customers using a membership system, large showrooms, customer advisors, and strong relationships with a wide range of suppliers. This strategy worked until the 2008 worldwide financial crisis, when the company started experiencing losses as customers sought out lower-priced rivals like IKEA. As a result, Mr. Otsuka put his daughter in charge as president of the company. Ms. Otsuka cut prices, renovated stores, and created a line of lower-priced walk-in stores, bringing the company back to profitability. Although customers apparently approved of Ms. Otsuka's actions, her father and many employees did not. So Mr. Otsuka fired his daughter and reverted to the company's original strategy. Mr. Otsuka even went so far as to call his daughter a "bad child" and label her marketing actions "terrorism." When the company's profitability once again suffered, shareholders voted to bring back Ms. Otsuka as president of the company.

2-11. Do you think Mr. Otsuka's demands to continue focusing on high-end customers are reasonable? (AACSB: Communication; Ethical Reasoning)

2-12. Discuss an example of a company that successfully changed its marketing strategy. (AACSB: Communication; Reflective Thinking)

Marketing by the Numbers Apple Versus Microsoft

In 2014, Apple reported profits of more than $50 billion on sales of $182 billion. For that same period, Microsoft posted a profit of almost $30 billion on sales of $88 billion. So Apple is a better marketer, right? Sales and profits provide information to compare the profitability of these two competitors, but between these numbers is information regarding the efficiency of marketing efforts in creating those sales and profits. Appendix 3, Marketing by the Numbers, discusses other marketing profitability measures beyond the return on marketing investment (marketing ROI) measure described in this chapter. Review the Appendix 2 to answer the questions using the following information from the two companies' incomes statements (all numbers are in thousands):

	Apple	Microsoft
Sales	$182,795,000	$86,833,000
Gross Profit	$70,537,000	$59,899,000
Marketing Expenses	$8,994,750	$15,474,000
Net Income (Profit)	$52,503,000	$27,759,000

2-13. Calculate profit margin, net marketing contribution, marketing return on sales (or marketing ROS), and marketing return on investment (or marketing ROI) for each company. Which company is performing better? (AACSB: Communication; Use of IT; Analytic Thinking)

2-14. Go to Yahoo! Finance (http://finance.yahoo.com/) and find the income statements for two other competing companies. Perform the same analyses for these companies that you performed for the previous question. Which company is doing better overall and with respect to marketing? For marketing expenses, use 75 percent of the company's reported "Selling General and Administrative" expenses, as not all of the expenses in that category are marketing expenses. (AACSB: Communication; Analytic Reasoning; Reflective Thinking)

Video Case Konica Minolta

Konica Minolta has been in business since 1873. For decades, it was a successful photo company selling cameras, equipment, and supplies primarily to final consumers. But dramatic changes in the marketing environment forced the company to reevaluate its marketing strategy and ultimately to abandon what had been its primary industry.

Today, Konica Minolta has a successful business-to-business strategy centered on office equipment and print products for commercial printers. The company has also developed a health-care and medical group, an optics group, and a division that produces components for mobile phones and televisions. With the advent and growth of social media, Konica Minolta's marketing strategy continues to evolve.

After viewing the video featuring Konica Minolta, answer the following questions:

2-15. What is Konica Minolta's mission?

2-16. What market conditions led Konica Minolta to reevaluate its marketing strategy?

2-17. How has Konica Minolta modified its marketing mix? Are these changes in line with its mission?

Company Cases 2 Samsung/1 FedEx/3 Sony

See Appendix 1 for cases appropriate for this chapter. **Case 2, Samsung: A Strategic Plan for Success.** Once an off-brand, strategic planning has made Samsung the number one consumer electronics company. **Case 1, FedEx: Making Every Customer Experience Outstanding.** From the time FedEx opened for business over 40 years ago, the company strategy has been built on a foundation of obsessive customer focus. **Case 3, Sony: Battling the Marketing Environment's "Perfect Storm."** Where Samsung has succeeded through sound strategic planning, Sony is struggling due to the lack thereof.

MyMarketingLab

If assigned by your instructor, complete these writing sections from your Assignments in the MyLab.

2-18. Explain the roles of market segmentation, market targeting, differentiation, and positioning in implementing an effective marketing strategy. (AACSB: Communication)

2-19. Marketers are increasingly held accountable for demonstrating marketing success. Research the various marketing metrics, in addition to those described in the chapter and Appendix 3, used by marketers to measure marketing performance. Write a brief report of your findings. (AACSB: Written and Oral Communication; Reflective Thinking)

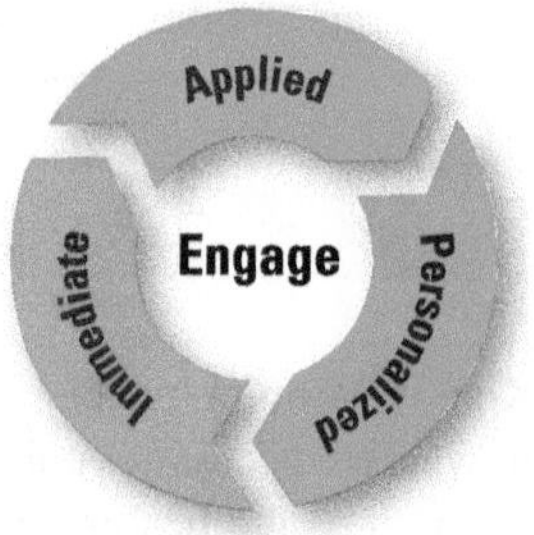

3 Analyzing the Marketing Environment

CHAPTER ROAD MAP Objective Outline

OBJECTIVE 3-1 **Describe the environmental forces that affect the company's ability to serve its customers.** The Microenvironment (68–72); The Macroenvironment (72)

OBJECTIVE 3-2 **Explain how changes in the demographic and economic environments affect marketing decisions.** The Demographic Environment (72–80); The Economic Environment (80–81)

OBJECTIVE 3-3 **Identify the major trends in the firm's natural and technological environments.** The Natural Environment (81–82); The Technological Environment (82–85)

OBJECTIVE 3-4 **Explain the key changes in the political and cultural environments.** The Political and Social Environment (85–88); The Cultural Environment (88–91)

OBJECTIVE 3-5 **Discuss how companies can react to the marketing environment.** Responding to the Marketing Environment (91–93)

Previewing the Concepts

So far, you've learned about the basic concepts of marketing and the steps in the marketing process for engaging and building profitable relationships with targeted consumers. Next, we'll begin digging deeper into the first step of the marketing process—understanding the marketplace and customer needs and wants. In this chapter, you'll see that marketing operates in a complex and changing environment. Other actors in this environment—suppliers, intermediaries, customers, competitors, publics, and others—may work with or against the company. Major environmental forces—demographic, economic, natural, technological, political, and cultural—shape marketing opportunities, pose threats, and affect the company's ability to engage customers and build customer relationships. To develop effective marketing strategies, a company must first understand the environment in which marketing operates.

To start, let's look at Kellogg, the world's largest cereal maker and one of its most recognized and respected brands. Kellogg's cereals have been staples in American homes for generations. However, as demographic, cultural, lifestyle, and other environmental shifts have changed how people eat breakfast, mighty Kellogg has had difficulty adapting. The storied company now finds itself battling to bring modern breakfast eaters back to its table.

First Stop

Kellogg: Losing Its Snap, Crackle, and Pop?

For more than 109 years, ever since the Kellogg brothers of Battle Creek, Michigan, first perfected the process of making toasted corn flakes, the morning bowl of cereal has been a daily ritual in U.S. homes. Generations of sleepy-eyed Americans have bellied up to the breakfast table, filled a bowl with crunchy goodness, and munched their way through enough fuel to fortify them until lunch.

That morning ritual has made Kellogg the world's largest cereal maker. For more than a century, the company's storied brands—such as Kellogg's Corn Flakes, Frosted Flakes, Froot Loops, Rice Krispies, Frosted Mini-Wheats, Raisin Bran, and Special K—have helped define the American breakfast experience.

For generations, Kellogg's storied cereal brands have helped to define the American breakfast experience. But as modern American lifestyles and breakfast-eating behaviors have changed, Kellogg has lost some of its snap, crackle, and pop.

Associated Press

From its origins, Kellogg has capitalized on environmental trends and shifts, even led them. Before Kellogg, most people ate leftovers for breakfast, a sure-fire path to late-morning indigestion. Then John and Will Kellogg patented the process for making a healthy alternative, "flaked cereal," leading to their first successful product, Kellogg's Corn Flakes. When television appeared in 1950s, Kellogg pioneered the pairing of its cereal brands with familiar animated mascots, such as Tony the Tiger for Frosted Flakes; Toucan Sam for Froot Loops; and Snap, Crackle, and Pop for Rice Krispies. And when cereal sales waned in the 1980s, Kellogg almost single-handedly grew the entire cereal category by 50 percent in just five years by targeting baby boomers with products positioned on nutrition and convenience.

But in recent years, amid a flurry of demographic, cultural, and lifestyle changes, Kellogg's bowl-of-cereal breakfast has lost a lot of its allure. Today, as people increasingly reach for granola bars or Greek yogurt, cold cereal consumption has dipped. As breakfast-eating behavior has changed, however, Kellogg has not. As a result, in recent years, Kellogg's overall revenues and profits have lost their snap, crackle, and pop. Its morning-foods sales—which account for the lion's share of its overall revenues—have been hardest hit. Last year, for example, sales of 19 of Kellogg's 25 top cereals dropped by as much as 14 percent.

Americans simply aren't eating as much cereal these days. Gone are the times when families gathered around the breakfast table before Dad headed off to work while Mom stayed home, made lunches, and got the kids off to school. Cold cereal fit well with that routine. But now, with both parents often working, it's a grab-and-go breakfast world, with little time to linger over a bowl of Raisin Bran and the morning newspaper. "For a while, breakfast cereal was convenience food," says one food historian. "But convenience is relative. It's more convenient [now] to grab a breakfast bar, yogurt, a piece of fruit, or a breakfast sandwich at some fast-food place than to eat a bowl of breakfast cereal." Kellogg does market some grab-and-go breakfast lines—such as Eggo frozen waffles, Pop-Tarts toaster pastries, and Nutri-Grain cereal bars. But the modest gains in those products have done little to offset the bigger losses from Kellogg's powerhouse cereals.

There's another major lifestyle trend affecting Kellogg's cereal business—Americans have become more health-conscious. Increasingly, consumers are looking for food with attributes such as "low-carb," "gluten-free," "organic," and "non-GMO" (genetically modified organisms). That presents a big problem for Kellogg, which churns out box after box of carb-heavy, processed foods made from corn, oats, wheat, and rice.

Increased health concerns also add new weight to long-standing claims by food activists that the cereal industry is peddling junk food to children. "Many of the kid-oriented cereals have a fair amount of sugar in them," says one Kellogg critic. "Their Eggo waffles are mostly white flour. Pop-Tarts are white flour and sugar. For a company that started out as a health-food company, they've turned into something very different." For some discerning breakfast eaters, says one analyst, "Tony the Tiger and Toucan Sam may seem less like friendly childhood avatars and more like malevolent sugar traffickers."

Kellogg is the world's largest cereal maker. But as demographic, cultural, lifestyle, and other shifts in the marketing environment change how people eat breakfast, mighty Kellogg finds itself battling to bring modern breakfast eaters back to its table.

Kellogg has responded to some of these concerns. Over the years it has lowered the amount of sugar in its top-selling children's cereals, added gluten-free and GMO-free cereal varieties, and added healthier extensions such as Raisin Bran with Cranberries and Special K Red Berries, a current best seller. In 2000, Kellogg also purchased Kashi, a California-based health-food cereal brand known for natural and organic ingredients. Leveraging Kellogg's resources and know-how, Kashi's annual revenues grew from $25 million to more than $600 million in less than a decade.

But moves toward a healthier Kellogg have been compromised by decisions that seemed at odds with shifting customer lifestyles and preferences. For example, at the same time that Kellogg was adding healthier options to its mainstream brands, it was weighing down its more wholesome brands like Special K and Kashi with less-than-healthy extensions—such as Special K Chocolately Pretzel Bars, Special K Fudge Brownie Bites, Kashi GoLean Vanilla Graham Clusters cereal, and Kashi Blueberry Frozen Waffles—all processed foods loaded with carbs and calories. Kashi also now sells cookies, crackers, pizzas, and frozen entrees in addition to breakfast foods. As a result, these "healthier" Kellogg brands have suffered setbacks. Last year, some Special K versions posted double-digit declines. And the Kashi brand is now struggling with both its identity and its sales. "Kashi is a brand that has lost its way," says an analyst. "Many of its varieties are not organic. Many have GMOs."

Kellogg has plans to reenergize its breakfast sales, such as restoring Kashi's credibility among health-food shoppers and repositioning Special K from a diet brand to one with broader appeal to health-conscious consumers. And the company is busy developing new on-trend breakfast products. Kellogg has also reduced its reliance on cereals with the acquisitions of big snack brands such as Pringles and Keebler—cereal now accounts for 45 percent of its business, down from 70 percent 15 years ago.

Still, some analysts wonder if Kellogg's heart is really into keeping up with new health and lifestyle trends. For example, its recent unveiling of a new gluten-free Special K was largely overshadowed by the enthusiastic introduction of peanut butter and jelly Pop-Tarts, a product largely out of sync with where the U.S. food culture is heading. And although Kellogg has already put 15 new GMO-free cereals on supermarket shelves, behind the scenes the company is spending millions to defeat ballot initiatives in three Western states that would require companies to identify GMO ingredients on their labels. Finally, the Pringles and Keebler acquisitions were more off-trend than on, and they moved the company farther away from its breakfast-foods core.

Despite its recent woes, Kellogg remains a strong, iconic brand. Kellogg's CEO doesn't seem all that worried: "The company has been around for 109 years," he says. "We have the time. We have a plan to turn it around." Some analysts, however, paint a more ominous picture. "Carbs, sugar, and stubbornness are killing Kellogg," says one. Whatever their views, all observers agree that Kellogg is at a critical juncture. As consumers change, Kellogg must change with them. The company's difficulties provide a cautionary tale of what can happen when a company—even a dominant market leader—fails to adapt to its changing marketing environment. Companies that understand and adapt well to their environments can thrive. Those that don't risk their very survival.[1]

Marketing environment
The actors and forces outside marketing that affect marketing management's ability to build and maintain successful relationships with target customers.

Microenvironment
The actors close to the company that affect its ability to engage and serve its customers—the company, suppliers, marketing intermediaries, customer markets, competitors, and publics.

Macroenvironment
The larger societal forces that affect the microenvironment—demographic, economic, natural, technological, political, and cultural forces.

A company's **marketing environment** consists of the actors and forces outside marketing that affect marketing management's ability to build and maintain successful relationships with target customers. Like Kellogg, companies must constantly watch and adapt to the changing environment—or, in many cases, lead those changes.

More than any other group in the company, marketers must be environmental trend trackers and opportunity seekers. Although every manager in an organization should watch the outside environment, marketers have two special aptitudes. They have disciplined methods—marketing research and marketing intelligence—for collecting information and developing insights about the marketing environment. They also spend more time in customer and competitor environments. By carefully studying the environment, marketers can adapt their strategies to meet new marketplace challenges and opportunities.

The marketing environment consists of a *microenvironment* and a *macroenvironment*. The **microenvironment** consists of the actors close to the company that affect its ability to engage and serve its customers—the company, suppliers, marketing intermediaries, customer markets, competitors, and publics. The **macroenvironment** consists of the larger societal forces that affect the microenvironment—demographic, economic, natural, technological, political, and cultural forces. We look first at the company's microenvironment.

Author Comment
The microenvironment includes all the actors close to the company that affect, positively or negatively, its ability to create value for and relationships with customers.

The Microenvironment

Marketing management's job is to build relationships with customers by creating customer value and satisfaction. However, marketing managers cannot do this alone. **>> Figure 3.1** shows the major actors in the marketer's microenvironment. Marketing success requires building relationships with other company departments, suppliers, marketing intermediaries, competitors, various publics, and customers, which combine to make up the company's value delivery network.

The Company

In designing marketing plans, marketing management takes other company groups into account—groups such as top management, finance, research and development (R&D), purchasing, operations, human resources, and accounting. All of these interrelated groups

Figure 3.1 Actors in the Microenvironment

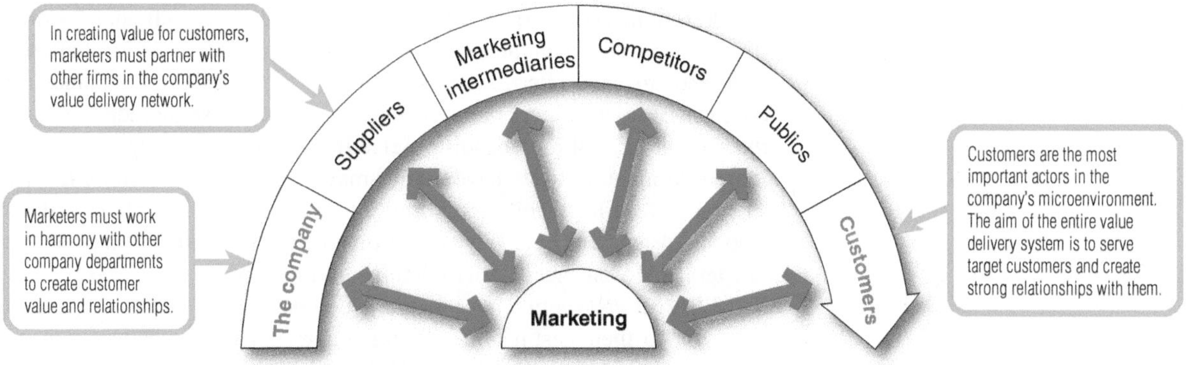

form the internal environment. Top management sets the company's mission, objectives, broad strategies, and policies. Marketing managers make decisions within these broader strategies and plans. Then, as we discussed in Chapter 2, marketing managers must work closely with other company departments. With marketing taking the lead, all departments—from manufacturing and finance to legal and human resources—share the responsibility for understanding customer needs and creating customer value.

Suppliers

Suppliers form an important link in the company's overall customer value delivery network. They provide the resources needed by the company to produce its goods and services. Supplier problems can seriously affect marketing. Marketing managers must watch supply availability and costs. Supply shortages or delays, natural disasters, and other events can cost sales in the short run and damage customer satisfaction in the long run. Rising supply costs may force price increases that can harm the company's sales volume.

Most marketers today treat their suppliers as partners in creating and delivering customer value. For example, Honda knows the importance of building close relationships with its extensive network of suppliers, who furnish everything from fuel tanks, brake controls, and seating systems to production equipment and office supplies.[2]

In the United States alone, American Honda purchases $23 billion worth of auto parts and materials annually from 530 strategic suppliers in 34 states. It spends billions of dollars more on maintenance, repair, and operations (MRO) supplies and services from another 13,900 suppliers. Outside purchases represent about 75 percent of the cost of making a Honda vehicle. So Honda views strategic suppliers as key players in its success and develops deep relationships and teamwork with them. "These suppliers are literally considered extensions of Honda," says one insider.

For example, Honda requires that strategic suppliers open up their books and give Honda full access to their financial information. This helps Honda purchasing associates, Honda engineers, and supplier engineers work as a team to achieve target costs and quality standards, often improving suppliers' performance and profit margins in the process. Supplier personnel also participate in Honda training programs on leadership, finance, quality, and other topics. And Honda meets formally each year with strategic suppliers to review the previous year's results and set goals for the coming year. As a result of such teamwork, Honda has developed healthy, long-term supplier relationships. "Almost 100 percent of the original suppliers selected in the late 1980s are still Honda suppliers today," says the insider. In a recent industry survey, automotive suppliers rated Honda the "most preferred" customer among the world's top six auto manufacturers.

Suppliers: Through close teamwork, Honda has developed healthy, long-term supplier relationships. Strategic suppliers are considered extensions of Honda, to the benefit of both partners.

(right) © Ian Dagnall/Alamy Stock Photo (left) Bloomberg via Getty Images

Marketing Intermediaries

Marketing intermediaries
Firms that help the company to promote, sell, and distribute its products to final buyers.

Marketing intermediaries help the company promote, sell, and distribute its products to final buyers. They include resellers, physical distribution firms, marketing services agencies, and financial intermediaries. *Resellers* are distribution channel firms that help the company find customers or make sales to them. These include wholesalers and retailers that buy and resell merchandise. Selecting and partnering with resellers is not easy. No longer do manufacturers have many small, independent resellers from which to choose. They now face large and growing reseller organizations, such as Walmart, Target, Home Depot, Costco, and Best Buy. These organizations frequently have enough power to dictate terms or even shut smaller manufacturers out of large markets.

Physical distribution firms help the company stock and move goods from their points of origin to their destinations. *Marketing services agencies* are the marketing research firms, advertising agencies, media firms, and marketing consulting firms that help the company target and promote its products to the right markets. *Financial intermediaries* include banks, credit companies, insurance companies, and other businesses that help finance transactions or insure against the risks associated with the buying and selling of goods.

Like suppliers, marketing intermediaries form an important component of the company's overall value delivery network. In its quest to create satisfying customer relationships, the company must do more than just optimize its own performance. It must partner effectively with marketing intermediaries to optimize the performance of the entire system.

Thus, today's marketers recognize the importance of working with their intermediaries as partners rather than simply as channels through which they sell their products. » For example, when Coca-Cola signs on as the exclusive beverage provider for a fast-food chain, such as McDonald's, Wendy's, or Subway, it provides much more than just soft drinks. It also pledges powerful marketing support:[3]

» **Partnering with intermediaries: Coca-Cola provides its retail partners with much more than just soft drinks. It also pledges powerful marketing support.**

Bloomberg via Getty Images

> Coca-Cola assigns cross-functional teams dedicated to understanding the finer points of each retail partner's business. It conducts a staggering amount of research on beverage consumers and shares these insights with its partners. It analyzes the demographics of U.S. zip code areas and helps partners determine which Coke brands are preferred in their areas. Coca-Cola has even studied the design of drive-through menu boards to better understand which layouts, fonts, letter sizes, colors, and visuals induce consumers to order more food and drink. Based on such insights, the Coca-Cola Foodservice group develops marketing programs and merchandising tools that help its retail partners improve their beverage sales and profits. Its Web site, www.CokeSolutions.com, provides retailers with a wealth of information, business solutions, merchandising tips, advice on digital and social media marketing, and techniques on how to go green. "At Coca-Cola we always strive to be our customers' most valued partner," says Coca-Cola's vice president of Foodservice Customer Marketing. Such intense partnering has made Coca-Cola a runaway leader in the U.S. fountain-soft-drink market.

Competitors

The marketing concept states that, to be successful, a company must provide greater customer value and satisfaction than its competitors do. Thus, marketers must do more than simply adapt to the needs of target consumers. They also must gain strategic advantage by positioning their offerings strongly against competitors' offerings in the minds of consumers.

No single competitive marketing strategy is best for all companies. Each firm should consider its own size and industry position compared with those of its competitors. Large firms with dominant positions in an industry can use certain strategies that smaller firms cannot afford. But being large is not enough. There are winning strategies for large firms, but there are also losing ones. And small firms can develop strategies that give them better rates of return than large firms enjoy.

Publics

Public
Any group that has an actual or potential interest in or impact on an organization's ability to achieve its objectives.

The company's marketing environment also includes various publics. A **public** is any group that has an actual or potential interest in or impact on an organization's ability to achieve its objectives. We can identify seven types of publics:

- ***Financial publics.*** This group influences the company's ability to obtain funds. Banks, investment analysts, and stockholders are the major financial publics.
- ***Media publics.*** This group carries news, features, editorial opinions, and other content. It includes television stations, newspapers, magazines, and blogs and other social media.
- ***Government publics.*** Management must take government developments into account. Marketers must often consult the company's lawyers on issues of product safety, truth in advertising, and other matters.
- ***Citizen-action publics.*** A company's marketing decisions may be questioned by consumer organizations, environmental groups, minority groups, and others. Its public relations department can help it stay in touch with consumer and citizen groups.
- ***Local publics.*** This group includes neighborhood residents and community organizations. Large companies usually work to become responsible members of the local communities in which they operate. »For example, Office Depot serves its communities through the Office Depot Foundation, an independent, nonprofit foundation that serves as Office Depot's primary charitable giving arm. The foundation supports a variety of programs that give children tools to succeed in school and in life, build the capacity of nonprofit organizations, and help communities prepare for and overcome disasters. The company backs its "Listen Learn Care" mission with several key community programs supporting children, parents, and teachers. Since 2001, the foundation's National Backpack Program has donated new backpacks containing essential school supplies to more than 3.3 million deserving children. The Office Depot Foundation works with the Kids In Need Foundation to fund Ready, Steady, GO! teacher grants that inspire innovative hands-on learning projects in primary and secondary classrooms. And the company's Be The Difference: Speak Up Against Bullying initiative sponsors school assemblies for students, along with antibullying education sessions for parents, teachers, and administrators conducted by nationally known experts.[4]
- ***General public.*** A company needs to be concerned about the general public's attitude toward its products and activities. The public's image of the company affects its buying behavior.
- ***Internal publics.*** This group includes workers, managers, volunteers, and the board of directors. Large companies use newsletters and other means to inform and motivate their internal publics. When employees feel good about the companies they work for, this positive attitude spills over to the external publics.

» **Publics: The Office Depot Foundation's "Listen Learn Care" mission calls for giving children tools to succeed in school...and in life. Its National Backpack Program has donated new backpacks containing essential school supplies to more than 3.3 million deserving children.**

Office Depot Foundation

A company can prepare marketing plans for these major publics as well as for its customer markets. Suppose the company wants a specific response from a particular public, such as goodwill, favorable word of mouth and social sharing, or donations of time or money. The company would have to design an offer to this public that is attractive enough to produce the desired response.

Customers

Customers are the most important actors in the company's microenvironment. The aim of the entire value delivery network is to engage target customers and create strong relationships with them. The company might target any or all of five types of customer markets. *Consumer markets* consist of individuals and households that buy goods and services for personal consumption. *Business markets* buy goods and services for further processing or use in their production processes, whereas *reseller markets* buy goods and services to resell at a profit. *Government markets* consist of government agencies that buy goods and services to produce public services or transfer the goods and services to others who need them. Finally, *international markets* consist of these buyers in other countries, including consumers, producers, resellers, and governments. Each market type has special characteristics that call for careful study by the seller.

Author Comment
The macroenvironment consists of broader forces that affect the actors in the microenvironment.

The Macroenvironment

Demography
The study of human populations in terms of size, density, location, age, gender, race, occupation, and other statistics.

The company and all of the other actors operate in a larger macroenvironment of forces that shape opportunities and pose threats to the company. **Figure 3.2** shows the six major forces in the company's macroenvironment. Even the most dominant companies can be vulnerable to the often turbulent and changing forces in the marketing environment. Some of these forces are unforeseeable and uncontrollable. Others can be predicted and handled through skillful management. Companies that understand and adapt well to their environments can thrive. Those that don't can face difficult times. One-time dominant market leaders such as Xerox, Sears, and Sony have learned this lesson the hard way. In the remaining sections of this chapter, we examine these forces and show how they affect marketing plans.

Author Comment
Changes in demographics mean changes in markets, so they are very important to marketers. We first look at the biggest demographic trend—the changing age structure of the population.

The Demographic Environment

Demography is the study of human populations in terms of size, density, location, age, gender, race, occupation, and other statistics. The demographic environment is of major interest to marketers because it involves people, and people make up markets. The world population is growing at an explosive rate. It now exceeds 7.2 billion people and is expected to grow to more than 8 billion by the year 2030.[5] The world's large and highly diverse population poses both opportunities and challenges.

Figure 3.2 Major Forces in the Company's Macroenvironment

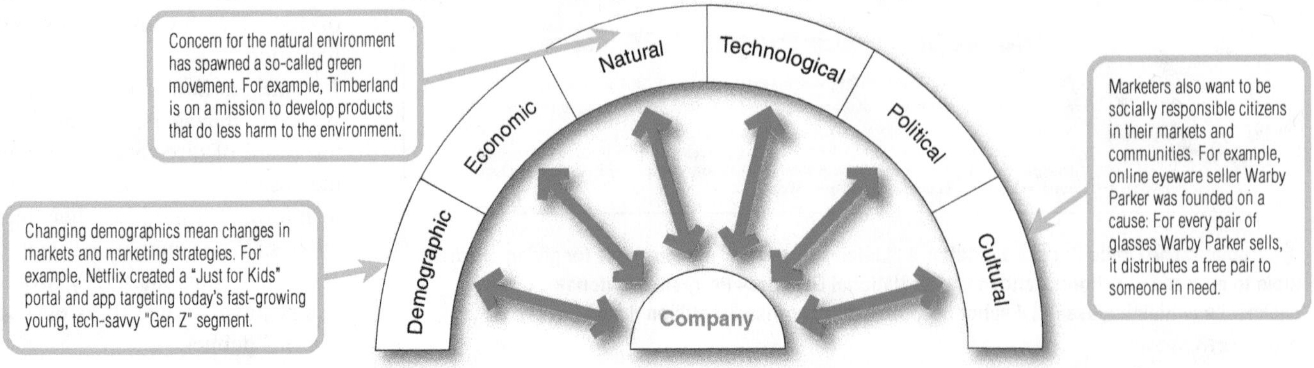

Changes in the world demographic environment have major implications for business. Thus, marketers keep a close eye on demographic trends and developments in their markets. They analyze changing age and family structures, geographic population shifts, educational characteristics, and population diversity. Here, we discuss the most important demographic trends in the United States.

The Changing Age Structure of the Population

The U.S. population currently stands at nearly 321 million and may reach almost 364 million by 2030.[6] The single most important demographic trend in the United States is the changing age structure of the population. Primarily because of falling birthrates and longer life expectancies, the U.S. population is rapidly getting older. In 1980, the median age was 23; by 2050, it is estimated to be 38.[7] This aging of the population will have a significant impact on markets and those who service them.

The U.S. population contains several generational groups. Here, we discuss the four largest groups—the baby boomers, Generation X, the Millennials, and Generation Z—and their impact on today's marketing strategies.

Baby boomers
The 78 million people born during the years following World War II and lasting until 1964.

The Baby Boomers. The post–World War II baby boom produced 78 million **baby boomers**, who were born between 1946 and 1964. Over the years, the baby boomers have been one of the most powerful forces shaping the marketing environment. The youngest boomers are now in their fifties; the oldest are in their late sixties and well into retirement.

The baby boomers are the wealthiest generation in U.S. history, what one analyst calls "a marketer's dream." Today's baby boomers account for about 35 percent of the U.S. population but control an estimated 70 percent of the nation's disposable income and half of all consumer spending.[8] The boomers constitute a lucrative market for financial services, new housing and home remodeling, new cars, travel and entertainment, eating out, health and fitness products, and just about everything else.

In a recent campaign aimed at convincing companies to advertise in its magazine, the AARP (formerly the American Association of Retired Persons) advises that brands focusing on younger demographics groups are missing a big opportunity. The AARP ads feature people in their 50s and 60s, with headlines such as "I may be creased, but my money is crisp" and "I may be gray, but my money is as green as it gets." The ads continue: "Why is it all about 18–34, when they barely have a dime of their own? The story is simple, AARP…reaches the best boomers, and 68 percent of those over 50 give money to their adult kids."

It would be a mistake to think of the older boomers as phasing out or slowing down. For example, the titles of many magazines targeting boomers suggest that these consumers are anything but the stereotypical faded, poverty-struck shut-ins. >> With titles such as *Everything Zoomer, WatchBoom,* and *BOOM! Magazine,* they appeal to an active boomer generation that is redefining the meaning of growing older:[9]

> *BOOM! Magazine* targets active 50-plus consumers, with an appeal to Live Smart—Live Well—Live Large." The magazine bills itself as "a lifestyle resource for active adults [that] inspires, educates, motivates, and delights readers with a vigorous new image of phase-two living." Monthly topics include health and wellness, travel and leisure, food and wine, history, visual and performing arts, and financial planning. Each issue features local personalities in a *Fifty & Fabulous* spotlight. Fodder for old folks? You won't find much of that in *BOOM! Magazine* or its online newsletter *Boom! Blast.*

>> **Targeting baby boomers: *BOOM! Magazine* targets active 50-plus consumers, urging them to "Live Smart—Live Well—Live Large."**
Boom! Magazine

Rather than viewing themselves that way, many of today's boomers see themselves as entering new life phases. The more active boomers—sometimes called zoomers—have no intention of abandoning their youthful lifestyles as they age. For example, adults over 50 now account for 80 percent of luxury travel spending in America. Boomers are also digitally active and increasingly social media savvy. They are the fastest-growing demographic online, and nine out of 10 boomers have made an online purchase. They are also the fastest-growing social media users, with an 80 percent surge in Facebook usage over the past four years.[10]

Thus, although the boomers buy lots of products that help them deal with issues of aging—from vitamins to blood pressure monitors to Good Grips kitchen tools—they also constitute a lucrative market for products and services that help them live life to the fullest. For example, Amazon created a site dedicated to customers over 50—called "50+ Active & Healthy Living." The site features four sections catering to health-care, medical, and dietary needs but five sections focused on products for travel and leisure, exercise and fitness, personal care, beauty, and entertainment.

Generation X. The baby boom was followed by a "birth dearth," creating another generation of 49 million people born between 1965 and 1976. Author Douglas Coupland calls them **Generation X** because they lie in the shadow of the boomers.

Generation X
The 49 million people born between 1965 and 1976 in the "birth dearth" following the baby boom.

Considerably smaller than the boomer generation that precedes them and the Millennials who follow, the Generation Xers are a sometimes overlooked consumer group. Although they seek success, they are less materialistic than the other groups; they prize experience, not acquisition. For many of the Gen Xers who are parents, family comes first—both children and their aging parents—and career second. From a marketing standpoint, the Gen Xers are a more skeptical bunch. They tend to research products heavily before they consider a purchase, prefer quality to quantity, and tend to be less receptive to overt marketing pitches. They are more likely to be receptive to irreverent ad pitches that make fun of convention and tradition.

The first to grow up in the Internet era, Generation X is a connected generation that embraces the benefits of new technology. Some 60 percent use a smartphone daily compared with 42 percent of baby boomers. Of the Xers on the Internet, 74 percent use the Internet for banking, 72 percent use it for researching companies or products, and 81 percent have made purchases online. Nearly two-thirds of Xers used Facebook in the last month and 30 percent use Pinterest.[11]

The Gen Xers, now middle-aged, have grown up and are taking over. They have increasingly displaced the lifestyles, culture, and values of the baby boomers. They are firmly into their careers, and many are proud homeowners with growing families. They are the most educated generation to date, and they possess hefty annual purchasing power.

With so much potential, many brands and organizations focus on Gen Xers as a prime target segment. For example, a full 82 percent of Gen Xers own their own homes, making them an important segment for home-and-hearth marketers. >> Home improvement retailer Lowe's markets heavily to Gen X homeowners, urging them to "Never Stop Improving." Through ads, online videos, and a substantial social media presence, Lowe's provides ideas and advice on a wide range of indoor and outdoor home improvement projects and problems, providing solutions that make life simpler for busy Gen X homeowners and their families. Its myLowe's app is like a 24/7 home improvement concierge that lets customers build room-by-room profiles of their homes, archive their Lowe's purchases, build product lists with photos, receive reminders for things like changing furnace filters, and even consult with store employees online as they plan out home improvement projects.[12]

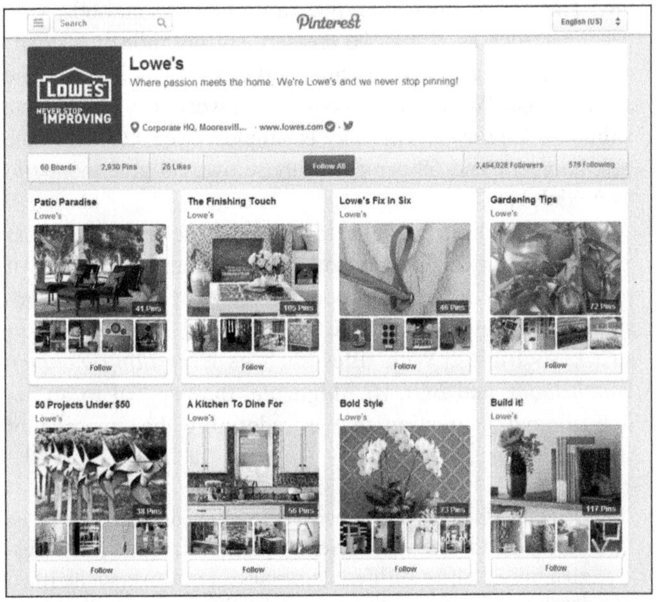

>> Targeting Gen Xers: Lowe's markets heavily to Gen X homeowners with ideas and advice on home improvement projects and problems, urging them to "Never Stop Improving." The Lowe's Pinterest page is loaded with tips for Gen Xers.

Millennials (or Generation Y)
The 83 million children of the baby boomers born between 1977 and 2000.

Millennials. Both the baby boomers and Gen Xers will one day be passing the reins to the **Millennials** (also called **Generation Y** or the echo boomers). Born between 1977 and 2000, these children of the baby boomers number 83 million or more, dwarfing the Gen Xers and becoming larger even than the baby boomer segment. In the postrecession era, the Millennials are the most financially strapped generation. Facing higher unemployment and saddled with more debt, many of these young consumers have near-empty piggy banks. Still, because of their numbers, the Millennials make up a huge and attractive market, both now and in the future.

One thing that all Millennials have in common is their comfort with digital technology. They don't just embrace technology; it's a way of life. The Millennials were the first generation to grow up in a world filled with computers, mobile phones, satellite TV, iPods and iPads, and online social media. As a result, they engage with brands in an entirely new way, such as with mobile or social media. More than sales pitches from marketers, Millennials seek authenticity and opportunities to shape their own brand experiences and share them with others. One AT&T marketer identifies what she calls "universal Millennial truths: being transparent, authentic, immediate and versatile."[13]

Many brands are now fielding specific products and marketing campaigns aimed at Millennial needs and lifestyles. » For example, GE has created a new entry-level line of stylish but affordable home appliances called GE Artistry. GE has traditionally focused its marketing and design on consumers ages 45 to 60, who boast fatter wallets and fancier kitchens. However, the GE Artistry line is designed to capture the fast-growing segment of tech-design-savvy but price-conscious Millennials who are buying and equipping their first homes.[14]

» **Targeting Millennials: GE's Artistry appliance line is designed to capture the fast-growing segment of tech-design-savvy but price-conscious Millennials who are buying and equipping their first homes.**
GE

Similarly, Marriott and IKEA recently joined forces to launch a new European hotel chain called Moxy Hotels. The innovative lifestyle hotel chain targets the fast-emerging market of young Millennial travelers by combining contemporary design, approachable service, high-tech features, and—perhaps most important—reasonable prices. Moxy hotels offer stylish, no-frills accommodations to keep prices down. But they feature plenty of the technologies that young Millennials favor, such as checking in via mobile devices, big-screen TVs, plenty of built-in USB ports in rooms, free Wi-Fi, and "Plug and Meet" common areas furnished with state-of-the-art computers, writing walls, and large TV screens for presentations.[15]

Generation Z
People born after 2000 (although many analysts include people born after 1995) who make up the kids, tweens, and teens markets.

Generation Z. Hard on the heels of the Millennials is **Generation Z**, young people born after 2000 (although many analysts include people born after 1995 in this group). The approximately 72 million Gen Zers make up important kids, tweens, and teens markets. They spend an estimated $44 billion annually of their own money and influence a total of almost $200 billion of their own and parents' spending.[16] These young consumers also represent tomorrow's markets—they are now forming brand relationships that will affect their buying well into the future.

Even more than the Millennials, the defining characteristic of Gen Zers is their utter fluency and comfort with digital technologies. Generation Z take smartphones, tablets, Internet-connected game consoles, wireless Internet, and digital and social media for granted—they've always had them—making this group highly mobile, connected, and social. On average, connected Gen Zers receive more than 3,000 texts per month. "If they're awake, they're online," quips one analyst. They have "digital in their DNA," says another.[17]

Gen Zers blend the online and offline worlds seamlessly as they socialize and shop. According to recent studies, despite their youth, more than half of all Generation Z tweens and teens do product research before buying a product or having their parents buy it for them. Of those who shop online, more than half *prefer* shopping online in categories ranging from electronics, books, music, sports equipment, and beauty products to clothes, shoes, and fashion accessories.

Targeting Generation Z: By themselves, U.S. "tweens" number 20 million girls and boys who spend billions of dollars annually of their own money and influence billions more of their parents' spending.

© Blend Images/Alamy

Companies in almost all industries market products and services aimed at Generation Z. For example, many retailers have created special lines or even entire stores appealing to Gen Z buyers and their parents—consider Abercrombie Kids, Gap Kids, Old Navy Kids, and Pottery Barn Kids. The Justice chain targets tween girls, with apparel and accessories laser-focused on their special preferences and lifestyles. Although these young buyers often have their mothers in tow, "the *last* thing a 10- or 12-year-old girl wants is to look like her mom," says Justice's CEO. Justice's stores, Web site, and social media pages are designed with tweens in mind. "You have to appeal to their senses," says the CEO. "They love sensory overload—bright colors, music videos, a variety of merchandise, the tumult of all of that." Justice now outsells even Walmart and Target in girl's apparel (that's impressive considering that Walmart has almost 4,000 U.S. stores compared with Justice's 1,000).[18]

Marketing to Gen Zers and their parents presents special challenges. Traditional media are still important to this group. Magazines such as J-14 and *Twist* are popular with some Gen Z segments, as are TV channels such as Nickelodeon and the Disney Channel. But marketers know they must meet Gen Zers where they hang out and shop. Increasingly, that's in the online and mobile worlds. Although the under-13 set remains barred from social media such as Facebook and Instagram, at least officially, the social media will play a crucial marketing role as the kids and tweens grow into teens.

Today's kids are notoriously fickle and hard to pin down, and they have short attention spans. The key is to engage these young consumers and let them help to define their brand experiences. Another Generation Z concern involves children's privacy and their vulnerability to marketing pitches. Companies marketing to this group must do so responsibly or risk the wrath of parents and public policy makers.

Generational Marketing. Do marketers need to create separate products and marketing programs for each generation? Some experts warn that marketers need to be careful about turning off one generation each time they craft a product or message that appeals effectively to another. Others caution that each generation spans decades of time and many socioeconomic levels. For example, marketers often split the baby boomers into three smaller groups—leading-edge boomers, core boomers, and trailing-edge boomers—each with its own beliefs and behaviors. Similarly, they split Generaton Z into kids, tweens, and teens.

Thus, marketers need to form more precise age-specific segments within each group. More important, defining people by their birth date may be less effective than segmenting them by lifestyle, life stage, or the common values they seek in the products they buy. We will discuss many other ways to segment markets in Chapters 5 and 6.

The Changing American Family

The traditional household consists of a husband, wife, and children (and sometimes grandparents). Yet the historic American ideal of the two-child, two-car suburban family has lately been losing some of its luster.

In the United States, fewer than half of today's households contain married couples, down from 76 percent in 1940. Married couples with children under 18 represent only 19 percent of the nation's 123 million households. Married couples without children represent 23 percent and single parents are another 14 percent. A full 34 percent are nonfamily households—singles living alone or unrelated adults of one or both sexes living together.[19]

More people are divorcing or separating, choosing not to marry, marrying later, remarrying, or marrying without intending to have children. One in 12 married couples is interracial. The number of same-sex couples raising children has increased 75 percent since 2000. The changing composition of today's modern American families is increasingly reflected in popular movies and televisions shows, such as *Modern Family*, the award-winning TV sitcom about an extended nontraditional family.

The American family: The changing composition of American families is increasingly reflected in popular movies and television shows, such as *Modern Family*, the award-winning TV sitcom about an extended nontraditional family.

Mitch Haddad/Getty Images

Marketers must consider the special needs of nontraditional households because they are now growing more rapidly than traditional households. Each group has distinctive needs and buying habits.

The number of working women has also increased greatly, growing from under 40 percent of the U.S. workforce in the late 1950s to 69 percent today. American women now make up 40 percent of primary family breadwinners. Among households made up of married couples with children, 60 percent are dual-income households; only the husband works in 28.5 percent. Meanwhile, more men are staying home with their children and managing the household while their wives go to work. Four percent of the stay-at-home-parent families have a full-time stay-at-home dad.[20]

Companies are now adapting their marketing to reflect the changing dynamics of American families. For example, whereas fathers were once ignored or portrayed as dolts in family-oriented ads, today's advertisers are showing more caring and capable dads. One recent Samsung Galaxy phone ad, for instance, features a dad swaddling and calming his newborn son while Mom runs errands. When the anxious mom calls home to check in, the newly minted swaddle master replies, "We're having a dudes' day here. We're fiiiine. You take the *weekend* if you want to."

Other ads reflect the evolving diversity in modern American households. For instance, one ad for Honey Maid graham crackers takes family diversity to a whole new level:[21]

> A single 30-second Honey Maid commercial features everything from a same-sex couple bottle-feeding their son, to an interracial couple and their three kids holding hands, to a Hispanic mother and an African-American father with their three mixed-race children. There's even a father covered in body tattoos. The century-old Honey Maid brand—owned by Mondelez, which also makes Oreos, Ritz, and Chips Ahoy—is reinventing itself as a wholesome but relevant snack for today's families. "No matter how things change," says the narrator in the ad, "what makes wholesome never will." The ad concludes: "Honey Maid everyday wholesome snacks. For every wholesome family." Says a Mondelez marketer, no matter what their skin color or sexual orientation, "these families that we portray all have wonderful parent and child connections. This is a recognition that the family dynamic in America is evolving...and we've evolved, too."

Geographic Shifts in Population

This is a period of great migratory movements between and within countries. Americans, for example, are a mobile people, with about 12 percent of all U.S. residents moving each year and 35 percent or more moving every five years. Over the past two decades, the U.S. population has shifted toward the Sunbelt states. The West and South have grown, whereas the Midwest and Northeast states have lost population.[22] Such population shifts interest marketers because people in different regions buy differently. For example, people in the Midwest buy more winter clothing than people in the Southeast.

Also, for more than a century, Americans have been moving from rural to metropolitan areas. In the 1950s, they made a massive exit from the cities to the suburbs. Today, the migration to the suburbs continues. And more and more Americans are moving to "micropolitan areas," small cities located beyond congested metropolitan areas, such as Minot, North Dakota; Boone, North Carolina; Traverse City, Michigan; and Concord, New Hampshire. These smaller micros offer many of the advantages of metro areas—jobs, restaurants, diversions, community organizations—but without the population crush, traffic jams, high crime rates, and high property taxes often associated with heavily urbanized areas. Ten percent of the U.S. population now resides in micropolitan areas.[23]

The shift in where people live has also caused a shift in where they work. For example, the migration toward micropolitan and suburban areas has resulted in a rapid increase in the number of people who "telecommute"—work at home or in a remote office and conduct business by phone or the Internet. This trend, in turn, has created a booming SOHO

Telecommuting: Applications like Citrix's GoToMeeting help people meet and collaborate online via computer, tablet, or smartphone, no matter what their work location.

Citrix Systems, Inc.

(small office/home office) market. Increasing numbers of people are working from home with the help of electronic conveniences such as PCs, smartphones, and broadband Internet access. One recent study estimates that 24 percent of employed individuals do some or all of their work at home.[24]

Many marketers are actively courting the lucrative telecommuting market. For example, online applications such as Citrix's GoToMeeting and Cisco's WebEx help connect people who telecommute or work remotely. With such applications, people can meet and collaborate online via computer, tablet, or smartphone, no matter what their work location. And companies ranging from Salesforce.com to Google and IBM offer cloud computing applications that let people collaborate anywhere and everywhere through the Internet and mobile devices.[25]

Additionally, for telecommuters who can't work fully at home, companies such as NextSpace, Grind, and Regus rent out fully equipped shared office space. For a daily, monthly, or yearly fee, telecommuters who work away from a main office can rent shared space that includes the same amenities of regular office, from networked computers, printers, and copiers to conference rooms and lounge spaces.[26]

A Better-Educated, More White-Collar, More Professional Population

The U.S. population is becoming better educated. For example, in 2012, 88 percent of the U.S. population over age 25 had completed high school and 32 percent had a bachelor's degree or better, compared with 66 percent and 16 percent, respectively, in 1980.[27] The workforce also is becoming more white collar. Job growth is now strongest for professional workers and weakest for manufacturing workers. Between 2010 and 2020, of 30 detailed occupations projected to have the fastest employment growth, 17 require some type of postsecondary education.[28] The rising number of educated professionals will affect not just what people buy but also how they buy.

Increasing Diversity

Countries vary in their ethnic and racial makeup. At one extreme is Japan, where almost everyone is Japanese. At the other extreme is the United States, with people from virtually all national origins. The United States has often been called a melting pot, where diverse groups from many nations and cultures have melted into a single, more homogenous whole. Instead, the United States seems to have become more of a "salad bowl" in which various groups have mixed together but have maintained their diversity by retaining and valuing important ethnic and cultural differences.

Marketers now face increasingly diverse markets, both at home and abroad, as their operations become more international in scope. The U.S. population is about 62.2 percent non-Hispanic white, with Hispanics at 17.4 percent and African Americans at 13.2 percent. The U.S. Asian American population now totals more than 5.4 percent of the total U.S. population, with the remaining groups being Native Hawaiian, Pacific Islander, American Indian, Eskimo, or Aleut. Moreover, one in eight people living in the United States—more than 13 percent of the population—was born in another country. The nation's ethnic populations are expected to explode in coming decades. By 2060, Hispanics will be about 28 percent of the population, African Americans will be about 14 percent, and Asian Americans will increase to 9 percent.[29]

Most large companies, from P&G, Walmart, Allstate, and Wells Fargo to McDonald's and Southwest Airlines, now target specially designed products, ads, and promotions to one or more of these groups. For example, Southwest Airlines' outreach to Asian Americans includes being the title sponsor for the Chinese New Year Festival and Parade

Serving diverse customer communities: Southwest Airlines reaches out to Asian American consumers through its title sponsorship of San Francisco's Chinese New Year Festival and Parade and through ads like this one, which pass along "cleverly constructed well wishes and cheerful nods to the community."

Southwest Airlines Co.

in San Francisco, the biggest nighttime parade in the United States and the second-biggest in North America after the Macy's Thanksgiving Day parade:[30]

> San Francisco's Chinese New Year Festival and Parade typically draws hundreds of thousands of spectators and is broadcast on English- and Asian-language TV stations to viewers around the world. Consumers in the affluent, fast-growing Asian American segment travel often. And they are concentrated in a few key areas such as California and New York, making them easy to pinpoint. That makes them an ideal target for Southwest. The Chinese New Year Festival and Parade event also aligns well with Southwest's preference for grassroots marketing programs that position it as a hometown carrier targeting local "passion points," in this case a cultural and family-related celebration. To support its title sponsorship, Southwest ties its brand to the Lunar New Year though promotional efforts ranging from floats and ticket-giveaway contests to "cleverly constructed well wishes and cheerful nods to the community" on street pole banners, bus shelters, billboards, and traditional broadcast and print ads. Something must be working right—Southwest has been the event's title sponsor for more than 15 years.

Diversity goes beyond ethnic heritage. For example, many major companies explicitly target gay and lesbian consumers. According to one estimate, the 6 to 7 percent of U.S. adults who identify themselves as lesbian, gay, bisexual, or transgender (LGBT) have buying power of more than $830 billion.[31] As a result of TV shows such as *Modern Family,* movies like *Brokeback Mountain* and *The Perks of Being a Wallflower,* and openly gay celebrities and public figures such as Neil Patrick Harris, Ellen DeGeneres, David Sedaris, and Apple CEO Tim Cook, the LGBT community has increasingly emerged in the public eye.

Numerous media now provide companies with access to this market. For example, Planet Out Inc., a leading global media and entertainment company that exclusively serves the LGBT community, offers several successful magazines (*Out, The Advocate, Out Traveler*) and Web sites (*Gay.com* and *PlanetOut.com*). In addition, media giant Viacom's MTV Networks offers LOGO, a cable television network aimed at gays and lesbians and their friends and family. LOGO is now available in more than 51 million U.S. households, and its Web site is number one in the LGBT category of digital, mobile, and video streaming. More than 100 mainstream marketers have advertised on LOGO, including Ameriprise Financial, Toyota, Anheuser-Busch, Dell, Levi Strauss, eBay, J&J, Orbitz, Sears, Sony, and Subaru.

Brands in a wide range of industries are now targeting the LGBT community with gay-specific ads and marketing efforts—from Amazon, American Airlines, Allstate, and Apple to luxury jewelry retailer Tiffany. Allstate recently ran an "Everyone deserves to be in good hands" campaign with ads featuring same-sex couples and the hashtag #OutHoldingHands. Brands ranging from Axe to Tiffany have sponsored similar ads. American Airlines has a dedicated LGBT "Rainbow Team," sponsors gay and lesbian community events, and offers a special Web site (www.aa.com/rainbow), Facebook pages, and a Twitter feed featuring LGBT-oriented travel deals, information, and discussion. The airline's focus on gay consumers has earned it double-digit revenue growth from the LGBT community each year for more than a decade.[32]

Another attractive diversity segment is the 57 million U.S. adults with disabilities—a market larger than African Americans or Hispanics—representing anywhere from $200 to $500 billion in annual spending power. Most individuals with disabilities are active consumers. For example, one study found that the segment spends $13.6 billion on 31.7 million business or leisure trips every year. And if certain needs were met, the amount spent on travel could double to $27 billion annually.[33]

How are companies trying to reach consumers with disabilities? Many marketers now recognize that the worlds of people with disabilities and those without disabilities are one in the same. Marketers such as McDonald's, Verizon Wireless, Nike, Samsung, Nordstrom, and Toyota have featured people with disabilities in their mainstream marketing. For instance, a recent Toyota Super Bowl commercial featured Paralympic snowboarder Amy Purdy (also a popular recent finalist on *Dancing with the Stars*) persevering as she trains on the slopes, performs on the dance floor, and poses for a photo shoot, using special prosthetic legs for each task. And, of course, she drives a Toyota.[34]

As the population in the United States grows more diverse, successful marketers will continue to diversify their marketing programs to take advantage of opportunities in fast-growing segments.

LINKING THE CONCEPTS

Stop here and think about how deeply these demographic factors affect all of us and, as a result, marketing strategies.

- Apply these demographic developments to your own life. Discuss some specific examples of how changing demographic factors affect you and your buying behavior.
- Identify a specific company that has done a good job of reacting to the shifting demographic environment—generational segments (baby boomers, Gen Xers, Millennials, or Gen Zers), the changing American family, and increased diversity. Compare this company with one that's done a poor job.

Author Comment The economic environment can offer both opportunities and threats. For example, in the post-Great Recession era of more sensible consumer spending, "value" has become the marketing watchword.

The Economic Environment

Economic environment Economic factors that affect consumer purchasing power and spending patterns.

Markets require buying power as well as people. The **economic environment** consists of economic factors that affect consumer purchasing power and spending patterns. Economic factors can have a dramatic effect on consumer spending and buying behavior. For example, until fairly recently, American consumers spent freely, fueled by income growth, a boom in the stock market, rapid increases in housing values, and other economic good fortunes. They bought and bought, seemingly without caution, amassing record levels of debt. However, the free spending and high expectations of those days were dashed by the Great Recession of 2008–2009.

As a result, as discussed in Chapter 1, consumers have now adopted a back-to-basics sensibility in their lifestyles and spending patterns that will likely persist for years to come. They are buying less and looking for greater value in the things they do buy. In turn, *value marketing* has become the watchword for many marketers. Marketers in all industries are looking for ways to offer today's more financially frugal buyers greater value—just the right combination of product quality and good service at a fair price.

You'd expect value pitches from the sellers of everyday products. For example, as Target has shifted emphasis toward the "Pay Less" side of its "Expect More. Pay Less." slogan, the once-chic headlines at the Target.com Web site have been replaced by more practical appeals such as "Our lowest prices of the season," "Fun, sun, save," and "Free shipping, every day." However, these days, even luxury-brand marketers are emphasizing good value. For example, Tiffany has long been known for selling high-end "fine jewelry" and "statement jewelry" at prices of $5,000 to $50,000 or more. However, when the Great Recession eroded Tiffany's high-end sales, the company began offering affordable luxury items—what it calls "fashion jewelry"—priced at as little as $100 to $500. Such relatively affordable items now account for about one-quarter of the Tiffany's sales.[35]

Economic environment: To serve the tastes of today's more financially frugal buyers, companies like Target are emphasizing the "pay less" side of their value propositions.

Associated Press

Marketers should pay attention to *income distribution* as well as income levels. Over the past several decades, the rich have grown richer, the middle class has shrunk, and the poor have remained poor. The top 5 percent of American earners get more than 22 percent of the country's adjusted gross income, and the top 20 percent of earners capture 51 percent of all

Natural environment
The physical environment and the natural resources that are needed as inputs by marketers or that are affected by marketing activities.

income. In contrast, the bottom 40 percent of American earners get just 11.5 percent of the total income.[36]

This distribution of income has created a tiered market. Many companies—such as Nordstrom and Neiman Marcus—aggressively target the affluent. Others—such as Dollar General, Five Below, and Family Dollar—target those with more modest means. In fact, dollar stores are now the fastest-growing retailers in the nation. Still other companies tailor their marketing offers across a range of markets, from the less affluent to the very affluent. For example, Ford offers cars ranging from the low-priced Ford Fiesta, starting at $13,965, to the luxury Lincoln Navigator SUV, starting at $61,920.

Changes in major economic variables, such as income, cost of living, interest rates, and savings and borrowing patterns, have a large impact on the marketplace. Companies watch these variables by using economic forecasting. Businesses do not have to be wiped out by an economic downturn or caught short in a boom. With adequate warning, they can take advantage of changes in the economic environment.

Author Comment
Today's enlightened companies are developing environmentally sustainable strategies in an effort to create a world economy that the planet can support indefinitely.

The Natural Environment

The **natural environment** involves the physical environment and the natural resources that are needed as inputs by marketers or that are affected by marketing activities. At the most basic level, unexpected happenings in the physical environment—anything from weather to natural disasters—can affect companies and their marketing strategies. For example, during a recent cold winter—in which the term *polar vortex* gusted into the American vocabulary—sales suffered across a wide range of businesses, from florists and auto dealers to restaurants, airlines, and tourist destinations. In contrast, the severe weather boosted demand for products such as salt, snow blowers, winter clothing, and auto repair centers.

Natural environment: Companies must prepare for unexpected happenings in the natural environment. For example, FedEx and UPS employ large staffs of meteorologists to anticipate weather conditions that might inhibit on-time deliveries around the world.
PAUL J. RICHARDS/AFP/GettyImages

Although companies can't prevent such natural occurrences, they should prepare for dealing with them. For example, shipping companies such as FedEx and UPS maintain corps of meteorologists on their staffs to anticipate weather conditions that might inhibit on-time deliveries around the world. "Someone awaiting a package in Bangkok doesn't care if it snowed in Louisville, Kentucky," says a UPS meteorologist. "They want their stuff."[37]

At a broader level, environmental sustainability concerns have grown steadily over the past three decades. In many cities around the world, air and water pollution have reached dangerous levels. World concern continues to mount about the possibilities of global warming, and many environmentalists fear that we soon will be buried in our own trash.

Marketers should be aware of several trends in the natural environment. The first involves growing *shortages of raw materials*. Air and water may seem to be infinite resources, but some groups see long-run dangers. Air pollution chokes many of the world's large cities, and water shortages are already a big problem in some parts of the United States and the world. By 2030, more than one in three people in the world will not have enough water to drink.[38] Renewable resources, such as forests and food, also have to be used wisely. Nonrenewable resources, such as oil, coal, and various minerals, pose a serious problem. Firms making products that require these scarce resources face large cost increases even if the materials remain available.

A second environmental trend is *increased pollution*. Industry will almost always damage the quality of the natural environment. Consider the disposal of chemical and nuclear wastes; the dangerous mercury levels in the ocean; the quantity of chemical pollutants in the soil and food supply; and the littering of the environment with nonbiodegradable bottles, plastics, and other packaging materials.

A third trend is *increased government intervention* in natural resource management. The governments of different countries vary in their concern and efforts to promote a clean environment. Some, such as the German government, vigorously pursue environmental quality. Others, especially many poorer nations, do little about pollution, largely because they lack the needed funds or political will.

In the United States, the Environmental Protection Agency (EPA) was created in 1970 to create and enforce pollution standards and conduct pollution research. In the future, companies doing business in the United States can expect continued strong controls from government and pressure groups. Instead of opposing regulation, marketers should help develop solutions to the materials and energy problems facing the world.

Environmental sustainability
Developing strategies and practices that create a world economy that the planet can support indefinitely.

Concern for the natural environment has spawned an **environmental sustainability** movement. Today, enlightened companies go beyond what government regulations dictate. They are developing strategies and practices that create a world economy that the planet can support indefinitely. Environmental sustainability means meeting present needs without compromising the ability of future generations to meet their needs.

Technological environment
Forces that create new technologies, creating new product and market opportunities.

Many companies are responding to consumer demands with more environmentally responsible products. Others are developing recyclable or biodegradable packaging, recycled materials and components, better pollution controls, and more energy-efficient operations. For example, Timberland's mission is about more than just making rugged, high-quality boots, shoes, clothes, and other outdoor gear. The VF brand is about doing everything it can to reduce the environmental footprint of its products and processes:[39]

> Timberland is on a mission to develop processes and products that cause less harm to the environment and to enlist consumers in the cause. For example, it has a solar-powered distribution center in California and a wind-powered factory in the Dominican Republic. It has installed energy-efficient lighting and equipment retrofits in its facilities and is educating workers about production efficiency. Timberland is constantly looking for and inventing innovative materials that allow it to reduce its impact on the planet while at the same time making better gear. Its Earthkeepers line of boots is made from recycled and organic materials, and the brand has launched footwear collections featuring outsoles made from recycled car tires. Plastic from recycled soda bottles goes into its breathable linings and durable shoe laces. Coffee grounds find a place in its odor-resistant jackets. Organic cotton without toxins makes it into its rugged canvas. To inspire consumers to make more sustainable decisions, Timberland puts Green Index tags on its products that rate each item's ecological footprint in terms of climate impact, chemicals used, and resources consumed. To pull it all together, Timberland launched an Earthkeepers campaign, an online social media effort that seeks to inspire people to take actions to lighten their environmental footprints.

Companies today are looking to do more than just good deeds. More and more, companies are making environmental sustainability a part of their core missions. And they are learning that what's good for customer well-being and the planet can also be good business. For example, Chipotle Mexican Grill has built a thriving business around an environmentally responsible mission of providing "Food With Integrity" (see Marketing at Work 3.1).

Author Comment
Technological advances are perhaps the most dramatic forces affecting today's marketing strategies. Just think about the tremendous impact on marketing of digital technologies—which have exploded in recent years. You'll see examples of the fast-growing world of online, mobile, and social media marketing throughout every chapter, and we'll discuss them in detail in Chapter 14.

The Technological Environment

The **technological environment** is perhaps the most dramatic force now shaping our destiny. Technology has released such wonders as antibiotics, robotic surgery, smartphones, and the Internet. It also has released such horrors as nuclear missiles and assault rifles. It has released such mixed blessings as the automobile, television, and credit cards. Our attitude toward technology depends on whether we are more impressed with its wonders or its blunders.

New technologies can offer exciting opportunities for marketers. For example, what would you think about having tiny little transmitters implanted in all the products you buy that would allow tracking of the products from their point of production through use and disposal? Or how about a bracelet with a chip inserted that would let you make and pay for purchases, receive personalized specials at retail locations, or even track your whereabouts or those of friends? On the one hand, such technology would provide many advantages to both buyers and sellers. On the other hand, it could be a bit scary. Either way, with the advent of radio-frequency identification (RFID) transmitters, it's already happening.

MARKETING AT WORK 3.1

Chipotle's Environmental Sustainability Mission: Food With Integrity

Envision this. You're sitting in a restaurant where the people—from the CEO on down to the kitchen crew—obsess over using only the finest ingredients. They come to work each morning inspired by all the "fresh produce and meats they have to marinate, rice they have to cook, and fresh herbs they have to chop," says the CEO. The restaurant prefers to use sustainable, naturally raised ingredients sourced from local family farms. It's on a mission not just to serve its customers good food but to change the way its entire industry produces food. This sounds like one of those high-falutin', gourmet specialty restaurants, right? Wrong. It's your neighborhood Chipotle Mexican Grill. That's right, it's a fast-food restaurant.

In an age when many fast-feeders seem to be using ever-cheaper ingredients and centralization of food preparation to cut costs and keep prices low, Chipotle is doing just the opposite. The chain's core sustainable mission is to serve "Food With Integrity." What does that mean? The company explains it this way:

> Chipotle is committed to finding the very best ingredients raised with respect for animals, the environment, and farmers. It means serving the very best sustainably raised food possible with an eye to great taste, great nutrition, and great value. It means that we support and sustain family farmers who respect the land and the animals in their care. It means that whenever possible we use meat from animals raised without the use of antibiotics or added hormones. And it means that we source organic and local produce when practical, and that we use dairy from cows raised without the use of synthetic hormones. In other words, "integrity" is kind of a funny word for "good."

When founder and CEO Steve Ells opened the first Chipotle in Denver in 1993, his primary goal was to make the best gourmet burrito around. However, as the chain grew, Ells found that he didn't like the way the ingredients Chipotle used were raised and processed. So, in 2000, Chipotle began developing a supply chain with the goal of producing and using naturally raised, organic, hormone-free, non–genetically modified ingredients. Pursuing this healthy-food mission was no easy task. As the fast-food industry increasingly moved toward low-cost, efficient food processing, factory farms were booming, whereas independent farms producing naturally raised and organic foods were in decline.

To obtain the ingredients it needed, Chipotle had to develop many new sources by supporting family farming and encouraging sustainable farming practices. Such efforts have paid off. For example, when Chipotle first started serving naturally raised pork in 2000, there were only 60 to 70 farms producing meat for the Niman Ranch pork cooperative, an important Chipotle supplier. Now, there are more than 700.

Today, 100 percent of Chipotle's pork and beef comes from producers that meet or exceed its "naturally raised" standards (the animals are raised in a humane way, fed a vegetarian diet, never given hormones, and allowed to display their natural tendencies). Chipotle's goal is to meet that same 100 percent mark for its chicken, its dairy, and even its produce. It then plans to tighten its standards even more.

Sourcing such natural and organic ingredients not only serves Chipotle's sustainability mission, it results in one of the most nutritious, best-tasting fast-food burritos on the market—something the company can brag about to customers. Whereas some fast-food companies intentionally obscure the sometimes less-than-appetizing truths about their ingredients, Chipotle doesn't play that game. Instead, it commits fast-food heresy: Proudly telling customers what's really inside its burritos.

Chipotle chose the "Food With Integrity" slogan because it sends the right message in an appetizing way. "Saying that we don't buy dairy from cows that are given the hormone rBGH is not an appetizing message," says Ells. So the company is building its marketing campaign around the more positive message that food production should be healthier and more ethical. Chipotle communicates this positioning via an integrated mix of traditional and digital promotion venues, ranging from its Farm Team invitation-only loyalty program—by which

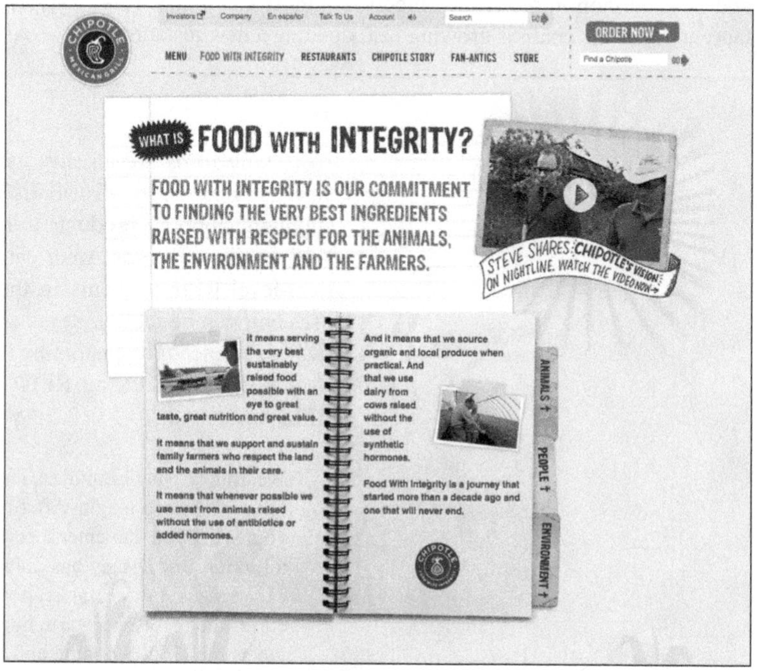

» **Environmental sustainability: What's good for customer well-being and the planet can also be good for business. Chipotle is thriving under its environmentally responsible mission of providing "Food With Integrity."**

© Chipotle Mexican Grill, Inc.

customers earn rewards based not on frequent buying but on knowledge about food and how it is produced—to its Pasture Pandemonium smartphone app, where players try to get their pig across a pasture without getting trapped in pens or pricked by antibiotic needles.

While Chipotle doesn't spend much on traditional media advertising, the company uses both traditional and nontraditional promotional methods to broadcast its message. Chipotle made a big splash a few years ago during the broadcast for the Grammy Awards with its first-ever national television ad, "Back to the Start"—a two-and-a-half-minute stop-motion animation film showing the negative effects of industrialized farming. The ad received critical acclaim and racked up millions of views online.

As a follow-up, Chipotle released "The Scarecrow," another animated video indicting the industrial food industry. Accompanied by Fiona Apple's cover of "Pure Imagination," the star character leaves his job at a factory farm and opens his own little shop selling freshly prepared food under the banner "Cultivate a better world." The online ad directed people to the campaign's centerpiece—an arcade-style game app. So far, the video has racked up more than 14 million views on YouTube and more than 9 million people have downloaded the app. Today, Chipotle has moved well beyond ads. The eco-conscious burrito maker is now producing sitcoms with a message. For example, it partnered with Hulu for the original comedy series *Farmed and Dangerous,* attacking the sins of big agriculture.

Companies with a socially responsible business model often struggle to grow and make profits. But Chipotle is proving that a company can do both. Last year, its 45,000 employees chopped, sliced, diced, and grilled their way to $4.1 billion in revenues and $445 million in profits at Chipotle's almost 1,800 U.S. restaurants. And the chain is growing fast, opening a new restaurant about every two days. In the past five years, Chipotle's stock price surged sixfold, suggesting that the company's investors are as pleased as its fast-growing corps of customers.

Founder and CEO Ells wants Chipotle to grow and make money. But ultimately, on a larger stage, he wants to change the way fast food is produced and sold—not just by Chipotle but by the entire industry. "We think the more people understand where their food comes from and the impact that has on independent family farmers [and] animal welfare, the more they're going to ask for better ingredients," says Ells. Whether customers stop by Chipotle's restaurants to support the cause, gobble down the tasty food, or both, it all suits Ells just fine. Chipotle's sustainability mission isn't an add-on, created just to position the company as "socially responsible." Doing good "is the company's ethos and ingrained in everything we do," says Chipotle's director of communications. "Chipotle is a very different kind of company where the deeper you dig into what's happening, the more there is to like and feel good about."

Sources: Based on information and quotes from Denise Lee Yohn, "How Chipotle Changed American Fast Food Forever," *Fast Company,* March 14, 2014, www.fastcompany.com/3027647/lessons-learned/how-chipotle-changed-american-fast-food-forever; Danielle Sacks, "Chipotle: For Exploding All the Rules of Fast Food," *Fast Company,* March 2012, pp. 125–126; John Trybus, "Chipotle's Chris Arnold and the Food With Integrity Approach to Corporate Social Responsibility," *The Social Strategist,* March 22, 2012, https://blogs.commons.georgetown.edu/socialimpact/2012/03/22/the-social-strategist-part-xvi-chipotle%E2%80%99s-chris-arnold-and-the-food-with-integrity-approach-to-corporate-social-responsibility/; Emily Bryson York, "Chipotle Ups the Ante on Its Marketing," *Chicago Tribune,* September 30, 2011, http://articles.chicagotribune.com/2011-09-30/business/ct-biz-chipotle-profile-20110930_1_chipotle-plans-executive-steve-ells-chipotle-founder; Kyle Stock and Venesa Wong, "Chipotle: The Definitive Oral History," *Bloomberg Business,* www.bloomberg.com/graphics/2015-chipotle-oral-history/, accessed June, 2015; and information from www.chipotle.com and www.chipotle.com/en-US/fwi/fwi.aspx, accessed September 2015.

Many firms are already using RFID technology to track products and customers at various points in the distribution channel. For example, Walmart has strongly encouraged suppliers shipping products to its distribution centers to apply RFID tags to their pallets. And retailers such as American Apparel, Macy's, and Bloomingdales are now installing item-level RFID systems in their stores. Fashion and accessories maker Burberry even uses chips imbedded in items and linked to smartphones to provide personalized, interactive experiences for customers in its stores and at runway shows.[40]

» Disney is taking RFID technology to new levels with its cool new MagicBand RFID wristband:[41]

> Wearing a MagicBand at The Walt Disney World Resort opens up a whole new level of Disney's famed magic. After registering for cloud-based MyMagic+ services, with the flick of your wrist you can enter a park or attraction, buy dinner or souvenirs, or even unlock your hotel room. But Disney has only begun to tap the MagicBand's potential for personalizing guest experiences. Future applications could be truly magical. Imagine, for example, the wonder of a child who receives a warm hug from Mickey Mouse or a bow from Prince Charming, who then greets the child by name and wishes her a happy birthday. Imagine animatronics that interact with nearby guests based on personal information supplied in advance. You get separated from family or friends? No problem. A quick scan of your MagicBand at a nearby directory could pinpoint the locations of your entire party. Linked to your Disney phone app, the MagicBand could trigger in-depth information about park features, ride wait times, FastPass check-in alerts, and your reservations schedule. Of course, the MagicBand also offers Disney a potential

Marketing technology: Disney is taking RFID technology to new levels with its cool new MagicBand RFID wristband.

Bob Croslin

mother lode of digital data on guest activities and movements in minute detail, helping to improve guest logistics, services, and sales. If all this seems too big-brotherish, there will be privacy options—for example, letting parents opt out of things like characters knowing children's names. In all, such digital technologies promise to enrich the Disney experience for both guests and the company.

The technological environment changes rapidly, creating new markets and opportunities. However, every new technology replaces an older technology. Transistors hurt the vacuum-tube industry, digital photography hurt the film business, and digital downloads and streaming are hurting the CD and DVD businesses. When old industries fight or ignore new technologies, their businesses decline. Thus, marketers should watch the technological environment closely. Companies that do not keep up will soon find their products outdated. If that happens, they will miss new product and market opportunities.

As products and technologies become more complex, the public needs to know that these items are safe. Thus, government agencies investigate and ban potentially unsafe products. In the United States, the Food and Drug Administration (FDA) has created complex regulations for testing new drugs. The Consumer Product Safety Commission (CPSC) establishes safety standards for consumer products and penalizes companies that fail to meet them. Such regulations have resulted in much higher research costs and longer times between new product ideas and their introduction. Marketers should be aware of these regulations when applying new technologies and developing new products.

Author Comment

Even the strongest free-market advocates agree that the system works best with at least some regulation. But beyond regulation, most companies *want* to be socially responsible.

The Political and Social Environment

Marketing decisions are strongly affected by developments in the political environment. The **political environment** consists of laws, government agencies, and pressure groups that influence or limit various organizations and individuals in a given society.

Political environment
Laws, government agencies, and pressure groups that influence or limit various organizations and individuals in a given society.

Legislation Regulating Business

Even the strongest advocates of free-market economies agree that the system works best with at least some regulation. Well-conceived regulation can encourage competition and ensure fair markets for goods and services. Thus, governments develop *public policy* to guide commerce—sets of laws and regulations that limit business for the good of society as a whole. Almost every marketing activity is subject to a wide range of laws and regulations.

Legislation affecting business around the world has increased steadily over the years. The United States and many other countries have many laws covering issues such as competition, fair-trade practices, environmental protection, product safety, truth in advertising, consumer privacy, packaging and labeling, pricing, and other important areas (see **Table 3.1**).

Understanding the public policy implications of a particular marketing activity is not a simple matter. In the United States, there are many laws created at the national, state, and local levels, and these regulations often overlap. For example, aspirin products sold in Dallas are governed by both federal labeling laws and Texas state advertising laws. Moreover, regulations are constantly changing; what was allowed last year may now be prohibited, and what was prohibited may now be allowed. Marketers must work hard to keep up with changes in regulations and their interpretations.

Business legislation has been enacted for a number of reasons. The first is to *protect companies* from each other. Although business executives may praise competition, they sometimes try to neutralize it when it threatens them. Therefore, laws are passed to define and prevent unfair competition. In the United States, such laws are enforced by the Federal Trade Commission (FTC) and the Antitrust Division of the Attorney General's office.

» Table 3.1 Major U.S. Legislation Affecting Marketing

Legislation	Purpose
Sherman Antitrust Act (1890)	Prohibits monopolies and activities (price-fixing, predatory pricing) that restrain trade or competition in interstate commerce.
Federal Food and Drug Act (1906)	Created the Food and Drug Administration (FDA). It forbids the manufacture or sale of adulterated or fraudulently labeled foods and drugs.
Clayton Act (1914)	Supplements the Sherman Act by prohibiting certain types of price discrimination, exclusive dealing, and tying clauses (which require a dealer to take additional products in a seller's line).
Federal Trade Commission Act (1914)	Established the Federal Trade Commission (FTC), which monitors and remedies unfair trade methods.
Robinson-Patman Act (1936)	Amends the Clayton Act to define price discrimination as unlawful. Empowers the FTC to establish limits on quantity discounts, forbid some brokerage allowances, and prohibit promotional allowances except when made available on proportionately equal terms.
Wheeler-Lea Act (1938)	Makes deceptive, misleading, and unfair practices illegal regardless of injury to competition. Places advertising of food and drugs under FTC jurisdiction.
Lanham Trademark Act (1946)	Protects and regulates distinctive brand names and trademarks.
National Traffic and Safety Act (1958)	Provides for the creation of compulsory safety standards for automobiles and tires.
Fair Packaging and Labeling Act (1966)	Provides for the regulation of the packaging and labeling of consumer goods. Requires that manufacturers state what the package contains, who made it, and how much it contains.
Child Protection Act (1966)	Bans the sale of hazardous toys and articles. Sets standards for child-resistant packaging.
Federal Cigarette Labeling and Advertising Act (1967)	Requires that cigarette packages contain the following statement: "Warning: The Surgeon General Has Determined That Cigarette Smoking Is Dangerous to Your Health."
National Environmental Policy Act (1969)	Establishes a national policy on the environment. The 1970 Reorganization Plan established the Environmental Protection Agency (EPA).
Consumer Product Safety Act (1972)	Establishes the Consumer Product Safety Commission (CPSC) and authorizes it to set safety standards for consumer products as well as exact penalties for failing to uphold those standards.
Magnuson-Moss Warranty Act (1975)	Authorizes the FTC to determine rules and regulations for consumer warranties and provides consumer access to redress, such as the class-action suit.
Children's Television Act (1990)	Limits the number of commercials aired during children's programs.
Nutrition Labeling and Education Act (1990)	Requires that food product labels provide detailed nutritional information.
Telephone Consumer Protection Act (1991)	Establishes procedures to avoid unwanted telephone solicitations. Limits marketers' use of automatic telephone dialing systems and artificial or prerecorded voices.
Americans with Disabilities Act (1991)	Makes discrimination against people with disabilities illegal in public accommodations, transportation, and telecommunications.
Children's Online Privacy Protection Act (2000)	Prohibits Web sites or online services operators from collecting personal information from children without obtaining consent from a parent and allowing parents to review information collected from their children.
Do-Not-Call Implementation Act (2003)	Authorizes the FTC to collect fees from sellers and telemarketers for the implementation and enforcement of a national Do-Not-Call Registry.
CAN-SPAM Act (2003)	Regulates the distribution and content of unsolicited commercial email.
Financial Reform Law (2010)	Created the Bureau of Consumer Financial Protection, which writes and enforces rules for the marketing of financial products to consumers. It is also responsible for enforcement of the Truth-in-Lending Act, the Home Mortgage Disclosure Act, and other laws designed to protect consumers.

The second purpose of government regulation is to *protect consumers* from unfair business practices. Some firms, if left alone, would make shoddy products, invade consumer privacy, mislead consumers in their advertising, and deceive consumers through their packaging and pricing. Rules defining and regulating unfair business practices are enforced by various agencies.

The third purpose of government regulation is to *protect the interests of society* against unrestrained business behavior. Profitable business activity does not always create a better quality of life. Regulation arises to ensure that firms take responsibility for the social costs of their production or products.

International marketers will encounter dozens, or even hundreds, of agencies set up to enforce trade policies and regulations. In the United States, Congress has established federal regulatory agencies, such as the FTC, the FDA, the Federal Communications Commission, the Federal Energy Regulatory Commission, the Federal Aviation Administration, the Consumer Product Safety Commission, the Environmental Protection Agency, and hundreds of others. Because such government agencies have some discretion in enforcing the laws, they can have a major impact on a company's marketing performance.

New laws and their enforcement will continue to increase. Business executives must watch these developments when planning their products and marketing programs. Marketers need to know about the major laws protecting competition, consumers, and society. They need to understand these laws at the local, state, national, and international levels.

Increased Emphasis on Ethics and Socially Responsible Actions

Written regulations cannot possibly cover all potential marketing abuses, and existing laws are often difficult to enforce. However, beyond written laws and regulations, business is also governed by social codes and rules of professional ethics.

Socially Responsible Behavior. Enlightened companies encourage their managers to look beyond what the regulatory system allows and simply "do the right thing." These socially responsible firms actively seek out ways to protect the long-run interests of their consumers and the environment.

Almost every aspect of marketing involves ethics and social responsibility issues. Unfortunately, because these issues usually involve conflicting interests, well-meaning people can honestly disagree about the right course of action in a given situation. Thus, many industrial and professional trade associations have suggested codes of ethics. And more companies are now developing policies, guidelines, and other responses to complex social responsibility issues.

The boom in online, mobile, and social media marketing has created a new set of social and ethical issues. Critics worry most about online privacy issues. There has been an explosion in the amount of personal digital data available. Users themselves supply some of it. They voluntarily place highly private information on social media sites, such as Facebook or LinkedIn, or on genealogy sites that are easily searched by anyone with a computer or a smartphone.

However, much of the information is systematically developed by businesses seeking to learn more about their customers, often without consumers realizing that they are under the microscope. Legitimate businesses track consumers' online browsing and buying behavior and collect, analyze, and share digital data from every move consumers make at their online sites. Critics worry that these companies may now know *too* much and might use digital data to take unfair advantage of consumers. Although most companies fully disclose their Internet privacy policies and most try to use data to benefit their customers, abuses do occur. As a result, consumer advocates and policy makers are taking action to protect consumer privacy. In Chapter 4, we discuss these and other societal marketing issues in greater depth.

Cause-Related Marketing. To exercise their social responsibility and build more positive images, many companies are now linking themselves to worthwhile causes. These days, every product seems to be tied to some cause. For example, the P&G "Tide Loads of Hope" program provides mobile laundromats and loads of clean laundry to families in disaster-stricken

» Cause-related marketing: AT&T joined forces with competitors Verizon, Sprint, and T-Mobile to spearhead the "It Can Wait" campaign, which urges people of all ages to take the pledge to never text and drive.

areas—P&G washes, dries, and folds clothes for these families for free. Shake Shack runs an annual Great American Shake Sale: If you donate at least $2 at the register to Share Our Strength's No Kid Hungry program dedicated to ending child hunger in America, you get a $5 shake free on your next visit. »And AT&T joined forces with competitors Verizon, Sprint, and T-Mobile to spearhead the "It Can Wait" campaign, which addresses the texting-while-driving epidemic by urging people of all ages to take the pledge to never text and drive. The campaign's cause-related message: "No text is worth the risk. It can wait."[42]

Some companies are founded on cause-related missions. Under the concept of "values-led business" or "caring capitalism," their mission is to use business to make the world a better place. For example, Warby Parker—the online marketer of low-priced prescription eyewear—was founded with the hope of bringing affordable eyewear to the masses. The company sells "eyewear with a purpose." For every pair of glasses Warby Parker sells, it distributes a free pair to someone in need. The company also works with not-for-profit organizations that train low-income entrepreneurs to sell affordable glasses. "We believe that everyone has the right to see," says the company.[43]

Cause-related marketing has become a primary form of corporate giving. It lets companies "do well by doing good" by linking purchases of the company's products or services with benefiting worthwhile causes or charitable organizations. Beyond being socially admirable, Warby Parker's Buy a Pair, Give a Pair program also makes good economic sense, for both the company and its customers. "Companies can do good in the world while still being profitable," says Warby Parker co-founder Neil Blumenthal. "A single pair of reading glasses causes, on average, a 20 percent increase in income. Glasses are one of the most effective poverty alleviation tools in the world."[44]

Cause-related marketing has also stirred some controversy. Critics worry that cause-related marketing is more a strategy for selling than a strategy for giving—that "cause-related" marketing is really "cause-exploitative" marketing. Thus, companies using cause-related marketing might find themselves walking a fine line between increased sales and an improved image and facing charges of exploitation. However, if handled well, cause-related marketing can greatly benefit both the company and the cause. The company gains an effective marketing tool while building a more positive public image. The charitable organization or cause gains greater visibility and important new sources of funding and support. Spending on cause-related marketing in the United States skyrocketed from only $120 million in 1990 to $1.92 billion in 2015.[45]

Author Comment
Cultural factors strongly affect how people think and how they consume, so marketers are keenly interested in the cultural environment.

The Cultural Environment

Cultural environment
Institutions and other forces that affect a society's basic values, perceptions, preferences, and behaviors.

The **cultural environment** consists of institutions and other forces that affect a society's basic values, perceptions, preferences, and behaviors. People grow up in a particular society that shapes their basic beliefs and values. They absorb a worldview that defines their relationships with others. The following cultural characteristics can affect marketing decision making.

The Persistence of Cultural Values

People in a given society hold many beliefs and values. Their core beliefs and values have a high degree of persistence. For example, most Americans believe in individual freedom, hard work, getting married, and achievement and success. These beliefs shape more specific attitudes and behaviors found in everyday life. *Core* beliefs and values are passed on from parents to children and are reinforced by schools, businesses, religious institutions, and government.

Secondary beliefs and values are more open to change. Believing in marriage is a core belief; believing that people should get married early in life is a secondary belief.

Marketers have some chance of changing secondary values but little chance of changing core values. For example, family-planning marketers could argue more effectively that people should get married later than not get married at all.

Shifts in Secondary Cultural Values

Although core values are fairly persistent, cultural swings do take place. Consider the impact of popular music groups, movie personalities, and other celebrities on young people's hairstyle and clothing norms. Marketers want to predict cultural shifts to spot new opportunities or threats. The major cultural values of a society are expressed in people's views of themselves and others, as well as in their views of organizations, society, nature, and the universe.

People's Views of Themselves. People vary in their emphasis on serving themselves versus serving others. Some people seek personal pleasure, wanting fun, change, and escape. Others seek self-realization through religion, recreation, or the avid pursuit of careers or other life goals. Some people see themselves as sharers and joiners; others see themselves as individualists. People use products, brands, and services as a means of self-expression, and they buy products and services that match their views of themselves.

For example, ads for Tetley tea focus on taste, appealing to tea drinkers with a more practical view and telling them to "Brew Up Something Brilliant." Its Classic Blend black tea offers "a deep amber color and delicious tea flavor." By contrast, Yogi Tea Company appeals to tea drinkers with a more transcendent, holistic view of themselves, their lives, and their teas. The brand offers more than 100 herbs and botanicals, blended "for both flavor and purpose." » Yogi's slogan, "How Good Can You Feel?," suggests that its teas not only taste good but also make you feel well, both physically and mentally. For example, Yogi Stress Relief tea is "a delicious, all-natural blend that helps soothe your body and mind." Yogi Sweet Tangerine Positive Energy tea "is a harmonizing and aromatic blend that energizes and elevates mood." A recent post at the Yogi Community online site invited everyone to have a "Happy Feel-Good Friday and a Happy Spring!"[46]

» **People's self-views: Yogi appeals to tea drinkers with a more spiritual view of themselves, their lives, and their teas. Yogi Sweet Tangerine Positive Energy tea "energizes and elevates mood." "How good can you feel?"**

Courtesy Yogi Tea. Photo in ad: Mark Laita, Absodels/Getty Images

People's Views of Others. People's attitudes toward and interactions with others shift over time. In recent years, some analysts have voiced concerns that the digital age would result in diminished human interaction, as people buried themselves in social media pages or emailed and texted rather than interacting personally. Instead, today's digital technologies seem to have launched an era of what one trend watcher calls "mass mingling." Rather than interacting less, people are using social media and mobile communications to connect more than ever. Basically, the more people meet, network, Tweet, and socialize online, the more likely they are to eventually meet up with friends and followers in the real world.

However, these days, even when people are together, they are often "alone together." Groups of people may sit or walk in their own little bubbles, intensely connected to tiny screens and keyboards. One expert describes the latest communication skill as "maintaining eye contact with someone while you text someone else; it's hard but it can be done," she says. "Technology-enabled, we are able to be with one another, and also elsewhere, connected to wherever we want to be."[47] Thus, whether the new technology-driven communication is a blessing or a curse is a matter of much debate.

This new way of interacting strongly affects how companies market their brands and communicate with customers. Consumers increasingly tap digitally into networks of friends and online brand communities to learn about and buy products and to shape and share brand experiences. As a result, it is important for brands to participate in these networks too.

People's Views of Organizations. People vary in their attitudes toward corporations, government agencies, trade unions, universities, and other organizations. By and large, people are willing to work for major organizations and expect them, in turn, to carry out society's work.

The past two decades have seen a sharp decrease in confidence in and loyalty toward America's business and political organizations and institutions. In the workplace, there has been an overall decline in organizational loyalty. Waves of company downsizings bred cynicism and distrust. In just the past decade, major corporate scandals, rounds of layoffs resulting from the Great Recession, the financial meltdown triggered by Wall Street bankers' greed and incompetence, and other unsettling activities have resulted in a further loss of confidence in big business. Many people today see work not as a source of satisfaction but as a required chore to earn money to enjoy their nonwork hours. This trend suggests that organizations need to find new ways to win consumer and employee confidence.

People's Views of Society. People vary in their attitudes toward their society—patriots defend it, reformers want to change it, and malcontents want to leave it. People's orientation to their society influences their consumption patterns and attitudes toward the marketplace.

American patriotism has been increasing gradually for the past two decades. Marketers respond with renewed "Made in America" pitches and patriotic products and promotions, offering everything from orange juice to computers to cars with patriotic themes. For example, Chrysler's patriotic "Imported from Detroit" campaign, which declared that "the world's going to hear the roar of our engines," resonated strongly with Americans consumers. And Apple recently kicked off a $100 million "Made in America" push with the introduction of a new high-end Mac Pro personal computer. The Mac Pro, "the most powerful Mac ever," is built in Austin, Texas, with components made domestically.[48]

Although most such marketing efforts are tasteful and well received, waving the red, white, and blue can sometimes prove tricky. Flag-waving promotions can be viewed as corny or as token attempts to cash in on the nation's emotions. For example, some critics note that, so far, Apple's "Made in America" push hasn't had much real impact. The Mac Pro contributes less than 1 percent of Apple's total revenues. More than 70 percent of the company's revenues come from its iPhone and iPad products, both built in China. Marketers must take care when appealing to patriotism and other strong national emotions.

People's Views of Nature. People vary in their attitudes toward the natural world—some feel ruled by it, others feel in harmony with it, and still others seek to master it. A long-term trend has been people's growing mastery over nature through technology and the belief that nature is bountiful. More recently, however, people have recognized that nature is finite and fragile; it can be destroyed or spoiled by human activities.

This renewed love of things natural has created a sizable market of consumers who seek out everything from natural, organic, and nutritional products to fuel-efficient cars and alternative medicines. These consumers make up a sizable and growing market. For example, food producers have also found fast-growing markets for natural and organic products. In total, the U.S. organic/natural food market generated $53.5 billion in retail sales last year, more than doubling over the past five years.[49]

Annie's Homegrown, a General Mills company, caters to this market with sustainable, all-natural food products—from mac and cheese to pizzas, pastas, snacks, and salad dressings—made and sold in a sustainable way:[50]

>> Annie's mission is "to cultivate a healthier and happier world by spreading goodness through nourishing foods, honest words, and conduct that is considerate and forever kind to the planet." Annie's products are made from simple, natural ingredients grown by its farm partners. The products contain "no artificial anything," says the company. "If it's not real, it's

not Annie's." The company works closely with its food supply-system partners to jointly raise the bar for sustainability and organics. Annie's also makes sustainable practices a top priority with its packaging—more than 90 percent of Annie's packaging by weight is recyclable. Finally, Annie's gives back to the community through programs such as sustainable agriculture scholarships, school garden programs, and support for like-minded organizations dedicated to making the planet a better place to live and eat.

>> Riding the trend toward all things natural: Annie's mission is "to cultivate a healthier and happier world by spreading goodness through nourishing foods, honest words, and conduct that is considerate and forever kind to the planet."

General Mills Marketing, Inc.

People's Views of the Universe. Finally, people vary in their beliefs about the origins of the universe and their place in it. Although most Americans practice religion, religious conviction and practice have been dropping off gradually through the years. According to a recent poll, one-fifth of Americans now say they are not affiliated with any particular faith, double the percentage in 1990. Among Americans ages 18 to 29, one-third say they are not currently affiliated with any particular religion.[51]

However, the fact that people are dropping out of organized religion doesn't mean that they are abandoning their faith. Some futurists have noted a renewed interest in spirituality, perhaps as a part of a broader search for a new inner purpose. People have been moving away from materialism and dog-eat-dog ambition to seek more permanent values—family, community, earth, faith—and a more certain grasp of right and wrong. Rather than calling it "religion," they call it "spirituality."[52] This changing spiritualism affects consumers in everything from the television shows they watch and the books they read to the products and services they buy.

Author Comment
Rather than simply watching and reacting to the marketing environment, companies should take proactive steps.

Responding to the Marketing Environment

Someone once observed, "There are three kinds of companies: those who make things happen, those who watch things happen, and those who wonder what's happened." Many companies view the marketing environment as an uncontrollable element to which they must react and adapt. They passively accept the marketing environment and do not try to change it. They analyze environmental forces and design strategies that will help the company avoid the threats and take advantage of the opportunities the environment provides.

Other companies take a *proactive* stance toward the marketing environment. Rather than assuming that strategic options are bounded by the current environment, these firms develop strategies to change the environment. Companies and their products often create and shape new industries and their structures, products such as Ford's Model T car, Apple's iPod and iPhone, and Google's search engine.

Even more, rather than simply watching and reacting to environmental events, proactive firms take aggressive actions to affect the publics and forces in their marketing environment. Such companies hire lobbyists to influence legislation affecting their industries and stage media events to gain favorable press coverage. They take to the social media and run blogs to shape public opinion. They press lawsuits and file complaints with regulators to keep competitors in line, and they form contractual agreements to better control their distribution channels.

By taking action, companies can often overcome seemingly uncontrollable environmental events. For example, whereas some companies try to hush up negative talk about their products, others proactively counter false information. McDonald's did this when a photo went viral showing unappetizing "mechanically separated chicken" (also known as "pink goop") and associating it with the company's Chicken McNuggets:[53]

McDonald's quickly issued statements disclaiming the pink goop photo as a hoax and noting that McNuggets are made using only boneless white breast meat chicken in a process that never produces anything remotely resembling the weird pink substance. But McDonald's took its response an important step further. It created its own nearly three-minute social media video giving a tour of a company processing plant in Canada, showing the step-by-step process by which McNuggets are made. In the process, fresh chicken breasts are ground and seasoned, stamped into four nugget shapes (balls, bells, boots, and bow ties), battered, flash-fried, frozen, packaged, and shipped out to local McDonald's restaurants where they are fully cooked. There's not a trace of the gross pink goop anywhere in the process. The proactive video itself went viral, garnering more than 3.5 million YouTube views in less than six weeks. As a follow-up, McDonald's launched an "Our Food. Your Questions." campaign inviting consumers to submit questions about its food-making processes via Facebook, Twitter, YouTube, and other social media. It then addressed the top concerns in a series of "behind-the-scenes" Webisodes.

Marketing management cannot always control environmental forces. In many cases, it must settle for simply watching and reacting to the environment. For example, a company would have little success trying to influence geographic population shifts, the economic environment, or major cultural values. But whenever possible, smart marketing managers take a *proactive* rather than *reactive* approach to the marketing environment (see Marketing at Work 3.2).

MARKETING AT WORK 3.2

In the Social Media Age: When the Dialogue Gets Nasty

Marketers have hailed the Internet and social media as the great new way to engage customers and nurture customer relationships. In turn, today's more-empowered consumers use the new digital media to share their brand experiences with companies and with each other. All of this back and forth helps both the company and its customers. But sometimes, the dialogue can get nasty. Consider the following examples:

- Upon receiving a severely damaged computer monitor via FedEx, YouTube user goobie55 posts footage from his security camera. The video clearly shows a FedEx delivery man hoisting the monitor package over his head and tossing it over goobie55's front gate without ever attempting to ring the bell, open the gate, or walk the package to the door. The video—with FedEx's familiar purple and orange logo prominently displayed on everything from the driver's shirt to the package and the truck—goes viral, with 5 million hits in just five days. TV news and talk shows go crazy discussing the clip.
- A young creative team at Ford's ad agency in India produces a Ford Figo print ad and releases it to the Internet without approval. The ad features three women—bound, gagged, and scantily clad—in the hatch of a Figo, with a caricature of a grinning Silvio Berlusconi (Italy's sex-scandal-plagued ex-prime minister) at the wheel. The ad's tagline: "Leave your worries behind with Figo's extra-large boot (trunk)." Ford quickly pulls the ad, but not before it goes viral. Within days, millions of people around the world have viewed the ad, causing an online uproar and giving Ford a global black eye.
- When 8-year-old Harry Winsor sends a crayon drawing of an airplane he's designed to Boeing with a suggestion that the company might want to manufacture it, the company responds with a stern, legal-form letter. "We do not accept unsolicited ideas," the letter states. "We regret to inform you that we have disposed of your message and retain no

» Today's empowered consumers: Boeing's embarrassing blunder over young Harry Winsor's airplane design made instant national news. However, Boeing quickly took responsibility and turned the potential PR disaster into a positive.

John Winsor

copies." The embarrassing blunder would probably go unnoticed were it not for the fact that Harry's father—John Winsor, a prominent ad exec—blogs and tweets about the incident, making it instant national news.

Extreme events? Not anymore. The Internet and social media have turned the traditional power relationship between businesses and consumers upside down. In the good old days, disgruntled consumers could do little more than bellow at a company service rep or shout out their complaints from a street corner. Now, armed with only a laptop or smartphone, they can take it public, airing their gripes to millions on blogs, social media sites, or even hate sites devoted exclusively to their least favorite corporations. "A consumer's megaphone is now [sometimes] more powerful than a brand's," says one ad agency executive. "Individuals can bring a huge company to its knees... simply by sharing their experiences and opinions on Facebook, Yelp, Twitter, Instagram, or other social forums."

"I hate" and "sucks" sites are almost commonplace. These sites target some highly respected companies with some highly disrespectful labels: Walmartblows.com, PayPalSucks.com (aka NoPayPal), IHateStarbucks.com, DeltaREALLYsucks.com, and UnitedPackageSmashers.com (UPS), to name only a few. "Sucks" videos on YouTube and other video sites also abound. For example, a search of "Apple sucks" on YouTube turns up more than 600,000 videos; a search for Microsoft finds 143,000 videos. An "Apple sucks" search on Facebook links to hundreds of groups. If you don't find one you like, try "Apple suks" or "Apple sux" for hundreds more.

Some of these sites, videos, and other online attacks air legitimate complaints that should be addressed. Others, however, are little more than anonymous, vindictive slurs that unfairly ransack brands and corporate reputations. Some of the attacks are only a passing nuisance; others can draw serious attention and create real headaches.

How should companies react to online attacks? The real quandary for targeted companies is figuring out how far they can go to protect their images without fueling the already raging fire. One point on which all experts seem to agree: Don't try to retaliate in kind. "It's rarely a good idea to lob bombs at the fire starters," says one analyst. "Preemption, engagement, and diplomacy are saner tools." Such criticisms are often based on real consumer concerns and unresolved anger. Hence, the best strategy might be to proactively monitor these sites and respond honestly to the concerns they express.

For example, Boeing quickly took responsibility for mishandling aspiring Harry Winsor's designs, turning a potential PR disaster into a positive. It called and invited young Harry to visit Boeing's facilities. On its corporate Twitter site, it confessed, "We're experts at airplanes but novices in social media. We're learning as we go." In response to its Figo ad fiasco, Ford's chief marketing officer issued a deep public apology, citing that Ford had not approved the ads and that it had since modified its ad review process. Ford's ad agency promptly fired the guilty creatives.

Similarly, FedEx drew praise by immediately posting its own YouTube video addressing the monitor-smashing incident. In the video, FedEx Senior Vice President of Operations Matthew Thornton stated that he had personally met with the aggrieved customer, who had accepted the company's apology. "This goes directly against all FedEx values," declared Thornton. The FedEx video struck a responsive chord. Numerous journalists and bloggers responded with stories about FedEx's outstanding package handling and delivering record.

Many companies have now created teams of specialists that monitor online conversations and engage unhappy consumers. For example, the social media team at Southwest Airlines includes a chief Twitter officer who tracks Twitter comments and monitors Facebook groups, an online representative who checks facts and interacts with bloggers, and another person who takes charge of the company's presence on sites such as YouTube, Instagram, Flickr, and LinkedIn. So if someone posts an online comment, the company can respond promptly in a personal way.

Not long ago, Southwest's team averted what could have been a major PR catastrophe when a hole popped open in a plane's fuselage on a flight from Phoenix to Sacramento. The flight had Wi-Fi, and the first passenger tweet about the incident, complete with a photo, was online in only nine minutes—11 minutes before Southwest's official dispatch channel report. But Southwest's monitoring team picked up the social media chatter and was able to craft a blog post and other social media responses shortly after the plane made an emergency landing in Yuma, Arizona. By the time the story hit the major media, the passenger who had tweeted initially was back on Twitter praising the Southwest crew for its professional handling of the situation.

Thus, by monitoring and proactively responding to seemingly uncontrollable events in the environment, companies can prevent the negatives from spiraling out of control or even turn them into positives. Who knows? With the right responses, Walmartblows.com might even become Walmartrules.com. Then again, probably not.

Sources: Quotes, excerpts, and other information based on Matt Wilson, "How Southwest Airlines Wrangled Four Social Media Crises," *Ragan.com*, February 20, 2013, www.ragan.com/Main/Articles/How_Southwest_Airlines_wrangled_four_social_media_46254.aspx#; Vanessa Ko, "FedEx Apologizes after Video of Driver Throwing Fragile Package Goes Viral," *Time*, December 23, 2011, http://newsfeed.time.com/2011/12/23/fedex-apologizes-after-video-of-driver-throwing-fragile-package-goes-viral/; Michelle Conlin, "Web Attack," *BusinessWeek*, April 16, 2007, pp. 54–56; "Boeing's Social Media Lesson," May 3, 2010, http://mediadecoder.blogs.nytimes.com/2010/05/03/boeings-social-media-lesson/; Brent Snavely, "Ford Marketing Chief Apologizes for Ads," *USA Today*, March 27, 2013; David Angelo, "CMOs, Agencies: It's Time to Live Your Brands," *Advertising Age*, October 2, 2013, http://adage.com/print/244524; and www.youtube.com/watch?v=C5uIH0VTg_o, accessed September 2015.

MyMarketingLab

If assigned by your instructor, complete the questions marked with the ✪ from the EOC Discussion Questions section in the MyLab. To complete the Marketing by the Numbers problems found in this section, go to your Assignments in the MyLab.

REVIEWING AND EXTENDING THE CONCEPTS

CHAPTER REVIEW AND CRITICAL THINKING

Objectives Review

In this and the next two chapters, you'll examine the environments of marketing and how companies analyze these environments to better understand the marketplace and consumers. Companies must constantly watch and manage the *marketing environment* to seek opportunities and ward off threats. The marketing environment consists of all the actors and forces influencing the company's ability to transact business effectively with its target market.

OBJECTIVE 3-1 Describe the environmental forces that affect the company's ability to serve its customers. (pp 68–72)

The company's *microenvironment* consists of actors close to the company that combine to form its value delivery network or that affect its ability to serve customers. It includes the company's *internal environment*—its several departments and management levels—as it influences marketing decision making. *Marketing channel firms*—suppliers, marketing intermediaries, physical distribution firms, marketing services agencies, and financial intermediaries—cooperate to create customer value. *Competitors* vie with the company in an effort to serve customers better. Various *publics* have an actual or potential interest in or impact on the company's ability to meet its objectives. Finally, five types of customer *markets* exist: consumer, business, reseller, government, and international markets.

The *macroenvironment* consists of larger societal forces that affect the entire microenvironment. The six forces making up the company's macroenvironment are demographic, economic, natural, technological, political/social, and cultural forces. These forces shape opportunities and pose threats to the company.

OBJECTIVE 3-2 Explain how changes in the demographic and economic environments affect marketing decisions. (pp 72–81)

Demography is the study of the characteristics of human populations. Today's *demographic environment* shows a changing age structure, shifting family profiles, geographic population shifts, a better-educated and more white-collar population, and increasing diversity. The *economic environment* consists of factors that affect buying power and patterns. The economic environment is characterized by more frugal consumers who are seeking greater value—the right combination of good quality and service at a fair price. The distribution of income also is shifting. The rich have grown richer, the middle class has shrunk, and the poor have remained poor, leading to a two-tiered market.

OBJECTIVE 3-3 Identify the major trends in the firm's natural and technological environments. (pp 81–85)

The *natural environment* shows three major trends: shortages of certain raw materials, higher pollution levels, and more government intervention in natural resource management. Environmental concerns create marketing opportunities for alert companies. The *technological environment* creates both opportunities and challenges. Companies that fail to keep up with technological change will miss out on new product and marketing opportunities.

OBJECTIVE 3-4 Explain the key changes in the political and cultural environments. (pp 85–91)

The *political environment* consists of laws, agencies, and groups that influence or limit marketing actions. The political environment has undergone changes that affect marketing worldwide: increasing legislation regulating business, strong government agency enforcement, and greater emphasis on ethics and socially responsible actions. The *cultural environment* consists of institutions and forces that affect a society's values, perceptions, preferences, and behaviors. The environment shows trends toward new technology-enabled communication, a lessening trust of institutions, increasing patriotism, greater appreciation for nature, a changing spiritualism, and the search for more meaningful and enduring values.

OBJECTIVE 3-5 Discuss how companies can react to the marketing environment. (pp 91–93)

Companies can passively accept the marketing environment as an uncontrollable element to which they must adapt, avoiding threats and taking advantage of opportunities as they arise. Or they can take a *proactive* stance, working to change the environment rather than simply reacting to it. Whenever possible, companies should try to be proactive rather than reactive.

Key Terms

Objective 3-1
Marketing environment (p 68)
Microenvironment (p 68)
Macroenvironment (p 68)
Marketing intermediaries (p 70)
Public (p 71)

Objective 3-2
Demography (p 72)
Baby boomers (p 73)
Generation X (p 74)
Millennials (Generation Y) (p 75)
Generation Z (p 75)
Economic environment (p 80)

Objective 3-3
Natural environment (p 81)
Environmental sustainability (p 82)
Technological environment (p 82)

Objective 3-4
Political environment (p 85)
Cultural environment (p 88)

Discussion Questions

3-1. Name and describe the types of publics in a company's marketing environment. (AASCB: Communication)

3-2. Who are the Millennials, and why are they of so much interest to marketers? (AACSB: Communication; Reflective Thinking)

3-3. Describe Generation Z. What differentiates it from other demographic groups, such as baby boomers, Generation X, and Millennials? (AACSB: Communication; Reflective Thinking)

3-4. Compare and contrast core beliefs/values and secondary beliefs/values. Provide an example of each and discuss the potential impact marketers have on each. (AACSB: Communication; Reflective Thinking)

3-5. How should marketers respond to the changing environment? (AACSB: Communication)

Critical Thinking Exercises

3-6. In 1965, more than 40 percent of American adults were smokers. That percentage has now fallen to less than 18 percent. Tobacco companies have dealt with this threat by developing new markets overseas and also developing alternative nicotine products such as electronic cigarettes (e-cigarettes). Research this product and the regulatory environment regarding this product, then write a report advising tobacco companies on the opportunities and threats posed by this technology. (AACSB: Communication; Reflective Thinking)

3-7. Form a small group and discuss cultural trends in the United States. Research one of them in depth and create a presentation on the trend's impact on marketing. (AACSB: Communication; Reflective Thinking)

3-8. Visit www.causemarketingforum.com to learn about companies that have won Halo Awards for outstanding cause-related marketing programs. Present an award-winning case study to your class. (AACSB: Communication; Use of IT)

MINICASES AND APPLICATIONS

Online, Mobile, and Social Media Marketing Sharing Economy

Changes in the technological environment have created amazing opportunities for new business models while at the same time threatening traditional ones. For example, Airbnb has shaken up the hospitality industry by allowing people to rent out spare rooms or their entire homes to strangers. The Uber and Lyft ride-sharing businesses allow consumers to find a ride from people looking to earn extra money with their vehicles. And with Uber you don't have to worry about having enough cash or giving your credit card to the driver—payments and tips are all done through the Uber app. Traditional hotel and cab companies are crying foul, claiming that these businesses are not playing by the same regulatory rules to which they are subject. Others are concerned about safety amid reports of riders allegedly being attacked, kidnappings, and driver accidents, questioning the thoroughness of background checks of the 160,000-plus Uber drivers around the world. Some countries, states, and cities have banned Uber because of these issues.

3-9. Describe how Uber's business model works and the role technology has played in its success. What are the arguments for banning these types of businesses? What are the arguments for defending them? (AACSB: Communication; Use of IT; Reflective Thinking)

3-10. Describe examples of two other businesses based on the sharing economy model and create a new business idea based on this concept. (AACSB: Communication; Reflective Thinking)

Marketing Ethics Mutant Loophole

Genetically modifying seeds to produce herbicide-resistant plants that increase crop yields has revolutionized modern agriculture. However, genetically modified organisms (GMOs) have come under fire in recent years, with consumer groups calling for mandatory GMO labeling on all food packages that contain GMO ingredients. GMO labeling laws have been in force in the European Union and other countries for several years, but the threat to the U.S. food industry is only now surfacing. Although bills requiring GMO labeling have been introduced in many state legislatures, Vermont is the only state where such a law has so far withstood the first round of legal battles from the industry. Leading chemical companies, including Monsanto, BASF, and DuPont, are the world's largest suppliers of seeds that grow the food that feeds the world. To counter the GMO labeling threat, they now are turning to mutagenesis as an alternative technique to create herbicide-resistant crops. Mutagenesis mimics the sun's irradiation of plants to create similar results to GMO techniques but with virtually no regulation. Some scientists claim mutant crops created from this process are likely to create even greater health risks than genetic modification. Seed companies see it as a way around the threat of GMO labeling requirements as consumer package-goods marketers put pressure on suppliers for non-GMO ingredients.

3-11. Debate whether it is ethical for seed manufacturers to replace one controversial technique (genetic engineering) with another (mutagenesis) to avoid regulatory threats. (AACSB: Communication; Reflective Thinking; Ethical Reasoning)

3-12. Is it wise for GMO manufacturers to fight mandatory labeling? Debate this issue. (AACSB: Communication; Reflective Thinking)

Marketing by the Numbers Demographic Trends

Marketers are interested in demographic trends related to variables such as age, ethnicity, and population. The U.S. Census Bureau provides considerable demographic information that is useful for marketers. For example, the following table provides a sample of such population data (see www.censusscope.org/2010Census/PDFs/RaceEth-States.pdf):

	2000		2010	
State	**Total**	**Hispanic**	**Total**	**Hispanic**
Georgia	8,186,453	435,227	9,687,653	853,689
Michigan	9,938,444	323,877	9,883,640	436,358
California	33,871,648	10,966,556	37,253,956	14,013,719

3-13. What percentage change in the total and Hispanic populations occurred in each state between 2000 and 2010? What conclusions can be drawn from this analysis? (AACSB: Communication; Analytical Reasoning; Reflective Thinking)

3-14. Research another demographic trend and create a presentation to marketers regarding the significance of the trend you analyzed. (AACSB: Communication; Reflective Thinking)

Video Case Burger King

In the fast-food burgers business, french fries are perhaps more important than the burgers themselves. System-wide, Burger King sells 56 million orders of french fries every month—one order of fries for every two customers. But nothing is exempt from the impact of marketing environment forces. As health trends drove some companies to cut back on fatty foods, Burger King saw its french fry sales dip.

So Burger King decided to let people have their fries and eat them to. To bring health-conscious customers back to the counter, Burger King introduced Satisfries—french fries with 30 percent less fat and 20 percent fewer calories than its regular fries. In a product category that has seen little if any innovation, Satisfries could be a big game changer. Still, reduced fat and calories may not be enough to make a difference to health-food lovers. And at 30 to 40 cents more per item, Satisfries may end up as little more than a fry fiasco.

After viewing the video featuring Burger King, answer the following questions:

3-15. Considering marketing environment forces, describe how Burger King went about developing its new Satisfries.

3-16. With Satisfries, has Burger King truly created customer value, or is it just chasing trends? Explain.

Company Cases 3 Sony/7 Target/9 Coach

See Appendix 1 for cases appropriate for this chapter. **Case 3, Sony: Battling the Marketing Environment's "Perfect Storm."** The many forces of the marketing environment have converged to take Sony from the global leader in consumer electronics to a company that is struggling to remain relevant. **Case 7, Target: Where Store Brands Offer More Than Low Prices.** In addition to carrying popular national brands, Target caters to current trends in consumer desire by building a portfolio of store brands. **Case 9, Coach: Riding the Wave of Premium Pricing.** Coach grew from a premium niche brand into a $5 billion powerhouse by pursuing popular trends of selling through outlet stores at a discount. But such tactics are taking a toll.

MyMarketingLab

If assigned by your instructor, complete these writing sections from your Assignments in the MyLab.

3-17. What is environmental sustainability and why has it grown in importance for marketers? (AACSB: Communication)

3-18. Discuss a recent change in the technological environment that impacts marketing. How has it affected buyer behavior and how has it changed marketing? (AACSB: Written and Oral Communication; Reflective Thinking)

Applied
Engage
Personalized
Immediate

4 Managing Marketing Information to Gain Customer Insights

CHAPTER ROAD MAP Objective Outline

- OBJECTIVE 4-1 **Explain the importance of information in gaining insights about the marketplace and customers.** Marketing Information and Customer Insights (100–101)
- OBJECTIVE 4-2 **Define the marketing information system and discuss its parts.** Assessing Marketing Information Needs (102); Developing Marketing Information (102–106)
- OBJECTIVE 4-3 **Outline the steps in the marketing research process.** Marketing Research (106–118)
- OBJECTIVE 4-4 **Explain how companies analyze and use marketing information.** Analyzing and Using Marketing Information (118–123)
- OBJECTIVE 4-5 **Discuss the special issues some marketing researchers face, including public policy and ethics issues.** Other Marketing Information Considerations (123–127)

Previewing the Concepts

In this chapter, we continue our exploration of how marketers gain insights into consumers and the marketplace. We look at how companies develop and manage information about important marketplace elements: customers, competitors, products, and marketing programs. To succeed in today's marketplace, companies must know how to turn mountains of marketing information into fresh customer insights that will help them deliver greater value to customers.

Let's start with a story about marketing research and customer insights in action. Over the past decade, The LEGO Group has used innovative marketing research to gain deep insights into how children really play and then used those insights to create compelling play experiences for children all over the world. In the process, it has rescued itself from near bankruptcy to become the world's biggest toy maker. As one analyst puts it, The LEGO Group has now become "the Apple of Toys."

First Stop

The LEGO Group: Digging Out Fresh Customer Insights

The LEGO Group's innovative marketing research produced lots of "Aha! Moments," helping the brand to recast its classic, colorful bricks into modern, tech-rich play experiences for children around the world.

Classic LEGO plastic bricks have been fixtures in homes around the world for more than 65 years. Last year, The LEGO Group (TLG) produced a record 55 *billion* LEGO bricks, enough to construct a continuous line stretching around the world more than 20 times. More than 78 million LEGO sets found their way into the eager hands of customers in 130 countries. TLG is now the world's second-largest toy company, ahead of Hasbro and neck and neck with market leader Mattel. And whereas Mattel and Hasbro are facing flat or declining sales, TLG's sales are exploding. In the past 10 years, its revenues have quadrupled to nearly $5 billion, up 25 percent last year alone.

But only a decade ago, TLG was near bankruptcy, spiraling downward and losing money at a rate of $1 million a day. The problem: The classic toy company had fallen out of touch with its customers. In the age of the Internet, video games, mobile devices, and high-tech playthings, traditional toys such as LEGO bricks had been pushed to the back of the closet. So, in 2004, the company set out to rebuild its aging products and approaches, brick by brick.

The LEGO makeover, however, didn't start with engineers working in design labs. First, TLG had to reconnect with customers. So it started with marketing research—lots and lots of it—listening to customers and learning in depth how children around the world really play. It created a Global Insights Team, a group of marketing researchers charged with finding innovative new ways to dig out fresh customer insights.

Beyond traditional research methods and data analytics, TLG used innovative immersive research approaches to understand the deeper motivations underlying LEGO purchases and play. For example, TLG research teams conducted up-close-and-personal ethnographic studies. They embedded researchers with families, observed children at play, interviewed their parents, shopped with families, and studied the inside workings of toy stores. This immersive research produced a lot of "Aha! Moments," customer insights that shattered many of the brand's decades-old traditions.

For example, TLG had long held fast to a "keep it simple" mantra. From the beginning, it had offered only basic play sets—bricks, building bases, beams, doors, windows, wheels, and slanting roof tiles—with few or no instructions. The philosophy was that giving children unstructured building sets would stimulate their imaginations and foster creativity. But the research showed that this concept just wasn't cutting it in today's modern, tech-rich world. Today's children get bored easily, and in the current fast-moving environment, they are exposed to many more characters, themes, and technologies. However, counter to previous assumptions that kids seek only instant gratification, TLG found that today's children welcome challenging tasks, such as putting together complex LEGO sets.

Responding to such insights, TLG shifted toward more-specialized, more-structured play experiences. It now churns out a seemingly endless assortment of themed product lines and specific building projects, complete with detailed instructions. So instead of just buying a set of basic square LEGO bricks and building their own houses or cars, children can now buy specialized kits to construct anything from fire trucks and helicopters to crave-worthy ninja castles. To add variety and familiarity, TLG also offers an ever-changing assortment of licensed lines based on everything from *Star Wars* and *DC Comics* to *Marvel Super Heroes* and *Disney Princesses*. And to satisfy children's needs for skill-mastery challenges, TLG has developed involving play experiences such as LEGO MINDSTORMS, a series of building sets complete with hardware and software for making customizable robots that are programmable from a smartphone app. The latest incarnation of LEGO MINDSTORMS, EV3, is a 601-piece kit that includes software, motors, and sensors that control robot movements and speech.

The LEGO Group uses innovative marketing research—lots and lots of it—to dig out fresh customer insights, then uses the insights to create irresistible play experiences for children around the world. LEGO is now neck and neck with Mattel as the world's number-one toy maker.

Another customer insight that emerged from the ethnographic research is that kids no longer draw meaningful distinctions between digital and physical play. "To them, it's not two separate worlds," says a LEGO Group product designer. "It's one world that blends together." This insight led to TLG's "One Reality" products, which combine digital and real-world play experiences that involve building with LEGO bricks alongside software running on a phone or tablet app. For example, the LEGO Fusion line lets children build physical models with actual LEGO bricks, scan their creations using a phone or tablet app, and bring them to life in a virtual world. In LEGO Fusion Town Master, for instance, kids create a miniature virtual LEGO city, then run the city as its mayor in an app. Town Master was one of last year's hottest-selling Christmas toys.

TLG's marketing researchers have also discovered important differences between how boys and girls play, leading to the launch of girl-focused lines such as LEGO Friends. Both boys and girls like the construction aspects of LEGO bricks. However, boys tend to be more drawn to narrative—as reflected in popular boy-focused, story-based product lines such as Ninjago and Legends of Chima. In contrast, girls tend to use their sets for role-play, as reflected in the pink- and purple-accented LEGO Friends, which focuses on community and friendship themes. The development of LEGO Friends took four years, based on research involving 3,500 girls and their mothers around the world, seeking to understand what girls who had not previously played with LEGO products might want in a construction toy. LEGO Friends has been a major hit with girls in markets ranging from the United States and Germany to China.

Of course, kids aren't the only ones playing with LEGO bricks. The classic brick sets have a huge fan base of adults who never got over the toys of their youth. Hundreds of thousands of AFOLs (Adult Fans of LEGO) around the globe spend large sums on LEGO products. These adults maintain thousands of LEGO fan sites and blogs and organize get-togethers such as the annual BrickFest fan festival. TLG actively taps into the AFOL community for new customer insights and ideas. It has created a roster of customer ambassadors who provide regular input, and it even invites customers to participate directly in the product-development process. For example, it once invited 250 LEGO train-set enthusiasts to visit its New York office to assess new designs. The result was the LEGO Santa Fe Super Chief set, which sold out the first 10,000 units in less than two weeks with virtually no marketing. Similarly, TLG used customer co-creation to develop its most popular product ever, LEGO MINDSTORMS.

Thus, over the past decade, thanks to customer insight-driven marketing research, The LEGO Group has reconnected with both its customers and the times. TLG probably knows as much about how children play as any organization on earth, and it has parlayed that knowledge into compelling, profitable play experiences for the world's children. As one analyst concludes, "In the last 10 years, LEGO has grown into nothing less than the Apple of Toys: a profit-generating, design-driven miracle built around premium, intuitive, highly covetable [play experiences that its young] fans can't get enough of."[1]

As the LEGO story highlights, good products and marketing programs begin with good customer information. Companies also need an abundance of information on competitors, resellers, and other actors and marketplace forces. But more than just gathering information, marketers must *use* the information to gain powerful *customer and market insights.*

Author Comment

Marketing information by itself has little value. The value is in the *customer insights* gained from the information and how marketers use these insights to make better decisions.

Marketing Information and Customer Insights

To create value for customers and build meaningful relationships with them, marketers must first gain fresh, deep insights into what customers need and want. Such customer insights come from good marketing information. Companies use these customer insights to develop a competitive advantage.

For example, when it began five years ago, social media site Pinterest needed to differentiate itself from the dozens, even hundreds, of existing social networking options.[2]

> Pinterest's research uncovered a key customer insight: Many people want more than just Twitter- or Facebook-like places to swap messages and pictures. They want a way to collect, organize, and share things on the Internet related to their interests and passions. So Pinterest created a social scrapbooking site, where people can create and share digital pinboards—theme-based image collections on things that inspire them. "Pinterest is your own little Internet of only the things you love," says the company.
>
> » Thanks to this unique customer insight, Pinterest has been wildly popular. Today, more than 70 million Pinterest users collectively pin more than 5 million articles a day and view more than 2.5 billion Pinterest pages a month. In turn, more than a half-million businesses use Pinterest to engage and inspire their customer communities. Nordstrom, for example, has more than 4.4 million Pinterest followers. Some 47 percent of U.S. online shoppers have purchased something as a result of a Pinterest recommendation.

Although customer and market insights are important for building customer value and engagement, these insights can be very difficult to obtain. Customer needs and buying motives are often anything but obvious—consumers themselves usually can't tell you exactly what they need and why they buy. To gain good customer insights, marketers must effectively manage marketing information from a wide range of sources.

Key customer insights have helped make social scrapbooking site Pinterest wildly successful with its 70 million users. In turn, more than a half-million brands use Pinterest to engage and inspire their customer communities.

Pinterest

Marketing Information and Today's "Big Data"

With the recent explosion of information technologies, companies can now generate and find marketing information in great quantities. The marketing world is filled to the brim with information from innumerable sources. Consumers themselves are now generating tons of marketing information. Through their smartphones, PCs, and tablets via online browsing and blogging, apps and social media interactions, texting and video, and geolocation data, consumers now volunteer a tidal wave of bottom-up information to companies and to each other.

Far from lacking information, most marketing managers are overloaded with data and often overwhelmed by it. This problem is summed up in the concept of **big data**. The term *big data* refers to the huge and complex data sets generated by today's sophisticated information generation, collection, storage, and analysis technologies. Every year, the people and systems of the world generate about a trillion gigabytes of information. That's enough data to fill 2.47 trillion good old CD-ROMs, a stack tall enough to go to the moon and back four times. A full 90 percent of all the data in the world has been created in just the past two years.[3]

Big data
The huge and complex data sets generated by today's sophisticated information generation, collection, storage, and analysis technologies.

Big data presents marketers with both big opportunities and big challenges. Companies that effectively tap this glut of big data can gain rich, timely customer insights. However, accessing and sifting through so much data is a daunting task. For example, when a large consumer brand such as Coca-Cola or Apple monitors online discussions about its brand in Tweets, blogs, social media posts, and other sources, it might take in a stunning 6 million public conversations a day, more than 2 billion a year. That's far more information than any manager can digest. Thus, marketers don't need *more* information; they need *better* information. And they need to make better *use* of the information they already have.

Managing Marketing Information

The real value of marketing information lies in how it is used—in the **customer insights** that it provides. Based on such thinking, companies ranging from Coca-Cola, Starbucks, and McDonald's to Google and GEICO are restructuring their marketing information and research functions. They are creating *customer insights teams*, headed by a senior marketing executive with representatives from all of the firm's functional areas. For example, GEICO's Customer Insights team analyzes data from dozens of sources to gain insights into the GEICO customer experience and then works with functional leaders across the organization to find ways to improve that experience.[4]

Customer insights
Fresh marketing information-based understandings of customers and the marketplace that become the basis for creating customer value, engagement, and relationships.

Customer insights groups collect customer and market information from a wide variety of sources, ranging from traditional marketing research studies to mingling with and observing consumers to monitoring social media conversations about the company and its products. They mine big data from sources far and wide. Then they *use* this information to develop important customer insights from which the company can create more value for its customers.

Thus, companies must design effective marketing information systems that give managers the right information, in the right form, at the right time and help them to use this information to create customer value, engagement, and stronger customer relationships. A **marketing information system (MIS)** consists of people and procedures dedicated to assessing information needs, developing the needed information, and helping decision makers use the information to generate and validate actionable customer and market insights.

Marketing information system (MIS)
People and procedures dedicated to assessing information needs, developing the needed information, and helping decision makers to use the information to generate and validate actionable customer and market insights.

Figure 4.1 shows that the MIS begins and ends with information users—marketing managers, internal and external partners, and others who need marketing information. First, it interacts with these information users to assess information needs. Next, it interacts with the marketing environment to develop needed information through internal company databases, marketing intelligence activities, and marketing research. Finally, the MIS helps users to analyze and use the information to develop customer insights, make marketing decisions, and manage customer engagement and relationships.

Figure 4.1 The Marketing Information System

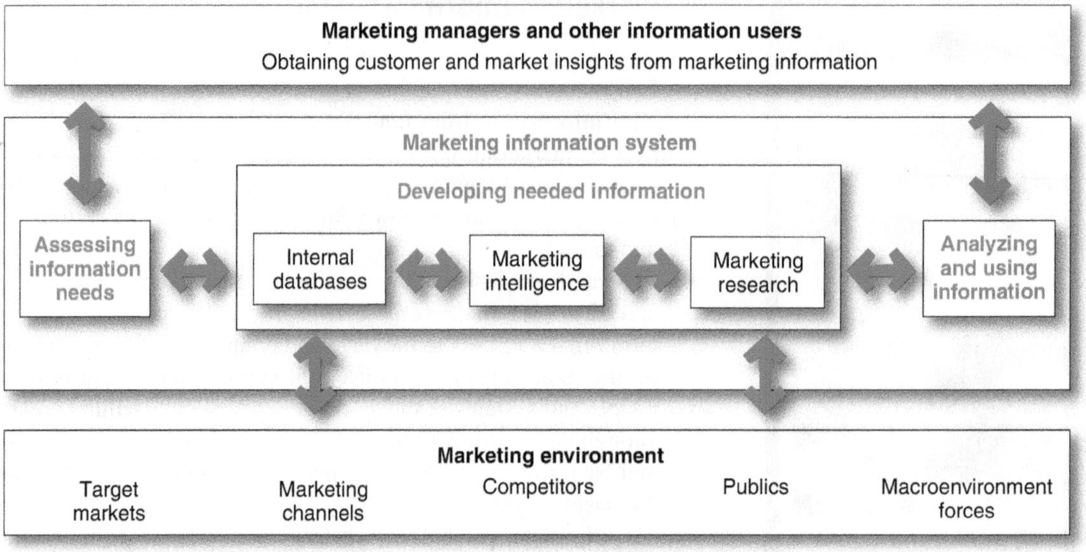

This chapter is all about managing marketing information to gain customer insights. And this important figure organizes the entire chapter. Marketers start by assessing user information needs. Then they develop the needed information using internal data, marketing intelligence, and marketing research processes. Finally, they make the information available to users in the right form at the right time.

Author Comment
The marketing information system begins and ends with users—assessing their information needs and then delivering information and insights that meet those needs.

Assessing Marketing Information Needs

The marketing information system primarily serves the company's marketing and other managers. However, it may also provide information to external partners, such as suppliers, resellers, or marketing services agencies. For example, Walmart's Retail Link system gives key suppliers access to information on everything from customers' buying patterns and store inventory levels to how many items they've sold in which stores in the past 24 hours.[5]

A good marketing information system balances the information users would *like* to have against what they really *need* and what is *feasible* to offer. Some managers will ask for whatever information they can get without thinking carefully about what they really need. And in this age of big data, some managers will want to collect and store vast amounts of digital data simply because technology lets them. But too much information can be as harmful as too little. In contrast, other managers may omit things they ought to know, or they may not know to ask for some types of information they should have. The MIS must monitor the marketing environment to provide decision makers with information they should have to make key marketing decisions.

Finally, the costs of obtaining, analyzing, storing, and delivering information can mount quickly. The company must decide whether the value of insights gained from additional information is worth the costs of providing it, and both value and cost are often hard to assess.

Author Comment
The problem isn't *finding* information; in this "big data" age, the world is bursting with information from a glut of sources. The real challenge is to find the *right* information—from inside and outside sources—and turn it into customer insights.

Developing Marketing Information

Marketers can obtain the needed information from *internal data, marketing intelligence,* and *marketing research.*

Internal Data

Internal databases
Collections of consumer and market information obtained from data sources within the company network.

Many companies build extensive **internal databases**, collections of consumer and market information obtained from data sources within the company's network. Information in an internal database can come from many sources. The marketing department furnishes information on customer characteristics, in-store and online sales transactions, and Web and social media site visits. The customer service department keeps records of customer satisfaction or service problems. The accounting department provides detailed records of sales, costs, and cash flows. Operations reports on production, shipments, and inventories. The sales force reports on reseller reactions and competitor activities, and marketing channel partners provide data on sales transactions. Harnessing such information can provide powerful customer insights and competitive advantage.

For example, as part of its MyMacy's customer-centricity program, Macy's uses its huge internal database to glean customer insights and personalize customer engagements:[6]

Through its MyMacy's program, Macy's digs deeply into its huge customer database and uses the resulting insights to hyper-personalize its customers' shopping experiences.

Bloomberg/Getty Images

Macy's has assembled a vast shopper database containing reams of information on 33 million customer households and 500 million shopper transactions a year. Individual customer data include demographics, in-store and online purchases, style preferences and personal motivations, and even browsing patterns at Macy's Web, mobile, and social media sites. Macy's then analyzes the data intensely and uses the resulting insights to coordinate and hyper-personalize each customer's shopping experiences.

For example, Macy's now sends out up to 500,000 unique versions of a single direct mail catalogue. "My book might look very different from [someone else's]," says Macy's chief marketer. "I'm not such a great homemaker, but I am a cosmetic, shoe, and jewelry person, so what you might see in my book would be all of those categories." Similarly, under its "Intelligent Display" initiative, Macy's can track what customers browse on the company Web or mobile sites, then have relevant display ads appear as they are browsing on other sites. Future MyMacy's actions will include data-informed email, mobile, and Web and social media site customizations. The ultimate goal of the massive internal database effort is to "put the customer at the center of all decisions."

Internal databases usually can be accessed more quickly and cheaply than other information sources, but they also present some problems. Because internal information is often collected for other purposes, it may be incomplete or in the wrong form for making marketing decisions. Data also age quickly; keeping the database current requires a major effort. Finally, managing and mining the mountains of information that a large company produces requires highly sophisticated equipment and techniques.

Competitive Marketing Intelligence

Competitive marketing intelligence
The systematic monitoring, collection, and analysis of publicly available information about consumers, competitors, and developments in the marketplace.

Competitive marketing intelligence is the systematic monitoring, collection, and analysis of publicly available information about consumers, competitors, and developments in the marketplace. The goal of competitive marketing intelligence is to improve strategic decision making by understanding the consumer environment, assessing and tracking competitors' actions, and providing early warnings of opportunities and threats. Marketing intelligence techniques range from observing consumers firsthand to quizzing the company's own employees, benchmarking competitors' products, online research, and monitoring social media buzz.

Good marketing intelligence can help marketers gain insights into how consumers talk about and engage with their brands. Many companies send out teams of trained observers to mix and mingle personally with customers as they use and talk about the company's products. Other companies—such as Dell, PepsiCo, Kraft, and MasterCard—have set up sophisticated digital command centers that routinely monitor brand-related online consumer and marketplace activity (see Marketing at Work 4.1).

Companies also need to actively monitor competitors' activities. They can monitor competitors' Web and social media sites. For example, Amazon's Competitive Intelligence arm routinely purchases merchandise from competing sites to analyze and compare their assortment, speed, and service quality. Companies can use the Internet to search specific competitor names, events, or trends and see what turns up. And tracking consumer conversations about competing brands is often as revealing as tracking conversations about the company's own brands.

Firms use competitive marketing intelligence to gain early insights into competitor moves and strategies and to prepare quick responses. For example, Samsung routinely

MARKETING AT WORK 4.1

Social Media Command Centers: Listening to and Engaging Customers in Social Space

Today's social space is alive with buzz about brands and related happenings and trends. As a result, many companies are now setting up state-of-the-art social media command centers with which they track or even help shape the constant barrage of social media activity surrounding their brands.

Some social media command centers are event-specific. For example, Jaguar set up "The Villain's Lair," a social media command center for the express purpose of managing engagement with its Super Bowl ads featuring famous movie villains. But many other organizations, ranging from financial institutions and consumer products companies to not-for-profit organizations, have opened permanent digital command centers to help them harness the power of today's burgeoning social media chatter.

For example, MasterCard's digital intelligence command center—called the Conversation Suite—monitors, analyzes, and responds in real time to millions of online conversations around the world. It monitors online brand-related conversations across 56 markets and 27 languages. It tracks social networks, blogs, online and mobile video, and traditional media—any and every digital place that might contain relevant content or commentary on MasterCard and its competitors.

At MasterCard's Purchase, New York, headquarters, Conversation Suite staff huddle with managers from various MasterCard departments and business units in front of a giant 40-foot LED screen that displays summaries of ongoing global brand conversations, refreshed every four minutes. A rotating group of marketing and customer service people spends two or three hours a day in the command center. "It's a real-time focus group," says a MasterCard communications executive. "We track all mentions of MasterCard and any of our products, plus the competition."

MasterCard uses what it sees, hears, and learns in the Conversation Suite to improve its products and marketing, track brand performance, and spark meaningful customer conversations and engagement. MasterCard is even training "social ambassadors," who can join online conversations and engage customers and brand influencers directly. "Today, almost everything we do [across the company] is rooted in insights we're gathering from the Conversation Suite," says another manager. "[It's] transforming the way we do business."

PepsiCo's Gatorade was one of the first brands to set up a social media command center, called Gatorade Mission Control. The center conducts extensive real-time monitoring of brand-related social media activity. Whenever someone mentions anything related to Gatorade (including competitors, Gatorade athletes, and sports nutrition–related topics) on major social media or blogs, it pops up in various visualizations and dashboards on one of six big screens. Gatorade Mission Control staffers also monitor digital ad, Web, and mobile site traffic, producing a consolidated picture of the brand's Internet image. Gatorade uses what it sees and learns at the center to improve its products, marketing, and interactions with customers.

Gatorade Mission Control also lets the brand engage consumers in real time, sometimes adding to or even shaping the online discourse. For example, during Game One of the 2014 NBA Finals, when then-Miami Heat forward LeBron James was carried off the court with leg cramps, Twitter exploded with comments that Gatorade had failed to prevent James's cramps. Although the former Gatorade spokesman had recently switched to rival Powerade, a Coca-Cola brand, most fans still associated King James with Gatorade. However, at the same time that fans were Tweeting concerns about the brand, the Gatorade Mission Control team was countering with its own humorous responses, such as "The person cramping isn't our client. Our athletes can take the Heat." When one fan Tweet asked where Gatorade was when LeBron James needed it, the team replied, "Waiting on the sidelines, but he prefers to drink something else." Thus, real-time social media monitoring

>> Competitive marketing intelligence: MasterCard's digital intelligence command center—called the Conversation Suite—monitors, analyzes, and responds in real time to millions of brand-related conversations across 56 markets and 27 languages around the world.

MasterCard

helped Gatorade turn potentially negative online chatter into a game-winning shot at the buzzer.

All kinds of organizations are now setting up social media command centers, even not-for-profits. For example, the American Red Cross partnered with Dell to create its Digital Operations Center in Washington, DC, which helps the humanitarian relief organization improve its responses to emergencies and natural disasters. The Red Cross got serious about monitoring social media after an opinion poll revealed that 80 percent of Americans expect emergency responders to monitor social networks, and one-third presumed that they could get help during a disaster within an hour if they posted or Tweeted a request. Modeled after Dell's own iconic social media center, the Red Cross Digital Operations Center broke new ground with an innovative digital volunteer program, adding thousands of trained volunteers around the country to help handle the massive volume of social media traffic that occurs during a disaster.

The Digital Operations Center helps improve the Red Cross's everyday relief efforts, such as responses to an apartment fire in a large metropolitan area. "Not only are we scanning the social media landscape looking for actionable intelligence," says a Red Cross manager, "we are also scanning the social space to see if there are people out there who need information and emotional support."

But it's the major disasters that highlight the center's biggest potential. For example, during the week of Hurricane Sandy, one of the biggest natural disasters in U.S. history, the Digital Operations Center played a crucial role in directing Red Cross relief efforts. In addition to the usual data from government partners, on-the-ground assessments, and damage reports from traditional media, the center pored through and acted on millions Tweets, Facebook posts, blog entries, and photos posted online. In all, it tracked more than 2 million posts and responded directly to thousands of people. In at least 88 cases, social media posts had a direct effect on Red Cross actions. "We put trucks in areas where we saw a greater need, we moved cots to a shelter where we needed more supplies," says the Red Cross manager. Even a lack of social media activity was an important indicator. A social media "black hole" in a specific area probably meant that factors were preventing people in that area from Tweeting and that they needed help.

So whether it's MasterCard, Gatorade, or the American Red Cross, a social media command center can help marketers scour the digital environment, analyze brand-related conversations in real time to gain marketing insights, and respond quickly and appropriately. Ultimately, social media listening gives consumers another voice, to the benefit of both customers and the brand. "It enables us to give the public a seat at our response table," says the Red Cross manager. Wells Fargo's Director of Social Media agrees: "Consumers want to be a part of how companies serve them," she says. "Our nirvana is that if someone offers us an idea, tip, or feedback that really helps us, we respond directly."

Sources: "MasterCard Conversation Suite Video," http://newsroom.mastercard.com/videos/mastercard-conversation-suite-video/, accessed September 2015; Sheila Shayon, "MasterCard Harnesses the Power of Social with Innovative Conversation Suite," *brandchannel,* May 7, 2013, www.brandchannel.com/home/post/2013/05/07/MasterCard-Conversation-Suite-050713.aspx; Giselle Abramovich, "Inside Mastercard's Social Command Center," *Digiday,* May 9, 2013, http://digiday.com/brands/inside-mastercards-social-command-center/; Anthony Shop, "Social Media Lessons from Gatorade Mission Control," *Socialmediadriver.com,* August 28, 2013, http://socialdriver.com/2013/08/28/social-media-lessons-from-gatorade-mission-control/; Evan Hanson, "PepsiCo Drinks In Gatorade's Social Media Performance at Game One of NBA Finals," *24/7 Wallstreet,* June 7, 2014, http://247wallst.com/general/2014/06/07/pepsico-drinks-in-gatorades-social-media-performance-at-game-one-of-nba-finals/#ixzz3O6SWtQJt; Ariel Schwartz, "How the Red Cross Used Tweets to Save Lives during Hurricane Sandy," *Fast Company,* October 31, 2013, www.fastcoexist.com/3020923/how-the-red-cross-used-tweets-to-save-lives-during-hurricane-sandy; and Scott Gulbransen, "Taking Back the Social-Media Command Center," *Forbes,* January 22, 2014, www.forbes.com/sites/onmarketing/2014/01/22/taking-back-the-social-media-command-center/.

---

monitors real-time social media activity surrounding the introduction of Apple's latest iPhones to quickly shape marketing responses for its own Galaxy S smartphones and tablets.[7]

At the same time that Apple CEO Tim Cook is on stage unveiling the latest much-anticipated new iPhone, Samsung marketing strategists are huddled around screens in a war room hundreds of miles away watching the introduction unfold. They carefully monitored not only each new iPhone feature as it is presented but also the gush of online consumer commentary flooding blogs and social media channels. Even as the real-time consumer and competitive data surge in, the Samsung team is drafting a response. Within only a few days, just as the new iPhones are hitting store shelves, Samsung is already airing TV, print, and social media response ads that rechannel the excitement surrounding the iPhone debut toward its own Galaxy line.

For example, during the iPhone 5 roll-out, Samsung launched an ad mocking iPhone fans lined up outside Apple stores buzzing about the features of the new iPhone, only to be upstaged by passersby and their Samsung Galaxy smartphones ("The next big thing is already here"). Lines in the ad were based on thousands of actual Tweets and other social media interactions concerning specific iPhone features. The real-time-insights-based ad became the tech-ad sensation of the year (grabbing more than 70 million online views). Similarly, during the iPhone 6 debut, Samsung quickly launched a series of "It doesn't take a genius" ads poking fun at various iPhone features announced at Apple's release event.

Much competitor intelligence can be collected from people inside the company—executives, engineers and scientists, purchasing agents, and the sales force. The company can also obtain important intelligence information from suppliers, resellers, and key customers. Intelligence seekers can also pour through any of thousands of online databases. Some are free. For example, the U.S. Security and Exchange Commission's database provides a huge stockpile of financial information on public competitors, and the U.S. Patent Office and Trademark database reveals patents that competitors have filed. For a fee, companies can also subscribe to any of the more than 3,000 online databases and information search services, such as Hoover's, LexisNexis, and Dun & Bradstreet. Today's marketers have an almost overwhelming amount of competitor information only a few keystrokes away.

The intelligence game goes both ways. Facing determined competitive marketing intelligence efforts by competitors, most companies take steps to protect their own information. One self-admitted corporate spy advises that companies should try conducting marketing intelligence investigations of themselves, looking for potentially damaging information leaks. They should start by "vacuuming up" everything they can find in the public record, including job postings, court records, company advertisements and blogs, Web pages, press releases, online business reports, social media postings by customers and employees, and other information available to inquisitive competitors.[8]

The growing use of marketing intelligence also raises ethical issues. Some intelligence-gathering techniques may involve questionable ethics. Clearly, companies should take advantage of publicly available information. However, they should not stoop to snoop. With all the legitimate intelligence sources now available, a company does not need to break the law or accepted codes of ethics to get good intelligence.

Author Comment
Whereas marketing intelligence involves actively scanning the general marketing environment, marketing research involves more focused studies to gain customer insights relating to specific marketing decisions.

Marketing Research

In addition to marketing intelligence information about general consumer, competitor, and marketplace happenings, marketers often need formal studies that provide customer and market insights for specific marketing situations and decisions. For example, Starbucks wants to know how customers would react to a new breakfast menu item. Yahoo! wants to know how Web searchers will react to a proposed redesign of its site. Or Samsung wants to know how many and what kinds of people will buy its next-generation, ultrathin televisions. In such situations, managers will need marketing research.

Marketing research
The systematic design, collection, analysis, and reporting of data relevant to a specific marketing situation facing an organization.

Marketing research is the systematic design, collection, analysis, and reporting of data relevant to a specific marketing situation facing an organization. Companies use marketing research in a wide variety of situations. For example, marketing research gives marketers insights into customer motivations, purchase behavior, and satisfaction. It can help them to assess market potential and market share or measure the effectiveness of pricing, product, distribution, and promotion activities.

Some large companies have their own research departments that work with marketing managers on marketing research projects. In addition, these companies—like their smaller counterparts—frequently hire outside research specialists to consult with management on specific marketing problems and to conduct marketing research studies. Sometimes firms simply purchase data collected by outside firms to aid in their decision making.

The marketing research process has four steps (see **>> Figure 4.2**): defining the problem and research objectives, developing the research plan, implementing the research plan, and interpreting and reporting the findings.

This first step is probably the most difficult but also the most important one. It guides the entire research process. It's frustrating and costly to reach the end of an expensive research project only to learn that you've addressed the wrong problem!

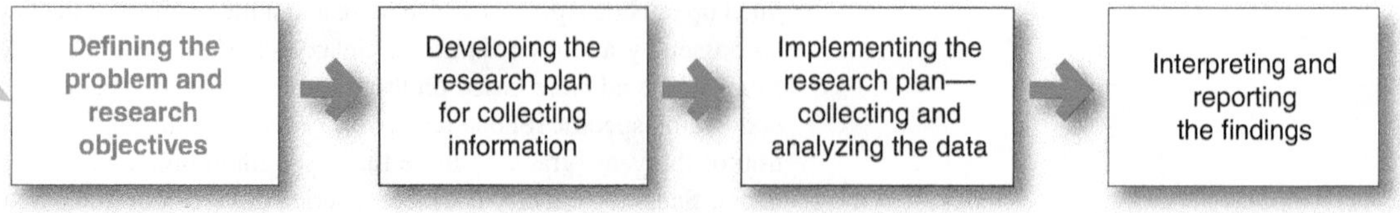

>> Figure 4.2 The Marketing Research Process

Defining the Problem and Research Objectives

Marketing managers and researchers must work together closely to define the problem and agree on research objectives. The manager best understands the decision for which information is needed, whereas the researcher best understands marketing research and how to obtain the information. Defining the problem and research objectives is often the hardest step in the research process. The manager may know that something is wrong without knowing the specific causes.

After the problem has been defined carefully, the manager and the researcher must set the research objectives. A marketing research project might have one of three types of objectives. The objective of **exploratory research** is to gather preliminary information that will help define the problem and suggest hypotheses. The objective of **descriptive research** is to describe things, such as the market potential for a product or the demographics and attitudes of consumers who buy the product. The objective of **causal research** is to test hypotheses about cause-and-effect relationships. For example, would a 10 percent decrease in tuition at a private college result in an enrollment increase sufficient to offset the reduced tuition? Managers often start with exploratory research and later follow with descriptive or causal research.

Exploratory research
Marketing research to gather preliminary information that will help define problems and suggest hypotheses.

Descriptive research
Marketing research to better describe marketing problems, situations, or markets, such as the market potential for a product or the demographics and attitudes of consumers.

Causal research
Marketing research to test hypotheses about cause-and-effect relationships.

The statement of the problem and research objectives guides the entire research process. The manager and the researcher should put the statement in writing to be certain that they agree on the purpose and expected results of the research.

Developing the Research Plan

Once researchers have defined the research problem and objectives, they must determine the exact information needed, develop a plan for gathering it efficiently, and present the plan to management. The research plan outlines sources of existing data and spells out the specific research approaches, contact methods, sampling plans, and instruments that researchers will use to gather new data.

Research objectives must be translated into specific information needs. For example, suppose that >> Chipotle Mexican Grill wants to know how consumers would react to the addition of drive-thru service to its restaurants. U.S. fast-food chains generate an estimated 24 percent of sales through drive-thrus. However, Chipotle—the sustainability-minded fast-casual restaurant that positions itself on "Food With Integrity"—doesn't offer drive-thru service. Adding drive-thrus might help Chipotle leverage its strong brand position and attract new sales. The proposed research might call for the following specific information:

- The demographic, economic, and lifestyle characteristics of current Chipotle customers: Do current counter-service customers also use drive-thrus? Are drive-thrus consistent with their needs and lifestyles? Or would Chipotle need to target a new segment of consumers?
- The characteristics and usage patterns of the broader population of fast-food and fast-casual diners: What do they need and expect from such restaurants? Where, when, and how do they use them,and what existing quality, price, and service levels do they value? The new Chipotle service would require trong, relevant, and distinctive positioning in the crowded fast-food market.
- Impact on the Chipotle customer experience: Would drive-thrus be consistent with a higher-quality fast-casual experience like the one Chipotle offers?
- Chipotle employee reactions to drive-thru service: Would restaurant employees support drive-thrus? Would adding drive-thrus disrupt operations and their ability to deliver high-quality food and service to inside customers?

>> A decision by Chipotle Mexican Grill to add drive-thru service would call for marketing research that provides lots of specific information.
Chipotle Mexican Grill, Inc.

- Forecasts of both inside and drive-thru sales and profits: Would the new drive-thru service create new sales and customers or simply take sales away from current operations?

Chipotle's marketers would need these and many other types of information to decide whether to introduce drive-thru service and, if so, the best way to do it.

The research plan should be presented in a *written proposal*. A written proposal is especially important when the research project is large and complex or when an outside firm carries it out. The proposal should cover the management problems addressed, the research objectives, the information to be obtained, and how the results will help management's decision making. The proposal also should include estimated research costs.

Secondary data
Information that already exists somewhere, having been collected for another purpose.

Primary data
Information collected for the specific purpose at hand.

To meet the manager's information needs, the research plan can call for gathering secondary data, primary data, or both. **Secondary data** consist of information that already exists somewhere, having been collected for another purpose. **Primary data** consist of information collected for the specific purpose at hand.

Gathering Secondary Data

Researchers usually start by gathering secondary data. The company's internal database provides a good starting point. However, the company can also tap into a wide assortment of external information sources.

Companies can buy secondary data from outside suppliers. For example, Nielsen sells shopper insight data from a consumer panel of more than 250,000 households in 25 countries worldwide, with measures of trial and repeat purchasing, brand loyalty, and buyer demographics. Experian Simmons carries out a full spectrum of consumer studies that provide a comprehensive view of the American consumer. The U.S. Yankelovich MONITOR service by The Futures Company sells information on important social and lifestyle trends. These and other firms supply high-quality data to suit a wide variety of marketing information needs.[9]

Using *commercial online databases*, marketing researchers can conduct their own searches of secondary data sources. >> General database services such as ProQuest and LexisNexis put an incredible wealth of information at the fingertips of marketing decision makers. Beyond commercial services offering information for a fee, almost every industry association, government agency, business publication, and news medium offers free information to those tenacious enough to find their Web sites or apps.

Internet search engines can also be a big help in locating relevant secondary information sources. However, they can also be very frustrating and inefficient. For example, a Chipotle marketer Googling "fast-food drive-thru" would come up with more than 2.8 million hits. Still, well-structured, well-designed online searches can be a good starting point to any marketing research project.

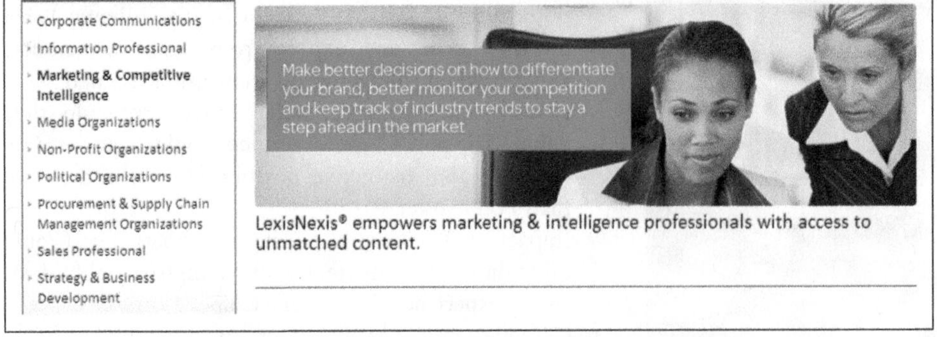

>> **General database services such as ProQuest and LexisNexis put an incredible wealth of information at the fingertips of marketing decision makers.**

Secondary data can usually be obtained more quickly and at a lower cost than primary data. Also, secondary sources can sometimes provide data an individual company cannot collect on its own—information that either is not directly available or would be too expensive to collect. For example, it would be too expensive for a consumer products brand such as Coca-Cola or Tide to conduct a continuing retail store audit to find out about the market shares, prices, and displays of its own and competitors' brands. But those marketers can buy the InfoScan service from SymphonyIRI Group, which provides this information based on scanner and other data from 34,000 retail stores in markets around the nation.[10]

Secondary data can also present problems. Researchers can rarely obtain all the data they need from secondary sources. For example, Chipotle will not find existing information regarding consumer reactions about new drive-thru service that it has not yet installed. Even when data can be found, the information might not be very usable. The researcher must evaluate secondary information carefully to make certain it is *relevant* (fits the research project's needs), *accurate* (reliably collected and reported), *current* (up-to-date enough for current decisions), and *impartial* (objectively collected and reported).

Primary Data Collection

Secondary data provide a good starting point for research and often help to define research problems and objectives. In most cases, however, the company must also collect primary data. **>>Table 4.1** shows that designing a plan for primary data collection calls for a number of decisions on *research approaches, contact methods*, the *sampling plan*, and *research instruments*.

Research Approaches

Research approaches for gathering primary data include observation, surveys, and experiments. We discuss each one in turn.

Observational research
Gathering primary data by observing relevant people, actions, and situations.

Observational Research. **Observational research** involves gathering primary data by observing relevant people, actions, and situations. For example, food retailer Trader Joe's might evaluate possible new store locations by checking traffic patterns, neighborhood conditions, and the locations of competing Whole Foods, Fresh Market, and other retail chains.

Researchers often observe consumer behavior to glean customer insights they can't obtain by simply asking customers questions. For instance, Fisher-Price has established an observation lab in which it can observe the reactions little tots have to new toys. The Fisher-Price Play Lab is a sunny, toy-strewn space where lucky kids get to test Fisher-Price prototypes under the watchful eyes of designers who hope to learn what will get them worked up into a new-toy frenzy. In the lab, some 3,500 kids participate each year testing 1,200 products annually. "Our designers watch and learn from how [children] play," says a Fisher-Price child research manager. "It really helps us make better products."[11]

Marketers not only observe what consumers do but also observe what consumers are saying. As discussed earlier, marketers now routinely listen in on consumer conversations on blogs, social networks, and Web sites. Observing such naturally occurring feedback can provide inputs that simply can't be gained through more structured and formal research approaches.

Ethnographic research
A form of observational research that involves sending trained observers to watch and interact with consumers in their "natural environments."

A wide range of companies now use **ethnographic research**. Ethnographic research involves sending observers to watch and interact with consumers in their "natural environments." The observers might be trained anthropologists and psychologists or company

>> Table 4.1 Planning Primary Data Collection

Research Approaches	Contact Methods	Sampling Plan	Research Instruments
Observation	Mail	Sampling unit	Questionnaire
Survey	Telephone	Sample size	Mechanical instruments
Experiment	Personal	Sampling procedure	
	Online		

researchers and managers. For example, Coors insights teams frequent bars and other locations in a top-secret small-town location—they call it the "Outpost"—within a day's drive of Chicago. The researchers use the town as a real-life lab, hob-knobbing anonymously with bar patrons, supermarket shoppers, restaurant diners, convenience store clerks, and other townspeople to gain authentic insights into how middle American consumers buy, drink, dine, and socialize around Coors and competing beer brands.[12]

Global branding firm Landor launched Landor Families, an ongoing ethnographic study that has followed 11 French families intensely for the past seven years. >> Landor researchers visit the families twice a year in their homes, peeking into their refrigerators and diving deeply into both their refrigerators and their food shopping behaviors and opinions. The researchers also shop with the families at their local supermarkets and look over their shoulders while they shop online. The families furnish monthly online reports detailing their shopping behaviors and opinions. The Landor Families study provides rich behavioral insights for Landor clients such as Danone, Kraft Foods, and Procter & Gamble. Today's big data analytics can provide important insights into the whats, whens, and wheres of consumer buying. The Landor Families program is designed to explore the whys. According to Landor, "There is no better way to understand people than to observe them in real life."[13]

>> The Landor Families ongoing ethnographic study has followed 11 French families intensely for the past seven years, diving deeply into both their refrigerators and their food shopping behaviors. Says Landor, "There is no better way to understand people than to observe them in real life."

Landor

Beyond conducting ethnographic research in physical consumer environments, many companies now routinely conduct *Netnography* research—observing consumers in a natural context in the Internet and mobile space. Observing people as they interact and move about in the online world can provide useful insights into both online and offline buying motives and behavior. And observing people's shopping patterns by tracking their mobile movement, both within and between stores, can provide retailers with valuable marketing information.

Observational and ethnographic research often yields the kinds of details that just don't emerge from traditional research questionnaires or focus groups. Whereas traditional quantitative research approaches seek to test known hypotheses and obtain answers to well-defined product or strategy questions, observational research can generate fresh customer and market insights that people are unwilling or unable to provide. It provides a window into customers' unconscious actions and unexpressed needs and feelings.

However, some things simply cannot be observed, such as attitudes, motives, or private behavior. Long-term or infrequent behavior is also difficult to observe. Finally, observations can be very difficult to interpret. Because of these limitations, researchers often use observation along with other data collection methods.

Survey research
Gathering primary data by asking people questions about their knowledge, attitudes, preferences, and buying behavior.

Survey Research. **Survey research**, the most widely used method for primary data collection, is the approach best suited for gathering descriptive information. A company that wants to know about people's knowledge, attitudes, preferences, or buying behavior can often find out by asking them directly.

The major advantage of survey research is its flexibility; it can be used to obtain many different kinds of information in many different situations. Surveys addressing almost any marketing question or decision can be conducted by phone or mail, in person, or online.

However, survey research also presents some problems. Sometimes people are unable to answer survey questions because they cannot remember or have never thought about what they do and why they do it. People may be unwilling to respond to unknown interviewers or about things they consider private. Respondents may answer survey questions even when they do not know the answer just to appear smarter or more informed. Or they may try to help the interviewer by giving pleasing answers. Finally, busy people may not take the time, or they might resent the intrusion into their privacy.

Experimental research
Gathering primary data by selecting matched groups of subjects, giving them different treatments, controlling related factors, and checking for differences in group responses.

Experimental Research. Whereas observation is best suited for exploratory research and surveys for descriptive research, **experimental research** is best suited for gathering causal information. Experiments involve selecting matched groups of subjects, giving them different treatments, controlling unrelated factors, and checking for differences in group responses. Thus, experimental research tries to explain cause-and-effect relationships.

For example, before adding a new sandwich to its menu, McDonald's might use experiments to test the effects on sales of two different prices it might charge. It could introduce the new sandwich at one price in one city and at another price in another city. If the cities are similar and if all other marketing efforts for the sandwich are the same, then differences in sales in the two cities could be related to the price charged.

Contact Methods

Information can be collected by mail, telephone, personal interview, or online. **>> Table 4.2** shows the strengths and weaknesses of each contact method.

Mail, Telephone, and Personal Interviewing. *Mail questionnaires* can be used to collect large amounts of information at a low cost per respondent. Respondents may give more honest answers to more personal questions on a mail questionnaire than to an unknown interviewer in person or over the phone. Also, no interviewer is involved to bias respondents' answers.

However, mail questionnaires are not very flexible; all respondents answer the same questions in a fixed order. Mail surveys usually take longer to complete, and the response rate—the number of people returning completed questionnaires—is often very low. Finally, the researcher often has little control over the mail questionnaire sample. Even with a good mailing list, it is hard to control *who* at a particular address fills out the questionnaire. As a result of the shortcomings, more and more marketers are now shifting to faster, more flexible, and lower-cost email, online, and mobile phone surveys.

Telephone interviewing is one of the best methods for gathering information quickly, and it provides greater flexibility than mail questionnaires. Interviewers can explain difficult questions and, depending on the answers they receive, skip some questions or probe on others. Response rates tend to be higher than with mail questionnaires, and interviewers can ask to speak to respondents with the desired characteristics or even by name.

However, with telephone interviewing, the cost per respondent is higher than with mail, online, or mobile questionnaires. Also, people may not want to discuss personal questions

>> Table 4.2 Strengths and Weaknesses of Contact Methods

	Mail	Telephone	Personal	Online
Flexibility	Poor	Good	Excellent	Good
Quantity of data that can be collected	Good	Fair	Excellent	Good
Control of interviewer effects	Excellent	Fair	Poor	Fair
Control of sample	Fair	Excellent	Good	Excellent
Speed of data collection	Poor	Excellent	Good	Excellent
Response rate	Poor	Poor	Good	Good
Cost	Good	Fair	Poor	Excellent

Source: Based on Donald S. Tull and Del I. Hawkins, *Marketing Research: Measurement and Method,* 7th ed. (New York: Macmillan Publishing Company, 1993). Adapted with permission of the authors.

with an interviewer. The method introduces interviewer bias—the way interviewers talk, how they ask questions, and other differences that may affect respondents' answers. Finally, in this age of do-not-call lists and promotion-harassed consumers, potential survey respondents are increasingly hanging up on telephone interviewers rather than talking with them.

Personal interviewing takes two forms: individual interviewing and group interviewing. *Individual interviewing* involves talking with people in their homes or offices, on the street, or in shopping malls. Such interviewing is flexible. Trained interviewers can guide interviews, explain difficult questions, and explore issues as the situation requires. They can show subjects actual products, packages, advertisements, or videos and observe reactions and behavior. However, individual personal interviews may cost three to four times as much as telephone interviews.

Group interviewing consists of inviting small groups of people to meet with a trained moderator to talk about a product, service, or organization. Participants normally are paid a small sum for attending. A moderator encourages free and easy discussion, hoping that group interactions will bring out actual feelings and thoughts. At the same time, the moderator "focuses" the discussion—hence the name **focus group interviewing**.

Focus group interviewing
Personal interviewing that involves inviting small groups of people to gather for a few hours with a trained interviewer to talk about a product, service, or organization. The interviewer "focuses" the group discussion on important issues.

In traditional focus groups, researchers and marketers watch the focus group discussions from behind a one-way mirror and record comments in writing or on video for later study. Focus group researchers often use videoconferencing and Internet technology to connect marketers in distant locations with live focus group action. Marketing executives in far-off locations can look in and listen, even participate, as a focus group progresses.

Along with observational research, focus group interviewing has become one of the major qualitative marketing research tools for gaining fresh insights into consumer thoughts and feelings. In focus group settings, researchers not only hear consumer ideas and opinions, they also can observe facial expressions, body movements, group interplay, and conversational flows. However, focus group studies present some challenges. They usually employ small samples to keep time and costs down, and it may be hard to generalize from the results. Moreover, consumers in focus groups are not always open and honest about their real feelings, behavior, and intentions in front of other people.

To overcome these problems, many researchers are tinkering with the focus group design. Some companies are changing the environments in which they conduct focus groups to help consumers relax and elicit more authentic responses. For example, Lexus hosts "An Evening with Lexus" dinners in customers' homes with groups of luxury car buyers to learn up close and personal why they did or did not buy a Lexus. Other companies use *immersion groups*—small groups of consumers who interact directly and informally with product designers without a focus group moderator present. >> Research and innovation consultancy The Mom Complex uses such immersion groups to help brand marketers from companies such as Unilever, Johnson & Johnson, Kimberly-Clark, Kellogg, Playskool, and Walmart understand and connect with their "mom customers":[14]

>> **New focus group designs: The Mom Complex uses "Mom Immersion Sessions" to help brand marketers understand and connect directly with their "mom customers" on important brand issues.**

© caia image/Alamy

> According to The Mom Complex, America's 80 million moms control 85 percent of household purchases, yet three out of four moms say marketers have no idea what it's like to be a mother. To change that, The Mom Complex arranges "Mom Immersion Sessions," in which brand marketers interact directly with groups of mothers, who receive $100 in compensation for a two-hour session. Rather than the usual focus group practice of putting the marketers behind a one-way mirror to observe groups of moms discussing their brands, the participants and marketers sit in the same room. Guided by a discussion facilitator, the moms begin by educating the marketers about the realities of motherhood—"the raw, real ugly truth about being a mom." Then the moms and marketers work together to address specific brand issues—whether it's new product ideas, current product problems, or positioning and communications strategy. The goal is to "turn the challenges of motherhood into growth opportunities for brands."

Individual and focus group interviews can add a personal touch as opposed to more numbers-oriented, big data research. They can provide rich insights into the motivations and feelings behind the numbers and analytics. "Focus groups are the most widely used qualitative research tool," says one analyst, "and with good reason. They foster fruitful discussion and can provide unique insight into customers' and potential customers' needs, wants, thoughts, and feelings." Things really come to life when you hear people say them.[15]

Online Marketing Research. The Internet has had a dramatic impact on how marketing research is conducted. Increasingly, researchers are collecting primary data through **online marketing research**: Internet and mobile surveys, online panels, experiments, and online focus groups and brand communities.

Online marketing research
Collecting primary data online through Internet surveys, online focus groups, Web-based experiments, or tracking of consumers' online behavior.

Online research can take many forms. A company can use the Internet or mobile technology as a survey medium: It can include a questionnaire on its Web or social media sites or use email or mobile devices to invite people to answer questions. It can create online panels that provide regular feedback or conduct live discussions or online focus groups. Researchers can also conduct online experiments. They can experiment with different prices, headlines, or product features on different Web or mobile sites or at different times to learn the relative effectiveness of their offers. They can set up virtual shopping environments and use them to test new products and marketing programs. Or a company can learn about the behavior of online customers by following their click streams as they visit the online site and move to other sites.

The Internet is especially well suited to *quantitative* research—for example, conducting marketing surveys and collecting data. More than 87 percent of all Americans now use the Internet, making it a fertile channel for reaching a broad cross-section of consumers.[16] As response rates for traditional survey approaches decline and costs increase, the Internet is quickly replacing mail and the telephone as the dominant data collection methodology.

Internet-based survey research offers many advantages over traditional phone, mail, and personal interviewing approaches. The most obvious advantages are speed and low costs. By going online, researchers can quickly and easily distribute surveys to thousands of respondents simultaneously via email or by posting them on selected online and mobile sites. Responses can be almost instantaneous, and because respondents themselves enter the information, researchers can tabulate, review, and share research data as the information arrives.

Online research also usually costs much less than research conducted through mail, phone, or personal interviews. Using the Internet eliminates most of the postage, phone, interviewer, and data-handling costs associated with the other approaches. Moreover, sample size and location have little impact on costs. Once the questionnaire is set up, there's little difference in cost between 10 respondents and 10,000 respondents on the Internet, or between local or globally distant respondents.

Its low cost puts online research well within the reach of almost any business, large or small. In fact, with the Internet, what was once the domain of research experts is now available to almost any would-be researcher. » Even smaller, less sophisticated researchers can use online survey services such as Snap Surveys (www.snapsurveys.com) and SurveyMonkey (www.surveymonkey.com) to create, publish, and distribute their own custom online or mobile surveys in minutes.

Internet-based surveys also tend to be more interactive and engaging, easier to complete, and less intrusive

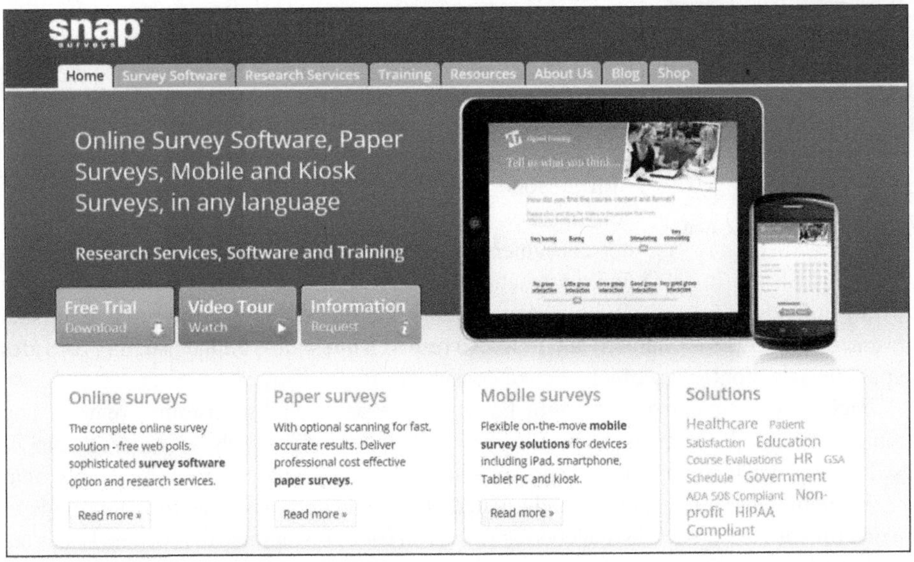

» **Online research: Thanks to survey services such as Snap Surveys, almost any business, large or small, can create, publish, and distribute its own custom online or mobile surveys in minutes.**

Reproduced with permission from Snap Surveys. www.snapsurveys.com

than traditional phone or mail surveys. As a result, they usually garner higher response rates. The Internet is an excellent medium for reaching the hard-to-reach consumer—for example, the often-elusive teen, single, affluent, and well-educated audiences. It's also good for reaching people who lead busy lives, from working mothers to on-the-go executives. Such people are well represented online, and they can respond in their own space and at their own convenience.

Just as marketing researchers have rushed to use the Internet for quantitative surveys and data collection, they are now also adopting *qualitative* Internet-based research approaches, such as online focus groups, blogs, and social networks. The Internet can provide a fast, low-cost way to gain qualitative customer insights.

Online focus groups
Gathering a small group of people online with a trained moderator to chat about a product, service, or organization and gain qualitative insights about consumer attitudes and behavior.

A primary qualitative Internet-based research approach is **online focus groups**. For example, online research firm FocusVision offers its InterVu service, which harnesses the power of the Internet to conduct focus groups with participants at remote locations, anywhere in the world, at any time. Using their own Webcams, InterVu participants can log on to focus sessions from their homes or offices and see, hear, and react to each other in real-time, face-to-face discussions.[17] Such focus groups can be conducted in any language and viewed with simultaneous translation. They work well for bringing together people from different parts of the country or world at low cost. Researchers can view the sessions in real time from just about anywhere, eliminating travel, lodging, and facility costs. Finally, although online focus groups require some advance scheduling, results are almost immediate.

Although growing rapidly, both quantitative and qualitative Internet-based research have some drawbacks. One major problem is controlling who's in the online sample. Without seeing respondents, it's difficult to know who they really are. To overcome such sample and context problems, many online research firms use opt-in communities and respondent panels. Alternatively, many companies have now developed their own custom social networks and are using them to gain customer inputs and insights. For example, in its relentless "Pursuit of Perfection," Lexus has built an extensive online research community called the Lexus Advisory Board, which consists of 20,000 invitation-only Lexus owners representing a wide range of demographics, psychographics, and model ownership. Similarly, NASCAR has built an online community of 12,000 core fans called the NASCAR Fan Council. Both companies survey these online communities regularly to obtain quick and relevant feedback from customers about everything from brand perceptions to proposed marketing initiatives.[18]

NASCAR has built an online research community of 12,000 core fans called the NASCAR Fan Council, which it surveys regularly for inputs and insights.
NASCAR

Online Behavioral and Social Tracking and Targeting. Thus, in recent years, the Internet has become an important tool for conducting research and developing customer insights. But today's marketing researchers are going even further—well beyond online surveys, focus groups, and Internet communities. Increasingly, they are listening to and watching consumers by actively mining the rich veins of unsolicited, unstructured, "bottom-up" customer information already coursing around the Internet. Whereas traditional marketing research provides more logical consumer responses to structured and intrusive research questions, online listening provides the passion and spontaneity of unsolicited consumer opinions.

Tracking consumers online might be as simple as scanning customer reviews and comments on the company's brand site or on shopping sites such as Amazon.com or BestBuy.com. Or it might mean using sophisticated online-analysis tools to deeply analyze the mountains of consumer brand–related comments and messages found in blogs or on social media sites, such as Facebook, Yelp, YouTube, Instagram, or Twitter. Listening to and engaging customers online can provide valuable insights into what consumers are saying or feeling about a brand. It can also provide opportunities for building positive brand experiences and relationships. Many companies now excel at listening online and responding quickly and appropriately. As noted previously, more and more companies are setting up social media command centers with which they scour the digital environment and analyze brand-related comments and conversations to gain marketing insights.

Information about what consumers do while trolling the vast digital expanse—what searches they make, the online and mobile sites they visit, how they shop, and what they buy—is pure gold to marketers. And today's marketers are busy mining that gold. Then, in a practice called **behavioral targeting**, marketers use the online data to target ads and offers to specific consumers. For example, if you place an Apple iPad in your Amazon.com shopping cart but don't buy it, you might expect to see some ads for that very type of tablet the next time you visit your favorite ESPN site to catch up on the latest sports scores.

Behavioral targeting
Using online consumer tracking data to target advertisements and marketing offers to specific consumers.

The newest wave of Web analytics and targeting takes online eavesdropping even further—from *behavioral* targeting to *social* targeting. Whereas behavioral targeting tracks consumer movements across online sites, social targeting also mines individual online social connections and conversations from social networking sites. Research shows that consumers shop a lot like their friends and are much more likely to respond to ads from brands friends use. So, instead of just having a Zappos.com ad for running shoes pop up because you've recently searched online for running shoes (behavioral targeting), an ad for a specific pair of running shoes pops up because a friend that you're connected to via Twitter just bought those shoes from Zappos.com last week (social targeting).

>> Marketers watch what consumers say and do online, then use the resulting insights to personalize online shopping experiences. Is it sophisticated online research or "just a little creepy"?
Andresr/Shutterstock.com

Online listening, behavioral targeting, and social targeting can help marketers to harness the massive amounts of consumer information swirling around the Internet. However, as marketers get more adept at trolling blogs, social networks, and other Internet and mobile domains, many critics worry about consumer privacy. >> At what point does sophisticated online research cross the line into consumer stalking? Proponents claim that behavioral and social targeting benefit more than abuse consumers by feeding back ads and products that are more relevant to their interests. But to many consumers and public advocates, following consumers online and stalking them with ads feels more than just a little creepy.

Regulators and others are stepping in. The Federal Trade Commission (FTC) has recommended the creation of a "Do Not Track" system (the online equivalent to the "Do Not Call" registry)—which would let people opt out of having their actions monitored online. However, progress has been mixed. Meanwhile, many major Internet browsers and social media have heeded the concerns by adding extended privacy features to their services.[19]

Sampling Plan

Marketing researchers usually draw conclusions about large groups of consumers by studying a small sample of the total consumer population. A **sample** is a segment of the population selected for marketing research to represent the population as a whole. Ideally, the sample should be representative so that the researcher can make accurate estimates of the thoughts and behaviors of the larger population.

Sample
A segment of the population selected for marketing research to represent the population as a whole.

Designing the sample requires three decisions. First, *who* is to be studied (what *sampling unit*)? The answer to this question is not always obvious. For example, to learn about the decision-making process for a family automobile purchase, should the subject be the husband, the wife, other family members, dealership salespeople, or all of these? Second, *how many* people should be included (what *sample size*)? Large samples give more reliable results than small samples. However, larger samples usually cost more, and it is not necessary to sample the entire target market or even a large portion to get reliable results.

Finally, *how* should the people in the sample be *chosen* (what *sampling procedure*)? >> **Table 4.3** describes different kinds of samples. Using *probability samples*, each population member has a known chance of being included in the sample, and researchers can calculate confidence limits for sampling error. But when probability sampling costs too much or takes too much time, marketing researchers often take *nonprobability samples* even though their sampling error cannot be measured. These varied ways of drawing samples have different costs and time limitations as well as different accuracy and statistical properties. Which method is best depends on the needs of the research project.

» Table 4.3 Types of Samples

Probability Sample	
Simple random sample	Every member of the population has a known and equal chance of selection.
Stratified random sample	The population is divided into mutually exclusive groups (such as age groups), and random samples are drawn from each group.
Cluster (area) sample	The population is divided into mutually exclusive groups (such as blocks), and the researcher draws a sample of the groups to interview.
Nonprobability Sample	
Convenience sample	The researcher selects the easiest population members from which to obtain information.
Judgment sample	The researcher uses his or her judgment to select population members who are good prospects for accurate information.
Quota sample	The researcher finds and interviews a prescribed number of people in each of several categories.

Research Instruments

In collecting primary data, marketing researchers have a choice of two main research instruments: *questionnaires* and *mechanical devices*.

Questionnaires. The questionnaire is by far the most common instrument, whether administered in person, by phone, by email, or online. Questionnaires are very flexible—there are many ways to ask questions. Closed-ended questions include all the possible answers, and subjects make choices among them. Examples include multiple-choice questions and scale questions. Open-ended questions allow respondents to answer in their own words. In a survey of airline users, Southwest Airlines might simply ask, "What is your opinion of Southwest Airlines?" Or it might ask people to complete a sentence: "When I choose an airline, the most important consideration is. . . ." These and other kinds of open-ended questions often reveal more than closed-ended questions because they do not limit respondents' answers.

Open-ended questions are especially useful in exploratory research, when the researcher is trying to find out *what* people think but is not measuring *how many* people think in a certain way. Closed-ended questions, on the other hand, provide answers that are easier to interpret and tabulate.

Researchers should also use care in the *wording* and *ordering* of questions. They should use simple, direct, and unbiased wording. Questions should be arranged in a logical order. The first question should create interest if possible, and difficult or personal questions should be asked last so that respondents do not become defensive.

Mechanical Instruments. Although questionnaires are the most common research instrument, researchers also use mechanical instruments to monitor consumer behavior. Nielsen Media Research attaches people meters to television sets, cable boxes, and satellite systems in selected homes to record who watches which programs. Retailers use checkout scanners to record shoppers' purchases. Mondelez International—maker of Chips Ahoy!, Ritz crackers, Oreos, and other goodies—is even building supermarket "smart shelves." » The shelves use sensors to analyze facial structures and other characteristics that identify a shopper's age and sex and determine if and when the shopper selects a product off the shelf. Along with supplying a wealth of insights into consumer shopping behavior, based on who's buying what, the smart shelves allow marketers to deliver real-time, personalized promotions via video screens on the shelves.[20]

Using mechanical instruments to monitor consumers: Some marketers are building supermarket "smart shelves" that track shopper demographics and purchases, supplying a wealth of insights into consumer shopping behavior.

Associated Press

Other mechanical devices measure subjects' physical responses to marketing offerings. Consider this example:[21]

> Time Warner's MediaLab at its New York headquarters looks more like a chic consumer electronics store than a research lab. But the lab employs a nifty collection of high-tech observation techniques to capture the changing ways that today's viewers are using and reacting to television and Web content. The MediaLab uses biometric measures to analyze every show subjects watch, every site they visit, and every commercial they skip. Meanwhile, mechanical devices assess viewer engagement via physiological measures of skin temperature, heart rate, sweat level, leaning in, and facial and eye movements. Observers behind two-way mirrors or using cameras that peer over each subject's shoulder make real-time assessments of Web browsing behavior. In all, the deep consumer insights gained from MediaLab observations are helping Time Warner prepare for marketing in today's rapidly changing digital media landscape.

Still other researchers apply *neuromarketing*, measuring brain activity to learn how consumers feel and respond. Marketing scientists using MRI scans and EEG devices have learned that tracking brain electrical activity and blood flow can provide companies with insights into what turns consumers on and off regarding their brands and marketing.

Companies ranging from PepsiCo and Disney to Google and Microsoft now hire neuromarketing research companies such as Neurons Inc., Sands Research, and Nielsen NeuroFocus to help figure out what people are really thinking. For example, PepsiCo's Frito-Lay worked with Nielsen NeuroFocus to assess consumer motivations underlying the success of its Cheetos snack brand. After scanning the brains of carefully chosen consumers, Nielsen NeuroFocus learned that part of what makes Cheetos a junk-food staple is the messy orange cheese dust—that's right, the neon stuff that gloms onto your fingers and then smears on your shirt or the couch cushions. As it turns out, the icky coating triggers a powerful brain response: a sense of "giddy subversion" that makes the messiness more than worth the trouble it causes. Using this finding, Frito-Lay successfully framed an entire advertising campaign—called "The Orange Underground"—around the mess Cheetos make. For its part, Nielsen NeuroFocus won an award for outstanding advertising research.[22]

Although neuromarketing techniques can measure consumer involvement and emotional responses second by second, such brain responses can be difficult to interpret. Thus, neuromarketing is usually used in combination with other research approaches to gain a more complete picture of what goes on inside consumers' heads.

Implementing the Research Plan

The researcher next puts the marketing research plan into action. This involves collecting, processing, and analyzing the information. Data collection can be carried out by the company's marketing research staff or outside firms. Researchers should watch closely to make sure that the plan is implemented correctly. They must guard against problems with data collection techniques and technologies, data quality, and timeliness.

Researchers must also process and analyze the collected data to isolate important information and insights. They need to check data for accuracy and completeness and code them for analysis. The researchers then tabulate the results and compute statistical measures.

Interpreting and Reporting the Findings

The market researcher must now interpret the findings, draw conclusions, and report them to management. The researcher should not try to overwhelm managers with numbers and fancy statistical techniques. Rather, the researcher should present important findings and insights that are useful in the major decisions faced by management.

However, interpretation should not be left only to researchers. Although they are often experts in research design and statistics, the marketing manager knows more about the problem and the decisions that must be made. The best research means little if the manager blindly accepts faulty interpretations from the researcher. Similarly, managers may be biased. They might tend to accept research results that show what they expected and reject those that they did not expect or hope for. In many cases, findings can be interpreted in different ways, and discussions between researchers and managers will help point to the best interpretations. Thus, managers and researchers must work together closely when interpreting research results, and both must share responsibility for the research process and resulting decisions.

LINKING THE CONCEPTS

Whew! We've covered a lot of territory. Hold up a minute, take a breather, and see if you can apply the marketing research process you've just studied.

- What specific kinds of research do Chipotle Mexican Grill's marketing managers use to learn more about its customers' preferences and buying behaviors? Sketch out a brief research plan for assessing potential reactions to a new drive-thru service.
- Could you use the marketing research process to analyze your career opportunities and job possibilities? (Think of yourself as a "product" and employers as potential "customers.") If so, what would your research plan look like?

Author Comment
We've talked generally about managing customer relationships throughout the book. But here, "customer relationship management" (CRM) has a much narrower data-management meaning. It refers to capturing and using customer data from all sources to manage customer interactions, engage customers, and build customer relationships.

Analyzing and Using Marketing Information

Information gathered from internal databases, competitive marketing intelligence, and marketing research usually requires additional analysis. Managers may need help applying the information to gain customer and market insights that will improve their marketing decisions. This help may include advanced analytics to learn more about the relationships within sets of data. Information analysis might also involve the application of analytical models that will help marketers make better decisions.

Once the information has been processed and analyzed, it must be made available to the right decision makers at the right time. In the following sections, we look deeper into analyzing and using marketing information.

Customer Relationship Management (CRM)

The question of how best to analyze and use individual customer data presents special problems. In the current *big data* era, most companies are awash in information about their customers and the marketplace. Still, smart companies capture information at every possible customer *touch point*. These touch points include customer purchases, sales force contacts, service and support calls, Web and social media site visits, satisfaction surveys, credit and payment interactions, market research studies—every contact between a customer and a company.

Unfortunately, this information is usually scattered widely across the organization or buried deep in separate company databases. To overcome such problems, many companies are now turning to **customer relationship management (CRM)** to manage detailed information about individual customers and carefully manage customer touch points to maximize customer loyalty.

Customer relationship management (CRM)
Managing detailed information about individual customers and carefully managing customer touch points to maximize customer loyalty.

CRM consists of sophisticated software and analysis tools from companies such as Salesforce.com, Oracle, Microsoft, and SAS that integrate customer and marketplace information from all sources, analyze it, and apply the results to build stronger customer relationships. CRM integrates everything that a company's sales, service, and marketing teams know about individual customers, providing a 360-degree view of the customer relationship. For example, MetLife recently developed a CRM system that it calls "The MetLife Wall":[23]

> One of the biggest customer service challenges for MetLife's sales and service reps used to be quickly finding and getting to customer information—different records, transactions, and interactions stored in dozens of different company data locations and formats. The MetLife Wall solves that problem. The Wall uses a Facebook-like interface to serve up a consolidated view of each MetLife customer's service experience. The innovative CRM system draws customer data from 70 different MetLife systems containing 45 million customer agreements and 140 million transactions. It puts all of a given customer's information and related links into a single record on a single screen, updated in near real time. Now, thanks to The MetLife Wall—with only a single click instead of the 40 clicks it used to take—sales and service reps can see a complete view of a given customer's various policies, transactions, and claims filed and paid, along with a history of all the interactions the customer has had with MetLife across the company's many touch points, all on a simple timeline. The Wall has given a big boost to MetLife's customer service and cross-selling efforts. According to a MetLife marketing executive, it's also had "a huge impact on customer satisfaction."

By using CRM to understand customers better, companies can provide higher levels of customer service and develop deeper customer relationships. They can use CRM to pinpoint high-value customers, target them more effectively, cross-sell the company's products, and create offers tailored to specific customer requirements.

Big Data and Marketing Analytics

Marketing analytics
The analysis tools, technologies, and processes by which marketers dig out meaningful patterns in big data to gain customer insights and gauge marketing performance.

Today's big data can yield big results. But simply collecting and storing huge amounts of data has little value. Marketers must sift through the mountains of data to mine the gems—the bits that yield customer insights. As one marketing executive puts it, "It's actually [about getting] *big insights* from big data. It's throwing away 99.999 percent of that data to find things that are actionable." Says another data expert, "*right* data trumps *big* data."[24] That's the job of *marketing analytics*.

Marketing analytics consists of the analysis tools, technologies, and processes by which marketers dig out meaningful patterns in big data to gain customer insights and gauge marketing performance.[25] Marketers apply marketing analytics to the large and complex sets of data they collect from Web, mobile, and social media tracking; customer transactions and engagements; and other big data sources. For example, Netflix maintains a bulging customer database and uses sophisticated marketing analytics to gain insights, which it then uses to fuel recommendations to subscribers, decide what programming to offer, and even develop its own exclusive content in the quest to serve its customers better (see Marketing at Work 4.2).

Another good example of marketing analytics in action comes from food products giant Kraft, whose classic brands—from JELL-O, Miracle Whip, and Kraft Macaroni and Cheese to Oscar Meyer, Philadelphia Cream Cheese, Lunchables, and Planters nuts—are found in 98 percent of all North American households:[26]

Marketing analytics: Food products giant Kraft reaps a treasure trove of data from customers of its classic brands, then applies high-level marketing analytics to mine nuggets of customer insights.
Bloomberg/Getty Images

> Kraft has a treasure trove of marketing data, gathered from years of interactions with customers and from its social media monitoring hub called Looking Glass. Looking Glass tracks consumer trends, competitor activities, and more than 100,000 brand-related conversations daily in social media and on blogs. Kraft also reaps data from customer interactions with its *Kraft Food & Family* magazine, email communications, and the more than 100 Web and social media sites that serve its large brand portfolio. In all, Kraft has 18 years' worth of customer data across 22,000 different attributes.

MARKETING AT WORK 4.2

Netflix Streams Success with Big Data and Marketing Analytics

Americans now watch more movies and TV programs streamed online than they watch on DVDs and Blu-ray discs. And with its rotating library of more than 60,000 titles, Netflix streams more movie and program content by far than any other video service. Netflix's 62 million paid subscribers watch more than 3.3 billion hours of movies and TV programs every month. During peak hours on any given day, a remarkable one-third of all downloads on the non-mobile Internet are devoted to streamed programming from Netflix.

All of this comes as little surprise to avid Netflixers. But members might be startled to learn that while they are busy watching Netflix videos, Netflix is busy watching *them*—watching them very, very closely. Netflix tracks and analyzes heaps of customer data in excruciating detail. Then it uses the big data insights to give customers exactly what they want. Netflix knows in depth what its audience wants to watch, and it uses this knowledge to fuel recommendations to subscribers, decide what programming to offer, and even develop its own exclusive content.

No company knows its customers better than Netflix. The company has mind-boggling access to real-time data on member viewing behavior and sentiments. Every day, Netflix tracks and parses member data on tens of millions of searches, ratings, and "plays." Netflix's bulging database contains every viewing detail for each individual subscriber—what shows they watch, at what time of day, on what devices, at what locations, even when they hit the pause, rewind, or fast-forward buttons during programs.

Netflix supplements this already-massive database with consumer information purchased from Nielsen, Facebook, Twitter, and other sources. Finally, the company employs experts to classify each video on hundreds of characteristics, such as talent, action, tone, genre, color, volume, scenery, and many, many others. Using this rich base of big data, Netflix builds detailed subscriber profiles based on individual viewing habits and preferences. It then uses these profiles to personalize each customer's viewing experience. According to Netflix, there are 53 million different versions of Netflix, one for each individual subscriber worldwide.

For example, Netflix uses data on viewing history to make personalized recommendations. Wading through 60,000 titles to decide what to watch can be overwhelming. So when new customers sign up, Netflix asks them to rate their interest in movie and TV genres and to rate specific titles they have already seen. It then cross-references what people like with other similar titles to predict additional movies or programs customers will enjoy.

But that's just the beginning. As customers watch and rate more and more video content, and as Netflix studies the details of their viewing behavior, the predictions become more and more accurate. Netflix often comes to know individual customer viewing preferences better than customers themselves do. How accurate are Netflix's recommendations? Seventy-five percent of viewing activity results from these suggestions. That's important. The more subscribers watch, the more likely they are to stay with Netflix—viewers who watch at least 15 hours of content each month are 75 percent less likely to cancel. Accurate recommendations increase average viewing time, keeping subscribers in the fold.

Increased viewing also depends on offering the right content in the first place. But adding new programming is expensive—content licensing fees constitute the lion's share of Netflix's cost of goods sold. With so many new and existing movies and TV programs on the market, Netflix must be very selective in what it adds to its content inventory. Once again, it's big data and marketing analytics to the rescue. Just as Netflix analyzes its database to come up with subscriber recommendations, it uses the data to assess what additional titles customers might enjoy and how much each is worth. The goal is to maximize subscriber "happiness-per-dollar-spent" on new titles. "We always use our in-depth knowledge about what our members love to watch to decide what's available on Netflix," says a Netflix marketer. "If you keep watching, we'll keep adding more of what you love."

>> Netflix, big data, and CRM: While members are busy watching Netflix videos, Netflix is busy watching *them*—watching them very, very closely. Then it uses the big data insights to give customers exactly what they want.

To get even more viewers watching even more hours, Netflix uses its extensive big data insights to add its own exclusive video content—things you can see only on Netflix. In its own words, Netflix wants "to become HBO faster than HBO can become Netflix." For example, Netflix stunned the media industry when it outbid both HBO and AMC by paying a stunning $100 million for exclusive rights to air the first two seasons of *House of Cards*, a U.S. version of a hit British political drama produced by Hollywood bigwigs David Fincher and Kevin Spacey.

To outsiders, the huge investment in *House of Cards* seemed highly risky. However, using its powerful database, Netflix was able to predict accurately which and how many existing members would watch the new *House of Cards* regularly and how many new members would sign up because of the show. Netflix also used its viewer knowledge to pinpoint and personalize promotion of the exclusive new series to just the right members. Before *House of Cards* premiered, based on their profiles, selected subscribers saw one of 10 different trailers of the show aimed at their specific likes and interests.

Thanks to Netflix's big data and marketing analytics prowess, *House of Cards* was a smash hit. It brought in 3 million new subscribers in only the first three months. These new subscribers alone covered almost all of the $100 million investment. More important, a Netflix survey revealed that for the average *House of Cards* viewer, 86 percent were less likely to cancel because of the new program. Such success came as no surprise to Netflix. Its data had predicted that the program would be a hit before the director ever shouted "action."

Since then, *House of Cards* has become Netflix's hottest program. Based on its success, Netflix developed a number of other original series, including *Hemlock Grove, Lillyhammer, Orange Is the New Black, Bad Samaritans, Marco Polo,* and the animated series *BoJack Horseman*. For traditional broadcast networks, the average success rate for new television shows is 35 percent. In contrast, Netflix is batting almost 70 percent. To continue the momentum, Netflix has committed $300 million a year to developing new original content. The digital video giant now has 12 exclusive or original shows on the air, with another 24 scheduled for the next two years, including drama series, comedy specials, movies, and documentaries.

Netflix's success has thrown a scare into competitors such as leading cable-subscription network HBO. Although Netflix still lags HBO in profits, its U.S. online-only membership has reached 36 million compared with HBO's 30 million cable subscribers, and Netflix recently passed HBO in U.S. revenues. Such numbers, along with its unconventional methods for producing content, have earned Netflix the nickname "The Red Menace" among competitors. It's no surprise, then, that HBO announced that it will soon start selling online-only subscriptions.

As more and more high-quality video streams out of Netflix, more success streams in. Netflix's sales have surged 53 percent during the past two years. Last year alone, membership grew by more than 20 percent. Netflix thrives on using big data and marketing analytics to know and serve its customers. The company excels at helping customers figure out just what they want to watch and offering just the right content profitably. Says Netflix's chief communications officer, "Because we have a direct relationship with consumers, we *know* what people like to watch, and that helps us [immeasurably]."

Sources: Nicole Laporte, "Netflix: The Red Menace," *Fast Company*, January 7, 2014, www.fastcompany.com/3024158/netflix-the-red-menace; Anders Bylund, "Netflix, Inc. Is Paying Huge Sums to Produce Original Shows," *Motley Fool*, October 6, 2014, www.fool.com/investing/general/2014/10/06/netflix-inc-is-paying-huge-sums-to-produce-origina.aspx; David Carr, "Giving Viewers What They Want," *New York Times*, February 25, 2013, p. B1; Zach Bulygo, "How Netflix Uses Analytics to Select Movies, Create Content, and Make Multimillion Dollar Decisions," *Kissmetrics*, September 6, 2013, blog.kissmetrics.com/how-netflix-uses-analytics/; Craig Smith, "By the Numbers: 40 Amazing Netflix Statistics and Facts," *Expanded Ramblings*, October 24, 2014, http://expandedramblings.com/index.php/netflix_statistics-facts/; Marcus Wohlsen, "Netflix Is Beating HBO in Revenue, but It's Still the Underdog," *Wired*, August 7, 2014, www.wired.com/2014/08/netflix-is-beating-hbo-in-revenue-but-its-still-the-underdog/; Lisa Richwine, "Netflix Beats Forecasts with 62 Million Streaming Subscribers," *Reuters,* April 15, 2015, http://www.reuters.com/article/2015/04/15/us-netflix-results-idUSKBN0N62HC20150415; and www.netflix.com, accessed September 2015.

Kraft applies high-level marketing analytics to this wealth of data to mine nuggets of customer insight. Then it uses these insights to shape big data–driven marketing strategies and tactics, from developing new products to creating more focused and personalized Web, mobile, and social media content. For example, Kraft's analytics have identified more than 500 custom target segments. Within these segments, Kraft knows in detail what consumers need and like. Says one analyst, it knows "their dietary [characteristics and] restrictions—gluten free, a diabetic, low calorie, big snacks, feeding a big family, whether they are new cooks." Kraft uses this knowledge to personalize digital interactions with individual customers, down to the fine details. "If Kraft knows you're not a bacon user," says the analyst, "you will never be served a bacon ad." Thus, sophisticated analytics let Kraft target the right customer with the right message in the right medium at the right moment.

The benefits of customer relationship management and big data analytics don't come without costs or risks. The most common mistake is to view CRM and marketing analytics as technology processes only. Yet technology alone cannot build profitable customer relationships. Companies can't improve customer relationships by simply installing some new software. Instead, marketers should start with the fundamentals of managing customer relationships and *then* employ high-tech data and analytics solutions. They should focus first on the R—it's the *relationship* that CRM is all about.

Distributing and Using Marketing Information

Marketing information has no value until it is used to make better marketing decisions. Thus, the marketing information system must make information readily available to managers and others who need it, when they need it. In some cases, this means providing managers with regular performance reports, intelligence updates, and reports on the results of research studies.

But marketing managers may also need access to nonroutine information for special situations and on-the-spot decisions. For example, a sales manager having trouble with a large customer may want a summary of the account's sales and profitability over the past year. Or a brand manager may want to get a sense of the amount of the social media buzz surrounding the recent launch of a new product. These days, therefore, information distribution involves making information available in a timely, user-friendly way.

Many firms use company *intranet* and internal CRM systems to facilitate this process. These systems provide ready access to research and intelligence information, customer transaction and experience information, shared reports and documents, and more. For example, the CRM system at phone and online gift retailer 1-800-Flowers.com gives customer-facing employees real-time access to customer information. When a repeat customer calls, the system immediately pulls up data on previous transactions and other contacts, helping reps make the customer's experience easier and more relevant. For instance, if a customer usually buys tulips for his wife, the rep can talk about the best tulip selections and related gifts. Such connections result in greater customer satisfaction and loyalty and greater sales for the company. "We can do it in real time," says a 1-800-Flowers.com executive, "and it enhances the customer experience."[27]

In addition, companies are increasingly allowing key customers and value-network members to access account, product, and other data on demand through *extranets*. Suppliers, customers, resellers, and select other network members may access a company's extranet to update their accounts, arrange purchases, and check orders against inventories to improve customer service. For example, online shoes and accessories retailer Zappos considers suppliers to be "part of the Zappos family" and a key component in its quest to deliver "WOW" through great customer service. So it treats suppliers as valued partners, including sharing information with them. Through its ZUUL extranet (Zappos Unified User Login), thousands of suppliers are given full access to brand-related Zappos' inventory levels, sales figures, and even profitability. Suppliers can also use ZUUL to interact with the Zappos creative team and to enter suggested orders for Zappos buyers to approve.[28]

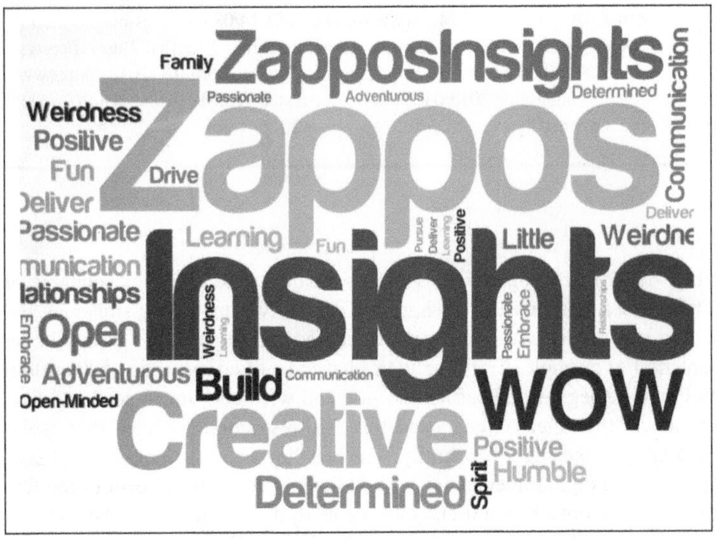

Extranets: Zappos shares marketing information and insights with suppliers through its ZUUL extranet. It considers suppliers to be "part of the Zappos family."

Zappos

Thanks to modern technology, today's marketing managers can gain direct access to a company's information system at any time and from virtually anywhere. They can tap into the system from a home office, customer location, airport, or the local Starbucks—anyplace they can connect on a laptop, tablet, or smartphone. Such systems allow managers to get the information they need directly and quickly and tailor it to their own needs.

LINKING THE CONCEPTS

Let's stop here, think back, and be certain that you've got the "big picture" concerning marketing information systems.

- What's the overall goal of a marketing information system? How are the individual components linked, and what does each contribute? Take another look at Figure 4.1—it provides a good organizing framework for the entire chapter.
- Apply the MIS framework to Converse (a Nike company). How might Converse go about assessing marketing managers' information needs, developing the needed information, and helping managers to analyze and use the information to gain actionable customer and market insights?

Author Comment
We finish this chapter by examining three special marketing information topics.

Other Marketing Information Considerations

This section discusses marketing information in two special contexts: marketing research in small businesses and nonprofit organizations and international marketing research. Then we look at public policy and ethics issues in marketing research.

Marketing Research in Small Businesses and Nonprofit Organizations

Just like larger firms, small organizations need market information and the customer insights that it can provide. Managers of small businesses and not-for-profit organizations often think that marketing research can be done only by experts in large companies with big research budgets. True, large-scale research studies are beyond the budgets of most small organizations. However, many of the marketing research techniques discussed in this chapter also can be used by smaller organizations in a less formal manner and at little or no expense. Consider how one small business owner conducted market research on a shoestring before even opening his doors:[29]

Before opening Bibbentuckers dry cleaner, owner Robert Byerley conducted research to gain insights into what customers wanted. First on the list: quality.

Bibbentuckers

After a string of bad experiences with his local dry cleaner, Robert Byerley decided to open his own dry-cleaning business. But before jumping in, he conducted plenty of market research. He needed a key customer insight: How would he make his business stand out from the others? To start, Byerley spent an entire week online, researching the dry-cleaning industry. To get input from potential customers, using a local marketing firm, Byerley held focus groups on the store's name, look, and brochure. He also took clothes to the 15 best competing cleaners in town and had focus group members critique their work. Based on his research, he made a list of features for his new business. First on his list: quality. His business would stand behind everything it did. Not on the list: cheap prices. Creating the perfect dry-cleaning establishment simply didn't fit with a discount operation.

With his research complete, Byerley opened Bibbentuckers, a high-end dry cleaner positioned on high-quality service and convenience. It featured a bank-like drive-through area with curbside delivery. A computerized barcode system read customer cleaning preferences and tracked clothes all the way through the cleaning process. Byerley added other differentiators, such as decorative awnings, TV screens, and refreshments (even "candy for the kids and a doggy treat for your best friend"). "I wanted a place...that paired five-star service and quality with an establishment that didn't look like a dry cleaner," he says. The market research yielded results. Today, Bibbentuckers is a thriving eight-store operation.

Thus, small businesses and not-for-profit organizations can obtain good marketing insights through observation or informal surveys using small convenience samples. Also, many associations, local media, and government agencies provide special help to small organizations. For example, the U.S. Small Business Administration offers dozens of free publications and a Web site (www.sba.gov) that give advice on topics ranging from starting, financing, and expanding a small business to ordering business cards. Other excellent research resources for small businesses include the U.S. Census Bureau (www.census.gov) and the Bureau of Economic Analysis (www.bea.gov). Finally, small businesses can collect a considerable amount of information at very little cost online. They can check out online product and service review sites, use Internet search engines to research specific companies and issues, and scour competitor and customer Web, mobile, and social media sites.

In summary, secondary data collection, observation, surveys, and experiments can all be used effectively by small organizations with small budgets. However, although these informal research methods are less complex and less costly, they still must be conducted with care. Managers must think carefully about the objectives of the research, formulate questions in advance, recognize the biases introduced by smaller samples and less skilled researchers, and conduct the research systematically.[30]

International Marketing Research

International marketing research has grown tremendously over the past few decades. International researchers follow the same steps as domestic researchers, from defining the research problem and developing a research plan to interpreting and reporting the results. However, these researchers often face more and different problems. Whereas domestic researchers deal with fairly homogeneous markets within a single country, international researchers deal with diverse markets in many different countries. These markets often vary greatly in their levels of economic development, cultures and customs, and buying patterns.

In many foreign markets, the international researcher may have a difficult time finding good secondary data. Whereas U.S. marketing researchers can obtain reliable secondary data from dozens of domestic research services, many countries have almost no research services at all. Some of the largest international research services operate in many countries. For example, The Nielsen Company (the world's largest marketing research company) has offices in more than 100 countries, from Schaumburg, Illinois, to Hong Kong to Nicosia, Cyprus.[31] However, most research firms operate in only a relative handful of countries. Thus, even when secondary information is available, it usually must be obtained from many different sources on a country-by-country basis, making the information difficult to combine or compare.

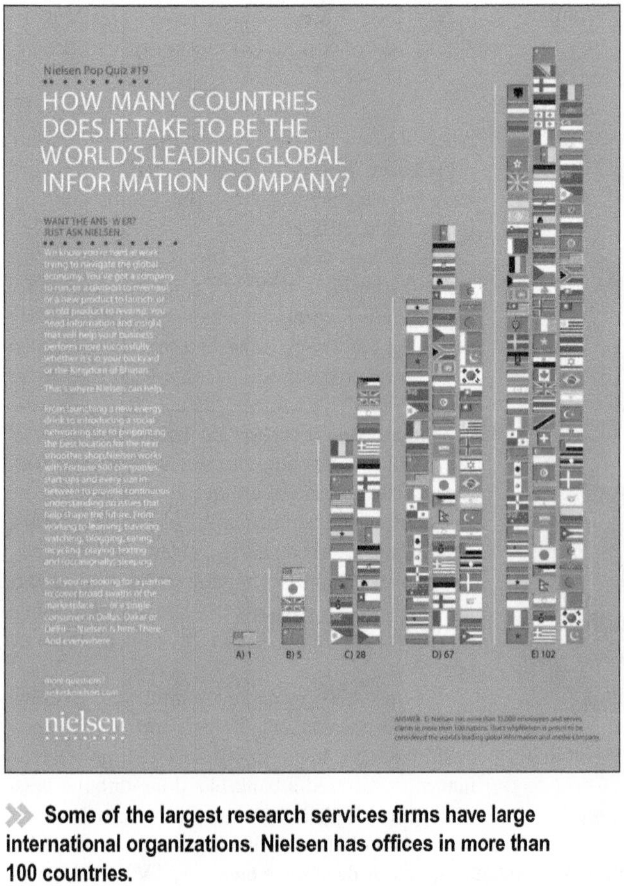

Some of the largest research services firms have large international organizations. Nielsen has offices in more than 100 countries.

Because of the scarcity of good secondary data, international researchers often must collect their own primary data. However, obtaining primary data may be no easy task. For example, it can be difficult simply to develop good samples. U.S. researchers can use current telephone directories, email lists, census tract data, and any of several sources of socioeconomic data to construct samples. However, such information is largely lacking in many countries.

Once the sample is drawn, the U.S. researcher usually can reach most respondents easily by phone, by mail, online, or in person. However, reaching respondents is often not so easy in other parts of the world. Researchers in Mexico cannot rely on phone, Internet, and mail data collection—most data collection is conducted door to door and concentrated in three or four of the largest cities. In some countries, few people have computers, let alone Internet access. For example, whereas there are 84 Internet users per 100 people in the United States, there are only 43 Internet users per 100 people in Mexico. In Madagascar, the number drops to 2 Internet users per 100 people. In some countries, the postal system is notoriously unreliable. In Brazil, for instance, an estimated 30 percent of the mail is never delivered; in Russia, mail delivery can take several weeks. In many developing countries, poor roads and transportation systems make certain areas hard to reach, making personal interviews difficult and expensive.[32]

Cultural differences from country to country cause additional problems for international researchers. Language is the most obvious obstacle. For example, questionnaires must be prepared in one language and then translated into the languages of each country researched. Responses then must be translated back into the original language for analysis and interpretation. This adds to research costs and increases the risks of error. Even within a given country, language can be a problem. For example, in India, English is the language of business, but consumers may use any of 14 "first languages," with many additional dialects.

Translating a questionnaire from one language to another is anything but easy. Many idioms, phrases, and statements mean different things in different cultures. For example, a Danish executive noted, "Check this out by having a different translator put back into English what you've translated from English. You'll get the shock of your life. I remember [an example in which] 'out of sight, out of mind' had become 'invisible things are insane.'"[33]

Consumers in different countries also vary in their attitudes toward marketing research. People in one country may be very willing to respond; in other countries, nonresponse can be a major problem. Customs in some countries may prohibit people from talking with strangers. In certain cultures, research questions often are considered too personal. For example, in many Muslim countries, mixed-gender focus groups are taboo, as is videotaping female-only focus groups. In some countries, even when respondents are *willing* to respond, they may not be *able* to because of high functional illiteracy rates.

Despite these problems, as global marketing grows, global companies have little choice but to conduct these types of international marketing research. Although the costs and problems associated with international research may be high, the costs of not doing it—in terms of missed opportunities and mistakes—might be even higher. Once recognized, many of the problems associated with international marketing research can be overcome or avoided.

Public Policy and Ethics in Marketing Research

Most marketing research benefits both the sponsoring company and its consumers. Through marketing research, companies gain insights into consumers' needs, resulting in more satisfying products and services and stronger customer relationships. However, the misuse of marketing research can also harm or annoy consumers. Two major public policy and ethics issues in marketing research are intrusions on consumer privacy and the misuse of research findings.

Intrusions on Consumer Privacy

Many consumers feel positive about marketing research and believe that it serves a useful purpose. Some actually enjoy being interviewed and giving their opinions. However, others strongly resent or even mistrust marketing research. They don't like being interrupted by researchers. They worry that marketers are building huge databases full of personal information about customers. Or they fear that researchers might use sophisticated techniques to probe our deepest feelings, track us as we use our mobile devices or browse and interact on the Internet, or peek over our shoulders as we shop and then use this knowledge to manipulate our buying. A recent survey showed that more than 90 percent of Americans feel that they have lost control over the collection and use by companies of their personal data and information they share on social media sites.[34]

For example, Target made some of its customers very uneasy recently when it used their buying histories to figure out that they had a baby on the way, including eerily accurate estimates of child gender and due date:[35]

> Target gives every customer a Guest ID number, tied to his or her name, credit card, or email address. It then tracks the customer's purchases in detail, along with demographic information

Consumer privacy: Target made some customers uneasy when it used their buying histories to figure out things about them that even their family and friends didn't know. The chain's bulls-eye logo may now "send a shiver... down the closely-watched spines of some Target shoppers.

from other sources. By studying the buying histories of women who'd previously signed up for its baby registries, Target found that it could develop a "pregnancy prediction" score for each customer based on her purchasing patterns across 25 product categories. It used this score to start sending personalized books of coupons for baby-related items to expectant parents, keyed to their pregnancy stages.

The strategy seemed to make good marketing sense—by hooking parents-to-be, Target could turn them into loyal buyers as their families developed. However, the strategy hit a snag when an angry man showed up at his local Target store, complaining that his high school–aged daughter was receiving Target coupons for cribs, strollers, and maternity clothes. "Are you trying to encourage her to get pregnant?" he demanded. The Target store manager apologized. But when he called to apologize again a few days later, he learned that Target's marketers had, in fact, known about the young woman's pregnancy before her father did. It turns out that many other customers were creeped out that Target knew about their pregnancies before they'd told even family and close friends. And they wondered what else Target might be tracking and profiling. As one reporter concluded: "The store's bulls-eye logo may now send a shiver... down the closely-watched spines of some [Target shoppers]."

When mining customer information, marketers must be careful not to cross over the privacy line. But there are no easy answers when it comes to marketing research and privacy. For example, is it a good or bad thing that marketers track and analyze consumers' online browsing or buying patterns to send them personalized promotions? Should we worry when marketers track consumer locations via their mobile phones to issue location-based information, ads, and offers? Should we care that some retailers use mannequins with cameras hidden in one eye to record customer demographics and shopping behavior? Similarly, should we applaud or resent companies that monitor consumer posts on Facebook, Twitter, Instagram, YouTube, or other social media in an effort to be more responsive?[36]

Increasing consumer privacy concerns have become a major problem for the marketing research industry. Companies face the challenge of unearthing valuable but potentially sensitive consumer data while also maintaining consumer trust. At the same time, consumers wrestle with the trade-offs between personalization and privacy. They want to receive relevant, personalized offers that meet their needs, but they worry or resent that companies may track them too closely. The key question: When does a company cross the line in gathering and using customer data? One recent study shows that nearly half of U.S. adults worry that they have little or no control over the personal information that companies gather about them online. Another survey found that 86 percent of Internet users have taken steps to remove or mask their digital footprints, such as removing cookies or encrypting email.

Failure to address privacy issues could result in angry, less cooperative consumers and increased government intervention. As a result, the marketing research industry is considering several options for responding to intrusion and privacy issues. One example is the Marketing Research Association's "Your Opinion Counts" and "Respondent Bill of Rights" initiatives to educate consumers about the benefits of marketing research and distinguish it from telephone selling and database building. The industry also has considered adopting broad standards, perhaps based on the International Chamber of Commerce's International Code of Marketing and Social Research Practice. This code outlines researchers' responsibilities to respondents and the general public. For example, it urges that researchers make their names and addresses available to participants and be open about the data they are collecting.[37]

Most major companies—including Facebook, Apple, Microsoft, IBM, American Express, and even the U.S. government—have now appointed a chief privacy officer (CPO), whose job is to safeguard the privacy of consumers who do business with the company. In the end, however, if researchers provide value in exchange for information, customers will gladly provide it. For example, Amazon.com's customers don't mind if the firm builds a database of products they buy as a way to provide future product recommendations. This saves time and provides value. The best approach is for researchers to ask only for the information they need, use it responsibly to provide customer value, and avoid sharing information without the customer's permission.

Misuse of Research Findings

Research studies can be powerful persuasion tools; companies often use study results as claims in their advertising and promotion. Today, however, many research studies appear to be little more than vehicles for pitching the sponsor's products. In fact, in some cases, research surveys appear to have been designed just to produce the intended effect. For example, a Black Flag survey once asked: "A roach disk...poisons a roach slowly. The dying roach returns to the nest and after it dies is eaten by other roaches. In turn these roaches become poisoned and die. How effective do you think this type of product would be in killing roaches?" Not surprisingly, 79 percent said effective.

However, few advertisers openly rig their research designs or blatantly misrepresent the findings—most abuses tend to be more subtle "stretches." Or disputes arise over the validity and use of research findings. >> Consider this example:

>> **Use of research findings: The FTC recently ruled against POM Wonderful's research-based advertising claims that the brand could improve a user's health. POM is appealing the ruling.**

Christopher Schall | Impact Photo

> The FTC recently charged POM Wonderful—the pomegranate juice sold in the distinctive curvy bottle—and its parent company with making false and unsubstantiated health claims in its advertising. The disputed ads suggest that POM Wonderful Pomegranate Juice can prevent or treat heart disease, prostate cancer, and even erectile dysfunction. For instance, one ad boasted that POM has "Super Health Powers!" while another proclaimed, "I'm off to saveprostates!" POM has stood behind its ad claims, asserting that they are backed by $35 million worth of company research showing that antioxidant-rich pomegranate products are good for you. The brand even retaliated during two years of legal wrangling with ads disputing the FTC and its allegations. But the FTC isn't buying the research behind POM's claims—it recently issued a final ruling ordering the brand to refrain from making claims that its products could improve a user's health unless backed by more stringent research. "When a company touts scientific research in its advertising, the research must squarely support the claims made," says the agency. "Contrary to POM Wonderful's advertising, the available scientific information does not prove that POM Juice...effectively treats or prevents these illnesses." POM Wonderful is currently appealing the FTC ruling.[38]

Recognizing that marketing research can be abused, several associations—including the American Marketing Association, the Marketing Research Association, and the Council of American Survey Research Organizations (CASRO)—have developed codes of research ethics and standards of conduct. For example, the CASRO Code of Standards and Ethics for Survey Research outlines researcher responsibilities to respondents, including confidentiality, privacy, and avoidance of harassment. It also outlines major responsibilities in reporting results to clients and the public.[39]

In the end, however, unethical or inappropriate actions cannot simply be regulated away. Each company must accept responsibility for policing the conduct and reporting of its own marketing research to protect consumers' best interests and its own.

> **MyMarketingLab**
>
> If assigned by your instructor, complete the questions marked with the ✪ from the EOC Discussion Questions section in the MyLab. To complete the Marketing by the Numbers problems found in this section, go to your Assignments in the MyLab.

REVIEWING AND EXTENDING THE CONCEPTS

CHAPTER REVIEW AND CRITICAL THINKING

Objectives Review

To create value for customers and build meaningful relationships with them, marketers must first gain fresh, deep insights into what customers need and want. Such insights come from good marketing information. As a result of the recent explosion of "big data" and marketing technology, companies can now obtain great quantities of information, sometimes even too much. Consumers themselves are now generating a tidal wave of bottom-up information through their smartphones, PCs, and tablets via online browsing and blogging, apps and social media interactions, and texting and video. The challenge is to transform today's vast volume of consumer information into actionable customer and market insights.

OBJECTIVE 4-1 Explain the importance of information in gaining insights about the marketplace and customers. (pp 100–101)

The marketing process starts with a complete understanding of the marketplace and consumer needs and wants. Thus, the company needs to turn sound consumer information into meaningful *customer insights* by which it can produce superior value for its customers. The company also requires information on competitors, resellers, and other actors and forces in the marketplace. Increasingly, marketers are viewing information not only as an input for making better decisions but also as an important strategic asset and marketing tool.

OBJECTIVE 4-2 Define the marketing information system and discuss its parts. (pp 102–106)

The *marketing information system* (MIS) consists of people and procedures for assessing information needs, developing the needed information, and helping decision makers use the information to generate and validate actionable customer and market insights. A well-designed information system begins and ends with users.

The MIS first *assesses information needs.* The MIS primarily serves the company's marketing and other managers, but it may also provide information to external partners. Then the MIS *develops information* from internal databases, marketing intelligence activities, and marketing research. *Internal databases* provide information on the company's own operations and departments. Such data can be obtained quickly and cheaply but often need to be adapted for marketing decisions. *Marketing intelligence* activities supply everyday information about developments in the external marketing environment, including listening and responding to the vast and complex digital environment. *Market research* consists of collecting information relevant to a specific marketing problem faced by the company. Last, the marketing information system helps users analyze and use the information to develop customer insights, make marketing decisions, and manage customer relationships.

OBJECTIVE 4-3 Outline the steps in the marketing research process. (pp 106–118)

The first step in the marketing research process involves *defining the problem and setting the research objectives*, which may be exploratory, descriptive, or causal research. The second step consists of *developing a research plan* for collecting data from primary and secondary sources. The third step calls for *implementing the marketing research plan* by gathering, processing, and analyzing the information. The fourth step consists of *interpreting and reporting the findings.* Additional information analysis helps marketing managers apply the information and provides them with sophisticated statistical procedures and models from which to develop more rigorous findings.

Both *internal* and *external* secondary data sources often provide information more quickly and at a lower cost than primary data sources, and they can sometimes yield information that a company cannot collect by itself. However, needed information might not exist in secondary sources. Researchers must also evaluate secondary information to ensure that it is *relevant, accurate, current,* and *impartial.*

Primary research must also be evaluated for these features. Each primary data collection method—*observational, survey,* and *experimental*—has its own advantages and disadvantages. Similarly, each of the various research contact methods—mail, telephone, personal interview, and online—has its own advantages and drawbacks.

OBJECTIVE 4-4 Explain how companies analyze and use marketing information. (pp 118–123)

Information gathered in internal databases and through marketing intelligence and marketing research usually requires more analysis. To analyze individual customer data, many companies have now acquired or developed special software and analysis techniques—called *customer relationship management* (CRM)—that integrate, analyze, and apply the mountains of individual customer data to gain a 360-degree view of customers and build stronger the customer relationships. They apply *marketing analytics* to dig out meaningful patterns in big data and gain customer insights and gauge marketing performance.

Marketing information has no value until it is used to make better marketing decisions. Thus, the MIS must make the information available to managers and others who make marketing decisions or deal with customers. In some cases, this means providing regular reports and updates; in other cases, it means making nonroutine information available for special situations and on-the-spot decisions. Many firms use company intranets and extranets to facilitate this process. Thanks to modern technology, today's marketing managers can gain direct access to marketing information at any time and from virtually any location.

OBJECTIVE 4-5 Discuss the special issues some marketing researchers face, including public policy and ethics issues. (pp 123–127)

Some marketers face special marketing research situations, such as those conducting research in small business, not-for-profit, or international situations. Marketing research can be conducted effectively by small businesses and nonprofit organizations with limited budgets. International marketing researchers follow the same steps as domestic researchers but often face more and different problems. All organizations need to act responsibly concerning major public policy and ethical issues surrounding marketing research, including issues of intrusions on consumer privacy and misuse of research findings.

Key Terms

Objective 4-1
Big data (p 101)
Customer insights (p. 101)
Marketing information system (MIS) (p. 101)

Objective 4-2
Internal databases (p 102)
Competitive marketing intelligence (p 103)

Objective 4-3
Marketing research (p 106)
Exploratory research (p 107)
Descriptive research (p 107)
Causal research (p 107)
Secondary data (p 108)
Primary data (p 108)
Observational research (p 109)
Ethnographic research (p 109)
Survey research (p 110)
Experimental research (p 111)
Focus group interviewing (p 112)
Online marketing research (p 113)
Online focus groups (p 114)
Behavioral targeting (p 115)
Sample (p 115)

Objective 4-4
Customer relationship management (CRM) (p 118)
Marketing analytics (p 119)

Discussion Questions

4-1. What is *big data,* and what opportunities and challenges does it provide for marketers? (AACSB: Communication; Reflective Thinking)

4-2. What is a marketing information system (MIS), and what characteristics should it possess? (AACSB: Communication)

4-3. Name and describe the three types of research objectives and give an example of a research study for each. (AACSB: Communication; Reflective Thinking)

4-4. What impact has the Internet had on how marketing research is conducted? What advantages does the Internet provide over traditional marketing data collection methods? (AACSB: Communication)

4-5. Why are marketing analytics so important in the age of big data? (AACSB: Communication)

Critical Thinking Exercises

4-6. In a small group, identify a problem faced by a local business or charitable organization and propose a research project addressing that problem. Develop a research proposal that implements each step of the marketing research process. Discuss how the research results will help the business or organization. (AACSB: Communication; Reflective Thinking)

4-7. Go to www.bized.co.uk/learn/business/marketing/research/index.htm and review the various resources available. Select one activity and present what you learned from that activity. (AACSB: Communication; Use of IT; Reflective Thinking)

4-8. Research the marketing research industry and develop a presentation describing various marketing research jobs and compensation for those jobs. Create a graphical representation to communicate your findings. (AACSB: Communication; Use of IT; Reflective Thinking)

MINICASES AND APPLICATIONS

Online, Mobile, and Social Media Marketing Social Data

People have been using Twitter's social media platform to Tweet short bursts of information in 140 characters or less since 2006 and now average 500 million Tweets a day. The full stream of Tweets is referred to as Twitter's fire hose. Various firms analyze data from the fire hose and sell the information gleaned from that analysis to other companies. Twitter recently purchased Gnip, the world's largest social data provider and one of the few companies that had access to the fire hose. Gnip also mines public data from Facebook, Google+, Tumblr, and other social media platforms. Analyzing social data has become a big business because companies such PepsiCo, Warner Brothers, and General Motors pay to learn about consumers' sentiments toward them. According to the CEO of social media analysis company BrandWatch, "We're at the bottom of the foothills in terms of the kind of global demand for social data." Twitter alone earned more than $70 million last year from licensing its data. Perhaps Mark Twain's character, Mulberry Sellers, summed it up nicely—"There's gold in them thar hills"—and Twitter and other social media platforms and data analytic companies are mining that gold.

4-9. Discuss the value of social data for marketers. (AACSB: Communication; Reflective Thinking)

4-10. A "dark social channel" refers to a private channel or a channel difficult to match with other digital channels. An example of a dark channel is email. However, Google routinely mines its roughly half-billion Gmail users' emails. Research how Google scans email data and the fallout from those actions, then summarize your findings. (AACSB: Communication; Use of IT; Reflective Thinking)

Marketing Ethics Metadata

Everyone generates metadata as they use technologies such as computers and mobile devices to search, post, Tweet, play, text, and talk. What many people don't realize, however, is that this treasure trove of date, time, and location information can be used to identify them without their knowledge. For example, in analyzing more than a million anonymous credit card transactions, researchers at the Massachusetts Institute of Technology were able to link 90 percent of the transactions to specific users with just four additional bits of metadata, such as user locations based on apps such as Foursquare, the timing of an activity such as a Tweet on Twitter, or playing a mobile game. Since there are more mobile devices than there are people in the United States and 60 percent of purchases are made with a credit card, marketing research firms are gobbling up all sorts of metadata that will let them tie a majority of purchase transactions to specific individuals.

4-11. Describe at least four applications you use that provide location, time, and date information that can be tied to your identity. (AACSB Communication; Reflective Thinking)

4-12. Debate whether it is ethical for marketers to use metadata to link individual consumers with specific credit card transactions. (AACSB: Communication; Ethical Reasoning)

Marketing by the Numbers The Value of Information

Conducting research is costly, and the costs must be weighed against the value of the information gathered. Consider a company faced with a competitor's price reduction. Should the company also reduce price in order to maintain market share, or should the company maintain its current price? The company has conducted some preliminary research showing the financial outcomes of each decision under two competitor responses: the competition maintains its price or the competition lowers its price further. The company feels pretty confident that the competitor cannot lower its price further and assigns that outcome a probability (p) of 0.7, which means the other outcome would have only a 30 percent chance of occurring ($1 - p = 0.3$). These outcomes are shown in the table below:

	Competitive Response	
Company action	**Maintain Price** $p = 0.7$	**Reduce Price** $(1 - p) = 0.3$
Reduce Price	$160,000	$120,000
Maintain Price	$180,000	$100,000

For example, if the company reduces its price and the competitor maintains its price, the company would realize $160,000, and so on. From this information, the expected monetary value (EMV) of each company action (reduce price or maintain price) can be determined using the following equation:

$$\text{EMV} = (p)(\text{financial outome}_p) + (1 - p)(\text{financial outcome}_{(1-p)})$$

The company would select the action expected to deliver the greatest EMV. More information might be desirable, but is it worth the cost of acquiring it? One way to assess the value of additional information is to determine the expected value of perfect information (EMV_{PI}), calculated using the following equation:

$$EMV_{PI} = EMV_{certainty} - EMV_{best\ alternative}$$

where

$$EMV_{certainty} = (p)\ (\text{highest financial outcome}_p) + (1 - p)\ (\text{highest financial outcome}_{(1-p)})$$

If the value of perfect information is more than the cost of conducting the research, then the research should be undertaken (that is, $EMV_{PI} >$ cost of research). However, if the value of the additional information is less than the cost of obtaining more information, the research should not be conducted.

4-13. Calculate the expected monetary value (EMV) of both company actions. Which action should the company take? (AACSB: Communication; Analytical Reasoning)

4-14. What is the expected value of perfect information (EMV_{PI})? Should the research be conducted? (AACSB: Communication; Analytical Reasoning)

Video Case Nielsen

Most people know Nielsen as the TV ratings company. In reality, however, Nielsen is a multiplatform market research company that has constantly been evolving since 1923. Its goal is to measure and track a wide range of consumer activity in order to establish a 360-degree view of individuals and market segments. To accomplish this, Nielsen has to follow consumers wherever they may be—watching TV, online, in their homes, or in stores.

How does Nielsen track all this activity? The veteran research firm has established effective methods of recording consumer activity, from retail scanner data to household panels to monitoring social networks. As data are captured, they are transferred to a Nielsen data warehouse, where they are matched to the right individual and added to the terabytes of information Nielsen already possesses. Through data sorting and analytics, Nielsen cuts through billions of daily transactions to deliver clear consumer insights to clients.

After viewing the video featuring Nielsen, answer the following questions:

4-15. What is Nielsen's expertise?

4-16. Providing a real-world example, describe how Nielsen might discover a consumer insight.

4-17. What kinds of partnerships might Nielsen need to form with other companies in order to accomplish its goals?

Company Cases 4 Campbell's/8 3M/14 Alibaba

See Appendix 1 for cases appropriate for this chapter.

Case 4, Campbell's: Watching What You Eat. The pillar of product development at Campbell's is deep dive research—field research where observations lead to consumer insight.

Case 8, 3M: Where Innovation Is a Way of Life. Few companies provide more support for research-based product development than 3M.

Case 14, Alibaba: The World's Largest E-Tailer Is Not Amazon. The largest customer base provides ecommerce giant with the largest database and endless possibilities.

MyMarketingLab

If assigned by your instructor, complete these writing sections from your Assignments in the MyLab.

4-18. What is neuromarketing and how is it useful in marketing research? Why is this research approach usually combined with other approaches? (AACSB: Communication)

4-19. Describe an example in which marketing research could cause harm to participants. Many companies have a review process similar to that required for following the government's "Common Rule." Write a brief report explaining this rule and how you would apply it to your example. (AACSB: Written and Oral Communication; Reflective Thinking)

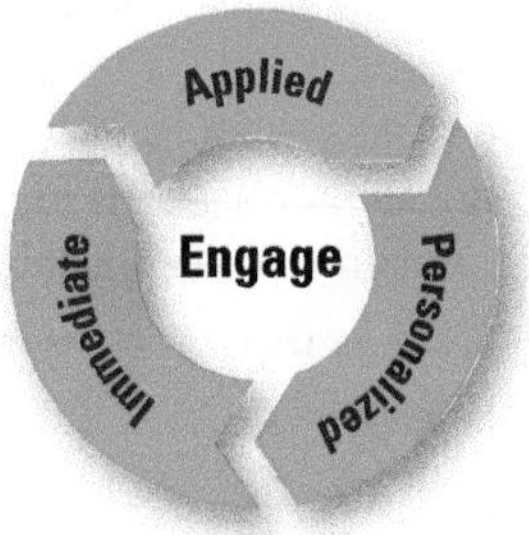

5 Understanding Consumer and Business Buyer Behavior

CHAPTER ROAD MAP Objective Outline

Previewing the Concepts

You've studied how marketers obtain, analyze, and use information to develop customer insights and assess marketing programs. In this chapter, we take a closer look at the most important element of the marketplace—customers. The aim of marketing is to engage customers and affect how they think and act. To affect the *whats, whens*, and *hows* of buyer behavior, marketers must first understand the *whys*. We first look at *final consumer* buying influences and processes and then at the buyer behavior of *business customers*. You'll see that understanding buyer behavior is an essential but very difficult task.

To get a better sense of the importance of understanding consumer behavior, we begin by looking at Harley-Davidson, maker of the nation's top-selling heavyweight motorcycles. Who rides these big Harley "Hogs"? What moves them to tattoo their bodies with the Harley-Davidson bar and shield logo, abandon home and hearth for the open road, and flock to Harley rallies by the hundreds of thousands? You might be surprised by the answers to these questions, but Harley-Davidson knows them *very* well.

First Stop

Harley-Davidson: Selling Freedom, Independence, Power, and Authenticity

For Harley-Davidson enthusiasts, it's all about the experience. More than just bikes, the iconic company is selling self-expression, lifestyle, aspirations, and dreams.

Scott Olson/Getty images

Few brands engender such intense loyalty as that found in the hearts of Harley-Davidson owners. Harley buyers are granitelike in their devotion to the brand. You don't see people tattooing "Yamaha" on their bodies, or "Kawasaki" or "Honda." Harley-Davidson riders don't want just any motorcycle—it's *got* to be a Harley. The iconic Harley-Davidson brand is that strong.

In August 2013, an estimated 100,000 to 200,000 people flocked to Harley-Davidson's 110th anniversary celebration in Milwaukee, the city where it all began. One reporter described the epic event's opening parade as "one of the greatest spectacles in America, . . . a thunder of Harley-Davidson pride you could literally feel as nearly 7,000 [riders] rolled through downtown Milwaukee." During the three days of rumbling fun, bikers from across the nation lounged on their low-slung Harley's, swapped biker tales, and sported T-shirts proclaiming things like "Screw it, let's ride!" and "I'd rather push a Harley than ride a Yamaha."

Riding such intense emotions, Harley-Davidson has long dominated the U.S. motorcycle market. The brand captures 30 percent of all U.S. bike sales and nearly 55 percent of the heavyweight segment, and its sales and profits are growing at a smooth-riding pace. Over the past three years, sales have grown more than 20 percent and profits have jumped sixfold.

Harley-Davidson's marketers have spent a great deal of time thinking about customers and their buying behavior. They want to know who their customers are, what they think and how they feel, and why they buy a Harley-Davidson Softail rather than a Yamaha or a Kawasaki or a big Honda Gold Wing. What is it that makes Harley buyers so fiercely loyal? These are difficult questions; even Harley owners themselves don't know exactly what motivates their buying. But Harley-Davidson management puts top priority on understanding customers and what makes them tick.

Who rides a Harley-Davidson? You might be surprised. It's not the outlaw bad-boy biker that some people still associate with Harleys. The brand's motorcycles attract a different breed of bikers—older, more affluent, and better educated. Remove the helmets and the leathers of a hard-core Harley enthusiast, and there's no telling whom you'll find. It might be a guy with tattoos and unruly hair, but it's just as likely to be a CEO, investment banker, or gourmet chef.

The average Harley customer is a 50-something male with a median household income of $87,000. More than 12 percent of Harley purchases today are made by women. "Harley brings together all walks of life," says Harley's chief marketing officer. "You'll find a neurosurgeon talking and riding with a janitor. It's a family." And a big family it is. The Harley Owners Group (H.O.G.)—the official riding club of "Harley owners around the world, bound by a passion to ride"—has more than a million members. The brand's Facebook site counts more the 7 million Likes.

In recent years, the company has been extending the Harley-Davidson family beyond the core segment of older Caucasian males who now account for about two-thirds of buyers. It has crafted products and programs specifically designed to attract what it calls "outreach customers," segments such as young adults ages 18 to 34, women, African Americans, and Hispanics. Last year, sales to those outreach groups grew at more than twice the rate of sales to its traditional core customers. For example, to broaden its reach, Harley-Davidson recently introduced its first all-new motorcycle platform in 13 years—its Street models—smaller, lighter, more agile, and more efficient motorcycles designed for the riding needs of young urban riders. Though smaller, these new motorcycles still carry the Harley mystique. "These new bikes are leaner, yet still have a mean streak," says Harley's CMO. "They're the real deal, made of real steel."

Harley-Davidson's market dominance market comes from a deep understanding of the emotions and motivations that underlie consumer behavior. Harley doesn't just sell motorcycles; its sells freedom, independence, power, and authenticity.

Harley-Davidson makes good bikes, and to keep up with its shifting market, the company has upgraded its showrooms and sales approaches. But Harley customers are buying a lot more than just a quality bike and a smooth sales pitch. To gain a better understanding of customers' deeper motivations, over the years Harley-Davidson has conducted seemingly endless surveys, focus groups, and interpretive studies that plumb the depths of customers' feelings about their Harleys. Beyond research, everyone connected with the Harley-Davidson brand—from the CEO and CMO to ad agency copywriters—attend biker events and immerse themselves deeply in the biker culture. They spend countless hours in the saddle to gain a first-hand understanding of what moves and motivates core customers.

All of the research yields strong and consistent results. No matter who they are, what they do, or where they come from, Harley-Davidson disciples share a common, deeply held attraction to the brand. The universal Harley appeals are these: freedom, independence, power, and authenticity. Harley-Davidson doesn't just sell motorcycles. It sells self-expression, lifestyles, aspirations, and dreams. "It's all about the *experience*," says an analyst, "one forged in heavy metal thunder, living free and peeling wheel down Route 66. It's an experience that allows middle-aged accountants to don black, studded leather and forget about debits and credits for a little while."

To hard-core enthusiasts, a Harley is much more than a machine. It's a part of who they are and where they want to go in life. A Harley renews your spirits and announces your freedom and independence. A popular line at Harley-Davidson is that "Thumbing the starter of a Harley does a lot more than fire the engine. It fires the imagination." The classic look, the throaty sound, the very idea of a Harley—all contribute to its mystique. Owning this "American legend" makes you a part of something bigger, a member of the Harley-Davidson family.

The strong emotions and motivations underlying Harley consumer behavior are captured in a classic old Harley-Davidson print advertisement. The ad shows a close-up of an arm, the bicep adorned with a Harley-Davidson tattoo. The headline asks, "When was the last time you felt this strongly about anything?" The ad copy outlines the problem and suggests a solution: "Wake up in the morning and life picks up where it left off. . . . What once seemed exciting has now become part of the numbing routine. It all begins to feel the same. Except when you've got a Harley-Davidson. Something strikes a nerve. The heartfelt thunder rises up, refusing to become part of the background. Suddenly things are different. Clearer. More real. As they should have been all along. Riding a Harley changes you from within. The effect is permanent. Maybe it's time you started feeling this strongly. Things are different on a Harley."[1]

Author Comment
In some ways, consumer and business markets are similar in their buyer behavior. But in many other ways, they differ a lot. We start by digging into consumer buyer behavior. Later in the chapter, we'll tackle business buyer behavior.

The Harley-Davidson example shows that factors at many levels affect consumer buying behavior. Buying behavior is never simple, yet understanding it is an essential task of marketing management. First we explore the dynamics of the consumer market and the consumer buyer behavior. We then examine business markets and the business buyer process.

Consumer Markets and Consumer Buyer Behavior

Consumer buyer behavior
The buying behavior of final consumers—individuals and households that buy goods and services for personal consumption.

Consumer buyer behavior refers to the buying behavior of final consumers—individuals and households that buy goods and services for personal consumption. All of these final consumers combine to make up the **consumer market**. The American consumer market consists of more than 320 million people who consume more than $11 trillion worth of goods and services each year, making it one of the most attractive consumer markets in the world.[2]

Consumers around the world vary tremendously in age, income, education level, and tastes. They also buy an incredible variety of goods and services. How these diverse consumers relate with each other and with other elements of the world around them affects their choices among various products, services, and companies. Here we examine the fascinating array of factors that affect consumer behavior.

Author Comment
Despite the simple-looking model in Figure 5.1, understanding the *whys* of buying behavior is very difficult. Says one expert, "The mind is a whirling, swirling, jumbled mass of neurons bouncing around. . . ."

Model of Consumer Behavior

Consumers make many buying decisions every day, and the buying decision is the focal point of the marketer's effort. Most large companies research consumer buying decisions in great detail to answer questions about what consumers buy, where they buy, how and how much they buy, when they buy, and why they buy. Marketers can study actual consumer purchases to find out what they buy, where, and how much. But learning about the *whys* behind consumer buying behavior is not so easy—the answers are often locked deep within the consumer's mind. Often, consumers themselves don't know exactly what influences their purchases.

The central question for marketers is this: How do consumers respond to various marketing efforts the company might use? The starting point is the stimulus-response model of buyer behavior shown in » **Figure 5.1**. This figure shows that marketing and other stimuli enter the consumer's "black box" and produce certain responses. Marketers must figure out what is in the buyer's black box.

Consumer market
All the individuals and households that buy or acquire goods and services for personal consumption.

Marketing stimuli consist of the four *P*s: product, price, place, and promotion. Other stimuli include major forces and events in the buyer's environment: economic, technological, social, and cultural. All these inputs enter the buyer's black box,

>> Figure 5.1 The Model of Buyer Behavior

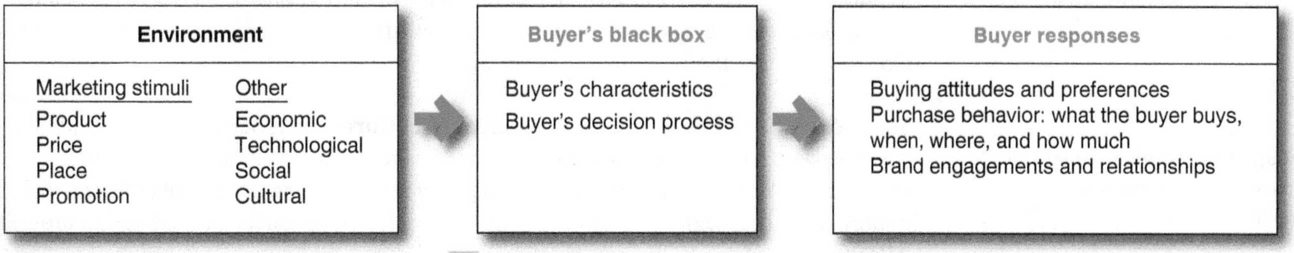

We can measure the whats, wheres, and whens of consumer buying behavior. But it's very diffcult to "see" inside the consumer's head and figure out the whys of buying behavior (that's why it's called the black box). Marketers spend a lot of energy and dollars trying to figure out what makes customers tick.

where they are turned into a set of buyer responses—the buyer's attitudes and preferences, brand engagements and relationships, and what he or she buys, when, where, and how much.

Marketers want to understand how the stimuli are changed into responses inside the consumer's black box, which has two parts. First, the buyer's characteristics influence how he or she perceives and reacts to the stimuli. Second, the buyer's decision process itself affects his or her behavior. We look first at buyer characteristics as they affect buyer behavior and then discuss the buyer decision process.

Author Comment Many levels of factors affect our buying behavior—from broad cultural and social influences to motivations, beliefs, and attitudes lying deep within us. For example, why *did* you buy *that* specific phone you're carrying?

Characteristics Affecting Consumer Behavior

Consumer purchases are influenced strongly by cultural, social, personal, and psychological characteristics, as shown in >> **Figure 5.2**. For the most part, marketers cannot control such factors, but they must take them into account.

Cultural Factors

Cultural factors exert a broad and deep influence on consumer behavior. Marketers need to understand the role played by the buyer's *culture, subculture*, and *social class.*

Culture
The set of basic values, perceptions, wants, and behaviors learned by a member of society from family and other important institutions.

Culture. **Culture** is the most basic cause of a person's wants and behavior. Human behavior is largely learned. Growing up in a society, a child learns basic values, perceptions, wants, and behaviors from his or her family and other important institutions. A child in the United States normally is exposed to the following values: achievement and success, freedom, individualism, hard work, activity and involvement, efficiency and practicality, material comfort, youthfulness, and fitness and health. Every group or society has a culture, and cultural influences on buying behavior may vary greatly from both county to county and country to country.

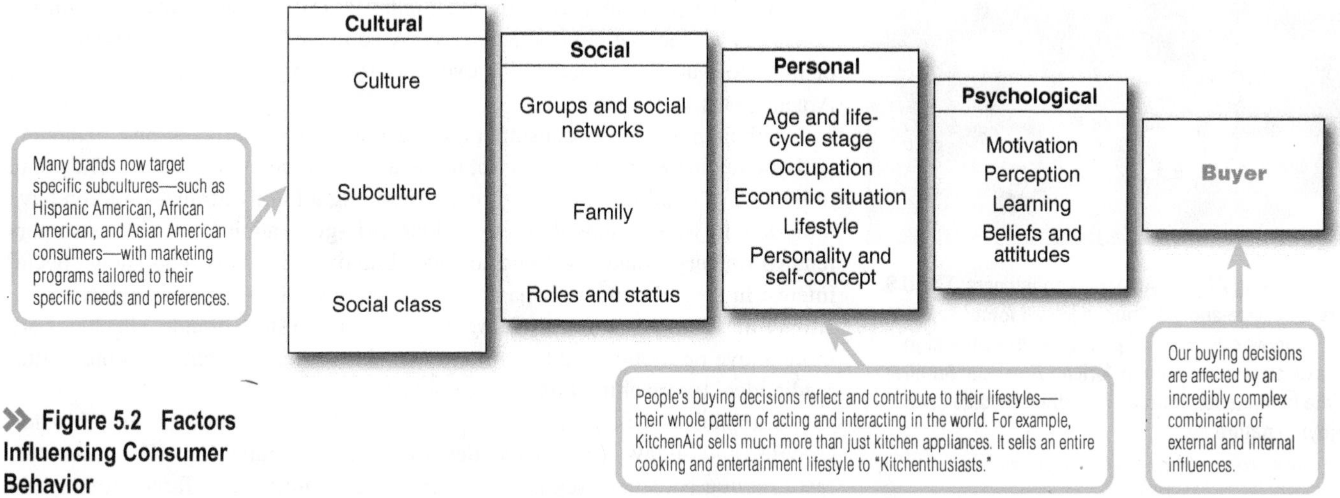

>> Figure 5.2 Factors Influencing Consumer Behavior

Marketers are always trying to spot *cultural shifts* so as to discover new products that might be wanted. For example, the cultural shift toward greater concern about health and fitness has created a huge industry for health-and-fitness services, exercise equipment and clothing, organic foods, and a variety of diets.

Subculture
A group of people with shared value systems based on common life experiences and situations.

Subculture. Each culture contains smaller **subcultures**, or groups of people with shared value systems based on common life experiences and situations. Subcultures include nationalities, religions, racial groups, and geographic regions. Many subcultures make up important market segments, and marketers often design products and marketing programs tailored to their needs. Examples of three such important subculture groups are African American, Hispanic American, and Asian American consumers.

The U.S. *African American* population is growing in affluence and sophistication. The nation's more than 42 million black consumers wield almost $1.2 trillion in annual buying power. Although more price conscious than other segments, blacks are also strongly motivated by quality and selection. Brands are important. African American consumers are heavy users of digital and social media, providing access through a rich variety of marketing channels.[3]

Many companies develop special products, appeals, and marketing programs for African American consumers—from carmakers like Ford and Hyundai to consumer products companies like P&G to even not-for-profits and government agencies such as the U.S. Forest Service. >> For example, the U.S. Forest Service and the Ad Council recently joined forces to create the "Discover the Forest" public service campaign to raise awareness among families of the benefits for children of getting outside and enjoying nature. One round of the campaign specifically targeted the parents of African American tweens:[4]

> Although more than 245 million Americans live within 100 miles of a national forest or grassland, research shows that a majority of children in some population segments are not spending active time outdoors. For example, only 37 percent of African American children ages six to twelve participate frequently in outdoor activities compared with 67 percent of the broader U.S. population in that age group. To help close that gap, the U.S. Forest Service and the Ad Council created the "Discover the Forest" campaign, a series of public service messages ranging from billboards and radio commercials to interactive social media and Web site content. With headlines such as "Unplug," "Where curiosity blooms," and "Where imagination sprouts," the ads targeting African American families promote the discovery and imagination wonders of connecting with the great outdoors and the resulting physical, mental health, and emotional well-being benefits. "The forest is one of those amazing places where kids can flex their imagination muscles through exploration and discovery," says a marketer associated with the campaign.

>> Targeting African American consumers: The U.S. Forest Service and Ad Council joined forces to create the "Discover the Forest" public service campaign to raise awareness among African American families of the benefits for children of getting outside and enjoying nature.

The Forest Service, an agency of the U.S. Department of Agriculture and the Ad Council.

Hispanics represent a large, fast-growing market. The nation's more than 55 million Hispanic consumers (almost one out of every six Americans) have total annual buying power of $1.7 trillion. The U.S. Hispanic population will surge to more than 120 million by 2060, close to one-third of the total U.S. population.[5] Within the Hispanic market, there exist many distinct subsegments based on nationality, age, income, and other factors. A company's product or message may be more relevant to one nationality over another, such as Mexicans, Costa Ricans, Argentineans, or Cubans.

Although Hispanic consumers share many characteristics and behaviors with the mainstream buying public, there are also distinct differences. They tend to be deeply family oriented and make shopping a family affair—children have a big say in what brands they buy. Older, first-generation Hispanic consumers tend to be very brand loyal and to favor brands and sellers who show special interest in them. Younger Hispanics, however, have shown increasing price sensitivity in recent years and a willingness to switch to store brands. Hispanics are more active on mobile and social networks than other segments, making digital media ideal for reaching this segment.[6]

Companies such as P&G, McDonald's, Walmart, State Farm, Chrysler, Google, and many others have developed special targeting efforts for this fast-growing consumer segment. For example, Walmart and Target both spend heavily to cultivate the Hispanic market. Both use Spanish-language ads and social media, place bilingual signs in stores, and stock their shelves with products that appeal to the special preferences of Hispanics. And Chrysler's successful three-year "A Todo, Con Todo" campaign markets the company's Ram trucks to the important Hispanic segment:[7]

> Pickup trucks are Ram's biggest market, and Hispanics are crucial to the brand's success in that segment. The "A Todo, Con Todo" Ram truck campaign targets Hispanic pickup-truck owners with Spanish- and English-language TV, magazine, radio, and digital ads in major Hispanic markets, such as Albuquerque, Miami, Phoenix, New York, Los Angeles, Denver, and numerous Texas communities. "A Todo, Con Todo"—which translates as "To everything, with everything" (or "Give it all you've got")—appeals to authentic Hispanic values. The first ads in the series featured two Hispanic truck owners—Ascension Banuelos and Arturo Barcelo—who use their Ram trucks day in and day out for work and recreation. Banuelos manages a horse training ranch in Jacksboro, Texas, and owns a Ram 3500; Barcelo drives a Ram 1500 and owns a home-improvement construction company in Dallas. In the ads, these truck owners give unscripted, real-life testimonials about values that are important to them and how their Ram trucks fit those values. An announcer concludes: "Finding a way to rise above, to push our limits further. The Ram 1500. Because success is not a destination, it's our journey. Ram. A Todo, Con Todo." Thanks largely to this campaign, Ram pickup-truck sales to the important Hispanics segment were up 33 percent last year.

Asian Americans are the most affluent U.S. demographic segment. A relatively well-educated segment, they now number more than 18 million (5 percent of the population), with annual buying power expected to approach $1 trillion by 2017. Asian Americans are the second-fastest-growing subsegment after Hispanic Americans. And like Hispanic Americans, they are a diverse group. Chinese Americans constitute the largest group, followed by Filipinos, Asian Indians, Vietnamese, Korean Americans, and Japanese Americans. Yet, unlike Hispanics who all speak various dialects of Spanish, Asians speak many different languages. For example, ads for the 2010 U.S. Census ran in languages ranging from Japanese, Cantonese, Khmer, Korean, and Vietnamese to Thai, Cambodian, Hmong, Hinglish, and Taglish.[8]

Total market strategy
Integrating ethnic themes and cross-cultural perspectives within a brand's mainstream marketing, appealing to consumer similarities across subcultural segments rather than differences.

As a group, Asian American consumers shop frequently and are the most brand conscious of all the ethnic groups. They can be fiercely brand loyal. As a result, many firms now target the Asian American market. » AT&T learned that young Asian Americans are more than just a lucrative technology market in themselves—they also influence other consumers. So it created an innovative marketing campaign aimed at improving perceptions in this influential young segment:[9]

> To raise perceptions of AT&T as an innovative and preferred brand among Asian-American youth, key influencers in its tech markets, AT&T created an engaging crowd-sourced, boy-meets-girl Web series called "Away We Happened." The low-cost series featured popular Asian youth celebrities Victor Kim and Jen Chae of Frmheadtotoe. AT&T partnered with Asian YouTube producer Wong Fu Productions to create the first episode. It then encouraged viewers to visit a Facebook app to submit their ideas for what happened next and vote on the best ideas for future episodes. The Effie-winning, six-episode series went viral, grabbing more than 13 million views over its six-week run and raising AT&T brand perceptions by 50 percent among young Asian American consumers.

» Targeting Asian American consumers: To improve perceptions among young Asian Americans, key influencers in its tech markets, AT&T created an engaging crowd-sourced, boy-meets-girl Web series called "Away We Happened."

Courtesy of AT&T Intellectual Property, interTrend Communications, Wong Fu Productions, Inc., and Rezonate Media. Female talent: Jen Chae (Jen of FrmHeadtoToe). Used with permission.

Beyond targeting segments such as Hispanics, African Americans, and Asian Americans with specially tailored efforts, many marketers now embrace a **total market strategy**—the practice of integrating ethnic themes and cross-cultural perspectives within their mainstream marketing. An example is general-market commercials for Cheerios and Swiffer that feature interracial families.[10] A total market strategy appeals to consumer similarities across subcultural segments rather than differences.

Many marketers are finding that insights gleaned from ethnic consumer segments can influence their broader markets. For example, today's youth-oriented lifestyle is influenced heavily by Hispanic and African American entertainers. So it follows that consumers expect to see many different cultures and ethnicities represented in the advertising and products they consume. For instance, McDonald's takes cues from African Americans, Hispanics, and Asians to develop menus and advertising in hopes of encouraging mainstream consumers to buy smoothies, mocha drinks, and snack wraps as avidly as they consume hip-hop and rock'n' roll. Or McDonald's might take an ad primarily geared toward African Americans and run it in general-market media.

Social class
Relatively permanent and ordered divisions in a society whose members share similar values, interests, and behaviors.

Social Class. Almost every society has some form of social class structure. **Social classes** are society's relatively permanent and ordered divisions whose members share similar values, interests, and behaviors. Social scientists have identified the seven American social classes: upper upper class, lower upper class, upper middle class, middle class, working class, upper lower class, and lower lower class.

Social class is not determined by a single factor, such as income, but is measured as a combination of occupation, income, education, wealth, and other variables. In some social systems, members of different classes are reared for certain roles and cannot change their social positions. In the United States, however, the lines between social classes are not fixed and rigid; people can move to a higher social class or drop into a lower one.

Marketers are interested in social class because people within a given social class tend to exhibit similar buying behavior. Social classes show distinct product and brand preferences in areas such as clothing, home furnishings, travel and leisure activity, financial services, and automobiles.

Social Factors

A consumer's behavior also is influenced by social factors, such as the consumer's *small groups, social networks, family*, and *social roles and status*.

Group
Two or more people who interact to accomplish individual or mutual goals.

Groups and Social Networks. Many small **groups** influence a person's behavior. Groups that have a direct influence and to which a person belongs are called *membership groups*. In contrast, *reference groups* serve as direct (face-to-face interactions) or indirect points of comparison or reference in forming a person's attitudes or behavior. People often are influenced by reference groups to which they do not belong. For example, an *aspirational group* is one to which the individual wishes to belong, as when a young basketball player hopes to someday emulate basketball star LeBron James and play in the NBA.

Marketers try to identify the reference groups of their target markets. Reference groups expose a person to new behaviors and lifestyles, influence the person's attitudes and self-concept, and create pressures to conform that may affect the person's product and brand choices. The importance of group influence varies across products and brands. It tends to be strongest when the product is visible to others whom the buyer respects.

Word-of-mouth influence
The impact of the personal words and recommendations of trusted friends, family, associates, and other consumers on buying behavior.

Word-of-mouth influence can have a powerful impact on consumer buying behavior. The personal words and recommendations of trusted friends, family, associates, and other consumers tend to be more credible than those coming from commercial sources, such as advertisements or salespeople. One recent study showed that 92 percent of consumers trust recommendations from friends and family above any form of advertising.[11] Most word-of-mouth influence happens naturally: Consumers start chatting about a brand they use or feel strongly about one way or the other. Often, however, rather than leaving it to chance, marketers can help to create positive conversations about their brands.

Opinion leader
A person within a reference group who, because of special skills, knowledge, personality, or other characteristics, exerts social influence on others.

Marketers of brands subjected to strong group influence must figure out how to reach **opinion leaders**—people within a reference group who, because of special skills, knowledge, personality, or other characteristics, exert social influence on others. Some experts call this group the *influentials* or *leading adopters*. When these influentials talk, consumers listen. Marketers try to identify opinion leaders for their products and direct marketing efforts toward them.

Buzz marketing involves enlisting or even creating opinion leaders to serve as "brand ambassadors" who spread the word about a company's products. Consider Mercedes-Benz's award-winning "Take the Wheel" influencer campaign:[12]

Creating word of mouth: Mercedes-Benz's "Take the Wheel" influencer campaign really got people buzzing about its all-new CLA model, helping to create millions of positive social conversations and record sales.

© Courtesy of Daimler AG

Mercedes-Benz wanted get more people talking about its all-new, soon-to-be-launched 2014 CLA model, priced at $29,900 and aimed at getting a new generation of younger consumers into the Mercedes brand. So it challenged five of Instagram's most influential photographers—everyday Gen Y consumers whose stunning imagery had earned them hundreds of thousands of fans—to each spend five days behind the wheel of a CLA, documenting their journeys in photos shared via Instagram. The photographer who got the most Likes got to keep the CLA. The short campaign really got people buzzing about the car, earning 87 million social media impressions and more than 2 million likes. Ninety percent of the social conversation was positive. And when Mercedes launched the CLA the following month, it broke sales records.

Sometimes, everyday customers become a brand's best evangelists. For instance, Alan Klein loves the McDonald's McRib—a sandwich made of a boneless pork patty molded into a rib-like shape, slathered in BBQ sauce and topped with pickles and onion. The McRib is sold for only short time periods each year at McDonald's restaurants around the nation. Klein loves it so much that he created the McRib Locator app and Web site (mcriblocator.com), where McRib fans buzz about locations where they've recently sighted the coveted sandwich.[13]

Online social networks
Online communities—blogs, social networking Web sites, and other online communities—where people socialize or exchange information and opinions.

Over the past several years, a new type of social interaction has exploded onto the scene—online social networking. **Online social networks** are online communities where people socialize or exchange information and opinions. Social networking communities range from blogs (Consumerist, Gizmodo, Zenhabits) and message boards (Craigslist) to social media sites (Facebook, Twitter, YouTube, Pinterest, and LinkedIn) and even communal shopping sites (Amazon.com and Etsy). These online forms of consumer-to-consumer and business-to-consumer dialogue have big implications for marketers.

Marketers are working to harness the power of these new social networks and other "word-of-Web" opportunities to promote their products and build closer customer relationships. Instead of throwing more one-way commercial messages at consumers, they hope to use the digital, mobile, and social media to *interact* with consumers and become a part of their conversations and lives.

For example, Red Bull has an astounding 46 million friends on Facebook; Twitter and Facebook are the primary ways it communicates with college students. JetBlue listens in on customers on Twitter and often responds; one consumer recently Tweeted "Thanks for taking me home for the holidays @JetBlue. And thanks to the crew in Austin for giving me a row to myself so I can sleep!" JetBlue Tweeted back "You're most welcome, Nancy! Thanks for letting us be your ride! Happy Holidays to you and your family! #VIPTreatmentForNancy." Even the Mayo Clinic uses social media extensively. It maintains Facebook, Pinterest, and Twitter pages; a YouTube channel; smartphone patient apps that "put Mayo in your pocket wherever you are"; and a Sharing Mayo Clinic blog on which patients share their Mayo Clinic experiences and employees offer a behind-the-scenes view.

Most brands have built a comprehensive social media presence. We will dig deeper into online and social media as marketing tools in Chapter 14. However, although much of the current talk about tapping social influence focuses on the digital, mobile, and social media, most brand conversations still take place the old-fashioned way—face to face. So most effective word-of-mouth marketing programs begin with generating person-to-person brand conversations and integrating both offline and online social influence strategies. The goal is to create opportunities for customers to get involved with brands and then help them share their brand passions and experiences with others in both their real and digital worlds (see Marketing at Work 5.1).

MARKETING AT WORK 5.1

Word-of-Mouth Marketing: Sparking Brand Conversations and Helping Them Catch Fire

People love talking with others about things that make them happy—including their favorite products and brands. Say you really like JetBlue Airways—it flies with flair and gets you there at an affordable price. Or you just plain love your new little GoPro HERO4 Black Edition video camera—it's too cool to keep to yourself. So you spread the good word about your favorite brands to anyone who will listen. In the old days, you'd have chatted up these brands with a few friends and family members. But these days, thanks to the online, mobile, and social media, anyone can share brand experiences with thousands, even millions, of other consumers digitally.

In response, marketers are now feverishly working to harness today's technologies and get people interacting with each other about their brands, both online and offline. The aim is to inspire, nurture, and amplify brand conversations. Whether it entails seeding a product among high-potential consumers to get them talking, creating brand ambassadors, tapping into existing influentials and the social media, or developing conversation-provoking events and videos, the idea is to get people involved with and talking about the brand.

Generating successful word of mouth might be as simple as prompting Facebook Likes and Shares, Twitter streams, Pinterest boards, online reviews, blog commentaries, or YouTube videos. Even companies with small budgets can earn global exposure in the social media. For example, little-known start-up DollarShaveClub.com—which ships quality razors directly to customers for as little as $1 a month—became an overnight sensation thanks largely to a single YouTube video. Founder Michael Dubin scraped together $4,500 to produce a clever video featuring himself, some corny props, a guy in a bear suit, and very salty language to pitch the new service. "Are the blades any good?" Dubin asked in the video. "No. Our blades are f***ing great," he answered. "So stop forgetting where you're going to buy your blades every month and start deciding where you're going to stack all those dollar bills I'm saving you." The edgy video went viral, and the word-of-mouth firestorm earned DollarShaveClub.com more than 17 million YouTube views, 60,000 Twitter followers, 1.5 million Likes on Facebook, dozens of response videos, and $10 million in venture capital funding. DollarShaveClub's success has even prompted giant Gillette to begin its own blade subscription program.

But most successful social influence campaigns go well beyond a YouTube video or Facebook Likes. For example, many companies start by creating their own brand evangelists. That's what Ford did to introduce its Fiesta subcompact model in the United States. Under its now-classic Fiesta Movement campaign, Ford handed out Fiestas to 100 young Millennial drivers—the target audience for the car—selected from 4,000 applicants. These "Fiesta Agents" lived with their cars for six months, all the while sharing their experiences via blogs, Tweets, Facebook updates, and YouTube and Flickr posts. The highly successful Fiesta Movement campaign generated 58 percent prelaunch brand awareness among Fiesta's under-30 target consumers. The Fiesta ambassadors posted 50,000 items, generating 28 million social media views, 52,000 test drives, and 10,000 online vehicle reservations. The Fiesta Movement was so successful that Ford created similar social media evangelist campaigns for the Ford Escape ("Escape Routes") and the Ford Fusion ("Random Acts of Fusion").

Beyond creating their own ambassadors, companies looking to harness influence can work with the army of self-made influencers already plying the Internet—independent bloggers. Believe it or not, there are now almost as many people making a living as bloggers as there are lawyers. No matter what the interest area, there are probably hundreds of bloggers covering it. Moreover, research shows that 90 percent of bloggers post about their favorite and least favorite brands.

>> Sparking word of mouth: Chubbies spreads its "shorts revolution" manifesto through both a booming social media presence and an army of face-to-face brand ambassadors on college campuses.

Chubbies Shorts

As a result, most companies try to form relationships with influential bloggers and online personalities. The key is to find bloggers who have strong networks of relevant readers, a credible voice, and a good fit with the brand. For example, companies ranging from P&G and McDonald's to Walmart work closely with influential "mommy bloggers." And you'll no doubt cross paths with the likes of climbers and skiers blogging for Patagonia, bikers blogging for Harley-Davidson, and foodies blogging for Whole Foods Market or Trader Joe's. Sometimes, bloggers and other social media mavens focus exclusively on a given brand. For example, StarbucksMelody.com is "an unofficial fan site for any and all Starbucks enthusiasts everywhere." TUAW is "The Unofficial Apple Weblog—a resource for all things Apple and beyond." Thanks to their independence, such blogs often generate more trustworthy buzz than a company's own blogs or online sites can.

Much of the word-of-mouth marketing frenzy today seems to center on creating online buzz. However, the majority of brand conversations still take place offline. According to one expert, some 93 percent of brand conversations still happen in the real world rather than the virtual one. So many marketers look beyond the digital world to create good old face-to-face brand conversations.

For example, Chubbies is a small but trendy and fast-growing startup that targets young men with a line of "anti-cargo shorts" (and a retro 5 1/2-inch inseam). So far, the brand has marketed itself only through its social media presence. Avid Chubsters actively swap influence via pictures, videos, and stories on YouTube, Facebook, Twitter, Instagram, Pinterest, and the Chubbies Web site and ChubsterNation blog. But now, Chubbies is building an army of face-to-face influencers in the form of 250 student ambassadors at college campuses across the country. The ambassadors—what it calls "thigh-liberating patriots"—spread the Chubster manifesto that "We don't do pants. We don't do cargos. We don't do capris. We do shorts and only shorts." "Pants are for work," they preach. Chubbies "are for having fun, or jumping off rocks, or playing beer pong, or climbing Everest." The ambassadors personally rally the faithful at tailgate parties and other campus events, expanding the ChubsterNation and sparking even more word of mouth for the irreverent brand.

Whether offline, online, or both, effective word-of-mouth marketing isn't something that just happens. And it's more than just building a following on Facebook. Marketers must build comprehensive programs that spark person-to-person brand conversations and then help them catch fire. The goal of word-of-mouth marketing is to find the company's best customers, give them opportunities to become more involved, and help them spread their brand passion and enthusiasm within their in-person and digital networks. It's all about sparking brand conversations and helping them catch fire.

Sources: Jefferson Graham, "Dollar Shave Club's Dubin: From YouTube Star to CEO," June 14, 2014, www.usatoday.com/story/money/business/2014/06/09/ceo-profile-dollar-shave-clubs-michael-dubin/9993045/; Giselle Abramovich, "Why Ford Credits Social Media in Turnaround," *Digiday*, October 10, 2012, www.digiday.com/brands/why-ford-credits-social-media-in-turnaround/; Iris Mansour, "The New Face of Word-of-Mouth," *CNNMoney*, August 2013, http://management.fortune.cnn.com/2013/08/28/word-of-mouth-marketing/; Nellie Bowles, "Chubbies Shorts Popular with Troops," June 28, 2013, www.sfgate.com/style/article/Chubbies-shorts-popular-with-troops-4634821.php; Jim Dougherty, "9 Ways to Improve Word-of-Mouth Communications," *Cision*, January 5, 2015, www.cision.com/us/2015/01/9-ways-to-improve-word-of-mouth-communication/; www.chubbiesshorts.com/pages/manifesto, www.dollarshaveclub.com, and www.chubbiesshorts.com/, accessed September 2015.

Family. Family members can strongly influence buyer behavior. The family is the most important consumer buying organization in society, and it has been researched extensively. Marketers are interested in the roles and influence of the husband, wife, and children on the purchase of different products and services.

Husband–wife involvement varies widely by product category and by stage in the buying process. Buying roles change with evolving consumer lifestyles. For example, in the United States, the wife traditionally has been considered the main purchasing agent for the family in the areas of food, household products, and clothing. But with 71 percent of all mothers now working outside the home and the willingness of husbands to do more of the family's purchasing, all this has changed in recent years. Recent surveys of men show that nearly half do at least 50 percent of their household's grocery shopping, 39 percent handle most of their household's laundry, and about one-quarter say they are responsible for all of their household's cooking. At the same time, today women outspend men three to two on new technology purchases and influence more than 80 percent of all new car purchases.[14]

Such shifting roles signal a new marketing reality. Marketers in industries that have traditionally sold their products to only women or only men—from groceries and personal care products to cars and consumer electronics—are now carefully targeting the opposite sex. Other companies are showing their products in "modern family" contexts. For example, » one General Mills ad shows a father packing Go-Gurt yogurt in his son's lunch as the child heads off to school in the morning, with the slogan "Dads who get it, get Go-Gurt." And the recent General Mills "How to Dad" campaign for Cheerios presents a

» Changing family buying influences: One Go-Gurt ad shows a father packing Go-Gurt yogurt in his son's lunch as the child heads off to school. "Dads who get it, get Go-Gurt."

Use with permission of General Mills Marketing Inc. (GMMI).

dad as a multitasking superhero around the house, a departure from the bumbling dad stereotypes often shown in food ads. This dad does all the right things, including feeding this children healthy Cheerios breakfasts. "Being a dad is awesome," he proclaims in one ad. "Just like Cheerios are awesome. That's why it's the Official Cereal of Dadhood."[15]

Children may also have a strong influence on family buying decisions. The nation's kids and tweens influence up to 80 percent of all household purchases, to the tune of $1.2 trillion of spending annually. Kids significantly influence family decisions about everything from clothing, cars, and entertainment to where they eat out and take vacations.[16]

Roles and Status. A person belongs to many groups—family, clubs, organizations, online communities. The person's position in each group can be defined in terms of both role and status. A role consists of the activities people are expected to perform according to the people around them. Each role carries a status reflecting the general esteem given to it by society.

People usually choose products appropriate to their roles and status. Consider the various roles a working mother plays. In her company, she may play the role of a brand manager; in her family, she plays the role of wife and mother; at her favorite sporting events, she plays the role of avid fan. As a brand manager, she will buy the kind of clothing that reflects her role and status in her company. At the game, she may wear clothing supporting her favorite team.

Personal Factors

A buyer's decisions also are influenced by personal characteristics such as the buyer's *occupation, age and life-cycle stage, economic situation, lifestyle*, and *personality and self-concept*.

Occupation. A person's occupation affects the goods and services bought. Blue-collar workers tend to buy more rugged work clothes, whereas executives buy more business suits. Marketers try to identify the occupational groups that have an above-average interest in their products and services. A company can even specialize in making products needed by a given occupational group. For example, Duluth Trading Company makes rugged, durable work clothes with a "no-bull" guarantee. From its "Ballroom Jeans" that give you "room to crouch without singing soprano" to its "Longtail T-shirts" that fix your "plumber's butt," Duluth's products are designed and tested by tradesmen. "Taking care of working guys is priority #1 at Duluth," says the company.

Age and Life Stage. People change the goods and services they buy over their lifetimes. Tastes in food, clothes, furniture, and recreation are often age related. Buying is also shaped by the stage of the family life cycle—the stages through which families might pass as they mature over time. Life-stage changes usually result from demographics and life-changing events—marriage, having children, purchasing a home, divorce, children going to college, changes in personal income, moving out of the house, and retirement. Marketers often define their target markets in terms of life-cycle stage and develop appropriate products and marketing plans for each stage.

One of the leading life-stage segmentation systems is the Nielsen PRIZM Lifestage Groups system. PRIZM classifies every American household into one of 66 distinct life-stage segments, which are organized into 11 major life-stage groups, based on affluence, age, and family characteristics. The classifications consider a host of demographic factors such as age, education, income, occupation, family composition, ethnicity, and housing; and behavioral and lifestyle factors, such as purchases, free-time activities, and media preferences.

The major PRIZM Lifestage groups carry names such as "Striving Singles," "Midlife Success," "Young Achievers," "Sustaining Families," "Affluent Empty Nests," and "Conservative Classics," which in turn contain subgroups such as "Brite Lites, Li'l City," "Kids & Cul-de-Sacs," "Gray Power," and "Big City Blues." The "Young Achievers" group consists of hip, single 20-somethings who rent apartments in or close to metropolitan neighborhoods. Their incomes range from working class to well-to-do, but the entire group tends to be politically liberal, listen to alternative music, and enjoy lively nightlife.[17]

Different life-stage groups exhibit different buying behaviors. Life-stage segmentation provides a powerful marketing tool for marketers in all industries to better find, understand, and engage consumers. Armed with data about the makeup of consumer life stages, marketers can create targeted, actionable, personalized campaigns based on how people consume and interact with brands and the world around them.

Economic Situation. A person's economic situation will affect his or her store and product choices. Marketers watch trends in spending, personal income, savings, and interest rates. In today's more value-conscious times, most companies have taken steps to create more customer value by redesigning, repositioning, and repricing their products and services. For example, in recent years, upscale discounter Target has put more emphasis on the "Pay Less" side of its "Expect More. Pay Less." positioning promise.

Similarly, in line with worldwide economic trends, smartphone makers who once offered only premium-priced phones are now offering lower-priced models for consumers both at home and in the world's emerging economies. Microsoft's Nokia division recently targeted emerging markets with lower-end Lumia models priced well under $100. And Apple introduced a lower-end, lower-priced version of its iPhone, the iPhone 5C. As their more affluent Western markets have become saturated and more competitive, the phone makers hope that their lower-priced phones will help them to compete effectively and grow in less-affluent emerging Eastern markets such as China and Southeast Asia.[18]

Lifestyle
A person's pattern of living as expressed in his or her activities, interests, and opinions.

Lifestyle. People coming from the same subculture, social class, and occupation may have quite different lifestyles. **Lifestyle** is a person's pattern of living as expressed in his or her psychographics. It involves measuring consumers' major AIO dimensions—*activities* (work, hobbies, shopping, sports, social events), *interests* (food, fashion, family, recreation), and *opinions* (about themselves, social issues, business, products). Lifestyle captures something more than the person's social class or personality. It profiles a person's whole pattern of acting and interacting in the world.

When used carefully, the lifestyle concept can help marketers understand changing consumer values and how they affect buyer behavior. Consumers don't just buy products; they buy the values and lifestyles those products represent. For example, you may know KitchenAid by its high-performance mixers and other kitchen appliances. But KitchenAid sells much more than just appliances. It sells an entire cooking and entertainment lifestyle:[19]

> KitchenAid cultivates "Kitchenthusiasts"—a lifestyle community of "hosts with the most" who thrive on cooking and entertainment challenges. Its Kitchenthusiast blog, Facebook pages, and 11 Pinterest boards are brimming with recipes, cooking challenges, tips and techniques, and coverage of the latest cooking lifestyle news and events by key contributors. KitchenAid's "There's So Much More to Make" marketing campaign highlights how the brand's appliances contribute to the lifestyles of passionate Kitchenthusiasts. Says one ad: "When entertaining elates you, when every machine does incredible things, there's so much more to make."

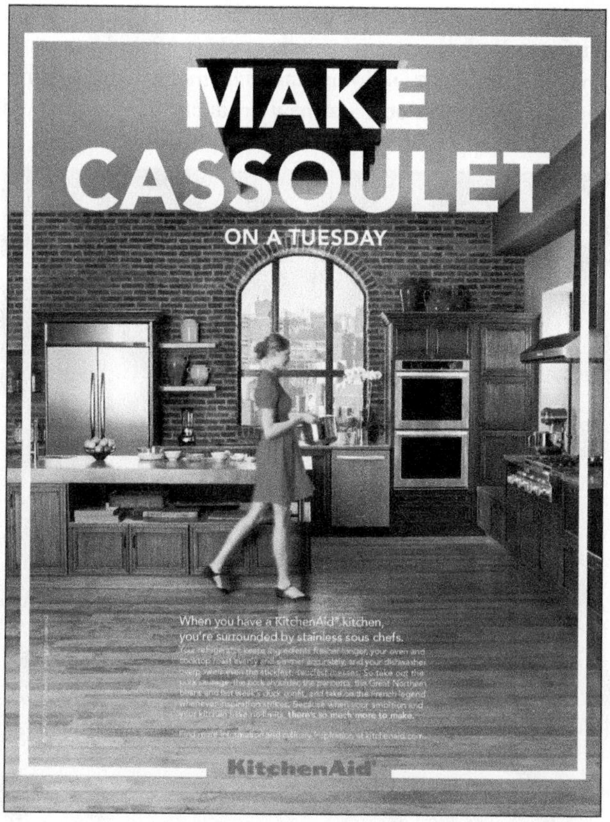

Lifestyles: KitchenAid sells much more than just high-performance kitchen appliances. It sells an entire cooking and entertainment lifestyle to "Kitchenthusiasts."

Courtesy of Whirlpool Corporation. Photo © Melanie Acevedo/Stockland Martel

Marketers look for lifestyle segments with needs that can be served through special products or marketing approaches. Such segments might be defined by anything from family characteristics or outdoor interests to the foods people eat. For example, fast-food chain Taco Bell recently repositioned itself as an experience brand, consistent with the lifestyles of its primary target customers, Millennials (see Marketing at Work 5.2).

MARKETING AT WORK 5.2

Taco Bell: More than Just Tacos, a "Live Más" Lifestyle

Years ago, Taco Bell practically invented the fast-food "value menu," with its "59¢-79¢-99¢" pricing structure. With slogans such as "The Cure for the Common Meal," "Make a Run for the Border," and "Think Outside the Bun," Taco Bell firmly established its affordable Mexican-inspired fare as a unique, "more-for-your-money" alternative to the mostly burgers and fries offered by dominant McDonald's and other fast-food competitors.

In the early 2000s, however, consumer tastes began to change. Americans were looking for fresher, better-tasting, healthier eating options and more contemporary fast-casual atmospheres. Taco Bell's "food-as-fuel" marketing philosophy—its "fill them up, move them out" thinking—made the chain seem out of step with the times. After three straight years of flat sales, Taco Bell ended 2011 with a 1.4-percent decline in systemwide revenues. These dire results called for a shift in Taco Bell's strategy.

The shift began with the realization that customers want more from a fast-food restaurant than just lots of food on the cheap. More than "calories per dollar," they are seeking a food-eating experience, one that fits with and enhances their lifestyles. So in early 2012, Taco Bell shifted its positioning from "food as fuel" to "food as experience and lifestyle." It crafted a new tagline—"Live Más" ("más" is Spanish for "more"). As part of its $280 million annual marketing budget, the "Live Más" slogan is designed as a lifestyle rallying cry for Taco Bell's core customers, Millennials—young adults who consume a disproportionate share of fast and fast-casual food.

Taco Bell's aspirational "Live Más" message is crafted to inspire Millennials to try new things and to live life to the fullest. The first "Live Más" ad, called "Pockets," showed a hip, 20-something man coming into a dim apartment as dawn breaks. He emptied his pockets onto a table as he thought back over the night he'd had. Along with the standard wallet, keys, and smartphone, he tossed out a concert ticket stub, a matchbook from a 24-hour psychic, a pair of Kanji dice, and a strip of photo-booth images of himself with a young woman. The last item he pulled out was a blister pack of Taco Bell Fire Sauce, adorned with the new "Live Más" logo and the message "You have chosen wisely." It was this last item that brought a smile to his face.

Support for the "Live Más" lifestyle tagline goes well beyond just advertising. For example, it includes new menu items aimed to please Millennial palates. In early 2012, Taco Bell unveiled cobranded Doritos Locos Tacos, like a standard Taco Bell taco or Taco Supreme but wrapped in a tasty shell made from Nacho Cheese Doritos. Hungry Millennials gobbled up 100 million Doritos Locos Tacos in just the first 10 weeks, at the time making it the most successful new-product launch in the company's 50-year history. The brand quickly added Cool Ranch and Fiery versions.

Recognizing that customers who want to "Live Más" might be looking to eat at just about any time of day, Taco Bell has focused on more day parts. For example, after a long absence from morning hours, Taco Bell has rolled out a 7 am (or earlier) to 11 am breakfast menu. Initial options included breakfast burritos, waffle tacos, the A.M. Crunchwrap, the A.M. Grilled Taco, and bite-size Cinnabon Delights. Similarly, Taco Bell's "Happier Hour" initiative targets between-meal-snack appetites from 2 pm to 5 pm daily, featuring new Mountain Dew Baja Blast and Dr Pepper frozen beverages and $1 Loaded Grillers. And for the late-night "Live Más" crowd, there's Fourthmeal, as in "You're out. You're hungry. You're doing Fourthmeal." In one ad—titled "After-Wedding Party"—a newlywed couple feasts on Taco Bell fare in the back of a limo along with their groomsmen and bridesmaids. The announcer concludes, "Fourthmeal—sometimes the best dinner is after the dinner."

To better engage targeted Millennials, Taco Bell now reaches them where they hang out—online, digital, and mobile. Befitting the Millennial lifestyle, it recently added a new mobile ordering app. And a significant portion of the "Live Más" promotion budget goes to social media, digital tools, and other nontraditional channels. Beyond the usual Facebook and Twitter, Taco Bell uses social media such as Vine, Instagram, and Snapchat for buzz-building announcements, limited-time promotions, and sneak peeks at new products. The revitalized

>> Taco Bell's innovative "Live Más" positioning targets the lifestyles of the brand's key target customers, Millennials.

Taco Bell Corporation

chain watches and participates in online brand conversations with its "Fishbowl"—Taco Bell's own command center for monitoring social media and generating digital dialogue. For example, the brand achieved more than 600 million social-media impressions for Cool Ranch Doritos Locos Tacos alone before the product even officially launched.

Some analysts suggest that with "Live Más," Taco Bell is stretching too far beyond its core affordable fast-food positioning. "They're trying to suggest a lifestyle aspiration, but this seems an overreach for Taco Bell," says one restaurant-marketing consultant. "A tagline should embrace the DNA of the brand, which for Taco Bell is extraordinary value." Not so, says Taco Bell. Rather than abandoning the brand's "value" roots, says the company, the new tagline and other elements of "Live Más" underscore brand values dating back to its founding—"value, quality, relevance, and an exceptional experience." The "value" message still resonates in the tagline, but "Live Más" also energizes the "relevance" and "experience" aspects of Taco Bell's long-standing value proposition.

The early results suggest that Taco Bell is right on track with the "Live Más" lifestyle positioning. The year following the introduction of the tagline saw sales soar 8 percent, more than twice the gain of industry leader McDonald's. And ad industry magazine *Advertising Age* recently named Taco Bell its Marketer of the Year for going "into innovation overdrive, churning out a string of hot new products, game-changing menus, and an aggressive mix of traditional, social, and digital media that's hitting the mark with Millennials."

But for Taco Bell, becoming an experience and lifestyle brand isn't just about reversing sales declines and reaping marketing honors. It's about building for the future. Taco Bell recently announced plans to nearly double its business to $14 billion by 2022 with 8,000 restaurants domestically. Accomplishing that lofty objective will have both Taco Bell's customers *and* Taco Bell marketers shouting "Live Más!"

Sources: Kate Taylor, "KFC, Pizza Hut, and Taco Bell Want Even More Millennial Customers in 2015," *Entrepreneur,* December 11, 2014, www.entrepreneur.com/article/240835; Maureen Morrison, "Sales Are Going Loco at Taco Bell, Ad Age's Marketer of the Year," *Advertising Age*, September 2, 2013, p. 2; Shirley Brady, "Taco Bell Promotes New 'Live Más' Tagline in New Campaign," *Brand Channel*, February 24, 2012, www.brandchannel.com/home/post/2012/02/24/Taco-Bell-Live-Mas-Doritos-Locos-Tacos-Spots-022412.aspx; Maureen Morrison, "Taco Bell to Exchange 'Think Outside the Bun' for 'Live Más,'" *Advertising Age*, February 21, 2012, adage.com/print/232849; Mark Brandau, "Yum Plans to Double U.S. Taco Bell Sales," *Restaurant News*, May 22, 2013, nrn.com/quick-service/analysts-yum-plans-double-us-taco-bell-sales; and various pages at www.tacobell.com and www.tacobell.com/livemas, accessed September 2015.

Personality
The unique psychological characteristics that distinguish a person or group.

Personality and Self-Concept. Each person's distinct personality influences his or her buying behavior. **Personality** refers to the unique psychological characteristics that distinguish a person or group. Personality is usually described in terms of traits such as self-confidence, dominance, sociability, autonomy, defensiveness, adaptability, and aggressiveness. Personality can be useful in analyzing consumer behavior for certain product or brand choices.

The idea is that brands also have personalities, and consumers are likely to choose brands with personalities that match their own. A *brand personality* is the specific mix of human traits that may be attributed to a particular brand. One researcher identified five brand personality traits: *sincerity* (down-to-earth, honest, wholesome, and cheerful), *excitement* (daring, spirited, imaginative, and up-to-date), *competence* (reliable, intelligent, and successful), *sophistication* (glamorous, upper class, charming), and *ruggedness* (outdoorsy and tough). "Your personality determines what you consume, what TV shows you watch, what products you buy, and [most] other decisions you make," says one consumer behavior expert.[20]

Most well-known brands are strongly associated with one particular trait: the Ford F150 with "ruggedness," Apple with "excitement," the *Washington Post* with "competence," Method with "sincerity," and Gucci with "class and sophistication." Hence, these brands will attract persons who are high on the same personality traits. JetBlue projects a "human" personality. Its recent "Air on the Side of Humanity" marketing campaign affirms that the airline cares about people. The airline is committed to award-winning customer service "for everyone, at every stage of the flying experience." ›› It has been "inspiring humanity since 2000."[21]

›› **Brand personality: Customers are likely to choose brands with personalities that match their own. JetBlue projects a "human" personality. It's been "inspiring humanity since 2000."**
JetBlue

Many marketers use a concept related to personality—a person's *self-concept* (also called *self-image*). The idea is that people's possessions contribute to and reflect their identities—that is, "we are what we consume." Thus, to understand consumer behavior, marketers must first understand the relationship between consumer self-concept and possessions.

Psychological Factors

A person's buying choices are further influenced by four major psychological factors: *motivation, perception, learning,* and *beliefs and attitudes*.

Motivation. A person has many needs at any given time. Some are biological, arising from states of tension such as hunger, thirst, or discomfort. Others are psychological, arising from the need for recognition, esteem, or belonging. A need becomes a motive when it is aroused to a sufficient level of intensity. A **motive** (or **drive**) is a need that is sufficiently pressing to direct the person to seek satisfaction. Psychologists have developed theories of human motivation. Two of the most popular—the theories of Sigmund Freud and Abraham Maslow—carry quite different meanings for consumer analysis and marketing.

Motive (drive)
A need that is sufficiently pressing to direct the person to seek satisfaction.

Sigmund Freud assumed that people are largely unconscious about the real psychological forces shaping their behavior. His theory suggests that a person's buying decisions are affected by subconscious motives that even the buyer may not fully understand. Thus, an aging baby boomer who buys a sporty BMW convertible might explain that he simply likes the feel of the wind in his thinning hair. At a deeper level, he may be trying to impress others with his success. At a still deeper level, he may be buying the car to feel young and independent again.

Consumers often don't know or can't describe why they act as they do. Thus, many companies employ teams of psychologists, anthropologists, and other social scientists to carry out *motivation research* that probes the subconscious motivations underlying consumers' emotions and behaviors toward brands. One ad agency routinely conducts one-on-one, therapy-like interviews to delve the inner workings of consumers. Another company asks consumers to describe their favorite brands as animals or cars (say, a Mercedes versus a Chevy) to assess the prestige associated with various brands. Still others rely on hypnosis, dream therapy, or soft lights and mood music to plumb the murky depths of consumer psyches.

Such projective techniques might seem pretty goofy, and some marketers dismiss such motivation research as mumbo jumbo. But many marketers use such touchy-feely approaches, now sometimes called *interpretive consumer research*, to dig deeper into consumer psyches and develop better marketing strategies.

Abraham Maslow sought to explain why people are driven by particular needs at particular times. Why does one person spend a lot of time and energy on personal safety and another on gaining the esteem of others? Maslow's answer is that human needs are arranged in a hierarchy, as shown in >> **Figure 5.3**, from the most pressing at the bottom to the least pressing at the top.[22] They include *physiological* needs, *safety* needs, *social* needs, *esteem* needs, and *self-actualization* needs.

A person tries to satisfy the most important need first. When that need is satisfied, it will stop being a motivator, and the person will then try to satisfy the next most important need. For example, starving people (physiological need) will not take an interest in the latest happenings in the art world (self-actualization needs) nor in how they are seen or esteemed by others (social or esteem needs) nor even in whether they are breathing clean air (safety needs). But as each important need is satisfied, the next most important need will come into play.

Perception. A motivated person is ready to act. How the person acts is influenced by his or her own perception of the situation. All of us learn by the flow of information through our five senses: sight, hearing, smell, touch, and taste. However, each of us receives, organizes, and interprets this sensory information in an individual way. **Perception** is the process by which people select, organize, and interpret information to form a meaningful picture of the world.

Perception
The process by which people select, organize, and interpret information to form a meaningful picture of the world.

People can form different perceptions of the same stimulus because of three perceptual processes: selective attention, selective distortion, and selective retention. People are exposed to a great amount of stimuli every day. For example, individuals are exposed to an estimated 3,000 to 5,000 ad messages daily. The cluttered digital environment adds 30 billion online display ads shown each day, 500 million Tweets sent daily, 144,000 hours of

Figure 5.3 Maslow's Hierarchy of Needs

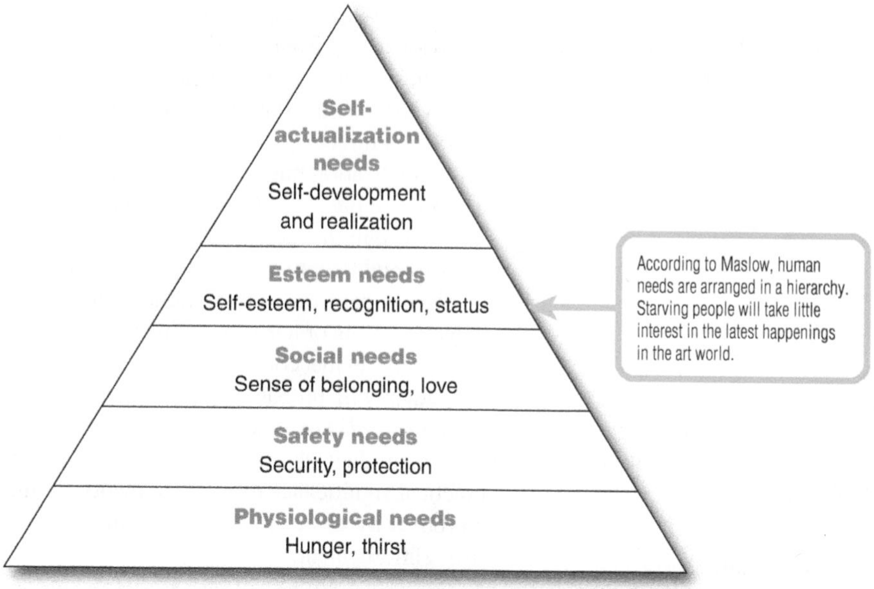

video uploaded daily on YouTube, and 4.75 billion pieces of content shared on Facebook every day.[23] People can't possibly pay attention to all the competing stimuli surrounding them. *Selective attention*—the tendency for people to screen out most of the information to which they are exposed—means that marketers must work especially hard to attract the consumer's attention.

Even noticed stimuli do not always come across in the intended way. Each person fits incoming information into an existing mindset. *Selective distortion* describes the tendency of people to interpret information in a way that will support what they already believe. People also will forget much of what they learn. They tend to retain information that supports their attitudes and beliefs. *Selective retention* means that consumers are likely to remember good points made about a brand they favor and forget good points made about competing brands. Because of selective attention, distortion, and retention, marketers must work hard to get their messages through.

Interestingly, although most marketers worry about whether their offers will be perceived at all, some consumers worry that they will be affected by marketing messages without even knowing it—through *subliminal advertising*. More than 50 years ago, a researcher announced that he had flashed the phrases "Eat popcorn" and "Drink Coca-Cola" on a screen in a New Jersey movie theater every five seconds for 1/300th of a second. He reported that although viewers did not consciously recognize these messages, they absorbed them subconsciously and bought 58 percent more popcorn and 18 percent more Coke. Suddenly advertisers and consumer-protection groups became intensely interested in subliminal perception. Although the researcher later admitted to making up the data, the issue has not died. Some consumers still fear that they are being manipulated by subliminal messages.

Numerous studies by psychologists and consumer researchers have found little or no link between subliminal messages and consumer behavior. Recent brain-wave studies have found that in certain circumstances, our brains may register subliminal messages. However, it appears that subliminal advertising simply doesn't have the power attributed to it by its critics. One classic ad from the American Association of Advertising Agencies pokes fun at subliminal advertising. "So-called 'subliminal advertising' simply doesn't exist," says the ad. "Overactive imaginations, however, most certainly do."

This classic ad from the American Association of Advertising Agencies pokes fun at subliminal advertising. "So-called 'subliminal advertising' simply doesn't exist," says the ad. "Overactive imaginations, however, most certainly do."

American Association of Advertising Agencies

Learning Changes in an individual's behavior arising from experience.

Learning. When people act, they learn. **Learning** describes changes in an individual's behavior arising from experience. Learning theorists say that most human behavior is learned. Learning occurs through the interplay of drives, stimuli, cues, responses, and reinforcement.

A *drive* is a strong internal stimulus that calls for action. A drive becomes a motive when it is directed toward a particular *stimulus object*. For example, a person's drive for self-actualization might motivate him or her to look into buying a camera. The consumer's response to the idea of buying a camera is conditioned by the surrounding cues. *Cues* are minor stimuli that determine when, where, and how the person responds. For example, the person might spot several camera brands in a shop window, hear of a special sale price, or discuss cameras with a friend. These are all cues that might influence a consumer's *response* to his or her interest in buying the product.

Suppose the consumer buys a Nikon camera. If the experience is rewarding, the consumer will probably use the camera more and more, and his or her response will be *reinforced*. Then the next time he or she shops for a camera, or for binoculars or some similar product, the probability is greater that he or she will buy a Nikon product. The practical significance of learning theory for marketers is that they can build up demand for a product by associating it with strong drives, using motivating cues, and providing positive reinforcement.

Belief A descriptive thought that a person holds about something.

Attitude A person's relatively consistently favorable or unfavorable evaluations, feelings, and tendencies toward an object or idea.

Beliefs and Attitudes. Through doing and learning, people acquire beliefs and attitudes. These, in turn, influence their buying behavior. A **belief** is a descriptive thought that a person holds about something. Beliefs may be based on real knowledge, opinion, or faith and may or may not carry an emotional charge. Marketers are interested in the beliefs that people formulate about specific products and services because these beliefs make up product and brand images that affect buying behavior. If some of the beliefs are wrong and prevent purchase, the marketer will want to launch a campaign to correct them.

People have attitudes regarding religion, politics, clothes, music, food, and almost everything else. **Attitude** describes a person's relatively consistent evaluations, feelings, and tendencies toward an object or idea. Attitudes put people into a frame of mind of liking or disliking things, of moving toward or away from them. Our camera buyer may hold attitudes such as "Buy the best," "The Japanese make the best camera products in the world," and "Creativity and self-expression are among the most important things in life." If so, the Nikon camera would fit well into the consumer's existing attitudes.

Attitudes are difficult to change. A person's attitudes fit into a pattern; changing one attitude may require difficult adjustments in many others. Thus, a company should usually try to fit its products into existing attitude patterns rather than attempt to change attitudes. Of course, there are exceptions. For example, trying to convince parents that their children would actually like onions—that's right, onions—seems like an uphill battle against prevailing attitudes. Convincing the children themselves seems like an even bigger challenge. However, the Vidalia Onion Committee (VOC), formed to promote one of Georgia's most important agricultural products, managed to do just that:[24]

> It can be hard selling children on the idea of eating onions. Onions have a strong smell, they can make you cry, and many kids simply refuse to eat them. So to help change these attitudes, the >> VOC employed Shrek, the famous ogre from the hugely popular animated films. The inspiration came from a scene in the first Shrek film, in which Shrek explains ogres to his friend, Donkey. "Onions have layers, ogres have layers," says Shrek. "Ogres are like onions. End of story." The result was a national now-classic "Ogres and Onions" marketing campaign, launched to coincide with both the onion harvest and the premiere of the latest Shrek film. The campaign featured giant Shrek placards in grocery store aisles alongside bags of Vidalia onions on which Shrek asked, "What do ogres and onions have in common?" At the VOC Web site, Shrek offered kid-friendly Vidalia onion recipes. The award-winning campaign soon had kids clamoring for onions, and surprised and delighted parents responded. Sales of bagged Vidalia onions increased almost 30 percent for the season.

>> Attitudes and beliefs are difficult to change; however, the Vidalia Onion Committee's award-winning Ogres and Onions campaign made believers of children and their delighted parents. Sales of bagged Vidalia onions shot up 30 percent.

Vidalia Onion Committee. Vidalia® is a registered certification mark of Georgia Department of Agriculture.

We can now appreciate the many forces acting on consumer behavior. The consumer's choice results from the complex interplay of cultural, social, personal, and psychological factors.

Author Comment
The actual purchase decision is part of a much larger buying process—from recognizing a need through how you feel after making the purchase. Marketers want to be involved throughout the entire buyer decision process.

The Buyer Decision Process

Now that we have looked at the influences that affect buyers, we are ready to look at how consumers make buying decisions. **Figure 5.4** shows that the buyer decision process consists of five stages: *need recognition, information search, evaluation of alternatives,* the *purchase decision*, and *postpurchase behavior*. Clearly, the buying process starts long before the actual purchase and continues long after. Marketers need to focus on the entire buying process rather than on the purchase decision only.

Figure 5.4 suggests that consumers pass through all five stages with every purchase in a considered way. But buyers may pass quickly or slowly through the buying decision process. And in more routine purchases, consumers often skip or reverse some of the stages. Much depends on the nature of the buyer, the product, and the buying situation. A person buying a regular brand of toothpaste would recognize the need and go right to the purchase decision, skipping information search and evaluation. However, we use the model in Figure 5.4 because it shows all the considerations that arise when a consumer faces a new and complex purchase situation.

Need recognition: This ad for *National Geographic Kids* reminds parents that, in these days of game consoles and social networking sites, they need to be certain that their children "make room for nature."

Courtesy National Geographic Society, Fox P2 Advertising, and Lung Animation

Need Recognition

The buying process starts with *need recognition*—the buyer recognizes a problem or need. The need can be triggered by *internal stimuli* when one of the person's normal needs—for example, hunger or thirst—rises to a level high enough to become a drive. A need can also be triggered by *external stimuli*. For example, an advertisement or a discussion with a friend might get you thinking about buying a new car. At this stage, the marketer should research consumers to find out what kinds of needs or problems arise, what brought them about, and how they led the consumer to this particular product.

Information Search

An interested consumer may or may not search for more information. If the consumer's drive is strong and a satisfying product is near at hand, he or she is likely to buy it then. If not, the consumer may store the need in memory or undertake an *information search* related to the need. For example, once you've decided you need a new car, at the least, you will probably pay more attention to car ads, cars owned by friends, and car conversations. Or you may actively search online, talk with friends, and gather information in other ways.

Consumers can obtain information from any of several sources. These include *personal sources* (family, friends, neighbors, acquaintances), *commercial sources* (advertising, salespeople, dealer and manufacturer Web and mobile sites, packaging, displays), *public sources* (mass media, consumer rating organizations, social media, online searches,

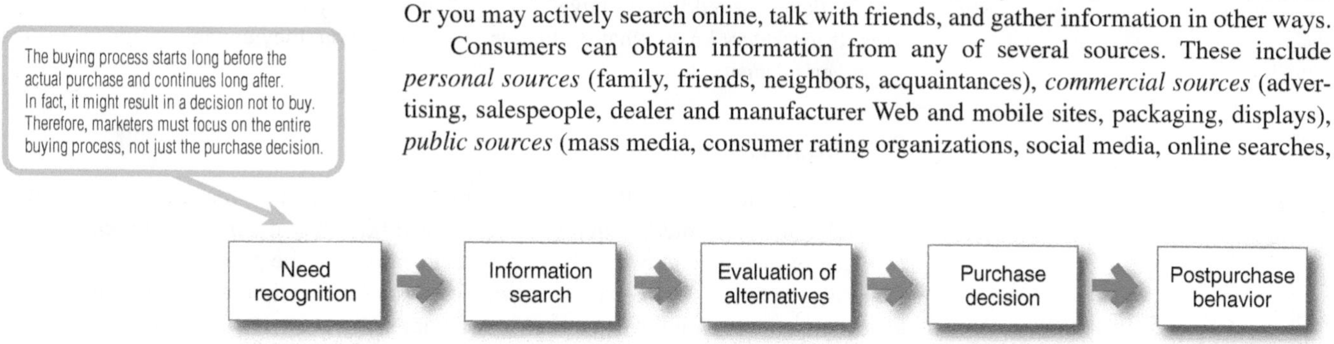

Figure 5.4 Buyer Decision Process

and peer reviews), and *experiential sources* (examining and using the product). The relative influence of these information sources varies with the product and the buyer.

Traditionally, consumers have received the most information about a product from commercial sources—those controlled by the marketer. The most effective sources, however, tend to be personal. Commercial sources normally *inform* the buyer, but personal sources *legitimize* or *evaluate* products for the buyer. Few advertising campaigns can be as effective as a next-door neighbor leaning over the fence and raving about a wonderful experience with a product you are considering.

Increasingly, that "neighbor's fence" is a digital one. Today, consumers share product opinions, images, and experiences freely across social media. And buyers can find an abundance of user-generated reviews alongside the products they are considering at sites ranging from Amazon.com or BestBuy.com to Yelp, TripAdvisor, Epinions, and Epicurious. Although individual user reviews vary widely in quality, an entire body of reviews often provides a reliable product assessment—straight from the fingertips of people like you who've actually purchased and experienced the product.

As more information is obtained, the consumer's awareness and knowledge of the available brands and features increase. In your car information search, you may learn about several brands that are available. The information might also help you to drop certain brands from consideration. A company must design its marketing mix to make prospects aware of and knowledgeable about its brand. It should carefully identify consumers' sources of information and the importance of each source.

Evaluation of Alternatives

We have seen how consumers use information to arrive at a set of final brand choices. Next, marketers need to know about *alternative evaluation*, that is, how consumers process information to choose among alternative brands. Unfortunately, consumers do not use a simple and single evaluation process in all buying situations. Instead, several evaluation processes are at work.

How consumers go about evaluating purchase alternatives depends on the individual consumer and the specific buying situation. In some cases, consumers use careful calculations and logical thinking. At other times, the same consumers do little or no evaluating. Instead, they buy on impulse and rely on intuition. Sometimes consumers make buying decisions on their own; sometimes they turn to friends, online reviews, or salespeople for buying advice.

Suppose you've narrowed your car choices to three brands. And suppose that you are primarily interested in four attributes—price, style, operating economy, and performance. By this time, you've probably formed beliefs about how each brand rates on each attribute. Clearly, if one car rated best on all the attributes, the marketer could predict that you would choose it. However, the brands will no doubt vary in appeal. You might base your buying decision mostly on one attribute, and your choice would be easy to predict. If you wanted style above everything else, you would buy the car that you think has the most style. But most buyers consider several attributes, each with different importance. By knowing the importance that you assigned to each attribute, the marketer could predict and affect your car choice more reliably.

Marketers should study buyers to find out how they actually evaluate brand alternatives. If marketers know what evaluative processes go on, they can take steps to influence the buyer's decision.

Purchase Decision

In the evaluation stage, the consumer ranks brands and forms purchase intentions. Generally, the consumer's *purchase decision* will be to buy the most preferred brand, but two factors can come between the purchase *intention* and the purchase *decision*. The first factor is the *attitudes of others*. If someone important to you thinks that you should buy the lowest-priced car, then the chances of you buying a more expensive car are reduced.

The second factor is *unexpected situational factors*. The consumer may form a purchase intention based on factors such as expected income, expected price, and expected product benefits. However, unexpected events may change the purchase intention. For example, the economy might take a turn for the worse, a close competitor might drop its price, or a friend might report being disappointed in your preferred car. Thus, preferences and even purchase intentions do not always result in an actual purchase choice.

Postpurchase Behavior

The marketer's job does not end when the product is bought. After purchasing the product, the consumer will either be satisfied or dissatisfied and will engage in *postpurchase behavior* of interest to the marketer. What determines whether the buyer is satisfied or dissatisfied with a purchase? The answer lies in the relationship between the *consumer's expectations* and the product's *perceived performance*. If the product falls short of expectations, the consumer is disappointed; if it meets expectations, the consumer is satisfied; if it exceeds expectations, the consumer is delighted. The larger the negative gap between expectations and performance, the greater the consumer's dissatisfaction. This suggests that sellers should promise only what their brands can deliver so that buyers are satisfied.

Cognitive dissonance
Buyer discomfort caused by postpurchase conflict.

Almost all major purchases, however, result in **cognitive dissonance**, or discomfort caused by postpurchase conflict. After the purchase, consumers are satisfied with the benefits of the chosen brand and are glad to avoid the drawbacks of the brands not bought. However, every purchase involves compromise. So consumers feel uneasy about acquiring the drawbacks of the chosen brand and about losing the benefits of the brands not purchased. Thus, consumers feel at least some postpurchase dissonance for every purchase.

Why is it so important to satisfy the customer? Customer satisfaction is a key to building profitable relationships with consumers—to keeping and growing consumers and reaping their customer lifetime value. Satisfied customers buy a product again, talk favorably to others about the product, pay less attention to competing brands and advertising, and buy other products from the company. >> Many marketers go beyond merely *meeting* the expectations of customers—they aim to *delight* customers.

>> Postpurchase cognitive dissonance: Postpurchase customer satisfaction is a key to building profitable customer relationships. Most marketers go beyond merely *meeting* the customer expectations—they aim to *delight* customers.

Dusit/Shutterstock

A dissatisfied consumer responds differently. Bad word of mouth often travels farther and faster than good word of mouth. It can quickly damage consumer attitudes about a company and its products. But companies cannot simply wait for dissatisfied customers to volunteer their complaints. Most unhappy customers never tell the company about their problems. Therefore, a company should measure customer satisfaction regularly. It should set up systems that *encourage* customers to complain. In this way, the company can learn how well it is doing and how it can improve.

By studying the overall buyer decision process, marketers may be able to find ways to help consumers move through it. For example, if consumers are not buying a new product because they do not perceive a need for it, marketing might launch advertising messages that trigger the need and show how the product solves customers' problems. If customers know about the product but are not buying because they hold unfavorable attitudes toward it, marketers must find ways to change either the product or consumer perceptions.

New product
A good, service, or idea that is perceived by some potential customers as new.

Author Comment
Here we look at some special considerations in *new product* buying decisions.

The Buyer Decision Process for New Products

We now look at how buyers approach the purchase of new products. A **new product** is a good, service, or idea that is perceived by some potential customers as new. It may have been around for a while, but our interest is in how consumers learn about products for the

Adoption process
The mental process through which an individual passes from first hearing about an innovation to final adoption.

first time and make decisions on whether to adopt them. We define the **adoption process** as the mental process through which an individual passes from first learning about an innovation to final adoption. *Adoption* is the decision by an individual to become a regular user of the product.[25]

Stages in the Adoption Process

Consumers go through five stages in the process of adopting a new product:

Awareness. The consumer becomes aware of the new product but lacks information about it.

Interest. The consumer seeks information about the new product.

Evaluation. The consumer considers whether trying the new product makes sense.

Trial. The consumer tries the new product on a small scale to improve his or her estimate of its value.

Adoption. The consumer decides to make full and regular use of the new product.

This model suggests that marketers should think about how to help consumers move through these stages. >> For example, if SodaStream finds that many consumers are evaluating its home soda makers favorably but are still tentative about buying one, it might work with Bed Bath & Beyond and other retailers to offer a sale price that gets consumers over the decision hump.

To help car buyers past purchase-decision hurdles following the economic meltdown in 2008, Hyundai offered a unique Hyundai Assurance Plan. It promised buyers who financed or leased new Hyundais that they could return them at no cost and with no harm to their credit rating if they lost their jobs or incomes within a year. Sales of the Hyundai Sonata surged 85 percent in the month following the start of the campaign.

>> The adoption process: To help get tentative consumers over the buying decision hump, SodaStream offers sales at retail, rebates, and other buying incentives—here a $20 cashback rebate offer.

Image courtesy of SodaStream

Individual Differences in Innovativeness

People differ greatly in their readiness to try new products. In each product area, there are "consumption pioneers" and early adopters. Other individuals adopt new products much later. People can be classified into the adopter categories shown in **>> Figure 5.5.**[26] As shown by the curve, after a slow start, an increasing number of people adopt the new product. As successive groups of consumers adopt the innovation, it eventually reaches its cumulative saturation level. Innovators are defined as the first 2.5 percent of buyers to adopt a new idea (those beyond two standard deviations from mean adoption time); the early adopters are the next 13.5 percent (between one and two standard deviations); and then come early mainstream, late mainstream, and lagging adopters.

The five adopter groups have differing values. *Innovators* are venturesome—they try new ideas at some risk. *Early adopters* are guided by respect—they are opinion leaders in their communities and adopt new ideas early but carefully. *Early mainstream* adopters are deliberate—although they rarely are leaders, they adopt new ideas before the average person. *Late mainstream* adopters are skeptical—they adopt an innovation only after a majority of people have tried it. Finally, *lagging adopters* are tradition bound—they are suspicious of changes and adopt the innovation only when it has become something of a tradition itself.

This adopter classification suggests that an innovating firm should research the characteristics of innovators and early adopters in their product categories and direct initial marketing efforts toward them.

Figure 5.5 Adopter Categories Based on Relative Time of Adoption of Innovations

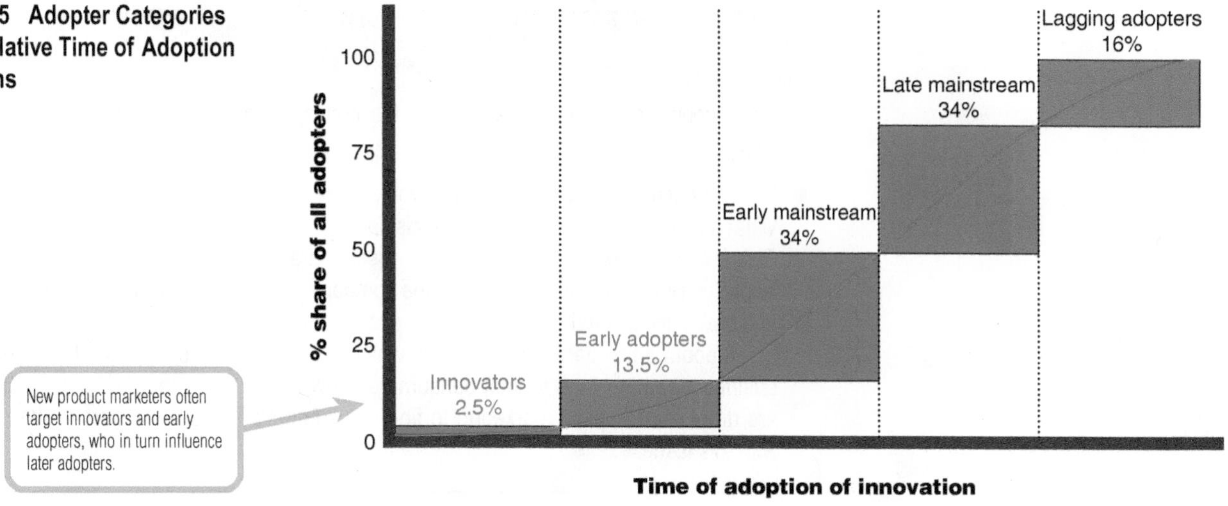

Influence of Product Characteristics on Rate of Adoption

The characteristics of the new product affect its rate of adoption. Some products catch on almost overnight. For example, Apple's iPod, iPhone, and iPad flew off retailers' shelves at an astounding rate from the day they were first introduced. Others take a longer time to gain acceptance. For example, all-electric cars were first introduced in the United States in 2010, led by models such as the Nissan Leaf and the Tesla Model S. However, electric vehicles still account for far less than 1 percent of total U.S. automobile sales. It will likely be years or even decades before they replace the gasoline-powered cars.[27]

Five characteristics are especially important in influencing an innovation's rate of adoption. For example, consider the characteristics of all-electric vehicles in relation to their rate of adoption:

Relative advantage. The degree to which the innovation appears superior to existing products. All-electric cars require no gas and use clean, less costly energy. This accelerated their rate of adoption. However, they have limited driving range before recharging and cost more initially, which will slow the adoption rate.

Compatibility. The degree to which the innovation fits the values and experiences of potential consumers. Electric cars are driven the same way as gas-powered cars. However, they are not compatible with the nation's current refueling network. Plug-in electric charging stations are few and far between. Increased adoption will depend on the development of a national network of recharging stations, which may take considerable time.

Complexity. The degree to which the innovation is difficult to understand or use. Electric cars are not different or complex to drive, which will help to speed up adoption. However, the "conceptual complexity" of the new technologies and concerns about how well they will likely work slow down the adoption rate.

Divisibility. The degree to which the innovation may be tried on a limited basis. Consumers can test-drive electric cars, a positive for the adoption rate. However, current high prices to own and fully experience these new technologies will likely slow adoption.

Communicability. The degree to which the results of using the innovation can be observed or described to others. To the extent that electric cars lend themselves to demonstration and description, their use will spread faster among consumers.

Other characteristics influence the rate of adoption, such as initial and ongoing costs, risk and uncertainty, and social approval. The new product marketer must research all these factors when developing the new product and its marketing program.

LINKING THE CONCEPTS

Here's a good place to pause and apply the concepts you've examined in the first part of this chapter.

- Think about a specific major purchase you've made recently. What buying process did you follow? What major factors influenced your decision?
- Pick a company or brand that we've discussed in a previous chapter—Nike, Starbucks, Netflix, Apple, JetBlue, or another. How does the company you chose use its understanding of customers and their buying behavior to build better customer relationships?
- Think about a company such as Intel, which sells its products to computer makers and other businesses rather than to final consumers. How would Intel's marketing to business customers differ from Apple's marketing to final consumers? The second part of the chapter deals with this issue.

Author Comment
Now that we've looked at consumer markets and buyer behavior, let's dig into business markets and buyer behavior. Thinking ahead, how are they the same? How are they different?

Business Markets and Business Buyer Behavior

In one way or another, most large companies sell to other organizations. Companies such as Boeing, DuPont, IBM, Caterpillar, and countless other firms sell *most* of their products to other businesses. Even large consumer-products companies, which make products used by final consumers, must first sell their products to other businesses. For example, General Mills makes many familiar consumer brands—Big G cereals (Cheerios, Wheaties, Trix, Chex, Total, Fiber One), baking products (Pillsbury, Betty Crocker, Bisquick, Gold Medal flour), snacks (Nature Valley, Bugles, Chex Mix), Yoplait yogurt, Häagen-Dazs ice cream, and many others. But to sell these products to consumers, General Mills must first sell them to its wholesaler and retailer customers, who in turn serve the consumer market.

Business buyer behavior
The buying behavior of organizations that buy goods and services for use in the production of other products and services that are sold, rented, or supplied to others.

Business buying process
The process by which business buyers determine which products and services their organizations need to purchase and then find, evaluate, and choose among alternative suppliers and brands.

Business buyer behavior refers to the buying behavior of organizations that buy goods and services for use in the production of other products and services that are sold, rented, or supplied to others. It also includes the behavior of retailing and wholesaling firms that acquire goods to resell or rent to others at a profit. In the **business buying process**, business buyers determine which products and services their organizations need to purchase and then find, evaluate, and choose among alternative suppliers and brands.

Business-to-business (B-to-B) marketers must do their best to understand business markets and business buyer behavior. Then, like businesses that sell to final buyers, they must engage business customers and build profitable relationships with them by creating superior customer value.

Author Comment
Business markets operate "behind the scenes" to most consumers. Most of the things you buy involve many sets of business purchases before you ever see them.

Business Markets

The business market is *huge*. In fact, business markets involve far more dollars and items than do consumer markets. For example, think about the large number of business transactions involved in the production and sale of a single set of Goodyear tires. Various suppliers sell Goodyear the rubber, steel, equipment, and other goods that it needs to produce tires. Goodyear then sells the finished tires to retailers, which in turn sell them to consumers. Thus, many sets of *business* purchases were made for only one set of *consumer* purchases. In addition, Goodyear sells tires as original equipment to manufacturers that install them on new vehicles and as replacement tires to companies that maintain their own fleets of company cars, trucks, or other vehicles.

In some ways, business markets are similar to consumer markets. Both involve people who assume buying roles and make purchase decisions to satisfy needs. However, business markets differ in many ways from consumer markets. The main differences are in *market structure and demand*, the *nature of the buying unit*, and the *types of decisions and the decision process* involved.

Market Structure and Demand

The business marketer normally deals with *far fewer but far larger buyers* than the consumer marketer does. Even in large business markets, a few buyers often account for most of the purchasing. For example, when Goodyear sells replacement tires to final consumers, its potential market includes millions of car owners around the world. But its fate in business markets depends on getting orders from only a handful of large automakers.

Further, many business markets have *inelastic and more fluctuating demand.* The total demand for many business products is not much affected by price changes, especially in the short run. A drop in the price of leather will not cause shoe manufacturers to buy much more leather unless it results in lower shoe prices that, in turn, increase consumer demand for shoes. And the demand for many business goods and services tends to change more—and more quickly—than does the demand for consumer goods and services. A small percentage increase in consumer demand can cause large increases in business demand.

Derived demand
Business demand that ultimately comes from (derives from) the demand for consumer goods.

Finally, business demand is **derived demand**—it ultimately derives from the demand for consumer goods. For example, demand for Gore-Tex fabrics derives from consumer purchases of outdoor apparel brands made from Gore-Tex. And consumers buy Corning's Gorilla Glass only when they buy laptops, tablets, and smartphones with Gorilla Glass screens from producers such as Apple, Samsung, Lenovo, Dell, HP, Sony, and Microsoft. If consumer demand for these end products increases, so does the demand for the Gore-Tex fabrics and the Gorilla Glass they contain.

Therefore, B-to-B marketers sometimes promote their products directly to final consumers to increase business demand. >> For example, Corning's long-running "Tough, yet beautiful" consumer marketing campaign features a family of gorillas who are out to convince final buyers that it makes sense to choose digital devices with screens made of Gorilla Glass rather than a less-tough competitor. Such advertising benefits both Corning and the partner brands that incorporate its durable, scratch-resistant glass. Thanks in part to the consumer marketing campaign, Corning's Gorilla Glass has to date been featured in more than 40 major brands and more than 3 billion devices worldwide.[28]

>> Derived demand: Corning's long-running "Tough, yet beautiful" consumer marketing campaign convinces final users that it makes sense to buy devices with screens made of Gorilla Glass, to the benefit of both Corning and its partner brands.

Photo courtesy Corning Incorporated.

Nature of the Buying Unit

Compared with consumer purchases, a business purchase usually involves *more decision participants* and a *more professional purchasing effort.* Often, business buying is done by trained purchasing agents who spend their working lives learning how to buy better. The more complex the purchase, the more likely it is that several people will participate in the decision-making process. Buying committees composed of technical experts and top management are common in the buying of major goods. Beyond this, B-to-B marketers now face a new breed of higher-level, better-trained supply managers. Therefore, companies must have well-trained marketers and salespeople to deal with these well-trained buyers.

Types of Decisions and the Decision Process

Business buyers usually face *more complex* buying decisions than do consumer buyers. Business purchases often involve large sums of money, complex technical and economic considerations, and interactions among people at many levels of the buyer's organization. The business buying process also tends to be *longer* and *more formalized.* Large business purchases usually call for detailed product specifications, written purchase orders, careful supplier searches, and formal approval.

Finally, in the business buying process, the buyer and seller are often much *more dependent* on each other. B-to-B marketers may roll up their sleeves and work closely with customers during all stages of the buying process—from helping customers define problems to finding solutions to supporting after-sale operation. In the short run, sales go to suppliers who meet buyers' immediate product and service needs. In the long run, however, business-to-business marketers keep customers by meeting current needs *and* by partnering with them to help solve their problems. For example, consider the buying process for GE's diesel locomotives:[29]

Business buyer decision process: In selling locomotives with an average list price of $2.2 million, GE's real challenge is to win buyers' business by building day-in, day-out, year-in, year-out partnerships with them based on close collaboration.

GE Transportation

> GE locomotives might not seem glamorous to you, but they are beautiful brutes to those who buy and use them. Performance plays an important role in the locomotive buyer's decision, and GE locomotives outperform competing engines on most important dimensions. But performance is only part of the buying equation. Selling locomotives with an average list price of $2.2 million involves a tortuously long buying process, dozens or even hundreds of decision makers, and layer upon layer of subtle and not-so-subtle buying influences.
>
> GE's real challenge is to win buyers' business by building day-in, day-out, year-in, year-out, problem-solving partnerships with them based on close collaboration. More than just "selling locomotives," GE wins contracts by partnering strategically with customers to help them translate performance into moving passengers and freight more efficiently and reliably. For example, CSX Transportation (CSXT), one of GE's largest customers, has purchased hundreds of GE locomotives in recent years. According to a CSXT purchasing executive, the company "evaluates many cost factors before awarding... a locomotive contract. Environmental impact, fuel consumption, reliability, serviceability [are] all key elements in this decision." But as important is "the value of our ongoing partnership with GE."

Supplier development
Systematic development of networks of supplier-partners to ensure a dependable supply of products and materials for use in making products or reselling them to others.

As in GE's case, in recent years, relationships between most customers and suppliers have been changing from downright adversarial to close and chummy. In fact, many customer companies are now practicing **supplier development**, systematically developing networks of supplier-partners to ensure a dependable supply of the products and materials that they use in making their own products or reselling to others. For example, Walmart doesn't have a "Purchasing Department"; it has a "Supplier Development Department." The giant retailer knows that it can't just rely on spot suppliers who might be available when needed. Instead, Walmart manages a huge network of supplier-partners that help provide the hundreds of billions of dollars of goods that it sells to its customers each year.

Author Comment
Business buying decisions can range from routine to incredibly complex, involving only a few or very many decision makers and buying influences.

Business Buyer Behavior

At the most basic level, marketers want to know how business buyers will respond to various marketing stimuli. **Figure 5.6** shows a model of business buyer behavior. In this model, marketing and other stimuli affect the buying organization and produce certain buyer responses. To design good marketing strategies, marketers must understand what happens within the organization to turn stimuli into purchase responses.

Within the organization, buying activity consists of two major parts: the *buying center*, composed of all the people involved in the buying decision, and the *buying decision process*. The model shows that the buying center and the buying decision process are influenced by internal organizational, interpersonal, and individual factors as well as external environmental factors.

The model in Figure 5.6 suggests four questions about business buyer behavior: What buying decisions do business buyers make? Who participates in the business buying process? What are the major influences on buyers? How do business buyers make their buying decisions?

Major Types of Buying Situations

Straight rebuy
A business buying situation in which the buyer routinely reorders something without any modifications.

There are three major types of buying situations.[30] In a **straight rebuy**, the buyer reorders something without any modifications. It is usually handled on a routine basis by the purchasing department. To keep the business, "in" suppliers try to maintain customer

Figure 5.6 A Model of Business Buyer Behavior

In some ways, business markets are similar to consumer markets—this model looks a lot like the model of consumer buyer behavior presented in Figure 5.1. But there are some major differences, especially in the nature of the buying unit, the types of decisions made, and the decision process.

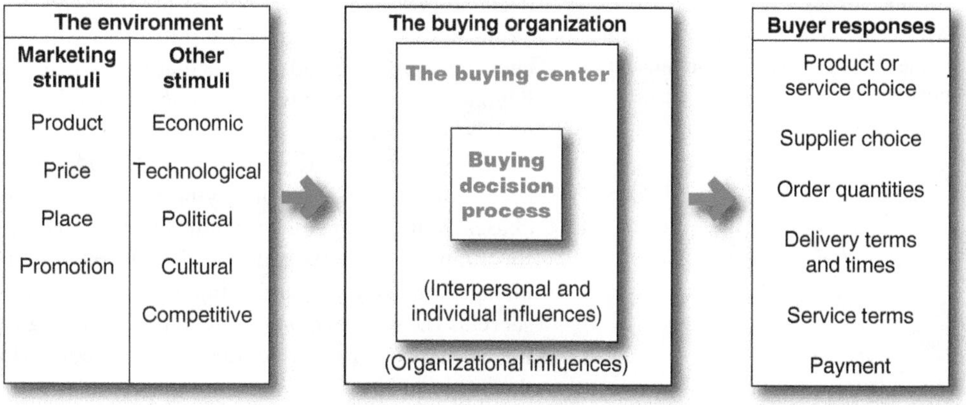

engagement and product and service quality. "Out" suppliers try to find new ways to add value or exploit dissatisfaction so that the buyer will consider them.

Modified rebuy
A business buying situation in which the buyer wants to modify product specifications, prices, terms, or suppliers.

New task
A business buying situation in which the buyer purchases a product or service for the first time.

Systems selling (or solutions selling)
Buying a complete solution to a problem from a single seller, thus avoiding all the separate decisions involved in a complex buying situation.

In a **modified rebuy**, the buyer wants to modify product specifications, prices, terms, or suppliers. The "in" suppliers may become nervous and feel pressured to put their best foot forward to protect an account. "Out" suppliers may see the modified rebuy situation as an opportunity to make a better offer and gain new business.

A company buying a product or service for the first time faces a **new task** situation. In such cases, the greater the cost or risk, the larger the number of decision participants and the greater the company's efforts to collect information. The new task situation is the marketer's greatest opportunity and challenge. The marketer not only tries to reach as many key buying influences as possible but also provides help and information. The buyer makes the fewest decisions in the straight rebuy and the most in the new task decision.

Many business buyers prefer to buy a complete solution to a problem from a single seller rather than buying separate products and services from several suppliers and putting them together. The sale often goes to the firm that engages business customers deeply and provides the most complete *system* for meeting a customer's needs and solving its problems. Such **systems selling** (or **solutions selling**) is often a key business marketing strategy for winning and holding accounts. Consider IBM and its customer Six Flags Entertainment Corporation:[31]

Solutions selling: Delivering a fun and safe experience for Six Flags guests requires careful and effective management of thousands of park assets across its 19 regional theme parks. IBM works hand in hand with Six Flags to provide not just software but a complete solution.

Mathew Imaging/WireImage/Getty Images

Six Flags operates 19 regional theme parks across North America featuring exciting rides and water attractions, world-class roller coasters, and special shows and concerts. To deliver a fun and safe experience for guests, Six Flags must carefully and effectively manage thousands of park assets—from rides and equipment to buildings and other facilities. Six Flags needed a tool for managing all those assets efficiently and effectively across its far-flung collection of parks. So it turned to IBM, which has software—called Maximo Asset Management software—that handles that very problem well.

But IBM didn't just hand the software over to Six Flags with best wishes for happy implementation. Instead, IBM's Maximo Professional Services group combined the software with an entire set of services designed to get and keep the software up and running. IBM worked hand in hand with Six Flags to customize the application and strategically implement and run it across Six Flags's far-flung facilities, along with on-site immersion training and planning workshops. Thus, IBM isn't just selling the software; it's selling a complete solution to Six Flags's complex asset management problem.

Participants in the Business Buying Process

Who does the buying of the trillions of dollars' worth of goods and services needed by business organizations? The

Buying center
All the individuals and units that play a role in the purchase decision-making process.

decision-making unit of a buying organization is called its **buying center**. It consists of all the individuals and units that play a role in the business purchase decision-making process. This group includes the actual users of the product or service, those who make the buying decision, those who influence the buying decision, those who do the actual buying, and those who control buying information.

The buying center is not a fixed and formally identified unit within the buying organization. It is a set of buying roles assumed by different people for different purchases. Within the organization, the size and makeup of the buying center will vary for different products and for different buying situations. For some routine purchases, one person—say, a purchasing agent—may assume all the buying center roles and serve as the only person involved in the buying decision. For more complex purchases, the buying center may include 20 or 30 people from different levels and departments in the organization.

The buying center concept presents a major marketing challenge. The business marketer must learn who participates in the decision, each participant's relative influence, and what evaluation criteria each decision participant uses. This can be difficult.

The buying center usually includes some obvious participants who are involved formally in the buying decision. For example, the decision to buy a corporate jet will probably involve the company's CEO, the chief pilot, a purchasing agent, some legal staff, a member of top management, and others formally charged with the buying decision. It may also involve less obvious, informal participants, some of whom may actually make or strongly affect the buying decision. Sometimes, even the people in the buying center are not aware of all the buying participants. For example, the decision about which corporate jet to buy may actually be made by a corporate board member who has an interest in flying and who knows a lot about airplanes. This board member may work behind the scenes to sway the decision. Many business buying decisions result from the complex interactions of ever-changing buying center participants.

Major Influences on Business Buyers

Business buyers are subject to many influences when they make their buying decisions. Some marketers assume that the major influences are economic. They think buyers will favor the supplier who offers the lowest price or the best product or the most service. They concentrate on offering strong economic benefits to buyers. Such economic factors are very important to most buyers, especially in a tough economy. However, business buyers actually respond to both economic and personal factors. Far from being cold, calculating, and impersonal, business buyers are human and social as well. They react to both reason and emotion.

Today, most B-to-B marketers recognize that emotion plays an important role in business buying decisions. Consider this example:[32]

>> **Emotions play a role in business buying. Ads like this one from USG's "It's Your World. Build It." corporate marketing campaign pack a decidedly emotional wallop.**
USG Corportion

>> USG Corporation is a leading manufacturer of gypsum wallboard and other building materials for the construction and remodeling industries. Given its construction contractor, architect, and builder audience, you might expect USG's B-to-B ads to focus heavily on performance features and benefits, such as strength, impact resistance, ease of installation, and costs. USG does promote these benefits. However, it's most recent corporate marketing campaign, built around its new "It's Your World. Build It." positioning, packs a decidedly more emotional wallop. The campaign focuses not on how USG's products perform but on what the company and its products stand for and mean. For example, one split-image ad shows excited children building a sand castle on one side and a worker at a construction site, hard hat in hand, on the other. The headline states: "As children we imagine great kingdoms. Build them." As one analyst concludes, "Building materials and emotion aren't something you would link immediately, but the [USG] campaign captures a powerful sentiment about the human need to build."

>> Figure 5.7 lists various groups of influences on business buyers—environmental, organizational, interpersonal, and individual. Business buyers are heavily influenced by factors in the current and expected *economic environment*, such as the level of primary demand, the economic outlook, and the cost of money. Another environmental factor is the *supply* of key materials. Business buyers also are affected by *supply, technological, political*, and *competitive* developments in the environment. Finally, *culture and customs* can strongly influence business buyer reactions to the marketer's behavior and strategies, especially in the international marketing environment. The business buyer must watch these factors, determine how they will affect the buyer, and try to turn these challenges into opportunities.

Organizational factors are also important. Each buying organization has its own objectives, strategies, structure, systems, and procedures, and the business marketer must understand these factors well. Questions such as these arise: How many people are involved in the buying decision? Who are they? What are their evaluative criteria? What are the company's policies and limits on its buyers?

The buying center usually includes many participants who influence each other, so *interpersonal factors* also influence the business buying process. However, it is often difficult to assess such interpersonal factors and group dynamics. Buying center participants do not wear tags that label them as "key decision maker" or "not influential." Nor do buying center participants with the highest rank always have the most influence. Participants may influence the buying decision because they control rewards and punishments, are well liked, have special expertise, or have a special relationship with other important participants. Interpersonal factors are often very subtle. Whenever possible, business marketers must try to understand these factors and design strategies that take them into account.

Each participant in the business buying decision process brings in personal motives, perceptions, and preferences. These *individual factors* are affected by personal characteristics such as age, income, education, professional identification, personality, and attitudes toward risk. Also, buyers have different buying styles. Some may be technical types who make in-depth analyses of competitive proposals before choosing a supplier. Other buyers may be intuitive negotiators who are adept at pitting the sellers against one another for the best deal.

The Business Buyer Decision Process

>> Figure 5.8 lists the eight stages of the business buyer decision process.[33] Buyers who face a new task buying situation usually go through all stages of the buying process. Buyers making modified or straight rebuys, in contrast, may skip some of the stages. We will examine these steps for the typical new task buying situation.

Problem Recognition. The buying process begins when someone in the company recognizes a problem or need that can be met by acquiring a specific product or service. *Problem recognition* can result from internal or external stimuli. Internally, the company may decide to launch a new product that requires new production equipment and materials. Or a machine may break down and need new parts. Perhaps a purchasing manager is unhappy with a current supplier's product quality, service, or prices. Externally, the buyer may get

>> Figure 5.7 Major Influences on Business Buyer Behavior

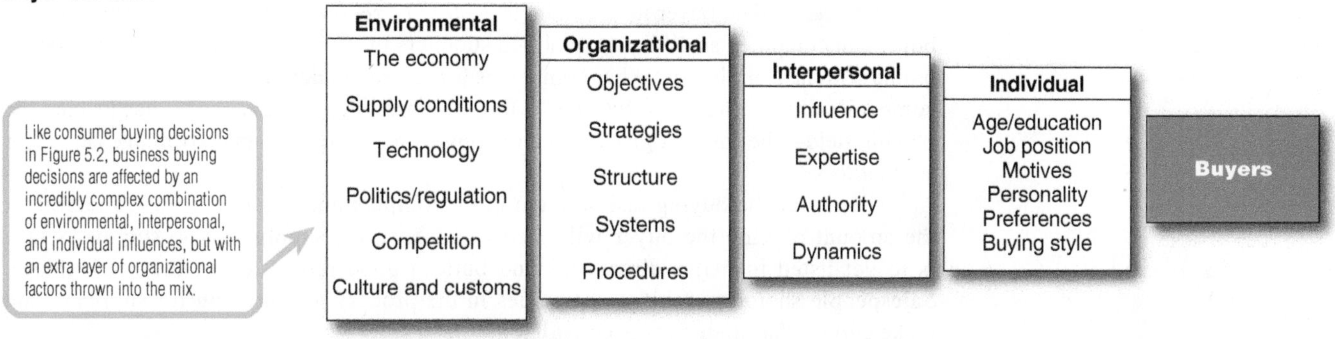

Figure 5.8 Stages of the Business Buyer Decision Process

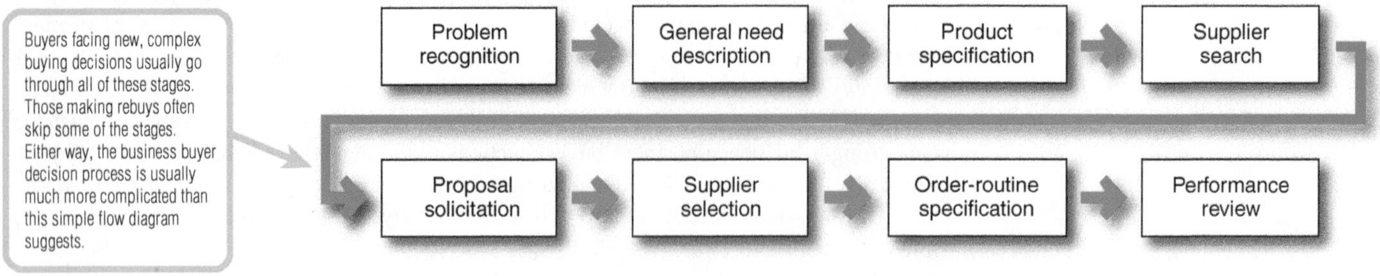

some new ideas at a trade show, see an ad or Web site, or receive a call from a salesperson who offers a better product or a lower price.

In fact, in their advertising, business marketers often alert customers to potential problems and then show how their products and services provide solutions. For example, consulting firm Accenture's award-winning "High Performance. Delivered." B-to-B ads do this. One Accenture ad points to the urgent need for a business to get up to speed with digital technology. "Accenture Digital can help you attract more customers." the ad states, showing moths drawn to a brightly lit smartphone screen. Accenture's solution: "Our industry expertise, coupled with our integrated capabilities across interactive, analytics, and mobility, can help you take advantage of the opportunity to innovate and compete." Other ads in the series tell success stories of how Accenture has helped client companies recognize and solve a variety of other problems.[34]

Problem recognition: This Accenture ad alerts customers to the problem of getting up to speed with digital technology, then suggests a solution. It promises "High Performance. Delivered."

Accenture

General Need Description. Having recognized a need, the buyer next prepares a *general need description* that describes the characteristics and quantity of the needed item. For standard items, this process presents few problems. For complex items, however, the buyer may need to work with others—engineers, users, consultants—to define the item. The team may want to rank the importance of reliability, durability, price, and other attributes desired in the item. In this phase, the alert business marketer can help the buyers define their needs and provide information about the value of different product characteristics.

Product Specification. The buying organization next develops the item's technical *product specifications*, often with the help of a value analysis engineering team. *Product value analysis* is an approach to cost reduction in which components are studied carefully to determine if they can be redesigned, standardized, or made by less costly methods of production. The team decides on the best product characteristics and specifies them accordingly. Sellers, too, can use value analysis as a tool to help secure a new account. By showing buyers a better way to make an object, outside sellers can turn straight rebuy situations into new task situations that give them a chance to obtain new business.

Supplier Search. The buyer now conducts a *supplier search* to find the best vendors. The buyer can compile a small list of qualified suppliers by reviewing trade directories, doing online searches, or phoning other companies for recommendations. Today, more and more companies are turning to the Internet to find suppliers. For marketers, this has leveled the playing field—the Internet gives smaller suppliers many of the same advantages as larger competitors.

The newer the buying task and the more complex and costly the item, the greater the amount of time the buyer will spend searching for suppliers. The supplier's task is to get listed in major directories and build a good reputation in the marketplace. Salespeople should watch for companies in the process of searching for suppliers and make certain that their firm is considered.

Proposal Solicitation. In the *proposal solicitation* stage of the business buying process, the buyer invites qualified suppliers to submit proposals. In response, some suppliers will refer the buyer to its Web site or promotional materials or send a salesperson to call on the prospect. However, when the item is complex or expensive, the buyer will usually require detailed written proposals or formal presentations from each potential supplier.

Business marketers must be skilled in researching, writing, and presenting proposals in response to buyer proposal solicitations. Proposals should be marketing documents, not just technical documents. Presentations should inspire confidence and should make the marketer's company stand out from the competition.

Supplier Selection. The members of the buying center now review the proposals and select a supplier or suppliers. During *supplier selection*, the buying center often will draw up a list of the desired supplier attributes and their relative importance. Such attributes include product and service quality, reputation, on-time delivery, ethical corporate behavior, honest communication, and competitive prices. The members of the buying center will rate suppliers against these attributes and identify the best suppliers.

Buyers may attempt to negotiate with preferred suppliers for better prices and terms before making the final selections. In the end, they may select a single supplier or a few suppliers. Many buyers prefer multiple sources of supplies to avoid being totally dependent on one supplier and to allow comparisons of prices and performance of several suppliers over time. Today's supplier development managers want to develop a full network of supplier-partners that can help the company bring more value to its customers.

Order-Routine Specification. The buyer now prepares an *order-routine specification.* It includes the final order with the chosen supplier or suppliers and lists items such as technical specifications, quantity needed, expected delivery time, return policies, and warranties. In the case of maintenance, repair, and operating items, buyers may use blanket contracts rather than periodic purchase orders. A blanket contract creates a long-term relationship in which the supplier promises to resupply the buyer as needed at agreed prices for a set time period.

Many large buyers now practice *vendor-managed inventory*, in which they turn over ordering and inventory responsibilities to their suppliers. Under such systems, buyers share sales and inventory information directly with key suppliers. The suppliers then monitor inventories and replenish stock automatically as needed. For example, most major suppliers to large retailers such as Walmart, Target, Home Depot, and Lowe's assume vendor-managed inventory responsibilities.

Performance Review. In this stage, the buyer reviews supplier performance. The buyer may contact users and ask them to rate their satisfaction. The *performance review* may lead the buyer to continue, modify, or drop the arrangement. The seller's job is to monitor the same factors used by the buyer to make sure that the seller is giving the expected satisfaction.

In all, the eight-stage buying-process model shown in Figure 5.8 provides a simple view of the business buying as it might occur in a new task buying situation. However, the actual process is usually much more complex. In the modified rebuy or straight rebuy situation, some of these stages would be compressed or bypassed. Each organization buys in its own way, and each buying situation has unique requirements.

Different buying center participants may be involved at different stages of the process. Although certain buying-process steps usually do occur, buyers do not always follow them in the same order, and they may add other steps. Often, buyers will repeat certain stages of the process. Finally, a customer relationship might involve many different types of purchases ongoing at a given time, all in different stages of the buying process. The seller must manage the total *customer relationship*, not just individual purchases.

Engaging Business Buyers with Digital and Social Marketing

As in every other area of marketing, the explosion of information technologies and online, mobile, and social media has changed the face of the B-to-B buying and marketing process. In the following sections, we discuss two important technology advancements: *e-procurement and online purchasing* and *B-to-B digital and social media marketing*.

E-procurement and Online Purchasing

E-procurement
Purchasing through electronic connections between buyers and sellers—usually online.

Advances in information technology have dramatically affected the face of the B-to-B buying process. Online and electronic purchasing, often called **e-procurement**, has grown rapidly in recent years. Virtually unknown two decades ago, online purchasing is standard procedure for most companies today. In turn, business marketers can connect with customers online to share marketing information, sell products and services, provide customer support services, and maintain ongoing customer relationships.

Companies can do e-procurement in any of several ways. They can conduct *reverse auctions*, in which they put their purchasing requests online and invite suppliers to bid for the business. Or they can engage in online *trading exchanges*, through which companies work collectively to facilitate the trading process. Companies also can conduct e-procurement by setting up their own *company buying sites*. For example, GE operates a company trading site on which it posts its buying needs and invites bids, negotiates terms, and places orders. Or companies can create *extranet links* with key suppliers. For instance, they can create direct procurement accounts with suppliers such as Dell or Staples through which company buyers can purchase equipment, materials, and supplies directly. »Staples operates a business-to-business procurement division called Staples Advantage, which serves the office supplies and services buying needs of businesses of any size, from 20 employees to the *Fortune* 1000.

Business-to-business e-procurement yields many benefits. First, it shaves transaction costs and results in more efficient purchasing for both buyers and suppliers. E-procurement reduces the time between order and delivery. And an online-powered purchasing program eliminates the paperwork associated with traditional requisition and ordering procedures and helps an organization keep better track of all purchases. Finally, beyond the cost and time savings, e-procurement frees purchasing people from a lot of drudgery and paperwork. Instead, they can focus on more-strategic issues, such as finding better supply sources and working with suppliers to reduce costs and develop new products.

» **Online buying: Staples operates a business-to-business procurement division called Staples Advantage, which serves the office supplies and services buying needs of business customers of any size.**

Staples the Office Superstore, LLC

The rapidly expanding use of e-procurement, however, also presents some problems. For example, at the same time that the Internet makes it possible for suppliers and customers to share business data and even collaborate on product design, it can also erode decades-old customer–supplier relationships. Many buyers now use the power of the Internet to pit suppliers against one another and search out better deals, products, and turnaround times on a purchase-by-purchase basis.

Business-to-Business Digital and Social Media Marketing

In response to customers' rapid shift toward online buying, today's B-to-B marketers are now using a wide range of digital and social media marketing approaches—from Web sites, blogs, mobile apps, e-newsletters, and proprietary online networks to mainstream social media such as Facebook, LinkedIn, YouTube, Google+, and Twitter—to engage customers and manage customer relationships anywhere, any time. The use of digital and social media channels in business marketing isn't just growing, it's exploding. Digital and social media marketing have rapidly become *the* new space for engaging

B-to-B social media: Machining tool manufacturer Makino engages its business customers through extensive digital and social marketing—everything from proprietary online communities and webinars to Facebook, YouTube, and Twitter.

Courtesy of Makino

business customers. Consider Makino, a leading manufacturer of metal cutting and machining technology:

> There's a hot new video on YouTube these days, featured at the Makino Machine Tools YouTube channel. It shows Makino's D500 five-axis vertical machining center in action, with metal chips flying as the machinery mills a new industrial part. Sound exciting? Probably not to you. But to the right industrial customer, the video is downright spellbinding. The video has been viewed more than 33,000 times, mostly by current or prospective Makino customers. For B-to-B marketer Makino, that's great exposure.[35]
>
> Makino employs a wide variety of digital and social media initiatives to engage customers. For example, it hosts an ongoing series of industry-specific webinars that position the company as an industry thought leader. It produces about three webinars each month and offers a library of more than 100 on topics ranging from optimizing machine tool performance to discovering new metal-cutting processes. The Webinars help to build Makino's customer database, generate leads, build customer relationships, and prepare the way for salespeople by providing relevant information and educating customers online. Makino also uses Twitter, Facebook, Google+, and YouTube extensively to engage customers and prospects with the latest Makino innovations and events and to vividly demonstrate the company's machines in action.

Compared with traditional media and sales approaches, digital and social media can create greater customer engagement and interaction. B-to-B marketers know that they aren't really targeting *businesses,* they are targeting *individuals* in those businesses who affect buying decisions. And today's business buyers are always connected via their digital devices—whether it's PCs, tablets, or smartphones.

Digital and social media play an important role in engaging these always-connected business buyers in a way that personal selling alone cannot. Instead of the old model of sales reps calling on business customers at work or maybe meeting up with them at trade shows, the new digital approaches facilitate anytime, anywhere connections between a wide range of people in the selling and customer organizations. It gives both sellers and buyers more control of and access to important information. B-to-B marketing has always been social network marketing, but today's digital environment offers an exciting array of new networking tools and applications.

MyMarketingLab

If assigned by your instructor, complete the questions marked with the ✪ from the EOC Discussion Questions section in the MyLab. To complete the Marketing by the Numbers problems found in this section, go to your Assignments in the MyLab.

REVIEWING AND EXTENDING THE CONCEPTS

CHAPTER REVIEW AND CRITICAL THINKING

Objectives Review

This chapter is the last of three chapters that address understanding the marketplace and consumers. Here, we've looked closely at *consumer* and *business buyer behavior.* The American consumer market consists of more than 320 million people who consume more than $11 trillion worth of goods and services each year, making it one of the most attractive consumer markets in the world. The business market involves even more dollars and items than the consumer market. Understanding buyer behavior is one of the biggest challenges marketers face.

OBJECTIVE 5-1 Understand the consumer market and the major factors that influence consumer buyer behavior. (pp 134–148)

The *consumer market* consists of all the individuals and households that buy or acquire goods and services for personal consumption. A simple model of consumer behavior suggests that marketing stimuli and other major forces enter the consumer's "black box." This black box has two parts: buyer characteristics and the buyer's decision process. Once in the black box, the inputs result in buyer responses, such as buying attitudes and preferences and purchase behavior.

Consumer buyer behavior is influenced by four key sets of buyer characteristics: cultural, social, personal, and psychological. Understanding these factors can help marketers to identify interested buyers and to shape products and appeals to serve consumer needs better. *Culture* is the most basic determinant of a person's wants and behavior. People in different cultural, subcultural, and social class groups have different product and brand preferences. *Social factors*—such as small group, social network, and family influences—strongly affect product and brand choices, as do *personal characteristics,* such as age, life stage, occupation, economic circumstances, lifestyle, and personality. Finally, consumer buying behavior is influenced by four major sets of *psychological factors*—motivation, perception, learning, and beliefs and attitudes. Each of these factors provides a different perspective for understanding the workings of the buyer's black box.

OBJECTIVE 5-2 Identify and discuss the stages in the buyer decision process. (pp 149–151)

When making a purchase, the buyer goes through a decision process consisting of need recognition, information search, evaluation of alternatives, purchase decision, and postpurchase behavior. During *need recognition,* the consumer recognizes a problem or need that could be satisfied by a product or service. Once the need is recognized, the consumer moves into the *information search* stage. With information in hand, the consumer proceeds to *alternative evaluation* and assesses brands in the choice set. From there, the consumer makes a *purchase decision* and actually buys the product. In the final stage of the buyer decision process, *postpurchase behavior,* the consumer takes action based on satisfaction or dissatisfaction. The marketer's job is to understand the buyer's behavior at each stage and the influences that are operating.

OBJECTIVE 5-3 Describe the adoption and diffusion process for new products. (pp 151–153)

The product *adoption process* is made up of five stages: awareness, interest, evaluation, trial, and adoption. New product marketers must think about how to help consumers move through these stages. With regard to the *diffusion process* for new products, consumers respond at different rates, depending on consumer and product characteristics. Consumers may be innovators, early adopters, early mainstream, late mainstream, or lagging adopters. Each group may require different marketing approaches. Marketers often try to bring their new products to the attention of potential early adopters, especially those who are opinion leaders.

OBJECTIVE 5-4 Define the business market and identify the major factors that influence business buyer behavior. (pp 154–159)

The *business market* is composed of all organizations that buy goods and services for use in the production of other products and services or for the purpose of reselling or renting them to others at a profit. Compared with consumer markets, business markets usually have fewer, larger buyers who are more geographically concentrated. Business demand is derived demand, and the business buying decision usually involves more, and more professional, buyers.

Business buyers make decisions that vary with the three types of *buying situations:* straight rebuys, modified rebuys, and new tasks. The decision-making unit of a buying organization—the *buying center*—can consist of many different persons playing many different roles. The business marketer needs to know the following: Who are the major buying center participants? In what decisions do they exercise influence and to what degree? What evaluation criteria does each decision participant use? The business marketer also needs to understand the major environmental, organizational, interpersonal, and individual influences on the buying process.

OBJECTIVE 5-5 List and define the steps in the business buyer decision process. (pp 159–163)

The *business buyer decision process* itself can be quite involved, with eight basic stages: problem recognition, general need description, product specification, supplier search, proposal solicitation, supplier selection, order-routine specification, and performance review. Buyers who face a new task buying situation usually go through all stages of the buying process. Buyers making modified or straight rebuys may skip some of the stages. Companies must manage the overall customer relationship, which often includes many different buying decisions in various stages of the buying decision process. Recent advances in information and digital technology have given birth to "e-procurement," by which business buyers are purchasing all kinds of products and services online. Business marketers are increasingly connecting with customers online and through digital, mobile, and social media to engage customers, share marketing information, sell products and services, provide customer support services, and maintain ongoing customer relationships.

Key Terms

Objective 5-1
Consumer buyer behavior (p 134)
Consumer market (p 134)

Objective 5-2
Culture (p 135)
Subculture (p 136)
Total market strategy (p 137)
Social class (p 138)
Group (p 138)
Word-of-mouth influence (p 138)
Opinion leader (p 138)
Online social networks (p 139)
Lifestyle (p 143)
Personality (p 145)
Motive (drive) (p 146)
Perception (p 146)
Learning (p 148)
Belief (p 148)
Attitude (p 148)
Cognitive dissonance (p 151)

Objective 5-3
New product (p 151)
Adoption process (p 152)

Objective 5-4
Business buyer behavior (p 154)
Business buying process (p 154)
Derived demand (p 155)
Supplier development (p 156)
Straight rebuy (p 156)
Modified rebuy (p 157)
New task (p 157)
Systems selling (solutions selling) (p 157)
Buying center (p 158)

Objective 5-5
E-procurement (p 162)

Discussion Questions

5-1. Discuss the stages of the consumer buyer decision process and describe how you or your family used this process to make a purchase. (AACSB: Communication; Reflective Thinking)

5-2. Name and describe the stages in the adoption process and discuss the importance of this model for marketers. (AACSB: Communication; Reflective Thinking)

5-3. How does the market structure and demand faced by business marketers differ from that faced by consumer marketers? (AACSB: Communication)

5-4. Compare and contrast the types of business buying situations. (AACSB: Communication; Reflective Thinking)

5-5. Describe how business-to-business marketers use digital and social media channels to engage customers, market their products, and manage customer relationships anywhere. (AACSB: Communication)

Critical Thinking Exercises

5-6. Researchers study the role of personality on consumer purchase behavior. One research project—Beyond the Purchase—offers a range of surveys consumers can take to learn more about their own personalities in general and their consumer personalities in particular. Register at www.beyondthepurchase.org/ and take the "Spending Habits" surveys along with any of the other surveys that interest you. What do these surveys tell you about your general and consumer personality? Do you agree with the findings? Why or why not? (AACSB: Communication; Use of IT; Diversity; Reflective Thinking)

5-7. *Kaizen. Seiri. Seiton. Seiso. Seiketsu. Shitsako. Jishuken.* These Japanese words are related to continuous quality improvement and are applied in supplier development programs, particularly Toyota's. Research Toyota's Production System (TPS) and describe how these concepts are applied in supplier development. (AACSB: Communication; Multicultural and Diversity)

5-8. Business buying occurs worldwide, so marketers need to be aware of cultural factors influencing business customers. In a small group, select a country and develop a multimedia presentation on proper business etiquette and manners, including appropriate appearance, behavior, and communication. Include a map showing the location of the country as well as a description of the country in terms of its demographics, culture, and economic history. (AACSB: Communication; Multicultural and Diversity; Use of IT)

MINICASES AND APPLICATIONS

Online, Mobile, and Social Media Marketing Digital Influencers

Jen Hsieh is a college student with a love for fashion who shares outfits and fashion sense on Jennifhsieh, her fashion blog. Her social influence earned her an invitation to Kate Spade's New York fashion week presentation, after which she blogged, "I had to keep myself from drooling" when describing the collection. Digital influencers like Jen are often paid to write product reviews on their blogs and to post pictures of themselves on sites such as Pinterest and Instagram wearing clothes given to them by the sponsor. Some are given all-expenses-paid trips to events. For example, Olivia Lopez, a personal-style blogger with a site called Lust for Life, was invited by Samsung to the South by Southwest and Lollapalloza music festivals and provided a phone with which to post pictures for her 90,000 Instagram followers. The hashtag "#thenextbigthing," which is used in Samsung's product promotions, was included in her posts. Otherwise, Olivia included no indication that Samsung provided sponsorship.

5-9. Find an example of a blog on a topic that interests you. Are there advertisements on the blog? Does the blogger appear to be sponsored by any companies? Is there information regarding sponsorship? Write a brief report of your observations. (AACSB: Use of IT; Communication; Reflective Thinking)

5-10. Summarize the FTC's disclosure rules on using social media to promote products and services. Does the blogger you reviewed in the previous question follow these rules? Explain. (AACSB: Communication; Reflective Thinking)

Marketing Ethics Business-to-Business Commercial Bribery

The CEO of FalconStor Software directed employees to bribe B-to-B customer JPMorgan Chase executives with more than $300,000 worth of stock options, golf-related perks, gift cards, and gambling vouchers in return for lucrative licensing contracts totaling more than $13 million that pumped up the company's stock price 22 percent. The Department of Justice filed charges under the Travel Act against FalconStor because a FalconStor sales representative traveled with a JPMorgan executive on a lavish entertainment and gambling junket to Hong Kong and Macau. FalconStor must pay $5.8 million in fines and institute corporate compliance reforms before criminal charges can be dropped. But that's not the end of it. The Securities and Exchange Commission (SEC) also filed a complaint claiming FalconStor misled investors by claiming the contracts with customer JPMorgan Chase as vindication of the quality of the company's product. In addition, since the bribery expenses were disguised as employee performance bonuses, promotional expenses, and entertainment expenses, the SEC filed charges under the Foreign Corrupt Practices Act (FCPA).

5-11. Research the Travel Act and the FCPA. Explain how the SEC could file charges under the FCPA if this was not a bribery case involving a foreign government. (AACSB: Communication; Reflective Thinking)

5-12. What would you do if your supervisor directed you to bribe other businesses to obtain contracts? Is there legal protection for employees who report employers' illegal behavior? (AACSB: Communication; Ethical Reasoning)

Marketing by the Numbers Evaluating Alternatives

One way consumers can evaluate alternatives is to identify important attributes and assess how purchase alternatives perform on those attributes. Consider the purchase of a tablet. Each attribute, such as screen size, is given a weight to reflect its level of importance to that consumer. Then the consumer evaluates each alternative on each attribute. For example, in the table below, price (weighted at 0.5) is the most important attribute for this consumer. The consumer believes that brand C performs best on price, rating it 7 (higher ratings indicate higher performance). Brand B is perceived as performing the worst on this attribute (rating of 3). Screen size and available apps are the consumer's next most important attributes. Operating system is least important.

Attributes	Importance Weight (e)	Alternative Brands A	B	C
Screen size	0.2	4	6	2
Price	0.5	6	3	7
Operating system	0.1	5	5	4
Apps available	0.2	4	6	7

A score can be calculated for each brand by multiplying the importance weight for each attribute by the brand's score on that attribute. These weighted scores are then summed to determine the score for that brand. For example, $\text{Score}_{\text{Brand A}} = (0.2\times4)+(0.5\times6)+(0.1\times5)+(0.2\times4)=0.8+3.0+0.5+0.8 = 5.1$. This consumer will select the brand with the highest score.

5-13. Calculate the scores for brands B and C. Which brand would this consumer likely choose? (AACSB: Communication; Analytic Reasoning)

5-14. Which brand is this consumer least likely to purchase? Discuss two ways the marketer of this brand can enhance consumer likelihood of purchasing its brand. (AACSB: Communication; Reflective Thinking; Analytic Reasoning)

Video Case IMG Worldwide

IMG Worldwide is the world's largest sports entertainment media company. In years past, IMG was all about professional golf and tennis marketing. But today, IMG handles sales and marketing activities for 70 to 80 colleges, making college sports marketing the company's highest-growth business. In short, IMG handles anything and everything that touches the college sports consumer short of actually playing games on the court or field.

Although you might think that all college sports fans are created equal, IMG finds that nothing could be further from the truth. How different fans consume sports and sports-related activities is affected by geographical, generational, and institutional factors. IMG focuses on comprehensively understanding the process that consumers go through to view or attend a sporting event. It then connects with consumers at each and every stage.

After viewing the video featuring IMG Worldwide, answer the following questions:

5-15. What "product" is a college athletics department selling?

5-16. Discuss how a college sports fan might go through the buying decision process, providing examples for each stage.

5-17. Of the four sets of factors affecting consumer behavior, which most strongly affects how college sports fans consume a sport?

Company Cases 5 UPS/1 FedEx/7 Target

See Appendix 1 for cases appropriate for this chapter. **Case 5, UPS: "We Love Logistics"—Put UPS to Work for You and You'll Love Logistics Too.** Business buying decisions are influenced by numerous factors that go way beyond dollars and cents. UPS recognizes the value business clients place on providing full-service logistics solutions. **Case 1, FedEx: Making Every Customer Experience Outstanding.** Businesses and consumers have various needs when it comes to shipping letters and packages. From the time FedEx opened for business more than 40 years ago, the company strategy has been built on a foundation of obsessive customer focus and meeting those needs at every stage. **Case 7, Target: Where Store Brands Offer More Than Low Prices.** So many factors influence the decisions consumers make. Target understands this and has focused on making the purchase decision easy with a comprehensive strategy based on store brands.

MyMarketingLab

If assigned by your instructor, complete these writing sections from your Assignments in the MyLab.

5-18. Discuss how lifestyle influences consumers' buying behavior and how marketers measure lifestyle. (AACSB: Communication; Reflective Thinking)

5-19. Describe the characteristics of a new product that affect its rate of adoption. Which characteristics will affect how quickly the new digital and social media services described above will be accepted by consumers in the United States? (AACSB: Written and Oral Communication; Reflective Thinking)

6 Customer Value-Driven Marketing Strategy

Creating Value for Target Customers

CHAPTER ROAD MAP Objective Outline

OBJECTIVE 6-1 Define the major steps in designing a customer value-driven marketing strategy: market segmentation, targeting, differentiation, and positioning. Customer Value-Driven Marketing Strategy (170)

OBJECTIVE 6-2 List and discuss the major bases for segmenting consumer and business markets. Market Segmentation (170–178)

OBJECTIVE 6-3 Explain how companies identify attractive market segments and choose a market-targeting strategy. Market Targeting (179–185)

OBJECTIVE 6-4 Discuss how companies differentiate and position their products for maximum competitive advantage. Differentiation and Positioning (187–196)

Previewing the Concepts

So far, you've learned what marketing is and about the importance of understanding consumers and the marketplace. With that as a background, you're now ready to delve deeper into marketing strategy and tactics. This chapter looks further into key customer value-driven marketing strategy decisions—dividing up markets into meaningful customer groups (*segmentation*), choosing which customer groups to serve (*targeting*), creating market offerings that best serve targeted customers (*differentiation*), and positioning the offerings in the minds of consumers (*positioning*). The chapters that follow explore the tactical marketing tools—the four Ps—by which marketers bring these strategies to life.

To open our discussion of segmentation, targeting, differentiation, and positioning, let's look at Dunkin' Donuts. Dunkin' has expanded rapidly in recent years into a national powerhouse, on par with Starbucks. But Dunkin' is no Starbucks. In fact, it doesn't want to be. It targets a very different kind of customer with a very different value proposition. Grab yourself a cup of coffee and read on.

First Stop

Dunkin' Donuts: Targeting the Average Joe

A few years back, Dunkin' Donuts paid dozens of faithful customers in cities around the country $100 a week to buy coffee at Starbucks instead. At the same time, the coffee chain paid Starbucks customers to make the opposite switch. When it later debriefed the two groups, Dunkin' says it found them so polarized that company researchers dubbed them "tribes," each of which loathed the very things that made the other tribe loyal to their coffee shop. Dunkin' fans viewed Starbucks as pretentious and trendy, whereas Starbucks loyalists saw Dunkin' as plain and unoriginal. "I don't get it," one Dunkin' regular told researchers after visiting Starbucks. "If I want to sit on a couch, I stay at home."

»» Dunkin' Donuts targets everyday Joes who just don't get what Starbucks is all about. Its targeting and positioning are pretty well summed up in its long-running ad slogan "America Runs on Dunkin'."

Tim Boyle/Getty Images

Dunkin' Donuts has rapidly expanded into a national coffee powerhouse, on par with Starbucks, the nation's largest coffee chain. But the research confirmed a simple fact: Dunkin' is *not* Starbucks. In fact, it doesn't want to be. To prosper, Dunkin' must have its own clear vision of just which customers it wants to serve and how. Dunkin' and Starbucks target very different customers who want very different things from their favorite coffee shops. Starbucks is strongly positioned as a sort of high-brow "third place"—outside the home and office—featuring couches, eclectic music, and art-splashed walls. Dunkin' has a decidedly more low-brow, "everyman" kind of appeal.

Dunkin' Donuts's research showed that its brand fans were largely bewildered and turned off by the atmosphere at Starbucks. They groused that crowds of laptop users made it difficult to find a seat. They didn't like Starbucks's "tall," "grande," and "venti" lingo for small, medium, and large coffees. And they couldn't understand why anyone would pay so much for a cup of coffee. "It was almost as though they were a group of Martians talking about a group of Earthlings," says an executive from Dunkin's advertising agency. The Starbucks customers that Dunkin' paid to switch were equally uneasy in Dunkin' shops. "The Starbucks people couldn't bear that they weren't special anymore," says the ad executive.

Such opposing opinions aren't surprising, given the differences in the two stores' customers. Dunkin's customers include more middle-income blue- and white-collar workers across all age, race, and income demographics. By contrast, Starbucks targets a higher income, more professional group. But Dunkin' researchers concluded that it was more the ideal, rather than income, that set the two tribes apart: Dunkin's tribe members want to be part of a crowd, whereas members of the Starbucks tribe want to stand out as individuals. "You could open a Dunkin' Donuts right next to Starbucks and get two completely different types of consumers," says one retailing expert.

Dunkin' Donuts built its positioning on serving simple fare at reasonable prices to working-class customers. It gained a reputation as a morning pit stop where everyday folks could get their daily donut and caffeine fix. But in recent years, to broaden its appeal and fuel expansion, the chain has been moving upscale—a bit, but not too far. It has spiffed up its stores and added new menu items, such as lattes and non-breakfast items like a steak sandwich and breaded chicken sandwich with barbecue sauce. Dunkin' has also made dozens of store and atmosphere redesign changes, big and small, ranging from adding free Wi-Fi, digital menu boards, and more electrical outlets for laptops and smartphones to playing relaxing background music. And Dunkin' franchisees can now redecorate their stores in any of four Starbucks-esque color schemes, including "Dark Roast," "Cappuccino Blend," and "Jazz Brew," which features "dark orange and brown cozy booth seating, as well as hanging light fixtures that lend a soft glow to wall murals printed with words such as 'break,' 'fresh' and 'quality.'"

As it inches upscale, however, Dunkin' Donuts is being careful not to alienate its traditional customer base. There are no couches in the remodeled stores. Dunkin' even renamed a new hot sandwich a "stuffed melt" after customers complained that calling it a "panini" was too fancy; it then dropped it altogether when faithful customers thought it was too messy. "We're walking [a fine] line," says the chain's vice president of consumer insights. "The thing about the Dunkin' tribe is, they see through the hype."

Dunkin' Donuts targets the "Dunkin' tribe"—not the Starbucks coffee snob but the average Joe. Dunkin' isn't like Starbucks; it doesn't want to be.

Over the past several years, both Dunkin' Donuts and Starbucks have grown rapidly, each targeting its own tribe of customers and riding the wave of America's growing thirst for coffee. Now, both are looking for more growth by convincing "grab-and-go" morning customers to visit later in the day and stick around longer. Although still smaller than Starbucks—which captures a 36 percent U.S. market share versus Dunkin's roughly 24 percent share—Dunkin' is currently the nation's fastest-growing snack and coffee chain. It hopes that the recent repositioning and upgrades will help keep that momentum going. Dunkin' plans to add at least 4,000 more U.S. stores in by 2020.

Again, however, in refreshing its stores and positioning, Dunkin' Donuts has stayed true to the needs and preferences of the Dunkin' tribe. Dunkin' is "not going after the Starbucks coffee snob," says one analyst, it's "going after the average Joe." So far so good. For seven years running, Dunkin' Donuts has ranked number one in the coffee category in a leading customer loyalty and engagement survey, ahead of number-two Starbucks. According to the survey, Dunkin' Donuts was the top brand for consistently meeting or exceeding customer expectations with respect to taste, quality, and customer service.

Dunkin' Donuts' targeting and positioning are pretty well summed up in its long-running ad slogan "America Runs on Dunkin'." No longer just a morning pit stop, Dunkin now bills itself as America's favorite all-day, everyday stop for coffee and baked goods. "We remain committed to keeping America running with our great coffee, baked goods, and snacks served in a friendly environment at a great value," says Dunkin's chief global marketing officer. Nothing too fancy—just meeting the everyday, all-day needs of the Dunkin' tribe.[1]

Market segmentation
Dividing a market into distinct groups of buyers who have different needs, characteristics, or behaviors and who might require separate marketing strategies or mixes.

Market targeting (targeting)
Evaluating each market segment's attractiveness and selecting one or more segments to serve.

Differentiation
Actually differentiating the market offering to create superior customer value.

Positioning
Arranging for a market offering to occupy a clear, distinctive, and desirable place relative to competing products in the minds of target consumers.

Companies today recognize that they cannot appeal to all buyers in the marketplace—or at least not to all buyers in the same way. Buyers are too numerous, widely scattered, and varied in their needs and buying practices. Moreover, companies themselves vary widely in their abilities to serve different market segments. Instead, like Dunkin' Donuts, companies must identify the parts of the market they can serve best and most profitably. They must design customer-driven marketing strategies that build the right relationships with the right customers. Thus, most companies have moved away from mass marketing and toward *target marketing:* identifying market segments, selecting one or more of them, and developing products and marketing programs tailored to each.

>> **Figure 6.1** shows the four major steps in designing a customer value-driven marketing strategy. In the first two steps, the company selects the customers that it will serve. **Market segmentation** involves dividing a market into distinct groups of buyers who have different needs, characteristics, or behaviors and who might require separate marketing strategies or mixes. The company identifies different ways to segment the market and develops profiles of the resulting market segments. **Market targeting** (or **targeting**) consists of evaluating each market segment's attractiveness and selecting one or more market segments to serve.

In the final two steps, the company decides on a value proposition—how it will create value for target customers. **Differentiation** involves actually differentiating the firm's market offering to create superior customer value. **Positioning** consists of arranging for a market offering to occupy a clear, distinctive, and desirable place relative to competing products in the minds of target consumers. We discuss each of these steps in turn.

Author Comment
Market segmentation addresses the first simple-sounding marketing question: What customers will we serve?

Market Segmentation

Buyers in any market differ in their wants, resources, locations, buying attitudes, and buying practices. Through market segmentation, companies divide large, diverse markets into smaller segments that can be reached more efficiently and effectively with products and services that match their unique needs. In this section, we discuss four important segmentation topics: segmenting consumer markets, segmenting business markets, segmenting international markets, and the requirements for effective segmentation.

>> **Figure 6.1 Designing a Customer Value-Driven Market Strategy**

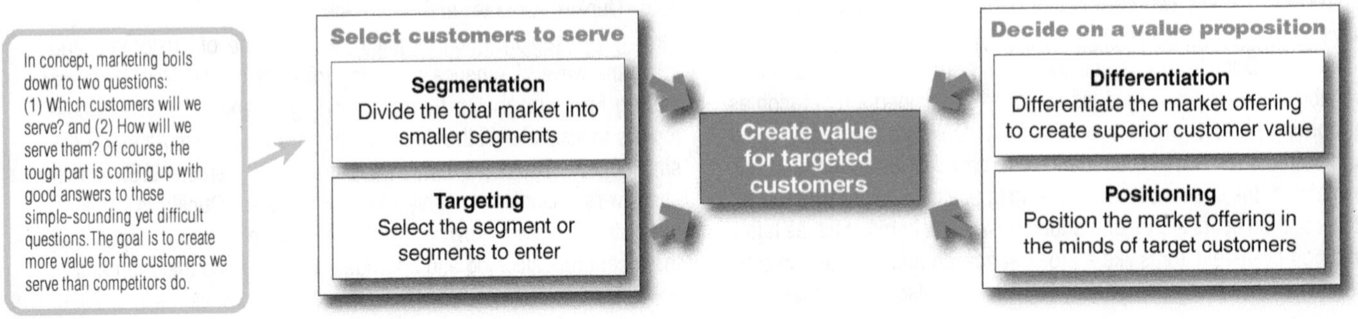

Segmenting Consumer Markets

There is no single way to segment a market. A marketer has to try different segmentation variables, alone and in combination, to find the best way to view market structure. **Table 6.1** outlines variables that might be used in segmenting consumer markets. Here we look at the major *geographic, demographic, psychographic,* and *behavioral* variables.

Geographic Segmentation

Geographic segmentation Dividing a market into different geographical units, such as nations, states, regions, counties, cities, or even neighborhoods.

Geographic segmentation calls for dividing the market into different geographical units, such as nations, regions, states, counties, cities, or even neighborhoods. A company may decide to operate in one or a few geographical areas or operate in all areas but pay attention to geographical differences in needs and wants. Moreover, many companies today are localizing their products, services, advertising, promotion, and sales efforts to fit the needs of individual regions, cities, and neighborhoods.

Geographic segmentation: Target is now opening smaller-format, conveniently located CityTarget and TargetExpress stores designed to fit into densely packed urban neighborhoods.

ZUMA Press, Inc/Alamy

For example, many large retailers—from Target and Walmart to Kohl's and Staples—are now opening smaller-format stores designed to fit the needs of densely packed urban neighborhoods not suited to their typical large suburban superstores. Target's CityTarget stores average about half the size of a typical Super Target; its TargetExpress stores are even smaller at about one-fifth the size of a big-box outlet. These smaller, conveniently located stores carry a more limited assortment of goods that meet the needs of urban residents and commuters, such as groceries, home essentials, beauty products, and consumer electronics. They also offer pick-up-in-store services and a pharmacy.[2]

Beyond adjusting store size, many retailers also localize product assortments and services. For example, department store chain Macy's has a localization program called MyMacy's in which merchandise is customized under 69 different geographical districts. At stores around the country, Macy's sales clerks record local shopper requests and pass them along to district managers. In turn, blending the customer requests with store transaction data, the district managers customize the mix of merchandise in their stores. So, for instance, Macy's stores in Michigan stock more locally made Sanders chocolate candies. In Orlando, Macy's carries more swimsuits in stores near waterparks and more twin bedding in stores near condominium rentals. The chain stocks extra coffee percolators in its Long Island stores, where it sells more of the 1960s must-haves than anywhere else in the country. In all, the "MyMacy's" strategy is to meet the needs of local markets, making the giant retailer seem smaller and more in touch.[3]

Table 6.1 Major Segmentation Variables for Consumer Markets

Segmentation Variable	Examples
Geographic	Nations, regions, states, counties, cities, neighborhoods, population density (urban, suburban, rural), climate
Demographic	Age, life-cycle stage, gender, income, occupation, education, religion, ethnicity, generation
Psychographic	Social class, lifestyle, personality
Behavioral	Occasions, benefits, user status, usage rate, loyalty status

Demographic Segmentation

Demographic segmentation Dividing the market into segments based on variables such as age, life-cycle stage, gender, income, occupation, education, religion, ethnicity, and generation.

Demographic segmentation divides the market into segments based on variables such as age, life-cycle stage, gender, income, occupation, education, religion, ethnicity, and generation. Demographic factors are the most popular bases for segmenting customer groups. One reason is that consumer needs, wants, and usage rates often vary closely with demographic variables. Another is that demographic variables are easier to measure than most other types of variables. Even when marketers first define segments using other bases, such as benefits sought or behavior, they must know a segment's demographic characteristics to assess the size of the target market and reach it efficiently.

Age and life-cycle segmentation Dividing a market into different age and life-cycle groups.

Age and Life-Cycle Stage. Consumer needs and wants change with age. Some companies use **age and life-cycle segmentation**, offering different products or using different marketing approaches for different age and life-cycle groups. For example, Kraft's Oscar Mayer brand markets Lunchables, convenient prepackaged lunches for children. To extend the substantial success of Lunchables, however, Oscar Mayer later introduced Lunchables Uploaded, a version designed to meet the tastes and sensibilities of teenagers. Most recently, the brand launched an adult version, but with the more adult-friendly name P3 (Portable Protein Pack). Now, consumers of all ages can enjoy what is rapidly becoming one of America's favorite noontime meals.

Other companies offer brands that target specific age or life-stage groups. For example, whereas most tablet makers have been busy marketing their devices to grown-ups, Amazon has spotted a tinier tablet market. Feedback from parents suggested that they were handing their entertainment-packed Kindle Fire tablet over to their young children for entertainment, education, and babysitting purposes. To tap this young-family market, Amazon introduced FreeTime Unlimited, a multimedia subscription service targeted toward three- to eight-year-olds. Complete with parental controls, the service features "Endless kid stuff. No grownup stuff." It provides access to a treasure trove of G-rated movies, games, and books, including premium content from Nickelodeon, Disney, Sesame Street, and DC Comics. Not only does FreeTime Unlimited generate revenues for Amazon, it helps sell more Kindle Fire tablets to young families.[4]

Gender segmentation Dividing a market into different segments based on gender.

Marketers must be careful to guard against stereotypes when using age and life-cycle segmentation. For example, although some 80-year-olds fit the stereotypes of doddering shut-ins with fixed incomes, others ski and play tennis. Similarly, whereas some 40-year-old couples are sending their children off to college, others are just beginning new families. Thus, age is often a poor predictor of a person's life cycle, health, work or family status, needs, and buying power.

Gender segmentation: GoldieBlox markets engineering toys for girls. "Move over Barbie, there's a new girl in town. And she's wearing overalls and construction boots."

GoldieBlox, Inc.

Gender. **Gender segmentation** has long been used in marketing clothing, cosmetics, toiletries, toys, and magazines. For example, P&G was among the first to use gender segmentation with Secret, a deodorant brand specially formulated for a woman's chemistry, packaged and advertised to reinforce the female image.

More recently, the men's personal care industry has exploded, and many cosmetics brands that previously catered mostly to women—from L'Oréal, Nivea, and Sephora to Unilever's Dove brand—now successfully market men's lines. For example, Dove's Men+Care line calls itself "The authority on man maintenance." The brand provides a full line of body washes ("skin care built in"), body bars ("fight skin dryness"), antiperspirants ("tough on sweat, not on skin"), face care ("take better care of your face"), and hair care ("3X stronger hair").[5]

Going in the other direction, GoldieBlox markets a collection of engineering toys for girls. Designed by a female engineer from Stanford University, the brand's goal is "to get girls building" and to inspire a future generation of female engineers. Aimed at girls 5 to 9 years old, GoldieBlox consists of storybooks and construction sets that require young girls to solve a series of construction challenges. Initially funded by more than $250,000 raised via crowdfunding platform Kickstarter, the innovative product has recently won two Toy Industry Foundation Toy of the Year awards—Educational and People's Choice. As one writer notes, "Move over Barbie, there's a new girl in town. And she's wearing overalls and construction boots."[6]

Income segmentation
Dividing a market into different income segments.

Income. The marketers of products and services such as automobiles, clothing, cosmetics, financial services, and travel have long used **income segmentation**. Many companies target affluent consumers with luxury goods and convenience services. Other marketers use high-touch marketing programs to court the well-to-do. Upscale retailer Saks Fifth Avenue provides exclusive services to its elite clientele of Fifth Avenue Club members, some of whom spend as much as $150,000 to $200,000 a year on clothing and accessories from Saks alone. For example, Fifth Avenue Club members have access to a Saks Personal Stylist. The fashion-savvy, well-connected personal consultant gets to know and helps to shape each client's personal sense of style, then guides her "through the maze of fashion must-haves." The Personal Stylist puts the customer first. For example, if Saks doesn't carry one of those must-haves that the client covets, the personal stylist will find it elsewhere at no added charge.[7]

However, not all companies that use income segmentation target the affluent. For example, many retailers—such as the Dollar General, Family Dollar, and Dollar Tree store chains—successfully target low- and middle-income groups. The core market for such stores is represented by families with incomes under $30,000. When Family Dollar real estate experts scout locations for new stores, they look for lower-middle-class neighborhoods where people wear less-expensive shoes and drive old cars that drip a lot of oil. With their low-income strategies, dollar stores are now the fastest-growing retailers in the nation.

Psychographic Segmentation

Psychographic segmentation
Dividing a market into different segments based on social class, lifestyle, or personality characteristics.

Psychographic segmentation divides buyers into different segments based on social class, lifestyle, or personality characteristics. People in the same demographic group can have very different psychographic characteristics.

In Chapter 5, we discussed how the products people buy reflect their *lifestyles*. As a result, marketers often segment their markets by consumer lifestyles and base their marketing strategies on lifestyle appeals. For example, retailer Anthropologie, with its whimsical, "French flea market" store atmosphere, sells a Bohemian-chic lifestyle to which its young women customers aspire. And VF Corporation offers a closet full of more than 30 premium lifestyle brands that "fit the lives of consumers the world over, from commuters to cowboys, surfers to soccer moms, sports fans to rock bands."[8]

Differentiated marketing: VF Corporation offers a closet full of more than 30 premium lifestyle brands, each of which "taps into consumer aspirations to fashion, status, and well-being" in a well-defined segment.

VF Corporation

VF is the nation's number-one jeans maker, with brands such as Lee, Riders, Rustler, and Wrangler. But jeans are not the only focus for VF. The company's brands are carefully separated into five major lifestyle segments—Jeanswear, Imagewear (workwear), Outdoor and Action Sports, Sportswear, and Contemporary. The North Face and Timberland brands, both part of the Outdoor unit, offer top-of-the-line gear and apparel for outdoor enthusiasts. From the Sportswear unit, Nautica focuses on people who enjoy high-end casual apparel inspired by sailing and the sea. Vans began as a skate shoemaker, and Reef features surf-inspired footwear and apparel. In the Contemporary unit, Lucy features upscale activewear, whereas 7 for All Mankind supplies premium denim and accessories sold in boutiques and high-end department stores such as Saks and Nordstrom. At the other end of the spectrum, Horace Small, part of the Imagewear unit, markets uniforms for police and fire departments and other first responders. No matter who you are, says the company, "We fit your life."

Marketers also use *personality* variables to segment markets. For example, different soft drinks target different personalities. On the one hand, Mountain Dew projects a youthful, rebellious, adventurous, go-your-own-way personality. Its ads remind customers that "It's different on the Mountain." By contrast, Coca-Cola Zero appears to target more mature, practical, and cerebral but good-humored personality types. Its subtly humorous ads promise "Real Coca-Cola taste and zero calories."

Marketers sometimes refer to brand-focused psychographic segments as *brand "tribes"*—communities of core customers with shared characteristics, brand experiences, and strong affinities for a particular brand.[9] For example, outfitter REI's core customers are passionate about the great outdoors and share this belief as members of the REI tribe. The Apple tribe consists of stylish, tech-savvy nonconformists. Home Depot targets a core psychographic segment of dedicated do-it-yourself enthusiasts; the Nike tribe consists of high-performance athletes. Often, brands in the same product category target very different tribes. For example, as discussed in the chapter-opening story, although both Dunkin' Donuts and Starbucks are snack and coffee shops, their brand tribes are as different as day and night.

Behavioral Segmentation

Behavioral segmentation divides buyers into segments based on their knowledge, attitudes, uses, or responses concerning a product. Many marketers believe that behavior variables are the best starting point for building market segments.

Behavioral segmentation
Dividing a market into segments based on consumer knowledge, attitudes, uses of a product, or responses to a product.

Occasion segmentation
Dividing the market into segments according to occasions when buyers get the idea to buy, actually make their purchase, or use the purchased item.

Benefit segmentation
Dividing the market into segments according to the different benefits that consumers seek from the product.

Occasions. Buyers can be grouped according to occasions when they get the idea to buy, actually make their purchases, or use the purchased items. **Occasion segmentation** can help firms build up product usage. Campbell's advertises its soups more heavily in the cold winter months. And for more than a decade, Starbucks has welcomed the autumn season with its Pumpkin Spice Latte (PSL). Sold only in the fall, to date, the coffee chain has sold more than 200 million cups of the eagerly anticipated concoction. "I've never been happier about burning my tongue with a hot beverage," Tweeted a Starbucks customer recently.[10]

Still other companies try to boost consumption by promoting usage during nontraditional occasions. For example, most consumers drink orange juice in the morning, but orange growers have promoted drinking orange juice as a cool, healthful refresher at other times of the day. Similarly, whereas consumers tend to drink soft drinks later in the day, Mountain Dew introduced Mtn Dew A.M. (a mixture of Mountain Dew and orange juice) to increase morning consumption. And Taco Bell's First Meal campaign attempts to build business by promoting Mtn Dew A.M. (available only at Taco Bell) along with the chain's A.M. Crunchwrap and other breakfast items as a great way to start the day.

Benefit segmentation: Schwinn makes bikes for every benefit segment. For example, Schwinn's urban bikes are "for riders who want a functional, durable, and stylish bike to commute or ride casually in urban areas."
Schwinn Bicycles

Benefits Sought. A powerful form of segmentation is grouping buyers according to the different *benefits* that they seek from a product. **Benefit segmentation** requires finding the major benefits people look for in a product class, the kinds of people who look for each benefit, and the major brands that deliver each benefit.

For example, people buying bicycles are looking for any number of benefits, from competitive racing and sports performance to recreation, fitness, touring, transportation, and just plain fun. To meet varying benefit preferences, Schwinn makes affordable, quality bikes in seven major benefit groups: cruisers, hybrid, bike path, mountain, road, urban, and kids. *Bike path* bikes are "Perfect for riders who want a comfortable and easy-riding bike with convenient features for casual riding over all surfaces." Schwinn's *urban* bikes are "for riders who want a functional, durable, and stylish bike to commute or ride casually in urban areas."

In all, Schwinn makes more than 50 different lines of bikes, each designed for a specific benefit segment or subsegment. For example, Schwinn's Lakeshore bike (priced at an affordable $170 to $220) is a steel frame classic cruiser bike with coaster brakes that sells at mass retailers. It allows for "relaxing exercise" and comes with a rack on the back, handy for running errands. In contrast, the high-tech Vestige bike (priced at $1,470) is a sustainably designed urban bike, with a frame made of natural, biodegradable flax fibers and coated in water-soluble paint. The Vestige's fenders and grips are made of bamboo, and the bike can be purchased only through select dealers. The Schwinn Vestige combines style with function and has a low carbon footprint.

User Status. Markets can be segmented into nonusers, ex-users, potential users, first-time users, and regular users of a product. Marketers want to reinforce and retain regular users, attract targeted nonusers, and reinvigorate relationships with ex-users. Included in the potential users group are consumers facing life-stage changes—such as new parents and newlyweds—who can be turned into heavy users. For example, to get new parents off to the right start, P&G makes certain that its Pampers Swaddlers are the diaper most U.S. hospitals provide for newborns and then promotes them as "the #1 choice of hospitals."

Usage Rate. Markets can also be segmented into light, medium, and heavy product users. Heavy users are often a small percentage of the market but account for a high percentage of total consumption. For instance, Carl's Jr. and Hardee's restaurants, both owned by parent company CKE Restaurants, focus on a target of "young, hungry men." These young male customers, ages 18 to 34, fully embrace the chain's "If you're gonna eat, eat like you mean it" positioning. That means they wolf down a lot more Thickburgers and other indulgent items featured on the chains' menus. » To attract this audience, the company is known for its steamy hot-models-in-bikinis commercials, featuring models such as Kate Upton, Padma Lakshmi, Nina Agdal, and Hannah Ferguson to heat up the brands' images. Such ads clearly show "what our target audience of young, hungry guys like," says CKE's chief executive.[11]

» Targeting heavy users: Sister chains Hardee's and Carl's, Jr. use steamy hot-models-in-bikinis commercials to attract an audience of "young, hungry men," who wolf down a lot more of the chains' featured Thickburgers and other indulgent items than consumers in other segments.

Audrina Patridge/CKE Restaurants/Splash News/Newscom

Loyalty Status. A market can also be segmented by consumer loyalty. Consumers can be loyal to brands (Tide), stores (Target), and companies (Apple). Buyers can be divided into groups according to their degree of loyalty. Some consumers are completely loyal—they buy one brand all the time and can't wait to tell others about it. For example, whether they own a MacBook Pro, an iPhone, or an iPad, Apple devotees are granitelike in their devotion to the brand. At one end are the quietly satisfied Apple users, folks who own one or several Apple devices and use them for browsing, texting, email, and social networking. At the other extreme, however, are the Apple zealots—the so-called MacHeads or Macolytes—who can't wait to tell anyone within earshot of their latest Apple gadget. Such loyal Apple devotees helped keep Apple afloat during the lean years a decade ago, and they are now at the forefront of Apple's huge iPhone, iPad, iPod, and iTunes empire.

Other consumers are somewhat loyal—they are loyal to two or three brands of a given product or favor one brand while sometimes buying others. Still other buyers show no loyalty to any brand—they either want something different each time they buy, or they buy whatever's on sale.

A company can learn a lot by analyzing loyalty patterns in its market. It should start by studying its own loyal customers. Highly loyal customers can be a real asset. They often promote the brand through personal word of mouth and social media. Some companies actually put loyalists to work for the brand. For example, Patagonia relies on its most tried-and-true customers—what it calls Patagonia ambassadors—to field-test products in harsh environments, provide input for "ambassador-driven" lines of apparel and gear, and share their product experiences with others.[12] In contrast, by studying its less-loyal buyers, a company can detect which brands are most competitive with its own. By looking at customers who are shifting away from its brand, the company can learn about its marketing weaknesses and take actions to correct them.

Using Multiple Segmentation Bases

Marketers rarely limit their segmentation analysis to only one or a few variables. Rather, they often use multiple segmentation bases in an effort to identify smaller, better-defined target groups. Several business information services—such as Nielsen, Acxiom, Esri, and Experian—provide multivariable segmentation systems that merge geographic, demographic, lifestyle, and behavioral data to help companies segment their markets down to zip codes, neighborhoods, and even households.

One of the leading consumer segmentation systems is Experian's Mosaic USA system. >> It classifies U.S. households into one of 71 lifestyle segments and 19 levels of affluence, based on specific consumer demographics, interests, behaviors, and passions. Mosaic USA segments carry exotic names such as Birkenstocks and Beemers, Bohemian Groove, Sports Utility Families, Colleges and Cafes, Heritage Heights, Small Town Shallow Pockets, and True Grit Americans.[13] Such colorful names help bring the segments to life.

>> Using Experian's mosaic USA segmentation system, marketers can paint a surprisingly precise picture of who you are and what you might buy. Mosiac USA segments carry colorful names such as Colleges and Cafes, Birkenstocks and Beemers, Bohemian Groove, Rolling the Dice, Small Town Shallow Pockets, and True Grit Americans that help bring the segments to life.

Zeljkodan/Shutterstock

For example, the Birkenstocks and Beemers group is located in the Middle Class Melting Pot level of affluence and consists of 40- to 65-year-olds who have achieved financial security and left the urban rat race for rustic and artsy communities located near small cities. They find spirituality more important than religion. Colleges and Cafes consumers are part of the Singles and Starters affluence level and are mainly white, under-35 college graduates who are still finding themselves. They are often employed as support or service staff related to a university. They don't make much money and tend to not have any savings.

Mosaic USA and other such systems can help marketers to segment people and locations into marketable groups of like-minded consumers. Each segment has its own pattern of likes, dislikes, lifestyles, and purchase behaviors. For example, Bohemian Groove consumers, part of the Significant Singles group, are urban singles ages 45 to 65 living in apartments in smaller cities such as Sacramento, CA, and Harrisburg, PA. They tend to be laid back, maintain a large circle of friends, and stay active in community groups. They enjoy music, hobbies, and the creative arts. When they go out to eat, they choose places such as the Macaroni Grill or Red Robin. Their favorite TV channels are Bravo, Lifetime, Oxygen, and TNT, and they watch two times more CSI than the average American. Using the Mosaic system, marketers can paint a surprisingly precise picture of who you are and what you might buy.

Such rich segmentation provides a powerful tool for marketers of all kinds. It can help companies identify and better understand key customer segments, reach them more efficiently, and tailor market offerings and messages to their specific needs.

Segmenting Business Markets

Consumer and business marketers use many of the same variables to segment their markets. Business buyers can be segmented geographically, demographically (industry, company size), or by benefits sought, user status, usage rate, and loyalty status. Yet business marketers also use some additional variables, such as customer *operating characteristics, purchasing approaches, situational factors*, and *personal characteristics*.

Almost every company serves at least some business markets. For example, Starbucks has developed distinct marketing programs for each of its two business segments: the office coffee segment and the food service segment. In the office coffee and vending segment, Starbucks Office Coffee Solutions markets a variety of workplace coffee services to businesses of any size, helping them to make Starbucks coffee and related products available to their employees in their workplaces. Starbucks helps these business customers design the best office solutions involving its coffees (the Starbucks or Seattle's Best brands), teas (Tazo), syrups, and branded paper products and methods of serving them—portion packs, single cups, or vending. The Starbucks Foodservice division teams up with businesses and other organizations—ranging from airlines, restaurants, colleges, and hospitals to baseball stadiums—to help them serve the well-known Starbucks brand to their own customers. Starbucks provides not only the coffee, tea, and paper products to its food service partners but also equipment, training, and marketing and merchandising support.[14]

Many companies establish separate systems for dealing with larger or multiple-location customers. For example, Steelcase, a major producer of office furniture systems, first divides customers into several segments: health-care, education, hospitality, legal, U.S. and Canadian governments, and state and local governments. Next, company salespeople work with independent Steelcase dealers to handle smaller, local, or regional Steelcase customers in each segment. But many national, multiple-location customers, such as ExxonMobil or IBM, have special needs that may reach beyond the scope of individual dealers. Therefore, Steelcase uses national account managers to help its dealer networks handle national accounts.

Segmenting International Markets

Few companies have either the resources or the will to operate in all, or even most, of the countries that dot the globe. Although some large companies, such as Coca-Cola or Unilever, sell products in more than 200 countries, most international firms focus on a smaller set. Different countries, even those that are close together, can vary greatly in their economic, cultural, and political makeup. Thus, just as they do within their domestic markets, international firms need to group their world markets into segments with distinct buying needs and behaviors.

Companies can segment international markets using one or a combination of several variables. They can segment by *geographic location*, grouping countries by regions such as Western Europe, the Pacific Rim, South Asia, or Africa. Geographic segmentation assumes that nations close to one another will have many common traits and behaviors. Although this is sometimes the case, there are many exceptions. For example, some U.S. marketers lump all Central and South American countries together. However, the Dominican Republic is no more like Brazil than Italy is like Sweden. Many Central and South Americans don't even speak Spanish, including more than 200 million Portuguese-speaking Brazilians and the millions in other countries who speak a variety of Indian dialects.

World markets can also be segmented based on *economic factors*. Countries might be grouped by population income levels or by their overall level of economic development. A country's economic structure shapes its population's product and service needs and therefore the marketing opportunities it offers. For example, many companies are now targeting the BRIC countries—Brazil, Russia, India, and China—which are fast-growing developing economies with rapidly increasing buying power.

Countries can also be segmented by *political and legal factors* such as the type and stability of government, receptivity to foreign firms, monetary regulations, and amount of bureaucracy. *Cultural factors* can also be used, grouping markets according to common languages, religions, values and attitudes, customs, and behavioral patterns.

Intermarket (cross-market) segmentation
Forming segments of consumers who have similar needs and buying behaviors even though they are located in different countries.

Segmenting international markets based on geographic, economic, political, cultural, and other factors presumes that segments should consist of clusters of countries. However, as new communications technologies, such as satellite TV and online and social media, connect consumers around the world, marketers can define and reach segments of like-minded consumers no matter where in the world they are. Using **intermarket segmentation** (also called **cross-market segmentation**), they

» **Intermarket segmentation: Coca-Cola targets teens the world over through universal teen themes, such as music.**

Shirlaine Forrest/Getty Images

form segments of consumers who have similar needs and buying behaviors even though they are located in different countries.

For example, retailer H&M targets fashion-conscious but frugal shoppers in 43 countries with its low-priced, trendy apparel and accessories. » And Coca-Cola creates special programs to target teens, core consumers of its soft drinks the world over. By 2020, one-third of the world's population—some 2.5 billion people—will be under 18 years of age. Coca-Cola reaches this important market through the universal teen themes, such as music. For example, it joined forces with Spotify to provide a global music network that helps teens discover new music, connect with other music-loving teens, and share their experiences with friends worldwide both online and offline. And it's teen-focused "The Aah Effect" digital campaign serves up "snackable pieces of content"—games, videos, and music—designed to engage the world's teens with the Coca-Cola brand.[15]

Requirements for Effective Segmentation

Clearly, there are many ways to segment a market, but not all segmentations are effective. For example, buyers of table salt could be divided into blonde and brunette customers. But hair color obviously does not affect the purchase of salt. Furthermore, if all salt buyers bought the same amount of salt each month, believed that all salt is the same, and wanted to pay the same price, the company would not benefit from segmenting this market.

To be useful, market segments must be

- ***Measurable.*** The size, purchasing power, and profiles of the segments can be measured.
- ***Accessible.*** The market segments can be effectively reached and served.
- ***Substantial.*** The market segments are large or profitable enough to serve. A segment should be the largest possible homogeneous group worth pursuing with a tailored marketing program. It would not pay, for example, for an automobile manufacturer to develop cars especially for people whose height is greater than seven feet.
- ***Differentiable.*** The segments are conceptually distinguishable and respond differently to different marketing mix elements and programs. If men and women respond similarly to marketing efforts for soft drinks, they do not constitute separate segments.
- ***Actionable.*** Effective programs can be designed for attracting and serving the segments. For example, although one small airline identified seven market segments, its staff was too small to develop separate marketing programs for each segment.

LINKING THE CONCEPTS

Pause for a bit and think about segmentation. How do the companies you do business with employ the segmentation concepts you're reading about here?

- Can you identify specific companies, other than the examples already mentioned, that practice the different types of segmentation just discussed?
- Using the segmentation bases you've just read about, segment the U.S. footwear market. Describe each of the major segments and subsegments. Keep these segments in mind as you read the next section on market targeting.

Author Comment
After dividing the market into segments, it's time to answer that first seemingly simple marketing strategy question we raised in Figure 6.1: Which customers will the company serve?

Market Targeting

Market segmentation reveals the firm's market segment opportunities. The firm now has to evaluate the various segments and decide how many and which segments it can serve best. We now look at how companies evaluate and select target segments.

Evaluating Market Segments

In evaluating different market segments, a firm must look at three factors: segment size and growth, segment structural attractiveness, and company objectives and resources. First, a company wants to select segments that have the right size and growth characteristics. But "right size and growth" is a relative matter. The largest, fastest-growing segments are not always the most attractive ones for every company. Smaller companies may lack the skills and resources needed to serve larger segments. Or they may find these segments too competitive. Such companies may target segments that are smaller and less attractive, in an absolute sense, but that are potentially more profitable for them.

The company also needs to examine major structural factors that affect long-run segment attractiveness.[16] For example, a segment is less attractive if it already contains many strong and aggressive *competitors* or if it is easy for *new entrants* to come into the segment. The existence of many actual or potential *substitute products* may limit prices and the profits that can be earned in a segment. The relative *power of buyers* also affects segment attractiveness. Buyers with strong bargaining power relative to sellers will try to force prices down, demand more services, and set competitors against one another—all at the expense of seller profitability. Finally, a segment may be less attractive if it contains *powerful suppliers* that can control prices or reduce the quality or quantity of ordered goods and services.

Even if a segment has the right size and growth and is structurally attractive, the company must consider its own objectives and resources. Some attractive segments can be dismissed quickly because they do not mesh with the company's long-run objectives. Or the company may lack the skills and resources needed to succeed in an attractive segment. For example, the economy segment of the automobile market is large and growing. But given its objectives and resources, it would make little sense for luxury-performance carmaker Mercedes-Benz to enter this segment. A company should only enter segments in which it can create superior customer value and gain advantages over its competitors.

Target market
A set of buyers sharing common needs or characteristics that the company decides to serve.

Undifferentiated (mass) marketing
A market-coverage strategy in which a firm decides to ignore market segment differences and go after the whole market with one offer.

Selecting Target Market Segments

After evaluating different segments, the company must decide which and how many segments it will target. A **target market** consists of a set of buyers who share common needs or characteristics that the company decides to serve. Market targeting can be carried out at several different levels. **>> Figure 6.2** shows that companies can target very broadly (*undifferentiated marketing*), very narrowly (*micromarketing*), or somewhere in between (*differentiated or concentrated marketing*).

Undifferentiated Marketing

Using an **undifferentiated marketing** (or **mass marketing**) strategy, a firm might decide to ignore market segment differences and target the whole market with one offer. Such a

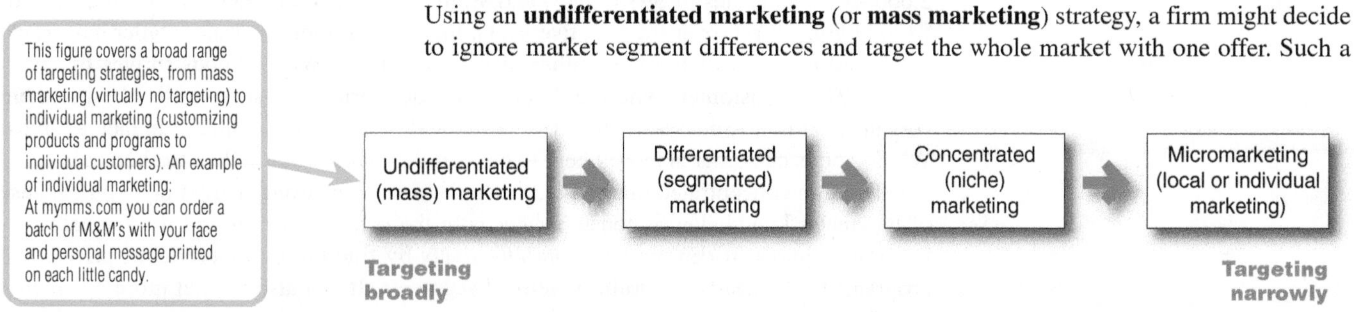

>> Figure 6.2 Market-Targeting Strategies

strategy focuses on what is *common* in the needs of consumers rather than on what is *different*. The company designs a product and a marketing program that will appeal to the largest number of buyers.

As noted earlier in the chapter, most modern marketers have strong doubts about this strategy. Difficulties arise in developing a product or brand that will satisfy all consumers. Moreover, mass marketers often have trouble competing with more-focused firms that do a better job of satisfying the needs of specific segments and niches.

Differentiated Marketing

Differentiated (segmented) marketing
A market-coverage strategy in which a firm decides to target several market segments and designs separate offers for each.

Using a **differentiated marketing** (or **segmented marketing**) strategy, a firm decides to target several market segments and designs separate offers for each. For example, P&G markets at least six different laundry detergent brands in the United States (Tide, Gain, Cheer, Era, Dreft, and Bold), which compete with each other on supermarket shelves. Then P&G further segments each detergent brand to serve even narrower niches. >> For example, you can buy any of dozens of versions of Tide—from Tide Original, Tide Coldwater, or Tide Pods to Tide Free & Gentle, Tide Vivid White + Bright, Tide Colorguard, Tide plus Febreze, or Tide with a Touch of Downy.

By offering product and marketing variations to segments, companies hope for higher sales and a stronger position within each market segment. Developing a stronger position within several segments creates more total sales than undifferentiated marketing across all segments. Thanks to its differentiated approach, P&G is really cleaning up in the $15 billion U.S. laundry detergent market. Incredibly, by itself, the Tide family of brands captures a 38 percent share of all North American detergent sales; the Gain brand pulls in another 15 percent. Even more incredible, all P&G detergent brands combined capture a 60 percent U.S. market share.[17]

>> Differentiated marketing: P&G markets multiple laundry detergent brands, then further segments each brand to service even narrower niches. As a result, it's really cleaning up in the U.S. laundry detergent market, with an almost 60 percent market share.

© Torontonian/Alamy Stock Photo

But differentiated marketing also increases the costs of doing business. A firm usually finds it more expensive to develop and produce, say, 10 units of 10 different products than 100 units of a single product. Developing separate marketing plans for separate segments requires extra marketing research, forecasting, sales analysis, promotion planning, and channel management. And trying to reach different market segments with different advertising campaigns increases promotion costs. Thus, the company must weigh increased sales against increased costs when deciding on a differentiated marketing strategy.

Concentrated Marketing

Concentrated (niche) marketing
A market-coverage strategy in which a firm goes after a large share of one or a few segments or niches.

When using a **concentrated marketing** (or **niche marketing**) strategy, instead of going after a small share of a large market, a firm goes after a large share of one or a few smaller segments or niches. For example, Whole Foods Market has little more than 400 stores and about $14 billion in sales, compared with goliaths such as Kroger (more than 2,600 stores and sales of $98 billion) and Walmart (more than 11,000 stores and sales of $476 billion).[18] Yet, over the past five years, the smaller, more upscale retailer has grown faster and more profitably than either of its giant rivals. Whole Foods thrives by catering to affluent customers who the Walmarts of the world can't serve well, offering them "organic, natural, and gourmet foods, all swaddled in Earth Day politics." In fact, a typical Whole Foods customer is more likely to boycott the local Walmart than to shop at it.

Through concentrated marketing, the firm achieves a strong market position because of its greater knowledge of consumer needs in the niches it serves and the special reputation it acquires. It can market more *effectively* by fine-tuning its products, prices, and programs to the needs of carefully defined segments. It can also market more *efficiently*, targeting its products or services, channels, and communications programs toward only consumers that it can serve best and most profitably.

Niching lets smaller companies focus their limited resources on serving niches that may be unimportant to or overlooked by larger competitors. Many companies start as nichers to get a foothold against larger, more resourceful competitors and then grow into broader competitors. For example, Southwest Airlines began by serving intrastate, no-frills commuters in Texas but is now one of the nation's largest airlines. And Enterprise Rent-A-Car began by building a network of neighborhood offices rather than competing with Hertz and Avis in airport locations. Enterprise is now the nation's largest car rental company.

Today, the low cost of setting up shop on the Internet makes it even more profitable to serve seemingly small niches. Small businesses, in particular, are realizing riches from serving niches on the Web. >> Consider online women's fashion retailer Stitch Fix:[19]

>> Concentrated marketing: Thanks to the power and personalization characteristics of online marketing, online women's fashion retailer Stitch Fix is attracting attention and growing fast.

STITCH FIX and FIX are trademarks of Stitch Fix, Inc.

> Stitch Fix offers affordable personal styling services online to busy women on the go. It positions itself as "Your partner in personal style." Although "personal service" and "online" might seem a contradiction, Stitch Fix pulls it off with a team of more than 1,500 personal stylists who apply a sophisticated algorithm to determine each customer's unique sense of style. A customer begins by filling out a detailed style profile that goes far beyond the usual sizing charts. It probes personal preferences with questions such as "What do you like to flaunt?" and "How adventurous do you want your Fix selections to be?" (One answer choice: "Frequently: Adventure is my middle name, bring it on!") The customer also rates photo montages of different fashions and can even submit links to her own Pinterest pages or other social media.
>
> Combining the algorithm with large doses of human judgment (the stylist may completely override the algorithm), the personal stylist assembles and ships the customer's first fashion "Fix"—a box containing five clothing or accessory items pegged to the customer's special tastes. "Our professional stylists will pick out items they think you'll love—sometimes a little out of your comfort zone, but that's part of the fun," says the company. The customer keeps what she likes and returns the rest, along with detailed feedback. The first Fix is the hardest because the stylist and algorithm are still learning. But after that, the Stitch Fix experience becomes downright addictive for many shoppers. Thanks to the power and personalization qualities of the Internet, Stitch Fix is attracting attention and growing fast. The online nicher has inspired a virtual army of pro-Stitch Fix blog and social media posters, and its revenues have skyrocketed.

Concentrated marketing can be highly profitable. At the same time, it involves higher-than-normal risks. Companies that rely on one or a few segments for all of their business will suffer greatly if the segment turns sour. Or larger competitors may decide to enter the same segment with greater resources. In fact, many large companies develop or acquire niche brands of their own. For example, Coca-Cola's Venturing and Emerging Brands unit markets a cooler full of niche beverages. Its brands include Honest Tea (the nation's number-one organic bottled tea brand), NOS (an energy drink popular among auto enthusiasts), FUZE (a fusion of tea, fruit, and other flavors), Zico (pure premium coconut water), Odwalla (natural beverage and bars that "bring goodness to your life"), Core Power (milk-based protein drink), and many others. Such brands let Coca-Cola compete effectively in smaller, specialized markets, and some will grow into future powerhouse brands.[20]

Micromarketing

Differentiated and concentrated marketers tailor their offers and marketing programs to meet the needs of various market segments and niches. At the same time, however, they do not customize their offers to each individual customer. **Micromarketing** is the practice of tailoring products and marketing programs to suit the tastes of specific individuals and locations. Rather than seeing a customer in every individual, micromarketers see the individual in every customer. Micromarketing includes *local marketing* and *individual marketing*.

Micromarketing
Tailoring products and marketing programs to the needs and wants of specific individuals and local customer segments; it includes *local marketing* and *individual marketing*.

Local marketing
Tailoring brands and marketing to the needs and wants of local customer segments—cities, neighborhoods, and even specific stores.

Local Marketing. **Local marketing** involves tailoring brands and promotions to the needs and wants of local customers. For example, Marriott's Renaissance Hotels has rolled out its Navigator program, which hyper-localizes guest experiences at each of its 155 lifestyle hotels around the world:[21]

» Geographic segmentation: Marriott's Renaissance Hotels' Navigators and "Live Life to Discover" programs help guests to experience "the hidden gems around the unique neighborhood of each hotel through the eyes of those who know it best."

Renaissance Hotels/Marriott International/Marriott Rewards

Renaissance Hotels' Navigator program puts a personal and local face on each location by "micro-localizing" recommendations for guests' food, shopping, entertainment, and cultural experiences at each destination. The program is anchored by on-site Renaissance Hotels "Navigators" at each location. Whether it's Omar Bennett, a restaurant-loving Brooklynite at the Renaissance New York Times Square Hotel, or James Elliott at the St. Pancras Renaissance London Hotel, a history buff and local pub expert, Navigators are extensively trained locals who are deeply passionate about the destination and often have a personal connection to the locale. » Based on their own personal experiences and ongoing research, they work with guests personally to help them experience "the hidden gems throughout the neighborhood of each hotel through the eyes of those who know it best."

In addition, Renaissance Hotels engages locals in each city to participate by inviting them to follow their local Navigator via social media as well as adding their own favorites to the system, creating each hotel's own version of Yelp. Navigators then cull through submitted tips and feature the best recommendations alongside their own for sharing within the hotel lobby or on its Web, mobile, and social media channels. Since introducing the hyper-localized Navigator program as part of Renaissance Hotels' "Live Life to Discover" campaign two years ago, the hotel's Web site traffic has grown more than 80 percent, Facebook Likes have exploded from 40,000 to more than 970,000, and Twitter followers have surged from 5,000 to 100,000.

Advances in communications technology have given rise to new high-tech versions of location-based marketing. Thanks to the explosion in smartphones and tablets that integrate geo-location technology, companies can now track consumers' whereabouts closely and engage them on the go with localized deals and information fast, wherever they may be. It's called *SoLoMo (social+local+mobile)* marketing. Services such as Foursquare and Shopkick and retailers ranging from REI and Starbucks to Walgreens and Macy's have jumped onto the SoLoMo bandwagon, primarily in the form of smartphone and tablet apps. Consider Shopkick:[22]

Mobile app Shopkick excels at SoLoMo. It sends special offers and rewards to shoppers simply for checking into client stores such as Target, Macy's, Best Buy, Old Navy, or Crate & Barrel and buying brands from Shopkick partners such as P&G, Unilever, Disney, Kraft, and L'Oréal. When shoppers are near a participating store, the Shopkick app on their phone picks up a signal from the store and spits out store coupons, deal alerts, and product information. When Shopkickers walk into their favorite retail stores, the app automatically checks them in and they rack up rewards points or "kicks." If they buy something, they get even more kicks. Users can use their kicks for discounted or free merchandise of their own choosing. Shopkick helps users get the most out of their efforts by mapping out potential kicks in a given geographic area. Shopkick has grown quickly to become one of the nation's top shopping apps, with more than 6 million users than and 200 brand partners.

Local marketing has some drawbacks, however. It can drive up manufacturing and marketing costs by reducing the economies of scale. It can also create logistics problems as companies try to meet the varied requirements of different local markets. Still, as companies face increasingly fragmented markets and as new supporting digital technologies develop, the advantages of local marketing often outweigh the drawbacks.

Individual marketing
Tailoring products and marketing programs to the needs and preferences of individual customers.

Individual Marketing. In the extreme, micromarketing becomes **individual marketing**—tailoring products and marketing programs to the needs and preferences of individual customers. Individual marketing has also been labeled one-to-one marketing, mass customization, and markets-of-one marketing.

The widespread use of mass marketing has obscured the fact that for centuries consumers were served as individuals: The tailor custom-made a suit, the cobbler designed shoes for an individual, and the cabinetmaker made furniture to order. Today, new technologies are permitting many companies to return to customized marketing. Detailed databases, robotic production and flexible manufacturing, and interactive technologies such as smartphones and online and social media have combined to foster mass customization. *Mass customization* is the process by which firms interact one to one with masses of customers to design products, services, and marketing programs tailor-made to individual needs.

Individual marketing has made relationships with customers more important than ever. Just as mass production was the marketing principle of the twentieth century, interactive marketing is becoming a marketing principle for the twenty-first century. The world appears to be coming full circle—from the good old days when customers were treated as individuals to mass marketing when nobody knew your name and then back again.

Companies these days are hyper-customizing everything from food to artwork, earphones, sneakers, and motorcycles:[23]

At mymms.com, candy lovers can buy M&M's embossed with images of their kids or pets; at mixmyown.com, nutrition-minded folks can create their own healthy cereal mix. JH Audio in Orlando makes music earphones based on molds of customers' ears to provide optimized fit and better and safer sound. The company even laser prints designs on the tiny ear buds—some people request a kid for each ear; others prefer a dog. The PUMA Factory sneaker customization Web site lets customers pick their own fabrics and tailor their PUMA shoes to taste. "It's a place for you to match your shoes to your favorite team or oldest t-shirt, paint by numbers, and innovate outside the lines," says PUMA. On a much larger scale, Harley-Davidson's H-D1 customization program lets customers go online, design their own Harley, and get it in as little as four weeks. It invites customers to explore some 8,000 ways to create their own masterpiece. "You dream it. We build it," says the company.

Individual marketing: The PUMA Factory sneaker customization Web site lets customers tailor their PUMA shoes to taste. "You know what works—what styles, what textures, what colors. Customize your sneakers whatever way you want."
PUMA SE

Beyond customizing products, marketers also customize their marketing messages to engage customers on a one-to-one basis. For example, Nike collected data on its most enthusiastic customers, those who train using FuelBands and apps such as Nike+ Running. It then used the data to create 100,000 customized animated videos based on each individual's actual workout activities. For example, one video might feature an animation of a person in Los Angeles running past the Hollywood sign; another might show a New Yorker running in the rain along the East River. Nike then emailed the unique customized videos to each of the 100,000 Nike+ users, challenging them to achieve new heights in the coming year. The videos not only engaged Nike's biggest fans, they also spread to the broader Nike community. "These are some of the most social people on the planet," says one campaign manager. "They share like crazy. So that becomes a pretty awesome flagship marketing move for Nike."[24]

Choosing a Targeting Strategy

Companies need to consider many factors when choosing a market-targeting strategy. Which strategy is best depends on the company's resources. When the firm's resources are limited, concentrated marketing makes the most sense. The best strategy also depends on the degree of product variability. Undifferentiated marketing is more suited for uniform products, such as grapefruit or steel. Products that can vary in design, such as cameras and cars, are more suited to differentiation or concentration. The product's life-cycle stage also must be considered. When a firm introduces a new product, it may be practical to launch one version only, and undifferentiated marketing or concentrated marketing may make the most sense. In the mature stage of the product life cycle, however, differentiated marketing often makes more sense.

Another factor is *market variability*. If most buyers have the same tastes, buy the same amounts, and react the same way to marketing efforts, undifferentiated marketing is appropriate. Finally, *competitors' marketing strategies* should be considered. When competitors use differentiated or concentrated marketing, undifferentiated marketing can be suicidal. Conversely, when competitors use undifferentiated marketing, a firm can gain an advantage by using differentiated or concentrated marketing, focusing on the needs of buyers in specific segments.

Socially Responsible Target Marketing

Smart targeting helps companies become more efficient and effective by focusing on the segments that they can satisfy best and most profitably. Targeting also benefits consumers—companies serve specific groups of consumers with offers carefully tailored to their needs. However, target marketing sometimes generates controversy and concern. The biggest issues usually involve the targeting of vulnerable or disadvantaged consumers with controversial or potentially harmful products.

For example, fast-food chains have generated controversy over the years by their attempts to target inner-city minority consumers. They've been accused of pitching their high-fat, salt-laden fare to low-income, urban residents who are much more likely than suburbanites to be heavy consumers. Similarly, big banks and mortgage lenders have been criticized for targeting consumers in poor urban areas with attractive adjustable-rate home mortgages that they can't really afford.

Children are seen as an especially vulnerable audience. Marketers in a wide range of industries—from cereal, soft drinks, and fast food to toys and fashion—have been criticized for their marketing efforts directed toward children. Critics worry that enticing premium offers and high-powered advertising appeals will overwhelm children's defenses. In recent years, for instance, McDonald's has been criticized by various health advocates and parent groups concerned that its popular Happy Meals offers—featuring trinkets and other items tied in with popular children's movies and TV shows—create a too-powerful connection between children and the often fat- and calorie-laden meals. Some critics have even asked McDonald's to retire its iconic Ronald McDonald character. >> McDonald's has responded by putting the Happy Meal on a diet, cutting the overall calorie count by 20 percent, adding fruit to every meal, and promoting Happy Meals only with milk, water, and juice. And for a two-week span during each of the past two years, McDonald's has replaced the toys in its Happy Meals with children's books.[25]

>> Socially responsible targeting: McDonald's has responded to the concerns of parents and children's health advocates by putting the Happy Meal on a diet, cutting the calorie count by 20 percent, adding fruit, and promoting Happy Meals only with milk, water, and juice.

Michael Neelon/Alamy

The digital era may make children even more vulnerable to targeted marketing messages. In all, according to one source, kids ages 2 to 11 see an average of 25,600 ads a year.[26] Traditional child-directed TV and print ads usually contain obvious pitches that are easily detected and controlled by parents. However, marketing in digital media may be subtly embedded within the content and viewed by children on personal, small-screen devices that are beyond even the most watchful parent's eye. Such marketing might take the form of immersive "advergames"—video games specifically designed to engage children with products. Or they might consist of embedded ads, quizzes, or product placements that let marketers cross-promote branded products, TV shows, popular characters, or other marketable entities.

For example, free video games offered at Barbie.com let children help Barbie "build 'n style" her "perf mansion" or play "princess charm school games" with her. At Nickelodeon's The Club—an "online virtual world for kids"—young children can create an avatar and immerse themselves in "Super Spongy Square Games" with SpongeBob SquarePants or browse the Power Rangers Samurai store. Kraft's free "Jiggle-It" app engages kids by letting them watch a JELL-O cube dance to their favorite songs; the brand's "Dinner, Not Art" app lets them create digital macaroni art, helping to promote the company's Kraft Macaroni and Cheese. Some watchers see such marketing as adding value for both the children and the marketers—promoting child creativity and entertainment while engaging the child in brand-related experiences. Others, however, worry that it constitutes "stealth marketing" that takes advantage of children who can't yet tell the difference between commercial and entertainment or educational content.[27]

To encourage responsible children's advertising, the Children's Advertising Review Unit, the advertising industry's self-regulatory agency, has published extensive children's advertising guidelines that recognize the special needs of child audiences. Still, critics feel that more should have been done, especially concerning online and digital marketing. Some have even called for a complete ban on advertising to children.

Not all attempts to target children, minorities, or other special segments draw such criticism. In fact, most provide benefits to targeted consumers. For example, Pantene markets Relaxed and Natural hair products to women of color. Samsung markets the Jitterbug, an easy-to-use phone, directly to seniors who need a simpler mobile phone with bigger buttons, large screen text, and a louder speaker. And Colgate makes a large selection of toothbrush shapes and toothpaste flavors for children—from Colgate SpongeBob SquarePants Mild Bubble Fruit toothpaste to Colgate Dora the Explorer character toothbrushes. Such products help make tooth brushing more fun and get children to brush longer and more often.

More broadly, the growth of the Internet, smartphones, and other carefully targeted direct media has raised fresh concerns about potential targeting abuses. The Internet and mobile marketing allow more precise targeting, letting the makers of questionable products or deceptive advertisers zero in on the most vulnerable audiences. Unscrupulous marketers can now send tailor-made, deceptive messages by email directly to millions of unsuspecting consumers. For example, the Federal Bureau of Investigation's Internet Crime Complaint Center Web site alone received more than 263,000 complaints last year.[28]

Today's marketers are also using sophisticated analytical techniques to track consumers' digital movements and to build detailed customer profiles containing highly personal information. Such profiles can then be used to hypertarget individual consumers with personalized brand messages and offers. Hypertargeting can benefit both marketers and consumers, getting the right brand information into the hands of the right customers. However, taken too far or used wrongly, hypertargeting can harm consumers more than benefit them. Marketers must use these new targeting tools responsibly (see Marketing at Work 6.1).

Thus, in target marketing, the issue is not really *who* is targeted but rather *how* and for *what*. Controversies arise when marketers attempt to profit at the expense of targeted segments—when they unfairly target vulnerable segments or target them with questionable products or tactics. Socially responsible marketing calls for segmentation and targeting that serve not just the interests of the company but also the interests of those targeted.

LINKING THE CONCEPTS

It's time to pause and take stock.

- At the last Linking the Concepts, you segmented the U.S. footwear market. Refer to Figure 6.2 and select two companies that serve the footwear market. Describe their segmentation and targeting strategies. Can you come up with a company that targets many different segments versus another that focuses on only one or a few segments?
- How does each company you chose differentiate its market offering and image? Has each done a good job of establishing this differentiation in the minds of targeted consumers? The final section in this chapter deals with such positioning issues.

MARKETING AT WORK 6.1

Hypertargeting: Walking a Fine Line between Serving Customers and Stalking Them

How well does your smartphone know you? What stories could your laptop tell? In truth, your digital devices probably know more about you than you know about yourself. Smartphones and other digital equipment have become fundamental extensions of our lives. Whatever you do—at work, at play, socializing, shopping—your phone, tablet, laptop, or desktop is almost always a part of the action. These devices go where you go, entertain you, connect you with friends, take you browsing and shopping, feed you news and information, and listen in on even your most intimate voice, text, and email conversations. They know where you live, with whom you interact, what you search for, what you buy, and what you do for fun. And more and more, these devices are sharing all that personal information with marketers, who in turn use it to create hypertargeted brand messages and promotions crafted just for you.

In the old days (really only a year or two ago) marketers gathered information about consumers' digital doings using cookies—those small bits of data sent from Web sites or third parties and stored in users' Web browsers. But cookies don't work with mobile devices and apps. So as mobile and app usage has soared and as cookie-blocking technologies have improved, marketers have sought new ways to track consumers as they move about digitally.

As a result, companies have now developed sophisticated new ways to extract intimate insights about consumers that border on wizardry. For example, a string of high-tech mobile advertising service start-ups—with intriguing names such as Drawbridge, Flurry, Velti, and SessionM—are developing technologies that can put together amazingly detailed profiles of smartphone users—who they are, where they go, what they do, whom they know, and what they like and don't like. For brands and marketers, such information is pure gold.

These mobile advertising companies use different methods to track consumers. Drawbridge creates partnerships with online publishers and advertising exchanges to track online activity—every time a user visits a Web site or uses a mobile app, the partners send a notification to Drawbridge. In contrast, Flurry works with publishers to embed its software directly into their apps—so far, its software can be found in 350,000 apps on more than 1.2 billion devices. The companies then apply statistical modeling to analyze the mountain of data they collect, assign identifiers to individual users, and ferret out user characteristics and behavior patterns.

And here's the real wizardry: By tracking individual digital activity, the services can link several different devices—a smartphone, home computer, work computer, and tablet—to the same person, even if the devices themselves aren't connected. Every person's data profile is unique—kind of like a fingerprint. So Drawbridge, Flurry, and the other services can use the profiles to identify individuals no matter what device they are using.

For example, suppose that you regularly check your Snapchat Snaps in bed every morning from your smartphone. Then, while eating breakfast at the kitchen table, you use your laptop to browse the latest entertainment news on TMZ and to check a few social media sites. Between your morning classes, you use your phone to text friends and your tablet to do a little online browsing. In the afternoon, during breaks at your job, you use a company desktop to monitor your favorite sites and make a purchase at Amazon.com. At home that evening, you catch up on your favorite TV shows, exchange messages with friends, and do some online research for a class project, jumping back and forth between your phone, tablet, and laptop.

>> Hypertargeting: Marketers have developed sophisticated new ways to extract intimate insights about consumers that border on wizardry. But hypertargeting walks a fine line between "serving" consumers and "stalking" them.

Andrew Bret Wallis/Photographer's Choice RF/Getty Images

The entire time, chances are good that the information brokers are peering over your shoulder. Based on your unique pattern of browsing and carousing, one of the data services may well have identified your unique digital fingerprint. Not surprisingly, when you're signed into Google, Facebook, or Amazon.com, those companies can track your activities on their sites across devices. But companies like Drawbridge, once they've figured you out, can follow you across all activities and devices even if you aren't logged in.

This uncanny ability to follow unique users across devices lets mobile advertising services like Drawbridge and Flurry help marketers craft mobile ads and promotions that reach carefully targeted users with exactly the right message at just the right moment. So if you use your work computer to check on airline tickets to travel home for the holidays, that night you might see an Expedia ad on your phone offering a low price on a ticket for that same route and date. Drawbridge can define user profiles so precisely that it can often distinguish between different family members using the same devices and then target ads accordingly. Such targeting accuracy has attracted a host of blue chip brands to Drawbridge and similar services, from Expedia, Ford, and Fidelity Investments to Quiznos and Groupon.

Marketers argue that all of this up-close-and-personal information and hypertargeting better serve both customers and a company. Customers receive tailored, relevant information and offers from brands that really interest them. However, many consumer privacy advocates are concerned that such intimate information in the hands of unscrupulous marketers or other parties could result in more harm or concern than benefit to consumers. Even responsible marketers worry that customers will be put off by what they view less as "getting to know me better to serve me better" and more as "stalking" and "profiling." Companies like Drawbridge are careful in how they position their services. They don't call it tracking. "Tracking is a dirty word," says a Drawbridge executive. Instead, Drawbridge is "observing your behaviors and connecting your profile to mobile devices," he says elliptically. Drawbridge's CEO talks more grandly about "trying to democratize identity so that rivals like Facebook aren't the only firms with access to consumers."

Some information seems far too sensitive for use in hypertargeting. For example, targeting based on health, financial, or personal activity profiles could cause consumers embarrassment, discomfort, or damage. Consider revelations about certain prescription drug medications, financial planning or debt counseling, or private leisure activities. For instance, imagine having a taboo ad pop up on your work computer while your boss is looking over your shoulder or while you are making a presentation to colleagues. Or consider that someone targeting customized ads based on your travel plans also knows when your home will likely be unattended. And who's to protect the privacy of children and other vulnerable groups and shield them from the advances of overzealous marketers? Although most consumers are willing to share some personal information if it means getting better service or deals, many consumers worry that marketers might go too far.

Thus, with today's super-sophisticated behavioral targeting tools, marketers walk a fine line between serving consumers and stalking them. Most marketers want to do the right thing with hypertargeting—focusing on the right customers with personalized offers that meet their exacting needs. They want to build trusted relationships with customers by serving them, not harming them. But responsible hypertargeting calls for proactively guarding the rights and sensitivities of those being targeted. Marketers who cross the line risk the wrath of advocates, legislators, and consumers themselves.

Sources: Kate Kay, "Three Big Privacy Changes to Plan for in 2014," *Advertising Age*, January 3, 2014, http://adage.com/print/290885/; Claire Cain Miller and Somini Sengupta, "Selling Secrets of Phone Users to Advertisers," *New York Times*, October 6, 2013, p. A1; George Fox, "When Online Marketers Target Mobile Device Users, Nothing's Out of Bounds," *ECN Magazine*, October 28, 2013, www.ecnmag.com/blogs/2013/10/when-online-marketers-target-mobile-device-users-nothing's-out-bounds; Katy Bachman, "FTC's Ad Regulator Plans to Focus Heavily on Native and Mobile," *Adweek*, January 5, 2014, www.adweek.com/print/154693; "12 Stars of Ad Tech Who Are Building the Future of the Industry Right Now," *Adweek*, November 2, 2014, www.adweek.com/news-gallery/advertising-branding/12-stars-ad-tech-who-are-building-future-industry-right-now-161164; and www.flurry.com/solutions/analytics and www.drawbrid.ge, accessed September 2015.

Author Comment
While a company is answering the first simple-sounding question (Which customers will we serve?), it must be asking the second question (How will we serve them?).

Differentiation and Positioning

Beyond deciding which segments of the market it will target, the company must decide on a *value proposition*—how it will create differentiated value for targeted segments and what positions it wants to occupy in those segments. A **product position** is the way a product is *defined by consumers* on important attributes—the place the product occupies in consumers' minds relative to competing products. Products are made in factories, but brands happen in the minds of consumers.

Product position
How a product is defined by consumers on important attributes—the place a product occupies in consumers' minds relative to competing products.

Method laundry detergent is positioned as a smarter, easier, and greener detergent; Tide is "a washing miracle," an all-purpose, heavy-duty family detergent that gets out grime and tough stains. At IHOP, you "Come hungry. Leave happy"; at Buffalo Wild Wings it's "Wings. Beer. Sports." In the automobile market, the Honda Fit and Nissan Versa are positioned on economy, Mercedes and Cadillac on luxury, and Porsche and BMW on

Positioning: IKEA does more than just sell affordable home furnishings; it's the "Life improvement store."

Used with the permission of Inter IKEA Systems B.V.

performance. Home-improvement store Lowe's helps you "Never stop improving." And IKEA does more than just sell affordable home furnishings; it's the "Life improvement store."

Consumers are overloaded with information about products and services. They cannot reevaluate products every time they make a buying decision. To simplify the buying process, consumers organize products, services, and companies into categories and "position" them in their minds. A product's position is the complex set of perceptions, impressions, and feelings that consumers have for the product compared with competing products.

Consumers position products with or without the help of marketers. But marketers do not want to leave their products' positions to chance. They must *plan* positions that will give their products the greatest advantage in selected target markets, and they must design marketing mixes to create these planned positions.

Positioning Maps

In planning their differentiation and positioning strategies, marketers often prepare *perceptual positioning maps* that show consumer perceptions of their brands versus those of competing products on important buying dimensions. **Figure 6.3** shows a positioning map for the U.S. large luxury SUV market.[29] The position of each circle on the map indicates the brand's perceived positioning on two dimensions: price and orientation (luxury versus performance). The size of each circle indicates the brand's relative market share.

Thus, customers view the market-leading Cadillac Escalade as a moderately priced, large, luxury SUV with a balance of luxury and performance. The Escalade is positioned on urban luxury, and, in its case, "performance" probably means power and safety performance. You'll find no mention of off-road adventuring in an Escalade ad.

By contrast, the Range Rover and the Land Cruiser are positioned on luxury with nuances of off-road performance. For example, the Toyota Land Cruiser began in 1951 as a four-wheel-drive, jeep-like vehicle designed to conquer the world's most grueling terrains and climates. In recent years, the Land Cruiser has retained this adventure and performance positioning but with luxury added. Its Web site brags of "legendary off-road capability," with off-road technologies such as an Acoustic Control Induction System to get the most out of the RPMs, "so you can make molehills out of mountains." Despite its

Figure 6.3 Positioning Map: Large Luxury SUVs

Source: Based on data provided by WardsAuto.com and Edmunds.com, 2015.

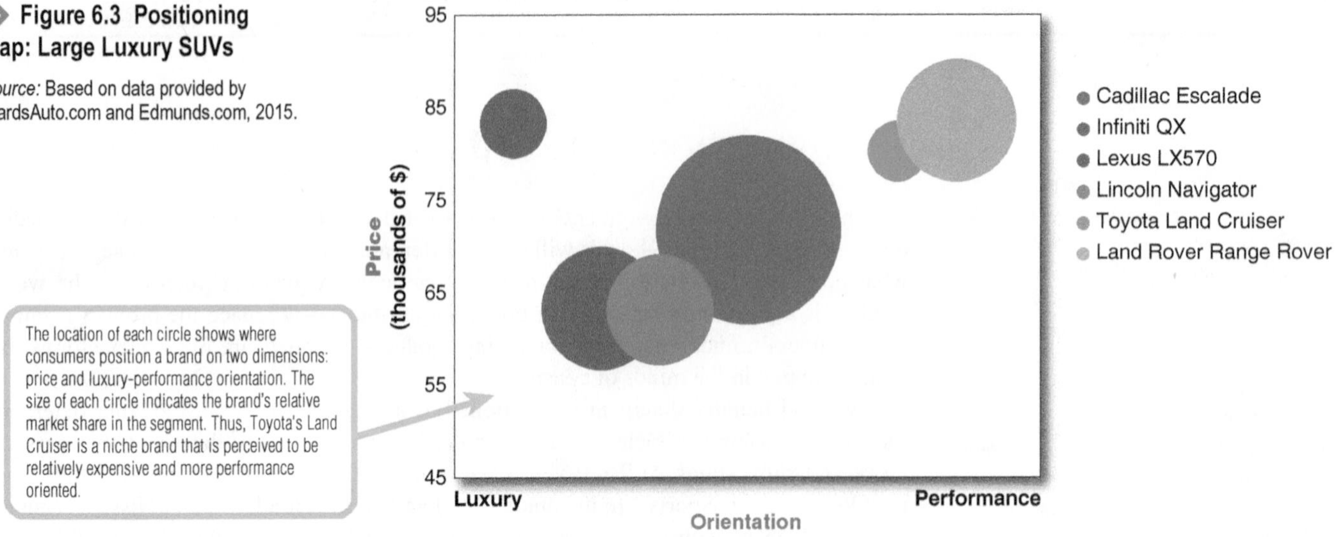

ruggedness, however, the company notes that "its Bluetooth hands-free technology, DVD entertainment, and a sumptuous interior have softened its edges."

Choosing a Differentiation and Positioning Strategy

Some firms find it easy to choose a differentiation and positioning strategy. For example, a firm well known for quality in certain segments will go after this position in a new segment if there are enough buyers seeking quality. But in many cases, two or more firms will go after the same position. Then each will have to find other ways to set itself apart. Each firm must differentiate its offer by building a unique bundle of benefits that appeal to a substantial group within the segment.

Above all else, a brand's positioning must serve the needs and preferences of well-defined target markets. For example, as discussed in the chapter-opening story, although both Dunkin' Donuts and Starbucks are coffee and snack shops, they target very different customers who want very different things from their favorite coffee seller. Starbucks targets more upscale professionals with more high-brow positioning. In contrast, Dunkin' Donuts targets the "average Joe" with a decidedly more low-brow, "everyman" kind of positioning. Yet each brand succeeds because it creates just the right value proposition for its unique mix of customers.

The differentiation and positioning task consists of three steps: identifying a set of differentiating competitive advantages on which to build a position, choosing the right competitive advantages, and selecting an overall positioning strategy. The company must then effectively communicate and deliver the chosen position to the market.

Identifying Possible Value Differences and Competitive Advantages

To build profitable relationships with target customers, marketers must understand customer needs and deliver more customer value better than competitors do. To the extent that a company can differentiate and position itself as providing superior customer value, it gains **competitive advantage**.

Competitive advantage
An advantage over competitors gained by offering greater customer value, either by having lower prices or providing more benefits that justify higher prices.

But solid positions cannot be built on empty promises. If a company positions its product as *offering* the best quality and service, it must actually differentiate the product so that it *delivers* the promised quality and service. Companies must do much more than simply shout out their positions with slogans and taglines. They must first *live* the slogan. For example, online shoes and accessories seller Zappos' "powered by service" positioning would ring hollow if not backed by truly outstanding customer care. Zappos aligns its entire organization and all of its people around providing the best possible customer service. The online seller's number-one core value: "Deliver WOW through service."[30]

To find points of differentiation, marketers must think through the customer's entire experience with the company's product or service. An alert company can find ways to differentiate itself at every customer contact point. In what specific ways can a company differentiate itself or its market offer? It can differentiate along the lines of *product, services, channels, people*, or *image*.

Through *product differentiation*, brands can be differentiated on features, performance, or style and design. Thus, premium audio brand Bose positions its audio products on the innovative, high-quality listening experiences it gives users. Bose promises "better sound through research." And SodaStream positions itself as an alternative to bottled carbonated waters and soft drinks. It promises a simple, convenient, ecofriendly process for turning home tap water into fresh, homemade soda with no heavy bottles to carry, store, and recycle. SodaStream gives you "Smart. Simple. Soda."

Beyond differentiating its physical product, a firm can also differentiate the services that accompany the product. Some companies gain *services differentiation* through speedy, convenient service. >> Jimmy John's doesn't just offer fast food; its gourmet sandwiches come "Freaky Fast." Other firms promise high-quality customer service. For example, in an age where customer satisfaction with airline service is in constant decline, Singapore Airlines sets itself apart through extraordinary customer care and the grace of its flight attendants.

Services differentiation: Jimmy John's doesn't just offer fast food; its gourmet sandwiches come "Freaky Fast."

Jimmy John's Sandwiches

Firms that practice *channel differentiation* gain competitive advantage through the way they design their channel's coverage, expertise, and performance. Amazon.com and GEICO, for example, set themselves apart with their smooth-functioning direct channels. Companies can also gain a strong competitive advantage through *people differentiation*—hiring and training better people than their competitors do. People differentiation requires that a company select its customer-contact people carefully and train them well. For example, East Coast supermarket chain Wegmans has long been recognized as a customer service champ with a cult-like loyalty among its shoppers. The secret to its extraordinary customer service lies in its carefully selected, superbly trained, happy employees, who personify Wegmans' commitment to customers: "Everyday You Get Our Best." For example, the chain's cashiers aren't allowed to interact with customers until they've had at least 40 hours of training. "Our employees are our number one asset," says the chain's vice president for human resources.[31]

Even when competing offers look the same, buyers may perceive a difference based on company or brand *image differentiation*. A company or brand image should convey a product's distinctive benefits and positioning. Developing a strong and distinctive image calls for creativity and hard work. A company cannot develop an image in the public's mind overnight by using only a few ads. If Ritz-Carlton means quality, this image must be supported by everything the company is, says, and does.

Symbols, such as the McDonald's golden arches, the colorful Google logo, the Twitter bird, the Nike swoosh, or Apple's "bite mark" logo, can provide strong company or brand recognition and image differentiation. The company might build a brand around a famous person, as Nike did with its Michael Jordan, Kobe Bryant, and LeBron James basketball shoe and apparel collections. Some companies even become associated with colors, such as Coca-Cola (red), IBM (blue), or UPS (brown). The chosen symbols, characters, and other image elements must be communicated through advertising that conveys the company's or brand's personality.

Choosing the Right Competitive Advantages

Suppose a company is fortunate enough to discover several potential differentiations that provide competitive advantages. It now must choose the ones on which it will build its positioning strategy. It must decide how many differences to promote and which ones.

How Many Differences to Promote. Many marketers think that companies should aggressively promote only one benefit to the target market. Former advertising executive Rosser Reeves, for example, said a company should develop a *unique selling proposition (USP)* for each brand and stick to it. Each brand should pick an attribute and tout itself as "number one" on that attribute. Buyers tend to remember number one better, especially in this overcommunicated society. Thus, Walmart promotes its unbeatable low prices and Burger King promotes personal choice—"have it your way."

Other marketers think that companies should position themselves on more than one differentiator. This may be necessary if two or more firms are claiming to be best on the same attribute. For example, with its "Expect More. Pay Less." positioning, Targets sets itself apart from Walmart by adding a touch of class to its low prices. And Microsoft differentiates its innovative Surface tablet as being both a laptop and tablet in one. It's the "One device for everything in your life"—lighter and thinner than a laptop but with a click-in keyboard and fuller features than competing tablets. It's "Powerful as a laptop, lighter than Air." Microsoft's challenge is to convince buyers that it's one brand can do it all.

Today, in a time when the mass market is fragmenting into many small segments, companies and brands are trying to broaden their positioning strategies to appeal to more segments. Today, in a time when the mass market is fragmenting into many small segments, companies and brands are trying to broaden their positioning strategies to appeal to more segments.

>> **Positioning on multiple competitive advantages: Microsoft's innovative Surface is positioned as "Powerful as a laptop, lighter than Air.**

Microsoft Corporation

Which Differences to Promote. Not all brand differences are meaningful or worthwhile, and each difference has the potential to create company costs as well as customer benefits. A difference is worth establishing to the extent that it satisfies the following criteria:

- ***Important.*** The difference delivers a highly valued benefit to target buyers.
- ***Distinctive.*** Competitors do not offer the difference, or the company can offer it in a more distinctive way.
- ***Superior.*** The difference is superior to other ways that customers might obtain the same benefit.
- ***Communicable.*** The difference is communicable and visible to buyers.
- ***Preemptive.*** Competitors cannot easily copy the difference.
- ***Affordable.*** Buyers can afford to pay for the difference.
- ***Profitable.*** The company can introduce the difference profitably.

Many companies have introduced differentiations that failed one or more of these tests. When the Westin Stamford Hotel in Singapore once advertised itself as the world's tallest hotel, it was a distinction that was not important to most tourists; in fact, it turned many off. Similarly, Coca-Cola's now classic product failure—New Coke—failed the superiority and importance tests among core Coca-Cola drinkers:

> Extensive blind taste tests showed that 60 percent of all soft drink consumers chose a new, sweeter Coca-Cola formulation over the original Coke, and 52 percent chose it over Pepsi. So the brand dropped its original-formula Coke and, with much fanfare, replaced it with New Coke, a sweeter, smoother version. However, in its research, Coca-Cola overlooked the many intangibles that have made Coca-Cola so popular for 125 years. To loyal Coke drinkers, the original beverage stands alongside baseball, apple pie, and the Statue of Liberty as an American institution. As it turns out, Coca-Cola differentiates its brand not just by taste but by tradition. By dropping the original formula, Coca-Cola trampled on the sensitivities of the huge core of loyal Coke drinkers who loved Coke just the way it was. After only three months, the company brought the classic Coke back.

Thus, choosing competitive advantages on which to position a product or service can be difficult, yet such choices are crucial to success. Choosing the right differentiators can help a brand stand out from the pack of competitors.

Selecting an Overall Positioning Strategy

Value proposition
The full positioning of a brand—the full mix of benefits on which it is differentiated and positioned.

The full positioning of a brand is called the brand's **value proposition**—the full mix of benefits on which a brand is differentiated and positioned. It is the answer to the customer's question "Why should I buy your brand?" BMW's "ultimate driving machine" value proposition hinges on performance but also includes luxury and styling, all for a price that is higher than average but seems fair for this mix of benefits.

>> **Figure 6.4** shows possible value propositions on which a company might position its products. In the figure, the five green cells on the top and right represent winning value propositions—differentiation and positioning that give the company a competitive advantage. The cells at the lower left, however, represent losing value propositions. The center cell represents at best a marginal proposition. In the following sections, we discuss the five winning value propositions: more for more, more for the same, the same for less, less for much less, and more for less.

More for More. *More-for-more* positioning involves providing the most upscale product or service and charging a higher price to cover the higher costs. A more-for-more market offering not only offers higher quality, it also gives prestige to the buyer. It symbolizes status and a loftier lifestyle. Four Seasons hotels, Rolex watches, Starbucks

Figure 6.4 Possible Value Propositions

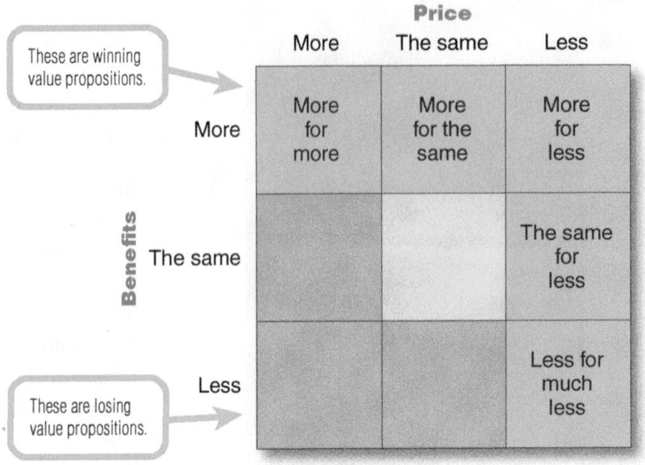

coffee, Louis Vuitton handbags, Mercedes automobiles, SubZero appliances—each claims superior quality, craftsmanship, durability, performance, or style and therefore charges a higher price.

Similarly, the marketers of Hearts On Fire diamonds have created a more-for-more niche as "The World's Most Perfectly Cut Diamond." Hearts On Fire diamonds have a unique "hearts and arrow" design. When viewed under magnification from the bottom, a perfect ring of eight hearts appears; from the top comes a perfectly formed Fireburst of light. Hearts On Fire diamonds aren't for everyone, says the company. "Hearts On Fire is for those who expect more and give more in return." The brand commands a 15 to 20 percent price premium over comparable competing diamonds.[32]

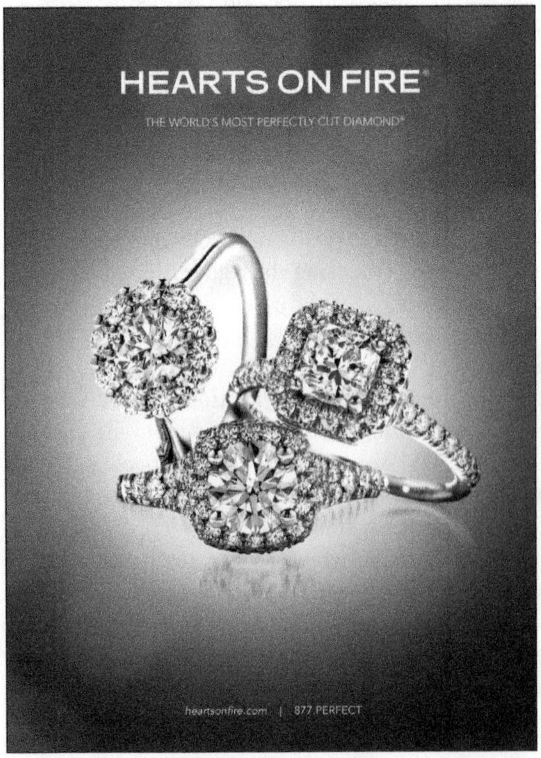

More-for-more positioning: Hearts On Fire diamonds have created a more-for-more niche as "The World's Most Perfectly Cut Diamond—for those who expect more and give more in return."

Used with permission of Hearts On Fire Company, LLC

Although more-for-more can be profitable, this strategy can also be vulnerable. It often invites imitators who claim the same quality but at a lower price. For example, more-for-more brand Starbucks now faces "gourmet" coffee competitors ranging from Dunkin' Donuts to McDonald's. Also, luxury goods that sell well during good times may be at risk during economic downturns when buyers become more cautious in their spending. The recent gloomy economy hit premium brands, such as Starbucks, the hardest.

More for the Same. A company can attack a competitor's value proposition by positioning its brand as offering more for the same price. For example, Target positions itself as the "upscale discounter." It claims to offer more in terms of store atmosphere, service, stylish merchandise, and classy brand image but at prices comparable to those of Walmart, Kohl's, and other discounters.

The Same for Less. Offering *the same for less* can be a powerful value proposition—everyone likes a good deal. Discount stores such as Walmart and "category killers" such as Best Buy, PetSmart, David's Bridal, and DSW Shoes use this positioning. They don't claim to offer different or better products. Instead, they offer many of the same brands as department stores and specialty stores but at deep discounts based on superior purchasing power and lower-cost operations. Other companies develop imitative but lower-priced brands in an effort to lure customers away from the market leader. For example, Amazon offers a line of Kindle Fire tablets, which sell for less than 40 percent of the price of the Apple iPad or Samsung Galaxy tablet. Amazon claims that it offers "Premium products at non-premium prices."

Less for Much Less. A market almost always exists for products that offer less and therefore cost less. Few people need, want, or can afford "the very best" in everything they buy. In many cases, consumers will gladly settle for less-than-optimal performance or give up some of the bells and whistles in exchange for a lower price. For example, many travelers seeking lodgings prefer not to pay for what they consider unnecessary extras, such as a pool, an attached restaurant, or mints on the pillow. Hotel chains such as Ramada Limited, Holiday Inn Express, and Motel 6 suspend some of these amenities and charge less accordingly.

Less-for-much-less positioning involves meeting consumers' lower performance or quality requirements at a much lower price. For example, Costco warehouse stores offer less merchandise selection and consistency and much lower levels of service; as a result, they charge rock-bottom prices. And under Spirit Airlines' "Bare Fare" pricing, you don't get much when you fly Spirit. Then again, with its super-cheap fares, you don't pay for what you don't get (see Marketing at Work 6.2).

More for Less. Of course, the winning value proposition would be to offer *more for less*. Many companies claim to do this. And, in the short run, some companies can actually achieve such lofty positions. For example, when it first opened for business, Home Depot had arguably the best product selection, the best service, *and* the lowest prices compared with local hardware stores and other home-improvement chains.

Yet in the long run, companies will find it very difficult to sustain such best-of-both positioning. Offering more usually costs more, making it difficult to deliver on the "for-less" promise. Companies that try to deliver both may lose out to more focused competitors. For example, facing determined competition from Lowe's stores, Home Depot must now decide whether it wants to compete primarily on superior service or on lower prices.

All said, each brand must adopt a positioning strategy designed to serve the needs and wants of its target markets. *More for more* will draw one target market, *less for much less* will draw another, and so on. In any market, there is usually room for many different companies, each successfully occupying different positions. The important thing is that each company must develop its own winning positioning strategy, one that makes the company special to its target consumers.

Positioning statement
A statement that summarizes company or brand positioning using this form: To (target segment and need) our (brand) is (concept) that (point of difference).

Developing a Positioning Statement

Company and brand positioning should be summed up in a **positioning statement**. The statement should follow the form: To (target segment and need) our (brand) is (concept) that (point of difference).[33] >> Here is an example using the popular digital information management application Evernote: "To busy multitaskers who need help remembering things, Evernote is a digital content management application that makes it easy to capture and remember moments and ideas from your everyday life using your computer, phone, tablet, and the Web."

Note that the positioning statement first states the product's membership in a category (digital content management application) and then shows its point of difference from other members of the category (easily capture moments and ideas and remember them later). Evernote helps you "remember everything" by letting you take notes, capture photos, create to-do lists, and record voice reminders and then makes them easy to find and access using just about any device, anywhere—at home, at work, or on the go.

Placing a brand in a specific category suggests similarities that it might

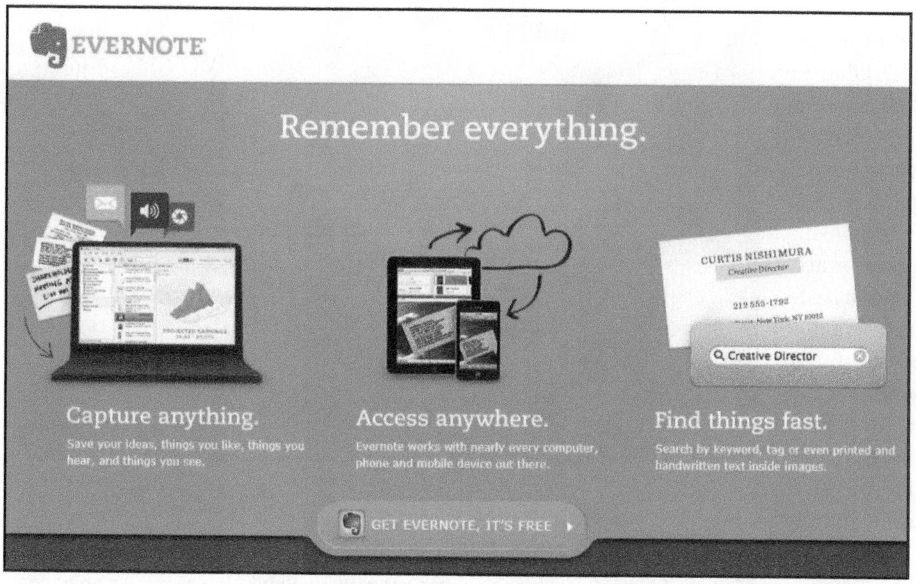

>> **Positioning statement: Evernote is positioned as a digital content management application that helps busy people to capture and remember moments and ideas and find them fast later.**
Evernote Corporation

MARKETING AT WORK 6.2

Spirit Airlines: Getting Less but Paying Much Less for It

"@SpiritAirlines worst, most devious, nickel-and-diming I've ever experienced. I will NEVER fly with you again. #lessonlearned."

This Tweet, and a flood of similar social media comments posted regularly by dissatisfied Spirit Airlines customers, isn't the kind of feedback most companies want to hear. What's more, adding to such negative social media testimonials, Spirit Airlines also recently earned the dubious distinction of being *Consumer Reports'* lowest-rated airline for the customer experience, receiving one of the lowest-ever overall scores given by the organization.

So Spirit Airlines must be headed down the path to bankruptcy and ruin, right? To the contrary—Spirit is one of the nation's fastest-growing carriers. It fills almost every available seat on every flight. And it turns a healthy profit every quarter—a difficult feat in the up-and-down airline industry. How does Spirit Airlines do it? By mastering the art and science of its less-for-much-less value proposition. Spirit's positioning promise: "Less money. More go."

Spirit Airlines is an unrivaled "ultra low-cost carrier," resulting in prices much lower than those of competitors—up to 90 percent lower in some cases. But to cash in on such rock-bottom fares, customers must accept less in return. Buying a ticket on a Spirit flight gets you one thing and one thing only—a seat on a plane to your destination. If you want more, you pay for it. Under what it calls "Bare Fare" pricing, Spirit charges extra for everything. *Everything.* You get only what you pay for—and not one peanut more.

For example, whereas most airlines provide free beverages, Spirit charges $3 for a bottle of water or can of soda. Want a pillow or a blanket? Glad to oblige—that'll be $7, please. Spirit offers no on-board entertainment or Wi-Fi. Getting a seat assignment costs $15, and it will cost you $10 extra to have a check-in agent print out your boarding pass. A full-size carry-on bag runs another $50. Adding insult to injury, seats on Spirit flights are crammed much closer together (what Spirit calls "a little cozier seating"), and the seats don't recline. If you do want a little more breathing room—you guessed it—for a fee you can get an exit row or front-row seat.

Spirit refers to its pricing practices as "Frill Control," claiming that it gives customers more control over what they pay for. It points out that the so-called free sodas and extra legroom on other airlines aren't really free. Customers pay for them in the ticket price whether they want them or not. On Spirit, passengers have the option. Although this approach sounds refreshing, some customers view it as cheap nickel-and-diming or, worse, as unfair and deceitful. The social media are filled with tales of unwary customers who say they ended up paying more for extras than they saved on the initial ticket.

Spirit Airlines takes a hardline approach in responding to customer complaints. When customers request pricing exceptions, Spirit agents stand their ground. The extra charges are optional, not mandatory, the airline explains. The base ticket price includes everything passengers need to get to their destinations. "We've rejected, for example, charging for bathrooms," says Spirit's CEO. "We're never going to do that. That's not an optional thing."

Rather than hiding from its poor customer service record, Spirit Airlines seems almost to wear it as a badge of honor. When one recent study showed that Spirit ranked dead last in complaints made to the U.S. Department of Transportation, Spirit turned it into bragging rights. Over the five years of the study, the airline averaged only eight complaints per 100,000 customers. Spirit celebrated by offering $24 discounts. "That's right, over 99.99 percent of our customers did not file a complaint with the Department of Transportation," Spirit declared in a press release. "To the 0.01 percent—that's OK, we know we aren't the airline for everyone (though we'd love for you to save by flying with us again!)."

The company further defends its pricing by noting that, for customers who take the time to look, it provides plenty

» Less-for-much-less positioning: Fast-growing Spirit Airlines thrives on giving customers less but charging them much less for it. You don't pay for what you don't get.

Spirit Airlines

of up-front information about what its fares cover. In fact, Spirit's online site offers "Spirit 101: Your Simple Guide to the Way We Fly," a detailed guide on what you get for what you pay and how to make the Spirit Bare Fare system work to your advantage. Despite the angst of the vocal few who think they are being fleeced, most Spirit customers seem to know exactly what they are getting and are happy with that. When asked if she resented paying $3 for water on a Spirit flight, one passenger replied, "Not at all. They're trying to cover their costs." That attitude is shared by most Spirit customers, who seem more than happy to give up the extras to get the super-cheap fares.

To see what all the fuss was about, one airline analyst put Spirit Airlines to the test, eyes wide open. After paying only $63 for a one-way flight from Detroit to LaGuardia—roughly $300 less than the same fare offered by Delta, American, or United—he reported on his experience. "After we landed I turned to my friend and said, 'I don't get it—what...are people complaining about?'" He concluded that most dissatisfaction stems from misconceptions—that if people are aware of Spirits' policies ahead of time, they can avoid unpleasant surprises and add-ons they don't want. If you want entertainment, he suggests, bring along your own on a mobile device. Plan ahead and buy snacks and beverages before boarding. Think ahead and add in the fees for carry-ons or checked bags to calculate the true fare. Or pack light and jam everything into a small carry-on bag or backpack you can take on for free. And prepare yourself mentally that you might "be able to determine the shampoo used by the person in the row ahead of you." For flights no longer than three hours, being a little squished isn't all that bad.

For those customers who complain that the extras add up to more than the savings, official numbers suggest otherwise. Spirit's total flight price (all fees included) is still the lowest in the industry—an average of 40 percent below competitors' prices. Even at those super-low prices, thanks to its industry-lowest cost per seat-mile, Spirit Airlines still reaps industry-leading profit margins. For example, Spirit's total revenue per passenger is less than half of what United Airlines needs per passenger just to break even. Over the past four years, Spirit's annual revenues shot up 46 percent to $1.7 billion; net income soared 250 percent.

Thus, Spirit Airlines is thriving with its less-for-much-less positioning approach. True, you don't get much when you fly Spirit. Then again, you don't pay for what you don't get. If paying for the extras bothers you, don't buy them. Or just fly another airline and pay the full up-front fare. But Spirit won't be giving away those extras for free anytime soon. "[We won't] add costs for things that most customers don't value as much as our low fares just to reduce the complaints of a few customers," says the CEO. "Doing that would raise prices for everyone, compromising our commitment to what our customers have continuously told us they truly value—the lowest possible price."

Sources: Based on information from "If Spirit Airlines Is So Unpopular, Why Are Its Flights So Full?" *CBS News*, March 23, 2014, www.cbsnews.com/news/if-spirit-airlines-is-so-unpopular-why-are-its-flights-so-full/; Justin Bachman, "Spirit Airlines Sees All Those Passenger Complaints as Mere Misunderstandings," *Bloomberg Businessweek*, April 18, 2014, www.businessweek.com/articles/2014-04-18/spirit-airlines-passenger-complaints-part-of-its-business-model; Jared Blank, "3 Myths about Spirit Airlines," *Online Travel Review*, September 10, 2012, www.onlinetravelreview.com/2012/09/10/3-myths-about-spirit-airlines-or-my-flight-on-spirit-was-perfectly-fine-really/; Adam Levine-Weinberg, "Why Houston Is Spirit Airlines' Next Big Growth Market," *The Motley Fool*, November 20, 2014, www.fool.com/investing/general/2014/11/20/why-houston-is-spirit-airlines-next-big-growth-mar.aspx; "Value Airline of the Year—Spirit Airlines," ATW, January 23, 2015, http://atwonline.com/airlines/value-airline-year-spirit-airlines; and http://marketing.spirit.com/how-to-fly-spirit-airlines/en/ and www.spirit.com, accessed September 2015.

share with other products in the category. But the case for the brand's superiority is made on its points of difference. For example, the U.S. Postal Service ships packages just like UPS and FedEx, but it differentiates its Priority Mail from competitors with convenient, low-price, flat-rate shipping boxes and envelopes. "If it fits, it ships," promises the Post Office.

Communicating and Delivering the Chosen Position

Once it has chosen a position, the company must take strong steps to deliver and communicate the desired position to its target consumers. All the company's marketing mix efforts must support the positioning strategy.

Positioning the company calls for concrete action, not just talk. If the company decides to build a position on better quality and service, it must first *deliver* that position. Designing the marketing mix—product, price, place, and promotion—involves working out the tactical details of the positioning strategy. Thus, a firm that seizes on a more-for-more position knows that it must produce high-quality products, charge a high price, distribute through high-quality dealers, and advertise in high-quality media. It must hire and train more service people, find retailers that have a good reputation for service, and develop sales and advertising messages that broadcast its superior service. This is the only way to build a consistent and believable more-for-more position.

Companies often find it easier to come up with a good positioning strategy than to implement it. Establishing a position or changing one usually takes a long time. In contrast, positions that have taken years to build can quickly be lost. Once a company has built the desired position, it must take care to maintain the position through consistent performance and communication. It must closely monitor and adapt the position over time to match changes in consumer needs and competitors' strategies. However, the company should avoid abrupt changes that might confuse consumers. Instead, a product's position should evolve gradually as it adapts to the ever-changing marketing environment.

MyMarketingLab

If assigned by your instructor, complete the questions marked with the ✪ from the EOC Discussion Questions section in the MyLab. To complete the Marketing by the Numbers problems found in this section, go to your Assignments in the MyLab.

REVIEWING AND EXTENDING THE CONCEPTS

CHAPTER REVIEW AND CRITICAL THINKING

Objectives Review

In this chapter, you learned about the major elements of a customer value-driven marketing strategy: segmentation, targeting, differentiation, and positioning. Marketers know that they cannot appeal to all buyers in their markets—or at least not to all buyers in the same way. Therefore, most companies today practice *target marketing*—identifying market segments, selecting one or more of them, and developing products and marketing mixes tailored to each.

OBJECTIVE 6-1 Define the major steps in designing a customer value-driven marketing strategy: market segmentation, targeting, differentiation, and positioning. (p 170)

A customer value-driven marketing strategy begins with selecting which customers to serve and determining a value proposition that best serves the targeted customers. It consists of four steps. *Market segmentation* is the act of dividing a market into distinct groups of buyers who have different needs, characteristics, or behaviors and who might require separate marketing strategies or mixes. Once the groups have been identified, *market targeting* evaluates each market segment's attractiveness and selects one or more segments to serve. *Differentiation* involves actually differentiating the market offering to create superior customer value. *Positioning* consists of positioning the market offering in the minds of target customers. A customer value-driven marketing strategy seeks to build the *right relationships* with the *right customers*.

OBJECTIVE 6-2 List and discuss the major bases for segmenting consumer and business markets. (pp 170–178)

There is no single way to segment a market. Therefore, the marketer tries different variables to see which give the best segmentation opportunities. For consumer marketing, the major segmentation variables are geographic, demographic, psychographic, and behavioral. In *geographic segmentation*, the market is divided into different geographical units, such as nations, regions, states, counties, cities, or even neighborhoods. In *demographic segmentation*, the market is divided into groups based on demographic variables, including age, life-cycle stage, gender, income, occupation, education, religion, ethnicity, and generation. In *psychographic segmentation*, the market is divided into different groups based on social class, lifestyle, or personality characteristics. In *behavioral segmentation*, the market is divided into groups based on consumers' knowledge, attitudes, uses, or responses concerning a product.

Business marketers use many of the same variables to segment their markets. But business markets also can be segmented by business *demographics* (industry, company size), *operating characteristics, purchasing approaches, situational factors*, and *personal characteristics*. The effectiveness of the segmentation analysis depends on finding segments that are *measurable, accessible, substantial, differentiable*, and *actionable*.

OBJECTIVE 6-3 Explain how companies identify attractive market segments and choose a market-targeting strategy. (pp 179–185)

To target the best market segments, the company first evaluates each segment's size and growth characteristics, structural attractiveness, and compatibility with company objectives and resources. It then chooses one of four market-targeting strategies—ranging from very broad to very narrow targeting. The seller can ignore segment differences and target broadly using *undifferentiated* (or *mass*) *marketing*. This involves mass producing, mass distributing, and mass promoting the same product in about the same way to all consumers. Or the seller can adopt *differentiated marketing*—developing different market offers for several segments. *Concentrated marketing* (or *niche marketing*) involves focusing on one or a few market segments only. Finally, *micromarketing* is the practice of tailoring products and marketing programs to suit the tastes of specific individuals and locations. Micromarketing includes *local marketing* and *individual marketing*. Which targeting strategy is best depends on company resources, product variability, product life-cycle stage, market variability, and competitive marketing strategies.

OBJECTIVE 6-4 Discuss how companies differentiate and position their products for maximum competitive advantage. (pp 187–196)

Once a company has decided which segments to enter, it must decide on its *differentiation and positioning strategy*. The differentiation and positioning task consists of three steps: identifying a set of possible differentiations that create competitive advantage, choosing advantages on which to build a position, and selecting an overall positioning strategy.

The brand's full positioning is called its *value proposition*—the full mix of benefits on which the brand is positioned. In general, companies can choose from one of five winning value propositions on which to position their products: more for more, more for the same, the same for less, less for much less, or more for less. Company and brand positioning are summarized in positioning statements that state the target segment and need, the positioning concept, and specific points of difference. The company must then effectively communicate and deliver the chosen position to the market.

Key Terms

Objective 6-1
Market segmentation (p 170)
Market targeting (targeting) (p 170)
Differentiation (p 170)
Positioning (p 170)

Objective 6-2
Geographic segmentation (p 171)
Demographic segmentation (p 172)
Age and life-cycle segmentation (p 172)
Gender segmentation (p 172)
Income segmentation (p 173)
Psychographic segmentation (p 173)
Behavioral segmentation (p 174)
Occasion segmentation (p 174)
Benefit segmentation (p 174)
Intermarket (cross-market) segmentation (p 177)

Objective 6-3
Target market (p 179)
Undifferentiated (mass) marketing (p 179)
Differentiated (segmented) marketing (p 180)
Concentrated (niche) marketing (p 180)
Micromarketing (p 181)
Local marketing (p 181)
Individual marketing (p 183)

Objective 6-4
Product position (p 187)
Competitive advantage (p 189)
Value proposition (p 191)
Positioning statement (p 193)

Discussion Questions

6-1. Name and briefly describe the four major steps in designing a customer value-driven marketing strategy. (AACSB: Communication)

6-2. How can marketers use behavioral segmentation in consumer markets? Give an example for each method of behavioral segmentation. (AACSB: Communication; Reflective Thinking)

6-3. Discuss the three factors firms consider when evaluating market segments. Which is most important? (AACSB: Communication; Reflective Thinking)

6-4. How can a company gain competitive advantage through differentiation? Describe an example of a company that illustrates each type of differentiation discussed in the chapter. (AACSB: Communication)

6-5. Discuss the criteria that should be evaluated in determining which differences a company should promote in its products. (AACSB: Communication)

Critical Thinking Exercises

6-6. The chapter describes many companies' individual marketing efforts that customize products for individual customers, such as M&Ms, PUMA, and Harley-Davidson. Find and describe another example and discuss whether the cost of customizing is worth the value provided to consumers. (AACSB: Communication; Reflective Thinking)

6-7. *Manfluencers* is a term that describes a new marketing trend. To what does this refer? Describe two examples of how marketers have responded to the manfluencers trend. (AACSB: Communication; Reflective Thinking)

6-8. In a small group, create an idea for a new business. Using the steps described in the chapter, develop a customer value-driven marketing strategy. Describe your strategy and conclude with a positioning statement for this business. (AACSB: Communication; Reflective Thinking)

MINICASES AND APPLICATIONS

Online, Mobile, and Social Media Marketing SoLoMo (social+local+mobile)

Imagine walking into a retail store that has very little merchandise on display. Technology company Hointer is allowing retailers to do just that. For example, the company's store in Seattle has only one of every style of clothing hanging on display, seemingly floating in the air. With the store app, customers simply scan the tag to get information about each product, read reviews by others, access media clips, and request that the product be added to their fitting room. Once in the fitting room, customers can request other sizes or styling advice via a tablet on the wall or through the mobile app on their phones. Customers return products they don't want through one chute and another size is delivered through another chute in about 30 seconds. With one click, customers can check out on a mobile device or at the sales counter, and they can share their purchases with others on Instagram, Facebook, or Twitter. Sales associates still exist, but they are likely using the associate's tools to monitor customers' choices and suggest matching items of clothing and accessories. All this is possible with Hointer's suite of SoLoMo tools for retailers—eTag, Digital Connections, Omnicart, Associate Tools, and Whoosh Fitting Room.

6-9. Search the Internet to find other examples of retailers using SoLoMo to target and engage potential customers, or describe how you have used a retailer's app in this manner. (AACSB: Communication; Use of IT; Reflective Thinking)

6-10. Do manufacturers use SoLoMo? Find examples of or make suggestions as to how manufacturers can use this type of targeting. (AACSB: Communication; Reflective Thinking)

Marketing Ethics Unrealistic Bodies

With more than a third of American children and adolescents overweight, you would think that Mattel's slender Barbie doll would be a good role model for little girls. Not so, according to some critics. If Barbie was a real woman, she would have less than 17 percent body fat, a neck too thin to hold her head up, a waist too small to house a full liver and intestines, and ankles and feet too tiny to walk. One group of researchers estimated the likelihood of a woman having Barbie's body at one in 100,000. Yet some women strive for impossible bodies, with more than 20 million suffering from eating disorders such as anorexia and bulimia. Other research has shown that 40 to 60 percent of preadolescent girls are concerned about their weight, and almost 70 percent of elementary-age girls who read magazines say the pictures of thin models influence their perceptions of an ideal weight. Statistics like these cause consumer advocacy groups such as the Campaign for a Commercial-Free Childhood (CCFC) to call for action, especially when targeting young girls. For example, the CCFC is concerned about Mattel's Barbie Be Anything, Do Everything partnership with the Girl Scouts, in which Daisy and Brownie scouts (that is, kindergarten through third-graders) can play an interactive game on the Girl Scouts' Web site and earn Barbie participation badges to wear on their uniforms.

6-11. Do you think it is wrong for Mattel and other doll manufacturers to market dolls with unrealistic body proportions to young girls? Explain why you think that way. Discuss other examples of marketers targeting females with unrealistic body concepts. (AACSB: Communication; Ethical Reasoning)

6-12. Give an example of a company that is countering this trend by offering more realistic dolls for young girls. (AACSB: Communication; Reflective Thinking)

Marketing by the Numbers USAA

USAA is a financial services company formed in 1922 by 25 Army officers who came together to insure each other's automobiles because they were deemed too high-risk to insure. USAA now has almost 25,000 employees and more than 9 million member customers. It consistently ranks in the top 10 automobile insurance companies and offers other types of insurance as well as banking, investment, retirement, and financial planning services. USAA practices a niche marketing strategy—it targets only active and former military personnel and their immediate families. Members earn the right to be customers by serving in the military and can pass that on to their spouses and children. The company was originally even more restrictive, targeting only military officers. However, in 1996, eligibility was extended to enlisted personnel and is now extended to anyone who served and was honorably discharged from the military and their immediate family members. The potential market represents all active duty military members, all veterans, and their families. According to the U.S. Department of Defense, as of December 31, 2014, there were 1,361,755 active duty personnel in all armed services. The veteran population totaled 21 million at the end of 2014.

6-13. Assuming the average cost of life insurance is $700 per year and that potential customers purchase one policy per year, use the chain ratio method described in Appendix 3: Marketing by the Numbers to calculate the market potential for life insurance in the military market.

6-14. Discuss the factors used to evaluate the usefulness of the military segment. (AACSB: Communication; Reflective Thinking)

Video Case Sprout

In the world of children's television programming, Sprout is a relative newcomer. Owned by NBCUniversal, Sprout airs PBS Kids programming as well as additional acquired material. A true multi-platform network, Sprout can be accessed as regular cable programming, as on-demand programming through Comcast, and online through Sproutonline.com.

Sprout does not target only kids, however. It targets preschool families—households that have one or more preschool-age children. Parents need to be involved with their children's viewing of interactive content, multiple access points, and 24-hour programming. For this reason, Sprout's promotional efforts are geared toward parents as well as children.

After viewing the video featuring Sprout, answer the following questions:

6-15. Why does Sprout target preschool families rather than focusing solely on children? Give examples.

6-16. Which target marketing strategy best describes Sprout's efforts? Support your choice.

6-17. How does Sprout use differentiation and positioning to build relationships with target customers?

Company Cases 6 Virgin America/7 Target/11 Sears

See Appendix 1 for cases appropriate for this chapter. **Case 6, Virgin America: Flight Service for the Tech Savvy.** Fighting since 2007 for a place in the air travel market, Virgin America has found a profitable niche by providing exceptional customer service for Silicon Valley clientele. **Case 7, Target: Where Store Brands Offer More than Low Prices.** In addition to carrying popular national brands, Target has built its own house for brands by moving store brands upscale. **Case 11, Sears: Why Should You Shop There?** Once "Where America Shops," the former largest retailer is struggling to find its place among Millennials and other shoppers in today's market.

MyMarketingLab

If assigned by your instructor, complete these writing sections from your Assignments in the MyLab.

6-18. Describe how marketers segment international markets. What is intermarket segmentation? (AACSB: Communication)

6-19. Discuss ideas for applications of the Google Glass device among the business and institutional markets. How can these applications be incorporated into online, mobile, and social media marketing? (AACSB: Written and Oral Communication; Information Technology; Reflective Thinking)

7 Products, Services, and Brands
Building Customer Value

CHAPTER ROAD MAP Objective Outline

OBJECTIVE 7-1 **Define *product* and describe the major classifications of products and services.** What Is a Product? (202–207)

OBJECTIVE 7-2 **Describe the decisions companies make regarding their individual products and services, product lines, and product mixes.** Product and Service Decisions (207–215)

OBJECTIVE 7-3 **Identify the four characteristics that affect the marketing of services and the additional marketing considerations that services require.** Services Marketing (215–221)

OBJECTIVE 7-4 **Discuss branding strategy—the decisions companies make in building and managing their brands.** Branding Strategy: Building Strong Brands (221–231)

Previewing the Concepts

After examining customer value-driven marketing strategy, we now take a deeper look at the marketing mix: the tactical tools that marketers use to implement their strategies, engage customers, and deliver superior customer value. In this and the next chapter, we will study how companies develop and manage products, services, and brands. Then, in the chapters that follow, we look at pricing, distribution, and marketing communication tools. The product and brand are usually the first and most basic marketing consideration. We start with a seemingly simple question: What *is* a product? As it turns out, the answer is not so simple.

To dig a little deeper into the question of "What is a product?", we begin by looking at GoPro. You may never have heard of GoPro, the fast-growing company that makes tiny, wearable HD video cameras. Yet few brands can match the avid enthusiasm and loyalty that GoPro has created in the hearts and minds of its customers. GoPro knows that, deep down, its products are much more than just durable little cameras. More than that, it gives customers a way to share action-charged moments and emotions with friends.

First Stop

GoPro: Be a HERO

>> **GoPro's amazing little cameras let even the rankest video amateurs take stunning videos, giving them a way to celebrate the action-charged moments and emotions of their lives with others.**

Used with permission of Mike Basich

A growing army of GoPro customers—many of them extreme sports enthusiasts—are now strapping amazing little GoPro cameras to their bodies or mounting them on anything from the front bumpers of race cars to the heels of skydiving boots in order to capture the extreme moments of their lives and lifestyles. Then they can't wait to share those emotion-packed GoPro moments with friends. In fact, the chances are good that you've seen many GoPro-created videos on YouTube, Facebook, and Instagram or even on TV.

Maybe it's the video shot by the skier who sets off an avalanche in the Swiss Alps and escapes by parachuting off a cliff—that amateur video received 2.6 million YouTube views in nine months. Or maybe you saw the one where a seagull picks up a tourist's camera and takes off with it, capturing a bird's-eye view of a castle in Cannes, France (3 million views in seven months). Or what about the video of the mountain biker in Africa who is ambushed by a full-grown gazelle (more than 13 million views in four months)? One promotional video featuring 5 minutes of video clips captured by fans with the latest GoPro model snared more than 16 million YouTube videos in only three months.

GoPro's avid customers have become evangelists for the brand. On average, they upload three new videos to YouTube every minute. In turn, the videos inspire new GoPro customers and even more video sharing. As a result, GoPro has become the world's hottest camera company. GoPro holds a 21.5 percent share of the digital camcorder market and an estimated 70 to 90 percent share of the wearable-camera market. The company went public in mid-2014, and its sales soared to an estimated $1.2 billion in 2015, a fivefold increase in only four years.

What makes GoPro so successful? Part of the formula is the physical product itself: GoPro cameras are marvels of technology, especially given their affordable starting price of only $200 to $400. A GoPro HD video camera looks like little more than a small gray box. But the lightweight, wearable or mountable GoPro is extremely versatile, and it packs amazing power for capturing stunning HD-quality video. A removable housing makes GoPro cameras waterproof to depths of 130 feet. And GoPro cameras are drop-proof from 3,000 feet (so claims one skydiver).

But GoPro knows that it sells much more than just a small metal box that takes action-sports videos. GoPro users don't just want to take videos. More than that, they want to tell the stories and share the adrenaline-pumped emotions of the extreme moments in their lives. "Enabling you to share your life through incredible photos and video is what we do," says GoPro. We "help people capture and share their lives' most meaningful experiences with others—to celebrate them together."

When people view a stunning GoPro video clip—like the one of New Zealand's Jed Mildon landing the first-ever BMX triple backflip captured by his helmet camera—to some degree, they experience what the subject experiences. They feel the passion and adrenaline. And when that happens, GoPro creates an emotional connection between the GoPro storyteller and the audience.

Thus, making good cameras is only the start of GoPro's success. GoPro founder Nick Woodman, himself an extreme sports junkie, talks about helping customers through four essential steps in their storytelling and emotion-sharing journeys: capture, creation, broadcast, and recognition. *Capture* is what the cameras do—shooting pictures and videos. *Creation* is the editing and production process that turns raw footage into compelling videos. *Broadcast* involves distributing the video content to an audience. *Recognition* is the payoff for the content creator. Recognition might come in the form of YouTube views or Likes and Shares on Facebook. More probably, it's the enthusiastic oohs and ahs that their videos evoke from friends and family. The company's slogan sums up what it's really selling: "GoPro: Be a HERO."

GoPro's runaway success comes from a deep-down understanding that it's selling much more than just tiny, wearable sports-action video cameras. GoPro helps people capture, share, and celebrate with others the most meaningful experiences in their lives.

Initially, GoPro focused primarily on the capture step of the customer storytelling experience. It offers a seemingly endless supply of rigs, mounts, harnesses, straps, and other accessories that make GoPro cameras wearable or mountable just about anywhere. Users can strap the little cameras to their wrists or mount them on helmets. They can attach them to the tip of a snow ski, the bottom of a skateboard, or the underside of an RC helicopter. In fact, rumor has it that GoPro will soon make drones that will let GoPro enthusiasts take breathtaking videos from on high. The handy little GoPro lets even the rankest video amateur capture some pretty incredible footage.

But Woodman knows that to keep growing, GoPro must broaden its offer to address the full range of customer needs and motivations—not just capture, but also creation, broadcast, and recognition. For example, on the creation side, GoPro offers free GoPro Studio software that makes it easier for users to create professional-quality videos from their GoPro content. On the broadcast side, with the GoPro app, users can view and play back photos and videos, then share their favorites with friends on the GoPro Channel, which is already distributed though social media platforms such as YouTube, Facebook, Twitter, Instagram, Vimeo, Pinterest, and GoPro.com/Channels. As for recognition, GoPro now airs TV commercials created from the best videos submitted by customers at its Web site. GoPro's future lies in enabling and integrating the full user experience, from capturing video to sharing stories and life's emotions with others.

GoPro's rich understanding of what product it's really selling is serving the company well. Its enthusiastic customers are among the most loyal and engaged of any brand. For example, GoPro's Facebook fan base is more than 8.4 million and growing fast. To put that in perspective, much larger Canon USA has only 1.2 million Facebook followers. Beyond uploading nearly half a million videos a year, GoPro fans interact heavily across a broad range of social media. "I think we have the most socially engaged online audience of any consumer brand in the world," claims Woodman.

All that customer engagement and enthusiasm has made GoPro the world's fastest-growing camera company. Today GoPro cameras are available in more than 35,000 stores in more than 100 countries, from small sports-enthusiast shops to REI, Best Buy, and Amazon.com. GoPro's remarkable little cameras have also spread beyond amateurs. They have become standard equipment for many professional filmmakers—whether it's the Discovery Channel or a news show team filming rescues, wildlife, and storms or the production crew of hit reality-TV shows such as *Deadliest Catch* taking pictures of underwater crab pots or the sides of ships in heavy seas. When stuntman Felix Baumgartner made his breathtaking 128,000-foot jump from the edge of space, he was wearing five GoPros. The use of GoPro equipment by professionals lends credibility that fuels even greater consumer demand.

The moral of this story: GoPro knows that it doesn't just sell cameras. More than that, it enables customers to share important moments and emotions. Says Woodman: "We spent a lot of time recently thinking about, What are we really doing here? We know that our cameras are arguably the most socially networked consumer devices of our time, so it's clear we're not just building hardware." The company sums it up this way: "Dream it. Do it. Capture it with your GoPro. Capture and share your world."[1]

As the GoPro story shows, in their quest to create customer relationships, marketers must build and manage products and brands that connect with customers. This chapter begins with a deceptively simple question: *What is a product?* After addressing this question, we look at ways to classify products in consumer and business markets. Then we discuss the important decisions that marketers make regarding individual products, product lines, and product mixes. Next, we examine the characteristics and marketing requirements of a special form of product—services. Finally, we look into the critically important issue of how marketers build and manage product and service brands.

Author Comment
As you'll see, this is a deceptively simple question with a very complex answer. For example, think back to the opening GoPro story. What is the GoPro "product"?

What Is a Product?

We define a **product** as anything that can be offered to a market for attention, acquisition, use, or consumption that might satisfy a want or need. Products include more than just tangible objects, such as cars, computers, or mobile phones. Broadly defined, *products* also include services, events, persons, places, organizations, and ideas or a mixture of these. Throughout this text, we use the term *product* broadly to include any or all of these entities. Thus, an Apple iPhone, a Toyota Camry, and a Caffé Mocha at Starbucks are products. But so are a trip to Las Vegas, Schwab online investment services, your Pinterest page, and advice from your family doctor.

Product
Anything that can be offered to a market for attention, acquisition, use, or consumption that might satisfy a want or need.

Service
An activity, benefit, or satisfaction offered for sale that is essentially intangible and does not result in the ownership of anything.

Because of their importance in the world economy, we give special attention to services. **Services** are a form of product that consists of activities, benefits, or satisfactions offered for sale that are essentially intangible and do not result in the ownership of anything. Examples include banking, hotel, airline travel, retail, wireless communication, and home-repair services. We will look at services more closely later in this chapter.

Products, Services, and Experiences

Products are a key element in the overall *market offering*. Marketing mix planning begins with building an offering that brings value to target customers. This offering becomes the basis on which the company builds profitable customer relationships.

A company's market offering often includes both tangible goods and services. At one extreme, the market offer may consist of a *pure tangible good*, such as soap, toothpaste, or salt; no services accompany the product. At the other extreme are *pure services*, for which the market offer consists primarily of a service. Examples include a doctor's exam and financial services. Between these two extremes, however, many goods-and-services combinations are possible.

Today, as products and services become more commoditized, many companies are moving to a new level in creating value for their customers. To differentiate their offers, beyond simply making products and delivering services, they are creating and managing customer *experiences* with their brands or companies.

Experiences have always been an important part of marketing for some companies. Disney has long manufactured dreams and memories through its movies and theme parks—it wants theme park cast members to deliver a thousand "small wows" to every customer. And Nike has long declared, "It's not so much the shoes but where they take you." Today, however, all kinds of firms are recasting their traditional goods and services to create experiences. For example, newly redesigned Verizon Wireless Smart Stores don't just sell phones. They create lifestyle experiences that encourage customers to visit more often, hang around, and experience the wonders of mobile technology:[2]

Creating customer experiences: Verizon's redesigned Smart Stores don't just sell phones. They create lifestyle experiences—a kind of "rec room for geeks" in which customers can hang around and experience the wonders of mobile technology.

Craig Lassig/AP Images

You probably don't much look forward to visiting your wireless carrier's retail store—you maybe stop by every few years to upgrade your phone in exchange for extending your contract. But Verizon Wireless is trying to change all that. It's remodeling some 1,700 retail stores nationwide, turning them into "Smart Stores"—what one observer calls "rec rooms for geeks." The aim is to create a new retail experience, one that helps customers to discover how Verizon technology can enhance their mobile lifestyles. These wireless lifestyle stores are organized into interactive mobile lifestyle zones where customers can try out gadgets, apps, and gear relevant to their lifestyle needs running on the Verizon network. For example, a "Get Fit" zone caters to active sports and fitness buffs; a "Have Fun" zone focuses on gamers; a "Home and On the Go" zone is for folks interested in home monitoring and energy management. In the "Workshop" area, Verizon specialists hold classes in front of a large digital display screen and share tips about getting the most out of mobile devices and Verizon's services. With the new stores, Verizon hopes to build deeper brand engagement and customer relationships by serving as a guide for its wireless customers. "We want to talk with them about all the ways they can use their devices," says a Verizon executive.

Levels of Product and Services

Product planners need to think about products and services on three levels (see **Figure 7.1**). Each level adds more customer value. The most basic level is the *core customer value*, which addresses the question: *What is the buyer really buying?* When designing products, marketers must first define the core, problem-solving benefits or services that consumers seek. A woman buying lipstick buys more than lip color. Charles Revson of Revlon saw this early: "In the factory, we make cosmetics; in the store, we sell hope." And people who buy an Apple iPad are buying much more than just a tablet computer. They are buying entertainment, self-expression, productivity, and connectivity with friends and family—a mobile and personal window to the world.

At the second level, product planners must turn the core benefit into an *actual product*. They need to develop product and service features, a design, a quality level, a brand

Figure 7.1 Three Levels of Product

name, and packaging. For example, the iPad is an actual product. Its name, parts, styling, operating system, features, packaging, and other attributes have all been carefully combined to deliver the core customer value of staying connected.

Finally, product planners must build an *augmented product* around the core benefit and actual product by offering additional consumer services and benefits. The iPad is more than just a digital device. It provides consumers with a complete connectivity solution. Thus, when consumers buy an iPad, Apple and its resellers also might give buyers a warranty on parts and workmanship, quick repair services when needed, and Web and mobile sites to use if they have problems or questions. Apple also provides access to a huge assortment of apps and accessories, along with an iCloud service that integrates buyers' photos, music, documents, apps, calendars, contacts, and other content across all of their devices from any location.

Core, actual, and augmented product: People who buy an iPad are buying much more than a tablet computer. They are buying entertainment, self-expression, productivity, and connectivity—a mobile and personal window to the world.

Betsie Van der Meer/Stone/Getty Images

Consumers see products as complex bundles of benefits that satisfy their needs. When developing products, marketers first must identify the *core customer value* that consumers seek from the product. They must then design the *actual* product and find ways to *augment* it to create customer value and a full and satisfying brand experience.

Product and Service Classifications

Products and services fall into two broad classes based on the types of consumers who use them: *consumer products* and *industrial products*. Broadly defined, products also include other marketable entities such as experiences, organizations, persons, places, and ideas.

Consumer Products

Consumer products are products and services bought by final consumers for personal consumption. Marketers usually classify these products and services further based on how consumers go about buying them. Consumer products include *convenience products, shopping products, specialty products*, and *unsought products*. These products differ in the ways consumers buy them and, therefore, in how they are marketed (see »Table 7.1).

Consumer product
A product bought by final consumers for personal consumption.

Convenience product
A consumer product that customers usually buy frequently, immediately, and with minimal comparison and buying effort.

Shopping product
A consumer product that the customer, in the process of selecting and purchasing, usually compares on such attributes as suitability, quality, price, and style.

Specialty product
A consumer product with unique characteristics or brand identification for which a significant group of buyers is willing to make a special purchase effort.

Unsought product
A consumer product that the consumer either does not know about or knows about but does not normally consider buying.

Convenience products are consumer products and services that customers usually buy frequently, immediately, and with minimal comparison and buying effort. Examples include laundry detergent, candy, magazines, and fast food. Convenience products are usually low priced, and marketers place them in many locations to make them readily available when customers need or want them.

Shopping products are less frequently purchased consumer products and services that customers compare carefully on suitability, quality, price, and style. When buying shopping products and services, consumers spend much time and effort in gathering information and making comparisons. Examples include furniture, clothing, major appliances, and hotel services. Shopping product marketers usually distribute their products through fewer outlets but provide deeper sales support to help customers in their comparison efforts.

Specialty products are consumer products and services with unique characteristics or brand identifications for which a significant group of buyers is willing to make a special purchase effort. Examples include specific brands of cars, high-priced photography equipment, designer clothes, gourmet foods, and the services of medical or legal specialists. A Lamborghini automobile, for example, is a specialty product because buyers are usually willing to travel great distances to buy one. Buyers normally do not compare specialty products. They invest only the time needed to reach dealers carrying the wanted products.

Unsought products are consumer products that the consumer either does not know about or knows about but does not normally consider buying. Most major new innovations are unsought until the consumer becomes aware of them through advertising. Classic examples of known but unsought products and services are life insurance, preplanned funeral services, and blood donations to the Red Cross. By their very nature, unsought products require a lot of advertising, personal selling, and other marketing efforts.

» Table 7.1 Marketing Considerations for Consumer Products

Marketing Considerations	Type of Consumer Product: Convenience	Shopping	Specialty	Unsought
Customer buying behavior	Frequent purchase; little planning, little comparison or shopping effort; low customer involvement	Less frequent purchase; much planning and shopping effort; comparison of brands on price, quality, and style	Strong brand preference and loyalty; special purchase effort; little comparison of brands; low price sensitivity	Little product awareness or knowledge (or, if aware, little or even negative interest)
Price	Low price	Higher price	High price	Varies
Distribution	Widespread distribution; convenient locations	Selective distribution in fewer outlets	Exclusive distribution in only one or a few outlets per market area	Varies
Promotion	Mass promotion by the producer	Advertising and personal selling by both the producer and resellers	More carefully targeted promotion by both the producer and resellers	Aggressive advertising and personal selling by the producer and resellers
Examples	Toothpaste, magazines, and laundry detergent	Major appliances, televisions, furniture, and clothing	Luxury goods, such as Rolex watches or fine crystal	Life insurance and Red Cross blood donations

Industrial Products

Industrial product
A product bought by individuals and organizations for further processing or for use in conducting a business.

Industrial products are those products purchased for further processing or for use in conducting a business. Thus, the distinction between a consumer product and an industrial product is based on the *purpose* for which the product is purchased. If a consumer buys a lawn mower for use around home, the lawn mower is a consumer product. If the same consumer buys the same lawn mower for use in a landscaping business, the lawn mower is an industrial product.

The three groups of industrial products and services are materials and parts, capital items, and supplies and services. *Materials and parts* include raw materials as well as manufactured materials and parts. Raw materials consist of farm products (wheat, cotton, livestock, fruits, vegetables) and natural products (fish, lumber, crude petroleum, iron ore). Manufactured materials and parts consist of component materials (iron, yarn, cement, wires) and component parts (small motors, tires, castings). Most manufactured materials and parts are sold directly to industrial users. Price and service are the major marketing factors; branding and advertising tend to be less important.

Capital items are industrial products that aid in the buyer's production or operations, including installations and accessory equipment. Installations consist of major purchases such as buildings (factories, offices) and fixed equipment (generators, drill presses, large computer systems, elevators). Accessory equipment includes portable factory equipment and tools (hand tools, lift trucks) and office equipment (computers, fax machines, desks). These types of equipment have shorter lives than do installations and simply aid in the production process.

The final group of industrial products is *supplies and services*. Supplies include operating supplies (lubricants, coal, paper, pencils) and repair and maintenance items (paint, nails, brooms). Supplies are the convenience products of the industrial field because they are usually purchased with a minimum of effort or comparison. Business services include maintenance and repair services (window cleaning, computer repair) and business advisory services (legal, management consulting, advertising). Such services are usually supplied under contract.

Organizations, Persons, Places, and Ideas

In addition to tangible products and services, marketers have broadened the concept of a product to include other market offerings: organizations, persons, places, and ideas.

Organizations often carry out activities to "sell" the organization itself. *Organization marketing* consists of activities undertaken to create, maintain, or change the attitudes and behavior of target consumers toward an organization. Both profit and not-for-profit organizations practice organization marketing.

Organization marketing: GE's long-running Imagination at Work campaign markets the industrial giant as a company whose imaginative products and technologies are making a difference in the world.
General Electric Company

Business firms sponsor public relations or *corporate image marketing* campaigns to market themselves and polish their images. For example, GE's long-running "Imagination at Work" campaign markets the industrial giant as a company whose imaginative products and technologies are making a difference in the world. Consider one recent award-winning TV spot, called "Childlike Imagination." The whimsical ad brings GE's products—from jet engines and diesel locomotives to giant wind turbines and hospital diagnostics machines—to life through the eyes of an amazed young girl whose mom works at GE. GE is "Building, powering, moving, and curing the world," says the company. "Not just imagining. Doing. GE works."[3]

People can also be thought of as products. *Person marketing* consists of activities undertaken to create, maintain, or change attitudes or behavior toward particular people. People ranging from presidents, entertainers, and sports figures to professionals such as doctors, lawyers, and architects use person marketing to build their reputations. And businesses, charities, and other organizations use well-known personalities to help sell their products or causes. For example, P&G's Cover Girl brand is represented by well-known celebrities such as Katy Perry, Janelle, and Sofia Vergara. The skillful use of marketing can turn a person's name into a powerhouse brand. For example, The Food Network's celebrity chef Rachael Ray is a one-woman marketing phenomenon, with her own daytime talk show, cookware and cutlery brands, dog food brand (Nutrish), and even her own brand of EVOO (extra virgin olive oil, for those not familiar with Rayisms).

Place marketing involves activities undertaken to create, maintain, or change attitudes or behavior toward particular places. Cities, states, regions, and even entire nations compete to attract tourists, new residents, conventions, and company offices and factories. The New Orleans city Web site shouts "Go NOLA" and markets annual events such as Mardi Gras festivities and the New Orleans Jazz and Heritage Festival. Tourism Australia advertises that "There's Nothing Like Australia" and provides a Web site and smartphone app complete with videos, holiday ideas, destination information, and about anything else travelers might need to plan an Australian vacation.[4]

Ideas can also be marketed. In one sense, all marketing is the marketing of an idea, whether it is the general idea of brushing your teeth or the specific idea that Crest toothpastes create "healthy, beautiful smiles for life." Here, however, we narrow our focus to the marketing of *social ideas*. This area has been called **social marketing** and consists of using traditional business marketing concepts and tools to create behaviors that will create individual and societal well-being.

Social marketing
Using traditional business marketing concepts and tools to create behaviors that will create individual and societal well-being.

Social marketing programs cover a wide range of issues. The Ad Council of America (www.adcouncil.org), for example, has developed dozens of social advertising campaigns involving issues ranging from health care, education, and environmental sustainability to human rights and personal safety. But social marketing involves much more than just advertising. It involves a broad range of marketing strategies and marketing mix tools designed to bring about beneficial social change.[5]

Author Comment
Now that we've answered the "What is a product?" question, we dig into the specific decisions that companies must make when designing and marketing products and services.

Product and Service Decisions

Marketers make product and service decisions at three levels: individual product decisions, product line decisions, and product mix decisions. We discuss each in turn.

Individual Product and Service Decisions

>> **Figure 7.2** shows the important decisions in the development and marketing of individual products and services. We will focus on decisions about *product attributes, branding, packaging, labeling*, and *product support services*.

Product and Service Attributes

Developing a product or service involves defining the benefits that it will offer. These benefits are communicated and delivered by product attributes such as *quality, features*, and *style and design*.

>> **Figure 7.2 Individual Product Decisions**

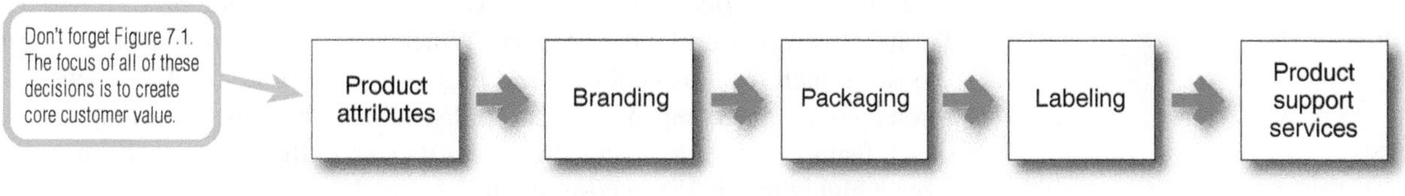

Product quality
The characteristics of a product or service that bear on its ability to satisfy stated or implied customer needs.

Product Quality. **Product quality** is one of the marketer's major positioning tools. Quality affects product or service performance; thus, it is closely linked to customer value and satisfaction. In the narrowest sense, quality can be defined as "no defects." But most marketers go beyond this narrow definition. Instead, they define quality in terms of creating customer value and satisfaction. The American Society for Quality defines quality as the characteristics of a product or service that bear on its ability to satisfy stated or implied customer needs. Similarly, Siemens defines quality this way: "Quality is when our customers come back and our products don't."[6]

Total quality management (TQM) is an approach in which all of the company's people are involved in constantly improving the quality of products, services, and business processes. For most top companies, customer-driven quality has become a way of doing business. Today, companies are taking a *return-on-quality* approach, viewing quality as an investment and holding quality efforts accountable for bottom-line results.

Product quality has two dimensions: level and consistency. In developing a product, the marketer must first choose a *quality level* that will support the product's positioning. Here, product quality means *performance quality*—the product's ability to perform its functions. For example, a Rolls-Royce provides higher performance quality than a Chevrolet: It has a smoother ride, lasts longer, and provides more hand craftsmanship, luxury, and "creature comforts." Companies rarely try to offer the highest possible performance quality level; few customers want or can afford the high levels of quality offered in products such as a Rolls-Royce automobile, a Viking range, or a Rolex watch. Instead, companies choose a quality level that matches target market needs and the quality levels of competing products.

Beyond quality level, high quality also can mean high levels of quality consistency. Here, product quality means *conformance quality*—freedom from defects and consistency in delivering a targeted level of performance. All companies should strive for high levels of conformance quality. In this sense, a Chevrolet can have just as much quality as a Rolls-Royce. Although a Chevy doesn't perform at the same level as a Rolls-Royce, it can just as consistently deliver the quality that customers pay for and expect.

>> **By consistently meeting or exceeding customers' quality expectations, Chick-fil-A has won a trophy case full of awards for top food and service quality, helping it build a fierce following of loyal customers.**

Bloomberg/Getty Images

>> Similarly, the Chick-fil-A fast-food chain doesn't aspire to provide gourmet dining experiences. However, by consistently meeting or exceeding customers' quality expectations, the chain has earned a trophy case full of awards for top food and service quality.[7] Last year, for instance, the chain was the only restaurant named to *24/7 Wall Street's* Customer Service Hall of Fame, based on a survey of 2,500 adults asked about the quality of customer service at 150 of America's best-known companies across 15 industries. Chick-fil-A placed fourth overall, alongside the likes of Amazon, Marriott, and Apple. Although it doesn't try to be Ritz-Carlton, it does send its managers to the Ritz-Carlton quality training program, where they learn things such as how to greet customers and how to probe for and serve unexpressed needs. Such consistency in meeting quality expectations has helped Chick-fil-A build a following of fiercely loyal customers.

Product Features. A product can be offered with varying features. A stripped-down model, one without any extras, is the starting point. The company can then create higher-level models by adding more features. Features are a competitive tool for differentiating the company's product from competitors' products. Being the first producer to introduce a valued new feature is one of the most effective ways to compete.

How can a company identify new features and decide which ones to add to its product? It should periodically survey buyers who have used the product and ask these questions: How do you like the product? Which specific features of the product do you like most? Which features could we add to improve the product? The answers to these questions provide the company with a rich list of feature ideas. The company can then assess each feature's *value* to customers versus its *cost* to the company. Features that customers value highly in relation to costs should be added.

Product Style and Design. Another way to add customer value is through distinctive *product style and design*. Design is a larger concept than style. *Style* simply describes the appearance of a product. Styles can be eye catching or yawn producing. A sensational style may grab attention and produce pleasing aesthetics, but it does not necessarily make the product *perform* better. Unlike style, *design* is more than skin deep—it goes to the very heart of a product. Good design contributes to a product's usefulness as well as to its looks.

Good design doesn't start with brainstorming new ideas and making prototypes. Design begins with observing customers, understanding their needs, and shaping their product-use experience. Product designers should think less about technical product specifications and more about how customers will use and benefit from the product. For example, using smart design based on consumer needs, Sonos created a wireless, Internet-enabled speaker system that's easy to use and fills a whole house with great sound.

> In the past, setting up a whole-house entertainment or sound system required routing wires through walls, floors, and ceilings, creating a big mess and lots of expense. And if you moved, you couldn't take it with you. Enter Sonos, which took home-audio and theater systems to a new level worthy of the digital age. The innovative company created a wireless speaker system that's not just stylish but also easy to set up, easy to use, and easy to move to meet changing needs. With Sonos, you can stream high-quality sound through a variety of stylish speakers anywhere in your home with just an app and a tap on your smartphone. Smart design has paid off handsomely for Sonos. Founded in 2002, over just the past two years the company's sales have nearly tripled to an estimated $1 billion a year.[8]

Branding

Brand
A name, term, sign, symbol, or design or a combination of these that identifies the products or services of one seller or group of sellers and differentiates them from those of competitors.

Perhaps the most distinctive skill of professional marketers is their ability to build and manage brands. A **brand** is a name, term, sign, symbol, or design or a combination of these that identifies the maker or seller of a product or service. Consumers view a brand as an important part of a product, and branding can add value to a consumer's purchase. Customers attach meanings to brands and develop brand relationships. As a result, brands have meaning well beyond a product's physical attributes. >> Consider this story:[9]

> One Tuesday evening in January, Joshua Bell, one of the world's finest violinists, played at Boston's stately Symphony Hall before a packed audience who'd paid an average of $100 a seat. Based on the well-earned strength of the "Joshua Bell brand," the talented musician routinely drew standing-room-only audiences at all of his performances around the world. Three days later, however, as part of a *Washington Post* social experiment, Bell found himself standing in a Washington, DC, metro station, dressed in jeans, a T-shirt, and a Washington Nationals baseball cap. As morning commuters streamed by, Bell pulled out his $4 million Stradivarius violin, set the open case at his feet, and began playing the same revered classics he'd played in

>> The meaning of a strong brand: The "branded" and "unbranded" Joshua Bell. The premier musician packs concert halls at an average of $100 or more a seat but made only $32 as a street musician at a Washington, DC, metro station.

(left) NBCUniversal/Getty Images; (right) The Washington Post/Getty Images

Boston. During the next 45 minutes, some 1,100 people passed by but few stopped to listen. Bell earned a total of $32. No one recognized the "unbranded" Bell, so few appreciated his artistry. What does that tell you about the meaning of a strong brand?

Branding has become so strong that today hardly anything goes unbranded. Salt is packaged in branded containers, common nuts and bolts are packaged with a distributor's label, and automobile parts—spark plugs, tires, filters—bear brand names that differ from those of the automakers. Even fruits, vegetables, dairy products, and poultry are branded—Cuties mandarin oranges, Dole Classic salads, Horizon Organic milk, Perdue chickens, and Eggland's Best eggs.

Branding helps buyers in many ways. Brand names help consumers identify products that might benefit them. Brands also say something about product quality and consistency—buyers who always buy the same brand know that they will get the same features, benefits, and quality each time they buy. Branding also gives the seller several advantages. The seller's brand name and trademark provide legal protection for unique product features that otherwise might be copied by competitors. Branding helps the seller to segment markets. For example, rather than offering just one general product to all consumers, Toyota can offer the different Lexus, Toyota, and Scion brands, each with numerous sub-brands—such as Avalon, Camry, Corolla, Prius, Yaris, Tundra, and Land Cruiser.

Finally, a brand name becomes the basis on which a whole story can be built about a product's special qualities. For example, the Cuties brand of pint-sized mandarins sets itself apart from ordinary oranges by promising "Kids love Cuties because Cuties are made for kids." They are a healthy snack that's "perfect for little hands": sweet, seedless, kid-sized, and easy to peel.[10] Building and managing brands are perhaps the marketer's most important tasks. We will discuss branding strategy in more detail later in the chapter.

Packaging
The activities of designing and producing the container or wrapper for a product.

Packaging

Packaging involves designing and producing the container or wrapper for a product. Traditionally, the primary function of the package was to hold and protect the product. In recent times, however, packaging has become an important marketing tool as well. Increased competition and clutter on retail store shelves means that packages must now perform many sales tasks—from attracting buyers to communicating brand positioning to closing the sale. Not every customer will see a brand's advertising, social media pages, or other promotions. However, all consumers who buy and use a product will interact regularly with its packaging. Thus, the humble package represents prime marketing space.

Distinctive packaging may become an important part of a brand's identity. An otherwise plain brown carton imprinted with only the familiar curved arrow from the Amazon.com logo—variously interpreted as "a to z" or even a smiley face—leaves no doubt as to who shipped the package sitting at your doorstep.

Lux Igitur/Alamy

Companies are realizing the power of good packaging to create immediate consumer recognition of a brand. For example, an average supermarket stocks about 44,000 items; the average Walmart supercenter carries 142,000 items. The typical shopper makes three out of four purchase decisions in stores and passes by some 300 items per minute. In this highly competitive environment, the package may be the seller's best and last chance to influence buyers. So the package itself has become an important promotional medium.[11]

Poorly designed packages can cause headaches for consumers and lost sales for the company. Think about all those hard-to-open packages, such as DVD cases sealed with impossibly sticky labels, packaging with finger-splitting wire twist-ties, or sealed plastic clamshell containers that cause "wrap rage" and send thousands of people to the hospital each year with lacerations and puncture wounds. Another packaging issue is overpackaging—as when a tiny USB flash drive in an oversized cardboard and plastic display package is delivered in a giant corrugated shipping carton. Overpackaging creates an incredible amount of waste, frustrating those who care about the environment.

Amazon now offers Frustration-Free Packaging to alleviate both wrap rage and overpackaging. The online retailer works with more than 2,000 companies, such as Fisher-Price, Mattel, Unilever, Microsoft, and others, to create smaller, easy-to-open, recyclable packages that use less packaging material and no frustrating plastic clamshells or wire ties. It currently offers more than 200,000 such items and to date has shipped more than 75 million of them to 175 countries. In the process, the initiative has eliminated nearly 60 million square feet of cardboard and 25 million pounds of packaging waste.[12]

Innovative packaging can give a company an advantage over competitors and boost sales. Distinctive packaging may even become an important part of a brand's identity. » For example, an otherwise plain brown carton imprinted with the familiar curved arrow from the Amazon.com logo—variously interpreted as "a to z" or even a smiley face—leaves no doubt as to who shipped the package sitting at your doorstep. And Tiffany's distinctive blue boxes have come to embody the exclusive jewelry retailer's premium legacy and positioning. As the company puts it, "Glimpsed on a busy street or resting in the palm of a hand, Tiffany Blue Boxes make hearts beat faster and epitomize Tiffany's great heritage of elegance, exclusivity, and flawless craftsmanship."[13]

In recent years, product safety has also become a major packaging concern. We have all learned to deal with hard-to-open "childproof" packaging. Due to the rash of product tampering scares in the 1980s, most drug producers and food makers now put their products in tamper-resistant packages. In making packaging decisions, the company also must heed growing environmental concerns. Fortunately, many companies have gone "green" by reducing their packaging and using environmentally responsible packaging materials.

Labeling

Labels range from simple tags attached to products to complex graphics that are part of the packaging. They perform several functions. At the very least, the label *identifies* the product or brand, such as the name Sunkist stamped on oranges. The label might also *describe* several things about the product—who made it, where it was made, when it was made, its contents, how it is to be used, and how to use it safely. Finally, the label might help to *promote* the brand and engage customers. For many companies, labels have become an important element in broader marketing campaigns.

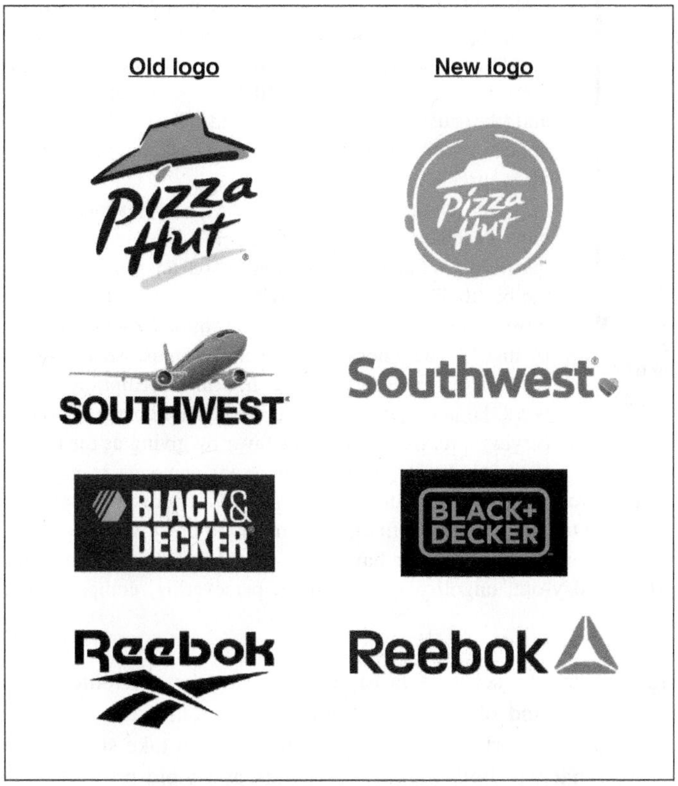

» Brand logos must be redesigned from time to time to keep them contemporary with the brand's positioning and to meet the needs of new digital media. The above brands recently made seemingly small but important logo changes.

Pizza Hut, Inc.; The Hershey Company; Southwest Airlines Co.; Reebok International Ltd; Black & Decker

Labels and brand logos can support the brand's positioning and add personality to the brand. In fact, brand labels and logos can become a crucial element in the brand–customer connection. Customers often become strongly attached to logos as symbols of the brands they represent. Consider the feelings evoked by the logos of companies such as Coca-Cola, Google, Twitter, Apple, and Nike.

Logos must be redesigned from time to time. » For example, brands ranging from Yahoo!, eBay, and Southwest Airlines to Wendy's, Pizza Hut, Black+Decker, and Hershey have successfully adapted their logos to keep them contemporary and to meet the needs of new interactive media such as the Web and mobile apps and browsers. Although important, such changes are often subtle and may even go largely unnoticed by customers.

However, companies must take care when changing such important brand symbols. Customer often form strong connections to the visual representations of their brands and may react strongly to changes. For example, a few years ago when Gap introduced a more contemporary redesign of its familiar old logo—the well-known white text on a blue square—customers went ballistic and imposed intense online pressure. Gap reinstated the old logo after only one week.

Along with the positives, there has been a long history of legal concerns about packaging and labels. The Federal Trade Commission Act of 1914 held that false, misleading, or deceptive labels or packages constitute unfair competition. Labels can mislead customers, fail to describe important ingredients, or fail to include needed safety warnings. As a result, several federal and state laws regulate labeling. The most prominent is the Fair Packaging and Labeling Act of 1966, which set mandatory labeling requirements, encouraged voluntary industry packaging standards, and allowed federal agencies to set packaging regulations in specific industries. The Nutritional Labeling and Educational Act of 1990 requires sellers to provide detailed nutritional information on food products, and recent sweeping actions by the Food and Drug Administration (FDA) regulate the use of health-related terms such as *low fat, light, high fiber,* and *organic*. Sellers must ensure that their labels contain all the required information.

Product Support Services

Customer service is another element of product strategy. A company's offer usually includes some support services, which can be a minor part or a major part of the total offering. Later in this chapter, we will discuss services as products in themselves. Here, we discuss services that augment actual products.

Support services are an important part of the customer's overall brand experience. For example, L.L.Bean—the iconic American outdoor apparel and equipment retailer—knows good marketing doesn't stop with making the sale. Keeping customers happy *after* the sale is the key to building lasting relationships.[14]

Year after year, L.L.Bean lands in the top 10 of virtually every list of top service companies, including J.D. Power's most recent list of "customer service champions." The customer-service culture runs deep at L.L.Bean. >> More than 100 years ago, Leon Leonwood Bean founded the company on a philosophy of complete customer satisfaction, expressed in the following guarantee: "I do not consider a sale complete until [the] goods are worn out and [the] customer [is] still satisfied." To this day, customers can return any item, no questions asked, even decades after purchase.

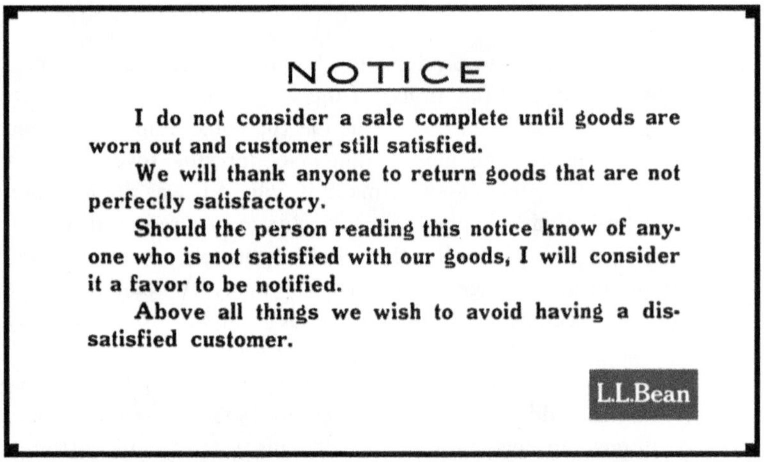
NOTICE

I do not consider a sale complete until goods are worn out and customer still satisfied.

We will thank anyone to return goods that are not perfectly satisfactory.

Should the person reading this notice know of anyone who is not satisfied with our goods, I will consider it a favor to be notified.

Above all things we wish to avoid having a dissatisfied customer.

L.L.Bean

>> **Customer service: For more than 100 years, L.L.Bean has been going the extra mile for customers. As founder Leon Leonwood Bean put it: "I do not consider a sale complete until goods are worn out and customer still satisfied."**

L.L.Bean Inc.

The company's customer-service philosophy is perhaps best summed up in founder L.L.'s answer to the question "What is a customer?" His answer still forms the backbone of the company's values: "A customer is the most important person ever in this company—in person or by mail. A customer is not dependent on us, we are dependent on him. A customer is not an interruption of our work, he is the purpose of it. We are not doing a favor by serving him, he is doing us a favor by giving us the opportunity to do so. A customer is not someone to argue or match wits with. Nobody ever won an argument with a customer. A customer is a person who brings us his wants. It is our job to handle them profitably to him and to ourselves." Adds former L.L.Bean CEO Leon Gorman: "A lot of people have fancy things to say about customer service, but it's just a day-in, day-out, ongoing, never-ending, persevering, compassionate kind of activity."

The first step in designing support services is to survey customers periodically to assess the value of current services and obtain ideas for new ones. Once the company has assessed the quality of various support services to customers, it can take steps to fix problems and add new services that will both delight customers and yield profits to the company.

Many companies now use a sophisticated mix of phone, email, online, social media, mobile, and interactive voice and data technologies to provide support services that were not possible before. For example, home improvement store Lowe's offers a vigorous dose of customer service at both its store and online locations that makes shopping easier, answers customer questions, and handles problems. Customers can access Lowe's extensive support by phone, email (CareTW@lowes.com), Web site, mobile app, and Twitter via @LowesCares. The Lowe's Web site and mobile app link to a buying guide and how-to library. In its stores, Lowe's has equipped employees with 42,000 iPhones filled with custom apps and add-on hardware, letting them perform service tasks such as checking inventory at nearby stores, looking up specific customer purchase histories, sharing how-to videos, and checking competitor prices—all without leaving the customer's side. Lowe's is even experimenting with putting interactive, talking, moving robots in stores that can greet customers as they enter, answer even their most vexing questions, and guide them to whatever merchandise they are seeking.[15]

Product Line Decisions

Product line
A group of products that are closely related because they function in a similar manner, are sold to the same customer groups, are marketed through the same types of outlets, or fall within given price ranges.

Beyond decisions about individual products and services, product strategy also calls for building a product line. A **product line** is a group of products that are closely related because they function in a similar manner, are sold to the same customer groups, are marketed through the same types of outlets, or fall within given price ranges. For example, Nike produces several lines of athletic shoes and apparel, and Marriott offers several lines of hotels.

The major product line decision involves *product line length*—the number of items in the product line. The line is too short if the manager can increase profits by adding items; the line is too long if the manager can increase profits by dropping items. Managers need to analyze their product lines periodically to assess each item's sales and profits and understand how each item contributes to the line's overall performance.

A company can expand its product line in two ways: by *line filling* or *line stretching*. *Product line filling* involves adding more items within the present range of the line. There are several reasons for product line filling: reaching for extra profits, satisfying dealers, using excess capacity, being the leading full-line company, and plugging holes to keep out competitors. However, line filling is overdone if it results in cannibalization (eating up sales of the company's own existing products) and customer confusion. The company should ensure that new items are noticeably different from existing ones.

Product line stretching occurs when a company lengthens its product line beyond its current range. The company can stretch its line downward, upward, or both ways. Companies located at the upper end of the market can stretch their lines *downward*. A company may stretch downward to plug a market hole that otherwise would attract a new competitor or to respond to a competitor's attack on the upper end. Or it may add low-end products because it finds faster growth taking place in the low-end segments. Companies can also stretch their product lines *upward*. Sometimes, companies stretch upward to add prestige to their current products. Or they may be attracted by a faster growth rate or higher margins at the higher end.

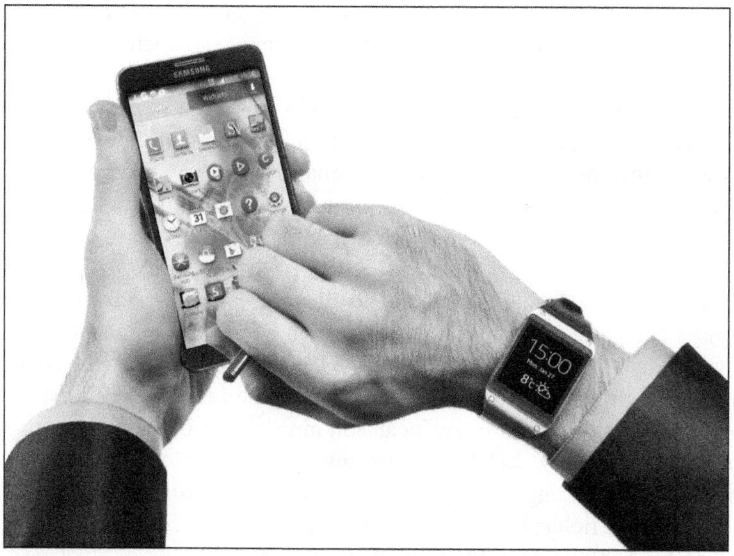

» Product line stretching and filling: Samsung's bulging Galaxy mobile devices line now offers a size for any need or preference, including smartphones, "phablets," tablets, and even a wristwatch-like wearable smartphone, the Galaxy Gear.

Oleksiy Maksymenko Photography/Alamy

» Over the past few years Samsung has both stretched and filled its Galaxy line of premium smartphone and tablet mobile devices:

> Samsung started the Galaxy line with a 4" smartphone, then quickly added a 10.1" tablet. It now offers a bulging Galaxy line that includes a size for any need or preference. The basic Galaxy smartphones come with 5" screens. The popular Galaxy Note "phablet" comes with a 5.7" screen in what Samsung calls "the best of both" between a phone and tablet. Galaxy Tab buyers can now choose among any

of four sizes—7", 8", 10" and 12". To top things off, Samsung offers the Galaxy Gear, a wristwatch-like wearable Galaxy smartphone, and the Galaxy Fit, a wearable activity-tracking device. The Galaxy line still caters heavily to the top end of its markets. But to address the fastest-growing smartphone segment—phones that sell for less than $300 contract-free—Samsung is rumored to have lower-priced Galaxy J1 models in the works. As a result, through artful stretching and filling, Samsung's successful Galaxy line has broadened its appeal, improved its competitive position, and boosted growth.

Product Mix Decisions

Product mix (or product portfolio) The set of all product lines and items that a particular seller offers for sale.

An organization with several product lines has a product mix. A **product mix** (or **product portfolio**) consists of all the product lines and items that a particular seller offers for sale. For example, The Clorox Company is best known for its CLOROX bleach. But, in fact, Clorox is a $5.6 billion firm that makes and markets a full product mix consisting of dozens of familiar lines and brands. Clorox divides its overall product mix into five major lines: Cleaning, Household, Lifestyle, Professional, and International.[16] Each product line consists of many brands and items.

The product mix: The Clorox Company has a nicely contained product mix consistent with its mission to "make everyday life better, every day."

All trademarks and logos appearing in this figure are owned by The Clorox Company and its subsidiaries and are used with permission. ©2016 The Clorox Company. Reprinted with permission.

A company's product mix has four important dimensions: width, length, depth, and consistency. Product mix *width* refers to the number of different product lines the company carries. For example, Clorox has a fairly contained product mix that fits its mission to "make everyday life better, every day." By contrast, GE manufactures as many as 250,000 items across a broad range of categories, from lightbulbs to medical equipment, jet engines, and diesel locomotives.

Product mix *length* refers to the total number of items a company carries within its product lines. Clorox carries several brands within each line. For example, its cleaning line includes CLOROX, FORMULA 409, LIQUID PLUMBER, SOS, PINE-SOL, TILEX, HANDI-WIPES, and others. The lifestyle line contains the KC MASTERPIECE, BRITA, HIDDEN VALLEY, and BURT'S BEES brands, among others.

Product mix *depth* refers to the number of versions offered for each product in the line. The Clorox brand contains a deep assortment of items and varieties, including disinfecting wipes, floor cleaners, stain removers, and bleach products. Each variety comes in a number of product forms, formulations, scents, and sizes. For example, you can buy CLOROX Regular Bleach, CLOROX Scented Bleach, CLOROX Bleach Foamer, CLOROX High Efficiency Bleach, CLOROX UltimateCare Bleach (gentle for delicate fabrics), or any of a dozen other varieties.

Finally, the *consistency* of the product mix refers to how closely related the various product lines are in end use, production requirements, distribution channels, or some other aspect. The Clorox Company's product lines are consistent insofar as they are primarily consumer products and go through the same distribution channels. The lines are less consistent insofar as they perform different functions for buyers.

These product mix dimensions provide the handles for defining the company's product strategy. A company can increase its business in four ways. It can add new product lines, widening its product mix. In this way, its new lines build on the company's reputation in its other lines. A company can lengthen its existing product lines to become a more full-line company. It can add more versions of each product and thus deepen its product mix. Finally, a company can pursue more product line consistency—or less—depending on whether it wants to have a strong reputation in a single field or in several fields.

From time to time, a company may also have to streamline its product mix to pare out marginally performing lines and to regain its focus. For example, P&G pursues a megabrand strategy built around 23 billion-dollar-plus brands in the household care and beauty and grooming categories. During the past decade, the consumer products giant has sold off dozens of major brands that no longer fit either its evolving focus or the billion-dollar threshold, ranging from Jif peanut butter, Crisco shortening, Folgers coffee, Pringles snack chips, and Sunny Delight drinks to Noxzema skin care products, Right Guard deodorant, and Aleve pain reliever. In its most dramatic product pruning move yet, P&G announced plans to cut or sell off as many as 90 to 100 of its remaining brands, resulting in the recent unloading of headliner brands such as Duracell batteries, CoverGirl and Max Factor cosmetics, Wella and Clairol hair care products, and its Iams and other pet food brands. These divestments will allow P&G to focus investment and energy on the 70 to 80 core brands that yield 90 percent of its sales and more than 95 percent of profits. "Less will be much more," says P&G's CEO.[17]

LINKING THE CONCEPTS

Slow down for a minute. To get a better sense of how large and complex a company's product offering can become, investigate Procter & Gamble's product mix.

- Using P&G's Web site (www.pg.com), its annual report, or other sources, develop a list of all the company's product lines and individual products. What surprises you about this list of products?
- Is P&G's product mix consistent? What products has P&G dropped or sold recently? What overall strategy or logic appears to have guided the shaping of this product mix?

Author Comment
As noted at the start of this chapter, services are "products," too—intangible ones. So all the product topics we've discussed so far apply to services as well as to physical products. However, in this section, we focus on the special characteristics and marketing needs that set services apart.

Services Marketing

Services have grown dramatically in recent years. Services now account for 80 percent of the U.S. gross domestic product (GDP). Services are growing even faster in the world economy, making up almost 64 percent of the gross world product.[18]

Service industries vary greatly. *Governments* offer services through courts, employment services, hospitals, military services, police and fire departments, the postal service, and schools. *Private not-for-profit organizations* offer services through museums, charities, churches, colleges, foundations, and hospitals. In addition, a large number of *business organizations* offer services—airlines, banks, hotels, insurance companies, consulting firms, medical and legal practices, entertainment and telecommunications companies, real estate firms, retailers, and others.

The Nature and Characteristics of a Service

A company must consider four special service characteristics when designing marketing programs: intangibility, inseparability, variability, and perishability (see **>> Figure 7.3**).

Service intangibility
Services cannot be seen, tasted, felt, heard, or smelled before they are bought.

Service intangibility means that services cannot be seen, tasted, felt, heard, or smelled before they are bought. For example, people undergoing cosmetic surgery cannot see the result before the purchase. Airline passengers have nothing but a ticket and a promise that they and their luggage will arrive safely at the intended destination, hopefully

>> Figure 7.3 Four Service Characteristics

Although services are "products" in a general sense, they have special characteristics and marketing needs. The biggest differences come from the fact that services are essentially intangible and that they are created through direct interactions with customers. Think about your experiences with an airline or Google versus Nike or Apple.

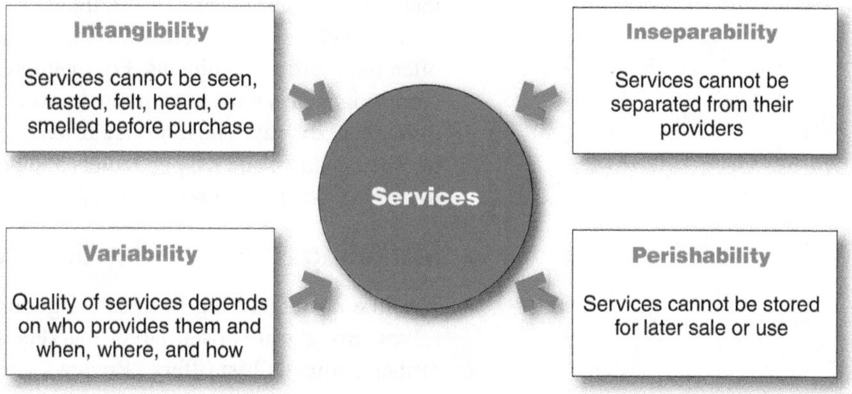

at the same time. To reduce uncertainty, buyers look for *signals* of service quality. They draw conclusions about quality from the place, people, price, equipment, and communications that they can see.

Therefore, the service provider's task is to make the service tangible in one or more ways and send the right signals about quality. » The Mayo Clinic does this well:[19]

> When it comes to hospitals, most patients can't really judge "product quality." It's a very complex product that's hard to understand, and you can't try it out before buying it. So when considering a hospital, most people unconsciously search for evidence that the facility is caring, competent, and trustworthy. The Mayo Clinic doesn't leave these things to chance. Rather, it offers patients organized and honest evidence of its dedication to "providing the best care to every patient every day."
>
> Inside, staff is trained to act in a way that clearly signals Mayo Clinic's concern for patient well-being. For example, doctors regularly follow up with patients at home to see how they are doing, and they work with patients to smooth out scheduling problems. The clinic's physical facilities also send the right signals. They've been carefully designed to offer a place of refuge, show caring and respect, and signal competence. Looking for external confirmation? Go online and hear directly from those who've been to the clinic or work there. The Mayo Clinic uses social networking—everything from blogs to Facebook, Twitter, YouTube, and Pinterest—to enhance the patient experience. For example, on the Sharing Mayo Clinic blog (http://sharing.mayoclinic.org), patients and their families retell their Mayo experiences, and Mayo employees offer behind-the-scenes views. The result? Highly loyal customers who willingly spread the good word to others, building one of the most powerful brands in health care.

» **By providing customers with organized, honest evidence of its capabilities, the Mayo Clinic has built one of the most powerful brands in health care. Its Sharing Mayo Clinic blog lets you hear directly from those who have been to the clinic or who work there.**

Mayo Clinic

Physical goods are produced, then stored, then later sold, and then still later consumed. In contrast, services are first sold and then produced and consumed at the same time. **Service inseparability** means that services cannot be separated from their providers, whether the providers are people or machines. If a service employee provides the service, then the employee becomes a part of the service. And customers don't just buy and use a service; they play an active role in its delivery. Customer coproduction makes *provider–customer interaction* a special feature of services marketing. Both the provider and the customer affect the service outcome.

Service inseparability
Services are produced and consumed at the same time and cannot be separated from their providers.

Service variability means that the quality of services depends on who provides them as well as when, where, and how they are provided. For example, some hotels—say, Marriott—have reputations for providing better service than others. Still, within a given Marriott hotel, one registration-counter employee may be cheerful and efficient, whereas another standing just a few feet away may be grumpy and slow. Even the quality of a single Marriott employee's service varies according to his or her energy and frame of mind at the time of each customer encounter.

Service variability
The quality of services may vary greatly depending on who provides them and when, where, and how they are provided.

Service perishability means that services cannot be stored for later sale or use. Some doctors charge patients for missed appointments because the service value existed only at that point and disappeared when the patient did not show up. The perishability of services is not a problem when demand is steady. However, when demand fluctuates, service firms often have difficult problems. For example, because of rush-hour demand, public transportation companies have to own much more equipment than they would if demand were even throughout the day. Thus, service firms often design strategies for producing a better match between demand and supply. Hotels and resorts charge lower prices in the off-season to attract more guests. And restaurants hire part-time employees to serve during peak periods.

Service perishability
Services cannot be stored for later sale or use.

Marketing Strategies for Service Firms

Just like manufacturing businesses, good service firms use marketing to position themselves strongly in chosen target markets. FedEx promises to take your packages "faster, farther"; Angie's List offers "Reviews you can trust." At Hampton, "We love having you here." And St. Jude Children's Hospital is "Finding cures. Saving children." These and other service firms establish their positions through traditional marketing mix activities. However, because services differ from tangible products, they often require additional marketing approaches.

The Service Profit Chain

Service profit chain
The chain that links service firm profits with employee and customer satisfaction.

In a service business, the customer and the front-line service employee *interact* to co-create the service. Effective interaction, in turn, depends on the skills of front-line service employees and on the support processes backing these employees. Thus, successful service companies focus their attention on both their customers and their employees. They understand the **service profit chain**, which links service firm profits with employee and customer satisfaction. This chain consists of five links:[20]

- ***Internal service quality.*** Superior employee selection and training, a quality work environment, and strong support for those dealing with customers, which results in...
- ***Satisfied and productive service employees.*** More satisfied, loyal, and hardworking employees, which results in...
- ***Greater service value.*** More effective and efficient customer value creation, engagement, and service delivery, which results in...
- ***Satisfied and loyal customers.*** Satisfied customers who remain loyal, make repeat purchases, and refer other customers, which results in...
- ***Healthy service profits and growth.*** Superior service firm performance.

For example, supermarket chain Wegmans—a perennial customer service champion—has developed a cult-like customer following by putting its employees first. Wegmans believes that happy, superbly trained employees create a superior customer experience. The resulting happy customers become tremendously loyal, give the firm more business, and convince other customers to do the same. That, in turn, results in happy investors. "Our employees are our number one asset, period," says a Wegmans executive. "The first question [we] ask is 'Is this the best thing for employees?'"[21] Similarly, customer-service all-star Zappos.com—the online shoes, clothing, and accessories retailers—knows that happy customers begin with happy, dedicated, energetic employees (see Marketing at Work 7.1).

Internal marketing
Orienting and motivating customer-contact employees and supporting service employees to work as a team to provide customer satisfaction.

Services marketing requires more than just traditional external marketing using the four Ps. **Figure 7.4** shows that services marketing also requires *internal marketing* and *interactive marketing*. **Internal marketing** means that the service firm must orient and motivate its customer-contact employees and supporting service people to work as a team to provide customer satisfaction. Marketers must get everyone in the organization to be customer centered. In fact, internal marketing must *precede* external marketing. For example, Zappos starts by hiring the right people and carefully orienting and inspiring them to give unparalleled customer service. The idea is to make certain that employees themselves believe in the brand so that they can authentically deliver the brand's promise to customers.

Figure 7.4 Three Types of Services Marketing

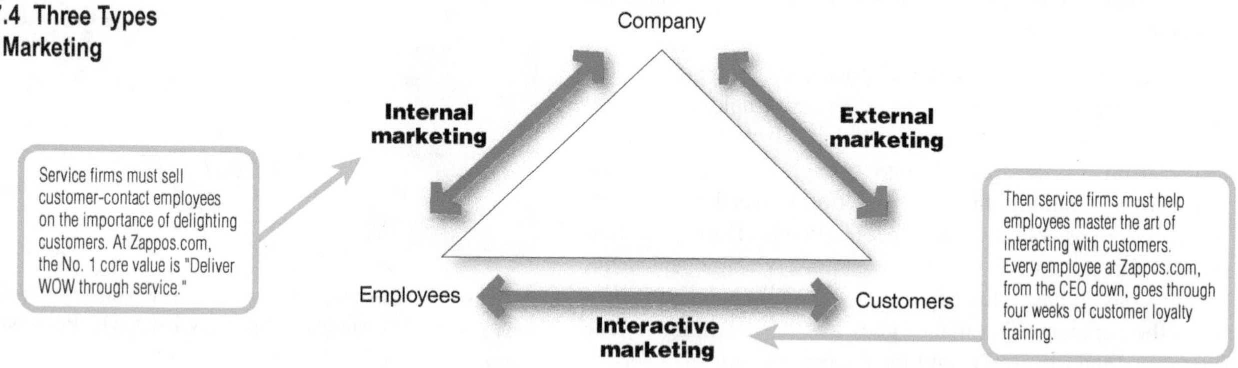

MARKETING AT WORK 7.1

Zappos.com: Taking Care of Those Who Take Care of Customers

Imagine a retailer with service so good its customers wish it would take over the Internal Revenue Service or start up an airline. It might sound like a marketing fantasy, but this scenario is a reality for customer-service all-star Zappos.com. At Zappos, the customer experience really does come first—it's a daily obsession. Says Zappos's understated CEO Tony Hsieh (pronounced "Shay"), "Our whole goal at Zappos is for the Zappos brand to be about the very best customer service and customer experience." Zappos is "Powered by Service."

From the start, the scrappy online retailer of shoes, clothing, handbags, and accessories made customer service a cornerstone of its marketing. As a result, Zappos grew astronomically. In fact, Zappos's online success and passion for customers made it an ideal match for another highly successful, customer-obsessed online retailer, Amazon.com, which purchased Zappos a few years ago and has allowed it to operate as an independent division.

At Zappos, customer care starts with a deep-down, customer-focused culture. How does Zappos turn this culture into a customer reality? It all starts with the company's customer-service reps—what the company calls its Customer Loyalty Team. Most of Zappos.com's business is driven by word-of-mouth and customer interactions with company employees. And Zappos knows that happy *customers* begin with happy, dedicated, and energetic *employees*. So the company starts by hiring the right people, training them thoroughly in customer-service basics, and inspiring them to new heights in taking care of customers.

"Getting customers excited about the service they had at Zappos has to come naturally," says one Zappos marketing executive. "You can't teach it; you have to hire for it." Hiring the right people starts with the application process. The invitation to apply on the Zappos Web site suggests the kind of people Zappos seeks:

> Please check out the Zappos Family's 10 Core Values before applying! They are the heart and soul of our culture and central to how we do business. If you are "fun and a little weird"—and think the other 9 Core Values fit you too—please take a look at our openings! PS: At the Zappos Family of Companies, over-sized egos are not welcome. Over-sized Eggos, however, are most welcome and appreciated!

Once hired, to make sure Zappos's customer obsession permeates the entire organization, each new employee—everyone from the CEO and chief financial officer to the children's footwear buyer—is required to go through four weeks of customer loyalty training. In fact, in an effort to weed out the half-hearted, Zappos actually bribes people to quit. During the four weeks of customer-service training, it offers employees a full month's pay in cash plus payment for the time worked if they *leave* the company. The theory goes that those willing to take the money and run aren't right for Zappos' culture anyway.

Once in place, Zappos treats employees as well as it treats customers. "It's not so much about what the company provides externally," says CEO Hsieh. "It's what the employees ultimately feel internally." The Zappos family culture emphasizes "a satisfying and fulfilling job...and a career you can be proud of. Work hard. Play hard. All the time!" Hsieh continues, "We think it's important for employees to have fun...it drives employee engagement." Zappos creates a relaxed, fun-loving, and close-knit family atmosphere, complete with free meals, a nap room, Nerf gun wars, and Oreo eating contests, not to mention full benefits, a 40 percent employee discount on all Zappos.com merchandise, and even a full-time life coach—all of which make it a great place to work. In fact, Zappos appears annually on *Fortune* magazine's "100 Best Companies to Work For" list.

The result is what one observer calls "1,550 perpetually chipper employees." Every year, the company publishes a "culture book," filled with unedited, often gushy testimonials from Zapponians about what it's like to work there. "Oh my gosh,"

» Zappos knows that delivering customer happiness begins with happy, dedicated, energetic employees. Zappos is "Powered by Service."

Zappos

says one employee, "this is my home away from home. . . . It's changed my life. . . . Our culture is the best reason to work here." Says another, "The most surprising thing about coming to work here is that there are no limits. So pretty much anything you are passionate about is possible." And what are the things about which Zapponians are most passionate? The Zappos family's No. 1 core value: "Deliver WOW through service."

Such enthusiastic employees, in turn, make outstanding brand ambassadors. Whereas many Web sites bury contact information several links deep because they don't really want to hear from customers, Zappos.com puts the number at the top of every single Web page and staffs its call center 24/7. Hsieh sees each customer contact as an opportunity: "We actually want to talk to our customers," he says. "If we handle the call well, we have an opportunity to create an emotional impact and lasting memory."

Hsieh insists that reps be helpful with anything that customers might call about—and he really means it. One customer called in search of a pizza joint open after midnight in Santa Monica, CA. Two minutes later, the Zappos rep found him one. And Zappos doesn't hold its reps accountable for call times. Its longest phone call lasted 10 hours. Another call, from a customer who wanted the rep's help while she looked at what seemed like thousands of pairs of shoes, lasted almost six hours.

At Zappos, each employee is like a little marketing department. Relationships—inside and outside the company—mean everything at Zappos. Hsieh and many other employees stay in direct touch with customers, with each other, and with just about anyone else interested in the company. They use social networking tools such as Facebook, Twitter, Pinterest, and blogs to share information, both good and bad. Such openness might worry some retailers, but Zappos embraces it.

Zappos even features employees in its marketing. For example, it uses associates in short videos to describe and explain its products. In one recent year, it turned out 100,000 such videos of staff—not professional models—showing off shoes, bags, and clothing. Zappos found that when the product includes a personal video explanation, purchases rise and returns decrease.

The moral: Just as the service-profit chain suggests, taking good care of customers begins with taking good care of those who take care of customers. The Zappos customer-driven philosophy is perhaps best summed up by the title of CEO Hsieh's book—*Delivering Happiness: A Path to Profits, Passion, and Purpose*. Zappos's enthusiasm and culture are infectious. Put Zappos happy reps together with happy customers and good things will result. "We've actually had customers ask us if we would please start an airline or run the IRS," Hsieh says, adding, "30 years from now I wouldn't rule out a Zappos airline that's all about the very best service."

Sources: Portions based on http://about.Zappos.com/jobs, accessed March 2015; and Natalie Zmuda, "Zappos: Customer Service First—and a Daily Obsession," *Advertising Age*, October 20, 2008, p. 36; with additional information and quotes from Jim Edwards, "Check Out the Insane Lengths Zappos Customer Service Reps Will Go To," *Business Insider*, January 9, 2012, www.businessinsider.com/zappos-customer-service-crm-2012-1; Tony Hsieh, "Zappos's CEO on Going to Extremes for Customers," *Harvard Business Review*, July–August 2010, pp. 41–44; "Zappos Corporate Culture: Innovating for Employees, Clients, and the Ecosystem," *Innovation Is Everywhere*, www.innovationiseverywhere.com/zappos-corporate-culture-innovating-employees-clients-ecosystem/, accessed March 2015; "100 Best Companies to Work For," *Fortune*, http://money.cnn.com/magazines/fortune/best-companies/, accessed September 2015; and www.youtube.com/users/zappos and www.zappos.com, accessed September 2015.

Interactive marketing
Training service employees in the fine art of interacting with customers to satisfy their needs.

Interactive marketing means that service quality depends heavily on the quality of the buyer–seller interaction during the service encounter. In product marketing, product quality often depends little on how the product is obtained. But in services marketing, service quality depends on both the service deliverer and the quality of delivery. Service marketers, therefore, have to master interactive marketing skills. Thus, Zappos selects only people with an innate "passion to serve" and instructs them carefully in the fine art of interacting with customers to satisfy their every need. All new hires—at all levels of the company—complete a four-week customer-loyalty training regimen.

Today, as competition and costs increase and as productivity and quality decrease, more services marketing sophistication is needed. Service companies face three major marketing tasks: They want to increase their *service differentiation, service quality*, and *service productivity*.

Managing Service Differentiation

In these days of intense price competition, service marketers often complain about the difficulty of differentiating their services from those of competitors. To the extent that customers view the services of different providers as similar, they care less about the provider than the price. The solution to price competition is to develop a differentiated offer, delivery, and image.

The *offer* can include innovative features that set one company's offer apart from competitors' offers. For example, some retailers differentiate themselves with offerings that take you well beyond the products they stock. Apple's highly successful stores offer a Genius Bar for technical support and a host of free workshops on everything from iPhone, iPad, and

Service differentiation: Apple differentiates its stores by offering extras such as free workshops on everything from iPhone, iPad, and Mac basics to the intricacies of using iMovie to turn home movies into blockbusters.

Mario Tama/Getty Images

Mac basics to the intricacies of using iMovie to turn home movies into blockbusters. At some Dick's Sporting Goods, customers can sample shoes on Dick's indoor footwear track, test golf clubs with an on-site golf swing analyzer and putting green, shoot bows in its archery range, and receive personalized fitness product guidance from an in-store team of fitness trainers.

Service companies can differentiate their service *delivery* by having more able and reliable customer-contact people, developing a superior physical environment in which the service product is delivered, or designing a superior delivery process. For example, many grocery chains now offer online shopping and home delivery as a better way to shop than having to drive, park, wait in line, and tote groceries home. And most banks offer mobile phone apps that allow you to more easily transfer money and check account balances. Many even allow mobile check deposits. "Sign, snap a photo, and submit a check from anywhere," says one Citibank ad. "It's easier than running to the bank."

Finally, service companies also can work on differentiating their *images* through symbols and branding. Aflac adopted the duck as its advertising symbol. Today, the duck is immortalized through stuffed animals, golf club covers, and free ringtones and screensavers. The well-known Aflac duck helped make the big but previously unknown insurance company memorable and approachable. Other well-known service characters and symbols include the GEICO gecko, Progressive Insurance's Flo, McDonald's golden arches, Allstate's "good hands," the Twitter bird, and the freckled, red-haired, pig-tailed Wendy's girl. Mr. Clean has amassed more than 1 million Facebook fans.

Managing Service Quality

A service firm can differentiate itself by delivering consistently higher quality than its competitors provide. Like manufacturers before them, most service industries have now joined the customer-driven quality movement. And like product marketers, service providers need to identify what target customers expect in regard to service quality.

Unfortunately, service quality is harder to define and judge than product quality. For instance, it is harder to agree on the quality of a haircut than on the quality of a hair dryer. Customer retention is perhaps the best measure of quality; a service firm's ability to hang onto its customers depends on how consistently it delivers value to them.

Top service companies set high service-quality standards. They watch service performance closely, both their own and that of competitors. They do not settle for merely good service—they strive for 100 percent defect-free service. A 98 percent performance standard may sound good, but using this standard, the U.S. Postal Service would lose or misdirect 361,000 pieces of mail each hour, and U.S. pharmacies would misfill 1.5 million prescriptions each week.[22]

Unlike product manufacturers who can adjust their machinery and inputs until everything is perfect, service quality will always vary, depending on the interactions between employees and customers. As hard as they may try, even the best companies will have an occasional late delivery, burned steak, or grumpy employee. However, good *service recovery* can turn angry customers into loyal ones. In fact, good recovery can win more customer purchasing and loyalty than if things had gone well in the first place.

For example, Southwest Airlines has a proactive customer communications team whose job is to find the situations in which something went wrong—a mechanical delay, bad weather, a medical emergency, or a berserk passenger—then remedy the bad experience quickly, within 24 hours if possible.[23] The team's communications to passengers, usually emails these days, have three basic components: a sincere apology, a brief explanation of what happened, and a gift to make it up, usually a voucher in dollars that can be used on their next Southwest flight. Surveys show that when Southwest handles a delay situation well, customers score it 14 to 16 points higher than on regular on-time flights.

These days, social media such as Facebook and Twitter can help companies root out and remedy customer dissatisfaction with service. As discussed in Chapter 4, many companies now monitor the digital space to spot customer issues quickly and respond in real time. A quick and thoughtful response can turn a dissatisfied customer into a brand advocate.[24]

» **Managing service productivity: Companies should be careful not to take things too far. For example, in their attempts to improve productivity, some airlines have mangled customer service.**

DPA/Stringer/Getty Images

Managing Service Productivity

With their costs rising rapidly, service firms are under great pressure to increase service productivity. They can do so in several ways. They can train current employees better or hire new ones who will work harder or more skillfully. Or they can increase the quantity of their service by giving up some quality. Finally, a service provider can harness the power of technology. Although we often think of technology's power to save time and costs in manufacturing companies, it also has great—and often untapped—potential to make service workers more productive.

However, companies must avoid pushing productivity so hard that doing so reduces quality. Attempts to streamline a service or cut costs can make a service company more efficient in the short run. But that can also reduce its longer-run ability to innovate, maintain service quality, or respond to consumer needs and desires. » For example, some airlines have learned this lesson the hard way as they attempt to economize in the face of rising costs. Passengers on most airlines now encounter "time-saving" check-in kiosks rather than personal counter service. And most airlines have stopped offering even the little things for free—such as in-flight snacks—and now charge extra for everything from checked luggage to aisle seats. The result is a plane full of disgruntled customers. In their attempts to improve productivity, many airlines have mangled customer service.

Thus, in attempting to improve service productivity, companies must be mindful of how they create and deliver customer value. They should be careful not to take *service* out of the service. In fact, a company may purposely lower service productivity in order to improve service quality, in turn allowing it to maintain higher prices and profit margins.

LINKING THE CONCEPTS

Let's pause here for a moment. We've said that although services are "products" in a general sense, they have special characteristics and marketing needs. To get a better grasp of this concept, select a traditional product brand, such as Nike or Honda. Next, select a service brand, such as JetBlue Airlines or McDonald's. Then compare the two.

- How are the characteristics and marketing needs of the product and service brands you selected similar?
- How do the characteristics and marketing needs of the two brands differ? How are these differences reflected in each brand's marketing strategy? Keep these differences in mind as we move into the final section of the chapter.

Author Comment
A brand represents everything that a product or service *means* to consumers. As such, brands are valuable assets to a company. For example, when you hear someone say "Coca-Cola," what do you think, feel, or remember? What about "Target"? Or "Google"?

Branding Strategy: Building Strong Brands

Some analysts see brands as *the* major enduring asset of a company, outlasting the company's specific products and facilities. John Stewart, former CEO of Quaker Oats, once said, "If this business were split up, I would give you the land and bricks and mortar, and I would keep the brands and trademarks, and I would fare better than you." A former CEO of McDonald's declared, "If every asset we own, every building, and every piece of equipment were destroyed in a terrible natural disaster, we would be able to borrow all the money to replace it very quickly because of the value of our brand. . . . The brand is more valuable than the totality of all these assets."[25]

Thus, brands are powerful assets that must be carefully developed and managed. In this section, we examine the key strategies for building and managing product and service brands.

Brand Equity and Brand Value

Brands are more than just names and symbols. They are a key element in the company's relationships with consumers. Brands represent consumers' perceptions and feelings about a product and its performance—everything that the product or the service *means* to consumers. In the final analysis, brands exist in the heads of consumers. As one well-respected marketer once said, "Products are created in the factory, but brands are created in the mind."[26]

Brand equity
The differential effect that knowing the brand name has on customer response to the product and its marketing.

A powerful brand has high *brand equity*. **Brand equity** is the differential effect that knowing the brand name has on customer response to the product and its marketing. It's a measure of the brand's ability to capture consumer preference and loyalty. A brand has positive brand equity when consumers react more favorably to it than to a generic or unbranded version of the same product. It has negative brand equity if consumers react less favorably than to an unbranded version.

Brands vary in the amount of power and value they hold in the marketplace. Some brands—such as Coca-Cola, Nike, Disney, GE, McDonald's, Harley-Davidson, and others—become larger-than-life icons that maintain their power in the market for years, even generations. Other brands—such as Google, Apple, ESPN, Instagram, and Wikipedia—create fresh consumer excitement and loyalty. These brands win in the marketplace not simply because they deliver unique benefits or reliable service. Rather, they succeed because they forge deep connections with customers. People really do have relationships with brands. » For example, to devoted Vespa fans around the world, the brand stands for much more than just a scooter. It takes them places, physically and emotionally. It stands for "La Vespa Vita," a carefree, stylish lifestyle. Colorful, cute, sleek, nimble, efficient—the Vespa brand represents the freedom to roam wherever you wish and "live life with passion."[27]

Ad agency Young & Rubicam's BrandAsset Valuator measures brand strength along four consumer perception dimensions: *differentiation* (what makes the brand stand out), *relevance* (how consumers feel it meets their needs), *knowledge* (how much consumers know about the brand), and *esteem* (how highly consumers regard and respect the brand). Brands with strong brand equity rate high on all four dimensions. The brand must be distinct, or consumers will have no reason to choose it over other brands. However, the fact that a brand is highly differentiated doesn't necessarily mean that consumers will buy it. The brand must stand out in ways that are relevant to consumers' needs. Even a differentiated, relevant brand is far from a shoe-in. Before consumers will respond to the brand, they must first know about and understand it. And that familiarity must lead to a strong, positive consumer–brand connection.[28]

» **Consumers' relationship with brands: To devoted Vespa fans, the brand stands for much more than just a scooter. It stands for "La Vespa Vita"—living life with passion.**

Courtesy of Piaggio Group

Thus, positive brand equity derives from consumer feelings about and connections with a brand. Consumers sometimes bond *very* closely with specific brands. As perhaps the ultimate expression of brand devotion, a surprising number of people—and not just Harley-Davidson fans—have their favorite brand tattooed on their bodies.

Whether it's contemporary new brands such as Facebook or Amazon or old classics like Harley or Converse, strong brands are built around an ideal of engaging consumers in some relevant way.

Brand value
The total financial value of a brand.

A brand with high brand equity is a very valuable asset. **Brand value** is the total financial value of a brand. Measuring such value is difficult. However, according to one estimate, the brand value of Google is a whopping $159 billion, with Apple at $148 billion, IBM at $108 billion, Microsoft at $90 billion, McDonald's at $86 billion, and Coca-Cola at $81 billion. Other brands rating among the world's most valuable include AT&T, China Mobile, GE, Walmart, and Amazon.[29]

High brand equity provides a company with many competitive advantages. A powerful brand enjoys a high level of consumer brand awareness and loyalty. Because consumers expect stores to carry the particular brand, the company has more leverage in bargaining with resellers. Because a brand name carries high credibility, the company can more easily launch line and brand extensions. A powerful brand also offers the company some defense against fierce price competition and other competitor marketing actions.

Above all, however, a powerful brand forms the basis for building strong and profitable customer engagement and relationships. The fundamental asset underlying brand equity is *customer equity*—the value of customer relationships that the brand creates. A powerful brand is important, but what it really represents is a profitable set of loyal customers. The proper focus of marketing is building customer equity, with brand management serving as a major marketing tool. Companies need to think of themselves not as portfolios of brands but as portfolios of customers.

Building Strong Brands

Branding poses challenging decisions to the marketer. **>> Figure 7.5** shows that the major brand strategy decisions involve *brand positioning, brand name selection, brand sponsorship*, and *brand development*.

Brand Positioning

Marketers need to position their brands clearly in target customers' minds. They can position brands at any of three levels.[30] At the lowest level, they can position the brand on *product attributes*. For example, P&G invented the disposable diaper category with its Pampers brand. Early Pampers marketing focused on attributes such as fluid absorption, fit, and disposability. In general, however, attributes are the least desirable level for brand positioning. Competitors can easily copy attributes. More important, customers are not interested in attributes as such—they are interested in what the attributes will do for them.

A brand can be better positioned by associating its name with a desirable *benefit*. Thus, Pampers can go beyond technical product attributes and talk about the resulting containment and baby skin-health benefits from staying dry. Some successful brands positioned on benefits are FedEx (guaranteed on-time delivery), Nike (performance), Walmart (save money), and Instagram (capturing and sharing moments).

The strongest brands go beyond attribute or benefit positioning. They are positioned on strong *beliefs and values*, engaging customers on a deep, emotional level. For example, to parents, Pampers mean much more than just containment and dryness. The Pampers Web site (www.pampers.com) positions Pampers as a "love, sleep, and play" brand that's concerned about happy babies, parent–child relationships, and total baby care. Says a former

Brands are powerful assets that must be carefully developed and managed. As this figure suggests, building strong brands involves many challenging decisions.

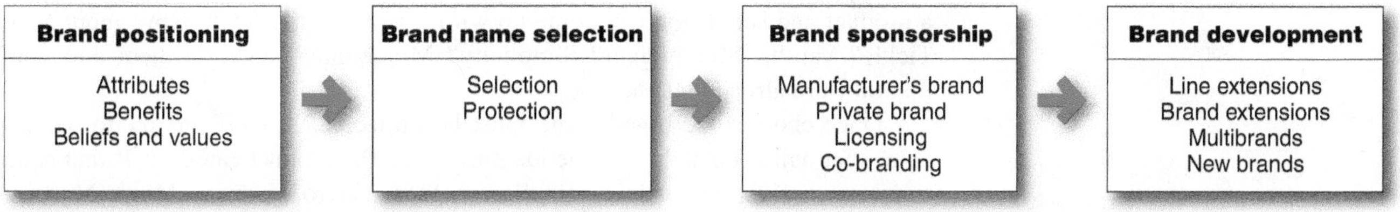

>> Figure 7.5 Major Brand Strategy Decisions

P&G executive, "Our baby care business didn't start growing aggressively until we changed Pampers from being about dryness to helping mom with her baby's development."[31]

Successful brands engage customers on a deep, emotional level. Advertising agency Saatchi & Saatchi suggests that brands should strive to become *lovemarks*, products or services that "inspire loyalty beyond reason." Brands ranging from Apple, Disney, Nike, and Coca-Cola to Trader Joe's, Google, and Pinterest have achieved this status with many of their customers. Lovemark brands pack an emotional wallop. Customers don't just like these brands; they have strong emotional connections with them and love them unconditionally.[32] Brands don't have to be big or legendary to be classified as lovemarks. Consider Shake Shack, which began 11 years ago as a lowly hot dog cart in Manhattan and grew into a small burger chain with a big, almost cult-like following. The occasionally epic lines at local Shake Shacks testify to its status as a lovemark brand.

When positioning a brand, the marketer should establish a mission for the brand and a vision of what the brand must be and do. A brand is the company's promise to deliver a specific set of features, benefits, services, and experiences consistently to buyers. The brand promise must be clear, simple, and honest. Motel 6, for example, offers clean rooms, low prices, and good service but does not promise expensive furnishings or large bathrooms. In contrast, the Ritz-Carlton offers luxurious rooms and a truly memorable experience but does not promise low prices.

Brands don't have to be big or legendary to be classified as lovemarks. The occasionally epic lines at local Shake Shacks testify to its lovemark status.

Chuck Solomon/Getty Images

Brand Name Selection

A good name can add greatly to a product's success. However, finding the best brand name is a difficult task. It begins with a careful review of the product and its benefits, the target market, and proposed marketing strategies. After that, naming a brand becomes part science, part art, and a measure of instinct.

Desirable qualities for a brand name include the following: (1) It should suggest something about the product's benefits and qualities: Beautyrest, Slimfast, Snapchat, Pinterest. (2) It should be easy to pronounce, recognize, and remember: iPad, Tide, Jelly Belly, Twitter, JetBlue. (3) The brand name should be distinctive: Panera, Swiffer, Zappos, Nest. (4) It should be extendable—Amazon.com began as an online bookseller but chose a name that would allow expansion into other categories. (5) The name should translate easily into foreign languages. The official name of Microsoft's Bing search engine in China is *bi ying,* which literally means "very certain to respond" in Chinese.[33] (6) It should be capable of registration and legal protection. A brand name cannot be registered if it infringes on existing brand names.

Choosing a new brand name is hard work. After a decade of choosing quirky names (Yahoo!, Google) or trademark-proof made-up names (Novartis, Aventis, Accenture), today's style is to build brands around names that have real meaning. For example, names like Silk (soy milk), Method (home products), Smartwater (beverages), and Snapchat (photo messaging app) are simple and make intuitive sense. But with trademark applications soaring, *available* new names can be hard to find. Try it yourself. Pick a product and see if you can come up with a better name for it. How about Moonshot? Tickle? Vanilla? Treehugger? Simplicity? Mindbender? Google them and you'll find that they are already taken.

Once chosen, the brand name must be protected. Many firms try to build a brand name that will eventually become identified with the product category. Brand names such as Kleenex, JELL-O, BAND-AID, Scotch Tape, Velcro, Formica, Magic Marker, Post-it Notes, and Ziploc have succeeded in this way. However, their very success may threaten the company's rights to the name. Many originally protected brand names—such as cellophane, aspirin, nylon, kerosene, linoleum, yo-yo, trampoline, escalator, thermos, and shredded wheat—are now generic names that any seller can use.

To protect their brands, marketers present them carefully using the word *brand* and the registered trademark symbol, as in "BAND-AID® Brand Adhesive Bandages." Even the long-standing "I am stuck on BAND-AID 'cause BAND-AID's stuck on me" jingle has now become "I am stuck on BAND-AID brand 'cause BAND-AID's stuck on me." Similarly, a recent Kleenex ad advises advertisers and others that the name Kleenex should always be followed by the registered trademark symbol and the words "Brand Tissue." "You may not realize it, but by using the name Kleenex® as a generic term for tissue," says the ad, "you risk erasing our coveted brand name that we've worked so hard for all these years."

Protecting the brand name: This ad asks advertisers and others to always add the registered trademark symbol and the words "Brand Tissue" to the Kleenex name, helping to keep from "erasing our coveted brand name that we've worked so hard for all these years."

Kimberly-Clark Worldwide, Inc. Reprinted with permission.

Brand Sponsorship

A manufacturer has four sponsorship options. The product may be launched as a *national brand* (or *manufacturer's brand*), as when Samsung and Kellogg sell their output under their own brand names (the Samsung Galaxy tablet or Kellogg's Frosted Flakes). Or the manufacturer may sell to resellers who give the product a *private brand* (also called a *store brand* or *distributor brand*). Although most manufacturers create their own brand names, others market licensed brands. Finally, two companies can join forces and *co-brand* a product. We discuss each of these options in turn.

National Brands versus Store Brands. National brands (or manufacturers' brands) have long dominated the retail scene. In recent times, however, increasing numbers of retailers and wholesalers have created their own **store brands** (or **private brands**). Store brands have been gaining strength for more than two decades, but recent tighter economic times have created a store-brand boom. Studies show that consumers are now buying even more private brands, which on average yield a 38 percent savings.[34] More frugal times give store brands a boost as consumers become more price-conscious and less brand-conscious.

Store brand (or private brand) A brand created and owned by a reseller of a product or service.

In fact, store brands have grown much faster than national brands in recent years. Private labels now account for almost 17 percent of drugstore dollar sales and 20 percent of supermarket dollar sales. One of every four supermarket products sold is private label. Similarly, for apparel sales, department store private-label brands have shot up. At Kohl's, for example, private label sales grew from 42 percent to 52 percent over the past five years.[35]

Many large retailers skillfully market a deep assortment of store-brand merchandise. For example, Kroger's private brands—the Kroger house brand, Private Selection, Heritage Farm, Simple Truth (natural and organic), Psst and Check This Out (savings), and others—add up to a whopping 25 percent of the giant grocery retailer's sales, nearly $25 billion worth annually. At thrifty grocery chain ALDI, more than 90 percent of sales come from private brands such as Baker's Choice, Friendly Farms, Simply Nature, and Mama Cozzi's Pizza Kitchen. Even online retailer Amazon has developed a stable of private brands, including Amazon Elements (diapers and other everyday essentials), AmazonBasics (electronics), Pinzon (kitchen gadgets), Strathwood (outdoor furniture), Pike Street (bath and home products), and Denali (tools).[36]

Store Brands: Kroger's store brands—from Private Selection to Simple Truth—account for 25 percent of the grocery retailer's sales.

Al Behrman/AP Images

Once known as "generic" or "no-name" brands, today's store brands are shedding their image as cheap knockoffs of national brands. Store brands now offer much greater selection, and they are rapidly achieving name-brand quality.

In fact, retailers such as Target and Trader Joe's are out-innovating many of their national-brand competitors. Kroger even offers a Kroger brand guarantee—"Try it, like it, or get the national brand free." As a result, consumers are becoming loyal to store brands for reasons besides price. Recent research showed that 9 out of 10 consumers believe that several store brands are just as good as national brands. "Sometimes I think they don't actually know what is a store brand," says one retail analyst.[37] In some cases, consumers are even willing to pay more for store brands that have been positioned as gourmet or premium items.

In the so-called *battle of the brands* between national and private brands, retailers have many advantages. They control what products they stock, where they go on the shelf, what prices they charge, and which ones they will feature in local promotions. Retailers often price their store brands lower than comparable national brands and feature the price differences in side-by-side comparisons on store shelves. Although store brands can be hard to establish and costly to stock and promote, they also yield higher profit margins for the reseller. And they give resellers exclusive products that cannot be bought from competitors, resulting in greater store traffic and loyalty. Fast-growing retailer Trader Joe's, which carries 85 percent store brands, largely controls its own brand destiny rather than relying on producers to make and manage the brands it needs to serve its customers best.[38]

To compete with store brands, national brands must sharpen their value propositions, especially when appealing to today's more frugal consumers. Many national brands are fighting back by rolling out more discounts and coupons to defend their market share. In the long run, however, leading brand marketers must compete by investing in new brands, new features, and quality improvements that set them apart. They must design strong advertising programs to maintain high awareness and preference. And they must find ways to partner with major distributors to find distribution economies and improve joint performance.

For example, in response to the surge in private-label sales, consumer product giant Procter & Gamble has redoubled its efforts to develop and promote new and better products, particularly at lower price points. "We invest $2 billion a year in research and development, $400 million on consumer knowledge, and about 10 percent of sales on advertising," says P&G's CEO. "Store brands don't have that capacity." As a result, P&G brands still dominate in their categories. For example, its Tide, Gain, Cheer, and other premium laundry detergent brands capture a combined 60 percent of the $7 billion U.S. detergent market.[39]

Licensing. Most manufacturers take years and spend millions to create their own brand names. However, some companies license names or symbols previously created by other manufacturers, names of well-known celebrities, or characters from popular movies and books. For a fee, any of these can provide an instant and proven brand name. For example, consider the Kodak brand with its familiar red and yellow colors, which has retained its value even after the company went bankrupt and discontinued its consumer products:[40]

> Consumer products carrying the Kodak name are no longer made by Eastman Kodak, which now focuses exclusively on printing-related commercial equipment and technology following its bankruptcy a few years ago. But the Kodak brand name and associated "Kodak moments" still resonate powerfully with consumers. So even though Eastman Kodak has dropped its consumer lines, we'll still be seeing a lot of Kodak-branded consumer products made by other companies under licensing agreements with Eastman Kodak. For example, Sakar International now makes Kodak cameras and accessories, and the Bullitt Group will soon launch a variety of Kodak electronics, including an Android smartphone and a tablet computer. Video monitoring company Seedonk makes and sells a Kodak Baby Monitoring System.
>
> Thus, the venerable old Kodak name still has value to both Eastman Kodak and the licensees who put it on their products. For Kodak, brand licensing agreements earn the company upwards of $200 million a year. In turn, licensees get a name that's immediately familiar and trusted—it will be a lot easier to market a Kodak phone than a Bullitt phone or a Kodak baby monitoring system than a Seedonk one. "It was difficult to find a brand that resonated—family values, taking care of loved ones," says a Seedonk executive. "Then the Kodak opportunity came up. Kodak Moments, these are things that are important to our customers."

Licensing: Nickelodeon has developed a stable full of hugely popular characters—such as SpongeBob SquarePants—that generate billions of dollars of retail sales each year.

AF Archive/Alamy

Apparel and accessories sellers pay large royalties to adorn their products—from blouses to ties and linens to luggage—with the names or initials of well-known fashion innovators such as Calvin Klein, Tommy Hilfiger, Gucci, or Armani. Sellers of children's products attach an almost endless list of character names to clothing, toys, school supplies, linens, dolls, lunch boxes, cereals, and other items. Licensed character names range from classics such as Sesame Street, Disney, Barbie, Star Wars, Scooby Doo, Hello Kitty, SpongeBob SquarePants, and Dr. Seuss characters to the more recent Doc McStuffins, Monster High, Angry Birds, and Ben 10. And currently, numerous top-selling retail toys are products based on television shows and movies.

Name and character licensing has grown rapidly in recent years. Annual retail sales of licensed products worldwide have grown from only $4 billion in 1977 to $55 billion in 1987 and more than $252 billion today. Licensing can be a highly profitable business for many companies. For example, Nickelodeon's hugely popular SpongeBob SquarePants character by itself has generated some $12 billion worth of endorsement deals over the past 15 years. Disney is the world's biggest licensor with a studio full of hugely popular characters, from the Disney Princesses and Disney Fairies to heroes from *Toy Story* and *Cars* and classic characters such as Mickey and Minnie Mouse. Disney characters reaped a reported $41 billion in worldwide merchandise sales last year.[41]

Co-branding
The practice of using the established brand names of two different companies on the same product.

Co-branding. **Co-branding** occurs when two established brand names of different companies are used on the same product. Co-branding offers many advantages. Because each brand operates in a different category, the combined brands create broader consumer appeal and greater brand equity. For example, Benjamin Moore and Pottery Barn joined forces to create a special collection of Benjamin Moore paint colors designed to perfectly coordinate with Pottery Barn's unique furnishings and accents. Taco Bell and Doritos teamed up to create the Doritos Locos Taco. Taco Bell sold more than 100 million of the tacos in just the first 10 weeks and quickly added Cool Ranch and Fiery versions and has since sold more than a billion. More than just co-branding, these companies are "co-making" these products.[42]

Co-branding can take advantage of the complementary strengths of two brands. It also allows a company to expand its existing brand into a category it might otherwise have difficulty entering alone. For example, Nike and Apple co-branded the Nike+iPod Sport Kit, which lets runners link their Nike shoes with their iPods to track and enhance running performance in real time. The Nike+iPod arrangement gave Apple a presence in the sports and fitness market. At the same time, it helps Nike bring new value to its customers.

Co-branding can also have limitations. Such relationships usually involve complex legal contracts and licenses. Co-branding partners must carefully coordinate their advertising, sales promotion, and other marketing efforts. Finally, when co-branding, each partner must trust that the other will take good care of its brand. If something damages the reputation of one brand, it can tarnish the co-brand as well.

Brand Development

A company has four choices when it comes to developing brands (see **Figure 7.6**). It can introduce *line extensions, brand extensions, multibrands*, or *new brands*.

Line extension
Extending an existing brand name to new forms, colors, sizes, ingredients, or flavors of an existing product category.

Line Extensions. **Line extensions** occur when a company extends existing brand names to new forms, colors, sizes, ingredients, or flavors of an existing product category. For example, over the years, KFC has extended its "finger lickin' good" chicken lineup well beyond original recipe, bone-in Kentucky fried chicken. It now offers grilled chicken, boneless fried chicken, chicken tenders, hot wings, chicken bites, and, most recently, KFC Go Cups—chicken and potato wedges in a handy car-cup holder that lets customers snack on the go.

Figure 7.6 Brand Development Strategies

Brand name \ Product category	Existing	New
Existing	Line extension	Brand extension
New	Multibrands	New brands

This is a very handy framework for analyzing brand development opportunities. For example, what strategy did Toyota use when it introduced the Toyota Camry Hybrid? When it introduced the Toyota Prius? The Scion?

A company might introduce line extensions as a low-cost, low-risk way to introduce new products. Or it might want to meet consumer desires for variety, use excess capacity, or simply command more shelf space from resellers. However, line extensions involve some risks. An overextended brand name might cause consumer confusion or lose some of its specific meaning.

For example, in its efforts to offer something for everyone—from basic burger buffs to practical parents to health-minded fast-food seekers—McDonald's has created a menu bulging with options. Some customers find the crowded menu a bit overwhelming, and offering so many choices has complicated the chain's food assembly process and slowed service at counters and drive-throughs. McDonald's has extended its menu by more than 40 percent in the past seven years, and average drive-thru wait times are the longest they've been in 15 years. As a result, McDonald's recently announced plans to cut items and simplify its menu.[43]

Brand extension
Extending an existing brand name to new product categories.

At some point, additional extensions might add little value to a line. For instance, the original Doritos Tortilla Chips have morphed into a U.S. roster of more than 20 different types of chips and flavors, plus dozens more in foreign markets. Flavors include everything from Nacho Cheese and Pizza Supreme to Blazin' Buffalo & Ranch, Fiery Fusion, and Salsa Verde. Or how about duck-flavored Gold Peking Duck Chips or wasabi-flavored Mr. Dragon's Fire Chips (Japan)? Although the line seems to be doing well with global sales of nearly $5 billion, the original Doritos chips now seem like just another flavor.[44] And how much would adding yet another flavor steal from Doritos' own sales versus those of competitors? A line extension works best when it takes sales away from competing brands, not when it "cannibalizes" the company's other items.

Brand extensions: Nest is now extending its brand to include "Works with Nest," applications developed with a variety of partners that let its smart devices interact with and control everything from video monitoring devices, smart door locks, and home lighting systems to home appliances and fitness tracking bands.
Nest Labs

Brand Extensions. A **brand extension** extends a current brand name to new or modified products in a new category. For example, Nest—the maker of stylish, connected, learning thermostats that can be controlled remotely from a phone—extended its line with an equally smart and stylish Nest Protect home smoke and carbon monoxide alarm. It's now extending the Nest line to include "Works with Nest," applications developed with a variety of partners that let its smart devices interact with and control everything from video monitoring devices, smart door locks, and home lighting systems to home appliances and fitness tracking bands. All of the extensions fit together under Nest's smart homes mission.[45]

A brand extension gives a new product instant recognition and faster acceptance. It also saves the high advertising costs usually required to build a new brand name. At the same time, a brand extension strategy involves some risk. The extension may confuse the image of the main brand—for example, how about Zippo perfume or Dr Pepper marinades? Brand extensions such as Cheetos lip balm, Heinz pet food, and Life Savers gum met early deaths.[46] And if a brand extension fails, it may harm consumer attitudes toward other products carrying the same brand name. Furthermore, a brand name may not be appropriate to a particular new product, even if it is well made and satisfying—would you consider flying on Hooters Air or wearing an Evian water-filled padded bra (both failed)? Thus, before transferring a brand name to a new product, marketers must research how well the extension fits the parent brand's associations as well as how much the parent brand will boost the extension's market success (see Marketing at Work 7.2).

Multibrands. Companies often market many different brands in a given product category. For example, in the United States, PepsiCo markets at least eight brands of soft drinks (Pepsi, Sierra Mist, Mountain Dew, Manzanita Sol, Mirinda, IZZE, Tropicana Twister, and Mug root beer), three brands of sports and energy drinks (Gatorade, AMP Energy, Starbucks Refreshers), four brands of bottled teas and coffees (Lipton, SoBe, Starbucks, and Tazo), three brands of bottled waters (Aquafina, H2OH!, and SoBe), and nine brands of fruit drinks (Tropicana, Dole, IZZE, Lipton, Looza, Ocean Spray, and others). Each brand includes a long list of sub-brands. For instance, SoBe consists of SoBe Teas & Elixers, SoBe Lifewater, SoBe Lean, and SoBe Lifewater with Coconut Water. Aquafina includes regular Aquafina, Aquafina Flavorsplash, and Aquafina Sparkling.

Multibranding offers a way to establish different features that appeal to different customer segments, lock up more reseller shelf space, and capture a larger market share. For example, although PepsiCo's many brands of beverages compete with one another on supermarket shelves, the combined brands reap a much greater overall market share than any single brand ever could. Similarly, by positioning multiple brands in multiple segments, Pepsi's eight soft drink brands combine to capture much more market share than any single brand could capture by itself.

A major drawback of multibranding is that each brand might obtain only a small market share, and none may be very profitable. The company may end up spreading its resources over many brands instead of building a few brands to a highly profitable level. These companies should reduce the number of brands they sell in a given category and set up tighter screening procedures for new brands. This happened to GM, which in recent years has cut numerous brands from its portfolio, including Saturn, Oldsmobile, Pontiac, Hummer, and Saab. Similarly, as part of its recent turnaround, Ford dropped its Mercury line, sold off Volvo, and pruned the number of Ford nameplates from 97 to fewer than 20.

New Brands. A company might believe that the power of its existing brand name is waning, so a new brand name is needed. Or it may create a new brand name when it enters a new product category for which none of its current brand names are appropriate. For example, Toyota created the separate Lexus brand aimed at luxury car consumers and the Scion brand, targeted toward Millennial consumers.

As with multibranding, offering too many new brands can result in a company spreading its resources too thin. And in some industries, such as consumer packaged goods, consumers and retailers have become concerned that there are already too many brands with too few differences between them. Thus, P&G, PepsiCo, Kraft, and other large marketers of consumer products are now pursuing megabrand strategies—weeding out weaker or slower-growing brands and focusing their marketing dollars on brands that can achieve the number-one or number-two market share positions with good growth prospects in their categories.

Managing Brands

Companies must manage their brands carefully. First, the brand's positioning must be continuously communicated to consumers. Major brand marketers often spend huge amounts on advertising to create brand awareness and build preference and loyalty. For example, worldwide, Coca-Cola spends almost $3 billion annually to advertise its many brands, GM spends nearly $3.4 billion, Unilever spends $7.9 billion, and P&G spends an astounding $11.5 billion.[47]

Such advertising campaigns can help create name recognition, brand knowledge, and perhaps even some brand preference. However, the fact is that brands are not maintained

MARKETING AT WORK 7.2

Brand Extensions: Consumers Say "Yeah!" or "Huh?"

These days, a large majority of new products—tens of thousands of them every year—are extensions of already-successful brands. Compared with building new brands, extensions can create immediate new-product familiarity and acceptance. For example, it's not just any new wireless charging mat for your mobile devices, it's a Duracell Powermat. And it's not just a new, no-name over-the-counter sleep-aid, it's Vicks ZzzQuil. Extensions such as the Duracell Powermat and Vicks ZzzQuil make good sense—they connect well with the core brand's values and build on its strengths.

But for every sensible and successful brand extension, there are puzzlers that leave you scratching your head and asking, "Huh? What were they thinking?" For example, how about Gerber food for adults (including a lip-smacking pureed sweet-and-sour pork and chicken Madeira)? Or how would you feel about quaffing a can of Exxon fruit punch or Kodak quencher? Other misbegotten attempts to stretch a good name include Cracker Jack cereal, Smucker's premium ketchup, Carnation pet food, and Fruit of the Loom laundry detergent. Not only were these extensions epic flops themselves, they threatened to sully the reputations of the base brands they extended. Huh? Really. What *were* they thinking?

What separates brand extension hits from misses? According to brand extension consultancy Parham | Santana, the success of a brand extension rests on three pillars: The extension should have a logical fit with the parent brand; the parent brand should give the extension a competitive advantage in a new category; and the extension should offer significant sales and profit potential.

It's the "fit factor" that seems to drive the other two pillars. The value of any brand is its good name, which it earns over time. People become loyal to it; they trust it to deliver a consistent set of attributes. You can't just take a familiar brand name and slap it on a product in another category. Instead, a good extension should fit logically with its parent brand. But brands are complex perceptual and emotional entities, so fit can be hard to define. One way to ensure fit is to focus on the brand's core product portfolio.

Consider the recent introduction of Planters Peanut Butter. For more than 100 years, the Planters brand has focused on one type of product—nuts. Cashews, almonds, pistachios, walnuts, sunflower seeds, and, of course, peanuts. No brand is more strongly associated with America's favorite nut. The company's mascot—the 100-year-old, monocled Mr. Peanut—is one of the best-known icons in advertising history. Given Planters' focus on nuts in general and on peanuts in particular, extending the brand to include peanut butter seems obvious. Consumers appear to agree. Only nine months after its introduction, Planters Peanut Butter had achieved a profitable, mid-single-digit share in a mature and highly competitive market.

Other well-known brands, however, have squandered consumer trust by attaching their good names to something totally out of character. For example, Louis Sherry No Sugar Added Gorgonzola Cheese Dressing was everything that the Louis Sherry brand—known for its rich chocolate candies and ice cream—shouldn't be: sugarless, cheese, and salad dressing. Similarly, Zippo, the company that's been making quality refillable lighters for more than 80 years, recently extended its brand with a perfume, named Zippo The Woman. The perfume has an attractive fruity and floral fragrance, and it comes in a frosted pink container that looks like a lighter, complete with the classic Zippo flip top. Unfortunately, however, no matter how good it smells, perfume has little to do with the Zippo brand's core competency of "all things flame." As a result, in a recent Parham | Santana survey, consumers voted Zippo The Woman as the worst brand extension of the past year. Zippo, what were you thinking?

Even when a new product seems to associate well with a brand's core values, consumers may not make the connection. For example, back in the early 1990s, Clorox investigated several cleaning-related extensions, from laundry detergents to carpet cleaners. That seemed to make sense, given Clorox's

>> Brand extensions: A good brand extension should fit the parent brand, and the parent brand should give the extension competitive advantage in its new category. Above, it's not just a new, no-name over-the-counter sleep-aid, it's Vicks ZzzQuil.

The Procter & Gamble Company

association with cleaning. But consumers rejected these new-product concepts, worried that cleaning products from a bleach company might damage the colors in their clothes or carpets. More than just "cleaning," consumers associated the Clorox brand with "cleaning, disinfecting, and stain fighting." So rather than trying to change those brand perceptions, Clorox leveraged them with products such as Clorox Toilet Bowl Cleaner, now the bestselling brand in its category with a 35 percent market share. Other successful brand extensions include Clorox Disinfecting Wipes, Clorox Clean-Up (designed to clean and disinfect stains on a variety of surfaces), and Clorox OxiMagic (a multi-purpose stain remover spray that works on both laundry and household stains).

Good fit goes both ways. Just as an extension should fit the parent brand, the parent brand should give the extension competitive advantage in its new category. The result is sales and profit success. For example, consumers have long associated the Vicks NyQuil brand with relieving cold symptoms so that they could get a better night's sleep. So the Vicks ZzzQuil name gave the extension a substantial boost in the sleep-aids segment. Similarly, when FedEx created FedEx TechConnect, a service that handles technology configuring, repairing, and refurbishing for businesses, the FedEx brand's established reputation for speed, reliability, and accessibility gave the new service immediate credibility over competitors.

Of course, when it comes to brand extensions, most consumers don't stop to think about the "three pillars" or other factors of success. Instead, they simply react. And according to Parham Santana's president, consumers usually have instantaneous, almost visceral responses to brand extensions. An extension either makes sense or it doesn't. In his words, "Some folks say 'Yeah!' and some just say 'Huh?'" What were they thinking?

Sources: Based on information from Robert Klara, "The Best (and Worst) Brand Extensions," *Adweek*, February 4, 2013, pp. 26–27; Robert Klara, "Best and Worst Brand Extension: Connecting with Consumers in a Meaningful Way," *Adweek,* January 14, 2014, www.adweek.com/news-gallery/advertising-branding/best-brand-extensions-2013-154948#intro: Brad Tuttle, "Why Some Brand Extensions Are Brilliant and Others Are Just Awkward," *Time*, February 7, 2013, http://business.time.com/2013/02/07/why-some-brand-extensions-are-brilliant-and-others-are-just-awkward/; Gary Belsky, "These Companies Stretched Their Brands to Make Even Bigger Bucks," *Time*, March 13, 2012, http://business.time.com/2012/03/14/the-10-best-brand-extensions-ever-according-to-me/; Denise Lee Yohn, "Great Brands Aim for Customers' Hearts, Not Their Wallets," *Forbes*, January 2014, www.forbes.com/sites/onmarketing/2014/01/08/great-brands-aim-for-customers-hearts-not-their-wallets/; and www.clorox.com/products, www.duracellpowermat.com, and www.zzzquil.com, accessed September 2015.

by advertising but by customers' *engagement* with brands and customers' *brand experiences*. Today, customers come to know a brand through a wide range of contacts and touch points. These include advertising but also personal experience with the brand, word of mouth and social media, company Web pages and mobile apps, and many others. The company must put as much care into managing these touch points as it does into producing its ads. » As one former Disney top executive put it: "A brand is a living entity, and it is enriched or undermined cumulatively over time, the product of a thousand small gestures."[48]

» **Managing brands requires managing touch points. Says a former Disney executive: "A brand is a living entity, and it is enriched or undermined cumulatively over time, the product of a thousand small gestures."**

Joe Raedle/Getty Images

The brand's positioning will not take hold fully unless everyone in the company lives the brand. Therefore, the company needs to train its people to be customer centered. Even better, the company should carry on internal brand building to help employees understand and be enthusiastic about the brand promise. Many companies go even further by training and encouraging their distributors and dealers to serve their customers well.

Finally, companies need to periodically audit their brands' strengths and weaknesses. They should ask: Does our brand excel at delivering benefits that consumers truly value? Is the brand properly positioned? Do all of our consumer touch points support the brand's positioning? Do the brand's managers understand what the brand means to consumers? Does the brand receive proper, sustained support? The brand audit may turn up brands that need more support, brands that need to be dropped, or brands that must be rebranded or repositioned because of changing customer preferences or new competitors.

MyMarketingLab

If assigned by your instructor, complete the questions marked with the ✪ from the EOC Discussion Questions section in the MyLab. To complete the Marketing by the Numbers problems found in this section, go to your Assignments in the MyLab.

REVIEWING AND EXTENDING THE CONCEPTS

CHAPTER REVIEW AND CRITICAL THINKING

Objectives Review

A product is more than a simple set of tangible features. Each product or service offered to customers can be viewed on three levels. The *core customer value* consists of the core problem-solving benefits that consumers seek when they buy a product. The *actual product* exists around the core and includes the quality level, features, design, brand name, and packaging. The *augmented product* is the actual product plus the various services and benefits offered with it, such as a warranty, free delivery, installation, and maintenance.

OBJECTIVE 7-1 Define *product* and describe the major classifications of products and services. (pp 202–207)

Broadly defined, a *product* is anything that can be offered to a market for attention, acquisition, use, or consumption that might satisfy a want or need. Products include physical objects but also services, events, persons, places, organizations, ideas, or mixtures of these entities. *Services* are products that consist of activities, benefits, or satisfactions offered for sale that are essentially intangible, such as banking, hotel, tax preparation, and home-repair services.

Products and services fall into two broad classes based on the types of consumers who use them. *Consumer products*—those bought by final consumers—are usually classified according to consumer shopping habits (convenience products, shopping products, specialty products, and unsought products). *Industrial products*—those purchased for further processing or for use in conducting a business—include materials and parts, capital items, and supplies and services. Other marketable entities—such as organizations, persons, places, and ideas—can also be thought of as products.

OBJECTIVE 7-2 Describe the decisions companies make regarding their individual products and services, product lines, and product mixes. (pp 207–215)

Individual product decisions involve product attributes, branding, packaging, labeling, and product support services. *Product attribute* decisions involve product quality, features, and style and design. *Branding* decisions include selecting a brand name and developing a brand strategy. *Packaging* provides many key benefits, such as protection, economy, convenience, and promotion. Package decisions often include designing *labels*, which identify, describe, and possibly promote the product. Companies also develop *product support services* that enhance customer service and satisfaction and safeguard against competitors.

Most companies produce a product line rather than a single product. A *product line* is a group of products that are related in function, customer-purchase needs, or distribution channels. All product lines and items offered to customers by a particular seller make up the *product mix*. The mix can be described by four dimensions: width, length, depth, and consistency. These dimensions are the tools for developing the company's product strategy.

OBJECTIVE 7-3 Identify the four characteristics that affect the marketing of services and the additional marketing considerations that services require. (pp 215–221)

Services are characterized by four key aspects: they are *intangible, inseparable, variable*, and *perishable*. Each characteristic poses problems and marketing requirements. Marketers work to find ways to make the service more tangible, increase the productivity of providers who are inseparable from their products, standardize quality in the face of variability, and improve demand movements and supply capacities in the face of service perishability.

Good service companies focus attention on *both* customers and employees. They understand the *service profit chain*, which links service firm profits with employee and customer satisfaction. Services marketing strategy calls not only for external marketing but also for *internal marketing* to motivate employees and *interactive marketing* to create service delivery skills among service providers. To succeed, service marketers must create *competitive differentiation*, offer high *service quality*, and find ways to increase *service productivity*.

OBJECTIVE 7-4 Discuss branding strategy—the decisions companies make in building and managing their brands. (pp 221–231)

Some analysts see brands as *the* major enduring asset of a company. Brands are more than just names and symbols; they embody everything that the product or the service *means* to consumers. *Brand equity* is the positive differential effect that knowing the brand name has on customer response to the product or the service. A brand with strong brand equity is a very valuable asset.

In building brands, companies need to make decisions about brand positioning, brand name selection, brand sponsorship, and brand development. The most powerful *brand positioning* builds around strong consumer beliefs and values. *Brand name selection* involves finding the best brand name based on a careful review of product benefits, the target market, and proposed marketing strategies. A manufacturer has four *brand sponsorship* options: it can launch a *national brand* (or manufacturer's brand), sell to resellers that use a *private brand*, market *licensed brands*, or join forces with another company to *co-brand* a product. A company also has four choices when it comes to developing brands. It can introduce *line extensions, brand extensions, multibrands*, or *new brands*.

Companies must build and manage their brands carefully. The brand's positioning must be continuously communicated to consumers. Advertising can help. However, brands are not maintained by advertising but by customers' *brand experiences*. Customers come to know a brand through a wide range of contacts and interactions. The company must put as much care into managing these touch points as it does into producing its ads. Companies must periodically audit their brands' strengths and weaknesses.

Key Terms

Objective 7-1
Product (p 202)
Service (p 202)
Consumer product (p 204)
Convenience product (p 205)
Shopping product (p 205)
Specialty product (p 205)
Unsought product (p 205)
Industrial product (p 206)
Social marketing (p 207)

Objective 7-2
Product quality (p 208)
Brand (p 209)
Packaging (p 210)
Product line (p 213)
Product mix (product portfolio) (p 214)

Objective 7-3
Service intangibility (p 215)
Service inseparability (p 216)
Service variability (p 216)
Service perishability (p 216)
Service profit chain (p 217)
Internal marketing (p 217)
Interactive marketing (p 219)

Objective 7-4
Brand equity (p 222)
Brand value (p 223)
Store brand (private brand) (p 225)
Co-branding (p 227)
Line extension (p 227)
Brand extension (p 228)

Discussion Questions

7-1. What is a product? Name, describe, and give an example of each type of consumer product. (AACSB: Communication; Reflective Thinking)

7-2. Compare and contrast the two dimensions of product quality. (AACSB: Communication)

7-3. What is a product line? Discuss the various product line decisions marketers make and how a company can expand its product line. (AACSB: Communication)

7-4. What is a product mix? Name and describe the four important dimensions of a product mix. (AACSB: Communication)

7-5. Discuss the four special characteristics of services. In terms of these characteristics, how do the services offered by a doctor's office differ from those offered by a bank? (AACSB: Communication, Reflective Thinking)

Critical Thinking Exercises

7-6. The Food and Drug Administration recently announced a proposal to change the standard nutrition label on food items. In a small group, research the proposed changes and create a report explaining them. Include history on nutrition labels in your presentation. (AACSB: Communication; Use of IT; Reflective Thinking)

7-7. List the names of the store brands found in the following stores: Walmart, Best Buy, and Whole Foods. Identify the private label brands of another retailer of your choice and compare the price and quality of one of the products to a comparable national brand. (AACSB: Communication; Reflective Thinking)

7-8. What is "genericide"? Discuss a recent case and make recommendations regarding how marketers can avoid it. (AACSB: Communication; Reflective Thinking)

MINICASES AND APPLICATIONS

Online, Mobile, and Social Media Marketing Keeping Tabs on Fido's Health

Want to monitor your dog's health and fitness? Now you can with devices like Whistle and Voyce, wearable bands placed around a dog's neck like a regular collar. Only this is no regular collar. It monitors your pooch's vital signs, such as heart and respiratory rates and calories burned. You can also learn if your dog is active or sleeps most of the day. Unlike humans, dogs do not exhibit symptoms and it is often too late when you notice something is wrong. Voyce gives dogs a "voice" by letting owners "connect the dots" to reveal anything that's amiss. Although the monitoring will not set off alarm bells, owners can track vital stats through a monthly subscription service synced with a computer, tablet, or smartphone and share those data with a veterinarian. Over time, the device gets to know a dog and sends owners customized articles, tips, and advice. Using a mobile device, owners can remotely access their pet's data anytime through www.MyDogsVoyce.com. Voyce also makes it easy to share your pup's milestones with friends and family through social media. Such devices are not cheap, however, ranging from $129.95 for similar product Whistle to $299 for Voyce in addition to a monthly service fee. The makers of Voyce also hope to introduce a device to fit even the smallest dogs, cats, and horses.

7-9. Describe the core, actual, and augmented levels of product associated with this product. What level does the monitoring service represent? Explain. (AACSB: Communication; Reflective Thinking)

7-10. Discuss two examples of similar types of wearable technology for humans. (AACSB: Communication; Reflective Thinking)

Marketing Ethics Geographical Indication (GI)

Scotch Whiskey, Champagne Sparkling Wine, Parmesan Cheese, Dijon Mustard—what do all of these have in common? They are not brand names but rather geographical indicators (GIs) of the origins of these foodstuffs. Europe has a long history of gastronomical delicacies that the European Union has been eager to protect for economic reasons. For example, not just any sparkling wine can be labeled *champagne* because only sparkling wine produced in the Champagne region of France can put that on the label. The British government is launching a registry of Scottish whiskey makers to protect its $4 billion industry from imitators who label their whiskey as Scotch. True Scotch must be aged in oak casks in Scotland for at least three years. Dijon mustard must be produced in Dijon, France, with chardonnay wine from the Burgundy wine region. Parmesan cheese was developed more than 2,000 years ago in Parma, Italy, which also boasts Parma ham (Prosciutto di Parma). True Swiss cheeses, such as Emmental, Gruyere, and other varieties, are produced in Switzerland following strict rules to guarantee purity, and the authorities there identify counterfeits with DNA fingerprinting based on the 10,000 strains of milk bacteria that are used for authentic Swiss cheeses. All of these come with a higher price tag for consumers. For example, Portugal Algarve Salt and French Fleur De Sel sea salt cost about $80 per pound compared with 30¢ per pound for regular table salt.

7-11. Do you think products with geographical indications are actually superior to other similar ones not originating from that geographical region? Is it ethical for makers of these products to command higher prices when others can make or grow them just as well? (AACSB: Communication; Reflective Thinking; Ethical Reasoning)

7-12. Do geographical indications (GIs) offer benefits to consumers? Are there disadvantages for sellers? Explain. (AACSB: Communication; Reflective Thinking)

Marketing by the Numbers Pop-Tarts Gone Nutty!

Kellogg's, maker of Pop-Tarts, recently introduced Pop-Tarts Gone Nutty! The new product includes flavors such as peanut butter and chocolate peanut butter. Although the new Gone Nutty! product will reap a higher wholesale price for the company ($1.20 per eight-count package of the new product versus $1.00 per package for the original product), it also comes with higher variable costs ($0.55 per eight-count package for the new product versus $0.30 per eight-count package for the original product).

7-13. What brand development strategy is Kellogg's undertaking? (AACSB: Communication; Reflective Thinking)

7-14. Assume the company expects to sell 5 million packages of Pop-Tarts Gone Nutty! in the first year after introduction but expects that 80 percent of those sales will come from buyers who would normally purchase existing Pop-Tart flavors (that is, cannibalized sales). Assuming the sales of regular Pop-Tarts are normally

300 million packages per year and that the company will incur an increase in fixed costs of $500,000 during the first year to launch Gone Nutty!, will the new product be profitable for the company? Refer to the discussion of cannibalization in Appendix 3: Marketing by the Numbers for an explanation regarding how to conduct this analysis. (AACSB: Communication; Analytical Reasoning)

Video Case Plymouth Rock Assurance

Plymouth Rock Assurance is an insurance company with a branding tale to tell. What started as a single Massachusetts-based auto insurance company in the early 1980s quickly grew into a group of separate companies that write and manage property and casualty insurance in various states. To streamline operations, cut costs, and better serve customers, the company undertook a rebranding process to combine three distinct auto insurance brands—Plymouth Rock, High Point, and Palisades—into one.

Rather than remaking the brand overnight, the company carried out a gradual transformation that retained existing brand equity and put customers' minds at ease. With Plymouth Rock as the parent brand and High Point and Palisades as sub-brands, the company transitioned the three into a single brand in incremental steps

After viewing the video featuring Plymouth Rock Assurance, answer the following questions:

7-15. What value proposition lies at the core of Plymouth Rock Assurance?)

7-16. What was the reasoning behind the decision to rebrand the three auto insurance brands as one brand?)

7-17. Describe the process that Plymouth Rock Assurance used to rebrand the company. How does this process differ from other options it could have pursued?

Company Cases 7 Target/10 Apple Pay/16 Adidas

See Appendix 1 for cases appropriate for this chapter. **Case 7, Target: Where Store Brands Offer More Than Low Prices**. In addition to carrying popular national brands, Target has built its own house for brands by moving store brands upscale. **Case 10, Apple Pay: Taking Mobile Payments Mainstream**. Apple may succeed where Google, Paypal, Visa, and others have failed in making mobile payments the go-to way to pay. **Case 16, Adidas: Athletic Apparel with Purpose**. Not just fashionable shoes and apparel, adidas is making a difference by focusing on a strategy of sustainability.

MyMarketingLab

If assigned by your instructor, complete these writing sections from your Assignments in the MyLab.

7-18. Describe how marketers manage service differentiation, other than through pricing, and describe an example of a service provider that has successfully differentiated its offering from competitors. (AACSB: Communication, Reflective Thinking)

7-19. A product's package must satisfy many criteria, such as sustainability, convenience, safety, efficiency, functionality, and marketing. Research "packaging awards" and develop a presentation analyzing an award-winning product packaging effort. Describe the organization hosting the award competition, the criteria for selecting winners, and one of the award-winning packages. (AACSB: Written and Oral Communication; Information Technology)

8 Developing New Products and Managing the Product Life Cycle

CHAPTER ROAD MAP Objective Outline

OBJECTIVE 8-1 **Explain how companies find and develop new product ideas.** New Product Development Strategy (238–239)

OBJECTIVE 8-2 **List and define the steps in the new product development process and the major considerations in managing this process.** The New Product Development Process (239–247); Managing New Product Development (247–249)

OBJECTIVE 8-3 **Describe the stages of the product life cycle and how marketing strategies change during a product's life cycle.** Product Life-Cycle Strategies (249–256)

OBJECTIVE 8-4 **Discuss two additional product issues: socially responsible product decisions and international product and services marketing.** Additional Product and Service Considerations (256–258)

Previewing the Concepts

In the previous chapter, you've learned how marketers manage and develop products and brands. In this chapter, we examine two additional product topics: developing new products and managing products through their life cycles. New products are the lifeblood of an organization. However, new product development is risky, and many new products fail. So, the first part of this chapter lays out a process for finding and growing successful new products. Once introduced, marketers then want their products to enjoy long and happy lives. In the second part of this chapter, you'll see that every product passes through several life-cycle stages, and each stage poses new challenges requiring different marketing strategies and tactics. Finally, we wrap up our product discussion by looking at two additional considerations: social responsibility in product decisions and international product and services marketing.

For openers, consider Google, one of the world's most innovative companies. Google seems to come up with an almost unending flow of knock-your-eye-out new technologies and services. If it has to do with finding, refining, or using information, there's probably an innovative Google solution for it. At Google, innovation isn't just a process; it's in the very spirit of the place.

First Stop

Google: The New Product Moonshot Factory

Google is wildly innovative. Over the past decade, it has become a top five fixture in every list of most-innovative companies. Google simply refuses to get comfortable with the way things are. Instead, it innovates constantly, plunging into new markets and taking on new competitors.

As a result, Google is also spectacularly successful. Despite formidable competition from giants such as Microsoft and Yahoo!, Google's U.S. share in its core business—online search—stands at a decisive 75 percent, more than six times the market shares of its next two competitors combined. The company also dominates in paid online and mobile search-related and other online and mobile advertising revenue, which accounted for 90 percent of Google's $66 billion in revenues last year. And Google is growing at a blistering rate—its revenues have more than doubled in just the past four years.

» Google is wildly innovative. Its innovation machine is renowned for producing new product "moonshots," futuristic longshots that, if successful, will profoundly change how people live.

Guy Corbishley/Alamy

But Google has rapidly become much more than just an online search and advertising company. Google's mission is "to organize the world's information and make it universally accessible and useful." In Google's view, information is a kind of natural resource—one to be mined, refined, and universally distributed. That idea unifies what would otherwise appear to be a widely diverse set of Google projects, such as mapping the world, creating wearable computer technology, amassing the world's largest video library, or even developing a fleet of stratospheric balloons to blanket the world with Internet access. If it has to do with harnessing and using information, Google's got it covered in some innovative way.

Google knows how to innovate. At many companies, new product development is a cautious, step-by-step affair that might take years to unfold. In contrast, Google's freewheeling new product development process moves at the speed of light. The nimble innovator implements major new products and services in less time than it takes competitors to refine and approve an initial idea. As one Google executive explains, "The hardest part about indoctrinating people into our culture is when engineers show me a prototype and I'm like, 'Great, let's go!' They'll say, 'Oh, no, it's not ready.' I tell them, 'The Googly thing is to launch it early [as a beta product] and then to iterate, learning what the market wants—and making it great.'"

When it comes to new product development at Google, there are no two-year plans. The company's new product planning looks ahead only four to five months. Google would rather see projects fail quickly than see a carefully planned, drawn-out project fail. As one Google executive puts it, "Why put off failing until tomorrow or next week if you can fail now?" Whereas even highly innovative companies such as Apple prefer the safety of a "perfect-it-before-you-sell-it" approach, at Google, it's all about "launching and iterating." When Google developers face two paths and aren't sure which one to take, they invariably take the quickest one.

Google's famously chaotic innovation process has unleashed a seemingly unending flurry of diverse products, most of which are market leaders in their categories. These include an email service (Gmail), a digital media store (Google Play), an online payment service (Google Wallet), a photo sharing service (Google Picasa), a mobile operating system (Google Android), an online social network (Google+), an ultrahigh-speed residential broadband network (Google Fiber), a cloud-friendly Internet browser (Chrome), affordable laptops with a browser for an operating system (Chromebooks), and even projects for mapping and exploring the world (Google Maps and Google Earth).

Google's most recent innovations are taking it well beyond simply organizing and searching for information. The company is now leading the way in harnessing the potential of the Internet to connect virtually everything in people's lives. For example, Google recently paid an eyeball-bending $3.2 billion—twice what it paid for YouTube—to acquire Nest Labs, a maker of smart thermostats and smoke alarms. Nest has reimagined these lowly home appliances into connected, digital devices worthy of the smartphone age, making them fun, easy, and efficient to use. And the fast-growing Nest is now moving quickly into the exploding "smart homes" arena with "Works with Nest" applications by which its devices interact with and control video monitoring devices, smart door locks, appliances, garage doors, and just about anything else around the house. Although it may seem like Google paid a lot for a little with Nest, with Google's substantial resources and innovation prowess, Nest may soon be helping you run your entire home, a huge potential market.

Google's famously chaotic, wild-eyed innovation process has unleashed a seemingly unending flurry of diverse new products. But at Google, innovation is more than a process. It's part of the company's DNA. "Where does innovation happen at Google? It happens everywhere."

If the concept of Internet-connected smart homes seems a bit far-fetched for Google, that's pretty tame next to some of the company's other grand ideas. Google's innovation machine is renowned for "moonshots"— futuristic, breathtakingly idealistic long shots that, if successful, will profoundly change how people live. To foster moonshots, Google created Google X—a secretive innovation lab and kind of nerd heaven charged with developing things that seem audacious even for Google. "Anything which is a huge problem for society we'll sign up for," says the innovation unit's director, whose official title is Captain of Moonshots.

Google X's most notable innovations so far have been in wearable smart devices, such as Google Glass virtual-reality eyewear, which jump-started the wearable technology trend. But behind the secret curtain are numerous other futuristic projects, such as those high-altitude Wi-Fi balloons, glucose-monitoring contact lenses, and Google's self-driving car—a project once thought to be pure science fiction but now surprisingly close to reality. Imagine buying something online, then having an automated Google Car pull up to your home and a Google Humanoid jump out to deliver the package to your door. Seem far-fetched? Maybe not. Google is now a leading robotics developer.

Google is open to new product ideas from just about any source. But the company also places responsibility for innovation on every employee. Google is famous for its Innovation Time-Off program, which encourages engineers and developers to spend 20 percent of their time—one day a week—developing their own "cool and wacky" new product ideas. In the end, at Google, innovation is more than a process—it's part of the company's DNA. "Where does innovation happen at Google? It happens everywhere," says a Google research scientist.

> Talk to Googlers at various levels and departments, one powerful theme emerges: These people feel that their work can change the world. The marvel of Google is its ability to continue to instill a sense of creative fearlessness and ambition in its employees. Prospective hires are often asked, "If you could change the world using Google's resources, what would you build?" But here, this isn't a goofy or even theoretical question: Google wants to know because thinking—and building—on that scale is what Google does. When it comes to innovation, Google is different. But the difference isn't tangible. It's in the air—in the spirit of the place.[1]

As the Google story suggests, companies that excel at developing and managing new products reap big rewards. Every product seems to go through a life cycle: It is born, goes through several phases, and eventually dies as newer products come along that create new or greater value for customers.

This product life cycle presents two major challenges: First, because all products eventually decline, a firm must be good at developing new products to replace aging ones (the challenge of *new product development*). Second, a firm must be good at adapting its marketing strategies in the face of changing tastes, technologies, and competition as products pass through stages (the challenge of *product life-cycle strategies*). We first look at the problem of finding and developing new products and then at the problem of managing them successfully over their life cycles.

Author Comment
New products are the lifeblood of a company. As old products mature and fade away, companies must develop new ones to take their place. For example, the iPhone and iPad have been around for less than a decade but are now Apple's two top-selling products.

New Product Development Strategy

A firm can obtain new products in two ways. One is through *acquisition*—by buying a whole company, a patent, or a license to produce someone else's product. The other is through the firm's own **new product development** efforts. By *new products* we mean original products, product improvements, product modifications, and new brands that the firm develops through its own research and development (R&D) efforts. In this chapter, we concentrate on new product development.

New product development
The development of original products, product improvements, product modifications, and new brands through the firm's own product development efforts.

New products are important to both customers and the marketers who serve them: They bring new solutions and variety to customers' lives, and they are a key source of growth for companies. In today's fast-changing environment, many companies rely on new products for the majority of their growth. For example, new products have almost completely transformed Apple in recent years. The iPhone and iPad—neither of which was available a decade ago—are now the company's two biggest-selling products, with the latest iPhone model bringing in more than two-thirds of Apple's total revenues shortly after its introduction.[2]

Yet innovation can be very expensive and very risky. New products face tough odds. For example, by one estimate, 60 percent of all new consumer packaged products introduced by established companies fail; two-thirds of new product concepts are never even launched.[3] Why do so many new products fail? There are several reasons. Although an idea may be good, the company may overestimate market size. The actual product may be poorly designed. Or it might be incorrectly positioned, launched at the wrong time, priced too high, or poorly advertised. A high-level executive might push a favorite idea despite poor marketing research findings. Sometimes the costs of product development are higher than expected, and sometimes competitors fight back harder than expected.

So, companies face a problem: They must develop new products, but the odds weigh heavily against success. To create successful new products, a company must understand its consumers, markets, and competitors and develop products that deliver superior value to customers.

Author Comment
Companies can't just hope that they'll stumble across good new products. Instead, they must develop a systematic new product development process.

The New Product Development Process

Rather than leaving new products to chance, a company must carry out strong new product planning and set up a systematic, customer-driven *new product development process* for finding and growing new products. **Figure 8.1** shows the eight major steps in this process.

Idea Generation

Idea generation
The systematic search for new product ideas.

New product development starts with **idea generation**—the systematic search for new product ideas. A company typically generates hundreds—even thousands—of ideas to find a few good ones. Major sources of new product ideas include internal sources and external sources such as customers, competitors, distributors and suppliers, and others.

Internal Idea Sources

Using *internal sources*, the company can find new ideas through formal R&D. For example, Ford operates an innovation and mobility center in Silicon Valley staffed by engineers, app developers, and scientists working on everything from driverless cars to Works with Nest apps that let consumers control home heating, lighting, and appliances from their vehicles. Chick-fil-A set up a large innovation center called Hatch, where its staff and partners explore new ideas in food, design, and service. Hatch is a place to "ideate, explore, and imagine the future," to hatch new food and restaurant ideas and bring them to life.[4]

Beyond its internal R&D process, a company can pick the brains of its own people—from executives to salespeople to scientists, engineers, and manufacturing staff. Many companies have developed successful internal social networks and *intrapreneurial* programs that encourage employees to develop new product ideas. For example, Google's Innovation Time-Off program has resulted in blockbuster product ideas ranging from Gmail and Ad Sense to Google News. A similar program at 3M, called Dream Days, has long encouraged employees to spend 15 percent of their working time on their own projects, resulting in Post-it Notes and many other successful products.[5]

Tech companies such as Facebook and Twitter sponsor periodic "hackathons," in which employees take a day or a week away from their day-to-day work to develop new ideas. LinkedIn, the 300 million–member professional social media network, holds "hackdays," a Friday each month when it encourages employees to work on whatever they want that will benefit the company. LinkedIn takes the process a step further with its InCubator program, under which employees can form teams each quarter that pitch innovative new ideas to LinkedIn executives. If approved, the team gets up to 90 days away from its regular work to develop the idea into reality.[6]

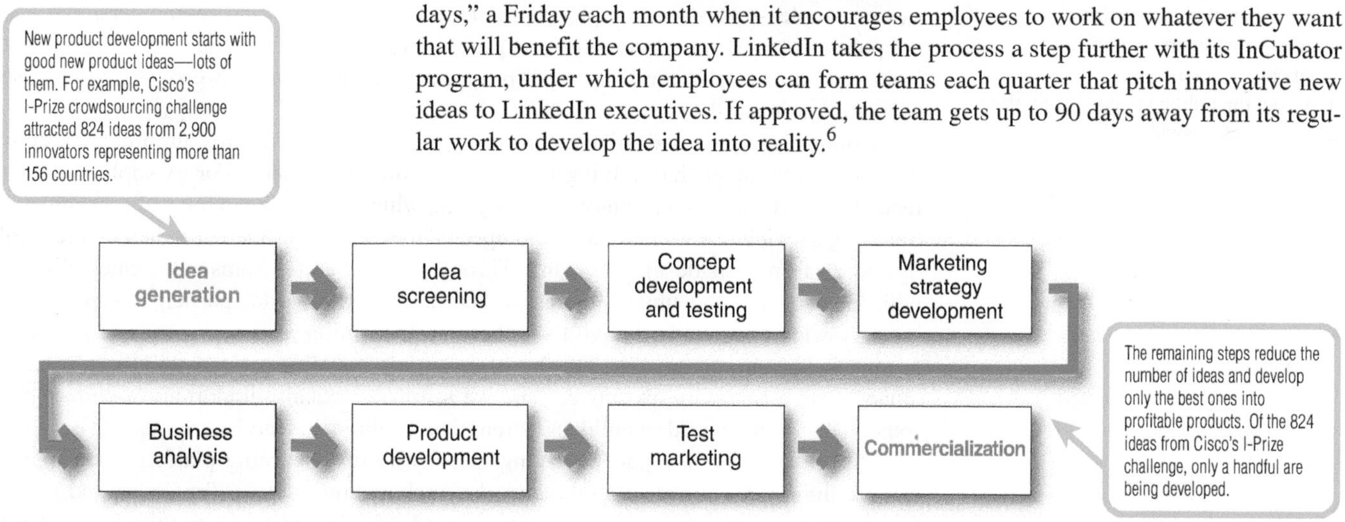

Figure 8.1 Major Stages in New Product Development

External Idea Sources

Companies can also obtain good new product ideas from any of a number of external sources. For example, *distributors and suppliers* can contribute ideas. Distributors are close to the market and can pass along information about consumer problems and new product possibilities. Suppliers can tell the company about new concepts, techniques, and materials that can be used to develop new products.

Competitors are another important source. Companies watch competitors' ads to get clues about their new products. They buy competing new products, take them apart to see how they work, analyze their sales, and decide whether they should bring out a new product of their own. Other idea sources include trade magazines, shows, Web sites, and seminars; government agencies; advertising agencies; marketing research firms; university and commercial laboratories; and inventors.

Perhaps the most important sources of new product ideas are *customers* themselves. The company can analyze customer questions and complaints to find new products that better solve consumer problems. Or it can invite customers to share suggestions and ideas. For example, the LEGO Group, maker of the classic LEGO® plastic bricks that have been fixtures in homes around the world for more than 60 years, systematically taps users for new product ideas and input via the LEGO Ideas Web site:[7]

> At the LEGO Ideas Web site, the giant toy maker turns user ideas into new LEGO building sets. The site invites customers to submit their ideas and to evaluate and vote on the ideas of others. Ideas supported by 10,000 votes head to the LEGO Review Board for an internal review by various departments including marketing and design. Ideas passing the review are made into official LEGO products. Customers whose ideas reach production earn 1 percent of total net sales of the product and receive credit as the LEGO Ideas set creator inside every set sold. So far, LEGO Ideas has resulted in 10 major new products, including the likes of LEGO Minecraft, LEGO Birds, LEGO *Big Bang Theory*, LEGO *Ghostbusters*, and LEGO *Back to the Future* DeLorean Time Machine.

New product ideas from customers: The LEGO Ideas Web site invites customer to submit and vote on new product ideas. So far, LEGO Ideas has resulted in 10 major new products.

Crowdsourcing

Crowdsourcing
Inviting broad communities of people—customers, employees, independent scientists and researchers, and even the public at large—into the new product innovation process.

More broadly, many companies are now developing crowdsourcing or open-innovation new product idea programs. Through **crowdsourcing**, a company invites broad communities of people—customers, employees, independent scientists and researchers, and even the public at large—into the innovation process. Tapping into a breadth of sources—both inside and outside the company—can produce unexpected and powerful new ideas (see Marketing at Work 8.1).

Companies large and small, across all industries, are crowdsourcing product innovation ideas rather than relying only on their own R&D labs. For example, Samsung recently launched an Open Innovation Program, which breaks down the walls surrounding Samsung's own innovation process and opens the doors to fresh new product and technology ideas from outside the company. Through the program, Samsung creates alliances with top industry and university researchers around the world, participates actively in industry-wide forums, works with suppliers on innovation, and seeks out and invests in promising start-up companies. "In the 21st century, no company can do all the research alone," says a Samsung executive, "and we see it as critically important to partner with [others] across the world to build and strengthen a vibrant research community."[8]

Rather than creating and managing their own crowdsourcing platforms, companies can use third-party crowdsourcing networks, such as InnoCentive, TopCoder, and jovoto. For example, organizations ranging from Audi, Microsoft, and Nestlé to Swiss Army Knife maker Victorinox have tapped into jovoto's network of 50,000 creative professionals for

MARKETING AT WORK 8.1

Crowdsourcing: Throwing the Innovation Doors Wide Open

Today, crowdsourcing is big business. You're probably most familiar with consumer-generated marketing efforts in which companies invite customers to help them create new advertising or product ideas. PepsiCo's Frito-Lay division is well known for doing this. For example, its annual Doritos Crash the Super Bowl ad competition generates award-winning, consumer-produced Super Bowl ads every year. And its Frito-Lay "Do Us a Flavor" competition invites consumers to submit and vote on new flavors for Lays potato chips. These highly successful crowdsourcing campaigns generate heaps of customer involvement and buzz. Last year's "Do Us a Flavor" contest alone produced more than 4 million new flavor ideas.

But today's crowdsourcing is about much more than just clever consumer contests that build buzz. Companies ranging from giants like P&G and Under Armour to small manufacturing start-ups like Quirky are throwing the innovation doors wide open, inviting broad communities of people—customers, employees, independent scientists and researchers, and even the public at large—into the new product innovation process. Consider the following examples.

Procter & Gamble

P&G has long set the gold standard for breakthrough innovation and new product development in its industry. P&G's Tide detergent was the first synthetic laundry detergent for automatic washing machines, its Pampers brand was the first successful disposable diaper, and P&G's Febreze was the first air freshener that eliminated odors rather than just covering them up. Such breakthrough innovations have been pivotal in P&G's incredible growth and success.

Until recently, most of P&G's innovations came from its own R&D labs. P&G employs more than 8,000 R&D researchers in 26 facilities around the globe, some of the best research talent in the world. But P&G's research labs alone simply can't provide the quantity of innovation required to meet the growth needs of the $84 billion company.

So about 12 years ago, P&G began inviting outside partners to help develop new products and technologies. It launched P&G Connect + Develop, a major crowdsourcing program that invites entrepreneurs, scientists, engineers, and other researchers—even consumers themselves—to submit ideas for new technologies, product designs, packaging, marketing models, research methods, engineering, or promotion—anything that has the potential to create better products that will help P&G meet its goal of "improving more consumers' lives."

P&G isn't looking to replace its 8,000 researchers; it wants to leverage them better. Through careful crowdsourcing, it can extend its inside people with millions of brilliant minds outside. Through Connect + Develop, says the company, "Together, we can do more than either of us could do alone."

Today, thanks to Connect + Develop, P&G has a truly global open-innovation network. More than 50 percent of its innovations involve some kind of external partner. So far, the program has resulted in more than 2,000 successful agreements. The long list of successful Connect + Develop products includes, among others, Tide Pods, Tide Total Care, Olay Regenerist, Swiffer Dusters, Glad ForceFlex Bags, CoverGirl Eyewear, the Oral B Pulsonic toothbrush, and Mr. Clean Magic Eraser. P&G Connect + Develop is "at the heart of how P&G innovates."

Under Armour

Sports apparel maker Under Armour knows that no matter how many top-notch developers it has inside, sometimes the only way to produce good outside-the-box ideas is by going outside the company. So Under Armour sponsors a semiannual Future Show Innovation Challenge, a competition that is part crowdsourcing and part new product *American Idol* but all business in its quest to find the Next Big Thing. The Future Show invites inventors from around the nation to submit new product ideas. From thousands of entries, an Under Armour team culls 12 finalists, who go before a panel of seven judges to pitch their products in a splashy, *Shark Tank*–like reality TV setting. The winner earns $50,000 and a contract to work with Under Armour to help develop the winning product.

>> **Crowdsourcing: New product start-up Quirky best illustrates the raw power of crowdsourcing in its purest form. "Nobody is innovating at the pace that Quirky is."**

Quirky

Under Armour founder and CEO Kevin Plank started the company with his innovative idea for a shirt that pulled moisture away from the body to keep athletes dry. Since then, the now-$2.3-billion-a-year company has built its reputation on innovative but pricy sports gear. The Future Show is one more way to keep Under Armour on the cutting edge of innovation. "We don't have all the good ideas," says Plank. The goal of the Future Show Challenge is to "cajole top innovators to come to Under Armour first with gee-whizzers."

The first winner, and Plank's favorite so far, is a made-for-athletes zipper—the UA MagZip—that can be zipped easily with only one hand. Under Armour's internal R&D team had been trying to develop a better zipper for two years, but "we couldn't get it to work," says the company's innovation chief. The crowdsourced zipper has now shown up in stores on Under Armour jackets and could eventually be used in all Under Armour outerwear. That simple zipper is just one of dozens of creative new product ideas from Future Show. But by itself, it makes the entire crowdsourcing effort worthwhile.

Quirky

It's not just big companies such as P&G and Under Armour that use crowdsourcing. Quirky is a promising $100 million company built solely around crowdsourcing. Based on the notion that ordinary people have extraordinary ideas, Quirky manufactures products from everyday inventors. It taps into an online community of 600,000 members—what one writer calls an "invention mob"—who submit inventive new product ideas in the form of "a napkin sketch, a sentence, or a fully baked product." The company receives more than 4,000 ideas a week. The community then votes for its favorites, and each week, in a live Webcast from Quirky's New York headquarters, company executives, industry experts, and community members debate the merits of submitted ideas and select three or four for development.

Quirky then handles all of the difficult design, production, legal, and marketing details in turning chosen ideas into marketable products. Crowdsourcing plays a role throughout—the Quirky community provides input on everything from design to the product's name, packaging, tagline, and price. Products that make it through development are shipped off to one of five global distribution centers, then to any of more than 35,000 retail locations, including Target, Bed Bath & Beyond, Home Depot, Best Buy, Amazon.com, Quirky's own Internet store, and even QVC.

Inventors whose ideas become products and people who contribute to improving those products share in royalties based on product sales. Of the more than 400 products that Quirky has put on store shelves in its brief history, not one has lost money. The company's top seller to date is a clever pivoting power strip called Pivot Power. Sales of the Pivot Power quickly surpassed a million units, making its young amateur inventor more than $1 million in royalties last year alone.

The P&Gs, PepsiCos, and Under Armours of the world operate on a scale that dwarfs the Quirkys. Yet small Quirky perhaps best illustrates the raw power of crowdsourcing, the democratization of product development in its purest form. As one Target representative concludes, "Nobody is innovating at the pace that Quirky is."

Sources: Based on information from Dale Buss, "P&G Enhances Connect + Develop Innovation Pipeline," *BrandChannel,* February 13, 2013, www.brandchannel.com/home/post/2013/02/13/PG-Connect-Develop-Website-021313.aspx; Larry Huston and Nabil Sakkab, "Connect and Develop: Inside Procter & Gamble's New Model for Innovation," *Harvard Business Review,* March 2006, pp. 2–9; Bruce Horovitz, "Under Armour Seeks Ideas for Its Next Big Thing," *USA Today,* October 20, 2013; Josh Dean, "Is This the World's Most Creative Manufacturer?" *Inc.,* October 2013, pp. 95–114; Kyle Stock, "Under Armour Holds a Game Show to Find Its Future," *Bloomberg Businessweek,* October 13, 2014, www.businessweek.com/articles/2014-10-13/under-armour-holds-a-game-show-to-find-its-future; Steve Lohr, "The Invention Mob, Brought to You by Quirky," *New York Times,* February 15, 2015, p. BU1; and www.pgconnectdevelop.com and www.quirky.com, accessed October 2015.

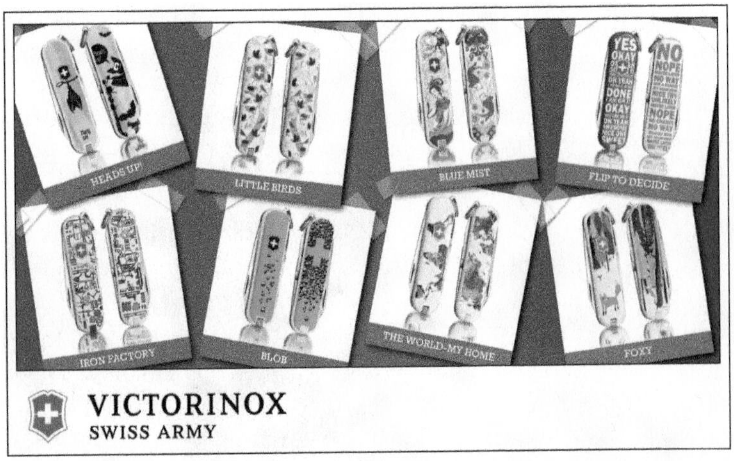

» **Victorinox used third-party crowdsourcing network jovoto to capture creative designs for limited fashion editions of its venerable Swiss Army Knife. The crowdsourced designed models had 20 percent better sales success than any previous internally created limited editions.**

Victorinox AG

ideas and solutions, offering prizes of $100 to $100,000. » For the past three years, Victorinox has used jovoto to capture new designs for a limited fashion edition of its Swiss Army Knife. The aim of the fashion designs is to attract younger buyers to the venerable old product. The first year, more than 1,000 artists submitted designs via jovoto. The limited edition, consisting of 10 designs selected after review by jovoto community members and voting on Facebook by Victorinox brand fans, had 20 percent better sales success than any previous internally created limited edition models.[9]

Crowdsourcing can produce a flood of innovative ideas. In fact, opening the floodgates to anyone and everyone can overwhelm the company with ideas—some good and some bad. For example, when Cisco Systems sponsored an open-innovation effort called I-Prize, soliciting ideas from external sources, it received more than 820 distinct ideas from more than 2,900 innovators from 156 countries. "The evaluation process was far more labor-intensive than we'd anticipated," says Cisco's chief technology officer. It required "significant investments of time, energy, patience, and imagination...to discern the gems hidden within rough stones." In the end, a team of six Cisco people worked full-time for three months to carve out 32 semifinalist ideas, as well as nine teams representing 14 countries in six continents for the final phase of the competition.[10]

Truly innovative companies don't rely only on one source or another for new product ideas. Instead, they develop extensive innovation networks that capture ideas and inspiration from every possible source, from employees and customers to outside innovators and multiple points beyond.

Idea Screening

Idea screening
Screening new product ideas to spot good ones and drop poor ones as soon as possible.

The purpose of idea generation is to create a large number of ideas. The purpose of the succeeding stages is to *reduce* that number. The first idea-reducing stage is **idea screening**, which helps spot good ideas and drop poor ones as soon as possible. Product development costs rise greatly in later stages, so the company wants to go ahead only with those product ideas that will turn into profitable products.

Many companies require their executives to write up new product ideas in a standard format that can be reviewed by a new product committee. The write-up describes the product or the service, the proposed customer value proposition, the target market, and the competition. It makes some rough estimates of market size, product price, development time and costs, manufacturing costs, and rate of return. The committee then evaluates the idea against a set of general criteria.

One marketing expert describes an R-W-W ("real, win, worth doing") new product screening framework that asks three questions. First, *Is it real?* Is there a real need and desire for the product, and will customers buy it? Is there a clear product concept, and will such a product satisfy the market? Second, *Can we win?* Does the product offer a sustainable competitive advantage? Does the company have the resources to make such a product a success? Finally, *Is it worth doing?* Does the product fit the company's overall growth strategy? Does it offer sufficient profit potential? The company should be able to answer yes to all three R-W-W questions before developing the new product idea further.[11]

Concept Development and Testing

Product concept
A detailed version of the new product idea stated in meaningful consumer terms.

An attractive idea must then be developed into a **product concept**. It is important to distinguish between a product idea, a product concept, and a product image. A *product idea* is an idea for a possible product that the company can see itself offering to the market. A *product concept* is a detailed version of the idea stated in meaningful consumer terms. A *product image* is the way consumers perceive an actual or potential product.

>> All-electric cars: This is Tesla's initial all-electric roadster. Later, more-affordable mass-market models will travel more than 300 miles on a single charge, recharge in 45 minutes from a normal 120-volt electrical outlet, and cost about one penny per mile to power.

Tesla

Concept Development

Suppose a car manufacturer has developed a practical battery-powered, all-electric car. Its initial model is a sleek, sporty roadster convertible that sells for more than $100,000.[12] >> However, in the near future it plans to introduce more-affordable, mass-market versions that will compete with recently introduced hybrid-electric or all-electric cars such as the Nissan Leaf, Chevy Volt, KIA Soul EV, and Chevy Bolt EV. This 100 percent plug-in electric car will accelerate from 0 to 60 miles per hour in four seconds, travel up to 300 miles on a single charge, recharge in 45 minutes from a normal 120-volt electrical outlet, and cost about one penny per mile to power.

Looking ahead, the marketer's task is to develop this new product into alternative product concepts, find out how attractive each concept is to customers, and choose the best one. It might create the following product concepts for this all-electric car:

- ***Concept 1.*** An affordably priced midsize car designed as a second family car to be used around town for running errands and visiting friends.
- ***Concept 2.*** A mid-priced sporty compact appealing to young singles and couples.
- ***Concept 3.*** A "green" car appealing to environmentally conscious people who want practical, no-polluting transportation.
- ***Concept 4.*** A high-end midsize utility vehicle appealing to those who love the space SUVs provide but lament the poor gas mileage.

Concept Testing

Concept testing
Testing new product concepts with a group of target consumers to find out if the concepts have strong consumer appeal.

Concept testing calls for testing new product concepts with groups of target consumers. The concepts may be presented to consumers symbolically or physically. Here, in more detail, is concept 3:

> An efficient, fun-to-drive, battery-powered compact car that seats four. This 100 percent electric wonder provides practical and reliable transportation with no pollution. It goes 300 miles on a single charge and costs pennies per mile to operate. It's a sensible, responsible alternative to today's pollution-producing gas-guzzlers. Its fully equipped base price is $28,800.

Many firms routinely test new product concepts with consumers before attempting to turn them into actual new products. For some concept tests, a word or picture description might be sufficient. However, a more concrete and physical presentation of the concept will increase the reliability of the concept test. After being exposed to the concept, consumers then may be asked to react to it by answering questions similar to those in » **Table 8.1**.

The answers to such questions will help the company decide which concept has the strongest appeal. For example, the last question asks about the consumer's intention to buy. Suppose 2 percent of consumers say they "definitely" would buy and another 5 percent say "probably." The company could project these figures to the full population in this target group to estimate sales volume. Even then, however, the estimate is uncertain because people do not always carry out their stated intentions.

Marketing Strategy Development

Marketing strategy development
Designing an initial marketing strategy for a new product based on the product concept.

Suppose the carmaker finds that concept 3 for the electric car tests best. The next step is **marketing strategy development**, designing an initial marketing strategy for introducing this car to the market.

» Table 8.1 Questions for the All-Electric Car Concept Test

1. Do you understand the concept of a battery-powered electric car?
2. Do you believe the claims about the car's performance?
3. What are the major benefits of an all-electric car compared with a conventional car?
4. What are its advantages compared with a hybrid gas-electric car?
5. What improvements in the car's features would you suggest?
6. For what uses would you prefer an all-electric car to a conventional car?
7. What would be a reasonable price to charge for the car?
8. Who would be involved in your decision to buy such a car? Who would drive it?
9. Would you buy such a car (definitely, probably, probably not, definitely not)?

The *marketing strategy statement* consists of three parts. The first part describes the target market; the planned value proposition; and the sales, market-share, and profit goals for the first few years. Thus:

> The target market is younger, well-educated, moderate- to high-income individuals, couples, or small families seeking practical, environmentally responsible transportation. The car will be positioned as more fun to drive and less polluting than today's internal combustion engine or hybrid cars. The company will aim to sell 50,000 cars in the first year, at a loss of not more than $15 million. In the second year, the company will aim for sales of 90,000 cars and a profit of $25 million.

The second part of the marketing strategy statement outlines the product's planned price, distribution, and marketing budget for the first year:

> The battery-powered all-electric car will be offered in three colors—red, white, and blue—and will have a full set of accessories as standard features. It will sell at a base retail price of $28,800, with 15 percent off the list price to dealers. Dealers who sell more than 10 cars per month will get an additional discount of 5 percent on each car sold that month. A marketing budget of $50 million will be split 40-30-30 among a national media campaign, online and social media marketing, and local event marketing. Advertising, the Web and mobile sites, and various social media content will emphasize the car's fun spirit and low emissions. During the first year, $100,000 will be spent on marketing research to find out who is buying the car and what their satisfaction levels are.

The third part of the marketing strategy statement describes the planned long-run sales, profit goals, and marketing mix strategy:

> We intend to capture a 3 percent long-run share of the total auto market and realize an after-tax return on investment of 15 percent. To achieve this, product quality will start high and be improved over time. Price will be raised in the second and third years if competition and the economy permit. The total marketing budget will be raised each year by about 10 percent. Marketing research will be reduced to $60,000 per year after the first year.

Business Analysis

Business analysis
A review of the sales, costs, and profit projections for a new product to find out whether these factors satisfy the company's objectives.

Once management has decided on its product concept and marketing strategy, it can evaluate the business attractiveness of the proposal. **Business analysis** involves a review of the sales, costs, and profit projections for a new product to find out whether they satisfy the company's objectives. If they do, the product can move to the product development stage.

To estimate sales, the company might look at the sales history of similar products and conduct market surveys. It can then estimate minimum and maximum sales to assess the range of risk. After preparing the sales forecast, management can estimate the expected costs and profits for the product, including marketing, R&D, operations, accounting, and finance costs. The company then uses the sales and cost figures to analyze the new product's financial attractiveness.

Product Development

Product development
Developing the product concept into a physical product to ensure that the product idea can be turned into a workable market offering.

For many new product concepts, a product may exist only as a word description, a drawing, or perhaps a crude mock-up. If the product concept passes the business test, it moves into **product development**. Here, R&D or engineering develops the product concept into a physical product. The product development step, however, now calls for a huge jump in investment. It will show whether the product idea can be turned into a workable product.

The R&D department will develop and test one or more physical versions of the product concept. R&D hopes to design a prototype that will satisfy and excite consumers and that can be produced quickly and at budgeted costs. Developing a successful prototype can take days, weeks, months, or even years depending on the product and prototype methods.

Often, products undergo rigorous tests to make sure that they perform safely and effectively or that consumers will find value in them. Companies can do their own product testing or outsource testing to other firms that specialize in testing.

Product testing: Carhartt has enlisted an army of Groundbreakers, volunteers who take part in live chats with Carhartt designers, review new product concepts, and field-test products that they helped to create.

Carhartt, Inc.

Marketers often involve actual customers in product development and testing. For example, Carhartt, maker of durable workwear and outerwear, has enlisted an army of Groundbreakers, "hard working men and women to help us create our next generation of products." These volunteers take part in live chats with Carhartt designers, review new product concepts, and field-test products that they helped to create.[13]

A new product must have the required functional features and also convey the intended psychological characteristics. The all-electric car, for example, should strike consumers as being well built, comfortable, and safe. Management must learn what makes consumers decide that a car is well built. To some consumers, this means that the car has "solid-sounding" doors. To others, it means that the car is able to withstand a heavy impact in crash tests. Consumer tests are conducted in which consumers test-drive the car and rate its attributes.

Test Marketing

Test marketing
The stage of new product development at which the product and its proposed marketing program are tested in realistic market settings.

If the product passes both the concept test and the product test, the next step is **test marketing**, the stage at which the product and its proposed marketing program are introduced into realistic market settings. Test marketing gives the marketer experience with marketing a product before going to the great expense of full introduction. It lets the company test the product and its entire marketing program—targeting and positioning strategy, advertising, distribution, pricing, branding and packaging, and budget levels.

The amount of test marketing needed varies with each new product. When introducing a new product requires a big investment, when the risks are high, or when management is not sure of the product or its marketing program, a company may do a lot of test marketing. For instance, Taco Bell took three years and 45 prototypes before introducing Doritos Locos Tacos, now the most successful product launch in the company's history. And Starbucks spent 20 years developing Starbucks VIA instant coffee—one of its most risky product rollouts ever—and several months testing the product in Starbucks shops in Chicago and Seattle before releasing it nationally. The testing paid off. The Starbucks VIA line now accounts for more than $300 million in sales annually.[14]

However, test marketing costs can be high, and testing takes time that may allow market opportunities to slip by or competitors to gain advantages. A company may do little or no test marketing when the costs of developing and introducing a new product are low or when management is already confident about the new product. For example, companies often do not test-market simple line extensions or copies of competitors' successful products.

Companies may also shorten or skip testing in the face of fast-changing market developments. For example, to take advantage of digital and mobile trends, Starbucks quickly introduced a less-than-perfect mobile payments app, then worked out the flaws during the six months after launch. The Starbucks app now accounts for 6 million transactions per week. "We don't think it is okay if things aren't perfect," says Starbucks' chief digital officer, "but we're willing to innovate and have speed to market trump a 100 percent guarantee that it'll be perfect."[15]

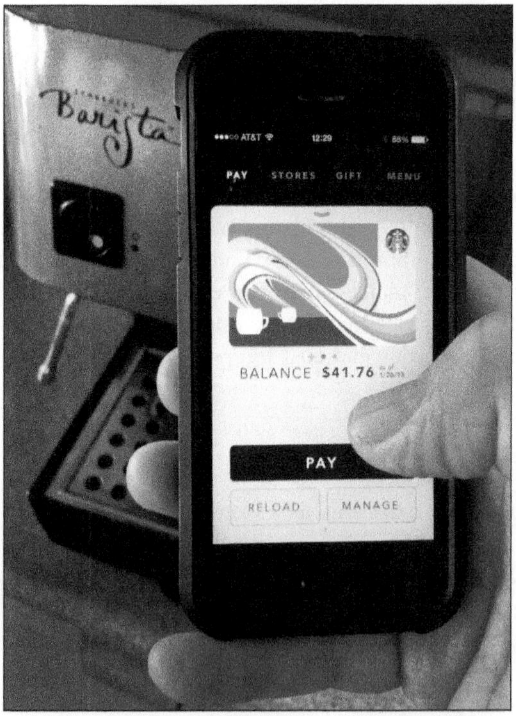

Companies sometimes shorten or skip test marketing to take advantage of fast-changing market developments, as Starbucks did with its hugely successful mobile payments app.

Kevin Schafer/Moment Mobile/Getty Images

As an alternative to extensive and costly standard test markets, companies can use controlled test markets or simulated test markets. In *controlled test markets*, such as SymphonyIRI's BehaviorScan, new products and tactics are tested among controlled panels of shoppers and stores.[16] By combining information on each test consumer's purchases with consumer demographic and TV viewing information, BehaviorScan can provide store-by-store, week-by-week reports on the sales of tested products and the impact of in-store and in-home marketing efforts. Using *simulated test markets*, researchers measure consumer responses to new products and marketing tactics in laboratory stores or simulated online shopping environments. Both controlled test markets and simulated test markets reduce the costs of test marketing and speed up the process.

Commercialization

Commercialization
Introducing a new product into the market.

Test marketing gives management the information needed to make a final decision about whether to launch the new product. If the company goes ahead with **commercialization**—introducing the new product into the market—it will face high costs. For example, the company may need to build or rent a manufacturing facility. And, in the case of a major new consumer product, it may spend hundreds of millions of dollars for advertising, sales promotion, and other marketing efforts in the first year. For instance, to introduce the Surface tablet, Microsoft spent close to $400 million on an advertising blitz that spanned TV, print, radio, outdoor, the Internet, events, public relations, and sampling. Similarly, Tide spent $150 million on a campaign to launch Tide Pods in the highly competitive U.S. laundry detergent market.[17]

A company launching a new product must first decide on introduction *timing*. If the new product will eat into the sales of other company products, the introduction may be delayed. If the product can be improved further or if the economy is down, the company may wait until the following year to launch it. However, if competitors are ready to introduce their own competing products, the company may push to introduce its new product sooner.

Next, the company must decide *where* to launch the new product—in a single location, a region, the national market, or the international market. Some companies may quickly introduce new models into the full national market. Companies with international distribution systems may introduce new products through swift global rollouts. For example, Apple launched its iPhone 6 and iPhone 6 Plus phones in its fastest-ever global rollout, making them available in 115 countries within less than three months of initial introduction.[18]

Author Comment
Above all else, new product development must focus on creating customer value. Says a senior Samsung executive, "We get our ideas from the market. The market is the driver."

Managing New Product Development

The new product development process shown in Figure 8.1 highlights the important activities needed to find, develop, and introduce new products. However, new product development involves more than just going through a set of steps. Companies must take a holistic approach to managing this process. Successful new product development requires a customer-centered, team-based, and systematic effort.

Customer-Centered New Product Development

Above all else, new product development must be customer centered. When looking for and developing new products, companies often rely too heavily on technical research in their R&D laboratories. But like everything else in marketing, successful new product development begins with a thorough understanding of what consumers need and value. **Customer-centered new product development** focuses on finding new ways to solve customer problems and create more customer-satisfying experiences.

Customer-centered new product development
New product development that focuses on finding new ways to solve customer problems and create more customer-satisfying experiences.

One study found that the most successful new products are ones that are differentiated, solve major customer problems, and offer a compelling customer value proposition. Another study showed that companies that directly engage their customers in the new product innovation process had twice the return on assets and triple the growth in operating income of firms that did not. Thus, customer involvement has a positive effect on the new product development process and product success.[19]

Intuit—maker of financial software such as TurboTax, QuickBooks, and Quicken—is a strong proponent of customer-driven new product development:[20]

> Intuit follows a "Design for Delight (D4D)" development philosophy that says products should delight customers by providing experiences that go beyond their expectations. Design for Delight starts with customer empathy—knowing customers better than they know themselves.

To that end, each year, Intuit conducts 10,000 hours of what it calls "follow-me-homes," in which design employees observe firsthand how customers use its products at home and at work. They look to understand problems and needs that even customers themselves might not recognize. Based on customer observations, the next D4D step is to "go broad, go narrow"—developing many customer-driven product ideas, then narrowing them down to one or a few great ideas for products that will solve customer problems. The final D4D step involves turning the great ideas into actual products and services that create customer delight, collecting customer feedback steadily throughout the development process.

Intuit works relentlessly to embed Design for Delight concepts deeply into its culture. "You've got to feel it," says the company's vice president of design innovation. "It can't be in your head. It's got to be in your heart. It's got to be in your gut. And we want to put it in our products." Thanks to customer-centered new product development, Intuit's revenues have grown to $4.5 billion annually, a 45 percent increase in just the past five years.

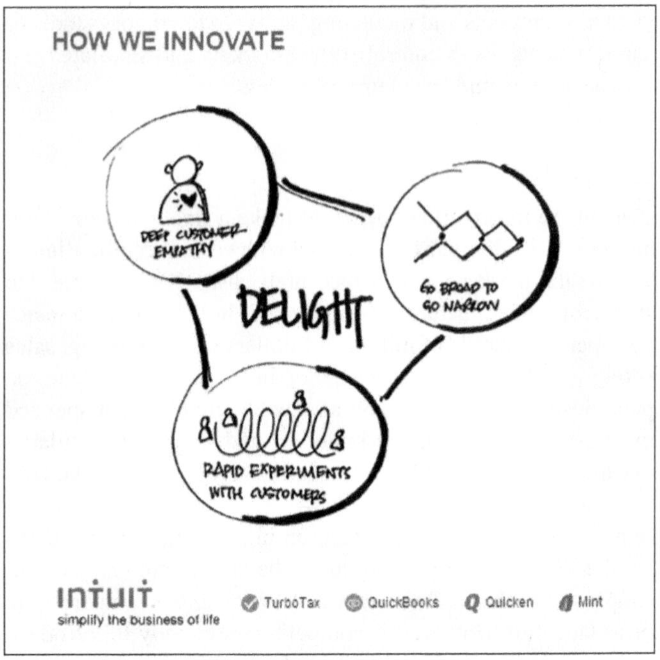

Customer-centered new product development: Financial software maker Intuit follows a "Design for Delight" philosophy that says products should delight customers by providing experiences that go beyond their expectations.

Thus, today's innovative companies get out of the research lab and connect with customers in search of fresh ways to meet customer needs. Customer-centered new product development begins and ends with understanding customers and involving them in the process.

Team-Based New Product Development

Good new product development also requires a total-company, cross-functional effort. Some companies organize their new product development process into the orderly sequence of steps shown in Figure 8.1, starting with idea generation and ending with commercialization. Under this *sequential product development* approach, one company department works individually to complete its stage of the process before passing the new product along to the next department and stage. This orderly, step-by-step process can help bring control to complex and risky projects. But it can also be dangerously slow. In fast-changing, highly competitive markets, such slow-but-sure product development can result in product failures, lost sales and profits, and crumbling market positions.

Team-based new product development
New product development in which various company departments work closely together, overlapping the steps in the product development process to save time and increase effectiveness.

To get their new products to market more quickly, many companies use a **team-based new product development** approach. Under this approach, company departments work closely together in cross-functional teams, overlapping the steps in the product development process to save time and increase effectiveness. Instead of passing the new product from department to department, the company assembles a team of people from various departments that stays with the new product from start to finish. Such teams usually include people from the marketing, finance, design, manufacturing, and legal departments and even supplier and customer companies. In the sequential process, a bottleneck at one phase can seriously slow an entire project. In the team-based approach, however, if one area hits snags, it works to resolve them while the team moves on.

The team-based approach does have some limitations, however. For example, it sometimes creates more organizational tension and confusion than the more orderly sequential approach. However, in rapidly changing industries facing increasingly shorter product life cycles, the rewards of fast and flexible product development far exceed the risks. Companies that combine a customer-centered approach with team-based new product development gain a big competitive edge by getting the right new products to market faster.

Systematic New Product Development

Finally, the new product development process should be holistic and systematic rather than compartmentalized and haphazard. Otherwise, few new ideas will surface, and many good ideas will sputter and die. To avoid these problems, a company can install an *innovation management system* to collect, review, evaluate, and manage new product ideas.

The company can appoint a respected senior person to be its innovation manager. It can set up Web-based idea management software and encourage all company stakeholders—employees, suppliers, distributors, dealers—to become involved in finding and developing new products. It can assign a cross-functional innovation management committee to evaluate proposed new product ideas and help bring good ideas to market. It can also create recognition programs to reward those who contribute the best ideas.

The innovation management system approach yields two favorable outcomes. First, it helps create an innovation-oriented company culture. It shows that top management supports, encourages, and rewards innovation. Second, it will yield a larger number of new product ideas, among which will be found some especially good ones. The good new ideas will be more systematically developed, producing more new product successes. No longer will good ideas wither for the lack of a sounding board or a senior product advocate.

Thus, new product success requires more than simply thinking up a few good ideas, turning them into products, and finding customers for them. It requires a holistic approach for finding new ways to create valued customer experiences, from generating and screening new product ideas to creating and rolling out want-satisfying products to customers.

More than this, successful new product development requires a whole-company commitment. At companies known for their new product prowess, such as Google, Samsung, Apple, 3M, P&G, and GE, the entire culture encourages, supports, and rewards innovation. >> Consider Samsung:[21]

>> Samsung's entire culture encourages and supports innovation. Every product has to pass the customer "Wow!" test, or it goes straight back to development.

Julie Jacobson/AP Images

> Not many years ago, Samsung was a copycat consumer electronics brand you bought if you couldn't afford Sony, then the world's most coveted consumer electronics brand. In the mid-1990s, however, Samsung made an inspired decision. It turned its back on cheap knockoffs and set out to overtake rival Sony. To dethrone the consumer electronics giant, however, Samsung first had to change its entire culture, from copycat to leading edge. To out-*sell* Sony, Samsung first had to out-*innovate* Sony.
>
> To make that happen, Samsung hired a crop of fresh, young designers and managers who unleashed a torrent of new products—not humdrum, me-too products but sleek, bold, and beautiful products targeted to high-end users. Samsung called them "lifestyle works of art." Every new product had to pass the "Wow!" test: If it didn't get a "Wow!" reaction during market testing, it went straight back to development. Beyond innovative technology and stylish designs, Samsung put the customer at the core of its innovation movement. Its primary goal was to improve the customer experience and bring genuine change to people's lives in everything it did.
>
> Today, thanks to its whole-company culture of innovation, the Samsung brand holds a high-end, cutting-edge aura that rivals or even exceeds that of Apple, long considered to be the keeper of all things cool. Samsung is now by far the world's largest consumer electronics company, with sales two and a half times those of Sony and 25 percent greater than Apple's.

Product life cycle (PLC)
The course of a product's sales and profits over its lifetime.

Author Comment
A company's products are born, grow, mature, and then decline, just as living things do. To remain vital, the firm must continually develop new products and manage them effectively throughout their life cycles.

Product Life-Cycle Strategies

After launching the new product, management wants that product to enjoy a long and happy life. Although it does not expect the product to sell forever, the company wants to earn a decent profit to cover all the effort and risk that went into launching it. Management is aware that each product will have a life cycle, although its exact shape and length is not known in advance.

>> Figure 8.2 shows a typical **product life cycle (PLC)**, the course that a product's sales and profits take over its lifetime. The PLC has five distinct stages:

1. ***Product development*** begins when the company finds and develops a new product idea. During product development, sales are zero, and the company's investment costs mount.

Figure 8.2 Sales and Profits over the Product's Life from Inception to Decline

Some products die quickly; others stay in the mature stage for a long, long time. For example, TABASCO sauce has been around for more than 140 years. Even then, to keep the product young, the company has added a full line of flavors (such as Sweet & Spicy and Chipotle) and a kitchen cabinet full of new TABASCO products (such as salsas, marinades, and a chili mix).

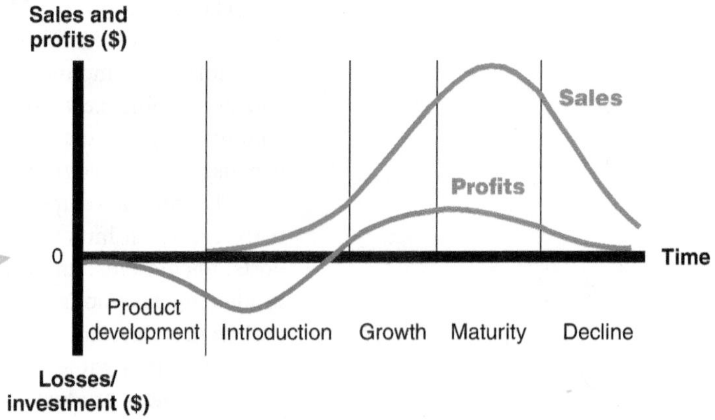

2. ***Introduction*** is a period of slow sales growth as the product is introduced in the market. Profits are nonexistent in this stage because of the heavy expenses of product introduction.
3. ***Growth*** is a period of rapid market acceptance and increasing profits.
4. ***Maturity*** is a period of slowdown in sales growth because the product has achieved acceptance by most potential buyers. Profits level off or decline because of increased marketing outlays to defend the product against competition.
5. ***Decline*** is the period when sales fall off and profits drop.

Not all products follow all five stages of the PLC. Some products are introduced and die quickly; others stay in the mature stage for a long, long time. Some enter the decline stage and are then cycled back into the growth stage through strong promotion or repositioning. It seems that a well-managed brand could live forever. Venerable brands like Coca-Cola, Gillette, Budweiser, Guinness, American Express, Wells Fargo, Kikkoman, and TABASCO® sauce, for instance, are still going strong after more than 100 years. Guinness beer has been around for more than 250 years, Life Savers Mints recently celebrated "100 years of keeping mouths feeling fresh," and TABASCO sauce brags that it's "over 140 years old and still able to totally whup your butt!"

Product life cycle: Some products die quickly; others stay in the mature stage for a long, long time. TABASCO® sauce is "over 140 years old and yet still able to totally whup your butt!"

TABASCO® is a registered trademark for sauces and other goods and services; TABASCO, the TABASCO bottle design and label designs are the exclusive property of and licensed by McIlhenny Company, Avery Island, Louisiana 70513. www.TABASCO.com

The PLC concept can describe a *product class* (gasoline-powered automobiles), a *product form* (SUVs), or a *brand* (the Ford Escape). The PLC concept applies differently in each case. Product classes have the longest life cycles; the sales of many product classes stay in the mature stage for a long time. Product forms, in contrast, tend to have the standard PLC shape. Product forms such as dial telephones, VHS tapes, and film cameras passed through a regular history of introduction, rapid growth, maturity, and decline.

A specific brand's life cycle can change quickly because of changing competitive attacks and responses. For example, although laundry soaps (product class) and powdered detergents (product form) have enjoyed fairly long life cycles, the life cycles of specific brands have tended to be much shorter. Today's leading U.S. brands of powdered laundry soap are Tide and Gain; the leading brands 100 years ago were Fels-Naptha, Octagon, and Kirkman.

The PLC concept also can be applied to what are known as styles, fashions, and fads. Their special life cycles are shown in **Figure 8.3**. A **style** is a basic and distinctive mode of expression. For example, styles appear in homes (colonial, ranch, transitional), clothing (formal, casual), and art (realist, surrealist, abstract). Once a style is invented, it may last for generations, passing in and out of vogue. A style has a cycle showing several periods of renewed interest.

A **fashion** is a currently accepted or popular style in a given field. For example, the more formal "business attire" look of corporate dress of the 1980s and 1990s gave way to the "business casual" look of the 2000s and 2010s. Fashions tend to grow slowly, remain popular for a while, and then decline slowly.

>> Figure 8.3 Styles, Fashions, and Fads

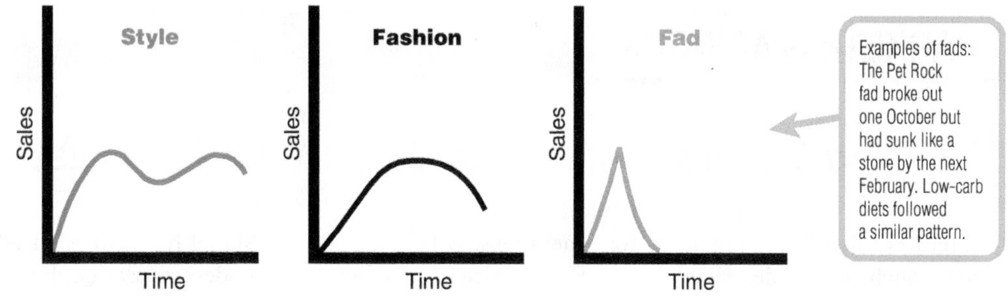

Style
A basic and distinctive mode of expression.

Fashion
A currently accepted or popular style in a given field.

Fad
A temporary period of unusually high sales driven by consumer enthusiasm and immediate product or brand popularity.

Fads are temporary periods of unusually high sales driven by consumer enthusiasm and immediate product or brand popularity.[22] A fad may be part of an otherwise normal life cycle, as in the case of recent surges in the sales of poker chips and accessories. Or the fad may comprise a brand's or product's entire life cycle. Pet Rocks are a classic example. Upon hearing his friends complain about how expensive it was to care for their dogs, advertising copywriter Gary Dahl joked about his pet rock. He soon wrote a spoof of a dog-training manual for it, titled *The Care and Training of Your Pet Rock*. Soon Dahl was selling some 1.5 million ordinary beach pebbles at $4 a pop. Yet the fad, which broke one October, had sunk like a stone by the next February. Dahl's advice to those who want to succeed with a fad: "Enjoy it while it lasts." Other examples of fads include Silly Bandz, Furbies, and Pogs.[23]

Marketers can apply the product life-cycle concept as a useful framework for describing how products and markets work. And when used carefully, the PLC concept can help in developing good marketing strategies for the different life-cycle stages. However, using the PLC concept for forecasting product performance or developing marketing strategies presents some practical problems. For example, in practice, it is difficult to forecast the sales level at each PLC stage, the length of each stage, and the shape of the PLC curve. Using the PLC concept to develop marketing strategy also can be difficult because strategy is both a cause and a result of the PLC. The product's current PLC position suggests the best marketing strategies, and the resulting marketing strategies affect product performance in later stages.

Moreover, marketers should not blindly push products through the traditional product life-cycle stages. Instead, marketers often defy the "rules" of the life cycle and position or reposition their products in unexpected ways. By doing this, they can rescue mature or declining products and return them to the growth phase of the life cycle. Or they can leapfrog obstacles that slow consumer acceptance and propel new products forward into the growth phase.

The moral of the product life cycle is that companies must continually innovate; otherwise, they risk extinction. No matter how successful its current product lineup, a company must skillfully manage the life cycles of existing products for future success. And to grow, the company must develop a steady stream of new products that bring new value to customers. Toy maker Mattel is learning this lesson the hard way. It has long dominated the world toy industry with classic brands such as Barbie, Hot Wheels, Fisher-Price, and American Girl. In recent years, however, as its core brands have matured, Mattel's sales have stagnated at the hands of nimbler, more innovative competitors (see Marketing at Work 8.2).

We looked at the product development stage of the PLC in the first part of this chapter. We now look at strategies for each of the other life-cycle stages.

Introduction Stage

Introduction stage
The PLC stage in which a new product is first distributed and made available for purchase.

The **introduction stage** starts when a new product is first launched. Introduction takes time, and sales growth is apt to be slow. Well-known products such as frozen foods and HDTVs lingered for many years before they entered a stage of more rapid growth.

In this stage, as compared to other stages, profits are negative or low because of the low sales and high distribution and promotion expenses. Much money is needed to attract distributors and build their inventories. Promotion spending is relatively high to inform

MARKETING AT WORK 8.2

Managing Mattel's Product Life Cycle: More Than Just Fun and Games

Mattel has ruled the toy industry for generations, with classic brands such as Barbie, Hot Wheels, Fisher-Price, American Girl, and a host of others. For more than 50 years, Mattel's toys have topped the wish lists of children across America.

Recently, however, Mattel's sales have fallen off as its core brands have matured. Venerable Barbie, now in her mid-50s, has experienced double-digit sales dips in each of the past two years. Sagging Fisher-Price and American Girl sales suggest that today's toy buyers are less enamored with those storied brands than previous generations were. And Mattel's Hot Wheels brand, while holding its own, now seems coveted more by nostalgic dads than by their young sons.

Mattel could blame its slump on broader toy industry trends—declining birthrates, rising costs, unfavorable economic conditions, and the boom in digital technologies that make many traditional toys now seem like relics from the past. The global toy industry has stagnated in recent years, with market leaders such as Mattel and Hasbro taking the biggest hits. Yet none of that has slowed Mattel's hottest competitor, The LEGO Group. In the past 10 years, despite the toy industry's doldrums, LEGO revenues have quadrupled, up 25 percent last year alone. LEGO recently surged past Mattel and Hasbro to become the world's largest toy maker.

LEGO's success suggests that Mattel's problems go beyond just industry ups and downs. Rather, the company appears to have a product life-cycle problem—lots of good old products but too few good new ones. In an industry facing a barrage of hot new playthings, Mattel has lagged in product development and failed to adapt to rapidly changing toy trends and tastes.

Consider Barbie, Mattel's biggest and oldest brand. Born in 1959, Barbie quickly became a must-have for young girls everywhere. By the late 1970s, 90 percent of U.S. girls between the ages of 5 and 10 owned at least one Barbie. For more than five decades, Barbie has remained Mattel's number-one moneymaker, accounting for as much as 30 percent of its revenues. But during the past few years, Barbie's popularity has spiraled downward. Although still one of the world's largest toy brands, Barbie's current annual revenues of $1 billion are little more than half of what they were at her peak. Barbie sales dropped a stomach-churning 16 percent last year, prompting one analyst to suggest that "it might be time for Mattel to roll out Retirement Barbie."

That won't happen anytime soon. But like many other Mattel brands, Barbie is showing her age. Designers work tirelessly on new Barbie models and features. An example is Entrepreneur Barbie, the first Barbie with her own smartphone and LinkedIn profile. Still, Barbie continues to lose relevance alongside trendier toy aisle juggernauts like Disney's *Frozen* line of toys and play sets.

Mattel has also misfired in some of its marketing attempts to modernize Barbie. For example, the Barbie "Unapologetic" campaign—with its "If you can dream it, you can be it" slogan—tried to strike a blow for female empowerment. Yet despite the fact that it targets 3- to 12-year-old girls and even after decades of criticism concerning Barbie's unrealistic figure and the standard of beauty she sets, Mattel kicked the campaign off by featuring Barbie on an advertising wrap on the cover of 1,000 issues of the 50th anniversary *Sports Illustrated* swimsuit edition. That move incurred the wrath of countless mothers across the nation.

Over the years, as Barbie has aged, Mattel has tried to round out its product portfolio with new, younger lines of dolls. In the late 1990s, the company purchased the wildly popular, premium-priced American Girl line. And more recently, it created runaway hit Monster High—a line of dolls and accessories composed of characters such as Draculaura, Ghoulia Yelps, and Abbey Bominable. However, much like Barbie, both American Girl and Monster High are now maturing and experiencing sales declines. Critics blame Mattel's uninspired designs, conservative innovation mindset, and inability to keep the brands fresh and relevant to the times.

With most of its core brands in mature or declining life-cycle stages, Mattel is fighting an uphill battle. Take Hot Wheels, long the market leader in toy cars. Mattel has had modest success in revitalizing the mature brand by taking it

>> Product life-cycle management: Like many other Mattel brands, Barbie is showing her age. Beyond revitalizing its classic brands, Mattel must create a steady stream of exciting new ones that stay ahead of changing consumer trends and tastes.

Mike Blake/Reuters

into hot pockets of the market. For example, as the popularity of remote control helicopters and drones has soared in recent years, Hot Wheels launched the Street Hawk, a flying remote control car. Street Hawk became one of the biggest hits during its first holiday season. Still, the hits have been too few and too far between. Even with its avid cross-generational collector base, the Hot Wheels brand is barely holding its own against the onslaught of new-age products from competitors with more inspired innovation processes.

As its own core brands have aged, Mattel has injected new life into its product lines by licensing hot characters from popular movies, TV shows, and comic books. Specifically, Mattel has made a small fortune with licensed Disney Princess and *Frozen* dolls and toys. It recently launched a line of Star Wars Hot Wheels cars, and it has partnered with Warner Bros. Entertainment on 10 upcoming films based on DC Comics characters. Although profitable, however, such licensed products can't compensate for Mattel's inability to revitalize its own brands and develop new ones. For example, Mattel recently lost its Disney character rights to rival Hasbro, leaving a huge revenue hole to fill.

Thus, to regain its prowess in today's turbulent, fast-changing toy market, Mattel must develop a faster, more nimble, more customer-focused process for developing relevant new products and guiding them profitably through their product life cycles. Beyond reinvigorating its classic brands, Mattel must create a steady stream of exciting new ones that stay ahead of changing consumer trends and tastes. For Mattel, mastering the product life cycle is more than just fun and games. It's a matter of growth, prosperity, and even long-run survival.

Sources: Jens Hansegard, "Oh, Snap! Lego Pushes Ahead of Mattel in Sales," *Wall Street Journal*, September 5, 2014, p. B5; Paul Ziobro, "Floundering Mattel Tries to Make Things Fun Again," *Wall Street Journal*, December 23, 2014, p. A1; Alexandra Petri, "The End of (Doll) History," *Washington Post*, May 4, 2013, P. A13; Shan Li, "Mattel's CEO Resigns as Toy Maker Struggles," *Los Angeles Times*, January 27, 2015, p. A1; John Kell, "Mattel's Barbie Sales Down for Third Consecutive Year," *Fortune*, January 30, 2015, http://fortune.com/2015/01/30/mattels-barbie-sales-drop-third-year/; "Shake-Up at Mattel as Barbie Loses Her Appeal," *New York Times*, January 27, 2015, p. B1; Laura Stampler, "Bye, Bye Barbie: 2015 Is the Year We Abandon Unrealistic Beauty Ideals," *Time*, January 30, 2015, http://time.com/3667580/mattel-barbie-earnings-plus-size-body-image/; and www.barbie.com and http://corporate.mattel.com, accessed October 2015.

---

consumers of the new product and get them to try it. Because the market is not generally ready for product refinements at this stage, the company and its few competitors produce basic versions of the product. These firms focus their selling on those buyers who are the most ready to buy.

A company, especially the *market pioneer*, must choose a launch strategy that is consistent with the intended product positioning. It should realize that the initial strategy is just the first step in a grander marketing plan for the product's entire life cycle. If the pioneer chooses its launch strategy to make a "killing," it may be sacrificing long-run revenue for the sake of short-run gain. The pioneer has the best chance of building and retaining market leadership if it plays its cards correctly from the start.

Growth Stage

Growth stage
The PLC stage in which a product's sales start climbing quickly.

If the new product satisfies the market, it will enter a **growth stage** in which sales will start climbing quickly. The early adopters will continue to buy, and later buyers will start following their lead, especially if they hear favorable word of mouth. Attracted by the opportunities for profit, new competitors will enter the market. They will introduce new product features, and the market will expand. The increase in competitors leads to an increase in the number of distribution outlets, and sales jump just to build reseller inventories. Prices remain where they are or decrease only slightly. Companies keep their promotion spending at the same or a slightly higher level. Educating the market remains a goal, but now the company must also meet the competition.

Profits increase during the growth stage as promotion costs are spread over a large volume and as unit manufacturing costs decrease. The firm uses several strategies to sustain rapid market growth as long as possible. It improves product quality and adds new product features and models. It enters new market segments and new distribution channels. It shifts some advertising from building product awareness to building product conviction and purchase, and it lowers prices at the right time to attract more buyers.

In the growth stage, the firm faces a trade-off between high market share and high current profit. By spending a lot of money on product improvement, promotion, and distribution, the company can capture a dominant position. In doing so, however, it gives up maximum current profit, which it hopes to make up in the next stage.

Maturity Stage

Maturity stage
The PLC stage in which a product's sales growth slows or levels off.

At some point, a product's sales growth will slow down, and it will enter the **maturity stage**. This maturity stage normally lasts longer than the previous stages, and it poses strong challenges to marketing management. Most products are in the maturity stage of the life cycle, and therefore most of marketing management deals with the mature product.

The slowdown in sales growth results in many producers with many products to sell. In turn, this overcapacity leads to greater competition. Competitors begin marking down prices, increasing their advertising and sales promotions, and upping their product development budgets to find better versions of the product. These steps lead to a drop in profit. Some of the weaker competitors start dropping out, and the industry eventually contains only well-established competitors.

Although many products in the mature stage appear to remain unchanged for long periods, most successful ones are actually evolving to meet changing consumer needs. Product managers should do more than simply ride along with or defend their mature products—a good offense is the best defense. They should consider modifying the market, product offering, and marketing mix.

In *modifying the market*, the company tries to increase consumption by finding new users and new market segments for its brands. For example, brands such as Harley-Davidson and Axe fragrances, which have typically targeted male buyers, are introducing products and marketing programs aimed at women. Conversely, Weight Watchers and Bath & Body Works, which have typically targeted women, have created products and programs aimed at men.

The company may also look for ways to increase usage among present customers. For example, 3M recently ran a marketing campaign to inspire more usage of its Post-it products:[24]

> The Post-it Brand's "Go Ahead" campaign aimed to convince customers that the sticky pieces of paper are good for much more than just scribbling temporary notes and reminders. Instead, it positioned Post-it Notes as a means of self-expression by showing creative, nontraditional ways that consumers around the world use them. In the past, 3M promoted mostly functional uses of Post-it products, but research showed that consumers have a surprisingly strong emotional relationship with the brand. "They're using it to communicate, using it to collaborate, using it to organize themselves," says a 3M marketing executive. The "Go Ahead" campaign was motivated by customers' "quirky and inspired uses of our product."
>
> An initial ad showed people on a college campus blanketing a wall outside a building with Post-it Notes answering the question "What inspires you?" "Share on a real wall," the announcer explained. Other scenes showed a young man filling a wall with mosaic artwork created from multiple colors of Post-it Notes, teachers using Post-it Notes to enliven their classrooms, and a man posting a "Morning, beautiful" note on the bathroom mirror as his wife is brushing her teeth. "Go ahead," said the announcer, "keep the honeymoon going." The ad ended with a hand peeling Post-it Notes off a pad one by one to reveal new, unexpected uses: "Go ahead, Connect," "Go ahead, Inspire," and "Go ahead, Explore."

The company might also try *modifying the product*—changing characteristics such as quality, features, style, packaging, or technology platforms to retain current users or attract new ones. Thus, to freshen up their products for today's technology-obsessed children, many classic toy and game makers are creating new digital versions or add-ons for old favorites. For example, the venerable Crayola brand has souped up its product line to meet the technology tastes of the new generation. With the Crayola My Virtual Fashion Show drawing kit and app, for instance, children first design fashions using the provided color pencils and sketchpad. They then take photos of the designs with their smartphones or tablets and watch their original creations magically come to life inside the app on 3D models who walk virtual runways in Milan, New York, and Paris.[25]

Finally, the company can try *modifying the marketing mix*—improving sales by changing one or more marketing mix elements. The company can offer new or improved services to buyers. It can cut prices to attract new users and competitors' customers. It can launch a better advertising campaign or use aggressive sales promotions—trade deals, cents-off, premiums, and contests. In addition to pricing and promotion, the company can also move into new marketing channels to help serve new users.

» **Managing the product life cycle: Thanks to the "Quaker Up" campaign, 137-year-old Quaker now has a more contemporary appeal as a lifestyle brand that helps give young families the fuel and energy needed to get through the day.**

Provided courtesy of The Quaker Oat Company.

PepsiCo used all of these market, product, and marketing mix modification approaches to reinvigorate its 137-year-old Quaker brand and keep it from sinking into decline. » To reawaken the brand, Quaker launched a major new "Quaker Up" marketing campaign, supported by an estimated $100 million budget:[26]

> The "Quaker Up" campaign targets a new market of young mothers under 35, positioning Quaker's lines of hot and cold cereals, snack bars, cookies, and other products as healthy lifestyle choices that help give a young family the fuel and energy needed to get through the day. The campaign advises families to "Quaker Up—with Quaker's good energy for the moments that matter." As part of the retargeting and repositioning effort, Quaker has modernized every element of the brand, from products and packaging to in-store displays and ad platforms. To start, it slimmed down the iconic Quaker man by 20 pounds and gave him a facelift to make him look healthier, stronger, and more contemporary. The brand added new energy-packed products, such as Quaker Medleys—a hearty blend of oats and grains with real fruit and nuts; Quaker Soft Baked Bars—high in fiber, protein, and B vitamins; and Quaker Protein—protein-packed instant oatmeal and baked energy bars. Befitting the more mobile and connected lifestyles of today's young parents, the "Quaker Up" campaign also incorporates and healthy dose of digital media, including banner ads, YouTube videos, a Facebook app, a Quaker Up community Web site, and a full slate of other digital content. In all, despite its age, the reenergized Quaker brand now has a much younger appeal. "People know the brand, people love the brand, but we needed to forge a stronger connection with contemporary moms," says Quaker's chief marketing officer.

Decline Stage

The sales of most product forms and brands eventually dip. The decline may be slow, as in the cases of stamps and oatmeal cereal, or rapid, as in the cases of VHS tapes. Sales may plunge to zero, or they may drop to a low level where they continue for many years. This is the **decline stage**.

Decline stage
The PLC stage in which a product's sales fade away.

Sales decline for many reasons, including technological advances, shifts in consumer tastes, and increased competition. As sales and profits decline, some firms withdraw from the market. Those remaining may prune their product offerings. In addition, they may drop smaller market segments and marginal trade channels, or they may cut the promotion budget and reduce their prices further.

Carrying a weak product can be very costly to a firm, and not just in profit terms. There are many hidden costs. A weak product may take up too much of management's time. It often requires frequent price and inventory adjustments. It requires advertising and sales-force attention that might be better used to make "healthy" products more profitable. A product's failing reputation can cause customer concerns about the company and its other products. The biggest cost may well lie in the future. Keeping weak products delays the search for replacements, creates a lopsided product mix, hurts current profits, and weakens the company's foothold on the future.

For these reasons, companies must identify products in the decline stage and decide whether to maintain, harvest, or drop them. Management may decide to *maintain* its brand, repositioning or reinvigorating it in hopes of moving it back into the growth stage of the product life cycle. P&G has done this with several brands, including Mr. Clean and Old Spice. Over the past decade, P&G has retargeted, repositioned, revitalized, and extended both of these old brands, taking each from near extinction to billion-dollar-brand status.

Management may decide to *harvest* the product, which means reducing various costs (plant and equipment, maintenance, R&D, advertising, sales force), hoping that sales hold up. If successful, harvesting will increase the company's profits in the short run. Finally, management may decide to *drop* the product from its line. The company can sell the product to another firm or simply liquidate it at salvage value. If the company plans to find a buyer, it will not want to run down the product through harvesting. In recent years, P&G has sold off several declining brands and brands that no longer fit strategically, such as Folgers coffee, Crisco oil, Comet cleanser, Sure deodorant, Duncan Hines cake mixes, Jif peanut butter, Duracell batteries, and Iams pet foods.[27]

Table 8.2 summarizes the key characteristics of each stage of the PLC. The table also lists the marketing objectives and strategies for each stage.[28]

Author Comment
Let's look at just a few more product topics, including regulatory and social responsibility issues and the special challenges of marketing products internationally.

Additional Product and Service Considerations

We wrap up our discussion of products and services with two additional considerations: social responsibility in product decisions and issues of international product and services marketing.

Product Decisions and Social Responsibility

Marketers should carefully consider public policy issues and regulations regarding acquiring or dropping products, patent protection, product quality and safety, and product warranties.

Regarding new products, the government may prevent companies from adding products through acquisitions if the effect threatens to lessen competition. Companies dropping products must be aware that they have legal obligations, written or implied, to their suppliers, dealers, and customers who have a stake in the dropped product. Companies

Table 8.2 Summary of Product Life-Cycle Characteristics, Objectives, and Strategies

	Introduction	Growth	Maturity	Decline
Characteristics				
Sales	Low sales	Rapidly rising sales	Peak sales	Declining sales
Costs	High cost per customer	Average cost per customer	Low cost per customer	Low cost per customer
Profits	Negative	Rising profits	High profits	Declining profits
Customers	Innovators	Early adopters	Mainstream adopters	Lagging adopters
Competitors	Few	Growing number	Stable number beginning to decline	Declining number
Marketing objectives				
	Create product engagement and trial	Maximize market share	Maximize profit while defending market share	Reduce expenditure and milk the brand
Strategies				
Product	Offer a basic product	Offer product extensions, service, and warranty	Diversify brand and models	Phase out weak items
Price	Use cost-plus	Price to penetrate market	Price to match or beat competitors	Cut price
Distribution	Build selective distribution	Build intensive distribution	Build more intensive distribution	Go selective: phase out unprofitable outlets
Advertising	Build product awareness among early adopters and dealers	Build engagement and interest in the mass market	Stress brand differences and benefits	Reduce to level needed to retain hard-core loyals
Sales Promotion	Use heavy sales promotion to entice trial	Reduce to take advantage of heavy consumer demand	Increase to encourage brand switching	Reduce to minimal level

Source: Based on Philip Kotler and Kevin Lane Keller, *Marketing Management*, 15th ed. (Upper Saddle River, NJ: Pearson Education, 2016), p. 358. © 2016. Printed and Electronically reproduced by permission of Pearson Education, Inc., Upper Saddle River, New Jersey.

must also obey U.S. patent laws when developing new products. A company cannot make its product illegally similar to another company's established product.

Manufacturers must comply with specific laws regarding product quality and safety. The Federal Food, Drug, and Cosmetic Act protects consumers from unsafe and adulterated food, drugs, and cosmetics. Various acts provide for the inspection of sanitary conditions in the meat- and poultry-processing industries. Safety legislation has been passed to regulate fabrics, chemical substances, automobiles, toys, and drugs and poisons. The Consumer Product Safety Act of 1972 established the Consumer Product Safety Commission, which has the authority to ban or seize potentially harmful products and set severe penalties for violation of the law.

If consumers have been injured by a product with a defective design, they can sue manufacturers or dealers. A recent survey of manufacturing companies found that product liability was the second-largest litigation concern, behind only labor and employment matters. Tens of thousands of product liability suits are now tried in U.S. district courts each year. Although manufacturers are found to be at fault in only a small percentage of all product liability cases, when they are found guilty, awards can run into the tens or even hundreds of millions of dollars. Class-action suits can run into the billions. For example, after it recalled 11 million vehicles for acceleration pedal–related issues, Toyota faced more than 100 class-action and individual lawsuits and ended up paying a $1.6 billion settlement to compensate owners for financial losses associated with the defect.[29]

This litigation phenomenon has resulted in huge increases in product liability insurance premiums, causing big problems in some industries. Some companies pass these higher rates along to consumers by raising prices. Others are forced to discontinue high-risk product lines. Some companies are now appointing *product stewards*, whose job is to protect consumers from harm and the company from liability by proactively ferreting out potential product problems.

International Product and Services Marketing

International product and services marketers face special challenges. First, they must figure out what products and services to introduce and in which countries. Then they must decide how much to standardize or adapt their products and services for world markets.

On the one hand, companies would like to standardize their offerings. Standardization helps a company develop a consistent worldwide image. It also lowers the product design, manufacturing, and marketing costs of offering a large variety of products. On the other hand, markets and consumers around the world differ widely. Companies must usually respond to these differences by adapting their product offerings. For example, by carefully tailoring its products to local tastes in China, PepsiCo has become the largest snack-and-beverage company in the world's second-biggest economy:[30]

» Global product adaptation: Lay's famously funky Chinese chip flavors include cucumber (a best-seller), iced lemon tea, "Numb & Spicy Hot Pot," and "Sha La Chui," a concoction that tastes like a baked salad.

Frito-Lay, Inc.

> PepsiCo has found that success in China's huge beverage and snack markets depends on carefully adapting its many brands—such as Pepsi, Lay's, Gatorade, and Quaker—to the tastes of Chinese consumers. Its large food-and-beverage innovation center in Shanghai employs consumer and food researchers, product developers, experimental kitchens, and even a pilot manufacturing plant, all devoted to pinpointing and pinging the unique palates of Chinese consumers. And before new product concepts ever hit the market, they are sampled extensively by local taste testers—often local homemakers.
>
> While not likely to be favorites in Western markets, PepsiCo's Chinese lineup includes lip-smackers such as hot and sour fish soup potato chips, white fungus oatmeal, and blueberry Gatorade. Lay's famously funky Chinese chip flavors include cucumber (a best-seller), iced lemon tea, "Numb & Spicy Hot Pot," » and "Sha La Cui," a concoction designed to taste like a baked salad.

The Chinese market holds huge potential for PepsiCo. For example, China's 1.35 billion people now consume an average of only about one small bag of potato chips every two to four weeks, compared with 15 bags in that period in the United States. Skillful product adaptation has helped PepsiCo achieve double-digit growth in this important market.

Service marketers also face special challenges when going global. Some service industries have a long history of international operations. For example, the commercial banking industry was one of the first to grow internationally. Banks had to provide global services to meet the foreign exchange and credit needs of their home-country clients who wanted to sell overseas. In recent years, many banks have become truly global. Germany's Deutsche Bank, for example, serves more than 28 million customers through 2,900 branches in more than 70 countries. For its clients around the world who wish to grow globally, Deutsche Bank can raise money not only in Frankfurt but also in Zurich, London, Paris, Tokyo, and Moscow.[31]

Professional and business services industries, such as accounting, management consulting, and advertising, have also globalized. The international growth of these firms followed the globalization of the client companies they serve. For example, as more clients employ worldwide marketing and advertising strategies, advertising agencies have responded by globalizing their own operations. McCann Worldgroup, a large U.S.-based advertising and marketing services agency, operates in 120 countries. It serves international clients such as Coca-Cola, GM, ExxonMobil, Microsoft, MasterCard, Johnson & Johnson, and Unilever in markets ranging from the United States and Canada to Korea and Kazakhstan. Moreover, McCann Worldgroup is one company in the Interpublic Group of Companies, an immense, worldwide network of advertising and marketing services companies.[32]

Retailers are among the latest service businesses to go global. As their home markets become saturated, American retailers such as Walmart, Office Depot, and Saks Fifth Avenue are expanding into faster-growing markets abroad. For example, Walmart now serves 250 million customers weekly in 27 countries; its international division's sales account for nearly 29 percent of total sales. Foreign retailers are making similar moves. Asian shoppers can now buy American products in French-owned Carrefour stores. Carrefour—the world's fourth-largest retailer behind Walmart, Costco, and the UK's Tesco—now operates more than 10,000 stores in 34 countries. It is the leading retailer in Europe, Brazil, and Argentina and the largest foreign retailer in China.[33]

The trend toward growth of global service companies will continue, especially in banking, airlines, telecommunications, and professional services. Today, service firms are no longer simply following their manufacturing customers. Instead, they are taking the lead in international expansion.

MyMarketingLab

If assigned by your instructor, complete the questions marked with the ✪ from the EOC Discussion Questions section in the MyLab. To complete the Marketing by the Numbers problems found in this section, go to your Assignments in the MyLab.

REVIEWING AND EXTENDING THE CONCEPTS

CHAPTER REVIEW AND CRITICAL THINKING

Objectives Review

A company's current products face limited life spans and must be replaced by newer products. But new products can fail—the risks of innovation are as great as the rewards. The key to successful innovation lies in a customer-focused, holistic, total-company effort; strong planning; and a systematic new product development process.

OBJECTIVE 8-1 Explain how companies find and develop new product ideas. (pp 238–239)

Companies find and develop new product ideas from a variety of sources. Many new product ideas stem from *internal sources*. Companies conduct formal R&D, or they pick the brains of their employees, urging them to think up and develop new product ideas. Other ideas come from *external sources*. Companies track *competitors'* offerings and obtain ideas from *distributors and suppliers* who are close to the market and can pass along information about consumer problems and new product possibilities.

Perhaps the most important sources of new product ideas are *customers* themselves. Companies observe customers, invite them to submit their ideas and suggestions, or even involve customers in the new product development process. Many companies are now developing *crowdsourcing* or *open-innovation* new product idea programs, which invite broad communities of people—customers, employees, independent scientists and researchers, and even the general public—into the new product innovation process. Truly innovative companies do not rely only on one source for new product ideas.

OBJECTIVE 8-2 List and define the steps in the new product development process and the major considerations in managing this process. (pp 239–249)

The new product development process consists of eight sequential stages. The process starts with *idea generation*. Next comes *idea screening,* which reduces the number of ideas based on the company's own criteria. Ideas that pass the screening stage continue through *product concept development,* in which a detailed version of the new product idea is stated in meaningful consumer terms. This stage includes *concept testing,* in which new product concepts are tested with a group of target consumers to determine whether the concepts have strong consumer appeal. Strong concepts proceed to *marketing strategy development,* in which an initial marketing strategy for the new product is developed from the product concept. In the *business-analysis* stage, a review of the sales, costs, and profit projections for a new product is conducted to determine whether the new product is likely to satisfy the company's objectives. With positive results here, the ideas become more concrete through *product development* and *test marketing* and finally are launched during *commercialization.*

New product development involves more than just going through a set of steps. Companies must take a systematic, holistic approach to managing this process. Successful new product development requires a customer-centered, team-based, systematic effort.

OBJECTIVE 8-3 Describe the stages of the product life cycle and how marketing strategies change during a product's life cycle. (pp 249–256)

Each product has a *life cycle* marked by a changing set of problems and opportunities. The sales of the typical product follow an S-shaped curve made up of five stages. The cycle begins with the *product development* stage in which the company finds and develops a new product idea. *The introduction stage* is marked by slow growth and low profits as the product is distributed to the market. If successful, the product enters a *growth stage,* which offers rapid sales growth and increasing profits. Next comes a *maturity stage* in which the product's sales growth slows down and profits stabilize. Finally, the product enters a *decline stage* in which sales and profits dwindle. The company's task during this stage is to recognize the decline and decide whether it should maintain, harvest, or drop the product. The different stages of the PLC require different marketing strategies and tactics.

OBJECTIVE 8-4 Discuss two additional product issues: socially responsible product decisions and international product and services marketing. (pp 256–258)

Marketers must consider two additional product issues. The first is *social responsibility*. This includes public policy issues and regulations involving acquiring or dropping products, patent protection, product quality and safety, and product warranties. The second involves the special challenges facing international product and services marketers. International marketers must decide how much to standardize or adapt their offerings for world markets.

Key Terms

Objective 8-1
New product development (p 238)

Objective 8-2
Idea generation (p 239)
Crowdsourcing (p 240)
Idea screening (p 243)
Product concept (p 243)
Concept testing (p 244)
Marketing strategy development (p 244)
Business analysis (p 245)
Product development (p 245)
Test marketing (p 246)
Commercialization (p 247)
Customer-centered new product development (p 247)
Team-based new product development (p 248)

Objective 8-3
Product life cycle (PLC) (p 249)
Style (p 250)
Fashion (p 250)
Fad (p 251)
Introduction stage (p 251)
Growth stage (p 253)
Maturity stage (p 254)
Decline stage (p 255)

Discussion Questions

8-1. Define crowdsourcing and describe an example not already presented in the chapter. (AACSB: Communication; Reflective Thinking)

8-2. What activities are performed in the marketing strategy development step of the new product development process? What is required in a good marketing strategy statement? (AACSB: Communication; Reflective Thinking)

8-3. What is performed in the business analysis step of the new product development process? How does a business carry out this step? (AACSB: Communication)

8-4. How can companies adopt a holistic approach to managing new product development? (AACSB: Communication).

8-5. Describe the options available to marketers of products in the decline stage of the product life cycle. (AACSB: Communication)

Critical Thinking Exercises

8-6. It appears that the sky is the limit regarding ideas for smartphone/tablet apps. In a small group, create an idea for new apps related to (1) business, (2) health, (3) education, (4) sports, and (5) shopping. (AACSB: Communication; Use of IT; Reflective Thinking)

8-7. Find an example of a company that launched a new consumer product within the past five years. Develop a presentation showing how the company implemented the 4*P*s in launching the product and report on the product's success since the launch. (AACSB: Communication; Reflective Thinking)

8-8. The "Internet of Things"—a term that refers to everyday objects being connected to the Internet—is growing. Thermostats, ovens, cars, toothbrushes, and even baby clothes are connecting to the Internet. Research this phenomenon and suggest five innovative product ideas connected to the Internet of Things. (AACSB: Communication; Use of IT; Reflective Thinking)

MINICASES AND APPLICATIONS

Online, Mobile, and Social Media Marketing Telemedicine

With the majority of health-care costs spent for the treatment of chronic diseases and the reason for most emergency room visits being nonemergencies, the time is ripe for telemedicine. Patients are tapping their phones, tablets, and keyboards instead of making an office visit or trip to the emergency room. Technology makes it possible for doctors to consult with patients through Skype or FaceTime on smartphones, access medical tests via electronic medical records, and send a prescription to a patient's local pharmacy—all from miles away. The telemedicine industry is still in its infancy, earning only $200 million in annual revenue, but it is predicted to increase to an almost $2 billion industry in just a few years. Technology isn't the only reason for this industry's growth. The HITECH Act encouraging electronic medical records is also adding fuel to this fire.

8-9. Research the telemedicine industry and describe two companies offering services. What are the pros and cons of offering medical services this way, and is there governmental or industry guidance for this industry? (AACSB: Communications; Reflective Thinking)

8-10. In what stage of the product life cycle is telemedicine? What role has mobile technology played in evolution of this industry? Explain (AACSB: Communication; Reflective Thinking)

Marketing Ethics Put On Your Thinking Caps!

For years, electrical current has been used to treat brain disorders such as depression, Parkinson's disease, and epilepsy. Traditional electrical treatment methods are invasive and require sending large currents or implanting devices in users' brains to achieve positive results. Recent studies have shown, however, that sending noninvasive low-dose electric current powered by a nine-volt battery through the brains of adults and children helps them to learn math and languages better. For as little as $55, you can purchase your own transcranial direct-current stimulation (tDCS) device to get better grades in school. The Brain Stimulator tDCS Basic Kit allows users to select between four different current levels and a nice blue headband or cap to hold the electrodes next to your skull. The buyer should beware, however, because these devices have been neither reviewed nor approved by the Food and Drug Administration as medical devices.

8-11. Discuss the ethical issues surrounding this type of product. Is there substantial research to support the claims and safety of these new products? (AACSB: Communication; Ethical Reasoning)

8-12. What is the Food and Drug Administration's stance on these types of devices and other products, such as herbal supplements, marketed as cognitive enhancers? (AACSB: Communication; Reflective Thinking)

Marketing by the Numbers Dental House Calls

With the population aging and patients who dread sitting in a sterile dental office, dentists are finding an opportunity in dental house calls. The Blende Dental Group has taken its service on the road in San Francisco and New York City, performing everything from routine exams and cleanings to root canals. Some patients are wealthy and prefer the personal service, whereas others are elderly homebounds who cannot get out to the dentist's office. Recreating a dental office in a home requires additional equipment, such as a portable X-ray machine that looks like a ray gun, sterile water tanks, a dental drill, lights, and a laptop. A portable X-ray machine alone costs $8,000. Refer to Appendix 3: Marketing by the Numbers to answer the following questions.

8-13. What types of fixed costs are associated with this service? Assuming fixed costs of adding this mobile service will increase by $20,000 and a desired contribution margin of 40 percent, determine the amount of sales necessary to break even on this increase in fixed costs to offer this additional service. (AACSB: Communication; Analytical Thinking)

8-14. What other factors must a dentist consider before offering this service in addition to his or her in-office service? (AACSB: Communication; Reflective Thinking)

Video Case Day2Night Convertible Heels

Many women love the fashionable looks and heightening effects of high-heeled shoes. But every woman knows the problems associated with wearing them. For example, they are very uncomfortable for anything more than light walking for short distances. For other activities, you'd better be packing a second pair of shoes.

That's where Day2Night Convertible Heels comes in. Created by a woman who had an epiphany after a hard night of dancing, Day2Night's shoes instantly convert to any one of four heel sizes, from low-heeled pumps to spiked-heeled stilettos. An interchangeable heel makes these high heels a high-tech proposition. Beyond launching a line of shoes, Day2Night is looking to license the technology to other shoe manufacturers.

After viewing the video featuring Day2Night Convertible Heels, answer the following questions:

8-15. Based on the stages of new product development, discuss how Day2Night was likely developed.

8-16. What stage of the product life cycle best applies to Day2Night's shoe line? As the company attempts to launch the shoes, how should it market them?

8-17. What challenges does Day2Night face?

Company Cases 8 3M/2 Samsung/10 Apple Pay

See Appendix 1 for cases appropriate for this chapter. **Case 8, 3M: Where Innovation Is a Way of Life**. Generally not considered high-tech, 3M is consistently one of the most innovative companies due to a culture of innovation. **Case 2, Samsung: A Strategic Plan for Success.** One of the most innovative companies in the world, Samsung consistently raises the bar with cutting-edge new products in numerous categories. **Case 10, Apple Pay: Taking Mobile Payments Mainstream.** While the Apple Watch was a highly anticipated new product, the real new product story may be Apple Pay—the mobile payment system that was initially seen as merely a feature of Apple's flashy hardware.

MyMarketingLab

If assigned by your instructor, complete these writing sections from your Assignments in the MyLab.

8-18. Discuss how a company can maintain success for products in the mature stage of the product life cycle and give examples not already described in the chapter. (AACSB: Communication)

8-19. What decisions must be made once a company decides to go ahead with commercialization for a new product? (AACSB: Written and Oral Communication)

Applied
Engage
Personalized
Immediate

9 Pricing
Understanding and Capturing Customer Value

CHAPTER ROAD MAP Objective Outline

OBJECTIVE 9-1 Identify the three major pricing strategies and discuss the importance of understanding customer-value perceptions, company costs, and competitor strategies when setting prices. What Is a Price? (264–265); Major Pricing Strategies (265–272)

OBJECTIVE 9-2 Identify and define the other important external and internal factors affecting a firm's pricing decisions. Other Internal and External Considerations Affecting Price Decisions (272–277)

OBJECTIVE 9-3 Describe the major strategies for pricing new products. New Product Pricing Strategies (277–278)

OBJECTIVE 9-4 Explain how companies find a set of prices that maximizes the profits from the total product mix. Product Mix Pricing Strategies (278–280)

OBJECTIVE 9-5 Discuss how companies adjust their prices to take into account different types of customers and situations. Price Adjustment Strategies (280–288)

OBJECTIVE 9-6 Discuss the key issues related to initiating and responding to price changes. Price Changes (288–291); Public Policy and Pricing (291–293)

Previewing the Concepts

In this chapter, we look at the second major marketing mix tool—pricing. If effective product development, promotion, and distribution sow the seeds of business success, effective pricing is the harvest. Firms successful at creating customer value with the other marketing mix activities must still capture some of this value in the prices they earn. In this chapter, we discuss the importance of pricing, dig into three major pricing strategies, and look at internal and external considerations that affect pricing decisions. Finally we examine some additional pricing considerations and approaches.

For openers, let's examine the importance of pricing in online retailing. In case you haven't noticed, there's a war going on—between Walmart, by far the world's largest retailer, and Amazon, the planet's largest online merchant. Each combatant brings an arsenal of potent weapons to the battle. For now, the focus is on price. But in the long run, it'll take much more than low prices to win this war. The spoils will go to the company that delivers the best overall online customer experience and value for the price.

First Stop

Amazon versus Walmart: A Price War for Online Supremacy

"Walmart to Amazon: Let's Rumble" read the headline. Ali had Frazier. Coke has Pepsi. The Yankees have the White Sox. And now, the two retail heavyweights are waging a war all their own. The objective? Online supremacy. The weapon of choice? Prices, at least for now—not surprising, given the two combatants' long-held low-cost positions.

Each side is formidable in its own right. Walmart dominates offline retailing. It's price-driven "Save money. Live better." positioning has made it far and away the world's biggest retailer, and the world's largest company to boot. In turn, Amazon is the "Walmart of the Web"—our online general store. Although Walmart's yearly sales total an incredible \$487 billion, more than 5.3 times Amazon's \$89 billion annually, Amazon's online sales are 7.5 times greater than Walmart's online sales. By one estimate, Amazon captures a full one-third of all U.S. online buying.

Why does Walmart worry about Amazon? After all, online sales currently account for only about 5 percent of total U.S. retail sales. Walmart captures most of its business through its 11,000 brick-and-mortar stores—online buying accounts for only a trifling 2.7 percent of its total sales. But this battle isn't about now, it's about the future. Although still a small market by Walmart's standards, online sales are growing at three times the rate of physical-world sales. Within the next decade, online and mobile buying will capture as much as a third of all retail sales. Because Amazon owns online, its revenues have soared 20 percent or more annually over the past three years. Meanwhile, Walmart's earthbound sales have grown at less than 5 percent a year during that period. At that rate, Amazon's revenues will reach \$100 billion within the next year, reaching that mark faster than any other company in history.

Amazon has shown a relentless ambition to offer more of almost everything online. It started by selling only books but now sells everything from books, movies, and music to consumer electronics, home and garden products, clothing, jewelry, toys, tools, and even groceries. Thus, Amazon's online prowess now looms as a significant threat to Walmart. If Amazon's expansion continues and online sales spurt as predicted, the digital merchant will eat further and further into Walmart's bread-and-butter store sales.

But Walmart isn't about to let that happen without a fight. Instead, it's taking the battle to Amazon's home territory—the Internet and mobile buying. It started with the tactics it knows best—low costs and prices. Through aggressive pricing, Walmart is now fighting for every dollar consumers spend online. If you compare prices at Walmart.com and Amazon.com, you'll find a price war raging across a broad range of products.

In a price war, Walmart would seem to have the edge. Low costs and prices are in the company's DNA. Through the years, Walmart has used its efficient operations and immense buying power to slash prices and thrash one competitor after another. But Amazon is not like most other competitors. Its network is optimized for online shopping, and the Internet seller isn't saddled with the costs of running physical stores. As a result, Amazon has been able to match or even beat Walmart at its own pricing game online. The two giants now seem

» Walmart versus Amazon online: Achieving online supremacy will take more than just waging and winning an online price war. The spoils will go to the company that delivers the best overall online customer experience and value for the price.

(top) Andrew Harrer/Bloomberg/Getty Images; (bottom) Digitallife/Alamy

pretty much stalemated on low prices, giving neither much of an advantage there. In fact, in the long run, reckless price cutting will likely do more damage than good to both Walmart and Amazon. So, although low prices will be crucial, they won't be enough to win over online buyers. Today's online shoppers want it all, low prices *and* selection, speed, convenience, and a satisfying overall shopping experience.

Walmart, the world's largest retailer, and Amazon, the world's largest online merchant, are fighting a war for online supremacy. The weapon of choice? Prices, at least for now. But in the long run, winning the war will take much more than low prices.

For now, Amazon seems to have the upper hand on most of the important nonprice buying factors. Its made-for-online distribution network speeds orders to buyers' homes quickly and efficiently—including same-day delivery in some markets. Amazon's online assortment outstrips even Walmart's, and the online and mobile shopping wizard is now moving into groceries, an area that currently accounts for 55 percent of Walmart's sales. As for Amazon's lack of physical stores—no problem. Amazon's heavily used mobile app lets customers shop Amazon.com even as they are browsing

Walmart's stores. Finally, Amazon's unmatched, big data–driven customer interface creates personalized, highly satisfying online buying experiences. Amazon regularly rates among the leaders in customer satisfaction across all industries.

By contrast, Walmart came late to online selling. It's still trying to figure out how to efficiently deliver goods into the hands of online shoppers. As its online sales have grown, the store-based giant has patched together a makeshift online distribution network out of unused corners of its store distribution centers. And the still–mostly store retailer has yet to come close to matching Amazon's online customer buying experience. So even with its impressive low-price legacy, Walmart finds itself playing catch-up online.

To catch up, Walmart is investing heavily to create a next-generation fulfillment network. Importantly, it's taking advantage of a major asset that Amazon can't match—an opportunity to integrate online buying with its massive network of brick-and-mortar stores. For example, Walmart now fulfills more than a fifth of Walmart.com orders more quickly and cheaply by having workers in stores pluck and pack items and mail or deliver them to customers' homes. Two-thirds of the U.S. population lives within five miles of a Walmart store, offering the potential for 30-minute delivery.

And by combining its online and offline operations, Walmart can provide some unique services, such as free and convenient pickup and returns of online orders in stores (Walmart.com gives you three buying options: "online," "in-store," and "site-to-store"). Using Walmart's Web site and mobile app can also smooth in-store shopping. They let customers prepare shopping lists in advance, locate products by aisle to reduce wasted shopping time, and use their smartphones at checkout with preloaded digital coupons applied automatically. Customers who pick up online orders in the store can pay with cash, opening up online shopping to the 20 percent of Walmart customers who don't have bank accounts or credit cards. For customers who do pay online, Walmart is testing in-store lockers where customers can simply go to an assigned locker for pickup.

Who will win the battle for the hearts and dollars of online buyers? Certainly, low prices will continue to be important. But achieving online supremacy will involve much more than just waging and winning an online price war. It will require delivering low prices *plus* selection, convenience, and a world-class online buying experience—something that Amazon perfected long ago. For Walmart, catching and conquering Amazon online will require time, resources, and skills far beyond its trademark everyday low prices. As Walmart's president of global e-commerce puts it, the important task of winning online "will take the rest of our careers and as much as we've got [to invest]. This isn't a project. It's about the future of the company."[1]

>> **Pricing: No matter what the state of the economy, companies should sell value, not price.**

Magicoven/Shutterstock

Companies today face a fierce and fast-changing pricing environment. Value-seeking customers have put increased pricing pressure on many companies. Thanks to tight economic times in recent years, the pricing power of the Internet, and value-driven retailers such as Walmart, today's more frugal consumers are pursuing spend-less strategies. In response, it seems that almost every company has been looking for ways to cut prices.

>>Yet cutting prices is often not the best answer. Reducing prices unnecessarily can lead to lost profits and damaging price wars. It can cheapen a brand by signaling to customers that price is more important than the customer value a brand delivers.Instead, in both good economic times and bad, companies should sell value, not price. In some cases, that means selling lesser products at rock-bottom prices. But in most cases, it means persuading customers that paying a higher price for the company's brand is justified by the greater value they gain.

What Is a Price?

Price
The amount charged for a product or service, or the sum of the values that customers exchange for the benefits of having or using the product or service.

In the narrowest sense, **price** is the amount of money charged for a product or a service. More broadly, price is the sum of all the values that customers give up to gain the benefits of having or using a product or service. Historically, price has been the major factor affecting buyer choice. In recent decades, however, nonprice factors have gained increasing importance. Even so, price remains one of the most important elements that determine a firm's market share and profitability.

Price is the only element in the marketing mix that produces revenue; all other elements represent costs. Price is also one of the most flexible marketing mix elements. Unlike product features and channel commitments, prices can be changed quickly. At the same time, pricing is the number-one problem facing many marketing executives, and many companies do not handle pricing well. Some managers view pricing as a big headache, preferring instead to focus on other marketing mix elements.

However, smart managers treat pricing as a key strategic tool for creating and capturing customer value. Prices have a direct impact on a firm's bottom line. A small percentage improvement in price can generate a large percentage increase in profitability. More important, as part of a company's overall value proposition, price plays a key role in creating customer value and building customer relationships. So, instead of shying away from pricing, smart marketers are embracing it as an important competitive asset.[2]

Author Comment
Setting the right price is one of the marketer's most difficult tasks. A host of factors come into play. But as the opening story about Walmart and Amazon illustrates, finding and implementing the right pricing strategy is critical to success.

Major Pricing Strategies

The price the company charges will fall somewhere between one that is too low to produce a profit and one that is too high to produce any demand. **Figure 9.1** summarizes the major considerations in setting prices. Customer perceptions of the product's value set the ceiling for its price. If customers perceive that the product's price is greater than its value, they will not buy the product. Likewise, product costs set the floor for a product's price. If the company prices the product below its costs, the company's profits will suffer. In setting its price between these two extremes, the company must consider several external and internal factors, including competitors' strategies and prices, the overall marketing strategy and mix, and the nature of the market and demand.

Figure 9.1 suggests three major pricing strategies: customer value-based pricing, cost-based pricing, and competition-based pricing.

Author Comment
Like everything else in marketing, good pricing starts with *customers* and their perceptions of value.

Customer Value-Based Pricing

In the end, the customer will decide whether a product's price is right. Pricing decisions, like other marketing mix decisions, must start with customer value. When customers buy a product, they exchange something of value (the price) to get something of value (the benefits of having or using the product). Effective customer-oriented pricing involves understanding how much value consumers place on the benefits they receive from the product and setting a price that captures that value.

Customer value-based pricing
Setting price based on buyers' perceptions of value rather than on the seller's cost.

Customer value-based pricing uses buyers' perceptions of value as the key to pricing. Value-based pricing means that the marketer cannot design a product and marketing program and then set the price. Price is considered along with all other marketing mix variables *before* the marketing program is set.

Figure 9.2 compares value-based pricing with cost-based pricing. Although costs are an important consideration in setting prices, cost-based pricing is often product driven. The company designs what it considers to be a good product, adds up the costs of making the product, and sets a price that covers costs plus a target profit. Marketing must then convince buyers that the product's value at that price justifies its purchase. If the price turns out to be too high, the company must settle for lower markups or lower sales, both resulting in disappointing profits.

Value-based pricing reverses this process. The company first assesses customer needs and value perceptions. It then sets its target price based on customer perceptions of value. The targeted value and price drive decisions about what costs can be incurred and the

Figure 9.1 Considerations in Setting Price

If customers perceive that a product's price is greater than its value, they won't buy it. If the company prices the product below its costs, profits will suffer. Between the two extremes, the "right" pricing strategy is one that delivers both value to the customer and profits to the company.

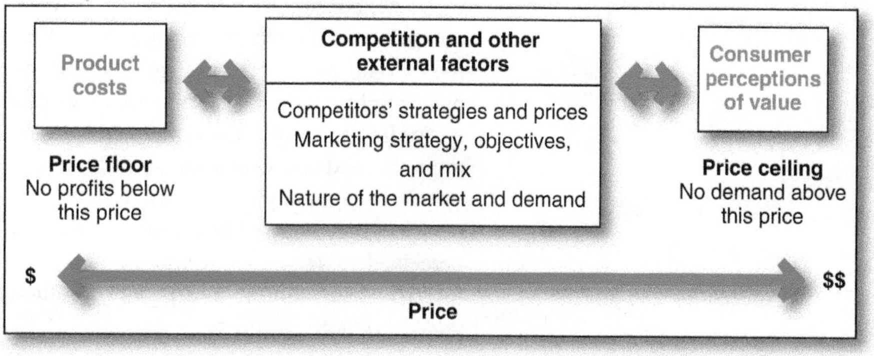

Figure 9.2 Value-Based Pricing versus Cost-Based Pricing

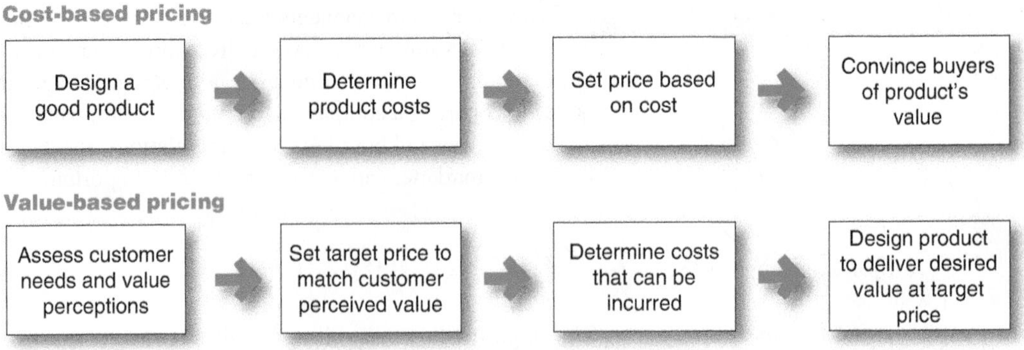

Costs play an important role in setting prices. But like everything else in marketing, good pricing starts with the customer.

resulting product design. As a result, pricing begins with analyzing consumer needs and value perceptions, and the price is set to match perceived value.

It's important to remember that "good value" is not the same as "low price." For example, some owners consider a luxurious Patek Philippe watch a real bargain, even at eye-popping prices ranging from \$20,000 to \$500,000:[3]

Perceived value: Some owners consider a luxurious Patek Philippe watch a real bargain, even at eye-popping prices ranging from \$20,000 to \$500,000. Every Patek Philippe watch is handmade by Swiss watchmakers and can take more than a year to make.

Fabrice Coffrini/AFP/Getty Images

Listen up here, because I'm about to tell you why a certain watch costing \$20,000, or even \$500,000, isn't actually expensive but is in fact a tremendous value. Every Patek Philippe watch is handmade by Swiss watchmakers from the finest materials and can take more than a year to make. Still not convinced? Beyond keeping precise time, Patek Philippe watches are also good investments. They carry high prices but retain or even increase their value over time. Many models achieve a kind of cult status that makes them the most coveted timepieces on the planet. But more important than just a means of telling time or a good investment is the sentimental and emotional value of possessing a Patek Philippe. Says the company's president: "This is about passion. I mean—it really is a dream. Nobody needs a Patek." These watches are unique possessions steeped in precious memories, making them treasured family assets. According to the company, "The purchase of a Patek Philippe is often related to a personal event—a professional success, a marriage, or the birth of a child—and offering it as a gift is the most eloquent expression of love or affection." A Patek Philippe watch is made not to last just one lifetime but many. Says one ad: "You never actually own a Patek Philippe, you merely look after it for the next generation." That makes it a real bargain, even at twice the price.

A company will often find it hard to measure the value customers attach to its product. For example, calculating the cost of ingredients in a meal at a fancy restaurant is relatively easy. But assigning value to other measures of satisfaction such as taste, environment, relaxation, conversation, and status is very hard. Such value is subjective; it varies both for different consumers and different situations.

Still, consumers will use these perceived values to evaluate a product's price, so the company must work to measure them. Sometimes, companies ask consumers how much they would pay for a basic product and for each benefit added to the offer. Or a company might conduct experiments to test the perceived value of different product offers. According to an old Russian proverb, there are two fools in every market—one who asks too much and one who asks too little. If the seller charges more than the buyers' perceived value, the company's sales will suffer. If the seller charges less, its products will sell very well, but they will produce less revenue than they would if they were priced at the level of perceived value.

We now examine two types of value-based pricing: *good-value pricing* and *value-added pricing*.

Good-value pricing: Even premium brands can launch good-value versions. The Mercedes CLA Class gives customers "The Art of Seduction. At a price reduction."

Courtesy of Daimler AG.

Good-Value Pricing

The Great Recession of 2008 to 2009 caused a fundamental and lasting shift in consumer attitudes toward price and quality. In response, many companies have changed their pricing approaches to bring them in line with changing economic conditions and consumer price perceptions. More and more, marketers have adopted the strategy of **good-value pricing**—offering the right combination of quality and good service at a fair price.

In many cases, this has involved introducing less-expensive versions of established brand name products or new lower-price lines. For example, Walmart launched an extreme-value store brand called Price First. Priced even lower than the retailer's already-low-priced Great Value brand, Price First offer thrift-conscious customers rock-bottom prices on grocery staples. Good-value prices are a relative thing—even premium brands can launch value versions. Mercedes-Benz recently released its CLA Class, entry-level models starting at $31,500. From its wing-like dash and diamond-block grille to its 208-hp turbo inline-4 engine, the CLA Class gives customers "The Art of Seduction. At a price reduction."[4]

Good-value pricing
Offering just the right combination of quality and good service at a fair price.

In other cases, good-value pricing involves redesigning existing brands to offer more quality for a given price or the same quality for less. Some companies even succeed by offering less value but at very low prices. For example, the ALDI supermarket chain has established an impressive good-value pricing position by which it gives customers "more 'mmm' for the dollar" (see Marketing at Work 9.1).

ALDI practices an important type of good-value pricing at the retail level called *everyday low pricing (EDLP)*. EDLP involves charging a constant, everyday low price with few or no temporary price discounts. Other retailers such as Costco and Lumber Liquidators practice EDLP. However, the king of EDLP is Walmart, which practically defined the concept. Except for a few sale items every month, Walmart promises everyday low prices on everything it sells. In contrast, *high-low pricing* involves charging higher prices on an everyday basis but running frequent promotions to lower prices temporarily on selected items. Department stores such as Kohl's and Macy's practice high-low pricing by having frequent sale days, early-bird savings, and bonus earnings for store credit-card holders.

Value-added pricing
Attaching value-added features and services to differentiate a company's offers and charging higher prices.

Value-Added Pricing

Value-based pricing doesn't mean simply charging what customers want to pay or setting low prices to meet competition. Instead, many companies adopt **value-added pricing** strategies. Rather than cutting prices to match competitors, they attach value-added features and services to differentiate their offers and thus support their higher prices. For example, even as frugal consumer spending habits linger, some movie theater chains are *adding* amenities and charging *more* rather than cutting services to maintain lower admission prices:[5]

Value-added pricing: Rather than cutting services to maintain lower admission prices, premium theaters such as AMC's Cinema Suites are adding amenities and charging more. "Once people experience it, ... they don't want to go anywhere else."

Courtesy of AMC Theaters.

> Some theater chains are turning their multiplexes into smaller, roomier luxury outposts. The premium theaters offer value-added features such as online reserved seating, high-backed leather executive or rocking chairs with armrests and footrests, the latest in digital sound and super-wide screens, dine-in restaurants serving fine food and drinks, and even valet parking. For example, AMC Theatres (the second-largest American theater chain) operates more than 75 theaters with some kind of enhanced food and beverage amenities, including Fork & Screen (upgraded leather seating, seat-side service, extensive menu including dinner offerings, beer, wine, and cocktails) and

MARKETING AT WORK 9.1

ALDI: Impressively High Quality at Impossibly Low Prices, Every Day

When asked to name the world's largest grocery chains, you'd probably come up with Walmart, the world's largest retailer; and maybe Kroger, the largest U.S. grocery-only merchant. One name that probably wouldn't come to mind is Germany-based discount grocer ALDI. Yet, surprisingly, with more than $81 billion in annual revenues and more than 10,000 stores in 17 countries, ALDI is the world's eighth-largest retailer overall and the second-largest grocery-only retailer behind Kroger. What's more, ALDI is taking the United States and other country markets by storm, growing faster than any of its larger rivals.

How does ALDI do it? Its simple formula for success is no secret. In fact, it's almost a cliché: Give customers a basic assortment of good-quality everyday items at everyday extra low prices. These days, many grocers brag about low prices. But at ALDI, they are an absolute fact. The rapidly expanding chain promises customers "Simply Smarter Shopping," driven by a long list of "ALDI Truths" by which it delivers "impressively high quality at impossibly low prices." (ALDI Truth #1: When deciding between eating well and saving money, always choose both.)

ALDI has redesigned the food shopping experience to reduce costs and give customers prices that it claims are up to 50 percent lower than those of rival supermarkets. To keep costs and prices down, ALDI operates smaller, energy-saving stores (about one-third the size of traditional supermarkets), and each store carries only about 1,800 of the fastest-moving grocery items (the typical supermarket carries about 40,000 items). Almost 95 percent of its items are ALDI store brands. So, ALDI claims, customers are paying for the product itself, not national brand advertising and marketing. Also, ALDI does no promotional pricing or price matching—it just sticks with its efficient everyday very low prices (ALDI Truth #12: We don't match other stores' prices because that would mean raising ours).

In trimming costs and passing savings along to customers, ALDI leaves no stone unturned. Even customers themselves help to keep costs low: They bring their own bags (or purchase them from ALDI for a small charge), bag their own groceries (ALDI provides no baggers), return shopping carts on their own (to get back a 25-cent deposit), and pay with cash or a debit card (no credit cards accepted at most ALDI stores). But to ALDI fans, the savings make it all worthwhile (ALDI Truth #14: You can't eat frills, so why pay for them?).

Whereas ALDI cuts operating costs to the bone, it doesn't scrimp on quality. With its preponderance of store brands, ALDI exercises complete control over the quality of the products on its shelves, and the chain promises that everything it sells is certifiably fresh and tasty. ALDI Truth #60—We make delicious cost a lot less—makes it clear that the chain promises more than just low prices. ALDI backs this promise with a Double Guarantee on all items: "If for any reason you are not 100-percent satisfied with any product, we will gladly replace the product AND refund your money."

To improve the quality of its assortment, ALDI has progressively added items that aren't usually associated with "discounted" groceries. Beyond the typical canned, boxed, and frozen food basics, ALDI carries fresh meat, baked goods, and fresh produce. It also carries an assortment of regular and periodic specialty goods, such as Mama Cozzi's Pizza Kitchen Meat Trio Focaccia, Appetitos Spinach Artichoke Dip, and All Natural Mango Salsa. ALDI even offers a selection of organic foods. With such items, and with its clean, bright stores, ALDI targets not just low-income customers, but frugal middle-class and upper-middle-class customers as well.

None of this is news to German shoppers, who have loved ALDI for decades. In Germany, the chain operates more than 4,200 stores, accounting for more than 28 percent of the market. That might explain why Walmart gave up in Germany just

» Good-value pricing: ALDI keeps costs low so that it can offer customers "impressively high quality at impossibly low prices" every day.

Keri Miksza

nine years after entering the market. Against competitors like ALDI, Walmart's normally low prices were just too expensive for frugal German consumers.

ALDI's no-frills basic approach isn't for everyone. Whereas some shoppers love the low prices, basic assortments, and simple store atmosphere, others can't imagine life without at least some of the luxuries and amenities offered by rivals. But most people who shop at ALDI quickly become true believers. Testimonials from converts litter the Internet. "I just recently switched to ALDI from a 'premium' grocery store ... and the savings blow me away!" proclaims one customer. "Shoot, I wish I had some pom-poms, because I am so totally team ALDI!" Says another fervent fan:

> I will probably never grocery shop anywhere else! As a family of three on a very strict budget, I usually scour the sale papers and coupons looking to save. I usually make two or three different stops on my grocery trips and do my shopping every two weeks. We budget $200 a month for groceries and I usually come in right under that amount. Today at ALDI I got everything on my list, plus about 20 extra items not on the list, and my total was only $86! I cannot believe how much I saved! ALDI is now my immediate go-to grocery store!

Many customers also wax enthusiastic about their favorite ALDI products, items they can't live without and can't get anywhere else.

With tradition behind it and its can't-lose operating and marketing model, ALDI plans for rapid U.S. expansion. The company has quickly grown to more than 1,300 stores in 32 states. That's a huge accomplishment compared with, say, British discount chain Tesco, the world's second-largest retailer, which exited the U.S. market with heavy losses after only seven years. ALDI still has plenty of room for more growth. It has a $3 billion plan to open 130 U.S. stores a year, expanding by 50 percent to 1,950 stores by 2018. With its proven everyday extra low pricing strategy, ALDI will likely accomplish or even exceed that goal. That's good news for the company but also for customers. When ALDI comes to your neighborhood, "Your wallet and taste buds are in for a treat" (ALDI Truth #34).

Sources: Walter Loeb, "Why Aldi and Lidl Have What It Takes to Beat the Best and the Biggest," *Forbes*, October 30, 2013, www.forbes.com/sites/walterloeb/2013/10/30/why-aldi-and-lidl-have-what-it-takes-to-beat-the-best-and-the-biggest/; Leslie Patton, "Aldi Plans to Expand U.S. Store Count by 50% in Next Five Years," *Businessweek*, December 20, 2013, www.businessweek.com/news/2013-12-20/aldi-plans-to-expand-u-dot-s-dot-store-count-by-50-percent-in-next-five-years; Bill Bishop, "ALDI Offers the Thrill of Discovery," *Supermarket News*, October 20, 2014, http://supermarketnews.com/limited-assortment/aldi-offers-thrill-discovery; "Top 250 Global Powers of Retailing 2015," Deloitte, https://nrf.com/2015/global250-table; and www.aldi.us, www.aldi.us/en/new-to-aldi/aldi-truths/, and www.aldi.us/en/new-to-aldi/switch-save/, accessed October 2015.

Cinema Suites (additional upscale food offerings in addition to premium cocktails and an extensive wine list, seat-side service, red leather reclining chairs, and eight to nine feet of spacing between rows).

So at the Cinema Suites at the AMC Easton 30 with IMAX in Columbus, Ohio, bring on the mango margaritas! For $9 to $15 a ticket (depending on the time and day), moviegoers are treated to reserved seating, a strict 21-and-over-only policy, reclining leather seats, and the opportunity to pay even more to have dinner and drinks brought to their seats. Such theaters are so successful that AMC plans to add more. "Once people experience it," says a company spokesperson, "more often than not they don't want to go anywhere else."

Cost-Based Pricing

Cost-based pricing
Setting prices based on the costs of producing, distributing, and selling the product plus a fair rate of return for effort and risk.

Whereas customer value perceptions set the price ceiling, costs set the floor for the price that the company can charge. **Cost-based pricing** involves setting prices based on the costs of producing, distributing, and selling the product plus a fair rate of return for the company's effort and risk. A company's costs may be an important element in its pricing strategy.

Some companies, such as Walmart or Spirit Airlines, work to become the *low-cost producers* in their industries. Companies with lower costs can set lower prices that result in smaller margins but greater sales and profits. However, other companies—such as Apple, BMW, and Steinway—intentionally pay higher costs so that they can add value and claim higher prices and margins. For example, it costs more to make a "handcrafted" Steinway piano than a Yamaha production model. But the higher costs result in higher quality, justifying an average $87,000 price. To those who buy a Steinway, prices is nothing; the Steinway experience is everything. The key is to manage the spread between costs and prices—how much the company makes for the customer value it delivers.

Types of Costs

Fixed costs (overhead)
Costs that do not vary with production or sales level.

A company's costs take two forms: fixed and variable. **Fixed costs** (also known as **overhead**) are costs that do not vary with production or sales level. For example, a company must pay each month's bills for rent, heat, interest, and executive salaries regardless

Variable costs
Costs that vary directly with the level of production.

Total costs
The sum of the fixed and variable costs for any given level of production.

of the company's level of output. **Variable costs** vary directly with the level of production. Each PC produced by HP involves a cost of computer chips, wires, plastic, packaging, and other inputs. Although these costs tend to be the same for each unit produced, they are called variable costs because the total varies with the number of units produced. **Total costs** are the sum of the fixed and variable costs for any given level of production. Management wants to charge a price that will at least cover the total production costs at a given level of production.

The company must watch its costs carefully. If it costs the company more than its competitors to produce and sell a similar product, the company will need to charge a higher price or make less profit, putting it at a competitive disadvantage.

Author Comment
Costs set the floor for price, but the goal isn't always to *minimize* costs. In fact, many firms invest in higher costs so that they can claim higher prices and margins (think back about Patek Philippe watches). The key is to manage the *spread* between costs and prices—how much the company makes for the customer value it delivers.

Cost-Plus Pricing

The simplest pricing method is **cost-plus pricing (or markup pricing)**—adding a standard markup to the cost of the product. For example, an electronics retailer might pay a manufacturer $20 for a flash drive and mark it up to sell at $30, a 50 percent markup on cost. The retailer's gross margin is $10. If the store's operating costs amount to $8 per flash drive sold, the retailer's profit margin will be $2. The manufacturer that made the flash drive probably used cost-plus pricing, too. If the manufacturer's standard cost of producing the flash drive was $16, it might have added a 25 percent markup, setting the price to the retailers at $20.

Cost-plus pricing (markup pricing)
Adding a standard markup to the cost of the product.

Break-even pricing (target return pricing)
Setting price to break even on the costs of making and marketing a product or setting price to make a target return.

Does using standard markups to set prices make sense? Generally, no. Any pricing method that ignores consumer demand and competitor prices is not likely to lead to the best price. Still, markup pricing remains popular for many reasons. First, sellers are more certain about costs than about demand. By tying the price to cost, sellers simplify pricing. Second, when all firms in the industry use this pricing method, prices tend to be similar and price competition is minimized.

Another cost-oriented pricing approach is **break-even pricing,** or a variation called **target return pricing**. The firm tries to determine the price at which it will break even or make the target return it is seeking. Target return pricing uses the concept of a *break-even chart*, which shows the total cost and total revenue expected at different sales volume levels. **>> Figure 9.3** shows a break-even chart for the flash drive manufacturer discussed previously. Fixed costs are $6 million regardless of sales volume, and variable costs are $5 per unit. Variable costs are added to fixed costs to form total costs, which rise with volume. The slope of the total revenue curve reflects the price. Here, the price is $15 (for example, the company's revenue is $12 million on 800,000 units, or $15 per unit).

>> Figure 9.3 Break-Even Chart for Determining Target Return Price and Break-Even Volume

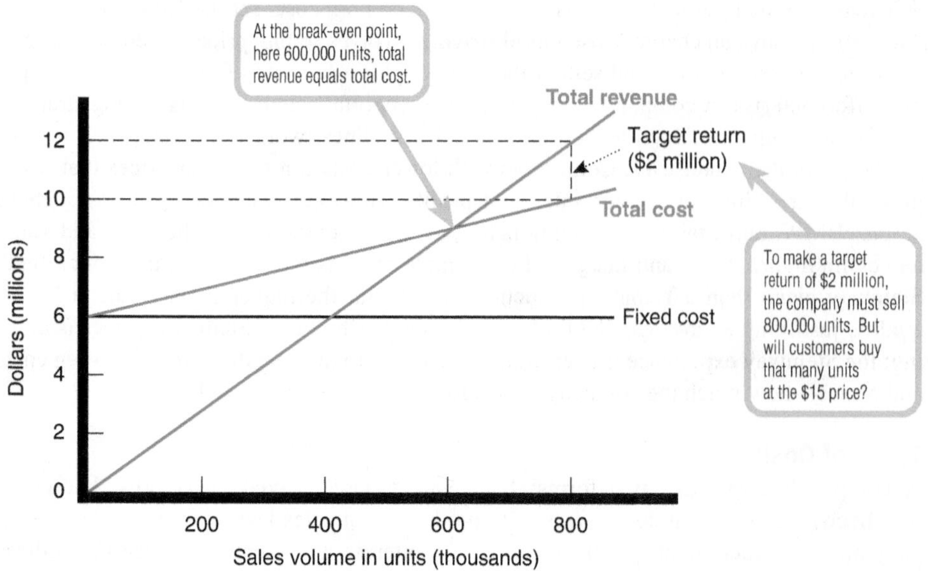

At the $15 price, the manufacturer must sell at least 600,000 units to *break even* (break-even volume = fixed costs ÷ [price – variable costs] = $6,000,000 ÷ [$15 – $5] = 600,000). That is, at this level, total revenues will equal total costs of $9 million, producing no profit. If the flash drive manufacturer wants a target return of $2 million, it must sell at least 800,000 units to obtain the $12 million of total revenue needed to cover the costs of $10 million plus the $2 million of target profits. In contrast, if the company charges a higher price, say, $20, it will not need to sell as many units to break even or to achieve its target profit. In fact, the higher the price, the lower the manufacturer's break-even point will be.

The major problem with this analysis, however, is that it fails to consider customer value and the relationship between price and demand.

As the *price* increases, *demand* decreases, and the market may not buy even the lower volume needed to break even at the higher price. For example, suppose the flash drive manufacturer calculates that, given its current fixed and variable costs, it must charge a price of $30 for the product in order to earn its desired target profit. But marketing research shows that few consumers will pay more than $25. In this case, the company must trim its costs in order to lower the break-even point so that it can charge the lower price consumers expect.

Thus, although break-even analysis and target return pricing can help the company to determine the minimum prices needed to cover expected costs and profits, they do not take the price–demand relationship into account. When using this method, the company must also consider the impact of price on the sales volume needed to realize target profits and the likelihood that the needed volume will be achieved at each possible price.

Author Comment
In setting prices, the company must also consider competitors' prices. No matter what price it charges—high, low, or in between—the company must be certain to give customers superior value for that price.

Competition-Based Pricing

Competition-based pricing Setting prices based on competitors' strategies, prices, costs, and market offerings.

Competition-based pricing involves setting prices based on competitors' strategies, costs, prices, and market offerings. Consumers will base their judgments of a product's value on the prices that competitors charge for similar products.

In assessing competitors' pricing strategies, the company should ask several questions. First, how does the company's market offering compare with competitors' offerings in terms of customer value? If consumers perceive that the company's product or service provides greater value, the company can charge a higher price. If consumers perceive less value relative to competing products, the company must either charge a lower price or change customer perceptions to justify a higher price.

Next, how strong are current competitors, and what are their current pricing strategies? If the company faces a host of smaller competitors charging high prices relative to the value they deliver, it might charge lower prices to drive weaker competitors from the market. If the market is dominated by larger, lower-price competitors, a company may decide to target unserved market niches by offering value-added products and services at higher prices.

Importantly, the goal is not to match or beat competitors' prices. Rather, the goal is to set prices according to the relative value created versus competitors. If a company creates greater value for customers, higher prices are justified. » For example, Caterpillar makes high-quality, heavy-duty construction and mining equipment. It dominates its industry despite charging higher prices than competitors such as Komatsu. When a commercial customer once asked a Caterpillar dealer why it should pay $500,000 for a big Caterpillar bulldozer when it could get an "equivalent" Komatsu dozer for $420,000, the Caterpillar dealer famously provided an analysis like the following:

$420,000	the Caterpillar's price if equivalent to the competitor's bulldozer
$50,000	the value added by Caterpillar's superior reliability and durability
$40,000	the value added by Caterpillar's lower lifetime operating costs
$40,000	the value added by Caterpillar's superior service
$20,000	the value added by Caterpillar's longer parts warranty
$570,000	the total value-added price for Caterpillar's bulldozer
–$70,000	discount
$500,000	final price

» **Pricing versus competitors: Despite Caterpillar's premium prices. Customers believe that Caterpillar gives them a lot more value for the price over the lifetime of its machines.**

Kristoffer Tripplaar/Alamy

Thus, although the customer pays an $80,000 price premium for the Caterpillar bulldozer, it's actually getting $150,000 in added value over the product's lifetime. The customer chose the Caterpillar bulldozer.

What principle should guide decisions about what price to charge relative to those of competitors? The answer is simple in concept but often difficult in practice: No matter what price you charge—high, low, or in between—be certain to give customers superior value for that price.

Author Comment

Now that we've looked at the three general pricing strategies—value-, cost-, and competitor-based pricing—let's dig into some of the many other factors that affect pricing decisions.

Other Internal and External Considerations Affecting Price Decisions

Beyond customer value perceptions, costs, and competitor strategies, the company must consider several additional internal and external factors. Internal factors affecting pricing include the company's overall marketing strategy, objectives, and marketing mix as well as other organizational considerations. External factors include the nature of the market and demand and other environmental factors.

Overall Marketing Strategy, Objectives, and Mix

Price is only one element of the company's broader marketing strategy. So, before setting price, the company must decide on its overall marketing strategy for the product or service. Sometimes, a company's overall strategy is built around its price and value story. For example, grocery retailer Trader Joe's unique price-value positioning has made it one of the nation's fastest-growing, most popular food stores:

> Trader Joe's has put its own special twist on the food price-value equation—call it "cheap gourmet." It offers gourmet-caliber, one-of-a-kind products at bargain prices, all served up in a festive, vacation-like atmosphere that makes shopping fun. Trader Joe's is a gourmet foodie's delight, featuring everything from kettle corn cookies, organic strawberry lemonade, creamy Valencia peanut butter, and fair-trade coffees to kimchi fried rice and triple-ginger ginger snaps. If asked, almost any customer can tick off a ready list of Trader Joe's favorites that he or she just can't live without—a list that quickly grows.
>
> The assortment is uniquely Trader Joe's—more than 85 percent of the store's brands are private labels. The prices aren't all that low in absolute terms, but they're a real bargain compared with what you'd pay for the same quality and coolness elsewhere. "It's not complicated," says Trader Joe's. "We just focus on what matters—great food + great prices = value. So you can afford to be adventurous without breaking the bank." Trader Joe's inventive price-value positioning has earned it an almost cult-like following of devoted customers who love what they get from Trader Joe's for the prices they pay.[6]

If a company has selected its target market and positioning carefully, then its marketing mix strategy, including price, will be fairly straightforward. For example, Amazon positions its Kindle Fire tablet as offering the same (or even more) for less and prices it at 40 percent less than Apple's iPads and Samsung's Galaxy tablets. It recently began targeting families with young children, positioning the Kindle Fire as the "perfect family tablet," with models priced as low as $99, bundled with Kindle FreeTime, an all-in-one subscription service starting at $2.99 per month that brings together books, games, educational apps, movies, and TV shows for kids ages 3 through 8. Thus, the Kindle pricing strategy is largely determined by decisions on market positioning.

Pricing may play an important role in helping to accomplish company objectives at many levels. A firm can set prices to attract new customers or profitably retain existing ones. It can set prices low to prevent competition from entering the market or set prices at competitors' levels to stabilize the market. It can price to keep the loyalty and support of resellers or avoid government intervention. Prices can be reduced temporarily to create excitement for a brand. Or one product may be priced to help the sales of other products in the company's line.

Price decisions must be coordinated with product design, distribution, and promotion decisions to form a consistent and effective integrated marketing mix program. Decisions made for other marketing mix variables may affect pricing decisions. For example, a decision to position the product on high-performance quality will mean that the seller must charge a higher price to cover higher costs. And producers whose resellers are expected to support and promote their products may have to build larger reseller margins into their prices.

Companies often position their products on price and then tailor other marketing mix decisions to the prices they want to charge. Here, price is a crucial product-positioning factor that defines the product's market, competition, and design. Many firms support such price-positioning strategies with a technique called **target costing**. Target costing reverses the usual process of first designing a new product, determining its cost, and then asking, "Can we sell it for that?" Instead, it starts with an ideal selling price based on customer value considerations and then targets costs that will ensure that the price is met. For example, when Honda initially designed the Honda Fit, it began with a $13,950 starting price point and highway mileage of 33 miles per gallon firmly in mind. It then designed a stylish, peppy little car with costs that allowed it to give target customers those values.

Target costing
Pricing that starts with an ideal selling price, then targets costs that will ensure that the price is met.

Other companies deemphasize price and use other marketing mix tools to create *nonprice* positions. Often, the best strategy is not to charge the lowest price but rather to differentiate the marketing offer to make it worth a higher price. » For example, luxury smartphone maker Vertu puts very high value into its products and charges premium prices to match that value. Vertu phones are made from high-end materials such as titanium and sapphire crystal, and each phone is hand-assembled by a single craftsman in England. Phones come with additional services such as Vertu Concierge, which helps create personal, curated user experiences and recommendations. Vertu phones sell for an average price of $6,000, with top models going for more than $20,000. But target customers recognize Vertu's very high quality and are willing to pay more to get it. With Vertu, "Every moment makes for an extraordinary story."[7]

» **Nonprice positioning: Luxury smartphone maker Vertu puts very high value into its products and charges sky-high prices to match that value. Average price: nearly $6,000.**

Vertu

Thus, marketers must consider the total marketing strategy and mix when setting prices. But again, even when featuring price, marketers need to remember that customers rarely buy on price alone. Instead, they seek products that give them the best value in terms of benefits received for the prices paid.

Organizational Considerations

Management must decide who within the organization should set prices. Companies handle pricing in a variety of ways. In small companies, prices are often set by top management rather than by the marketing or sales departments. In large companies, pricing is typically handled by divisional or product managers. In industrial markets, salespeople may be allowed to negotiate with customers within certain price ranges. Even so, top management sets the pricing objectives and policies, and it often approves the prices proposed by lower-level management or salespeople.

In industries in which pricing is a key factor (airlines, aerospace, steel, railroads, oil companies), companies often have pricing departments to set the best prices or help others set them. These departments report to the marketing department or top management. Others who have an influence on pricing include sales managers, production managers, finance managers, and accountants.

The Market and Demand

As noted earlier, good pricing starts with an understanding of how customers' perceptions of value affect the prices they are willing to pay. Both consumer and industrial buyers balance the price of a product or service against the benefits of owning it. Thus, before setting prices, the marketer must understand the relationship between price and demand for the company's product. In this section, we take a deeper look at the price–demand relationship and how it varies for different types of markets. We then discuss methods for analyzing the price–demand relationship.

Pricing in Different Types of Markets

The seller's pricing freedom varies with different types of markets. Economists recognize four types of markets, each presenting a different pricing challenge.

Under *pure competition*, the market consists of many buyers and sellers trading in a uniform commodity, such as wheat, copper, or financial securities. No single buyer or seller has much effect on the going market price. In a purely competitive market, marketing research, product development, pricing, advertising, and sales promotion play little or no role. Thus, sellers in these markets do not spend much time on marketing strategy.

Under *monopolistic competition*, the market consists of many buyers and sellers trading over a range of prices rather than a single market price. A range of prices occurs because sellers can differentiate their offers to buyers. Because there are many competitors, each firm is less affected by competitors' pricing strategies than in oligopolistic markets. Sellers try to develop differentiated offers for different customer segments and, in addition to price, freely use branding, advertising, and personal selling to set their offers apart. Thus, Wrigley sets its Skittles candy brand apart from the profusion of other candy brands not by price but by brand building—clever "Taste the Rainbow" positioning built through quirky advertising and a heavy presence in social media such as Tumblr, Instagram, YouTube, Facebook, and Twitter. The social media-savvy brand boasts nearly 27 million Facebook Likes and 258,000 Twitter followers.

Under *oligopolistic competition*, the market consists of only a few large sellers. » For example, only a handful of providers—Comcast, Time Warner, AT&T, and Dish Network—control a lion's share of the cable/satellite television market. Because there are few sellers, each seller is alert and responsive to competitors' pricing strategies and marketing moves. In the battle for subscribers, price becomes a major competitive tool. For example, to woo customers away from Comcast, TimeWarner, and other cable companies, AT&T's DirecTV unit offers low-price "Cable Crusher" offers, lock-in prices, and free HD. In a *pure monopoly*, the market is dominated by one seller. The seller may be a government monopoly (the U.S. Postal Service), a private regulated monopoly (a power company), or a private unregulated monopoly (De Beers and diamonds). Pricing is handled differently in each case.

» Pricing in oligopolistic markets: Price is an important competitive tool for AT&T's DirecTV unit and other cable/satellite television providers. Here, DirecTV woos cable customers with low lock-in prices and free HD.

NetPhotos/Alamy Stock Photo

Analyzing the Price–Demand Relationship

Demand curve
A curve that shows the number of units the market will buy in a given time period at different prices that might be charged.

Each price the company might charge will lead to a different level of demand. The relationship between the price charged and the resulting demand level is shown in the **demand curve** in **» Figure 9.4**. The demand curve shows the number of units the market will buy in a given time period at different prices that might be charged. In the normal case, demand and price are inversely related—that is, the higher the price, the lower the demand. Thus, the company would sell less if it raised its price from P_1 to P_2. In short, consumers with limited budgets probably will buy less of something if its price is too high.

Figure 9.4 Demand Curve

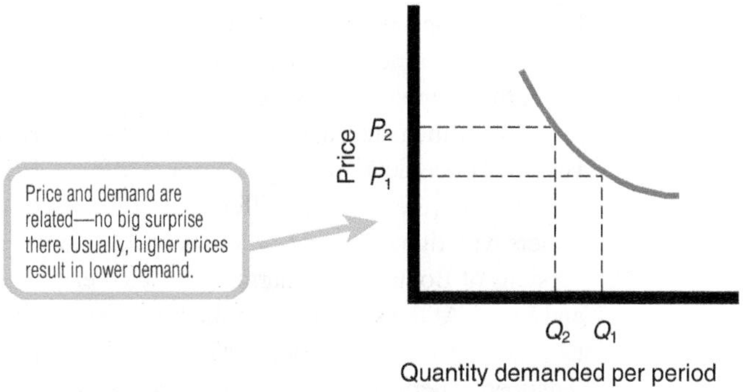

Understanding a brand's price–demand curve is crucial to good pricing decisions. ConAgra Foods learned this lesson when pricing its Banquet frozen dinners:[8]

> When ConAgra tried to cover higher commodity costs by raising the list price of Banquet dinners from $1 to $1.25, consumers turned up their noses to the higher price. Sales dropped, forcing ConAgra to sell off excess dinners at discount prices. It turns out that "the key component for Banquet dinners—the key attribute—is you've got to be at $1," says ConAgra's CEO Gary Rodkin. "Everything else pales in comparison to that." Banquet dinner prices are now back to a buck a dinner. To make money at that price, ConAgra has done a better job of managing costs by shrinking portions and substituting less expensive ingredients for costlier ones. More than just Banquet dinners, ConAgra prices all of its frozen and canned products at under $1 per serving. Consumers are responding well to the brand's efforts to keep prices down. After all, where else can you find dinner for $1?

Most companies try to measure their demand curves by estimating demand at different prices. The type of market makes a difference. In a monopoly, the demand curve shows the total market demand resulting from different prices. If the company faces competition, its demand at different prices will depend on whether competitors' prices stay constant or change with the company's own prices.

Price Elasticity of Demand

Price elasticity
A measure of the sensitivity of demand to changes in price.

Marketers also need to know **price elasticity**—how responsive demand will be to a change in price. If demand hardly changes with a small change in price, we say demand is *inelastic*. If demand changes greatly, we say the demand is *elastic*.

If demand is elastic rather than inelastic, sellers will consider lowering their prices. A lower price will produce more total revenue. This practice makes sense as long as the extra costs of producing and selling more do not exceed the extra revenue. At the same time, most firms want to avoid pricing that turns their products into commodities. In recent years, forces such as deregulation and the instant price comparisons afforded by the Internet and other technologies have increased consumer price sensitivity, turning products ranging from phones and computers to new automobiles into commodities in some consumers' eyes.

The Economy

Economic conditions can have a strong impact on the firm's pricing strategies. Economic factors such as a boom or recession, inflation, and interest rates affect pricing decisions because they affect consumer spending, consumer perceptions of the product's price and value, and the company's costs of producing and selling a product.

In the aftermath of the Great Recession of 2008 to 2009, many consumers rethought the price–value equation. They tightened their belts and become more value conscious. Consumers have continued their thriftier ways well beyond the economic recovery. As a result, many marketers have increased their emphasis on value-for-the-money pricing strategies.

The most obvious response to the new economic realities is to cut prices and offer discounts. Thousands of companies have done just that. Lower prices make products more affordable and help spur short-term sales. However, such price cuts can have undesirable long-term consequences. Lower prices mean lower margins. Deep discounts may cheapen a brand in consumers' eyes. And once a company cuts prices, it's difficult to raise them again when the economy recovers.

Rather than cutting prices on their main-market brands, many companies have instead developed "price tiers," adding both more affordable lines and premium lines that span the varied means and preferences of different customer segments. For example, for cost-conscious customers with tighter budgets, P&G has added lower-price versions of its brands, such as "Basic" versions of Bounty and Charmin and a lower-priced version of Tide called Tide Simply Clean and Fresh. At the same time, at the higher end, P&G has launched upscale versions of some of its brands, such as Bounty DuraTowel and Cascade Platinum dishwasher detergent, which offer superior performance at up to twice the price of the middle-market versions.

Other companies are holding their price positions but redefining the "value" in their value propositions. » Consider upscale grocery retailer Whole Foods Market:[9]

> Whole Foods Market practically invented the upscale, socially responsible supermarket concept, and it grew rapidly and profitably under its "Whole Foods. Whole People. Whole Planet." mission. However, the high-margin chain faced setbacks following the 2008 financial crisis, as even well-heeled consumers cut their food budgets. It also felt increasing price pressures from swarms of new, lower-priced competitors—from specialty supermarkets such as Trader Joe's and Sprouts Farmers Market to traditional chains such as Walmart and Kroger—that rushed to add organics to their shelves.
>
> In response, Whole Foods has worked to shed its "Whole Foods. Whole Paycheck." image. The chain has reduced costs, passed the savings along to customers, and subtly increased its emphasis on affordable options. At the same time, however, Whole Foods has reinforced its core up-market positioning by convincing shoppers that, when it comes to quality food, bargain prices aren't everything. Whole Foods' new marketing campaign—called Values Matter—emphasizes that "value" is inseparable from "values." When shopping at Whole Foods, customers can be confident about "where their food comes from and how it was grown, raised, or made." The retailer's produce is "responsibly grown." Thus, Whole Foods Market is meeting pricing challenges in a way that preserves what has made it special to customers through the years. "We have the ability to compete on price, and we will do that," says the chain's co-CEO. "But this is not just a race to the bottom. We are also going to start a new race to the top, with better-quality food, higher standards, richer experiences for our customers, and new levels of transparency and accountability in the marketplace." Even if that means a little higher prices.[10]

» Whole Foods Market's new "Values Matter" campaign emphasizes that there is more to value than just bargain prices. "Value" is inseparable from "values."

Justin Sullivan/Getty Images

Remember, even in tough economic times, consumers do not buy based on prices alone. They balance the price they pay against the value they receive. For example, despite selling its shoes for as much as $150 a pair, Nike commands the highest consumer loyalty of any brand in the footwear segment. Customers perceive the value of Nike's products and the Nike ownership experience to be well worth the price. Thus, no matter what price they charge—low or high—companies need to offer great *value for the money*.

Other External Factors

Beyond the market and the economy, the company must consider several other factors in its external environment when setting prices. It must know what impact its prices will have on other parties in its environment. How will *resellers* react to various prices? The company should set prices that give resellers a fair profit, encourage their support, and help them to sell the product effectively. The *government* is another important external influence on pricing decisions. Finally, *social concerns* may need to be taken into account. In setting prices, a company's short-term sales, market share, and profit goals may need to be tempered by broader societal considerations. We will examine public policy issues later in this chapter.

LINKING THE CONCEPTS

The concept of customer value is critical to good pricing and to successful marketing in general. Pause for a minute and be certain that you appreciate what value really means.

- An earlier example states that although the average Steinway piano costs $87,000, to those who own one, a Steinway is a great value. Does this fit your idea of value?
- Pick two competing brands from a familiar product category (watches, perfume, consumer electronics, restaurants)—one low-priced and the other high-priced. Which, if either, offers the greatest value?
- Does "value" mean the same thing as "low price"? How do these concepts differ?

Author Comment
Pricing new products can be especially challenging. Just think about all the things you'd need to consider in pricing a new smartphone, say, the first Apple iPhone. Even more, you need to start thinking about the price—along with many other marketing considerations—at the very beginning of the design process.

New Product Pricing Strategies

Pricing strategies usually change as the product passes through its life cycle. The introductory stage is especially challenging. Companies bringing out a new product face the challenge of setting prices for the first time. They can choose between two broad strategies: *market-skimming pricing* and *market-penetration pricing*.

Market-Skimming Pricing

Market-skimming pricing (price skimming)
Setting a high price for a new product to skim maximum revenues layer by layer from the segments willing to pay the high price; the company makes fewer but more profitable sales.

Many companies that invent new products set high initial prices to *skim* revenues layer by layer from the market. Apple frequently uses this strategy, called **market-skimming pricing** (or **price skimming**). When Apple first introduced the iPhone, its initial price was as high as $599 per phone. The phones were purchased only by customers who really wanted the sleek new gadget and could afford to pay a high price for it. Six months later, Apple dropped the price to $399 for an 8-GB model and $499 for the 16-GB model to attract new buyers. Within a year, it dropped prices again to $199 and $299, respectively, and you can now get a basic 8-GB model for free with a wireless phone contract. In this way, each new iPhone model starts at a high price, then works its way down as new models are introduced. Apple skims the maximum amount of revenue from the various segments of the market.

Market skimming makes sense only under certain conditions. First, the product's quality and image must support its higher price, and enough buyers must want the product at that price. Second, the costs of producing a smaller volume cannot be so high that they cancel the advantage of charging more. Finally, competitors should not be able to enter the market easily and undercut the high price.

Market-Penetration Pricing

Market-penetration pricing
Setting a low price for a new product in order to attract a large number of buyers and a large market share.

Rather than setting a high initial price to skim off small but profitable market segments, some companies use **market-penetration pricing**. Companies set a low initial price to *penetrate* the market quickly and deeply—to attract a large number of buyers quickly and win a large market share. The high sales volume results in falling costs, allowing companies to cut their prices even further. For example, Samsung has used penetration pricing to quickly build demand for its mobile devices in fast-growing emerging markets:[11]

> In Kenya, Nigeria, and other African countries, Samsung recently unveiled an affordable yet full-function Samsung Galaxy Pocket Neo model that sells for only about $113 with no contract. »The Samsung Pocket is designed and priced to encourage millions of first-time

>> **Penetration pricing: Samsung has used low initial prices to make quick and deep inroads into emerging mobile device markets such as Africa and India.**

Trevor Snapp/Bloomberg/Getty Images

African buyers to trade up to smartphones from their more basic handsets. Samsung also offers a line of Pocket models in India, selling for as little as $87. Through penetration pricing, the world's largest smartphone maker hopes to make quick and deep inroads into India's exploding mobile device market, which consists of mostly first-time users and accounts for nearly one-quarter of all smartphones sold globally each year. Low prices are also required in emerging markets to compete with super-cheap phones from competitors such as Chinese phone maker Xiaomi. Samsung's penetration pricing has set off price wars with Apple, which has responded in emerging markets with heavy discounts and more affordable models of its own. Apple iPhones have typically sold for more than $300 in India, limiting Apple's market share to only about 2 percent there.

Several conditions must be met for this low-price strategy to work. First, the market must be highly price sensitive so that a low price produces more market growth. Second, production and distribution costs must decrease as sales volume increases. Finally, the low price must help keep out the competition, and the penetration pricer must maintain its low-price position. Otherwise, the price advantage may be only temporary.

Author Comment
Most individual products are part of a broader product mix and must be priced accordingly. For example, Gillette prices its Fusion razors low. But once you buy the razor, you're a captive customer for its higher-margin replacement cartridges.

Product Mix Pricing Strategies

The strategy for setting a product's price often has to be changed when the product is part of a product mix. In this case, the firm looks for a set of prices that maximizes its profits on the total product mix. Pricing is difficult because the various products have related demand and costs and face different degrees of competition. We now take a closer look at the five product mix pricing situations summarized in >> **Table 9.1**: *product line pricing, optional-product pricing, captive-product pricing, by-product pricing*, and *product bundle pricing*.

Product Line Pricing

Product line pricing
Setting the price steps between various products in a product line based on cost differences between the products, customer evaluations of different features, and competitors' prices.

Companies usually develop product lines rather than single products. In **product line pricing**, management must determine the price steps to set between the various products in a line. The price steps should take into account cost differences between products in the line. More important, they should account for differences in customer perceptions of the value of different features.

For example, at a Mr. Clean car wash, you can choose from any of six wash packages, ranging from a basic exterior-clean-only "Bronze" wash for $5; to an exterior clean, shine,

>> Table 9.1 Product Mix Pricing

Pricing Situation	Description
Product line pricing	Setting prices across an entire product line
Optional-product pricing	Pricing optional or accessory products sold with the main product
Captive-product pricing	Pricing products that must be used with the main product
By-product pricing	Pricing low-value by-products to get rid of or make money on them
Product bundle pricing	Pricing bundles of products sold together

and protect "Gold" package for $12; to an interior-exterior "Signature Shine" package for $27 that includes the works, from a thorough cleaning inside and out to a tire shine, underbody rust inhibitor, surface protectant, and even air freshener. The car wash's task is to establish perceived value differences that support the price differences.

Optional-Product Pricing

Optional-product pricing
The pricing of optional or accessory products along with a main product.

Captive-product pricing
Setting a price for products that must be used along with a main product, such as blades for a razor and games for a video-game console.

By-product pricing
Setting a price for by-products in order to make the main product's price more competitive.

Many companies use **optional-product pricing**—offering to sell optional or accessory products along with the main product. For example, a car buyer may choose to order a navigation system and premium entertainment system. Refrigerators come with optional ice makers. And when you order a new computer, you can select from a bewildering array of processors, hard drives, docking systems, software options, and service plans. Pricing these options is a sticky problem. Companies must decide which items to include in the base price and which to offer as options.

Captive-Product Pricing

Companies that make products that must be used along with a main product are using **captive-product pricing**. Examples of captive products are razor blade cartridges, video games, printer cartridges, single-serve coffee pods, and e-books. Producers of the main products (razors, video-game consoles, printers, single-cup coffee brewing systems, and tablet computers) often price them low and set high markups on the supplies. For example, Amazon makes little or no profit on its Kindle readers and tablets. It hopes to more than make up for thin margins through sales of digital books, music, movies, subscription services, and other content for the devices. "We want to make money when people use our devices, not when they buy our devices," declares Amazon CEO Jeff Bezos.[12]

» Captive product pricing: Nearly 77 percent of Keurig's sales come from its K-Cup portion packs. The brand must find the right balance between main-product and captive-product prices.

Toby Talbot/AP Images

Captive products can account for a substantial portion of a brand's sales and profits. » For example, only a relatively small percentage of Keurig's revenues come from the sale of its single-cup brewing systems. The bulk of the brand's revenues—nearly 77 percent—comes from captive sales of its K-Cup portion packs.[13] However, companies that use captive-product pricing must be careful. Finding the right balance between the main-product and captive-product prices can be tricky. Even more, consumers trapped into buying expensive captive products may come to resent the brand that ensnared them.

For example, customers of single-cup coffee brewing systems may cringe at what they must pay for those handy little coffee portion packs. Although they might seem like a bargain when compared on a cost-per-cup basis versus Starbucks, the pods' prices can seem like highway robbery when broken down by the pound. One investigator calculated the cost of pod coffee at a shocking $51 per pound.[14] At those prices, you'd be better off cost-wise brewing a big pot of premium coffee and pouring out the unused portion. For many buyers, the convenience and selection offered by single-cup brewing systems outweigh the extra costs. However, such captive product costs might make others avoid buying the device in the first place or cause discomfort during use after purchase.

In the case of services, captive-product pricing is called *two-part pricing*. The price of the service is broken into a *fixed fee* plus a *variable usage rate*. Thus, at Six Flags and other amusement parks, you pay a daily ticket or season pass charge plus additional fees for food and other in-park features.

By-Product Pricing

Producing products and services often generates by-products. If the by-products have no value and if getting rid of them is costly, this will affect the pricing of the main product. Using **by-product pricing**, the company seeks a market for these by-products to help offset the costs of disposing of them and help make the price of the main product more competitive.

The by-products themselves can even turn out to be profitable—turning trash into cash. For example, cheese makers in Wisconsin have discovered a use for their leftover brine, a salt solution used in the cheese-making process. Instead of paying to have it disposed of, they now sell it to local city and county highway departments, which use it in conjunction with salt to melt icy roads. It doesn't stop there. In New Jersey, pickle makers sell their leftover brine for similar uses. In Tennessee, distilleries sell off potato juice, a by-product of vodka distillation. And on many highways across the nation, highway crews use a product called Beet Heet, which is made from—you guessed it—beet juice brine by-products. The only side effect of these brine solutions is a slight odor. Says one highway department official about cheese brine, "If you were behind a snow plow, you'd immediately smell it."[15]

Product Bundle Pricing

Product bundle pricing
Combining several products and offering the bundle at a reduced price.

Using **product bundle pricing**, sellers often combine several products and offer the bundle at a reduced price. For example, fast-food restaurants bundle a burger, fries, and a soft drink at a "combo" price. Bath & Body Works offers "three-fer" deals on its soaps and lotions (such as three antibacterial soaps for $10). And Comcast, AT&T, Verizon, and other telecommunications companies bundle TV service, phone service, and high-speed Internet connections at a low combined price. Price bundling can promote the sales of products consumers might not otherwise buy, but the combined price must be low enough to get them to buy the bundle.

Author Comment
Setting the base price for a product is only the start. The company must then adjust the price to account for customer and situational differences. When was the last time you paid the full suggested retail price for something?

Price Adjustment Strategies

Companies usually adjust their basic prices to account for various customer differences and changing situations. Here we examine the seven price adjustment strategies summarized in » **Table 9.2**: *discount and allowance pricing, segmented pricing, psychological pricing, promotional pricing, geographical pricing, dynamic pricing*, and *international pricing*.

Discount and Allowance Pricing

Most companies adjust their basic price to reward customers for certain responses, such as paying bills early, volume purchases, and off-season buying. These price adjustments—called *discounts* and *allowances*—can take many forms.

» Table 9.2 Price Adjustments

Strategy	Description
Discount and allowance pricing	Reducing prices to reward customer responses such as volume purchases, paying early, or promoting the product
Segmented pricing	Adjusting prices to allow for differences in customers, products, or locations
Psychological pricing	Adjusting prices for psychological effect
Promotional pricing	Temporarily reducing prices to spur short-run sales
Geographical pricing	Adjusting prices to account for the geographic location of customers
Dynamic pricing	Adjusting prices continually to meet the characteristics and needs of individual customers and situations
International pricing	Adjusting prices for international markets

Discount
A straight reduction in price on purchases during a stated period of time or of larger quantities.

One form of **discount** is a *cash discount*, a price reduction to buyers who pay their bills promptly. A typical example is "2/10, net 30," which means that although payment is due within 30 days, the buyer can deduct 2 percent if the bill is paid within 10 days. A *quantity discount* is a price reduction to buyers who buy large volumes. A seller offers a *functional discount* (also called a *trade discount*) to trade-channel members who perform certain functions, such as selling, storing, and record keeping. A *seasonal discount* is a price reduction to buyers who buy merchandise or services out of season.

Allowance
Promotional money paid by manufacturers to retailers in return for an agreement to feature the manufacturer's products in some way.

Allowances are another type of reduction from the list price. For example, *trade-in allowances* are price reductions given for turning in an old item when buying a new one. Trade-in allowances are most common in the automobile industry, but they are also given for other durable goods. *Promotional allowances* are payments or price reductions that reward dealers for participating in advertising and sales-support programs.

Segmented Pricing

Segmented pricing
Selling a product or service at two or more prices, where the difference in prices is not based on differences in costs.

Companies will often adjust their basic prices to allow for differences in customers, products, and locations. In **segmented pricing**, the company sells a product or service at two or more prices, even though the difference in prices is not based on differences in costs.

Segmented pricing takes several forms. Under *customer-segment pricing*, different customers pay different prices for the same product or service. Museums and movie theaters, for example, may charge a lower admission for students and senior citizens. Under *product form pricing*, different versions of the product are priced differently but not according to differences in their costs. For instance, a round-trip economy seat on a flight from New York to London might cost $1,100, whereas a business-class seat on the same flight might cost $3,400 or more. Although business-class customers receive roomier, more comfortable seats and higher-quality food and service, the differences in costs to the airlines are much less than the additional prices to passengers. >> However, to passengers who can afford it, the additional comfort and services are worth the extra charge.

Using *location-based pricing*, a company charges different prices for different locations, even though the cost of offering each location is the same. For instance, state universities charge higher tuition for out-of-state students, and theaters vary their seat prices because of audience preferences for certain locations. Finally, using *time-based pricing*, a firm varies its price by the season, the month, the day, and even the hour. For example, movie theaters charge matinee pricing during the daytime, and resorts give weekend and seasonal discounts.

>> Product-form pricing: A roomier business-class seat on a flight from New York to London is several times the price of an economy seat on the same flight. To customers who can afford it, the extra comfort and service are worth the extra charge.

Stewart Cohen/Photolibrary/Getty Images

For segmented pricing to be an effective strategy, certain conditions must exist. The market must be segmentable, and segments must show different degrees of demand. The costs of segmenting and reaching the market cannot exceed the extra revenue obtained from the price difference. Of course, the segmented pricing must also be legal.

Most important, segmented prices should reflect real differences in customers' perceived value. Consumers in higher price tiers must feel that they're getting their extra money's worth for the higher prices paid. By the same token, companies must be careful not to treat customers in lower price tiers as second-class citizens. Otherwise, in the long run, the practice will lead to customer resentment and ill will. For example, in recent years, the airlines have incurred the wrath of frustrated customers at both ends of the airplane. Passengers paying full fare for business- or first-class seats often feel that they are being gouged. At the same time, passengers in lower-priced coach seats feel that they're being ignored or treated poorly.

Psychological Pricing

Price says something about the product. For example, many consumers use price to judge quality. A $100 bottle of perfume may contain only $3 worth of scent, but some people are willing to pay the $100 because this price indicates something special.

Psychological pricing
Pricing that considers the psychology of prices and not simply the economics; the price is used to say something about the product.

In using **psychological pricing**, sellers consider the psychology of prices, not simply the economics. For example, consumers usually perceive higher-priced products as having higher quality. When they can judge the quality of a product by examining it or by calling on past experience with it, they use price less to judge quality. But when they cannot judge quality because they lack the information or skill, price becomes an important quality signal. For instance, who's the better lawyer, one who charges $50 per hour or one who charges $500 per hour? You'd have to do a lot of digging into the respective lawyers' credentials to answer this question objectively; even then, you might not be able to judge accurately. Most of us would simply assume that the higher-priced lawyer is better.

Reference prices
Prices that buyers carry in their minds and refer to when they look at a given product.

Another aspect of psychological pricing is **reference prices**—prices that buyers carry in their minds and refer to when looking at a given product. The reference price might be formed by noting current prices, remembering past prices, or assessing the buying situation. Sellers can influence or use these consumers' reference prices when setting price. For example, a grocery retailer might place its store brand of bran flakes and raisins cereal priced at $2.49 next to Kellogg's Raisin Bran priced at $3.79. Or a company might offer more expensive models that don't sell very well to make its less expensive but still-high-priced models look more affordable by comparison. For example, Williams-Sonoma once offered a fancy bread maker at the steep price of $279. However, it then added a $429 model. The expensive model flopped, but sales of the cheaper model doubled.[16]

Promotional pricing
Temporarily pricing products below the list price, and sometimes even below cost, to increase short-run sales.

For most purchases, consumers don't have all the skill or information they need to figure out whether they are paying a good price. They don't have the time, ability, or inclination to research different brands or stores, compare prices, and get the best deals. Instead, they may rely on certain cues that signal whether a price is high or low. Interestingly, such pricing cues are often provided by sellers, in the form of sales signs, price-matching guarantees, loss-leader pricing, and other helpful hints.

>> Psychological pricing: What do the prices marked on these tags suggest about the products and buying situations?

Jamie Grill/Tetra Images/Alamy

Even small differences in price can signal product differences. A 9 or 0.99 at the end of a price often signals a bargain. You see such prices everywhere. For example, browse the online sites of top discounters such as Target, Best Buy, or Overstock.com, where almost every price ends in 9. In contrast, high-end retailers might favor prices ending in a whole number (for example, $6, $25, or $200). Others use 00-cent endings on regularly priced items and 99-cent endings on discount merchandise.

>> Although actual price differences might be small, the impact of such psychological tactics can be big. For example, in one study, people were asked how likely they were to choose among LASIK eye surgery providers based only on the prices they charged: $299 or $300. The actual price difference was only $1, but the study found that the psychological difference was much greater. Preference ratings for the providers charging $300 were much higher. Subjects perceived the $299 price as significantly less, but the lower price also raised stronger concerns about quality and risk. Some psychologists even argue that each digit has symbolic and visual qualities that should be considered in pricing. Thus, eight (8) is round and even and creates a soothing effect, whereas seven (7) is angular and creates a jarring effect.[17]

Promotional Pricing

With **promotional pricing**, companies will temporarily price their products below list price—and sometimes even below cost—to create buying excitement and urgency. Promotional pricing takes several forms. A seller may simply offer *discounts* from normal prices to increase sales and reduce inventories. Sellers also use *special-event pricing* in certain seasons to draw more customers. Thus, TVs and other consumer electronics are promotionally priced in November and

December to attract holiday shoppers into the stores. *Limited-time offers*, such as online *flash sales*, can create buying urgency and make buyers feel lucky to have gotten in on the deal.

Manufacturers sometimes offer *cash rebates* to consumers who buy the product from dealers within a specified time; the manufacturer sends the rebate directly to the customer. Rebates have been popular with automakers and producers of mobile phones and small appliances, but they are also used with consumer packaged goods. Some manufacturers offer *low-interest financing, longer warranties*, or *free maintenance* to reduce the consumer's "price." This practice has become another favorite of the auto industry.

Promotional pricing can help move customers over humps in the buying decision process. For example, to encourage Apple customers to switch from their Apple laptops to its Surface tablets, Microsoft recently offered buyers up to $650 toward a Surface Pro 3 when they traded in a MacBook Air. Such aggressive price promotions can provide powerful buying and switching incentives.

Promotional pricing: To Encourage Apple customers to switch from their Apple laptops to its Surface tablets, Microsoft recently offered buyers up to $650 toward a Surface Pro 3 when they traded in a MacBook Air. Such aggressive price promotions can provide powerful buying incentives.

Microsoft

Promotional pricing, however, can have adverse effects. During most holiday seasons, for example, it's an all-out bargain war. Marketers carpet-bomb consumers with deals, causing buyer wear-out and pricing confusion. Used too frequently, price promotions can create "deal-prone" customers who wait until brands go on sale before buying them. In addition, constantly reduced prices can erode a brand's value in the eyes of customers.

Marketers sometimes become addicted to promotional pricing, especially in tight economic times. They use price promotions as a quick fix instead of sweating through the difficult process of developing effective longer-term strategies for building their brands. Consider JCPenney:

> Over the past two decades, JCPenney has steadily lost ground to discounters and department store rivals such as Walmart, Kohl's, and Macy's on the one hand and to nimbler specialty store retailers on the other. To compete, the 110-year-old retailer increasingly relied on deep and frequent discounts to drive sales, even at the expense of profitability. By 2012, almost 75 percent of JCPenney's merchandise was being sold at discounts of 50 percent or more, and less than 1 percent was sold at full price.
>
> To reverse declining sales and profits, Penney's implemented a bold new everyday-low-pricing strategy, called "Fair and Square" pricing. It ditched deep discounts and endless rounds of sales, instead cutting regular retail prices by 40 percent across the board. The goal was to offer fair, predictable prices for the value received while at the same time boosting the chain's margins. However, the new pricing strategy turned out to be an absolute disaster. JCPenney's deal-prone core customers, accustomed to deep discounts, didn't want just "fair" prices; they wanted rock-bottom prices. Penney's sales plunged to the lowest levels in 25 years. To win back core customers, JCPenney soon reverted to pricing as usual, once again featuring regular sale prices, discounts, and coupons. Moving forward, as sales and profits continue to suffer, JCPenney faces a desperate struggle to find the right pricing formula. It can't live with sale prices, but it can't live without them, either.[18]

Geographical Pricing

A company also must decide how to price its products for customers located in different parts of the United States or the world. Should the company risk losing the business of more-distant customers by charging them higher prices to cover the higher shipping costs? Or should the company charge all customers the same prices regardless of location? We will look at five *geographical pricing* strategies for the following hypothetical situation:

> The Peerless Paper Company is located in Atlanta, Georgia, and sells paper products to customers all over the United States. The cost of freight is high and affects the companies from which customers buy their paper. Peerless wants to establish a geographical pricing policy. It is trying to determine how to price a $10,000 order to three specific customers: Customer A (Atlanta), Customer B (Bloomington, Indiana), and Customer C (Compton, California).

One option is for Peerless to ask each customer to pay the shipping cost from the Atlanta factory to the customer's location. All three customers would pay the same factory price of $10,000, with Customer A paying, say, $100 for shipping; Customer B, $150; and Customer C, $250. Called *FOB-origin pricing*, this practice means that the goods are placed *free on board* (hence, FOB) a carrier. At that point, the title and responsibility pass to the customer, who pays the freight from the factory to the destination. Because each customer picks up its own cost, supporters of FOB pricing feel that this is the fairest way to assess freight charges. The disadvantage, however, is that Peerless will be a high-cost firm to distant customers.

Uniform-delivered pricing is the opposite of FOB pricing. Here, the company charges the same price plus freight to all customers, regardless of their location. The freight charge is set at the average freight cost. Suppose this is $150. Uniform-delivered pricing therefore results in a higher charge to the Atlanta customer (who pays $150 freight instead of $100) and a lower charge to the Compton customer (who pays $150 instead of $250). Although the Atlanta customer would prefer to buy paper from another local paper company that uses FOB-origin pricing, Peerless has a better chance of capturing the California customer.

Zone pricing falls between FOB-origin pricing and uniform-delivered pricing. The company sets up two or more zones. All customers within a given zone pay a single total price; the more distant the zone, the higher the price. For example, Peerless might set up an East Zone and charge $100 freight to all customers in this zone, a Midwest Zone in which it charges $150, and a West Zone in which it charges $250. In this way, the customers within a given price zone receive no price advantage from the company. For example, customers in Atlanta and Boston pay the same total price to Peerless. The complaint, however, is that the Atlanta customer is paying part of the Boston customer's freight cost.

Using *basing-point pricing*, the seller selects a given city as a "basing point" and charges all customers the freight cost from that city to the customer location, regardless of the city from which the goods are actually shipped. For example, Peerless might set Chicago as the basing point and charge all customers $10,000 plus the freight from Chicago to their locations. This means that an Atlanta customer pays the freight cost from Chicago to Atlanta, even though the goods may be shipped from Atlanta. If all sellers used the same basing-point city, delivered prices would be the same for all customers, and price competition would be eliminated.

Finally, the seller who is anxious to do business with a certain customer or geographical area might use *freight-absorption pricing*. Using this strategy, the seller absorbs all or part of the actual freight charges to get the desired business. The seller might reason that if it can get more business, its average costs will decrease and more than compensate for its extra freight cost. Freight-absorption pricing is used for market penetration and to hold on to increasingly competitive markets.

Dynamic and Online Pricing

Throughout most of history, prices were set by negotiation between buyers and sellers. *Fixed-price* policies—setting one price for all buyers—is a relatively modern idea that arose with the development of large-scale retailing at the end of the nineteenth century. Today, most prices are set this way. However, some companies are now reversing the fixed-pricing trend. They are using **dynamic pricing**—adjusting prices continually to meet the characteristics and needs of individual customers and situations.

Dynamic pricing
Adjusting prices continually to meet the characteristics and needs of individual customers and situations.

Dynamic pricing is especially prevalent online, where the Internet seems to be taking us back to a new age of fluid pricing. Such pricing offers many advantages for marketers. For example, online sellers such as L.L.Bean, Amazon.com, and Dell can mine their databases to gauge a specific shopper's desires, measure his or her means, check out competitors' prices, and instantaneously tailor offers to fit that shopper's situation and behavior, pricing products accordingly.

Services ranging from retailers, airlines, and hotels to sports teams change prices on the fly according to changes in demand, costs, or competitor pricing, adjusting what they charge for specific items on a daily, hourly, or even continuous basis. Done well, dynamic pricing can help sellers to optimize sales and serve customers better. However, done poorly, it can trigger margin-eroding price wars and damage customer relationships and trust. Companies must be careful not to cross the fine line between smart dynamic pricing strategies and damaging ones (see Marketing at Work 9.2).

MARKETING AT WORK 9.2

Dynamic Pricing: The Wonders and Woes of Real-Time Price Adjustments

These days, it seems every seller knows what prices competitors are charging—for anything and everything it sells, minute by minute, and down to the penny. What's more, today's technologies give sellers the flexibility to adjust their own prices on the fly. This often results in some pretty zany pricing dynamics.

For example, during a recent Black Friday weekend, the prices charged for the latest version of an Xbox game, Dance Central, experienced some head-spinning dips and dives. The day before Thanksgiving, Amazon marked the game down to $49.96, matching Walmart's price and beating Target's price by three cents. On Thanksgiving Day, Amazon slashed that price in half to just $24.99, matching Best Buy's Thanksgiving Day special. Walmart responded quickly with a rock-bottom price of $15, which Amazon matched immediately. "What kind of pricing lunacy is this?" you ask. Welcome to the wonders and woes of dynamic pricing.

On the plus side, dynamic pricing can help sellers optimize sales and serve customers better by aligning prices with market conditions. For example, airlines routinely use dynamic pricing to constantly adjust fares for specific flights, depending on competitor pricing and anticipated seat availability. As any frequent flyer knows, if you call now to book a seat on a flight to sunny Florida next week, you'll get one price. Try again an hour later and you'll get a different price—maybe higher, maybe lower. Book the same seat a month in advance, and you'll probably pay a lot less.

Dynamic pricing isn't just about sellers optimizing their returns. It also puts pricing power into the hands of consumers, as alert shoppers take advantage of the constant price skirmishes among sellers. By using online price checkers and shopping apps to monitor prices, consumers can snap up good deals or leverage retailer price-matching policies. In fact, today's fluid pricing sometimes gives buyers too much of an upper hand. With price checking and online ordering now at the shopper's fingertips, even giant retailers such as Target, Walmart, and Best Buy have fallen victim to "showrooming"—whereby shoppers check merchandise and prices in store-retailer showrooms, then buy the goods online.

Stores like Best Buy are in turn using dynamic pricing to combat showrooming or even turn it into an advantage. For example, Best Buy Canada provides its sales associates with mobile price checkers of their own that they can use with every transaction to check the competing prices in real time. Associates can often show customers that Best Buy actually has the best prices on most items. When Best Buy's price isn't lowest, associates are instructed to beat the lower-priced competitor—online or offline—by 10 percent. Once it has neutralized price as a buying factor, Best Buy reasons, it can convert showroomers into in-store buyers with its nonprice advantages of service, immediacy, convenient locations, and easy returns.

As the Best Buy example illustrates, dynamic pricing doesn't just happen in the fast-shifting online environment. For example, discount department store Kohl's has replaced static price tags with digital ones. These digital tags can be centrally controlled to change prices dynamically on individual items within a given store or across the entire chain. The technology lets Kohl's apply Internet-style dynamic pricing, changing prices as conditions dictate without the time and costs of changing physical tags.

Beyond using dynamic pricing to match competitors, many sellers use it to adjust prices based on customer characteristics or buying situations. Some sellers vary prices they charge different customers based on customer purchase histories or personal data. Some companies offer special discounts to customers with more items in their shopping carts. Online travel agent Orbitz has even been reported to charge higher prices to Mac and iPad users because Apple fans have higher average household incomes.

Most consumers are surprised to learn that it's perfectly legal under most circumstances to charge different prices to different customers based on their buying behaviors. In fact, one survey found that two-thirds of online shoppers thought the practice was illegal. When they learned that it was not illegal, nearly nine out of ten thought it should be.

Legal or not, dynamic pricing doesn't always sit well with customers. Done poorly, it can cause customer confusion, frustration, or even resentment, damaging hard-won customer relationships. For example, according to one source, Amazon's automated dynamic pricing system changes the price on as

>> Dynamic pricing: Amazon's automated dynamic pricing system reportedly changes the price on as many as 80 million items on its site in a given day based on a host of marketplace factors.

Webpics/Alamy

many as 80 million items on its site throughout a given day, based on a host of marketplace factors. Consider this Amazon shopper's experience:

> Nancy Plumlee had just taken up mahjong, a Chinese game of tiles similar to rummy. She browsed Amazon.com and, after sifting through several pages of options, settled on a set for $54.99. She placed it in her [shopping cart] and continued shopping for some scorecards and game accessories. A few minutes later, she scanned the cart and noticed the $54.99 had jumped to $70.99. Plumlee thought she was going crazy. She checked her computer's viewing history and, indeed, the game's original price was listed at $54.99. Determined, she cleared out the cart and tried again. [This time,] the game's price jumped from $54.99 to $59.99. "That just doesn't feel like straight-up business honesty. Shame on Amazon," said Plumlee, who called [Amazon] and persuaded the online retailer to refund her $5.

It is sometimes difficult to locate the fine line between a smart dynamic pricing strategy and one that crosses the line, doing more damage to customer relationships than good to the company's bottom line. Consider Uber, an app-based car dispatch service serving many major U.S. cities that lets customers summon taxis, cars, or other transportation using texts or the company's phone app:

> Uber uses a form of dynamic pricing called "surge pricing." Under normal circumstances, Uber customers pay reasonable fares. However, using Uber in periods of surging demand can result in shocking price escalations. For example, on one recent stormy, holiday-Saturday night in Manhattan, Uber charged—and got—fares that were more than eight times the usual. Although Uber's app warned customers of heightened fares before processing their requests, many customers were outraged. One customer shared an Instagram photo of a taxi receipt for $415. "That is robbery!" Tweeted another. However, despite the protests, Uber experienced no subsequent drop in demand in the New York City area. It seems that, to most people who can afford Uber, convenience and prestige are the deciding factors, not price.

Thus, used well, dynamic pricing can help sellers to optimize sales and profits by keeping track of competitor pricing and quickly adjusting to marketplace changes. Used poorly, however, it can trigger margin-eroding price wars and damage customer relationships and trust. Too often, dynamic pricing takes the form of a pricing "arms race" among sellers, putting too much emphasis on prices at the expense of other important customer value-building elements. Companies must be careful to keep pricing in balance. As one Best Buy marketer states, pricing—dynamic or otherwise—remains "just one part of the equation. There's the right assortment, convenience, expedited delivery, customer service, warranty. All of these things matter to the customer."

Sources: Andrew Nusca, "The Future of Retail Is Dynamic Pricing. So Why Can't We Get It Right?," *ZDNet,* October 2, 2013, www.zdnet.com/the-future-of-retail-is-dynamic-pricing-so-why-cant-we-get-it-right-7000021444/; Laura Gunderson, "Amazon's 'Dynamic' Prices Get Some Static," *The Oregonian,* May 5, 2012, http://blog.oregonlive.com/complaintdesk/2012/05/amazons_dynamic_prices_get_som.html; David P; Schulz, "Changing Direction," *Stores,* March 2013, www.stores.org/STORES%20Magazine%20March%202013/changing-direction; Jessi Hempel, "Why Surge-Pricing Fiasco Is Great for Uber," *CNNMoney,* December 30, 2013, http://tech.fortune.cnn.com/2013/12/30/why-the-surge-pricing-fiasco-is-great-for-uber/; Alison Griswold, "Everybody Hates Surge Pricing," *Slate,* April 24, 2014, www.slate.com/articles/business/moneybox/2014/04/uber_style_surge_pricing_does_the_system_make_sense_for_d_c_cabs.html; and Mike Murphy, "Amazon Changed the Price of the Bible Over 100 Times in Five Years," *Quartz,* January 21, 2015, http://qz.com/327835/amazon-dynamic-pricing-changed-the-price-of-the-bible-over-100-times-in-five-years/.

In the extreme, some companies customize their offers and prices based on the specific characteristics and behaviors of individual customers, mined from online browsing and purchasing histories. These days, online offers and prices might well be based on what specific customers search for and buy, how much they pay for other purchases, and whether they might be willing and able to spend more. For example, a consumer who recently went online to purchase a first-class ticket to Paris or customize a new Mercedes coupe might later get a higher quote on a new Bose Wave Radio. By comparison, a friend with a more modest online search and purchase history might receive an offer of 5 percent off and free shipping on the same radio.[19]

Although such dynamic pricing practices seem legally questionable, they're not. Dynamic pricing is legal as long as companies do not discriminate based on age, gender, location, or other similar characteristics. Dynamic pricing makes sense in many contexts—it adjusts prices according to market forces and consumer preferences. But marketers need to be careful not to use dynamic pricing to take advantage of certain customer groups, thereby damaging important customer relationships.

The practice of online pricing, however, goes both ways, and consumers often benefit from online and dynamic pricing. Thanks to the Internet, the centuries-old art of haggling is suddenly back in vogue. For example, consumers can negotiate prices at online auction sites and exchanges. Want to sell that antique pickle jar that's been collecting dust for generations? Post it on eBay or Craigslist. Want to name your own price for a hotel room or rental car? Visit Priceline.com or another reverse auction site. Want to bid on a ticket to a hot show or sporting event? Check out Ticketmaster.com, which offers an online auction service for event tickets.

Dynamic and Internet pricing: Using mobile apps such as Amazon's Price Check, consumers can get instant product and price comparisons. Just "Scan it," "Snap it," or "Say it."

Andrew Harrer/Bloomberg/Getty Images

Also thanks to the Internet, consumers can get instant product and price comparisons from thousands of vendors at price comparison sites such as Yahoo! Shopping, Epinions.com, and PriceGrabber.com or using mobile apps such as TheFind, eBay's RedLaser, or Amazon's Price Check. For example, the RedLaser mobile app lets customers scan barcodes or QR codes (or search by voice or image) while shopping in stores. It then searches online and at nearby stores to provide thousands of reviews and comparison prices, and even offers buying links for immediate online purchasing. Armed with this information, consumers can often negotiate better in-store prices.

In fact, many retailers are finding that ready online access to comparison prices is giving consumers *too* much of an edge. Store retailers ranging from Target and Best Buy to Brookstone and GNC are now devising strategies to combat the consumer practice of *showrooming*. Consumers armed with smartphones now routinely come to stores to see an item, compare prices online while in the store, and then buy the item online at a lower price. Such behavior is called showrooming because consumers use retailers' stores as de facto "showrooms" for online resellers such as Amazon.com.

This past holiday season, Best Buy launched an advertising campaign—called "Your Ultimate Holiday Showroom"—designed to directly combat showrooming:[20]

> In the campaign, a host of popular celebrities pitched Best Buy as a better shopping experience than buying from online-only retailers like Amazon.com. They touted Best Buy advantages, such as assistance by well-trained associates, the ability to order online and pick up in store, and Best Buy's low-price guarantee. "Showrooming ... is not the ideal experience," says a Best Buy marketer, "...to do research at home, go to the store, do more research, then hit pause, go home and order and hope it arrives on time. There's a better way." That better way would be shopping and buying at Best Buy, the ultimate holiday showroom. Most consumers reacted positively to the light-hearted campaign, which helped lift holiday store traffic. However, the real challenge for Best Buy is to convert shoppers to buyers. Some customers remained skeptics. As one consumer Tweeted regarding the "Ultimate Showroom" ads: "Dear Best Buy, I'm glad you know your place as a showroom. Love, everyone who shops at Amazon."

International Pricing

Companies that market their products internationally must decide what prices to charge in different countries. In some cases, a company can set a uniform worldwide price. For example, Boeing sells its jetliners at about the same price everywhere, whether the buyer is in the United States, Europe, or a third-world country. However, most companies adjust their prices to reflect local market conditions and cost considerations.

The price that a company should charge in a specific country depends on many factors, including economic conditions, competitive situations, laws and regulations, and the nature of the wholesaling and retailing system. Consumer perceptions and preferences also may vary from country to country, calling for different prices. Or the company may have different marketing objectives in various world markets, which require changes in pricing strategy. For example, Apple introduces sophisticated, feature-rich, premium smartphones in carefully segmented mature markets in highly developed countries using a market-skimming pricing strategy. By contrast, it's now under pressure to discount older models and develop cheaper, more basic phone models for sizable but less affluent markets in developing countries, where even discounted older Apple phones sell at prices three to five times those of those of competing low-price models.

Costs play an important role in setting international prices. Travelers abroad are often surprised to find that goods that are relatively inexpensive at home may carry outrageously higher price tags in other countries. A pair of Levi's selling for $30 in the United States might go for $63 in Tokyo and $88 in Paris. A McDonald's Big Mac selling for a modest $4.20 in the United States might cost $7.85 in Norway or $5.65 in Brazil, and an Oral-B toothbrush selling for $2.49 at home may cost $10 in China. Conversely, a Gucci handbag going for only $140 in Milan, Italy, might fetch $240 in the United States.

>> International prices: Travelers are often surprised to find that product price tags vary greatly from country to country. For example, thanks to Chinese import tariffs and consumption taxes, Western luxury goods bought in mainland China carry prices as much as 50 percent higher than in Europe.

James McCauley/Harrods/Getty Images

In some cases, such *price escalation* may result from differences in selling strategies or market conditions. In most instances, however, it is simply a result of the higher costs of selling in another country—the additional costs of operations, product modifications, shipping and insurance, exchange-rate fluctuations, and physical distribution. Import tariffs and taxes can also add to costs. >> For example, China imposes duties as high as 25 percent on imported Western luxury products such as watches, designer dresses, shoes, and leather handbags. It also levies consumption taxes of 30 percent for cosmetics and 20 percent on high-end watches. As a result, Western luxury goods bought in mainland China carry prices as much as 50 percent higher than in Europe.[21]

Price has become a key element in the international marketing strategies of companies attempting to enter less affluent emerging markets. Typically, entering such markets has meant targeting the exploding middle classes in developing countries such as China, India, Russia, and Brazil, whose economies have been growing rapidly. More recently, however, as the weakened global economy has slowed growth in both domestic and emerging markets, many companies are shifting their sights to include a new target—the so-called "bottom of the pyramid," the vast untapped market consisting of the world's poorest consumers.

Not long ago, the preferred way for many brands to market their products in developing markets—whether consumer products or cars, computers, and smartphones—was to paste new labels on existing models and sell them at higher prices to the privileged few who could afford them. However, such a pricing approach put many products out of the reach of the tens of millions of poor consumers in emerging markets. As a result, many companies developed smaller, more basic and affordable product versions for these markets. For example, Unilever—the maker of such brands as Dove, Sunsilk, Lipton, and Vaseline—shrunk its packaging and set low prices that even the world's poorest consumers could afford. It developed single-use packages of its shampoo, laundry detergent, face cream, and other products that it could sell profitably for just pennies a pack. As a result, today, more than half of Unilever's revenues come from emerging economies.[22]

Although this strategy has been successful for Unilever, most companies are learning that selling profitably to the bottom of the pyramid requires more than just repackaging or stripping down existing products and selling them at low prices. Just like more well-to-do consumers, low-income buyers want products that are both functional *and* aspirational. Thus, companies today are innovating to create products that not only sell at very low prices but also give bottom-of-the-pyramid consumers more for their money, not less.

International pricing presents many special problems and complexities. We discuss international pricing issues in more detail in Chapter 15.

Author Comment
When and how should a company change its price? What if costs rise, putting the squeeze on profits? What if the economy sags and customers become more price sensitive? Or what if a major competitor raises or drops its prices? As Figure 9.5 suggests, companies face many price-changing options.

Price Changes

After developing their pricing structures and strategies, companies often face situations in which they must initiate price changes or respond to price changes by competitors.

Initiating Price Changes

In some cases, the company may find it desirable to initiate either a price cut or a price increase. In both cases, it must anticipate possible buyer and competitor reactions.

Initiating Price Cuts

Several situations may lead a firm to consider cutting its price. One such circumstance is excess capacity. Another is falling demand in the face of strong price competition or a weakened economy. In such cases, the firm may aggressively cut prices to boost sales and market share. But as the airline, fast-food, automobile, retailing, and other industries have learned in recent years, cutting prices in an industry loaded with excess capacity may lead to price wars as competitors try to hold on to market share.

A company may also cut prices in a drive to dominate the market through lower costs. Either the company starts with lower costs than its competitors, or it cuts prices in the hope of gaining market share that will further cut costs through larger volume. For example, computer and electronics maker Lenovo uses an aggressive low-cost, low-price strategy to increase its share of the PC market in developing countries. Similarly, Chinese low-price phone maker Xiaomi has now become China's smartphone market leader, and the low-cost producer is making rapid inroads into India and other emerging markets.

Initiating Price Increases

A successful price increase can greatly improve profits. For example, if the company's profit margin is 3 percent of sales, a 1 percent price increase will boost profits by 33 percent if sales volume is unaffected. A major factor in price increases is cost inflation. Rising costs squeeze profit margins and lead companies to pass cost increases along to customers. Another factor leading to price increases is over-demand: When a company cannot supply all that its customers need, it may raise its prices, ration products to customers, or both—consider today's worldwide oil and gas industry.

When raising prices, the company must avoid being perceived as a *price gouger*. >> For example, when gasoline prices rise rapidly, angry customers often accuse the major oil companies of enriching themselves at the expense of consumers. Customers have long memories, and they will eventually turn away from companies or even whole industries that they perceive as charging excessive prices. In the extreme, claims of price gouging may even bring about increased government regulation.

There are some techniques for avoiding these problems. One is to maintain a sense of fairness surrounding any price increase. Price increases should be supported by company communications telling customers why prices are being raised.

Wherever possible, the company should consider ways to meet higher costs or demand without raising prices. For example, it might consider more cost-effective ways to produce or distribute its products. It can "unbundle" its market offering, removing features, packaging, or services and separately pricing elements that were formerly part of the offer. Or it can shrink the product or substitute less-expensive ingredients instead of raising the price. P&G recently did this with Tide by holding price while shrinking 100-ounce containers to 92 ounces and 50-ounce containers to 46 ounces, creating a more than 8 percent price increase per ounce without changing package prices. Similarly, Kimberly-Clark raised Kleenex prices by "desheeting"—reducing the number of sheets of toilet paper or facial tissues in each package. And a regular Snickers bar now weighs 1.86 ounces, down from 2.07 ounces in the past, effectively increasing prices by 11 percent.[23]

>> Initiating price increases: When gasoline prices rise rapidly, angry consumers often accuse the major oil companies of enriching themselves by gouging customers.

Jerry/Marcy Monkman/EcoPhotography.com/Alamy

Buyer Reactions to Price Changes

Customers do not always interpret price changes in a straightforward way. A price *increase*, which would normally lower sales, may have some positive meanings for buyers. For example, what would you think if Rolex *raised* the price of its latest watch model? On the one hand, you might think that the watch is even more exclusive or better made. On the other hand, you might think that Rolex is simply being greedy by charging what the traffic will bear.

Similarly, consumers may view a price *cut* in several ways. For example, what would you think if Rolex were to suddenly cut its prices? You might think that you are getting a better deal on an exclusive product. More likely, however, you'd think that quality had been reduced, and the brand's luxury image might be tarnished. A brand's price and image are often closely linked. A price change, especially a drop in price, can adversely affect how consumers view the brand.

Competitor Reactions to Price Changes

A firm considering a price change must worry about the reactions of its competitors as well as those of its customers. Competitors are most likely to react when the number of firms involved is small, when the product is uniform, and when the buyers are well informed about products and prices.

How can the firm anticipate the likely reactions of its competitors? The problem is complex because, like the customer, the competitor can interpret a company price cut in many ways. It might think the company is trying to grab a larger market share or that it's doing poorly and trying to boost its sales. Or it might think that the company wants the whole industry to cut prices to increase total demand.

The company must assess each competitor's likely reaction. If all competitors behave alike, this amounts to analyzing only a typical competitor. In contrast, if the competitors do not behave alike—perhaps because of differences in size, market shares, or policies—then separate analyses are necessary. However, if some competitors will match the price change, there is good reason to expect that the rest will also match it.

Responding to Price Changes

Here we reverse the question and ask how a firm should respond to a price change by a competitor. The firm needs to consider several issues: Why did the competitor change the price? Is the price change temporary or permanent? What will happen to the company's market share and profits if it does not respond? Are other competitors going to respond? Besides these issues, the company must also consider its own situation and strategy and possible customer reactions to price changes.

>> **Figure 9.5** shows the ways a company might assess and respond to a competitor's price cut. Suppose a company learns that a competitor has cut its price and decides that this price cut is likely to harm its sales and profits. It might simply decide to hold its current price and profit margin. The company might believe that it will not lose too much market share or that it would lose too much profit if it reduced its own price. Or it might decide that it should wait and respond when it has more information on the effects of the competitor's price change. However, waiting too long to act might let the competitor get stronger and more confident as its sales increase.

If the company decides that effective action can and should be taken, it might make any of four responses. First, it could *reduce its price* to match the competitor's price. It may decide that the market is price sensitive and that it would lose too much market share to the lower-priced competitor. However, cutting the price will reduce the company's profits in the short run. Some companies might also reduce their product quality, services,

>> Figure 9.5 Responding to Competitor Price Changes

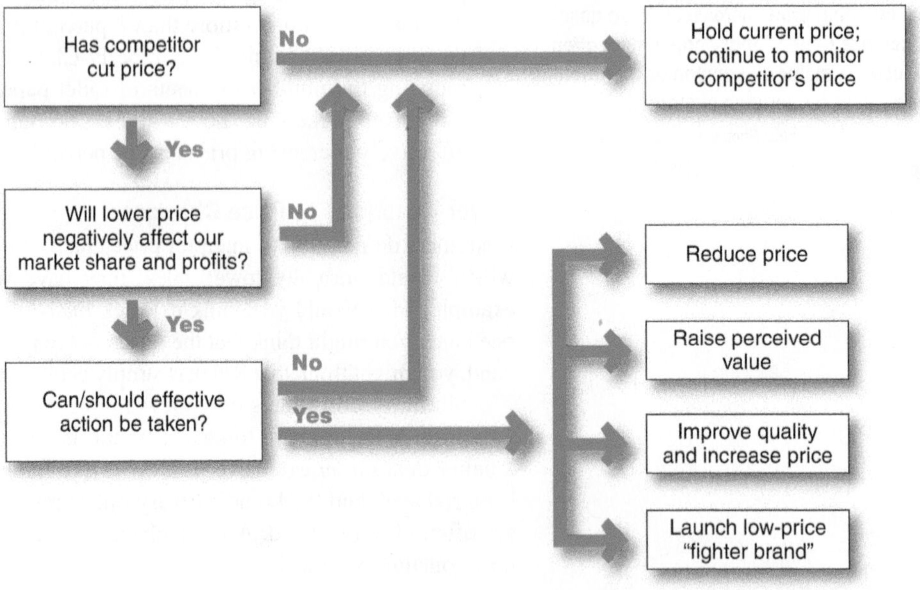

When a competitor cuts prices, a company's first reaction may be to drop its prices as well. But that is often the wrong response. Instead, the firm may want to emphasize the "value" side of the price–value equation.

and marketing communications to retain profit margins, but this will ultimately hurt long-run market share. The company should try to maintain its quality as it cuts prices.

Alternatively, the company might maintain its price but *raise the perceived value* of its offer. It could improve its communications, stressing the relative value of its product over that of the lower-price competitor. The firm may find it cheaper to maintain price and spend money to improve its perceived value than to cut price and operate at a lower margin. Or the company might *improve quality* and *increase price*, moving its brand into a higher price–value position. The higher quality creates greater customer value, which justifies the higher price. In turn, the higher price preserves the company's higher margins.

Finally, the company might launch a *low-price "fighter brand"*—adding a lower-price item to the line or creating a separate lower-price brand. This is necessary if the particular market segment being lost is price sensitive and will not respond to arguments of higher quality. » Starbucks did this when it acquired Seattle's Best Coffee, a brand positioned with working-class, "approachable-premium" appeal compared to the more professional, full-premium appeal of the main Starbucks brand. Seattle's Best coffee is generally cheaper than the parent Starbucks brand. As such, at retail, it competes more directly with Dunkin' Donuts, McDonald's, and other mass-premium brands through its franchise outlets and through partnerships with Subway, Burger King, Delta, AMC theaters, Royal Caribbean cruise lines, and others. On supermarket shelves, it competes with store brands and other mass-premium coffees such as Folgers Gourmet Selections and Millstone.

» **Fighter brands: Starbucks has positioned its Seattle's Best Coffee unit to compete more directly with the "mass-premium" brands sold buy Dunkin' Donuts, McDonald's, and other lower-priced competitors.**

Curved Light USA/Alamy

To counter store brands and other low-price entrants in a tighter economy, P&G turned a number of its brands into fighter brands. Luvs disposable diapers give parents "premium leakage protection for less than pricier brands." And P&G offers popular budget-priced basic versions of several of its major brands. For example, Charmin Basic "holds up at a great everyday price," and Puffs Basic gives you "Everyday softness. Everyday value." Tide Simply Clean & Fresh is about 35 percent cheaper than regular Tide detergent. However, companies must use caution when introducing fighter brands, as such brands can tarnish the image of the main brand. In addition, although they may attract budget buyers away from lower-priced rivals, they can also take business away from the firm's higher-margin brands.

Author Comment
Pricing decisions are often constrained by social and legal issues. For example, think about the pharmaceuticals industry. Are rapidly rising prescription drug prices justified? Or are the drug companies unfairly lining their pockets by gouging consumers who have few alternatives? Should the government step in?

Public Policy and Pricing

Price competition is a core element of our free-market economy. In setting prices, companies usually are not free to charge whatever prices they wish. Many federal, state, and even local laws govern the rules of fair play in pricing. In addition, companies must consider broader societal pricing concerns. In setting their prices, for example, pharmaceutical firms must balance their development costs and profit objectives against the sometimes life-and-death needs of drug consumers.

The most important pieces of legislation affecting pricing are the Sherman Act, the Clayton Act, and the Robinson-Patman Act, initially adopted to curb the formation of monopolies and regulate business practices that might unfairly restrain trade. Because these federal statutes can be applied only to interstate commerce, some states have adopted similar provisions for companies that operate locally.

Figure 9.6 Public Policy Issues in Pricing

Source: Adapted from Dhruv Grewal and Larry D. Compeau, "Pricing and Public Policy: A Research Agenda and Overview of the Special Issue," *Journal of Public Policy and Marketing*, Spring 1999, pp. 3–10.

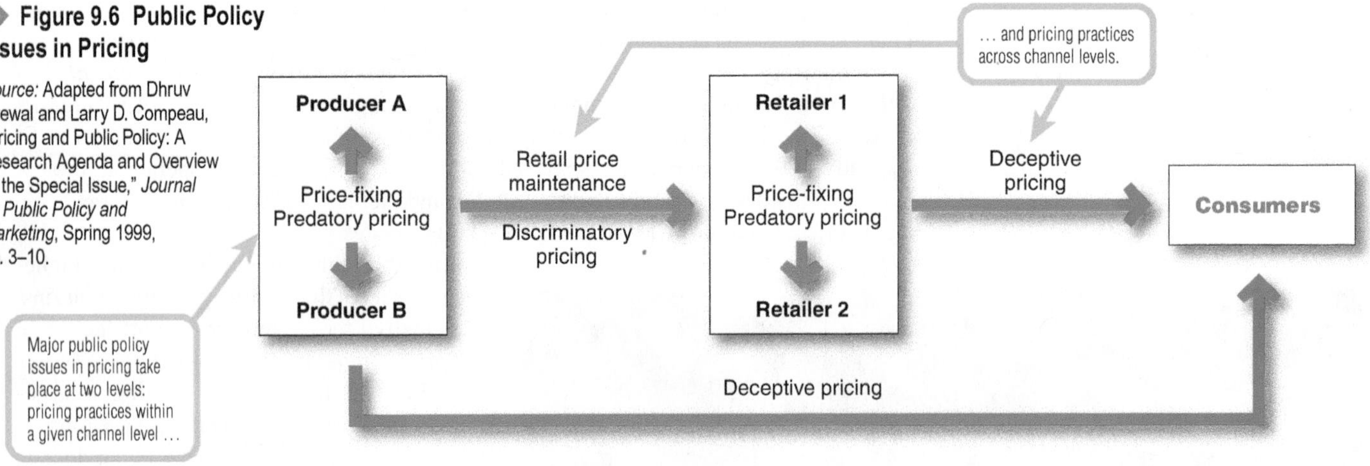

Figure 9.6 shows the major public policy issues in pricing. These include potentially damaging pricing practices within a given level of the channel (price-fixing and predatory pricing) and across levels of the channel (retail price maintenance, discriminatory pricing, and deceptive pricing).[24]

Pricing within Channel Levels

Federal legislation on *price-fixing* states that sellers must set prices without talking to competitors. Otherwise, price collusion is suspected. Price-fixing is illegal per se—that is, the government does not accept any excuses for price-fixing. As such, companies found guilty of these practices can receive heavy fines. Recently, governments at the state and national levels have been aggressively enforcing price-fixing regulations in industries ranging from gasoline, insurance, and concrete to credit cards, CDs, computer chips, and e-books. For example, in recent years, the U.S. Department of Justice has brought charges against Apple for colluding with publishers to fix prices on e-books. Price-fixing is also prohibited in many international markets. For example, Apple was recently fined $670,000 on price-fixing charges for its iPhones in Taiwan.[25]

Sellers are also prohibited from using *predatory pricing*—selling below cost with the intention of punishing a competitor or gaining higher long-run profits by putting competitors out of business. This protects small sellers from larger ones that might sell items below cost temporarily or in a specific locale to drive them out of business. The biggest problem is determining just what constitutes predatory pricing behavior. Selling below cost to unload excess inventory is not considered predatory; selling below cost to drive out competitors is. Thus, a given action may or may not be predatory depending on intent, and intent can be very difficult to determine or prove.

Predatory pricing: Some industry critics have accused Amazon.com of pricing books at fire-sale prices that harm competing booksellers. But is it predatory pricing or just plain good competitive marketing?

Iain Masterton/Alamy

In recent years, several large and powerful companies have been accused of predatory pricing. However, turning an accusation into a lawsuit can be difficult. For example, many publishers and booksellers have expressed concerns about Amazon.com's predatory practices, especially its book pricing:[26]

> Many booksellers and publishers complain that Amazon's book pricing policies are destroying their industry. During past holiday seasons, Amazon has sold top 10 best-selling hardback books as loss leaders at cut-rate prices of less than $10 each. And Amazon now sells e-books at fire-sale prices in order to win customers for its Kindle e-reader. Such very low book prices have caused considerable damage to competing booksellers, many of whom view Amazon's pricing actions as predatory. Says one observer, "The word 'predator' is pretty strong, and I don't use it loosely, but ... I could have sworn we had laws against predatory pricing. I just don't understand why [Amazon's pricing] is not an issue." Still, no predatory pricing charges have ever been filed against Amazon. It would be extremely difficult to prove that such loss-leader pricing is purposefully predatory as opposed to just plain good competitive marketing.

Pricing across Channel Levels

The Robinson-Patman Act seeks to prevent unfair *price discrimination* by ensuring that sellers offer the same price terms to customers at a given level of trade. For example, every retailer is entitled to the same price terms from a given manufacturer, whether the retailer is REI or a local bicycle shop. However, price discrimination is allowed if the seller can prove that its costs are different when selling to different retailers—for example, that it costs less per unit to sell a large volume of bicycles to REI than to sell a few bicycles to the local dealer.

The seller can also discriminate in its pricing if the seller manufactures different qualities of the same product for different retailers. The seller has to prove that these differences are proportional. Price differentials may also be used to "match competition" in "good faith," provided the price discrimination is temporary, localized, and defensive rather than offensive.

Laws also prohibit *retail (or resale) price maintenance*—a manufacturer cannot require dealers to charge a specified retail price for its product. Although the seller can propose a manufacturer's *suggested* retail price to dealers, it cannot refuse to sell to a dealer that takes independent pricing action, nor can it punish the dealer by shipping late or denying advertising allowances. For example, the Florida attorney general's office investigated Nike for allegedly fixing the retail price of its shoes and clothing. It was concerned that Nike might be withholding items from retailers who were not selling its most expensive shoes at prices the company considered suitable.

Deceptive pricing occurs when a seller states prices or price savings that mislead consumers or are not actually available to consumers. This might involve bogus reference or comparison prices, as when a retailer sets artificially high "regular" prices and then announces "sale" prices close to its previous everyday prices. For example, Overstock.com came under scrutiny for inaccurately listing manufacturer's suggested retail prices, often quoting them higher than the actual prices. Such comparison pricing is widespread.

Although comparison pricing claims are legal if they are truthful, the Federal Trade Commission's "Guides against Deceptive Pricing" warn sellers not to advertise (1) a price reduction unless it is a savings from the usual retail price, (2) "factory" or "wholesale" prices unless such prices are what they are claimed to be, and (3) comparable value prices on imperfect goods.[27]

Other deceptive pricing issues include *scanner fraud* and price confusion. The widespread use of scanner-based computer checkouts has led to increasing complaints of retailers overcharging their customers. Most of these overcharges result from poor management, such as a failure to enter current or sale prices into the system. Other cases, however, involve intentional overcharges.

Many federal and state statutes regulate against deceptive pricing practices. For example, the Automobile Information Disclosure Act requires automakers to attach a statement on new vehicle windows stating the manufacturer's suggested retail price, the prices of optional equipment, and the dealer's transportation charges. However, reputable sellers go beyond what is required by law. Treating customers fairly and making certain that they fully understand prices and pricing terms are an important part of building strong and lasting customer relationships.

MyMarketingLab

If assigned by your instructor, complete the questions marked with the ✪ from the EOC Discussion Questions section in the MyLab. To complete the Marketing by the Numbers problems found in this section, go to your Assignments in the MyLab.

REVIEWING AND EXTENDING THE CONCEPTS

CHAPTER REVIEW AND CRITICAL THINKING

Objectives Review

Price can be defined as the sum of all the values that customers give up in order to gain the benefits of having or using a product or service. Pricing decisions are subject to an incredibly complex array of company, environmental, and competitive forces.

OBJECTIVE 9-1 Identify the three major pricing strategies and discuss the importance of understanding customer-value perceptions, company costs, and competitor strategies when setting prices. (pp 264–272)

The three major pricing strategies include customer value-based pricing, cost-based pricing, and competition-based pricing. Good pricing begins with a complete understanding of the value that a product or service creates for customers and setting a price that captures that value.

Customer perceptions of the product's value set the ceiling for prices. If customers perceive that the price is greater than the product's value, they will not buy the product. At the other extreme, company and product costs set the floor for prices. If the company prices the product below its costs, its profits will suffer. Between these two extremes, consumers will base their judgments of a product's value on the prices that competitors charge for similar products. Thus, in setting prices, companies need to consider all three factors: customer perceived value, costs, and competitors pricing strategies.

Costs are an important consideration in setting prices. However, cost-based pricing is often product driven. The company designs what it considers to be a good product and sets a price that covers costs plus a target profit. If the price turns out to be too high, the company must settle for lower markups or lower sales, both resulting in disappointing profits. Value-based pricing reverses this process. The company assesses customer needs and value perceptions and then sets a target prices to match targeted value. The targeted value and price then drive decisions about product design and what costs can be incurred. As a result, price is set to match customers' perceived value.

OBJECTIVE 9-2 Identify and define the other important external and internal factors affecting a firm's pricing decisions. (pp 272–277)

Other *internal* factors that influence pricing decisions include the company's overall marketing strategy, objectives, and marketing mix as well as organizational considerations. Price is only one element of the company's broader marketing strategy. If the company has selected its target market and positioning carefully, then its marketing mix strategy, including price, will be fairly straightforward. Common pricing objectives might include customer retention and building profitable customer relationships, preventing competition, supporting resellers and gaining their support, or avoiding government intervention. Price decisions must be coordinated with product design, distribution, and promotion decisions to form a consistent and effective marketing program. Finally, in order to coordinate pricing goals and decisions, management must decide who within the organization is responsible for setting price.

Other *external* pricing considerations include the nature of the market and demand and environmental factors such as the economy, reseller needs, and government actions. Ultimately, the customer decides whether the company has set the right price. The customer weighs the price against the perceived values of using the product—if the price exceeds the sum of the values, consumers will not buy. So the company must understand concepts like demand curves (the price-demand relationship) and price elasticity (consumer sensitivity to prices).

Economic conditions can have a major impact on pricing decisions. The Great Recession caused consumers to rethink the price-value equation. Marketers have responded by increasing their emphasis on value-for-the-money pricing strategies. Even in tight economic times, however, consumers do not buy based on prices alone. Thus, no matter what price they charge—low or high—companies need to offer superior value for the money.

OBJECTIVE 9-3 Describe the major strategies for pricing new products. (pp 277–278)

Pricing is a dynamic process. Companies design a *pricing structure* that covers all their products. They change this structure over time and adjust it to account for different customers and situations. Pricing strategies usually change as a product passes through its life cycle. In pricing innovative new products, a company can use *market-skimming pricing* by initially setting high prices to "skim" the maximum amount of revenue from various segments of the market. Or it can use *market-penetrating pricing* by setting a low initial price to penetrate the market deeply and win a large market share.

OBJECTIVE 9-4 Explain how companies find a set of prices that maximizes the profits from the total product mix. (pp 278–280)

When the product is part of a product mix, the firm searches for a set of prices that will maximize the profits from the total mix. In *product line pricing*, the company decides on price steps for the entire set of products it offers. In addition, the company must set prices for *optional products* (optional or accessory products included with the main product), *captive products* (products that are required for use of the main product), *by-products* (waste or residual products produced when making the main product), and *product bundles* (combinations of products at a reduced price).

OBJECTIVE 9-5 Discuss how companies adjust their prices to take into account different types of customers and situations. (pp 280–288)

Companies apply a variety of *price adjustment strategies* to account for differences in consumer segments and situations. One is *discount and allowance pricing*, whereby the company establishes cash, quantity, functional, or seasonal discounts or varying types of allowances. A second strategy is *segmented pricing*, where the company sells a product at two or more prices to accommodate different customers, product forms, locations, or times. Sometimes companies consider more than economics in their pricing decisions, using *psychological pricing* to better communicate a product's intended position. In *promotional pricing*, a company offers discounts or temporarily sells a product below list price as a special event, sometimes even selling below cost as a loss leader. Another approach is *geographical pricing*, whereby the company decides how to price to near or distant customers. In *dynamic pricing*, companies adjust prices continually to meet the characteristics and needs of individual customers and situations. Finally, *international pricing* means that the company adjusts its price to meet different conditions and expectations in different world markets.

OBJECTIVE 9-6 Discuss the key issues related to initiating and responding to price changes. (pp 288–293)

When a firm considers initiating a *price change*, it must consider customers' and competitors' reactions. There are different implications to *initiating price cuts* and *initiating price increases*. Buyer reactions to price changes are influenced by the meaning customers see in the price change. Competitors' reactions flow from a set reaction policy or a fresh analysis of each situation.

There are also many factors to consider in responding to a competitor's price changes. The company that faces a price change initiated by a competitor must try to understand the competitor's intent as well as the likely duration and impact of the change. If a swift reaction is desirable, the firm should preplan its reactions to different possible price actions by competitors. When facing a competitor's price change, the company might sit tight, reduce its own price, raise perceived quality, improve quality and raise price, or launch a fighting brand.

Key Terms

Objective 9-1
Price (p 264)
Customer value-based pricing (p 265)
Good-value pricing (p 267)
Value-added pricing (p 267)
Cost-based pricing (p 269)
Fixed costs (overhead) (p 269)
Variable costs (p 270)
Total costs (p 270)
Cost-plus pricing (markup pricing) (p 270)
Break-even pricing (target return pricing) (p 270)
Competition-based pricing (p 271)

Objective 9-2
Target costing (p 273)
Demand curve (p 274)
Price elasticity (p 275)

Objective 9-3
Market-skimming pricing (price skimming) (p 277)
Market-penetration pricing (p 277)

Objective 9-4
Product line pricing (p 278)
Optional-product pricing (p 279)
Captive-product pricing (p 279)
By-product pricing (p 279)
Product bundle pricing (p 280)

Objective 9-5
Discount (p 281)
Allowance (p 281)
Segmented pricing (p 281)
Psychological pricing (p 282)
Reference prices (p 282)
Promotional pricing (p 282)
Dynamic pricing (p 284)

Discussion Questions

9-1. Name and describe the two types of value-based pricing methods. (AACSB: Communication)

9-2. Name and describe the four types of markets and the challenges they pose with respect to setting prices. (AACSB: Communication)

9-3. What is captive-product pricing? What is this pricing tactic called in the case of services? Give examples. (AACSB: Communication; Reflective Thinking)

9-4. Name and describe the two broad new product pricing strategies. When would each be appropriate? (AACSB: Communication)

9-5. Compare and contrast price discounts and allowances, describing the types of each. (AACSB: Communication)

Critical Thinking Exercises

9-6. If you've ever traveled to another country, such as Germany, you may have noticed that the price on a product is the total amount you actually pay when you check out. That is, no sales tax is added to the purchase price at the checkout as it is in the United States. That is because many countries impose a Value Added Tax (VAT). In a small group, research value added taxes and debate whether such taxes benefit consumers. Do marketers support or dislike these types of taxes? (AACSB: Communication; Reflective Thinking)

9-7. In a small group, research the legal requirements regarding orders resulting from an online pricing mistake. Must sellers honor such orders? Write a report of what you learned. Then describe an example of an online pricing glitch and summarize what the company did to respond to the glitch. (AACSB: Communication; Reflective Thinking)

9-8. Bridgestone Corporation, the world's largest tire and rubber producer, recently agreed to plead guilty to price-fixing along with 25 other automotive suppliers. What is price-fixing? Discuss other recent examples of price-fixing. (AACSB: Communication; Reflective Thinking)

MINICASES AND APPLICATIONS

Online, Mobile, and Social Media Marketing Online Price Tracking

Got your eye on a new 32-inch Samsung television? Well, you better not purchase it in December—that's when the price was highest on Amazon.com ($500 versus $400 in November or February). Most consumers know that prices fluctuate throughout the year, but did you know they even fluctuate hourly? You probably can't keep up with that, but there's an app that can. Camelcamelcamel is a tool that tracks Amazon's prices for consumers and sends alerts when a price hits the sweet spot. This app allows users to import entire Amazon wishlists and to set desired price levels at which emails or tweets are sent to inform them of the prices. All of this is free. Camel makes its money from an unlikely partner—Amazon—which funnels price data directly to Camel. Camel is a member of Amazon's Affiliate program, kicking back 8.5 percent of sales for each customer Camel refers. It would seem that Amazon would want customers to buy when prices are higher, not lower. But the online behemoth sees this as a way to keep the bargain hunters happy while realizing more profitability from less price-sensitive customers. This is an improvement over Amazon's earlier pricing tactics, which charged different customers different prices based on their buying behavior.

9-9. Go to http://us.camelcamelcamel.com/ and set up a free account. Track 10 products that interest you. Did any of the products reach your desired price? Write a report on the usefulness of this type of app for consumers. (AACSB: Communication; Use of IT)

9-10. Camel is not the only Amazon tracking or online price-tracking application. Find and describe an example of another online price-tracking tool for consumers. (AACSB: Communication; Use of IT)

Marketing Ethics Psychology of Mobile Payments

Consumers love to play games on their mobile devices, and Japanese consumers seem to be the most passionate. Mobile game publishers in Japan have mastered the art of getting as much revenue as possible from players—some earning more than $4 million per day. The makers of Puzzle & Dragons have seemingly cracked the revenue code by using the psychology of mobile payments to squeeze more revenue by encouraging players to play longer. One Puzzle & Dragons secret was to issue its own virtual currency, called magic stones, so consumers don't feel like they are spending real money for chances to enhance play. Then the game offers a little reward at the end with a reminder of what is lost if the player doesn't take the offer. Limited-time sales offer monsters to use in battle for just a few magic stones, and if players run out of space, the game reminds them that they will lose their monsters if they don't purchase more space. All the while, mathematicians and statisticians work behind the scenes to track game play and make it easier or more challenging to keep players engaged and spending. One expert called Puzzle & Dragons "truly diabolical" in convincing players to pay and play more. These and other game producers' tactics have propelled Japan's game revenue alone to exceed revenue from all apps in the United States.

9-11. Is it ethical for game producers to use game-playing data to encourage consumers to spend more? Explain why or why not. (AACSB: Communication; Ethical Reasoning)

9-12. Is this similar to the "freemium" model used by many U.S. game producers? Explain the "freemium" model and discuss examples of games that use this model. (AACSB: Communication; Reflective Thinking; Ethical Reasoning)

Marketing by the Numbers Breakeven on Price Reduction

Abercrombie & Fitch, once the favorite of loyal teens, is considering lowering prices on all items it sells in an effort to win them back after several years of sales declines. A&F's total sales were $4 billion last year, but they have been declining in the face of a weak economy and an intensively competitive retail environment. Price reductions are often effective in increasing sales, but marketers need to analyze how much sales must go up before a price reduction pays off and increases revenue enough to make the it worth doing. Refer to Appendix 3: Marketing by the Numbers to answer the following questions.

9-13. Assuming A&F's gross profit margin is 60 percent and cost of goods sold represents the only variable cost, by how much must sales increase to maintain the same gross profit margin in terms of absolute dollars if A&F lowers prices by 10 percent? (AACSB: Communication; Analytical Reasoning)

9-14. By what percentage must costs decrease if A&F wants to maintain the gross margin percentage of 60 percent? (AACSB: Communication; Analytical Reasoning)

Video Case Fast-Food Discount Wars

Fast-food chains are locked in a fierce battle that has them practically giving food away. McDonald's, Wendy's, Burger King, and others are constantly trying to lure customers at the low end of the price spectrum with tempting menu options that can serve as a snack or a meal. Although this technique is nothing new, it's more popular today than ever. The tactic has even found its way into full-service restaurant chains such as Olive Garden.

But are bargain-basement options a sustainable path for restaurant chains? This video takes a look at the various ways discount menus are executed. It also considers the reasons for using discount menu tactics as well as the possible negative outcomes.

After viewing the video featuring restaurant discount menu wars, answer the following questions:

9-15. Can discount menu strategies like those featured in the video be classified as "value pricing"? Explain.

9-16. Discuss why a restaurant chain might employ a discount menu as a pricing option.

9-17. What are the possible negative outcomes of employing a discount menu strategy?

Company Cases 9 Coach/11 Sears

See Appendix 1 for cases appropriate for this chapter. **Case 9, Coach: Riding the Wave of Premium Pricing.** After years of high-growth revenues, discount tactics are taking a toll on this premium brand. **Case 11, Sears: Why Should You Shop There?** Sears is a perfect example of why it takes more than low prices to succeed in discount retail.

MyMarketingLab

If assigned by your instructor, complete these writing sections from your Assignments in the MyLab.

9-18. Describe the cost-plus pricing method and discuss why marketers use it even if it is not the best method for setting prices. (AACSB: Communication)

9-19. Compare and contrast fixed costs and variable costs and discuss their importance in setting prices. (AACSB: Written and Oral Communication; Reflective Thinking)

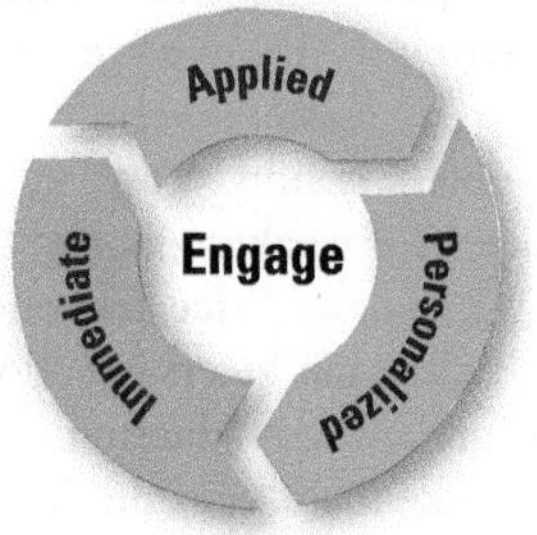

10 Marketing Channels

Delivering Customer Value

CHAPTER ROAD MAP Objective Outline

- OBJECTIVE 10-1 **Explain why companies use marketing channels and discuss the functions these channels perform.** Supply Chains and the Value Delivery Network (300–301); The Nature and Importance of Marketing Channels (301–303)
- OBJECTIVE 10-2 **Discuss how channel members interact and how they organize to perform the work of the channel.** Channel Behavior and Organization (304–311)
- OBJECTIVE 10-3 **Identify the major channel alternatives open to a company.** Channel Design Decisions (311–315)
- OBJECTIVE 10-4 **Explain how companies select, motivate, and evaluate channel members.** Channel Management Decisions (315–318); Public Policy and Distribution Decisions (319)
- OBJECTIVE 10-5 **Discuss the nature and importance of marketing logistics and integrated supply chain management.** Marketing Logistics and Supply Chain Management (319–326)

Previewing the Concepts

We now look at the third marketing mix tool—distribution. Companies rarely work alone in creating value for customers and building profitable customer relationships. Instead, most are only a single link in a larger supply chain and marketing channel. As such, a firm's success depends not only on how well *it* performs but also on how well its *entire marketing channel* competes with competitors' channels. The first part of this chapter explores the nature of marketing channels and the marketer's channel design and management decisions. We then examine physical distribution—or logistics—an area that has grown dramatically in importance and sophistication. In the next chapter, we'll look more closely at two major channel intermediaries: retailers and wholesalers.

We start by looking at Uber, the fast-growing, app-based car-hailing service that has recently sprouted up in cities around the world. Uber has radically reinvented urban transportation channels, posing a serious threat to conventional taxi cab and car service companies. As Uber grows, traditional competitors must innovate or risk being pushed aside.

First Stop

Uber: Radically Reshaping Urban Transportation Channels

>> Uber lets passengers hail the nearest cab from any location using its smartphone app, then track the vehicle on a map as it approaches.

PAUL J. RICHARDS/AFP/Getty Images

It's rare. But every now and then a company comes along that completely disrupts the traditional ways of distributing a product or service. FedEx revolutionized small package delivery channels; Amazon.com radically transformed online selling; and Apple's iTunes and iPod turned music distribution on its ear. Now comes Uber, the app-based ride service that is revolutionizing urban transportation. Fast-growing Uber is giving conventional taxi cab and car services a real ride for their money. In just five short years, Uber has revved up operations in 270 major cities in 55 countries, already booking more than $1 billion in rides annually.

Why are so many customers around the world bypassing good old taxi cabs in favor of newcomer Uber? It's all about convenience, ease of use, and peace of mind. No more stepping out into busy city streets to wave down a passing cab. Instead, Uber's smartphone app lets passengers hail the nearest cab or limo from any location with the touch of a button, then track the vehicle on a map as it approaches. The Uber app gives riders an accurate estimate in advance of the fare to their destinations (usually less than that charged by a regular cab), eliminating guesswork and uncertainty. After the ride, passengers simply exit and walk away. Uber automatically pays the driver (including tip) from the passenger's prepaid Uber account, eliminating the often inconvenient and awkward moment of payment. And it's the same process all over the world, from San Francisco, London, Paris, or Abu Dhabi to Ashville, North Carolina, or Athens, Georgia.

Compare the Uber experience to the uncertain and often unsettling experience of using a standard taxi cab. One business reporter describes waiting in line at a taxi stand while a driver tried to convince another would-be passenger—a total stranger—to share the cab, thereby increasing his fare. The cab itself was ancient and filthy, with ripped and worn seats. During the entire ride, the cabbie carried on a phone conversation in a foreign language via his headset, causing safety concerns while distractedly navigating busy city streets. The driver spoke only poor, hard-to-understand English. "That turned out to be a good thing," says the reporter, "because I couldn't understand what he was trying to say when he insulted me for not tipping him enough." The reporter's conclusion: "I stepped out of the taxi in front of my house and realized I just don't have to put up with this garbage anymore. Uber has changed my life, and as God is my witness, [wherever Uber is available] I will never take a taxi again."

Uber actually began as a ride-sharing service. Current Uber drivers range from professional drivers who've switched over from conventional cab and transportation companies to regular people looking for a little adventure and some extra income in their spare time. All Uber drivers go through an orientation that requires proficiency in a market area's dominant language, ensuring that they can communicate effectively with customers. Uber vehicles must be at least 2007-year models or newer, and customers can often choose the type of car they want, from an entry-level Prius to a stretch Mercedes S-Class. A two-way rating system—by which riders rate drivers and drivers rate riders in return—helps keep both sides on their best behavior. Poorly rated drivers risk being rejected by future passengers; poorly rated passengers risk rejection by drivers, who can choose which fares they accept.

Uber's disruptive innovation has brought a breath of fresh air to an industry begging for change. Urban transportation channels have long been characterized by cartel-like relationships between cab companies and local governments, high fixed fares, poor service, and little accountability. As one economics professor points out, the taxi cab industry "was ripe for entry [by startups] because everybody hates it." The business reporter puts it more plainly: "If service at Starbucks was as routinely disappointing as service from taxis, Starbucks would have gone out of business long ago."

Like any innovator, upstart Uber faces some significant challenges. For example, Uber has been criticized for exercising too little control over driver quality and security. So far, the company has ridden beneath the radar of industry regulators by not directly employing drivers (all Uber drivers are independent contractors) and not owning any vehicles (all vehicles are driver-owned). However, although some municipalities have passed ordinances favorable to Uber's operations, others are imposing new regulatory restrictions and licensing requirements.

Uber—the fast-growing app-based ride service—is revolutionizing urban transportation channels in cities around the globe. As Uber grows, traditional taxi cab services must innovate or risk extinction.

Uber has also been criticized for its "surge pricing" practices—a dynamic pricing mechanism that kicks in to raise prices when demand exceeds supply, sometimes resulting in shockingly high fares and accusations of price gouging. Uber justifies surge pricing by pointing to the very foundation of its business model—allowing the forces of supply and demand to work. Surge pricing provides an incentive for more drivers to be available during periods when passengers need them most. According to Uber, if a passenger faces a higher-than-normal fare because of surge pricing, the alternative without Uber would more than likely be no taxi at all. Moreover, Uber informs passengers in advance what the fares will be. If they don't like the fare, they can find another cab, take public transportation, or walk.

As Uber expands within a given market, Uber founder and CEO Travis Kalanick envisions the increased likelihood of what he calls "a perfect day"—a day when there is a ride available for everyone who needs one and no surge pricing results. Such a scenario is no pipe dream. In New York City recently, Uber riders experienced seven such "perfect days" in a row.

Uber's huge success has attracted a garage full of competitors, such as Lyft, Sidecar, Gett, Carma, and Curb. Even Google (itself a major Uber investor) is rumored to be readying the launch of its own ride-sharing service, one that would eventually utilize the driverless vehicles Google is developing. Uber still has a huge first-to-market advantage. It has an estimated seven times the riders and 12 times the revenues of nearest competitor Lyft, and it's adding new customers at an estimated five times faster.

Beyond the numbers, however, for now, Uber has little to fear from like-minded competitors. In fact, the more competitors adopt the new model, the more the revolutionary channel will grow and thrive versus traditional channels, creating opportunities for all new entrants. Instead, the new distribution model poses the biggest threat to traditional taxi cab and car-for-hire companies, who are now losing both customers and drivers to Uber and its competitors.

Uber-mania is even catching on in other industries. It seems like there's an app-based on-demand "Uber" for almost anything these days—laundry and dry cleaning (Washio), in-home massage (Zeel), 24/7 delivery services (Postmates), and even booze (Minibar). In fact, CEO Kalanick sees no end of future applications for Uber's services, well beyond just delivering people to their destinations. Once Uber has established a dense network of cars in every city, he predicts using the network to deliver everything from packages from retailers to takeout food. As Kalanick puts it, "Once you're delivering cars in five minutes, there are a lot of other things you can deliver in five minutes."[1]

As the Uber story shows, good distribution strategies can contribute strongly to customer value and create competitive advantage for a firm. But firms cannot bring value to customers by themselves. Instead, they must work closely with other firms in a larger value delivery network.

Author Comment

These are pretty hefty terms for a really simple concept: A company can't go it alone in creating customer value. It must work within a broader network of partners to accomplish this task. Individual companies and brands don't compete; their entire value delivery networks do.

Supply Chains and the Value Delivery Network

Producing a product or service and making it available to buyers requires building relationships not only with customers but also with key suppliers and resellers in the company's *supply chain*. This supply chain consists of upstream and downstream partners. Upstream from the company is the set of firms that supply the raw materials, components, parts, information, finances, and expertise needed to create a product or service. Marketers, however, have traditionally focused on the downstream side of the supply chain—the *marketing channels* (or *distribution channels*) that look toward the customer. Downstream marketing channel partners, such as wholesalers and retailers, form a vital link between the firm and its customers.

Value delivery network: In making and marketing even just its classic colas, Pepsi manages a huge network of people within the company plus thousands of outside suppliers, bottlers, retailers, and marketing service firms that must work together to create customer value and establish the brand's "Pepsi: Live for Now" positioning.

Vasiliy Baziuk/AP Images

The term *supply chain* may be too limited, as it takes a *make-and-sell* view of the business. It suggests that raw materials, productive inputs, and factory capacity should serve as the starting point for market planning. A better term would be *demand chain* because it suggests a *sense-and-respond* view of the market. Under this view, planning starts by identifying the needs of target customers, to which the company responds by organizing a chain of resources and activities with the goal of creating customer value.

Yet, even a demand chain view of a business may be too limited because it takes a step-by-step, linear view of purchase-production-consumption activities. Instead, most large companies today are engaged in building and managing a complex, continuously evolving value delivery network. As defined in Chapter 2, a **value delivery network** is made up of the company, suppliers, distributors, and, ultimately, customers who "partner" with each other to improve the performance of the entire system. For example, Pepsi makes great beverages. But to make and market just one of its many lines—say, its classic colas—Pepsi manages a huge network of people

Value delivery network
A network composed of the company, suppliers, distributors, and, ultimately, customers who partner with each other to improve the performance of the entire system in delivering customer value.

within the company, from marketing and sales people to folks in finance and operations. It also coordinates the efforts of thousands of suppliers, bottlers, retailers ranging from Kroger and Walmart to Papa John's Pizza, and advertising agencies and other marketing service firms. The entire network must function together to create customer value and establish the brand's "Pepsi: Live for Now" positioning.

This chapter focuses on marketing channels—on the downstream side of the value delivery network. We examine four major questions concerning marketing channels: What is the nature of marketing channels, and why are they important? How do channel firms interact and organize to do the work of the channel? What problems do companies face in designing and managing their channels? What role do physical distribution and supply chain management play in attracting and satisfying customers? In the next chapter, we will look at marketing channel issues from the viewpoints of retailers and wholesalers.

Author Comment
In this section, we look at the downstream side of the value delivery network—the marketing channel organizations that connect the company and its customers. To understand their value, imagine life without retailers—say, without grocery stores or department stores.

The Nature and Importance of Marketing Channels

Marketing channel (distribution channel)
A set of interdependent organizations that help make a product or service available for use or consumption by the consumer or business user.

Few producers sell their goods directly to final users. Instead, most use intermediaries to bring their products to market. They try to forge a **marketing channel** (or **distribution channel**)—a set of interdependent organizations that help make a product or service available for use or consumption by the consumer or business user.

A company's channel decisions directly affect every other marketing decision. Pricing depends on whether the company works with national discount chains, uses high-quality specialty stores, or sells directly to consumers online. The firm's sales force and communications decisions depend on how much persuasion, training, motivation, and support its channel partners need. Whether a company develops or acquires certain new products may depend on how well those products fit the capabilities of its channel members.

Companies often pay too little attention to their distribution channels—sometimes with damaging results. In contrast, many companies have used imaginative distribution systems to gain a competitive advantage. Enterprise Rent-A-Car revolutionized the car-rental business by setting up off-airport rental offices. Apple turned the retail music business on its head by selling music for the iPod via the Internet on iTunes. FedEx's creative and imposing distribution system made it a leader in express package delivery. And Amazon.com forever changed the face of retailing and became the Walmart of the Internet by selling anything and everything without using physical stores.

Distribution channel decisions often involve long-term commitments to other firms. For example, companies such as Ford, McDonald's, or Nike can easily change their advertising, pricing, or promotion programs. They can scrap old products and introduce new ones as market tastes demand. But when they set up distribution channels through contracts with franchisees, independent dealers, or large retailers, they cannot readily replace these channels with company-owned stores or Internet sites if the conditions change. Therefore, management must design its channels carefully, with an eye on both today's likely selling environment and tomorrow's as well.

How Channel Members Add Value

Why do producers give some of the selling job to channel partners? After all, doing so means giving up some control over how and to whom they sell their products. Producers use intermediaries because they create greater efficiency in making goods available to target markets. Through their contacts, experience, specialization, and scale of operation, intermediaries usually offer the firm more than it can achieve on its own.

»**Figure 10.1** shows how using intermediaries can provide economies. Figure 10.1A shows three manufacturers, each using direct marketing to reach three customers. This system requires nine different contacts. Figure 10.1B shows the three manufacturers working through one distributor, which contacts the three customers. This system requires only

Marketing channel intermediaries make buying a lot easier for consumers. Again, think about life without grocery retailers. How would you go about buying that 12-pack of Coke or any of the hundreds of other items that you now routinely drop into your shopping cart?

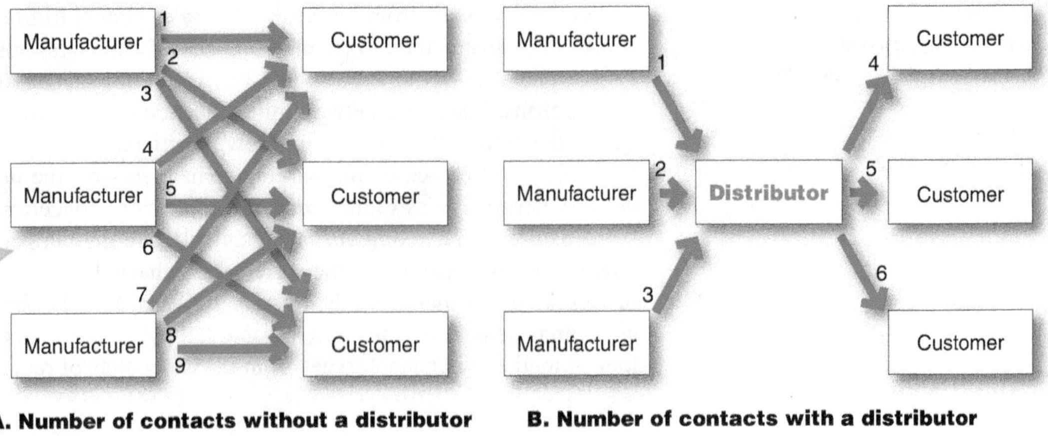

» Figure 10.1 How a Distributor Reduces the Number of Channel Transactions

six contacts. In this way, intermediaries reduce the amount of work that must be done by both producers and consumers.

From the economic system's point of view, the role of marketing intermediaries is to transform the assortments of products made by producers into the assortments wanted by consumers. Producers make narrow assortments of products in large quantities, but consumers want broad assortments of products in small quantities. Marketing channel members buy large quantities from many producers and break them down into the smaller quantities and broader assortments desired by consumers.

For example, Unilever makes millions of bars of Lever 2000 hand soap each week. However, you most likely only want to buy a few bars at a time. Therefore, big food, drug, and discount retailers, such as Safeway, Walgreens, and Target, buy Lever 2000 by the truckload and stock it on their stores' shelves. In turn, you can buy a single bar of Lever 2000 along with a shopping cart full of small quantities of toothpaste, shampoo, and other related products as you need them. Thus, intermediaries play an important role in matching supply and demand.

In making products and services available to consumers, channel members add value by bridging the major time, place, and possession gaps that separate goods and services from those who use them. Members of the marketing channel perform many key functions. Some help to complete transactions:

- ***Information.*** Gathering and distributing information about consumers, producers, and other actors and forces in the marketing environment needed for planning and aiding exchange.
- ***Promotion.*** Developing and spreading persuasive communications about an offer.
- ***Contact.*** Finding and engaging customers and prospective buyers.
- ***Matching.*** Shaping offers to meet the buyer's needs, including activities such as manufacturing, grading, assembling, and packaging.
- ***Negotiation.*** Reaching an agreement on price and other terms so that ownership or possession can be transferred.

Others help to fulfill the completed transactions:

- ***Physical distribution.*** Transporting and storing goods.
- ***Financing.*** Acquiring and using funds to cover the costs of the channel work.
- ***Risk taking.*** Assuming the risks of carrying out the channel work.

The question is not *whether* these functions need to be performed—they must be—but rather *who* will perform them. To the extent that the manufacturer performs these functions, its costs go up; therefore, its prices must be higher. When some of these functions are shifted to intermediaries, the producer's costs and prices may be lower, but the intermediaries must charge more to cover the costs of their work. In dividing the work of the channel, the various functions should be assigned to the channel members that can add the most value for the cost.

Number of Channel Levels

Channel level
A layer of intermediaries that performs some work in bringing the product and its ownership closer to the final buyer.

Direct marketing channel
A marketing channel that has no intermediary levels.

Indirect marketing channel
A marketing channel containing one or more intermediary levels.

Companies can design their distribution channels to make products and services available to customers in different ways. Each layer of marketing intermediaries that performs some work in bringing the product and its ownership closer to the final buyer is a **channel level**. Because both the producer and the final consumer perform some work, they are part of every channel.

The *number of intermediary levels* indicates the *length* of a channel. **>> Figure 10.2** shows both consumer and business channels of different lengths. Figure 10.2A shows several common consumer distribution channels. Channel 1, called a **direct marketing channel**, has no intermediary levels—the company sells directly to consumers. For example, Mary Kay Cosmetics and Amway sell their products through home and office sales parties and online Web sites and social media; companies ranging from GEICO insurance to Omaha Steaks sell directly to customers via the Internet, mobile, and telephone. The remaining channels in Figure 10.2A are **indirect marketing channels**, containing one or more intermediaries.

Figure 10.2B shows some common business distribution channels. The business marketer can use its own sales force to sell directly to business customers. Or it can sell to various types of intermediaries, which in turn sell to these customers. Although consumer and business marketing channels with even more levels can sometimes be found, these are less common. From the producer's point of view, a greater number of levels means less control and greater channel complexity. Moreover, all the institutions in the channel are connected by several types of *flows*. These include the *physical flow* of products, the *flow of ownership*, the *payment flow*, the *information flow*, and the *promotion flow*. These flows can make even channels with only one or a few levels very complex.

>> Figure 10.2 Consumer and Business Marketing Channels

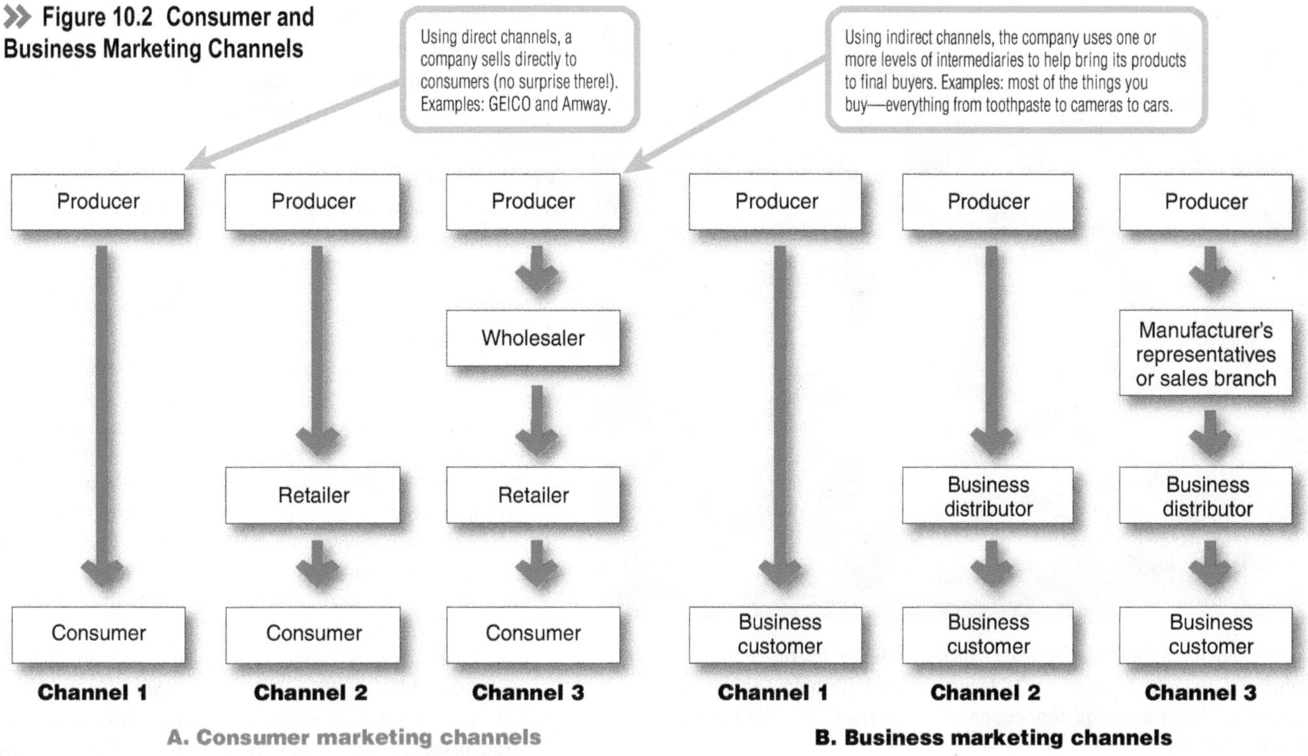

Author Comment

Channels are made up of more than just boxes and arrows on paper. They are behavioral systems consisting of real companies and people who interact to accomplish their individual and collective goals. Like groups of people, sometimes they work well together and sometimes they don't.

Channel Behavior and Organization

Distribution channels are more than simple collections of firms tied together by various flows. They are complex behavioral systems in which people and companies interact to accomplish individual, company, and channel goals. Some channel systems consist of only informal interactions among loosely organized firms. Others consist of formal interactions guided by strong organizational structures. Moreover, channel systems do not stand still—new types of intermediaries emerge and whole new channel systems evolve. Here we look at channel behavior and how members organize to do the work of the channel.

Channel Behavior

A marketing channel consists of firms that have partnered for their common good. Each channel member depends on the others. For example, a Ford dealer depends on Ford to design cars that meet customer needs. In turn, Ford depends on the dealer to engage customers, persuade them to buy Ford cars, and service the cars after the sale. Each Ford dealer also depends on other dealers to provide good sales and service that will uphold the brand's reputation. In fact, the success of individual Ford dealers depends on how well the entire Ford marketing channel competes with the channels of Toyota, GM, and other auto manufacturers.

Each channel member plays a specialized role in the channel. For example, Samsung's role is to produce electronics products that consumers will covet and create demand through national advertising. Best Buy's role is to display these Samsung products in convenient locations, answer buyers' questions, and complete sales. The channel will be most effective when each member assumes the tasks it can do best.

Channel conflict
Disagreements among marketing channel members on goals, roles, and rewards—who should do what and for what rewards.

Ideally, because the success of individual channel members depends on the overall channel's success, all channel firms should work together smoothly. They should understand and accept their roles, coordinate their activities, and cooperate to attain overall channel goals. However, individual channel members rarely take such a broad view. Cooperating to achieve overall channel goals sometimes means giving up individual company goals. Although channel members depend on one another, they often act alone in their own short-run best interests. They often disagree on who should do what and for what rewards. Such disagreements over goals, roles, and rewards generate **channel conflict**.

Horizontal conflict occurs among firms at the same level of the channel. For instance, some Ford dealers in Chicago might complain that other dealers in the city steal sales from them by pricing too low or advertising outside their assigned territories. Or Holiday Inn franchisees might complain about other Holiday Inn operators overcharging guests or giving poor service, hurting the overall Holiday Inn image.

Vertical conflict, conflict between different levels of the same channel, is even more common. » For example, McDonald's has recently faced growing conflict with its corps of almost 3,000 independent franchisees:[2]

> In a recent company Webcast, based on rising customer complaints that service isn't fast or friendly enough, McDonald's told its franchisees that their cashiers need to smile more. At the same time, it seems, the franchisees weren't very happy with McDonald's, either. A recent survey of franchise owners reflected growing franchisee discontent with the corporation. Much of the conflict stems from a recent slowdown in systemwide sales that has both sides on edge. The most basic conflicts are financial. McDonald's makes its money from franchisee royalties based on total system sales. In contrast, franchisees make money on margins—what's left over after their costs.

» **Channel conflict: Growing McDonald's franchisee discontent may explain the increasing lack of smiles on the faces of both McDonald's cashiers and customers. "There's a huge connection" between franchisee satisfaction and customer service.**

Seth Perlman/AP Images

To reverse the sales slump, McDonald's has increased emphasis on Dollar Menu items, a strategy that increases corporate sales but squeezes franchisee margins. Franchisees are also grumbling about adding popular but more complex menu items, such as Snack Wraps, that increase the top line for McDonald's but add preparation and staffing costs for franchisees while slowing down service. McDonald's is also asking franchisees to make costly restaurant upgrades and overhauls. As one survey respondent summarized, there's "too much reliance on price-pointing and discounting to drive top-line sales, which is where the corporate cow feeds." In all, the survey rates McDonald's current franchisee relations at a decade-low 1.93 out of a possible 5, in the "fair" to "poor" range. That fact might explain both the lack of smiles and the increasing customer complaints. According to one restaurant consultant, "there's a huge connection" between franchisee satisfaction and customer service.

Some conflict in the channel takes the form of healthy competition. Such competition can be good for the channel; without it, the channel could become passive and noninnovative. For example, the McDonald's conflict with its franchisees might represent normal give-and-take over the respective rights of the channel partners. However, severe or prolonged conflict can disrupt channel effectiveness and cause lasting harm to channel relationships. McDonald's should manage the channel conflict carefully to keep it from getting out of hand.

Vertical Marketing Systems

Conventional distribution channel
A channel consisting of one or more independent producers, wholesalers, and retailers, each a separate business seeking to maximize its own profits, perhaps even at the expense of profits for the system as a whole.

Vertical marketing system (VMS)
A channel structure in which producers, wholesalers, and retailers act as a unified system. One channel member owns the others, has contracts with them, or has so much power that they all cooperate.

For the channel as a whole to perform well, each channel member's role must be specified, and channel conflict must be managed. The channel will perform better if it includes a firm, agency, or mechanism that provides leadership and has the power to assign roles and manage conflict.

Historically, *conventional distribution channels* have lacked such leadership and power, often resulting in damaging conflict and poor performance. One of the biggest channel developments over the years has been the emergence of *vertical marketing systems* that provide channel leadership. **>> Figure 10.3** contrasts the two types of channel arrangements.

A **conventional distribution channel** consists of one or more independent producers, wholesalers, and retailers. Each is a separate business seeking to maximize its own profits, perhaps even at the expense of the system as a whole. No channel member has much control over the other members, and no formal means exists for assigning roles and resolving channel conflict.

In contrast, a **vertical marketing system (VMS)** consists of producers, wholesalers, and retailers acting as a unified system. One channel member owns the others, has

>> Figure 10.3 Comparison of Conventional Distribution Channel with Vertical Marketing System

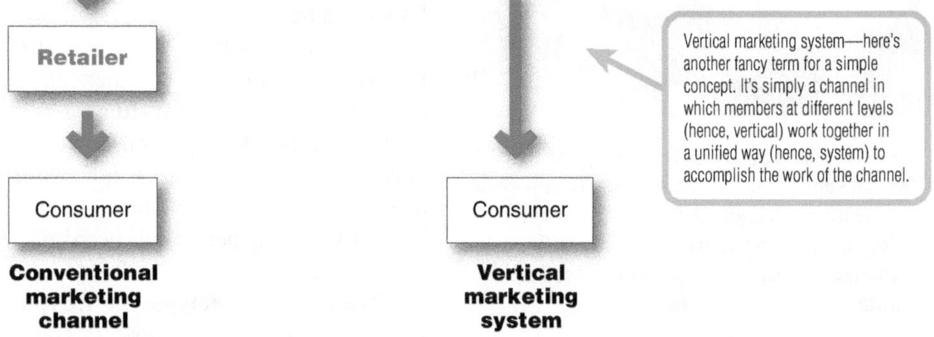

contracts with them, or wields so much power that they must all cooperate. The VMS can be dominated by the producer, the wholesaler, or the retailer.

We look now at three major types of VMSs: *corporate, contractual*, and *administered*. Each uses a different means for setting up leadership and power in the channel.

Corporate VMS

A **corporate VMS** integrates successive stages of production and distribution under single ownership. Coordination and conflict management are attained through regular organizational channels. For example, Sherwin-Williams, the largest U.S. coatings manufacturer, sells its Sherwin-Williams-branded products exclusively through more than 4,000 company-owned retail paint stores. And grocery giant Kroger owns and operates 38 manufacturing plants—17 dairies, 6 bakery plants, 5 grocery plants, 2 frozen dough plants, 2 beverage plants, 2 cheese plants, 2 ice cream plants, and 2 meat plants—that give it factory-to-store channel control over 40 percent of the more than 11,000 private-label items found on its shelves.[3]

Corporate VMS
A vertical marketing system that combines successive stages of production and distribution under single ownership—channel leadership is established through common ownership.

Contractual VMS
A vertical marketing system in which independent firms at different levels of production and distribution join together through contracts.

Franchise organization
A contractual vertical marketing system in which a channel member, called a franchisor, links several stages in the production-distribution process.

Integrating the entire distribution chain—from its own design and manufacturing operations to distribution through its own managed stores—has turned Spanish clothing chain Zara into the world's fastest-growing fast-fashion retailer:[4]

> In recent years, fashion retailer Zara has attracted an army of loyal shoppers swarming to buy its "cheap chic"—stylish designs that resemble those of big-name fashion houses but at moderate prices. However, Zara's amazing success comes not just from *what* it sells but from *how fast* its cutting-edge distribution system *delivers* what it sells. Zara delivers fast fashion—*really* fast fashion. Thanks to vertical integration, Zara can take a new fashion concept through design, manufacturing, and store-shelf placement in as little as three weeks, whereas competitors such as H&M, Gap, or Benetton often take six months or more. And the resulting low costs let Zara offer the very latest midmarket chic at downmarket prices.
>
> Speedy design and distribution allow Zara to introduce a copious supply of new fashions—at three times the rate of competitor introductions. Then Zara's distribution system supplies its stores with small shipments of new merchandise twice a week, compared with competing chains' outlets, which get large shipments seasonally, usually just four to six times per year. The combination of a large number of timely new fashions delivered in frequent small batches gives Zara stores a continually updated merchandise mix that brings customers back more often. Fast turnover also results in less outdated and discounted merchandise. Rather than guessing about tomorrow's fashions, Zara can wait to see what customers are actually buying and then make that.

Franchising systems: Through franchising, Two Men and a Truck—"Movers Who Care"—grew quickly from two high school students with a pickup truck to an international network of 330 franchise locations that's experienced record growth over the past six years.

Two Men and a Truck International

Contractual VMS

A **contractual VMS** consists of independent firms at different levels of production and distribution that join together through contracts to obtain more economies or sales impact than each could achieve alone. Channel members coordinate their activities and manage conflict through contractual agreements.

The **franchise organization** is the most common type of contractual relationship. In this system, a channel member called a *franchisor* links several stages in the production-distribution process. In the United States alone, some 780,000 franchise outlets account for more than $889 billion of economic output. Industry analysts estimate that a new franchise outlet opens somewhere in the United States every eight minutes and that about one out of every 12 retail business outlets is a franchised business.[5]

Almost every kind of business has been franchised—from motels and fast-food restaurants to dental centers and dating services, from wedding consultants and handyman services to funeral homes, fitness centers, and moving services. For example, through franchising, Two Men and a Truck moving services—"Movers Who Care"—grew quickly from two high school students looking to make extra money with a pickup truck to an international network of 330 franchise locations that's experienced record growth over the past six years and completed more than 5.5 million moves.[6]

There are three types of franchises. The first type is the *manufacturer-sponsored retailer franchise system*—for example, Ford and its network of independent franchised dealers. The second type is the *manufacturer-sponsored wholesaler franchise system*—Coca-Cola licenses bottlers (wholesalers) in various world markets that buy Coca-Cola syrup concentrate and then bottle and sell the finished product to retailers locally. The third type is the *service-firm-sponsored retailer franchise system*—for example, Burger King and its nearly 12,100 franchisee-operated restaurants around the world. Other examples can be found in everything from auto rentals (Hertz, Avis), apparel retailers (The Athlete's Foot, Plato's Closet), and motels (Holiday Inn, Hampton Inn) to supplemental education (Huntington Learning Center, Mathnasium) and personal services (Great Clips, Mr. Handyman, Anytime Fitness).

The fact that most consumers cannot tell the difference between contractual and corporate VMSs shows how successfully the contractual organizations compete with corporate chains. The next chapter presents a fuller discussion of the various contractual VMSs.

Administered VMS
A vertical marketing system that coordinates successive stages of production and distribution through the size and power of one of the parties.

Horizontal marketing system
A channel arrangement in which two or more companies at one level join together to follow a new marketing opportunity.

Administered VMS

In an **administered VMS**, leadership is assumed not through common ownership or contractual ties but through the size and power of one or a few dominant channel members. Manufacturers of a top brand can obtain strong trade cooperation and support from resellers. For example, GE, P&G, and Apple can command unusual cooperation from many resellers regarding displays, shelf space, promotions, and price policies. In turn, large retailers such as Walmart, Home Depot, Kroger, and Walgreens can exert strong influence on the many manufacturers that supply the products they sell.

For example, in the normal push and pull between Walmart and its consumer goods suppliers, giant Walmart—the biggest grocer in the United States with nearly 30 percent share of all U.S. grocery sales—usually gets its way. Take supplier Clorox, for instance. Although The Clorox Company's strong consumer brand preference gives it significant negotiating power, Walmart simply holds more cards. Sales to Walmart make up 26 percent of Clorox's sales, whereas Clorox products account for only one-third of 1 percent of Walmart's purchases, making Walmart by far the dominant partner. Things get even worse for Cal-Maine Foods and its Eggland's Best brand, which relies on Walmart for nearly one-third of its sales but tallies only about one-tenth of 1 percent of Walmart's volume. For such brands, maintaining a strong relationship with the giant retailer is crucial.[7]

Horizontal marketing systems: General Mills and Nestlé operate a joint venture—Cereal Partners Worldwide—that markets General Mills Big G cereal brands outside North America.

Sonny Meddle/Rex Features/Presselect/Alamy

Horizontal Marketing Systems

Another channel development is the **horizontal marketing system**, in which two or more companies at one level join together to follow a new marketing opportunity. By working together, companies can combine their financial, production, or marketing resources to accomplish more than any one company could alone.

Companies might join forces with competitors or noncompetitors. They might work with each other on a temporary or permanent basis, or they may create a separate company. For example, competing big media companies Fox Broadcasting, Disney-ABC, and NBCUniversal (Comcast) jointly own and market Hulu, the successful online subscription service that provides on-demand streaming of TV shows, movies, and other video content. Together, they compete more effectively against digital streaming competitors such as Netflix. Walmart partners with noncompetitor McDonald's to place "express" versions of McDonald's restaurants in Walmart stores. McDonald's benefits from Walmart's heavy store traffic, and Walmart keeps hungry shoppers from needing to go elsewhere to eat.

Such channel arrangements also work well globally. For example, competitors General Mills and Nestlé operate a joint venture—Cereal Partners Worldwide—to market General Mills Big G cereal brands in 130 countries outside North America. General Mills supplies a kitchen cabinet full of quality cereal brands, whereas Nestlé contributes its extensive international distribution channels and local market knowledge. The 25-year-old alliance produces $1.1 billion in revenues for General Mills.[8]

Multichannel Distribution Systems

Multichannel distribution system
A distribution system in which a single firm sets up two or more marketing channels to reach one or more customer segments.

In the past, many companies used a single channel to sell to a single market or market segment. Today, with the proliferation of customer segments and channel possibilities, more and more companies have adopted **multichannel distribution systems**. Such multichannel marketing occurs when a single firm sets up two or more marketing channels to reach one or more customer segments.

>> **Figure 10.4** shows a multichannel marketing system. In the figure, the producer sells directly to consumer segment 1 using catalogs, online, and mobile channels and reaches consumer segment 2 through retailers. It sells indirectly to business segment 1 through distributors and dealers and to business segment 2 through its own sales force.

These days, almost every large company and many small ones distribute through multiple channels. For example, John Deere sells its familiar green-and-yellow lawn and garden tractors, mowers, and outdoor power products to consumers and commercial users through several channels, including John Deere retailers, Lowe's home improvement stores, and online. It sells and services its tractors, combines, planters, and other agricultural equipment through its premium John Deere dealer network. And it sells large construction and forestry equipment through selected large, full-service John Deere dealers and their sales forces.

Multichannel distribution systems offer many advantages to companies facing large and complex markets. With each new channel, the company expands its sales and market coverage and gains opportunities to tailor its products and services to the specific needs of diverse customer segments. But such multichannel systems are harder to control, and they can generate conflict as more channels compete for customers and sales. For example, when John Deere first began selling selected consumer products through Lowe's home improvement stores, many of its independent dealers complained loudly. To avoid such conflicts in its online marketing channels, the company routes all of its online sales to John Deere dealers.

Changing Channel Organization

Disintermediation
The cutting out of marketing channel intermediaries by product or service producers or the displacement of traditional resellers by radical new types of intermediaries.

Changes in technology and the explosive growth of direct and online marketing are having a profound impact on the nature and design of marketing channels. One major trend is toward **disintermediation**—a big term with a clear message and important consequences.

>> Figure 10.4 Multichannel Distribution System

Most large companies distribute through multiple channels. For example, you could buy a familiar green-and-yellow John Deere lawn tractor from a neighborhood John Deere dealer or from Lowe's. A large farm or forestry business would buy larger John Deere equipment from a premium full-service John Deere dealer and its sales force.

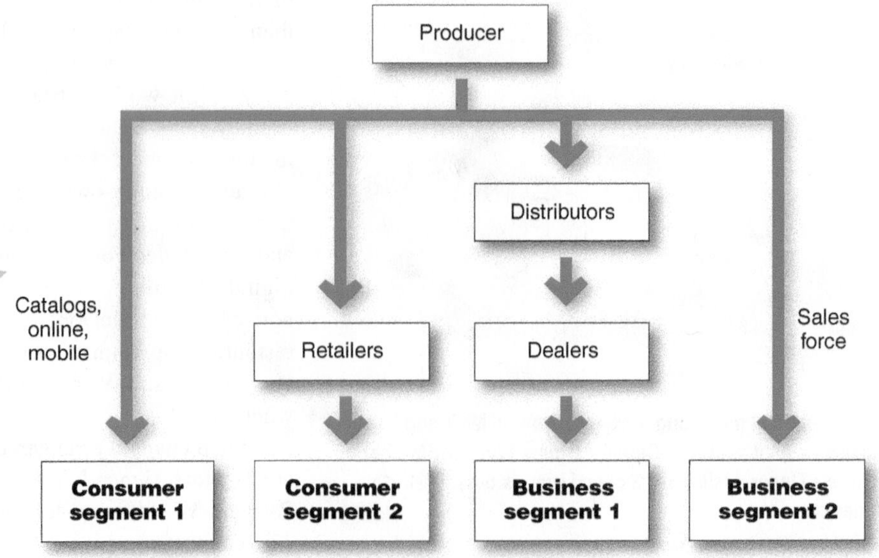

Disintermediation occurs when product or service producers cut out intermediaries and go directly to final buyers or when radically new types of channel intermediaries displace traditional ones.

Thus, in many industries, traditional intermediaries are dropping by the wayside, as is the case with online marketers taking business from traditional brick-and-mortar retailers. For example, online music download services such as iTunes and Amazon MP3 have pretty much put traditional music-store retailers out of business. » In turn, streaming music services such as Spotify and Vevo are now disintermediating digital download services—digital downloads peaked last year while music streaming increased 32 percent.

» **Disintermediation: Streaming music services such as Spotify are rapidly disintermediating both traditional music-store retailers and even music download services such as iTunes.**

Dado Ruvic/Reuters/Corbis

Disintermediation presents both opportunities and problems for producers and resellers. Channel innovators who find new ways to add value in the channel can displace traditional resellers and reap the rewards. In turn, traditional intermediaries must continue to innovate to avoid being swept aside. For example, when Netflix pioneered online DVD-by-mail video rentals, it sent traditional brick-and-mortar video stores such as Blockbuster into ruin. Then Netflix itself faced disintermediation threats from an even hotter channel—video streaming. But instead of simply watching developments, Netflix has led them (see Marketing at Work 10.1).

Similarly, superstore booksellers Borders and Barnes & Noble pioneered huge book selections and low prices, shutting down most small independent bookstores. Then along came Amazon.com, which threatened even the largest brick-and-mortar bookstores. Amazon.com almost single-handedly bankrupted Borders in less than 10 years. Now, both offline and online sellers of physical books are being threatened by digital book downloads and e-readers. Rather than yielding to digital developments, however, Amazon.com is leading them with its highly successful Kindle e-readers and tablets. By contrast, Barnes & Noble—the giant that put so many independent bookstores out of business—was a latecomer with its struggling Nook e-reader and now finds itself locked in a battle for survival.[9]

Like resellers, to remain competitive, product and service producers must develop new channel opportunities, such as the Internet and other direct channels. However, developing these new channels often brings them into direct competition with their established channels, resulting in conflict. To ease this problem, companies often look for ways to make going direct a plus for the entire channel.

For example, Volvo Car Group (now owned by Chinese car maker Geeley) recently announced plans to start selling Volvo vehicles online in all of its markets. Some 80 percent of Volvo buyers already shop online for other goods, so cars seem like a natural extension. Few auto makers have tried selling directly, with the exception of Tesla, which sells its all-electric cars online, bypassing dealers altogether. Other car companies worry that selling directly would alienate their independent dealer networks. "If you say e-commerce, initially dealers get nervous," says Volvo's head of marketing. So, to avoid channel conflicts, Volvo will pass all online sales through established dealers for delivery. In that way, boosting sales through direct marketing will benefit both Volvo and its channel partners.[10]

LINKING THE CONCEPTS

Stop here for a moment and apply the distribution channel concepts we've discussed so far.

- Compare the Zara and Ford channels. Draw a diagram that shows the types of intermediaries in each channel. What kind of channel system does each company use?
- What are the roles and responsibilities of the members in each channel? How well do these channel members work together toward overall channel success?

MARKETING AT WORK 10.1

Netflix: Disintermediate or Be Disintermediated

Baseball great Yogi Berra, known more for his mangled phrasing than for his baseball prowess, once said, "The future ain't what it used to be." For Netflix, the world's largest video subscription service, no matter how you say it, figuring out the future is challenging and a bit scary. Netflix faces dramatic changes in how video entertainment will be distributed. The question is: Will Netflix be among the disintermediators or among the disintermediated?

Time and again, Netflix has innovated its way to the top in the distribution of video entertainment. In the early 2000s, Netflix's revolutionary DVD-by-mail service put all but the most powerful movie-rental stores out of business. In 2007, Netflix's then-groundbreaking move into digital streaming once again revolutionized how people accessed movies and other video content. Now, with Netflix leading the pack, video distribution has become a roiling pot of emerging technologies and high-tech competitors, one that offers both mind-bending opportunities and stomach-churning risks.

Just ask Blockbuster. Less than a decade ago, the giant brick-and-mortar movie-rental chain flat-out owned the industry. Then along came Netflix, the fledgling DVD-by-mail service. First thousands, then millions, of subscribers were drawn to Netflix's innovative distribution model. In 2010, as Netflix surged, once-mighty Blockbuster fell into bankruptcy.

The Blockbuster riches-to-rags disintermediation story underscores the turmoil that typifies today's video distribution business. In only the past few years, a glut of video access options has materialized. At the same time that Netflix ascended and Blockbuster plunged, Coinstar's Redbox came out of nowhere to build a novel national network of $1-a-day DVD-rental kiosks. Then high-tech start-ups such as Hulu—with its high-quality, ad-supported free access to movies and current TV shows—began pushing digital streaming via the Internet.

All along the way, Netflix has acted boldly to stay ahead of the competition. For example, by 2007, Netflix had mailed out its one-billionth DVD. But rather than rest on success, Netflix and its CEO, Reed Hastings, set their sights on a then-revolutionary new video distribution model: Deliver Netflix to any and every Internet-connected screen—from laptops to Internet-ready TVs to smartphones and other Wi-Fi–enabled devices. Netflix launched a new Watch Instantly service, which let members stream movies to their computers as part of their monthly fee, even if it came at the expense of the company's still-hot DVD-by-mail business.

Although Netflix didn't pioneer digital streaming, it poured resources into improving the technology and building the largest streaming library. It built a huge subscriber base, and sales and profits soared. With its massive physical DVD library and a streaming library of more than 20,000 high-definition movies accessible via 200 different Internet-ready devices, it seemed that nothing could stop Netflix.

But Netflix's stunning success drew a slew of resourceful competitors. Video giants such as Google's YouTube and Apple's iTunes began renting movie downloads, and Hulu introduced subscription-based Hulu Plus. To stay ahead, even to survive, Netflix needed to keep the innovation pedal to the metal. So in the summer of 2011, in an ambitious but risky move, CEO Hastings made an all-in bet on digital streaming. He split off Netflix's still-thriving DVD-by-mail service into a separate business named Qwikster and required separate subscriptions for DVD rentals and streaming (at a startling 60 percent price increase for customers using both). The Netflix name would now stand for nothing but digital streaming, which would be the primary focus of the company's future growth.

Although perhaps visionary, Netflix's abrupt changes didn't sit well with customers. Some 800,000 subscribers dropped the service, and Netflix's stock price plummeted by almost two-thirds. Within only weeks, Netflix admitted its blunder and reversed its decision to set up a separate Qwikster operation. Despite the setback, however, Netflix retained its separate, higher pricing for DVDs by mail. The company rebounded quickly, soon replacing all of its lost subscribers and then some. What's more, with a 60 percent higher price, revenues and profits rose as well. Netflix's stock price was once again skyrocketing.

Now more than ever, Netflix's focus is on streaming video. Although customers can still access Netflix's world's-biggest DVD library, the DVD operation is now located at a separate DVD.Netflix Web site, with a separate subscription fee. Nearly

» Netflix's innovative distribution strategy: From DVDs by mail to Watch Instantly to video streaming on almost any device, Netflix has stayed ahead of the howling pack by doing what it does best—revolutionize distribution. What's next?

Mike Blake/Reuters

80 percent of Netflix's revenues now come from streaming. Its current 62 million paid subscribers stream an astounding 3.3 billion hours of movies and TV programs every month. On an average weeknight, Netflix commands more than a third of all Internet traffic in North American homes.

Despite its continuing success, Netflix knows that it can't rest its innovation machine. Competition continues to move at a blurring rate. For example, Amazon's Prime Instant Video offers streaming of thousands of movies and TV shows to Amazon Prime members at no extra cost. Google has moved beyond its YouTube rental service with Google Play, an all-media entertainment portal for movies, music, e-books, and apps. Comcast offers Xfinity Streampix, which lets subscribers stream older movies and television programs via their TVs, laptops, tablets, or smartphones. And Apple and Samsung are creating smoother integration with streaming content via smart TVs.

Moving ahead, as the industry settles into streaming as the main delivery model, content—not just delivery—will be a key to distancing Netflix from the rest of the pack. Given its head start, Netflix remains well ahead in the content race. However, Amazon, Hulu Plus, and other competitors are working feverishly to sign contracts with big movie and TV content providers. But so is Netflix. It recently scored a big win with a Disney exclusive—soon, Netflix will be the only place viewers can stream Disney's deep catalog and new releases from Walt Disney Animation, Marvel, Pixar, and Lucasfilm.

But as content-licensing deals with movie and television studios become harder to get, in yet another innovative video distribution twist, Netflix and its competitors are now developing their own original content at a feverish pace. Once again, Netflix appears to have the upper hand. For example, it led the way with the smash hit *House of Cards,* a U.S. version of a hit British political drama series produced by Hollywood bigwigs David Fincher and Kevin Spacey. Based on its huge success with *House of Cards,* Netflix developed a number of other original series, including *Hemlock Grove, Lillyhammer, Marco Polo,* and *Orange Is the New Black*, its most successful release to date. Such efforts have left the rest of the video industry scrambling to keep up. And Netflix is just getting started. It plans to invest $300 million a year in developing new original content, adding at least five original titles annually.

Thus, from DVDs by mail, to Watch Instantly, to video streaming on almost any device, to developing original content, Netflix has stayed ahead of the howling pack by doing what it does best—innovate and revolutionize distribution. What's next? No one really knows. But one thing seems certain: Whatever's coming, if Netflix doesn't lead the change, it risks being left behind—and quickly. Netflix must continue to disintermediate its own distribution model before competitors can. As Netflix's slower-moving competitors have learned the hard way, it's disintermedi*ate* or be disintermediat*ed*.[i]

[i] See Susan Young, "2014 SUCCESS Achiever of the Year: Reed Hastings," SUCCESS, February 10, 2015, www.success.com/article/2014-success-achiever-of-the-year-reed-hastings; Brian Stelter, "Netflix Grabs a Slice of Star Wars," *CNNMoney,* February 13, 2014, http://money.cnn.com/2014/02/13/technology/netflix-star-wars/; Mike Snider, "Netflix, Adding Customers and Profits, Will Raise Prices," *USA Today,* April 22, 2014, www.usatoday.com/story/tech/2014/04/21/netflix-results/7965613/; Michael Leidtke, "With 'House of Cards,' Netflix Got a Winning Hand," *Boston Globe,* February 27, 2015, www.bostonglobe.com/business/2015/02/27/house-cards-dealt-netflix-winning-hand/M5kBWc916HP1XMQyjdAd8N/story.html; Lisa Richwine, "Netflix Beats Forecasts with 62 Million Streaming Subscribers," *Reuters,* April 15, 2015, http://www.reuters.com/article/2015/04/15/us-netflix-results-idUSKBN0N62HC20150415; and annual reports and information at www.netflix.com, accessed October 2015.

Channel Design Decisions

Author Comment
Like everything else in marketing, good channel design begins with analyzing customer needs. Remember, marketing channels are really *customer value delivery networks.*

We now look at several channel design decisions manufacturers face. In designing marketing channels, manufacturers struggle between what is ideal and what is practical. A new firm with limited capital usually starts by selling in a limited market area. In this case, deciding on the best channels might not be a problem: The problem might simply be how to convince one or a few good intermediaries to handle the line.

If successful, the new firm can branch out to new markets through existing intermediaries. In smaller markets, the firm might sell directly to retailers; in larger markets, it might sell through distributors. In one part of the country, it might grant exclusive franchises; in another, it might sell through all available outlets. Then it might add an online store that sells directly to hard-to-reach customers. In this way, channel systems often evolve to meet market opportunities and conditions.

Marketing channel design
Designing effective marketing channels by analyzing customer needs, setting channel objectives, identifying major channel alternatives, and evaluating those alternatives.

For maximum effectiveness, however, channel analysis and decision making should be more purposeful. **Marketing channel design** calls for analyzing consumer needs, setting channel objectives, identifying major channel alternatives, and evaluating those alternatives.

Analyzing Consumer Needs

As noted previously, marketing channels are part of the overall *customer value delivery network.* Each channel member and level adds value for the customer. Thus, designing the marketing channel starts with finding out what target consumers want from the channel. Do consumers want to buy nearby, or are they willing to travel to more centralized locations? Would customers rather buy in person, by phone, or online? Do they value breadth of assortment, or do they prefer specialization? Do consumers want many add-on services (delivery, installation, repairs), or will they obtain these services elsewhere? The faster the delivery, the greater the assortment provided, and the more add-on services supplied, the greater the channel's service level.

Providing the fastest delivery, the greatest assortment, and the most services, however, may not be possible, practical, or desired. The company and its channel members may not have the resources or skills needed to provide all the desired services. Also, higher levels of service result in higher costs for the channel and higher prices for consumers. The success of modern discount retailing shows that consumers often accept lower service levels in exchange for lower prices.

>> Meeting customers' channel service needs: Ace Hardware positions itself as "The helpful place." To loyal Ace customers, the convenience of smaller stores and the personal service they receive are well worth Ace's somewhat higher prices.

ZUMA Press, Inc/Alamy

Many companies, however, position themselves on higher service levels, and customers willingly pay the higher prices. >> For example, your local independently owned Ace Hardware store probably provides more personalized service, a more convenient location, and less shopping hassle than the nearest huge Home Depot or Lowe's store. As a result, it also charges somewhat higher prices. To loyal Ace customers, the convenience and higher service levels are well worth the price. Ace positions itself as "The helpful place." Says the company: "While others have become large and impersonal, at Ace, we've remained small and very personal. That's why we say a visit to Ace is like a visit to your neighbor." In his review on Yelp, one loyal Ace customer agrees:[11]

> I have become a convert from Lowe's/Home Depot to Ace for two reasons. For one, it's much easier to get in and out of and it's closer to my house. Second, and most importantly, upon entering the store a knowledgeable employee will greet me and ask how they may help. Then they will lead me to where I need to go and boom, I'm done. At Lowe's I end up wandering around the caverns of that building—back and forth, is it here? down there? did I pass it?—until I'm exhausted. At Ace, the time and energy saved more than makes up for an increase in cost. Plus, they're very friendly.

Thus, companies must balance consumer needs not only against the feasibility and costs of meeting these needs but also against customer price preferences.

Setting Channel Objectives

Companies should state their marketing channel objectives in terms of targeted levels of customer service. Usually, a company can identify several segments wanting different levels of service. The company should decide which segments to serve and the best channels to use in each case. In each segment, the company wants to minimize the total channel cost of meeting customer service requirements.

The company's channel objectives are also influenced by the nature of the company, its products, its marketing intermediaries, its competitors, and the environment. For example, the company's size and financial situation determine which marketing functions it can handle itself and which it must give to intermediaries. Companies selling perishable products, for example, may require more direct marketing to avoid delays and too much handling.

In some cases, a company may want to compete in or near the same outlets that carry competitors' products. For example, Maytag and other appliance makers want their products displayed alongside competing brands to facilitate comparison shopping. In other cases, companies may avoid the channels used by competitors. The Pampered Chef, for instance, sells high-quality kitchen tools directly to consumers through its corps of more than 60,000 consultants worldwide rather than going head-to-head with other kitchen tool makers for scarce positions in retail stores. And Stella & Dot sells quality jewelry through more than 30,000 independent reps—called stylists—who hold Tupperware-like in-home "trunk shows."[12] GEICO and USAA primarily market insurance and banking products to consumers via phone and Internet channels rather than through agents.

Finally, environmental factors such as economic conditions and legal constraints may affect channel objectives and design. For example, in a depressed economy, producers will want to distribute their goods in the most economical way, using shorter channels and dropping unneeded services that add to the final price of the goods.

Identifying Major Alternatives

When the company has defined its channel objectives, it should next identify its major channel alternatives in terms of the *types* of intermediaries, the *number* of intermediaries, and the *responsibilities* of each channel member.

Types of Intermediaries

A firm should identify the types of channel members available to carry out its channel work. Most companies face many channel member choices. For example, until recently, Dell sold directly to final consumers and business buyers only through its sophisticated phone and online marketing channel. It also sold directly to large corporate, institutional, and government buyers using its direct sales force. However, to reach more consumers and match competitors such as Samsung and Apple, Dell now sells indirectly through retailers such as Best Buy, Staples, and Walmart. It also sells indirectly through *value-added resellers*, independent distributors and dealers that develop computer systems and applications tailored to the special needs of small and medium-sized business customers.

Using many types of resellers in a channel provides both benefits and drawbacks. For example, by selling through retailers and value-added resellers in addition to its own direct channels, Dell can reach more and different kinds of buyers. However, these are more difficult to manage and control. In addition, the direct and indirect channels compete with each other for many of the same customers, causing potential conflict. In fact, Dell often finds itself "stuck in the middle," with its direct sales reps complaining about competition from retail stores, whereas its value-added resellers complain that the direct sales reps are undercutting their business.

Number of Marketing Intermediaries

Companies must also determine the number of channel members to use at each level. Three strategies are available: intensive distribution, exclusive distribution, and selective distribution. Producers of convenience products and common raw materials typically seek **intensive distribution**—a strategy in which they stock their products in as many outlets as possible. These products must be available where and when consumers want them. For example, toothpaste, candy, and other similar items are sold in millions of outlets to provide maximum brand exposure and consumer convenience. Kraft, Coca-Cola, Kimberly-Clark, and other consumer goods companies distribute their products in this way.

Intensive distribution
Stocking the product in as many outlets as possible.

By contrast, some producers purposely limit the number of intermediaries handling their products. The extreme form of this practice is **exclusive distribution**, in which the producer gives only a limited number of dealers the exclusive right to distribute its products in their territories. Exclusive distribution is often found in the distribution of luxury brands. Breitling watches—positioned as "Instruments for Professionals" and selling at prices from $5,000 to more than $100,000—are sold by only a few authorized dealers in any given market area. For example, the brand sells through only one jeweler in Chicago and only six jewelers in the entire state of Illinois. Exclusive distribution enhances Breitling's distinctive positioning and earns greater dealer support and customer service.

Exclusive distribution
Giving a limited number of dealers the exclusive right to distribute the company's products in their territories.

Between intensive and exclusive distribution lies **selective distribution**—the use of more than one but fewer than all of the intermediaries who are willing to carry a

Selective distribution
The use of more than one but fewer than all of the intermediaries that are willing to carry the company's products.

Selective distribution: STIHL sells its chain saws, blowers, hedge trimmers, and other products through a select corps of independent hardware and lawn and garden retailers. "We count on them every day and so can you."

STIHL Incorporated

company's products. Most consumer electronics, furniture, and home appliance brands are distributed in this manner. For example, outdoor power equipment maker STIHL doesn't sell its chain saws, blowers, hedge trimmers, and other products through mass merchandisers such as Lowe's, Home Depot, or Sears. Instead, it sells through a select corps of independent hardware and lawn and garden dealers. By using selective distribution, STIHL can develop good working relationships with dealers and expect a better-than-average selling effort. Exclusive distribution also enhances the STIHL brand's image and allows for higher markups resulting from greater value-added dealer service. "We count on our select dealers every day and so can you," says one STIHL ad.

Responsibilities of Channel Members

The producer and intermediaries need to agree on the terms and responsibilities of each channel member. They should agree on price policies, conditions of sale, territory rights, and the specific services to be performed by each party. The producer should establish a list price and a fair set of discounts for the intermediaries. It must define each channel member's territory, and it should be careful about where it places new resellers.

Mutual services and duties need to be spelled out carefully, especially in franchise and exclusive distribution channels. For example, McDonald's provides franchisees with promotional support, a record-keeping system, training at Hamburger University, and general management assistance. In turn, franchisees must meet company standards for physical facilities and food quality, cooperate with new promotion programs, provide requested information, and buy specified food products.

Evaluating the Major Alternatives

Suppose a company has identified several channel alternatives and wants to select the one that will best satisfy its long-run objectives. Each alternative should be evaluated against economic, control, and adaptability criteria.

Using *economic criteria*, a company compares the likely sales, costs, and profitability of different channel alternatives. What will be the investment required by each channel alternative, and what returns will result? The company must also consider *control issues*. Using intermediaries usually means giving them some control over the marketing of the product, and some intermediaries take more control than others. Other things being equal, the company prefers to keep as much control as possible. Finally, the company must apply *adaptability criteria*. Channels often involve long-term commitments, yet the company wants to keep the channel flexible so that it can adapt to environmental changes. Thus, to be considered, a channel involving long-term commitments should be greatly superior on economic and control grounds.

Designing International Distribution Channels

International marketers face many additional complexities in designing their channels. Each country has its own unique distribution system that has evolved over time and changes very slowly. These channel systems can vary widely from country to country. Thus, global marketers must usually adapt their channel strategies to the existing structures within each country.

In some markets, the distribution system is complex, competitive, and hard to penetrate. For example, many Western companies find India's distribution system difficult to navigate. Large discount, department store, and supermarket retailers still account for only a small portion of the huge Indian market. Instead, most shopping is done in small neighborhood stores called *kirana* shops, run by their owners and popular because they offer personal service and credit. In addition, large Western retailers have difficulty dealing with India's complex government regulations and poor infrastructure.

>> International distribution: In the huge Indian market, most shopping is done in small neighborhood stores call *kirana* shops, run by their owners and popular because they offer personal service and credit.

Frank Bienewald/imageBROKER/Alamy

Distribution systems in developing countries may be scattered, inefficient, or altogether lacking. For example, China's rural markets are highly decentralized, made of many distinct submarkets, each with its own subculture. And, because of inadequate distribution systems, most companies can profitably access only the small portion of China's massive population located in affluent cities. China's distribution system is so fragmented that logistics costs to wrap, bundle, load, unload, sort, reload, and transport goods amount to 18 percent of the nation's GDP, far higher than in most other countries. (In comparison, U.S. logistics costs account for about 8.5 percent of the nation's GDP.) After years of effort, even Walmart executives admit that they have been unable to assemble an efficient supply chain in China.[13]

Sometimes local conditions can greatly influence how a company distributes products in global markets. For example, in low-income neighborhoods in Brazil where consumers have limited access to supermarkets, Nestlé supplements its distribution with thousands of self-employed salespeople who sell Nestlé products from refrigerated carts door to door. And in big cities in Asia and Africa, where crowded streets and high real estate costs make drive-thrus impractical, fast-food restaurants such as McDonald's and KFC offer delivery. Legions of motorbike delivery drivers in colorful uniforms dispense Big Macs and buckets of chicken to customers who call in. More than 30 percent of McDonald's total sales in Egypt and 12 percent of its Singapore sales come from delivery. Similarly, for KFC, delivery accounts for nearly half of all sales in Kuwait and a third of sales in Egypt.[14]

Thus, international marketers face a wide range of channel alternatives. Designing efficient and effective channel systems between and within various country markets poses a difficult challenge. We discuss international distribution decisions further in Chapter 15.

Author Comment
Now it's time to implement the chosen channel design and work with selected channel members to manage and motivate them.

Channel Management Decisions

Once the company has reviewed its channel alternatives and determined the best channel design, it must implement and manage the chosen channel. **Marketing channel management** calls for selecting, managing, and motivating individual channel members and evaluating their performance over time.

Marketing channel management
Selecting, managing, and motivating individual channel members and evaluating their performance over time.

Selecting Channel Members

Producers vary in their ability to attract qualified marketing intermediaries. Some producers have no trouble signing up channel members. For example, when Toyota first introduced its Lexus line in the United States, it had no trouble attracting new dealers. In fact, it had to turn down many would-be resellers.

At the other extreme are producers that have to work hard to line up enough qualified intermediaries. For example, when Timex first tried to sell its inexpensive watches through regular jewelry stores, most jewelry stores refused to carry them. The company then managed to get its watches into mass-merchandise outlets. This turned out to be a wise decision because of the rapid growth of mass merchandising.

Even established brands may have difficulty gaining and keeping their desired distribution, especially when dealing with powerful resellers. For example, you won't find Marlboro, Winston, Camel, or any other cigarette brand at your local CVS pharmacy store. >> CVS Caremark recently announced that it will no longer sell cigarettes in its stores, despite the resulting loss of more than $2 billion in annual sales. "This is the right thing to do," says the company. "We came to the decision that cigarettes and providing healthcare

Selecting channels: Even established brands may have difficulty keeping desired channels. CVS Caremark's decision to stop selling cigarettes leaves tobacco companies seeking new sales channels.

CVS Caremark Corporation

just don't go together in the same setting." Target dropped cigarettes nearly 20 years ago, and public advocates are pressuring Walmart to do the same. If the major discount stores and other drugstore chains such as Walgreens and Rite Aid follow suit, Philip Morris, R.J. Reynolds, and other tobacco companies will have to seek new channels for selling their brands.[15]

When selecting intermediaries, the company should determine what characteristics distinguish the better ones. It will want to evaluate each channel member's years in business, other lines carried, location, growth and profit record, cooperativeness, and reputation.

Managing and Motivating Channel Members

Once selected, channel members must be continuously managed and motivated to do their best. The company must sell not only *through* the intermediaries but also *to* and *with* them. Most companies see their intermediaries as first-line customers and partners. They practice strong *partner relationship management* to forge long-term partnerships with channel members. This creates a value delivery system that meets the needs of both the company *and* its marketing partners.

In managing its channels, a company must convince suppliers and distributors that they can succeed better by working together as a part of a cohesive value delivery system. Companies must work in close harmony with others in the channel to find better ways to bring value to customers. Thus, Amazon and P&G work closely to accomplish their joint goal of selling consumer package goods profitably online. Through its Vendor Flex program, Amazon operates within P&G warehouses to reduce distribution costs and speed up delivery, benefiting both the partnering companies and the customers they jointly serve (see Marketing at Work 10.2).

Similarly, heavy-equipment manufacturer Caterpillar works hand-in-hand with its superb dealer network—together they dominate the world's construction, mining, and logging equipment business:

> Heavy-equipment manufacturer Caterpillar produces innovative, high-quality industrial equipment products. But ask anyone at Caterpillar, and they'll tell you that the most important reason for Caterpillar's dominance is its outstanding distribution network of 189 independent dealers in more than 180 countries. Dealers are the ones on the front line. Once the product leaves the factory, the dealers take over. They're the ones that customers see. So rather than selling to or through its dealers, Caterpillar treats dealers as inside partners. When a big piece of Caterpillar equipment breaks down, customers know that they can count on both Caterpillar and its dealer network for support. A strong dealer network makes for a strong Caterpillar, and the other way around. On a deeper level, dealers play a vital role in almost every aspect of Caterpillar's operations, from product design and delivery to service and support. As a result of its close partnership with dealers, the big Cat is purring. Caterpillar dominates the world's markets for heavy construction, mining, and logging equipment. Its familiar yellow tractors, crawlers, loaders, bulldozers, and trucks capture well over a third of the worldwide heavy-equipment business, more than twice that of number-two Komatsu.

Many companies are now installing integrated high-tech partnership relationship management (PRM) systems to coordinate their whole-channel marketing efforts. Just as they use customer relationship management (CRM) software systems to help manage relationships with important customers, companies can now use PRM and supply chain management (SCM) software to help recruit, train, organize, manage, motivate, and evaluate relationships with channel partners.

MARKETING AT WORK 10.2

Amazon and P&G: Taking Channel Partnering to a New Level

Until recently, if you ordered Bounty paper towels, Pampers diapers, Charmin toilet paper, or any of the dozens of other P&G consumer products from Amazon.com, they probably came to your doorstep by a circuitous distribution route. The paper towels, for example, might well have been produced in P&G's large northeastern Pennsylvania factory and shipped by the trailer-truck load to its nearby Tunkhannock warehouse, where they were unloaded and repacked with other P&G goods and shipped to Amazon's Dinwiddie, Virginia, fulfillment center. At the fulfillment center, they were unloaded and shelved and then finally picked and packed by Amazon employees for shipment to you via UPS, FedEx, or the USPS.

But these days, in a move that could turn consumer package goods distribution upside down, Amazon and P&G are quietly blazing a new, simpler, lower-cost distribution trail for such goods. Now, for example, at the Pennsylvania warehouse, rather than reloading truckloads of P&G products and shipping them to Amazon fulfillment centers, P&G employees simply cart the goods to a fenced-off area inside their own warehouse. The fenced-in area is run by Amazon. From there, Amazon employees pack, label, and ship items directly to customers who've ordered them online. Amazon calls this venture Vendor Flex—and it's revolutionizing how people buy low-priced, low-margin everyday household products.

Amazon's Vendor Flex program offers big potential for both Amazon and supplier–partners like P&G. Americans currently buy only about 2 percent of their nonfood consumer package goods online. Boosting online sales of these staples to 6 percent—the percentage that the Internet now captures of overall retail sales—would give Amazon an additional $10 billion a year in revenues, up from the current $2 billion.

But there's a reason why household staples have lagged behind other kinds of products in online sales. Such goods have long been deemed too bulky or too cheap to justify the high shipping costs involved with Internet selling. To sell household staples profitably online, companies like Amazon and P&G must work together to streamline the distribution process and reduce costs. That's where Vendor Flex comes in.

Vendor Flex takes channel partnering to an entirely new level. Co-locating "in the same tent" creates advantages for both partners. For Amazon, Vendor Flex reduces the costs of storing bulky items, such as diapers and toilet paper, in its own distribution centers, and it frees up space in Amazon's centers for more higher-margin goods. The sharing arrangement lets Amazon extend its consumer package goods selection without building more distribution center space. For example, the P&G warehouse also stocks other popular P&G household brands, from Gillette razors to Pantene shampoo to Tide laundry detergent. Finally, locating at the source guarantees Amazon immediate availability and facilitates quick delivery of P&G products to customers.

P&G also benefits from the Vendor Flex partnership. It saves money by cutting out the costs of transporting goods to Amazon's fulfillment centers, which in turn lets it charge more competitive prices to the e-commerce giant. And although P&G is a superb in-store brand marketer, it is still a relative newcomer to online selling, one of the company's top priorities. By partnering more closely with Amazon, P&G gets Amazon's expert help in moving its brands online.

Amazon considers household staples to be one of its next big frontiers for Internet sales. Its presence inside the P&G Pennsylvania warehouse is just the tip of the iceberg for Vendor Flex. Amazon and P&G quietly began sharing warehouse space three years ago, and the online merchant has set up shop inside at least seven other P&G distribution centers worldwide, including facilities in Japan and Germany. Amazon is also inside or talking with other major consumer goods suppliers—from Kimberly Clark to Georgia Pacific to Seventh Generation—about co-locating distribution facilities. Moreover, Amazon has invested heavily to build an infrastructure for profitably selling all kinds

>> **Partnering in the distribution channel: Under Amazon's Vendor Flex program, P&G and Amazon share warehouse facilities, creating distribution cost and delivery advantages for both partners.**

Raywoo/Fotolia; Grzegorz Knec/Alamy; Grzegorz Knec/Alamy

of everyday household items to consumers online. For example, in late 2010, Amazon acquired Quidsi, the owner of Diapers.com and Soap.com, online retailers of baby products and household essentials. Since the Amazon acquisition, Quidsi has added a half-dozen new sites selling, among other things, toys (YoYo.com), pet supplies (Wag.com), premium beauty products (BeautyBar.com), and home products (Casa.com).

Vendor Flex looks like a win-win for everyone involved—Amazon, P&G, and final consumers. However, the close Amazon–P&G partnership has caused some grumbling among other important channel participants. For example, what about Walmart, P&G's largest customer by far? The giant store retailer is locked in a fierce online battle with Amazon, yet one of its largest suppliers appears to be giving Amazon preferential treatment. At the same time, Amazon's courtship of P&G may upset other important suppliers that compete with P&G on Amazon's site. Both P&G and Amazon must be careful that their close Vendor Flex relationship doesn't damage other important channel partnerships.

More broadly, some analysts assert that even with Vendor Flex, Amazon won't be able to sell products such as paper towels, detergent, or shaving cream profitably online. They reason that the margins on such items are simply too low to cover shipping costs. Amazon is already losing an estimated $1 billion to $2 billion annually on its Amazon Prime shipping program. And, they suggest, if there is money to be made by shipping a heavy jug of Tide or a bulky three-pack of Bounty paper towels from P&G's warehouse to your front door, P&G would have been doing that long ago.

However, such doom-and-gloom predictions seem to overlook recent rapid changes in the distribution landscape, especially in online retailing. Mega-shippers like UPS and FedEx are continuing to drive down small-package delivery times and costs. And Amazon is moving aggressively toward same-day delivery in major market areas, including grocery and related items. The Vendor Flex program seems to align well with such distribution trends.

As for the Amazon–P&G Vendor Flex partnership, it looks like an ideal match for both companies. If P&G wants to be more effective in selling its brands online, what better partner could it have than Amazon, the undisputed master of online retailing? If Amazon wants to be more effective in selling household staples, what better partner could it have than P&G, the acknowledged master of consumer package goods marketing? Together, under Amazon's Vendor Flex, these respective industry leaders can flex their distribution muscles to their own benefit—and to the benefit of the consumers they jointly serve.

Sources: Serena Ng, "Soap Opera: Amazon Moves In with P&G," *Wall Street Journal*, October 15, 2013, p. A1; Andre Mouton, "Amazon Considers 'Co-Creation' with Procter & Gamble," *USA Today*, October 21, 2013, www.usatoday.com/story/tech/2013/10/21/amazon-proctor-gamble-products/3143773/; David Streitfeld, "Amazon to Raise Fees as Revenue Disappoints," *New York Times*, January 31, 2014, p. B1; and Bridget Bergin, "Amazon's Involvement with Manufacturing: When Is It Too Much?" *Manufacturing.net*, September 25, 2014, www.manufacturing.net/blogs/2014/09/amazon%E2%80%99s-involvement-with-manufacturing-when-is-it-too-much.

Evaluating Channel Members

The company must regularly check channel member performance against standards such as sales quotas, average inventory levels, customer delivery time, treatment of damaged and lost goods, cooperation in company promotion and training programs, and services to the customer. The company should recognize and reward intermediaries that are performing well and adding good value for consumers. Those that are performing poorly should be assisted or, as a last resort, replaced.

Finally, companies need to be sensitive to the needs of their channel partners. Those that treat their partners poorly risk not only losing their support but also causing some legal problems. The next section describes various rights and duties pertaining to companies and other channel members.

LINKING THE CONCEPTS

Time for another pause. This time, compare the Caterpillar and KFC channel systems.

- Diagram the Caterpillar and KFC channel systems. How do they compare in terms of channel levels, types of intermediaries, channel member roles and responsibilities, and other characteristics? How well is each system designed?
- Assess how well Caterpillar and KFC have managed and supported their channels. With what results?

Public Policy and Distribution Decisions

For the most part, companies are legally free to develop whatever channel arrangements suit them. In fact, the laws affecting channels seek to prevent the exclusionary tactics of some companies that might keep another company from using a desired channel. Most channel law deals with the mutual rights and duties of channel members once they have formed a relationship.

Many producers and wholesalers like to develop exclusive channels for their products. When the seller allows only certain outlets to carry its products, this strategy is called *exclusive distribution*. When the seller requires that these dealers not handle competitors' products, its strategy is called *exclusive dealing*. Both parties can benefit from exclusive arrangements: The seller obtains more loyal and dependable outlets, and the dealers obtain a steady source of supply and stronger seller support. But exclusive arrangements also exclude other producers from selling to these dealers. This situation brings exclusive dealing contracts under the scope of the Clayton Act of 1914. They are legal as long as they do not substantially lessen competition or tend to create a monopoly and as long as both parties enter into the agreement voluntarily.

Exclusive dealing often includes *exclusive territorial agreements*. The producer may agree not to sell to other dealers in a given area, or the buyer may agree to sell only in its own territory. The first practice is normal under franchise systems as a way to increase dealer enthusiasm and commitment. It is also perfectly legal—a seller has no legal obligation to sell through more outlets than it wishes. The second practice, whereby the producer tries to keep a dealer from selling outside its territory, has become a major legal issue.

Producers of a strong brand sometimes sell it to dealers only if the dealers will take some or all of the rest of its line. This is called *full-line forcing*. Such *tying agreements* are not necessarily illegal, but they violate the Clayton Act if they tend to lessen competition substantially. The practice may prevent consumers from freely choosing among competing suppliers of these other brands.

Finally, producers are free to select their dealers, but their right to terminate dealers is somewhat restricted. In general, sellers can drop dealers "for cause." However, they cannot drop dealers if, for example, the dealers refuse to cooperate in a doubtful legal arrangement, such as exclusive dealing or tying agreements.

Author Comment
Marketers used to call this plain-old "physical distribution." But as these titles suggest, the topic has grown in importance, complexity, and sophistication.

Marketing Logistics and Supply Chain Management

In today's global marketplace, selling a product is sometimes easier than getting it to customers. Companies must decide on the best way to store, handle, and move their products and services so that they are available to customers in the right assortments, at the right time, and in the right place. Logistics effectiveness has a major impact on both customer satisfaction and company costs. Here we consider the nature and importance of logistics management in the supply chain, the goals of the logistics system, major logistics functions, and the need for integrated supply chain management.

Nature and Importance of Marketing Logistics

Marketing logistics (physical distribution)
Planning, implementing, and controlling the physical flow of goods, services, and related information from points of origin to points of consumption to meet customer requirements at a profit.

To some managers, marketing logistics means only trucks and warehouses. But modern logistics is much more than this. **Marketing logistics**—also called **physical distribution**—involves planning, implementing, and controlling the physical flow of goods, services, and related information from points of origin to points of consumption to meet customer requirements at a profit. In short, it involves getting the right product to the right customer in the right place at the right time profitably.

In the past, physical distribution planners typically started with products at the plant and then tried to find low-cost solutions to get them to customers. However, today's *customer-centered* logistics starts with the marketplace and works backward to the factory

Figure 10.5 Supply Chain Management

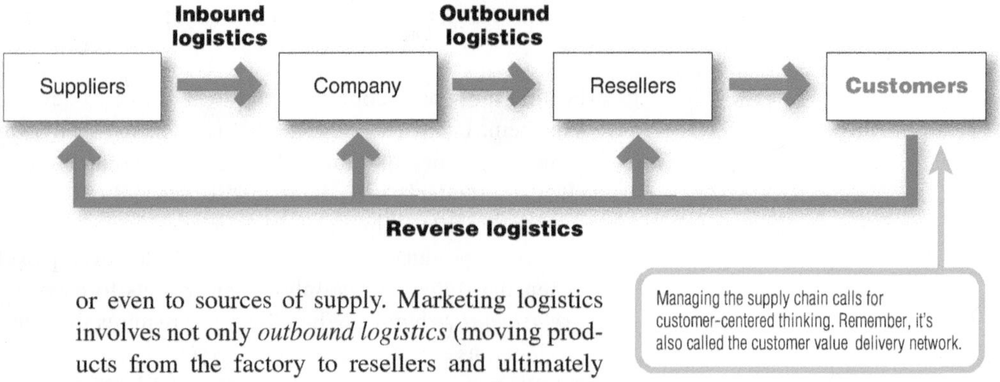

or even to sources of supply. Marketing logistics involves not only *outbound logistics* (moving products from the factory to resellers and ultimately to customers) but also *inbound logistics* (moving products and materials from suppliers to the factory) and *reverse logistics* (reusing, recycling, refurbishing, or disposing of broken, unwanted, or excess products returned by consumers or resellers). That is, it involves the entirety of **supply chain management**—managing upstream and downstream value-added flows of materials, final goods, and related information among suppliers, the company, resellers, and final consumers, as shown in **Figure 10.5**.

Supply chain management
Managing upstream and downstream value-added flows of materials, final goods, and related information among suppliers, the company, resellers, and final consumers.

The logistics manager's task is to coordinate the activities of suppliers, purchasing agents, marketers, channel members, and customers. These activities include forecasting, information systems, purchasing, production planning, order processing, inventory, warehousing, and transportation planning.

Companies today are placing greater emphasis on logistics for several reasons. First, companies can gain a powerful competitive advantage by using improved logistics to give customers better service or lower prices. Second, improved logistics can yield tremendous cost savings to both a company and its customers. As much as 20 percent of an average product's price is accounted for by shipping and transport alone. This far exceeds the cost of advertising and many other marketing costs. American companies spend $1.39 trillion each year—about 8.2 percent of GDP—to wrap, bundle, load, unload, sort, reload, and transport goods. That's more than the total national GDPs of all but 12 countries worldwide.[16]

Shaving off even a small fraction of logistics costs can mean substantial savings. For example, Walmart is currently implementing a program of logistics improvements through more efficient sourcing, greater supply chain productivity, and better management of its more than $51 billion worth of owned inventory, and that will reduce supply chain costs by 5 to 15 percent over five years—that's a whopping $4 billion to $12 billion.[17]

Third, the explosion in product variety has created a need for improved logistics management. For example, in 1916 the typical Piggly Wiggly grocery store carried only 605 items. Today, a Piggly Wiggly carries a bewildering stock of between 20,000 and 35,000 items, depending on store size. A Walmart Supercenter store carries more than 140,000 products, 30,000 of which are grocery products.[18] Ordering, shipping, stocking, and controlling such a variety of products presents a sizable logistics challenge.

Improvements in information technology have also created opportunities for major gains in distribution efficiency. Today's companies are using sophisticated supply chain management software, Internet-based logistics systems, point-of-sale scanners, RFID tags, satellite tracking, and electronic transfer of order and payment data. Such technology lets them quickly and efficiently manage the flow of goods, information, and finances through the supply chain.

Logistics: As this huge container ship suggests, American companies spent $1.39 trillion last year—8.2 percent of U.S. GDP—to wrap, bundle, load, unload, sort, reload, and transport goods.

E.G.Pors/Shutterstock

Finally, more than almost any other marketing function, logistics affects the environment and a firm's environmental sustainability efforts. Transportation, warehousing, packaging, and other logistics functions are typically the biggest supply chain contributors to the company's environmental footprint. So many companies are now developing *green supply chains.*

Sustainable Supply Chains

Companies have many reasons for reducing the environmental impact of their supply chains. For one thing, if they don't green up voluntarily, a host of sustainability regulations enacted around the world will soon require them to. For another, many large customers—from Walmart and Nike to the federal government—are demanding it. Environmental sustainability has become an important factor in supplier selection and performance evaluation. But perhaps even more important than *having* to do it, designing sustainable supply chains is simply the *right* thing to do. It's one more way that companies can contribute to saving our world for future generations.

But that's all pretty heady stuff. As it turns out, companies have a more immediate and practical reason for turning their supply chains green. Not only are sustainable channels good for the world, they're also good for a company's bottom line. The very logistics activities that create the biggest environmental footprint—such as transportation, warehousing, and packaging—also account for a lion's share of logistics costs. Companies green up their supply chains through greater efficiency, and greater efficiency means lower costs and higher profits. In other words, developing a sustainable supply chain is not only environmentally responsible, it can also be profitable. Consider Nike:[19]

Nike, the iconic sports shoe and apparel company, has developed a sweeping strategy for greening every phase of its supply chain. »For example, Nike recently teamed with Levi's, REI, Target, and other members of the Sustainable Apparel Coalition to develop the Higg Index—a tool that measures how a single apparel product affects the environment across the entire supply chain. Nike uses the Higg Index to work with suppliers and distributors to reduce its supply chain's environmental footprint. For instance, during just the past three years, the more than 900 contract factories that make Nike footwear worldwide have reduced their carbon emissions by 6 percent, despite production increases of 20 percent. That's equivalent to an emissions savings equal to more than 1 billion car-miles.

Nike has found that even seemingly simple supply chain adjustments can produce big benefits. For example, the company sources its shoes in Asia, but most are sold in North America. Until about a decade ago, the shoes were shipped from factory to store by air freight. After analyzing distribution costs more carefully, Nike shifted a sizable portion of its cargo to ocean freight. That simple shoes-to-ships shift reduced emissions per product by 4 percent, making environmentalists smile. But it also put a smile on the faces of Nike's accountants by saving the company some $8 million a year in shipping costs.

» Green supply chains: Nike has developed a sweeping strategy for greening its supply chain. The Higg Index lets Nike work with suppliers and distributors to reduce the supply chain's environmental footprint while at the same time reducing its logistics costs.

Sergio Azenha/Alamy

Goals of the Logistics System

Some companies state their logistics objective as providing maximum customer service at the least cost. Unfortunately, as nice as this sounds, no logistics system can *both* maximize customer service *and* minimize distribution costs. Maximum customer service implies rapid delivery, large inventories, flexible assortments, liberal returns policies, and other services—all of which raise distribution costs. In contrast, minimum distribution costs imply slower delivery, smaller inventories, and larger shipping lots—which represent a lower level of overall customer service.

The goal of marketing logistics should be to provide a *targeted* level of customer service at the least cost. A company must first research the importance of various distribution services to customers and then set desired service levels for each segment. The objective is to maximize *profits*, not sales. Therefore, the company must weigh the benefits of providing higher levels of service against the costs. Some companies offer less service than their competitors and charge a lower price. Other companies offer more service and charge higher prices to cover higher costs.

Major Logistics Functions

Given a set of logistics objectives, the company designs a logistics system that will minimize the cost of attaining these objectives. The major logistics functions are *warehousing, inventory management, transportation*, and *logistics information management*.

Warehousing

Production and consumption cycles rarely match, so most companies must store their goods while they wait to be sold. For example, Snapper, Toro, and other lawn mower manufacturers run their factories all year long and store up products for the heavy spring and summer buying seasons. The storage function overcomes differences in needed quantities and timing, ensuring that products are available when customers are ready to buy them.

Distribution center
A large, highly automated warehouse designed to receive goods from various plants and suppliers, take orders, fill them efficiently, and deliver goods to customers as quickly as possible.

A company must decide on *how many* and *what types* of warehouses it needs and *where* they will be located. The company might use either *storage warehouses* or *distribution centers*. Storage warehouses store goods for moderate to long periods. In contrast, **distribution centers** are designed to move goods rather than just store them. They are large and highly automated warehouses designed to receive goods from various plants and suppliers, take orders, fill them efficiently, and deliver goods to customers as quickly as possible.

For example, Amazon operates more than 50 giant distribution centers, called fulfillment centers, which fill online orders and handle returns. These centers are huge and highly automated. For example, the Amazon fulfillment center in Tracy, California, covers 1.2 million square feet (equivalent to 27 football fields). At the center, 4,000 employees control an inventory of 21 million items and ship out up to 700,000 packages a day to Amazon customers in Northern California and parts of the Pacific Northwest. During last year's Cyber Monday, Amazon's fulfillment center network filled customer orders at a rate of 426 items per second globally.[20]

Like almost everything else these days, warehousing has seen dramatic changes in technology in recent years. Outdated materials-handling methods are steadily being replaced by newer, computer-controlled systems requiring fewer employees. Computers and scanners read orders and direct lift trucks, electric hoists, or robots to gather goods, move them to loading docks, and issue invoices. For example, to improve efficiency in its massive fulfillment centers, Amazon recently purchased robot maker Kiva Systems:[21]

High-tech distribution centers: Amazon employs teams of super-retrievers—day-glo orange Kiva robots—to keep its fulfillment centers humming.
David Paul Morris/Bloomberg/Getty Images

> When you buy from Amazon, the chances are still good that your order will be plucked and packed by human hands. However, the humans in Amazon's fulfillment centers are increasingly being assisted by an army of squat, ottoman-size, day-glo orange robots. The Tracy, California, fulfillment center has 3,000 of them, "let out of their cage to scurry hither and yon bearing 6-foot-high...movable shelves." The robots bring racks of merchandise to workers, who in turn fill boxes. Dubbed the "magic shelf," racks of items simply materialize in front of workers, with red lasers pointing to items to be picked. The robots then drive off and new shelves appear. The super-efficient robots work tirelessly 16 hours a day, seven days a week. They

never complain about the workload or ask for pay raises, and they are pretty much maintenance free. "When they run low on power, they head to battery-charging terminals," notes one observer, "or, as warehouse personnel say, 'They get themselves a drink of water.'"

Inventory Management

Inventory management also affects customer satisfaction. Here, managers must maintain the delicate balance between carrying too little inventory and carrying too much. With too little stock, the firm risks not having products when customers want to buy. To remedy this, the firm may need costly emergency shipments or production. Carrying too much inventory results in higher-than-necessary inventory-carrying costs and stock obsolescence. Thus, in managing inventory, firms must balance the costs of carrying larger inventories against resulting sales and profits.

Many companies have greatly reduced their inventories and related costs through *just-in-time* logistics systems. With such systems, producers and retailers carry only small inventories of parts or merchandise, often enough for only a few days of operations. New stock arrives exactly when needed rather than being stored in inventory until being used. Just-in-time systems require accurate forecasting along with fast, frequent, and flexible delivery so that new supplies will be available when needed. However, these systems result in substantial savings in inventory-carrying and inventory-handling costs.

Marketers are always looking for new ways to make inventory management more efficient. In the not-too-distant future, handling inventory might even become fully automated. For example, in Chapter 3 we discussed RFID or "smart tag" technology, by which small transmitter chips are embedded in or placed on products and packaging for everything from flowers and razors to tires. Such "smart" products could make the entire supply chain—which accounts for nearly 75 percent of a product's cost—intelligent and automated.

Companies using RFID know, at any time, exactly where a product is located physically within the supply chain. "Smart shelves" would not only tell them when it's time to reorder but also place the order automatically with their suppliers. Such exciting new information technology is revolutionizing distribution as we know it. Many large and resourceful marketing companies, such as Walmart, Macy's, P&G, Kraft, and IBM, are investing heavily to make the full use of RFID technology a reality.

Transportation

The choice of transportation carriers affects the pricing of products, delivery performance, and the condition of goods when they arrive—all of which will affect customer satisfaction. In shipping goods to its warehouses, dealers, and customers, the company can choose among five main transportation modes: truck, rail, water, pipeline, and air, along with an alternative mode for digital products—the Internet.

Trucks have increased their share of transportation steadily and now account for 40 percent of total cargo ton-miles (a ton of freight moved one mile) transported in the United States. U.S. trucks travel more than 397 billion miles a year—more than double the distance traveled 25 years ago—carrying 9.2 billion tons of freight. According to the U.S. Department of Transportation, 70 percent of all the freight tonnage moved in the United States goes on trucks. Trucks are highly flexible in their routing and time schedules, and they can usually offer faster service than railroads. They are efficient for short hauls of high-value merchandise. Trucking firms have evolved in recent years to become full-service providers of global transportation services. For example, large trucking firms now offer everything from satellite tracking, Internet-based shipment management, and logistics planning software to cross-border shipping operations.[22]

Railroads account for 26 percent of the total cargo ton-miles moved. They are one of the most cost-effective modes for shipping large amounts of bulk products—coal, sand, minerals, and farm and forest products—over long distances. In recent years, railroads have increased their customer services by designing new equipment to handle special categories of goods, providing flatcars for carrying truck trailers by rail (piggyback), and providing in-transit services such as the diversion of shipped goods to other destinations en route and the processing of goods en route.

Multimodal transportation
Combining two or more modes of transportation.

Water carriers, which account for 7 percent of the cargo ton-miles, transport large amounts of goods by ships and barges on U.S. coastal and inland waterways. Although the cost of water transportation is very low for shipping bulky, low-value, nonperishable products such as sand, coal, grain, oil, and metallic ores, water transportation is the slowest mode and may be affected by the weather. *Pipelines*, which account for 17 percent of the cargo ton-miles, are a specialized means of shipping petroleum, natural gas, and chemicals from sources to markets. Most pipelines are used by their owners to ship their own products.

Although *air* carriers transport less than 1 percent of the cargo ton-miles of the nation's goods, they are an important transportation mode. Airfreight rates are much higher than rail or truck rates, but airfreight is ideal when speed is needed or distant markets have to be reached. Among the most frequently airfreighted products are perishables (such as fresh fish, cut flowers) and high-value, low-bulk items (technical instruments, jewelry). Companies find that airfreight also reduces inventory levels, packaging costs, and the number of warehouses needed.

The *Internet* carries digital products from producer to customer via satellite, cable, phone wire, or wireless signal. Software firms, the media, music and video companies, and education all make use of the Internet to transport digital products. The Internet holds the potential for lower product distribution costs. Whereas planes, trucks, and trains move freight and packages, digital technology moves information bits.

>> Shippers also use **multimodal transportation**—combining two or more modes of transportation. Eight percent of the total cargo ton-miles are moved via multiple modes. *Piggyback* describes the use of rail and trucks; *fishyback*, water and trucks; *trainship*, water and rail; and *airtruck*, air and trucks. Combining modes provides advantages that no single mode can deliver. Each combination offers advantages to the shipper. For example, not only is piggyback cheaper than trucking alone, but it also provides flexibility and convenience. Numerous logistics companies provide single-source multi-modal transportation solutions.

>> Transportation: In shipping goods to their warehouses, dealers, and customers, companies can choose among many transportation modes, including truck, rail, water, pipeline, and air. Much of today's shipping requires multiple modes.
Thanapun/Shutterstock

Most logistics carriers now recognize the importance of multimodal transportation, regardless of their main line of activity. For example, Union Pacific, primarily a rail carrier, offers "door-to-door shipping" coordination for its business customers. According to one Union Pacific ad: "The end of the tracks is just the beginning of our capabilities. Every day, we coordinate rail, trucks, and ocean carriers for thousands of companies—many without tracks to their doors. That would be a challenge if we were just a railroad, but we're not. We're logistics experts."

Logistics Information Management

Companies manage their supply chains through information. Channel partners often link up to share information and make better joint logistics decisions. From a logistics perspective, flows of information, such as customer transactions, billing, shipment and inventory levels, and even customer data, are closely linked to channel performance. Companies need simple, accessible, fast, and accurate processes for capturing, processing, and sharing channel information.

Information can be shared and managed in many ways, but most sharing takes place through *electronic data interchange* (EDI), the digital exchange of data between organizations, which primarily is transmitted via the Internet. Walmart, for example, requires EDI links with its more than 100,000 suppliers through its Retail Link sales data system. If new suppliers don't have the required EDI capability, Walmart will work with them to find and implement the needed tools.[23]

In some cases, suppliers might actually be asked to generate orders and arrange deliveries for their customers. Many large retailers—such as Walmart and Home Depot—work closely with major suppliers such as P&G or Moen to set up *vendor-managed inventory (VMI)* systems or *continuous inventory replenishment* systems. Using VMI, the customer shares real-time data on sales and current inventory levels with the supplier. The supplier then takes full responsibility for managing inventories and deliveries. Some retailers even go so far as to shift inventory and delivery costs to the supplier. Such systems require close cooperation between the buyer and seller.

Integrated Logistics Management

Integrated logistics management
The logistics concept that emphasizes teamwork—both inside the company and among all the marketing channel organizations—to maximize the performance of the entire distribution system.

Today, more and more companies are adopting the concept of **integrated logistics management**. This concept recognizes that providing better customer service and trimming distribution costs require *teamwork*, both inside the company and among all the marketing channel organizations. Inside, the company's various departments must work closely together to maximize its own logistics performance. Outside, the company must integrate its logistics system with those of its suppliers and customers to maximize the performance of the entire distribution network.

Cross-Functional Teamwork inside the Company

Most companies assign responsibility for various logistics activities to many different departments—marketing, sales, finance, operations, and purchasing. Too often, each function tries to optimize its own logistics performance without regard for the activities of the other functions. However, transportation, inventory, warehousing, and information management activities interact, often in an inverse way. Lower inventory levels reduce inventory-carrying costs. But they may also reduce customer service and increase costs from stockouts, backorders, special production runs, and costly fast-freight shipments. Because distribution activities involve strong trade-offs, decisions by different functions must be coordinated to achieve better overall logistics performance.

The goal of integrated supply chain management is to harmonize all of the company's logistics decisions. Close working relationships among departments can be achieved in several ways. Some companies have created permanent logistics committees composed of managers responsible for different physical distribution activities. Companies can also create supply chain manager positions that link the logistics activities of functional areas. For example, P&G has created product supply managers who manage all the supply chain activities for each product category. Many companies have a vice president of logistics or a supply chain VP with cross-functional authority.

Finally, companies can employ sophisticated, system-wide supply chain management software, now available from a wide range of software enterprises large and small, from SAP and Oracle to Infor and Logility. » For example, Oracle's supply chain management software solutions help companies to "gain sustainable advantage and drive innovation by transforming their traditional supply chains into integrated value chains." It coordinates every aspect of the supply chain, from value chain collaboration to inventory optimization to transportation and logistics management. The important thing is that the company must coordinate its logistics, inventory investments, demand forecasting, and marketing activities to create high market satisfaction at a reasonable cost.

» **Integrated logistics management: Oracle's supply chain management software solutions help companies to "gain sustainable advantage and drive innovation by transforming their traditional supply chains into integrated value chains."**

Oracle Corporation

Building Logistics Partnerships

Companies must do more than improve their own logistics. They must also work with other channel partners to improve whole-channel distribution. The members of a marketing channel are linked closely in creating customer value and building customer relationships. One company's distribution system is another company's supply system. The success of each channel member depends on the performance of the entire supply chain. For example, furniture retailer IKEA can create its stylish but affordable furniture and deliver the "IKEA lifestyle" only if its entire supply chain—consisting of thousands of merchandise designers and suppliers, transport companies, warehouses, and service providers—operates at maximum efficiency and with customer-focused effectiveness.

Smart companies coordinate their logistics strategies and forge strong partnerships with suppliers and customers to improve customer service and reduce channel costs. Many companies have created *cross-functional, cross-company teams*. For example, Nestlé's Purina pet food unit has a team of dozens of people working in Bentonville, Arkansas, the home base of Walmart. The Purina Walmart team members work jointly with their counterparts at Walmart to find ways to squeeze costs out of their distribution system. Working together benefits not only Purina and Walmart but also their shared, final consumers.

Other companies partner through *shared projects*. For example, many large retailers conduct joint in-store programs with suppliers. Home Depot allows key suppliers to use its stores as a testing ground for new merchandising programs. The suppliers spend time at Home Depot stores watching how their product sells and how customers relate to it. They then create programs specially tailored to Home Depot and its customers. Clearly, both the supplier and the customer benefit from such partnerships. The point is that all supply chain members must work together in the cause of bringing value to final consumers.

Third-Party Logistics

Although most big companies love to make and sell their products, many loathe the associated logistics "grunt work." They detest the bundling, loading, unloading, sorting, storing, reloading, transporting, customs clearing, and tracking required to supply their factories and get products to their customers. They hate it so much that many firms outsource some or all of their logistics to **third-party logistics (3PL) providers** such as Ryder, Penske Logistics, BAX Global, DHL Logistics, FedEx Logistics, and UPS Business Solutions.

Third-party logistics (3PL) provider
An independent logistics provider that performs any or all of the functions required to get a client's product to market.

For example, UPS knows that, for many companies, logistics can be a real nightmare. But logistics is exactly what UPS does best. To UPS, logistics is today's most powerful force for creating competitive advantage. "We ♥ logistics," proclaims UPS. "It makes running your business easier. It can make your customers happier. It's a whole new way of thinking." As one UPS ad concludes: "We love logistics. Put UPS to work for you and you'll love logistics too."

At one level, UPS can simply handle a company's package shipments. But on a deeper level, UPS can help businesses sharpen their own logistics systems to cut costs and serve customers better. At a still deeper level, companies can let UPS take over and manage part or all of their logistics operations. For example, consumer electronics maker Toshiba lets UPS handle its entire laptop PC repair process—lock, stock, and barrel. And UPS not only delivers packages for online shoe and accessories marketer Zappos, it also manages Zappos's important and complex order returns process in an efficient, customer-pleasing way.[24]

3PL providers like UPS can help clients tighten up sluggish, overstuffed supply chains; slash inventories; and get products to customers more quickly and reliably. According to one report, 86 percent of *Fortune* 500 companies use 3PL (also called *outsourced logistics* or *contract logistics*) services. General Motors, P&G, and Walmart each use 50 or more 3PLs.[25]

Companies use third-party logistics providers for several reasons. First, because getting the product to market is their main focus, using these providers makes the most sense, as they can often do it more efficiently and at lower cost. Outsourcing typically results in a 10 to 25 percent cost savings.[26] Second, outsourcing logistics frees a company to focus more intensely on its core business. Finally, integrated logistics companies understand increasingly complex logistics environments.

> **MyMarketingLab**
>
> If assigned by your instructor, complete the questions marked with the ✪ from the EOC Discussion Questions section in the MyLab. To complete the Marketing by the Numbers problems found in this section, go to your Assignments in the MyLab.

REVIEWING AND EXTENDING THE CONCEPTS

CHAPTER REVIEW AND CRITICAL THINKING

Objectives Review

Some companies pay too little attention to their distribution channels; others, however, have used imaginative distribution systems to gain a competitive advantage. A company's channel decisions directly affect every other marketing decision. Management must make channel decisions carefully, incorporating today's needs with tomorrow's likely selling environment.

OBJECTIVE 10-1 Explain why companies use marketing channels and discuss the functions these channels perform. (pp 300–303)

In creating customer value, a company can't go it alone. It must work within an entire network of partners—a value delivery network—to accomplish this task. Individual companies and brands don't compete; their entire value delivery networks do.

Most producers use intermediaries to bring their products to market. They forge a *marketing channel* (or *distribution channel*)—a set of interdependent organizations involved in the process of making a product or service available for use or consumption by the consumer or business user. Through their contacts, experience, specialization, and scale of operation, intermediaries usually offer the firm more than it can achieve on its own.

Marketing channels perform many key functions. Some help *complete transactions* by gathering and distributing *information* needed for planning and aiding exchange, developing and spreading persuasive *communications* about an offer, performing *contact* work (finding and communicating with prospective buyers), *matching* (shaping and fitting the offer to the buyer's needs), and entering into *negotiation* to reach an agreement on price and other terms of the offer so that ownership can be transferred. Other functions help to *fulfill* the completed transactions by offering *physical distribution* (transporting and storing goods), *financing* (acquiring and using funds to cover the costs of the channel work), and *risk taking* (assuming the risks of carrying out the channel work.

OBJECTIVE 10-2 Discuss how channel members interact and how they organize to perform the work of the channel. (pp 304–311)

The channel will be most effective when each member assumes the tasks it can do best. Ideally, because the success of individual channel members depends on overall channel success, all channel firms should work together smoothly. They should understand and accept their roles, coordinate their goals and activities, and cooperate to attain overall channel goals. By cooperating, they can more effectively sense, serve, and satisfy the target market.

In a large company, the formal organization structure assigns roles and provides needed leadership. But in a distribution channel composed of independent firms, leadership and power are not formally set. Traditionally, distribution channels have lacked the leadership needed to assign roles and manage conflict. In recent years, however, new types of channel organizations have appeared that provide stronger leadership and improved performance.

OBJECTIVE 10-3 Identify the major channel alternatives open to a company. (pp 311–315)

Channel alternatives vary from direct selling to using one, two, three, or more intermediary *channel levels*. Marketing channels face continuous and sometimes dramatic change. Three of the most important trends are the growth of *vertical, horizontal,* and *multichannel marketing systems*. These trends affect channel cooperation, conflict, and competition.

Channel design begins with assessing customer channel service needs and company channel objectives and constraints. The company then identifies the major channel alternatives in terms of the *types* of intermediaries, the *number* of intermediaries, and the *channel responsibilities* of each. Each channel alternative must be evaluated according to economic, control, and adaptive criteria. *Channel management* calls for selecting qualified intermediaries and motivating them. Individual channel members must be evaluated regularly.

OBJECTIVE 10-4 Explain how companies select, motivate, and evaluate channel members. (pp 315–319)

Producers vary in their ability to attract qualified marketing intermediaries. Some producers have no trouble signing up channel members, whereas others have to work hard to line up enough qualified intermediaries. When selecting intermediaries, the company should evaluate each channel member's qualifications and select those that best fit its channel objectives.

Once selected, channel members must be continuously motivated to do their best. The company must sell not only *through* the intermediaries but also *with* them. It should forge strong partnerships with channel members to create a marketing system that meets the needs of both the manufacturer *and* the partners.

OBJECTIVE 10-5 Discuss the nature and importance of marketing logistics and integrated supply chain management. (pp 319–326)

Marketing logistics (or *physical distribution*) is an area of potentially high cost savings and improved customer satisfaction. Marketing logistics addresses not only *outbound logistics* but also *inbound logistics* and *reverse logistics*. That is, it involves the entire *supply chain management*—managing value-added flows between suppliers, the company, resellers, and final users. No logistics system can both maximize customer service and minimize distribution costs. Instead, the goal of logistics management is to provide a *targeted* level of service at the least cost. The major logistics functions are *warehousing, inventory management, transportation*, and *logistics information management*.

The *integrated supply chain management concept* recognizes that improved logistics requires teamwork in the form of close working relationships across functional areas inside the company and across various organizations in the supply chain. Companies can achieve logistics harmony among functions by creating cross-functional logistics teams, integrative supply manager positions, and senior-level logistics executive positions with cross-functional authority. Channel partnerships can take the form of cross-company teams, shared projects, and information-sharing systems. Today, some companies are outsourcing their logistics functions to third-party logistics (3PL) providers to save costs, increase efficiency, and gain faster and more effective access to global markets.

Key Terms

Objective 10-1
Value delivery network (p 300)
Marketing channel (distribution channel) (p 301)
Channel level (p 303)
Direct marketing channel (p 303)
Indirect marketing channel (p 303)

Objective 10-2
Channel conflict (p 304)
Conventional distribution channel (p 305)
Vertical marketing system (VMS) (p 305)
Corporate VMS (p 306)
Contractual VMS (p 306)
Franchise organization (p 306)
Administered VMS (p 307)
Horizontal marketing system (p 307)
Multichannel distribution system (p 308)
Disintermediation (p 308)

Objective 10-3
Marketing channel design (p 311)
Intensive distribution (p 313)
Exclusive distribution (p 313)
Selective distribution (p 313)

Objective 10-4
Marketing channel management (p 315)

Objective 10-5
Marketing logistics (physical distribution) (p 319)
Supply chain management (p 320)
Distribution center (p 322)
Multimodal transportation (p 324)
Integrated logistics management (p 325)
Third-party logistics (3PL) provider (p 326)

Discussion Questions

10-1. Compare and contrast upstream and downstream partners in a company's supply chain. Explain why *value delivery network* might be a better term to use than *supply chain*. (AACSB: Communication)

10-2. Compare direct marketing channels and indirect marketing channels. Name the various types of resellers in marketing channels. (AACSB: Communication)

10-3. Name and describe the three strategies available when determining the number of marketing intermediaries. (AACSB: Communication; Reflective Thinking)

10-4. List and briefly describe the major logistics functions. Provide an example of a decision a logistics manager would make for each major function. (AACSB: Communication; Reflective Thinking)

10-5. What are third-party logistics providers, and why do companies use them? (AACSB: Communication)

Critical Thinking Exercises

10-6. The most common type of contractual vertical marketing system is the franchise organization. Visit the International Franchise Association at www.franchise.org and find a franchise that interests you. Write a report describing the franchise. Identify what type of franchise it represents and research the market opportunities for that product or service. (AACSB: Communication; Use of IT; Reflective Thinking)

10-7. Form a small group and research the distribution challenges faced by companies expanding into emerging international markets such as China, Africa, and India. Develop a multimedia presentation on how one company overcame these challenges. (AACSB: Communication; Reflective Thinking; Use of IT)

10-8. The term *last mile* is often used in the telecommunications industry. Research what is going on in this industry and how the *last mile* has evolved in recent years, and then predict where it is heading in the future. What companies are major players in the *last mile,* and how does the concept of *net neutrality* fit in? (AACSB: Communication; Reflective Thinking)

MINICASES AND APPLICATIONS

Online, Mobile, and Social Media Marketing Self-Publishing

Do you think that you have what it takes to write a best-selling novel? In the past, authors had to go through traditional publishing houses to print and distribute their work, but technology has turned the publishing industry on its head. Although aspiring authors could always self-publish a book, selling it through the traditional channels—bookstores—was only a pipe dream for most. But that has all changed thanks to the Internet and social media. Amazon's Kindle Direct Publishing is a popular platform for self-publishers, but others such as Smashwords, Author Solutions, and Fast-Pencil offer similar services with hundreds of thousands of authors and titles. For example, Amanda Hocking's self-published e-book sales caught the attention of a publisher, and now the former social worker is a millionaire. Self-published books have grown nearly 300 percent in less than 10 years, with the majority being e-books. Almost 40 percent of readers now own e-readers, such as Kindles and iPads. That creates opportunities for anyone wanting to distribute their works to these avid readers. For example, after being turned away by traditional publishers, author Christine Bronstein created her own online social network to promote her book, *Nothing but the Truth, So Help Me God: 51 Women Reveal the Power of Positive Female Connection*, which launched on Amazon and Barnes & Noble sites.

10-9. Visit a self-publishing site such as Amazon's Kindle Direct (https://kdp.amazon.com) and create a presentation to give to aspiring authors about distributing their works this way. (AACSB: Communication; Use of IT; Reflective Thinking)

10-10. What other industries' channels of distribution have been affected dramatically by online, mobile, and social media? (AACSB: Communication; Reflective Thinking)

Marketing Ethics Trucker Rest Rules

Large trucks are an important piece of the logistics chain. However, there were 333,000 large truck crashes in 2012, resulting in almost 3,800 fatalities, the majority being drivers or passengers of other vehicles, not the truck driver. One accident in 2014 caused a public uproar when a Walmart truck driver fell asleep at the wheel after being awake for 24 hours and crashed into another car, killing one person and critically injuring others, one being a well-known comedian. The U.S. Department of Transportation's Federal Motor Carrier Safety Administration enacted tougher hours-of-service rules that went into effect in July 2013. One report claimed that the industry would lose $1 billion in lost productivity as a result of these rules, while another concluded the industry would realize almost $500 million in benefit from reduced driver mortality. The new rules have caused considerable controversy and have caused hardships for drivers. As one driver put it, "If the wheels aren't turning, you're not earning."

10-11. Research the DOT's trucker hours-of-service rules and write a brief report outlining the rules. What is the current status of the 2013 rules? (AACSB: Communication; Reflective Thinking)

10-12. Do you think it is ethical that the trucking industry wants the rules repealed? Explain why or why not. (AACSB: Communication; Reflective Thinking; Ethical Reasoning)

Marketing by the Numbers Tyson Expanding Distribution

Tyson Foods is the largest U.S. beef and chicken supplier, processing more than 100,000 head of cattle and 40-plus million chickens weekly. Primary distribution channels are supermarket meat departments. However, the company is now expanding distribution into convenience stores. There are almost 150,000 gas stations and convenience stores where the company would like to sell hot Buffalo chicken bites near the checkout. This is a promising channel, as sales are growing considerably at these retail outlets and profit margins on prepared foods are higher than selling raw meat to grocery stores. Tyson will have to hire 10 more sales representatives at a salary of $45,000 each to expand into this distribution channel because many of these types of stores are independently owned. Each convenience store is expected to generate an average of $50,000 in revenue for Tyson. Refer to Appendix 3: Marketing by the Numbers to answer the following questions.

10-13. If Tyson's contribution margin is 30 percent on this product, what increase in sales will it need to break even on the increase in fixed costs to hire the new sales reps? (AACSB: Communication; Analytical Reasoning)

10-14. How many new retail accounts must the company acquire to break even on this tactic? What average number of accounts must each new rep acquire? (AACSB: Communication; Analytical Reasoning)

Video Case Progressive

Progressive has attained top-tier status in the insurance industry by focusing on innovation. Progressive was the first company to offer drive-in claims service, installment payment of premiums, and 24/7 customer service. But perhaps Progressive's most innovative moves involve its channels of distribution. Whereas most insurance companies distribute via intermediary agents or direct-to-consumer methods, Progressive was one of the first to see value in doing both. In the late 1980s, it augmented its agency distribution with a direct 800-number channel.

Two decades ago, Progressive moved into the digital future by becoming the first major insurer to launch a Web site. Soon after, it allowed customers to buy auto insurance policies online in real time. Today, customers can use Progressive's Web site to do everything from managing their own account information to reporting claims directly. Progressive even offers one-stop concierge claim service.

After viewing the Progressive video segment, answer the following questions about marketing channels.

10-15. Apply the concept of the supply chain to Progressive.

10-16. Using the model of consumer and business channels found in the chapter, sketch out as many channels for Progressive as you can. How does each of these channels meet distinct customer needs?

10-17. Discuss the various ways that Progressive has had an impact on the insurance industry.

Company Cases 10 Apple Pay/15 7-Eleven

See Appendix 1 for cases appropriate for this chapter. **Case 10, Apple Pay: Taking Moble Payments Mainstream.** In the past, Apple has disrupted marketing channels with revolutionary products. With Apple Pay, Apple is proving once again that it can deliver. **Case 15, 7-Eleven: Adapting to The World's Many Cultures.** Just a convenience store in the U.S., 7-Eleven has a strong global presence by catering to different distribution strategies throughout the world.

MyMarketingLab

If assigned by your instructor, complete these writing sections from your Assignments in the MyLab.

10-18. Why does channel conflict occur? Name and describe the various types of channel conflict. (AACSB: Communication)

10-19. Should retailers be responsible for safety conditions in garment supplier factories in other countries? Discuss. (AACSB: Written and Oral Communication; Reflective Thinking; Ethical Understanding and Reasoning)

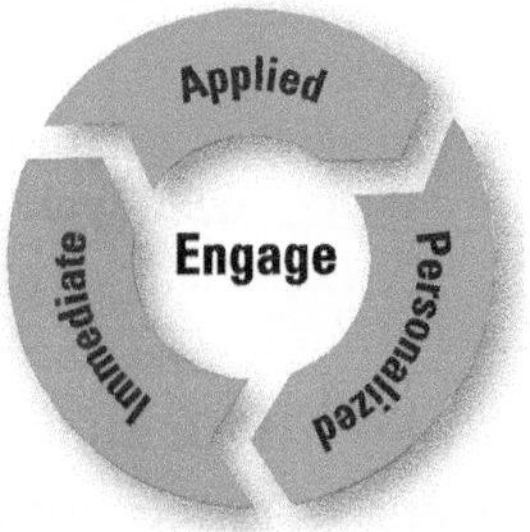

11 Retailing and Wholesaling

CHAPTER ROAD MAP Objective Outline

Previewing the Concepts

We now look more deeply into the two major intermediary marketing channel functions: retailing and wholesaling. You already know something about retailing—retailers of all shapes and sizes serve you every day, both in stores and online. However, you probably know much less about the hoard of wholesalers working behind the scenes. In this chapter, we examine the characteristics of different kinds of retailers and wholesalers, the marketing decisions they make, and trends for the future.

When it comes to retailers, you have to start with Walmart. This megaretailer's phenomenal success has resulted from an unrelenting focus on bringing value to its customers. Day in and day out, Walmart lives up to its promise: "Save money. Live better." That focus on customer value has made Walmart the world's largest retailer, the world's largest company. Yet, despite its huge success, Walmart still faces plenty of fresh opportunities and some daunting challenges as well.

First Stop

Walmart: The World's Largest *Retailer*—the World's Largest *Company*

» At Walmart: "Save money. Live better." Says Walmart's CEO, "We're obsessed with delivering value to customers."

Beth Hall/Bloomberg/Getty Images

Walmart is almost unimaginably big. It's the world's largest retailer—the world's largest *company*. It rang up an incredible $487 billion in sales last year—more than double the sales of competitors Costco, Target, Macy's, Sears, Kmart, JCPenney, and Kohl's *combined*.

Walmart is the number-one seller in many categories of consumer products, including groceries, clothing, toys, and pet care products. It sells nearly 2.7 times as many groceries as Kroger, the leading grocery-only food retailer, and its clothing and shoe sales alone exceed the total revenues of Macy's Inc., parent of both Macy's and Bloomingdale's department stores. Incredibly, Walmart sells an estimated 30 percent of the disposable diapers purchased in the United States each year, 30 percent of the hair care products, 30 percent of all health and beauty products, 26 percent of the toothpaste, 25 percent of all groceries, and 20 percent of the pet food. On average, worldwide, Walmart serves more than 250 million customers per week through more than 11,000 stores in 27 countries and online in 10 countries.

It's also hard to fathom Walmart's impact on the U.S. economy. It's the nation's largest employer—one out of every 246 men, women, and children in the United States is a Walmart associate. The chain's average profit is $3.1 million per *hour*. If Walmart were a separate country, it would be the world's 26th largest economy. By one estimate, through its own low prices and impact on competitors' prices, Walmart saves the average American household $2,500 each year, equivalent to more than six months' worth of groceries for the average family.

What's behind this spectacular success? First and foremost, Walmart is passionately dedicated to its long-time, low-price value proposition and what its low prices mean to customers: "Save money. Live better." To accomplish this mission, Walmart offers a broad selection of goods at "unbeatable low prices," day in and day out. No other retailer has come nearly so close to mastering the concepts of everyday low prices and one-stop shopping. Sam Walton himself summed up Walmart's mission best when he said, "If we work together, we'll lower the cost of living for everyone ... we'll give the world an opportunity to see what it's like to save and have a better life."

How does Walmart make money with such low prices? Walmart is a lean, mean distribution machine—it has the lowest cost structure in the industry. Low costs let the giant retailer charge lower prices while remaining profitable. Lower prices attract more shoppers, producing more sales, making the company more efficient, and enabling it to lower prices even more.

Walmart's low costs result from superior operations management, sophisticated information technology, and good-old "tough buying." Its huge, fully automated distribution centers supply stores efficiently. It employs an information technology system that the U.S. Department of Defense would envy, giving managers around the world instant access to sales and operating information. And Walmart is known for using its massive scale to wring low prices from suppliers. "Don't expect a greeter and don't expect friendly," said one supplier's sales executive after a visit to Walmart's buying offices. "Once you are ushered into one of the spartan little buyers' rooms, expect a steely eye across the table and be prepared to cut your price. They are very, very focused people, and they use their buying power more forcefully than anyone else in America."

Despite its incredible success over the past five decades, mighty Walmart faces some weighty challenges ahead. Having grown so big, the maturing giant is having difficulty maintaining the rapid growth rates of its youth. Think about this: To grow just 7 percent next year, Walmart will have to add more than $33 billion in new sales. That's a sales *increase* greater than the *total* sales of all but the top 96 companies on the *Fortune* 500, including companies such as McDonald's, Macy's, American Express, Xerox, Goodyear, Nike, or nearly three JCPenneys. The bigger Walmart gets, the harder it is to maintain a high rate of growth.

Day in and day out, giant Walmart lives up to its promise: "Save money. Live better." Its obsession with customer value has made Walmart not only the world's largest retailer but also the world's largest *company*.

To keep growing, Walmart has pushed into new, faster-growing product and service lines, including organic foods, store brands, in-store health clinics, and consumer financial services. To combat trendier competitors such as Target, Walmart even gave itself a modest image face-lift. It spruced up its stores with a cleaner, brighter, more open look and less clutter to make them more shopper friendly. In search of broader appeal, it has added new, higher-quality products. Many Walmart stores now carry a selection of higher-end consumer electronics products, from Samsung ultra-thin televisions to Dell and Toshiba laptops to Apple iPhones and iPads.

Despite its massive presence, Walmart still has room to expand geographically. Believe it or not, there are plenty of places in the United States that still don't have a Walmart. And the giant retailer is expanding rapidly in international markets, where sales grew to nearly 19 percent of total sales at $136 billion. Walmart also faces substantial growth opportunities—and challenges—in online, mobile, and social media commerce (see the Chapter 9 opening story on Walmart versus Amazon). Its online sales of an estimated $14 billion account for only about 2.7 percent of total sales, making it a distant online also-ran next to Amazon.com, which last year topped $89 billion in online sales. Walmart lists "winning in global e-commerce" as one of its top priorities for the future.

As Walmart continues to adapt and grow, however, one thing seems certain. The giant retailer may add new product lines and services. It might go digital and global. It might brush up its look and image. But Walmart has no intention of ever giving up its core low-price value proposition. After all, Walmart is and always will be a discounter. "I don't think Walmart's . . . ever going to be edgy," says a Walmart marketer. "I don't think that fits our brand. Our brand is about saving people money" so that they can live better.[1]

The Walmart story sets the stage for examining the fast-changing world of today's resellers. This chapter looks at *retailing* and *wholesaling*. In the first section, we look at the nature and importance of retailing, the major types of store and nonstore retailers, the decisions retailers make, and the future of retailing. In the second section, we discuss these same topics as they apply to wholesalers.

Author Comment
You already know a lot about retailers. You deal with them every day—store retailers, service retailers, online and mobile retailers, and others.

Retailing

Retailing
All the activities involved in selling products or services directly to final consumers for their personal, nonbusiness use.

Retailer
A business whose sales come *primarily* from retailing.

Shopper marketing
Focusing the entire marketing process on turning shoppers into buyers as they approach the point of sale, whether during in-store, online, or mobile shopping.

What is retailing? We all know that Costco, Home Depot, Macy's, and Target are retailers, but so are Amazon.com, the local Hampton Inn, and a doctor seeing patients. **Retailing** includes all the activities involved in selling products or services directly to final consumers for their personal, nonbusiness use. Many institutions—manufacturers, wholesalers, and retailers—do retailing. But most retailing is done by **retailers**, businesses whose sales come *primarily* from retailing. Retailing plays a very important role in most marketing channels. Last year, retailers accounted for more than $5 trillion of sales to final consumers.[2]

Retailing: Connecting Brands with Consumers

Retailers connect brands with consumers in the final phases of the buying process and at the point of purchase. In fact, many marketers are now embracing the concept of **shopper marketing**, focusing the entire marketing process—from product and brand development to logistics, promotion, and merchandising—toward turning shoppers into buyers as they approach the point of sale. Of course, every well-designed marketing effort focuses on customer buying behavior. What differentiates the concept of shopper marketing is the suggestion that these efforts should be coordinated around the shopping process itself.

>> Shopper marketing: The dramatic growth in online and mobile shopping has added new dimensions to "point of purchase." Influencing consumers' buying decisions as they shop now involves omni-channel efforts aimed at integrating in-store, online, and mobile shopping.
Betsie Van der Meer/Getty Images

Shopper marketing builds around what P&G calls the "First Moment of Truth"—the critical three to seven seconds that a shopper considers a product on a store shelf.[3] >> However, the dramatic growth of online and mobile shopping has added new dimensions to shopper marketing. The retailing "moment of truth" no longer takes place only in stores. Instead, Google defines a "zero moment of truth," when consumers begin the buying process by searching for and learning about products online.

Today's consumers are increasingly *omni-channel buyers,* who make little distinction between in-store and online shopping and for whom the path to a retail purchase runs across multiple channels. For these buyers, a particular purchase might consist of researching a product online and buying it from an online retailer, without ever setting foot in a retail store. Alternatively, they might use a smartphone to research a purchase on the fly, or even while in retail store aisles. For example, it's common to see a consumer examining an item

Omni-channel retailing
Creating a seamless cross-channel buying experience that integrates in-store, online, and mobile shopping.

on a shelf at Target while at the same time using a mobile app to look for coupons or check product reviews and prices at Amazon.com.

Thus, these days, shopper marketing and the "point of purchase" go well beyond in-store buying. They involve consumers working across multiple channels as they shop. Influencing consumers' buying decisions calls for **omni-channel retailing**, creating a seamless cross-channel buying experience that integrates in-store, online, and mobile shopping.[4]

Although most retailing is still done in retail stores, in recent years direct and online retailing have been growing much faster than store retailing. We discuss direct, online, and omni-channel retailing in detail later in this chapter and in Chapter 14. For now, we will focus on store retailing.

Types of Retailers

Retail stores come in all shapes and sizes—from your local hairstyling salon or family-owned restaurant to national specialty chain retailers such as REI or Williams-Sonoma to megadiscounters such as Costco or Walmart. The most important types of retail stores are described in **»Table 11.1** and discussed in the following sections. They can be classified in terms of several characteristics, including the *amount of service* they offer, the breadth and depth of their *product lines*, the *relative prices* they charge, and how they are *organized.*

Amount of Service

Different types of customers and products require different amounts of service. To meet these varying service needs, retailers may offer one of three service levels: self-service, limited service, and full service.

» Table 11.1 Major Store Retailer Types

Type	Description	Examples
Specialty store	A store that carries a narrow product line with a deep assortment, such as apparel stores, sporting-goods stores, furniture stores, florists, and bookstores.	REI, Sunglass Hut, Sephora, Williams-Sonoma
Department store	A store that carries several product lines—typically clothing, home furnishings, and household goods—with each line operated as a separate department managed by specialist buyers or merchandisers.	Macy's, Sears, Neiman Marcus
Supermarket	A relatively large, low-cost, low-margin, high-volume, self-service operation designed to serve the consumer's total needs for grocery and household products.	Kroger, Safeway, SuperValu, Publix
Convenience store	A relatively small store located near residential areas, open 24/7, and carrying a limited line of high-turnover convenience products at slightly higher prices.	7-Eleven, Circle K, Speedway, Sheetz
Discount store	A store that carries standard merchandise sold at lower prices with lower margins and higher volumes.	Walmart, Target, Kohl's
Off-price retailer	A store that sells merchandise bought at less-than-regular wholesale prices and sold at less than retail. These include *factory outlets* owned and operated by manufacturers; *independent off-price retailers* owned and run by entrepreneurs or by divisions of larger retail corporations; and *warehouse (or wholesale) clubs* selling a limited selection of goods at deep discounts to consumers who pay membership fees.	Mikasa (factory outlet); TJ Maxx (independent off-price retailer); Costco, Sam's Club, BJ's (warehouse clubs)
Superstore	A very large store that meets consumers' total needs for routinely purchased food and nonfood items. This includes *supercenters*, combined supermarket and discount stores, and *category killers*, which carry a deep assortment in a particular category.	Walmart Supercenter, SuperTarget, Meijer (discount stores); Best Buy, Petco, Staples, Bed Bath & Beyond (category killers)

Self-service retailers serve customers who are willing to perform their own *locate-compare-select* process to save time or money. Self-service is the basis of all discount operations and is typically used by retailers selling convenience goods (such as supermarkets) and nationally branded, fast-moving shopping goods (such as Target or Kohl's). *Limited-service retailers*, such as Sears or JCPenney, provide more sales assistance because they carry more shopping goods about which customers need information. Their increased operating costs result in higher prices.

Full-service retailers, such as high-end specialty stores (for example, Tiffany or Williams-Sonoma) and first-class department stores (such as Nordstrom or Neiman Marcus) assist customers in every phase of the shopping process. Full-service stores usually carry more specialty goods for which customers need or want assistance or advice. They provide more services, which results in much higher operating costs. These higher costs are passed along to customers as higher prices.

Product Line

Retailers can also be classified by the length and breadth of their product assortments. Some retailers, such as **specialty stores**, carry narrow product lines with deep assortments within those lines. Today, specialty stores are flourishing. The increasing use of market segmentation, market targeting, and product specialization has resulted in a greater need for stores that focus on specific products and segments.

Specialty store
A retail store that carries a narrow product line with a deep assortment within that line.

Department store
A retail store that carries a wide variety of product lines, each operated as a separate department managed by specialist buyers or merchandisers.

Supermarket
A large, low-cost, low-margin, high-volume, self-service store that carries a wide variety of grocery and household products.

By contrast, **department stores** carry a wide variety of product lines. In recent years, middle-market department stores have been squeezed between more focused and flexible specialty stores on the one hand and more efficient, lower-priced discounters on the other. In response, many have added promotional pricing to meet the discount threat. Others have stepped up the use of store brands and single-brand *designer shops* to compete with specialty stores. Still others are trying direct and online selling. Service remains the key differentiating factor. Retailers such as Nordstrom, Saks, Neiman Marcus, and other high-end department stores are doing well by emphasizing exclusive merchandise and high-quality service.

Supermarkets are the most frequently visited type of retail store. Today, however, they are facing slow sales growth because of slower population growth and an increase in competition from discounters (Walmart, Costco, and Dollar General) on the one hand and specialty food stores (Whole Foods Market, Trader Joe's, ALDI, Sprouts) on the other. Supermarkets' share of U.S. packaged foods sales slipped from 53 percent in 1998 to 37 percent in 2012.[5] Supermarkets also have been hit hard by the rapid growth of out-of-home eating over the past two decades.

In the battle for "share of stomachs," some supermarkets have moved upscale, providing improved store environments and higher-quality food offerings, such as from-scratch bakeries, gourmet deli counters, natural foods, and fresh seafood departments. Others, however, are competing head-on with large discounters such as Costco and Walmart by cutting costs, establishing more-efficient operations, and lowering prices. » WinCo, a fast-growing regional discount-grocery chain in the western United States, has done this successfully:[6]

» **In the battle for "share of stomach," regional supermarket chain WinCo successfully competes head-on with large discounters such as Costco and Walmart. It's rapidly becoming "Walmart's worst nightmare."**

WinCo Foods, Inc.

> You probably haven't heard of WinCo yet. But you can bet that Walmart and Costco are keeping a close eye on the small discount-grocery chain. In fact, according to one supermarket-retailing expert, WinCo is fast becoming "Walmart's worst nightmare." In its markets, WinCo (short for "Winning Company") positions itself directly against mighty Walmart as "The Supermarket Low Price Leader." And that's more than just a slogan—WinCo doesn't just match Walmart's prices; it often undercuts them. WinCo keeps prices low through low-cost, efficient operations. The chain often cuts out distributors and buys goods at lower costs directly from farms and factories. Its large, efficient, no-frills stores carry a limited assortment of basic fast-moving merchandise. WinCo's customers help to keep costs down by bagging their own groceries and paying cash (no credit cards accepted). Finally, the employee-owned chain has a reputation for treating its

employees right in terms of pay, benefits, and pensions. The result is a cheerful, highly motivated, productive workforce that genuinely contributes to the company's low-cost success. Why should Walmart and Costco worry about WinCo? The rapidly growing chain expects to double in size every five to seven years. According to the retailing expert, "WinCo is really unstoppable at this point."

Convenience store
A small store, located near a residential area, that is open long hours seven days a week and carries a limited line of high-turnover convenience goods.

Convenience stores are small stores that carry a limited line of high-turnover convenience goods. After several years of stagnant sales, these stores are now experiencing growth. Many convenience store chains have tried to expand beyond their primary market of young, blue-collar men by redesigning their stores to attract female shoppers. They are shedding the image of a "truck stop" where men go to buy gas, beer, cigarettes, or shriveled hotdogs on a roller grill and are instead offering freshly prepared foods and cleaner, safer, more-upscale environments.

For example, consider 7-Eleven, long known as a haven for Slurpees, Big Gulps, hot dogs spinning on a roller, self-serve nachos, smokes, beer, and bags of chips. The convenience chain now employs a team of culinary and food science experts who are stocking its shelves with an expanding menu of healthier snack and meal items under 400 calories, such as yogurt parfaits, salads, bags of carrots and celery, fresh subs, Smart turkey sandwiches on whole wheat bread, and a Bistro Snack Protein Pack—carrots, hummus, pita rounds, cheddar cheese, and grapes in a meal-to-go box. The chain is also resizing and single-sizing existing products. Over the next three years, 7-Eleven plans to boost its sales of high-margin fresh foods to 20 percent, twice the current level.[7]

Superstore
A store much larger than a regular supermarket that offers a large assortment of routinely purchased food products, nonfood items, and services.

Superstores are much larger than regular supermarkets and offer a large assortment of routinely purchased food products, nonfood items, and services. Walmart, Target, Meijer, and other discount retailers offer *supercenters*, very large combination food and discount stores. Whereas a traditional grocery store brings in about $482,000 a week in sales, a supercenter brings in about $1.4 million a week. Walmart, which opened its first supercenter in 1988, now has more than 3,400 supercenters in the United States and is opening new ones at a rate of about 120 per year.[8]

Category killer
A giant specialty store that carries a very deep assortment of a particular line.

Recent years have also seen the rapid growth of superstores that are actually giant specialty stores, the so-called **category killers** (for example, Best Buy, Home Depot, Petco, and Bed Bath & Beyond). They feature stores the size of airplane hangars that carry a very deep assortment of a particular line. Category killers are found in a wide range of categories, including electronics, home-improvement products, books, baby gear, toys, home goods, party goods, sporting goods, and even pet supplies.

Service retailer
A retailer whose product line is actually a service; examples include hotels, airlines, banks, colleges, and many others.

Finally, for many retailers, the product line is actually a service. **Service retailers** include hotels and motels, banks, airlines, restaurants, colleges, hospitals, movie theaters, tennis clubs, bowling alleys, repair services, hair salons, and dry cleaners. Service retailers in the United States are growing faster than product retailers.

Relative Prices

Retailers can also be classified according to the prices they charge (see Table 11.1). Most retailers charge regular prices and offer normal-quality goods and customer service. Others offer higher-quality goods and service at higher prices. Retailers that feature low prices are discount stores and "off-price" retailers.

Discount store
A retail operation that sells standard merchandise at lower prices by accepting lower margins and selling at higher volume.

Discount Stores. A **discount store** (for example, Target, Kohl's, or Walmart) sells standard merchandise at lower prices by accepting lower margins and selling at higher volume. The early discount stores cut expenses by offering few services and operating in warehouse-like facilities in low-rent, heavily traveled districts. Today's discounters have improved their store environments and increased their services while at the same time keeping prices low through lean, efficient operations.

Leading "big-box" discounters, such as Walmart and Target, now dominate the retail scene. However, even "small-box" discounters are thriving in the current economic environment. For example, dollar stores are now today's fastest-growing retail format. Back in the day, dollar stores sold mostly odd-lot assortments of novelties, factory overruns, closeouts, and outdated merchandise—most priced at $1. Not anymore. Dollar General, the

Discounter Dollar General, the nation's largest small-box discount retailer, makes a powerful value promise for the times: "Save time. Save money. Every day."

Daniel Acker/Bloomberg/Getty Images

nation's largest small-box discount retailer, makes a powerful value promise for the times: "Save time. Save money. Every day":[9]

Dollar General's slogan isn't just for show. It's a careful statement of the store's value promise. The retailer's goal is to keep shopping simple by offering only a selected assortment of popular brands at everyday low prices in small and convenient locations. Dollar General's slimmed-down product line and smaller stores (you could fit more than 25 Dollar General stores inside the average Walmart supercenter) add up to a quick trip—the average customer is in and out of the store in less than 10 minutes. And its prices on the popular brand name products it carries are an estimated 20 to 40 percent lower than grocery store prices. Put it all together, and things are sizzling right now at Dollar General. Moreover, the fast-growing retailer is well positioned for the future. We "see signs of a new consumerism," says Dollar General's CEO, "as people shift where they shop, switch to lower-cost brands, and stay generally more frugal." Convenience and low prices, it seems, never go out of style.

Off-price retailer
A retailer that buys at less-than-regular wholesale prices and sells at less than retail.

Off-Price Retailers. As the major discount stores traded up, a new wave of **off-price retailers** moved in to fill the ultralow-price, high-volume gap. Ordinary discounters buy at regular wholesale prices and accept lower margins to keep prices down. By contrast, off-price retailers buy at less-than-regular wholesale prices and charge consumers less than retail. Off-price retailers can be found in all areas, from food, clothing, and electronics to no-frills banking and discount brokerages.

Independent off-price retailer
An off-price retailer that is independently owned and operated or a division of a larger retail corporation.

The three main types of off-price retailers are *independents, factory outlets*, and *warehouse clubs*. **Independent off-price retailers** either are independently owned and run or are divisions of larger retail corporations. Although many off-price operations are run by smaller independents, most large off-price retailer operations are owned by bigger retail chains. Examples include store retailers such as TJ Maxx, Marshalls, and HomeGoods, all owned by TJX Companies, and online sellers such as Overstock.com. TJ Maxx promises brand name and designer fashions for 20 to 60 percent off department store prices. How does it fulfill this promise? Its buyers are constantly on the lookout for deals. "So when a designer overproduces and department stores overbuy," says the company, "we swoop in, negotiate the lowest possible price, and pass the savings on."[10]

Factory outlet
An off-price retailing operation that is owned and operated by a manufacturer and normally carries the manufacturer's surplus, discontinued, or irregular goods.

Factory outlets—manufacturer-owned and operated stores by firms such as J.Crew, Gap, Levi Strauss, and others—sometimes group together in *factory outlet malls* and *value-retail centers*. At these centers, dozens of outlet stores offer prices as much as 50 percent below retail on a wide range of mostly surplus, discounted, or irregular goods. Whereas outlet malls consist primarily of manufacturers' outlets, value-retail centers combine manufacturers' outlets with off-price retail stores and department store clearance outlets.

These malls in general are now moving upscale—and even dropping *factory* from their descriptions. A growing number of outlet malls now feature luxury brands such as Coach, Polo Ralph Lauren, Dolce & Gabbana, Giorgio Armani, Burberry, and Versace. As consumers become more value-minded, even upper-end retailers are accelerating their factory outlet strategies, placing more emphasis on outlets such as Nordstrom Rack, Neiman Marcus Last Call, Bloomingdale's Outlets, and Saks Off 5th. Many companies now regard outlets not simply as a way of disposing of problem merchandise but as an additional way of gaining business for fresh merchandise. For example, 90 percent of the merchandise sold in Neiman Marcus's Last Call outlets is made specifically for those stores.[11] The combination of highbrow brands and lowbrow prices found at outlets provides powerful shopper appeal, especially in thriftier times.

» **Off-price retailers: Independent off-price retailer TJX Companies negotiates the lowest prices on brand name goods and passes the savings on to customers.**

Matthew Staver/Bloomberg/Getty Images

Warehouse clubs (also known as *wholesale clubs* or *membership warehouses*), such as Costco, Sam's Club, and BJ's, operate in huge, drafty, warehouse-like facilities and offer few frills. However, they offer ultralow prices and surprise deals on selected branded merchandise. Warehouse clubs have grown rapidly in recent years. These retailers appeal not only to low-income consumers seeking bargains on bare-bones products but also to all kinds of customers shopping for a wide range of goods, from necessities to extravagances.

Consider Costco, now the world's second-largest retailer, behind only Walmart. Low price is an important part of Costco's equation, but what really set Costco apart are the products it carries and the sense of urgency that it builds into the Costco shopper's store experience:[12]

> Costco is a retail treasure hunt, where both low-end and high-end products meet deep-discount prices. Alongside the gallon jars of peanut butter and 2,250-count packs of Q-Tips, Costco offers an ever-changing assortment of high-quality products—even luxuries—all at tantalizingly low margins. Last year, Costco sold more than 109 million hot dog and soda combinations (still only $1.50, as they have been for more than 27 years). At the same time, it sold more than 100,000 carats of diamonds. It is the nation's biggest baster of poultry (nearly 70,000 rotisserie chickens a year at $4.99) but also the country's biggest seller of fine wines (including the likes of a Chateau Cheval Blanc Premier Grand Cru Classe at $1,750 a bottle).
>
> Each Costco store is a theater of retail that creates buying urgency and excitement. Mixed in with its regular stock of staples, Costco features a glittering, constantly shifting array of one-time specials, such as discounted Prada bags, Calloway golf clubs, or Kenneth Cole bags—deals you just won't find anywhere else. In fact, of the 3,600 items that Costco carries, 1,000 are designated as "treasure items" (Costco's words). The changing assortment and great prices keep people of all kinds coming back, wallets in hand. There was a time when only the great, unwashed masses shopped at off-price retailers, but Costco has changed all that. Now, even people who don't have to pinch pennies shop there.

Warehouse club
An off-price retailer that sells a limited selection of brand name grocery items, appliances, clothing, and other goods at deep discounts to members who pay annual membership fees.

Corporate chains
Two or more outlets that are commonly owned and controlled.

Organizational Approach

Although many retail stores are independently owned, others band together under some form of corporate or contractual organization. » **Table 11.2** describes four major types of retail organizations—*corporate chains, voluntary chains, retailer cooperatives*, and *franchise organizations*.

Corporate chains are two or more outlets that are commonly owned and controlled. They have many advantages over independents. Their size allows them to buy in large quantities at lower prices and gain promotional economies. They can hire specialists to deal with areas such as pricing, promotion, merchandising, inventory control, and sales forecasting.

» Table 11.2 Major Types of Retail Organizations

Type	Description	Examples
Corporate chain	Two or more outlets that are commonly owned and controlled. Corporate chains appear in all types of retailing but they are strongest in department stores, discount stores, food stores, drugstores, and restaurants.	Macy's (department stores), Target (discount stores), Kroger (grocery stores), CVS (drugstores)
Voluntary chain	Wholesaler-sponsored group of independent retailers engaged in group buying and merchandising.	Independent Grocers Alliance (IGA), Western Auto (auto supply), True Value (hardware)
Retailer cooperative	Group of independent retailers who jointly establish a central buying organization and conduct joint promotion efforts.	Associated Grocers (groceries), Ace Hardware (hardware)
Franchise organization	Contractual association between a franchisor (a manufacturer, wholesaler, or service organization) and franchisees (independent businesspeople who buy the right to own and operate one or more units in the franchise system).	McDonald's, Subway, Pizza Hut, Jiffy Lube, Meineke Mufflers, 7-Eleven

The great success of corporate chains caused many independents to band together in one of two forms of contractual associations. One is the *voluntary chain*—a wholesaler-sponsored group of independent retailers that engages in group buying and common merchandising. Examples include the Independent Grocers Alliance (IGA), Western Auto, and True Value hardware stores. The other type of contractual association is the *retailer cooperative*—a group of independent retailers that bands together to set up a jointly owned, central wholesale operation and conduct joint merchandising and promotion efforts. Examples are Associated Grocers and Ace Hardware. These organizations give independents the buying and promotion economies they need to meet the prices of corporate chains.

Franchise
A contractual association between a manufacturer, wholesaler, or service organization (a franchisor) and independent businesspeople (franchisees) who buy the right to own and operate one or more units in the franchise system.

Another form of contractual retail organization is a **franchise**. The main difference between franchise organizations and other contractual systems (voluntary chains and retail cooperatives) is that franchise systems are normally based on some unique product or service; a method of doing business; or the trade name, goodwill, or patent that the franchisor has developed. Franchising has been prominent in fast-food restaurants, motels, health and fitness centers, auto sales and service dealerships, and real estate agencies.

However, franchising covers a lot more than just burger joints and fitness centers. Franchises have sprung up to meet just about any need. For example, Mad Science Group franchisees put on science programs for schools, scout troops, and birthday parties. H&R Block provides tax-preparation services, and Supercuts offers affordable, anytime, walk-in haircuts. Mr. Handyman provides repair services for homeowners, while Merry Maids tidies up their houses. >> And Soccer Shots offers programs that give kids ages two to eight an introduction to basic soccer skills at daycare centers, schools, and parks.

>> **Franchising covers a lot more than just burger joints and fitness centers. For example, Soccer Shots franchisees offer programs that give kids ages two to eight an introduction to basic soccer skills.**

Soccer Shots Franchising

Franchises now command about 45 percent of all retail sales in the United States. These days, it's nearly impossible to stroll down a city block or drive on a city street without seeing a McDonald's, Subway, Jiffy Lube, or Holiday Inn. One of the best-known and most successful franchisers, McDonald's, now has more than 36,000 stores in more than 100 countries, including more than 14,000 in the United States. It serves 70 million customers a day and racks up more than \$98 billion in annual system-wide sales. More than 80 percent of McDonald's restaurants worldwide are owned and operated by franchisees. Gaining fast is Subway, one of the fastest-growing franchise restaurants, with system-wide sales of \$18.8 billion and more than 43,000 shops in 110 countries, including more than 27,000 in the United States.[13]

LINKING THE CONCEPTS

Pause here and think about all the different kinds of retailers you deal with regularly, many of which overlap in the products they carry.

- Pick a familiar product: a camera, microwave oven, lawn tool, or something else. Shop for this product at two very different store types, say, a discount store or category killer on the one hand and a department store or smaller specialty store on the other. Then shop for it online. Compare the three shopping outlets on product assortment, services, and prices. If you were going to buy the product, where would you buy it and why?
- What does your shopping trip suggest about the futures of the competing store formats that you sampled?

Retailer Marketing Decisions

Retailers are always searching for new marketing strategies to attract and hold customers. In the past, retailers attracted customers with unique product assortments and more or better services. Today, the assortments and services of various retailers are looking more and more alike. You can find most consumer brands not only in department stores but also in mass-merchandise discount stores, off-price discount stores, and all over the Internet. Thus, it's now more difficult for any one retailer to offer exclusive merchandise.

Service differentiation among retailers has also eroded. Many department stores have trimmed their services, whereas discounters have increased theirs. In addition, customers have become smarter and more price sensitive. They see no reason to pay more for identical brands, especially when service differences are shrinking. For all these reasons, many retailers today are rethinking their marketing strategies.

As shown in >> **Figure 11.1**, retailers face major marketing decisions about *segmentation and targeting, store differentiation and positioning*, and the *retail marketing mix*.

Segmentation, Targeting, Differentiation, and Positioning Decisions

Retailers must first segment and define their target markets and then decide how they will differentiate and position themselves in these markets. Should they focus on upscale, midscale, or downscale shoppers? Do target shoppers want variety, depth of assortment, convenience, or low prices? Until they define and profile their markets, retailers cannot make consistent decisions about product assortment, services, pricing, advertising, store décor, online and mobile site design, or any of the other decisions that must support their positions.

Too many retailers, even big ones, fail to clearly define their target markets and positions. For example, what market does Sears target? For what is the department store known? What is its value proposition versus, say, Walmart on one hand and Macy's or Nordstrom on the other? If you're having trouble answering those questions, you're not alone—so is Sears's management:

> For well over a century, Sears was America's iconic retailer. Its well-known slogan, "Where America Shops," was more than just an advertising tagline—it was a meaningful positioning statement. Almost every American relied on Sears for everything from basic apparel and home goods to appliances and tools. But during the past two decades, once-mighty Sears has lost its way. Squeezed between lower-priced big-box discount stores on the one hand and trendier, more targeted upscale department and specialty stores on the other, Sears has gotten lost in the murky middle. Its old "Where America Shops" positioning has

>> **Figure 11.1 Retailer Marketing Strategies**

As with other types of marketers, the name of the game for retailers is to find the customer value-driven marketing strategy and mix that will let them create value for customers and capture value in return. Think of Target's "Expect More. Pay Less." value proposition. And Olive Garden's "When you're here, you're family."

little meaning these days for a store with little more than one-twentieth the sales of competitor Walmart. It seems that about the only thing Sears has going for it these days is that everything it sells is always on sale. However, price is not a convincing value proposition for Sears, which has trouble matching the low prices of competitors such as Walmart, Target, or Kohl's. Now in a financial tailspin, some analysts even predict that once-dominant Sears will soon disappear entirely. To once again position Sears as the place "Where America Shops," the retailer must first answer the question "Why should people shop at Sears?"

By contrast, successful retailers define their target markets well and position themselves strongly. For example, Trader Joe's has established its "cheap gourmet" value proposition. Walmart is powerfully positioned on low prices and what those always-low prices mean to its customers. And highly successful outdoor products retailer Bass Pro Shops positions itself strongly as being "as close to the Great Outdoors as you can get indoors!"

With solid targeting and positioning, a retailer can compete effectively against even the largest and strongest competitors. For example, compare little Which Wich Superior Sandwiches to giant Subway. Which Wich has only about 300 stores and $175 million in sales; Subway has nearly 43,000 stores worldwide and system-wide sales of $18.8 billion. How does Which Wich compete with one of the world's largest franchise chains? It doesn't—at least not directly. >> Which Wich succeeds by carefully positioning itself *away* from Subway:[14]

>> **Retail targeting and positioning: Which Wich Superior Sandwiches succeeds by positioning itself strongly *away* from larger competitors. It offers more than 50 varieties of unique customizable "wiches" and a "positive energy" from being in the store—both unlike anything you'll find at Subway.**

Courtesy of Which Wich® Superior Sandwiches. www.WhichWich.com

Sandwiches are where it's at these days. If you're craving something between two slices of bread, you have no end of choices, from a basic Subway sub to more exotic creations from Panera Bread, McAlister's Deli, Au Bon Pain, or Potbelly Sandwich Shop. But Which Wich Superior Sandwiches stands out from the pack as the ultimate "have it your way" sandwich place. Which Wich invites you to "Crave something interesting." It offers more than 50 varieties of customizable "wiches"—unlike anything you'll find at Subway—from the signature Wicked (loaded with five meats and three cheeses) to unique items such as the Thank You Turkey (with stuffing and cranberry sauce) and the Elvis Wich (peanut butter, bacon, sweet honey, and fresh banana). Customers use red Sharpies to mark up preprinted menus on sandwich bags, starting with one of the 50 sandwich bases and customizing it with their choices of everything from breads to mustards to veggies. The possibilities for personalization are endless. And instead of standing in a cafeteria-style line as you would at Subway, at Which Wich you hand your bag to the cashier, grab a drink and chips, have a seat, and wait to hear your name called. While you're eating, use the red Sharpie to draw on your bag, then hang your "artwork" on the community wall. It's not just the food that sets Which Wich apart, says the company, "it's a feeling, that positive energy you get from being in our store."

So, Which Wich can't match Subway's massive economies of scale, incredible volume purchasing power, ultraefficient logistics, and low prices. But then again, it doesn't even try. By positioning itself away from Subway and other large competitors, Which Wich has become one of the nation's fastest-growing fast-casual restaurant chains.

Product Assortment and Services Decision

Retailers must decide on three major product variables: product assortment, services mix, and store atmosphere.

The retailer's *product assortment* should differentiate it while matching target shoppers' expectations. One strategy is to offer a highly targeted product assortment: Lane Bryant carries plus-size clothing, Brookstone offers an unusual assortment of gadgets and gifts, and BatteryDepot.com offers about every imaginable kind of replacement battery. Alternatively, a retailer can differentiate itself by offering merchandise that no other competitor carries, such as store brands or national brands on which it holds exclusive rights. For example, Kohl's gets exclusive rights to carry well-known labels such as Simply Vera by Vera Wang and a Food Network-branded line of kitchen tools, utensils, and appliances. Kohl's also offers its own private-label lines, such as Sonoma, Croft & Barrow, Candies, and Apt. 9.

The *services mix* can also help set one retailer apart from another. For example, some retailers invite customers to ask questions or consult service representatives in person or via phone or keyboard. Home Depot offers a diverse mix of services to do-it-yourselfers, from "how-to" classes and "do-it-herself" and kid workshops to a proprietary credit card. Nordstrom delivers top-notch service and promises to "take care of the customer, no matter what it takes."

The *store's atmosphere* is another important element in the reseller's product arsenal. Retailers want to create a unique store experience, one that suits the target market and moves customers to buy. Many retailers practice *experiential retailing*. » For example, L.L.Bean has turned its flagship retail store in Freeport, Maine, into an adventure center where customers can experience the store's goods before buying them:[15]

Customers don't just shop at L.L.Bean's flagship store in Freeport; they *experience* it. Sure, the company's several stores on the Freeport campus offer a full assortment of outdoor apparel and gear. But more than that, they create outdoor experiences. For example, along with selling camping, fishing, hiking, boating, home furnishings, and other goods, L.L.Bean offers a slate of free in-store, hands-on clinics in which knowledgeable experts share tips and techniques to help customers prepare for their own outdoor adventures. Clinics cover everything from tying knots and fishing flies to roadside bike repair to compass navigation and even stargazing. Customers seeking more depth can sign up for one of L.L.Bean's Outdoor Discovery Schools programs in snowshoeing, cross-country skiing, stand-up paddleboarding, fly fishing, biking, birdwatching, canoeing, hunting, or any of a dozen other outdoor activities.

L.L.Bean has turned the Freeport campus into a full-fledged outdoor adventure center, where customers can hike, bike, golf, kayak, or even go seal watching or fishing at nearby Cisco Bay. The adventure center pulls in more customers, who in turn buy more goods. L.L.Bean's flagship store and Freeport campus attract more than 3 million visitors a year, making them Maine's second-most popular tourist destination behind Acadia National Park. In addition, the Freeport campus has become a model for additional L.L.Bean adventure centers in other states from Vermont to Illinois.

» Experiential retailing: L.L.Bean has turned its flagship retail store in Freeport, Maine, into an adventure center where customers can experience goods before buying them.

Photos courtesy of L.L.Bean

Today's digital technologies present many new challenges and opportunities for shaping retail experiences. The surge in online and mobile shopping has changed retail customer behaviors and expectations. As a result, a wide range of store retailers—from high-tech sellers such as AT&T to high-touch sellers like Audi and Build-A-Bear—are digitizing the in-store experience. They are merging the physical and digital worlds to create new-age experiential retailing environments (see Marketing at Work 11.1).

Successful retailers carefully orchestrate virtually every aspect of the consumer store experience. The next time you step into a retail store—whether it sells consumer electronics, hardware, or high fashion—stop and carefully consider your surroundings. Think about the store's layout and displays. Listen to the background music. Check out the colors. Smell the smells. Chances are good that everything in the store, from the layout and lighting to the music and even the colors and smells, has been carefully orchestrated to help shape the customers' shopping experiences—and open their wallets.

For example, retailers choose the colors in their logos and interiors carefully: Black suggests sophistication, orange is associated with fairness and affordability, white signifies

MARKETING AT WORK 11.1

Digitizing the In-Store Retail Experience

There's a flashy new store on Michigan Avenue in downtown Chicago's high-end retail district known as the Magnificent Mile. The store is bright and inviting, with sights and sounds designed to pull people in and get them to linger longer. Customers sit at any of dozens of stations, sampling the latest phone apps and electronic gadgetry. Enthusiastic, iPad-wielding associates mingle with customers, talking tech and dispensing hands-on help and advice. With 130 digital screens and an 18-foot video wall, every aspect of the open space is designed to engage customers about future wireless technologies and services. It feels more like a techy neighborhood hangout than a place to buy products.

A gleaming new Apple store? Think again. This is AT&T's new flagship store. But the resemblance to Apple's groundbreaking retail concept is no mistake. Dozens of diverse retail chains—from high-tech sellers like AT&T to high-touch merchants such as Audi and Build-A-Bear—are remaking their stores in the image of Apple's open marketplace prototypes. But even more, with the surge in digital, online, and mobile technologies invading the retail space, these store chains are blazing new ground. They are digitizing in-store retail—transforming the traditional in-store experience by infusing digital and online technologies into their physical store environments. It's the future of store retailing, but it's already happening.

When they first walk into AT&T's new store, customers quickly realize that it's like nothing they've seen before. "One of my favorite comments from a recent patron ... was that it was like walking into a Web site," says AT&T's president of retail. Organized into zones and stations, the store's technology immerses customers in multimedia and interpersonal experiences. In the Explorer Lounge, customers can play with and learn about the latest apps. At the App Bar, "apptenders" give one-on-one or group demos, which are displayed on the Apps Wall for others to follow along. The 18-foot-high Connect Wall features a giant interactive video screen that displays customer interactions with content and product information, visible to the entire store and to passersby outside. Lifestyle Boutiques organize products, apps, and accessories by customer needs, such as Get Fit, Be Productive, and Share Your Life. At the Experience Platform, customers can interact with AT&T products for home security and automation, entertainment, music, and automobiles.

Although it might seem that the store is all about products and technologies, the real focus is on the customer experience. The store is designed to let customers interact with devices and services, understand how they work, and experience the impact the devices can have on their lives. In one store area, for example, customers can experience how Jawbone's Up Bracelet integrates with a smartphone app to monitor health and fitness by tracking sleep, eating, and movement patterns. In another, a Nissan Leaf is set up to interactively demonstrate various auto-based apps that help customers solve problems, such as monitoring how fast their teenagers are driving. The store is a physical manifestation of AT&T's "It's what you do with what we do" marketing campaign. "We used to sell phones," says the AT&T executive. "Now we've shifted to offering solutions."

Digitizing in-store retail is an obvious fit for a technology retailer like AT&T. But companies in a wide range of other industries are also pioneering the concept. Take German automaker Audi, for instance. In the lead-up to the XXX Summer Olympics in London, Audi threw open the doors to its first Audi City, a stunningly innovative digitized showroom in London's busy Piccadilly Circus area.

Rather than displaying a sea of shiny new vehicles, the Audi City showroom contains very few actual cars, and future Audi showrooms may have none at all. Instead, Audi City is all-digital. Prospective customers use touchscreens and Kinect-style cameras to design and manipulate virtual, life-size cars of their dreams displayed on massive screens surrounding the showroom space. When they've finished, a video shows the car they've designed in action, complete with the exact sound of the chosen engine in full stereo fidelity. The car is then loaded onto a memory stick that the customer can take for later remembering and sharing.

The idea of buying a car without actually seeing it flies in the face of auto retailing tradition. But these car-buying times are anything but traditional. Audi sees digitization as a way to fit showrooms into smaller urban settings and to overcome the limitations of physical dealerships. With 12 different models, each

» Digitizing in-store retail: AT&T's flagship Chicago showroom infuses digital and online technologies into a physical store environment to let customers experience the impact of its devices and services on their lives. It's "like walking into a Web site."

with up to six different trim levels, all with numerous options, no physical dealership can have every possible model on hand. Virtual showrooms, however, can present every model in Audi's extensive portfolio in every possible permutation. Moreover, customers can call them up instantly and make changes on the fly.

So far, the Audi City virtual experience is producing very real-world results. Audi City showrooms in London, Beijing, and Dubai are outselling their traditional counterparts by 70 percent, with an average increase in margin per vehicle of 30 percent. And the digitized auto lounges are bringing more new customers through the doors. Ninety percent of Audi City visitors are new to the brand.

The digitized showroom is finding its way into every industry imaginable. Consider Build-A-Bear Workshop. No stranger to retail innovation, Build-A-Bear revolutionized the in-store experience when it burst into America's malls almost 20 years ago with unique stores that were part showroom, part factory, and part theme park. With the original Build-A-Bear format, children moved from station to station, constructing and customizing their stuffed bears and watching them come to life before their very eyes.

But as smartphones, tablets, and other digital devices changed the way children play, Build-A-Bear saw its sales decline and losses mount. Now, however, rather than fighting digital-age developments, Build-A-Bear is deploying them. Today's Build-A-Bear stores are designed to engage the new generation of digitally adept children. A large video screen at the front of the store uses movement technology to greet children, engage them with interactive games, and introduce store features. From there, each of the eight stations in the bear-building process is enhanced by touchscreens and digital features that give young bear-builders more hands-on involvement and more design options. Kids can even give their finished bear a virtual bath before fluffing it with real air.

For AT&T, Audi, and Build-A-Bear, retailing is nothing new. Each has been in brick-and-mortar retailing for years, with hundreds of showrooms worldwide. But these forward-looking retailers are now betting on a digitized in-store future. AT&T plans to roll out six or seven elements of its Michigan Avenue store to each of its 2,300 other stores. Audi plans to open 20 more Audi City showrooms within a year. And Build-A-Bear has already updated each of its more than 400 stores with its new digital workstations. As AT&T's president of retail points out, digitization is more than just electronic whizbang. "It's all about creating [relevant customer experiences and] interactions rather than just transactions."

Sources: *Jacqueline Renfrow, "AT&T Turns Michigan Avenue Flagship into a Museum," Fierce Retail, March 11, 2015,* www.fierceretail.com/story/att-turns-michigan-avenue-flagship-museum/2015-03-11; Christopher Heine, "The Store of the Future Has Arrived," *Adweek*, June 3, 2013, www.adweek.com/print/149900; Nicole Giannopoulos, "A 'Magnificent' In-Store Experience," *Retail Info Systems News*, June 10, 2013, http://risnews.edgl.com/magazine/June-2013/A-Magnificent-In-Store-Experience86772; Elizabeth Olson, "Build-A-Bear Goes High Tech," *New York Times*, September 27, 2012, p. B3; Rajesh Setty, "Re-Imagining the Retail Experience: The Audi City Store," *Huffington Post*, December 29, 2013, www.huffingtonpost.com/rajesh-setty/re-imagining-the-retail-e_b_4514046.html; and www.callison.com/projects/att-%E2%80%93-michigan-avenue and www.youtube.com/watch?v=GDdPN6mVLPM, accessed October 2015.

---

simplicity and purity (think Apple stores), and blue connotes trust and dependability (financial institutions use it a lot). And most large retailers have developed signature scents that you smell only in their stores:[16]

> Anytime Fitness pipes in "Inspire," a eucalyptus-mint fragrance to create a uniform scent from store to store and mask that "gym" smell. Bloomingdale's uses different essences in different departments: the soft scent of baby powder in the baby store, coconut in the swimsuit area, lilacs in intimate apparel, and sugar cookies and evergreen scent during the holiday season. Luxury men's fashion brand Hugo Boss chose a signature smooth, musky scent for all of its stores. "We wanted it to feel like coming home," says a Hugo Boss marketer. Scents can subtly reinforce a brand's imagery and positioning. For example, the Hard Rock Café Hotel in Orlando added a scent of the ocean in its lobby to help guests imagine checking into a seaside resort (even though the hotel is located an hour from the coast). To draw customers into the hotel's often-overlooked downstairs ice cream shop, the hotel put a sugar cookie aroma at the top of the stairs and a whiff of waffle cone at the bottom. Ice cream sales jumped 45 percent in the following six months.

Such *experiential retailing* confirms that retail stores are much more than simply assortments of goods. They are environments to be experienced by the people who shop in them.

Price Decision

A retailer's price policy must fit its target market and positioning, product and service assortment, the competition, and economic factors. All retailers would like to charge high markups and achieve high volume, but the two seldom go together. Most retailers seek *either* high markups on lower volume (most specialty stores) *or* low markups on higher volume (mass merchandisers and discount stores).

Thus, 110-year-old Bergdorf Goodman caters to the upper crust by selling apparel, shoes, and jewelry created by designers such as Chanel, Prada, Hermes, and Jimmy Choo. The upmarket retailer pampers its customers with services such as a personal shopper and in-store showings of the upcoming season's trends with cocktails and hors d'oeuvres. By contrast, TJ Maxx sells brand name clothing at discount prices aimed at middle-class Americans. As it stocks new products each week, the discounter provides a treasure hunt for bargain shoppers. "No sales. No gimmicks." says the retailer. "Just brand name and designer fashions for you . . . for up to 60 percent off department store prices."

Retailers must also decide on the extent to which they will use sales and other price promotions. Some retailers use no price promotions at all, competing instead on product and service quality rather than on price. For example, it's difficult to imagine Bergdorf Goodman holding a two-for-the-price-of-one sale on Chanel handbags, even in a tight economy. Other retailers—such as Walmart, Costco, ALDI, and Family Dollar—practice *everyday low pricing (EDLP)*, charging constant, everyday low prices with few sales or discounts.

Still other retailers practice *high-low pricing*—charging higher prices on an everyday basis coupled with frequent sales and other price promotions to increase store traffic, create a low-price image, or attract customers who will buy other goods at full prices. Recent tighter economic times caused a rash of high-low pricing, as retailers poured on price cuts and promotions to coax bargain-hunting customers into their stores. Which pricing strategy is best depends on the retailer's overall marketing strategy, the pricing approaches of its competitors, and the economic environment.

Promotion Decision

Retailers use various combinations of the five promotion tools—advertising, personal selling, sales promotion, public relations, and direct and social media marketing—to reach consumers. They advertise in newspapers and magazines and on radio and television. Advertising may be supported by newspaper inserts and catalogs. Store salespeople greet customers, meet their needs, and build relationships. Sales promotions may include in-store demonstrations, displays, sales, and loyalty programs. PR activities, such as new-store openings, special events, newsletters and blogs, store magazines, and public service activities, are also available to retailers.

Most retailers also interact digitally with customers using Web sites and digital catalogs, online ads and video, social media, mobile ads and apps, blogs, and email. Almost every retailer, large or small, maintains a full social media presence. For example, giant Walmart leads the way with a whopping 35 million Facebook Likes, 41,000 Pinterest followers, 664,000 Twitter followers, and 66,000 YouTube subscribers. By contrast, Fairway Market, the small but fast-growing metropolitan New York grocery chain that carries a huge product assortment—from "sky-high piles" of produce to overflowing bins of fresh seafood to hand-roasted coffee—has only 114,000 Facebook Likes. But Fairway isn't complaining—that's twice as many Facebook Likes per million dollars of sales as mighty Walmart.[17]

Digital promotions let retailers reach individual customers with carefully targeted messages. » For example, to compete more effectively against rivals online, CVS distributes personalized versions of its weekly circulars to the chain's ExtraCare loyalty program members. Called myWeekly Ad, customers can view their circulars by logging into their personal accounts at CVS.com on computers, tablets, or smartphones. Based on ExtraCare members' characteristics and previous purchases, the personalized promotions highlight sales items and special offers of special interest to each specific customer. With the myWeekly Ad program, "We're trying to get people to change

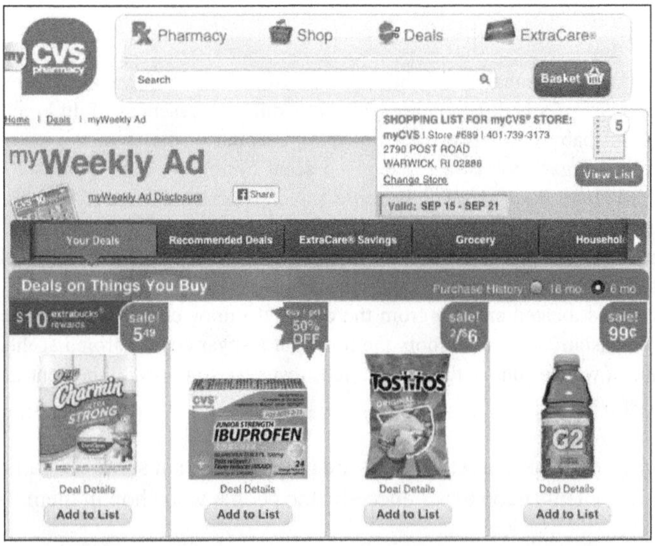

» **Retailer promotion: Most retailers interact digitally with customers using Web sites and digital catalogs, mobile and social media, and other digital platforms. CVS's myWeekly Ad program distributes personalized versions of its weekly circulars to the chain's ExtraCare loyalty program members.**

CVS Caremark Corporation

their behavior," says the CVS marketer heading up the effort, "going online for a much more personalized experience" rather than checking weekly circulars.[18]

Place Decision

Retailers often point to three critical factors in retailing success: location, location, and location! It's very important that retailers select locations that are accessible to the target market in areas that are consistent with the retailer's positioning. For example, Apple locates its stores in high-end malls and trendy shopping districts—such as the Magnificent Mile on Chicago's Michigan Avenue or Fifth Avenue in Manhattan—not low-rent strip malls on the edge of town. By contrast, to keep costs down and support its "cheap gourmet" positioning, Trader Joe's places its stores in lower-rent, out-of-the-way locations. Small retailers may have to settle for whatever locations they can find or afford. Large retailers, however, usually employ specialists who use advanced methods to select store locations.

Most stores today cluster together to increase their customer pulling power and give consumers the convenience of one-stop shopping. Central business districts were the main form of retail cluster until the 1950s. Every large city and town had a central business district with department stores, specialty stores, banks, and movie theaters. When people began moving to the suburbs, however, many of these central business districts, with their traffic, parking, and crime problems, began to lose business. In recent years, many cities have joined with merchants to revive downtown shopping areas, generally with only mixed success.

Shopping center
A group of retail businesses built on a site that is planned, developed, owned, and managed as a unit.

A **shopping center** is a group of retail businesses built on a site that is planned, developed, owned, and managed as a unit. A *regional shopping center*, or *regional shopping mall*, the largest and most dramatic shopping center, has from 50 to more than 100 stores, including two or more full-line department stores. It is like a covered mini-downtown and attracts customers from a wide area. A *community shopping center* contains between 15 and 50 retail stores. It normally contains a branch of a department store or variety store, a supermarket, specialty stores, professional offices, and sometimes a bank. Most shopping centers are *neighborhood shopping centers* or *strip malls* that generally contain between 5 and 15 stores. These centers, which are close and convenient for consumers, usually contain a supermarket, perhaps a discount store, and several service stores—dry cleaner, drugstore, hardware store, local restaurant, or other stores.[19]

A newer form of shopping center is the so-called power center. *Power centers* are huge unenclosed shopping centers consisting of a long strip of retail stores, including large, freestanding anchors such as Walmart, Home Depot, Costco, Best Buy, Michaels, PetSmart, and Office Depot. Each store has its own entrance with parking directly in front for shoppers who wish to visit only one store.

In contrast, *lifestyle centers* are smaller, open-air malls with upscale stores, convenient locations, and nonretail activities, such as a playground, skating rink, hotel, dining establishments, and a movie theater complex. The most recent lifestyle centers often consist of *mixed-use* developments, with ground-floor retail establishments and apartments or condominiums above, combining shopping convenience with the community feel of a neighborhood center. Meanwhile, traditional regional shopping malls are adding lifestyle elements—such as fitness centers, common areas, and multiplex theaters—to make themselves more social and welcoming. In all, today's centers are more like places to hang out rather than just places to shop. "The line between shopping, entertainment, and community building has blurred," says one analyst. "Shopping centers aren't just places to buy things. They're social centers, places for entertainment, and employment hubs."[20]

The past few years have brought hard times for shopping centers. Many experts suggest that the country has long been "overmalled." Not surprisingly, the Great Recession and its aftermath hit shopping malls hard. Consumer spending cutbacks forced many retailers—small and large—out of business, and vacancy rates at the nation's enclosed malls soared.[21] Power centers were also hard hit as their big-box retailer tenants such as Circuit City, Borders, Mervyns, and Linens N Things went out of business and others such as Best Buy, Barnes & Noble, and Office Depot reduced the number or size of their stores. Some of the pizzazz has also gone out of lifestyle centers, whose upper-middle-class shoppers suffered most during the recession.

As the economy has improved, however, malls of all types have rebounded a bit. Many power centers, for example, are filling their empty space with a broader range of retailers, from the likes of Ross Dress for Less, Boot Barn, Nordstrom Rack, and other off-price retailers to dollar stores, warehouse grocers, and traditional discounters like Walmart and Target.

Retailing Trends and Developments

Retailers operate in a harsh and fast-changing environment, which offers threats as well as opportunities. Consumer demographics, lifestyles, and spending patterns are changing rapidly, as are retailing technologies. To be successful, retailers need to choose target segments carefully and position themselves strongly. They need to take the following retailing developments into account as they plan and execute their competitive strategies.

Tighter Consumer Spending

Following many years of good economic times for retailers, the Great Recession of 2008–2009 turned many retailers' fortunes from boom to bust. Even as the economy has recovered, retailers will feel the effects of changed consumer spending patterns well into the future.

Value positioning: Facing tighter consumer spending, Home Depot adopted a thriftier theme: "More saving. More doing."

iofoto/Shutterstock; The Home Depot, Inc.

Some retailers actually benefit from a down economy. For example, as consumers cut back and looked for ways to spend less on what they bought, big discounters such as Costco scooped up new business from bargain-hungry shoppers. And price-oriented and off-price retailers such as ALDI, Dollar General, and TJ Maxx have attracted greater shares of more frugal buyers.

For other retailers, however, tighter consumer spending meant tough times. During and following the recession, several large and familiar retailers declared bankruptcy or closed their doors completely—including household names such as Linens N Things, Circuit City, KB Toys, Borders Books, and Sharper Image, to name a few. Other retailers, from Macy's and Home Depot to Starbucks, laid off employees, cut their costs, and offered deep price discounts and promotions aimed at luring cash-strapped customers back into their stores.

As the economy has improved and as consumers have retained their more frugal spending ways, many retailers have added new value pitches to their positioning. For example, Home Depot replaced its older "You can do it. We can help." theme with a thriftier one: "More saving. More doing." And retailers ranging from Walmart to Macy's to Kroger and Whole Foods Market are boosting their emphasis on more economical private-label brands.

When reacting to economic difficulties, retailers must be careful that their short-run actions don't damage their long-run images and positions. For example, drastic price discounting can increase immediate sales but damage brand loyalty. One analyst calls this "death by discount" and suggests that "virtually every retailer—at both the high and the low end—has fallen so deeply into the trap that discounting has become an expectation of customers rather than a bonus."[22] A stroll through your local shopping mall confirms this assessment. However, instead of relying on cost-cutting and price reductions, retailers should focus on building greater customer value within their long-term store positioning strategies.

New Retail Forms, Shortening Retail Life Cycles, and Retail Convergence

New retail forms continue to emerge to meet new situations and consumer needs, but the life cycle of new retail forms is getting shorter. Department stores took about 100 years to reach the mature stage of the life cycle; more recent forms, such as warehouse stores, reached maturity in about 10 years. In such an environment, seemingly solid retail positions can crumble quickly. Of the top 10 discount retailers in 1962 (the year that the first Walmart, Kmart, Target, and Kohl's stores opened), not one still exists today. Even the most successful retailers can't sit back with a winning formula. To remain successful, they must keep adapting.

New retail forms: Many retailers, such as Brazilian sandal maker Havaianas, use temporary pop-up shops to promote their brands to seasonal shoppers and create buzz in busy areas.

Havaianas

New retail forms are always emerging. The most recent blockbuster retailing trend is the advent of online retailing, by both online-only and store retailers, via Web sites, mobile apps, and social media. But lesser innovations occur regularly. For example, many retailers are now using limited-time *pop-up stores* that let them promote their brands to seasonal shoppers and create buzz in busy areas. During an NBA All-Star weekend at the Barclays Center in Brooklyn, New York, Nike opened a Jordan-themed pop-up shop across the street. Brazilian sandal maker Havaianas is known for opening temporary seasonal pop-up shops at beaches, festivals, and other summer hot spots around the world.[23]

The online and mobile equivalent is *flash sales* sites, such as Nordstrom's HauteLook and Amazon's MyHabit, which host time-limited sales events on top fashion and lifestyle brands. Similarly, Gilt.com flashes member-only, 70 percent discounts on designer-label clothing; and Groupon offers flash deals on travel through Groupon Getaways. Zulily flashes sales on products for moms, babies, and kids, offering limited-time sales "events" that quickly "scoot away to make room for new events." Flash sales add excitement and urgency to buying. Says Zulily, "Shopping here is like opening a new treasure chest every day. You never know exactly what you'll uncover, but you know gems are waiting."[24]

Today's retail forms appear to be converging. Increasingly, different types of retailers now sell the same products at the same prices to the same consumers. For example, you can buy brand name home appliances at department stores, discount stores, home-improvement stores, off-price retailers, electronics superstores, and a slew of online sites that all compete for the same customers. If you can't find the microwave oven you want at Sears, you can step across the street and find one for a better price at Lowe's or Best Buy—or just order one online from Amazon.com or even RitzCamera.com. This merging of consumers, products, prices, and retailers is called *retail convergence*. Such convergence means greater competition for retailers and greater difficulty in differentiating the product assortments of different types of retailers.

The Rise of Megaretailers

The rise of huge mass merchandisers and specialty superstores, the formation of vertical marketing systems, and a rash of retail mergers and acquisitions have created a core of superpower megaretailers. With their size and buying power, these giant retailers can offer better merchandise selections, good service, and strong price savings to consumers. As a result, they grow even larger by squeezing out their smaller, weaker competitors.

The megaretailers have shifted the balance of power between retailers and producers. A small handful of retailers now controls access to enormous numbers of consumers, giving them the upper hand in their dealings with manufacturers. For example, you may never have heard of specialty coatings and sealants manufacturer RPM International, but you've probably used one or more of its many familiar do-it-yourself brands—such as Rust-Oleum paints, Plastic Wood and Dap fillers, Mohawk and Watco finishes, and Testors hobby cements and paints—all of which you can buy at your local Home Depot store. Home Depot is a very important customer to RPM, accounting for a significant share of its consumer sales. However, Home Depot's sales of $78 billion are almost 20 times RPM's sales of $4.3 billion. As a result, the giant retailer can, and often does, use this power to wring concessions from RPM and thousands of other smaller suppliers.[25]

Growth of Direct, Online, Mobile, and Social Media Retailing

Most consumers still make a majority of their purchases the old-fashioned way: They go to a store, find what they want, plunk down their cash or credit cards, and bring home the goods. However, consumers now have a broad array of nonstore alternatives, including direct and digital shopping via Web sites, mobiles apps, and social media. As we'll discuss in Chapter 14, direct and digital marketing are currently the fastest-growing forms of marketing.

Today, thanks to advanced technologies, easier-to-use and enticing online sites and mobile apps, improved online services, and the increasing sophistication of search technologies, online retailing is thriving. In fact, although it currently accounts for only about 7 percent of total U.S. retail sales, online buying is growing at a much brisker pace than retail buying as a whole. Last year's U.S. online retail sales grew 117 percent over the previous year versus a 4 percent increase in overall retail sales.[26]

Retailer online sites, mobile apps, and social media also influence a large amount of in-store buying. An estimated 52 percent of total U.S. retail sales were either transacted directly or influenced by online research. An estimated 15 percent of all online sales now take place on mobile devices, a number that will grow to 25 percent by 2017. Retailers of all kinds rely on social media to engage their buyer communities. For example, whereas Walmart leads among retailers in Facebook Likes, L.L.Bean is tops in Pinterest followers. Victoria's Secret leads in Twitter followers, but H&M comes in a close second. And Victoria's Secret has the most YouTube subscribers.[27]

The spurt in online, mobile, and social media retailing is both a blessing and a curse to store retailers. Although it gives them new channels for engaging and selling to customers, it also creates more competition from online-only retailers. To the dismay of some store retailers, many shoppers now check out merchandise at physical-store showrooms but then buy it online using a computer or mobile device, sometimes while in the store—a process called **showrooming.** »These days, 75 percent of smartphone-carrying shoppers use their phones while shopping in stores. And as many as half of all shoppers who buy products online check them out first at a traditional store.[28] Store retailers such as Target, Walmart, Best Buy, Bed Bath & Beyond, and Toys "R" Us have been hit hard by showrooming.

Showrooming
The shopping practice of coming into retail store showrooms to check out merchandise and prices but instead buying from an online-only rival, sometimes while in the store.

Today, however, many store retailers are developing effective strategies to counter showrooming. Others are even embracing it as an opportunity to highlight the advantages of shopping in stores versus online-only retailers. The flip side of showrooming is *webrooming,* by which consumers first check out merchandise online, then buy it in a store. The key for store retailers is to convert showrooming shoppers into buyers when they visit the store.

However, it's no longer a matter of customers deciding whether to shop in a store *or* shop online. The Internet and digital devices have spawned a whole new breed of shopper and way of shopping. Today's omni-channel buyers shift seamlessly across online and in-store channels during the buying process. They've gotten used to researching and buying anywhere, anytime—whether it's in the store, online, on the go, or even online while in the store. To meet the needs of these omni-channel buyers, store retailers must master *omni-channel retailing,* integrating store and online channels into a single shopper experience (see Marketing at Work 11.2).

» **Showrooming: The now-common practice of viewing products in stores but buying them online presents serious challenges to store retailers. But rather than fighting showrooming, retailers are now embracing it as a way to showcase their omni-channel strengths.**
Kumar Sriskandan/Alamy

An increasing share of the growth in online sales is being captured by omni-channel retailers who successfully merge the virtual and physical worlds. In a recent ranking of the top 10 online retailers, five were store-based retail chains. Another study showed that, among the top 500 online retailers, online sales by store chains were growing 8 percent faster than those of online-only retailers and 40 percent faster than overall e-commerce.[29]

For example, thanks largely to rapid growth in online sales, upscale home products retailer Williams-Sonoma now captures more than half of its total revenues from its direct-to-consumer channel. Like many retailers, Williams-Sonoma has discovered that many of its best customers visit and shop both online and offline. Beyond just offering online shopping, the retailer engages customers through its Web site, online communities, social media, mobile apps, a blog, and special online programs. "The Internet has changed the way

MARKETING AT WORK 11.2

Omni-Channel Retailing: Creating a Seamless Shopping Experience

The shopping process has changed radically in recent years. Not all that long ago, shopping consisted mostly of going store to store—or perhaps flipping through catalogs—to gather product information, make price comparisons, and purchase goods. That was then. Now—in this age of the Internet, computers, smartphones, and other digital devices—shopping typically involves a dazzling array of channels and platforms.

Today's omni-channel consumers readily research products and prices online, shopping digitally from home, from work, in stores, or anywhere in between. They scour retailer Web sites and social media for buying ideas, inspiration, and advice. They might see products in stores and order them online, see products online then buy them in stores, or even buy goods online for in-store pickup. This massive shift in how people shop calls for massive changes in how store retailers operate. Omni-channel *buying* calls for omni-channel *retailing*, integrating all available shopping channels and devices into a seamless customer shopping experience.

At first, as online and mobile shopping caught fire, store retailers worried about *showrooming*—smartphone-wielding customers researching products online while examining them in stores, then jumping ship to catch lower online prices. But most store retailers have now adjusted to the showrooming threat with price-matching and other in-store tactics. In fact, smart retailers now see phone-toting customers not as a threat but as an opportunity.

For example, Best Buy has found that omni-channel shoppers have a higher-than-average propensity to purchase. One study showed that shoppers who use mobile devices in stores are almost twice as likely to purchase from the same retailer in-store or online than to buy elsewhere. "We love being used as the Internet's showroom," says Best Buy's CEO. Where Best Buy once fought showrooming, the chain now facilitates the process, converting showroomers into buyers. Best Buy sales associates are trained to proactively cross-check prices against both their own and other retailer's online offers, including online retailers like Amazon. Employees can then price-match competitors, putting the price question to rest and letting associates focus on areas where Best Buy has the advantage—such as personal advice and service, immediacy, convenient locations, and easy returns. Best Buy's new tagline highlights this strategy: "Best Buy: Expert Service. Unbeatable Prices."

Retailers have learned that shoppers with smartphones are doing far more than just checking online prices. More often, they are filling in the information gap. "The consumer has never been more informed, and that information comes from their phone," says a senior marketer at outdoor-gear retailer REI. "We love when someone enters the store holding their phone saying, 'I want this tent. I want this bike. Help me find this.'" This type of activity shows how digital and store retailing can come together to make a sale, even without cutting price.

But omni-channel retailing goes way beyond just helping in-store customers as they cross-shop on digital devices. It requires carefully integrating the entire range of available shopping channels, both in-store and out, from discovery to purchase in the buying process. For example, most large retailers are now boosting their own online and digital selling options and linking them with stores. One popular way to do that is by letting customers order online and pick up in the store. The "click-and-collect" experience merges the attractions of digital and in-store shopping. For example, Walmart has upped its emphasis on in-store pickups. It tells customers that they can order from its Walmart.com site, often pick up items on the same day, avoid shipping fees, and easily return items to the store if not satisfied. Customers now pick up half of all Walmart.com purchases in stores, often buying additional merchandise during the visit.

Some customers even use mobile devices to place online orders with a given retailer while visiting that retailer's store. Ten percent of Walmart purchases via mobile devices are made from inside a Walmart store. GAP Inc.—which operates the GAP, Old Navy, and Banana Republic chains—actively promotes in-store online ordering. Sales associates with tablets help customers search company-wide store and online inventories to find out-of-stock items. "It gives the team in the store the full capability

» **Foot Locker has mastered omni-channel retailing. It skillfully integrates its in-store environment, high-powered Web sites, and extensive social media presence to create the seamless, anytime-anywhere, omni-channel shopping experience that today's customers seek.**

Luke Sharrett/Bloomberg/Getty Images

to ... meet your needs without you having to go home and do it yourself," says a Banana Republic marketer.

In addition to Web sites, omni-channel retailers are integrating other digital shopping channels. Walmart, Target, Macy's, and other major retailers offer handy mobile apps that pull customers to both their Web sites and stores, let them prepare shopping lists, help them locate merchandise inside stores, and, in Target's case, received daily alerts and exclusive discounts sent to their phones. Macy's uses Shopkick's shopBeacon technology, by which in-store sensors detect opted-in customers as they enter a Macy's store, welcome them via the Macy's app on their phones, and pass along personalized shopping information and "only-for-you" deals.

Social media also play an important part in omni-channel retailing. Thirty percent of shoppers made purchases via social media last year, 44 percent discovered new products via social networks, and 49 percent made purchases based on referrals from social media. In turn, most large store retailers now use social media extensively to engage customers, build community, and link buyers to their Web sites and stores.

But simply creating a digital-friendly store, high-powered Web site, and extensive social media presence doesn't constitute good omni-channel retailing. The key is to integrate these elements to create that critical seamless, anywhere-anytime, omni-channel shopping experience that today's customers seek. Consider athletic footwear and apparel giant Foot Locker, which operates several chains, including Foot Locker and Champs Sports:

> Foot Locker has mastered omni-channel retailing. It now gets 12 percent of its sales online, half of that from mobile buying, and its online sales are growing at an eye-popping 40 percent annually. Its online and mobile efforts link seamlessly with store operations, offering options such as "buy online, ship from store" and "buy online, reserve in store" for pickup. And you'll find Foot Locker everywhere in social media, with more than 150 million total followers across Instagram, Facebook, Snapchat, Twitter, YouTube, and Pinterest, where it builds customer community and pulls customers to its online and store locations.
>
> Foot Locker's omni-channel prowess comes to life inside its Foot Locker, Champs Sports, and other stores. The chain gives sales associates the same mobile research capabilities that customers have. Tablets in hand, using online information about products and competitor offers, associates work with and educate customers. Foot Locker trains store employees to go beyond prices and engage customers in ways that add value through personal touches. With 3,500 stores and Foot Locker's own substantial online presence, the store retailer can help customers to shape almost any kind of shopping experience, including a broad choice of service, payment, and delivery options not available from online-only retailers. Thanks to its omni-channel mastery, whereas other shoe and apparel retailers have had trouble fending off Web-only sellers like online star Zappos, Foot Locker is thriving in the new omni-channel shopping environment. Over the past four years, the retailer's sales have zoomed 40 percent and profits have tripled.

Sources: Tim Simmons, "The Keys to Unlocking the Retail Omni-Channel Advantage," *Forbes*, January 2, 2015, www.forbes.com/sites/teradata/2015/01/02/the-keys-to-unlocking-the-retail-omni-channel-advantage/; Sarah Halzack, "Online or In-Store? How about a Little of Both?", *Washington Post*, November 28, 2014, p. A01; Christine Birkner, "Good Tidings for Retail," *Marketing News*, December 2014, p. 14; Kyle Stock, "Does Foot Locker Have Too Many Nikes?" *Bloomberg Businessweek*, March 7, 2014, www.bloomberg.com/bw/articles/2014-03-07/does-foot-locker-have-too-many-nikes; Laura Heller, "How Foot Locker Is Using Mobile to Reach Millennials," *FierceMobileRetail*, August 4, 2014, www.fierceretail.com/mobileretail/story/how-foot-locker-using-mobile-reach-millennials/2014-08-04; Brian Sozzi, "Foot Locker Transforming Its Stores as It Seeks to Keep Sales on Fire," *TheStreet*, March 17, 2015, www.thestreet.com/story/13081277/1/foot-locker-transforming-its-stores-as-it-seeks-to-keep-sales-on-fire.html; and www.footlocker-inc.com and www.footlocker.com, accessed October 2015.

our customers shop," says Williams-Sonoma CEO Laura Alber, "and the online brand experience has to be inspiring and seamless."[30]

Growing Importance of Retail Technology

Retail technologies have become critically important as competitive tools. Progressive retailers are using advanced information technology and software systems to produce better forecasts, control inventory costs, interact electronically with suppliers, send information between stores, and even sell to customers within stores. They have adopted sophisticated systems for checkout scanning, RFID inventory tracking, merchandise handling, information sharing, and customer interactions.

Perhaps the most startling advances in retail technology concern the ways in which retailers are connecting with consumers. Increasingly, retailers are bringing online and digital technologies into their physical stores. Many retailers now routinely use technologies ranging from touchscreen kiosks and handheld shopping assistants to interactive dressing-room mirrors and virtual sales associates. Macy's uses Shopkick's shopBeacon indoor positioning system to engage customers digitally as they shop around its stores. » When opted-in customers enter a Macy's store, a Bluetooth signal wakes up the shopBeacon app on their smartphone or tablet, which welcomes them and alerts them to location-specific rewards, deals, discounts, and personalized product recommendations within the store. The technology can also link in-store and at-home browsing; if the customer "likes" a specific product online, shopBeacon can remind them where to find it in the store, pop up a brief product video, and maybe pass along a for-you-only deal. The goal of

>> **Retail technology: Macy's uses Shopkick's shopBeacon to engage consumers in the store and personalize their shopping experiences.**

Shopkick, Inc.

shopBeacon is to engage Macy's tech-savvy and social customers as a trusted companion and to personalize their in-store shopping experience.[31]

The future of technology in retailing is to blend the new technologies with traditional services. For example, Walmart's goal is to merge in-store and online, social media, and mobile innovations to give customers an enhanced shopping experience:

> To augment in-store shopping, Walmart formed @ WalmartLabs, which develops mobile and social media platforms that make shopping easier, more accessible, and more fun. For example, the retailer's Walmart Gifts gift-finder app applies data from users' Facebook Likes, comments, status updates, and other data to recommend the best products for customers and gifts for their friends. The retailer's feature-rich mobile apps let customers create smart shopping lists, scan barcodes and check prices, access product information, and scan coupons in real time—all from a smartphone or tablet, at home, at work, in the store, or anywhere in between. Walmart's "Savings Catcher" app lets customers scan their store receipt to compare prices at competing stores—if the app finds cheaper prices elsewhere, shoppers get money back in the form of a gift card. And Walmart customers will soon be able to use their smartphones in self-checkout lines. The Walmart SocialStore team at @WalmartLabs is exploring other new in-store social media, mobile, and kiosk technologies that will both assist customers as they shop and help stores get to know and serve their customers better.[32]

Green Retailing

Today's retailers are increasingly adopting environmentally sustainable practices. They are greening up their stores and operations, promoting more environmentally responsible products, launching programs to help customers be more responsible, and working with channel partners to reduce their environmental impact.

At the most basic level, most large retailers are making their stores more environmentally friendly through sustainable building design, construction, and operations. >> For example, under its "People & Planet Positive" sustainability strategy, home furnishings retailer IKEA's long-term goal is to become 100 sustainable:[33]

> The "People & Planet Positive" strategy begins with making IKEA's 315 giant stores in 27 countries more energy independent and efficient. To power its stores, IKEA has committed to owning and operating 224 wind turbines and has installed 700,000 solar panels—90 percent of its U.S. stores have solar panels. By 2020, IKEA will generate as much energy as it uses from renewable sources. Inside its stores, IKEA uses only energy-efficient LED lighting. Most stores also sort food waste from in-store customer restaurants for composting or send it to treatment centers where it is turned into animal feed or biogas to fuel cars and buses. Some IKEAs offer customer recycling centers for products such as plastic, paper, CFL light bulbs, batteries, and even end-of-life appliances.

>> **Green retailing: Under its "People & Planet Positive" sustainability strategy, IKEA's long-term goal is to become 100 sustainable.**

Used with the permission of Inter IKEA Systems B.V

Retailers are also greening up their product assortments. For example, IKEA now sells only LED lighting products in its stores, and a growing proportion of the home furnishing products it sells are made from sustainable and renewable cotton, wood, and other resources. IKEA suppliers must adhere the retailer's IWAY supplier code of conduct sustainability standards. IKEA's goal is have all of its home furnishings made from renewable, recyclable, or recycled materials. "At IKEA, sustainability is central to our business," says the company, "to ensure that we have a positive impact on people and the planet."

Many retailers have also launched programs that help consumers make more environmentally responsible decisions. Staples's Easy on the Planet program "makes it easier to make a difference" by helping customers to identify green products sold in its stores and to recycle printer cartridges, mobile phones, computers, and other office technology products. Staples recycles some 30 million printer cartridges and 10 million pounds of old technology each year.[34]

Finally, many large retailers are joining forces with suppliers and distributors to create more sustainable products, packaging, and distribution systems. For example, Amazon.com works closely with the producers of many of the products it sells to reduce and simplify their packaging. And beyond its own substantial sustainability initiatives, Walmart wields its huge buying power to urge its army of suppliers to improve their environmental impact and practices. The retailer has even developed a worldwide Sustainable Product Index by which it rates suppliers. It plans to translate the index into a simple rating for consumers to help them make more sustainable buying choices.

Green retailing yields both top- and bottom-line benefits. Sustainable practices lift a retailer's top line by attracting consumers looking to support environmentally friendly sellers and products. They also help the bottom line by reducing costs. For example, Amazon.com's reduced-packaging efforts increase customer convenience and eliminate "wrap rage" while at the same time saving packaging costs. And IKEA's more energy-efficient buildings not only appeal to customers and help save the planet but also cost less to operate.

Global Expansion of Major Retailers

Retailers with unique formats and strong brand positions are increasingly moving into other countries. Many are expanding internationally to escape saturated home markets. Over the years, some giant U.S. retailers, such as McDonald's, have become globally prominent as a result of their marketing prowess. Others, such as Walmart, are rapidly establishing a global presence. Walmart, which now operates more than 6,100 stores in 26 non-U.S. markets, sees exciting global potential. Its international division alone last year racked up sales of more than $136 billion, almost 86 percent more than rival Target's *total* sales of $73 billion.[35]

However, most U.S. retailers are still significantly behind Europe and Asia when it comes to global expansion. Although nine of the world's top 20 retailers are U.S. companies, only four of these retailers have set up stores outside North America (Walmart, Home Depot, Costco, and Best Buy). Of the 12 non-U.S. retailers in the world's top 20, eight have stores in at least 10 countries. Foreign retailers that have gone global include France's Carrefour, Groupe Casino, and Auchan chains; Germany's Metro, Lidl, and ALDI chains; Britain's Tesco; and Japan's Seven & I.[36]

International retailing presents challenges as well as opportunities. Retailers can face dramatically different retail environments when crossing countries, continents, and cultures. Simply adapting the operations that work well in the home country is usually not enough to create success abroad. Instead, when going global, retailers must understand and meet the needs of local markets.

LINKING THE CONCEPTS

Time out! So-called experts have long predicted that online retailing eventually will replace store retailing as our primary way to shop. What do you think?

- Shop for a good book at the Barnes & Noble Web site (www.bn.com), taking time to browse the site and see what it has to offer. Next, shop at a nearby Barnes & Noble or other bookstore. Compare the two shopping experiences. Where would you rather shop? On what occasions? Why?
- A Barnes & Noble store creates an ideal "community" where people can "hang out." How does its Web site compare on this dimension?
- Do Barnes & Noble's various social media efforts create community for the retailer and its customers? For example, see www.facebook.com/barnesandnoble, https://twitter.com/bnbooks, and http://pinterest.com/barnesandnoble/followers/.

Author Comment

Whereas retailers primarily sell goods and services directly to final consumers for personal use, wholesalers sell primarily to those buying for resale or business use. Because wholesalers operate behind the scenes, they are largely unknown to final consumers. But they are very important to their business customers.

Wholesaling

Wholesaling includes all the activities involved in selling goods and services to those buying them for resale or business use. Firms engaged *primarily* in wholesaling activities are called **wholesalers**.

Wholesaling
All the activities involved in selling goods and services to those buying for resale or business use.

Wholesaler
A firm engaged *primarily* in wholesaling activities.

Wholesalers buy mostly from producers and sell mostly to retailers, industrial consumers, and other wholesalers. As a result, many of the nation's largest and most important wholesalers are largely unknown to final consumers. For example, Sysco is a huge $46 billion wholesale food distribution company that operates behind the scenes to supply boxes of seafood, chicken, pasta, vegetables, baked goods, condiments, napkins, and other goods to more than 425,000 restaurants, schools, hospitals, colleges, and other commercial customers that prepare meals away from home. Wholesaler Arrow Electronics supplies $23 billion worth of computer chips, capacitors, and other electronics and computer components annually to more than 100,000 original equipment manufacturers and commercial customers through a global network of more than 460 locations in 56 countries. And you may never have heard of a company called Grainger, even though it is very well known and much valued by its more than 2 million business and institutional customers in more than 150 countries:[37]

> Grainger may be the biggest market leader you've never heard of. It's a $10 billion business that offers more than 1.4 million maintenance, repair, and operating (MRO) products from more than 4,500 manufacturers to over 2 million active customers. Through its branch network, service centers, sales reps, catalog, and online and social media sites, Grainger links customers with the supplies they need to keep their facilities running smoothly and their people safe—everything from lightbulbs, cleaners, and display cases to nuts and bolts, motors, valves, power tools, test equipment, and safety supplies. Grainger's nearly 700 branches, 33 strategically located distribution centers, more than 23,700 employees, and innovative Web sites handle more than 115,000 transactions a day. Grainger's customers include organizations ranging from factories, garages, and grocers to schools and military bases.
>
> Grainger operates on a simple value proposition: to make it easier and less costly for customers to find and buy MRO supplies. It starts by acting as a one-stop shop for products needed to maintain facilities. On a broader level, it builds lasting relationships with customers by helping them find *solutions* to their overall MRO problems. Acting as consultants, Grainger sales reps help buyers with everything from improving their supply chain management to reducing inventories and streamlining warehousing operations.
>
> So, how come you've never heard of Grainger? Perhaps it's because the company operates in the not-so-glamorous world of MRO supplies, which are important to every business but not so important to consumers. More likely, it's because Grainger is a wholesaler. And like most wholesalers, it operates behind the scenes, selling mostly to other businesses.

Wholesaling: Many of the nation's largest and most important wholesalers—like Grainger—are largely unknown to final consumers. But they are very well known and much valued by the business customers they serve.

W. W. Grainger, Inc.

Why are wholesalers important to sellers? For example, why would a producer use wholesalers rather than selling directly to retailers or consumers? Simply put, wholesalers add value by performing one or more of the following channel functions:

- ***Selling and promoting.*** Wholesalers' sales forces help manufacturers reach many small customers at a low cost. The wholesaler has more contacts and is often more trusted by the buyer than the distant manufacturer.
- ***Buying and assortment building.*** Wholesalers can select items and build assortments needed by their customers, thereby saving much work.
- ***Bulk breaking.*** Wholesalers save their customers money by buying in carload lots and breaking bulk (breaking large lots into small quantities).
- ***Warehousing.*** Wholesalers hold inventories, thereby reducing the inventory costs and risks of suppliers and customers.

- ***Transportation.*** Wholesalers can provide quicker delivery to buyers because they are closer to buyers than are producers.
- ***Financing.*** Wholesalers finance their customers by giving credit, and they finance their suppliers by ordering early and paying bills on time.
- ***Risk bearing.*** Wholesalers absorb risk by taking title and bearing the cost of theft, damage, spoilage, and obsolescence.
- ***Market information.*** Wholesalers give information to suppliers and customers about competitors, new products, and price developments.
- ***Management services and advice.*** Wholesalers often help retailers train their salesclerks, improve store layouts and displays, and set up accounting and inventory control systems.

Types of Wholesalers

Merchant wholesaler
An independently owned wholesale business that takes title to the merchandise it handles.

Wholesalers fall into three major groups (see >> Table 11.3): *merchant wholesalers, brokers and agents*, and *manufacturers' and retailers' branches and offices*. **Merchant wholesalers** are the largest single group of wholesalers, accounting for roughly 50 percent of all wholesaling. Merchant wholesalers include two broad types: full-service wholesalers and limited-service wholesalers. *Full-service wholesalers* provide a full set of services, whereas the various *limited-service wholesalers* offer fewer services to their suppliers and customers. The different types of limited-service wholesalers perform varied specialized functions in the distribution channel.

>> Table 11.3 Major Types of Wholesalers

Type	Description
Merchant wholesalers	Independently owned businesses that take title to all merchandise handled. There are full-service wholesalers and limited-service wholesalers.
Full-service wholesalers	Provide a full line of services: carrying stock, maintaining a sales force, offering credit, making deliveries, and providing management assistance. Full-service wholesalers include wholesale merchants and industrial distributors.
Wholesale merchants	Sell primarily to retailers and provide a full range of services. General merchandise wholesalers carry several merchandise lines, whereas general line wholesalers carry one or two lines in great depth. Specialty wholesalers specialize in carrying only part of a line.
Industrial distributors	Sell to manufacturers rather than to retailers. Provide several services, such as carrying stock, offering credit, and providing delivery. May carry a broad range of merchandise, a general line, or a specialty line.
Limited-service wholesalers	Offer fewer services than full-service wholesalers. Limited-service wholesalers are of several types:
Cash-and-carry wholesalers	Carry a limited line of fast-moving goods and sell to small retailers for cash. Normally do not deliver.
Truck wholesalers (or truck jobbers)	Perform primarily a selling and delivery function. Carry a limited line of semiperishable merchandise (such as milk, bread, snack foods), which is sold for cash as deliveries are made to supermarkets, small groceries, hospitals, restaurants, factory cafeterias, and hotels.
Drop shippers	Do not carry inventory or handle the product. On receiving an order, drop shippers select a manufacturer, who then ships the merchandise directly to the customer. Drop shippers operate in bulk industries, such as coal, lumber, and heavy equipment.
Rack jobbers	Serve grocery and drug retailers, mostly in nonfood items. Rack jobbers send delivery trucks to stores, where the delivery people set up toys, paperbacks, hardware items, health and beauty aids, or other items. Rack jobbers price the goods, keep them fresh, set up point-of-purchase displays, and keep inventory records.
Producers' cooperatives	Farmer-owned members that assemble farm produce for sale in local markets. Producers' cooperatives often attempt to improve product quality and promote a co-op brand name, such as Sun-Maid raisins, Sunkist oranges, or Diamond nuts.
Mail-order or Web wholesalers	Send catalogs to or maintain Web sites for retail, industrial, and institutional customers featuring jewelry, cosmetics, specialty foods, and other small items. Its primary customers are businesses in small outlying areas.

Brokers and agents	**Do not take title to goods. The main function is to facilitate buying and selling, for which they earn a commission on the selling price. Generally specialize by product line or customer type.**
Brokers	Bring buyers and sellers together and assist in negotiation. Brokers are paid by the party who hired the broker and do not carry inventory, get involved in financing, or assume risk. Examples include food brokers, real estate brokers, insurance brokers, and security brokers.
Agents	Represent either buyers or sellers on a more permanent basis than brokers do. There are four types:
Manufacturers' agents	Represent two or more manufacturers of complementary lines. Often used in such lines as apparel, furniture, and electrical goods. A manufacturer's agent is hired by small manufacturers who cannot afford their own field sales forces and by large manufacturers who use agents to open new territories or cover territories that cannot support full-time salespeople.
Selling agents	Have contractual authority to sell a manufacturer's entire output. The selling agent serves as a sales department and has significant influence over prices, terms, and conditions of sale. Found in product areas such as textiles, industrial machinery and equipment, coal and coke, chemicals, and metals.
Purchasing agents	Generally have a long-term relationship with buyers and make purchases for them, often receiving, inspecting, warehousing, and shipping the merchandise to buyers. Purchasing agents help clients obtain the best goods and prices available.
Commission merchants	Take physical possession of products and negotiate sales. Used most often in agricultural marketing by farmers who do not want to sell their own output. Take a truckload of commodities to a central market, sell it for the best price, deduct a commission and expenses, and remit the balance to the producers.
Manufacturers' and retailers' branches and offices	**Wholesaling operations conducted by sellers or buyers themselves rather than operating through independent wholesalers. Separate branches and offices can be dedicated to either sales or purchasing.**
Sales branches and offices	Set up by manufacturers to improve inventory control, selling, and promotion. Sales branches carry inventory and are found in industries such as lumber and automotive equipment and parts. Sales offices do not carry inventory and are most prominent in the dry goods and notions industries.
Purchasing offices	Perform a role similar to that of brokers or agents but are part of the buyer's organization. Many retailers set up purchasing offices in major market centers, such as New York and Chicago.

Brokers and *agents* differ from merchant wholesalers in two ways: They do not take title to goods, and they perform only a few functions. Like merchant wholesalers, they generally specialize by product line or customer type. A **broker** brings buyers and sellers together and assists in negotiation. **Agents** represent buyers or sellers on a more permanent basis. *Manufacturers' agents* (also called *manufacturers' representatives*) are the most common type of agent wholesaler. The third major type of wholesaling is that done in **manufacturers' and retailers' branches and offices** by sellers or buyers themselves rather than through independent wholesalers.

Broker
A wholesaler who does not take title to goods and whose function is to bring buyers and sellers together and assist in negotiation.

Agent
A wholesaler who represents buyers or sellers on a relatively permanent basis, performs only a few functions, and does not take title to goods.

Manufacturers' and retailers' branches and offices
Wholesaling by sellers or buyers themselves rather than through independent wholesalers.

Wholesaler Marketing Decisions

Wholesalers now face growing competitive pressures, more-demanding customers, new technologies, and more direct-buying programs on the part of large industrial, institutional, and retail buyers. As a result, they have taken a fresh look at their marketing strategies. As with retailers, their marketing decisions include choices of segmentation and targeting, differentiation and positioning, and the marketing mix—product and service assortments, price, promotion, and distribution (see **Figure 11.2**).

Segmentation, Targeting, Differentiation, and Positioning Decisions

Like retailers, wholesalers must segment and define their target markets and differentiate and position themselves effectively—they cannot serve everyone. They can choose a target group by size of customer (for example, large retailers only), type of customer (convenience stores only), the need for service (customers who need credit), or other factors. Within the target

Figure 11.2 Wholesaler Marketing Strategies

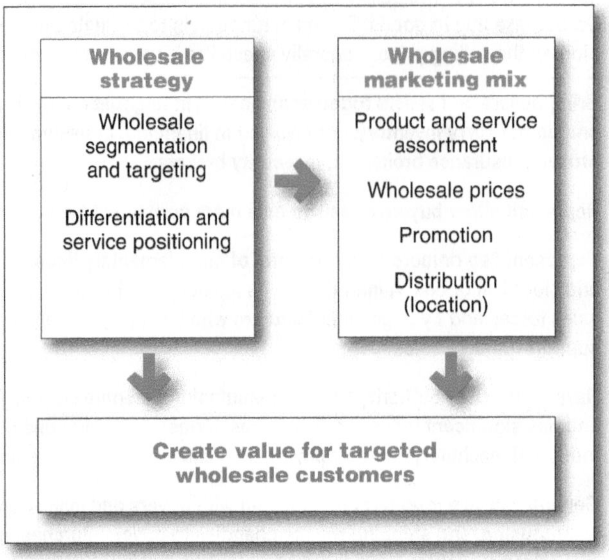

Why does this figure look so much like Figure 11.1? You guessed it. Like retailers, wholesalers must develop customer-driven marketing strategies and mixes that create value for customers and capture value in return. For example, Grainger helps its business customers "save time and money by providing them with the right products and solutions to keep their facilities up and running."

group, they can identify the more profitable customers, design stronger offers, and build better relationships with them. They can propose automatic reordering systems, establish management-training and advisory systems, or even sponsor a voluntary chain. They can discourage less-profitable customers by requiring larger orders or adding service charges to smaller ones.

Marketing Mix Decisions

Like retailers, wholesalers must decide on product and service assortments, prices, promotion, and place. Wholesalers add customer value though the *products and services* they offer. They are often under great pressure to carry a full line and stock enough for immediate delivery. But this practice can damage profits. Wholesalers today are cutting down on the number of lines they carry, choosing to carry only the more profitable ones. They are also rethinking which services count most in building strong customer relationships and which should be dropped or paid for by the customer. The key for companies is to find the mix of services most valued by their target customers.

Price is also an important wholesaler decision. Wholesalers usually mark up the cost of goods by a standard percentage—say, 20 percent. Expenses may run 17 percent of the gross margin, leaving a profit margin of 3 percent. In grocery wholesaling, the average profit margin is often less than 2 percent. The recent recession put heavy pressure on wholesalers to cut their costs and prices. As their retail and industrial customers face sales and margin declines, these customers turn to wholesalers, looking for lower prices. Wholesalers may, in turn, cut their margins on some lines to keep important customers. They may also ask suppliers for special price breaks in cases when they can turn them into an increase in the supplier's sales.

Although *promotion* can be critical to wholesaler success, most wholesalers are not promotion minded. They use largely scattered and unplanned trade advertising, sales promotion, personal selling, and public relations. Many are behind the times in personal selling; they still see selling as a single salesperson talking to a single customer instead of as a team effort to sell, build, and service major accounts. Wholesalers also need to adopt some of the nonpersonal promotion techniques used by retailers. They need to develop an overall promotion strategy and make greater use of supplier promotion materials and programs. Digital and social media are playing an increasingly important role. For example, Grainger maintains an active presence on Facebook, YouTube, Twitter, LinkedIn, and Google+. It also provides a feature-rich mobile app. On its YouTube channel, Grainger lists more than 500 videos on topics ranging from the company and its products and services to keeping down inventory costs.

Finally, *distribution* (location) is important. Wholesalers must choose their locations, facilities, and Web locations carefully. There was a time when wholesalers could locate in low-rent, low-tax areas and invest little money in their buildings, equipment, and systems. Today, however, as technology zooms forward, such behavior results in outdated systems for material handling, order processing, and delivery.

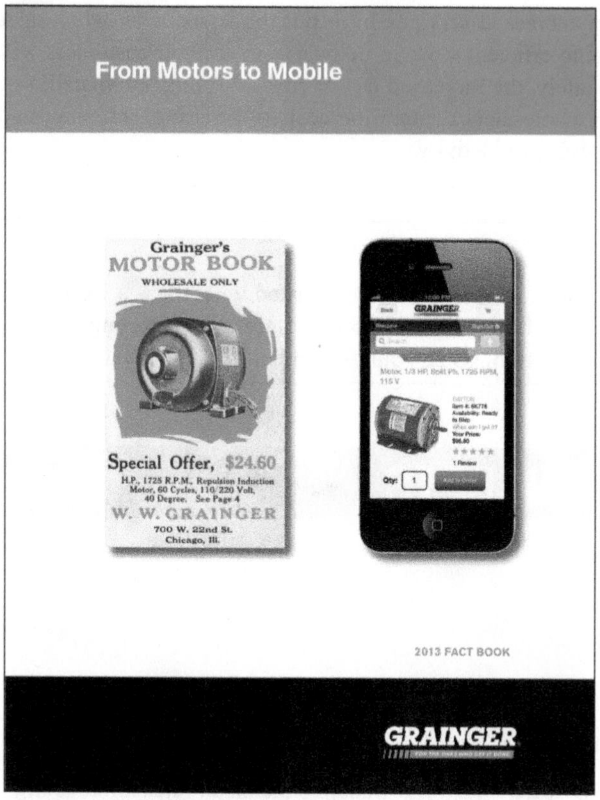

Wholesaler marketing: Progressive wholesalers like Grainger maintain an active presence in online, mobile, and social media. For example, online and mobile purchasing now account for 80 percent of Grainger's total sales.

W. W. Grainger, Inc.

Instead, today's large and progressive wholesalers have reacted to rising costs by investing in automated warehouses and IT systems. Orders are fed from the retailer's information system directly into the wholesaler's, and the items are picked up by mechanical devices and automatically taken to a shipping platform where they are assembled. Most large wholesalers use technology to carry out accounting, billing, inventory control, and forecasting. Modern wholesalers are adapting their services to the needs of target customers and finding cost-reducing methods of doing business. They are also transacting more business online. For example, e-commerce is Grainger's fastest-growing sales channel, making Grainger the 13th-largest online seller in the United States and Canada. Online and mobile purchasing now account for 36 percent of the wholesaler's total sales.[38]

Trends in Wholesaling

Today's wholesalers face considerable challenges. The industry remains vulnerable to one of its most enduring trends—the need for ever-greater efficiency. Recent tighter economic conditions have led to demands for even lower prices and the winnowing out of suppliers who are not adding value based on cost and quality. Progressive wholesalers constantly watch for better ways to meet the changing needs of their suppliers and target customers. They recognize that their only reason for existence comes from adding value, which occurs by increasing the efficiency and effectiveness of the entire marketing channel.

As with other types of marketers, the goal is to build value-adding customer relationships. McKesson provides an example of progressive, value-adding wholesaling. The company is a diversified health-care-services provider and the nation's leading wholesaler of pharmaceuticals, health and beauty care, home health-care, and medical supply and equipment products. To survive, especially in a tight economic environment, McKesson has to be more cost effective than manufacturers' sales branches. Thus, the company has built efficient automated warehouses, established direct computer links with drug manufacturers, and created extensive online supply management and accounts receivable systems for customers. It offers retail pharmacists a wide range of online resources, including supply management assistance, catalog searches, real-time order tracking, and an account management system. It has also created solutions such as automated pharmaceutical-dispensing machines that assist pharmacists by reducing costs and improving accuracy. Retailers can even use the McKesson systems to maintain prescription histories and medical profiles on their customers.

McKesson's medical-surgical supply and equipment customers receive a rich assortment of online solutions and supply management tools, including an online order management system and real-time information on products and pricing, inventory availability, and order status. According to McKesson, it adds value in the channel by providing "supply, information, and health care management products and services designed to reduce costs and improve quality across healthcare."[39]

The distinction between large retailers and large wholesalers continues to blur. Many retailers now operate formats such as wholesale clubs and supercenters that perform many wholesale functions. In return, some large wholesalers are setting up their own retailing operations. For example, SuperValu is the nation's largest food wholesaler, and it's also one of the country's largest food retailers. About half of the company's sales come from its Cub Foods, Save-A-Lot, Farm Fresh, Hornbacher's, Shop 'n Save, and Shoppers stores. In fact, SuperValu now bills itself as "America's neighborhood grocer."[40]

Wholesalers will continue to increase the services they provide to retailers—retail pricing, cooperative advertising, marketing and management information services, accounting services, online transactions, and others. However, both the more value-focused environment and the demand for increased services have put the squeeze on wholesaler profits. Wholesalers that do not find efficient ways to deliver value to their customers will soon drop by the wayside. Fortunately, the increased use of computerized, automated, and Internet-based systems will help wholesalers contain the costs of ordering, shipping, and inventory holding, thus boosting their productivity.

MyMarketingLab

If assigned by your instructor, complete the questions marked with the ✪ from the EOC Discussion Questions section in the MyLab. To complete the Marketing by the Numbers problems found in this section, go to your Assignments in the MyLab.

REVIEWING AND EXTENDING THE CONCEPTS

CHAPTER REVIEW AND CRITICAL THINKING

Objectives Review

Retailing and wholesaling consist of many organizations bringing goods and services from the point of production to the point of use. In this chapter, we examined the nature and importance of retailing, the major types of retailers, the decisions retailers make, and the future of retailing. We then examined these same topics for wholesalers.

OBJECTIVE 11-1 Explain the role of retailers in the distribution channel and describe the major types of retailers. (pp 334–340)

Retailing includes all the activities involved in selling goods or services directly to final consumers for their personal, nonbusiness use. Retailers play an important role in connecting brands to consumers in the final phases of the buying process. *Shopper marketing* involves focusing the entire marketing process on turning shoppers into buyers as they approach the point of sale. These days, shopper marketing and the "point of purchase" go well beyond in-store buying. Today's buyers are omni-channel consumers who work across multiple channels as they shop. Thus, influencing consumers' buying decisions calls for *omni-channel retailing*, creating a seamless cross-channel buying experience that integrates in-store, online, and mobile shopping

Retail stores come in all shapes and sizes, and new retail types keep emerging. Store retailers can be classified by the *amount of service* they provide (self-service, limited service, or full service), *product line sold* (specialty stores, department stores, supermarkets, convenience stores, superstores, and service businesses), and *relative prices* (discount stores and off-price retailers). Today, many retailers are banding together in corporate and contractual *retail organizations* (corporate chains, voluntary chains, retailer cooperatives, and franchise organizations).

OBJECTIVE 11-2 Describe the major retailer marketing decisions. (pp 341–348)

Retailers are always searching for new marketing strategies to attract and hold customers. They face major marketing decisions about segmentation and targeting, store differentiation and positioning, and the retail marketing mix.

Retailers must first segment and define their target markets and then decide how they will differentiate and position themselves in these markets. Those that try to offer "something for everyone" end up satisfying no market well. By contrast, successful retailers define their target markets well and position themselves strongly.

Guided by strong targeting and positioning, retailers must decide on a retail marketing mix—product and services assortment, price, promotion, and place. Retail stores are much more than simply an assortment of goods. Beyond the products and services they offer, today's successful retailers carefully orchestrate virtually every aspect of the consumer store experience. A retailer's price policy must fit its target market and positioning, products and services assortment, and competition. Retailers use various combinations of the five promotion tools—advertising, personal selling, sales promotion, PR, and direct marketing—to reach consumers. Online, mobile, and social media tools are playing an ever-increasing role in helping retailers to engage customers. Finally, it's very important that retailers select locations that are accessible to the target market in areas that are consistent with the retailer's positioning.

OBJECTIVE 11-3 Discuss the major trends and developments in retailing. (pp 348–354)

Retailers operate in a harsh and fast-changing environment, which offers threats as well as opportunities. Following years of good economic times, retailers have now adjusted to the new economic realities and more thrift-minded consumers. New retail forms continue to emerge. At the same time, however, different types of retailers are increasingly serving similar customers with the same products and prices (retail convergence), making differentiation more difficult. Other trends in retailing include the rise of megaretailers; the rapid growth of direct, online, mobile, and social media retailing; the growing importance of retail technology; a surge in green retailing; and the global expansion of major retailers.

OBJECTIVE 11-4 Explain the major types of wholesalers and their marketing decisions. (pp 355–360)

Wholesaling includes all the activities involved in selling goods or services to those who are buying for the purpose of resale or business use. Wholesalers fall into three groups. First, *merchant wholesalers* take possession of the goods. They include *full-service wholesalers* (wholesale merchants and industrial distributors) and *limited-service wholesalers* (cash-and-carry wholesalers, truck wholesalers, drop shippers, rack jobbers, producers' cooperatives, and mail-order wholesalers). Second, *brokers* and *agents* do not take possession of the goods but are paid a commission for aiding companies in buying and selling. Finally, *manufacturers' and retailers' branches and offices* are wholesaling operations conducted by non-wholesalers to bypass the wholesalers.

Like retailers, wholesalers must target carefully and position themselves strongly. And, like retailers, wholesalers must decide on product and service assortments, prices, promotion, and place. Progressive wholesalers constantly watch for better ways to meet the changing needs of their suppliers and target customers. They recognize that, in the long run, their only reason for existence comes from adding value, which occurs by increasing the efficiency and effectiveness of the entire marketing channel. As with other types of marketers, the goal is to build value-adding customer relationships.

Key Terms

Objective 11-1
Retailing (p 334)
Retailer (p 334)
Shopper marketing (p 334)
Omni-channel retailing (p 335)
Specialty store (p 336)
Department store (p 336)
Supermarket (p 336)
Convenience store (p 337)
Superstore (p 337)
Category killer (p 337)
Service retailer (p 337)
Discount store (p 337)
Off-price retailer (p 338)
Independent off-price retailer (p 338)
Factory outlet (p 338)
Warehouse club (p 339)
Corporate chains (p 339)
Franchise (p 340)

Objective 11-2
Shopping center (p 347)

Objective 11-3
Showrooming (p 350)

Objective 11-4
Wholesaling (p 355)
Wholesaler (p 355)
Merchant wholesaler (p 356)
Broker (p 357)
Agent (p 357)
Manufacturers' and retailers' branches and offices (p 357)

Discussion Questions

11-1. Define the concept of *shopper marketing* and explain why it has grown in prominence. (AACSB: Communication)

11-2. Explain how retailers can be classified based by the amount of service offered and discuss an example of each retailer type. (AACSB: Communication; Reflective Thinking)

11-3. Name and describe the three types of off-price retailers. How do off-price retailers differ from discount stores? (AACSB: Communication)

11-4. Name and describe the three major groups of wholesalers. (AACSB: Communication; Reflective Thinking)

11-5. Compare and contrast brokers and agents with merchant wholesalers. (AACSB: Communication; Reflective Thinking)

Critical Thinking Exercises

11-6. In a small group, present a plan for a new retail store. Who is the target market? Describe the merchandise, atmospherics, price points, services provided, location, and how you would promote your retail store. Describe how you will differentiate your store from competitors. (AACSB: Communication; Reflective Thinking)

11-7. Visit a local mall and evaluate five stores. What type of retailer is each of these stores? What is the target market for each? How is each store positioned? Do the retail atmospherics of each store enhance this positioning effectively to attract and satisfy the target market? (AACSB: Communication; Reflective Thinking)

11-8. Identify a retailer that is currently struggling. Discuss why it is having difficulties and suggest ways to turn things around. (AACSB: Communication; Reflective Thinking)

MINICASES AND APPLICATIONS

Online, Mobile, and Social Media Marketing Local Retailers

It seems you can't get away from the buzz of online, mobile, and social media marketing from the likes of Amazon, Walmart, Nordstrom, and other large retailers. But what about the small independent retailers? Are they also getting on the online, mobile, and social media bandwagon? Some independent retailers are using these tools. For example, a convenience store owner in Miami Tweets a picture to 7,000 followers of a new beer he just stocked that morning, and by late afternoon customers come streaming in to check it out. Emerson Salon in Seattle sources 75 percent of its business from Facebook, Twitter, and its blog. Butter Lane cupcake bakery in New York City has found success using social media as well. Although these retailers have embraced online, mobile, and social media marketing, to most small retailers, using Facebook, Twitter, Pinterest, Tumblr, Groupon, Instagram, Yelp, Foursquare, and other digital media can seem downright intimidating.

11-9. Find an example of a local retailer in your community that uses online, mobile, and social media marketing. Interview the owner of the store or restaurant and ask about the challenges and successes they've experienced when implementing this strategy. (AACSB: Communication; Use of IT; Reflective Thinking)

11-10. Create a presentation to give to local retailers explaining how they can effectively use online, mobile, and social media marketing to engage customers and enhance their business. (AACSB: Communication; Reflective Thinking)

Marketing Ethics Lilly for Target

The Lilly Pulitzer brand of brightly colored dresses and resort-themed designer items is the uniform of the preppy, Palm Beach set. Indeed, only select young women belonging to certain sororities in certain communities are allowed discounts on the $100 to $500 items. But Target created a buying frenzy by debuting its Lilly for Target collection in April 2015. Target's Pulitzer line was composed of 250 items, such as Lilly dresses at $40, which sold out within minutes of launch, crashed the store's Web site, and created a firestorm of negative online comments from customers. The long lines outside stores caused one manager to name the event "Preppy Black Friday," likening it to the frenzied shopping day after Thanksgiving known as Black Friday. Most shoppers went home empty-handed because others scooped up as much as they could, emptying the racks within minutes. Items then sold on eBay for much higher prices. This type of launch is not new for Target. In 2011, the retailer launched a line of Missoni items priced at $30 to $40. Missoni's distinctive zigzag and geometric-patterned knitwear, shoes, and houseware items normally sell for hundreds of dollars at retailers such as Bloomingdale's and Saks Fifth Avenue. During the Missoni event, shoppers grabbed goods by the armload, even poaching items from other shoppers' carts. While some shoppers went away happy, many more were not. In both merchandise promotions, Target officials announced the sold-out items would not be replenished.

11-11. Is it ethical for retailers to create a promotion but not have sufficient merchandise for all shoppers who want to buy the items? (AACSB: Communication; Ethical Reasoning)

11-12. Is it smart for Target to create such shopping frenzies even though some customers are dissatisfied? Explain why or why not. (AACSB: Communication; Reflective Thinking)

Marketing by the Numbers Stockturn Rate

Retailers need merchandise to make sales. In fact, a retailer's inventory is its biggest asset. Not stocking enough merchandise can result in lost sales, but carrying too much inventory increases costs and lowers margins. Both circumstances reduce profits. One measure of a reseller's inventory management effectiveness is its *stockturn rate* (also called *inventory turnover rate* for manufacturers). The key to success in retailing is realizing a large volume of sales on as little inventory as possible while maintaining enough stock to meet customer demands.

11-13. Refer to Appendix 3: Marketing by the Numbers, and determine the stockturn rate of a retailer carrying an average inventory at cost of $850,000, with a cost of goods sold of $1,800,000. (AACSB: Communication; Analytical Reasoning)

11-14. If this company's stockturn rate was 4.5 last year, is the stockturn rate calculated above better or worse? Explain. (AACSB: Communication; Reflective Thinking)

Video Case Kmart

Once the leader in discount retailing, Kmart long ago took a back seat to Walmart, Target, and others discount chains. But recent efforts to provide value to customers through innovation show that the veteran retailer may still have its edge. To gain a competitive one-up, Kmart started a unique program that combined the benefits of online and brick-and-mortar shopping. When an item that customers wanted to purchase was not in stock at one of its stores, Kmart would ship the item to the customer's home for free.

To launch this program, Kmart unveiled an ad campaign that illustrated an uncharacteristic relevance to younger, tech-savvy customers. With the slight-of-mouth message that customers could "ship their pants" (or any of the other 65 million items in Kmart's inventory) for free, the ad went viral. As a result, Kmart got its message out in spades, entertaining many while offending a few along the way.

After viewing the video featuring Kmart, answer the following questions:

11-15. Consider the retail marketing mix. How did Kmart differentiate itself from other retailers with its free shipping program?

11-16. What kind of customer does the "Ship My Pants" campaign target? How is this significant?

11-17. Discuss what will be the ultimate effects of this Kmart campaign.

Company Cases 11 Sears/14 Alibaba/15 7-Eleven

See Appendix 1 for cases appropriate for this chapter. **Case 11, Sears: Why Should You Shop There?** Once "Where America Shops", the former leading retailer now has customers scratching their heads. **Case 14, Alibaba: The World's Largest E-Tailer Is Not Amazon**. Hardly known in the U.S., Alibaba has become the fastest growing e-tailer in the world by expanding into just about every consumer business imaginable. **Case 15, 7-Eleven: Adapting to The World's Many Cultures.** Just a convenience store in the U.S., 7-Eleven has a strong global presence by adapting its retail marketing mix to fit the unique needs of consumers worldwide.

MyMarketingLab

If assigned by your instructor, complete these writing sections from your Assignments in the MyLab.

11-18. Describe the types of shopping centers and identify specific examples in your community or a nearby city. (AACSB: Communication; Reflective Thinking)

11-19. The atmosphere in a retail store is carefully crafted to influence shoppers. Select a retailer that has both a physical store and an online store. Describe the elements of the physical store's atmosphere, such as the colors, lighting, music, scents, and décor. What image is the store's atmosphere projecting? Is that image appropriate given the merchandise assortment and target market of the store? Which elements of the physical store's atmosphere are part of its online store atmosphere? Does the retailer integrate the physical store's atmosphere with its online presence? Explain. (AACSB: Written and Oral Communication; Information Technology; Reflective Thinking)

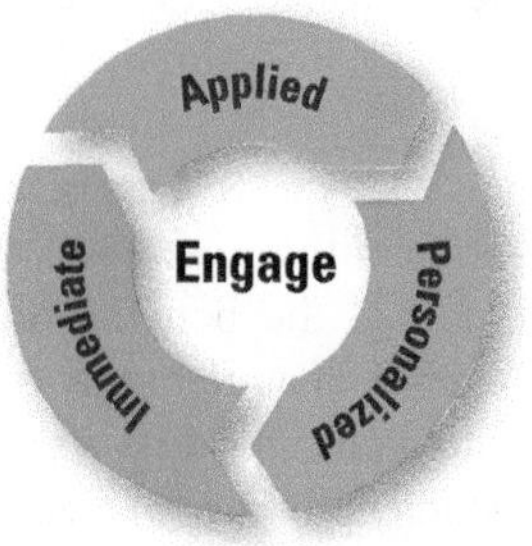

12 Engaging Consumers and Communicating Customer Value

Advertising and Public Relations

CHAPTER ROAD MAP Objective Outline

- OBJECTIVE 12-1 **Define the five promotion mix tools for communicating customer value.** The Promotion Mix (366–367)
- OBJECTIVE 12-2 **Discuss the changing communications landscape and the need for integrated marketing communications.** Integrated Marketing Communications (367–374)
- OBJECTIVE 12-3 **Describe and discuss the major decisions involved in developing an advertising program.** Advertising (375–392)
- OBJECTIVE 12-4 **Explain how companies use public relations to communicate with their publics.** Public Relations (392–394)

Previewing the Concepts

In this and the next two chapters, we'll examine the last of the marketing mix tools—promotion. Companies must do more than just create customer value. They must also clearly and persuasively communicate that value. Promotion is not a single tool but rather a mix of several tools. Ideally, under the concept of *integrated marketing communications,* a company will carefully coordinate these promotion elements to engage customers and build a clear, consistent, and compelling message about an organization and its products. We'll begin by introducing the various promotion mix tools. Next, we'll examine the rapidly changing communications environment—especially the addition of digital, mobile, and social media—and the need for integrated marketing communications. Finally, we'll look more closely at two of the promotion tools—advertising and public relations. In the next chapter, we'll visit two other promotion mix tools—sales promotion and personal selling. Then, in Chapter 14, we'll explore direct, online, mobile, and social media marketing.

Let's start by looking at an outstanding advertising campaign. Two decades ago, GEICO was a little-known nicher in the U.S. auto-insurance industry. But now, thanks in large part to an industry-changing, big-budget advertising program, featuring an enduring tagline and a likeable but unlikely spokes-lizard, GEICO has muscled its way to the number-two position in its ultra-competitive industry. The message: Good advertising really does matter. Here's the story.

First Stop

GEICO: From Bit Player to Behemoth through Good Advertising

For nearly 20 years, GEICO's advertising and charismatic gecko have creatively and relentlessly driven home the brand's value proposition: "15 minutes could save you 15 percent or more on car insurance."

Founded in 1936, GEICO initially targeted a select customer group of government employees and noncommissioned military officers with exceptional driving records. Unlike its competitors, GEICO had no agents. Instead, the auto insurer marketed directly to customers, keeping its costs low and passing on the savings in the form of lower premiums. For nearly 60 years, GEICO's marketing relied almost entirely on direct mail and telephone advertising.

In 1994, however, when GEICO decided to expand its customer base, it knew that it must also expand its marketing. So it entered the world of mass media, a shift that would dramatically change the face of insurance advertising. GEICO started slowly, spending a paltry $10 million to launch its first national TV, radio, and print ads. Then, in 1996, billionaire investor Warren Buffett bought the company and famously told the marketing group "money is no object" when it comes to growing the business, so "speed things up." Did it ever. Over the next 10 years, GEICO's ad spending jumped 50-fold, to more than $500 million a year.

By now, you know a lot about GEICO and its smooth-talking gecko. But at the start, the insurer faced a tough task—introducing a little-known brand with a funny name to a national audience. Like all good advertising, the GEICO campaign began with a simple but compelling theme, one that highlights the convenience and savings advantages of GEICO's direct-to-customers system. To this day, every single one of the hundreds of ads and other content pieces in the GEICO campaign has driven home the now-familiar pitch: "15 minutes could save you 15 percent or more on car insurance."

But what really set GEICO's advertising apart was the inspired way the company chose to bring its value proposition to life. At the time, competitors were using serious and sentimental pitches—"You're in good hands with Allstate" or "Like a good neighbor, State Farm is there." To make its advertising stand out, GEICO decided to deliver its punch line with humor. The creative approach worked, and sales began to climb.

In trying to grow the brand, it become apparent that customers had difficulty pronouncing the GEICO name (which stands for Government Employees Insurance Company). Too often, GEICO became "gecko." Enter the charismatic green lizard. In 1999, GEICO ran a 15-second spot in which the now-famous, British-accented gecko called a press conference and pleaded: "I am a gecko, not to be confused with GEICO, which could save you hundreds on car insurance. So stop calling me." The ad was supposed to be a one-time "throwaway," but consumers quickly flooded the company with calls and letters begging to see more of the gecko. The rest, as they say, is history.

Although the gecko remains GEICO's iconic spokesman, one lizard could take the company only so far. So over the years, to keep its pitch fresh and entertaining, GEICO has supplemented the gecko ads with a continuous flow of clever, buzzworthy new executions telling the brand's value story. Early on, when GEICO first went online, the campaign employed a clutch of cultured cavemen, insulted by the company's advertising slogan, "It's so easy to use GEICO.com, even a caveman could do it." Later, in response to the question, "Can switching to GEICO really save you 15 percent or more on car insurance?," the "Rhetorical Questions" campaign responded, "Is Ed 'Too Tall' Jones too tall?," "Was Abe Lincoln honest?," and "Did the little piggy cry 'wee wee wee' all the way home?" That last ad introduced the world to Maxwell, the talking pig who went on to star in his own GEICO campaign, emphasizing GEICO's growing digital, social, and mobile advances.

Another ad series promoted yet another GEICO character to pop culture icon status—the wildly popular Caleb the Camel who struts through the office every Wednesday rejoicing "It's hump day," suggesting that GEICO customers are "Happier than a camel on hump day." The swaggering Caleb went on to star in other GEICO commercials and even appeared in a string of pre-game Super Bowl commercials with Terry Bradshaw. In GEICO's more recent "It's what you do" campaign, among another fresh batch of creative ads and characters, one episode features Caleb and a friend at the zoo, nonchalantly accepting the taunts of people imitating his best "it's hump day" lines from previous commercials. The ad concludes, "If you're a camel, you put up with this all the time. It's what you do. And if you want to save 15 percent or more on car insurance, you switch to GEICO. It's what you do."

Thanks in large part to an industry-changing, big-budget advertising program, featuring an enduring tagline and a likeable but unlikely spokes-lizard, GEICO has muscled its way to the number-two position in its ultra-competitive industry.

"No matter how many GEICO ads you've seen over the years—and it's a bunch—they never seem to grow stale," observes one expert. The company's chief marketing officer explains, "We're trying to stay ever-present in the consumer's mind but not bore them and have them just tune out yet another GEICO ad." However, no matter how varied, each minicampaign has a distinctly GEICO flavor, and every single ad closes strongly with the crucial "15 minutes could save you 15 percent" tagline.

The GEICO tagline is now so well-recognized that in one minicampaign—"Did you know?"—the brand even poked a little fun at itself. The commercials showed one person reading a GEICO "15 percent" ad while a second person observed, "Everybody knows that." The first person then responded, "Well, did you know ..." followed by a humorous (though fictional) fact. For instance, after revealing that "Old MacDonald was a really bad speller," one ad showed a farmer participant being eliminated from a spelling bee when he spells *cow* "C-O-W ... E-I-E-I-O." Each ad concluded, "GEICO: 15 minutes could save you, well ... you know."

Along with fresh content, GEICO has also adapted its content delivery to the fast-changing digital times. The brand was one of the first in its industry to provide customers with mobile apps and options for obtaining quotes, buying policies, and managing their accounts. The company is also an acknowledged leader in the use of online and social media, ranking third in the insurance industry behind only full-line insurers Allstate and State Farm in social media performance and digital customer engagement. The company's ads and Web-only videos are heavily viewed favorites online.

GEICO continues to invest heavily in advertising and content marketing, outspending every other insurance company in measured media by a nearly two-to-one margin. Its annual advertising budget, now more than $1 billion, makes GEICO the third-most-advertised U.S. megabrand, ahead of big spenders such as McDonald's, Toyota, and Walmart. The brand's creative and relentless advertising messaging, plus its heavy investment, has paid big dividends. The once little-known GEICO brand now enjoys well over 90 percent awareness among insurance shoppers. And after years of double-digit market share gains, GEICO recently passed Allstate to move into second place in the ultra-competitive U.S. car-insurance market.

Moreover, beyond spurring GEICO's spectacular growth, the brand's advertising has changed the way the entire insurance industry markets its products. In what was once a yawn-provoking category, competitors ranging from Allstate (with "Mayhem") to Progressive (with "Flo") are now injecting humor and interest in their own advertising campaigns. "This strategy is absolutely working for GEICO," asserts one analyst. It's "a testament to how GEICO has used advertising to evolve from a bit player to a behemoth," says another.[1]

Author Comment
The promotion mix is the marketer's bag of tools for engaging and communicating with customers and other stakeholders. To deliver a clear and compelling message, each tool must be carefully coordinated under the concept of integrated marketing communications (IMC).

Building good customer relationships calls for more than just developing a good product, pricing it attractively, and making it available to target customers. Companies must also *engage* consumers and *communicate* their value propositions to customers, and what they communicate should not be left to chance. All communications must be planned and blended into carefully integrated programs. Just as good communication is important in building and maintaining any other kind of relationship, it is a crucial element in a company's efforts to engage customers and build profitable customer relationships.

The Promotion Mix

A company's total **promotion mix**—also called its **marketing communications mix**—consists of the specific blend of advertising, public relations, personal selling, sales promotion, and direct marketing tools that the company uses to engage consumers, persuasively communicate customer value, and build customer relationships. The five major promotion tools are defined as follows:[2]

- **Advertising**. Any paid form of nonpersonal presentation and promotion of ideas, goods, or services by an identified sponsor.
- **Sales promotion**. Short-term incentives to encourage the purchase or sale of a product or service.
- **Personal selling**. Personal customer interactions by the firm's sales force for the purpose of engaging customers, making sales, and building customer relationships.
- **Public relations (PR)**. Building good relations with the company's various publics by obtaining favorable publicity, building up a good corporate image, and handling or heading off unfavorable rumors, stories, and events.
- **Direct and digital marketing**. Engaging directly with carefully targeted individual consumers and customer communities to both obtain an immediate response and build lasting customer relationships.

Promotion mix (marketing communications mix)
The specific blend of promotion tools that the company uses to engage customers, persuasively communicate customer value, and build customer relationships.

Advertising
Any paid form of nonpersonal presentation and promotion of ideas, goods, or services by an identified sponsor.

Sales promotion
Short-term incentives to encourage the purchase or sale of a product or a service.

Personal selling
Personal customer interactions by the firm's sales force for the purpose of engaging customers, making sales, and building customer relationships.

Each category involves specific promotional tools that are used to communicate with customers. For example, *advertising* includes broadcast, print, online, mobile, outdoor, and other forms. *Sales promotion* includes discounts, coupons, displays, and demonstrations. *Personal selling* includes sales presentations, trade shows, and incentive programs. *Public relations* includes press releases, sponsorships, events, and Web pages. And *direct and digital marketing* includes direct mail, catalogs, online and social media, mobile marketing, and more.

At the same time, marketing communication goes beyond these specific promotion tools. The product's design, its price, the shape and color of its package, and the stores that sell it—*all* communicate something to buyers. Thus, although the promotion mix is the company's primary engagement and communications activity, the entire marketing mix—promotion, *and* product, price, and place—must be coordinated for greatest impact.

Author Comment
Integrated marketing communications—IMC—is a really hot topic these days. No other area of marketing is changing so quickly and profoundly. A big part of the reason is the huge surge in customer engagement through digital media—online, mobile, and social media marketing.

Integrated Marketing Communications

In past decades, marketers perfected the art of mass marketing: selling highly standardized products to masses of customers. In the process, they developed effective mass-media communication techniques to support these strategies. Large companies now routinely invest millions or even billions of dollars in television, magazine, or other mass-media advertising, reaching tens of millions of customers with a single ad. Today, however, marketing managers face some new marketing communications realities. Perhaps no other area of marketing is changing so profoundly as marketing communications, creating both exciting and challenging times for marketing communicators.

The New Marketing Communications Model

Several major factors are changing the face of today's marketing communications. First, *consumers* are changing. In this digital, wireless age, consumers are better informed and more communications empowered. Rather than relying on marketer-supplied information, they can use the Internet, social media, and other technologies to find information on their own. They can connect easily with other consumers to exchange brand-related information or even create their own brand messages and experiences.

Second, *marketing strategies* are changing. As mass markets have fragmented, marketers are shifting away from mass marketing. More and more, they are developing focused marketing programs designed to engage customers and build customer relationships in more narrowly defined micromarkets.

Finally, sweeping advances in *digital technology* are causing remarkable changes in the ways companies and customers communicate with each other. The digital age has spawned a host of new information and communication tools—from smartphones and tablets to satellite and cable television systems to the many faces of the Internet (brand Web sites, email, blogs, social media and online communities, the mobile Web, and so much more). Just as mass marketing once gave rise to a new generation of mass-media communications, the new digital and social media have given birth to a more targeted, social, and engaging marketing communications model.

Although network television, magazines, newspapers, and other traditional mass media remain very important, their dominance is declining. In their place, advertisers are now adding a broad selection of more-specialized and highly targeted media to engage smaller customer communities with more personalized, interactive content. The new media range from specialty cable television channels and made-for-the-Web videos to online ads, email and texting, blogs, mobile catalogs and coupons, and a burgeoning list of social media. Such new media have taken marketing by storm.

Some advertising industry experts even predict that the old mass-media communications model will eventually become obsolete. Mass-media costs are rising, audiences are shrinking, ad clutter is increasing, and viewers are gaining control of message exposure through technologies such as video streaming or DVRs that let them skip disruptive television commercials. As a result, the skeptics suggest, marketers are shifting ever-larger portions of their marketing budgets away from old-media mainstays and moving them to online, social, mobile, and other new-age media.

In recent years, although TV still dominates as an advertising medium with a 38 percent share of U.S. ad spending, its growth has stagnated. Spending in magazines, newspapers, and radio has lost ground. Meanwhile, digital media have come from nowhere during the

Public relations (PR)
Building good relations with the company's various publics by obtaining favorable publicity, building up a good corporate image, and handling or heading off unfavorable rumors, stories, and events.

Direct and digital marketing
Engaging directly with carefully targeted individual consumers and customer communities to both obtain an immediate response and build lasting customer relationships.

past several years to account for about 30 percent of U.S. advertising spending, second only to TV. By far the fastest-growing ad-spending category, digital's share is expected to grow to 36 percent by 2019. P&G, the world's biggest advertiser, now spends as much as one-third of its marketing budget on digital media. By one estimate, companies around the world now invest an average of 24 percent of their media budgets on digital.[3]

Some marketers now rely almost entirely on digital and social media. >> For example, eco-friendly household products maker Method employs a full but mostly digital promotional campaign themed "Clean happy":[4]

> Method is known for offbeat campaigns using slogans like "People against dirty" and "For the love of clean." But the most notable thing about the "Clean happy" campaign is that it at first used zero ads in traditional media like TV or magazines. Instead, the centerpiece of the campaign was brand videos aired only on YouTube and on the Method Facebook page. The campaign also employed online media ads as well as a major presence in social media that included, in addition to YouTube and Facebook, the Method Twitter feed and blogs. The "Clean happy" campaign fit both Method's personality and its budget. Method is the kind of grassroots brand that benefits from social media–type word of mouth. Moreover, "Clean happy" ran a first-year budget of only about $3.5 million, compared with the whopping $150 million or so that rival P&G might spend just to bring out a single new product, such as Tide Pods detergent packets.
>
> Method ran the digital-only campaign for a full year before beginning to bring it to TV. Even now, the "Clean happy" campaign relies heavily on digital and social media, supported only by carefully targeted regional cable TV in selected markets. More recent campaign installments include "Life's Messy Moments," a romantic comedy-style series of TV and online ads and other social media content that follow a young couple and their relatable messes from their first kiss to first kid to a clean, happy ending. To kick off the campaign on Facebook, Method hosted a photo contest called Clean Happy Awards, asking fans to submit their best pet, kid, and party messes. "We're embracing this grassroots movement," says a Method ad executive. "When you don't have 150 million bucks, that's what you have to do."

>> The new marketing communications model: Method's successful and long-running "Clean happy" campaign began as an online-only effort and still relies heavily on digital and social media, supported only by carefully targeted regional cable TV ads in selected markets.

Method Products PBC

In the new marketing communications world, rather than using old approaches that interrupt customers and force-feed them mass messages, new media formats let marketers reach smaller communities of consumers in more engaging ways. For example, think about television viewing these days. Consumers can now watch their favorite programs on just about anything with a screen—on televisions but also laptops, smartphones, or tablets. And they can choose to watch programs whenever and wherever they wish, often without commercials. Increasingly, some programs, ads, and videos are being produced only for online viewing.

Despite the shift toward digital media, however, traditional mass media still capture a sizable share of the promotion budgets of most major marketing firms, a fact that probably won't change quickly. Thus, rather than the old-media model collapsing completely, most marketers foresee a shifting mix of both traditional mass media and online, mobile, and social media that engage more-targeted consumer communities in a more personalized way. In the end, regardless of the communications channel, the key is to integrate all of these media in a way that best engages customers, communicates the brand message, and enhances the customer's brand experiences.

Content marketing
Creating, inspiring, and sharing brand messages and conversations with and among consumers across a fluid mix of paid, owned, earned, and shared channels.

As the marketing communications environment shifts, so will the role of marketing communicators. Rather than just creating and placing "TV ads" or "print ads" or "Snapchat branded story ads," many marketers now view themselves more broadly as **content marketing** managers. As such, they create, inspire, and share brand messages and conversations with and among customers across a fluid mix of *paid, owned, earned,* and *shared* communication channels. These channels include media that are both traditional and new as well as controlled and not controlled (see Marketing at Work 12.1).

MARKETING AT WORK 12.1

Just Don't Call It Advertising: It's Content Marketing

In the good old days, life seemed so simple for advertisers. When a brand needed an advertising campaign, everybody knew what that meant. The brand team and ad agency came up with a creative strategy, developed a media plan, produced and placed a set of TV commercials and magazine or newspaper ads, and maybe issued a press release to stir up some news. But in these digital times, the old practice of placing "advertisements" in well-defined "media" within the tidy framework of a carefully managed "advertising campaign" just doesn't work anymore.

Instead, the lines are rapidly blurring between traditional advertising and new digital content. To be relevant, today's brand messages must be social, mobile, interactively engaging, and multi-platformed. Says one industry insider: "Today's media landscape keeps getting more diverse—it's broadcast, cable, and streaming; it's online, tablet, and smartphone; it's video, rich media, social media, branded content, banners, apps, in-app advertising, and interactive technology products."

The new digital landscape has called into question the very definition of advertising. "What Is Advertising Anyway?" asks one provocative headline. Call it whatever you want, admonishes another, but "Just *Don't* Call It Advertising." Instead, according to many marketers these days, it's "content marketing," creating and distributing a broad mix of compelling content that engages customers, builds relationships with and among them, and moves them to action. To feed today's digital and social media machinery and to sustain "always-on" consumer conversations, brands need a constant supply of fresh content across a breadth of traditional and digital platforms.

Many advertisers and marketers now view themselves more broadly as *content marketing managers* who create, inspire, share, and curate marketing content—both their own content and that created by consumers and others. Rather than using traditional media breakdowns, they subscribe to a new framework that builds on how and by whom marketing content is created, controlled, and distributed. The new classification identifies four major types of media: paid, owned, earned, and shared (POES):

Paid media—promotional channels paid for by the marketer, including traditional media (such as TV, radio, print, or outdoor) and online and digital media (paid search ads, mobile ads, email marketing, or Web and social media display ads and sponsored content).

Owned media—promotional channels owned and controlled by the company, including company Web sites, corporate blogs, owned social media sites, proprietary brand communities, sales forces, and events.

Earned media—PR media channels, such as television, newspapers, blogs, online video sites, and other media not directly paid for or controlled by the marketer but that incorporate the content because of viewer, reader, or user interest.

Shared media—media shared by consumers with other consumers, such as social media, blogs, mobile media, and viral channels as well as traditional word of mouth.

In the past, advertisers have focused on traditional paid (broadcast, print) or earned (public relations) media. Now, however, content marketers are rapidly adding the new digital generation of owned (Web sites, blogs, brand communities) and shared (online social, mobile, email) media. Whereas a successful paid ad used to be an end in itself, marketers are now developing integrated marketing content that leverages the combined power of all the POES channels. Thus, many TV ads often aren't just TV ads anymore. They're "video content" you might see anywhere—on a TV screen but also on a tablet or phone. Other video content looks a lot like TV advertising but was never intended for TV, such as made-for-online videos posted on Web sites or social media. Similarly, printed brand messages and pictures no longer appear only in carefully crafted magazine ads or catalogs. Instead, such content, created by a variety of sources, pops up in anything from formal ads and online brand pages to mobile and social media and independent blogs.

>> Content marketing: Intel and Toshiba's award-winning "Inside" social media film series blurs the line between advertising, social media, and entertainment, creating high levels of customer–brand engagement for the two brands.

Courtesy Intel and Toshiba American Information Systems, Inc.

The new "content marketing" campaigns look a lot different from the old "advertising" campaigns. For example, to move beyond its long-running, traditional "Intel Inside" advertising, Intel recently teamed with computer maker Toshiba to produce an award-winning social media film series called "Inside." Enlisting the talents of Hollywood directors and actors, the engaging series blurs the lines between advertising, social media, and entertainment. One series, a comedy/sci-fi adventure called "The Power Inside," chronicled the efforts of a Scooby-Doo squad of 20-somethings to foil the plans of aliens intent on taking over the world by disguising themselves as mustaches and unibrows. Intel-powered Toshiba Ultrabooks play a central role, but the subtle product placement doesn't come across as an ad.

"The Power Inside" was released in six episodes on YouTube, with traffic driven through Facebook and Twitter (shared media), a dedicated microsite (owned media), and ads placed on Skype and Spotify (paid media). Awareness and popularity of the series were driven higher by mentions and articles in independent blogs and the press (earned media). "The Power Inside" earned even more publicity when its launch coincided perfectly with the awarding of a Daytime Emmy and the coveted Cannes Grand Prix award to the previous Intel/Toshiba series, "The Beauty Inside." In all, the integrated, multiplatform content marketing campaign created high levels of customer–brand engagement for the Intel and Toshiba brands. Based on the success of its partnership with Toshiba, Intel recently launched yet another social film series, "What Lives Inside," this time partnering with Dell.

Careful integration across the POES channels can produce striking communications results. Consider Samsung's "Life's a Photo. Take It." campaign to launch its Web-connected Galaxy Camera in 18 regions worldwide. To show how easily images taken by the camera can be shared instantly anytime, anyplace, Samsung chose 32 prominent Instagramers ("the world's most social photographers") and challenged them to use the new camera to prove that their cities—from London, Amsterdam, Berlin, Madrid, and Milan to Paris, Sydney, and San Francisco—were the most photogenic in the world. Their photos were uploaded to Tumblr, and fans voted for their favorites via Tumblr, Facebook, Twitter, and Pinterest. The winning city—Berlin—hosted a massive final event, where influencers invited from across Europe took photos with the connected camera and saw them projected onto giant, inflatable, 3D-projection cubes.

The "Life's a Photo. Take It." campaign, with its rich mix of marketing content, was an unqualified success. During its three-month run, the campaign reached more than 79 million people worldwide. Awareness of the Galaxy Camera rose 58 percent; purchase intent jumped 115 percent. The campaign won an Interactive Advertising Bureau MIXX award for content marketing, sparking a flurry of additional publicity. Finally, the social media campaign served as a foundation for a series of paid television ads. In the end, Samsung reignited a product category that many considered to be waning—dedicated digital cameras—and became the market leader in Web-connected digital imaging.

So, we can't just call it "advertising" anymore. Today's shifting and sometimes chaotic marketing communications environment calls for more than simply creating and placing ads in well-defined and controlled media spaces. Rather, today's marketing communicators must be marketing content strategists, creators, connectors, and catalysts who manage brand conversations with and among customers and help those conversations catch fire across a fluid mix of channels. That's a tall order, but with today's new thinking, anything is POES-ible!

Sources: Randall Rothenberg, "What Is Advertising Anyway?" *Ad Week*, September 16, 2013, p. 15; Joan Voight, "Intel and Toshiba Peddle Product Placement in Branded Film 'The Power Inside,'" *Ad Week*, July 29, 2013, www.adweek.com/print/151476; Patrick Darling, "Chip Shot: Dell and Intel Debut New Social Film 'What Lives Inside' on Hulu," March 23, 2015, http://newsroom.intel.com/community/intel_newsroom/blog/2015/03/23/chip-shot-dell-and-intel-debut-new-social-film-what-lives-inside-on-hulu; Peter Himler, "Paid, Earned & Owned: Revisited," *The Flack*, June 21, 2011, http://flatironcomm.com/2011/06/paid-earned-owned-revisited/; "Samsung's Galaxy Camera," 2013 AIB MIXX Awards Winners Gallery, www.iab.net/mixxawards/gallery2013/strategies-and-objectives/content-marketing.html; http://samsungcamera.tumblr.com/latest; "Life's a Photo, Take It," Jam, www.spreadingjam.com/our-work/samsung/life-s-a-photo-take-it, accessed June 2015; and "'Life's a Photo. Take It'—Campaign Overview," *Vice*, www.vice.com/sgc/lifes-a-photo-take-it-campaign-overview, accessed October 2015.

The Need for *Integrated* Marketing Communications

The shift toward a richer mix of media and content approaches poses a problem for marketers. Consumers today are bombarded by brand messages from a broad range of sources. But all too often, companies fail to integrate their various communication channels. Mass-media ads say one thing, whereas company's Internet site, emails, social media pages, or videos posted on YouTube say something altogether different.

One problem is that marketing content often comes from different parts of the company. Advertising messages are prepared by the advertising department or an ad agency. Other company departments or agencies prepare public relations messages, sales promotion events, and online or social media content. However, consumers don't distinguish between content sources the way marketers do. In the consumer's mind, brand-related content from different sources—whether it's a Super Bowl ad, in-store display, mobile app, or friend's social media post—all merge into a single message about the brand or

Figure 12.1 Integrated Marketing Communications

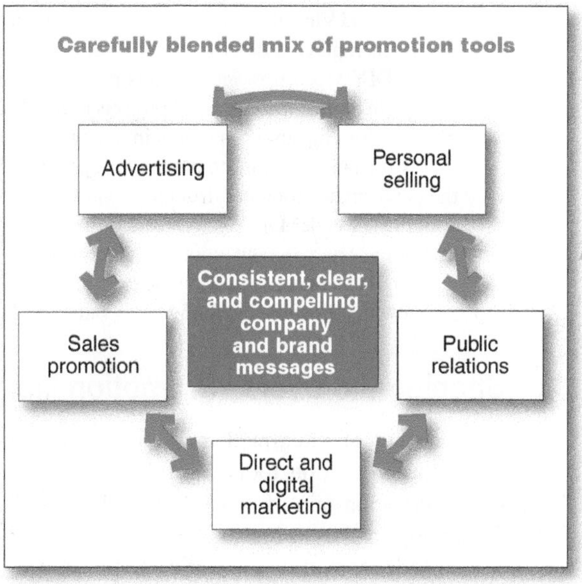

Today's customers are bombarded by brand content from all directions. For example, think about all the ways you interact with companies such as Nike, Apple, or Coca-Cola. Integrated marketing communications means that companies must carefully coordinate all of these customer touch points to ensure clear brand messages.

company. Conflicting content from these different sources can result in confused company images, brand positions, and customer relationships.

Thus, the explosion of online, mobile, and social media marketing presents tremendous opportunities but also big challenges. It gives marketers rich new tools for understanding and engaging customers. At the same time, it complicates and fragments overall marketing communications. The challenge is to bring it all together in an organized way. To that end, more companies today are adopting the concept of **integrated marketing communications (IMC)**. Under this concept, as illustrated in **Figure 12.1**, the company carefully integrates and coordinates its many communication channels to deliver a clear, consistent, and compelling message about the organization and its brands.

Integrated marketing communications (IMC)
Carefully integrating and coordinating the company's many communications channels to deliver a clear, consistent, and compelling message about the organization and its brands.

Often, different media play unique roles in engaging, informing, and persuading consumers. For example, a recent study showed that more than two-thirds of advertisers and their agencies are planning video ad campaigns that stretch across multiple viewing platforms, such as traditional TV and digital, mobile, and social media. Such *video convergence*, as it's called, combines TV's core strength—vast reach—with digital's better targeting, interaction, and engagement.[5] These varied media and roles must be carefully coordinated under the overall integrated marketing communications plan.

One good example of a well-integrated marketing communications effort is home-improvement retailer Lowe's "Never Stop Improving" campaign, which integrates the clout of big-budget traditional media with the power of social media to create personalized, real-time customer engagement:[6]

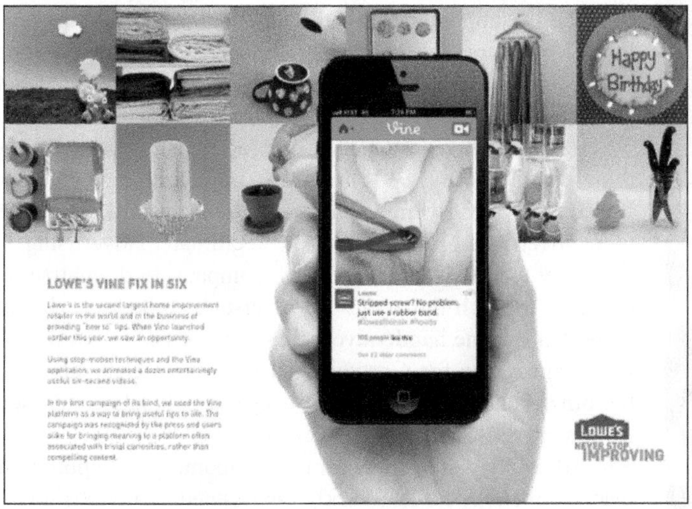

Integrated marketing communications: The Lowe's "Never Stop Improving" campaign integrates the clout of big-budget traditional media with the power of social media to create personalized, real-time customer engagement.

> To be sure, Lowe's runs a full slate of big-budget television spots and other traditional media ads that drive home its "Never Stop Improving" positioning. But in recent years, the company has added a rich flow of engaging, carefully integrated social media content that personalizes and enriches the Lowe's customer experience in ways that traditional media can't. Just one example is the Lowe's "Fix in Six" Vine video campaign. "Fix in Six" features dozens of clever six-second looping videos showing quick-fix solutions to home-improvement problems—everything from removing stripped screws to keeping squirrels away from plants. The award-winning series was a huge success from the start, generating 28,000 social media mentions within just the first week and earning millions of total campaign impressions to date.

Beyond Vine, the Lowe's "Never Stop Improving" campaign integrates a broad mix of social media, each playing its own unique role. Lowe's uses its heavily subscribed YouTube channel for longer DIY video tips and tutorials to supplement the quick hits on Vine. It uses Pinterest and Instagram to inspire customers' projects to life through high-impact imagery. Facebook provides a platform for engaging customers in dialogue—every Facebook comment gets an answer. Twitter serves for posting short comments or spreading the word about special offers. No matter what the platform, all content—from television spots to online videos to Facebook posts—is carefully coordinated under Lowe's "Never Stop Improving" mantra and its mission of helping customers find home-improvement solutions. According to one Lowe's marketer, the integrated marketing campaign is less about making the cash register ring and more about "making sure that customers ... know that Lowe's is offering them value and [about keeping them] engaged with the brand."

Author Comment
In this section, we'll look at how marketers blend the various marketing communication tools into a smooth-functioning integrated promotion mix.

Shaping the Overall Promotion Mix

The concept of integrated marketing communications suggests that the company must blend the promotion tools carefully into a coordinated *promotion mix*. But how does it determine what mix of promotion tools to use? Companies within the same industry differ greatly in the design of their promotion mixes. For example, cosmetics maker Mary Kay spends most of its promotion funds on personal selling and direct marketing, whereas competitor CoverGirl spends heavily on consumer advertising. We now look at factors that influence the marketer's choice of promotion tools.

The Nature of Each Promotion Tool

Each promotion tool has unique characteristics and costs. Marketers must understand these characteristics in shaping the promotion mix.

Advertising. Advertising can reach masses of geographically dispersed buyers at a low cost per exposure, and it enables the seller to repeat a message many times. Television advertising can reach huge audiences. For example, more than 114 million Americans watched the most recent Super Bowl, and as many as 18 million avid fans tuned in each week for the latest season of NCIS. What's more, a popular TV ad's reach can be extended through online and social media. » For example, consider Microsoft's inspiring and effective Super Bowl XLIX "Empowering" ad, featuring six-year-old Braylon O'Neill excelling on prosthetic legs and showing how technology empowers us all to make the impossible possible. In addition to 100-plus million TV viewers, the ad drew more than 6.2 million YouTube views during the ensuing two months. For companies that want to reach a mass audience, TV is the place to be.[7]

» **TV advertising has vast reach. Microsoft's inspiring Super Bowl XLIX "Empowering" ad—about how technology improves our lives—drew 100-plus million TV viewers and triggered millions of online views and shares.**
Microsoft Corporation

Beyond its reach, large-scale advertising says something positive about the seller's size, popularity, and success. Because of advertising's public nature, consumers tend to view advertised products as more legitimate. Advertising is also very expressive; it allows the company to dramatize its products through the artful use of visuals, print, sound, and color. On the one hand, advertising can be used to build up a long-term image for a product (such as Coca-Cola ads). On the other hand, advertising can trigger quick sales (as when Kohl's advertises weekend specials).

Advertising also has some shortcomings. Although it reaches many people quickly, mass-media advertising is impersonal and lacks the direct persuasiveness of company salespeople. For the most part, advertising can carry on only a one-way communication with an audience, and the audience does not feel that it has to pay attention or respond. In addition, advertising can be very costly. Although some advertising forms—such as newspaper, radio, or online advertising—can be done on smaller budgets, other forms, such as network TV advertising, require very large budgets. For example, the one-minute Microsoft "Empowering" Super Bowl ad discussed above cost $9 million for media time alone, not counting the costs of producing the ad.

Personal Selling. Personal selling is the most effective tool at certain stages of the buying process, particularly in building up buyers' preferences, convictions, and actions. It involves personal interaction between two or more people, so each person can observe the other's needs and characteristics and make quick adjustments. Personal selling also allows all kinds of customer relationships to spring up, ranging from matter-of-fact selling relationships to personal friendships. An effective salesperson keeps the customer's interests at heart to build a long-term relationship by solving a customer's problems. Finally, with personal selling, the buyer usually feels a greater need to listen and respond, even if the response is a polite "No, thank you."

These unique qualities come at a cost, however. A sales force requires a longer-term commitment than does advertising—advertising can be turned up or down, but the size of a sales force is harder to change. Personal selling is also the company's most expensive promotion tool, costing companies on average $600 or more per sales call, depending on the industry.[8] U.S. firms spend up to three times as much on personal selling as they do on advertising.

Sales Promotion. Sales promotion includes a wide assortment of tools—coupons, contests, discounts, premiums, and others—all of which have many unique qualities. They attract consumer attention, engage consumers, offer strong incentives to purchase, and can be used to dramatize product offers and boost sagging sales. Sales promotions invite and reward quick response. Whereas advertising says, "Buy our product," sales promotion says, "Buy it now." Sales promotion effects can be short lived, however, and often are not as effective as advertising or personal selling in building long-run brand preference and customer relationships.

Public Relations. Public relations is very believable—news stories, features, sponsorships, and events seem more real and believable to readers than ads do. PR can also reach many prospects who avoid salespeople and advertisements—the message gets to buyers as "news and events" rather than as a sales-directed communication. And, as with advertising, public relations can dramatize a company or product. Marketers tend to underuse public relations or use it as an afterthought. Yet a well-thought-out public relations campaign used with other promotion mix elements can be very effective and economical.

Direct and Digital Marketing. The many forms of direct and digital marketing—from direct mail, catalogs, and telephone marketing to online, mobile, and social media—all share some distinctive characteristics. Direct marketing is more targeted: It's usually directed to a specific customer or customer community. Direct marketing is immediate and personalized: Messages can be prepared quickly—even in real time—and tailored to appeal to individual consumers or brand groups. Finally, direct marketing is interactive: It allows a dialogue between the marketing team and the consumer, and messages can be altered depending on the consumer's response. Thus, direct and digital marketing are well suited to highly targeted marketing efforts, creating customer engagement, and building one-to-one customer relationships.

Promotion Mix Strategies

Marketers can choose from two basic promotion mix strategies: *push* promotion or *pull* promotion. >> **Figure 12.2** contrasts the two strategies. The relative emphasis given to the specific promotion tools differs for push and pull strategies. A **push strategy** involves "pushing" the product through marketing channels to final consumers. The producer directs its marketing activities (primarily personal selling and trade promotion) toward channel members to induce them to carry the product and promote it to final consumers. For example, John Deere does very little promoting of its lawn mowers, garden tractors, and other residential consumer products to final consumers. Instead, John Deere's sales force works with Lowe's, Home Depot, independent dealers, and other channel members, who in turn push John Deere products to final consumers.

Push strategy
A promotion strategy that calls for using the sales force and trade promotion to push the product through channels. The producer promotes the product to channel members who in turn promote it to final consumers.

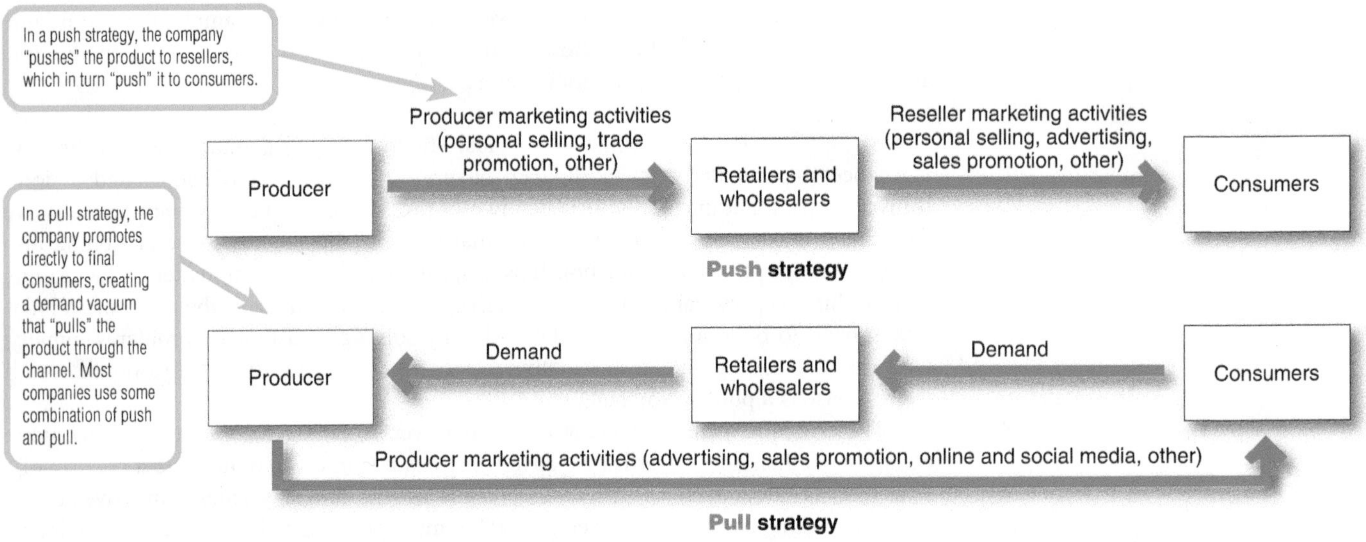

Figure 12.2 Push versus Pull Promotion Strategy

Pull strategy
A promotion strategy that calls for spending a lot on consumer advertising and promotion to induce final consumers to buy the product, creating a demand vacuum that "pulls" the product through the channel.

Using a **pull strategy**, the producer directs its marketing activities (primarily advertising, consumer promotion, and direct and digital media) toward final consumers to induce them to buy the product. For example, Unilever promotes its Axe grooming products directly to its young male target market using TV and print ads, Web and social media brand sites, and other channels. If the pull strategy is effective, consumers will then demand the brand from retailers such as CVS, Walgreens, or Walmart, which will in turn demand it from Unilever. Thus, under a pull strategy, consumer demand "pulls" the product through the channels.

Some industrial-goods companies use only push strategies; likewise, some direct marketing companies use only pull strategies. However, most large companies use some combination of both. For example, Unilever spends nearly $8 billion worldwide each year on consumer marketing and sales promotions to create brand preference and pull customers into stores that carry its products.[9] At the same time, it uses its own and distributors' sales forces and trade promotions to push its brands through the channels so that they will be available on store shelves when consumers come calling.

Companies consider many factors when designing their promotion mix strategies, including the type of product and market. For example, the importance of different promotion tools varies between consumer and business markets. Business-to-consumer companies usually pull more, putting more of their funds into advertising, followed by sales promotion, personal selling, and then public relations. In contrast, business-to-business marketers tend to push more, putting more of their funds into personal selling, followed by sales promotion, advertising, and public relations.

Now that we've examined the concept of integrated marketing communications and the factors that firms consider when shaping their promotion mixes, let's look more closely at the specific marketing communications tools.

LINKING THE CONCEPTS

Pause here for a few minutes. Flip back through and link the parts of the chapter you've read so far.

- How does the *integrated marketing communications (IMC)* concept relate to the *promotion mix* concept?
- How has the changing communications environment affected the ways in which companies communicate with you about their products and services? If you were in the market for a new car, where might you hear about various available models? Where would you *search* for information?

Author Comment
You already know a lot about advertising—you are exposed to it every day. But here we'll look behind the scenes at how companies make advertising decisions.

Advertising

Advertising can be traced back to the very beginnings of recorded history. Archaeologists working in countries around the Mediterranean Sea have dug up signs announcing various events and offers. The Romans painted walls to announce gladiator fights, and the Phoenicians painted pictures on large rocks to promote their wares along parade routes. During the golden age in Greece, town criers announced the sale of cattle, crafted items, and even cosmetics. An early "singing commercial" went as follows: "For eyes that are shining, for cheeks like the dawn/For beauty that lasts after girlhood is gone/For prices in reason, the woman who knows/Will buy her cosmetics from Aesclyptos."

Modern advertising, however, is a far cry from these early efforts. U.S. advertisers now run up an estimated annual bill of nearly $183 billion on measured advertising media; worldwide ad spending is an estimated $545 billion. P&G, the world's largest advertiser, spent more than $4.6 billion on U.S. advertising and $11.5 billion worldwide.[10]

Although advertising is used mostly by business firms, a wide range of not-for-profit organizations, professionals, and social agencies also use advertising to promote their causes to various target publics. In fact, the 39th-largest U.S. advertising spender is a not-for-profit organization—the U.S. government, which advertises in many ways. For example, its Centers for Disease Control spent $68 million on the third year of an anti-smoking advertising campaign titled "Tips from a Former Smoker," showing people who have paid dearly due to smoking-related diseases.[11] Advertising is a good way to engage, inform, and persuade, whether the purpose is to sell Coca-Cola worldwide, help smokers kick the habit, or educate people in developing nations on how to lead healthier lives.

Marketing management must make four important decisions when developing an advertising program (see **Figure 12.3**): *setting advertising objectives, setting the advertising budget, developing advertising strategy (message decisions and media decisions),* and *evaluating advertising effectiveness.*

Setting Advertising Objectives

Advertising objective
A specific communication *task* to be accomplished with a specific *target* audience during a specific period of *time*.

The first step is to set *advertising objectives*. These objectives should be based on past decisions about the target market, positioning, and the marketing mix, which define the job that advertising must do in the total marketing program. The overall advertising objective is to help engage customers and build customer relationships by communicating customer value. Here, we discuss specific advertising objectives.

An **advertising objective** is a specific communication *task* to be accomplished with a specific *target* audience during a specific period of *time*. Advertising objectives can be classified by their primary purpose—to *inform, persuade,* or *remind*. **Table 12.1** lists examples of each of these specific objectives.

Don't forget—advertising is only part of a broader set of marketing and company decisions. Its job is to help communicate the brand's value proposition to target customers. Advertising must blend well with other promotion and marketing mix decisions.

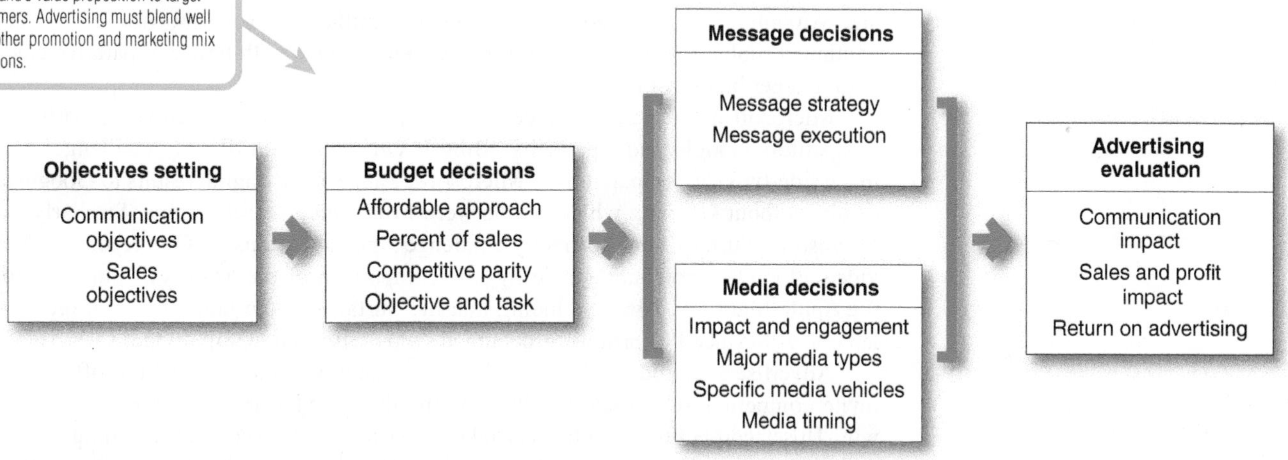

Figure 12.3 Major Advertising Decisions

Table 12.1 Possible Advertising Objectives

Informative Advertising	
Communicating customer value	Suggesting new uses for a product
Building a brand and company image	Informing the market of a price change
Telling the market about a new product	Describing available services and support
Explaining how a product works	Correcting false impressions
Persuasive Advertising	
Building brand preference	Persuading customers to purchase now
Encouraging switching to a brand	Creating customer engagement
Changing customer perceptions of product value	Building brand community
Reminder Advertising	
Maintaining customer relationships	Reminding consumers where to buy the product
Reminding consumers that the product may be needed in the near future	Keeping the brand in a customer's mind during off-seasons

Informative advertising is used heavily when introducing a new product category. In this case, the objective is to build primary demand. Thus, early producers of HDTVs first had to inform consumers of the image quality and size benefits of the new product. *Persuasive advertising* becomes more important as competition increases. Here, the company's objective is to build selective demand. For example, once HDTVs became established, Samsung began trying to persuade consumers that *its* brand offered the best quality for their money. Such advertising wants to engage customers and create brand community.

Some persuasive advertising has become *comparative advertising* (or *attack advertising*), in which a company directly or indirectly compares its brand with one or more other brands. You see examples of comparative advertising in almost every product category, ranging from sports drinks and fast food to car rentals, credit cards, and wireless phone services. For example, Taco Bell's initial ads introducing its then-new breakfast menu took a direct poke at fast-food breakfast leader McDonald's. Taco Bell ads employed a slew of actual people named Ronald McDonald as Taco Bell spokespeople. "It's not surprising these guys are loving Taco Bell," says one ad. "What's surprising is who they are." An online "behind-the-scenes" video drew millions of YouTube views. Taco Bell has continued rubbing its breakfast fare in McDonald's face with new comparative ads introducing other breakfast items.[12]

Microsoft has run several recent ad campaigns featuring head-on comparisons with competitors Google and Apple. Its "Bing It On" campaign directly challenged users to make side-by-side comparisons of Microsoft's Bing search engine results to Google search results without knowing which results were from which search engine. Similarly, ads for Microsoft's Surface tablets directly challenge Apple's laptops. » One recent Surface Pro video ad made a convincing side-by-side comparison of the Microsoft Surface Pro with the Apple MacBook Air, concluding that the Surface is "the tablet that can replace your laptop." A Surface Pro print ad proclaimed, "Powerful as a laptop, lighter than Air."[13]

Advertisers should use comparative advertising with caution. All too often, such ads invite competitor responses, resulting in an advertising war that neither competitor can win. Upset competitors might also take more drastic action, such as filing complaints with the self-regulatory National Advertising Division of the Council of Better Business Bureaus or even filing false-advertising lawsuits.

Reminder advertising is important for mature products; it helps to maintain customer relationships and keep consumers thinking about the product. Expensive Coca-Cola television ads primarily build and maintain the Coca-Cola brand relationship rather than inform consumers or persuade them to buy it in the short run.

Advertising's goal is to help move consumers through the buying process. Some advertising is designed to move people to immediate action. For example, a direct-response television ad by Weight Watchers urges consumers to go online and sign up right away, and a Best Buy newspaper insert for a weekend sale encourages immediate store visits. However, many ads focus on building or strengthening long-term customer relationships. For example, a Nike television ad in which well-known athletes work through extreme challenges in their Nike gear never directly asks for a sale. Instead, the goal is to engage customers and somehow change the way they think or feel about the brand.

>> **Comparative advertising: Many Microsoft ads feature head-on comparisons with competitors like Apple. The above video compared the Microsoft Surface Pro with the Apple MacBook Air, concluding that the Surface is "the tablet that can replace your laptop."**

Microsoft Corporation

Setting the Advertising Budget

After determining its advertising objectives, the company next sets its **advertising budget** for each product. Here, we look at four common methods used to set the total budget for advertising: the *affordable method*, the *percentage-of-sales method*, the *competitive-parity method*, and the *objective-and-task method*.

Affordable Method

Some companies use the **affordable method**: They set the promotion budget at the level they think the company can afford. Small businesses often use this method, reasoning that a company cannot spend more on advertising than it has. They start with total revenues, deduct operating expenses and capital outlays, and then devote some portion of the remaining funds to advertising.

Unfortunately, this method of setting budgets completely ignores the effects of promotion on sales. It tends to place promotion last among spending priorities, even in situations in which advertising is critical to the firm's success. It leads to an uncertain annual promotion budget, which makes long-range market planning difficult. Although the affordable method can result in overspending on advertising, it more often results in underspending.

Advertising budget
The dollars and other resources allocated to a product or a company advertising program.

Affordable method
Setting the promotion budget at the level management thinks the company can afford.

Percentage-of-sales method
Setting the promotion budget at a certain percentage of current or forecasted sales or as a percentage of the unit sales price.

Percentage-of-Sales Method

Other companies use the **percentage-of-sales method**, setting their promotion budget at a certain percentage of current or forecasted sales. Or they budget a percentage of the unit sales price. The percentage-of-sales method has advantages. It is simple to use and helps management think about the relationships between promotion spending, selling price, and profit per unit.

Despite these claimed advantages, however, the percentage-of-sales method has little to justify it. It wrongly views sales as the *cause* of promotion rather than as the *result*. Although studies have found a positive correlation between promotional spending and brand strength, this relationship often turns out to be effect and cause, not cause and effect. Stronger brands with higher sales can afford the biggest ad budgets.

Thus, the percentage-of-sales budget is based on availability of funds rather than on opportunities. It may prevent the increased spending sometimes needed to turn around falling sales. Because the budget varies with year-to-year sales, long-range planning is difficult. Finally, the method does not provide any basis for choosing a *specific* percentage, except what has been done in the past or what competitors are doing.

Competitive-Parity Method

Competitive-parity method
Setting the promotion budget to match competitors' outlays.

Still other companies use the **competitive-parity method**, setting their promotion budgets to match competitors' outlays. They monitor competitors' advertising or get industry promotion spending estimates from publications or trade associations and then set their budgets based on the industry average.

Two arguments support this method. First, competitors' budgets represent the collective wisdom of the industry. Second, spending what competitors spend helps prevent promotion wars. Unfortunately, neither argument is valid. There are no grounds for believing that the competition has a better idea of what a company should be spending on promotion than does the company itself. Companies differ greatly, and each has its own special promotion needs. Finally, there is no evidence that budgets based on competitive parity prevent promotion wars.

Objective-and-Task Method

Objective-and-task method
Developing the promotion budget by (1) defining specific promotion objectives, (2) determining the tasks needed to achieve these objectives, and (3) estimating the costs of performing these tasks. The sum of these costs is the proposed promotion budget.

The most logical budget-setting method is the **objective-and-task method**, whereby the company sets its promotion budget based on what it wants to accomplish with promotion. This budgeting method entails (1) defining specific promotion objectives, (2) determining the tasks needed to achieve these objectives, and (3) estimating the costs of performing these tasks. The sum of these costs is the proposed promotion budget.

The advantage of the objective-and-task method is that it forces management to spell out its assumptions about the relationship between dollars spent and promotion results. But it is also the most difficult method to use. Often, it is hard to figure out which specific tasks will achieve stated objectives. For example, suppose Microsoft wants 75 percent awareness for the latest version of its Surface tablet during the three-month introductory period. What specific advertising messages and media schedules should Microsoft use to attain this objective? How much would these messages and media schedules cost? Microsoft management must consider such questions, even though they are hard to answer.

No matter what method is used, setting the advertising budget is no easy task. John Wanamaker, the department store magnate, once said, "I know that half of my advertising is wasted, but I don't know which half. I spent $2 million for advertising, and I don't know if that is half enough or twice too much." For example, Coca-Cola spends hundreds of millions of dollars annually on advertising, but is that too little, just right, or too much?

Setting the promotion budget is one of the hardest decisions facing a company. Coca-Cola spends hundreds of millions of dollars annually, but is that "half enough or twice too much"?
Migstock/Alamy

As a result of such thinking, advertising is one of the easiest budget items to cut when economic times get tough. Cuts in brand-building advertising appear to do little short-term harm to sales. For example, in the wake of the recent Great Recession, U.S. advertising expenditures plummeted 12 percent over the previous year. In the long run, however, slashing ad spending risks long-term damage to a brand's image and market share. In fact, companies that can maintain or even increase their advertising spending while competitors are decreasing theirs can gain competitive advantage.

For example, during the Great Recession, while competitors were cutting back, car maker Audi actually increased its marketing and advertising spending. Audi "kept its foot on the pedal while everyone else is pulling back," said an Audi ad executive at the time. "Why would we go backwards now when the industry is generally locking the brakes and cutting spending?" As a result, Audi's brand awareness and buyer consideration reached record levels during the recession, outstripping those of BMW, Mercedes, and Lexus and positioning Audi strongly for the post-recession era. In the post-recession economy, Audi is now one of the hottest auto brands on the market.[14]

Developing Advertising Strategy

Advertising strategy
The strategy by which the company accomplishes its advertising objectives. It consists of two major elements: creating advertising messages and selecting advertising media.

Advertising strategy consists of two major elements: creating advertising *messages* and selecting advertising *media*. In the past, companies often viewed media planning as secondary to the message-creation process. After the creative department created good advertisements, the media department then selected and purchased the best media for carrying those advertisements to the desired target audiences. This often caused friction between creatives and media planners.

Today, however, soaring media costs, more-focused target marketing strategies, and the blizzard of new online, mobile, and social media have promoted the importance of the media-planning function. The decision about which media to use for an ad campaign—television, newspapers, magazines, video, a Web site, social media, mobile devices, or email—is now sometimes more critical than the creative elements of the campaign. Also, brand content is now often co-created through interactions with and among consumers. As a result, more and more advertisers are orchestrating a closer harmony between their messages and the media that deliver them. As discussed in the previous chapter, the goal is to create and manage brand content across a full range of media, whether they are paid, owned, earned, or shared.

Creating the Advertising Message and Brand Content

No matter how big the budget, advertising can succeed only if it engages consumers and communicates well. Good advertising messages and content are especially important in today's costly and cluttered advertising environment.

Today, the average household receives about TV 189 channels, and consumers have more than 7,200 magazines from which to choose.[15] Add in the countless radio stations and a continuous barrage of catalogs, direct mail, out-of-home media, email, and online, mobile, and social media exposures, and consumers are being bombarded with ads and brand content at home, work, and all points in between. For example, Americans are exposed to a cumulative 5.3 trillion online ad impressions each year and a daily diet of 500 million Tweets, 432,000 hours of uploaded YouTube video, 70 million photos shared on Instagram, 5 million article pins on Pinterest, and 4.75 billion pieces of shared content on Facebook.[16]

» **Advertising clutter: Today's consumers, armed with an arsenal of weapons, can choose what they watch and don't watch. Increasingly, they are choosing not to watch ads.**
Piotr Marcinski/Shutterstock

Breaking through the Clutter. If all this clutter bothers some consumers, it also causes huge headaches for marketers. Take the situation facing network television advertisers. They pay an average of $354,000 to produce a single 30-second commercial. Then, each time they show it, they pay an average of $112,100 for 30 seconds of advertising time during a popular primetime program. They pay even more if it's an especially popular program, such as *Sunday Night Football* ($627,000), *The Big Bang Theory* ($345,000), or a mega-event such as the Super Bowl (averaging $4.5 million per 30 seconds!). Then their ads are sandwiched in with a clutter of other commercials, network promotions, and other nonprogram material totaling as much as 20 minutes per primetime hour, with long commercial breaks coming every six minutes on average. Such clutter in television and other ad media has created an increasingly hostile advertising environment.[17]

Until recently, television viewers were pretty much a captive audience for advertisers. But today's digital wizardry has given viewers a rich new set of information and entertainment options—the Internet, video streaming, social and mobile media, tablets and smartphones, and others. Digital technology has also armed consumers with an arsenal of weapons for choosing what they watch or don't watch and when. » Increasingly, thanks to the growth of DVR systems and digital streaming, consumers are choosing *not* to watch ads. For example, 76 percent of U.S. homes have a DVR, subscribe to Netflix, or use video-on-demand from a cable or telecommunications provider. Forty-seven percent of American TV homes have DVRs, and two-thirds of DVR owners use the device to skip commercials.[18]

Thus, advertisers can no longer force-feed the same old cookie-cutter messages and content to captive consumers through traditional media. Simply interrupting or disrupting consumers no longer works. Unless ads provide content that is engaging, useful, or entertaining, many consumers will simply ignore or skip them.

Madison & Vine
A term that has come to represent the merging of advertising and entertainment in an effort to break through the clutter and create new avenues for reaching customers with more engaging messages.

Merging Advertising and Entertainment. To break through the clutter, many marketers have subscribed to a new merging of advertising and entertainment, dubbed "**Madison & Vine**." You've probably heard of Madison Avenue, the New York City street that houses the headquarters of many of the nation's largest advertising agencies. You may also have heard of Hollywood & Vine, the intersection of Hollywood Avenue and Vine Street in Hollywood, California, long the symbolic heart of the U.S. entertainment industry. Now, Madison Avenue and Hollywood & Vine have come together to form a new intersection—Madison & Vine—that represents the merging of advertising and entertainment in an effort to create new avenues for reaching consumers with more engaging messages.[19]

This merging of advertising and entertainment takes one of two forms: advertainment or brand integrations. The aim of *advertainment* is to make ads and brand content themselves so entertaining, or so useful, that people *want* to watch them. There's no chance that you'd watch ads on purpose, you say? Think again. For example, the Super Bowl has become an annual advertainment showcase. Tens of millions of people tune in to the Super Bowl each year, as much to watch the entertaining ads as to see the game. And ads and related content posted online before and after the big game draw tens of millions of views. These days, it's common to see an entertaining ad on YouTube before you see it on TV.

Advertisers are also creating new content forms that look less like ads and more like short films or shows. A range of new brand messaging platforms—from Webisodes and blogs to online videos and social media posts—now blur the line between ads and other consumer content. For example, as part of its long-running, highly successful Campaign for Real Beauty, Unilever's Dove brand created a thought-provoking three-minute video, called "Dove Real Beauty Sketches," about how women view themselves. The video compares images of women drawn by an FBI-trained sketch artist based on their self-descriptions versus strangers' descriptions of them. Side-by-side comparisons show that the stranger-described images are invariably more accurate and more flattering, creating strong reactions from the women. The tagline concludes, "You're more beautiful than you think." Although the award-winning video was never shown on TV, it drew more than 163 million global YouTube views within just two months, making it the most-watched video ever.[20]

Marketers have tested all kinds of novel ways to break through today's clutter and engage consumers. For example, Hostess Brands—maker of those yummy Twinkies, Ho Hos, Ding Dongs, and cream-filled cupcakes—recently shared a Tweet celebrating the opening day of the Major League Baseball season. The Tweet contained a picture of baseball-decorated cupcakes but also the bold headline TOUCHDOWN. As expected, the Tweet grabbed plenty of attention, as droves of Twitter followers pounced to point out the mistake, just the reaction Hostess intended. "The 'touchdown' line was intentional," says the marketing director of Hostess Brands. "It's fun and aimed at young audiences who are in on the running joke." Other brands have also "tested the stupid waters," as one analyst puts it. >> For example, JCPenney once posted incoherent Tweets, grabbing widespread attention and leading to speculation that the retailer's social media person was either drunk or had been hacked. Instead, says JCPenney, the person was Tweeting with mittens on to promote its winter merchandise.[21]

Brand integrations (or *branded entertainment*) involve making the brand an inseparable part of some other form of entertainment or content. The most common form of brand integration is product placements—embedding brands as props within other programming. It might be a brief glimpse of Starbucks coffee products on *Morning Joe* on MSNBC or of Microsoft's Surface tablet and Bing search engine in episodes of *Elementary* or *Arrow*.

It might be scenes from *Captain America: The Winter Soldier* in which our superhero rides a Harley-Davidson Street 750.

Or the product placement might be scripted into an episode. For example, an entire episode of *Modern Family,* called "Lost Connection," was built around and told through character Claire Dunphy's Apple MacBook Pro. The episode was shot completely with Apple MacBook Pros, iPhones, and iPads and told using familiar Apple apps—such as FaceTime, Messaging, Safari, iTunes, Reminders, iPhoto, and the iCloud—all seamlessly integrated within the show's theme of searching for missing daughter Haley. Other *Modern Family* episodes have been built around products ranging from Oreos and Target to the Toyota Prius.[22]

» Branded entertainment: The highly acclaimed *The LEGO Movie* was pretty much a 100-minute product placement for iconic LEGO construction bricks, what one writer calls "product-placement perfection.

Pictorial Press Ltd/Alamy

Originally created with TV in mind, brand integration has spread quickly into other sectors of the entertainment industry. If you look carefully, you'll see product placements in movies, video games, comic books, Broadway musicals, and even pop music. For example, last year's top 35 movies contained 464 identifiable brand placements.[23] »The highly acclaimed film *The LEGO Movie* was pretty much a 100-minute product placement for iconic LEGO construction bricks. According to one writer, "The audience happily sits through a cinematic sales pitch ... that shows off the immense versatility of the product while placing it in a deeply personal context. The majority of the film is a breathtaking display of what LEGO bricks are capable of as creative tools, but the personal element is what really elevates this film to product-placement perfection." *The LEGO Movie* boosted The LEGO Group's sales by 11 percent in the six months after it opened.[24]

A related form of brand integration is so-called *native advertising,* advertising or other brand-produced online content that appears to be "native to" the Web or social media site in which it is placed. That is, the brand content looks in form and function like the other natural content surrounding it on a Web or social media platform. It might be an article on a Web site such as *The Huffington Post, BuzzFeed, Mashable,* or even *The New York Times* or *The Wall Street Journal* that is paid for, written by, and placed by an advertiser but uses the same format as articles written by the editorial staff. Or it might be brand-prepared videos, pictures, posts, or pages integrated into social media such as Facebook, YouTube, Instagram, Pinterest, or Twitter that match the form and feel of native content on those media. Examples include Twitter's promoted Tweets, Facebook's promoted stories, *BuzzFeed*'s sponsored posts, or Snapchat's "brand story" ads, branded posts that appear in the app's "Stories" feed. Native advertising is an increasingly popular form of brand content. It lets advertisers create relevant associations between brand and consumer content. According to a recent study by the Association of National Advertisers, "given today's media landscape, where consumers can avoid ads more than ever, advertisers are looking for new ways to get their messages noticed and acted upon."[25]

Thus, Madison & Vine is now the meeting place for advertising, brand content, and entertainment. The goal is to make brand messages a part of the broader flow of consumer content and conversation rather than an intrusion or interruption of it. As advertising agency JWT puts it, "We believe advertising needs to stop *interrupting* what people are interested in and *be* what people are interested in." However, advertisers must be careful that the new intersection itself doesn't become too congested. With all the new brand content formats and integration, Madison & Vine threatens to create even more of the very clutter that it was designed to break through. At that point, consumers might decide to take yet a different route.

Message and Content Strategy. The first step in creating effective advertising content is to plan a *message strategy*—the general message that will be communicated to consumers. The purpose of advertising is to get consumers to engage with or react to the product or company in a certain way. People will engage and react only if they believe they will benefit from doing so. Thus, developing an effective message strategy begins with identifying customer *benefits* that can be used as advertising appeals. Ideally, the message strategy will follow directly from the company's broader positioning and customer value-creation strategies.

Message strategy statements tend to be plain, straightforward outlines of benefits and positioning points that the advertiser wants to stress. The advertiser must next develop a compelling **creative concept**—or *big idea*—that will bring the message strategy to life in a distinctive and memorable way. At this stage, simple message ideas become great ad campaigns. Usually, a copywriter and an art director will team up to generate many creative concepts, hoping that one of these concepts will turn out to be the big idea. The creative concept may emerge as a visualization, a phrase, or a combination of the two.

Distinctive advertising appeals: GE sets its Café refrigerator apart as one that gives users an in-the-door filtered hot water dispenser and Keurig K-Cup single-serve brewing system. It's "Brewing up the next big thing in refrigeration."

Courtesy of General Electric

The creative concept will guide the choice of specific appeals to be used in an advertising campaign. *Advertising appeals* should have three characteristics. First, they should be *meaningful*, pointing out benefits that make the product more desirable or interesting to consumers. Second, appeals must be *believable*. Consumers must believe that the product or service will deliver the promised benefits.

However, the most meaningful and believable benefits may not be the best ones to feature. Appeals should also be *distinctive*. They should tell how the product is better than competing brands. For example, the most meaningful benefit of a refrigerator is that it keeps foods cold. But GE sets its Café refrigerator apart as one that gives users an in-the-door filtered hot water dispenser and a Keurig K-Cup single-serve brewing system for making cups of coffee, tea, and other hot beverages at the fridge. It's "Brewing up the next big thing in refrigeration." Similarly, the most meaningful benefit of owning a wristwatch is that it keeps accurate time, yet few watch ads feature this benefit. Instead, watch advertisers might select any of a number of advertising themes. For years, Timex has been the affordable watch that "takes a licking and keeps on ticking." In contrast, Rolex ads talk about the brand's "obsession with perfection" and the fact that "Rolex has been the preeminent symbol of performance and prestige for more than a century."

Creative concept
The compelling "big idea" that will bring an advertising message strategy to life in a distinctive and memorable way.

Execution style
The approach, style, tone, words, and format used for presenting an advertising message.

Message Execution. The advertiser now must turn the big idea into an actual ad execution that will capture the target market's attention and interest. The creative team must find the best approach, style, tone, words, and format for executing the message. The message can be presented in various **execution styles**, such as the following:

- ***Slice of life.*** This style shows one or more "typical" people using the product in a normal setting. For example, a Silk Soymilk "Rise and Shine" ad shows a young professional starting the day with a healthier breakfast and high hopes.
- ***Lifestyle.*** This style shows how a product fits in with a particular lifestyle. For example, an ad for Athleta active wear shows a woman in a complex yoga pose and states: "If your body is your temple, build it one piece at a time."
- ***Fantasy.*** This style creates a fantasy around the product or its use. For example, a Calvin Klein "Drive in to Fantasy" ad shows a woman floating blissfully above a surf-strewn beach at sunset in her Calvin Klein Nightwear.
- ***Mood or image.*** This style builds a mood or image around the product or service, such as beauty, love, intrigue, serenity, or pride. Few claims are made about the product or service except through suggestion. For example, Dodge Ram Truck's moving Super Bowl XLVII commercial—"To the Farmer in Us All"—added poignant pictures to radio-broadcast-legend Paul Harvey's "So God Made a Farmer"

speech, pulling down the number-two spot in *USA Today's* Ad Meter ratings that year. Except for a few brief frames and a closing picture, the two-minute ad never directly mentioned or showed sponsor Dodge Ram Trucks. However, it associated the brand with strong emotions and basic American values.

- ***Musical.*** This style shows people or cartoon characters singing about the product. For example, the M&M's "Love Ballad" ad, part of the Better with M campaign, featured Red singing Meat Loaf's "I'd Do Anything for Love," showcasing his commitment to actress Naya Rivera. Red has second thoughts, however, when Rivera can't resist adding Red to some of her favorite treats, including cookies, cake, and ice cream. To all of that, Red answers with the lyric, "But I won't do that ... or that ... or that ... or that."
- ***Personality symbol.*** This style creates a character that represents the product. The character might be animated (Mr. Clean, the GEICO Gecko, or the Michelin Man) or real (perky Progressive Insurance spokeswoman Flo, Allstate's Mayhem, Ronald McDonald).
- ***Technical expertise.*** This style shows the company's expertise in making the product. Thus, Jim Koch of the Boston Beer Company tells about his many years of experience in brewing Samuel Adams beer.
- ***Scientific evidence.*** This style presents survey or scientific evidence that the brand is better or better liked than one or more other brands. For years, Crest toothpaste has used scientific evidence to convince buyers that Crest is better than other brands at fighting cavities.
- ***Testimonial evidence or endorsement.*** This style features a highly believable or likable source endorsing the product. It could be ordinary people saying how much they like a given product. For example, Whole Foods features a variety of real customers in its Values Matter marketing campaign. Or it might be a celebrity presenting the product, such as Beyoncé or Sofia Vergara speaking for Diet Pepsi.

The advertiser also must choose a *tone* for the ad. For example, P&G always uses a positive tone: Its ads say something very positive about its products. Other advertisers now use edgy humor to break through the commercial clutter. Bud Light commercials are famous for this.

The advertiser must use memorable and attention-getting *words* in the ad. For example, rather than just saying that its prescription sunglass lenses protect your eyes and look good at the same time, a LensCrafters ad announces, "Sunblock Never Looked So Good." Similarly, rather than claiming simply that its laundry detergent is "superconcentrated," Method asks customers, "Are you jug addicted?" The solution: "Our patent-pending formula that's so fricken' concentrated, 50 loads fits in a teeny bottle. ... With our help, you can get off the jugs and get clean."

Finally, *format* elements make a difference in an ad's impact as well as in its cost. A small change in an ad's design can make a big difference in its effect. In a print or display ad, the *illustration* is the first thing the reader notices—it must be strong enough to draw attention. Next, the *headline* must effectively entice the right people to read the copy. Finally, the *copy*—the main block of text in the ad—must be simple but strong and convincing. Moreover, these three elements must effectively work *together* to engage customers and persuasively present customer value. However, novel formats can help an ad stand out from the clutter. »For example, in one striking ad from Volkswagen, the illustration does most of the work in catching relevant attention for the car maker's precision parking assist feature. It shows a porcupine "parked" in a tight space between goldfish in water-filled plastic bags. The small-print headline says only, "Precision Parking. Park Assist by Volkswagen." Enough said!

» Novel formats can help an advertisement stand out. In this Volkswagen ad, the illustration does most of the work in illustrating the car maker's parking assist feature.

Used with permission of Volkswagen Aktiengesellschaft. Creative studio - The Operators

Consumer-Generated Content. Taking advantage of today's digital and social media technologies, many companies are now tapping consumers for marketing content, message ideas, or even actual ads and videos. Sometimes the results are outstanding; sometimes they are forgettable. If done well, however, user-generated content can incorporate the voice of the customer into brand messages and generate greater customer engagement.

Perhaps the best-known consumer-generated content effort is the long-running annual "Crash the Super Bowl Challenge" held annually by PepsiCo's Doritos brand. Doritos invites consumers to create their own 30-second video ads, and winners receive large cash awards and have their ads run during the Super Bowl. But brands across a wide range of industries—from automakers and fast-food chains to apparel brands and pet food marketers—are inviting customers to participate in generating marketing content.

For example, Chevrolet held an Oscars Program Video Contest last year that produced 72 imaginative ad videos for its Chevy Cruze model. The winner—a delightfully quirky one-minute video called "Speed Chaser"—was shot in an open field for only $4,000. Similarly, Purina conducted a video contest on its YouTube page, inviting owners of everyday dogs to submit videos showing "How is your dog great?" Using a compilation of clips from more than 500 submitted videos, Purina created a 60-second "How I'm Great" commercial and aired it during the broadcast of the Westminster Kennel Club Dog Show. And to help boost digital and social media engagement, » Taco Bell invited YouTube stars and influencers to create video content for its new Fiery Doritos Locos Tacos. Taco Bell ended up choosing 65 video ads to distribute online through Twitter feeds and social networks and used one clever video—featuring a "3D Doritos Taco printer"—in subsequent paid online advertising.[26]

» **Consumer-generated content: Taco Bell boosted digital and social media coverage of the introduction of its Fiery Doritos Locos Tacos with consumer-generated videos distributed through Twitter feeds, social networks, and online advertising buys.**

Taco Bell

Consumer-generated content can make customers an everyday part of the brand conversation. Yogawear company Lululemon launched its #TheSweatLife campaign, in which it invited customers to Tweet or Instagram photos of themselves "getting their sweat on" in Lululemon gear. "Your perspiration is our inspiration," said the brand at its Web site. Within only a few months, the brand had received more than 7,000 photos, which it featured in a #TheSweatLife online gallery, quickly drawing more than 40,000 unique visitors. The user-generated content campaign created substantial customer engagement for Lululemon. "We created the program as a way to connect with our guests and showcase how they're authentically sweating in our product offline," says a Lululemon brand manager. "We see it as a unique way to bring their offline experiences into our online community."[27]

Not all consumer-generated content efforts, however, are so successful. As many big companies have learned, ads and other content made by amateurs can be ... well, pretty amateurish. If done well, however, consumer-generated content efforts can produce new creative ideas and fresh perspectives on the brand from consumers who actually experience it. Such campaigns can boost consumer engagement and get customers talking and thinking about a brand and its value to them.

Selecting Advertising Media

Advertising media
The vehicles through which advertising messages are delivered to their intended audiences.

The major steps in **advertising media** selection are (1) determining *reach, frequency, impact,* and *engagement*; (2) choosing among major *media types*; (3) selecting specific *media vehicles*; and (4) choosing *media timing*.

Determining Reach, Frequency, Impact, and Engagement. To select media, the advertiser must determine the reach and frequency needed to achieve the advertising objectives. *Reach* is a measure of the *percentage* of people in the target market who are exposed to an ad campaign during a given period of time. For example, the advertiser might try to reach

70 percent of the target market during the first three months of a campaign. *Frequency* is a measure of how many *times* the average person in the target market is exposed to a message. For example, the advertiser might want an average exposure frequency of three.

But advertisers want to do more than just reach a given number of consumers a specific number of times. The advertiser also must determine the desired *media impact*—the *qualitative value* of message exposure through a given medium. For example, the same message in one magazine (say, *Time*) may be more believable than in another (say, the *National Enquirer*). For products that need to be demonstrated, television ads or online videos may have more impact than radio messages because they use sight, motion, *and* sound. Products for which consumers provide input on design or features might be better promoted at an interactive Web site or social media page than in a direct mailing.

More generally, an advertiser wants to choose media that will *engage* consumers rather than simply reach them. Using any medium, the relevance of ad content for its audience is often much more important than how many people it reaches. >> For example, when Mazda wanted to preannounce the sale of 100 25th-anniversary models of its iconic Mazda MX-5 Miata car at last year's New York International Auto show, it didn't use big-budget, high-reach media. Instead, it began churning out Facebook, Twitter, and Google+ posts directly to its large MX-5 Miata fan base, directing them to a microsite where they could preorder the sporty little car. Engaging the right audience in the right media worked well for Mazda. The microsite opened a month later to a flood of responses, and the limited-edition Miata model sold out within only 10 minutes.[28]

>> Engaging the right consumers with the right media worked well for Mazda. Using a highly targeted digital campaign, it sold out 100 25th-anniversary models of its iconic Mazda MX-5 Miata car in only 10 minutes.

Special thanks to those at Mazda North America Operations. Here's to 26 years of the MX-5 Miata and beyond. Long live the roadster.

Although Nielsen is beginning to measure *media engagement* levels for some television, radio, and social media, such measures are still hard to find in most cases. Current media measures are things such as ratings, readership, listenership, and click-through rates. However, engagement happens inside the consumer. It's hard enough to measure how many people are exposed to a given television ad, video, or social media post, let alone measuring the depth of engagement with that content. Still, marketers need to know how customers connect with an ad and brand idea as a part of the broader brand relationship.

Engaged consumers are more likely to act upon brand messages and even share them with others. Thus, rather than simply tracking *consumer impressions* for a media placement—how many people see, hear, or read an ad—Coca-Cola now also tracks the *consumer expressions* that result, such as a comment, a "Like," uploading a photo or video, or sharing brand content on social networks. Today's empowered consumers often generate more messages about a brand than a company can.

For example, Coca-Cola estimates that of the hundreds of millions of views of Coca-Cola–related content on YouTube each year, only about 18 percent are of content created by Coca-Cola. The other 82 percent are of content created by engaged consumers. So, many Coca-Cola marketing campaigns are aimed at sparking brand-related consumer expressions rather than just impressions. For example, the brand's recent "Ahh Effect" campaign called for teens to share the "ahh moments" they experience while drinking Coke at a www.AHH.com Web site and via social media using the hashtag #ThisisAHH. It then featured the user-generated personal expressions in "This is AHH" commercials on youth-oriented TV channels.[29]

Choosing among Major Media Types. As summarized in >> **Table 12.2**, the major media types are television; digital, mobile, and social media; newspapers; direct mail; magazines; radio; and outdoor. Each medium has its advantages and its limitations. Media planners want to choose a mix of media that will effectively and efficiently present the advertising message to target customers. Thus, they must consider each medium's impact, message effectiveness, and cost.

» Table 12.2 Profiles of Major Media Types

Medium	Advantages	Limitations
Television	Good mass-marketing coverage; low cost per exposure; combines sight, sound, and motion; appealing to the senses	High absolute costs; high clutter; fleeting exposure; less audience selectivity
Digital, mobile, and social media	High selectivity; low cost; immediacy; engagement capabilities	Potentially low impact; high audience control of content and exposure
Newspapers	Flexibility; timeliness; good local market coverage; broad acceptability; high believability	Short life; poor reproduction quality; small pass-along audience
Direct mail	High audience selectivity; flexibility; no ad competition within the same medium; allows personalization	Relatively high cost per exposure; "junk mail" image
Magazines	High geographic and demographic selectivity; credibility and prestige; high-quality reproduction; long life and good pass-along readership	Long ad purchase lead time; high cost; no guarantee of position
Radio	Good local acceptance; high geographic and demographic selectivity; low cost	Audio only; fleeting exposure; low attention ("the half-heard" medium); fragmented audiences
Outdoor	Flexibility; high repeat exposure; low cost; low message competition; good positional selectivity	Little audience selectivity; creative limitations

As discussed earlier in the chapter, traditional mass media still dominate today's media mixes. However, as mass-media costs rise and audiences shrink, many companies are now adding digital, mobile, and social media that cost less, target more effectively, and engage consumers more fully. Today's marketers want to assemble a full mix of *paid, owned, earned, and shared media* that create and deliver engaging brand content to target consumers.

In addition to the explosion of online, mobile, and social media, cable and satellite television systems are thriving. Such systems allow narrow programming formats, such as all sports, all news, nutrition, arts, home improvement and gardening, cooking, travel, history, finance, and others that target select groups. Comcast and other cable operators are even testing systems that will let them target specific types of ads to TVs in specific neighborhoods or individually to specific types of customers. For example, ads for a Spanish-language channel would run in only Hispanic neighborhoods, or only pet owners would see ads from pet food companies.

» Marketers have discovered a dazzling array of alternative media, like this heated Caribou Coffee bus shelter.

Caribou Coffee

Finally, in their efforts to find less costly and more highly targeted ways to reach consumers, advertisers have discovered a dazzling collection of *alternative media*. These days, no matter where you go or what you do, you will probably run into some new form of advertising:

> Tiny billboards attached to shopping carts urge you to buy Pampers while ads roll by on the store's checkout conveyor touting your local Chevy dealer. Step outside and there goes a city trash truck sporting an ad for Glad trash bags or a school bus displaying a Little Caesar's pizza ad. A nearby fire hydrant is emblazoned with advertising for KFC's "fiery" chicken wings. You escape to the ballpark, only to find billboard-size video screens running Budweiser ads while a blimp with an electronic message board circles lazily overhead. » In midwinter, you wait in a city bus shelter that looks like an oven—with heat coming from the coils—shouting out Caribou Coffee's lineup of hot breakfast sandwiches.

These days, you're likely to find ads—well—anywhere. Taxi cabs sport electronic messaging signs tied to GPS location sensors that can pitch local stores and restaurants wherever they roam. Ad space is being sold on parking-lot tickets, airline boarding passes, subway turnstiles, highway toll booth gates, ATMs, municipal garbage cans, and even police cars, doctors' examining tables, and church bulletins. One company even sells space on toilet paper furnished free to restaurants, stadiums, and malls—the paper carries advertiser logos, coupons, and codes you can scan with your smartphone to download digital coupons or link to advertisers' social media pages. Now that's a captive audience.

Such alternative media seem a bit far-fetched, and they sometimes irritate consumers who resent it all as "ad nauseam." But for many marketers, these media can save money and provide a way to hit selected consumers where they live, shop, work, and play.

Another important trend affecting media selection is the rapid growth in the number of *media multitaskers*, people who absorb more than one medium at a time. For example, it's not uncommon to find someone watching TV with a smartphone in hand, Tweeting, Snapchatting with friends, and chasing down product information on Google. One recent survey found that 35 percent of all screen time involves simultaneous use of TV and a digital device. Although some of this multitasking is related to TV viewing—such as looking up related product and program information—most multitasking involves tasks unrelated to the shows or ads being watched. Marketers need to take such media interactions into account when selecting the types of media they will use.[30]

Selecting Specific Media Vehicles. Media planners must also choose the best media vehicles—specific media within each general media type. For example, television vehicles include *Modern Family* and *ABC World News Tonight*. Magazine vehicles include *Time, Real Simple*, and *ESPN The Magazine*. Online and mobile vehicles include Twitter, Facebook, Instagram, and YouTube.

Media planners must compute the cost per 1,000 persons reached by a vehicle. For example, if a full-page, four-color advertisement in the U.S. national edition of *Forbes* costs $148,220 and *Forbes*'s readership is 900,000 people, the cost of reaching each group of 1,000 persons is about $164. The same advertisement in *Bloomberg Businessweek*'s Northeast U.S. regional edition may cost only $48,100 but reach only 155,000 people—at a cost per 1,000 of about $310.[31] The media planner ranks each magazine by cost per 1,000 and favors those magazines with the lower cost per 1,000 for reaching target consumers. In the previous case, if a marketer is targeting Northeast business managers, *Businessweek* might be the more cost-effective buy, even at a higher cost per thousand.

Media planners must also consider the costs of producing ads for different media. Whereas newspaper ads may cost very little to produce, flashy television ads can be very costly. Many online and social media ads cost little to produce, but costs can climb when producing made-for-the-Web video and ad series.

In selecting specific media vehicles, media planners must balance media costs against several media effectiveness factors. First, the planner should evaluate the media vehicle's audience quality. For a Huggies disposable diapers ad, for example, *Parents* magazine would have a high exposure value; men's lifestyle magazine *Maxim* would have a low exposure value. Second, the media planner should consider audience engagement. Readers of *Vogue*, for example, typically pay more attention to ads than do *Time* readers. Third, the planner should assess the vehicle's editorial quality. *Time* and *The Wall Street Journal* are more believable and prestigious than *Star* or the *National Enquirer*.

Deciding on Media Timing. An advertiser must also decide how to schedule the advertising over time. Suppose sales of a product peak in December and drop in March (for winter outdoor gear, for instance). The firm can vary its advertising to follow the seasonal pattern, oppose the seasonal pattern, or be the same all year. Most firms do some seasonal advertising. For example, Mars currently runs M&M's special ads for almost every holiday and "season," from Easter, Fourth of July, and Halloween to the Super Bowl season and the Oscar season. And weight-loss product and service marketers tend to heavy-up after the first of the year, targeting consumers who let their appetites get the better of them

>> **Media timing: Today's social media let advertisers respond to events in real-time. Arby's "Hey @Pharrell, can we have our hat back?" Tweet during the Grammy Awards earned the brand more than 75,000 re-Tweets and 40,000 Favorites.**

Kevin Winter/WireImage/Getty Images; Arby's Restaurant Group, Inc.

over the holiday season. Weight Watchers, for instance, spends more than a quarter of its annual advertising budget in January. Some marketers do *only* seasonal advertising: For instance, P&G advertises its Vicks NyQuil only during the cold and flu season.[32]

Today's online and social media let advertisers create ads that respond to events in real time. For example, Lexus recently introduced a new model through live streaming from the North American International Auto Show via Facebook's News Feed. Some 100,000 people watched the introduction live in only the first 10 minutes; another 600,000 viewed it online within the next few days. Oreos reacted in a timely way to a power outage during Super Bowl XLVII with an outage-related "You can still dunk in the dark" Tweet ad. The fast-reaction ad was re-Tweeted and Favorited thousands of times in only 15 minutes. Similarly, Arby's created big buzz during last year's Grammy Awards with a real-time Tweet responding to Pharrell Williams' infamous Vivienne Westwood hat, which looks a bit like the hat in the familiar Arby's logo. >> The Tweet "Hey @Pharrell, can we have our hat back?" earned more than 75,000 re-Tweets and 40,000 Favorites.[33]

Evaluating Advertising Effectiveness and the Return on Advertising Investment

Return on advertising investment The net return on advertising investment divided by the costs of the advertising investment.

Measuring advertising effectiveness and the **return on advertising investment** has become a hot issue for most companies. Top management at many companies is asking marketing managers, "How do we know that we're spending the right amount on advertising?" and "What return are we getting on our advertising investment?"

Advertisers should regularly evaluate two types of advertising results: the communication effects and the sales and profit effects. Measuring the *communication effects* of an ad or ad campaign tells whether the ads and media are communicating the ad message well. Individual ads can be tested before or after they are run. Before an ad is placed, the advertiser can show it to consumers, ask how they like it, and measure message recall or attitude changes resulting from it. After an ad is run, the advertiser can measure how the ad affected consumer recall or product awareness, engagement, knowledge, and preference. Pre- and post-evaluations of communication effects can be made for entire advertising campaigns as well.

Advertisers have gotten pretty good at measuring the communication effects of their ads and ad campaigns. However, *sales and profit* effects of advertising and other content are often much harder to measure. For example, what sales and profits are produced by an ad campaign that increases brand awareness by 20 percent and brand preference by 10 percent? Sales and profits are affected by many factors other than advertising—such as product features, price, and availability.

One way to measure the sales and profit effects of advertising is to compare past sales and profits with past advertising expenditures. Another way is through experiments. For example, to test the effects of different advertising spending levels, Coca-Cola could vary the amount it spends on advertising in different market areas and measure the differences in the resulting sales and profit levels. More complex experiments could be designed to include other variables, such as differences in the ads or media used.

However, because so many factors affect advertising effectiveness, some controllable and others not, measuring the results of advertising spending remains an inexact science. For example, dozens of advertisers spend lavishly on high-profile Super Bowl ads each year. Although they sense that the returns are worth the sizable investment, few could actually measure or prove it (see Marketing at Work 12.2). Managers often must rely on large doses of judgment along with quantitative analysis when assessing advertising performance.

MARKETING AT WORK 12.2

The Super Bowl: The Mother of All Advertising Events—But Is It Worth the Price?

The Super Bowl is the mother of all advertising events. Each year, dozens of blue-chip advertisers showcase some of their best work to huge audiences around the world. But all this doesn't come cheap. Last year, major advertisers plunked down an average of $4.5 million per 30-second spot—that's $150,000 per second! Throw in ad production costs—which can run millions more per ad—and running even a single Super Bowl ad becomes a super-expensive proposition.

So each year, up pops the big debate: Is Super Bowl advertising worth all that money? Super Bowl stalwarts such as Anheuser-Busch, Doritos, Coca-Cola, and GM must think it's a good investment—they come back year after year. But for every big brand that invests in the Super Bowl, there are lots of others that just don't think the returns justify the costs.

The naysayers make some pretty good arguments. Super Bowl advertising is outrageously expensive. And, beyond the costs, the competition for attention during the Super Bowl is fierce. Every single ad represents the best efforts of a major marketer trying to design a knock-your-socks-off spectacular. Many advertisers feel they can get more for their dollar in venues that aren't so crowded with bigger-than-life commercials. For example, the cost of just one Super Bowl ad would buy more than 40 regular prime-time TV commercials, 6.4 million clicks on search ads, 50 million views on Facebook, a full week's worth of advertising on Snapchat, or a whopping 3.5 billion display ads across the Internet.

Still, the Super Bowl has much to offer advertisers. It plays to a huge and receptive audience. Super Bowl XLIV drew nearly 115 million U.S. viewers, making it the most-watched television event in history. What's more, during a typical Super Bowl, the ads draw as much or more viewership than the game. As a result, according to one study, the ROI for one Super Bowl ad can equal that of as many as 250 regular TV ads.

Perhaps more important, more and more these days, a Super Bowl ad itself is only the centerpiece of something much, much bigger. Long before the game begins and long after it ends, consumers, ad critics, media pundits, and advertisers are previewing, reviewing, sharing, rating, and rehashing the commercials. What used to be a one-time showing with some postgame "watercooler" chat is now a full eight- to 12-week experience.

In this digital, mobile, and social media age, rather than surprising viewers with their blockbuster ads during the game, most sponsors now flood online and social media channels weeks in advance with teasers or often entire ads. Weeks and days before the Super Bowl XLIX kick-off, ads posted by Budweiser, Doritos, BMW, Morphie, Snickers, Dove Men+Care, and many other brands had already grabbed hundreds of millions of online views. In fact, YouTube activity for Super Bowl XLIX ads and teaser videos produced 4 million hours of viewing before the game even started. Rather than stealing from a blockbuster ad, the previews seem to make them even more effective on game day. According to one study, 60 percent of the most-shared Super Bowl spots of all time were introduced before the game was broadcast. And on average, commercials uploaded to YouTube before the game generated 3.4 times more views than commercials released on game day.

Consider Anheuser-Busch's pregame activities for Super Bowl XLIX. The company released its Budweiser "Lost Dog" ad—a heartwarming tale featuring a lost Golden Retriever puppy rescued in the nick of time by the Clydesdales—on YouTube four days before the game. By game time, "Lost Dog" had already garnered 41.8 million YouTube views, 10 million more than the brand's ever-so-popular "Puppy Love" prequel the previous year. Aided by the previews, during the game, the endearing ad became the runaway leader in almost every major Super Bowl ad rating.

Super Bowl advertisers also work hard these days to create ads that engage consumers interactively during the game itself. Half of this year's Super Bowl ads incorporated hashtags, and many ads prominently mentioned Facebook, Twitter, YouTube, and other social media. All those digital nods made Super Bowl XLIX the most social Super Bowl ever. Viewers exchanged more than 28 million game-related Tweets during the event. Sixty-five million Facebook users generated 265 million actions, most related to the ads. Budweiser scored the big win—"Lost Dog" was shared more than 2 million times and inspired off nearly 200,000 Tweets during the game. Skittles, Nationwide, Doritos, and McDonald's rounded out the top-five most-talked-about ads on social media.

>> The Doritos Crash the Super Bowl contest and ads generate substantial consumer engagement before, during, and after the Big Game, extending the brand's return on its hefty Super Bowl advertising investment

Frito-Lay Inc.

Finally, for most Super Bowl advertisers, long after the game ends, the marketing content machine is still cranking. Next-day watercooler discussions about Super Bowl ads have been going on for decades. But digital, mobile, and social media have taken post-game buzz into the stratosphere. For days or even weeks following the game, online social channels hum with ad views and reviews, Likes, Shares, and comments. Becoming a part of all that online conversation and sharing can substantially extend a company's return on the game-day investment.

PepsiCo's Doritos brand begins its Super Bowl campaign each year a full four months prior to the event with its "Crash the Super Bowl" contest. Doritos invites consumers to submit their own 30-second commercials and, based on fan votes, runs the best ones during the game. The contest and ads ensure several months of heavy consumer involvement. Now in its ninth year, "Crash the Super Bowl" has produced numerous top-place finishers in the *USA Today* Ad Meter rankings. Last year's contest attracted 4,900 entries from 29 countries. The winner, "Middle Seat"—a clever ad about a man who uses a bag of Doritos to entice a pretty woman to sit next to him on a plane flight only to find that she has a fussy baby in tow —placed fifth in the Ad Meter rankings and earned its amateur creators a $1 million prize plus a "dream job" working at Universal Studios. The ad created buzz well beyond the actual game-day broadcast, as did the runner-up ad, "When Pigs Fly"—a chuckler in which a farm kid straps a rocket on a pig and makes the impossible happen in order to score a bag of Doritos.

So—back to the original question: Is Super Bowl advertising really worth the huge investment? The Super Bowl is certainly not for every brand. But for the right brands—and the brands that do it right—the answer is a resounding "yes." It's not just about running an ad or two during the big game. Instead, it's about consumers by the millions watching, streaming, sharing, commenting, debating, and buzzing about ads and brands before the game, in the moment, and after the main event. For the Super Bowl, says one marketing executive, "We are fundamentally playing a different game. [It's] no longer about 30 seconds [but] about a month long, really, really meaningful program." Says another Super Bowl regular: "Not only does the broadcast itself bring great value, but if you just look at the explosion in the social-media value and digital value in recent years, it's a terrific return on investment."

Sources: Julia Boorstin, "Who Won the Social Super Bowl," CNBC, February 2, 2015, www.cnbc.com/id/102389530; Drew Beechler, "Super Bowl XLIX Social Media Trends and Analysis #Infographic," *Salesforce.com*, February 2, 2015, www.salesforce.com/blog/2015/02/super-bowl-xlix-social-media-trends-and-analysis.html; Stuart Elliott, "Super Bowl Ads Get Their Own Pregame Show," *New York Times*, January 17, 2014; "Pepsi Alters Super Bowl Strategy, Takes Masterbrand Approach," *Advertising Age*, January 24, 2014, http://adage.com/print/291271; "How Marketers Can Bring Their A-Game to the Super Bowl," *Advertising Age*, November 4, 2013, http://adage.com/print/291177; John McDermott, "What the Cost of a Super Bowl Ad Can Buy Online," *Digiday*, January 30, 2015, http://digiday.com/platforms/cost-super-bowl-ad-can-buy-online/; and Jeanine Poggi, "Is the Super Bowl Worth the Price?" *Advertising Age*, February 9, 2015, p. 8.

Other Advertising Considerations

In developing advertising strategies and programs, the company must address two additional questions. First, how will the company organize its advertising function—who will perform which advertising tasks? Second, how will the company adapt its advertising strategies and programs to the complexities of international markets?

Organizing for Advertising

Different companies organize in different ways to handle advertising. In small companies, advertising might be handled by someone in the sales department. Large companies have advertising departments whose job it is to set the advertising budget, work with ad agencies, and handle other advertising not done by an agency. However, most large companies use outside advertising agencies because they offer several advantages.

Advertising agency
A marketing services firm that assists companies in planning, preparing, implementing, and evaluating all or portions of their advertising programs.

How does an **advertising agency** work? Advertising agencies originated in the mid- to late 1800s from salespeople and brokers who worked for the media and received a commission for selling advertising space to companies. As time passed, the salespeople began to help customers prepare their ads. Eventually, they formed agencies and grew closer to the advertisers than to the media.

Today's agencies employ specialists who can often perform advertising and brand content tasks better than the company's own staff can. Agencies also bring an outside point of view to solving the company's problems, along with lots of experience from working with different clients and situations. So, today, even companies with strong advertising departments of their own use advertising agencies.

Some ad agencies are huge; the largest U.S. agency, Y&R, has annual gross U.S. revenues of $1.69 billion. In recent years, many agencies have grown by gobbling up other agencies, thus creating huge agency holding companies. The largest of these megagroups, WPP, includes several large advertising, PR, digital, and promotion agencies with combined worldwide revenues of more than $17 billion.[34]

Most large advertising agencies have the staff and resources to handle all phases of an advertising campaign for their clients, from creating a marketing plan to developing ad and content campaigns and preparing, placing, and evaluating ads and content. Large brands commonly employ several agencies that handle everything from mass-media advertising campaigns to shopper marketing and social media content.

International Advertising Decisions

International advertisers face many complexities not encountered by domestic advertisers. The most basic issue concerns the degree to which global advertising should be adapted to the unique characteristics of various country markets.

Some advertisers have attempted to support their global brands with highly standardized worldwide advertising, with campaigns that work as well in Bangkok as they do in Baltimore. >> For example, McDonald's unifies its creative elements and brand presentation under the familiar "i'm lovin' it" theme in all its 100-plus markets worldwide. Visa coordinates its $500 million worldwide advertising efforts for its debit and credit cards under the "Everywhere you want to be" creative platform, which works as well in Korea as it does in the United States or Brazil.[35] And Snickers runs similar versions of its "You're not you when you're hungry" ads in 80 different countries, from the United States and the United Kingdom to Mexico, Australia, and even Russia. No matter what the country, the ads strike a common human emotion that everyone can relate to—people get out of sorts and do uncharacteristic things when they need nutrition. A Snickers bar can help them get back to being their real selves. Snickers let's local markets make adjustments for local languages and personalities. Otherwise, the ads are similar worldwide.[36]

>> International advertising: McDonald's unifies its global advertising under the familiar "i'm lovin' it" theme in all its 100-plus markets worldwide, here China.

TED ALJIBE/AFP/Getty Images

In recent years, the increased popularity of online marketing and social media sharing has boosted the need for advertising standardization for global brands. Most big marketing and advertising campaigns include a large online presence. Connected consumers can now zip easily across borders via the Internet and social media, making it difficult for advertisers to roll out adapted campaigns in a controlled, orderly fashion. As a result, at the very least, most global consumer brands coordinate their Web sites internationally. For example, Coca-Cola Web sites around the world, from Australia and Argentina to France, Romania, and Russia, are surprisingly uniform. All feature splashes of familiar Coke red, iconic Coke bottle shapes, and Coca-Cola's music and "open happiness" themes.

Standardization produces many benefits—lower advertising costs, greater global advertising coordination, and a more consistent worldwide image. But it also has drawbacks. Most important, it ignores the fact that country markets differ greatly in their cultures, demographics, and economic conditions. Thus, most international advertisers "think globally but act locally." They develop global advertising *strategies* that make their worldwide efforts more efficient and consistent. Then they adapt their advertising *programs* to make them more responsive to consumer needs and expectations within local markets. For example, although Visa employs its "Everywhere you want to be" theme globally, ads in specific locales employ local language and inspiring local imagery that make the theme relevant to the local markets in which they appear.

Global advertisers face several special problems. For instance, advertising media costs and availability differ vastly from country to country. Countries also differ in the extent to which they regulate advertising practices. Many countries have extensive systems of laws restricting how much a company can spend on advertising, the media used, the nature of advertising claims, and other aspects of the advertising program. Such restrictions often require advertisers to adapt their campaigns from country to country.

Thus, although advertisers may develop global strategies to guide their overall advertising efforts, specific advertising programs must usually be adapted to meet local cultures and customs, media characteristics, and regulations.

LINKING THE CONCEPTS

Think about what goes on behind the scenes for the ads we all tend to take for granted.

- Pick a favorite print or television ad. Why do you like it? Do you think that it's effective? Can you think of an ad that people like that may not be effective?
- Dig a little deeper and learn about the campaign *behind* your ad. What are the campaign's objectives? What is its budget? Assess the campaign's message and media strategies. What other brand content does the campaign contain? Looking beyond your own feelings about the ad, is the campaign likely to be effective?

Author Comment
Not long ago, public relations was considered a marketing stepchild because of its limited marketing use. That situation is changing fast, however, as more marketers recognize PR's brand-building, customer engagement, and social power.

Public Relations

Another major mass-promotion tool, public relations, consists of activities designed to engage and build good relations with the company's various publics. PR departments may perform any or all of the following functions:[37]

- ***Press relations or press agency.*** Creating and placing newsworthy information in the news media to attract attention to a person, product, or service.
- ***Product publicity.*** Publicizing specific products.
- ***Public affairs.*** Building and maintaining national or local community relationships.
- ***Lobbying.*** Building and maintaining relationships with legislators and government officials to influence legislation and regulation.
- ***Investor relations.*** Maintaining relationships with shareholders and others in the financial community.
- ***Development.*** Working with donors or members of nonprofit organizations to gain financial or volunteer support.

MilkPEP's "Built With Chocolate Milk" public relations campaign is repositioning chocolate milk as a sports recovery "after" beverage for both everyday and well-known adults, here Ironman World Champion Chris Lieto.

Bob Levey/WireImage/Getty images

Public relations is used to promote products, people, places, ideas, activities, organizations, and even nations. Companies use PR to build good relations with consumers, investors, the media, and their communities. Trade associations have used PR to rebuild interest in commodities, such as eggs, apples, potatoes, onions, and even chocolate milk. For example, the Milk Processor Education Program (MilkPEP), known for its successful "Got Milk?" campaign in previous years, created a strong PR campaign to promote the health benefits and boost consumption of chocolate milk:[38]

MilkPEP launched an extensive, integrated PR campaign to reposition chocolate milk—the traditional children's favorite—as a post-workout, sports recovery beverage for adults. Backed by more than 20 research studies that support the refueling benefits of chocolate milk, MilkPEP's "Built With Chocolate Milk" campaign enlists important influencers—such as athletes, sports nutritionists, fitness bloggers, and health researchers—to help change perceptions of chocolate milk from just a kid's drink to a legitimate sports drink, one that's "Trusted by Athletes. Backed by Science." Ads and social media content feature both everyday and well-known athletes, such as 12-time swimming medalist Dara Torres, pro hockey's Zach Parise, Ironman World Champions Chris Lieto and Mirinda Carfrae, and NBA basketball star Carmelo Anthony. For example, MilkPEP sponsored Pittsburgh Steelers football player Hines Ward to train and compete in the Ironman. The chocolate milk team followed Hines through workouts and meetings with dieticians, showing the science behind chocolate milk as a recovery drink, then posted videos and other accounts on YouTube, Twitter, and Facebook. Hines's experience with chocolate milk inspired both fans and fellow athletes to try the beverage. Beyond working with professional athletes, MilkPEP also participates in hundreds of local events across the country, such as California's Big

Sur Marathon, passing out free chocolate milk at finish lines. Thanks to strong PR, chocolate milk is now making a comeback, with 6 to 12 percent sales increases among targeted adults.

The Role and Impact of PR

Public relations can have a strong impact on public awareness at a much lower cost than advertising can. When using public relations, the company does not pay for the space or time in the media. Rather, it pays for a staff to develop and circulate information and manage events. If the company develops an interesting story or event, it could be picked up by several different media and have the same effect as advertising that would cost millions of dollars. What's more, public relations has the power to engage consumers and make them a part of the brand story and its telling.

PR results can sometimes be spectacular. Consider the launch of Apple's iPad:[39]

> Apple's iPad was one of the most successful new product launches in history. The funny thing: Whereas most big product launches are accompanied by huge prelaunch advertising campaigns, Apple pulled this one off with no advertising. None at all. Instead, it simply fed the PR fire. It built buzz months in advance by distributing iPads for early reviews, feeding the offline and online press with tempting tidbits and offering fans an early online peek at thousands of new iPad apps that would be available. At launch time, it fanned the flames with a cameo on the TV sitcom *Modern Family*, a flurry of launch-day appearances on TV talk shows, and other launch-day events. In the process, through PR alone, the iPad launch generated unbounded consumer excitement, a media frenzy, and long lines outside retail stores on launch day. Apple sold more than 300,000 of the sleek gadgets on the first day alone and more than 2 million in the first two months—even as demand outstripped supply. Apple repeated the feat a year later with the equally successful launch of iPad 2, which sold close to 1 million devices the weekend of its launch.

Despite its potential strengths, public relations is occasionally described as a marketing stepchild because of its sometimes limited and scattered use. The PR department is often located at corporate headquarters or handled by a third-party agency. Its staff is so busy dealing with various publics—stockholders, employees, legislators, and the press—that PR programs to support product marketing objectives may be ignored. Moreover, marketing managers and PR practitioners do not always speak the same language. Whereas many PR practitioners see their jobs as simply communicating, marketing managers tend to be much more interested in how advertising and PR affect brand building, sales and profits, and customer engagement and relationships.

This situation is changing, however. Although public relations still captures only a small portion of the overall marketing budgets of many firms, PR can be a powerful brand-building tool. Especially in this digital age, the lines between advertising, PR, and other content are becoming more and more blurred. For example, are brand Web sites, blogs, brand videos, and social media activities advertising, PR, or something else? All are marketing content. And as the use of earned and shared digital content grows rapidly, PR may play a bigger role in marketing content management. More than any other department, PR has always been responsible for creating relevant marketing content that draws consumers to a brand rather than pushing messages out. "PR pros are an organization's master storytellers. In a word, they *do* content," says one expert. "The rise of social media [is] moving public relations professionals from the backroom, crafting press releases and organizing events, to the forefront of brand development and customer engagement," says another.[40] The point is that PR should work hand in hand with advertising within an integrated marketing communications program to help build customer engagement and relationships.

Major Public Relations Tools

Public relations uses several tools. One of the major tools is *news*. PR professionals find or create favorable news about the company and its products or people. Sometimes news stories occur naturally; sometimes the PR person can suggest events or activities that would create news. Another common PR tool is *special events*, ranging from news conferences and speeches, brand tours, and sponsorships to laser light shows, multimedia presentations, or educational programs designed to reach and interest target publics.

Public relations people also prepare *written materials* to reach and influence their target markets. These materials include annual reports, brochures, articles, and company newsletters and magazines. *Audiovisual materials*, such as DVDs and online videos, are being used increasingly as communication tools. *Corporate identity materials* can also help create a corporate identity that the public immediately recognizes. Logos, stationery, brochures, signs, business forms, business cards, buildings, uniforms, and company cars and trucks all become marketing tools when they are attractive, distinctive, and memorable. Finally, companies can improve public goodwill by contributing money and time to *public service activities*.

As previously discussed, the Web and social media are also important PR channels. Web sites, blogs, and social media such as YouTube, Facebook, Instagram, Snapchat, Pinterest, and Twitter are providing new ways to reach and engage people. As noted, storytelling and engagement are core PR strengths, and that plays well into the use of online, mobile, and social media.

As with the other promotion tools, in considering when and how to use product public relations, management should set PR objectives, choose the PR messages and vehicles, implement the PR plan, and evaluate the results. The firm's PR should be blended smoothly with other promotion activities within the company's overall integrated marketing communications effort.

MyMarketingLab

If assigned by your instructor, complete the questions marked with the ✪ from the EOC Discussion Questions section in the MyLab. To complete the Marketing by the Numbers problems found in this section, go to your Assignments in the MyLab.

REVIEWING AND EXTENDING THE CONCEPTS

CHAPTER REVIEW AND CRITICAL THINKING

Objectives Review

In this chapter, you've learned how companies use integrated marketing communications (IMC) to engage customers and communicate customer value. You've also explored two of the major marketing communications mix elements—advertising and public relations. Modern marketing calls for more than just creating customer value by developing a good product, pricing it attractively, and making it available to target customers. Companies also must clearly and persuasively *communicate* that value to current and prospective customers. To do this, they must blend five communication mix tools, guided by a well-designed and implemented integrated marketing communications strategy.

OBJECTIVE 12-1 Define the five promotion mix tools for communicating customer value. (pp 366–367)

A company's total *promotion mix*—also called its *marketing communications mix*—consists of the specific blend of *advertising, personal selling, sales promotion, public relations,* and *direct and digital marketing* tools that the company uses to engage customers, persuasively communicate customer value, and build customer relationships. Advertising includes any paid form of nonpersonal presentation and promotion of ideas, goods, or services by an identified sponsor. In contrast, public relations focuses on building good relations with the company's various publics. Personal selling is personal presentation by the firm's sales force for the purpose of making sales and building customer relationships. Firms use sales promotion to provide short-term incentives to encourage the purchase or sale of a product or service. Finally, firms seeking immediate response from targeted individual consumers and consumer communities use direct, digital, and social media marketing tools to engage consumers and cultivate relationships with them.

OBJECTIVE 12-2 Discuss the changing communications landscape and the need for integrated marketing communications. (pp 367–374)

The explosive developments in communications technology and changes in marketer and customer communication strategies have had a dramatic impact on marketing communications. The new digital and social media have given birth to a more targeted, social, and engaging marketing communications model. Along with traditional media, advertisers are now adding a broad selection of more-specialized and highly targeted media to engage smaller customer segments with more-personalized, interactive content. As they adopt richer but more fragmented media and promotion mixes to reach their diverse markets, however, they risk creating a communications hodgepodge for consumers. To prevent this, companies are adopting the concept of *integrated marketing communications (IMC)*. Guided by an overall IMC strategy, the company works out the roles that the various promotional tools will play and the extent to which each will be used. It carefully coordinates the promotional activities and the timing of when major campaigns take place.

OBJECTIVE 12-3 Describe and discuss the major decisions involved in developing an advertising program. (pp 375–392)

Advertising—the use of paid, owned, earned, and shared media by a seller to inform, persuade, and remind about its products or organization—is a strong promotion tool that takes many forms and has many uses. *Advertising decision making* involves decisions about the objectives, the budget, the message, the media, and, finally, the evaluation of results. Advertisers should set clear *objectives* as to whether the advertising is supposed to inform, persuade, or remind buyers. The advertising *budget* can be based on what is affordable, on sales, on competitors' spending, or on advertising objectives and tasks. The *message decision* calls for planning a creative concept (or "big idea") and message strategy and executing it effectively. The *media decision* involves defining reach, frequency, impact, and engagement goals; choosing major media types; selecting media vehicles; and deciding on media timing. Message and media decisions must be closely coordinated for maximum campaign effectiveness. Finally, *evaluation* calls for evaluating the communication and sales effects of advertising and other brand content before, during, and after it is placed and measuring advertising return on investment.

OBJECTIVE 12-4 Explain how companies use public relations to communicate with their publics. (pp 392–394)

Public relations involves building good relations with the company's various publics. Its functions include *press agency, product publicity, public affairs, lobbying, investor relations,* and *development.* Public relations can have a strong impact on public awareness at a much lower cost than advertising can, and PR results can sometimes be spectacular. Despite its potential strengths, however, PR sometimes sees only limited and scattered use. Public relations tools include *news, special events, written materials, audiovisual materials, corporate identity materials,* and *public service activities*. A company's Web site and online social media can be good PR vehicles. In considering when and how to use product PR, management should set PR objectives, choose the PR messages and vehicles, implement the PR plan, and evaluate the results. Public relations should be blended smoothly with other promotion activities within the company's overall integrated marketing communications effort.

Key Terms

Objective 12-1
Promotion mix (marketing communications mix) (p 366)
Advertising (p 366)
Sales promotion (p 366)
Personal selling (p 366)
Public relations (PR) (p 366)
Direct and digital marketing (p 366)
Content marketing (p 368)

Objective 12-2
Integrated marketing communications (IMC) (p 371)
Push strategy (p 373)
Pull strategy (p 374)

Objective 12-3
Advertising objective (p 375)
Advertising budget (p 377)
Affordable method (p 377)
Percentage-of-sales method (p 377)
Competitive-parity method (p 378)
Objective-and-task method (p 378)
Advertising strategy (p 379)
Madison & Vine (p 380)
Creative concept (p 382)
Execution style (p 382)
Advertising media (p 384)
Return on advertising investment (p 388)
Advertising agency (p 390)

Discussion Questions

12-1. Name and describe the five major promotion tools used in marketing. (AASCB: Communication)

12-2. What is integrated marketing communications (IMC), and how does a company go about implementing it? (AACSB: Communication)

12-3. Compare and contrast push and pull promotion strategies and discuss the factors marketers consider when deciding which one to use. (AACSB: Communication; Reflective Thinking)

12-4. What are the role and functions of public relations within an organization? (AACSB: Communication)

12-5. Discuss the major public relations tools and the roles played by the Internet and social media. (AACSB: Communication)

Critical Thinking Exercises

12-6. Marketers use Q Scores to determine a celebrity's appeal to their target audience. Research Q Scores and write a report on a specific celebrity's Q Score for the past several years. If the score changed considerably, what could be the reason? What other types of Q Scores are there besides scores for celebrities? (AACSB: Communication; Reflective Thinking)

12-7. Find three examples of advertisements that incorporate socially responsible marketing in their messages. Some companies are criticized for exploiting social issues or organizations by promoting them for their own gain. Do the examples you found do that? Explain. (AACSB: Communication; Ethical Reasoning; Reflective Thinking)

12-8. The Public Relations Society of America (PRSA) awards the best public relations campaigns with Silver Anvil Awards. Visit www.prsa.org/Awards/Search and review several case reports on previous winners. What does the field of public relations encompass? Write a report on one of the award winners focusing on marketing-related activities. (AACSB: Communication; Use of IT; Reflective Thinking)

MINICASES AND APPLICATIONS

Online, Mobile, and Social Media Marketing Native Advertising

Marketers have always advertised in traditional media such as newspapers, television, and magazines, but today they are increasingly creating content for the online platforms of these media through *native advertising*, also called sponsored content. This form of promotion is not new. It dates back to the late 1880s as "reading notices" that placed information about brands and companies in news stories, usually without indicating sponsorship. However, sponsorship of today's native advertising is often clearly labeled. Native advertising is growing quickly. It is now offered by 73 percent of online publishers, and more than 40 percent of brands now use it. For example, *Forbes*'s BrandVoice lets companies such as IBM and CenturyLink place content both in the print magazine and on its digital platform at Forbes.com. Readers can learn from CenturyLink about how big data will change travel marketing or from Samsung about how to close the gender gap in science, technology, engineering, and math (STEM) education. Other publisher sites, such as *The Huffington Post*, help marketers create sponsored content. Its HuffPost Partner Studio provides writers, designers, and editors who assist business partners in creating relevant content about their brands in the familiar HuffPost voice. Fiber One tells readers "11 Diet 'Rules' You Can Absolutely Break," IBM explains how businesses can use social media, and Cottonelle tells readers how to fix the mistakes they are making in the bathroom. Social media are also getting in on the action. For example, Facebook reaped more than $1 billion in mobile native advertising alone in just one quarter. The rapid growth of native advertising has also caught the attention of the Federal Trade Commission. The FTC recently held a conference, "Blurred Lines: Advertising or Content? An FTC Workshop on Native Advertising" to discuss the issues of blending advertising with news and other content, leaving some to wonder if further regulations are forthcoming.

12-9. Find examples of native advertising on various publishers' Web and mobile sites. Create a presentation with screenshots showing the content and how it is identified. Has the content been shared with others via social media? (AACSB: Communication; Use of IT)

12-10. Debate whether the FTC's current regulations and guidelines regarding online advertising are adequate for this nature of advertising promotions. Will the FTC likely issue new guidelines or regulations? (AACSB Communication; Reflective Thinking)

Marketing Ethics Amazon's Dronerama

On the eve of the biggest e-commerce shopping day of the year in 2013, Amazon's normally secretive founder and CEO, Jeff Bezos, scored a public relations home run by going on CBS's *60 Minutes* program to unveil the company's Prime Air unmanned aircraft project to deliver packages to consumers' doorsteps. Forget that it couldn't be implemented because the Federal Aviation Administration does not allow such use of drones and that it will likely be 2026 before drone delivery might even be possible. The interview set off "Dronerama," as some have called it. The next morning—Cyber Monday—the media were abuzz about drone delivery, with news organizations and Internet sites replaying the video of Amazon's cool drone delivering a package. The normally hard-hitting *60 Minutes* interview has been criticized because the interviewer, the famous Charlie Rose, seemed to gush all over Bezos and ignore other controversial issues, such as working conditions at Amazon. Rose further gushed over Amazon during the *60 Minutes Overtime* digital supplement to the show. Critics believe the normally unattainable Bezos called the shots in return for appearing on the show. "Dronerama" not only got Amazon on every cyber shoppers' lips on that all-important online shopping day, it seemed to take some of the wind out of the sails of a recently released book critical of Bezos at a time when Amazon needed customers the most.

12-11. Watch the *60 Minutes* interview at www.cbsnews.com/news/amazons-jeff-bezos-looks-to-the-future/. Is it ethical for companies to use the media in this way to gain favorable exposure? Did Jeff Bezos acknowledge the fact that drones were not feasible at the time of the interview? (AACSB: Communication; Ethical Reasoning; Reflective Thinking)

12-12. Create a presentation on the publicity Amazon received as a result of the *60 Minutes* interview and continues to receive over drone delivery. Would you judge this campaign a success or failure? (AACSB: Communication; Use of IT; Reflective Thinking)

Marketing by the Numbers Advertising-to-Sales Ratios

Using the percent-of-sales method, an advertiser sets its advertising budget at a certain percentage of current or forecasted sales. However, determining what percentage to use is not always clear. Many marketers look at industry averages and competitor spending for comparisons. Web sites and trade publications publish data regarding industry averages to guide marketers in setting the percentage to use. For example, firms competing in the toy and apparel industries spend 10 percent or more of sales on advertising, whereas firms competing in the mortgage servicing and insulation industries spend less than 1 percent of sales on advertising. You read about GEICO at the beginning of the chapter. It is the number-two auto insurer with $17 billion in revenue last year. It spent $1.1 billion on advertising that year and plans to continue spending the same percentage of sales on advertising next year. The average advertising-to-sales ratio for the insurance industry is 0.1 percent of sales.

12-13. If GEICO projects $19 billion in sales next year, using the percentage-of-sales method of advertising budgeting, how much will the company budget for advertising if basing it on projected sales? (AACSB: Communication; Analytical Reasoning; Reflective Thinking)

12-14. How much would GEICO budget if the company based its advertising spending on the industry advertising-to-sales ratio? Is GEICO consistent with average industry ad spending? (AACSB: Communication; Analytical Reasoning; Reflective Thinking)

Video Case Kmart

On the heels of its wildly popular "Ship My Pants" ads, Kmart struck again with an ad that was considered hilarious by some, offensive by others, and a stroke of genius by advertising critics. Its latest ad, "Big Gas Savings," was launched on YouTube prior to airing on television. And like its "Ship My Pants" predecessor, the ad also went viral.

In addition to relying on potty humor to pull its sales out of the toilet, Kmart struck a very timely note in the tune of customer value—saving money on gasoline. Customers could save 30 cents a gallon on gas by spending $50 or more in its stores. Millions of customers took advantage of the offer, driving traffic into Kmart stores.

After viewing the video featuring Kmart, answer the following questions:

12-15. What is the advertising message in the Kmart "Big Gas Savings" ad?

12-16. Why did Kmart choose to air this video on YouTube?

12-17. Is this Kmart ad effective? Explain.

Company Cases 12 Allstate/5 GoldieBlox

See Appendix 1 for cases appropriate for this chapter. **Case 12, Allstate: Bringing Mayhem to the Auto Insurance Advertising Wars.** With an endlessly flexible advertising mascot, Allstate is driving its message to consumers and keeping competitors on their toes. **Case 5, GoldieBlox: Swimming Upstream Against Consumer Perceptions.** A new toy company, GoldieBlox is out to change how people think of toys for girls with the message that success comes not from playing with dollhouses, but from building them.

MyMarketingLab

If assigned by your instructor, complete these writing sections from your Assignments in the MyLab.

12-18. Name and describe the various execution styles for presenting messages and provide an example of each style different from the ones in the chapter. (AACSB: Communication)

12-19. Discuss the major advertising objectives and describe an advertisement that is attempting to achieve each objective. (AACSB: Written and Oral Communication; Reflective Thinking)

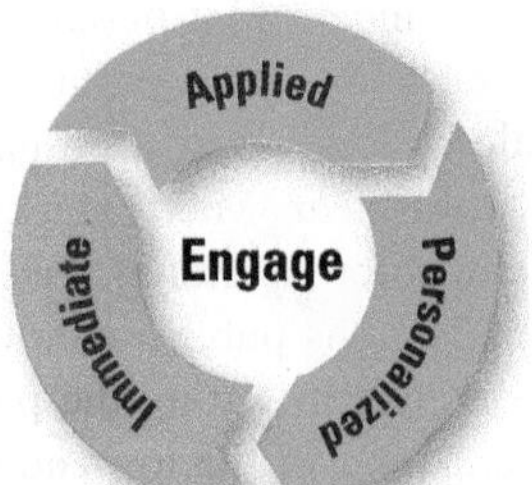

13 Personal Selling and Sales Promotion

CHAPTER ROAD MAP Objective Outline

OBJECTIVE 13-1 **Discuss the role of a company's salespeople in creating value for customers and building customer relationships.** Personal Selling (400–402)

OBJECTIVE 13-2 **Identify and explain the six major sales force management steps.** Managing the Sales Force (402–410); Social Selling: Online, Mobile, and Social Media Tools (410–413)

OBJECTIVE 13-3 **Discuss the personal selling process, distinguishing between transaction-oriented marketing and relationship marketing.** The Personal Selling Process (414–417)

OBJECTIVE 13-4 **Explain how sales promotion campaigns are developed and implemented.** Sales Promotion (417–424)

Previewing the Concepts

In the previous two chapters, you learned about engaging customers and communicating customer value through integrated marketing communications (IMC) and two elements of the promotion mix: advertising and public relations. In this chapter, we examine two more IMC elements: personal selling and sales promotion. Personal selling is the interpersonal arm of marketing communications, in which the sales force engages customers and prospects to build relationships and make sales. Sales promotion consists of short-term incentives to encourage the purchase or sale of a product or service. Although this chapter presents personal selling and sales promotion as separate tools, they must be carefully integrated with the other elements of the promotion mix.

First, let's look at a real-life sales force. When you think of salespeople, perhaps you think of pushy retail sales clerks, "yell and sell" TV pitchmen, or the stereotypical glad-handing "used-car salesman." But such stereotypes don't fit the reality of most of today's salespeople—sales professionals who succeed not by taking advantage of customers but by listening to their needs and helping to forge solutions. Consider Salesforce—the industry leader in customer relationship management solutions. Salesforce not only produces market-leading sales management software, it also excels at practicing what it preaches—effective personal selling.

First Stop

Salesforce: You Need a Great Sales Force to Sell Salesforce

Salesforce is way out in front of the $20 billion market for customer relationship management (CRM) solutions. The Salesforce logo, set inside the image of a puffy cloud, underscores Salesforce's highly successful cloud-based computing model (no software to install or own). Cloud-based systems are common today, but they were state-of-the-art when Salesforce pioneered the concept more than 15 years ago. Since then, the company has established itself as a leading innovator, constantly finding new ways to help client companies connect with customers and achieve greater sales force effectiveness using the latest online, mobile, social, and cloud technologies.

» Salesforce's cloud-based "Customer Success Platform" provides a wide array of customer relationship management tools that help its customers "supercharge their sales."

webpics/Alamy

Salesforce helps businesses to "supercharge their sales." It supplies what it calls a "Customer Success Platform," a wide array of cloud-based sales force automation and customer relationship management tools that gather, organize, analyze, and disseminate in-depth data about a company's customers, sales, and individual sales rep and overall sales force performance. From its home in the cloud, Salesforce makes all these data and analysis readily available anytime, from anywhere, on any device with online access—desktops, laptops, tablets, or smartphones. Salesforce also integrates with major social media, providing tools for social media monitoring and real-time customer engagement and collaboration on its Salesforce Chatter platform, a kind of Facebook for enterprises.

Salesforce's innovative products have made it the world's number-one and fastest-growing CRM platform, ahead of blue-chip competitors such as Microsoft, Oracle, SAP, and IBM. The company's revenues hit $5.4 billion last year, up an impressive 32 percent over the previous year and more than triple what they were just four years ago. Salesforce has been named by *Forbes* as the World's Most Innovative Company in any industry for four straight years.

Innovative products and platforms have played a major role in Salesforce's stunning success. But even the best products don't sell themselves. You need a great sales force to sell Salesforce, and the company excels at practicing what it preaches—effective personal selling. Like the companies that buy its services, Salesforce has its own army of experienced, well-trained, highly motivated sales reps who take the company's products to customers. In many respects, Salesforce's own sales force serves as a model for the products and services it sells—not just for using the Salesforce cloud but more generally for achieving the "supercharged" sales force results that the company promises its clients.

At Salesforce, developing an outstanding sale force starts with recruiting and hiring top-notch salespeople. Salesforce's aggressive but highly selective recruiting program skims the cream off the top of the global sales rep candidate pool. Last year, Salesforce hired only 4.5 percent of the more than 100,000 candidates who applied. Experience counts. Salesforce expects a minimum of two years of prior sales experience for small-business sales reps and up to two decades of experience for sales execs assigned to major accounts. To find such experienced candidates, Salesforce freely raids rival companies for new hires, counting on its high-energy culture and strong compensation packages to lure successful salespeople into the Salesforce fold.

Once hired, as you might expect, Salesforce salespeople have access to all the latest high-tech selling tools. In fact, the first major assignment of new hires is to study 20 hours of at-home video that teaches them the ins and outs of the Salesforce technologies that they won't be just selling but also using. But Salesforce would be the first to tell you that, although its cloud wizardry can help to optimize customer contact and the selling process, it doesn't take the place of good personal selling skills. So in training and fine-tuning its own sales force, the company starts by preaching tried-and-true selling fundamentals, tempered by its own modern twists.

Salesforce leads the market in sales force automation and customer relationship management solutions. But even Salesforce's innovative products won't sell themselves. The company knows that it needs a great sales force to sell Salesforce.

The first fundamental of good selling at Salesforce is to *listen and learn*. As new recruits go through Salesforce's week-long selling boot camp, taught at the company's Salesforce U, they learn that they should begin building customer relationships by asking probing questions and getting customers to talk, seeking to understand everything they can about a customer's situation and needs. "Eighty-five percent of salespeople don't slow down enough to really understand their customer's business," says a senior Salesforce sales executive.

Understanding the customer leads to a second selling fundamental: *empathize*—let customers know that you understand their issues and feel their pain. Empathy builds rapport and trust, an important step toward closing sales and building long-term customer relationships. Listening, learning, and empathizing are important first steps, but more is needed. "If all you are is responsive and helpful, then all you are is an administrative assistant," says the Salesforce sales executive.

So the next important step is to *offer solutions*—to show how Salesforce's cloud-based solutions will help clients make their sales forces more effective and productive in connecting with and selling to customers. Salesforce believes that the best way to offer solutions is by telling good stories that highlight other customers' successes with its products. "Storytelling is very, very important," says Salesforce's sales productivity manager. "It can be the foundation of things like the corporate pitch and your interactions with your customers and prospects." When it comes to handling objections—such as "I don't trust putting our data in the cloud," or "My current system is working fine," or "It costs too much"—Salesforce tells its salespeople that stories can be the most powerful tools they have. "When faced with objections, we always relate it back to a customer story," says a Salesforce marketing manager. "We're not the hero in our customer's stories," says another manager. "It's how the customer succeeded, not how we saved them."

When it comes to competitors, Salesforce's salespeople are ferocious. But Salesforce reps are trained to take the high road—to sell Salesforce's strengths, not competitors' weaknesses. "Internally, we have these posters: Crush Microsoft and Obliterate Oracle," says the Salesforce marketing manager. But, he adds "when you go out to your customers, you have to be careful that you're guiding them and not just stepping on Microsoft. Even though we all want to."

Thus, effective professional selling is about much more than glad-handing and back-slapping on the one hand or plying high-tech CRM tools and data analytics on the other. Even though Salesforce boasts the best sales and customer connection tools in the business, backed by big data and combined with plenty of new-school techniques, its sales reps stay focused on old-school selling principles. At Salesforce—or anywhere else—good selling starts with the fundamentals of engaging and listening to customers, understanding and empathizing with their problems, and building relationships by offering meaningful solutions for mutual gain. That's how you build an incredibly successful sales force and Salesforce.[1]

In this chapter, we examine two more promotion mix tools: *personal selling* and *sales promotion*. Personal selling consists of interpersonal interactions with customers and prospects to make sales and maintain customer relationships. Sales promotion involves using short-term incentives to encourage customer purchasing, reseller support, and sales force efforts.

Author Comment

Personal selling is the interpersonal arm of the promotion mix. A company's sales force creates and communicates customer value by personally engaging customers and building customer relationships.

Personal Selling

Robert Louis Stevenson once noted, "Everyone lives by selling something." Companies around the world use sales forces to sell products and services to business customers and final consumers. But sales forces are also found in many other kinds of organizations. For example, colleges use recruiters to attract new students, and churches use membership committees to attract new members. Museums and fine arts organizations use fundraisers to contact donors and raise money. Even governments use sales forces. The U.S. Postal Service, for instance, uses a sales force to sell Express Mail and other shipping and mailing solutions to corporate customers. In the first part of this chapter, we examine personal selling's role in the organization, sales force management decisions, and the personal selling process.

The Nature of Personal Selling

Personal selling

Personal presentations by the firm's sales force for the purpose of engaging customers, making sales, and building customer relationships.

Personal selling is one of the oldest professions in the world. The people who do the selling go by many names, including salespeople, sales representatives, agents, district managers, account executives, sales consultants, and sales engineers.

People hold many stereotypes of salespeople—including some unfavorable ones. *Salesman* may bring to mind the image of Dwight Schrute, the opinionated Dunder Mifflin paper salesman from the old TV show *The Office*, who lacks both common sense and social skills. Or they may think of the real-life "yell-and-sell" TV pitchmen, who hawk everything from the Flex Seal to the FOCUS T25 Workout and the Ove Glove in infomercials. However, the majority of salespeople are a far cry from these unfortunate stereotypes.

As the opening Salesforce story shows, most salespeople are well-educated and well-trained professionals who add value for customers and maintain long-term customer relationships. They listen to their customers, assess customer needs, and organize the company's efforts to solve customer problems. The best salespeople are the ones who work closely with customers for mutual gain. »Consider Boeing, the aerospace giant competing in the rough-and-tumble worldwide commercial aircraft market. It takes more than fast talk and a warm smile to sell expensive airplanes:

> Selling high-tech aircraft at $150 million or more a copy is complex and challenging. A single big sale to an airline, air-freight carrier, government, and military customer can easily run into billions of dollars. Boeing salespeople head up an extensive team of company specialists—sales and service technicians, financial analysts, planners, engineers—all dedicated to finding ways to satisfy a large customer's needs. On the customer side, buying a batch of jetliners involves dozens or even hundreds of decision-makers from all levels of the buying organization and layer upon layer of subtle and not-so-subtle buying influences. The selling process is nerve-rackingly slow—it can take two or three years from the first sales presentation to the day the sale is announced. After getting the order, salespeople then must stay in almost constant touch to keep track of the account's equipment needs and to make certain the customer stays satisfied. The real challenge is to win buyers' business by building day-in, day-out, year-in, year-out partnerships with them based on superior products and close collaboration.

» Professional selling: It takes more than fast talk and a warm smile to sell expensive airplanes. Boeing's real challenge is to win business by building partnerships—day-in, day-out, year-in, year-out—with its customers.

Kin Cheung/AP Images

Salesperson
An individual who represents a company to customers by performing one or more of the following activities: prospecting, communicating, selling, servicing, information gathering, and relationship building.

The term **salesperson** covers a wide range of positions. At one extreme, a salesperson might be largely an *order taker*, such as the department store salesperson standing behind the counter. At the other extreme are *order getters*, whose positions demand *creative selling, social selling,* and *relationship building* for products and services ranging from appliances, industrial equipment, and airplanes to insurance and IT services. In this chapter, we focus on the more creative types of selling and the process of building and managing an effective sales force.

The Role of the Sales Force

Personal selling is the interpersonal arm of the promotion mix. It involves interpersonal interactions and engagement between salespeople and individual customers—whether face to face, by phone, via email or social media, through video or online conferences, or by other means. Personal selling can be very effective in complex selling situations. Salespeople can probe customers to learn more about their problems and then adjust the marketing offer and presentation to fit each customer's special needs.

The role of personal selling varies from company to company. Some firms have no salespeople at all—for example, companies that sell only online, or companies that sell through manufacturers' reps, sales agents, or brokers. In most firms, however, the sales force plays a major role. In companies that sell business products and services, such as IBM, DuPont, or Boeing, salespeople work directly with customers. In consumer product companies such as P&G or Nike, the sales force plays an important behind-the-scenes role. It works with wholesalers and retailers to gain their support and help them be more effective in selling the company's products to final buyers.

Linking the Company with Its Customers

The sales force serves as a critical link between a company and its customers. In many cases, salespeople serve two masters—the seller and the buyer. First, they *represent the company to customers*. They find and develop new customers and communicate information about

Salespeople link the company with its customers. To many customers, the salesperson is the company.

Tim Robbins/Mint Images Limited/Alamy

the company's products and services. They sell products by engaging customers, presenting their offerings, answering objections, negotiating prices and terms, closing sales, servicing accounts, and maintaining account relationships.

At the same time, salespeople *represent customers to the company*, acting inside the firm as "champions" of customers' interests and managing the buyer–seller relationship. Salespeople relay customer concerns about company products and actions back inside to those who can handle them. They learn about customer needs and work with other marketing and nonmarketing people in the company to develop greater customer value.

In fact, to many customers, the salesperson *is* the company—the only tangible manifestation of the company that they see. Hence, customers may become loyal to salespeople as well as to the companies and products they represent. This concept of *salesperson-owned loyalty* lends even more importance to the salesperson's customer-relationship-building abilities. Strong relationships with the salesperson will result in strong relationships with the company and its products. Conversely, poor salesperson relationships will probably result in poor company and product relationships.

Coordinating Marketing and Sales

Ideally, the sales force and other marketing functions (marketing planners, brand managers, marketing content managers, and researchers) should work together closely to jointly create value for customers. Unfortunately, however, some companies still treat sales and marketing as separate functions. When this happens, the separate sales and marketing groups may not get along well. When things go wrong, marketers blame the sales force for its poor execution of what they see as an otherwise splendid strategy. In turn, the sales team blames the marketers for being out of touch with what's really going on with customers. Neither group fully values the other's contributions. However, if not repaired, such disconnects between marketing and sales can damage customer relationships and company performance.

A company can take several actions to help bring its marketing and sales functions closer together. At the most basic level, it can increase communications between the two groups by arranging joint meetings and spelling out communication channels. It can create opportunities for salespeople and marketers to work together. Brand managers and researchers can tag along on sales calls or sit in on sales planning sessions. In turn, salespeople can sit in on marketing planning sessions and share their firsthand customer knowledge.

Sales force management
Analyzing, planning, implementing, and controlling sales force activities.

A company can also create joint objectives and reward systems for sales and marketing teams or appoint marketing–sales liaisons—people from marketing who "live with the sales force" and help coordinate marketing and sales force programs and efforts. Finally, it can appoint a high-level marketing executive to oversee both marketing and sales. Such a person can help infuse marketing and sales with the common goal of creating value for customers to capture value in return.[2]

Author Comment
Here's another definition of sales force management: "planning, organizing, leading, and controlling personal contact programs designed to achieve profitable customer relationships." Once again, the goal of every marketing activity is to create customer value, engage customers, and build profitable customer relationships.

Managing the Sales Force

We define **sales force management** as analyzing, planning, implementing, and controlling sales force activities. It includes designing sales force strategy and structure as well as recruiting, selecting, training, compensating, supervising, and evaluating the firm's salespeople. These major sales force management decisions are shown in **Figure 13.1** and discussed in the following sections.

Designing the Sales Force Strategy and Structure

Marketing managers face several sales force strategy and design questions. How should salespeople and their tasks be structured? How big should the sales force be? Should salespeople sell alone or work in teams with other people in the company? Should they sell in the field, by phone, or using online and social media? We address these issues next.

Figure 13.1 Major Steps in Sales Force Management

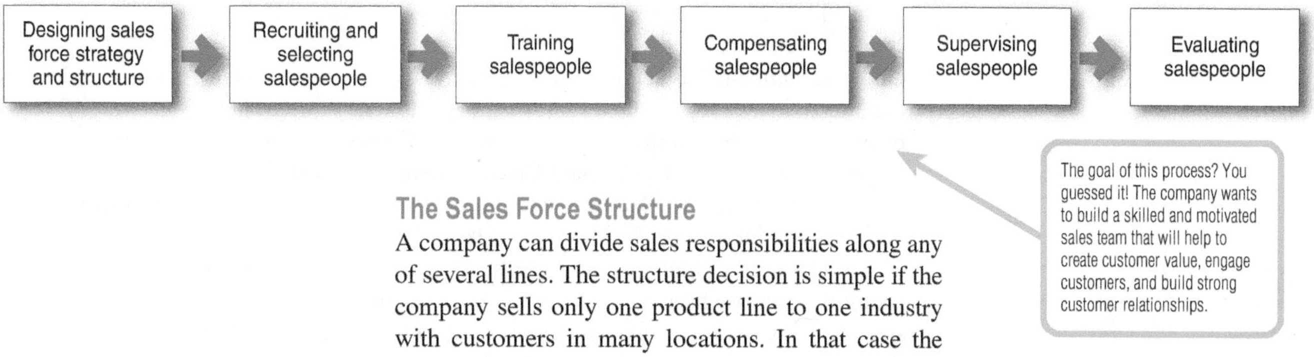

The Sales Force Structure

A company can divide sales responsibilities along any of several lines. The structure decision is simple if the company sells only one product line to one industry with customers in many locations. In that case the company would use a *territorial sales force structure*. However, if the company sells many products to many types of customers, it might need a *product sales force structure*, a *customer sales force structure*, or a combination of the two.

Territorial sales force structure
A sales force organization that assigns each salesperson to an exclusive geographic territory in which that salesperson sells the company's full line.

Product sales force structure
A sales force organization in which salespeople specialize in selling only a portion of the company's products or lines.

Customer (or market) sales force structure
A sales force organization in which salespeople specialize in selling only to certain customers or industries.

In the **territorial sales force structure**, each salesperson is assigned to an exclusive geographic area and sells the company's full line of products or services to all customers in that territory. This organization clearly defines each salesperson's job and fixes accountability. It also increases the salesperson's desire to build local customer relationships that, in turn, improve selling effectiveness. Finally, because each salesperson travels within a limited geographic area, travel expenses are relatively small. A territorial sales organization is often supported by many levels of sales management positions. For example, individual territory sales reps may report to area managers, who in turn report to regional managers who report to a director of sales.

If a company has numerous and complex products, it can adopt a **product sales force structure**, in which the sales force specializes along product lines. For example, GE employs different sales forces within different product and service divisions of its major businesses. Within GE Infrastructure, for instance, the company has separate sales forces for aviation, energy, transportation, and water processing products and technologies. No single salesperson can become expert in all of these product categories, so product specialization is required. Similarly, GE Healthcare employs different sales forces for diagnostic imaging, life sciences, and integrated IT products and services. In all, a company as large and complex as GE might have dozens of separate sales forces serving its diverse product and service portfolio.

Using a **customer (or market) sales force structure**, a company organizes its sales force along customer or industry lines. Separate sales forces may be set up for different industries, serving current customers versus finding new ones, and serving major accounts versus regular accounts. Organizing the sales force around customers can help a company build closer relationships with important customers. Many companies even have special sales forces to handle the needs of individual large customers. For example, GE Aviation has a special Boeing sales team. And appliance maker Whirlpool assigns individual teams of salespeople to big retail customers such as Sears, Lowe's, Best Buy, and Home Depot. Each Whirlpool sales team aligns with the large customer's buying team.

Sales force structure: Whirlpool specializes its sales force by customer and by territory for each key customer group.
Paul Sancya/AP Images

When a company sells a wide variety of products to many types of customers over a broad geographic area, it often employs a *complex sales force structure,* which combines several types of organization. Salespeople can be specialized by customer and territory; product and territory; product and customer; or territory, product, and customer. For example, Whirlpool specializes its sales force by customer (with different sales teams for Sears, Lowe's, Best Buy, Home Depot, and smaller independent retailers) *and* by territory for each key customer group (territory representatives, territory managers, regional managers, and so on). No single structure is best for all companies and situations. Each company should select a sales force structure that best serves the needs of its customers and fits its overall marketing strategy.

Sales Force Size

Once the company has set its structure, it is ready to consider *sales force size*. Sales forces may range in size from only a few salespeople to tens of thousands. Some sales forces are huge—for example, in the United States, PepsiCo employs 36,000 salespeople; American Express, 23,400; GE, 16,400; and Cisco Systems, 14,000.[3] Salespeople constitute one of the company's most productive—and most expensive—assets. Therefore, increasing their numbers will increase both sales and costs.

A company might use some form of *workload approach* to set sales force size. Using this approach, a company first groups accounts into different classes according to size, account status, or other factors related to the amount of effort required to maintain the account. It then determines the number of salespeople needed to call on each class of accounts the desired number of times.

The company might think as follows: Suppose we have 1,000 A-level accounts and 2,000 B-level accounts. A-level accounts require 36 calls per year, and B-level accounts require 12 calls per year. In this case, the sales force's *workload*—the number of calls it must make per year—is 60,000 calls $[(1{,}000 \times 36) + (2{,}000 \times 12) = 36{,}000 + 24{,}000 = 60{,}000]$. Suppose our average salesperson can make 1,000 calls a year. Thus, we need 60 salespeople $(60{,}000 \div 1{,}000)$.

Other Sales Force Strategy and Structure Issues

Sales management must also determine who will be involved in the selling effort and how various sales and sales-support people will work together.

Outside sales force (or field sales force)
Salespeople who travel to call on customers in the field.

Inside sales force
Salespeople who conduct business from their offices via telephone, online and social media interactions, or visits from buyers.

Outside and Inside Sales Forces. A company may have an **outside sales force (or field sales force)**, an **inside sales force**, or both. Outside salespeople travel to call on customers in the field. In contrast, inside salespeople conduct business from their offices via telephone, online and social media interactions, or visits from buyers. The use of inside sales has grown in recent years as a result of increased outside selling costs and the surge in online, mobile, and social media technologies.

Some inside salespeople provide support for the outside sales force, freeing them to spend more time selling to major accounts and finding new prospects. For example, *technical sales-support people* provide technical information and answers to customers' questions. *Sales assistants* provide research and administrative backup for outside salespeople. They track down sales leads, call ahead and confirm appointments, follow up on deliveries, and answer customers' questions when outside salespeople cannot be reached. Using such combinations of inside and outside salespeople can help serve important customers better. The inside rep provides daily access and support, whereas the outside rep provides face-to-face collaboration and relationship building.

Other inside salespeople do more than just provide support. *Telemarketers* and *online sellers* use the phone, Internet, and social media to find new leads, learn about customers and their business, and sell and service accounts directly. Telemarketing and online selling can be very effective, less costly ways to sell to smaller, harder-to-reach customers. Depending on the complexity of the product and customer, for example, a telemarketer can make from 20 to 33 decision-maker contacts a day, compared with the average of four that an outside salesperson can make. In addition, whereas the cost of a business-to-business (B-to-B) field sales call can average close to $600, a routine industrial telemarketing or online contact might average only $20 to $30.[4]

Although the federal government's Do Not Call Registry put a dent in telephone sales to consumers, telemarketing remains a vital tool for most B-to-B marketers. For some smaller companies, telephone and online selling may be the primary sales approaches. However, most of the larger companies also use these tactics extensively, either to sell directly to small and midsize customers or to assist their sales forces in selling to larger ones.

In addition to costs savings, in today's digital, mobile, and social media environments, many buyers are more receptive to—or even prefer—phone and online contact versus the high level of face-to-face contact once required. Today's customers are more inclined to gather their own information online—one study showed that a typical buyer reports contacting a sales rep only after independently completing about 60 percent of the buying process. Then buyers routinely use the phone, online meetings, and social media interactions to engage sellers and close deals. "With virtual meeting software such as GoToMeeting.com and WebEx, communications tools such as Skype, and social media sites such as Twitter, Facebook, and LinkedIn, it's become easier to sell with few if any face-to-face meetings," says an inside sales consultant.[5]

As a result of these trends, telephone and online selling are growing much faster than in-person selling. One recent study found that inside sales positions are growing 300 times faster than outside sales positions. Another study also notes the emergence of the "hybrid sales rep," a modern cross between a field sales rep and an inside rep, who often works from a remote location. Some 41 percent of outside sales activity is now done over the phone or a mobile device, from either a home office or a company office or on the go.[6]

For many types of products and selling situations, >> phone or online selling can be as effective as a personal sales call:[7]

> Climax Portable Machining and Welding Systems Company, which manufactures portable maintenance tools for the metal cutting industry, has proven that telephone and online marketing can save money and still lavish attention on buyers. Under the old system, Climax sales engineers spent one-third of their time on the road, training distributor salespeople and accompanying them on calls. They could make about four contacts a day. Now, each sales engineers on Climax's inside sales team calls about 30 prospects a day, following up on leads generated by ads, emails, and the company's Facebook, LinkedIn, Twitter, YouTube, and other social media sites. Because it takes about five calls to close a sale, the sales engineers update a prospect's profile after each contact, noting the degree of commitment, requirements, next call date, and personal comments. "If anyone mentions he's going on a fishing trip, our sales engineer enters that in the sales information system and uses it to personalize the next call," says Climax's president, noting that this is one way to engage customers and build good relations.
>
> Another is that the first contact with a prospect includes the sales engineer's business card with his or her picture on it. Climax's customer sales system also gives inside reps instant access to customer information entered by the outside sales force and service people. Armed with all the information, inside reps can build surprisingly strong and personal customer relationships. Of course, it takes more than friendliness to sell $15,000 machine tools without face-to-face contact (special orders may run $200,000), but the telephone and online approach works well. When Climax customers were asked, "Do you see the sales engineer often enough?" the response was overwhelmingly positive. Obviously, many people didn't realize that the only contact they had with Climax had been on the phone or Internet.

>> For many types of selling situations, phone or Web selling can be as effective as a personal sales call. At Climax Portable Machine Tools, phone reps build surprisingly strong and personal customer relationships.

Image Source/Getty Images

Team selling
Using teams of people from sales, marketing, engineering, finance, technical support, and even upper management to service large, complex accounts.

Team Selling. As products become more complex and as customers grow larger and more demanding, a single salesperson simply can't handle all of a large customer's needs. Instead, most companies now use **team selling** to service large, complex accounts. Sales teams can unearth problems, solutions, and sales opportunities that no individual salesperson could. Such teams might include experts from any area or level of the selling firm—sales, marketing, technical and support services, research and development, engineering, operations, finance, and others.

In many cases, the move to team selling mirrors similar changes in customers' buying organizations. Many large customer companies have implemented team-based purchasing, requiring marketers to employ equivalent team-based selling. When dealing with large, complex accounts, one salesperson can't be an expert in everything the customer needs. Instead, selling is done by strategic account teams, quarterbacked by senior account managers or customer business managers.

Some companies, such as IBM and P&G, have used teams for a long time. P&G sales reps are organized into Customer Business Development (CBD) teams. Each CBD team is assigned to a major P&G customer, such as Walmart, Safeway, or CVS Health. The CBD organization places the focus on serving the complete needs of each major customer. It lets P&G "grow business by working as a 'strategic partner' with our accounts," not just as a supplier.[8]

Team selling does have some pitfalls, however. For example, salespeople are by nature competitive and have often been trained and rewarded for outstanding individual performance. Salespeople who are used to having customers all to themselves may have trouble learning to work with and trust others on a team. In addition, selling teams can confuse or overwhelm customers who are used to working with only one salesperson. Finally, difficulties in evaluating individual contributions to the team-selling effort can create some sticky compensation issues.

Recruiting and Selecting Salespeople

At the heart of any successful sales force operation is the recruitment and selection of good salespeople. The performance difference between an average salesperson and a top salesperson can be substantial. In a typical sales force, the top 30 percent of the salespeople might bring in 60 percent of the sales. Thus, careful salesperson selection can greatly increase overall sales force performance. Beyond the differences in sales performance, poor selection results in costly turnover. When a salesperson quits, the costs of finding and training a new salesperson—plus the costs of lost sales—can be very high. One sales consulting firm calculates the total costs of a bad sales hire at a whopping $616,000.[9] Also, a sales force with many new people is less productive, and turnover disrupts important customer relationships and sales team morale.

What sets great salespeople apart from all the rest? In an effort to profile top sales performers, Gallup Consulting, a division of the well-known Gallup polling organization, has interviewed hundreds of thousands of salespeople. Its research suggests that the best salespeople possess four key talents: intrinsic motivation, a disciplined work style, the ability to close a sale, and, perhaps most important, the ability to build relationships with customers.[10]

Super salespeople are motivated from within—they have an unrelenting drive to excel. Some salespeople are driven by money, a desire for recognition, or the satisfaction of competing and winning. Others are driven by the desire to provide service and build relationships. The best salespeople possess some of each of these motivations. However, another analysis found that the best salespeople are driven by a strong sense of purpose: "The salespeople who sold with noble purpose, who truly want to make a difference to customers, consistently outsold the salespeople focused on sales goals and money." Selling with such a sense of customer-related purpose is not only more successful, it's also more profitable and more satisfying to salespeople.[11]

Super salespeople also have a disciplined work style. They lay out detailed, organized plans and then follow through in a timely way. But motivation and discipline mean little unless they result in closing more sales and building better customer relationships. Super salespeople build the skills and knowledge they need to get the job done. » Perhaps most important, top salespeople are excellent customer problem solvers and relationship builders. They understand their customers' needs. Talk to sales executives and they'll describe top performers in these terms: good listeners, empathetic, patient, caring, and responsive. Top performers can put themselves on the buyer's side of the desk and see the world through their customers' eyes. They don't want just to be liked; they want to add value for their customers.

» Great salespeople: The best salespeople possess intrinsic motivation, a disciplined work style, the ability to close a sale, and, perhaps most important, the ability to build relationships with customers.

Paul Bradbury/OJO Images Ltd/Alamy

That said, there is no one right way to sell. Each successful salesperson uses a different approach, one that best applies his or her unique strengths and talents. For example, some salespeople enjoy the thrill of a harder sell in confronting challenges and winning people over. Others might apply "softer" talents to reach the same goal. "The truth is, no two great sales reps are alike," says one sales consultant. "You might thrive on fierce competition, while a colleague wins by being a super-analytical problem solver. Or maybe you have a tremendous talent for building relationships, while your fellow top performer is a brilliant strategist. What's most important is that you win business your way."[12]

When recruiting, a company should analyze the sales job itself and the characteristics of its most successful salespeople to identify the traits needed by a successful salesperson in their industry. Then it must recruit the right salespeople. The human resources department looks for applicants by getting names from current salespeople, using employment agencies, searching the Internet and online social media, posting ads and notices on its Web site and industry media, and working through college placement services. Another source is to attract top salespeople from other companies. Proven salespeople need less training and can be productive immediately.

Recruiting will attract many applicants from which the company must select the best. The selection procedure can vary from a single informal interview to lengthy testing and interviewing. Many companies give formal tests to sales applicants. Tests typically measure sales aptitude, analytical and organizational skills, personality traits, and other characteristics. But test scores provide only one piece of information in a set that includes personal characteristics, references, past employment history, and interviewer reactions.

Training Salespeople

New salespeople may spend anywhere from a few weeks or months to a year or more in training. After the initial training ends, most companies provide continuing sales training via seminars, sales meetings, and online learning throughout the salesperson's career. According to one source, American firms spent approximately $15 billion on sales training each year. Although training can be expensive, it can also yield dramatic returns. For instance, one recent study showed that sales training conducted by ADP, an administrative services firm, resulted in a return on investment of nearly 340 percent in only 90 days.[13]

Training programs have several goals. First, salespeople need to know about customers and how to build relationships with them. Therefore, the training program must teach them about different types of customers and their needs, buying motives, and buying habits. It must also teach them how to sell effectively and train them in the basics of the selling process. Salespeople also need to know and identify with the company, its products, and its competitors. Therefore, an effective training program teaches them about the company's objectives, organization, products, and the strategies of major competitors.

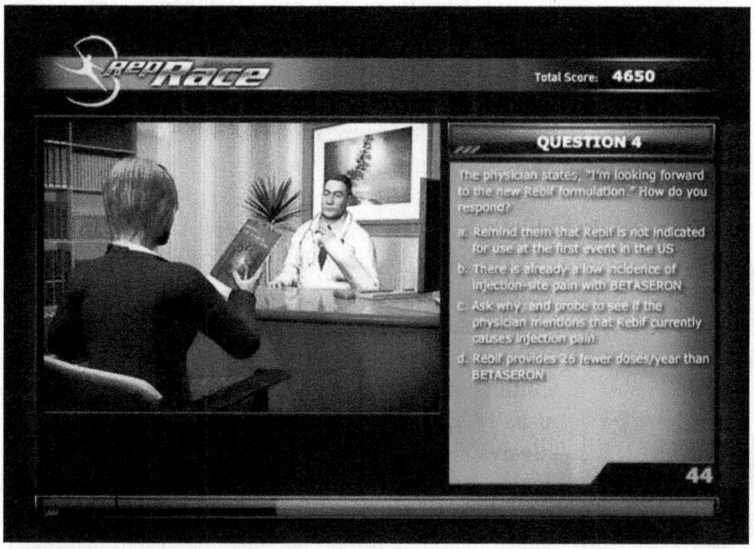

» E-training can make sales training more efficient—and more fun. Bayer HealthCare Pharmaceuticals' role-playing video game—Rep Race—helped improve sales rep effectiveness by 20 percent.

Concentric Pharma Advertising

Today, many companies are adding digital e-learning to their sales training programs. Online training may range from simple text- and video-based product training and Internet-based sales exercises that build sales skills to sophisticated simulations that re-create the dynamics of real-life sales calls. One of the most basic forms is virtual instructor-led training (VILT). Using this method, a small group of salespeople at remote locations logs on to an online conferencing site, where a sales instructor leads training sessions using online video, audio, and interactive learning tools.

»Training online instead of on-site can cut travel and other training costs, and it takes up less of a salesperson's selling time. It also makes on-demand training available to salespeople, letting them train as little or as much as needed, whenever and wherever needed. Although most e-learning is Web-based, many companies now offer on-demand training from anywhere via almost any mobile digital device.

Many companies are now using imaginative and sophisticated e-learning techniques to make sales training more efficient—and sometimes even more fun. For example, Bayer HealthCare Pharmaceuticals worked with Concentric Pharma Advertising, a health-care marketing agency, to create a role-playing simulation video game to train its sales force on a new drug marketing program:[14]

> Most people don't usually associate fast-paced rock music and flashy graphics with online sales training tools. But Concentric Pharma Advertising's innovative role-playing video game—Rep Race: The Battle for Office Supremacy—has all that and a lot more. Rep Race gives Bayer sales reps far more entertainment than the staid old multiple-choice skills tests it replaces. The game was created to help breathe new life into a mature Bayer product—Betaseron, an 18-year-old multiple sclerosis (MS) therapy treatment. The aim was to find a fresh, more active way to help Bayer sales reps apply the in-depth information they learned about Betaseron to actual selling and objections-handling situations. Bayer also wanted to increase rep engagement through interactive learning and feedback through real-time results. Bayer reps liked Rep Race from the start. According to Bayer, when the game was first launched, reps played it as many as 30 times. In addition to its educational and motivational value, Rep Race allowed Bayer to measure sales reps' individual and collective performance. In the end, Bayer calculated that the Rep Race simulation helped improve the Betaseron sales team's effectiveness by 20 percent.

Compensating Salespeople

To attract good salespeople, a company must have an appealing compensation plan. Compensation consists of four elements: a fixed amount, a variable amount, expenses, and fringe benefits. The fixed amount, usually a salary, gives the salesperson some stable income. The variable amount, which might be commissions or bonuses based on sales performance, rewards the salesperson for greater effort and success.

A sales force compensation plan can both motivate salespeople and direct their activities. » Compensation should direct salespeople toward activities that are consistent with the overall sales force and marketing objectives.[15] For example, if the strategy is to acquire new business, grow rapidly, and gain market share, the compensation plan might include a larger commission component, coupled with a new-account bonus to encourage high sales performance and new account development. In contrast, if the goal is to maximize current account profitability, the compensation plan might contain a larger base-salary component with additional incentives for current account sales or customer satisfaction.

In fact, more and more companies are moving away from high-commission plans that may drive salespeople to make short-term grabs for business. They worry that a salesperson who is pushing too hard to close a deal may ruin the customer relationship. Instead, companies are designing compensation plans that reward salespeople for building customer relationships and growing the long-run value of each customer.

When times get tough economically, some companies are tempted to cut costs by reducing sales compensation. However, although some cost-cutting measures make sense when business is sluggish, cutting sales force compensation across the board is usually an action of last resort. Top salespeople are always in demand, and paying them less might mean losing them at a time when they are most needed. Thus, short-changing key salespeople can result in short-changing important customer relationships. If the company must reduce its compensation expenses, rather than making across-the-board cuts, companies should continue to pay top performers well while turning loose low performers.

» **Sales force compensation: A good compensation plan both motivates salespeople and directs their activities.**

Amble Design/Shutterstock

Supervising and Motivating Salespeople

New salespeople need more than a territory, compensation, and training—they need supervision and motivation. The goal of *supervision* is to help salespeople "work smart" by doing the right things in the right ways. The goal of *motivation* is to encourage salespeople to "work hard" and energetically toward sales force goals. If salespeople work smart and work hard, they will realize their full potential—to their own and the company's benefit.

Supervising Salespeople

Companies vary in how closely they supervise their salespeople. Many help salespeople identify target customers and set call objectives. Some may also specify how much time the sales force should spend prospecting for new accounts and set other time management priorities. One tool is the weekly, monthly, or annual *call plan* that shows which customers and prospects to call on and which activities to carry out. Another tool is *time-and-duty analysis*. In addition to time spent selling, the salesperson spends time traveling, waiting, taking breaks, and doing administrative chores.

»Figure 13.2 shows how salespeople spend their time. On average, active selling time accounts for only 37 percent of total working time.[16] Companies are always looking for ways to save time—simplifying administrative duties, developing better sales-call and routing plans, supplying more and better customer information, and using phone, email, online, or mobile conferencing instead of traveling.

Many firms have adopted *sales force automation systems*: computerized, digitized sales force operations that let salespeople work more effectively anytime, anywhere. Companies now routinely equip their salespeople with laptops or tablets, smartphones, wireless connections, videoconferencing technologies, and customer-contact and relationship management software. Armed with these technologies, salespeople can more effectively and efficiently profile customers and prospects, analyze and forecast sales, engage customers, make presentations, prepare sales and expense reports, and manage account relationships. The result is better time management, improved customer service, lower sales costs, and higher sales performance. In all, technology has reshaped the ways in which salespeople carry out their duties and engage customers.

Motivating Salespeople

Beyond directing salespeople, sales managers must also motivate them. Some salespeople will do their best without any special urging from management. To them, selling may be the most fascinating job in the world. But selling can also be frustrating. Salespeople often work alone, and they must sometimes travel away from home. They may also face aggressive competing salespeople and difficult customers. Therefore, salespeople often need special encouragement to do their best.

Management can boost sales force morale and performance through its organizational climate, sales quotas, and positive incentives. *Organizational climate* describes the feeling that salespeople have about their opportunities, value, and rewards for a good performance. Some companies treat salespeople as if they are not very important, so performance suffers accordingly. Other companies treat their

» Figure 13.2 How Salespeople Spend Their Time

Source: "2014 Sales Performance Optimization Study," *CSO Insights*, www.csoinsights.com. Used with permission.

salespeople as valued contributors and allow virtually unlimited opportunity for income and promotion. Not surprisingly, these companies enjoy higher sales force performance and less turnover.

Sales quota
A standard that states the amount a salesperson should sell and how sales should be divided among the company's products.

Many companies motivate their salespeople by setting **sales quotas**—standards stating the amount they should sell and how sales should be divided among the company's products. Compensation is often related to how well salespeople meet their quotas. Companies also use various *positive incentives* to increase the sales force effort. *Sales meetings* provide social occasions, breaks from the routine, chances to meet and talk with "company brass," and opportunities to air feelings and identify with a larger group. Companies also sponsor *sales contests* to spur the sales force to make a selling effort above and beyond what is normally expected. Other incentives include honors, merchandise and cash awards, trips, and profit-sharing plans.

Evaluating Salespeople and Sales Force Performance

We have thus far described how management communicates what salespeople should be doing and how it motivates them to do it. This process requires good feedback, which means getting regular information about salespeople to evaluate their performance.

Management gets information about its salespeople in several ways. The most important source is *sales reports*, including weekly or monthly work plans and longer-term territory marketing plans. Salespeople also write up their completed activities on *call reports* and turn in *expense reports* for which they are partly or wholly reimbursed. The company can also monitor the sales and profit performance data in the salesperson's territory. Additional information comes from personal observation, customer surveys, and talks with other salespeople.

Using various sales force reports and other information, sales management evaluates the members of the sales force. It evaluates salespeople on their ability to "plan their work and work their plan." Formal evaluation forces management to develop and communicate clear standards for judging performance. It also provides salespeople with constructive feedback and motivates them to perform well.

On a broader level, management should evaluate the performance of the sales force as a whole. Is the sales force accomplishing its customer relationship, sales, and profit objectives? Is it working well with other areas of the marketing and company organization? Are sales force costs in line with outcomes? As with other marketing activities, the company wants to measure its *return on sales investment*.

Author Comment
Like just about everything else these days, digital technologies have affected selling big time. Today's sales forces are mastering the use of online, mobile, and social media tools to engage business customers, build relationships, and make sales.

Social Selling: Online, Mobile, and Social Media Tools

Social selling
Using online, mobile, and social media to engage customers, build stronger customer relationships, and augment sales performance.

The fastest-growing sales trend is the explosion in **social selling**—the use of online, mobile, and social media to engage customers, build stronger customer relationships, and augment sales performance. New digital sales force technologies are creating exciting new avenues for connecting with and engaging customers in the digital and social media age. Some analysts even predict that the Internet will mean the death of person-to-person selling, as salespeople are ultimately replaced by Web sites, online social media, mobile apps, video and conferencing technologies, and other tools that allow direct customer contact. "Don't believe it," says one sales expert. "There may be less face-to-face selling," says another. "But on the seller's side, there needs to be someone in charge of that (customer) interaction. That will remain the role of the salesperson" (see Marketing at Work 13.1).[17] Thus, online and social media technologies won't likely make salespeople obsolete. Used properly, however, they will make salespeople more productive and effective.

The new digital technologies are providing salespeople with powerful tools for identifying and learning about prospects, engaging customers, creating customer value, closing sales, and nurturing customer relationships. Social selling technologies can produce big organizational benefits for sales forces. They help conserve salespeople's valuable time, save travel dollars, and give salespeople new vehicles for selling and servicing accounts.

MARKETING AT WORK 13.1

B-to-B Salespeople: In This Digital and Social Media Age, Who Needs Them Anymore?

It's hard to imagine a world without salespeople. But according to some analysts, there will be a lot fewer of them a decade from now. With the explosion of the Internet, mobile devices, social media, and other technologies that link customers directly with companies, they reason, who needs face-to-face selling anymore? According to the doubters, salespeople are rapidly being replaced by Web sites, email, blogs, mobile apps, video sharing, virtual trade shows, social media such as LinkedIn and Facebook, and a host of other digital-age interaction tools.

Research firm Forrester predicts a 22 percent decline in the number of B-to-B sales reps in the United States over the next five years. That means that one in five sales reps will be out of a job by 2020. "The world no longer needs salespeople," one doomsayer boldly proclaims. "Sales is a dying profession and soon will be as outmoded as oil lamps and the rotary phone." Says another, "If we don't find and fill a need faster than a computer, we won't be needed."

So, is business-to-business selling really dying? Will the Internet, mobile technologies, and social media replace the age-old art of selling face to face? To answer these questions, *SellingPower* magazine called together a panel of sales experts and asked them to weigh in on the future of B-to-B sales. The panel members agreed that technology is radically transforming the selling profession. Today's revolutionary changes in how people communicate are affecting every aspect of business, and selling is no exception.

But is B-to-B selling dead in this digital and social media age? Don't believe it, says the *SellingPower* panel. Technology and the Internet won't soon be replacing person-to-person buying and selling. Selling has changed, agrees the panel, and the technology can greatly enhance the selling process. But it can't replace many of the functions that salespeople perform. "The Internet can take orders and disseminate content, but what it can't do is discover customer needs," says one panelist. "It can't build relationships, and it can't prospect on its own." Adds another panelist, "Someone must define the company's value proposition and unique message and communicate it to the market, and that person is the sales rep."

What is dying, however, is what one panelist calls the account-maintenance role—the order taker who stops by the customer's office on Friday and says, "Hey, got anything for me?" Likewise, there's not much of a future for explainers, reps who simply convey product and service information that can be obtained more quickly and easily online. Such salespeople are not creating value and can easily be replaced by automation. However, salespeople who excel at new customer acquisition, relationship management, problem solving, and account growth with existing customers will always be in high demand.

There's no doubt about it—technology is transforming the selling profession. Instead of relying on salespeople for basic information and education, customers can now do much of their own prepurchase research via Web sites, online searches, phone apps, social media contacts, and other venues. Many customers now start the sales process online and do their homework about problems, competing products, and suppliers before the first sales meeting ever takes place. They don't need basic information or product education; they need solutions and new insights. According to one recent survey, business buyers are at least 57 percent of the way through the buying process by the time they reach out to a vendor. So today's salespeople need "to move into the discovery and relationship-building phase, uncovering pain points and focusing on the prospect's business," says a panelist. In fact, jobs for such consultant-type sales reps are expected to increase by one-half million during the next five years.

Rather than replacing salespeople, technology is augmenting them. Today's salespeople aren't really doing anything fundamentally new. They've always done customer research and social networking. Today, however, they are doing it on steroids, using a new kit of high-tech digital tools and applications.

For example, many companies have moved rapidly into online-community-based selling. Case in point: Enterprise-software company SAP, which six years ago set up EcoHub, its

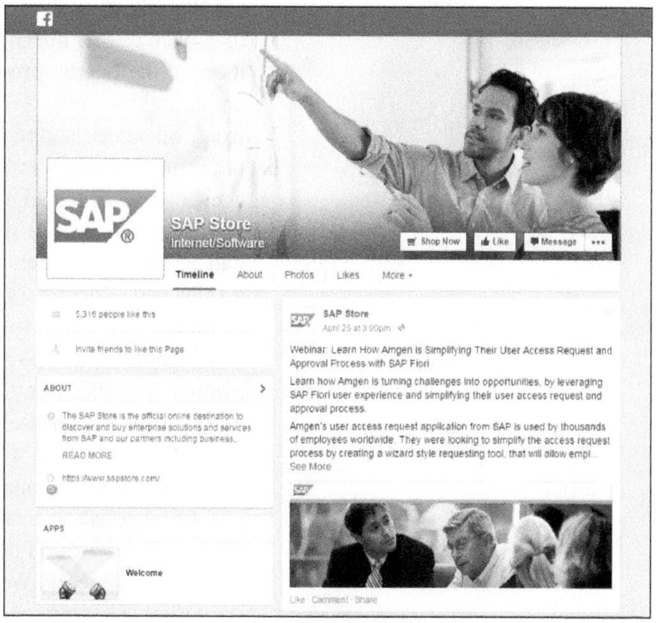

>> Online selling tools, such as SAP's EcoHub and SAP Store online community-based marketplaces, can help to build customer engagement and generate buying interest and sales. But rather than replacing salespeople, such efforts extend their reach and effectiveness.

own online, community-powered social media and mobile marketplace consisting of customers, SAP software experts, partners, and almost anyone else who wanted to join. The EcoHub community grew quickly to more than 2 million users in 200 countries, extending across a broad online spectrum—a dedicated Web site, mobile apps, Twitter channels, LinkedIn groups, Facebook and Google+ pages, YouTube channels, and more. EcoHub grew to more than 600 "solution storefronts," where visitors could "discover, evaluate, and buy" software solutions and services from SAP and its partners. EcoHub also let users rate and share the solutions and advice they got from other community members.

SAP was surprised to learn that what it had originally seen as a place for customers to discuss issues, problems, and solutions turned into a significant point of sale. The information, give-and-take discussions, and conversations at the site drew in customers, even for big-ticket sales of $20 to $30 million or more. In fact, EcoHub has now evolved into SAP Store, a gigantic SAP marketplace where customers can engage with SAP, its partners, and each other to share information, post comments and reviews, discover problems, and evaluate and buy SAP solutions.

However, although the SAP Store draws in new potential customers and takes them through many of the initial stages of product discovery and evaluation, it doesn't replace SAP's or its partners' salespeople. Instead, it extends their reach and effectiveness. Its real value is the flood of sales leads it creates for the SAP and partner sales forces. Once prospective customers have discovered, discussed, and evaluated SAP solutions online, SAP invites them to initiate contact, request a proposal, or start the negotiation process. That's where the person-to-person selling begins.

All this suggests that B-to-B selling isn't dying, it's just changing. The tools and techniques may be different as sales forces leverage and adapt to selling in the digital and social media age. But the panelists agree strongly that B-to-B marketers will never be able to do without strong sales teams. Salespeople who can engage customers, discover customer needs, solve customer problems, and build relationships will be needed and successful, regardless of what else changes. Especially for those big-ticket B-to-B sales, "all the new technology may make it easier to sell by building strong ties to customers even before the first sit-down, but when the signature hits the dotted line, there will be a sales rep there."

Sources: Based on information from Tom Pisello, "Death of a Salesman? Forrester Says Yes (at Least 1 in 5 at Risk)!" *Alinean*, March 12, 2015, http://blog.alinean.com/2015/03/death-of-salesman-forrester-says-yes.html; Tony J. Hughes, "Back to the Future of Sales in 2015," *LinkedIn*, December 27, 2014, www.linkedin.com/pulse/back-future-sales-2015-tony-j-hughes; Lain Chroust Ehmann, "Sales Up!" *SellingPower*, January/February 2011, p. 40; Paul Nolan, "Mapping the Buyer's Journey," *Sales and Marketing Management*, March 27, 2015, www.salesandmarketing.com/content/mapping-buyer's-journey; "Getting Started with SAP EcoHub," http://ecohub.sap.com/getting-started, accessed June 2015; "SAP EcoHub to the SAP Store: The Evolution of the Online Channel at SAP," YouTube, www.youtube.com/watch?v=WADFf6k34V8, accessed June 2015; and https://store.sap.com/ and https://scn.sap.com, accessed September 2015.

Social selling hasn't really changed the fundamentals of selling. Sales forces have always taken the primary responsibility for reaching out to and engaging customers and managing customer relationships. Now, more of that is being done digitally. However, online and social media are dramatically changing the customer buying process. As a result, they are also changing the selling process. In today's digital world, many customers no longer rely as much as they once did on information and assistance provided by salespeople. Instead, they carry out more of the buying process on their own—especially the early stages. Increasingly, they use online and social media resources to analyze their own problems, research solutions, get advice from colleagues, and rank buying options before ever speaking to a salesperson. A recent study of business buyers found that 92 percent of buyers start their searches online and that, on average, buyers completed nearly 60 percent of the buying process before contacting a supplier.[18]

Thus, today's customers have much more control over the sales process than they had in the days when brochures, pricing, and product advice were available only from a sales rep. Customers can now browse corporate Web sites, blogs, and YouTube videos to identify and qualify sellers. They can hobnob with other buyers on social media such as LinkedIn, Google+, Twitter, or Facebook to share experiences, identify solutions, and evaluate products they are considering. As a result, if and when salespeople do enter the buying process, customers often know almost as much about a company's products as the salespeople do. And when customers do call in salespeople, they are more often doing it digitally, with the expectation of real-time engagement.

In response to this new digital buying environment, sellers are reorienting their selling processes around the new customer buying process. They are "going where customers are"—social media, Web forums, online communities, blogs—in order to engage customers earlier. They are engaging customers not just where and when they are buying but also where and when they are learning about and evaluating what they will buy.

Salespeople now routinely use digital tools that monitor customer social media exchanges to spot trends, identify prospects, and learn what customers would like to buy, how they feel about a vendor, and what it would take to make a sale. They generate lists of prospective customers from online databases and social networking sites, such as

InsideView, Hoovers, and LinkedIn. They create dialogues when prospective customers visit their Web and social media sites through live chats with the sales team. They use Internet conferencing tools such as WebEx, Zoom, GoToMeeting, or TelePresence to talk live with customers about products and services. They provide videos and other information on their YouTube channels and Facebook pages.

Today's sales forces are also ramping up their own use of social media to engage customers throughout the buying process. A recent survey of business-to-business marketers found that, although they have recently cut back on traditional media and event spending, they are investing more in social media, ranging from proprietary online customer communities to Webinars and social media and mobile applications.[19] Consider industrial and consumer products giant GE:[20]

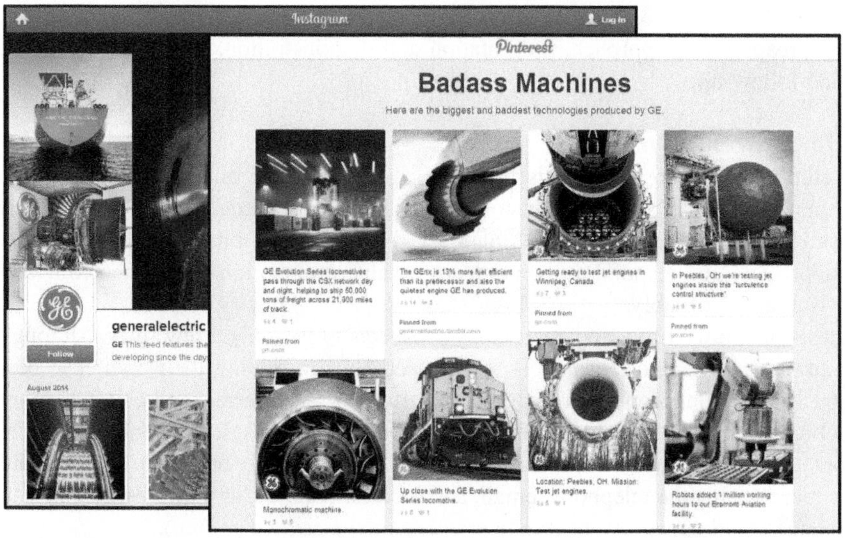

Social selling: GE complements its sales force efforts through a wide variety of social media that inform and engage business customers, connect them with GE salespeople, and promote customer purchasing and relationships. "We want to get our sales team 100 percent digitized."

GE

GE complements its sales force efforts through a wide variety of digital and social media that inform and engage business customers, connect them with GE salespeople, and promote customer purchasing and relationships. For example, GE's various divisions—from GE Aviation to GE Healthcare and GE Energy—offer dozens of industry-specific Web sites, containing thousands of individual site areas and tens of thousands of pages that provide B-to-B customers with purchasing solutions, product overviews, detailed technical information, online videos and Webinars, live chats, and real-time customer support. GE also builds brand awareness and helps its sales force engage business customers deeply through a comprehensive presence in major social media, such as Facebook, Twitter, LinkedIn, Google+, Salesforce.com, and even Instagram, Pinterest, and Vine. "We have a core belief that business is social," says GE's chief marketing officer. "If you're in business you need social because it's going to get you closer to your customers. We want to get our sales team 100 percent digitized."

Ultimately, social selling technologies are helping to make sales forces more efficient, cost-effective, and productive. The technologies help salespeople do what good salespeople have always done—build customer relationships by solving customer problems—but do it better, faster, and cheaper.

However, social selling also has some drawbacks. For starters, it's not cheap. In addition, such systems can intimidate low-tech salespeople or clients. Even more, there are some things you just can't present or teach via the Internet—things that require personal engagement and interaction. For these reasons, some high-tech experts recommend that sales executives use online and social media technologies to spot opportunities, provide information, maintain customer contact, and make preliminary client sales presentations but resort to old-fashioned, face-to-face meetings when the time draws near to close a big deal.

LINKING THE CONCEPTS

Take a break and reexamine your thoughts about salespeople and sales management.

- Again, when someone says "salesperson," what image comes to mind? Have your perceptions of salespeople changed after what you've read in the chapter so far? If so, how? Be specific.
- Find and talk with someone employed in professional sales. Ask about and report on how this salesperson's company designs its sales force and recruits, selects, trains, compensates, supervises, and evaluates its salespeople. Would you like to work as a salesperson for this company?

Author Comment
So far, we've examined how sales management develops and implements overall sales force strategies and programs. In this section, we'll look at how individual salespeople and sales teams sell to customers and build relationships with them.

The Personal Selling Process

We now turn from designing and managing a sales force to the personal selling process. The **selling process** consists of several steps that salespeople must master. These steps focus on the goal of getting new customers and obtaining orders from them. However, most salespeople spend much of their time maintaining existing accounts and building long-term customer relationships. We will discuss the relationship aspect of the personal selling process in a later section.

Steps in the Selling Process

Selling process
The steps that salespeople follow when selling, which include prospecting and qualifying, preapproach, approach, presentation and demonstration, handling objections, closing, and follow-up.

Prospecting
The sales step in which a salesperson or company identifies qualified potential customers.

As shown in »**Figure 13.3**, the selling process consists of seven steps: prospecting and qualifying, preapproach, approach, presentation and demonstration, handling objections, closing, and follow-up.

Prospecting and Qualifying

The first step in the selling process is **prospecting**—identifying qualified potential customers. Approaching the right customers is crucial to selling success. Salespeople don't want to call on just any potential customers. They want to call on those who are most likely to appreciate and respond to the company's value proposition—those the company can serve well and profitably.

A salesperson must often approach many prospects to get only a few sales. Although the company supplies some leads, salespeople need skill in finding their own. The best source is referrals. Salespeople can ask current customers for referrals and cultivate other referral sources, such as suppliers, dealers, noncompeting salespeople, and online or social media contacts. They can also search for prospects in directories or on the Internet and track down leads using the telephone, email, and social media. Or, as a last resort, they can drop in unannounced on various offices (a practice known as *cold calling*).

Salespeople also need to know how to *qualify* leads—that is, how to identify the good ones and screen out the poor ones. Prospects can be qualified by looking at their financial ability, volume of business, special needs, location, and possibilities for growth.

Preapproach

Preapproach
The sales step in which a salesperson learns as much as possible about a prospective customer before making a sales call.

Before calling on a prospect, the salesperson should learn as much as possible about the organization (what it needs, who is involved in the buying) and its buyers (their characteristics and buying styles). This step is known as **preapproach**. A successful sale begins long before the salesperson makes initial contact with a prospect. Preapproach begins with good research and preparation. The salesperson can consult standard industry and online sources, acquaintances, and others to learn about the company. He or she can scour the prospect's Web and social media sites for information about its products, buyers, and buying processes. Then the salesperson must apply the research gathered to develop a customer strategy.

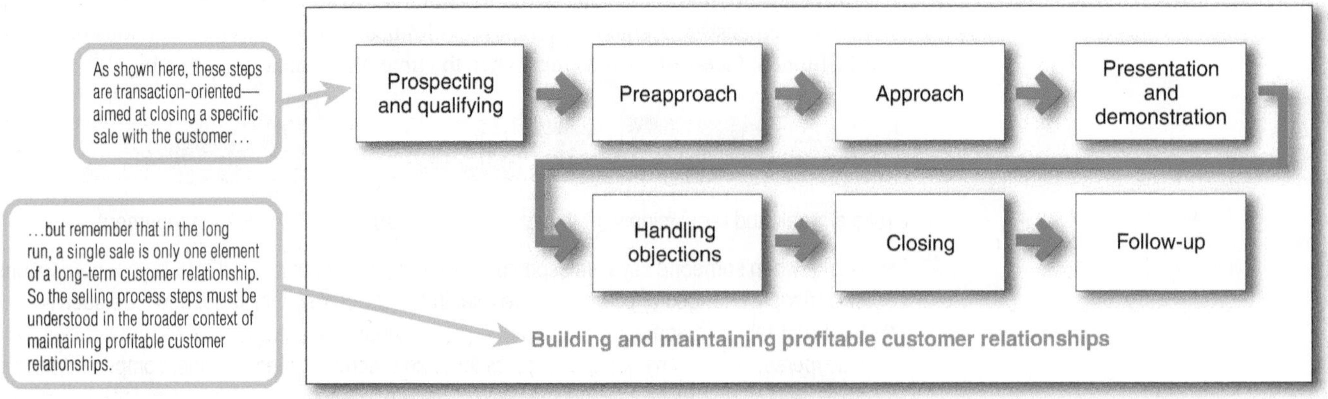

» **Figure 13.3 Steps in the Selling Process**

The salesperson should set *call objectives*, which may be to qualify the prospect, gather information, or make an immediate sale. Another task is to determine the best approach, which might be a personal visit, a phone call, an email, or a text or Tweet. The ideal timing should be considered carefully because many prospects are busiest at certain times of the day or week. Finally, the salesperson should give thought to an overall sales strategy for the account.

Approach
The sales step in which a salesperson meets the customer for the first time.

Approach

During the **approach** step, the salesperson should know how to meet and greet the buyer and get the relationship off to a good start. The approach might take place offline or online, in-person or via digital conferencing or social media. This step involves the salesperson's appearance, opening lines, and follow-up remarks. The opening lines should be positive to build goodwill from the outset. This opening might be followed by some key questions to learn more about the customer's needs or by showing a display or sample to attract the buyer's attention and curiosity. As in all stages of the selling process, listening to the customer is crucial.

Presentation
The sales step in which a salesperson tells the "value story" to the buyer, showing how the company's offer solves the customer's problems.

Presentation and Demonstration

During the **presentation** step of the selling process, the salesperson tells the "value story" to the buyer, showing how the company's offer solves the customer's problems. The *customer-solution approach* fits better with today's relationship marketing focus than does a hard sell or glad-handing approach.

The goal should be to show how the company's products and services fit the customer's needs. Buyers today want insights and solutions, not smiles; results, not razzle-dazzle. Moreover, buyers don't want just products; they want to know how those products will add value to their businesses. They want salespeople who listen to their concerns, understand their needs, and respond with the right products and services.

But before salespeople can *present* customer solutions, they must *develop* solutions to present. The solutions approach calls for good listening and problem-solving skills. The qualities that buyers *dislike most* in salespeople include being pushy, late, deceitful, unprepared, disorganized, or overly talkative. The qualities they *value most* include good listening, empathy, honesty, dependability, thoroughness, and follow-through. >> Great salespeople know how to sell, but more important, they know how to listen and build strong customer relationships. According to an old sales adage, "You have two ears and one mouth. Use them proportionally." A classic ad from office products maker Boise Cascade makes the listening point. It shows a Boise salesperson with huge ears drawn on. "With Boise, you'll notice a difference right away, especially with our sales force," says the ad. "At Boise ... our account representatives have the unique ability to listen to your needs."

>> Great salespeople know how to sell, but more important, they know how to listen and build strong customer relationships.

Tony Garcia/The Image Bank/Getty Images

Finally, salespeople must also plan their presentation methods. Good interpersonal communication skills count when it comes to engaging customers and making effective sales presentations. However, the current media-rich and cluttered communications environment presents many new challenges for sales presenters. Today's information-overloaded customers demand richer presentation experiences. For their part, presenters now face multiple distractions during presentations from mobile phones, text messages, and other digital competition. As a result, salespeople must deliver their messages in more engaging and compelling ways.

Thus, today's salespeople are employing advanced presentation technologies that allow for full multimedia presentations to only one or a few people. The venerable old sales presentation flip chart has been replaced with tablets, sophisticated presentation software, online presentation technologies, interactive whiteboards, and digital projectors.

Handling Objections

Handling objections
The sales step in which a salesperson seeks out, clarifies, and overcomes any customer objections to buying.

Customers almost always have objections during the presentation or when asked to place an order. The objections can be either logical or psychological, and they are often unspoken. In **handling objections**, the salesperson should use a positive approach, seek out hidden objections, ask the buyer to clarify any objections, take objections as opportunities to provide more information, and turn the objections into reasons for buying. Every salesperson needs training in the skills of handling objections.

Closing

Closing
The sales step in which a salesperson asks the customer for an order.

After handling the prospect's objections, the salesperson next tries to close the sale. However, some salespeople do not get around to **closing** or don't handle it well. They may lack confidence, feel guilty about asking for the order, or fail to recognize the right moment to close the sale. Salespeople should know how to recognize closing signals from the buyer, including physical actions, comments, and questions. For example, the customer might sit forward and nod approvingly or ask about prices and credit terms.

Salespeople can use any of several closing techniques. They can ask for the order, review points of agreement, offer to help write up the order, ask whether the buyer wants this model or that one, or note that the buyer will lose out if the order is not placed now. The salesperson may offer the buyer special reasons to close, such as a lower price, an extra quantity at no charge, or additional services.

Follow-Up

Follow-up
The sales step in which a salesperson follows up after the sale to ensure customer satisfaction and repeat business.

The last step in the selling process—**follow-up**—is necessary if the salesperson wants to ensure customer satisfaction and repeat business. Right after closing, the salesperson should complete any details on delivery time, purchase terms, and other matters. The salesperson then should schedule a follow-up call after the buyer receives the initial order to make sure proper installation, instruction, and servicing occur. This visit would reveal any problems, assure the buyer of the salesperson's interest, and reduce any buyer concerns that might have arisen since the sale.

Personal Selling and Managing Customer Relationships

The steps in the just-described selling process are *transaction oriented*—their aim is to help salespeople close a specific sale with a customer. But in most cases, the company is not simply seeking a sale. Rather, it wants to engage the customer over the long haul in a mutually profitable *relationship*. The sales force usually plays an important role in customer relationship building. Thus, as shown in Figure 13.3, the selling process must be understood in the context of building and maintaining profitable customer relationships. Moreover, as discussed in a previous section, today's buyers are increasingly moving through the early stages of the buying process themselves, before ever engaging sellers. Salespeople must adapt their selling process to match the new buying process. That means discovering and engaging customers on a relationship basis rather than a transaction basis.

Successful sales organizations recognize that winning and keeping accounts requires more than making good products and directing the sales force to close lots of sales. If the company wishes only to close sales and capture short-term business, it can do this by simply slashing its prices to meet or beat those of competitors. Instead, most companies want their salespeople to practice *value selling*—demonstrating and delivering superior customer value and capturing a return on that value that is fair for both the customer and the company.

Unfortunately, in the heat of closing sales, salespeople too often take the easy way out by cutting prices rather than selling value. » Sales management's challenge is to transform salespeople from customer advocates for price cuts into company advocates for value. Here's how Rockwell Automation sells value and relationships rather than price:[21]

Under pressure from Walmart to lower its prices, a condiment producer asked several competing supplier representatives—including Rockwell Automation sales rep Jeff Policicchio—to help it find ways to reduce its operating costs. After spending a day in the customer's plant,

» **Value selling: Sales management's challenge is to transform salespeople from customer advocates for price cuts into company advocates for value.**

Almagami/123rf

Policicchio quickly put his finger on the major problem: Production was suffering because of down time due to poorly performing pumps on the customer's 32 large condiment tanks. Quickly gathering cost and usage data, Policicchio used his Rockwell Automation laptop value-assessment tool to develop an effective solution for the customer's pump problem.

The next day, as he and competing reps presented their cost-reduction proposals to plant management, Policicchio offered the following value proposition: "With this Rockwell Automation pump solution, through less downtime, reduced administrative costs in procurement, and lower spending on repair parts, your company will save at least $16,268 per pump—on up to 32 pumps—relative to our best competitor's solution." Compared with competitors' proposals, Policicchio's solution carried a higher initial price. However, no competing rep offered more than fuzzy promises about possible cost savings. Most simply lowered their prices.

Impressed by Policicchio's value proposition—despite its higher initial price—the plant managers opted to buy and try one Rockwell Automation pump. When the pump performed even better than predicted, the customer ordered all of the remaining pumps. By demonstrating tangible value rather than simply selling on price, Policicchio not only landed the initial sale but also earned a loyal future customer.

Thus, value selling requires listening to customers, understanding their needs, and carefully coordinating the whole company's efforts to create lasting relationships based on customer value.

Author Comment
Sales promotion is the most short-term of the promotion mix tools. Whereas advertising or personal selling says "buy," sales promotions say "buy now."

Sales Promotion

Personal selling and advertising often work closely with another promotion tool: sales promotion. **Sales promotion** consists of short-term incentives to encourage the purchase or sales of a product or service. Whereas advertising offers reasons to buy a product or service, sales promotion offers reasons to buy *now*.

Sales promotion
Short-term incentives to encourage the purchase or sale of a product or a service.

» Examples of sales promotions are found everywhere. A freestanding insert in the Sunday newspaper contains a coupon offering $1 off Meow Mix Tender Centers food for your cat. A Sunday newspaper ad from your local Orange Leaf frozen yogurt store offers "Buy 1 Get 1 Free" and "20% off your next purchase." The end-of-the-aisle display in the local supermarket tempts impulse buyers with a wall of Coca-Cola cases—four 12-packs for $12. Buy a new Samsung tablet and get a free memory upgrade. A hardware store chain receives a 10 percent discount on selected Stihl power lawn and garden tools if it agrees to advertise them in local newspapers. Sales promotion includes a wide variety of promotion tools designed to stimulate earlier or stronger market response.

The Rapid Growth of Sales Promotion

Sales promotion tools are used by most organizations, including manufacturers, distributors, retailers, and not-for-profit institutions. They are targeted toward final buyers (*consumer promotions*), retailers and wholesalers (*trade promotions*), business customers (*business promotions*), and members of the sales force (*sales force promotions*). Today, in the average consumer packaged-goods company, sales promotion accounts for 60 percent of all marketing budgets.[22]

Several factors have contributed to the rapid growth of sales promotion, particularly in consumer markets. First, inside the company, product managers face greater pressures to increase current sales, and they view promotion as an effective short-run sales tool. Second, externally, the company faces more competition, and competing brands are less differentiated. Increasingly, competitors are using sales promotion to help differentiate their offers. Third, advertising efficiency has declined because of rising costs, media clutter, and legal restraints.

Sales promotions are found everywhere. For example, your Sunday newspaper or favorite magazine is loaded with offers like this one that promote a strong and immediate response.

Orange Leaf Frozen Yogurt

Finally, consumers have become more deal oriented. In the current economy, consumers are demanding lower prices and better deals. Sales promotions can help attract today's more thrift-oriented consumers.

The growing use of sales promotion has resulted in *promotion clutter*, which is similar to advertising clutter. With so many products being sold on deal these days, a given promotion runs the risk of being lost in a sea of other promotions, weakening its ability to trigger an immediate purchase. Manufacturers are now searching for ways to rise above the clutter, such as offering larger coupon values, creating more dramatic point-of-purchase displays, or delivering promotions through new digital media—such as the Internet or mobile phones. According to one study, 88 percent of retailers now see digital promotions—such as mobile coupons, shopper emails, and online deals—as an important part of their shopper marketing efforts.[23]

In developing a sales promotion program, a company must first set sales promotion objectives and then select the best tools for accomplishing these objectives.

Sales Promotion Objectives

Sales promotion objectives vary widely. Sellers may use *consumer promotions* to urge short-term customer buying or boost customer–brand engagement. Objectives for *trade promotions* include getting retailers to carry new items and more inventory, buy ahead, or promote the company's products and give them more shelf space. *Business promotions* are used to generate business leads, stimulate purchases, reward customers, and motivate salespeople. For the sales force, objectives include getting more sales force support for current or new products and getting salespeople to sign up new accounts.

Sales promotions are usually used together with advertising, personal selling, direct marketing, or other promotion mix tools. Consumer promotions must usually be advertised and can add excitement and pulling power to ads and other marketing content. Trade and business sales promotions support the firm's personal selling process.

When the economy tightens and sales lag, it's tempting to offer deep promotional discounts to spur consumer spending. In general, however, rather than creating only short-term sales or temporary brand switching, sales promotions should help to reinforce the product's position and build long-term customer relationships. If properly designed, every sales promotion tool has the potential to build both short-term excitement and long-term consumer engagement and relationships. Marketers should avoid "quick fix," price-only promotions in favor of promotions that are designed to build brand equity. Examples include the various *frequency marketing programs* and loyalty cards that have mushroomed in popularity in recent years. Most hotels, supermarkets, and airlines offer frequent-guest/buyer/flier programs that give rewards to regular customers to keep them coming back. Such promotional programs can build loyalty through added value rather than discounted prices.

Customer loyalty programs: Bloomingdale's Loyallist program works well because of its simplicity. "Become a Loyallist," says the company. "It's better on the list."

Bloomingdale's, Inc.

For example, department store Bloomingdale's offers its Loyallist program for loyal shoppers. Loyallist members earn points for every dollar they spend, in-store or online, no matter how they pay. They also receive special opportunities to earn double, triple, or even quadruple points at special times, along with free shipping and a

$25 Bloomingdale's gift card every time they reach 5,000 points. Loyallists can use any of a variety of apps to access their cards and balances wherever they are. The Loyallist program's success lies in its simplicity. According to one analyst, the program "is winning because it delivers well on the main goal of all loyalty programs: when members spend money, they are rewarded by points that they can turn around and use like money, which incentivizes future purchases for happy shoppers to spend—you guessed it—more money."[24]

Major Sales Promotion Tools

Many tools can be used to accomplish sales promotion objectives. Descriptions of the main consumer, trade, and business promotion tools follow.

Consumer Promotions

Consumer promotions
Sales promotion tools used to boost short-term customer buying and engagement or enhance long-term customer relationships.

Consumer promotions include a wide range of tools—from samples, coupons, refunds, premiums, and point-of-purchase displays to contests, sweepstakes, and event sponsorships.

Samples are offers of a trial amount of a product. Sampling is the most effective—but most expensive—way to introduce a new product or create new excitement for an existing one. Some samples are free; for others, the company charges a small amount to offset its cost. The sample might be sent by mail, handed out in a store or at a kiosk, attached to another product, or featured in an ad, email, or mobile offer. Samples are sometimes combined into sample packs, which can then be used to promote other products and services. Sampling can be a powerful promotional tool. For example, a bevy of big-name food marketers—from Papa John's Pizza and Pizza Hut to Campbell Soup and PepsiCo—descended upon Super Bowl XLVIII–related events in New York and New Jersey, handing out free samples. Pizza Hut handed out more than 10,000 slices of its hand-tossed pizza. "It's a massive opportunity to sample our new product," said a Pizza Hut marketer.[25]

Coupons are certificates that save buyers money when they purchase specified products. Most consumers love coupons. U.S. consumer packaged goods companies distributed 310 billion coupons with an average face value of $1.72 last year. Consumers redeemed more than 2.75 billion of them for a total savings of about $3.6 billion.[26] Coupons can promote early trial of a new brand or stimulate sales of a mature brand. However, to combat the increase in coupon clutter, most major consumer goods companies are issuing fewer coupons and targeting them more carefully.

Marketers are also cultivating new outlets for distributing coupons, such as supermarket shelf dispensers, electronic point-of-sale coupon printers, and online and mobile coupon programs. Digital coupons represent today's fastest-growing coupon segment. Digital coupons can be individually targeted and personalized in ways that print coupons can't. Digital coupons accounted for nearly 11 percent of all coupons redeemed last year; about 7 percent were printed from a computer at home, and 4 percent were redeemed via smartphone or other mobile devices. According to one study, an estimate 40 percent of smartphone users will redeem a mobile coupon this year.[27]

As mobile phones become appendages that many people can't live without, businesses are increasingly eyeing them as prime real estate for coupons, offers, and other marketing messages. » For example, drugstore chain Walgreens makes coupons available to its customers through several mobile channels:[28]

» Coupons: Drugstore chain Walgreens makes coupons available to customers through numerous channels, including its weekly ads, Web site, and mobile app.

Courtesy of Walgreen Co.

> Using the Walgreens smartphone app, customers can instantly download coupons ranging in value from 50 cents to $5, good toward anything from health and beauty products to everyday essentials such as diapers. The coupons are conveniently scannable—no clipping or printing required. Customers simply pull up the coupons on the Walgreens app and cashiers scan them straight from the customer's phone. Walgreens also Tweets mobile coupons to customers who check in to any of its 8,100 stores nationwide using check-in apps such as Foursquare, Yelp, or Shopkick. Walgreens has mobile scanning capabilities available at all of its stores, giving it the nation's largest retail mobile coupon program. Through its mobile app, "Walgreens is using technology to go above and beyond," says one analyst. "They're thinking about the customer."

Rebates (or *cash refunds*) are like coupons except that the price reduction occurs after the purchase rather than at the retail outlet. The customer sends proof of purchase to the manufacturer, who then refunds part of the purchase price by mail. For example, Toro ran a clever preseason promotion on some of its snowblower models, offering a rebate if the snowfall in the buyer's market area turned out to be below average. Competitors were not able to match this offer on such short notice, and the promotion was very successful.

Price packs (also called *cents-off deals*) offer consumers savings off the regular price of a product. The producer marks the reduced prices directly on the label or package. Price packs can be single packages sold at a reduced price (such as two for the price of one) or two related products banded together (such as a toothbrush and toothpaste). Price packs are very effective—even more so than coupons—in stimulating short-term sales.

Premiums are goods offered either free or at low cost as an incentive to buy a product, ranging from toys included with kids' products to phone cards and DVDs. A premium may come inside the package (in-pack), outside the package (on-pack), or through the mail. For example, over the years, McDonald's has offered a variety of premiums in its Happy Meals—from *My Little Pony* characters to Beanie Boos and LEGO hologram drink cups. Customers can visit www.happymeal.com to play games, read e-books, and watch commercials associated with the current Happy Meal sponsor.[29]

Advertising specialties, also called *promotional products*, are useful articles imprinted with an advertiser's name, logo, or message that are given as gifts to consumers. Typical items include T-shirts and other apparel, pens, coffee mugs, calendars, key rings, tote bags, coolers, golf balls, and caps. U.S. marketers spent nearly $20 billion on advertising specialties last year. Such items can be very effective. The "best of them stick around for months, subtly burning a brand name into a user's brain," notes a promotional products expert.[30]

Point-of-purchase (POP) promotions include displays and demonstrations that take place at the point of sale. Think of your last visit to the local Costco, Walmart, or Bed Bath & Beyond. Chances are good that you were tripping over aisle displays, promotional signs, "shelf talkers," or demonstrators offering free tastes of featured food products. Unfortunately, many retailers do not like to handle the hundreds of displays, signs, and posters they receive from manufacturers each year. Manufacturers have therefore responded by offering better POP materials, offering to set them up, and tying them in with television, print, or online messages.

Contests, sweepstakes, and *games* give consumers the chance to win something, such as cash, trips, or goods, by luck or through extra effort. A *contest* calls for consumers to submit an entry—a jingle, guess, suggestion—to be judged by a panel that will select the best entries. A *sweepstakes* calls for consumers to submit their names for a drawing. A *game* presents consumers with something—bingo numbers, missing letters—every time they buy, which may or may not help them win a prize.

All kinds of companies use sweepstakes and contests to create brand attention and boost consumer involvement. For example, Google's "Doodle 4 Google" contest invites kids to design a Google logo based on the theme "If I could invent one thing to make the world a better place . . . ," with prizes ranging from T-shirts and tablets to a $30,000 college scholarship. The "OXO I Do Sweepstakes" invites soon-to-be-married couples to "Like" OXO's Facebook page and earn a chance to win $500 toward their Amazon wedding registry. Enter the Coleman Camping Kit Giveaway and you win a gear prize pack worth more than $1,000. And if your recipe wins the annual Pillsbury Bake-Off, you could take home a $1 million prize.

Event marketing (or event sponsorships)
Creating a brand-marketing event or serving as a sole or participating sponsor of events created by others.

Finally, marketers can promote their brands through **event marketing** (or **event sponsorships**). They can create their own brand-marketing events or serve as sole or participating sponsors of events created by others. The events might include anything from mobile brand tours to festivals, reunions, marathons, concerts, or other sponsored gatherings. Event marketing is huge, and it may be the fastest-growing area of promotion. Effective event marketing links events and sponsorships to a brand's value proposition. And with the social sharing power of today's digital media, even local events can have far-reaching impact. For example, P&G's recent "Everyday Effect" takeover event in Manhattan illustrates how companies are now blending old-school promotional techniques with new-school social sharing technologies to enhance the impact of both (see Marketing at Work 13.2).

All kinds of brands now hold events. One week, it might be the National Football League (NFL) filling the southern tip of Times Square with NFL players to promote new

MARKETING AT WORK 13.2

P&G's "Everyday Effect" Event: A Great Marriage between Old-School Promotions and New-School Social Sharing

It was a hot, sunny June day in Manhattan, and pedestrians bustled along at 33rd Street and 7th Avenue near Madison Square Garden. But on this day, something special happened. In the middle of the sidewalk stood a glass shower stall, emblazoned with colorful Old Spice signage, causing even normally jaded New York City passersby to take notice. An Old Spice brand rep handed out samples of Old Spice bar soap and extended an unusual invitation—jump in the shower and give it a try. Surprisingly, many people accepted, including a well-dressed executive who lathered up while still in his finely tailored business suit.

Just another sales promotion gimmick? Not this time. The Old Spice Constant Shower was just one small piece of a live mega-promotion—P&G's "Everyday Effect" event—in which brand representatives and celebrities handed out more than 50,000 samples of 25 different P&G brands at multiple Manhattan locations in a single day. With street teams and exhibits all over town, the Everyday Effect takeover extravaganza was by far the biggest "consumer experience" event in P&G's 175-year history.

Visitors to the Gillette Man Cave "experience box" in Washington Square Park were pampered with free shaves and visits from actor Laz Alonso and New York Jets center Nick Mangold. At the Covergirl Beauty box near Times Square, *Fast and Furious* actress Jordana Brewster helped with free beauty and nail touch-ups. The Iam's Loving Home box at Riverside Park on the Upper West Side featured *Dancing with the Stars* heartthrob Val Chmerkovskiy posing for photos with pets and handing out Iam's product samples. And in Harlem, P&G's "My Black Is Beautiful" reps served up beauty tips and free mini-makeovers. All day long, brand ambassadors and characters such as the Charmin Bears fanned out across city streets giving out product samples, high-value coupons, advice, and even special P&G pedicab rides. They dispensed Scope mouthwash samples to coffee drinkers, Febreze car vent clips to taxi drivers, and personal care products to barber shops and salons.

By itself, the massive Manhattan giveaway produced substantial benefits for P&G in terms of brand trial and experience. "Simply getting someone to try a product remains the holy grail for consumer-goods companies," says one analyst. The event also reinforced P&G's broader, ongoing Everyday Effect campaign showcasing the effects of its products on the lives of real people. "We're making a deliberate effort to demonstrate to consumers how our brands improve their everyday life in small yet meaningful ways," says P&G's North American group president. "That's what we call the P&G 'Everyday Effect.'"

However, some experts question whether the returns on such a massive—and expensive—local event could ever justify the investment. Beyond the costs of product samples, P&G had to rent pricy Manhattan real estate, employ hundreds of reps, erect expensive facilities and props, provide incentives for celebrities, and put a sizable security detail in place to keep things orderly.

But the impact of the Everyday Effect event went far beyond the city limits of New York City. What made the event extra special was the skillful way that P&G used social media channels to turbocharge consumer engagement, not just in Manhattan but around the nation and world. Throughout the day, video of live events was streamed across P&G brand and social media sites. Nearly every element of the event was hashtagged, and visitors to event sites were given incentives to upload photos to their personal feeds. Followers of PGEveryday on Twitter and Facebook had opportunities to win Visa and Amazon gift cards. Participating celebrities not only helped draw coverage from more than 100 media outlets, they also reached out personally to their own fans through Twitter, Facebook, Instagram, and other social media.

"We chose New York as the world's largest stage," says a P&G brand executive. "At the end of the day, [we wanted to reach] as many New Yorkers as possible [but also] touch consumers we couldn't physically reach that day." Mission accomplished. By evening, the Everyday Effect event had scored some impressive social sharing results. The opt-in rate at the PGEveryday.com coupon and sampling site jumped 20 percent;

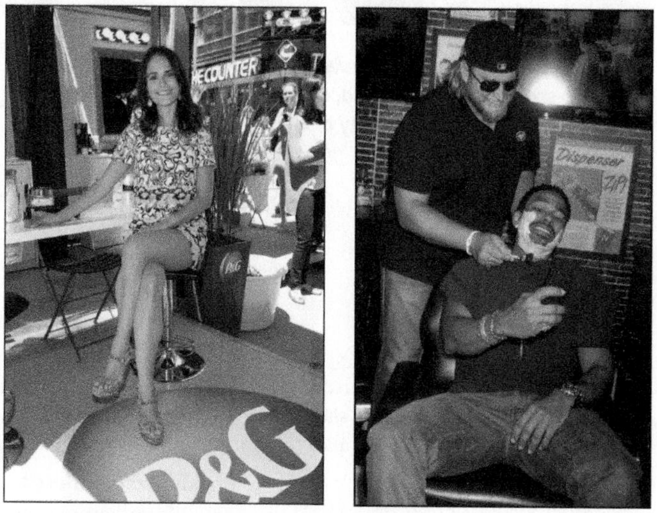

P&G's star-studded Everyday Effect event blended old-school live event marketing with new-school social sharing. Visitors to the Gillette Man Cave box were pampered with free shaves and visits from actor Laz Alonso and New York Jets center Nick Mangold. At the CoverGirl Beauty box, actress Jordana Brewster helped with free beauty and nail touch-ups. Such celebrities helped draw substantial social and traditional media coverage.

Everett Collection/Newscom (left); Dennis Van Tine/ABACAUSA.COM/Newscom (right) the engagement rate for visitors to the PGEveryday Facebook page soared 151 percent. And the social media were abuzz with pictures and posts of the day's happenings. #EverydayEffect became the day's number-two trending topic on Twitter.

P&G's Everyday Effect event is an example of how companies these days are blending old-school promotion techniques, such as samples and pop-ups, with new-school social sharing technologies to enhance the impact of both. Increasingly, the two promotional approaches form an important symbiotic relationship: A live event creates special face-to-face brand engagements that generate needed social media content. In turn, the social media help amplify and extend the event's impact.

"On the one hand, social is extending the reach of events to intensify their impact beyond those in attendance," says one event marketing expert. "On the other, events are becoming crucial content sources for brands' Facebook, Twitter, and Instagram feeds." Says another expert, "Social media in isolation is sort of like a long distance relationship; the human contact piece is missing." In contrast, an "experiential [event], as a deep engagement thing, can be very satisfying but you can't get scale behind it." His conclusion: "Together they're a great marriage."

Sources: Stuart Feil, "All the World Is a Stage," *Adweek*, July 22, 2013, www.adweek.com/print/151231; Kyle Stock, "The Logic behind P&G's Old-School Manhattan Giveaway," *Businessweek*, June 19, 2013, www.businessweek.com/articles/2013-06-19/the-logic-behind-p-and-gs-old-school-manhattan-giveaway; Barry Silverstein, "P&G Hosts Massive Everyday Effect Giveaway Event in New York City," *Brand Channel*, June 19, 2013, www.brandchannel.com/home/post/2013/06/19/PG-Everyday-Effect-Event-061913.aspx; "Tweeting the #EverydayEffect," www.pgeveryday.com/beauty/get-the-look/article/tweeting-the-everydayeffect, accessed June 2015; and "Everyday Effect," *P&G Newsroom*, http://news.pg.com/category/tags/everyday-effectandwww.pgeveryday.com/tag/everydayeffect, accessed September 2015.

>> Event marketing: Red Bull hosts hundreds of events each year in dozens of sports around the world, designed to bring the high-octane world of Red Bull to its community of enthusiasts.

Max Rossi/Reuters

NFL jersey designs. The next week, it's a mob of Russian models on the northern triangle of Times Square (called Duffy Square), using it as a fashion runway for Maybelline. But according to one business reporter, energy drink maker Red Bull is the "mother of all event marketers":[31]

> Event pioneer Red Bull holds hundreds of events each year in dozens of sports around the world. >> Each event features off-the-grid experiences designed to bring the high-octane world of Red Bull to its community of enthusiasts. The brand even hosts a "Holy S**t" tab on its Web site, featuring videos of everything from 27-meter ocean cliff dives at its Cliff Diving Series event in Grimstad, Norway, to daredevil freeskiing feats at its Red Bull Cold Rush event in the Colorado mountain peaks to absolutely breathtaking wing suit flights at Red Bull events staged in exotic locations from Monterrey, Mexico, to Hunan Province, China. The Red Bull Final Descent series is a mountain biking challenge that pushes riders to the brink and back, over some of the most technically challenging terrain in North America. Red Bull events draw large crowds and plenty of media coverage. But it's about more than just the events—it's about customer engagement. It's about creating face-to-face experiences in which customers can actually feel the excitement and live the brand. "It's about deepening and enhancing relationships," says one analyst.

Trade Promotions

Trade promotions
Sales promotion tools used to persuade resellers to carry a brand, give it shelf space, promote it in advertising, and push it to consumers.

Manufacturers direct more sales promotion dollars toward retailers and wholesalers (79 percent of all promotions dollars) than to final consumers (21 percent).[32] **Trade promotions** can persuade resellers to carry a brand, give it shelf space, promote it in advertising, and push it to consumers. Shelf space is so scarce these days that manufacturers often have to offer price-offs, allowances, buy-back guarantees, or free goods to retailers and wholesalers to get products on the shelf and, once there, to keep them on it.

Manufacturers use several trade promotion tools. Many of the tools used for consumer promotions—contests, premiums, displays—can also be used as trade promotions. Or the manufacturer may offer a straight *discount* off the list price on each case purchased during a stated period of time (also called a *price-off, off-invoice*, or *off-list*). Manufacturers also may offer an *allowance* (usually so much off per case) in return for the retailer's agreement to feature the manufacturer's products in some way. For example, an advertising allowance compensates retailers for advertising the product, whereas a display allowance compensates them for using special displays.

Manufacturers may offer *free goods*, which are extra cases of merchandise, to resellers who buy a certain quantity or who feature a certain flavor or size. They may also offer *push money*—cash or gifts to dealers or their sales forces to "push" the manufacturer's goods. Manufacturers may give retailers free *specialty advertising items* that carry the company's name, such as pens, calendars, memo pads, flashlights, and tote bags.

Business Promotions

Companies spend billions of dollars each year on promotion geared toward industrial customers. **Business promotions** are used to generate business leads, stimulate purchases, reward customers, and motivate salespeople. Business promotions include many of the same tools used for consumer or trade promotions. Here, we focus on two additional major business promotion tools: conventions and trade shows and sales contests.

Business promotions
Sales promotion tools used to generate business leads, stimulate purchases, reward customers, and motivate salespeople.

Many companies and trade associations organize *conventions and trade shows* to promote their products. Firms selling to the industry show their products at the trade show. Vendors at these shows receive many benefits, such as opportunities to find new sales leads, contact customers, introduce new products, meet new customers, sell more to present customers, and educate customers with publications and audiovisual materials. Trade shows also help companies reach many prospects that are not reached through their sales forces.

Some trade shows are huge. For example, at this year's International Consumer Electronics Show, 3,673 exhibitors attracted some 165,000 professional visitors. >> Even more impressive, at the Bauma mining and construction equipment trade show in Munich, Germany, more than 3,400 exhibitors from 57 countries presented their latest product innovations to more than 530,000 attendees from more than 200 countries. Total exhibition space equaled about 6.1 million square feet (more than 127 football fields).[33]

>> Some trade shows are huge. At this year's Bauma mining and construction equipment trade show in Munich, Germany, more than 3,400 exhibitors from 57 countries presented their latest product innovations to more than 530,000 attendees from more than 200 countries.

Messe Munchen

A *sales contest* is a contest for salespeople or dealers to motivate them to increase their sales performance over a given period. Sales contests motivate and recognize good company performers, who may receive trips, cash prizes, or other gifts. Some companies award points for performance, which the receiver can turn in for any of a variety of prizes. Sales contests work best when they are tied to measurable and achievable sales objectives (such as finding new accounts, reviving old accounts, or increasing account profitability).

Developing the Sales Promotion Program

Beyond selecting the types of promotions to use, marketers must make several other decisions in designing the full sales promotion program. First, they must determine the *size of the incentive*. A certain minimum incentive is necessary if the promotion is to succeed; a larger incentive will produce more sales response. The marketer also must set *conditions for participation*. Incentives might be offered to everyone or only to select groups.

Marketers must determine how to *promote and distribute the promotion* program itself. For example, a $2-off coupon could be given out in a package, in an advertisement, at the store, via the Internet, or in a mobile download. Each distribution method involves a different level of reach and cost. Increasingly, marketers are blending several media into a total campaign concept. The *length of the promotion* is also important. If the sales promotion period is too short, many prospects (who may not be buying during that time) will miss it. If the promotion runs too long, the deal will lose some of its "act now" force.

Evaluation is also very important. Marketers should work to measure the returns on their sales promotion investments, just as they should seek to assess the returns on other marketing activities. The most common evaluation method is to compare sales before, during, and after a promotion. Marketers should ask: Did the promotion attract new customers or more purchasing from current customers? Can we hold onto these new customers and purchases? Will the long-run customer relationship and sales gains from the promotion justify its costs?

Clearly, sales promotion plays an important role in the total promotion mix. To use it well, the marketer must define the sales promotion objectives, select the best tools, design the sales promotion program, implement the program, and evaluate the results. Moreover, sales promotion must be coordinated carefully with other promotion mix elements within the overall IMC program.

MyMarketingLab

If assigned by your instructor, complete the questions marked with the ✪ from the EOC Discussion Questions section in the MyLab. To complete the Marketing by the Numbers problems found in this section, go to your Assignments in the MyLab.

REVIEWING AND EXTENDING THE CONCEPTS

CHAPTER REVIEW AND CRITICAL THINKING

Objectives Review

This chapter is the second of three chapters covering the final marketing mix element—promotion. The previous chapter dealt with overall integrated marketing communications and with advertising and public relations. This chapter investigated personal selling and sales promotion. Personal selling is the interpersonal arm of the communications mix. Sales promotion consists of short-term incentives to encourage the purchase or sale of a product or service.

OBJECTIVE 13-1 Discuss the role of a company's salespeople in creating value for customers and building customer relationships. (pp 400–402)

Most companies use salespeople, and many companies assign them an important role in the marketing mix. For companies selling business products, the firm's sales force works directly with customers. Often, the sales force is the customer's only direct contact with the company and therefore may be viewed by customers as representing the company itself. In contrast, for consumer product companies that sell through intermediaries, consumers usually do not meet salespeople or even know about them. The sales force works behind the scenes, dealing with wholesalers and retailers to obtain their support and helping them become more effective in selling the firm's products.

As an element of the promotion mix, the sales force is very effective in achieving certain marketing objectives and carrying out such activities as prospecting, communicating, selling and servicing, and information gathering. But with companies becoming more market oriented, a customer-focused sales force also works to produce both customer satisfaction and company profit. The sales force plays a key role in engaging customers and developing and managing profitable customer relationships.

OBJECTIVE 13-2 Identify and explain the six major sales force management steps. (pp 402–413)

High sales force costs necessitate an effective sales management process consisting of six steps: designing sales force strategy and structure, recruiting and selecting, training, compensating, supervising, and evaluating salespeople and sales force performance.

In designing a sales force, sales management must address various issues, including what type of sales force structure will work best (territorial, product, customer, or complex structure), sales force size, who will be involved in selling, and how various salespeople and sales-support people will work together (inside or outside sales forces and team selling).

Salespeople must be recruited and selected carefully. In recruiting salespeople, a company may look to the job duties and the characteristics of its most successful salespeople to suggest the traits it wants in new salespeople. It must then look for applicants through recommendations of current salespeople, ads, and the Internet and social media as well as college recruitment/placement centers. After the selection process is complete, training programs familiarize new salespeople not only with the art of selling but also with the company's history, its products and policies, and the characteristics of its customers and competitors.

The sales force compensation system helps to reward, motivate, and direct salespeople. In addition to compensation, all salespeople need supervision, and many need continuous encouragement because they must make many decisions and face many frustrations. Periodically, the company must evaluate their performance to help them do a better job. In evaluating salespeople, the company relies on information gathered from sales reports, personal observations, customer surveys, and conversations with other salespeople.

The fastest-growing sales trend is the explosion in social selling—using online, mobile, and social media in selling. The new digital technologies are providing salespeople with powerful tools for identifying and learning about prospects, engaging customers, creating customer value, closing sales, and nurturing customer relationships. Many of today's customers no longer rely as much on assistance provided by salespeople. Instead, increasingly, they use online and social media resources to analyze their own problems, research solutions, get advice from colleagues, and rank buying options before ever speaking to a salesperson. In response, sellers are reorienting their selling processes around the new customer buying process. They are using social media, mobile devices, Web forums, online communities, blogs, and other digital tools to engage customers earlier and more fully. Ultimately, online, mobile, and social media technologies are helping to make sales forces more efficient, cost-effective, and productive.

OBJECTIVE 13-3 Discuss the personal selling process, distinguishing between transaction-oriented marketing and relationship marketing. (pp 414–417)

Selling involves a seven-step process: prospecting and qualifying, preapproach, approach, presentation and demonstration, handling objections, closing, and follow-up. These steps help marketers close a specific sale and, as such, are transaction oriented. However, a seller's dealings with customers should be guided by the larger concept of relationship marketing. The company's sales force should help to orchestrate a whole-company effort to develop profitable long-term relationships with key customers based on superior customer value and satisfaction.

OBJECTIVE 13-4 Explain how sales promotion campaigns are developed and implemented. (pp 417–424)

Sales promotion campaigns call for setting sales promotion objectives (in general, sales promotions should be *consumer relationship building*); selecting tools; and developing and implementing the sales promotion program by using *consumer promotion tools* (from coupons, refunds, premiums, and point-of-purchase promotions to contests, sweepstakes, and events), *trade promotion tools* (from discounts and allowances to free goods and push money), and *business promotion tools* (conventions, trade shows, and sales contests) as well as determining such things as the size of the incentive, the conditions for participation, how to promote and distribute the promotion package, and the length of the promotion. After this process is completed, the company must evaluate its sales promotion results.

Key Terms

Objective 3-1
Personal selling (p 400)
Salesperson (p 401)

Objective 3-2
Sales force management (p 402)
Territorial sales force structure (p 403)
Product sales force structure (p 403)
Customer (or market) sales force structure (p 403)
Outside sales force (or field sales force) (p 404)
Inside sales force (p 404)
Team selling (p 405)
Sales quota (p 410)
Social selling (p 410)

Objective 3-3
Selling process (p 414)
Prospecting (p 414)
Preapproach (p 414)
Approach (p 415)
Presentation (p 415)
Handling objections (p 416)
Closing (p 416)
Follow-up (p 416)

Objective 3-4
Sales promotion (p 417)
Consumer promotions (p 419)
Event marketing (or event sponsorships) (p 420)
Trade promotions (p 422)
Business promotions (p 423)

Discussion Questions

13-1. Describe the roles that a salesperson and the sales force perform in marketing. (AASCB: Communication; Reflective Thinking)

13-2. What traits and behaviors should an ethical salesperson possess? What role does the sales manager play in ethical selling behavior? (AACSB: Ethical Understanding and Reasoning)

13-3. Name and describe the four sales compensation elements. What are the various compensation combinations, and how can they be used to achieve the company's marketing objectives? (AACSB: Communication; Reflective Thinking)

13-4. Define *sales promotion* and discuss its objectives. (AACSB: Communication)

13-5. Discuss the different types of trade sales promotions and distinguish these types of promotions from business promotions. (AACSB: Communication)

Critical Thinking Exercises

13-6. There are considerable free sales training resources available on the Internet. Search "free sales training" to find some of these resources and access one of them. Create a presentation highlighting what you learned. (AACSB: Communication; Use of IT; Reflective Thinking)

13-7. Select a product or service and role-play a sales call—from the approach to the close—with another student. Have one member of the team act as the salesperson with the other member acting as the customer, raising at least three objections. Select another product or service and perform this exercise again with your roles reversed. (AACSB: Communication; Reflective Thinking)

13-8. In a small group, design a sales promotion campaign using online, social media, and mobile marketing for a small business or organization in your community. Develop a presentation to pitch your campaign to the business or organization and incorporate what you've learned about the selling process. (AACSB: Communication; Reflective Thinking)

MINICASES AND APPLICATIONS

Online, Social Media, and Mobile Marketing Snap It and Redeem It!

More than 300 billion coupons are distributed each year, with more than 90 percent of them printed on paper. Consumers redeem only about 1 percent of coupons distributed, often because they clip them but forget to use them in the store. SnipSnap has a solution for consumers. Hailed as the Best Shopping App by About.com and winning Media Post's Apply Awards for Best Finance App, this app has mobilized those paper coupons for consumers. SnipSnap now boasts 4 million users and more than 50 national retail partners. The app allows consumers to snap a photo of retailers' paper coupons and redeem them at the store. Users can share with friends on Facebook and Twitter and follow others' couponing. SnipSnap is the first mobile app that scans the text, images, logos, and barcodes in printed coupons and creates a mobile coupon. It also sends expiration date reminders and location-based notifications. Retailer Lord & Taylor installed iBeacon technology and partnered with SnipSnap to send shoppers targeted coupons based on where they are in the store. So if you want a good deal on a Michael Kors purse, it knows you are looking at the item and might send you a coupon through the app. SnipSnap employees noticed consumers were snapping pictures of "coupons" they created to send to friends and family that were good for some special treatment, so the company created a spin-off app called GoodFor. Now, if you want to send a special someone a coupon good for a 30-minute massage or your kid a "get out of chores free" coupon, GoodFor allows you to do it!

13-9. Research other types of apps that rely on smartphone cameras to redeem a sales promotion offer. Explain how they work and how they are similar to and different from SnipSnap. (AACSB: Communication; Use of IT; Reflective Thinking)

13-10. The profitable growth potential for SnipSnap is in the enterprise market where it provides mobile promotion services to retailers. SnipSnap is working with retailers to create and manage geo-conquesting campaigns. Research what this is and create a presentation explaining how it works. (AACSB: Communication; Use of IT; Reflective Thinking)

Marketing Ethics "Dollars for Docs"?

The pharmaceutical industry is innovating at a dizzying pace, but it is getting more difficult for pharmaceutical sales reps to reach doctors to inform them of new or improved products. One option is to host educational seminars. However, many educational seminars are held at lavish restaurants or destinations underwritten by pharmaceutical companies, and doctors providing the education are paid consulting and speaking fees to the tune of more than $2 billion since 2009. In some cases, speakers are given scripts developed by the pharmaceutical company, leading to the criticism that this is company-scripted marketing and the distinguished speaker is merely a "paid parrot" selling drugs for the company. Critics also claim that such promotion results in needlessly increased prescriptions for expensive branded drugs that are no better than generic alternatives. Many drug makers are reducing expenditures for such product promotions because of the Physician Payment Sunshine Act, a provision of the Affordable Care Act of 2010. *Pro Publica* has a "Dollars for Docs" searchable database, and as part of the Sunshine Act, a searchable government Web site is available to the public to shed light on pharmaceutical sales practices.

13-11. Is it wrong for pharmaceutical companies to explain the benefits of their products to physicians this way? Suggest other alternatives for reaching doctors to inform them of the benefits of a company's products. (AACSB: Communication; Ethical Reasoning; Reflective Thinking)

13-12. Learn about the Physician Payment Sunshine Act. Search *Pro Publica's* "Dollars for Docs" database (http://projects.propublica.org/docdollars/) for local physicians to see if they have received payments from pharmaceutical companies. Search the government's Web site (https://openpaymentsdata.cms.gov/) and compare your findings with those of *Pro Publica's* database. Write a report on what you found. (AACSB: Communication; Use of IT; Reflective Thinking)

Marketing by the Numbers Salesforce Analysis

Wheels, Inc. manufactures bicycles sold through retail bicycle shops in the southeastern United States. The company has two salespeople that do more than just sell the products—they manage relationships with the bicycle shops to enable them to better meet consumers' needs. The company's sales reps visit the shops several times per year, often for hours at a time. The owner of Wheels is considering expanding to the rest of the country and would like to have distribution through 1,000 bicycle shops. To do so, however, the company would have to hire more salespeople. Each salesperson earns $40,000 plus 2 percent commission on all sales annually. Another alternative is to use the services of sales agents instead of its own sales force. Sales agents would be paid 5 percent of sales.

13-13. Refer to Appendix 3 to answer this question. Determine the number of salespeople Wheels needs if it has 1,000 bicycle shop accounts that need to be called on four times per year. Each sales call lasts approximately 2.5 hours, and each sales rep has approximately 1,250 hours per year to devote to customers. (AACSB: Communication; Analytical Reasoning)

13-14. At what level of sales would it be more cost efficient for Wheels to use to sales agents compared with its own sales force? To determine this, consider the fixed and variable costs for each alternative. What are the pros and cons of using a company's own sales force versus independent sales agents? (AACSB: Communication; Analytical Reasoning; Reflective Thinking)

Video Case First Flavor

First Flavor is a start-up company with a unique product. It manufactures great-tasting edible film that can replicate the flavor of just about anything, from an eight-topping pizza to an alcoholic beverage. If you're wondering why a company would make such a product, think of the endless possibilities it allows for consumers to sample the taste of a food or beverage before purchasing it.

Although First Flavor first replicated flavors on thin film in order to market the product as a new method for product sampling, the company is now evaluating many other applications of the technology. This video demonstrates how one product can be marketed in multiple ways.

After viewing the video featuring First Flavor, answer the following questions:

13-15. Classify First Flavor's core business as a sales promotion element.

13-16. Brainstorm a list of the ways that First Flavor's edible film might be used to sample products.

13-17. Can First Flavor successfully in pursue consumer product opportunities in addition to its promotional services? Explain.

Company Cases 13 Sungard/8 3M

See Appendix 1 for cases appropriate for this chapter. **Case 13, Sungard: Building Sustained Growth by Selling the SunGard Way.** Consistently one of the top companies to sell for, Sungard is out to stay that way through a complete transformation of its sales force model. **Case 8, 3M: Where Innovation Is a Way of Life.** Although it has many consumer products, 3M is truly a B2B company that relies on a strong sales force.

MyMarketingLab

If assigned by your instructor, complete these writing sections from your Assignments in the MyLab.

13-18. What is social selling, and how is it affecting the sales function in organizations? (AACSB: Communication; Reflective Thinking)

13-19. What is team selling, and why has it become more important? Are there any pitfalls to this approach? (AACSB: Communication; Reflective Thinking)

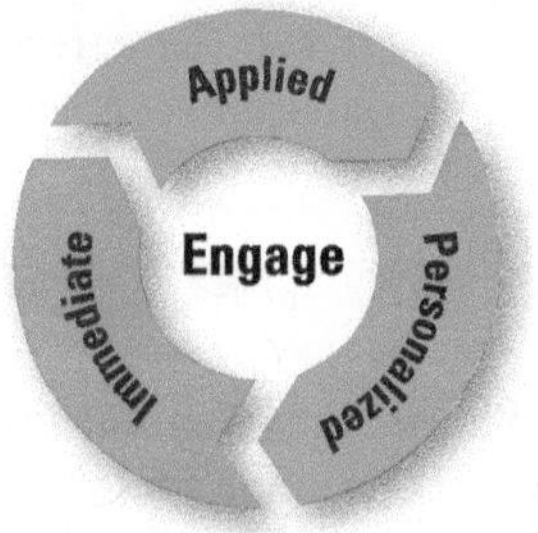

14 Direct, Online, Social Media, and Mobile Marketing

CHAPTER ROAD MAP Objective Outline

- OBJECTIVE 14-1 **Define *direct and digital marketing* and discuss their rapid growth and benefits to customers and companies.** Direct and Digital Marketing (430–432)
- OBJECTIVE 14-2 **Identify and discuss the major forms of direct and digital marketing.** Forms of Direct and Digital Marketing (432–433); Digital and Social Media Marketing (433)
- OBJECTIVE 14-3 **Explain how companies have responded to the Internet and the digital age with various online marketing strategies.** Marketing, the Internet, and the Digital Age (433–434); Online Marketing (434–439)
- OBJECTIVE 14-4 **Discuss how companies use social media and mobile marketing to engage consumers and create brand community.** Social Media Marketing (439–443); Mobile Marketing (443–447)
- OBJECTIVE 14-5 **Identify and discuss the traditional direct marketing forms and overview public policy and ethical issues presented by direct marketing.** Traditional Direct Marketing Forms (447–451); Public Policy Issues in Direct and Digital Marketing (451–453)

Previewing the Concepts

In the previous two chapters, you learned about engaging consumers and communicating customer value through integrated marketing communication, and about four elements of the marketing communications mix: advertising, publicity, personal selling, and sales promotion. In this chapter, we examine direct marketing and its fastest-growing form: digital marketing (online, social media, and mobile marketing). Today, spurred by the surge in Internet usage and buying as well as rapid advances in digital technologies—from smartphones, tablets, and other digital devices to the spate of online mobile and social media—direct marketing has undergone a dramatic transformation. As you read this chapter, remember that although direct and digital marketing are presented as separate tools, they must be carefully integrated with each other and with other elements of the promotion and marketing mixes.

Let's start by looking at Amazon, a company that markets *only* directly and digitally. In little over 20 years, Amazon has blossomed from an obscure dot-com upstart into one of the most powerful names on the Internet. According to one estimate, an incredible 30 percent of all online shoppers research Amazon.com first before buying. How has Amazon become such an incredibly successful direct and online marketer in such a short time? It's all about creating customer engagement, value, and relationships through personal and satisfying online customer experiences. Few online marketers do that as well as Amazon.com.

First Stop

Amazon.com: The Poster Child for Direct and Digital Marketing

» Amazon does much more than just sell goods online. It engages customers and creates direct, personalized, and highly satisfying customer online buying experiences.

Philippe Huguen/AFP/Getty Images

When you think of shopping online, chances are good that you think first of Amazon. The online pioneer first opened its virtual doors in 1995, selling books out of founder Jeff Bezos's garage in suburban Seattle. Amazon still sells books—lots and lots of books. But it now sells just about everything else as well, from music, electronics, tools, housewares, apparel, and groceries to fashions, loose diamonds, and Maine lobsters. Most analysts view Amazon as *the* model for direct marketing in the digital age.

From the start, Amazon has grown explosively. Its annual sales have rocketed from a modest $150 million in 1997 to $89 billion today. During just the past five years, Amazon's revenues have more than tripled. On last year's Cyber Monday alone, Amazon.com sold 37 million items to its 270 million active customers worldwide—that's 428 items per second. Amazon's revenues will likely reach $100 billion within the next year, faster to that mark than any other company in history (it took Walmart 34 years). That would make it the nation's second-largest retailer, trailing only Walmart.

What has made Amazon such an amazing success story? Founder and CEO Bezos puts it in three simple words: "Obsess over customers." To its core, the company is relentlessly customer driven. "The thing that drives everything is creating genuine value for customers," says Bezos. Amazon believes that if it does what's good for customers, profits will follow. So the company starts with the customer and works backward. Rather than asking what it can do with its current capabilities, Amazon first asks: Who are our customers? What do they need? Then it develops whatever capabilities are required to meet those customer needs.

At Amazon, every decision is made with an eye toward improving the Amazon.com customer experience. In fact, at many Amazon meetings, the most influential figure in the room is "the empty chair"—literally an empty chair at the table that represents the all-important customer. At times, the empty chair isn't empty but is occupied by a "Customer Experience Bar Raiser," an employee who is specially trained to represent customers' interests.

Amazon's obsession with serving the needs of its customers drives the company to take risks and innovate in ways that other companies don't. For example, when it noted that its book-buying customers needed better access to e-books and other digital content, Amazon developed the Kindle e-reader, its first-ever original product. The Kindle took more than four years and a whole new set of skills to develop. But Amazon's start-with-the-customer thinking paid off handsomely. The Kindle is one of the company's best-selling products, and Amazon.com now sells more e-books than hardcovers and paperbacks combined. What's more, the company's growing line of Kindle Fire tablets now leads the market for low-priced tablet computers. Thus, what started as an effort to improve the customer experience now gives Amazon a powerful presence in the burgeoning world of digital, mobile, and social media. Not only does the Kindle allow access to e-books, music, videos, and apps sold by Amazon, it makes interacting online with the digital giant easier than ever. Customers use their Kindle tablets to shop at Amazon.com and interact with the company on its blogs and social media pages.

Amazon wants to deliver a special online experience to every customer. Most Amazon.com regulars feel a surprisingly strong relationship with the company, especially given the almost complete lack of actual human interaction. Amazon obsesses over making each customer's experience uniquely personal. For example, the Amazon.com site greets customers with their very own home pages, complete with personalized recommendations. Amazon was the first company to sift through each customer's past purchases and browsing histories and the purchasing patterns of customers with similar profiles to come up with personalized site content. Amazon wants to personalize the shopping experience for each individual customer. If it has 270 million customers, it reasons, it should have 270 million stores.

Amazon's deep-down passion for creating superb online customer experiences has made it one of the most powerful names on the Internet. Amazon is *the* model for successful direct and digital marketing.

Visitors to Amazon.com receive a unique blend of benefits: huge selection, good value, low prices, and convenience. But it's the "discovery" factor that makes the buying experience really special. Once on the Amazon.com site, you're compelled to stay for a while—looking, learning, and discovering. To create even greater selection and discovery for customers, Amazon allows competing retailers—from mom-and-pop operations to Marks & Spencer—to sell their products on Amazon.com through the Amazon Marketplace, creating a virtual shopping mall of incredible proportions. The broader selection attracts more customers, and everyone benefits. Last year, Amazon customers bought more than 2 billion items from 2 million third-party

Amazon Marketplace sellers worldwide, accounting for 40 percent of Amazon's unit sales.

Amazon also makes the order delivery experience a whiz with its Amazon Prime service. For $99 a year, Prime members can receive free two-day shipping for all eligible purchases plus unlimited streaming of movies and TV shows with Prime Instant Video and access to borrowing e-books from the Kindle Owners' Lending Library. Amazon is moving rapidly toward same-day delivery. It recently launched Prime Now, which offers speedy two-*hour* free delivery of tens of thousands of items in several large metropolitan areas (or one-hour delivery for a $7.99 fee). "In the past six weeks my husband and I have made an embarrassing number of orders through Amazon Prime Now," says one excited customer. "It's cheap, easy, and insanely fast."

More than just a place to buy things, Amazon.com has become a kind of online community in which customers can browse for products, research purchase alternatives, share opinions and reviews with other visitors, and chat online with authors and experts. In this way, Amazon does much more than just sell goods online. It engages customers and creates direct, personalized customer relationships and satisfying online experiences. Year after year, Amazon places at or near the top of almost every customer satisfaction ranking, regardless of industry.

Based on its powerful growth, many analysts have speculated that Amazon will become the Walmart of the Web. In fact, some argue, it already is. Although Walmart's total sales of $487 billion dwarf Amazon's $89 billion in sales, Amazon's online sales are 7.5 times greater than Walmart's. So online, it's Walmart that's chasing Amazon. Put another way, Walmart wants to become the Amazon of the Web, not the other way around. However, despite its mammoth proportions, to catch Amazon online, Walmart will have to match the superb Amazon .com online customer experience, and that won't be easy.

Thus, Amazon has become the poster child for direct and digital marketing. "The reason I'm so obsessed with . . . the customer experience is that I believe [our success] has been driven exclusively by that experience," says Jeff Bezos. It all starts with customer value. If Amazon creates superior value for customers, it will earn their business and loyalty, and success will follow in terms of company sales and returns. As Bezos puts it, "When things get complicated, we simplify them by asking, 'What's best for the customer?' We believe that if we do that, things will work out in the long term."[1]

Many of the marketing and promotion tools that we've examined in previous chapters were developed in the context of *mass marketing*: targeting broad markets with standardized messages and offers distributed through intermediaries. Today, however, with the trend toward narrower targeting and the surge in digital and social media technologies, many companies are adopting *direct marketing*, either as a primary marketing approach or as a supplement to other approaches. In this section, we explore the exploding world of direct marketing and its fastest-growing form—digital marketing using online, social media, and mobile marketing channels.

Author Comment

For most companies, direct and digital marketing are supplemental channels or media. But for many other companies today—such as Amazon, GEICO, or Priceline—direct marketing is a complete way of doing business.

Direct and Digital Marketing

Direct and digital marketing involve engaging directly with carefully targeted individual consumers and customer communities to both obtain an immediate response and build lasting customer relationships. Companies use direct marketing to tailor their offers and content to the needs and interests of narrowly defined segments or individual buyers. In this way, they build customer engagement, brand community, and sales.

Direct and digital marketing
Engaging directly with carefully targeted individual consumers and customer communities to both obtain an immediate response and build lasting customer relationships.

For example, Amazon.com interacts directly with customers via its Web site or mobile app to help them discover and buy almost anything and everything online. Similarly, GEICO interacts directly with customers—by telephone, through its Web site or smartphone app, or on its Facebook, Twitter, and YouTube pages—to build individual brand relationships, give insurance quotes, sell policies, or service customer accounts.

The New Direct Marketing Model

Early direct marketers—catalog companies, direct mailers, and telemarketers—gathered customer names and sold goods mainly by mail and telephone. Today, however, spurred by the surge in Internet usage and buying, and by rapid advances in digital technologies—from smartphones, tablets, and other digital devices to the spate of online social and mobile media—direct marketing has undergone a dramatic transformation.

In previous chapters, we discussed direct marketing as direct distribution—as marketing channels that contain no intermediaries. We also included direct and digital marketing elements of the promotion mix—as an approach for engaging consumers directly and creating brand community. In actuality, direct marketing is both of these things and much more.

Most companies still use direct marketing as a supplementary channel or medium. Thus, most department stores, such as Sears or Macy's, sell the majority of their merchandise off their store shelves, but they also sell through direct mail, online catalogs, and social media pages. Pepsi's Mountain Dew brand markets heavily through mass-media advertising and its retail partners' channels. However, it also supplements these channels with a heavy dose of direct marketing. Mountain Dew's marketing mix consists of 55 percent television advertising and 45 percent digital. It uses its several brand Web sites and a long list of social media to engage its digitally connected customer community in everything from designing their own Mountain Dew lifestyle pages to deciding which limited-edition flavors should be launched or retired. Through such direct interactions, Mountain Dew has created one of the most passionately loyal fan bases of any brand, who in turn have made it the nation's fourth-largest soft drink brand.[2]

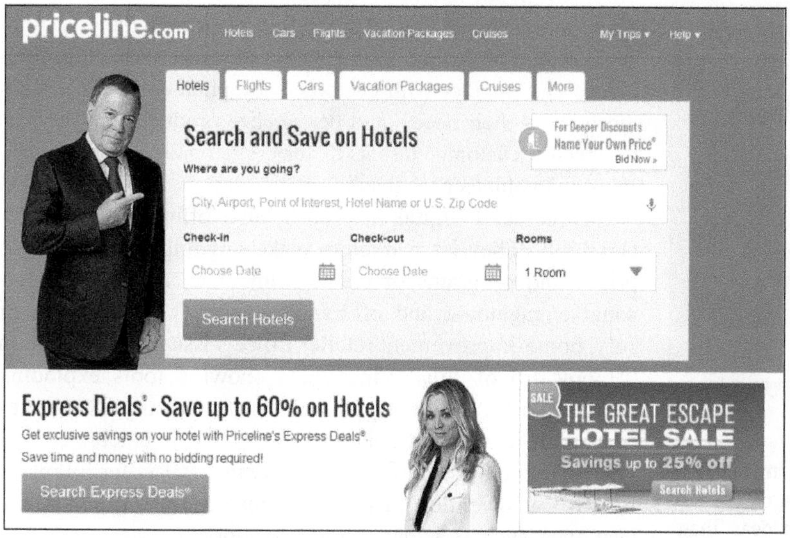

The new direct marketing model: Online travel agency Priceline.com sells its services exclusively through online, mobile, and social media channels. Along with other online competitors, Priceline.com has pretty much driven traditional offline travel agencies to extinction.

Priceline.com

However, for many companies today, direct and digital marketing are more than just supplementary channels or advertising media—they constitute a complete model for doing business. Firms employing this direct model use it as the only approach. Companies such as Amazon, Google, Facebook, eBay, Netflix, GEICO, and Priceline.com have successfully built their entire approach to the marketplace around direct and digital marketing. For example, Priceline.com, the online travel company, sells its services exclusively through online, mobile, and social media channels. Priceline.com and other online travel agency competitors such as Expedia and Orbitz have pretty much driven traditional offline travel agencies to extinction.[3]

Rapid Growth of Direct and Digital Marketing

Direct and digital marketing have become the fastest-growing form of marketing. According to one source, U.S. companies spent an estimated $157 billion on direct and digital marketing last year, up more than 11 percent over the previous year. As a result, direct-marketing-driven sales now amount to more than $2 trillion, accounting for 12 percent of the U.S. economy.[4]

Direct marketing continues to become more Internet-based, and digital direct marketing is claiming a surging share of marketing spending and sales. For example, U.S. marketers spent an estimated $64 billion on digital advertising alone last year, up a blistering 26 percent over the previous year. Total digital advertising spending—including online display and search advertising, social media, mobile, video, email, and other—now accounts for the second-largest share of media spending, behind only television, which it's expected to overtake by 2018. And as consumers spend more and more time on their tablets and smartphones, spending on mobile advertising is exploding. Next year alone, mobile ad spending is expected to grow by 50 percent, and by 2018 it will account for an expected 25 percent of all U.S. ad spending.[5]

Benefits of Direct and Digital Marketing to Buyers and Sellers

For buyers, direct and digital marketing are convenient, easy, and private. They give buyers anywhere, anytime access to an almost unlimited assortment of goods and a wealth of product and buying information. For example, on its Web site and mobile app, Amazon.com offers more information than most of us can digest, ranging from top 10 product lists, extensive product descriptions, and expert and user product reviews to recommendations based on customers' previous searches and purchases. Through direct marketing, buyers can interact with sellers by phone or on the seller's Web site or mobile

>> Direct and digital marketing lets brands create immediate and timely customer engagement, as when GE celebrated last year's National Inventors' Day by asking Twitter followers for offbeat invention ideas, then created illustrations of the best ones.

GE

app to create exactly the configuration of information, products, or services they want and then order them on the spot. Finally, for consumers who want it, digital marketing through online, mobile, and social media provides a sense of brand engagement and community—a place to share brand information and experiences with other brand fans.

For sellers, direct marketing often provides a low-cost, efficient, speedy alternative for reaching their markets. Today's direct marketers can target small groups or individual customers. Because of the one-to-one nature of direct marketing, companies can interact with customers by phone or online, learn more about their needs, and personalize products and services to specific customer tastes. In turn, customers can ask questions and volunteer feedback.

Direct and digital marketing also offer sellers greater flexibility. They let marketers make ongoing adjustments to prices and programs or create immediate, timely, and personal engagement and offers. For example, last Fourth of July, home-improvement retailer Lowe's issued a stop-motion "Happy 4th of July" Vine video showing tools exploding into fireworks, a nice supplement to its ongoing Vine series of "Fix in Six" do-it-yourself videos. >> GE celebrated last year's National Inventors' Day by asking its Twitter followers for offbeat invention ideas, then created illustrations of the best ones, such as a "hand-holding robot."

Especially in today's digital environment, direct marketing provides opportunities for *real-time marketing* that links brands to important moments and trending events in customers' lives. It is a powerful tool for moving customers through the buying process and for building customer engagement, community, and personalized relationships.

Author Comment
Direct marketing is rich in tools, from traditional favorites such as direct mail and catalogs to dazzling new digital tools—online, mobile, and social media.

Forms of Direct and Digital Marketing

The major forms of direct and digital marketing are shown in **>> Figure 14.1**. Traditional direct marketing tools include face-to-face selling, direct-mail marketing, catalog marketing, telemarketing, direct-response television marketing, and kiosk marketing. In recent years, however, a dazzling new set of digital direct marketing tools has burst onto the marketing scene, including online marketing (Web sites, online ads and promotions, email, online videos, and blogs), social media marketing, and mobile marketing. We'll begin by examining the new direct digital and social media marketing tools that have received so much attention lately. Then we'll look at the still heavily used and very important traditional direct marketing tools. As always, however, it's important to remember that all of these tools—both the new digital and the more traditional forms—must be blended into a fully integrated marketing communications program.

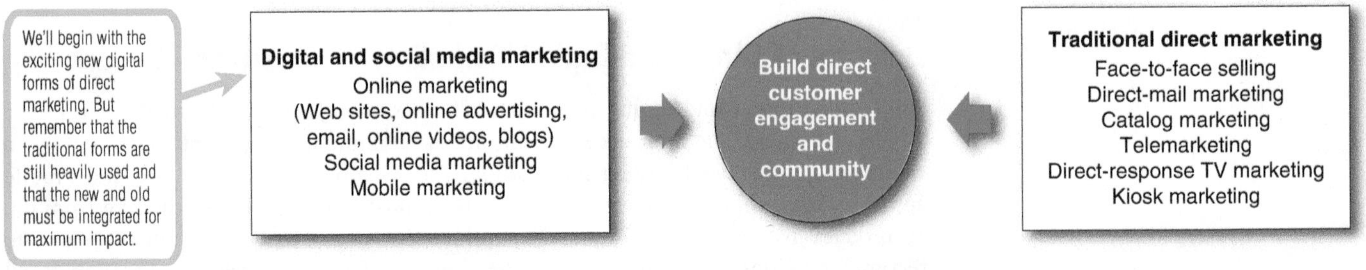

>> Figure 14.1 Forms of Direct and Digital Marketing

LINKING THE CONCEPTS

Hold up a moment and think about the impact of direct and digital marketing on your life.

- When was last time that you bought something via direct or digital marketing? What did you buy, and why did you buy it direct? When was the last time that you *rejected* a direct or digital marketing offer? Why did you reject it? Based on these experiences, what advice would you give to direct marketers?
- For the next week, keep track of all the direct and digital marketing offers that come your way via direct mail and catalogs, email and mobile ads, online and social media marketing offers, and others. Then analyze the offers by type, source, and what you liked or disliked about each offer and the way it was delivered. Which offer best hit its target (you)? Which missed by the widest margin?

Author Comment
Direct digital and social media marketing is surging and grabbing all the headlines these days, so we'll start with it. But the traditional direct marketing tools are still heavily used. We'll dig into them later in the chapter.

Digital and Social Media Marketing

As noted earlier, **digital and social media marketing** is the fastest-growing form of direct marketing. It uses digital marketing tools such as Web sites, online video, email, blogs, social media, mobile ads and apps, and other digital platforms to directly engage consumers anywhere, anytime via their computers, smartphones, tablets, Internet-ready TVs, and other digital devices. The widespread use of the Internet and digital technologies is having a dramatic impact on both buyers and the marketers who serve them.

Digital and social media marketing
Using digital marketing tools such as Web sites, social media, mobile apps and ads, online video, email, and blogs to engage consumers anywhere, anytime via their digital devices.

Marketing, the Internet, and the Digital Age

Much of the world's business today is carried out over digital networks that connect people and companies. These days, people connect digitally with information, brands, and each other at almost any time and from almost anywhere. The digital age has fundamentally changed customers' notions of convenience, speed, price, product information, service, and brand interactions. As a result, it has given marketers a whole new way to create customer value, engage customers, and build customer relationships.

Digital usage and impact continues to grow steadily. More than 87 percent of all U.S. adults use the Internet, and the average U.S. Internet user spends almost six hours a day using digital media, primarily via mobile devices. Worldwide, 40 percent of the population has Internet access. And 23 percent has access to the mobile Internet, a number that's expected to double over the next five years as mobile becomes an ever-more-popular way to get online.[6]

As a result, more than half of all U.S. households now regularly shop online, and digital buying continues to grow at a healthy double-digit rate. U.S. online retail sales were an estimated $305 billion last year, 6.5 percent of total retail sales. By 2018 as consumers continue to shift their spending from physical to digital stores, that number is expected to grow to almost $500 billion (8.9 percent of total retail sales). Perhaps even more important, it's estimated that nearly half of all U.S. retail sales were either transacted directly online or influenced by Internet research.[7] As today's omni-channel consumers become more and more adept at blending online and in-store shopping, digital channels will come into play for an ever-larger proportion of their purchases.

To reach this burgeoning market, most companies now market online. Some companies operate *only* online. They include a wide array of firms, from *e-tailers* such as Amazon and Expedia.com that sell products and services directly to final buyers via the Internet to *search engines and portals* (such as Google, Yahoo!, Bing, and DuckDuckGo), *transaction sites* (eBay, Craigslist), *content sites* (the *New York Times* on the Web, ESPN.com, and *Encyclopædia Britannica*), and *online social media* (Facebook, Twitter, YouTube, Pinterest, Instragram, and Snapchat).

Today, however, it's hard to find a company that doesn't have a substantial online presence. Even companies that have traditionally operated offline have now created their own

Omni-channel retailing
Creating a seamless cross-channel buying experience that integrates in-store, online, and mobile shopping.

online sales, marketing, and brand community channels. In fact, **omni-channel retailing** companies are having as much online success as their online-only competitors. A recent ranking of the nation's 10 largest online retail sites contained only three online-only retailers (Amazon.com, which was ranked number one, Netflix, and Liberty Interactive). Number two was a manufacturer—Apple. All of the rest were omni-channel retailers.[8]

For example, number three on the list of online retail sites is Staples, the $22 billion office supply retailer. Staples operates more than 1,675 North American superstores. But you might be surprised to learn that almost half of Staples's sales are generated online from its Web site and mobile app; its presence on social media such as Facebook, Google+, Twitter, YouTube, and LinkedIn; and its own Staples.com community.[9]

Multichannel marketing: Almost half of Staples's sales come from its online marketing operations, including its Web site and mobile app, its presence on social media, and its own Staples.com community.

Courtesy of Staples the Office Superstore, LLC & Staples, Inc.

Selling online lets Staples build deeper, more personalized relationships with customers large and small. A large customer, such as GE or P&G, can create lists of approved office products at discount prices and then let company departments or even individuals do their own online and mobile purchasing. This reduces ordering costs, cuts through the red tape, and speeds up the ordering process for customers. At the same time, it encourages companies to use Staples as a sole source for office supplies. Even the smallest companies and individual consumers find 24/7 online ordering via the Web, Staples mobile app, or social media sites easier and more efficient.

In addition, Staples' online, mobile, and social media efforts complement store sales by engaging customers, enlarging product assortments, offering hot deals, and helping customers find a local store and check stock and prices. In return, local stores promote online buying through in-store kiosks. If customers don't find what they need on the shelves, they can quickly order it via the kiosk. Thus, Staples backs its "make more happen" positioning by offering a full range of contact points and delivery modes—online, social media, mobile, catalogs, phone, and in the store. No online-only or store-only seller can match that kind of call, click, or visit convenience and support. "We're offering more products, more ways to buy, and more great value," summarizes Staples's vice president of global marketing.

Direct digital and social media marketing takes any of the several forms shown in Figure 14.1. These forms include online marketing, social media marketing, and mobile marketing. We discuss each in turn, starting with online marketing.

Online Marketing

Online marketing
Marketing via the Internet using company Web sites, online ads and promotions, email, online video, and blogs.

Online marketing refers to marketing via the Internet using company Web sites, online advertising and promotions, email marketing, online video, and blogs. Social media and mobile marketing also take place online and must be closely coordinated with other forms of digital marketing. However, because of their special characteristics, we discuss the fast-growing social media and mobile marketing approaches in separate sections.

Web Sites and Branded Web Communities

Marketing Web site
A Web site that engages consumers to move them closer to a direct purchase or other marketing outcome.

For most companies, the first step in conducting online marketing is to create a Web site. Web sites vary greatly in purpose and content. Some Web sites are primarily **marketing Web sites**, designed to engage consumers and move them closer to a direct purchase or other marketing outcome.

For example, GEICO operates a marketing Web site at www.geico.com. Once a potential customer clicks in, GEICO wastes no time trying to turn the inquiry into a sale and then into a long-term relationship. A bold headline urges potential customers to "Get a quote," and the site provides all the information and tools needed to do just that, complete with an auto insurance calculator to help buyers estimate the right insurance

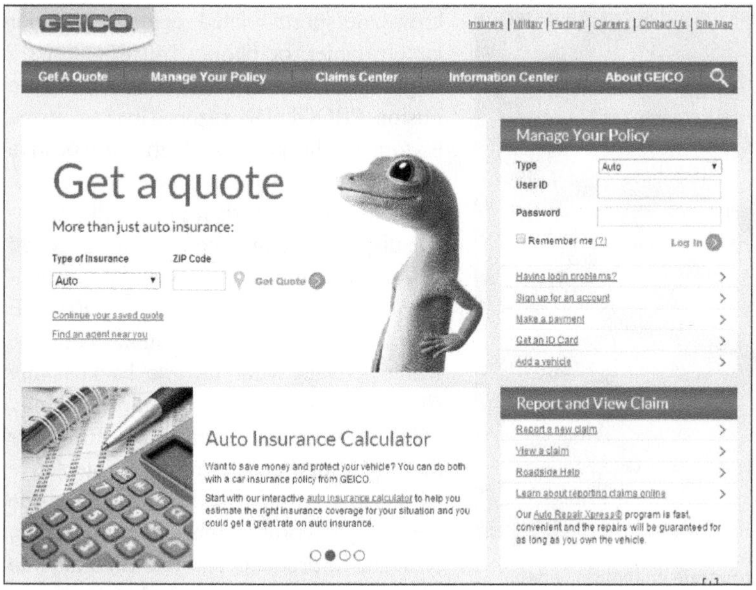

Marketing Web sites: Once a potential customer clicks in, GEICO's Web site wastes no time trying to turn the inquiry into a sale and then into a long-term relationship.
GEICO

coverage, rates, and savings. The straightforward site also makes it easy for current customers to manage their accounts and policies, add or replace vehicles, and make and view claims, all under the watchful eye of the familiar GEICO Gecko. Customers can also use GEICO's mobile app to access the brand's mobile Web site, where they can pay bills, get account and coverage information, view their ID cards, and even watch the latest GEICO ads and chat with Lily, their GEICO insurance voice assistant.

In contrast, **branded community Web sites** don't try to sell anything at all. Instead, their primary purpose is to present brand content that engages consumers and creates customer–brand community. Such sites typically offer a rich variety of brand information, videos, blogs, activities, and other features that build closer customer relationships and generate engagement with and between the brand and its customers.

Branded community Web site
A Web site that presents brand content that engages consumers and creates customer community around a brand.

For example, consider ESPN's Web site. You can't buy anything at ESPN.com. Instead, the site creates a vast branded sports community:[10]

> At ESPN.com, sports fans can access an almost overwhelming repository of sports information, statistics, and game updates. They can customize site content by sport, team, players, and authors to match their own special sports interests and team preferences. The site engages fans in contests and fantasy games (everything from fantasy football, baseball, basketball, and hockey to poker). Sports fans from around the world can participate in discussions with other fans and celebrities before, during, and after sporting events. They can friend and message other users and post comments on message boards and blogs. By downloading various widgets and apps, fans can customize their ESPN experience and carry it with them wherever they go. In all, ESPN's Web site creates a virtual brand community without walls, a must-have experience that keeps fans coming back again and again.

Creating a Web site is one thing; getting people to *visit* the site is another. To attract visitors, companies aggressively promote their Web sites in offline print and broadcast advertising and through ads and links on other sites. But today's Web users are quick to abandon any Web site that doesn't measure up. The key is to create enough engaging and valued content to get consumers to come to the site, stick around, and come back again.

At the very least, a Web site should be easy to use and visually appealing. Ultimately, however, Web sites must also be *useful*. When it comes to online browsing and shopping, most people prefer substance over style and function over flash. For example, ESPN's site isn't all that flashy, and it's pretty heavily packed and congested. But it connects customers quickly and effectively to all the sports information and involvement they are seeking. Thus, effective Web sites contain deep and useful information, interactive tools that help find and evaluate content of interest, links to other related sites, changing promotional offers, and entertaining features that lend relevant excitement.

Online Advertising

Online advertising
Advertising that appears while consumers are browsing online, including display ads and search-related ads.

As consumers spend more and more time online, companies are shifting more of their marketing dollars to **online advertising** to build brand sales or attract visitors to their Internet, mobile, and social media sites. Online advertising has become a major promotional medium. The main forms of online advertising are display ads and search-related ads. Together, display and search-related ads account for the largest portion of firms' digital marketing budgets.

Online display ads might appear anywhere on an Internet user's screen and are often related to the information being viewed. Such display ads have come a long way in recent years in terms of engaging consumers and moving them along the path to purchase. Today's *rich media* ads incorporate animation, video, sound, and interactivity. For example, while

Online display advertising: Today's dynamic rich media ads incorporate animation, video, sound, and interactivity, engaging consumers and moving them along the path to purchase.

The Procter & Gamble Company

browsing sports-related content on your laptop, tablet, or phone, you might see a bright blue and green banner ad for Gillette Fusion PROGLIDE razors floating at the bottom of the page, with the provocative headline "Our Gentlest Shave." A click on the banner expands it into a full interactive display ad, complete with an embedded 15-second demonstration video plus click-throughs to the Gillette Fusion PROGLIDE microsite and a buy-now link. Similarly, while perusing your favorite backpacking site, you might see an attention-grabbing video ad from The North Face. Roll over the brand logo and up pops an interactive ad panel, with the video continuing in the upper right corner alongside information on featured products and real-time links to The North Face Web site and a store locator. Such dynamic ads can engage consumers and deliver substantial impact.[11]

Using *search-related ads* (or *contextual advertising*), text- and image-based ads and links appear atop or alongside search engine results on sites such as Google, Yahoo!, and Bing. For example, search Google for "LCD TVs." At the top and side of the resulting search list, you'll see inconspicuous ads for 10 or more advertisers, ranging from Samsung and Panasonic to Best Buy, Amazon.com, Walmart.com, Crutchfield, and CDW. Almost 90 percent of Google's $66 billion in revenues last year came from ad sales. Search is an always-on kind of medium, and the results are easily measured.[12]

A search advertiser buys search terms from the search site and pays only if consumers click through to its site. For instance, type "Coke" or "Coca-Cola" or even just "soft drinks" or "rewards" into your search engine and almost without fail "My Coke Rewards" comes up as one of the top options, perhaps along with a display ad and link to Coca-Cola's official Google+ page. This is no coincidence. Coca-Cola supports its popular online loyalty program largely through search buys. The soft drink giant started first with traditional TV and print advertising but quickly learned that search was the most effective way to bring consumers to its www.mycokerewards.com Web site to register. Now, any of dozens of purchased search terms will return mycokerewards.com at or near the top of the search list.

Email Marketing

Email marketing
Sending highly targeted, tightly personalized, relationship-building marketing messages via email.

Email marketing remains an important and growing digital marketing tool. "Social media is the hot new thing," says one observer, "but email is still the king."[13] By one estimate, 91 percent of all U.S. consumers use email every day. What's more, email is no longer limited to PCs and workstations; 66 percent of all emails are now opened on mobile devices. Not surprisingly, then, a recent study found that email is 40 times more effective at capturing customers than Facebook and Twitter combined.

According to one recent survey, during the latest holiday season, 90 percent of marketers said that their holiday campaigns included email marketing. U.S. companies spent $2.3 billion on email marketing last year, up from only $243 million 12 years earlier. Despite all the email clutter, thanks to its low costs, email marketing still brings one of the highest marketing returns on investment. According to the Direct Marketing Association, marketers get a return of $42 on every $1 they spend on email.[14]

When used properly, email can be the ultimate direct marketing medium. Email lets these marketers send highly targeted, tightly personalized, relationship-building messages. And today's emails are anything but the staid, text-only messages of the past. Instead, they are colorful, inviting, personalized, and interactive. For example, one recent CVS Pharmacy email, sent to the chain's ExtraCare Rewards Program members

Email marketing: Today's emails are colorful, inviting, personalized, and interactive, like the CVS Pharmacy "Prepare for the Scare" email coupon offer.

CVS Caremark Corporation

prior to Halloween, contained a colorful, attention-getting coupon offering 30 percent off an in-store purchase. Clicking the "Get Coupon" button gave customers a choice of printing the coupon or simply having it zapped onto their loyalty cards for later automatic redemption. The CVS "Prepare for the Scare" email also contained a "View myWeekly Ad" button, by which ExtraCare members could link through to a Web page loaded with personalized deals based on things they buy most. Thus, the much-viewed email promoted both immediate store visits and customer loyalty.

But there's a dark side to the growing use of email marketing. The explosion of **spam**—unsolicited, unwanted commercial email messages that clog up our email boxes—has produced consumer irritation and frustration. According to one research company, spam now accounts for 64 percent of the billions of emails sent worldwide each day, almost two out of every three emails. Workers in American businesses send and receive nearly 109 billion emails per day and spend nearly one-third of their workweek managing email.[15] Email marketers walk a fine line between adding value for consumers and being intrusive and annoying.

To address these concerns, most legitimate marketers now practice *permission-based email marketing*, sending email pitches only to customers who "opt in." Many companies use configurable email systems that let customers choose what they want to get. Amazon.com targets opt-in customers with a limited number of helpful "we thought you'd like to know" messages based on their expressed preferences and previous purchases. Few customers object, and many actually welcome such promotional messages. Amazon.com benefits through higher return rates and by avoiding alienating customers with emails they don't want.

Spam
Unsolicited, unwanted commercial email messages.

Online Videos

Another form of online marketing is posting digital video content on brand Web sites or on social media sites such as YouTube, Facebook, Vine, and others. Some videos are made specifically for the Web and social media. Such videos range from "how-to" instructional videos and public relations (PR) pieces to brand promotions and brand-related entertainment. Other videos are ads that a company makes primarily for TV and other media but posts online before or after an advertising campaign to extend their reach and impact.

Good online videos can engage consumers by the tens of millions. The online video audience is soaring, with more than 60 percent of the U.S. population now streaming video.[16] Marketers hope that some of their videos will go viral. **Viral marketing**, the digital version of word-of-mouth marketing, involves creating videos, ads, and other marketing content that are so infectious that customers will seek them out or pass them along to their friends. Because customers find and pass along the message or promotion, viral marketing can be very inexpensive. And when a video or other information comes from a friend, the recipient is much more likely to view or read it.

Viral marketing
The digital version of word-of-mouth marketing: videos, ads, and other marketing content that is so infectious that customers will seek it out or pass it along to friends.

All kinds of videos can go viral, producing engagement and positive exposure for a brand. For example, in one simple but honest McDonald's video, the director of marketing at McDonald's Canada answered an online viewer's question about why McDonald's products look better in ads than in real life by conducting a behind-the-scenes tour of how a McDonald's ad is made. The award-winning three-and-a-half-minute video pulled almost 15 million views and 15,000 shares, earning the company praise for its honesty and transparency. As another example, P&G's Always brand launched an inspiring #LikeAGirl video campaign, which set out to replace the negative connotations of what it means "to do something like a girl" with the message "Let's make #LikeAGirl mean amazing things." The initial three-minute video was an instant viral hit, garnering 8 million YouTube views in the first week alone and more than 57 million views to date.[17]

Viral marketing: adidas's recent "Take It" campaign featuring famous adidas athletes (here international soccer star Lionel Messi) gutting it out in practice and on game day began on TV but quickly zoomed to the top of the viral charts.

adidas

Many brands produce multi-platform video campaigns that bridge traditional TV, online, and mobile media. For example, Adidas's recent "Take It" campaign—a series of action-packed 60-second video ads featuring famous Adidas athletes gutting it out in practice and on game day—began on TV but quickly zoomed to the top of the viral charts. The campaign drove home a captivating motivational message: "Do something, and be remembered. Or do nothing, and be forgotten. No one owns today. Take it." The initial "Take It" ad broke during NBA All-Star Weekend, but that was only the beginning. The video ad went on to capture a whopping 21 million YouTube views in just the first week and 40 million in the first two months. Additional videos in the ad series grabbed millions more views, making "Take It" one of the most successful viral campaigns of the decade.[18]

Despite these viral successes, it's important to note that marketers usually have little control over where their viral messages end up. They can seed content online, but that does little good unless the message itself strikes a chord with consumers. Says one creative director, "You hope that the creative is at a high enough mark where the seeds grow into mighty oaks. If they don't like it, it ain't gonna move. If they like it, it'll move a little bit; and if they love it, it's gonna move like a fast-burning fire through the Hollywood hills."[19]

Blogs
Online forums where people and companies post their thoughts and other content, usually related to narrowly defined topics.

Blogs and Other Online Forums

Brands also conduct online marketing through various digital forums that appeal to specific special-interest groups and brand communities. **Blogs** (or Web logs) are online forums where people and companies post their thoughts and other content, usually related to narrowly defined topics. Blogs can be about anything, from politics or baseball to haiku, car repair, brands, or the latest television series. Many bloggers use social networks such as Twitter, Facebook, Tumblr, and Instagram to promote their blogs, giving them huge reach. Such reach can give blogs—especially those with large and devoted followings—substantial influence.

Most marketers are now tapping into the blogosphere with their own brand-related blogs that reach customer communities. For example, on the Coca-Cola Unbottled blog, Coke fans and company insiders can "look at what's beyond the bottle," sharing posts on everything from new products and sustainability initiatives to fun and inspiring "what's bubbling" fan stories about "spreading happiness." On the Netflix Blog, members of the Netflix team (themselves rabid movie fans) tell about the latest Netflix features, share tricks for getting the most out of the Netflix experience, and collect feedback from subscribers. And the creative Nuts About Southwest blog, written by Southwest Airline employees, fosters a two-way dialogue that gives customers a look inside the company's culture and operations. At the same time, it lets Southwest engage customers directly and get feedback from them.

Tapping into blogs: The creative Nuts About Southwest blog, written by Southwest employees, fosters a two-way dialogue that gives customers a look inside the company's culture and operations.

Southwest Airlines Co.

Beyond their own brand blogs, many marketers use third-party blogs to help get their messages out. For example, McDonald's systematically reaches out to key "mommy bloggers," those who influence the nation's homemakers, who in turn influence their families' eating-out choices:[20]

> McDonald's recently hosted 15 influential bloggers on an all-expenses-paid tour of its headquarters in Oak Brook, Illinois. The bloggers toured the facilities (including the company's test kitchens), met McDonald's USA president, and had their pictures taken with Ronald at a nearby Ronald McDonald House. McDonald's knows that these mommy bloggers have loyal followings and talk a lot about McDonald's in their blogs. So it's turning the bloggers into believers by giving them a behind-the-scenes view. McDonald's doesn't try to tell the bloggers what to say in their posts about the visit. It simply asks them to write one honest recap of their trip. However, the resulting posts (each acknowledging the blogger's connection with McDonald's) were mostly very positive. Thanks to this and other such efforts, mommy bloggers around the country are now more informed about and connected with McDonald's. "I know they have smoothies and they have yogurt and they have other things that my kids would want," says one prominent blogger. "I really couldn't tell you what Burger King's doing right now," she adds. "I have no idea."

As a marketing tool, blogs offer some advantages. They can offer a fresh, original, personal, and cheap way to enter into consumer online and social media conversations. However, the blogosphere is cluttered and difficult to control. And although companies can sometimes leverage blogs to engage customers in meaningful relationships, blogs remain largely a consumer-controlled medium. Whether or not they actively participate in the blogs, companies should monitor and listen to them. Marketers can use insights from consumer online conversations to improve their marketing programs.

Author Comment
As in about every other area of our lives, social media and mobile technologies have taken the marketing world by storm. They offer some amazing marketing possibilities. But truth be told, many marketers are still sweating over how to use them most effectively.

Social Media Marketing

As we've discussed throughout the text so far, the surge in Internet usage and digital technologies and devices has spawned a dazzling array of online **social media** and digital communities. Countless independent and commercial social networks have arisen where people congregate to socialize and share messages, opinions, pictures, videos, and other content. These days, it seems, almost everyone is buddying up on Facebook or Google+, checking in with Twitter, tuning into the day's hottest videos at YouTube, pinning images on social scrapbooking site Pinterest, or sharing photos with Instagram and Snapchat. And, of course, wherever consumers congregate, marketers will surely follow.

Social media
Independent and commercial online social networks where people congregate to socialize and share messages, opinions, pictures, videos, and other content.

Most marketers are now riding the huge social media wave. According to one survey, 92 percent of U.S. companies now claim that social media marketing is important for their businesses.[21] Interestingly, just as marketers are now learning how to use social media to engage customers, the social media themselves are learning how to make their communities a suitable platform for marketing content, in a way that benefits both social media users and brands. Most social media, even the most successful ones, still face a monetization issue: How can they profitably tap the marketing potential of their massive communities to make money without driving off loyal users (see Marketing at Work 14.1)?

Using Social Media

Marketers can engage in social media in two ways: They can use existing social media or they can set up their own. Using existing social media seems the easiest. Thus, most brands—large and small—have set up shop on a host of social media sites. Check the Web sites of brands ranging from Coca-Cola, Nike, and Victoria's Secret to the Chicago Bulls or even the U.S. Forest Service and you'll find links to each brand's Facebook, Google+, Twitter, YouTube, Flickr, Instagram, or other social media pages. Such social media can create substantial brand communities. For example, the Bulls have more the 17 million Facebook fans; Coca-Cola has an eye-popping 90 million Facebook fans.

Some of the major social networks are huge. Nearly 1.4 billion people access Facebook every month, nearly 4.4 times the population of the United States. Similarly, Twitter has more than 288 million active monthly users. And YouTube's more than 1 billion users upload 300 hours of video every minute of every day. The list goes on: Google+ has 359 million active users, Instagram 300 million, LinkedIn 187 million, and Pinterest 40 million.[22]

MARKETING AT WORK 14.1

Social Media Monetization: Making Money without Driving Fans Away

As the world has rapidly gone social and mobile, social media have played a huge role. Whether it's on massive networks such as Facebook, Twitter, YouTube, Instagram, and Snapchat or lesser-known niche sites such as Blurty, Dogster, and Reddit, it's common to see people everywhere these days, heads down with devices in hand, connecting, posting, and sharing. On Facebook alone, every day, a mind-blowing 936 million of the network's 1.4 billion active users worldwide upload 350 million photos, generate 4.5 billion "Likes," and share 4.75 billion pieces of content.

However, although social media networks have achieved incredible success in terms of numbers of users, sheer volume of content and activity, and even company valuations, a nagging problem still plagues them. It's called *monetization*. How can social media profitably tap the marketing potential of their massive communities to make money without driving off their legions of loyal users? Most social media still struggle to make a profit, and even the most popular ones are only beginning to tap their full financial potential.

The first and best bet for converting the social-sharing potential of a social network's gigantic user community into real dollars is online advertising. For marketers, the targeting and customer engagement potential of social media is a dream come true, and advertisers willingly pay for access via ads and other paid brand content. However, placing commercial content in social media is still in its infancy, for both marketers and the social media networks. Successfully injecting brand content alongside user content can be tricky and risky. Social media users often cherish the free (and commercial-free) sharing cultures of their online communities. If not well conceived, commercial content becomes an unwelcome intrusion that can alienate users and potentially drive them away.

Thus, although social media have exploded in popularity, most are still having trouble making money. Even Facebook—far and away the most financially successful social network, which earned $2.9 billion in profits on $12.5 billion in revenues last year—has yet to scratch the surface of its vast financial potential.

To illustrate the monetization difficulties that social media face, let's dig deeper into one of today's most successful ones, Snapchat, the wildly popular messaging app. Snapchat serves a fast-growing community of more than 100 million users, heavily weighted toward young Millennials. As on other social media, Snapchat users share pictures or videos—known as Snaps—with friends and family. But unlike images shared on other networks, Snaps disappear without a trace in only seconds.

Snapchat exploded onto the scene only about five years ago. By the end of its first year, 1 billion photos had been shared through Snapchat's servers; after only two years, the Snapchat community was sharing 700 million photos every single day. As Snapchat's popularity soared, so did its valuation. Two years in, Facebook made Snapchat's founders a startling $3 billion buyout offer; the founders politely declined. A year later, Snapchat had raised more than $200 million in venture capital funding and was valued at $10 billion. Yet in its rise to glory, Snapchat had yet to make even a dime of revenues or profits.

Snapchat's financial story is typical for successful social media: modest beginnings as a start-up, followed by meteoric growth in popularity and use, leading to outrageously high valuation—all with little or no income. Then comes that difficult question: How can they monetize their massive user bases to make profits and sustain themselves? For Snapchat, that's especially difficult. The very feature that makes Snapchat unique and so popular—content lasting only seconds—means that it can't track and analyze users for targeting purposes, a turnoff to marketers. "In an era where big data rules, how does Snapchat, which collects no data on the user, sell itself to marketers?" asks one online advertiser. Snapchat's challenge is to persuade marketers that the benefits of reaching its young Millennials community outweigh user anonymity and lack of pinpoint targeting potential.

Careful not to ruffle its community's sensitivities or disrupt the user experience, Snapchat didn't introduce its first advertising platform until October 2014. Called Brand Stories, the platform let marketers share brand-related photo and video posts with users via its sponsored Stories feed, at rates of up to $750,000 per ad unit. The first client was Universal Pictures, which sent a 20-second video trailer for its upcoming fright film *Ouija*. A growing number of other brands—from Taco Bell and frozen-yogurt chain 16 Handles to the New Orleans Saints—soon began creating Snapchat handles and dabbling with Snaps to users. Although advertisers seemed eager to pay for the ad units, Snapchat halted Brand Stories after only six

>> Wildly popular messaging app Snapchat and other social media face a nagging *monetization* issue: How can they profitably tap the marketing potential of their massive communities to make money without driving off their legions of loyal users?

Jens Büttner/AP Images

months, apparently concerned about the feature's impact on the Snapchat user experience. The company suggested that it might reintroduce the feature later in a new form.

Meanwhile, Snapchat has focused on two other advertising formats: a magazine-like platform called "Discover" and a sponsored feeds platform dubbed "Our Story." Discover is a Snapchat content area where publishers ranging from ESPN, CNN, Comedy Central, and Food Channel to *Cosmopolitan, National Geographic,* and *People* post daily collections of their best content. Snapchat users can share Discover news stories and video with personalized comments or emoji. Advertisers pay as much as $100,000 a day to advertise alongside the Discover content.

Snapchat's Our Story feeds are TV-like streams of an event such as New Year's Eve, March Madness, an important football game, or the Macy's Thanksgiving Parade, featuring user-generated content curated by Snapchat. Advertisers can buy sponsorship rights for an Our Story feed for $400,000 to $500,000, which includes a brand mention in the opening title as well as branded snaps interspersed throughout the feed. For example, Macy's sponsors the Macy's Thanksgiving Parade feed, weaving its own brand content in with user content. Advertisers can also pay $100,000 for a single 10-second brand snap woven into a feed. Our Story feeds garner an estimated 20 million daily views within the Snapchat community.

All this leaves Snapchat's revenue model in a state of constant flux, as it tinkers to find the best monetization formula. In fact, features like Discover and Our Story may well have morphed into something else by the time you read this story. For example, word leaked recently that Snapchat would soon change the name of its Our Story feature to Live Story, Live Event, or even just Live, more in line with the evolving nature of the platform. "Snapchat, like social platforms before it, is making the bumpy transition from startup to big media company," says an analyst. "Ad products—and the clients who love them—are often affected by that change."

In its quest to monetize, Snapchat has a lot at stake. Will increased advertising and brand content alienate avid Snapchat fans? If they're done right, probably not. Studies show that social media users readily accept—even welcome—well-targeted brand content. A recent Snapchat survey found that 60 percent of Snapchat users actually like Our Story ads.

But that's the catch—doing it right. Like its own disappearing photo feature, Snapchat's soaring popularity could vanish quickly if overly aggressive monetization causes resentment within its highly mobile and typically fickle fan base. Snapchat must move forward carefully. As one Snapchat marketer concludes, "We're always fine tuning to ensure we deliver the best possible experience for our community."

Sources: Julia Greenberg, "Snapchat Allows Users to (Finally!) Share News," *Wired,* May 5, 2015, www.wired.com/2015/05/snapchat-news-business-discover-share/; "By the Numbers: 200+ Amazing Facebook User Statistics," http://expandedramblings.com/index.php/by-the-numbers-17-amazing-facebook-stats/#.U2F1gtxH38u, accessed June 2015; Kurt Wagner, "Snapchat Is No Longer Selling Its Original Ad Unit, Brand Stories," *re/code,* April 13, 2015, http://recode.net/2015/04/13/snapchat-is-no-longer-selling-its-original-ad-unit-brand-stories/; Jessi Hempel and Adam Lashinsky, "Countdown to the Snapchat Revolution," *Fortune,* January 1, 2014, pp. 82-87; James O'Toole, "Could Snapchat Really Be Worth $10 billion?" *CNNMoney,* August 1, 2014, http://money.cnn.com/2014/08/01/technology/social/snapchat-10-billion/index.html; Garrett Sloane, "Snapchat Persuades Brands to Go Vertical with Their Video," *Adweek,* April 27, 2015, pp. 20–22; and Tim Peterson, "With Snapchat's First Ad Format on Hold, Focus Shifts to Live Event Feeds," *Advertising Age,* April 16, 2015, www.adage.com/print/298082.

Although these large social media networks grab most of the headlines, countless niche social media have also emerged. Niche online social networks cater to the needs of smaller communities of like-minded people, making them ideal vehicles for marketers who want to target special interest groups. There's at least one social media network for just about every interest, hobby, or group. Kaboodle.com is for shopaholics, whereas moms share advice and commiseration at CafeMom.com. FarmersOnly.com provides online dating for down-to-earth "country folks" who enjoy "blue skies, living free and at peace in wide open spaces, raising animals, and appreciating nature"—"because city folks just don't get it." At Birdpost.com, avid bird watchers can keep an online list of birds they've seen and share bird sightings with other members using modern satellite maps.[23]

Countless niche social media have emerged, catering to needs of smaller communities of like-minded people. CafeMom is a "Meeting Place for Moms," where they can share conversations, advice, and entertainment.

CafeMom.com

Beyond these independent social media, many companies have created their own online brand communities. For example, in Nike's Nike+ running community—consisting of more than 20 million runners who together have logged more than 1 billion running miles worldwide—members join together online to upload, track, and compare their performances. Due to its success, Nike has expanded Nike+ to both basketball and general training, each with its own unique community site, app, and corresponding products.[24]

Social Media Marketing Advantages and Challenges

Using social media presents both advantages and challenges. On the plus side, social media are *targeted* and *personal*—they allow marketers to create and share tailored brand content with individual consumers and customer communities. Social media are *interactive,* making them ideal for starting and participating in customer conversations and listening to customer feedback. For example, Whole Foods Market hosts regular Thursday evening Twitter chats using the #WFMDish hashtag hosted by the @wholefoods account. The chats bring together the Whole Foods community of health-minded eaters to discuss themes such as what to eat during the winter months or how to host a healthy (but tasty) Super Bowl party. Chat participants share recipes, ideas, and opinions, while Whole Foods tweets links to blog posts and multimedia content.[25]

Social media are also *immediate* and *timely.* They can be used to reach customers anytime, anywhere with timely and relevant marketing content regarding brand happenings and activities. As discussed earlier in the chapter, the rapid growth in social media usage has caused a surge in *real-time marketing*, allowing marketers to create and join consumer conversations around situations and events as they occur. Marketers can now watch what's trending and create content to match.

Social media can be very *cost-effective.* Although creating and administering social media content can be costly, many social media are free or inexpensive to use. Thus, returns on social media investments are often high compared with those of expensive traditional media such as television or print. The low cost of social media puts them within easy reach of even small businesses and brands that can't afford the high costs of big-budget marketing campaigns.

Perhaps the biggest advantage of social media is their *engagement and social sharing capabilities.* Social media are especially well suited to creating customer engagement and community—for getting customers involved with the brand and with each other. More than any other channels, social media can involve customers in shaping and sharing brand content, experiences, information, and ideas.

>> For example, consider Etsy—the online craft marketplace that's "Your place to buy and sell all things handmade." Etsy uses its Web and mobile sites and a host of social media to create an Etsy lifestyle community, where buyers congregate to learn about, explore, exchange, and share ideas about handmade and vintage products and related topics. In addition to its active Facebook, Twitter, and YouTube pages, Etsy engages 334,000 brand followers on photo-sharing site Instagram, where the Etsy community shares photos of creative ideas and projects. It also engages 580,000 followers on social scrapbooking site Pinterest, with 113 boards on topics ranging from "DIY Projects," "Entertaining," and "Stuff We Love" to "Etsy Weddings" and even "Yum! Recipes to Share," where the community posts favorite recipes. Etsy sells few of the ingredients that go into the recipes, but it's all part of the Etsy lifestyle. Through its extensive online and social media presence, Etsy has created an active and engaged worldwide community of 19.8 million buyers and 1.4 million sellers worldwide in what it calls "The marketplace we make together."[26]

>> Through its extensive online and social media presence, Etsy has created an active and engaged worldwide brand community of buyers and sellers in what it calls "The marketplace we make together."

Etsy, Inc.

Social media marketing also presents challenges. First, many companies are still experimenting with how to use them effectively, and results are hard to measure. Second, such social networks are largely user controlled. The company's goal in using social media is to make the brand a part of consumers' conversations and their lives. However, marketers can't simply muscle their way into consumers' digital interactions—they need to earn the right to be there. Rather than intruding, marketers must become a valued part of the online experience by developing a steady flow of engaging content.

Because consumers have so much control over social media content, even the seemingly most harmless social media campaign can backfire. For example, Frito-Lay recently launched an annual Do Us a Flavor contest, in which it asks people to come up with new potato chip flavors, submit them to its Web or Facebook site, and design bag art for their creations. Many consumers take the annual contest (and the $1 million grand prize) seriously, submitting flavors that people would truly want to eat. However, others recently hijacked the contest by submitting sometimes hilarious but completely bogus flavors, ranging from Crunchy Frog and Blue Cheese, Toothpaste and Orange Juice, and 7th Grade Locker Room to Bandaid in a Public Pool and "90% Air and Like 4 Chips." Unfortunately, for each submission, no matter how bogus, the Web site responded cheerfully with a colorful rendition of the bag and flavor name, along with a message like the following: "7th Grade Locker Room? That does sound yummy as a chip! Keep those tasty ideas coming for your next chance to win $1 million."

Frito-Lay and its customers took the hijacking with good humor, and the Do Us a Flavor contest continues on its successful way. However, there's a clear message. With social media, "you're going into the consumer's backyard. This is their place," warns one social marketer. "Social media is a pressure cooker," says another. "The hundreds of thousands, or millions, of people out there are going to take your idea, and they're going to try to shred it or tear it apart and find what's weak or stupid in it."[27]

Integrated Social Media Marketing

Using social media might be as simple as posting some messages and promotions on a brand's Facebook or Twitter pages or creating brand buzz with videos or images on YouTube, Vine, or Pinterest. However, most large companies are now designing full-scale social media efforts that blend with and support other elements of a brand's marketing content strategy and tactics. More than making scattered efforts and chasing "Likes" and Tweets, companies that use social media successfully are integrating a broad range of diverse media to create brand-related social sharing, engagement, and customer community.

Managing a brand's social media efforts can be a major undertaking. For example, Starbucks, one of the most successful social media marketers, manages 51 Facebook pages (including 43 in other countries), 31 Twitter handles (19 of them international), and 22 Instagram names (14 international) plus Google+, Pinterest, YouTube, and Foursquare accounts. Managing and integrating all that social media content is challenging, but the results are worth the investment. Customers can and do engage with Starbucks by the tens of millions digitally, without ever setting foot in a store.

But more than just creating online engagement and community, Starbucks' social media presence also drives customers into its stores. For example, in its first big social media promotion six years ago, Starbucks offered a free pastry with a morning drink purchase. A million people showed up. Its more recent "Tweet-a-Coffee" promotion, which let customers give a $5 gift card to a friend by putting both #tweetacoffee and the friend's handle in a Tweet, resulted in $180,000 in purchases within little more than one month. Social media "are not just about engaging and telling a story and connecting," says Starbucks's head of global digital marketing. "They can have a material impact on the business."[28]

Mobile Marketing

Mobile marketing
Marketing messages, promotions, and other marketing content delivered to on-the-go consumers through mobile phones, smartphones, tablets, and other mobile devices.

Mobile marketing features marketing messages, promotions, and other marketing content delivered to on-the-go consumers through their mobile devices. Marketers use mobile marketing to engage customers anywhere, anytime during the buying and relationship-building processes. The widespread adoption of mobile devices and the surge in mobile Web traffic have made mobile marketing a must for most brands.

With the recent proliferation of mobile phones, smartphones, and tablets, mobile device penetration is now greater than 100 percent in the United States (many people possess more than one mobile device). Almost 40 percent of U.S. households are currently mobile-only households with no landline phone. About 65 percent of people in the United States own a smartphone, and more than 60 percent of smartphone users use them to access the mobile Internet. They not only browse the mobile Internet but are also avid mobile app users. The mobile apps market has exploded globally: There are more than 2 million apps available, and the average smartphone has 26 apps installed on it.[29]

Most people love their phones and rely heavily on them. According to one study, nearly 90 percent of consumers who own smartphones, tablets, computers, and TVs would give up all of those other screens before giving up their phones. On average, Americans check their phones 150 times a day—once every six-and-a-half minutes—and spend two hours and 51 minutes a day on their smartphones and other mobile devices talking, texting, and visiting Web sites. Thus, although TV is still a big part of people's lives, mobile is rapidly becoming their "first screen." Away from home, it's their only screen.[30]

For consumers, a smartphone or tablet can be a handy shopping companion. It can provide on-the-go product information, price comparisons, advice and reviews from other consumers, and access to instant deals and digital coupons. One recent study by Google found that 87 percent of mobile device owners use mobile to pre-shop and research purchases before getting to a store, and 75 percent of smartphone-toting shoppers use their phones in-store.[31] Not surprisingly, then, mobile devices provide a rich platform for engaging consumers more deeply as they move through the buying process with tools ranging from mobile ads, coupons, and texts to apps and mobile Web sites.

Mobile advertising spending in the United States is surging; it more than doubled last year alone and is expected to double again by next year. Almost every major marketer—from P&G and Macy's to your local bank or supermarket to nonprofits such as the ASPCA—is now integrating mobile marketing into its direct marketing programs. Such efforts can produce very positive outcomes. For example, 49 percent of mobile users search for more information after seeing a mobile ad.[32]

Companies use mobile marketing to stimulate immediate buying, make shopping easier, enrich the brand experience, or all of these. It lets marketers provide consumers with information, incentives, and choices at the moment they are expressing an interest or when they are in a position to make a buying choice. For example, McDonald's uses mobile marketing to promote new menu items, announce special promotions, and drive immediate traffic at its restaurants. One recent interactive ad on Pandora's mobile app read "Taste buds. Any size soft drink or sweet tea for $1. Tap to visit site." A tap on the mobile ad took customers to a mobile site promoting McDonald's ongoing summer promotion. Another McDonald's mobile campaign used a word scrabble game to entice customers to try the fast feeder's dollar menu items. Such efforts create both customer engagement and store traffic. Using a game "inside a mobile campaign is all about finding and maintaining engagement," says a McDonald's marketer.[33]

Today's rich-media mobile ads can create substantial engagement and impact. For example, JetBlue recently created a voice-activated mobile ad that interacts with customers and talks back. It starts with a JetBlue mobile banner ad that says, "Click here to learn how to speak pigeon." A click expands the ad, which then instructs users by voice to repeat words on the screen, such as "coo, coo, coo." When they've completed two full sentences in pigeon, users receive a virtual medal and the option to play again. Hitting "Learn more" takes users to the JetBlue Landing Perch, where they can explore and send messages to friends via digital carrier pigeons. The mobile ad is part of JetBlue's "Air on the Side of Humanity" campaign, which features pigeons—the ultimate frequent fliers. Rather than making direct sales pitches, the voice ad aims simply to enrich the JetBlue experience. The airline hopes people will "watch the ads, play with the pigeons, and remember us when they want to book tickets," says JetBlue's advertising manager.[34]

Retailers can use mobile marketing to enrich the customer's shopping experience at the same time that they stimulate buying. For example, Macy's built its recent "Brasil: A Magical Journey" promotion around a popular and imaginative smartphone app. The campaign featured apparel from Brazilian designers and in-store experiences celebrating Brazilian culture. By using their smartphones to scan codes throughout the store, shoppers could learn about featured fashions and experience Brazilian culture through virtual tours, such as a trip to the Amazon, a visit to Rio de Janeiro during Carnival, or attending a Brazilian soccer match.

Many marketers have created their own mobile online sites, optimized for specific phones and mobile service providers. Others have created useful or entertaining mobile apps to engage customers with their brands and help them shop (see Marketing at Work 14.2).

MARKETING AT WORK 14.2

Mobile Marketing: Smartphones Are Changing How People Live—and How They Buy

Armed only with a smartphone or other mobile device, you can learn, do, or buy almost anything these days, from anywhere, and at any time. Google's Waze app does more than just help you navigate—it pinpoints traffic jams, accidents, speed traps, and gas prices in real time, all updated by members of the Waze community. Is that Redbox kiosk too slow? Download the Redbox app—it lets you find and reserve a DVD using your mobile device and have it waiting for you at the kiosk. REI's Snow Report app, with its snowy fresh look and feel, gives you ski slope information for locations throughout the United States and Canada, such as snow conditions, number of open lifts, trail maps, and Webcam views. The app even helps you share resort information with friends via Twitter and Facebook, and it links you to "Shop REI" for times "when you decide you can't live without a new set of K2 skis or a two-man Hubba Hubba tent."

Welcome to the world of mobile marketing. Today's smartphones and other mobile devices are changing how people live, becoming indispensable hubs for communication, information, and entertainment. They are also revolutionizing the way people shop and buy, giving marketers new opportunities to engage customers in more effective and satisfying ways.

Marketers are responding to the huge growth in mobile access and use. Mobile ad spending has skyrocketed by more than 400 percent in the past three years and is expected to double in the next three. And the mobile app market has outright exploded. Just six years ago, Apple's App Store had a then-astounding 10,000 apps. But by last year, it boasted 1.2 million apps; Android's Google Play took the lead with more than 1.3 million apps. Mobile has become today's brave new marketing frontier, especially for brands courting younger consumers. Mobile devices are very personal, ever-present, and always on. That makes them an ideal medium for obtaining quick responses to individualized, time-sensitive offers.

Some marketers are still just warming up to mobile, and most are still learning how to use it effectively. Successful mobile marketing goes beyond just giving people a coupon and a link to buy. Instead, it enhances brand engagement and creates a "frictionless" buying experience. For example, with Amazon's mobile app—thanks to "1-click" purchasing, Prime membership, and other features—customers located anywhere, anytime can have products delivered to practically any location in less than 24 hours with nothing more than a smartphone, a simple search or scan, and the click of a button.

Consumers have come to expect such frictionless mobile buying experiences from marketing giants like Amazon. But with recent rapid advances in mobile capabilities, from location-based technologies to mobile payment systems, more and more companies are becoming the Amazons of their industries. Consider mobile app-based car-sharing service Getaround.

In the United States alone, personal cars sit idle for 6 billion car-hours every day. Peer-to-peer car-sharing service Getaround lets car owners earn money by sharing those unused hours with others in the Getaround community for a fee. The young company has already developed a fast-growing base of 25,000 car-sharing owners, who receive 60 percent of the rental fees—an average of $500 to $1,000 per month depending on the car. Getaround takes care of everything—customer contact and support, insurance, roadside assistance, and payment. To use Getaround, you just download the mobile app and supply credit card and driver's license information. Then you can use the app to search among and view thousands of cars available in the neighborhood and rent one by the hour or day, right when you need it. You locate the car with your phone's GPS, unlock it with the app, and get in and drive it away. Pay with a credit card on file or using Apple Pay with a single tap. It's that simple. The Getaround app even provides trip management tools for planning getaways on the go.

Mobile marketing can do much more than simply ease the buying process. It can also take ads, coupons, and other promotions to new levels. Mobile marketers can personalize promotions and weave them into relevant everyday customer experiences. For example, Kiip, a mobile reward network, specializes in helping brands provide customers with just the right reward at just the right time based on their everyday activities. The agency started by embedding its technology into video game apps such as Zombie Farm and Mega Jump. Gamers who

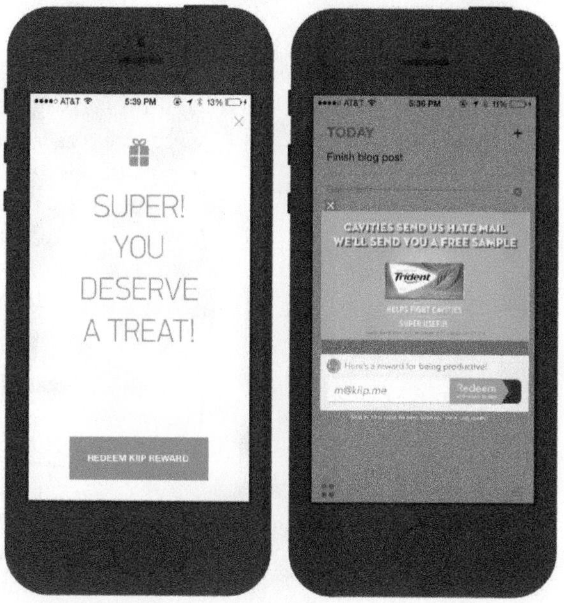

» Mobile marketing: Mobile promotions agency Kiip helps client brands link mobile offers to relevant customer experiences and positive moments. "We want to capitalize on happiness," says Kiip's CEO.

Kiip, inc.

reach a new game level or meet some other goal get a coupon to one of their favorite retailers, such as American Apparel.

Kiip now boasts a network of 2,500 apps and 60 million users across games, fitness, productivity, music, and cooking categories. It showcases more than 500 million reward moments every month for clients like McDonald's, Propel, Sour Patch Kids, P&G, and MasterCard. For fitness apps like MapMyRun and productivity apps like Any.do, Kiip ties rewards to real-life achievements. When users cross things off their to-do lists or achieve a running goal, they get a reward from a relevant brand. For example, P&G's Secret deodorant recently rewarded female MapMyRun users with free song downloads for their workout playlists. And snack giant Mondelez rewarded Any.do users with free packs of Trident when they set new personal records.

Kiip helps marketers reach targeted users at positive moments with rewards relevant to their real-time doings and accomplishments. Readers who finish a certain number of pages in a reading app receive a free magazine subscription. People using a couple's app to stay in touch receive credits toward a purchase from 1-800-Flowers. Kiip is even working with connected-car company Mojio, whose 4G telematic device plugs into a car's diagnostic port, tracks information about the car's status, and keeps the owner connected to favorite people, places, and things. Through Mojio, Kiip helps clients—from insurance companies and car repair shops to parking meter and garage operators—provide rewards tied to specific driver locations and behaviors.

Unlike typical banner ads, pop-ups, or emails, Kiip offers enhance a user's regular activities rather than interrupting them. According to Kiip's founder and CEO, Kiip "is less about real-time marketing and more about real-time-needs addressing." In fact, he asserts, Kiip isn't really in the mobile ad business at all—it's in the happiness business. "We want to capitalize on happiness," he says. "Everything's better when you're happy." Mobile timeliness, relevance, and happiness pay off in terms of consumer response. Users redeem Kiip's mobile promotions at a 22-percent clip, compared with the 0.3 percent for typical app ad engagement. Kiip's offers also increase mobile app revisits by 30 percent and more than double average app length of use.

Many consumers are initially skeptical about mobile marketing. But they often change their minds if mobile offers deliver useful brand and shopping information, entertaining content, or timely coupons and discounted prices. Most mobile efforts target only consumers who voluntarily opt in or download apps. In the increasingly cluttered mobile marketing space, customers just won't do that unless they see real value in it. The challenge for marketers: develop valued mobile offers, ads, and apps that make customers come calling.

Sources: Robert Hof, "Mobile Ads Will Smash $100 Billion Mark Worldwide in 2016," *Forbes*, April 2, 2015, www.forbes.com/sites/roberthof/2015/04/02/mobile-ads-will-smash-100-billion-mark-worldwide-in-2016/; Lindsay Harrison, "Kiip: For Making Mobile Ads That People Want," *Fast Company*, February 11, 2013, www.fastcompany.com/most-innovative-companies/2013/kiip; Christina Chaey, "How Kiip Ties Brand Rewards to Game and Life Achievements to Make Mobile Ads Engaging," *Fast Company*, July 23, 2012, www.fastcocreate.com/1681287; Neil Undgerleider, "Advertisers Are about to Enter Your Connected Car," *Fast Company*, April 11, 2014, www.fastcompany.com/3028744/most-innovative-companies/advertisers-are-about-to-enter-your-connected-car; Jason Ankeny, "Young Millionaires: How These Entrepreneurs under 30 Are Changing the World," *Entrepreneur*, August 20, 2014, www.entrepreneur.com/article/236621; and www.kiip.com/me, www.getaround.com/mobile, www.getaround.com/tour, and www.getaround.com/tour/benefits, accessed September 2015.

Mobile marketing: The Benjamin Moore Color Capture app engages customers and helps them shop.

Benjamin Moore, Color Capture and the triangle "M" are registered trademarks licensed to Benjamin Moore & Co.

For example, the Benjamin Moore Color Capture app lets customers take photos of colorful objects, then match them to any of 3,500 Benjamin Moore paint colors. Starbucks's mobile app lets customers use their phones as a Starbucks card to make fast and easy purchases. And Charles Schwab's mobile apps let customers get up-to-the-minute investment news, monitor their accounts, and make trades at any time from any location—it helps you "stay connected with your money."

As with other forms of direct marketing, however, companies must use mobile marketing responsibly or risk angering already ad-weary consumers. Most people don't want to be interrupted regularly by advertising, so marketers must be smart about how they engage people on mobile devices. The key is to provide genuinely useful information and offers that will make consumers want to engage. And many marketers target mobile ads on an opt-in-only basis.

In all, digital direct marketing—online, social media, and mobile marketing—offers both great promise and many challenges for the future. Its most ardent apostles still envision a time when the Internet and digital marketing will replace magazines, newspapers, and even stores as sources for information, engagement, and buying. Most marketers, however, hold a more realistic view. For most companies, digital and social media marketing will remain just one important approach to the marketplace that works alongside other approaches in a fully integrated marketing mix.

Although the fast-growing digital marketing tools have grabbed most of the headlines lately, traditional direct marketing tools are very much alive and still heavily used. We now examine the traditional direct marketing approaches shown on the right side of Figure 14.1.

LINKING THE CONCEPTS

Stop now and think about how online, social media, and mobile marketing affect your brand buying behavior and preferences.

- How much of your product research, shopping, and actual buying take place online? How much of that is conducted on a mobile device? How and how much do your digital and in-store buying activities interact?
- How much and what kinds of online, social media, and mobile marketing do you encounter? Do you benefit from such marketing, or is it more of an unwelcome intrusion? In what ways?
- Do you engage directly with any brands or brand communities through online sites, social media, or phone apps? Do your online, social media, or mobile interactions influence your brand preferences and buying? Discuss.

Author Comment
Again, although online, social media, and mobile direct marketing seem to be getting much of the attention these days, traditional direct media still carry a lot of the direct marketing freight. Just think about your often overstuffed mailbox.

Traditional Direct Marketing Forms

The major traditional forms of direct marketing—as shown in Figure 14.1—are face-to-face or personal selling, direct-mail marketing, catalog marketing, telemarketing, direct-response television (DRTV) marketing, and kiosk marketing. We examined personal selling in depth in Chapter 13. Here, we look into the other forms of traditional direct marketing.

Direct-Mail Marketing

Direct-mail marketing
Marketing that occurs by sending an offer, announcement, reminder, or other item directly to a person at a particular address.

Direct-mail marketing involves sending an offer, announcement, reminder, or other item directly to a person at a particular address. Using highly selective mailing lists, direct marketers send out millions of mail pieces each year—letters, catalogs, ads, brochures, samples, videos, and other "salespeople with wings." U.S. marketers spent an estimated $46 billion on direct mail last year (including both catalog and noncatalog mail), which accounted for 29 percent of all direct marketing spending. According to the Direct Mail Marketing Association, every dollar spent on direct mail generates $12.53 in sales.[35]

Direct mail is well suited to direct, one-to-one communication. It permits high target-market selectivity, can be personalized, is flexible, and allows the easy measurement of results. Although direct mail costs more per thousand people reached than mass media such as television or magazines, the people it reaches are much better prospects. Direct mail has proved successful in promoting all kinds of products, from books, insurance, travel, gift items, gourmet foods, clothing, and other consumer goods to industrial products of all kinds. Charities also use direct mail heavily to raise billions of dollars each year.

Some analysts predict a decline in the use of traditional forms of direct mail in the coming years as marketers switch to newer digital forms, such as email and online, social media, and mobile marketing. The newer digital direct marketing approaches deliver messages at incredible speeds and lower costs compared to the U.S. Post Office's "snail mail" pace.

However, even though new digital forms of direct marketing are bursting onto the scene, traditional direct mail is still heavily used by most marketers. Mail marketing offers some distinct advantages over digital forms. It provides something tangible for people to hold and keep, and it can be used to send samples. "Mail makes it real," says one analyst. It "creates an emotional connection with customers that digital cannot. They hold it, view it, and engage with it in a manner entirely different from their [digital] experiences." In contrast, email and other digital forms are easily filtered or trashed. "[With] spam filters and spam folders

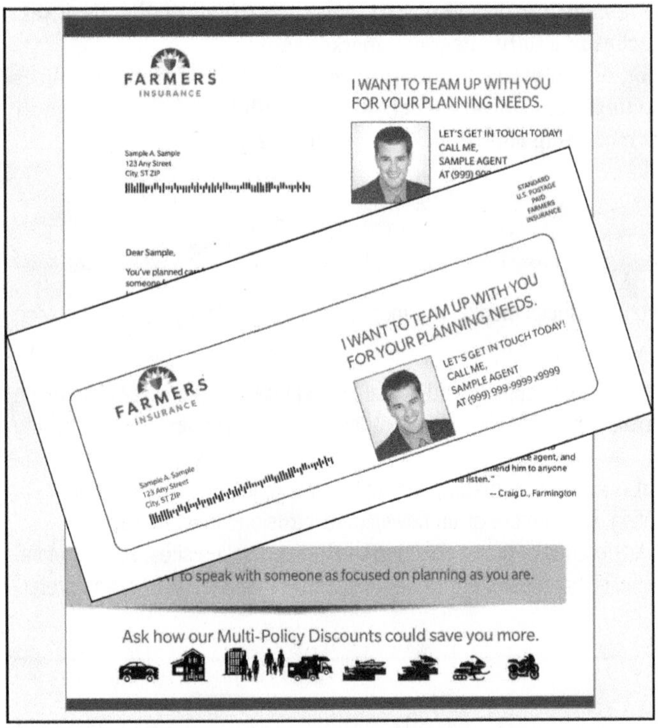

Direct mail marketing: Insurance companies like Farmers Insurance rely heavily on TV advertising to establish broad customer awareness. However, they also use lots of good old direct mail to communicate with consumers in a more direct and personalized way.

Farmers Group, Inc.

to keep our messaging away from consumers' inboxes," says a direct marketer, "sometimes you have to lick a few stamps."[36]

Traditional direct mail can be an effective component of a broader integrated marketing campaign. For example, most large insurance companies rely heavily on TV advertising to establish broad customer awareness and positioning. However, the insurance companies also use lots of good old direct mail to break through the glut of insurance advertising on TV. Whereas TV advertising talks to broad audiences, direct mail communicates in a more direct and personal way. "Mail is a channel that allows all of us to find the consumer with a very targeted, very specific message that you can't do in broadcast," says John Ingersoll, vice president of marketing communications for Farmers Insurance. And "most people are still amenable to getting marketing communications in their mailbox, which is why I think direct mail will grow."[37]

Direct mail may be resented as *junk mail* if sent to people who have no interest in it. For this reason, smart marketers are targeting their direct mail carefully so as not to waste their money and recipients' time. They are designing permission-based programs that send direct mail only to those who want to receive it.

Catalog Marketing

Catalog marketing
Direct marketing through print, video, or digital catalogs that are mailed to select customers, made available in stores, or presented online.

Advances in technology, along with the move toward personalized, one-to-one marketing, have resulted in exciting changes in **catalog marketing**. *Catalog Age* magazine used to define a *catalog* as "a printed, bound piece of at least eight pages, selling multiple products, and offering a direct ordering mechanism." Today, the definition must be revamped to meet the changing times.

With the stampede to the Internet and digital marketing, more and more catalogs are going digital. A variety of online-only catalogers have emerged, and most print catalogers have added Web-based catalogs and smartphone catalog shopping apps to their marketing mixes. For example, apps such as Catalog Spree put a mall full of classic catalogs from retailers such as Macy's, Anthropologie, L.L. Bean, Hammacher Schlemmer, Coldwater Creek, or West Elm only a swipe of the finger away on a smartphone or tablet. And days before the latest Eddie Bauer catalog arrives in the mail, customers can access it digitally on a laptop or mobile device at eddiebauer.com or catch highlights via social media outlets such as Pinterest. Eddie Bauer's mobile catalog gives customers the convenience of on-the-go browsing and purchasing.

Digital catalogs eliminate printing and mailing costs. And whereas space is limited in a print catalog, online catalogs can offer an almost unlimited amount of merchandise. They also offer a broader assortment of presentation formats, including search and video. Finally, online catalogs allow real-time merchandising; products and features can be added or removed as needed, and prices can be adjusted instantly to match demand. Customers can carry digital catalogs anywhere they go, even when shopping at physical stores.

Despite the advantages of digital catalogs, however, as your overstuffed mailbox may suggest, printed catalogs are still thriving. U.S. direct marketers mailed out some 12 billion catalogs last year—more than 97 per American household.[38] Why aren't companies ditching their old-fashioned paper catalogs in this new digital era? For one thing, printed catalogs are one of the best ways to drive online and mobile sales, making them more important than ever in digital time. According to one study, about 58 percent of online shoppers browse physical catalogs for ideas, and 31 percent have a retailer's catalog with them when they make a purchase online. Catalog users look at more than double the number of online pages per visit to the company's site than the average visitor and spend twice the amount of time there.[39]

But beyond their ability to drive immediate sales, paper catalogs create emotional connections with customers. Somehow, turning actual catalog pages engages consumers in a way that digital images simply can't. And many sellers are revamping their catalogs, making them much more than just big books full of product pictures and prices. For example, Anthropologie calls its catalogs "journals" and fills them with lifestyle images. "Of course we're trying to sell clothes and accessories," says Anthropologie's CMO, "but it's more to inspire and engage." Similarly, in addition to the 10 or so traditional catalogs that it publishes each year, Patagonia sends out other catalogs built around themes. One recent catalog featured falconry, with images of children with condors in Chile and wildlife volunteers in California releasing rehabilitated red-tailed hawks. The catalog included only a handful of products, placed on the last four pages of the 43-page book. Such catalogs are "a way we're speaking to our closest friends and people who know the brand really well," says a Patagonia marketer. "Years ago, [a catalog] was a selling tool, and now it's become an inspirational source," says another direct marketer. "We know our customers love a tactile experience."[40]

Catalogs: Even in the digital era, printed catalogs are still thriving. In addition to its traditional catalogs, Patagonia sends out catalogs built around lifestyle themes, as "a way we're speaking to our closest friends and people who know the brand really well."

Patagonia, Inc.

Telemarketing

Telemarketing involves using the telephone to sell directly to consumers and business customers. U.S. marketers spent an estimated $43 billion on telemarketing last year, almost as much as on direct mail.[41] We're all familiar with telephone marketing directed toward consumers, but business-to-business (B-to-B) marketers also use telemarketing extensively. Marketers use *outbound* telephone marketing to sell directly to consumers and businesses. They also use *inbound* toll-free numbers to receive orders from television and print ads, direct mail, or catalogs.

Telemarketing
Using the telephone to sell directly to customers.

Properly designed and targeted telemarketing provides many benefits, including purchasing convenience and increased product and service information. However, the explosion in unsolicited outbound telephone marketing over the years annoyed many consumers, who objected to the almost daily "junk phone calls." In 2003, U.S. lawmakers responded with the National Do Not Call Registry, which is managed by the Federal Trade Commission (FTC). The legislation bans most telemarketing calls to registered phone numbers (although people can still receive calls from nonprofit groups, politicians, and companies with which they have recently done business). Consumers responded enthusiastically. To date, more than 217 million home and mobile phone numbers have been registered at www.donotcall.gov or by calling 888-382-1222.[42] Businesses that break do-not-call laws can be fined up to $16,000 per violation. As a result, the program has been very successful.

Do-not-call legislation has hurt parts of the consumer telemarketing industry. However, two major forms of telemarketing—inbound consumer telemarketing and outbound B-to-B telemarketing—remain strong and growing. Telemarketing also remains a major fundraising tool for nonprofit and political groups. Interestingly, do-not-call regulations appear to be helping some direct marketers more than they're hurting them. Rather than making unwanted calls, many of these marketers are developing "opt-in" calling systems, in which they provide useful information and offers to customers who have invited the company to contact them by phone or email. The opt-in model provides better returns for marketers than the formerly invasive one.

Direct-Response Television Marketing

Direct-response television (DRTV) marketing
Direct marketing via television, including direct-response television advertising (or infomercials) and interactive television (iTV) advertising.

Direct-response television (DRTV) marketing takes one of two major forms: direct-response television advertising and interactive TV (iTV) advertising. Using *direct-response television advertising*, direct marketers air television spots, often 60 or 120 seconds in length, which persuasively describe a product and give customers a toll-free number or an online site for ordering. It also includes full 30-minute or longer advertising programs, called *infomercials*, for a single product.

Successful direct-response television advertising campaigns can ring up big sales. For example, little-known infomercial maker Guthy-Renker has helped propel its Proactiv

Solution acne treatment and other "transformational" products into power brands that pull in $1.8 billion in sales annually to 5 million active customers (compare that to only about $150 million in annual drugstore sales of acne products in the United States). Guthy-Renker now combines DRTV with social media campaigns using Facebook, Pinterest, Google+, Twitter, and YouTube to create a powerful integrated direct marketing channel that builds consumer involvement and buying.[43]

DRTV ads are often associated with somewhat loud or questionable pitches for cleaners, stain removers, kitchen gadgets, and nifty ways to stay in shape without working very hard at it. For example, over the past few years yell-and-sell TV pitchmen like Anthony Sullivan (Swivel Sweeper, Awesome Auger) and Vince Offer (ShamWow, SlapChop) have racked up billions of dollars in sales of "As Seen on TV" products. Brands like OxiClean, ShamWow, and the Snuggie (a blanket with sleeves) have become DRTV cult classics. And direct marketer Beachbody brings in more than $32 million annually via an army of workout videos—from P90X and T-25 to Insanity and Hip Hop Abs—that it advertises on TV using before-and-after stories, clips of the workout, and words of encouragement from the creators.

In recent years, however, a number of large companies—from P&G, Disney, Revlon, and Apple to Toyota, Coca-Cola, Anheuser-Busch, and even the U.S. Navy—have begun using infomercials to sell their wares, refer customers to retailers, recruit members, or attract buyers to their online, mobile, and social media sites.

A more recent form of direct-response television marketing is *interactive TV (iTV)*, which lets viewers interact with television programming and advertising. Thanks to technologies such as interactive cable systems, Internet-ready smart TVs, and smartphones and tablets, consumers can now use their TV remotes, phones, or other devices to obtain more information or make purchases directly from TV ads. For example, fashion retailer H&M recently ran ads that let viewers with certain Samsung smart TVs use their remotes to interact directly with the commercials. A small pop-up menu, shown as the ads ran, offered product information, the ability to send that information to another device, and the option to buy directly.[44]

Also, increasingly, as the lines continue to blur between TV screens and other video screens, interactive ads and infomercials are appearing not just on TV, but also on mobile, online, and social media platforms, adding even more TV-like interactive direct marketing venues.

Kiosk marketing: Redbox operates more than 42,000 DVD rental kiosks in supermarkets, fast-food restaurants, and other retail outlets.

Images-USA/Alamy

Kiosk Marketing

As consumers become more and more comfortable with digital and touchscreen technologies, many companies are placing information and ordering machines—called *kiosks* (good old-fashioned vending machines but so much more)—in stores, airports, hotels, college campuses, and other locations. Kiosks are everywhere these days, from self-service hotel and airline check-in devices, to unmanned product and information kiosks in malls, to in-store ordering devices that let you order merchandise not carried in the store. Many modern "smart kiosks" are now wireless-enabled. And some machines can even use facial recognition software that lets them guess gender and age and make product recommendations based on that data.

In-store Kodak, Fuji, and HP kiosks let customers transfer pictures from memory cards, mobile phones, and other digital storage devices; edit them; and make high-quality color prints. Seattle's Best kiosks in grocery, drug, and mass merchandise stores grind and brew fresh coffee beans and serve coffee, mochas, and lattes to on-the-go customers around the clock. Redbox operates more than 42,000 DVD rental kiosks in McDonald's, Walmart, Walgreens, CVS, Family Dollar, and other retail outlets—customers make their selections on a touchscreen, then swipe a credit or debit card to rent DVDs for less than $2 a day.

ZoomSystems creates small, free-standing kiosks called ZoomShops for retailers ranging from Apple, Sephora, and The Body Shop to Macy's and Best Buy. For example, 100 Best Buy Express ZoomShop kiosks across the country—conveniently located in airports, busy malls, military bases, retail stores, and resorts—automatically dispense an assortment of portable media players, digital cameras, gaming consoles, headphones, phone chargers, travel gadgets, and other popular products. According to ZoomSystems, today's automated retailing "offers [consumers] the convenience of online shopping with the immediate gratification of traditional retail."[45]

Author Comment
Although we mostly benefit from direct and digital marketing, like most other things in life, they have a dark side as well. Marketers and customers alike must guard against irritating or harmful direct and digital marketing practices.

Public Policy Issues in Direct and Digital Marketing

Direct marketers and their customers usually enjoy mutually rewarding relationships. Occasionally, however, a darker side emerges. The aggressive and sometimes shady tactics of a few direct marketers can bother or harm consumers, giving the entire industry a black eye. Abuses range from simple excesses that irritate consumers to instances of unfair practices or even outright deception and fraud. The direct marketing industry has also faced growing privacy concerns, and online marketers must deal with Internet and mobile security issues.

Irritation, Unfairness, Deception, and Fraud

Direct marketing excesses sometimes annoy or offend consumers. For example, most of us dislike direct-response TV commercials that are too loud, long, and insistent. Our mailboxes fill up with unwanted junk mail, our email inboxes bulge with unwanted spam, and our computer, phone, and tablet screens flash with unwanted online or mobile display ads, pop-ups, or pop-unders.

Beyond irritating consumers, some direct marketers have been accused of taking unfair advantage of impulsive or less-sophisticated buyers. Television shopping channels, enticing Web sites, and program-long infomercials targeting television-addicted shoppers seem to be the worst culprits. They feature smooth-talking hosts, elaborately staged demonstrations, claims of drastic price reductions, "while they last" time limitations, and unequaled ease of purchase to inflame buyers who have low sales resistance.

Fraudulent schemes, such as investment scams or phony collections for charity, have also multiplied in recent years. *Internet fraud*, including identity theft and financial scams, has become a serious problem. >> According to the Internet Crime Complaint Center, since 2005, Internet scam complaints have more than tripled to almost 300,000 per year. Last year, the monetary loss of scam complaints exceeded $800 million.[46]

One common form of Internet fraud is *phishing*, a type of identity theft that uses deceptive emails and fraudulent online sites to fool users into divulging their personal data. For example, consumers may receive an email, supposedly from their bank or credit card company, saying that their account's security has been compromised. The sender asks them to log on to a provided Web address and confirm their account number, password, and perhaps even their Social Security number. If they follow the instructions, users are actually turning this sensitive information over to scam artists. Although many consumers are now aware of such schemes, phishing can be extremely costly to those caught in the net. It also damages the brand identities of legitimate online marketers who have worked to build user confidence in Web, email, and other digital transactions.

Many consumers also worry about *online and digital security*. They fear that unscrupulous snoopers will eavesdrop on their online transactions and social media postings, picking up personal information or intercepting credit and debit card numbers. Although online shopping has grown rapidly, one recent study indicated that 70 percent of participants were still concerned about identity theft.[47]

Another Internet marketing concern is that of *access by vulnerable or unauthorized groups*. For example, marketers of adult-oriented materials and sites have found it difficult to restrict access by minors. Although Facebook allows no children under age 13 to have a profile, it has an estimated 5.6 million underage accounts. It removed some 800,000 underage accounts last year. And it's not just Facebook. Young users are logging onto social media

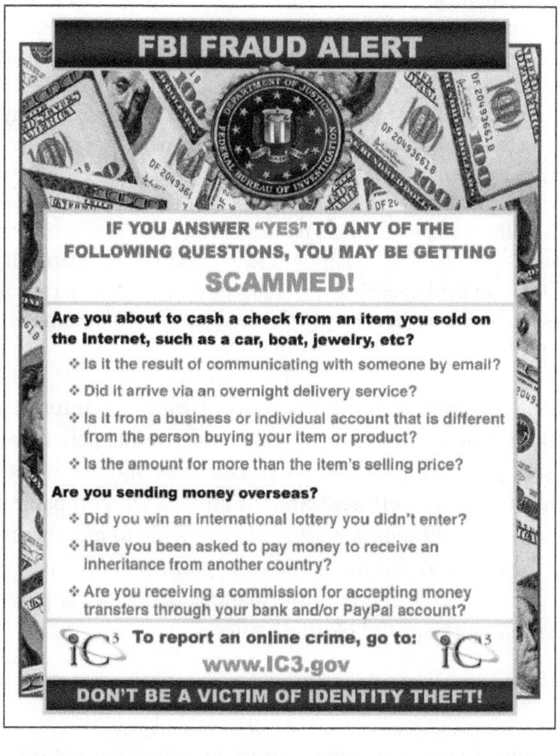

>> **Internet fraud has multiplied in recent years. The FBI's Internet Crime Complaint Center provides consumers with a convenient way to alert authorities to suspected violations.**
FBI

such as Formspring, Tweeting their locations to the Web, and making friends with strangers on Disney and other game sites. Concerned state and national lawmakers are currently debating bills that would help better protect children online. Unfortunately, this requires the development of technology solutions, and as Facebook puts it, "That's not so easy."[48]

Consumer Privacy

Invasion of privacy is perhaps the toughest public policy issue now confronting the direct marketing industry. Consumers often benefit from database marketing; they receive more offers that are closely matched to their interests. However, many critics worry that marketers may know *too* much about consumers' lives and that they may use this knowledge to take unfair advantage of consumers. At some point, they claim, the extensive use of databases intrudes on consumer privacy. Consumers, too, worry about their privacy. Although they are now much more willing to share personal information and preferences with marketers via digital and social media, they are still nervous about it. One recent survey found that 92 percent of U.S. Internet users worry about their privacy online. Another found that more than 90 percent of Americans feel they have lost control over the collection and use by companies of their personal data and information they share on social media sites.[49]

In these days of "big data," it seems that almost every time consumers post something on social media or send a Tweet, visit a Web site, enter a sweepstakes, apply for a credit card, or order products by phone or online, their names are entered into some company's already bulging database. Using sophisticated big data analytics, direct marketers can mine these databases to "microtarget" their selling efforts. Most marketers have become highly skilled at collecting and analyzing detailed consumer information both online and offline. Even the experts are sometimes surprised by how much marketers can learn. Consider this account by one *Advertising Age* reporter:[50]

> I'm no neophyte when it comes to targeting—not only do I work at *Ad Age*, but I cover direct marketing. Yet even I was taken aback when, as an experiment, we asked the database-marketing company to come up with a demographic and psychographic profile of me. Was it ever spot-on. Using only publicly available information, it concluded my date of birth, home phone number, and political-party affiliation. It gleamed that I was a college graduate, that I was married, and that one of my parents had passed away. It found that I have several bank, credit, and retail cards at "low-end" department stores. It knew not just how long I've lived at my house but how much it cost, how much it was worth, the type of mortgage that's on it, and—within a really close ballpark guess—how much is left to pay on it. It estimated my household income—again nearly perfectly—and determined that I am of British descent.
>
> But that was just the beginning. The company also nailed my psychographic profile. It correctly placed me into various groupings such as: someone who relies more on their own opinions than the recommendations of others when making a purchase; someone who is turned off by loud and aggressive advertising; someone who is family-oriented and has an interest in music, running, sports, computers, and is an avid concert-goer; someone who is never far from an Internet connection, generally used to peruse sports and general news updates; and someone who sees health as a core value. Scary? Certainly.

Some consumers and policy makers worry that the ready availability of information may leave consumers open to abuse. For example, they ask, should online sellers be allowed to plant cookies in the browsers of consumers who visit their sites and use tracking information to target ads and other marketing efforts? Should credit card companies be allowed to make data on their millions of cardholders worldwide available to merchants who accept their cards? Or is it right for states to sell the names and addresses of driver's license holders, along with height, weight, and gender information, allowing apparel retailers to target tall or overweight people with special clothing offers?

A Need for Action

To curb direct marketing excesses, various government agencies are investigating not only do-not-call lists but also do-not-mail lists, do-not-track-online lists, and Can Spam legislation. In response to online privacy and security concerns, the federal government has considered numerous legislative actions to regulate how online, social media, and mobile operators obtain and use consumer information. For example, Congress is drafting legislation that would give consumers more control over how online information is used. In addition, the FTC is taking a more active role in policing online privacy.

All of these concerns call for strong actions by marketers to monitor and prevent privacy abuses before legislators step in to do it for them. For example, to head off increased government regulation, six advertiser groups—the American Association of Advertising Agencies, the American Advertising Federation, the Association of National Advertisers, the Direct Marketing Association, the Interactive Advertising Bureau, and the Network Advertising Initiative—recently issued a set of online advertising principles through the Digital Advertising Alliance. Among other measures, the self-regulatory principles call for online marketers to provide transparency and choice to consumers if online viewing data are collected or used for targeting interest-based advertising. The ad industry uses an *advertising option icon*—a little "i" inside a triangle—that it adds to behaviorally targeted online ads to tell consumers why they are seeing a particular ad and allowing them to opt out.[51]

Consumer privacy: The ad industry has agreed on an *advertising option icon* that will tell consumers why they are seeing a particular ad and allow them to opt out.

Digital Advertising Alliance

Of special concern are the privacy rights of children. In 2000, Congress passed the Children's Online Privacy Protection Act (COPPA), which requires online operators targeting children to post privacy policies on their sites. They must also notify parents about any information they're gathering and obtain parental consent before collecting personal information from children under age 13. With the subsequent advent of online social media, mobile phones, and other digital technologies, Congress in 2013 extended COPPA to include "identifiers such as cookies that track a child's activity online, as well as geolocation information, photos, videos, and audio recordings." The main concern is the amount of data mined by third parties from social media as well as social media's own hazy privacy policies.[52]

Many companies have responded to consumer privacy and security concerns with actions of their own. Still others are taking an industry-wide approach. For example, TRUSTe, a nonprofit self-regulatory organization, works with many large corporate sponsors, including Microsoft, Yahoo!, AT&T, Facebook, Disney, and Apple, to audit privacy and security measures and help consumers navigate the Internet safely. According to the company's Web site, "TRUSTe believes that an environment of mutual trust and openness will help make and keep the Internet a free, comfortable, and richly diverse community for everyone." To reassure consumers, the company lends its TRUSTe privacy seal to Web sites, mobile apps, email marketing, and other online and social media channels that meet its privacy and security standards.[53]

The direct marketing industry as a whole is also addressing public policy issues. For example, in an effort to build consumer confidence in shopping direct, the Direct Marketing Association—the largest association for businesses practicing direct, database, and interactive marketing, including nearly half of the *Fortune* 100 companies—launched a "Privacy Promise to American Consumers." The Privacy Promise requires that all DMA members adhere to a carefully developed set of consumer privacy rules. Members must agree to notify customers when any personal information is rented, sold, or exchanged with others. They must also honor consumer requests to opt out of receiving further solicitations or having their contact information transferred to other marketers. Finally, they must abide by the DMA's Preference Service by removing the names of consumers who do not wish to receive mail, phone, or email offers.[54]

Direct marketers know that, if left untended, such direct marketing abuses will lead to increasingly negative consumer attitudes, lower response and engagement rates, and calls for more restrictive state and federal legislation. Most direct marketers want the same things that consumers want: honest and well-designed marketing offers targeted only toward consumers who will appreciate and respond to them. Direct marketing is just too expensive to waste on consumers who don't want it.

MyMarketingLab

If assigned by your instructor, complete the questions marked with the from the EOC Discussion Questions section in the MyLab. To complete the Marketing by the Numbers problems found in this section, go to your Assignments in the MyLab.

REVIEWING AND EXTENDING THE CONCEPTS

CHAPTER REVIEW AND CRITICAL THINKING

Objectives Review

This chapter is the last of three chapters covering the final marketing mix element—promotion. The previous chapters dealt with advertising, public relations, personal selling, and sales promotion. This one investigates the burgeoning field of direct and digital marketing, including online, social media, and mobile marketing.

OBJECTIVE 14-1 Define *direct and digital marketing* and discuss their rapid growth and benefits to customers and companies. (pp 430–432)

Direct and digital marketing involve engaging directly with carefully targeted individual consumers and customer communities to both obtain an immediate response and build lasting customer relationships. Companies use direct marketing to tailor their offers and content to the needs and interests of narrowly defined segments or individual buyers to build direct customer engagement, brand community, and sales. Today, spurred by the surge in Internet usage and buying and by rapid advances in digital technologies—from smartphones, tablets, and other digital devices to the spate of online social and mobile media—direct marketing has undergone a dramatic transformation.

For buyers, direct and digital marketing are convenient, easy to use, and private. They give buyers anywhere, anytime access to an almost unlimited assortment of products and buying information. Direct marketing is also immediate and interactive, allowing buyers to create exactly the configuration of information, products, or services they desire and then order them on the spot. Finally, for consumers who want it, digital marketing through online, mobile, and social media provides a sense of brand engagement and community—a place to share brand information and experiences with other brand fans. For sellers, direct and digital marketing are powerful tools for building customer engagement and close, personalized, interactive customer relationships. They also offer greater flexibility, letting marketers make ongoing adjustments to prices and programs or make immediate, timely, and personal announcements and offers.

OBJECTIVE 14-2 Identify and discuss the major forms of direct and digital marketing. (pp 432–433)

The main forms of direct and digital marketing include traditional direct marketing tools and the new digital marketing tools. Traditional direct approaches are face-to-face personal selling, direct-mail marketing, catalog marketing, telemarketing, DRTV marketing, and kiosk marketing. These traditional tools are still heavily used and very important in most firms' direct marketing efforts. In recent years, however, a dazzling new set of direct digital marketing tools has burst onto the marketing scene, including online marketing (Web sites, online ads and promotions, email, online videos, and blogs), social media marketing, and mobile marketing. The chapter first discusses the fast-growing new digital direct marketing tools and then examines the traditional tools.

OBJECTIVE 14-3 Explain how companies have responded to the Internet and the digital age with various online marketing strategies. (pp 433–439)

The Internet and digital age have fundamentally changed customers' notions of convenience, speed, price, product information, service, and brand interactions. As a result, they have given marketers a whole new way to create customer value, engage customers, and build customer relationships. The Internet now influences a staggering 50 percent of total sales—including sales transacted online plus those made in stores but encouraged by online research. To reach this burgeoning market, most companies now market online.

Online marketing takes several forms, including company Web sites, online advertising and promotions, email marketing, online video, and blogs. Social media and mobile marketing also take place online. But because of their special characteristics, we discuss these fast-growing digital marketing approaches in separate sections. For most companies, the first step in conducting online marketing is to create a Web site. The key to a successful Web site is to create enough value and engagement to get consumers to come to the site, stick around, and come back again.

Online advertising has become a major promotional medium. The main forms of online advertising are display ads and search-related ads. Email marketing is also an important form of digital marketing. Used properly, email lets marketers send highly targeted, tightly personalized, relationship-building messages. Another important form of online marketing is posting digital video content on brand Web sites or social media. Marketers hope that some of their videos will go viral, engaging consumers by the tens of millions. Finally, companies can use blogs as effective means of reaching customer communities. They can create their own blogs and advertise on existing blogs or influence content there.

OBJECTIVE 14-4 Discuss how companies use social media and mobile marketing to engage consumers and create brand community. (pp 439–447)

In the digital age, countless independent and commercial social media have arisen that give consumers online places to congregate, socialize, and exchange views and information. Most marketers are now riding this huge social media wave. Brands can use existing social media or they can set up their own. Using existing social media seems the easiest. Thus, most brands—large and small—have set up shop on a host of social media sites. Some of the major social networks are huge; other niche social media cater to the needs of smaller communities of like-minded people. Beyond these independent social media, many companies have created their own online brand communities. More than making just scattered efforts and chasing "Likes" and Tweets, most companies are integrating a broad range of diverse media to create brand-related social sharing, engagement, and customer community.

Using social media presents both advantages and challenges. On the plus side, social media are targeted and personal, interactive, immediate and timely, and cost-effective. Perhaps the biggest advantage is their engagement and social sharing capabilities, making them ideal for creating customer community. On the down side, consumers' control over social media content makes social media difficult to control.

Mobile marketing features marketing messages, promotions, and other content delivered to on-the-go consumers through their mobile devices. Marketers use mobile marketing to engage customers anywhere, anytime during the buying and relationship-building processes. The widespread adoption of mobile devices and the surge in mobile Web traffic have made mobile marketing a must for most brands, and almost every major marketer is now integrating mobile marketing into its direct marketing programs. Many marketers have created their own mobile online sites. Others have created useful or entertaining mobile apps to engage customers with their brands and help them shop.

OBJECTIVE 14-5 Identify and discuss the traditional direct marketing forms and overview the public policy and ethical issues presented by direct marketing. (pp 447–453)

Although the fast-growing digital marketing tools have grabbed most of the headlines lately, traditional direct marketing tools are very much alive and still heavily used. The major forms are face-to-face or personal selling, direct-mail marketing, catalog marketing, telemarketing, direct-response television (DRTV) marketing, and kiosk marketing.

Direct-mail marketing consists of the company sending an offer, announcement, reminder, or other item to a person at a specific address. Some marketers rely on catalog marketing—selling through catalogs mailed to a select list of customers, made available in stores, or accessed online. Telemarketing consists of using the telephone to sell directly to consumers. DRTV marketing has two forms: direct-response advertising (or infomercials) and interactive television (iTV) marketing. Kiosks are information and ordering machines that direct marketers place in stores, airports, hotels, and other locations.

Direct marketers and their customers usually enjoy mutually rewarding relationships. Sometimes, however, direct marketing presents a darker side. The aggressive and sometimes shady tactics of a few direct marketers can bother or harm consumers, giving the entire industry a black eye. Abuses range from simple excesses that irritate consumers to instances of unfair practices or even outright deception and fraud. The direct marketing industry has also faced growing concerns about invasion-of-privacy and Internet security issues. Such concerns call for strong action by marketers and public policy makers to curb direct marketing abuses. In the end, most direct marketers want the same things that consumers want: honest and well-designed marketing offers targeted only toward consumers who will appreciate and respond to them.

Key Terms

Objective 14-1
Direct and digital marketing (p 430)

Objective 14-2
Digital and social media marketing (p 433)

Objective 14-3
Omni-channel retailing (p 434)
Online marketing (p 434)
Marketing Web site (p 434)
Branded community Web site (p 435)
Online advertising (p 435)
Email marketing (p 436)
Spam (p 437)
Viral marketing (p 437)
Blogs (p 438)

Objective 14-4
Social media (p 439)
Mobile marketing (p 443)

Objective 14-5
Direct-mail marketing (p 447)
Catalog marketing (p 448)
Telemarketing (p 449)
Direct-response television (DRTV) marketing (p 449)

Discussion Questions

14-1. Discuss the benefits of direct and digital marketing to buyers and sellers. (AACSB: Communication)

14-2. What are blogs, and how are marketers using them to market their products and services? What advantages and disadvantages do blogs pose for marketers? (AACSB: Communication)

14-3. Discuss the advantages and challenges of social media marketing. (AASCB: Communication)

14-4. List and briefly describe the major traditional forms of direct marketing. (AACSB: Communication)

14-5. What is phishing, and how does it affect Internet marketing? (AACSB: Communication; Reflective Thinking)

Critical Thinking Exercises

14-6. In a small group, design and deliver a direct response television (DRTV) ad for a national brand not normally associated with this type of promotion, such as an athletic shoe, automobile, or food product. (AACSB: Communication; Reflective Thinking)

14-7. Review the Telephone Consumer Protection Act and discuss a recent case in which a marketer was fined for violating the act. (AACSB: Communication; Use of IT; Reflective Thinking)

14-8. Although mobile advertising makes up a small percentage of online advertising, it is one of the fastest-growing advertising channels. But one obstacle is measuring return on investment in mobile advertising. How are marketers doing so? Develop a presentation suggesting metrics marketers should use to measure effectiveness of mobile advertising. (AACSB: Communication; Use of IT; Reflective Thinking)

MINICASES AND APPLICATIONS

Online, Social Media, and Mobile Marketing "Buy" Buttons

Amazon is the big gun in e-commerce that has disrupted traditional retailing. But now, it seems, Amazon is in for some disruptive competition itself. With global e-commerce sales expected to reach almost $2 trillion a year, Google and social media sites such as Facebook, Twitter, Pinterest, and Instagram want to get in on the action. Several social media sites are experimenting with "Buy" buttons on their sites that let consumers purchase directly through the social medium. Google is experimenting with "Buy" buttons on search results to counter the almost 40 percent of consumers who now start their shopping searches on Amazon instead of search engines like Google. The biggest game changer, however, might be Pinterest. Pinterest started in 1999 as a sharable bulletin board where participants "pin" pictures of things they like. It is now a multibillion-dollar company with 70 million monthly visitors who have saved more than 50 billion objects on a billion Pinterest bulletin boards. Lots of people would like to be able to buy some of those pinned objects, so Pinterest has added a "Buy" button to its mobile app. Users had already been able to click through to a marketer's Web site, but now they can purchase any of more than 2 million products from retailers such as Macy's, Bloomingdales, and Nordstrom directly through Pinterest without leaving the site. Payments are processed through Pinterest's partners Stripe, Brainstorm, or Apply Pay, but the seller provides the order fulfillment. In the future, Pinterest users may see an appetizing recipe, click the "Buy" button to order the ingredients from Fresh Direct, and have them delivered to their homes in less than an hour.

14-9. What competitive advantage does Pinterest (www.pinterest.com) have over other social media that might make its "Buy" button more successful? (AACSB: Communication; Reflective Thinking)

14-10. Discuss advantages and disadvantages of "Buy" buttons for social media sites like Pinterest and search engines like Google. What are the advantages and disadvantages for marketers making their goods available through "Buy" buttons on these sites? (AACSB Communication; Reflective Thinking)

Marketing Ethics Tracking in "Meat Space"

By now, you know about behavioral targeting—marketers tracking consumers' online behavior in cyberspace to send them targeted advertising. Krux Digital reports that the average visit to a Web page generated 56 instances of data collection, a fivefold increase in just one year. An investigation by *The Wall Street Journal* found that the 50 most popular U.S. Web sites installed more than 3,000 tracking files on the computer used in the study. The total was even higher—4,123 tracking files—for the top 50 sites that are popular with children and teens. Many sites installed more than 100 tracking tools each during the tests. Tracking tools include files placed on users' computers and on Web sites. Marketers use this information to target online advertisements. But now, wearable and mobile devices allow marketers to track consumer movements in the physical world. The term *meat space* refers to the physical world in which our bodies move and do things, and marketers are using information obtained from wearable and mobile devices to personalize offers while consumers move around their space. With the growing trend in smartphone tracking and wearable technology such as smartwatches, fitness bands, and smart garments that are part of the "Internet of Things," tracking consumers in meat space is only going to grow.

14-11. Debate whether it is ethical to track consumers' physical movements, especially children's movements. (AACSB: Communication; Ethical Reasoning)

14-12. Discuss other ways marketers can track consumers in meat space. (AACSB: Communication; Reflective Thinking)

Marketing by the Numbers Field Sales versus Telemarketing

Many companies are realizing the efficiency of telemarketing in the face of soaring sales force costs. Whereas a business-to-business sales call by an outside salesperson on average costs $600, the cost of a telemarketing sales call can be as little as $20 to $30. And telemarketers can make 20 to 33 decision-maker contacts per day to a salesperson's four per day. This has gotten the attention of many business-to-business marketers, where telemarketing can be very effective.

14-13. Refer to Appendix 3: Marketing by the Numbers to determine the marketing return on sales (marketing ROS) and return on marketing investment (marketing ROI) for company A and company B in the chart below. Which company is performing better? Explain. (AACSB: Communication; Analytical Reasoning; Reflective Thinking)

	Company A (sales force only)	Company B (telemarketing only)
Net sales	$1,000,000	$850,000
Cost of goods sold	$500,000	$425,000
Sales expenses	$300,000	$100,000

14-14. Should all companies consider reducing their sales forces in favor of telemarketing? Discuss the pros and cons of this action. (AACSB: Communication; Reflective Thinking)

Video Case Nutrisystem

You've probably heard of Nutrisystem, a company that produced $800 million in revenues last year by selling weight-loss products. What started as a small effort based on an e-commerce marketing plan has evolved into a multipronged marketing campaign that not only has expanded the business but also provides substantial return-on-investment potential.

The key to Nutrisystem's efforts is its direct-to-consumer platform. Using various advertising outlets, from magazines to television, Nutrisystem's promotions all have one thing in common—they let customers make direct contact with the company. Inserting a unique URL or 800 number in every ad also lets Nutrisystem track the success of each and every effort.

After viewing the video featuring Nutrisystem, answer the following questions:

14-15. In what different ways does Nutrisystem engage in direct marketing?

14-16. What advantages does Nutrisystem's marketing campaign have over selling through intermediary channels?

14-17. In addition to its direct-to-consumer distribution and promotional efforts, what is essential to the success of Nutrisystem?

Company Cases 14 Alibaba/10 Apple Pay/11 Sears

See Appendix 1 for cases appropriate for this chapter. **Case 14, Alibaba: The World's Largest E-Tailer Is Not Amazon.** Selling more than Amazon and EBay combined, Alibaba's rapid growth may keep it out in front for good. **Case 10, Apple Pay: Taking Mobile Payments Mainstream.** Apple may succeed where Google, Paypal, Visa, and others have failed in making mobile payments the go-to way to pay. **Case 11, Sears: Why Should You Shop There?** Formerly the leading retailer, Sears struggles for survival by trying everything, including building an ecommerce presence.

MyMarketingLab

If assigned by your instructor, complete these writing sections from your Assignments in the MyLab.

14-18. Compare and contrast a marketing Web site and a branded community Web site. (AACSB: Communication)

14-19. Review the FTC's guidelines on disclosure in online, social media, and mobile advertisements at www.ftc.gov/os/2013/03/130312dotcomdisclosures.pdf. Will the FTC's requirements regarding ads and endorsements make Twitter less effective as an advertising medium?

15 The Global Marketplace

CHAPTER ROAD MAP Objective Outline

OBJECTIVE 15-1 **Discuss how the international trade system and the economic, political-legal, and cultural environments affect a company's international marketing decisions.** Global Marketing Today (460–462); Looking at the Global Marketing Environment (462–470); Deciding Whether to Go Global (470); Deciding Which Markets to Enter (471–472)

OBJECTIVE 15-2 **Describe three key approaches to entering international markets.** Deciding How to Enter the Market (472–475)

OBJECTIVE 15-3 **Explain how companies adapt their marketing strategies and mixes for international markets.** Deciding on the Global Marketing Program (475–482)

OBJECTIVE 15-4 **Identify the three major forms of international marketing organization.** Deciding on the Global Marketing Organization (483)

Previewing the Concepts

You've now learned the fundamentals of how companies develop competitive marketing strategies to engage customers, create customer value, and build lasting customer relationships. In this chapter, we extend these fundamentals to global marketing. Although we've discussed global topics in each previous chapter—it's difficult to find an area of marketing that doesn't contain at least some international elements—here we'll focus on special considerations that companies face when they market their brands globally. Advances in communication, transportation, and digital technologies have made the world a much smaller place. Today, almost every firm, large or small, faces international marketing issues. In this chapter, we will examine six major decisions marketers make in going global.

To start our exploration of global marketing, let's look at L'Oréal, the French cosmetics and beauty care giant. L'Oréal and its brands are truly global in scope and appeal. But the company's outstanding international success comes from achieving a global–local balance, one that adapts and differentiates L'Oréal's well-known brands to meet local needs while also integrating them across world markets to optimize their global impact. You can think of L'Oréal as a kind of "United Nations of beauty."

First Stop

L'Oréal: "The United Nations of Beauty"

» Global–local balance: Cosmetics and beauty care giant L'Oréal balances local brand responsiveness and global brand impact, making it "The United Nations of Beauty."

Marc Piasecki/Stringer/Getty images

How does a French company successfully market an American version of a Korean skin-beautifier under a French brand name in Australia? Ask L'Oréal, which sells more than $25 billion worth of cosmetics, hair care products, skin care concoctions, and fragrances each year in 130 countries, making it the world's biggest cosmetics marketer. L'Oréal sells its brands globally by understanding how they appeal to varied cultural nuances of beauty in specific local markets. Then it finds the best balance between standardizing its brands for global impact and adapting them to meet local needs and desires.

L'Oréal is as global as a company gets. With offices spread across 130 nations and more than half of its sales coming from markets outside Europe and North America, the company no longer has a clearly defined home market. L'Oréal's well-known brands originated in a half dozen or more different cultures, including French (L'Oréal Paris, Garnier, Lancôme), American (Maybelline, Kiehl's, SoftSheen-Carson, Ralph Lauren, Urban Decay, Clarisonic, Redken), British (The Body Shop), Italian (Giorgio Armani), and Japanese (Shu Uemura). With these and many other well-known brands, the master global marketer is the uncontested world leader in makeup, skin care, and hair coloring and second only to P&G in hair care.

L'Oréal's global mastery starts with a corps of highly multicultural managers. The company is famous for building global brand teams around managers who have deep backgrounds in several cultures. L'Oréal managers around the world bring diverse cultural perspectives to their brands as if they were, say, German or American or Chinese—or all three at once. As explained by one Indian-American-French manager of a team that launched a men's skin care line in Southeast Asia: "I cannot think about things one way. I have a stock of references in different languages: English, Hindi, and French. I read books in three different languages, meet people from different countries, eat food from different [cultures], and so on."

For example, a French-Irish-Cambodian skin care manager noticed that, in Europe, face creams tended to be either "tinted" (and considered makeup) or "lifting" (considered skin care). In Asia, however, many face creams combine both traits. Recognizing the growing popularity of Asian beauty trends in Europe, the manager and his team developed a tinted lifting cream for the French market, a product that proved highly successful.

L'Oréal digs deep to understand what beauty means to consumers in different parts of the world. It outspends all major competitors on R&D, painstakingly researching beauty and personal care behaviors unique to specific locales. L'Oréal has set up R&D centers all over the world, perfecting a local observation approach it calls "geocosmetics." This science is fueled with insights gained through everything from in-home visits to observations made in "bathroom laboratories" equipped with high-tech gadgetry. L'Oréal's research produces precise information about regional beauty and hygiene rituals and about local conditions and constraints that affect the use of its products, such as humidity and temperature:

> How many minutes does a Chinese woman devote to her morning beauty routine? How do people wash their hair in Bangkok? How many brush strokes does a Japanese woman or a French woman use to apply mascara? These beauty rituals, repeated thousands of times, are inherently cultural. Passed on by tradition, influenced by climate and by local living conditions, they strive to achieve an ideal of perfection that is different from one country and from one continent to the next. They provide an incredibly rich source of information for L'Oréal. Behind these rituals, there are physiological realities: fine, straight, and short eyelashes cannot be made up the same way as thick, curled, and long lashes.

L'Oréal uses such detailed insights to create products and positioning for brands in local markets. "Beauty is less and less one size fits all," says a L'Oréal executive in China. "You have to have an answer for very different needs." For example, more than 260 scientists now work in L'Oréal's Shanghai research center, tailoring products ranging from lipstick to herbal cleaners to cucumber toners for Chinese tastes.

Cosmetic and beauty care giant L'Oréal and its brands are truly global. But the company's huge international success comes from a global–local balance that adapts brands to local markets while optimizing their impact globally.

At the same time that understanding the minute details of local customer behavior helps L'Oréal be responsive to specific market needs, it also lets the company achieve global scale by integrating brands across world cultures. For example, consider Elséve Total Reparação, a hair care line initially developed at L'Oréal's labs in Rio de Janeiro to address specific hair problems described by Brazilian women. In Brazil, more than half of all women have long, dry, dull, and very curly hair, resulting from the humid Brazilian climate, exposure to the sun, frequent washing, and smoothing and straightening treatments. Elséve Total Reparação was an immediate hit in Brazil, and L'Oréal quickly rolled it out to other South American and Latin American markets. The company then tracked down other global locales with

Companies that ignore cultural norms and differences can make some very expensive and embarrassing mistakes. Here are two examples:

> Nike inadvertently offended Chinese officials when it ran an ad featuring LeBron James crushing a number of culturally revered Chinese figures in a kung fu–themed television ad. The Chinese government found that the ad violated regulations to uphold national dignity and respect the "motherland's culture" and yanked the multimillion-dollar campaign. With egg on its face, Nike released a formal apology. Burger King made a similar mistake when it created in-store ads in Spain showing Hindu goddess Lakshmi atop a ham sandwich with the caption "a snack that is sacred." Cultural and religious groups worldwide objected strenuously—Hindus are vegetarian. Burger King apologized and pulled the ads.[19]

Business norms and behaviors also vary from country to country. For example, American executives like to get right down to business and engage in fast and tough face-to-face bargaining. However, Japanese and other Asian businesspeople often find this behavior offensive. They prefer to start with polite conversation, and they rarely say no in face-to-face conversations. As another example, firm handshakes are a common and expected greeting in most Western countries; in some Middle Eastern countries, however, handshakes might be refused if offered. Microsoft founder Bill Gates once set off a flurry of international controversy when he shook the hand of South Korea's president with his right hand while keeping his left hand in his pocket, something that Koreans consider highly disrespectful. In some countries, when being entertained at a meal, not finishing all the food implies that it was somehow substandard. In other countries, in contrast, wolfing down every last bite might be taken as a mild insult, suggesting that the host didn't supply enough quantity.[20] American business executives need to understand these kinds of cultural nuances before conducting business in another country.

By the same token, companies that understand cultural nuances can use them to their advantage in the global markets. For example, furniture retailer IKEA's stores are a big draw for up-and-coming Chinese consumers. » But IKEA has learned that customers in China want a lot more from its stores than just affordable Scandinavian-designed furniture:[21]

» The impact of culture on marketing strategy: IKEA customers in China want a lot more from its stores than just affordable Scandinavian-designed furniture.
ZUMA Press, Inc./Alamy

> In Chinese, IKEA is known as Yi Jia. Translated, it means "comfortable home," a concept taken literally by the millions of consumers who visit one of IKEA's 18 huge Chinese stores each year. "Customers come on family outings, hop into display beds and nap, pose for snapshots with the décor, and hang out for hours to enjoy the air conditioning and free soda refills," notes one observer. On a typical Saturday afternoon, for example, display beds and other furniture in a huge Chinese IKEA store are occupied with customers of all ages lounging or even fast asleep. One Chinese IKEA has even hosted several weddings. IKEA managers encourage such behavior, figuring that familiarity with the store will result in later purchasing when shoppers' incomes eventually rise to match their aspirations. "Maybe if you've been visiting IKEA, eating meatballs, hot dogs, or ice cream for 10 years, then maybe you will consider IKEA when you get yourself a sofa," says the company's Asia-Pacific president. Thanks to such cultural understandings coupled with competitively low prices, China was IKEA's fastest-growing market last year. What do Chinese consumers think of Swedish meatballs? "They love them," says IKEA China's marketing director.

Thus, understanding cultural traditions, preferences, and behaviors can help companies not only avoid embarrassing mistakes but also take advantage of cross-cultural opportunities.

The Impact of Marketing Strategy on Cultures

Whereas marketers worry about the impact of global cultures on their marketing strategies, others may worry about the impact of marketing strategies on global cultures. For example, social critics contend that large American multinationals, such as McDonald's, Coca-Cola, Starbucks, Nike, Google, Disney, and Facebook, aren't just globalizing their brands; they are Americanizing the world's cultures. Other elements of American culture have become pervasive worldwide. For instance, more people now study English in China than speak it in the United States. If you assemble businesspeople from Brazil, Germany, and China, they'll likely transact in English. And the thing that binds the world's teens together in a kind of global community, notes one observer, "is American culture—the music, the Hollywood fare, the electronic games, Google, Facebook, American consumer brands. The . . . rest of the world is becoming [evermore] like us—in ways good and bad."[22]

"Today, globalization often wears Mickey Mouse ears, eats Big Macs, drinks Coke or Pepsi, and does its computing with Windows," says Thomas Friedman in his book *The Lexus and the Olive Tree: Understanding Globalization.* "Some Chinese kids' first English word [is] Mickey," notes another writer.[23]

Critics worry that, under such "McDomination," countries around the globe are losing their individual cultural identities. Teens in Turkey watch MTV, connect with others globally through Facebook and Twitter, and ask their parents for more Westernized clothes and other symbols of American pop culture and values. Grandmothers in small European villas no longer spend each morning visiting local meat, bread, and produce markets to gather the ingredients for dinner. Instead, they now shop at Walmart. Women in Saudi Arabia see American films, question their societal roles, and shop at any of the country's growing number of Victoria's Secret boutiques. In China, most people never drank coffee before Starbucks entered the market. Now Chinese consumers rush to Starbucks stores because it symbolizes a new kind of lifestyle. Similarly, in China, where McDonald's operates more than 80 restaurants in Beijing alone, nearly half of all children identify the chain as a domestic brand.

Such concerns have sometimes led to a backlash against American globalization. Well-known U.S. brands have become the targets of boycotts and protests in some international markets. As symbols of American capitalism, companies such as Coca-Cola, McDonald's, Nike, and KFC have been singled out by protestors and governments in hot spots around the world, especially when anti-American sentiment peaks. For example, following Russia's annexation of Crimea and the resulting sanctions by the West, Russian authorities initiated a crackdown on McDonald's franchises (even though most were Russian-owned), forcing some to close for uncertain reasons. The three McDonald's in Crimea were shuttered, with at least one becoming a nationalist chain outlet called Rusburger, serving "Czar Cheeseburgers" where Quarter Pounders once flowed.[24]

Despite such problems, defenders of globalization argue that concerns of Americanization and the potential damage to American brands are overblown. U.S. brands are doing very well internationally. In the most recent Millward Brown BrandZ brand value survey of global consumer brands, 19 of the top 25 global brands were American owned, including megabrands such as Google, Apple, IBM, Microsoft, McDonald's, Coca-Cola, GE, Amazon.com, and Walmart.[25]

Many iconic American brands are soaring globally. For example, most international markets covet American fast food. Consider KFC in Japan. On the day that KFC introduced its outrageous Double Down sandwich—bacon, melted cheese, and a "secret sauce" between two deep-fried chicken patties—in one of its restaurants in Japan, fans formed long lines and slept on the sidewalks outside to get a taste. "It was like the iPhone," says the CMO of KFC International, "people [were] crazy." The U.S. limited-time item has since become a runaway success worldwide, from Canada to Australia, the Philippines, and Malaysia. >> More broadly, KFC has become its own cultural institution in Japan. For instance, the brand has long been one of Japan's leading Christmas dining traditions, with the iconic Colonel Sanders standing in as a kind of Japanese Father Christmas:[26]

>> American brands in other cultures: KFC has become one of Japan's leading Christmas dining traditions, with the iconic Colonel Sanders standing in as a kind of Japanese Father Christmas.

Anthea Freshwater

> Japan's KFC Christmas tradition began more than 40 years ago when the company unleashed a "Kentucky for Christmas" advertising campaign in Japan to help the brand get off the ground. Now, eating Kentucky Fried Chicken has become one of the country's most popular

holiday traditions. Each KFC store displays a life-size Colonel Sanders statue, adorned in a traditional fur-trimmed red suit and Santa hat. A month in advance, Japanese customers order their special Christmas meal—a special bucket of fried chicken with wine and cake for about US $40. Those who don't preorder risk standing in lines that snake around the block or having to go without KFC's coveted blend of 11 herbs and spices altogether. Christmas Eve is KFC's most successful sales day of the year in Japan, and December monthly sales run as much as 10 times greater than sales in other months.

More fundamentally, the cultural exchange goes both ways: America gets as well as gives cultural influence. True, Hollywood dominates the global movie market, but British TV originated the programming that was Americanized into such hits as *House of Cards* and *Dancing with the Stars*. Although Chinese and Russian youth are donning NBA superstar jerseys, the increasing popularity of soccer in America has deep international roots.

Even American childhood has been increasingly influenced by European and Asian cultural imports. Most kids know all about imports such as Hello Kitty, the Bakugan Battle Brawler, or any of a host of Nintendo or Sega game characters. And J. K. Rowling's so-very-British Harry Potter books shaped the thinking of a generation of American youngsters, not to mention the millions of American oldsters who fell under their spell as well. For the moment, English remains the dominant language of the Internet, and having Web and mobile access often means that third-world youth have greater exposure to American popular culture. Yet these same technologies let Eastern European students studying in the United States hear Webcast news and music from Poland, Romania, or Belarus.

Thus, globalization is a two-way street. If globalization has Mickey Mouse ears, it is also talking on a Samsung smartphone, buying furniture at IKEA, driving a Toyota Camry, and watching a British-inspired show on a Panasonic LED TV.

Deciding Whether to go Global

Not all companies need to venture into international markets to survive. For example, most local businesses need to market well only in their local marketplaces. Operating domestically is easier and safer. Managers don't need to learn another country's language and laws. They don't have to deal with unstable currencies, face political and legal uncertainties, or redesign their products to suit different customer expectations. However, companies that operate in global industries, where their strategic positions in specific markets are affected strongly by their overall global positions, must compete on a regional or worldwide basis to succeed.

Any of several factors might draw a company into the international arena. For example, global competitors might attack the company's home market by offering better products or lower prices. The company might want to counterattack these competitors in their home markets to tie up their resources. The company's customers might be expanding abroad and require international servicing. Or, most likely, international markets might simply provide better opportunities for growth. For example, as note previously, Coca-Cola has emphasized international growth in recent years to offset stagnant or declining U.S. soft drink sales. Today, non-U.S. sales account for 57 percent of Coca-Cola's total revenues and 83 percent of its net income, and the company is making major pushes into 90 emerging markets, such as China, India, and the entire African continent.[27]

Before going abroad, the company must weigh several risks and answer many questions about its ability to operate globally. Can the company learn to understand the preferences and buyer behavior of consumers in other countries? Can it offer competitively attractive products? Will it be able to adapt to other countries' business cultures and deal effectively with foreign nationals? Do the company's managers have the necessary international experience? Has management considered the impact of regulations and the political environments of other countries?

Deciding Which Markets to Enter

Before going abroad, the company should try to define its international *marketing objectives and policies*. It should decide what *volume* of foreign sales it wants. Most companies start small when they go abroad. Some plan to stay small, seeing international sales as a small part of their business. Other companies have bigger plans, however, seeing international business as equal to—or even more important than—their domestic business.

The company also needs to choose in *how many* countries it wants to market. Companies must be careful not to spread themselves too thin or expand beyond their capabilities by operating in too many countries too soon. Next, the company needs to decide on the *types* of countries to enter. A country's attractiveness depends on the product, geographical factors, income and population, political climate, and other considerations. In recent years, many major new markets have emerged, offering both substantial opportunities and daunting challenges.

Entering new global markets: Netflix's decision to expand into new European markets seems like a no-brainer. But despite its huge market potential, Europe presents Netflix with some formidable challenges.

PSL Images/Alamy (logo)/Abstract images/Alamy (map)

After listing possible international markets, the company must carefully evaluate each one. It must consider many factors. For example, Netflix's decision to expand into European markets such as Germany, France, Austria, and Switzerland seems like a no-brainer. Netflix needs to grow its subscriber base to cover rapidly rising content costs, and Europe offers huge opportunities. Western Europe boasts 134 million broadband homes, compared with 94 million in the United States. The as-yet-largely-untapped European video-services market is expected to grow by 67 percent to more than $1.1 billion by 2017. Netflix has already entered the UK and the Nordic nations and is the leading video service in Sweden after only two years.[28]

However, as Netflix considers expanding into new European markets, it must ask some important questions. Can it compete effectively on a country-by-country basis with local competitors? Can it master the varied cultural and buying differences of European consumers? Will it be able to meet environmental and regulatory hurdles in each country? For example, Netflix's expansion has been slow and difficult in Latin America, where e-commerce is less established.

In entering new European markets, Netflix will face many challenges. For example, Europe is now crowded with formidable competitors. More than a dozen local Netflix-like rivals have sprung up there during the past few years—services such as Snap in Germany, Infinity in Italy, and CanalPlay in France have been busy locking in subscribers and content rights. And Amazon.com's Prime Instant Video is already the leading streaming service in Germany.

Content is another major consideration. Although Netflix is building its own portfolio of international content rights, European competitors already own exclusive in-country rights to many popular U.S. and non-U.S. shows. Netflix may also encounter local regulatory obstacles. Regulations in France, for instance, restrict services like Netflix from airing films until three years after they open nationally in theaters, and video services there are usually required to invest in film production in the country. Despite these challenges, however, Netflix CEO Reed Hastings seems unfazed. "We can still build a very successful business [in these new markets]," he says. Wherever Netflix goes, "I think the key is having unique content, a great reputation, and a good value proposition," things at which Netflix excels.

Possible global markets should be ranked on several factors, including market size, market growth, the cost of doing business, competitive advantage, and risk level. The goal is to determine the potential of each market, using indicators such as those shown in **Table 15.1**. Then the marketer must decide which markets offer the greatest long-run return on investment.

» Table 15.1 Indicators of Market Potential

Demographic Characteristics	Sociocultural Factors
Education Population size and growth Population age composition	Consumer lifestyles, beliefs, and values Business norms and approaches Cultural and social norms Languages
Geographic Characteristics	**Political and Legal Factors**
Climate Country size Population density—urban, rural Transportation structure and market accessibility	National priorities Political stability Government attitudes toward global trade Government bureaucracy Monetary and trade regulations
Economic Factors	
GDP size and growth Income distribution Industrial infrastructure Natural resources Financial and human resources	

Author Comment
A company has many options for entering an international market, from simply exporting its products to working jointly with foreign companies to setting up its own foreign-based operations.

Deciding How to Enter the Market

Once a company has decided to sell in a foreign country, it must determine the best mode of entry. Its choices are *exporting, joint venturing*, and *direct investment*. **»Figure 15.2** shows the three market entry strategies along with the options each one offers. As the figure shows, each succeeding strategy involves more commitment and risk but also more control and potential profits.

Exporting

Exporting
Entering foreign markets by selling goods produced in the company's home country, often with little modification.

The simplest way to enter a foreign market is through **exporting**. The company may passively export its surpluses from time to time, or it may make an active commitment to expand exports to a particular market. In either case, the company produces all its goods in its home country. It may or may not modify them for the export market. Exporting involves the least change in the company's product lines, organization, investments, or mission.

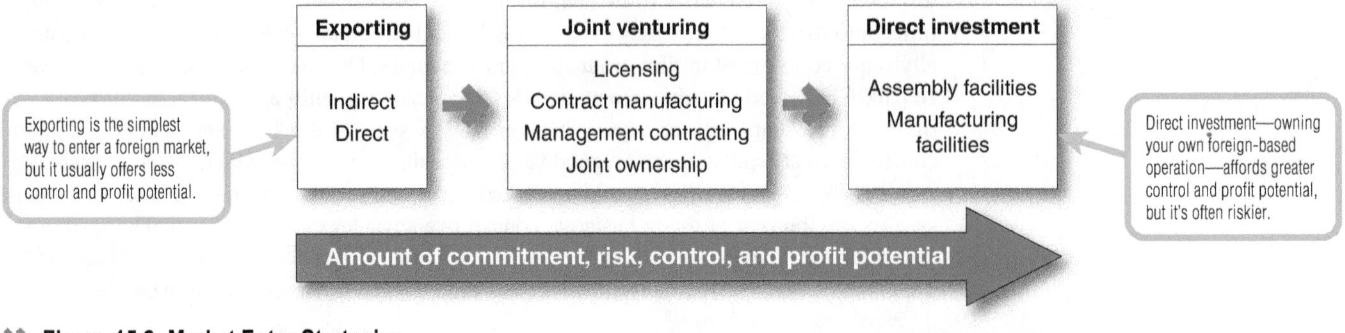

» Figure 15.2 Market Entry Strategies

Companies typically start with *indirect exporting*, working through independent international marketing intermediaries. Indirect exporting involves less investment because the firm does not require an overseas marketing organization or network. It also involves less risk. International marketing intermediaries bring know-how and services to the relationship, so the seller normally makes fewer mistakes. Sellers may eventually move into *direct exporting*, whereby they handle their own exports. The investment and risk are somewhat greater in this strategy, but so is the potential return.

Joint Venturing

Joint venturing
Entering foreign markets by joining with foreign companies to produce or market products or services.

A second method of entering a foreign market is by **joint venturing**—joining with foreign companies to produce or market products or services. Joint venturing differs from exporting in that the company joins with a host country partner to sell or market abroad. It differs from direct investment in that an association is formed with someone in the foreign country. There are four types of joint ventures: *licensing, contract manufacturing, management contracting*, and *joint ownership.*

Licensing

Licensing
Entering foreign markets through developing an agreement with a licensee in the foreign market.

Licensing is a simple way for a manufacturer to enter international marketing. The company enters into an agreement with a licensee in the foreign market. For a fee or royalty payments, the licensee buys the right to use the company's manufacturing process, trademark, patent, trade secret, or other item of value. The company thus gains entry into a foreign market at little risk; at the same time, the licensee gains production expertise or a well-known product or name without having to start from scratch.

In Japan, Budweiser beer flows from Kirin breweries, and Mizkan produces Sunkist lemon juice, drinks, and dessert items. >> Tokyo Disney Resort is owned and operated by Oriental Land Company under license from The Walt Disney Company. The 45-year license gives Disney licensing fees plus a percentage of admissions and food and merchandise sales. And Coca-Cola markets internationally by licensing bottlers around the world and supplying them with the syrup needed to produce the product. Its global bottling partners range from the Coca-Cola Bottling Company of Saudi Arabia to Europe-based Coca-Cola Hellenic, which bottles and markets 136 Coca-Cola brands to 589 million people in 28 countries, from Italy and Greece to Nigeria and Russia.[29]

>> **International licensing: The Tokyo Disney Resort is owned and operated by Oriental Land Company (a Japanese development company) under license from The Walt Disney Company.**

David Harding/Alamy

Licensing has potential disadvantages, however. The firm has less control over the licensee than it would over its own operations. Furthermore, if the licensee is very successful, the firm has given up these profits, and if and when the contract ends, it may find it has created a competitor.

Contract Manufacturing

Contract manufacturing
A joint venture in which a company contracts with manufacturers in a foreign market to produce its product or provide its service.

Another option is **contract manufacturing**, in which the company makes agreements with manufacturers in the foreign market to produce its product or provide its service. For example, P&G serves 650 million consumers across India with the help of nine contract manufacturing sites there. And Volkswagen contracts with Russia's largest auto manufacturer, GAZ Group, to make Volkswagen Jettas for the Russian market as well as its Škoda (VW's Czech Republic subsidiary) Octavia and Yeti models sold there.[30] The drawbacks of contract manufacturing are decreased control over the manufacturing process and loss of potential profits on manufacturing. The benefits are the chance to start faster, with less risk, and the later opportunity either to form a partnership with or buy out the local manufacturer. Contract manufacturing can also reduce plant investment, transportation, and tariff costs while at the same time helping to meet the host country's local manufacturing requirements.

Management Contracting

Management contracting
A joint venture in which the domestic firm supplies the management know-how to a foreign company that supplies the capital; the domestic firm exports management services rather than products.

Under **management contracting**, the domestic firm provides the management know-how to a foreign company that supplies the capital. In other words, the domestic firm exports management services rather than products. Hilton uses this arrangement in managing hotels around the world. For example, the hotel chain operates DoubleTree by Hilton hotels in countries ranging from the UK and Italy to Peru and Costa Rica to China, Russia, and Tanzania. The properties are locally owned, but Hilton manages the hotels with its world-renowned hospitality expertise.[31]

Management contracting is a low-risk method of getting into a foreign market, and it yields income from the beginning. The arrangement is even more attractive if the contracting firm has an option to buy some share in the managed company later on. The arrangement is not sensible, however, if the company can put its scarce management talent to better uses or if it can make greater profits by undertaking the whole venture. Management contracting also prevents the company from setting up its own operations for a period of time.

Joint Ownership

Joint ownership
A cooperative venture in which a company creates a local business with investors in a foreign market who share ownership and control.

Joint ownership ventures consist of one company joining forces with foreign investors to create a local business in which they share possession and control. A company may buy an interest in a local firm, or the two parties may form a new business venture. Joint ownership may be needed for economic or political reasons. For example, the firm may lack the financial, physical, or managerial resources to undertake the venture alone. Alternatively, a foreign government may require joint ownership as a condition for entry.

» **Joint ownership and direct investment: To increase its understanding and influence in China's huge mobile device market, Intel has invested heavily there in joint ownership ventures and its own manufacturing facilities.**
Jing Wei/Imaginechina/AP Images

Often, companies form joint ownership ventures to merge their complementary strengths in developing a global m arketing opportunity. » For example, to increase its presence and local influence in China's mobile phone and tablets markets, chipmaker Intel recently paid $1.5 billion for 20 percent ownership in China's state-run Tsinghua Unigroup, which controls two domestic mobile chipmakers. The joint ownership investment will help Intel to better understand Chinese consumers. It may also help to earn more favorable treatment from Chinese regulators. So far, Intel has gone untouched by China's recent crackdown on foreign technology companies such as competitor Qualcomm and software makers Microsoft and Symantec.[32]

Joint ownership has certain drawbacks, however. The partners may disagree over investment, marketing, or other policies. Whereas many U.S. firms like to reinvest earnings for growth, local firms often prefer to take out these earnings; whereas U.S. firms emphasize the role of marketing, local investors may rely on selling.

Direct Investment

Direct investment
Entering a foreign market by developing foreign-based assembly or manufacturing facilities.

The biggest involvement in a foreign market comes through **direct investment**—the development of foreign-based assembly or manufacturing facilities. For example, in addition to joint ownership ventures in China, Intel has also made substantial investments in its own manufacturing and research facilities there. It recently spent $1.6 billion upgrading its decade-old chip factory in the central Chinese city of Chengdu and another $2.5 billion to build a shiny new fabrication plant in Dalian, a port city in China's northeast. "China is our fastest-growing major market," says Intel's CEO, "and we believe it's critical that we invest in markets that will provide for future growth to better serve our customers."[33]

If a company has gained experience in exporting and if the foreign market is large enough, foreign production facilities offer many advantages. The firm may have lower costs in the form of cheaper labor or raw materials, foreign government investment incentives, and freight savings. The firm may also improve its image in the host country because it creates jobs. Generally, a firm develops a deeper relationship with the government, customers, local suppliers, and distributors, allowing it to adapt its products to the local market better.

Finally, the firm keeps full control over the investment and therefore can develop manufacturing and marketing policies that serve its long-term international objectives.

The main disadvantage of direct investment is that the firm faces many risks, such as restricted or devalued currencies, falling markets, or government changes. In some cases, a firm has no choice but to accept these risks if it wants to operate in the host country.

LINKING THE CONCEPTS

Slow down here and think about McDonald's global marketing issues.

- To what extent can McDonald's standardize for the Chinese market? What marketing strategy and program elements can be similar to those used in the United States and other parts of the Western world? Which ones must be adapted? Be specific.
- To what extent can McDonald's standardize its strategy, products, and programs for the Canadian market? What elements can be standardized, and which must be adapted?
- To what extent are McDonald's "globalization" efforts contributing to "Americanization" of countries and cultures around the world? What are the positives and negatives of such cultural developments?

Author Comment
The major global marketing decision usually boils down to this: How much, if at all, should a company adapt its marketing strategy and programs to local markets? How might the answer differ for Boeing versus McDonald's?

Deciding on the Global Marketing Program

Companies that operate in one or more foreign markets must decide how much, if at all, to adapt their marketing strategies and programs to local conditions. At one extreme are global companies that use **standardized global marketing**, essentially using the same marketing strategy approaches and marketing mix worldwide. At the other extreme is **adapted global marketing**. In this case, the producer adjusts the marketing strategy and mix elements to each international target market, resulting in more costs but hopefully producing a larger market share and return.

Standardized global marketing
A global marketing strategy that basically uses the same marketing strategy and mix in all of the company's international markets.

Adapted global marketing
A global marketing approach that adjusts the marketing strategy and mix elements to each international target market, which creates more costs but hopefully produces a larger market share and return.

The question of whether to adapt or standardize the marketing strategy and program has been much debated over the years. On the one hand, some global marketers believe that technology is making the world a smaller place, and consumer needs around the world are becoming more similar. This paves the way for global brands and standardized global marketing. Global branding and standardization, in turn, result in greater brand power and reduced costs from economies of scale.

On the other hand, the marketing concept holds that marketing programs will be more engaging if tailored to the unique needs of each targeted customer group. If this concept applies within a country, it should apply even more across international markets. Despite global convergence, consumers in different countries still have widely varied cultural backgrounds. They still differ significantly in their needs and wants, spending power, product preferences, and shopping patterns. Because these differences are hard to change, most marketers today adapt their products, prices, channels, and promotions to fit consumer desires in each country.

However, global standardization is not an all-or-nothing proposition. It's a matter of degree. Most international marketers suggest that companies should "think globally but act locally." They should seek a balance between standardization and adaptation, leveraging global brand recognition but adapting their marketing, products, and operations to specific markets. For example, as discussed in the story at the start of this chapter, cosmetics and beauty care giant L'Oréal and its brands are truly global. But the company's outstanding international success comes from achieving a global–local balance that adapts and differentiates brands to make them responsive to local needs while also integrating them across world markets to optimize their global impact.

Collectively, local brands still account for the overwhelming majority of consumer purchases. Most consumers, wherever they live, lead very local lives. So a global brand must engage consumers at a local level, respecting the culture and becoming a part of it. Starbucks operates this way. The company's overall brand strategy provides global strategic direction. Then regional or local units focus on adapting the strategy and brand to specific local markets. >> For example, when Starbucks entered China in 1998, given the strong Chinese tea-drinking culture, few observers expected success. But Starbucks quickly proved the doubters wrong:[34]

> Starbucks's success in China results from building on its global brand identity and values while at the same time adapting its brand strategy to the unique characteristics of Chinese consumers. Rather than forcing U.S. products on the Chinese, Starbucks developed new flavors—such as green tea–flavored coffee drinks—that appeal to local tastes. Rather than just charging U.S.-style premium prices in China, Starbucks boosted prices even higher, positioning the brand as a status symbol for the rapidly growing Chinese middle and upper classes. And rather than pushing takeout orders, which account for most of its U.S. revenues, Starbucks promoted dine-in services—making its stores the perfect meeting place for Chinese professionals and their friends. Whereas U.S. locations do about 70 percent of their business before 10 am, China stores do more than 70 percent of their business in the afternoon and evening. "It's a lifestyle to the Chinese," says the head of Starbucks's China and Asia Pacific operations. "It's much more of a gathering place for social occasions." Under this adapted strategy, Starbucks China is thriving. China is now Starbucks's largest market outside of the United States, with more than 1,700 current stores and 1,700 more stores in 70 cities planned by 2020. "We're trying to build a different kind of company in China and are mindful of how we grow while maintaining the heart and soul of what Starbucks stands for," says the Starbucks executive.

>> Think globally, act locally: Starbucks's outstanding success in China results from building on its global brand identity and values while at the same time adapting its brand strategy to the unique characteristics of Chinese consumers.

Chris Willson/Alamy

Product

Five strategies are used for adapting product and marketing communication strategies to a global market (see **>> Figure 15.3**).[35] We first discuss the three product strategies and then turn to the two communication strategies.

Straight product extension means marketing a product in a foreign market without making significant changes to the product. Top management tells its marketing people, "Take the product as is and find customers for it." The first step, however, should be to find out whether foreign consumers use that product and what form they prefer.

Straight product extension
Marketing a product in a foreign market without making significant changes to the product.

Straight extension has been successful in some cases and disastrous in others. Apple iPads, Gillette razors, Black & Decker tools, and even 7-Eleven Slurpees are all sold successfully in about the same form around the world. But when General Foods introduced its standard powdered JELL-O in the British market, it discovered that British consumers prefer a solid wafer or cake form. Likewise, Philips began to make a profit in Japan only after it reduced the size of its coffeemakers to fit into smaller Japanese kitchens and its shavers to fit smaller Japanese hands. And Panasonic's refrigerator sales in China surged 10-fold in a single year after it shaved the width of its appliances by 15 percent to fit smaller Chinese kitchens.[36] Straight extension is tempting because it involves no additional product development costs, manufacturing changes, or new promotion. But it can be costly in the long run if products fail to satisfy consumers in specific global markets.

Product adaptation
Adapting a product to meet local conditions or wants in foreign markets.

Product adaptation involves changing the product to meet local requirements, conditions, or wants. For example, McDonald's operates in more than 100 countries, with sometimes widely varying local food preferences. So although you'll find its

>> Figure 15.3 Five Global Product and Communications Strategies

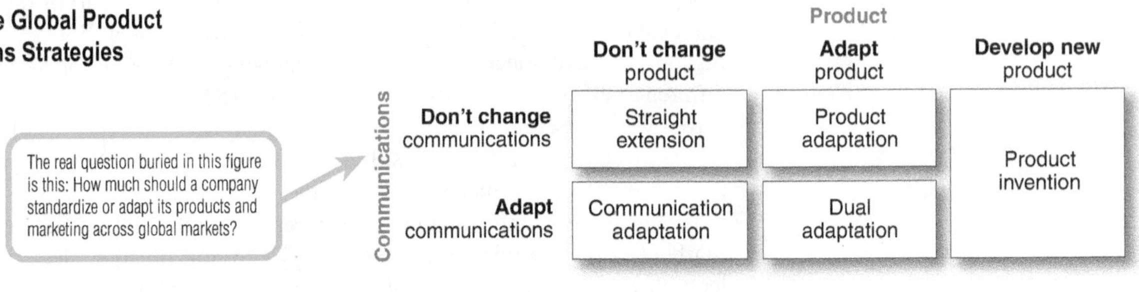

signature burgers and fries in most locations around the world, the chain has added menu items that meet the unique taste buds of customers in local markets. McDonald's serves salmon burgers in Norway, mashed-potato burgers in China, shrimp burgers in Japan, a Samurai Pork Burger in Thailand, chicken porridge in Malaysia, and Spam and eggs in Hawaii. In a German McDonald's, you'll find the Nürnburger (three large bratwurst on a soft roll with lots of mustard, of course); in Israel, there's the McFalafel (chickpea fritters, tomatoes, cucumber, and cheese topped with tahini and wrapped in lafa). And menus in Turkey feature a chocolate orange fried pie (Brazil adds banana, Egypt taro, and Hawaii pineapple).

In many major global markets, McDonald's adapts more than just its menu. It also adjusts its restaurant design and operations. For example, McDonald's France has redefined itself as a French company that adapts to the needs and preferences of French consumers:[37]

"France—the land of haute cuisine, fine wine, and cheese—would be the last place you would expect to find a thriving [McDonald's]," opines one observer. Yet the fast-food giant has turned France into its second-most-profitable world market. Although a McDonald's in Paris might at first seem a lot like one in Chicago, McDonald's has carefully adapted its French operations to the preferences of local customers. At the most basic level, although a majority of revenues still come from burgers and fries, McDonald's France has changed its menu to please the French palate. For instance, it offers up burgers with French cheeses such as chevre, cantel, and bleu, topped off with whole-grain French mustard sauce. »And French consumers love baguettes, so McDonald's bakes them fresh in its restaurants and sells them in oh-so-French McBaguette sandwiches.

But perhaps the biggest difference isn't in the food, but in the design of the restaurants themselves, which have been adapted to suit French lifestyles. For example, French meal times tend to be longer, with more food consumed per sitting. So McDonald's has refined its restaurant interiors to create a comfortable, welcoming environment where customers want to linger and perhaps order an additional coffee or dessert. McDonald's even provides table-side service. As a result, the average French McDonald's customer spends about four times what an American customer spends per visit.

» Product adaptation: By leveraging the power of its global brand but constantly adapting to the needs and preferences of French consumers and their culture, McDonald's has turned France into its second-most-profitable world market.

AFP/Getty Images

Product invention
Creating new products or services for foreign markets.

Product invention consists of creating something new to meet the needs of consumers in a given country. As markets have gone global, companies ranging from appliance manufacturers and carmakers to candy and soft drink producers have developed products that meet the special purchasing needs of low-income consumers in developing economies.

For example, Chinese appliance producer Haier developed sturdier washing machines for rural users in emerging markets, where it found that lighter-duty machines often became clogged with mud when farmers used them to clean vegetables as well as clothes. And solar lighting manufacturer d.light Solar has developed affordable solar-powered home lighting systems for the hundreds of millions of people in the developing world who don't have access to reliable power. d.light's hanging lamps and portable lanterns require no energy source other than the sun and can last up to 15 hours on one charge. The company has already reached 49 million users, is adding 1 million users per month and plans to reach 100 million users by 2020.[38]

Promotion

Companies can either adopt the same communication strategy they use in the home market or change it for each local market. Consider advertising messages. Some global companies use a standardized advertising theme around the world. For example, Chevrolet recently

Communication standardization: With nearly two-thirds of its sales now outside the United States, Chevy recently switched to a new, more global "Find New Roads" positioning and advertising theme that has meaning in all markets worldwide, here Russia.

General Motors, LLC

swapped out its previous, American-focused "Chevy Runs Deep" positioning and advertising theme with a more global "Find New Roads" theme. The new theme is one "that works in all markets," says a GM marketing executive. "The theme has meaning in mature markets like the U.S. as well as emerging markets like Russia and India, where the potential for continued growth is the greatest." The time is right for a more globally consistent Chevy brand message. Chevrolet sells cars in more than 140 countries, and nearly two-thirds of its sales are now outside the United States, compared with only about one-third a decade ago.[39]

Of course, even in highly standardized communications campaigns, some adjustments might be required for language and cultural differences. For example, ads for Pepsi's youthful "Live for Now" campaign have a similar look worldwide but are adapted in different global markets to feature local consumers, languages, and events. Similarly, in Western markets, fast-casual clothing retailer H&M runs fashion ads with models showing liberal amounts of bare skin. But in the Middle East, where attitudes toward public nudity are more conservative, the retailer runs the same ads digitally adapted to better cover its models.

Global companies often have difficulty crossing the language barrier, with results ranging from mild embarrassment to outright failure. Seemingly innocuous brand names and advertising phrases can take on unintended or hidden meanings when translated into other languages. For example, Interbrand of London, the firm that created household names such as Prozac and Acura, recently developed a brand name "hall of shame" list, which contained these and other foreign brand names you're never likely to see inside the local Kroger supermarket: Krapp toilet paper (Denmark), Plopp chocolate (Scandinavia), Crapsy Fruit cereal (France), Poo curry powder (Argentina), and Pschitt lemonade (France). Similarly, advertising themes often lose—or gain—something in the translation. In Chinese, the KFC slogan "finger-lickin' good" came out as "eat your fingers off." And Motorola's Hellomoto ringtone sounds like "Hello, Fatty" in India.

Marketers must be watchful to avoid such mistakes, taking great care when localizing their brand names and messages to specific global markets. In important but culturally different markets such as China, finding just the right name can make or break a brand (see Marketing at Work 15.2).

Communication adaptation
A global communication strategy of fully adapting advertising messages to local markets.

Rather than standardizing their advertising globally, other companies follow a strategy of **communication adaptation**, fully adapting their advertising messages to local markets. For example, in the United States and most Western countries, where running is accepted as a positive, healthful activity, Nike advertising focuses on products and personal performance. In China, however, running is viewed as a boring sport or even a punishment—something rigorous and painful. It's not something that most people in Asia's polluted cities choose to do, especially on streets jammed with pedestrians, bicycles, cars, and even rickshaws. "The joke is that when there's a person running in the city (and it's often a Westerner), people turn to see who's chasing him," quips one observer.

However, China is the largest footwear market in the world, offering huge untapped potential for Nike. So, in China, rather than pushing products and performance, Nike's advertising focuses on just trying to get more Chinese to put on running shoes. Ads and social media feature ordinary people who choose to run on city streets, letting them relate their reasons in their own words. "I run to make the hidden visible," says one young woman. "I run to get lost," says another. Salad—a stressed-out office worker who lives and runs in Shanghai—relates: "The city is always noisy and busy. This adds even more pressure to my day. I guess for me, running is about shutting down the noise." To make running a more social activity, Nike also sponsors nighttime "Lunar Runs" in big cities like Beijing and marathons in Shanghai, featuring fitness instructors, live music, and

MARKETING AT WORK 15.2

Localizing Chinese Brand Names: Very Important but Notoriously Tricky

After a long day's work, an average upscale Beijinger can't wait to dash home, lace on a comfortable pair of Enduring and Persevering, pop the top on a refreshing can of Tasty Fun, then hop into his Dashing Speed and head to the local tavern for a frosty glass of Happiness Power with friends. Translation? In China, those are the brand-name meanings for Nike, Coca-Cola, Mercedes, and Heineken, respectively.

To Westerners, such names sound pretty silly, but to brands doing business in China, the world's biggest and fastest-growing consumer market, they are no laughing matter. Perhaps more than anywhere else in the world, brand names in China take on deep significance. Finding just the right name can make or break a brand. "Often, a company's most important marketing decision in China is localizing its name," asserts one global branding analyst. "It's also a notoriously tricky one."

Ideally, to maintain global consistency, the Chinese name should sound similar to the original, while at the same time conveying the brand's benefits in meaningful symbolic terms. Nike's Chinese brand name, Nai ke, does this well. Not only does it sound the same when pronounced in Chinese, its "Enduring and Persevering" meaning powerfully encapsulates the "Just Do It" essence of the Nike brand the world over. Similarly, P&G's Tide is Taizi in China, which translates to "gets out the dirt," a perfect moniker for a tough-acting detergent. Coca-Cola's Chinese name—Ke kou ke le—dates all the way back to 1928. It not only sounds much like the English name, the Chinese symbols convey happiness in the mouth, a close fit to Coca-Cola's current "open happiness" positioning. Other names that wear well on Chinese ears while also conveying a brand's essence include Lay's snack foods—Le shi ("happy things"); Reebok—Rui bu ("quick steps"); and Colgate—Gau lu jie ("revealing superior cleanliness").

Chinese brand names can convey subtle meanings that might not be apparent to Western sensibilities. For example, "Dashing Speed" seems appropriate enough for an upscale automobile brand like Mercedes. So does BMW's name—Bao Ma—which translates to "Precious Horse." However, in China, "precious" has a feminine connotation, whereas "dashing speed" is more masculine. This works out well for both car makers, which target different genders among China's upper crust. For instance, BMW is a market leader among affluent Chinese women.

Some brand names translate naturally. For example, when Garnier introduced its Clear shampoo in China, it lucked out. The Chinese word for "clear"—Qing—is one of a select few Chinese words with unusually positive associations that are used in many brand names. Garnier added the word *yang*, which means "flying" or "scattering to the wind." According to the director of Garnier's brand consultancy, the Qing Yang brand name connotes "very light, healthy, and happy—think of hair in the air," just what the brand intends. Other universally positive Chinese words commonly found in brand names include "le" and "xi" (happy), "li" (strength or power), "ma" (horse), and "fu" (lucky). Thus, Kia sells one model in China named Qian li ma, or "thousand kilometer horse," suggesting unusual strength.

There was a time when Western companies entering China simply created a brand name that was phonetically similar to the domestic name, even if it had no meaning in the Chinese language. In fact, such obviously foreign-looking and sounding names often communicated a sense of Western cache. For example, Cadillac went with Ka di la ke—a meaningless group of sounds that gave status to the luxury brand. And McDonald's got away with Mai dang lao, a term that sounds

>> **Brand names in China take on deep significance. Coca-Cola's Chinese name, when pronounced, sounds much like the English name, and the Chinese symbols convey "tasty fun" or "happiness in the mouth," a close fit to Coca-Cola's current worldwide "open happiness" positioning.**

Zhang Peng/Getty Images

like the English version but whose characters translate into gibberish—"wheat," "should," and "labor." Other global companies with short names such as IBM or Gap simply expect consumers to learn their Western names.

Today, however, with so many foreign brands entering the crowded Chinese market, most companies expect more of their Chinese brand names. If Chinese consumers can't pronounce a name or don't know what it stands for, they are much less likely to buy it or talk about it with others, in person or in social media. Instead, with some work, companies can come up with names that will engage and inspire buyers. In China, it's not Subway, it's Sai bai wei—"better than 100 tastes." It's not Marriott but Wan Hao, or "10,000 wealthy elites."

However, finding the right names and characters can be a daunting challenge. Brand name development in China has become more of a science than an art, involving global branding consultants, computer software, linguistic analysis, and extensive consumer testing. Some global names require careful recrafting. For example, Microsoft had to rethink the introduction of its Bing search engine in China, where the most common translations of the character pronounced "bing" are words like "defect" or "virus," not good associations for a digital product. Microsoft changed the name of its product in China to Bi ying, which means "very certain to respond." Still, the brand is having difficulty shaking the resemblance to the original name.

Similarly, S.C. Johnson belatedly renamed its popular Mr. Muscle line of cleaners to Mr. Powerful (Weimeng xiansheng) in China, where Mr. Muscle had a less compelling second meaning—"Mr. Chicken Meat." And French automaker Peugeot thought it had a winning brand name with Biao zhi, only to learn too late that it was too close to biaozi, slang for prostitute. It's no surprise that the brand generated more off-color jokes than sales.

Sources: "Lost in Translation? Pick Your Chinese Brand Name Carefully," *Shanghalist*, March 28, 2014, http://shanghaiist.com/2014/03/28/hutong-school-pick-your-chinese-brand-name-carefully.php; Michael Wines, "Picking Brand Names in China Is a Business Itself," *New York Times*, November 12, 2011, p. A4; Carly Chalmers, "12 Amazing Translations of Chinese Brand Names," *todaytranslations*, August 27, 2013, www.todaytranslations.com/blog/12-amazing-translations-of-chinese-brand-names/; Angela Doland, "Why Western Companies Like LinkedIn Need Chinese Brand Names," *Advertising Age*, March 5, 2014, www.adage.com/print/291960/; and Alfred Maskeroni, "Can You Identify All These Famous Logos Redesigned by an Artist into Chinese?" *Adweek*, February 10, 2015, www.adweek.com/print/162867.

celebrities to introduce Chinese students and young professionals to running as a fun and rewarding after-class or after-work activity. The goal is to get more people to at least give running a try. But changing basic perceptions of the sport won't be easy. "It's a very long road for us," says a Nike China marketer.[40]

Media also need to be adapted internationally because media availability and regulations vary from country to country. TV advertising time is very limited in Europe, for instance, ranging from four hours a day in France to none in Scandinavian countries. Advertisers must buy time months in advance, and they have little control over airtimes. However, mobile phone ads are much more widely accepted in Europe and Asia than in the United States. Magazines also vary in effectiveness. For example, magazines are a major medium in Italy but a minor one in Austria. Newspapers are national in the United Kingdom but only local in Spain.[41]

Price

Companies also face many considerations in setting their international prices. For example, how might Makita price its power tools globally? It could set a uniform price globally, but this amount would be too high of a price in poor countries and not high enough in rich ones. It could charge what consumers in each country would bear, but this strategy ignores differences in the actual costs from country to country. Finally, the company could use a standard markup of its costs everywhere, but this approach might price Makita out of the market in some countries where costs are high.

Regardless of how companies go about pricing their products, their foreign prices probably will be higher than their domestic prices for comparable products. An Apple iPad Air that sells for $499 in the United States goes for $609 in the United Kingdom. Why? Apple faces a *price escalation* problem. It must add the cost of transportation, tariffs, importer margin, wholesaler margin, and retailer margin to its factory price. Depending on these added costs, a product may have to sell for two to five times as much in another country to make the same profit.

To overcome this problem when selling to less-affluent consumers in developing countries, many companies make simpler or smaller versions of their products that

>> International pricing: Lenovo's Motorola division developed the ultra-cheap Moto G smartphone intended primarily for emerging markets where consumers want low-cost phones.
ChinaFotoPress/Getty Images

can be sold at lower prices. Others have introduced new, more affordable brands for global markets. >> For example, Lenovo's Motorola division developed the ultra-cheap Moto G smartphone. Although not a flashy, high-tech gadget, the full-function device sells for only $179.99 in the United States with no contract. Motorola first introduced the phone in Brazil, one of the largest and fastest-growing emerging markets, then in other parts of South America, the Middle East, India, and more of Asia. Intended primarily for emerging markets where consumers want low-cost phones, the Moto G may also sell well to cost-conscious consumers in major developed markets, such as the United States and Europe. The Moto G phone puts pressure on Apple, which has focused on selling older models at reduced prices rather than developing cheaper models. The extremely affordable Moto G is now the most popular smartphone in Brazil, where it holds a sizable 18 percent market share, making Motorola the country's second-largest smartphone maker. The low-end phone also helped catapult a then-flagging Motorola into the number-four position in the huge Indian smartphone market.[42]

Recent economic and technological forces have had an impact on global pricing. For example, the Internet is making global price differences more obvious. When firms sell their wares over the Internet, customers can see how much products sell for in different countries. They can even order a given product directly from the company location or dealer offering the lowest price. This is forcing companies toward more standardized international pricing.

Distribution Channels

Whole-channel view
Designing international channels that take into account the entire global supply chain and marketing channel, forging an effective global value delivery network.

An international company must take a **whole-channel view** of the problem of distributing products to final consumers. >> **Figure 15.4** shows the two major links between the seller and the final buyer. The first link, *channels between nations*, moves company products from points of production to the borders of countries within which they are sold. The second link, *channels within nations*, moves products from their market entry points to the final consumers. The whole-channel view takes into account the entire global supply chain and marketing channel. It recognizes that to compete well internationally, the company must effectively design and manage an entire *global value delivery network*.

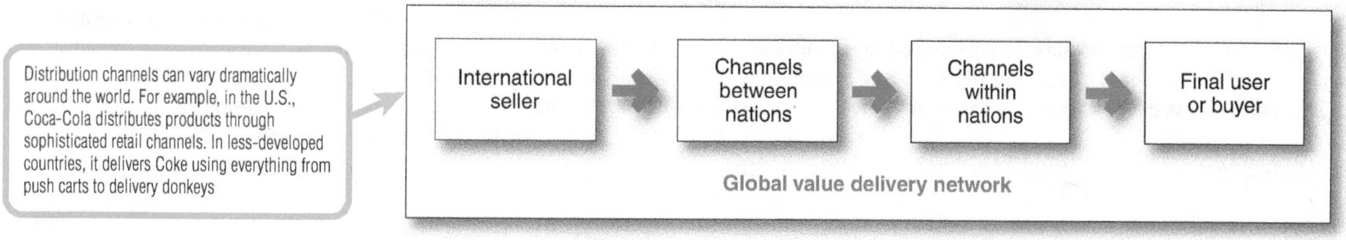

>> **Figure 15.4 Whole-Channel Concept for International Marketing**

Channels of distribution within countries vary greatly from nation to nation. There are large differences in the numbers and types of intermediaries serving each country market and in the transportation infrastructure serving these intermediaries. For example, whereas large-scale retail chains dominate the U.S. scene, most of the retailing in other countries is done by small, independent retailers. In India or Indonesia, millions of retailers operate tiny shops or sell in open markets.

Even in world markets containing similar types of sellers, retailing practices can vary widely. For example, you'll find plenty of Walmarts, Carrefours, Tescos, and other retail superstores in major Chinese cities. But whereas consumer brands sold in such stores in Western markets rely largely on self-service, brands in China hire armies of uniformed in-store promoters—called "promoter girls" or "push girls"—to dispense samples and pitch their products person to person. In a Beijing Walmart, on any given weekend, you'll find 100 or more such promoters acquainting customers with products from Kraft, Unilever, P&G, Johnson & Johnson, and a slew of local competitors. "Chinese consumers know the brand name through media," says the director of a Chinese retail marketing service, "but they want to feel the product and get a detailed understanding before they make a purchase."[43]

When selling in emerging markets, companies must often overcome distribution infrastructure and supply challenges. For example, in Nigeria, Domino's Pizza has had to dig wells and install water-treatment plants behind many of its restaurants to obtain clean water. And after having difficulty sourcing quality beef in South Africa, rather than buying scarce beef from scrawny cattle raised by local herdsmen, Burger King finally invested $5 million in its own local cattle ranch.[44]

Brazil's northeast region is its poorest, and many residents there lack access to basics such as roads and running water. But as it happens, northeast Brazil is also the region with the greatest growth in household income. So marketers are finding innovative ways to meet the distribution challenges in these regions to capture the growing potential there. Consider Nestlé:[45]

To tap the potential in less-developed regions of Brazil, Nestlé developed its "até Você" ("Reaching You") program, by which its reps go door to door with push carts—a method residents find very appealing—selling "kits" full of dairy products, cookies, yogurt, and desserts. More than just selling products, these Nestlé vendors are trained to serve as nutrition consultants, helping customers to develop healthier diets. >> To serve consumers in northeast Brazil's Amazon River basin, which lacks a solid network of roads and highways, Nestlé has even launched a floating supermarket that takes goods directly to consumers. Setting sail from Belem, Brazil's biggest city along the Amazon, the boat serves 1.5 million consumers in 27 riverside towns with 300 different Nestlé products. It spends one day at each stop. Customers can check the floating store's schedule at nestleatevoce.com.br, call a toll-free number, or text for more information and plan their shopping accordingly. This and other innovative até Você marketing initiatives are paying off for Nestlé. "Demand for our products has more than doubled in the north and northeast compared to other Brazilian regions," says Nestlé's marketing manager in Brazil.

>> Marketing in emerging markets: To tap the growing potential in Brazil's less developed regions, Nestlé's "Ate Voce" ("Reaching You") program includes innovative distribution approaches, such as this floating supermarket that serves customers in the country's Amazon River basin.

Bloomberg via Getty Images

Author Comment
Many large companies, regardless of their "home country," now think of themselves as truly *global* organizations. They view the entire world as a single borderless market. For example, although headquartered in Chicago, Boeing is as comfortable selling planes to Lufthansa or Air China as to American Airlines.

Deciding on the Global Marketing Organization

Companies manage their international marketing activities in at least three different ways: Most companies first organize an export department, then create an international division, and finally become a global organization.

A firm normally gets into international marketing by simply shipping out its goods. If its international sales expand, the company will establish an *export department* with a sales manager and a few assistants. As sales increase, the export department can expand to include various marketing services so that it can actively go after business. If the firm moves into joint ventures or direct investment, the export department will no longer be adequate.

Many companies get involved in several international markets and ventures. A company may export to one country, license to another, have a joint ownership venture in a third, and own a subsidiary in a fourth. Sooner or later it will create *international divisions* or subsidiaries to handle all its international activity.

International divisions are organized in a variety of ways. An international division's corporate staff consists of marketing, manufacturing, research, finance, planning, and personnel specialists. It plans for and provides services to various operating units, which can be organized in one of three ways. They can be *geographical organizations*, with country managers who are responsible for salespeople, sales branches, distributors, and licensees in their respective countries. Or the operating units can be *world product groups*, each responsible for worldwide sales of different product groups. Finally, operating units can be *international subsidiaries*, each responsible for their own sales and profits.

Many firms have passed beyond the international division stage and are truly *global organizations*. For example, as discussed in the chapter-opening story, despite its French origins, L'Oréal no longer has a clearly defined home market. Nor does it have a home-office staff. Instead, multicultural managers operate out of facilities located all around the world, bringing diverse cultural perspectives to their brands and operations.

Global organizations don't think of themselves as national marketers that sell abroad but as global marketers. The top corporate management and staff plan worldwide manufacturing facilities, marketing policies, financial flows, and logistical systems. The global operating units report directly to the chief executive or the executive committee of the organization, not to the head of an international division. Executives are trained in worldwide operations, not just domestic *or* international operations. Global companies recruit management from many countries, buy components and supplies where they cost the least, and invest where the expected returns are greatest.

Today, major companies must become more global if they hope to compete. As foreign companies successfully invade their domestic markets, companies must move more aggressively into foreign markets. They will have to change from companies that treat their international operations as secondary to companies that view the entire world as a single borderless market.

MyMarketingLab

If assigned by your instructor, complete the questions marked with the ✪ from the EOC Discussion Questions section in the MyLab. To complete the Marketing by the Numbers problems found in this section, go to your Assignments in the MyLab.

REVIEWING AND EXTENDING THE CONCEPTS

CHAPTER REVIEW AND CRITICAL THINKING

Objectives Review

Companies today can no longer afford to pay attention only to their domestic market, regardless of its size. Many industries are global industries, and firms that operate globally achieve lower costs and higher brand awareness. At the same time, global marketing is risky because of variable exchange rates, unstable governments, tariffs and trade barriers, and several other factors. Given the potential gains and risks of international marketing, companies need a systematic way to make their global marketing decisions.

OBJECTIVE 15-1 Discuss how the international trade system and the economic, political-legal, and cultural environments affect a company's international marketing decisions. (pp 460–472)

A company must understand the *global marketing environment*, especially the international trade system. It should assess each foreign market's *economic, political-legal*, and *cultural characteristics*. The company can then decide whether it wants to go abroad and consider the potential risks and benefits. It must decide on the volume of international sales it wants, how many countries it wants to market in, and which specific markets it wants to enter. These decisions call for weighing the probable returns against the level of risk.

OBJECTIVE 15-2 Describe three key approaches to entering international markets. (pp 472–475)

The company must decide how to enter each chosen market—whether through *exporting, joint venturing*, or *direct investment*. Many companies start as exporters, move to joint ventures, and finally make a direct investment in foreign markets. In *exporting*, the company enters a foreign market by sending and selling products through international marketing intermediaries (indirect exporting) or the company's own department, branch, or sales representatives or agents (direct exporting). When establishing a *joint venture*, a company enters foreign markets by joining with foreign companies to produce or market a product or service. In *licensing*, the company enters a foreign market by contracting with a licensee in the foreign market and offering the right to use a manufacturing process, trademark, patent, trade secret, or other item of value for a fee or royalty.

OBJECTIVE 15-3 Explain how companies adapt their marketing strategies and mixes for international markets. (pp 475–482)

Companies must also decide how much their marketing strategies and their products, promotion, price, and channels should be adapted for each foreign market. At one extreme, global companies use *standardized global marketing* worldwide. Others use *adapted global marketing*, in which they adjust the marketing strategy and mix to each target market, bearing more costs but hoping for a larger market share and return. However, global standardization is not an all-or-nothing proposition. It's a matter of degree. Most international marketers suggest that companies should "think globally but act locally"—that they should seek a balance between globally standardized strategies and locally adapted marketing mix tactics.

OBJECTIVE 15-4 Identify the three major forms of international marketing organization. (p 483)

The company must develop an effective organization for international marketing. Most firms start with an *export department* and graduate to an *international division*. Large companies eventually become *global organizations*, with worldwide marketing planned and managed by the top officers of the company. Global organizations view the entire world as a single, borderless market.

Key Terms

Objective 15-1
Global firm (p 461)
Economic community (p 463)

Objective 15-2
Exporting (p 472)
Joint venturing (p 473)
Licensing (p 473)
Contract manufacturing (p 473)
Management contracting (p 474)
Joint ownership (p 474)
Direct investment (p 474)

Objective 15-3
Standardized global marketing (p 475)
Adapted global marketing (p 475)
Straight product extension (p 476)
Product adaptation (p 476)
Product invention (p 477)
Communication adaptation (p 478)
Whole-channel view (p 481)

Discussion Questions

15-1. Explain what is meant by the term *global firm* and list the major decisions involved in international marketing. (AASCB: Communication)

15-2. Discuss the four types of country industrial structures and the opportunities each offers to international marketers. (AACSB: Communication)

15-3. What factors do companies consider when deciding on possible global markets to enter? (AACSB: Communication; Reflective Thinking)

15-4. Name and describe the four types of joint ventures as methods for entering another country. How does joint venturing differ from other methods of entering a foreign market? (AACSB: Communication; Reflective Thinking)

15-5. Explain what is meant by a whole-channel view and why it is important in international marketing. (AACSB: Communication; Reflective Thinking)

Critical Thinking Exercises

15-6. Visit www.transparency.org and find the most recent Corruption Perceptions Index (CPI) report. What is the most recent CPI for the following countries: Argentina, Denmark, Jamaica, Myanmar, New Zealand, Somali, and the United States? What are the implications of this index for U.S.-based companies doing business in these countries? (AACSB: Communication; Use of IT; Reflective Thinking)

15-7. In a small group, identify and research an environmental threat—such as a regulatory threat, a cultural threat, or and economic threat—posed to global marketers. Analyze the issues related to this threat, discuss how affected companies are reacting, and make recommendations regarding how these companies should address the threat. (AACSB: Communication; Reflective Thinking)

15-8. One way to analyze the cultural differences among countries is to conduct a Hofstede analysis. Visit www.geert-hofstede.com/ to learn what this analysis involves. Develop a presentation explaining how three countries of your choice differ from the United States. (AACSB: Communication; Use of IT; Reflective Thinking)

MINICASES AND APPLICATIONS

Online, Mobile, and Social Media Marketing Russian E-commerce

Russia is emerging as the next big e-commerce frontier with a population of 143 million, 70 million of whom are Internet users. Although online sales in Russia are not has high as U.S. online sales, they have grown rapidly in the past few years. That fact has caught the attention of global e-commerce firms such as the U.S.'s Amazon and eBay and China's equivalent of Amazon, Alibaba. The leading local online retailer in Russia is Ozon Group, often referred to as "Russia's Amazon." Ozon's sales last year were close to $500 million, an almost 70 percent increase in just two years. There are obstacles to e-commerce in Russia, however. The majority of consumers do not have credit cards because many do not trust them to pay for purchases online or offline, making Russia a heavily cash-based marketplace. Delivery is another problem. To combat these barriers, Ozon developed its own courier system, and drivers not only collect cash payments, they even offer style advice on apparel orders when delivered. Russian consumers ordering items from international e-commerce sites such as Amazon may never receive their packages. In fact, officials at Moscow airport reported having 500 metric tons of unprocessed packages in one month alone. Seeing an opportunity for revenue, Russia's Customs Service is considering import duties on packages ordered from foreign Web sites.

15-9. What types of barriers are present in Russia that might slow the expansion of international e-commerce there? (AACSB: Communication; Reflective Thinking)

15-10. Suggest the best ways companies such as eBay and Amazon can enter this market. (AACSB: Communication; Reflective Thinking)

Marketing Ethics Global Safety Standards

India is home to some of the world's deadliest roads. However, international automobile makers do not provide standard safety features in entry-level cars sold in India that are required in other developed countries. India's death toll on the roads has ranked top in the world for eight straight years, exceeding 130,000 fatalities a year. Despite this, automakers strip safety features such as air bags and antilock brakes out of the cars most people in India drive. They argue that Indian consumers cannot afford or are not willing to pay for safety features that could increase the cost of the car by 30 percent or more. Some manufacturers have begun to offer more safety features as standard in their models. But other producers are offering them only as an option, and some are not offering them at all to maintain price competitiveness.

15-11. Is it right for manufacturers to include product safety features that are known to save lives in countries that require them but not to include such features in a country where they are not specifically required? (AACSB: Communication; Ethical Reasoning)

15-12. Discuss world organizations that assist companies in developing and abiding by global standards to protect consumers worldwide. (AACSB: Communication; Reflective Thinking)

Marketing by the Numbers Netflix Global Expansion

Video streaming service Netflix is expanding rapidly around the globe. It is currently available in 50 countries with the goal of expanding to 200 countries by the end of 2016. Netflix's international slogan is "Have content, will travel." There are challenges to international expansion for this type of service, such as inadequate disposable household income and a low percentage of households with high-speed Internet needed to stream videos. And even though almost half of France's TV-owning households have Internet-connected TVs, cultural restrictions limit English-language program content, requiring Netflix to invest in local content for French customers. The next countries to get Netflix are Italy, Spain, and Portugal. Similar to Netflix's other European offerings, service will be offered at a price of €7.99 per month, which converts to U.S. $8.97 during the time of expansion.

15-13. Refer to Appendix 3: Marketing by the Numbers to calculatethe annual market sales potential for Spain in euros and U.S. dollars. There are 18,217,300 television households in Spain, with 75 percent having high-speed Internet. Assume 50 percent of the households are willing and able to purchase the service and would purchase one subscription at an average price of €7.99 per month ($8.97). (AACSB: Communication; Analytical Reasoning; Reflective Thinking)

15-14. Calculate the market sales potential using the current exchange rate between euros and U.S. dollars (see www.xe.com/currencyconverter/). Is the dollar currently strong or weak compared with the euro? Why are U.S.-based international companies concerned when the U.S. dollar is strong compared to other currencies? (AACSB: Communication; Analytic Reasoning; Reflective Thinking)

Video Case Monster Worldwide

Monster.com is one of the most visited employment sites in the United States and one of the largest in the world. Now a part of parent company Monster Worldwide, Monster.com pioneered job recruiting on the Internet. Today, it is the only online recruitment provider that can service job seekers and job posters on a truly global basis. With a presence in 50 countries around the world, Monster has unparalleled international reach. Even through tough economic times, Monster continued to invest heavily in order to maintain and expand its global presence.

Monster's international expansion included the purchase of ChinaHR.com, giving it a strong presence in the world's largest country. Monster already gets about 45 percent of its annual revenue of $1.3 billion from outside the United States. But it expects to become even more global in the coming years. To back that geographic expansion, Monster is also investing heavily in search technologies and Web design in order to appeal to clients everywhere.

After viewing the video featuring Monster Worldwide, answer the following questions:

15-15. Which of the five strategies for adapting products and promotion for global markets does Monster employ?

15-16. Which factors in the global marketing environment have challenged Monster's global marketing activities most? How has Monster met those challenges?

Company Cases 15 7-Eleven/14 Alibaba/16 Adidas

See Appendix 1 for cases appropriate for this chapter. **Case 15, 7-Eleven: Adapting to The World's Many Cultures.** Just a convenience store in the U.S., 7-Eleven has a strong global presence by adapting its model to fit the unique needs of consumers worldwide. **Case 14, Alibaba: The World's Largest E-Tailer Is Not Amazon.** Alibaba quickly became the world's largest e-tailer by selling to the world's largest consumer market. Now, as the company sets it sights on growth outside of China, there may be no stopping it. **Case 16, Adidas: Athletic Apparel With Purpose.** A strategy of sustainability may just give Adidas the global edge that it is looking for.

MyMarketingLab

If assigned by your instructor, complete these writing sections from your Assignments in the MyLab.

15-17. What is the World Trade Organization? What is its purpose, and what has it accomplished? (AACSB: Communication)

15-18. Visit www.ikea.com and compare a catalog from one country to that of another. Note the prices of some of the products. Convert some of the foreign prices to U.S. dollars and compare them to the prices in the U.S. catalog. Are the prices equivalent? Are they consistently higher or lower? (AACSB: Written and Oral Communication; Reflective Thinking)

Appendix 1 Company Cases

Company Case 1

FedEx: Making Every Customer Experience Outstanding

When you have a package that absolutely must arrive at a distant location within 24 hours, what's the first company that comes to mind? More than likely, it's FedEx. Just as Google is used as a verb for Internet search, FedEx is often synonymous with overnight shipping, as in "I'll FedEx it to you." From its humble beginnings in 1971, FedEx has grown into a $46-billion-a-year global giant. Every day, 325,000 FedEx employees deliver 11 million packages via 673 aircraft and 100,000 motor vehicles, connecting more than 99 percent of world's GDP. How did FedEx become so successful? Through its single-minded focus on the customer experience.

Starting with a Customer Need

Even in this era when Internet start-ups get all the press for amazing entrepreneurial stories, FedEx still stands as one of the greatest business success stories of the past 40 years. It all started in the 1960s when Fred Smith, FedEx's founder and current chairman and CEO, was an undergraduate student at Yale, paying his way through school working as a charter pilot. As he crossed paths with corporate pilots, the young Smith saw a trend emerging. Computers and other high-tech components were rapidly finding their way into the business world. But when those things broke down, companies had difficulty getting urgently needed parts to the right places quickly. There were no services for regional or national overnight shipping. In fact, companies often used their own corporate planes as internal courier systems—at great expense—to cart around parts in an effort to minimize downtime.

Smith wrote a paper for an economics class at Yale, proposing the idea of a national overnight-delivery service (reportedly, the professor gave him a C on the paper, calling the idea infeasible). But it wasn't until after college and a tour of duty in the Marine Corps that Smith decided to actually do something about the idea. Smith knew that the need for businesses to move packages fast would only grow with time. With that insight, the FedEx Corporation (Federal Express back then) was born, with eight aircraft providing overnight delivery service to 35 cities.

Putting the Customer First

More than just a good idea at the right time, one thing has kept FedEx growing and thriving over the past four decades. From the beginning, FedEx was built on a foundation of obsessive customer focus. "If people were going to use FedEx in lieu of having incalculable amounts of money tied up in inventories, it 'absolutely, positively' had to be there when promised," said Smith in a recent interview. Hence came FedEx's first positioning slogan—FedEx: When it absolutely, positively has to be there overnight.

To ensure that FedEx could deliver on that promise, Smith pursued the goal with a "no holds barred" vigor. He began FedEx with a nationwide clearinghouse infrastructure and its own fleet of planes and trucks, giving the company complete control. But while complex and expensive, those attributes were conventional. It was the unconventional elements that characterized the boundless pursuit of customer service that formed the core of the FedEx brand.

For example, when FedEx first started shipping packages, no one had ever printed "multiform, sequentially numbered" labels that could be attached to items and machine-read. And no other shipper had even contemplated using small, hand-held computers with barcode-scanning capabilities to communicate shipping information on a real-time basis. No company was tracking inventory on the move, let alone coordinating it with stationary inventory. It was these kinds of innovative capabilities that allowed Smith and FedEx to reliably move packages from one city to another in such a short time. These technologies not only made FedEx's service possible, they also gave rise to companies such as Walmart, Dell, and countless others.

The tenacious pursuit of fulfilling customer needs in FedEx's early days led to what is known at the company today as the "Purple Promise," a promise committed to memory by every FedEx employee: "I will make every FedEx experience outstanding." Fulfilling this promise requires elements of good service, such as treating "customers in a professional, competent, polite, and caring manner" and handling "every customer transaction with the precision required to achieve the highest quality service." But the Purple Promise goes far beyond traditional service. It requires all employees, regardless of their job titles, to recognize that what they do affects how customers perceive the FedEx brand.

Consider how FedEx fixed the problem of its "leaning tower of packages." For years, FedEx management thought of the majority of customers at its World Service Centers and FedEx Office locations as "Frisbees"—customers who step in, drop off packages, and step back out as quickly as possible. Management also thought it was doing a good job of serving these customers. However, recently, company satisfaction surveys began to reveal that not all customers were pleased with their experiences when dropping off packages.

FedEx quickly commissioned a study, which revealed that only about 10 percent of its drop-off customers were, in fact,

"Frisbees." The other 90 percent fell evenly into three different behavioral groups. The most intriguing of these groups was the "Confirmers." In a word, Confirmers were "uneasy." They entered a FedEx location well-prepared, with packages wrapped and ready to go. They had a clear sense of how much shipments would cost and how long they would take to deliver. Still, as they dropped off packages, they were filled with worry that something could go wrong with the shipment. That worry was compounded by the "leaning tower of packages"—FedEx-speak for the piles of packages already stacked behind the counter. For employees, there was no concern in the world that these packages would reach their destination on time. For the Confirmers, however, seemingly haphazard piles of packages sent a visual cue that something in the process was broken, increasing the chances that their packages might get lost. These uneasy customers were on the verge of taking their shipping business elsewhere.

FedEx's Purple Promise drove the company to make a simple, system-wide change that put the minds of Confirmers at ease. The company placed a wall behind the counter with five presort windows. Employees were then trained to thank the customer, turn around, and slip the package through the window that corresponded to the type of service the customer had purchased. For the Confirmers, this careful and organized processing of packages was a visible confirmation that packages were safely on their way.

The Purple Promise Today

A customer-centric culture requires that a company be flexible and dynamic, modifying its strategies and tactics to fit consumer trends. One example of how FedEx remains open to customer-centered change is the degree to which it has embraced social media. At FedEx, the customer service function is responsible for delighting customers through excellent and timely service. Given the omnipresence of mobile devices and social media in consumers' lives these days, the customer service function at FedEx often pursues the goal of delighting customers through social channels, including social networks such as Facebook and Twitter, blogs, and live chat.

Marketing through social and mobile media is all the rage these days. But at FedEx, it's more action than talk. And FedEx goes beyond just listening to customers; it engages them and helps solve their problems. Take the example of Nicole Snow, a now-loyal FedEx customer who owns a small business in Maine called "Darn Good Yarn."

> [Nicole Snow] is in a remote area with few shipping options, and extreme weather makes running her home business more difficult. One day she reached out to FedEx on social networks and asked for help in getting her supply chain set up. The team responded immediately and helped her solve the problem.
>
> Snow's story is fascinating. She hires women in India and Nepal to make yarn out of reclaimed materials like silk. She is nurturing a supply chain that reaches halfway across the globe as well as sourcing from local businesses in Maine. She is highly engaged in the community through activities like teaching knitting classes. "I take materials that otherwise would be thrown out in India and Nepal and import them into Maine and then FedEx them all over the world to my customers. I know that I can get something from India and to my house in the middle of Maine in three days. That's amazing!" Snow is now a huge FedEx fan and advocate. She shares stories of excellent FedEx support everywhere she goes.

Chinks in the Armor

Despite FedEx's obsessive customer focus, with 11 million packages flying all over the planet every day, there are bound to be some glitches now and then. And while social media have been a tremendous blessing, they can also be a curse. In the past few years, FedEx has had its share of videos go viral showing employees mishandling packages. For example, there's the one of a Maryland FedEx driver, captured by the resident's security camera, throwing a package onto a front porch from a distance of about 20 feet. Then there's the FedEx truck driving down a Colorado highway two days before Christmas with its rear door wide open and packages falling out onto the highway. And who can forget the FedEx driver who tossed a package containing a Samsung computer monitor over a six-foot iron fence onto a customer's driveway, with the FedEx truck clearly visible in the background.

As if employees caught on video aren't bad enough, a Philadelphia FedEx driver was caught stealing iPhones out of customers' packages. He was charged, tried, and found guilty to the tune of $40,000 worth of stolen merchandise. On a corporate level, FedEx was caught overcharging some business customers by as much as $3 per package over a three-year period. The company settled the ensuing lawsuit for $21.5 million.

Although none of these actions are justifiable, the fallout would have been far worse had it not been for similar bad press for competitor UPS, including videos of drivers throwing packages, making obscene gestures at a security camera, and even stealing iPads off porches (delivered by FedEx, no less). In FedEx's case, the company took responsibility when it needed to, fired offending employees, and made restitution for damages. In the case of the Samsung monitor–throwing incident, the aggrieved customer even received a personal visit and apology from FedEx's senior vice president of operations. "This goes directly against all FedEx values," declared the executive.

Today, FedEx continues to focus on its goal to "make every FedEx experience outstanding." According to one recent company statement, "Everyone at FedEx is committed to placing customer needs at the center of everything we do." The pledge seems to receive more than just lip service. FedEx routinely ranks among the top 10 of both *MSN Money*'s "Customer Service Hall of Fame" and *Fortune's* "World's Most Admired Companies." With founder Fred Smith still at the helm after more than 40 years, it appears that FedEx intends to be around for the long haul by putting customers first.

Questions for Discussion

1. Give examples of needs, wants, and demands that FedEx customers demonstrate, differentiating these three concepts.
2. Describe FedEx in terms of the value it provides customers. How does FedEx engage customers?

3. Evaluate FedEx's performance relative to customer expectations. What is the outcome of this process?
4. Which of the five marketing management orientations best applies to FedEx?
5. With increased competition today, how can FedEx continue to be competitive?

Sources: Christopher Tkaczyk, "World's Most Admired Companies," *Fortune*, March 1, 2015, pp. 97–104; "Driver Alerts FedEx Delivery Man to Packages Spilling from Open Truck," *CBS Local*, December 23, 2014, http://denver.cbslocal.com/2014/12/22/driver-alerts-fedex-delivery-man-to-packages-spilling-from-open-truck/; Karen Aho, "2013 Customer Service Hall of Fame," *MSN Money*, http://money.msn.com/investing/2013-customer-service-hall-of-fame; Ekaterina Walter, "The Big Brand Theory: How FedEx Achieves Social Customer Service Success," *Social Media Today*, May 27, 2013, www.socialmediatoday.com/ekaterinawalter/1494726/big-brand-theory-how-fedex-achieves-social-customer-service-success; Harley Manning and Kerry Bodine, "How FedEx Revamped Its Brand by Fixing Its 'Leaning Tower of Packages,'" *Fast Company*, August 21, 2012, www.fastcompany.com/3000554/how-fedex-revamped-its-brand-fixing-its-leaning-tower-packages; "Online Extra: Fred Smith on the Birth of FedEx," *Business Week*, September 19, 2004, www.businessweek.com/stories/2004-09-19/online-extra-fred-smith-on-the-birth-of-fedex; and http://about.van.fedex.com, September 2015.

Company Case 2

Samsung: A Strategic Plan for Success

You're probably familiar with Samsung. Maybe you have one of the company's hot new Galaxy smartphones or tablets that track your eye movements to help you navigate the screen. You might be doing your homework on one of its cutting-edge laptops. Or perhaps you've seen one of its dazzling new ultra-high-definition curved-screen smart TVs with Nano-crystal technology.

Chances are good that you or someone you know owns a Samsung product. After all, Samsung is the world's largest consumer electronics manufacturer, producing "gotta have" products in just about every electronics category, including TVs, DVD players, home theaters, digital cameras and camcorders, mobile devices, smartwatches, home appliances, laptops, printers, and LED lighting.

But only 20 years ago, Samsung was little known, and it was anything but cutting-edge. Back then, Samsung was a Korean copycat brand that you bought off a shipping pallet at Costco if you couldn't afford a Sony, then the world's most coveted consumer electronics brand. However, in 1993 Samsung made an inspired decision. It turned its back on cheap knockoffs and set out to overtake rival Sony. At the time, no one outside of Samsung believed that was possible. But the Korean manufacturer passed Sony in just 10 years, and Samsung has been widening the gap that separates it from the former market leader ever since.

The New Management Strategy

How did Samsung move so far so fast? The dramatic shift came about as a result of a top-down mandate to reform Samsung's business model and culture. In 1993, CEO Lee Kun-hee unveiled a new strategy. The goal: Dethrone Sony as the biggest and most desirable consumer electronics brand in the world. Turn Samsung into a premier brand and a trailblazing product leader. To that end, the company hired a crop of fresh, young designers and managers who unleashed a torrent of new products—not humdrum, me-too products, but sleek, bold, and beautiful products targeted to high-end users. Samsung called them "lifestyle works of art." Every new product had to pass the "Wow!" test: If it didn't get a "Wow!" reaction during market testing, it went straight back to the design studio.

Beyond just seeking cutting-edge technology and stylish designs, Samsung put the customer at the core of this innovation movement. "Put simply, our differentiation is centered on producing innovative technology that brings genuine change to people's lives," said Sue Shim, Samsung's chief marketing officer. "We do this by bringing a relentless focus on consumer experience and product innovation in everything we do."

With its fresh customer-centered focus, Samsung made quick work of surpassing Sony. Today, Samsung's annual revenues of $196 billion are more than two and a half times Sony's $75 billion. And over the past five years, as Samsung's sales and profits have seen double-digit growth, Sony's revenues have declined and losses have compounded. According to brand tracker Interbrand, Samsung is now the world's seventh most valuable brand—ahead of megabrands like Disney, Pepsi, Nike, and Toyota—and one of the fastest-growing brands in the world. And Sony? It has fallen from grace as the value of its brand has declined as dramatically as Samsung's has risen.

But more than growth, Samsung has achieved the new product Wow! factor it sought. As evidence, Samsung is a dominant force at the annual International Design Excellence Awards (IDEA) presentations—the Academy Awards of the design world—which judge new products based on appearance, functionality, and inspirational thinking. Year after year, Samsung emerges as the top corporate winner. Last year, Samsung claimed 10 awards, more than three times as many as the runners-up.

When New Becomes Old

Good companies achieve their strategic goals. Great companies modify their strategic plans as goals are met, always looking to the future and positioning themselves to remain in front. After Lee was named top CEO of the Decade by *Fortune Korea*, he announced that the "new management" plan was old news. After 17 years of remarkable success, Lee admitted that Samsung's main products would likely become obsolete within the next 10 years. He then unveiled the underpinnings of a new strategic direction based on the Chinese axiom *mabuljungje*—meaning "horse that does not stop." In a memo to Samsung employees, Lee said, "The 'new management' doctrine for the past 17 years helped catapult the company into being one of the world's best electronics makers. Now is not a time to be complacent but a time to run."

Although Samsung doesn't claim to know what will replace today's products as they become obsolete, it is investing heavily to ensure that it is the company that develops them. Even with its new product systems in place, CEO Lee stresses the need for Samsung to completely overhaul its business model or risk losing market share. Fortunately for Samsung, profits have been so good that it has the funds to support its quest to remain at the top of the innovation heap. Year after year, Samsung boosts its innovation investment budget to record highs, even as its competition makes cuts. Its most recent research and development expense of $13.4 billion was second only to Volkswagen's $13.5 billion and more than double that of Amazon, IBM, or Cisco. Sony, Toshiba, Sharp, and Hitachi—Samsung's more traditional competitors in the past—didn't even come close.

The folks at Samsung know that future success will require much more than flashy hardware gadgets. For that reason, Samsung isn't really paying attention to Sony anymore. Samsung knows that it cannot thrive in the long term by merely offering sharper colors, better sound quality, or even "Wow!" designs. Over the past half-decade, Samsung has focused on competing with the likes of Apple for dominance of the mobile device market and for the content and advertising that go along with such devices.

That focus has paid off, and Samsung has surged to the top of the smartphone market. Just a few years ago, Samsung's goal was to double its share of the smartphone market from 5 percent to 10 percent. But the success of the Galaxy line catapulted Samsung into the position of market leader, besting Apple with a global market share of more than 30 percent. And although Apple has the jump on controlling content with more than 100 billion downloads through its App Store, Samsung's Galaxy App Store is holding its own.

The Internet of Things

Despite its indisputable success in smartphones, Samsung knows that that success can be short-lived. Although it still maintains the lead in the market, Samsung's fortunes have waned in the past year as the latest rendition of the iPhone cut its market share in China in half, reducing its global market share to 25 percent. In a saturated and cut-throat market, Samsung knows that future growth will not come from a bigger, better smartphone.

Rather, Samsung is again shifting its strategic direction. Samsung wants to take the lead in "the Internet of Things"—a global environment where all electronic devices, appliances, vehicles, and even static items such as clothing will be digitally connected with each other, with the people who use them, and with the companies that make them.

In recent years, Samsung has quietly gone about creating a foundation for establishing an interconnective web between all of its products and linking them with the rest of the world. It already makes products in just about every imaginable category of home devices. Not many years ago, it dove into semiconductors, a business that has been growing rapidly for the company in terms of size, innovation, and profitability. And last year, it purchased SmartThings, a smart-home start-up company.

But at the recent Internet of Things World event in San Francisco, Young Sohn, Samsung's chief strategy officer, blew things wide open. He unveiled a plan that makes Samsung's intentions clear. The company is committing a funding pool of $100 million to start-ups that want to help build the ecosystem. Committing to a policy of openness and collaboration, Sohn unveiled a new line of semiconductor chips—state-of-the-art processors that combine hardware and software—that are now available for sale, helping companies large and small quickly and easily build Internet-connected devices. And to meet what it expects will be enormous demand for these and future chips, Samsung is investing $14 billion in a massive semiconductor manufacturing complex.

To accomplish its goal of becoming a leader in the Internet of Things market, Samsung is taking on its biggest challenge yet. For starters, this shift in strategy broadens Samsung's list of competitors from an already daunting set to one that includes just about every company in every field of high technology and even some beyond that. Adding to that challenge, there are no common standards for technologies required to connect the many devices of the world—technologies that involve networking, software, and hardware. As a result, there are thousands of companies—from Google and Apple to myriad start-ups—trying to move their products toward interconnectivity but not getting much closer to a state of universal compatibility.

To add to this challenge, the many participants in the Internet of Things game don't see eye to eye, a competitive dynamic that makes the process much more difficult. As the many players work toward compatibility, they employ numerous and often incompatible approaches. And whereas Samsung and many others have committed to collaboration and an open ecosystem, others intend to go it alone and develop their own systems. For example, Apple is developing its HomeKit platform—a proprietary system that allows users to command the devices in their homes through Apple TV using Siri. Remember "Intel Inside"? Picture a "Made for iPhone" logo on devices that would ensure shoppers of interoperability under the Apple system.

But these challenges are not dousing Samsung's fire. The company's motivations go beyond greater financial performance. According to Alex Hawkinson, CEO for SmartThings, Samsung is trying to lead by example and trying to "do what is right by the customers" by giving them more choice and flexibility. "We will focus on creating amazing experiences in both software and hardware, and win through the power of our innovation rather than trying to win by locking others out or limiting choice," Hawkinson says.

So far as the Internet of Things goes, the ultimate goal is to build artificial intelligence technology that can gather data from smart homes, cars, and wearable devices and turn them into useful insights. That might sounds just a little too Big Brother-ish, but the wheels are already in motion. According to one conservative estimate, the number of networked devices will surge from about a billion today to 26 billion by 2020, representing a $3 trillion market. By that time, Samsung claims that 100 percent of the products it makes will be Internet-connected.

Twenty years ago, few people would have predicted that Samsung could have transformed itself so quickly and completely from a low-cost copycat manufacturer into a world-leading innovator of stylish, high-performing, premium products. But through savvy strategic planning, that's exactly what Samsung has done. And not so long ago, few if any would have predicted that Samsung would be one of the driving forces behind creating a world that is entirely interconnected. Yet, while that much remains to be seen, Samsung certainly seems to have all the right ingredients. And, based on it record of success, Yoon may have waxed prophetic as he unveiled Samsung's new strategic direction: "We have to show consumers what's in it for them and what the Internet of Things can achieve—to transform our economy, society, and how we live our lives."

Questions for Discussion

1. How was Samsung able to go from a copycat brand to an innovation leader?
2. In recent years, how has Samsung achieved its goals in markets where it had little presence, such as smartphones?
3. What challenges does Samsung face with such a diverse product portfolio? What benefits?
4. Is Samsung's current and future strategy customer focused? Why or why not?
5. Will Samsung be successful in achieving its goal of becoming a leader in the Internet of Things market?

Sources: Jared Newman, "Samsung's $100 Million Internet of Things Bet Is Even Crazier Than You Think," *Fast Company*, January 28, 2015, www.fastcompany.com/3041104/app-economy/samsungs-100-million-internet-of-things-bet-is-even-crazier-than-you-think; Parmy Olson, "Samsung Set to Unveil New Chips to Power Internet of Things," *Forbes*, May 12, 2015, www.forbes.com/sites/parmyolson/2015/05/12/samsung-artik-system-on-a-chip-internet-of-things/; Brian X. Chen, "Samsung Emerges as a Potent Rival to Apple's Cool," *New York Times*, February 11, 2013, p. B1; Laurie Burkitt, "Samsung Courts Consumers, Marketers," *Forbes*, June 7, 2010, p. 27; Choi He-suk, "Samsung Renews Resolve to Reform," *Korea Herald*, June 8, 2010, www.koreaherald.com/view.php?ud=20100607001598; Max Chafkin, "Samsung: For Elevating Imitation to an Art Form," *Fast Company*, March 2013, p. 108; Shara Tibken, "Samsung Launches Artik Chips for the Internet of Things," *CNet*, May 12, 2015, www.cnet.com/news/samsung-launches-artik-chips-for-internet-of-things/; and information from www.samsung.com, accessed September 2015.

Company Case 3

Sony: Battling the Marketing Environment's "Perfect Storm"

With all the hype these days about companies such as Apple, Google, Amazon, and Samsung, it's hard to remember that companies like Sony once ruled. In fact, not all that long ago, Sony was a high-tech rock star, a veritable merchant of cool. Not only was it the world's largest consumer electronics company, its history of innovative products—such as Trinitron TVs, Walkman portable music players, Handycam video recorders, and PlayStation video game consoles—had revolutionized entire industries. Sony's innovations drove pop culture, earned the adoration of the masses, and made money for the company. The Sony brand was revered as a symbol of innovation, style, and high quality.

Today, however, Sony is more a relic than a rock star, lost in the shadows of today's high-fliers. While Sony is still an enormous company with extensive global reach, Samsung overtook the former market leader as the world's largest consumer electronics company more than a decade ago and has been pulling away ever since. Likewise, Apple has pounded Sony with one new product after another. "When I was young, I had to have a Sony product," summarizes one analyst, "but for the younger generation today it's Apple." The company's latest slogan is "Be Moved." But that seems only to be pointing to the migration of Sony's customers to other brands.

Sony's declining popularity among consumers is reflected in its financial situation. For the most recent year, Samsung and Apple each tallied revenues exceeding $180 billion—more than double Sony's top line. Samsung's profits have surged in recent years while Sony's losses reached catastrophic levels. And whereas stock prices and brand values have skyrocketed for competitors, Sony's have reached new lows. Adding insult to injury, Moody's Investors Service recently cut Sony's credit rating to "junk" status.

How did Sony fall so hard so fast? The answer is a complex one. Sony never lost the capabilities that made it great. In fact, throughout the past decade, Sony was poised to sweep the markets for mp3 players, smartphones, online digital stores, and many other hit products that other companies have marketed successfully. But Sony was caught in the middle of a perfect storm of environmental forces that inhibited its growth and success. Some factors were beyond Sony's control. However, at the core of it all, Sony took its eye off the market, losing sight of the future by failing to adapt to important changes occurring all around it.

Hit on All Sides

For starters, Sony fell behind in technology. The company built its once-mighty empire based on the innovative engineering and design of standalone electronics—TVs, CD players, and video game consoles. However, as Internet and digital technologies surged, creating a more connected and mobile world, standalone hardware was rapidly replaced by new connecting technologies, media, and content. As the world of consumer entertainment gave way to digital downloads and shared content accessed through PCs, iPods, smartphones, tablets, and Internet-ready TVs, Sony was late to adapt.

Behaving as though its market leadership could never be challenged, an arrogant Sony clung to successful old technologies rather than embracing new ones. For example, for three years prior to the launch of Apple's first iPod in 2001, Sony had been selling devices that could download and play digital music files. Sony had everything it needed to create an iPod/iTunes-type world, including its own recording company. But it passed up that idea in favor of continued emphasis on its then-highly successful CD business. "[Apple's] Steve Jobs figured it out, we figured it out, we didn't execute," said Sir Howard Stringer, former Sony CEO. "The music guys didn't want to see the CD go away."

Similarly, as the world's largest TV producer, Sony clung to its cherished Trinitron cathode-ray-tube technology. Meanwhile, Samsung, LG, and other competitors were moving rapidly ahead with flat screens. Sony eventually responded. But today, both Samsung and LG sell more TVs than Sony. Sony's TV business, once its main profit center, has lost $8 billion over the last 11 years. In an effort to get back on its feet, Sony spun off its TV division into a standalone unit. But it faces a daunting uphill battle in a competitive landscape that is far different from the one in Sony's heyday. Not only does Sony continue to lose market share to Samsung and LG, but Chinese TV makers such as Haier, Hisense, and TCL are producing cutting-edge flat-panel offerings with a cost advantage that significantly undercuts Sony.

It was a similar story for Sony's PlayStation consoles, once the undisputed market leader and accounting for one-third of Sony's profits. Sony yawned when Nintendo introduced its innovative motion-sensing Nintendo Wii, dismissing it as a "niche game device." Instead, Sony engineers loaded up the PS3 with pricey technology that produced a loss of $300 per unit sold. Wii became a smash hit and the best-selling game console; the PS3 lost billions for Sony, dropping it from first place to third.

Even as a money loser, the PlayStation system, with its elegant blending of hardware and software, had all the right ingredients to make Sony a leader in the new world of digital entertainment distribution and social networking. Executives inside Sony even recognized the PlayStation platform as the "epitome of convergence," with the potential to create "a fusion of computers and entertainment." In other words, Sony could have made a strong competitive response to Apple's iTunes. But that vision never materialized, and Sony has lagged in the burgeoning business of connecting people to digital entertainment.

There are plenty of other examples of Sony's failure to capitalize on market trends despite the fact that it had the products to do so. Consider the Sony MYLO (or MY Life Online), a clever device released a year before the first iPhone that had the essence of everything that would eventually define the smartphone—a touch screen, Skype, a built-in camera, even apps. Or how about the long line of Sony Reader devices, the first of which was released a year before Amazon took the world by storm with its first Kindle.

The Turnaround

As Sony awoke to the reality of flattening revenues and plummeting profits, it made efforts to turn things around. In 2005, then-CEO Stringer moved in to put Sony back on track. To his credit, Stringer made a credible effort to reignite company, developing a turnaround plan aimed at changing the Sony mindset and moving the company into the new connected and mobile digital age. Stringer's efforts were slow to take root, meeting resistance within Sony's hardware-worshipping culture. "Whenever I mentioned content," he says, "people would roll their eyes because, 'This is an electronics company, and content is secondary.'" But even with its rigid structure and inflexible culture working against it, Sony's strengths kept it in the game. In fact, just a few years into Stringer's tenure, the once-great consumer electronics giant began to show signs of life, as Sony's profits jumped 200 percent to $3.3 billion on rising revenue.

But if Sony didn't already have enough challenges, this uptick occurred just as the Great Recession hit. A year later, Sony was right back where it started with a billion-dollar loss. Stringer was quick to point out that if not for the global financial collapse and the yen trading near a post-war high, Sony would have been comfortably profitable. After a few more years of negative profits, Sony was again poised for success. Its best batch of new products in more than a decade was heading for store shelves. Perhaps more important, the company was ready to launch the Sony Entertainment Network—an iTunes-like global network that would finally combine Sony's strengths in movies, music, and video games with all its televisions, PCs, phones, and tablets. Analysts forecasted a profit of $2 billion.

But on March 11, 2011, Stringer received a text message at 4:30 am, after having just arrived in New York City. Eastern Japan had been devastated by an earthquake and tsunami. Nobody at Sony was hurt. In fact, Sony's employees dove into rescue efforts, fashioning rescue boats from foam shipping containers to assist in saving victims and ferrying supplies. But in the aftermath of the destruction, Sony shuttered 10 plants, disrupting the flow of Blu-ray discs, batteries, and many other Sony items.

In the wake of the extreme economic and natural disasters, Sony's miseries had only just begun. A month later, a hacking attack invaded the company's Internet entertainment services. In what was determined to be the second-largest online data breach in U.S. history, Sony was forced to shut down the PlayStation Network. A short four months later, fires set by rioters in London destroyed a Sony warehouse and an estimated 25 million CDs and DVDs, gutting the inventory of 150 independent labels. And to round out the year, floods in Thailand shut down component plants, disrupting production and distribution of Sony cameras.

Sony's big comeback turned out to be big all right, but for all the wrong reasons. The projected $2 billion profit ended up as a $3.1 billion loss, marking a three-year losing streak. As Stringer prepared to fade away into retirement, Kazuo Hirai, Sony's emerging CEO, began speaking publicly of Sony's "sense of crisis." Indeed, Sony entered the record books the following year with a net loss of $6 billion—its biggest ever.

Assessing the Damage

So, in the end, just what is it that has caused Sony's dramatic fall from grace? Was it an addiction to hardware, an uncompetitive cost structure, the global financial crisis, natural disasters, computer hacking, or riots? In retrospect, all these elements of the marketing environment combined to deliver blow after blow. Sony's encounter with a perfect storm of environmental forces illustrates the havoc such forces can wreak—whether unforeseeable natural and economic events or more predictable turns in technology.

Throughout Sony's recent turbulent existence, a few things remain clear. Sony is a company with a long history and strong legacy that refuses to give up. Even now, CEO Hirai and others at Sony are firmly resolved to save the company. In addition to spinning off the TV division, Hirai sold Sony's Vaio PC operation and cut thousands of jobs as part of a restructuring plan with the purpose of cutting costs and making Sony profitable again. But as revenues continue to slide and seven-figure annual losses continue to mount, there are few lifelines in sight. Sony hasn't had a breakout product in more than a decade. Even now, the most innovative items in development are a mobile payment device and smart glasses, products that competitors have already brought to the market. With its existing portfolio of products and the Sony Entertainment Network, the company still has all the ingredients needed to become a total entertainment provider in today's connected market. But so far, Sony doesn't seem to be making the kinds of changes needed to bring those ingredients together. And even if it does, can the Sony brand regain the allure that will bring consumers calling?

Questions for Discussion

1. What microenvironmental factors have affected Sony's performance since 2000?
2. What macroenvironmental factors have affected Sony's performance during that period?
3. What stands in the way of Sony's success today?
4. Given Sony's current situation, what recommendations would you make to Hirai for the future of the company?

Sources: Ewan Spence, "Sony's Lost Confidence Will Doom the Xperia Z4," *Forbes*, April 24, 2015, www.forbes.com/sites/ewanspence/2015/04/24/sony-xperia-z4-pr-fail/; Will Ripley and Charles Riley, "Can Anything Save Sony?" *CNNMoney*, October 31, 2014, http://money.cnn.com/2014/10/30/technology/sony/; James McQuivey, "Sony Should Have Been a Digital Contender," *Forbes*, February 6, 2014, www.forbes.com/sites/forrester/2014/02/06/sony-should-have-been-a-digital-contender/; Cliff Edwards and Mariko Yasu, "Sony's Search for Cool. The Old-Fashioned Way," *Bloomberg Businessweek*, February 24, 2013, pp. 20–21; and information from www.sony.net, accessed September 2015.

Company Case 4

Campbell Soup Company: Watching What You Eat

You might think that a well-known, veteran consumer products company like the Campbell Soup Company has it made. After all, when people think of soup, they think of Campbell's. Selling products under such an iconic brand name should be a snap. But if you ask Denise Morrison, CEO of Campbell, she'll tell you a different story. Just a few years ago, when Morrison took over as head of the world's oldest and best-known soup company, she faced a big challenge—reverse the declining market share of a 144-year-old brand in a mature, low-growth, and fickle market characterized by shifting consumer preferences, ever-expanding tastes, and little tolerance for price increases. Turning things around would require revitalizing the company's brands in a way that would attract new customers without alienating the faithful who had been buying Campbell products for decades.

Morrison had a plan. A core element of that plan was to maintain a laser-like focus on consumers. "The consumer is our boss," Morrison said. "[Maintaining a customer focus] requires a clear, up-to-the-minute understanding of consumers in order to create more relevant products." Morrison's plan involved transforming the traditional stagnant culture of a corporate dinosaur into one that embraces creativity and flexibility. But it also involved employing innovative methods that would allow brand managers and product developers to establish the customer understanding that was so desperately needed. In other words, marketing research at the Campbell Soup Company was about to change.

Reading Consumers' Minds

Soup is a well-accepted product found in just about everyone's pantry in the United States. However, not long ago, Campbell researchers discovered that marketing soups presents unique problems. People don't covet soup. Sure, a steaming bowl of savory soup really hits the spot after coming in out of a bitingly cold rain. But soup is not a top-of-mind meal or snack choice, and it's typically a prelude to a more interesting main course. The bottom line—consumers don't really think much about soup, making meaningful marketing research difficult.

For years, Campbell researchers relied on good old paper-and-pencil surveys and traditional interviews to gain consumer insights for making ads, labels and packaging, and the products themselves more effective. But Campbell's experience with such traditional marketing research showed that traditional methods failed to capture important subconscious thoughts, emotions, and behaviors that consumers experience when shopping for soup.

So instead, to get closer to what was really going on inside consumers' hearts and minds, Campbell researchers began employing state-of-the-art neuroscience methods. They outfitted shoppers with special vests that measured skin-moisture levels, heart rates, depth and pace of breathing, and postures. Sensors tracked eye movements and pupil width. Then, to aid interpretation, such biometric data was combined with interviews and videos that captured each shopper's experiences.

The high-tech research produced some startling insights. Campbell knew that people hold strong emotions associated with eating soup. After all, who doesn't remember getting a hot bowl of soup from Mom when they were sick or cold? But the new biometric testing revealed that all that warmth and those positive emotions evaporated when consumers confronted the sea of nearly identical red and white Campbell's cans found on a typical grocery store soup aisle.

In the past, the top of a typical store shelf display featured a large Campbell's logo with a bright-red background. But the new research showed that such signs made all varieties of Campbell's Soup blend together, creating an overwhelming browsing situation and causing shoppers to spend less time at the aisle. The biometric research methods also revealed that the soup can labels themselves were lacking—the big bowl of soup on a Campbell's label was not perceived warmly, and the large spoon filled with soup provoked no emotional response.

Bases on these research insights, in an attempt to prompt and preserve important consumer emotions surrounding soup consumption, Campbell's began evaluating specific aspects of its displays, labels, and packaging. This led to seemingly small but important changes. For starters, the Campbell's logo is now smaller and lower on the shelf, minimizing the overwhelming "sea of cans" effect. To further encourage browsing, can labels now fall into different categories, each with distinguishing visual cues. Varieties like Beef Broth and Broccoli Cheese, which are typically used as ingredients in recipes, feature a narrow blue swath across the middle of the can with a "Great for Cooking" label. A green swath and the label "98% Fat Free" characterize reduced-fat varieties. Tomato Chipotle & Olive Oil, part of Campbell's "Latin Inspired" line, features a black background rather than the traditional white. And top-sellers such as Chicken Noodle, Tomato, and Cream of Mushroom feature the plain traditional label with the center medallion, immortalized by Andy Warhol's larger-than-life recreations of Campbell's soup cans. As for bringing out those warm emotions, Campbell's labels are now adorned with steam rising off a larger, more vibrant picture of the featured soup in a more modern white bowl. The nonemotional spoons are gone as well.

Can such minor label changes make a real difference? Yes, they can. Campbell's claims that its sales of condensed soups are up by 2 percent since making the changes. That may not sound like much, but even a small sales bump applied to a $2 billion consumer brand means real money. The sales jump also indicates that consumers are receiving greater value through a more fulfilling shopping experience.

Diving Deeper for Insights

Although the insights from Campbell's biometric marketing research have proven valuable, it will take more to capture the attention of a new generation of customers and stay attuned to the changing nature of consumer food tastes and preferences. Additionally, the Campbell Soup Company makes and markets much more than just soup these days. Over the years, the company has added or created such brands as Pepperidge Farms, Swanson, Pace, Prego, V8, Bolthouse Farms, and Plum Organics. Today, Campbell's house of packaged food brands includes something for just about everyone. With that kind of product portfolio, maintaining and creating relevant products based on a clear, up-to-the-minute understanding of consumers is an especially daunting proposition.

To capture clear and contemporary customer insights, Campbell's researchers turn to deep dive marketing research—qualitative methods employed in the fields of anthropology and other social sciences for up-close-and-personal study. Campbell's researchers and marketers dive in and spend time with consumers on their own turf. "We're in their homes," says Charles Vila, Campbell's vice president of consumer and customer insights. "We are cooking with them; we're eating with them; we're shopping with them." By spending hours at a time with consumers and observing them in their natural environments, researchers can unlock deep consumer insights of which customers themselves are often not aware.

By employing deep dive marketing research methods, Campbell researchers have identified six different consumer groups, each with an extensive profile. For each of these groups, Campbell has created six fully equipped kitchens at its Camden, New Jersey, headquarters, each designed to mirror the homes of consumers in the six groups. Each kitchen has a unique design, with different appliances, different features, and, most importantly, different food in the cabinets and refrigerators.

At one end of the spectrum is the group called "Uninvolved Quick Fixers." These are individuals and families who are not acquainted with or into cooking. Their kitchens are strewn with pizza boxes, and collections of takeout menus adorn their fridges. Their stoves and ovens often look like they've never been touched. "They're doing a lot of microwaving and frozen foods," explains the manager of Campbell's test facilities.

At the other end of the spectrum is group six, the "Passionate Kitchen Masters." Their kitchens tend to be filled with well-used, high-end appliances. Their refrigerators are stuffed with fresh produce, dairy, and meats. Gourmet sauces and artisanal breads and pastas are complemented by a wide variety of spices.

Such levels of detail help Campbell marketers discover and understand existing and developing trends in each consumer group as well as in the general market. For example, ginger is in. Only a few years ago, this herb was something found only in ethnic restaurants or in obscure recipes. But now its popularity is soaring. Campbell expects that it will soon be an important ingredient for each of the six consumer segments, a valuable insight for developing new products.

Another conclusion from Campbell's deep dive is that although Passionate Kitchen Masters consume far fewer prepared and packaged foods than other consumers, they still buy a lot of ingredients—such as broth. Broth flies under the radar of most consumers. But for people who like to cook, it's a sturdy component of soups, sauces, and braised meats.

Under both the Campbell's and Swanson brands, broth is also a $400 million business for the Campbell Soup Company. Applying the 2 percent sales boost resulting from the label changes discussed earlier translates to $8 million sales gains in broth alone. That's why Campbell's researchers are so interested in consumer trends, big and small.

The main goal is to enhance the customer's food experience. For example, Thai dishes are becoming more popular for foodies. But coming up with key ingredients like lemongrass is both time consuming and expensive. "Even for confident cooks, to bring those together, to go and purchase them, and actually blend them in such a way that it actually works, that's not easy," says Campbell's vice president Dale Clemiss, who oversees the Swanson and other Campbell brands. Add that to other insights that Campbell's research has uncovered, and a new broth is born—Swanson Thai Ginger, a broth "infused with flavors of lime, soy sauce, coconut, lemongrass, cilantro, and ginger—a simple way to make delicious restaurant inspired global dishes at home."

Every marketing research method has pitfalls. So Campbell combines multiple research methods. In addition to neuroscience and deep dive research, the company still employs traditional methods of surveys and interviews. The triangulation of data across methods allows for greater accuracy as well as the ability to cover larger consumer samples.

In the packaged foods business, every little bit helps. It's all about staying in tune with consumers and keeping up with the changes—large and small—in consumer preferences. That philosophy has worked well for the Campbell Soup Company in the past. And as Campbell has dug deeper through multiple marketing research methods, the proof is in the pudding. Last year, Campbell's corporate revenues were up 2.4 percent, following a 5.1 percent increase the year before. Net profits are steady at 8 to 10 percent. Campbell's stock price has also increased by nearly 50 percent in the past few years. As the company Web site states, "For generations, people have trusted Campbell to provide authentic, flavorful, and readily available foods and beverages that connect them to each other, to warm memories, and to what's important today." With the help of Campbell's marketing research program, it looks like consumers will continue to trust Campbell for generations to come.

Questions for Discussion

1. What are the strengths and weaknesses of the Campbell Soup Company's marketing information system?
2. What objectives does Campbell have for the marketing research efforts described in this case?
3. Compare the effectiveness of Campbell's biometric research with its deep dive research.
4. Describe how traditional marketing research could be integrated with Campbell's research efforts from this case.

Sources: Mark Garrison, "How Food Companies Watch What You Eat," *Marketplace*, December 2, 2013, www.marketplace.org/topics/business/how-food-companies-watch-what-you-eat; Ilan Brat, "The Emotional Quotient of Soup Shopping," *Wall Street Journal*, February 17, 2010, p. B1; Bonnie Marcus, "Campbell Soup CEO Denise Morrison Stirs the Pot to Create Cultural Change," *Forbes*, April 25, 2015, www.forbes.com/sites/bonniemarcus/2014/04/25/campbell-soup-ceo-denise-morrison-stirs-the-pot-to-create-cultural-change/; and information from www.campbellsoupcompany.com/about-campbell/, accessed September 2015.

Company Case 5

GoldieBlox: Swimming Upstream against Consumer Perceptions

When Debbie Sterling was in high school, her math teacher recognized her quantitative talent and suggested she pursue engineering as a college major. At the time, Sterling couldn't figure out why her teacher thought she should drive trains for a living. But the suggestion was enough to get her started down the right path. After four years at Stanford, Sterling graduated with a degree in mechanical engineering. But throughout the course of her studies, Sterling noticed the lack of women in her engineering program—a characteristic phenomenon in field where men outnumber women 86 percent to 14 percent. This observation ignited an obsession in Sterling. She set out on a mission to inspire a future generation of female engineers by disrupting the pink aisle in toy stores.

During the past few years, Sterling has been named *Time*'s "Person of the Moment" and one of *Business Insider*'s "30 Women Who Are Changing the World" among other accolades. Why? Because Sterling is the founder and CEO of GoldieBlox, a toy company that is making Sterling's mission a reality.

A Different Kind of Toy Company

After graduating, Sterling started researching everything from childhood development to gender roles. One of her findings was that in order to gain interest in and pursue a given field, a person must be exposed to the right inputs at an early age. This fact became particularly bothersome as Sterling became more and more familiar with the contents of the average toy aisle in stores. Toys for girls are in the pink aisle, dominated by dolls, stuffed animals, and princesses, whereas toys for boys are found in the blue aisle, filled with macho action figures, various toy weapons, and a huge variety of building block sets. Most experts agree that the toys served up to young girls do little to encourage an interest in science, technology, engineering, and math (STEM) subjects. This knowledge led Sterling to develop a plan to create a different kind of toy for girls.

As she began developing ideas for toys, another research finding struck her—girls possess stellar verbal skills and tend to learn better by interacting with stories. That insight was instrumental in the creation of the GoldieBlox line of construction sets. Part Erector Set and part storybook, the combination was designed to engage girls through their verbal skills and encourage them to build through narratives that feature the adventures of Goldie, a freckled-faced blonde girl donning overalls and a tool belt. Although Goldie comes off as a bit of a tomboy, she's still girlish. Skinny, blonde, and cute, she favors pinks and purples. The toys and stories feature animals and ribbons, and characters are more likely to help others than to succeed on their own.

After her innovative toy sets received little interest at the American International Toy Fair in New York City, Sterling started her own company. That decision sparked more interest than she could have ever imagined. To raise the $150,000 needed for the first round of production, Sterling launched a Kickstarter crowd-sourced funding campaign. Her funding goal was reached in just four days, and the funding topped out at $285,000.

With little to spend on traditional advertising, Sterling first promoted her inventive toys with some YouTube ads, including "Princess Machine," featuring young girls who take their stereotypically girly toys and create a sophisticated Rube Goldberg device. That video went viral to the tune of 8 million views in little more than a week. Shortly thereafter, GoldieBlox's first two products became Amazon's top two selling toys during the industry's busiest month of December. And if all that wasn't enough, GoldieBlox beat out 15,000 contenders in Intuit's "Small Business Big Game" Super Bowl ad contest, winning a $4 million spot during the big game.

Today, less than three years after the launch of its first product, GoldieBlox's toys are sold at Target, Toys "R" Us, Amazon, and 6,000 other retailers worldwide. The brand features more than a dozen play sets, the Bloxtown interactive Web site and app, a Goldie action figure, a "More Than Just a Princess" line of T-shirts and hoodies, and an original music video. GoldieBlox has won numerous industry awards, and its toys have succeeded in raising awareness about the lack of women in technical and scientific fields as well as the issues associated with the traditional pink aisle.

All That Glitters Is Not Goldie

With all this success, you would think that GoldieBlox would be heralded by anyone and everyone wanting to change gender-based stereotypes in toys. But GoldieBlox has sparked substantial debate over whether it is really helping the cause it claims to be serving. The opposition, led by many feminist voices, claims that GoldieBox's approach is little more than window dressing. The debate got really ugly after the launch of GoldieBlox and the Parade Float, a construction set based on a new challenge faced by Goldie and her friends—to create a float to transport the winner of a beauty pageant. "You cannot create a toy meant to break down stereotypes when you start off with the ideal that 'we know all girls love princesses,'" argues author Melissa Atkins Wardy. Those in the opposition camp call for toys that are gender-neutral. "When we use princess culture, pinkification, and beauty norms to sell STEM toys to girls and fool ourselves that we are amazing and progressive and raising an incredible generation of female engineers, we continue to sell our girls short." Additionally, while the toys are designed to stir interest in girls by having them build and create, critics have raised concerns that GoldieBlox toys are too simplistic.

But Sterling is quick to respond to all such arguments and show that GoldieBlox isn't just trying to hook parents with a gimmick that doesn't deliver. "There's nothing wrong with being a princess," says the 32-year-old entrepreneur. "We just think girls can build their own castles too." This idea is backed by many advocates who recognize that to disrupt the pink aisle, you can't start out by trying to obliterate it.

To influence through play the types of hobbies and academic fields that women pursue, a company first must penetrate a very competitive market. Creating toys that are void of things that girls find appealing will only send girls scrambling for the nearest Bratz doll or Disney princess. GoldieBlox toys may incorporate traditional gender stereotypes, but they tweak and reframe them. GoldieBlox spent years researching gender differences, seeking significant input from Harvard neuroscientists, and observing children's play patterns. "Our stories leverage girls' advanced verbal skills to help develop and build self-confidence in their spatial skills," says Sterling with confidence.

Whether or not these two sides will resolve their differences in trying to achieve the same goal, there is no question that GoldieBlox has taken the toy industry by storm. And Sterling is far from finished. While clearly motivated to put an end to the stereotypes that have been generated by the toy and entertainment industries, she makes it clear that the goal is to become a multi-platform character brand à la Disney. "We want to be the brand that kids are whining for."

If the next three years are anything like GoldieBlox's first three, it's easy to envision a new kind of toy aisle at the local supercenter—one that heavily features Goldieblox's multi-platform brand.

Questions for Discussion

1. Of the factors that influence consumer behavior, which category or categories (cultural, social, personal, or psychological) best explain the existence of a blue toy aisle and a pink toy aisle? Why?
2. Choose the specific factor (for example, culture, family, occupation, attitudes) that you think most accounts for the blue/pink toy aisle phenomenon. Explain the challenges faced by GoldieBlox in attempting to market toys that "swim against the stream" or push back against the forces of that factor.
3. To what degree is GoldieBlox bucking the blue/pink toy aisle system?
4. If GoldieBlox succeeds at selling lots of its toys, will that accomplish the mission of increasing the presence of females in the field of engineering?

Sources: Lisa Wirthman, "4 Innovation Lessons Entrepreneurs Can Learn from GoldieBox," *Forbes*, March 2, 2015, www.forbes.com/sites/northwesternmutual/2015/03/02/disrupting-pink-how-goldieblox-changes-the-way-girls-think-about-toys/; Katy Waldman, "GoldieBlox: Great for Girls? Terrible for Girls? Or Just Selling Toys?" *Slate*,

November 26, 2013, www.slate.com/blogs/xx_factor/2013/11/26/goldieblox_disrupting_the_pink_aisle_or_just_selling_toys.html; Jennifer Reingold, "Watch Out Disney: This Toy Startup's Coming for You," *Fortune*, November 26, 2014, http://fortune.com/2014/11/26/goldieblox-toy-startup/; "Meet the Toymaker Who Is Disrupting the Pink Aisle," *American Association of University Women*, February 26, 2015, www.nccwsl.org/2015/02/26/debbie-sterling/; and information from www.goldieblox.com, accessed September 2015.

Company Case 6

Virgin America: Flight Service for the Tech Savvy

After an exceptionally frustrating day at the office, Jessica set out to unwind in one of her favorite third places. The mood lighting immediately brought her blood pressure down as she walked in and took a deep, relaxing breath. She was happy that her favorite spot was available—a comfy leather chair in the back corner of the room, where she used the touchscreen at the table in front of her to order her favorite drink. Then, putting on a set of noise-canceling headphones, Jessica began catching up on her favorite TV show with her own personal entertainment portal.

If this sounds like a local Starbucks or trendy nightclub, think again. Jessica had just boarded a flight on Virgin America, one of the youngest airlines in the United States. It's also the hottest airline, besting all competition in various industry and customer surveys. And after just six years in business, Virgin America is also profitable—one of the fastest launch-to-profitability postings in all of airdom.

How does a start-up airline break into one of the most competitive industries in the world, notorious for barriers to entry? For Virgin America, the answer is twofold—by putting customers first and by targeting the right customer segment.

Targeting the Right Customers

Virgin America first took to the skies in 2007. This wouldn't be the first shot at starting an airline for Richard Branson—founder of parent company Virgin Group. Virgin's international airline, Virgin Atlantic, had been crossing the pond between the United States and Europe since 1984. But Virgin America would be an entirely independent enterprise. And while Branson and other Virgin Group executives make no day-to-day decisions at Virgin America, the unorthodox Virgin culture—fun, creative, even whacky—is unmistakable.

One of Branson's core values that permeates Virgin America is this: Take care of your people first and profits will follow. In an industry characterized by customer complaints about service, it would seem that a customer-centric approach would be enough to gain a foothold in the market. But when Virgin started air service in the United States, at least a few other airlines had already established themselves based on a "customer first" mantra, including industry leader Southwest Airlines. And Virgin America knew that it could not expect to succeed by playing the low-price game. Not only was Southwest the reigning champion on value, but the bulk of airline competitors were already beating each other up for low-price dominance.

Virgin America found a different competitive hook. It targeted a segment of frequent fliers who were young, savvy, influential, and willing to pay just a little bit more for an airline that would take care of them—the Silicon Valley faction. By providing exceptional service and amenities that appeal to this particular slice of airline customers, Virgin America has been able to charge slightly higher fares and still establish a growing base of fiercely loyal patrons.

Honing In on the Details

Offering unique amenities in the airline business is a challenge for any company. But from the beginning, the Virgin America experience was designed with its target customer in mind. Its fleet consists of 53 Airbus A320s, each brand new when it went into service, minimizing the unexpected delays due to maintenance and repairs. Custom-designed leather seats are roomier and more comfortable than average coach seating. And that mood lighting? Not only does it bathe the aircraft cabin in an appealing purplish glow, it automatically adjusts to one of 12 different shades based on outside light.

To appeal to tech gurus, Virgin America focused on equipping its planes with the latest hardware and software. From day one, Virgin was the only domestic carrier to offer fleetwide in-flight WiFi—a distinction that it maintains to this day, even as it has stayed ahead of the competition by upgrading the network to ensure the fastest in-flight speeds available. Every seat has its own power outlet, USB port, and nine-inch video touchscreen with a QWERTY keyboard/remote control.

That touchscreen provides access to the most advanced entertainment and information system in U.S. skies. Virgin America's proprietary Red system allows each guest to choose on-demand movies, TV programs, music, or video games. Red also allows patrons to track their flight on interactive Google Maps, engage in seat-to-seat chat with other customers, and order food and drinks for themselves or anyone else on board. It's a system designed to give passengers a feeling of control during an experience that is otherwise mostly out of their control.

Many of these ideas came by way of Virgin America's techy clientele. It's no accident that the company's headquarters are located in Burlingame, California, just a few short miles from the San Francisco airport. In fact, Virgin America is the only airline based in Silicon Valley. Not only is the company constantly experimenting with every aspect of the business, it has made strong efforts to involve Silicon Valley entrepreneurs and executives in the process, helping Virgin to think like its disruptive clientele. "We see ourselves as more of an incubator," says Luanne Calvert, Virgin America's chief marketing officer.

Take VX Next, for example—a group of 30 or so frequent fliers who act as a brain trust for Virgin America, generating ideas for the company at no charge. Among other winning ideas, this group was instrumental in developing the company's recent interactive promotional campaign. At the center of the campaign is a slick cinematic site that provides viewers with a virtual tour of a Virgin America flight. Demonstrating the airline's in-flight perks are founders and CEOs of companies such as Pandora, Gilt, and Pitchfork. As part of the tour, visitors to the site discover that several of the passengers on board are Virgin America frequent fliers and Silicon Valley celebrities who have made creative contributions to the airline's services with things such as curating in-flight music and menu items.

Virgin America's home-brewed tech panel was also instrumental in creating the company's latest safety video. When the company started operations, it delighted customers with a safety video like none other—an animated short featuring a techie nun and a matador with his bull. Posted online as well, the video racked up millions of views and cemented Virgin America's image as a company that could find creative alternatives to just about anything, even a federally mandated reminder to wear seatbelts. That image has carried over to Virgin America's new safety video—one created by a top Hollywood director and world-class choreographers that features 10 *So You Think You Can Dance* alums, two former Olympians, and one *American Idol* finalist. Debuting in Times Square and getting plenty of coverage from the press, the new safety video racked up 6 million views in less than two weeks.

Above the Clouds

Although there is plenty of anecdotal evidence that Virgin America's customers are thrilled with its service, it's the industry quality ratings that count. Virgin America is coming through with flying colors there as well. In the most recent annual Airline Quality Report—a survey that ranks airlines based on mishandled baggage, customer complaints, denied boardings, and on-time percent—Virgin America was number one. Virgin America is also in the top spot for customer satisfaction on *Consumer Reports*. In fact, Virgin America came away with the highest score achieved by any U.S. airline in many years.

Not to get too cocky, Virgin knows that maintaining such high rankings will be a challenge. In the coming years, the airline will expand service to more cities with cold climates, a factor that will increase the likelihood of canceled or delayed flights. It will also increase the number of passengers on flights, which will lead to longer boarding and deplaning times, affecting multiple customer service metrics. And with Virgin's techy and connected clientele, any screwup is likely to be texted, Tweeted, or otherwise broadcast for all the world to see. Playing the features and amenities game is also problematic. Things that delight customers today become ho hum tomorrow, especially when competitors are constantly trying to improve their offerings.

That's why Virgin America views its operations as a work in progress, continually changing and improving, no matter how good current operations are. "If we stand still, they'll catch us," says David Cush, Virgin America's CEO. And Virgin America sees all those Tweeting customers as an opportunity to address customer service issues in real time, not to mention a powerful source of word of mouth.

With all its success, after six years, Virgin America still had not achieved an annual profit. With still-skeptical experts looking on, however, the company has now crossed that threshold, posting net profits for the past two years. For the most recent year, Virgin America achieved $84 million in profit—the highest ever for a young airline—on $1.5 billion in revenues. The company also went public in the second-largest airline IPO in history. Although the company is far from being out of the woods, Virgin America will continue to slowly expand its services by doing what it has done for its first eight years—wow every customer with exceptional service while giving the tech community a little something extra. It's a formula that Virgin aims to keep applying, even after it grows up.

Questions for Discussion

1. Using the full spectrum of segmentation variables, describe how Virgin America segments and targets the market for airline services.
2. Which market targeting strategy is Virgin America following? Justify your answer.
3. Write a positioning statement for Virgin America.
4. Will Virgin America succeed in the long run? Why or why not?

Sources: Lauren Schwartzberg, "Most Innovative Companies: 2015, Virgin America," *Fast Company*, March, 2015, pp. 135–137; Joe Berkowitz, "Silicon Valley Celebs Star in New Virgin America Campaign," *Fast Company*, September 5, 2012, www.fastcocreate.com/1681551/silicon-valley-celebs-star-in-new-virgin-america-campaign; Grant Martin, "America's Best Airlines," *Forbes*, April 15, 2015, www.forbes.com/sites/grantmartin/2015/04/15/americas-best-airlines/; Matt Richtel, "At Virgin America, a Fine Line between Pizazz and Profit," *New York Times*, September 8, 2013, p. BU1; Charisse Jones, "Virgin America Posts Record Profit for 2014," *USA Today*, February 18, 2015, www.usatoday.com/story/money/2015/02/18/virgin-america-posts-record-profit/23608205/; and information from www.virginamerica.com/cms/about-our-airline/corporate-facts.html, accessed September 2015.

Company Case 7

Target: Where Store Brands Offer More Than Low Prices

When it comes to discount retailing, Target doesn't need to make many excuses. In little more than 50 years, the Minnesota-based company has dotted the United States and Canada with more than 1,800 stores bearing the famous red-and-white bull's-eye. With $72 billion in annual sales, Target plays second fiddle in the U.S. discount retail market only to Walmart—the world's biggest corporation. And although it is only one-seventh Walmart's size, Target has managed to keep its much larger rival on its toes with a "cheap chic" image that has revolutionized discount retailing with heavy doses of style and fashion.

Throughout the past decade, however, Target has experienced its share of ups and downs. Whereas it outpaced Walmart in growth during the early 2000s, that growth has cooled as even the trendiest value shoppers have been drawn to the more-low-price positioning of Walmart and dollar stores. Through several years of changes that have included cost-cutting, store remodeling, and inventory restructuring, Target has better positioned itself strategically to fulfill its mission to deliver "outstanding value, continuous innovation and exceptional guest experiences by consistently fulfilling our 'Expect More. Pay Less.' brand promise."

One of the ways Target is carrying out this mission is through a strong portfolio of private brands. Although store brands are nothing new for Target, it has sought not only to expand its portfolio of store brands but also to raise the perceived value of those brands in the minds of consumers. Target still sells plenty of national brands. But as customers snatch up dozens of owned and exclusive brands that can be found only in Target stores, the chain has set a benchmark for retailers of every stripe to follow when it comes to executing a store-brand strategy.

Bringing Designer Labels to Discount Retail

Not that long ago, store brands everywhere carried a "low quality" and "bland" stigma. With those less-than-attractive perceptions, such brands were purchased primarily because they were priced much lower than comparable name-brand products. Perhaps more than any other retailer, Target has fought to establish its exclusive brands as anything but traditional. In fact, Target has clung to two mission-supporting corporate values to guide store brand development: "design and innovation" and "value as more for less."

As part its private-brand strategy, Target is forging collaborative relationships with high-end designers to create exclusive product lines. Since 1999, when it introduced design partners Michael Graves and Sonia Kashuk, Target has covered just about every category of goods with designer labels. It has signed more than 50 different designers to Target-exclusive agreements, from Graves's housewares line to Mulberry for Target handbags to Isaac Mizrahi's lines of clothing, accessories, bedding, and pet products. In the last year alone, Target introduced collections by Adam Lippes (plaid apparel, accessories, home furnishings, and pet goods), Eddie Borgo (jewelry and wall art), and Lilly Pulitzer (outdoor and beach apparel, shoes, and accessories).

With these alliances, everybody benefits. The designers get tremendous exposure, a large customer base, and the power and deep pockets of a mass retailer. Target gets brand cachet that enhances the chicness of its image, and customers get style at affordable prices. As products with a designer label that might normally adorn goods with a three- or four-figure price tag, Target's designer items have been huge hits. Tales have circulated of Target customers fighting over apparel items and filling their carts to the brim on days when new items go on sale. Sellouts are common, and Target's designer labels have been known to show up on eBay with significantly higher prices.

Setting a High Bar for Store Brands

As popular as Target's designer lines have been, they represent the smaller portion of the company's exclusive store brand efforts. Rather, Target has applied its value philosophy and design expertise to creating more than a dozen store brands. The most pervasive of these is "Up & Up," which replaced the main "Target" store brand a few years ago. Instead of the familiar bull's-eye, the Up & Up lines come in white packages with big, colorful, upward-pointing arrows. With more than 800 different products in more than 50 different categories, the Up & Up brand can be found in every department of a Target store.

While Up & Up follows the more traditional approach of store brands that provide budget-friendly basics, Target has taken great care to match the quality levels of national brands wherever possible. For certain basics such as hand sanitizer ($1.74 versus $2.69 for Purell), napkins ($2.66 versus $2.99 for Bounty), and cotton swabs ($2.99 versus $4.79 for Q-tips), it's tough to tell the difference. And even when customers can see a difference, the savings are worth it. On average, Up & Up products are priced about 30 percent lower than comparable name-brand products.

But as with its designer labels, Target does not pursue a singularly low-price positioning for its store brands. This is perhaps most evident in grocery aisles, where Target now has not one but three distinct in-house food brands. Like Up & Up, Target's own Market Pantry brand covers basic staples such as cheese, milk, eggs, baking ingredients, juices, snacks, and prepared meal options. And like Up & Up, the positioning is also similar to national brands—the same quality and taste but for a lot less money.

Target's other two food brands, however, go beyond just offering customers a lower-priced option. Archer Farms is a "healthier" choice that promises no artificial flavors, artificial sweeteners, or trans fats. And although it is a "budget-friendly" brand, that budget friendliness is relative only to the types of foods that carry the Archer Farms label—items that would typically interest food snobs and gourmets. To that end, Archer Farms products are noticeably fancier.

For example, why settle for a basic variety of trail mix from Planters when you can get Caramel Cashew, Sunny Cranberry, Tex Mex, or Cinnamon Raisin Nut Breakfast from Archer Farms? As with many Archer Farms categories, Target offers far more varieties with its store brands than it does with national brands. It also focuses on flavors that consumers won't find anywhere else. "One of the best-selling Archer Farms' chips is a blue corn chip with flax seed," says Annette Miller, who oversees Target's grocery business. "One of our best-selling Archer Farms pizzas is a goat cheese, potato, and spinach pizza." Priced 10 to 30 percent lower than name brands, Archer Farms products are still cheaper. And with options such as Key Lime Cookie Straws and organic milk, Archer Farms is very much in keeping with Target's "cheap chic" image.

If Archer Farms products still aren't fancy enough for some shoppers, Target has them covered with its third and latest food brand, Simply Balanced—a mostly organic line of more than 250 products originally launched as an Archer Farms subbrand. Claiming 40 percent organic content, Simply Balanced also claims to be mostly free of genetically modified organisms. This newest Target brand is hardly cheap, but its prices compare favorably with those of other organic upscale brands that Target doesn't even stock.

With its food brands, Target focuses on products that customers are more inclined to try, such as snacks, coffee, and dairy. Especially with its two upper-tier brands, Target's store brand foods are expected to be at least as good if not better than those made by national brands. To keep costs down and maintain quality, Target focuses on developing its own food products rather than sourcing them out to other companies. In its Minneapolis test kitchens, Target employees prepare, cook, and taste-test every product before it makes it onto Target's grocery shelves.

Capitalizing on Trends

The fact that Target pushes three separate in-house food brands clearly indicates that store brands have come a long way. Similar to trends for store brands in general, Target's brands are benefiting from—if not contributing to—a national trend in acceptance and consumption of private-label foods. According to recent studies, store brands are increasingly found in U.S. kitchens. Fewer consumers feel that they are sacrificing when they purchase store food brands, and fewer consumers indicate an intention to purchase fewer store brands in the future. In fact, a surprisingly high 80 percent of all shoppers believe that private-label brands are equal to or better than national brands in terms of quality. "I'll buy Target brand and not have any qualms about the product," said one budget-minded college student. "It is a bit cheaper, and it's still really good quality." And it's not just lower-income consumers who are turning to store brands. Fortunately for Target, the greatest surge in store-brand purchases is among more affluent shoppers.

Similar to the path that Target has pursued with its private-label food brands, the company has covered many other product categories as well. Target's Cherokee brand offers "classically cool kidswear at prices that make moms and dads everywhere smile." The Xhilaration brand helps juniors to "stay on top of the latest trends." Mossimo Supply Co. "boasts funkier, more laid-back casual looks for both women and men," and Merona is "Modern classic style ... shoes, accessories, and separates." Circo covers infants and children, and Gilligan & O'Malley has women's sleepwear and lingerie covered. When it comes to furniture and household accessories, RE (Room Essentials) appeals to the needs of young adults, whereas Threshold's claim of "quality & design" is more for the established household.

In many ways, Target's store-brand strategy is paying off. About one-third of Target's sales volume comes from its private brands, and that number is rising. "We've grown our own brand foods faster than our total food growth over the past five years, as we've continued to expand our product offering into new product categories that we hadn't developed before," says Target's Miller. Additionally, 10 of Target's private-label brands generate more than $1 billion a year. Not one to rest on its laurels, Target recently extended the return window for many of its private-label brands from 90 days to one year, a bold move that signals confidence in brand quality.

But Target continues to face a tough battle in the highly competitive discount retail sector. Net revenues have remained flat over the past few years, while Walmart's have been increasing by low single digits. Target's net profits have languished as well. This tepid financial performance seems to be despite Target's store-brand efforts rather than because of them. As Target deals with various factors in the marketing environment in its struggles to get financials back on track, its store brands have staved off higher losses and provide promise for the future. If general growth trends of store brands continue, you will likely see more and more Target brands on the retailer's shelves. Fortunately for Target, it is far better prepared for such developments than many of its competitors.

Questions for Discussion

1. What benefits does Target receive from its store brands?
2. Is Target's store brand strategy working? Explain.
3. What could Target do in the future to further develop its strengths in store brands?
4. What potential problems does Target face in continuing its focus on store brands?

Sources: Paul Ziobro, "Target Extends Return Window for Private-Label Brands," *Wall Street Journal*, March 18, 2015, www.wsj.com/articles/target-extends-return-window-for-private-label-brands-1426692941; Brad Tuttle, "The Rise of the Swanky No-Name Brand," *Time*, June 11, 2013, http://business.time.com/2013/06/11/the-rise-of-the-swanky-no-name-brand/; Martin Moylan, "Target Benefits from Popularity of Store Brands," *MPR News*, November 19, 2010, www.mprnews.org/story/2010/11/19/store-brands; and additional information from www.corporate.target.com/about/design-innovation/owned-brands/# and www.corporate.target.com/about/mission-values, accessed September 2015.

Company Case 8

3M: Where Innovation Is a Way of Life

In recent years, companies topping the world's "most innovative" lists are typically high-tech leaders such as Google, Apple, Samsung, and Amazon. When thinking of companies that set the world on fire with one revolutionary product after another, the image of a stodgy company that originated in the mining industry more than 100 years ago is hardly the icon. But while 3M may not be as flashy as today's high-tech headliners, it's anything but stodgy.

3M—the Minnesota Mining and Manufacturing Company—is a multinational powerhouse with more than $31 billion in annual sales. Year after year, with machine-like precision, 20 percent of 3M's sales filter down as operating profits, allowing the company to increase its dividend to shareholders—something it has done every year for the past 57 years.

3M sells more than 50,000 products in nearly 200 countries across dozens of industries, including office products, construction, telecommunications, electronics, health care, aerospace, and automotive. Among its products are some of the world's most recognizable consumer brands, such as Scotch Tape, Nexcare first aid products, Filtrete home filtration products, Command mounting products, and Post-it Notes. But 3M's portfolio is also packed with hundreds of brands that most people have never heard of—like Peltor hearing protection equipment or Pruven waste bags for picking up dog poop.

The unusual breadth of 3M's product portfolio is both a blessing and a curse for the company. Having a hand in so many industries shields the company from overreliance on any given market. Even when multiple industries are down, many more are doing just fine. That explains 3M's financial strength. But it also explains why 3M has a hard time thrilling Wall Street. Even a hit new product doesn't make much of a difference in 3M's steady but unspectacular growth rate—one that is consistently in the low single digits.

Like 3M, the company's current CEO, Inge Thulin, is methodical and understated. He keeps a long-term focus and places strong emphasis on maintaining 3M's reliable profitability. But Thulin is also interested in stoking the fire just a bit, to put a little more heat under sales growth. One of the first things Thulin did when he took over as CEO a few years ago was to trim 3M's annual sales growth goal from 7 or 8 percent—a goal the company consistently missed—to between 4 and 6 percent. Then, as the world watched, 3M's organic sales growth grew to 5.8 percent. And under Thulin's leadership, 3M is now on track to maintain that stronger growth rate.

How did Thulin do it? By doing the same thing 3M has been doing it for decades. At the core of 3M's success is its business model—organic growth comes from innovation and the creation of market-changing products. Such market-changing products have at times created entirely new industries. 3M has sustained this type of innovation decade after decade by fostering a deep culture of innovation, encouraging collaboration, and maintaining a dedication to research and development.

Culture of Innovation

From its earliest days, 3M created a culture of innovation by allowing team members to take risks in a protected environment. 3M knows that it must try thousands of product ideas to hit the new product jackpot. One well-worn slogan at 3M is "You have to kiss a lot of frogs to find a prince." "Kissing frogs" often means making mistakes, but 3M accepts blunders and dead ends as a normal part of creativity and innovation. In fact, its philosophy seems to be "If you aren't making mistakes, you probably aren't doing anything."

As it turns out, "blunders" have turned into some of 3M's most successful products. Old-timers at 3M love to tell the story about the chemist who accidentally spilled a new chemical on her sneakers. Some days later, she noticed that the spots hit by the chemical had not gotten dirty—an attractive benefit. It was that discovery that eventually led to the creation of Scotchgard fabric protector. They tell about the early 3M scientist who had a deathly fear of shaving with a straight razor. So he invented a very fine, waterproof sandpaper, which he used to sand the stubble from his face each morning. Although this invention never caught on as a shaving solution, it became one of 3M's best-selling products—wet-dry sandpaper, now used for a wide variety of commercial and industrial applications.

And then there's the one about 3M scientist Spencer Silver. Silver started out to develop a super-strong adhesive; instead he came up with one that didn't stick very well at all. He sent the apparently useless substance on to other 3M researchers to see whether they could find something to do with it. Nothing happened for several years. Then 3M scientist Arthur Fry had an idea. As a choir member in a local church, Mr. Fry was having trouble marking places in his hymnal—the little scraps of paper he used kept falling out. He tried dabbing some of Mr. Silver's weak glue on one of the scraps. It stuck nicely and later peeled off without damaging the book. Thus were born 3M's Post-it Notes, a product that is now one of the top-selling office supply products in the world.

One of the ways 3M fosters a culture of innovation is by encouraging everyone to look for new products. The company's renowned "15 percent rule" allows all employees to spend up to 15 percent of their time "bootlegging"—working on projects of personal interest whether those projects directly benefit the company or not. And yet there is a vibe throughout the company regarding these precious six hours a week. Who knows where the next Post-it Note will come from? "It's one of the things that sets 3M apart as an innovative company … giving every one of our employees the ability to follow their instincts to take advantage of opportunities for the company," says Kurt Beinlich, a technical director who oversees a 70-person lab team. "It's really shaped what and who 3M is."

Encouraging Collaboration

Although 3M's 15 percent program has inspired other companies to follow suit (both Google and HP apply their own versions), it's a rare perk in the corporate world. Not only is it an expense, but to be successful it takes a lot more than simply giving employees the time. Experts suggest that this kind of program works best at companies where there is a high level of collaboration across employees and departments.

3M has created that collaboration in spades. One example is an annual event that is simple but has a huge impact. The event resembles a middle school science fair, as employees from dozens of 3M divisions make cardboard posters describing their 15-percent-time project. Employees hang out next to their posters, await feedback, and look for potential collaborators. Wayne Maurer, an R&D manager in 3M's abrasives division, refers to it as a chance for people to unhinge their "inner geek." "For technical people, it's the most passionate and engaged event we have at 3M."

The event is more than just an opportunity to show off; it has actually moved projects through the development phase to commercialization. Past projects that have made it to market include clear bandages, optical films that reflect light, and painter's tape that prevents bleeding. The event has even put new life in projects that have sat on a back burner for years.

One employee had an idea for creating a sandpaper with reshaped grit particles that wouldn't dull so quickly. But after playing around with the idea for a while, he shelved it and moved on to other things. Fifteen years later, the employee resurrected the project during his 15 percent time and made a poster in hopes of getting some ideas that would move the project along. With the help of new employees and new technology, 3M discovered that a particle's sharp, pyramid-like shape became more durable with a change in the mixing order of the ingredients. That discovery led to the launch of Cubitron II, sandpaper that acts more like a cutting tool. On the market since 2009, it still stumps other companies trying to create copycat products.

Emphasis on R&D

Few companies provide more support for research and development than 3M. For years, 3M invested 6 percent of sales every year in R&D. But in recent years, that spending had been cut to just 5.5 percent—a small difference on paper, but one that Thulin believes is significant. "Those long-term investments are needed to get the growth engine up and going." If such investments are reduced, Thulin believes, "you will kill the business." That's why 3M's R&D expenditures are once again up to 6 percent. Thulin believes R&D "is the heartbeat of this company and it's a competitive advantage for us." By comparison, the average of R&D expenses across corporations is about 3 percent. For the most recent year, Apple spent $4.5 billion on R&D, a company record that still amounted to only 2.6 percent of sales.

But it isn't just the amount of money invested that is important for a successful R&D program. It's how the money is used. In addition to increasing 3M's R&D allotment, Thulin is putting more priority on the 3M technologies that have the most potential for growth. Among these technologies are films designed to protect everything from smartphones to kitchen appliances and a construction wrap that will outperform DuPont's Tyvek as a weather-resistant barrier for homes and buildings.

But Thulin's plan for allocating R&D funds also includes eliminating 3M units with poor financial performance or those that aren't a good fit with the company's core strengths. For Thulin, it's nothing personal; it's strictly business. Over the past two years, 3M sold Scientific Anglers—which makes fishing line and other related products—and its Static Control business. Thulin believed there was little symbiosis between developments in the product lines of these two divisions and other 3M technologies.

Although Thulin's plan focuses on high-tech areas, it also recognizes the importance of a broad portfolio that includes low-tech items—such as doggie doo bags. In fact, 3M is committed to a broad range of pet care supplies. "You cannot have only high-tech in every category because then you will not get space in the shops," says Thulin, recognizing that mass retailers want to purchase full lines of products within and across categories from manufacturers.

This is all reflected in 3M's first promotional campaign in more than 25 years, "3M Science. Applied to Life." This global campaign is a fully digital promotional effort designed to showcase 3M's technologies and the ways that they improve everyday life. The company hopes that the campaign will bring greater exposure to many of its products that have become ubiquitous. "Like any great company, we're looking at how we can improve and continue to invest in our strengths," says Jesse Singh, 3M's senior VP of marketing and sales. "We are continuing to invest in R&D, and likewise we felt it important that we continue to take steps to emphasize the brand."

3M will likely never have growth rates matching those of Apple, Facebook, or even Microsoft in its heyday. But it will also likely never experience the potential downturns that even the biggest companies eventually face. That's why 3M's net profits hum along at about 15 percent of sales year after year. It's also why 3M's stock price has doubled over the past four years. 3M's long-term dedication to innovative new products and technologies has sustained the company for decades, and there's no reason to expect that this will change. Who knows—the next "big thing" may just have "3M" stamped on it instead of "Apple."

Questions for Discussion

1. Based on concepts discussed in Chapter 8, describe the factors that have contributed to 3M's new product success.
2. Is 3M's product development process customer centered? Why or why not?
3. Considering the product life cycle, what challenges does 3M face in managing its product portfolio?
4. Are there limits to how broad 3M's product portfolio can grow? Explain.
5. Is it possible for 3M to maintain steady growth and profitability *and* raise that growth to much higher levels?

Sources: Jennifer Rooney, "Inside 3M's First Global Brand Campaign in More than 25 Years," *Forbes*, March 11, 2015, www.forbes.com/sites/jenniferrooney/2015/03/11/inside-3ms-first-global-brand-campaign-in-more-than-25-years/; "Here Is Why We Think 3M Is Worth $140," *Forbes*, March 6, 2014, www.forbes.com/sites/greatspeculations/2014/03/06/here-is-why-we-think-3m-is-worth-140/; James R. Hagerty, "50,000 Products but 3M Still Searching for Growth," *Wall Street Journal*, November 18, 2013, p. B1; Kaomi Goetz, "How 3M Gave Everyone Days Off and Created an Innovation Dynamo," *Fast Company*, February 1, 2011, www.fastcodesign.com/1663137/how-3m-gave-everyone-days-off-and-created-an-innovation-dynamo; and additional information from www.3m.com/3M/en_US/company-us/, accessed September, 2015.

Company Case 9

Coach: Riding the Wave of Premium Pricing

Victor Luis stood looking out the window of his office on 34th Street in Manhattan's Hell's Kitchen neighborhood. It had been just over a year since he had taken over as CEO of Coach, Inc., a position that had previously been held by Lewis Frankfort for 28 years. Under Frankfort's leadership, it seemed Coach could do no wrong. Indeed, over the previous decade, the 73-year-old company had seen its revenues skyrocket from about $1 billion to more than $5 billion as its handbags became one of the most coveted luxury items for women in the United States and beyond. On top of that, the company's $1 billion bottom line—a 20 percent net margin—was a common annual outcome. Coach's revenues made it the leading handbags seller in the nation. The brand's premium price and profit margins made the company a Wall Street darling.

Right around the time Luis took over, however, Coach's fortunes had begun to stumble. Although the company had experienced promising results with expansion into men's lines and international markets, it had just recorded the fourth straight quarter of declining revenues in the United States, a market that accounts for 70 percent of its business. North American comparable sales were down by a whopping 21 percent over the previous year. Once the trendsetter, Coach lost market share to younger and more nimble competitors for two years in a row. Investors were jittery, causing Coach's stock price to drop nearly 50 percent during that time. After years of success, it now seemed that Coach could do little right.

Artisanal Origins

In a Manhattan loft in 1941, six artisans formed a partnership called Gail Leather Products and ran it as a family-owned business. Employing skills handed down from generation to generation, the group handcrafted a collection of leather goods, primarily wallets and billfolds. Five years later, the company hired Miles and Lillian Cahn—owners of a leather handbag manufacturing firm—and by 1950, Miles was running things.

As the business grew, Cahn took particular interest in the distinctive properties of the leather in baseball gloves. The gloves were stiff and tough when new, but with use they became soft and supple. Cahn developed a method that mimicked the wear-and-tear process, making a leather that was stronger, softer, and more flexible. As an added benefit, the worn leather also absorbed dye to a greater degree, producing deep, rich tones. When Lillian Cahn suggested that the company add women's handbags to the company's low-margin line of wallets, the Coach brand was born.

Over the next 20 years, Coach's uniquely soft and feminine cowhide bags developed a reputation for durability. Coach bags also became known for innovative features and bright colors rather than the usual browns and tans. As the Coach brand expanded into shoes and accessories, it also became known for attractive integrated hardware pieces—particularly the silver toggle that remains an identifying feature of the Coach brand today. In 1985, the Cahns sold Coach to the Sara Lee Corporation, which housed the brand within its Hanes Group. Frankfort became Coach's director and took the brand into a new era of growth and development.

Under Frankfort's leadership, Coach grew from a relatively small company to a widely recognized global brand. This growth included not only new designs for handbags and new product lines but a major expansion of outlets as well. When Frankfort assumed the top position, Coach had only six boutiques located within department stores and a flagship Coach store on Madison Avenue. By the time Frankfort stepped down, there were more than 900 Coach stores in North America, Asia, and Europe, with hundreds of Coach boutiques in department stores throughout those same markets as well as in Latin America, the Middle East, and Australia. In addition to the brick-and-mortar outlets, Coach had developed a healthy stream of online sales through its Web sites.

High Price Equals High Sales

With the expansion in Coach's product lines and distribution outlets, women everywhere were drawn to the brand's quality and style. But perhaps more than anything, they were attracted to the brand as a symbol of luxury, taste, and success. Over the years, Coach had taken great care to find an optimal price point, well above that of ordinary department store brands. Whereas stores that carried Coach products also sold mid-tier handbag brands for moderate prices, Coach bags were priced as much as five times higher.

It might seem that such a high price would scare buyers off. To the contrary. As Coach's reputation grew, women aspired to own its products. And although the price of a Coach bag is an extravagance for most buyers, it is still within reach for even middle-class women who want to splurge once in a while. And with comparable bags from Gucci, Fendi, or Prada priced five to ten times higher, a Coach bag is a relative bargain.

With its image as an accessible status symbol, Coach was one of the few luxury brands that maintained steady growth and profits throughout the Great Recession. And it did so without discounting its prices. Fearing that price cuts would damage the brand's image, Coach instead introduced its "Poppy" line at prices about 30 percent lower than regular Coach bags. Coach concentrated on its factory stores in outlet malls. And it maintained an emphasis on quality to drive perceptions of value. As a result, Coach's devoted customer base remained loyal throughout the tough times.

At about the same time, Coach also invested in new customers. It opened its first men's-only store, stocked with small leather goods, travel accessories, footwear, jewelry, and swimsuits. Coach also expanded men's collections in other stores. As a result, its revenue from men's products doubled in one year. The company saw similar success with international customers, pressing hard into Europe, China, and other Asian markets.

But just as it seemed that Coach was untouchable, the brand showed signs of frailty. Coach's U.S. handbag business started slowing down. During Luis's first year on the job, Coach's share of the U.S. handbag market fell from 19 percent to 17.5 percent—the second straight year for such a loss. During that same period, Michael Kors, Coach's biggest competitive threat, saw its market share increase from 4.5 percent to 7 percent. Up-and-comers Kate Spade and Tory Burch also saw increases. Because the U.S. market accounted for such a large portion of the company's business, overall revenue took a dip despite the brand's growth in new markets.

What's the Problem?

Many factors could be blamed for Coach's U.S. decline. During the most recent holiday season, Coach had to contend with the same problem many other retailers faced—less traffic in shopping malls. But Kate Spade and Michael Kors, which operate their own stores and sell through department stores in malls just as Coach does, experienced double-digit gains during the same period. Coach's performance also ran counter to the dynamics of the handbag and accessory market as a whole, which grew by nearly 10 percent over the previous year.

The differences in sales trends between Coach and its competitors have led some analysts to speculate that the long-time leader has lost its eye for fashion. "These guys are definitely losing share," said analyst Brian Yarbrough. "Fashion-wise, they're missing the beat." Yarbrough isn't alone. Many others assert that, under the same creative direction for 17 years, Coach's designs have grown stale.

Then there is the issue of Coach's price structure—in short, Coach may have taken the premium price point too far. "Coach tried to eliminate coupon promotions tied directly to its discount outlets, which are the company's biggest source of revenue, and which attract customers looking to stretch their dollars," said one luxury retail expert. "The number of people willing and able to pay a premium for luxury brands, like Coach, is getting small as this weak economy continues." However, price alone would not explain why Coach's business slid at the same time that sales by comparably priced competitors rose. Additionally, while Coach's North American revenues were down last year, sales of its high-end handbags (priced above $400) actually increased.

Some analysts have also questioned the effect of Coach's popularity on its image of exclusivity. A luxury brand's image and customer aspirations often rest on the fact that not everyone can afford it. But Coach has become so accessible, anyone that wants a Coach product can usually find a way to buy one. This availability has been fostered by Coach's outlet stores—company-owned stores that carry prior season merchandise, seconds, and lower-quality lines at much lower prices. With the number of customers drawn in by low prices, Coach's outlet stores now account for a sizable 60 percent of revenues and an even higher percentage of unit sales. Outlet sales, combined with a healthy secondary market through eBay and other Web sites, mean that Coach products are no longer as exclusive as they once were.

Although new as CEO, Luis has been with Coach for the past eight years and oversaw Coach's international expansion. And although Frankfort has stepped down, he is still involved as chairman of the board. Led by these seasoned fashion executives, Coach has a turnaround plan. For starters, the company hired a new creative director. Stuart Vevers brings to Coach the same magic that he worked for brands like Louis Vuitton, Givenchy, Bottega Veneta, and Mulberry. According to Luis, Vevers is "providing a fashion relevance for the brand like we have never had."

In addition to the creative and design changes, Coach is rebalancing its product portfolio. To win back shoppers, Coach will be positioned as a lifestyle brand with greater expansion into footwear, clothing, and accessories. Additionally, the company will increase the number of handbag offerings priced at $400 or more, a move that could raise the average price point of Coach's handbags.

The initial fruit of Coach's turnaround plan appears promising. The first lines under Vevers's direction show evidence of a complete transformation while still remaining true to the core elements of the brand. Bold new shapes and colors abound in the handbag lines. But the real changes are apparent in Coach's other lines—black leather biker jackets festooned with pins and zippers, suede coats and parkas, and urban hiker boots, all accented liberally with shearling pieces. Vevers was going for "a Coach approach to luxury, even an American approach to luxury—not too precious ... not too perfect." Based on reviews from the fashion world and the public, Vevers seems to have dialed in the right combination. "Coach is cool again, and not in a way that's appealing only to fashion insiders," says Lauren Indvik, editor in chief of *Fashionista*.

Every company gets things wrong now and then. What distinguishes good companies from bad ones is the fact that good companies are able to see their mistakes and correct them. It's clear that those in charge at Coach have recognized their mistakes. But it remains to be seen if the turnaround plan is the antidote. With all that Coach has at stake, Luis, Frankfort, and the others will not give up easily. The question is, will the new strategy restore Coach to its former glory days?

Questions for Discussion

1. What challenges does Coach face in pricing its vast product line?
2. Based on principles from the chapter, explain how price affects customer perceptions of the Coach brand.
3. How has increased competition at Coach's price points affected the brand's performance?
4. Will the plan proposed by current Coach's leadership be successful in reversing the brand's slide in market share? Why or why not?
5. What recommendations would you make to Coach?

Sources: Lauren Indvik, "Stuart Vevers Is Creating Luxury That's 'Not Too Precious' for Coach," *Fashionista*, February 13, 2015, http://fashionista.com/2015/02/coach-fall-2015; Andrew Marder, "Coach, Inc. Can't Get It Together," *Motley Fool*, April 30, 2014, www.fool.com/investing/general/2014/04/30/coach-inc-cant-get-it-together.aspx; Phil Wahba, "Coach Sales in North America Plummet as Market Share Erodes," *Reuters*, January 22, 2014, http://in.reuters.com/article/2014/01/22/coach-results-idINL3N0KW3V920140122; and additional information taken from www.coach.com/aboutus?contentObject=about-us, accessed September, 2015.

Company Case 10

Apple Pay: Taking Mobile Payments Mainstream

After leaving his office in Manhattan, Tag stopped at a nearby Panera to grab a Frontega Chicken Panini and Green Passion Power Smoothie as a quick dinner on his way to see some friends in Soho. Upon ordering, he held his Apple Watch to the contactless reader near the register, gently pressed his finger to the TouchID fingerprint sensor on the small screen, and let Apple Pay do the rest.

Wanting to get across town as soon as possible, Tag used his Uber app to summon an UberX car. During the car ride, he remembered that he needed a couple of new dress shirts. With a few quick clicks on his watch, he selected the shirts through his Macy's app. With a simple tap, he used Apple Pay to seamlessly complete the transaction. As he neared his destination, Tag added a tip to the bill for the ride through the Uber app, which he'd already configured to use Apple Pay as the default. With one simple press of his finger to TouchID on his watch, he exited the cab.

Three purchases—offline, online, and, well, sort of in between—no wallet required. No traditional wallet, that is. This new reality—one that many early adopters are already living—is rapidly expanding toward what some experts predict will become the future for everyone. Folks like Tag don't even carry traditional wallets anymore, only their mobile devices and perhaps an ID and a backup credit card for retailers that don't accept mobile payments—yet. After years of predictions that mobile payments would replace cash and credit cards, there are finally signs that it might actually be happening. And Apple is leading the way.

Hardly New

The ability to pay for transactions with a mobile device is hardly new. In fact, the first technology for mobile payments was invented by Sony way back in 1989. It was first put into use in Hong Kong's subway system in 1997 and began taking root in Japan in 2001. The tech-savvy Japanese warmed to the idea quickly, and mobile wallet apps were being used on mobile phones throughout Japan by 2004. Ever since, more than 245 million Japanese mobile phones have been equipped with the capability to make mobile payments, and Japanese consumers use mobile payments for everything from transportation to food and household purchases.

So it seems odd that a similar system has not taken root in the United States, although it hasn't been for lack of trying. Companies have been experimenting with different approaches for years. PayPal was the first to take advantage of the smartphone revolution by creating a payment app that gave just about every smartphone the potential for mobile payments. About a year later, Google entered the mobile payment game with the launch of Google Wallet. In the past five years, numerous other companies, from small start-ups to electronics and retailing giants, have tried to gain market acceptance in mobile payments. They include the likes of Samsung, Square, and CurrentC, a mobile wallet app backed by a consortium of U.S. retailers (with Walmart leading the way) that hope to cut credit card companies and their fees out of the buying loop.

But none of these players—individually or together—have made much of a dent in replacing traditional credit cards and cash as a form of payment in the multi-trillion-dollar U.S. retail market. Although the mobile payments concept may seem like a no-brainer for convenience-loving American consumers, numerous barriers on both the buyer and seller sides have kept the concept from gaining momentum. With its recent launch of Apple Pay, Apple is clearly a market follower. But it's a feat that the innovative company has performed to perfection time and again—take a new technology, make it better than any of the initial offerings, then watch the market explode as the Apple version becomes the runaway market leader.

Overcoming Negative Consumer Perceptions

As with every new technology that involves paying for things, consumers have concerns about the security of mobile payments. Paypal, Google, and the others took significant measures to design secure systems. However, most consumers just weren't comfortable with the idea that their phone might be used as a portal to their credit cards and bank accounts if it fell into the wrong hands. Never mind that the same could be said of a wallet or handbag, far less secure devices.

Recognizing consumer reluctance to place digital versions of their financial devices in one app, Apple took security to a higher level. Requiring a fingerprint makes the process much more secure than the more common safeguard of entering a passcode. And if a mobile device is ever lost or stolen, the owner can use its Find My iPhone feature to immediately lock down Apple Pay or even wipe the device completely clean.

Additionally, every compatible Apple device is assigned a unique Device Account Number. This is encrypted and securely stored in a dedicated security chip on the device. That and a transaction-specific security code are the only numbers that Apple transmits to merchants. In fact, the merchant doesn't even need to know the customer's name. Credit and debit card numbers are stored only on the local device, not on Apple servers. This makes Apple Pay even more secure and more private than paying by credit card.

Beyond consumer security concerns, previous adoption of mobile payment apps has been slowed by perceptions of a clunky user experience. If convenience is the biggest draw for consumers, then anything more arduous than the already convenient swipe of a credit card simply won't cut it. Setting up any of the existing mobile payment apps takes time and effort. Using such apps at the point of purchase is far from seamless, especially if the technology isn't working quite right. "I don't want to be that guy holding up the line while we fumble around to get it all to work," says one business columnist, "just like I don't want to be the guy who holds up the line boarding an airplane because his mobile boarding pass can't be read." Mobile apps that hit the market prior to Apple Pay required entering a passcode and—in some cases—hitting multiple buttons. That took longer than the traditional swipe of the card, even if everything worked as intended.

With Apple Pay, users still need to configure the app. But Apple already has 800 million credit cards on file with its existing iTunes store. Not only can this facilitate a set up that is already streamlined compared with existing apps, it's a sign that iTunes users may be more comfortable with using the app given that they have already given their credit card information to Apple. And with the TouchID sensor, Apple has the transaction down to a one-touch process. That's quicker than swiping a card and going through the typical menu, not to mention quicker than inputting a passcode.

Establishing Points of Acceptance

For mobile payments to penetrate the market, consumer acceptance is necessary. But companies face a twofold challenge in making such a technology successful. Consumers won't adopt it if retailers don't accept it, and retailers won't invest the resources necessary to accept it unless there is sufficient consumer demand. And the lack of consumer demand is the biggest factor that has kept retailers from jumping onto the mobile payments bandwagon. As a result, there are currently too few retailers that accept mobile payments to convince people that they can leave their credit cards at home.

But thanks to Apple, that situation is changing rapidly. It may be because of Apple's clout or because of the company's massive and loyal user base. But in less than a year, Apple has signed up far more retailers than all the previous mobile payment providers combined. "You need so many points of acceptance to make mobile payments work," says a mobile payments analyst for Forrester Research. "Apple has made that happen, striking partnerships with top national brands across a variety of categories that will give consumers plenty of opportunity to use the service." Apple has also signed up enough credit card issuing banks and credit unions to cover 83 percent of charge volume. In fact, Apple Pay has gained enough steam that Best Buy and Meijer will soon be accepting the payment app, despite having signed exclusivity agreements as part of the CurrentC consortium.

But Apple still faces many challenges. For example, even though Apple Pay is now technically accepted at more than 700,000 U.S. retail outlets, many of those outlets don't yet have the hardware installed that will recognize Apple's app. That fact can be discouraging to early adopters, hurting repeat usage. One recent survey showed that 66 percent of iPhone 6 owners had signed up for Apple Pay, but nearly half of them had visited a store listed as an Apple Pay merchant only to find that the location wasn't set up yet to process mobile payments through the app. Additionally, although Apple's penetration of the market far exceeds that of the competition and continues to grow each month, the mobile payments leader has a long way to go before reaching critical mass with 8 million retail outlets. And this doesn't even take into account online and in-app payments.

Still, Apple remains confident. "We are more convinced than ever that 2015 will be the year of Apple Pay," says Tim Cook, Apple's CEO. While there are still plenty of doubters that mobile payments will replace plastic as the go-to method for purchasing goods and services, there are also plenty of believers. And while Apple is clearly ahead in this game, its success also bodes well for the competition. As the concept catches on and technologies become more compatible, demand among non-Apple users will increase as well.

There is no shortage of options in the mobile payments field. And improvements designed to make the apps more convenient are being made continually, including the integration of loyalty cards and other promotional mechanisms. But even as other companies' offerings get better, expect Apple to be more competitive than ever. After all, nothing is stopping it from creating Apple Pay for Android devices.

Questions for Discussion

1. As completely as possible, sketch the value delivery network for Apple Pay.
2. With respect to Apple Pay, is Apple a producer, a consumer, or an intermediary? Explain.
3. Identify all the reasons why Apple's partnerships are essential to the success of Apple Pay.
4. With respect to marketing channels, what are some threats to Apple Pay's future?

Sources: Robert Hof, "Apple Pay Starts to Take Off, Leaving Competition in the Dust," *Forbes*, January 27, 2015, www.forbes.com/sites/roberthof/2015/01/27/apple-pay-starts-to-take-off-leaving-competition-in-the-dust/; Robert Hof, "Apple Pay Momentum Keeps Growing Despite Challenges in Stores," *Forbes*, April 27, 2015, www.forbes.com/sites/roberthof/2015/04/27/apple-pay-momentum-keeps-growing-despite-challenges-in-stores/; Cade Metz, "How Apple Pay Will Destroy the Online-Offline Shopping Divide," *Wired*, September 10, 2014, www.wired.com/2014/09/how-apple-pay-will-become-the-easy-way-to-buy-everything/; and information from www.apple.com/apple-pay/, accessed September 2015.

Company Case 11

Sears: Why Should You Shop There?

After working late one evening, Joan stopped off at Sears to return some items she had purchased online from Lands' End—a Sears-affiliated brand since 2002. She couldn't remember the last time she'd set foot in a Sears store, instead usually shopping at other department stores or discount retailers. As she walked in, she noticed that the store felt old and a bit run-down. She also noticed that she was one of few people in the entire store. The store seemed to stock a hodgepodge of products and brands, arranged in a pedestrian way. On her way out of the store, she wondered to herself, "Who shops at Sears? Why?"

Younger shoppers might find it hard to believe, but until the 1980s, Sears was America's largest retailer—the Walmart of its day. It's once-famous slogan, "Where America Shops," wasn't just a clever tagline conjured up by Madison Avenue. It was a positioning statement with power. Sears catered to all, selling merchandise in just about every category to just about every customer segment.

But the once-dominant Sears has since fallen so hard and fast that some analysts are now predicting its complete demise within the next few years. Its once-famous slogan seems almost comical now, as its stores are often deserted, even during peak times. What caused this decline? Sears lost its focus. Whereas many retail brands have forged strong positioning strategies targeting specific segments, Sears no longer stands for much of anything. Mention Walmart and people think "Save money. Live better." Bring up Target and they know to "Expect more. Pay less." At Macy's you get "the magic of Macy's," and Nordstrom promises to "take care of customers no matter what it takes." But say Sears and most customers draw a blank. The chain has neither an image nor an apparent value proposition that gives people a compelling reason to shop at its stores.

The Fall of an Icon

Founded in 1886, during the next century, Sears grew to become America's iconic retailer. It began as a mail-order catalog company in the 1880s, grew into a national chain of urban department stores during the early to mid-1900s, and became an important anchor store in the fast-growing suburban malls of the 1960s and 1970s. Through the 1980s, Sears was the nation's largest retail chain. Almost every American relied on Sears for everything from basic apparel and home goods to appliances and tools. But during the past two decades, as the retail landscape has shifted, once-mighty Sears has lost its way. Sears has failed to refresh its positioning to make itself relevant in today's marketplace.

A look at Sears advertising or a visit to the Sears Web site testifies to the retailer's almost complete lack of current positioning. Headlines scream "Buy more, save more on appliances," "50% off your favorite apparel brands," "Lowest prices on Craftsman lawn and garden," and "Big brand sale: great values, top brands." It seems that about the only thing Sears has going for it these days is that everything it sells is always on sale. However, price is not a convincing value proposition for Sears, which has trouble matching the low prices of competitors such as Walmart, Target, or Kohl's.

In 2005, a struggling Sears merged with an even more distressed Kmart to become Sears Holding Corporation. The merger of the two failing retailers left analysts scratching their heads and customers even more confused about the value propositions of the respective chains. Following the merger, the corporation jumped from one questionable tactic to another. For example, Kmart stores began carrying well-known Sears brands such as Craftsman tools, Kenmore appliances, and Diehard batteries, diluting one of Sears's only remaining differentiating assets.

Sears Holding has also tried a variety of store formats. For instance, it converted 400 Kmart stores to Sears Essentials stores, which it later changed to Sears Grand stores—Walmart-like outlets that carry regular Sears merchandise plus everything from health and beauty brands, toys, and baby products to party supplies and groceries. It has also dabbled with a confusing assortment of other formats carrying the Sears name, such as Sears Hometown stores (a franchised smaller version of full-sized Sears stores), Sears Hardware stores, Sears Home Appliance Showrooms, Sears Outlet stores, and Sears Auto Centers.

Despite the variety of store formats, Sears has done little to refresh its positioning. "A lot of traditional department stores have reinvigorated themselves through merchandising. You haven't seen that from Sears," says one analyst. To make matters worse, whereas most competing retailers have invested heavily to spruce up their stores, Sears has spent less than one-quarter of the industry average on store maintenance and renovation, leaving many of its outlets looking old and shabby. "There's no reason to shop at Sears," concludes a retailing expert. "It offers a depressing shopping experience and uncompetitive prices."

Once a Retailer, Now a Hedge Fund

Many critics place the blame for Sears's lack of sound marketing and positioning on Sears Holding Company chairman Edward Lampert, a hedge fund manager and the driving force behind the Sears/Kmart merger. Lampert and his funds own about 60 percent of Sears Holding's stock. Critics claim that since the 2005 merger, Lampert has run the company more as a portfolio of financial assets than as a retail chain. A fierce advocate of free-market economics, Lampert restructured Sears into approximately 40 business units, each set up to operate as an independent business with its own set of c-suite officers, boards of directors, and profit-and-loss statements. The intention was for the decentralized structure to foster independence and competitiveness and to make each part of the corporation more accountable.

It had other, less appealing effects. For example, because the appliance unit could make more money selling products manufactured by outside brands, it began featuring brands like LG over Sears's own Kenmore. A similar problem arose when the Sears Craftsman brand unit proposed a tool co-branded with the Sears DieHard brand. But under the new structure, Craftsman would have had to pay DieHard royalties, making the cost of the item prohibitive. Craftsman tools and Kenmore appliances still lead their categories, and the DieHard brand of automotive batteries remains strong. But the infighting has had a negative effect on the market positions and fortunes of these and other Sears brands.

The decentralized structure also created barriers to pricing Sears and Kmart products competitively relative to competing chains. After studying the company's prices, a newly appointed president of retail services surmised that Kmart's food and drugs were more expensive than those at Walmart and Target. He proposed reducing prices on these product lines, bringing them in line with competitors. The presidents of various business units agreed with the proposal. But no unit was willing to cough up the $2 million needed to fund the project. Corporate headquarters rejected a request for a loan. So prices remained at uncompetitive levels.

As day-to-day operations played out, cooperation and collaboration gave way to a "warring tribes" culture that made the lack of a solid marketing message even worse. As chief marketing officers fought over advertising space in the weekly Sears circular, the circular turned into what one former executive referred to as a "Frankenstein" promotion—a hodgepodge of product combinations with no overall cohesion. Screwdrivers were advertised next to lingerie, and lawnmowers sat next to ladies' shoes. For the cover of one Mother's Day circular, the sporting-goods unit purchased space for a Doodle Bug minibike—an item popular with young boys.

All of this speaks to a lack of leadership at the top. Since the 2005 merger, Lampert has hired four CEOs, not a single one with any retailing experience. After the last CEO left more than a year ago, Lampert assumed CEO responsibilities himself. But "being a successful hedge fund manager doesn't make you a good retailer," says one Sears watcher.

The Only Hope?

There are a few signs of a prosperous future for the nation's once-greatest retailer. To streamline operations and free up cash, Sears is selling off parts of the company. Last year, Sears Holdings spun off Sears Hometown and Sears Outlet stores. Lampert also facilitated the sale of a portion of Sears's stake in Sears Canada. Most recently, the company sold Lands' End—now an independent company, although still located within Sears—in a transaction that put more than $1 billion in Sears's coffers. Lampert is eying similar deals for other Sears businesses. Although some see this as a way to strengthen the company by focusing on its core business, others see it as little more than "continuing to burn the furniture to stay warm."

One potential bright spot for Sears is online sales. As the company's revenues continued to drop, its online sales have been on the uptick. With a strategy to become a fully integrated omni-channel retailer, revenue from e-commerce has been growing by an average of 10 percent over the past few years. In fact, Sears is the sixth-largest online retailer in the United States. This is no accident. Lampert is a believer in selling online. In a recent statement that accompanied a financial update to the press, Lampert came as close as he ever has to issuing a statement of corporate strategy. "We are transitioning from a business that has historically focused on running a store network into a business that provides and delivers value by serving its members in the manner most convenient for them: whether in stores, at home, or through digital devices."

To support this assertion, Sears has developed the Shop Your Way loyalty program—a hybrid between Amazon and Facebook that allows customers to accumulate and spend rewards online or off. Sears has also experimented with a store pickup service, MyGofer—an initiative that essentially turns Kmart stores into a same-day pickup location for all Sears and Kmart brands and merchandise ordered online. With the omni-channel model very much in vogue, this strategy seems to put Sears right on target in terms of where the retail industry is headed.

But while Sears is apparently investing in the digital side of its business, it is neglecting the brick-and-mortar side. The chain hasn't opened a new store in years. In fact, it's selling off locations—235 this year alone. "Our stores are often in the wrong place and are often too large for our needs" was all that Lampert could say when questioned about the high rate of store closures. And Sears's remaining stores are progressively becoming less appealing. One retail analyst, once a big Sears fan, remembers growing up in Chicago at a time when his family wouldn't think of shopping anywhere but Sears. Now things are different. "I shopped for back-to-school clothes at a store [that's] now so dark and depressing, I can't bear to go in," he says, "even though it's [just] blocks from my home—a home that sits on a street that shares a name with an iconic Sears brand."

Although Lampert and his team continue to claim that turnaround efforts will soon bear fruit, things don't look promising for Sears. The lack of customer thinking and marketing strategy has taken a devastating toll. Sears Holding Corporation's revenues have fallen for 29 consecutive quarters. Total sales for the most recent year were $31.2 billion, down 14 percent from the previous year and a far cry from a peak of $53 billion just eight years prior. Profits also paint a grim picture—the company lost $1.7 billion last year, more than it made from selling off Lands' End. As a result, Sears's stock price has fallen nearly 80 percent since 2007.

In a letter to shareholders after the release of the most recent year's financials, Lampert boasted of his e-commerce plan, saying that otherwise, "we would be stuck on the same path that has claimed Circuit City, Borders, Radio Shack, and others," all iconic retailers that have gone out of business. And yet, with no cogent marketing plan and seemingly no way out of its financial tailspin, many analysts predict that once-dominant Sears will soon follow the same fate and disappear entirely.

Questions for Discussion

1. According to the principles of retail strategy, how did Sears once become the nation's biggest retailer?
2. According to those same principles, how did Sears lose its once-commanding market position?
3. What is the relationship between the current Sears corporate strategy and its marketing struggles?
4. Assess Sears' efforts to become a true bricks-and-clicks retailer.
5. Can anything save Sears? Support your position.

Sources: James Covert, "Sears Posts $548 million loss, Plans to Close 235 Stores," *New York Post*, December 4, 2014, http://nypost.com/2014/12/04/sears-posts-wider-q3-loss-on-13-revenue-drop/; Phil Wahba, "Eddie Lampert's Incredible Shrinking Empire," *Fortune*, February 26, 2015, http://fortune.com/2015/02/26/sears-earnings/; Lauren Coleman-Lochner and Carol Hymowitz, "A Money Man's Trials in Retailing," *Bloomberg Businessweek*, January 5, 2012, pp. 24–25; and various pages at www.sears.com, accessed September 2015.

Company Case 12

Allstate: Bringing Mayhem to the Auto Insurance Advertising Wars

In the spring of 1950, the teenage daughter of Allstate general sales manager Davis Ellis was stricken with hepatitis shortly before she was to graduate from high school. The worried executive arrived home from work one evening just as his wife returned from the hospital where their daughter was admitted. As he met her at the front door, his wife reported, "The hospital said not to worry ... we're in good hands with the doctor."

Later that year, Ellis became part of a team charged with developing the first major national advertising campaign for the Allstate Insurance Company. As the team discussed the message they wanted the brand to convey, Ellis recalled his wife's "we're in good hands" remark and how good it made him feel. The phrase projected security, reassurance, and responsibility, exactly the traits the team wanted customers to associate with Allstate. Thus was born the slogan "You're in good hands with Allstate."

By the early 2000s, a study by Northwestern University found that the long-standing Allstate catchphrase was the most recognized slogan in the United States. For years, Allstate held the position as the second-largest personal lines insurer, trailing only State Farm. In 2003, Allstate hired actor Dennis Haysbert as the brand's spokesperson. After starring in dozens of Allstate commercials—each culminating with the question "Are you in good hands?—Haysbert's deep voice became a comforting familiarity to television viewers. Today, the "Good Hands" slogan is the oldest surviving slogan for a paid campaign.

An Advertising Shakeup

Although Allstate's advertising served it well for decades, by the late 1990s, the company had fallen into the same routine as the rest of its industry. Big auto insurance companies were spending modestly on sleepy ad campaigns featuring touchy-feely, reassuring messages such as Allstate's "You're in good hands" or State Farm's "Like a good neighbor." In an industry characterized by low budgets and even lower-key ads, no brand's marketing stood out.

However, the advertising serenity ended with the first appearance of the now-iconic GEICO Gecko in 1999, backed by a big budget and pitching direct sales and low prices. That single GEICO ad campaign sparked a frenzy of ad spending and creativity in the insurance industry that quickly escalated into a full-scale advertising war. Once-conservative car insurance ads became creative showstoppers, as edgy and creative as ads found in any industry. Here are a few highlights:

- ***GEICO:*** GEICO got the auto insurance advertising wars rolling when it was acquired by billionaire Warren Buffet's Berkshire-Hathaway company in 1996 and given a blank check to aggressively increase market share. That led to an onslaught of advertising the likes of which the auto insurance industry had never seen. A string of creative GEICO campaigns featured everything from civilized cavemen to cash with googly eyes. But it was the GEICO Gecko that had the biggest impact. With his signature English accent, the Gecko made GEICO's simple message clear—"15 minutes can save you 15 percent or more on car insurance." More than any other industry spokesperson, the Gecko lent personality and pizzazz to the previously sleepy insurance industry and its staid brands.
- ***Progressive:*** Following GEICO's lead, in 2008 Progressive created its own perky and endearing personality—Flo. Progressive created the ever-upbeat, ruby-lipped salesclerk to help convince consumers who are already in the market that they can get an even better price deal from Progressive. Flo helped put Progressive hot on the heels of rising GEICO as the fourth-largest auto insurer. Flo assists people when they are ready to shop. Progressive later introduced a complementary campaign featuring the Messenger—the mustachioed, leather-jacket-wearing stranger—and Brad—the easy-going, self-assured man with an absurdly funny sense of self-esteem who refers to himself only in the third person.

Like the GEICO Gecko, Flo, the Messenger, and Brad pitch price savings as their primary appeal.

- ***State Farm:*** As GEICO and Progressive shook up the industry with their direct, low-price, high-profile selling models, conventional agent-based auto insurers were forced to respond. Ninety-year-old State Farm, the long-time industry leader, was hardly a stranger to advertising. Like Allstate, State Farm had a long-standing, widely recognized slogan—"Like a good neighbor, State Farm is there"—a jingle written by pop music icon Barry Manilow in 1971. Sensing the threat from the rising newcomers, State Farm fought back vigorously with a new campaign centered on its enduring jingle. In its "magic jingle" campaign, State Farm agents magically appear when summoned with the jingle by young drivers in trouble—including the likes of LeBron James. The campaign's goal—to convince consumers that they still need the services of one of State Farm's 18,000 agents. To help make the point more forcefully, State Farm doubled its ad budget.

"Good Hands" Meets Mayhem

Amid this surge in competition and advertising creativity, Allstate struggled just to hold its own, let alone to grow. In the wake of the Gecko and Flo, Allstate had lost market share for two years running, even with Haysbert's presence as company pitchman. The brand needed its own over-the-top personality. So Allstate brought mayhem to life—literally. With the new creepy Mayhem character played by actor Dean Winters, Allstate created a villainous counterpart to Haysbert's soothing hero. The campaign's goal: to convince consumers that there is more to buying car insurance than just price. Put more bluntly, says an ad agency executive involved with the campaign, "We wanted to kick Flo's ass."

Mayhem portrays all of the unlikely events that can lead to a major auto insurance claim. As a deer, he jumps into the path of a moving car at night "because that's what we deer do." As a torrential downpour, he loves leaky sunroofs. As a malfunctioning GPS, he sends a driver swerving into another car. As snow, he weighs down the roof of a garage until it collapses, smashing the car within. Each quirky ad ends with the statement and question "If you have cut-rate insurance, you could be paying for this yourself. Are you in good hands?"

Through such clever ads, Allstate's creative and award-winning "Mayhem. It's Everywhere." campaign has put a contemporary, attention-grabbing twist on the company's long-standing "You're in good hands with Allstate" slogan, helping to position the brand as a superior alternative to price-oriented competitors. Even with its long-standing "Good Hands" campaign, Allstate needed something unconventional. In fact, mayhem didn't just describe the Allstate campaign—it characterized the entire world of auto insurance advertising.

The Mayhem campaign quickly won many top ad industry awards. But perhaps a bigger indication of the campaign's impact is the extent to which the character has become ingrained in the pop culture. Although Mayhem has just more than a third of Flo's 4.9 million Facebook fans, he commands an engagement score nearly eight times that of Progressive's perky spokeswoman. And when the character's creator recently saw a Mayhem-costumed trick-or-treater walking down her street, she called it "a career highlight that gave her chills."

More than just popular, Mayhem is right on message. At the end of each ad, he warns, "If you've got cut-rate insurance, you could be paying for this yourself." Then a reassuring Haysbert provides the solution: "Are you in good hands?" he asks. "Get Allstate. You can save money and be better protected from Mayhem." This "worth-paying-a-little-more" message puts Allstate back at the top in terms of customer value.

Mayhem Redux

Allstate's ads were not only creative, they were effective. After a few years of Mayhem ads complementing Haysbert's Good Hands ads, Allstate's unaided brand awareness of 74 percent trailed State Farm's by only a slight margin, despite State Farm's 60 percent greater ad spending. And for a time, the Mayhem campaign halted Allstate's market share slide. According to Allstate CEO Thomas Wilson, "It's working. If you look at our quotes and our new business, it's way up." All this prompted Allstate to extend the campaign, including the introduction of Mayhem's Hispanic cousin, Mala Suerte (bad luck), aimed at Hispanic consumers.

In extending the campaign, Allstate took Mayhem to the next level, giving the character his own Twitter account. Seemingly late to the Twitter party, Allstate executives indicated that the delay was intentional. "We've been very careful about not overdoing Mayhem and not overexposing [him]," said Jennifer Egeland, Allstate's director of advertising. "[We wanted] the right idea for launching him in the Twitter space."

The right idea was to conform to Mayhem's persona. As a recent football season dawned, Mayhem polled followers about what he should portray in the next ad—a charcoal grill or a cheap bungee cord. Consumers voted for the cord. Mayhem disobeyed, Tweeting: "Too bad I'm a tailgate grill. Who's got a light?" He followed that up with Vine videos of a car set on fire from a grill mishap. Allstate then released two new Mayhem ads—"Tailgate Grill Fire" and "Cheap Bungee Cord," making everyone happy. Similar antics ensued for the ensuing March Madness kickoff of the NCAA playoffs, helping drive more than 61,000 followers to the @Mayhem Twitter account.

With all this activity and public response, Allstate thought it had a surefire weapon for maintaining its market position. But the all-out auto insurance advertising war illustrates just how critical it is to stay one step ahead of the competition. For the most recent year, Allstate increased its ad budget to $887 million, outdoing even market leader State Farm's $802 million effort. However, both companies were eclipsed by GEICO's eye-popping $1.1 billion advertising spending. Today, no fewer than 11 car insurance brands are running national TV advertising campaigns. Combined, the auto insurers now spend more than $6 billion each year to get their messages out. That makes things confusing for consumers, who struggle under the deluge of clever ads for the respective brands.

The intense competition, big budgets, and focus on consumer advertising have kept industry market share dynamic. In fact, in the last year, GEICO moved into the number-two spot behind State Farm and is pulling away with a 10.8 percent share of the auto insurance market to Allstate's 10.0 percent. Allstate has grown its auto insurance business in recent years. But GEICO's growth has been consistently stronger. With that development, Allstate is left to reconsider the value that it is getting out of its advertising investments and just how it might slow GEICO down GEICO and retake its number-two market position.

Questions for Discussion

1. Why has Allstate's "good hands" slogan withstood the test of time to become advertising's longest-running slogan?
2. Analyze Mayhem ads based on the process of creating an advertising message as outlined in the text (for Mayhem ads, check out www.allstate.com/mayhem-is-everywhere.aspx).
3. Discuss issues of selecting advertising media for the Mayhem campaign. How might this process differ from that of campaigns for other companies?
4. Based on the information in this case, how might Allstate measure the effectiveness of the Mayhem campaign?
5. Has the Mayhem campaign been effective? Support your answer.

Sources: Ashley Rodriguez, "How Allstate's Mayhem Disrupted the Chatter around Insurance," *Advertising Age*, June 10, 2015, http://adage.com/print/298779; Steve Daniels, "GEICO Overtakes Allstate as No. 2 Auto Insurer," *Advertising Age*, March 3, 2014, http://adage.com/print/291947; E.J. Schultz, "Allstate's Mayhem Joins Twitter ... Now What," *Advertising Age*, October 14, 2013, p. 28; Anthony Crup, "Allstate's Marketing Boss Talks Up 'March Mayhem,'" *Ad Week*, March 25, 2014, www.adweek.com/print/156471; and advertisements and other information accessed at www.allstatenewsroom.com and www.allstate.com/mayhem-is-everywhere.aspx, accessed September 2015.

Company Case 13

SunGard: Building Sustained Growth by Selling the SunGard Way

If asked what company topped the most recent *Selling Power* magazine list of "50 Best Companies to Sell For," you'd probably guess IBM, P&G, or maybe Xerox, companies long known for their outstanding sales forces. But number one on this year's list is a company you probably know less about—software and technology services company SunGard.

What makes SunGard such a good place to work as a salesperson? For starters, SunGard has strong name recognition and a solid reputation in its industry. SunGard has long provided excellent compensation and training to its salespeople. And the company has consistently delivered strong customer growth and retention. However, although SunGard has long been good in these areas, what has made it outstanding and put it at the top of *Selling Power*'s list is a recent complete transformation of SunGard's sales force model.

Pioneering a New Industry

In the late 1970s, the computer services division of the Sun Oil Company (today Sunoco) pioneered a service now considered indispensable by virtually every company in the world. Sun and 20 other Philadelphia-area companies entered an agreement to act as backups for each others' data systems. To create the needed capacity, the group developed a designated disaster recovery backup center. But when member companies were slow to pay their shares of the expenses, Sun Oil took over the backup operation and began selling computer services. In 1983, Sun Oil spun off the computer division and SunGard was born.

Since then, with the help of a few acquisitions, SunGard has grown steadily. It's now one of the world's leading software and technology services companies, with nearly $3 billion in annual revenues. SunGard now provides processing solutions for the financial services industry, K–12 education, and public sector organizations. It serves 16,000 customers in more than 70 countries. As a business-to-business service provider, that requires a substantial sales force.

Good, but Not Great

When Russell Fradin took over as the CEO of SunGard in 2011, business was good. But the company faced some issues of concern. For starters, the Internet increasingly provided SunGard clients and potential clients with the information they needed to solve their own problems. For both its private and public sector businesses, compliance with government regulations was also increasing. And increasing globalization made it more and more challenging for SunGard's sales reps to meet client needs. SunGard was not alone in facing these issues. But that just added to the pressure—any company finding effective ways to meet these challenges would gain considerable strategic advantage.

SunGard also faced plenty of internal issues. The company sold multiple product lines, and Fradin felt that the SunGard sales force wasn't achieving its potential in terms of selling the optimal mix of products. The company's thousands of sales reps spent most of their time and effort selling licensed software rather than developing broader solutions to customer problems. Moreover, with multiple divisions and product lines and a fragmented go-to-market approach, SunGard often had multiple sales reps pursuing the same clients, sapping productivity and even driving some customers away.

Based on these assessments, Fradin asked himself, "How can SunGard make its sales force—one of the company's biggest and most important investments—perform more effectively?" SunGard had decent systems in place for recruiting, hiring, and training its salespeople. And SunGard's sales executives did a reasonable job of making incremental changes. But Fradin felt that the company needed to do more in order to improve its growth and performance. If more drastic changes weren't made, the mounting challenges would likely limit future sales and profits. To Fradin's thinking, SunGard needed a complete sales force transformation.

According to a report by global sales consulting firm ZA Associates, companies that move sales force effectiveness from good to excellent by virtue of a sales force transformation can increase profitable growth by as much as 20 percent. But that kind of transformation would require a major effort, many months to plan and execute, and even longer to take hold. It would demand nothing less than a total commitment from everyone in the organization—those at the lowest rung on the corporate ladder up to senior management and executives. It would also require that everyone have a clear vision of the benefits, for both themselves and for the organization as a whole. Disruptions from implementing such a sweeping change would likely mean losing good people and clients. It might also result in a short-term dip in performance before the benefits began to kick in.

Setting Transformation in Motion

In early 2012, Fradin hired Jim Neve and Ken Powell to head up SunGard's global sales efforts. The two-person team had worked on other successful large-scale sales force transformations, and they planned to carry out the same process at SunGard. "We needed to maximize our channels, sell the broadest set of solutions possible, and go to market in a coordinated manner," said Powell. "We needed to build a sustainable growth engine."

Neve and Powell branded the sales force transformation initiative as "Selling the SunGard Way." More than just a fancy title, "Selling the SunGard Way" was a philosophy defined by specific goals and characteristics. First and foremost, the transformation would shift the basic sales approach from selling based on meeting customer needs to selling based on insights. SunGard reps needed to thoroughly understand the client buying decision process, anticipate needs before even customers themselves were aware of them, and tailor the client relationship to meet shifting concerns. Focusing on product functionality and price just wouldn't cut it anymore. And sales interactions would need to draw from technology and services across all SunGard business units, not just within specific divisions or product lines. In order to achieve these skills, SunGard's sales personnel would need greater knowledge and expertise of the full line of company products as well as the nature of each client's business.

After thoroughly surveying the needs of SunGard sales associates, Neve and Powell drafted a detailed transformation plan. Sales reps needed better training, detailed competitive analyses, and more effective sales campaigns. They needed better data, fewer administrative tasks, and a simplified interface for its Salesforce CRM sales management tool. To achieve such goals, Neve and Powell set out to overhaul SunGard's core sales functions, including recruiting, training, managing, and compensating sales force personnel.

This transformation would take time and effort, and it would cost millions. But by the time the plan was revealed, there was support throughout the company. "The whole organization gravitated toward change," said Powell. "[Everyone] knew it had to happen." To help cover costs, the company shifted budgets, reallocating funds from ineffective programs to the transformation project.

On the recruiting front, SunGard adopted a new talent-assessment tool that defined ideal job profiles and evaluated skills and performance patterns of potential hires. The company also hired a team of sales development managers, charged with increasing the productivity of first-year sales reps. It was their job to make sure that new sales reps received all the training and exposure necessary to understand the company's structure, strategic plans, products, and sales tools. That relieved front-line sales managers of these tasks, letting them focus more on selling. Sales development manager compensation hinged on the performance of first-year sales reps.

For existing sales personnel, SunGard revised procedures, metrics, training, and tools to make them consistent across the organization. It also made major revisions to its Salesforce CRM and sales management tool, with an eye toward providing salespeople with all the information they needed for every aspect of the sales process. The important tool now provided easy and immediate access to content such as case studies, customer information, and market data. Additional tools were made available to guide people through the necessary steps of effectively closing a sale.

But to improve effectiveness for both new and existing sales personnel, SunGard needed to make even more changes in how performance was measured and tracked. For example, prior to the transformation, the company tracked incentives and commissions manually, and they were not readily accessible by relevant stakeholders. Under the new scheme, metrics such as individual goals and forecasts, as well as how often sales were made or lost, became part of an automated system, accessible by sales reps and managers via mobile interface at any time. They could even run "what-if" scenarios to determine potential earnings of different situations. This capability motivated sales reps by increasing accountability and promoting a competitive spirit.

From Transformation to Results

As the new sales structure and tools took root, it wasn't long before they began to bear fruit. "There was a tremendous product suite that had yet to capture its full market share," says Todd Albright, who joined SunGard as senior vice president of sales for the Americas after the transformation was under way. That market share will soon be achieved. "There were tremendous assets locked up at SunGard," Neve summarizes. "We put a road map in place to unlock those assets, translating them into new sales and revenue growth."

With its billion-dollar sales plan now in place, SunGard is on target. As one example, consider the productivity improvements for first-year reps. Prior to the transformation, about

75 percent of new reps booked their first sale before the end of their first year at an average of about $400,000. Through the new policies, that sales productivity will soon double, adding an incremental $30 to $40 million to annual sales.

If boosting sales force effectiveness was easy, every company would achieve optimal sales force productivity. SunGard was willing to pay the price. In the first year following the implementation of the transformation, as expected, SunGard revenues decreased over the previous year—down by about 16 percent. However, profits rose by nearly 35 percent, thanks in part to reduced costs from more efficient operations. By the end of the second year, revenues were back on the rise. Fradin was notably pleased. "Clients are responding positively to these initiatives, knowing that our offerings help their businesses be more competitive. We [are] particularly pleased with our sales momentum and our organic revenue growth."

Importantly, SunGard's sales force is now much more coordinated and collaborative. It's better trained and equipped to sell based on insights. Its products and services are bundled across product lines rather than within lines. And reps are developing partnerships with customers, assisting them in streamlining operations, accelerating growth, and complying with regulations. By transforming its sales force to "Selling the SunGard Way," SunGard is on a path to sustainable, organic growth for years to come.

Questions for Discussion

1. Compare SunGard's sales force structure before and after the transformation.
2. What are the positive and negative aspects of SunGard's new sales force structure?
3. How would the challenges faced by SunGard have affected sales productivity had the company not initiated its transformational plan?
4. Identify specific ways SunGard's transformational plan addresses the different steps of managing the sales force.
5. Will "Selling the SunGard Way" really work? Why or why not?

Sources: Henry Canaday, "Selling the New SunGard Way," *Selling Power*, www.sellingpower.com/content/article/?a=10217/selling-the-new-sungard-way&page=1, accessed June 2015; "50 Companies to Sell For in 2014," *Selling Power*, www.sellingpower.com/2014/50-best-companies-to-sell-for/, accessed June 2015; Andris Zoltners, P. K. Sinha, and Sally Lorimer, "Improving Your Sales Force: Fine-tune or Transform?" *Harvard Business Review*, November 13, 2012, http://blogs.hbr.org/2012/11/improving-your-sales-force-fin/; and information from www.sungard.com/about-us and www.sungard.com/financials, accessed September 2015.

Company Case 14

Alibaba: The World's Largest E-tailer Is Not Amazon

There's a new king of e-commerce, and it dwarfs Amazon. Introducing Alibaba, the China-based behemoth that racked up $420 billion in revenues last year and is rapidly building an online empire that will include businesses ranging from a traditional online marketplace to online investment services. With annual sales that already place it much closer to Walmart ($487 billion) than to Amazon ($89 billion), Alibaba is growing so rapidly that by the end of the year it will comfortably pass Walmart to become the world's largest company. How is this Chinese upstart pulling off such a startling Internet feat? Let's start by taking a look at Alibaba's founder, Jack Ma.

Unlikely Beginnings

Jack Ma is an unlikely figure to be atop of one of the world's most powerful companies. Time and again, U.S. tech start-ups have emerged from California garages. However, perhaps none of those start-ups were founded by individuals as seemingly unprepared as Ma. Growing up in Shanghai, Ma did poorly in school. He failed the college entrance exam twice before getting in and completing a teaching degree. He learned to speak English by hanging out around tourists and listening to radio broadcasts. Ma was rejected for a number of jobs—including being a manager for KFC—before finally landing a job teaching English for $12 a month.

But Ma was animated and energetic, and he had lofty goals and ambitions, a combination that earned him the nickname "Crazy Jack." During China's export boom in the 1990s, Ma started a translation company. On a business trip to the United States, he was exposed to the World Wide Web and was surprised to find almost no Chinese content. After a failed attempt at starting an Internet company in China, Ma corralled 17 friends in his apartment in 1999 and set out to build an online marketplace. Substituting vision and charisma for coding skills, Ma started Alibaba.com, only a few years after legendary e-commerce marketers Amazon and eBay got their starts.

Feeding the Masses

It's difficult to examine Alibaba without making comparisons to the more globally familiar online sellers. In fact, Alibaba is often referred to as the "Amazon of China." But it's the differences between Alibaba and the Amazons, eBays, Googles, Walmarts, Costcos, Sears, and thousands of other successful e-tailers that explain how the Chinese company has grown so big and will grow so much bigger in the future.

For starters, consider the respective domestic markets. Amazon and the others got their starts in the United States, home to roughly 320 million people. This market serves up the most developed retail industry and the highest standard of living in the world. As the tech boom took off, numerous ambitious upstarts competed fiercely to transfer America's retail businesses into the quickly developing space. Tech-savvy U.S.

consumers scrambled to convert some of their buying from brick-and-mortar stores to online purchases.

Contrast this with China. With 1.3 billion people and the fastest-growing economy in the world, the Chinese market has tremendous power and potential. But perhaps more important, China's retail sector was still in the Dark Ages when Alibaba got its start. "E-commerce in the U.S. is like a dessert. It's just supplementary to your main business," Ma said recently. "In China, because the infrastructure of [traditional retail] commerce is [so] bad, e-commerce becomes the main course."

As many Chinese move from poverty to middle-class status, their exposure to buying online coincided with their exposure to any kind of buying. Relative to the U.S. market, there were relatively few competitors. The size and nature of China's market have Alibaba boasting of 300 million registered customers, a base that comfortably exceeds the size of the entire purchasing population of the United States. And Internet penetration in China is still only 47 percent, compared with the much more saturated 87 percent in the United States, providing enormous growth potential.

In adapting traditional retail to an online environment, Amazon and the other U.S. e-tailers operate a "managed marketplace"—they own their own distribution centers, sell a majority of their products directly, and even market their own brands, all characteristics that mimic traditional retail structures. This allows U.S. e-tailers to benefit from established distribution channels and to maintain a great deal of control over their operations. But it also requires massive investments in infrastructure and armies of employees, both of which result in wafer-thin profit margins. In fact, for two of the past four years, Amazon has lost money. For the other two years, the biggest profit it could muster was only 1.3 percent of sales. Walmart's profit margin percentages for both online and offline sales are typically in the low single digits.

But Alibaba does not own or operate massive distribution centers. It doesn't own the items sold on its sites. And it only employs about 25,000 people, a fraction of Amazon's 132,000 employees. Instead, Alibaba's open market platform simply connects buyers with sellers. That might sound like an eBay approach, but Ma insists that it is not. "Amazon and eBay are e-commerce companies, and Alibaba is not an e-commerce company," Ma said recently. "Alibaba helps others to do e-commerce. We do not sell things." While this gives Alibaba less control over the customer experience, Ma sleeps easier at night without the burden of obsessing over keeping prices low. As market forces work to set price points, Alibaba sits back and watches the cash pour in. Its profit margin over the past two years averaged almost 40 percent.

A Little of Everything

The continuous influx of cash has allowed Alibaba to invest in just about every kind of business imaginable. In its infancy, Alibaba.com primarily matched Chinese exporters with businesses throughout the rest of the world. But the company quickly shifted focus, catering to the growing purchase power of its domestic market. Unlike its Western counterparts, Alibaba developed and acquired different online sites and established major divisions. For example, Taobao.com is a site that helps small businesses and private parties sell merchandise to customers. But unlike eBay's commission structure, Taobao sellers pay only for the advertised promotion. From a shopping standpoint, Alibaba's Tmall.com is more similar Amazon, pairing customers with big corporations, including many global corporations such as Nike, P&G, Apple, and even retailers like Costco.

But Alibaba's development has taken it down numerous other paths as well. And although it may seem that the surging Chinese conglomerate is simply playing copycat, Ma's vision plays out creatively in every case. For example, Alipay is similar to PayPal. But starved for investment opportunities in an environment dominated by state-run banks, Alipay customers have access to financial products that pay attractive returns. In the first year of making such options available, Alipay customers tucked away $82 billion.

In another example of "follow-the-Silicon-Valley-guru," the soon-to-be-launched Tmall Box Office—or TBO—"aims to become [the equivalent] of Netflix in the U.S.," including plans to run original content produced by Alibaba's own Alibaba Pictures. But in an environment where TV viewers aren't accustomed to the pay-to-watch model, Alibaba is a true pioneer. And that pioneering effort extends to a crowd-sourced film investment fund, a model that threatens to upend traditional film financing in China by allowing regular folks to become producers with less risk.

During the past six months alone, Alibaba has spent $8 billion investing in start-up firms. Today, the Alibaba Group spreads out over a constellation of services, including music, gaming, blogs, social networks (the company just dropped $200 million on Snapchat), event ticket sales, shipping, ridesharing, and smartphones.

As Alibaba's list of businesses grows, Ma's vision and innovation seem unbounded. After all, how many U.S. Internet veterans can say they started their own holiday? Just six years ago, Ma enthusiastically launched Singles Day on November 11. What started as a sort of anti-Valentine's Day for single people is now one of the biggest blockbuster sales holidays in the world. Last year, it resulted in $9.3 billion in sales in a 24-hour period, almost double what fanatical U.S. residents spent during the five-day Thanksgiving shopping spree across all companies combined.

As Alibaba continues to grow, one frontier looms large—global expansion. Although China's biggest dot.com success certainly has global ambitions, it has so far chosen to focus on the massive potential of its home market. That will certainly change. "We plan to invest more in [the U.S. and U.K. markets] to get more traffic and ... build brand awareness," says Joe Yan, director of international B2C at Alibaba's export division. "Our biggest advantage is abundance, with 100 million products, we have more options for customers who can buy our products cheaper and at high quality." And while it remains to be seen how Alibaba will attack global markets, one analyst recently predicted a future marriage down the road of Alibaba and eBay.

At the same time, U.S. companies like Netflix and Amazon are exploring ways to expand their small presence in China. However, although the massive markets on both sides of the pond represent opportunities too tempting to pass up, only time will tell whether any of these successful U.S. companies can export the models they have applied so successfully in their home markets.

As U.S. competitors try to counter Alibaba, they will face one more particularly big hurdle. The Chinese love Jack Ma. For their own part, U.S. tech founders such as Bezos, Zuckerberg, Brin and Page, and certainly the late Steve Jobs are considered visionaries who have shaped the world's digital ecosystem. But the Chinese revere Mr. Ma, the man who turned a local underdog into a dominant giant with revenues bigger than Amazon, Facebook, Google, and Apple combined. Those kinds of patriotic emotions will be tough to crack.

Questions for Discussion

1. As a digital retailer, how does Alibaba provide value to Chinese consumers? What sets of values are unique to the Chinese market?
2. Given that Alibaba does not own or distribute any of the merchandise exchanged on its sites, describe what factors had to develop for the company to succeed.
3. Analyze Alibaba's business model relative to all the different forms of digital and online marketing covered in this chapter.
4. Can Alibaba succeed in countries outside of China? Why or why not?

Sources: Aaron Back, "Alibaba Dreams of E-commerce Globally but Acts Locally," *Wall Street Journal (Eastern Edition)*, June 24, 2015, p. C12; "Alibaba Plans Subscription Video Service," *Wall Street Journal*, June 14, 2015, www.wsj.com/articles/alibaba-plans-subscription-video-service-1434310742; Jillian D'Onfro, "How Jack Ma Went from Being a Poor School Teacher to Turning Alibaba into a $160 Billion Behemoth," *Business Insider*, September 14, 2014, www.businessinsider.com/the-story-of-jack-ma-founder-of-alibaba-2014-9#ixzz3dqFm4M9B; Angela Doland, "Five Takeaways from Alibaba's Record-Busting $9.3 Billion Shopping Fest," *Advertising Age*, November 11, 2014, http://adage.coverleaf.com/advertisingage/20141117?pg=42#pg42; Julie Makinen, "Alibaba: For Helping Consumers Save, Spend, and Be Entertained," www.fastcompany.com/3039571/most-innovative-companies-2015/alibaba; Charles Riley, "Alibaba Is Not the Amazon of China," *CNNMoney*, September 16, 2014, http://money.cnn.com/2014/09/15/investing/alibaba-amazon-china/; and Mohanbir Sawhney and Sanjay Khosla, "Alibaba vs. Amazon: Who Will Win the Global E-commerce War?" *Forbes*, September 22, 2014, www.forbes.com/sites/forbesleadershipforum/2014/09/22/alibaba-vs-amazon-who-will-win-the-global-e-commerce-war/.

Company Case 15

7-Eleven: Adapting to the World's Many Cultures

Americans love convenience stores. There's one on every corner, or so it seems. They open early and stay open late. And while you can't get everything at a convenience store, you can get what matters most—gas, beer, cigarettes ... and lots of snack foods! Snickers, Twinkies, Mountain Dew, Funyuns, Slim Jim, or Good Humor—the list goes on. Although new convenience store designs are serving up made-to-order hot meals for breakfast, lunch, and dinner, the presentation of America's favorite snack foods has risen to shrine-like status.

In an age of national brands, convenience store chains remain somewhat regional in the United States. At the same time, the top chains represent some of the country's biggest retailers—Circle K, Speedway, Casey's, QuikTrip, and Sheetz. Or maybe you prefer the small chains like Nebraska-based Bucky's, Moto-Mart in Illinois, or Minnesota's own Pump 'N Munch. While there is still no U.S. convenience store chain that comes close to covering all 50 states, there are hundreds of chains and more than 150,000 convenience store locations. Given the regional nature of domestic convenience store chains, it's hard to imagine any of them as global brands akin to Nike, McDonald's, or Coca-Cola. And because nearly all U.S.-based convenience stores adhere so closely to a prescribed formula, it's hard to imagine a convenience store being anything else.

But one convenience store chain is sweeping the planet. 7-Eleven, America's largest convenience store chain with more than 10,000 U.S. stores in 34 states, is also the world's biggest, with more than 55,000 stores in 16 countries, including North America, Asia, and Europe. That number grows every year. And as 7-Eleven expands, it provides a great example of how to adapt a successful business model to differences across global markets.

It All Started with Ice

In 1927, "Uncle Johnny" Jefferson Green started selling milk, bread, and eggs from the dock of the Southland Ice Company where he worked, often on Sundays and evenings when regular grocery stores were closed. Trying to make a little extra money, Uncle Johnny had no idea that he was inventing what would become one of the biggest and longest-standing retail concepts. His boss, Joe C. Thompson Jr., took notice. Within 10 years, Thompson's Southland Ice Company had 60 such retail outlets that sold the basic staples—everything from canned goods to cold watermelon. As the chain slowly grew, the convenience store concept took root—a small store (2,000 to 3,000 square feet) carrying 2,500 high-demand products, convenient locations, fair prices, speedy transactions, and friendly service.

Thompson's chain continued to grow and innovate. In 1946, the chain boldly established longer business hours than any other store had yet dared. Open from 7 a.m. to 11 p.m., the company changed its name to cement the convenience of its long hours into its brand image. In 1963, the first 7-Eleven open 24/7 emerged, and another revolution began. When the chain reached 1,500 locations in the mid-1960s, it unleashed a brain-freeze plague on the nation with the introduction of the Slurpee. Coffee-to-go, the 32-ounce Big Gulp, and the larger-than-normal Big Bite hot dog are among other innovations that would quickly become convenience store staples. But in 1969, 7-Eleven would launch another first that would become the template for its future. It was the first convenience store chain to begin opening outlets in other countries—first Canada, then Mexico, and soon Japan and other Asian markets.

Keeping up with such rapid expansion is challenging for any company. Shortly before it opened its first international store, 7-Eleven adopted a franchise model that would allow it to grow at a breakneck pace by requiring franchisees to shoulder some of the financial and operational burdens. The company also gave franchisees flexibility, within certain parameters, to customize product offerings in any given store in order to cater to local tastes, what 7-Eleven today refers to as "retailer initiative." The chain considers local initiative to be an important competitive advantage.

That idea of catering to local tastes would become the cornerstone of 7-Eleven's international expansion. Certain aspects of the corporate marketing mix would remain standard—such as the small-store format and the concept of selling products and services that local customers want most and most often. But as the company opened more international stores, it became obvious that each market possessed differences that changed the meaning of convenience.

The Japanese Invasion

Consider Japan, one of 7-Eleven's first international markets. U.S. tourists visiting Japan today notice a stark contrast between 7-Eleven stores in the Land of the Rising Sun and those they are familiar with at home. For starters, the stores are everywhere. There are more than 17,000 7-Eleven stores in Japan, 2,300 in Tokyo alone. That makes Japan by far the company's largest market.

But the large number of stores is only the beginning. The reason there are so many 7-Elevens in Japan is that the chain has become the country's most popular eatery. Around mealtime, the aisles at every 7-Eleven are packed and the lines are long. But the Japanese aren't lining up for potato chips and Slurpees. Instead, in Japan, 7-Eleven patrons are treated to some of the finest prepared foods in the world. Typical offerings include salmon on rice with butter and soy sauce, hashed beef doria in a red wine demi-glace, and ground chicken with ginger and a side of spinach coleslaw. Fresh sushi abounds, the ongiri (rice balls with seaweed) is wrapped in a way that keeps the seaweed crispy and the rice moist, and a perfectly cooked unshelled boiled egg somehow has an already salted yoke. 7-Eleven also offers a wide selection of beverages, including soft drinks, beer, sake, champagne, single-malt scotch, wine, and more than 20 varieties of iced coffee. This is not your typical U.S. 7-Eleven.

But it isn't just the selection of food that sets Japan's 7-Elevens apart. Stores receive two to five deliveries of food goods per day, keeping shelves stocked, making the food fresh, and ensuring that everything is made locally. Open display cases—both cold and hot—serve food in a manner that is more Trader Joe's than convenience store. And if all those stores aren't convenient enough, Japanese customers can order food and groceries online and have them delivered by a single-seat electric car.

If all this sounds too good to be true, there's more. Japan's number-one convenience store chain is also designed to meet the service needs of locals. At 7-Eleven, customers can pay their phone or utility bills, pick up their mail and parcel deliveries, and even buy baseball tickets from the copy machine.

For 7-Eleven, Japan represents far more than just a booming international market. Since the early 1990s, Japan has become 7-Eleven's domestic market. That's right. When Dallas-based 7-Eleven, Inc. went bankrupt in 1991, its own Japanese subsidiary bailed it out, buying a majority stake, debt and all. In 2005, Seven & I Holdings was created and the remaining shares of 7-Eleven, Inc. were acquired. Then, in a case of the student becoming the master, the directives were reversed as the new parent corporation increased investment in merchandising, store renovation, distribution and logistics systems, and information systems. What 7-Eleven Japan had mastered over the previous 40 years was used to strengthen "retailer initiative" in the U.S. division.

The Third Place of Convenience Stores

While it wouldn't be the first time that a Japanese company took a U.S. business concept, perfected it, then brought it back to the United States (think Honda automobiles, Sony televisions, or Toshiba computers), the core strategy remained the same—give the people what they want in every market. Many features established in 7-Eleven Japan worked well in other rapidly expanding Asian markets, including Taiwan, Singapore, China, and the Philippines. But the new parent company continues to adapt the model masterfully.

Nowhere is that more apparent than in one of 7-Eleven's newest markets, Indonesia. Picture this—on a Saturday night, thousands of young Indonesians gather at one of 200 7-Eleven stores to sip coffee or beer at sidewalk tables, listen to live music, and engage in their newest passion—the Internet. If that sounds more like Starbucks, it's no accident. As Seven & I Holdings analyzed the Indonesian market, certain insights became apparent.

For starters, Indonesia has a growing economy and a population of 240 million people. Until a few years ago, however, the country had largely been overlooked by global corporations. This meant that as consumer buying power began to increase, there were few options to satisfy local needs. That made Indonesia one of the world's most attractive international growth opportunities.

Although certain things in the Indonesian culture were common to other countries, the market also exhibited unique traits. For starters, hanging out and doing nothing—something the locals refer to as "nongkrong"—is a favorite pastime. People gather at street markets, roadside food stalls, and Western fast-food outlets simply to pass the time and share stories. But the demand for hangouts exceeded the supply, and few options provided wireless connectivity, an ever-increasing need.

In response, the concept for 7-Eleven stores in Indonesia focused more on the "third place" concept pioneered by Starbucks than on the convenience store concept found elsewhere. The chain still offers basic convenience store products, such as inexpensive ready-made food, snacks, and a variety of popular beverages. And 24-hour operations are perfect for a culture not bound by time. But to drive traffic into stores, 7-Eleven Indonesia also provides hassle-free parking (a premium feature in the traffic-choked island nation), a venue for local bands (the bands sometimes pay a fee for the privilege of playing), air-conditioning, free wireless connectivity, and lots of space to hang out. The target customer is between 18 and 35. And rather than putting stores on every corner, the target for locations is on big hubs in the country that consists of 17,000 islands.

The 7-Eleven local initiative formula is working once again. Even as the company strategically applies the 7-Eleven concept to each global market, franchisees and managers customize the offerings in each store to get even closer to fulfilling local consumer needs. As the company Website points out, "At 7-Eleven, our purpose and mission is to make life a little easier for our guests by being where they need us, whenever they need us." While it still has a way to go before conquering the world, 7-Eleven is accomplishing its mission well in markets where it does business.

Questions for Discussion

1. Of the five global product and communications strategies, which best describes 7-Eleven's approach?
2. On a scale of one to five, to what degree does 7-Eleven adapt its offering in each global market? Support your answer.
3. Which strategy does 7-Eleven employ for entering a new market? How does the company benefit from this approach?
4. Will 7-Eleven continue to succeed in Indonesia? How about the rest of the markets where it does business? Why or why not?

Sources: Taryn Stenvei, "What 7-Elevens in Tokyo Taught Me about Japan," *AWOL*, September 11, 2014, http://awol.com.au/what-7-elevens-in-tokyo-taught-me-about-japan/98; Justin Moyer, "In Honor of 7/11: How Japan Slurped Up 7-Eleven," *Washington Post*, July 11, 2014, www.washingtonpost.com/news/morning-mix/wp/2014/07/11/in-honor-of-711-how-japan-slurped-up-7-eleven/; Margot Huber, "Hang-out Haven," *Business Today*, May 26, 2013, http://businesstoday.intoday.in/story/london-business-school-case-study-on-7-eleven/1/194769.html; and information from http://corp.7-eleven.com/corp/7-eleven-profile, accessed September 2015.

Appendix 2: Marketing Plan

The Marketing Plan: An Introduction

As a marketer, you will need a good marketing plan to provide direction and focus for your brand, product, or company. With a detailed plan, any business will be better prepared to launch a new product or build sales for existing products. Nonprofit organizations also use marketing plans to guide their fundraising and outreach efforts. Even government agencies put together marketing plans for initiatives such as building public awareness of proper nutrition and stimulating area tourism.

The Purpose and Content of a Marketing Plan

Unlike a business plan, which offers a broad overview of the entire organization's mission, objectives, strategy, and resource allocation, a marketing plan has a more limited scope. It serves to document how the organization's strategic objectives will be achieved through specific marketing strategies and tactics, with the customer as the starting point. It is also linked to the plans of other departments within the organization. Suppose, for example, a marketing plan calls for selling 200,000 units annually. The production department must gear up to make that many units, the finance department must arrange funding to cover the expenses, the human resources department must be ready to hire and train staff, and so on. Without the appropriate level of organizational support and resources, no marketing plan can succeed.

Although the exact length and layout will vary from company to company, a marketing plan usually contains the sections described in Chapter 2. Smaller businesses may create shorter or less formal marketing plans whereas corporations frequently require highly structured marketing plans. To guide implementation effectively, every part of the plan must be described in considerable detail. Sometimes a company will post its marketing plans on an intranet site, which allows managers and employees in different locations to consult specific sections and collaborate on additions or changes.

The Role of Research

Marketing plans are not created in a vacuum. To develop successful strategies and action programs, marketers need up-to-date information about the environment, the competition, and the market segments to be served. Often, analysis of internal data is the starting point for assessing the current marketing situation, supplemented by marketing intelligence and research investigating the overall market, the competition, key issues, and threats and opportunities. As the plan is put into effect, marketers use a variety of research techniques to measure progress toward objectives and identify areas for improvement if results fall short of projections.

Finally, marketing research helps marketers learn more about their customers' requirements, expectations, perceptions, and satisfaction levels. This deeper understanding provides a foundation for building competitive advantage through well-informed segmenting, targeting, differentiating, and positioning decisions. Thus, the marketing plan should outline what marketing research will be conducted and how the findings will be applied.

The Role of Relationships

The marketing plan shows how the company will engage customers and build profitable customer relationships. In the process, however, it also shapes a number of internal and external relationships. First, it affects how marketing personnel work with each other and with other departments to deliver value and satisfy customers. Second, it affects how the company works with suppliers, distributors, and strategic alliance partners to achieve the objectives listed in the plan. Third, it influences the company's dealings with other stakeholders, including government regulators, the media, and the community at large. All of these relationships are important to the organization's success, so they should be considered when a marketing plan is being developed.

From Marketing Plan to Marketing Action

Companies generally create yearly marketing plans, although some plans cover a longer period. Marketers start planning well in advance of the implementation date to allow time for marketing research, thorough analysis, management review, and coordination between departments. Then, after each action program begins, marketers monitor ongoing results, compare them with projections, analyze any differences, and take corrective steps as needed. Some marketers also prepare contingency plans for implementation if certain conditions emerge. Because of inevitable and sometimes unpredictable environmental changes, marketers must be ready to update and adapt marketing plans at any time.

For effective implementation and control, the marketing plan should define how progress toward objectives will be measured. Managers typically use budgets, schedules, and performance standards for monitoring and evaluating results. With budgets, they can compare planned expenditures with actual expenditures for a given week, month, or other period. Schedules allow management to see when tasks were supposed to be completed—and when they were actually completed. Performance standards track the outcomes of marketing programs to see whether the company is moving toward its objectives. Some examples of performance standards are market share, sales volume, product profitability, and customer satisfaction.

Sample Marketing Plan: Chill Beverage Company

Executive Summary

The Chill Beverage Company is preparing to launch a new line of vitamin-enhanced water called NutriWater. Although the bottled water market is maturing, the vitamin-enhanced water category is still growing. NutriWater will be positioned by the slogan "Expect more"—indicating that the brand offers more in the way of desirable product features and benefits at a competitive price. Chill Beverage is taking advantage of its existing experience and brand equity among its loyal current customer base of Millennials who consume its Chill Soda soft drink. NutriWater will target similar Millennials who are maturing and looking for an alternative to soft drinks and high-calorie sugared beverages.

The primary marketing objective is to achieve first-year U.S. sales of $35 million, roughly 2 percent of the enhanced water market. Based on this market share goal, the company expects to sell more than 20 million units the first year and break even in the final period of the year.

Current Marketing Situation

The Chill Beverage Company was founded in 2007 by an entrepreneur who had successfully built a company that primarily distributed niche and emerging products in the beverage industry. Its Chill Soda soft drink brand hit the market with six unique flavors in glass bottles. A few years later, the Chill Soda brand introduced an energy drink as well as a line of natural juice drinks. The company now markets dozens of Chill Soda flavors, many unique to the brand. Chill Beverage has grown its business every year since it was founded. In the most recent year, it achieved $185 million in revenue and net profits of $14.5 million. As part of its future growth strategy, Chill Beverage is currently preparing to enter a new beverage category with a line of vitamin-enhanced waters.

For years, U.S. consumers drank more carbonated soft drinks than any other beverage. But recently, water once again became the number-one beverage of choice as concerns over health and obesity caused the soda market to go flat. On average, people in the U.S. drink 58 gallons of water each year compared with 44 gallons of soda. While those water numbers include tap water, bottled water consumption has grown tremendously since the 1990s. Currently, the average person in the United States consumes more than 34 gallons of bottled water every year, more than double the figure just 15 years prior. Bottled water consumption is second only to soft drink consumption, ahead of milk, beer, and coffee. As a beverage category, bottled water is growing at a robust rate of 5 to 7 percent annually, a figure that is expected to increase in years to come. Most other beverage categories have experienced declines. In the most recent year, 10.8 billion gallons of bottled water were sold in the United States with a value of approximately $13 billion.

Competition is more intense now than ever as demand slows, industry consolidation continues, and new types of bottled water emerge. The U.S. market is dominated by three global corporations. With a portfolio of 12 brands (including Poland Spring, Nestlé Pure Life, Arrowhead, Deer Park, and Ice Mountain), Nestlé leads the market for "plain" bottled water. However, when all subcategories of bottled water are included (enhanced water, flavored water, and so on), Coca-Cola leads the U.S. market with a 22.9 percent share. Nestlé markets only plain waters but is number two at 21.5 percent of the total bottled water market. PepsiCo is third with 16.2 percent of the market.

To break into this market, dominated by huge global corporations and littered with dozens of other small players, Chill Beverage must carefully target specific segments with features and benefits valued by those segments.

Market Description

The bottled water market consists of many different types of water. Varieties of plain water include spring, purified, mineral, and distilled. Although these different types of water are sold as consumer products, they also serve as the core ingredient for other types of bottled waters including enhanced water, flavored water, sparkling water, or any combination of those categories.

Although some consumers may not perceive much of a difference between brands, others are drawn to specific product features and benefits provided by different brands. For example, some consumers may perceive spring water as healthier than other types of water. Some may look for water that is optimized for hydration. Others seek additional nutritional benefits claimed by bottlers that enhance their brands with vitamins, minerals, herbs, and other additives. Still other consumers make selections based on flavor. The industry as a whole has positioned bottled water of all kinds as a low-calorie, healthy alternative to soft drinks, sports drinks, energy drinks, and other types of beverages.

Bottled water brands also distinguish themselves by size and type of container, multipacks, and refrigeration at point-of-sale. Chill Beverage's market for NutriWater consists of consumers of single-serving-sized bottled beverages who are looking for a healthy yet flavorful alternative. "Healthy" in this context means both low-calorie and enhanced nutritional content. This market includes traditional soft drink consumers who want to improve their health as well as non-soft-drink consumers who want an option other than plain bottled water. Specific segments that Chill Beverage will target during the first year include athletes, the health conscious, the socially responsible, and Millennials who favor independent corporations. The Chill Soda brand has established a strong base of loyal customers, primarily among Millennials. This generational segment is becoming a prime target as it matures and seeks alternatives to full-calorie soft drinks. **»Table A2.1** shows how NutriWater addresses the needs of targeted consumer segments.

Product Review

Chill Beverage's new line of vitamin-enhanced water—called NutriWater—offers the following features:

- Six new-age flavors including Peach Mango, Berry Pomegranate, Kiwi Dragonfruit, Mandarin Orange, Blueberry Grape, and Key Lime.
- Single-serving size, 20-ounce, PET recyclable bottles.
- Formulated for wellness, replenishment, and optimum energy.
- Full Recommended Daily Allowance (RDA) of essential vitamins and minerals (including electrolytes).

» Table A2.1 Segment Needs and Corresponding Features/Benefits of NutriWater

Targeted Segment	Customer Need	Corresponding Features/Benefits
Athletes	• Hydration and replenishment of essential minerals • Energy to maximize performance	• Electrolytes and carbohydrates • B vitamins, carbohydrates
Health conscious	• Maintain optimum weight • Optimize nutrition levels • Avoid harmful chemicals and additives • Desire to consume a tastier beverage than water	• Half the calories of fully sugared beverages • Higher levels of vitamins A, B, C, E, Zinc, Chromium, and Folic Acid than other products; vitamins unavailable in other products • All natural ingredients • Six new-age flavors
Socially conscious	• Support causes that help solve world's social problems	• 25-cent donation from each purchase to Vitamin Angels
Millennials	• Aversion to mass-media advertising/ technologically savvy • Counter-culture attitude • Diet enhancement due to fast-paced lifestyle	• Less-invasive online and social networking promotional tactics • Small, privately held company • Full RDA levels of essential vitamins and minerals

- Higher vitamin concentration—vitamin levels are two to ten times higher than market-leading products, with more vitamins and minerals than any other brand.
- Additional vitamins—vitamins include A, E, and B2 as well as folic acid—none of which are contained in the market-leading products.
- All natural—no artificial flavors, colors, or preservatives.
- Sweetened with pure cane sugar and Stevia, a natural zero-calorie sweetener.
- Twenty-five cents from each purchase will be donated to Vitamin Angels, a nonprofit organization with a mission to prevent vitamin deficiency in at-risk children.

Competitive Review

As sales of bottled waters entered a strong growth phase in the 1990s, the category began to expand. In addition to the various types of plain water, new categories emerged. These included flavored waters—such as Aquafina's Flavorsplash—as well as enhanced waters. Enhanced waters emerged to bridge the gap between soft drinks and waters, appealing to people who knew they should drink more water and fewer soft drinks but still wanted flavor. Initially, development of brands for this product variation occurred primarily in start-up and boutique beverage companies like Sobe and Glacéau, creator of Vitaminwater. In the 2000s, major beverage corporations acquired the most successful smaller brands, providing the bigger firms with a solid market position in this category and diversification in bottled waters in general. At that point, enhanced waters grew at a rate that exceeded that of plain water.

To demonstrate the strength of the enhanced water segment, Coca-Cola's Vitaminwater became the fourth-largest bottled water brand, behind plain water brands Nestlé Pure Life, Coca-Cola's Dasani, and Pepsi's Aquafina. In recent years, vitamin-enhanced waters have taken a hit in the wake of some bad press focusing on the low amount of vitamins and high amount of sugar contained in most brands. Nonetheless, enhanced water sales account for approximately 13 percent of the total bottled water market, and industry insiders expect sales to return to a growth trajectory in coming years.

The fragmentation of this category, combined with domination by the market leaders, has created a severely competitive environment. Although there is indirect competition posed by all types of bottled waters and even other types of beverages (soft drinks, energy drinks, juices, teas, and flavor drops), this competitive analysis focuses on direct competition from enhanced water brands. For the purposes of this analysis, enhanced water is bottled water with additives that are intended to provide health and wellness benefits. The most common additives include vitamins, minerals (including electrolytes), and herbs. Most commonly, enhanced waters are sweetened, flavored, and colored. This definition distinguishes enhanced water from sports drinks that have the primary purpose of maximizing hydration by replenishing electrolytes.

Enhanced water brands are typically sweetened with a combination of some kind of sugar and a zero-calorie sweetener, resulting in about half the sugar content, carbohydrates, and calories of regular soft drinks and other sweetened beverages. The types of sweeteners used create a point of differentiation. Many brands, including the market leaders, sell both regular and zero-calorie varieties.

Pricing for this product is consistent across brands and varies by type of retail outlet, with convenience stores typically charging more than grocery stores. The price for a 20-ounce bottle ranges from $1.00 to $1.89, with some niche brands costing slightly more. Key competitors to Chill Beverage's NutriWater line include the following:

- ***Vitaminwater:*** Created in 2000 as a new product for Energy Brands' Glacéau, which was also the developer of Smartwater (distilled water with electrolytes). Coca-Cola purchased Energy Brands for $4.1 billion in 2007. Vitaminwater is sold in regular and zero-calorie versions. With 19 bottled varieties—11 regular and 8 zero-calorie—as well as availability in fountain form and drops, Vitaminwater offers more options than any brand on the market. Whereas Vitaminwater varieties are distinguished by flavor, they are named to evoke perceptions of benefits such as Essential, Defense, Focus, and Revive. The brand's current slogan is "Hydrate the Hustle." Vitaminwater is vapor distilled, deionized, and/or filtered and is sweetened with crystalline fructose (corn syrup) and erythritol all-natural sweetener. Vitaminwater exceeds $700 million in annual sales and commands 63 percent of the enhanced water market.
- ***Propel:*** Gatorade created Propel in 2000, just one year prior to PepsiCo's purchase of this leading sports drink marketer. Marketed as "The Workout Water," Propel was originally available in regular and zero-calorie varieties. However, it is now available only as a zero-calorie beverage. Propel comes in nine flavors, each containing the same blend of B vitamins, vitamin C, vitamin E, antioxidants, and electrolytes. It is sweetened with sucralose. Propel is available in a wide variety of sizes, with 16.9-, 20-, and 24-ounce PET bottles and multipacks. Propel is also marketed in powder form and as a liquid enhancer to be added to bottled water. With $171 million in revenues, Propel is the number-two enhanced water brand with a 15 percent share of the enhanced water market.
- ***SoBe Lifewater:*** PepsiCo bought SoBe in 2000. SoBe introduced Lifewater in 2008 with a hit Super Bowl ad as an answer to Coca-Cola's Vitaminwater. The Lifewater line includes 13 regular and zero-calorie varieties. Each variety is infused with a formulation of vitamins, minerals, and herbs designed to provide a claimed benefit. Sweetened with a combination of sugar and erythritol, Lifewater makes the claim to be "all natural." It contains no artificial flavors or colors. However, some analysts debate the "natural" designation for erythritol. Lifewater is sold in 20-ounce PET bottles and multipacks as well as one-liter PET bottles. With more than $200 million in annual revenues, Lifewater is the number-three enhanced water brand with a 12 percent share.
- ***Niche brands:*** The market for enhanced waters includes at least four companies that market their wares on a small scale through independent retailers: Assure, Ex Aqua Vitamins, Ayala Herbal Water, and Skinny Water. Some brands feature exotic additives and/or artistic glass bottles.

Despite the strong competition, NutriWater believes it can create a relevant brand image and gain recognition among the targeted segments. The brand offers strong points of differentiation with higher and unique vitamin content, all-natural ingredients, and support for a relevant social cause. With other strategic assets, Chill Beverage is confident that it can establish a competitive advantage that will allow NutriWater to grow in the market. >> **Table A2.2** shows a sample of competing products.

Channels and Logistics Review

With the three main brands now owned by Coca-Cola and PepsiCo, there is a huge hole in the independent distributor system. NutriWater will be distributed through an independent distributor to a network of retailers in the United States. This strategy will avoid some of the head-on competition for shelf space with the Coca-Cola and PepsiCo brands and will

>> Table A2.2 Sample of Competitive Products

Competitor	Brand	Features
Coca-Cola	Vitaminwater	Regular and zero-calorie versions; 15 varieties; each flavor provides a different function based on blend of vitamins and minerals; vapor distilled, deionized, and/or filtered; sweetened with crystalline fructose and erythritol; 20-ounce single-serve or multipack, fountain, and drops.
PepsiCo	Propel	Zero-calorie only; seven flavors; fitness positioning based on "Replenish + Energize + Protect"; B vitamins, vitamin C, vitamin E, antioxidants, and electrolytes; sweetened with sucralose; 16.9-ounce, 20-ounce, and 24-ounce PET bottles and multipacks; powdered packets; liquid enhancer.
PepsiCo	SoBe Lifewater	Regular and zero-calorie versions; 15 varieties; six different functional categories; vitamins, minerals, and herbs; Pure—mildly flavored, unsweetened water; sweetened with sugar and erythritol; "all natural"; 20-ounce single-serve and multipacks as well as one-liter bottles.

also directly target likely NutriWater customers. As with the rollout of the core Chill Soda brand, this strategy will focus on placing coolers in retail locations that will exclusively hold NutriWater. These retailers include:

- ***Grocery chains:*** Regional grocery chains such as HyVee in the Midwest, Wegman's in the East, and WinCo in the West.
- ***Health and natural food stores:*** Chains such as Whole Foods Market as well as local health food co-ops.
- ***Fitness centers:*** National fitness center chains such as 24 Hour Fitness, Gold's Gym, and other regional chains.

As the brand gains acceptance, channels will expand into larger grocery chains, convenience stores, and unique locations relevant to the target customer segment.

Strengths, Weaknesses, Opportunities, and Threats Analysis

NutriWater has several powerful strengths on which to build, but its major weakness is lack of brand awareness and image. Major opportunities include a growing market and consumer trends targeted by NutriWater's product traits. Threats include barriers to entry posed by limited retail space as well as image issues for the bottled water industry. **>> Table A2.3** summarizes NutriWater's main strengths, weaknesses, opportunities, and threats.

Strengths

NutriWater can rely on the following important strengths:

1. ***Superior quality:*** NutriWater boasts the highest levels of added vitamins of any enhanced water, including full RDA levels of many vitamins. It is all natural with no artificial flavors, colors, or preservatives. It is sweetened with both pure cane sugar and the natural zero-calorie sweetener Stevia.
2. ***Expertise in alternative beverage marketing:*** The Chill Soda brand went from nothing to a successful and rapidly growing soft drink brand with fiercely loyal customers in a matter of only one decade. This success was achieved by starting small and focusing on gaps in the marketplace.
3. ***Social responsibility:*** Every customer will have the added benefit of helping malnourished children throughout the world. Although the price of NutriWater is in line with other competitors, low promotional costs allow for the substantial charitable donation of 25 cents per bottle while maintaining profitability.
4. ***Antiestablishment image:*** The big brands have decent products and strong distribution relationships. But they also carry the image of the large, corporate establishments. Chill Beverage has achieved success with an underdog image while remaining privately held. Vitaminwater and SoBe were built on this same image, but both are now owned by major multinational corporations.

Table A2.3 NutriWater's Strengths, Weaknesses, Opportunities, and Threats

Strengths	Weaknesses
• Superior quality • Expertise in alternative beverage marketing • Social responsibility • Antiestablishment image	• Lack of brand awareness • Limited budget
Opportunities	**Threats**
• Market growth • Gap in the distribution network • Health trends • Antiestablishment image	• Limited shelf space • Image of enhanced waters • Environmental issues

Weaknesses

1. ***Lack of brand awareness:*** As an entirely new brand, NutriWater will enter the market with limited or no brand awareness. The affiliation with Chill Soda will be kept at a minimum in order to prevent associations between NutriWater and soft drinks. This issue will be addressed through promotion and distribution strategies.
2. ***Limited budget:*** As a smaller company, Chill Beverage has much smaller funds available for promotional and research activities.

Opportunities

1. ***Market growth:*** Bottled water as a category is growing at a rate of about 7 percent annually. While the enhanced water subcategory has decreased in overall sales, that is expected to reverse as the enhanced water brands move past the negative associations of the past. Of the top six beverage categories, soft drinks, beer, milk, and fruit drinks experienced declines. The growth for coffee was less than 1 percent.
2. ***Gap in the distribution network:*** The market leaders distribute directly to retailers. This gives them an advantage in large national chains. However, no major enhanced water brands are currently being sold through independent distributors.
3. ***Health trends:*** Weight and nutrition continue to be issues for consumers in the United States. The country has the highest obesity rate for developed countries at 34 percent, with well over 60 percent of the population officially "overweight." Those numbers continue to rise. Additionally, Americans get 21 percent of their daily calories from beverages, a number that has tripled in the last three decades. Consumers still desire flavored beverages but look for lower-calorie alternatives.
4. ***Antiestablishment image:*** Millennials (born between 1977 and 2000) maintain a higher aversion to mass marketing messages and global corporations than do Gen Xers and baby boomers.

Threats

1. ***Limited shelf space:*** Whereas competition is generally a threat for any type of product, competition in retail beverages is particularly high because of limited retail space. Carrying a new beverage product requires retailers to reduce shelf or cooler space already occupied by other brands.
2. ***Image of enhanced waters:*** The image of enhanced waters took a hit as Coca-Cola recently fought a class-action lawsuit accusing it of violating FDA regulations by promoting the health benefits of Vitaminwater. The lawsuit exposed the number-one bottled water brand as basically sugar water with minimal nutritional value. Each of the major brands is strengthening its zero-calorie lines. They no longer promote health benefits on the labels. While this is potentially a threat, it is also an opportunity for Chill to exploit.

3. ***Environmental issues:*** Environmental groups continue to educate the public on the environmental costs of bottled water, including landfill waste, carbon emissions from production and transportation, and harmful effects of chemicals in plastics.

Objectives and Issues

Chill Beverage has set aggressive but achievable objectives for NutriWater for the first and second years of market entry.

First-Year Objectives

During the initial year on the market, Chill Beverage aims for NutriWater to achieve a 2 percent share of the enhanced water market, or approximately $35 million in sales, with break-even achieved in the final period of the year. With an average retail price of $1.69, that equates with a sales goal of 20,710,059 bottles.

Second-Year Objectives

During the second year, Chill Beverage will unveil additional NutriWater flavors, including zero-calorie varieties. The second-year objective is to double sales from the first year, to $70 million.

Issues

In launching this new brand, the main issue is the ability to establish brand awareness and a meaningful brand image based on positioning that is relevant to target customer segments. Chill Beverage will invest in nontraditional means of promotion to accomplish these goals and to spark word of mouth. Establishing distributor and retailer relationships will also be critical in order to make the product available and provide point-of-purchase communications. Brand awareness and knowledge will be measured in order to adjust marketing efforts as necessary.

Marketing Strategy

NutriWater's marketing strategy will involve developing a "more for the same" positioning based on extra benefits for the price. The brand will also establish channel differentiation, as it will be available in locations where major competing brands are not. The primary target segment is Millennials. This segment is composed of late teens (15 to 18) and young adults (19 to 38). NutriWater will focus specifically on the young adult market. Subsets of this generational segment include athletes, the health conscious, and the socially responsible.

Positioning

NutriWater will be positioned on an "Expect more" value proposition. This will allow for differentiating the brand based on product features (expect more vitamin content and all-natural ingredients), desirable benefits (expect greater nutritional benefits), and values (do more for a social cause). Marketing will focus on conveying that NutriWater is more than just a beverage: It gives customers much more for their money in a variety of ways.

Product Strategy

NutriWater will be sold with all the features described in the Product Review section. As awareness takes hold and retail availability increases, more varieties will be made available. A zero-calorie version will be added to the product line, providing a solid fit with the health benefits sought by consumers. Chill Beverage's considerable experience in brand building will be applied as an integral part of the product strategy for NutriWater. All aspects of the marketing mix will be consistent with the brand.

Pricing

There is little price variation in the enhanced waters category, particularly among leading brands. For this reason, NutriWater will follow a competition-based pricing strategy. Given that NutriWater claims superior quality, it must be careful not to position itself as a lower-cost alternative. Manufacturers do not quote list prices on this type of beverage, and prices vary considerably based on type of retail outlet and whether the product is refrigerated. Regular prices for single 20-ounce bottles of competing products are as low as $1.00 in discount-retailer stores and as high as $1.89 in convenience stores. Because NutriWater will not be targeting discount retailers and convenience stores initially, this will allow Chill Beverage to set prices at the average to higher end of the range for similar products in the same outlets. For grocery chains, this should be approximately $1.49 per bottle, with that price rising to $1.89 at health food stores and fitness centers, where prices tend to be higher.

Distribution Strategy

NutriWater will employ a selective distribution strategy with well-known regional grocers, health and natural food stores, and fitness centers. This distribution strategy will be executed through a network of independent beverage distributors, as there are no other major brands of enhanced water following this strategy. Chill Beverage gained success for its core Chill Soda soft drink line using this method. It also placed coolers with the brand logo in truly unique venues such as skate, surf, and snowboarding shops; tattoo and piercing parlors; fashion stores; and music stores—places that would expose the brand to target customers. Then the soft drink brand expanded by getting contracts with retailers such as Panera, Barnes & Noble, Target, and Starbucks. This same approach will be taken with NutriWater by starting small, then expanding into larger chains. NutriWater will not target all the same stores used originally by Chill Soda, as many of those outlets were unique to the positioning and target customer for the Chill Soda soft drink brand.

Marketing Communication Strategy

As with the core Chill Soda brand, the marketing communication strategy for NutriWater will not follow a strategy based on traditional mass-communication advertising. Initially, there will be no broadcast or print advertising. Promotional resources for NutriWater will focus on three areas:

- ***Online and mobile marketing:*** The typical target customer for NutriWater spends more time online than with traditional media channels. A core component for this strategy will be building Web and mobile brand sites and driving traffic to those sites by creating a presence on social networks, including Facebook, Google+, and Twitter. The NutriWater brand will also incorporate location-based services by Foursquare and Facebook to help drive traffic to retail locations. A mobile phone ad campaign will provide additional support to the online efforts.
- ***Trade promotions:*** Like the core Chill Soda brand, NutriWater's success will rely on relationships with retailers to create product availability. Primary incentives to retailers will include point-of-purchase displays, branded coolers, and volume incentives and contests. This push marketing strategy will combine with the other pull strategies.
- ***Event marketing:*** NutriWater will deploy teams in brand-labeled RVs to distribute product samples at events such as skiing and snowboarding competitions, golf tournaments, and concerts.

Marketing Research

To remain consistent with the online promotional approach as well as using research methods that will effectively reach target customers, Chill Beverage will monitor online discussions via services such as Radian6. In this manner, the company will gauge customer perceptions of the brand, the products, and general satisfaction. For future development of the product and new distribution outlets, crowdsourcing methods will be utilized.

Action Programs

NutriWater will be introduced in February. The following are summaries of action programs that will be used during the first six months of the year to achieve the stated objectives.

January: Chill Beverage representatives will work with both independent distributors and retailers to educate them on the trade promotional campaign, incentives, and advantages for selling NutriWater. Representatives will also ensure that distributors and retailers are educated on product features and benefits as well as instructions for displaying point-of-purchase materials and coolers. The brand Web site and other sites such as Facebook will present teaser information about the product as well as availability dates and locations. Buzz will be enhanced by providing product samples to selected product reviewers, opinion leaders, influential bloggers, and celebrities.

February: On the date of availability, product coolers and point-of-purchase displays will be placed in retail locations. The full brand Web site and social network campaign will launch with full efforts on Facebook, Google+, and Twitter. This campaign will drive the "Expect more" slogan as well as illustrate the ways that NutriWater delivers more than expected on product features, desirable benefits, and values by donating to Vitamin Angels and the social cause of battling vitamin deficiency in children.

March: To enhance the online and social marketing campaign, location-based services Foursquare and Facebook Places will be employed to drive traffic to retailers. Point-of-purchase displays and signage will be updated to support these efforts and to continue supporting retailers. The message of this campaign will focus on all aspects of "Expect more."

April: A mobile phone ad campaign will provide additional support, driving Web traffic to the brand Web site and social network sites as well as driving traffic to retailers.

May: A trade sales contest will offer additional incentives and prizes to the distributors and retailers that sell the most NutriWater during a four-week period.

June: An event marketing campaign will mobilize a team of NutriWater representatives in NutriWater RVs to concerts and sports events. This will provide additional visibility for the brand as well as give customers and potential customers the opportunity to sample products.

Budgets

Chill Beverage has set a first-year retail sales goal of \$35 million with a projected average retail price of \$1.69 per unit for a total of 20,710,059 units sold. With an average wholesale price of 85 cents per unit, this provides revenues of \$17.6 million. Chill Beverage expects to break even during the final period of the first year. A break-even analysis assumes per-unit wholesale revenue of 85 cents per unit, a variable cost per unit of 14 cents, and estimated first-year fixed costs of \$12,500,000. Based on these assumptions, the break-even calculation is:

$$\frac{\$12{,}500{,}000}{\$0.85/\text{unit} - \$0.14/\text{unit}} = 17{,}605{,}634$$

Controls

Chill Beverage is planning tight control measures to closely monitor product quality, brand awareness, brand image, and customer satisfaction. This will enable the company to react quickly in correcting any problems that may occur. Other early warning signals that will be monitored for signs of deviation from the plan include monthly sales (by segment and channel) and monthly expenses. Given the market's volatility, contingency plans are also in place to address fast-moving environmental changes such as shifting consumer preferences, new products, and new competition.

Sources: "Channel Check," *Bevnet*, January/February 2015, p. 18; "Channel Check," *Bevnet*, July/August 2015, p. 26; "The Heat Is On for U.S. Bottled Water Market," *PR Newswire*, July 21, 2015, www.prnewswire.com/news-releases/report-the-heat-is-on-for-us-bottled-water-market-300115888.html; Jeffrey Klineman, "Restoring an Icon," *Beverage Spectrum Magazine*, December 2010, pp. 16–18; Matt Casey, "Enhanced Options Divide a Category," *Beverage Spectrum Magazine*, December 2008, p. 74; "Water Becomes America's Favorite Drink Again," *USA Today*, March 11, 2013, www.usatoday.com/story/news/nation/2013/03/11/water-americas-favorite-drink/1978959/; and product and market information obtained from www.sobe.com, www.vitaminwater.com, and www.nestle-waters.com, accessed September 2015.

Appendix 3 Marketing by the Numbers

Marketing managers are facing increased accountability for the financial implications of their actions. This appendix provides a basic introduction to measuring marketing financial performance. Such financial analysis guides marketers in making sound marketing decisions and in assessing the outcomes of those decisions.

The appendix is built around a hypothetical manufacturer of consumer electronics products—HD. The company is introducing a device that plays videos and television programming streamed over the Internet on multiple devices in a home, including high-definition televisions, tablets, and mobile phones. In this appendix, we will analyze the various decisions HD's marketing managers must make before and after the new product launch.

The appendix is organized into *three sections*. The *first section* introduces pricing, break-even, and margin analysis assessments that will guide the introduction of HD's new product. The *second section* discusses demand estimates, the marketing budget, and marketing performance measures. It begins with a discussion of estimating market potential and company sales. It then introduces the marketing budget, as illustrated through a *pro forma* profit-and-loss statement followed by the actual profit-and-loss statement. Next, we discuss marketing performance measures, with a focus on helping marketing managers to better defend their decisions from a financial perspective. In the *third section,* we analyze the financial implications of various marketing tactics.

Each of the three sections ends with a set of quantitative exercises that provide you with an opportunity to apply the concepts you learned to situations beyond HD.

Pricing, Break-Even, and Margin Analysis

Pricing Considerations

Determining price is one of the most important marketing mix decisions. The limiting factors are demand and costs. Demand factors, such as buyer-perceived value, set the price ceiling. The company's costs set the price floor. In between these two factors, marketers must consider competitors' prices and other factors such as reseller requirements, government regulations, and company objectives.

Most current competing Internet streaming products sell at retail prices between $100 and $500. We first consider HD's pricing decision from a cost perspective. Then we consider consumer value, the competitive environment, and reseller requirements.

Determining Costs

Fixed costs
Costs that do not vary with production or sales level.

Variable costs
Costs that vary directly with the level of production.

Total costs
The sum of the fixed and variable costs for any given level of production.

Recall from Chapter 9 that there are different types of costs. **Fixed costs** do not vary with production or sales level and include costs such as rent, interest, depreciation, and clerical and management salaries. Regardless of the level of output, the company must pay these costs. Whereas total fixed costs remain constant as output increases, the fixed cost per unit (or average fixed cost) will decrease as output increases because the total fixed costs are spread across more units of output. **Variable costs** vary directly with the level of production and include costs related to the direct production of the product (such as costs of goods sold—COGS) and many of the marketing costs associated with selling it. Although these costs tend to be uniform for each unit produced, they are called variable because their total varies with the number of units produced. **Total costs** are the sum of the fixed and variable costs for any given level of production.

HD has invested $10 million in refurbishing an existing facility to manufacture the new video streaming product. Once production begins, the company estimates that it will incur fixed costs of $20 million per year. The variable cost to produce each device is estimated to be $125 and is expected to remain at that level for the output capacity of the facility.

Setting Price Based on Costs

Cost-plus pricing (or markup pricing)
A standard markup to the cost of the product.

HD starts with the cost-based approach to pricing discussed in Chapter 9. Recall that the simplest method, **cost-plus pricing (or markup pricing)**, simply adds a standard markup to the cost of the product. To use this method, however, HD must specify expected unit sales so that total unit costs can be determined. Unit variable costs will remain constant regardless of the output, but *average unit fixed costs* will decrease as output increases.

To illustrate this method, suppose HD has fixed costs of $20 million, variable costs of $125 per unit, and expects unit sales of 1 million players. Thus, the cost per unit is given by:

$$\text{Unit cost} = \text{variable cost} + \frac{\text{fixed costs}}{\text{unit sales}} = \$125 + \frac{\$20{,}000{,}000}{1{,}000{,}000} = \$145$$

Relevant costs
Costs that will occur in the future and that will vary across the alternatives being considered.

Note that we do *not* include the initial investment of $10 million in the total fixed cost figure. It is not considered a fixed cost because it is not a *relevant* cost. **Relevant costs** are those that will occur in the future and that will vary across the alternatives being considered. HD's investment to refurbish the manufacturing facility was a one-time cost that will not reoccur in the future. Such past costs are *sunk costs* and should not be considered in future analyses.

Break-even price
The price at which total revenue equals total cost and profit is zero.

Also notice that if HD sells its product for $145, the price is equal to the total cost per unit. This is the **break-even price**—the price at which total revenue equals total cost and profit is zero.

Suppose HD does not want to merely break even but rather wants to earn a 25% markup on sales. HD's markup price is:[i]

$$\text{Markup price} = \frac{\text{unit cost}}{(1 - \text{desired return on sales})} = \frac{\$145}{1 - .25} = \$193.33$$

This is the price at which HD would sell the product to resellers such as wholesalers or retailers to earn a 25% profit on sales.

Return on investment (ROI) pricing (or target-return pricing)
A cost-based pricing method that determines price based on a specified rate of return on investment.

Another approach HD could use is called **return on investment (ROI) pricing (or target-return pricing)**. In this case, the company *would* consider the initial $10 million investment, but only to determine the dollar profit goal. Suppose the company wants a 30% return on its investment. The price necessary to satisfy this requirement can be determined by:

$$\text{ROI price} = \text{unit cost} + \frac{\text{ROI} \times \text{investment}}{\text{unit sales}} = \$145 + \frac{0.3 \times \$10{,}000{,}000}{1{,}000{,}000} = \$148$$

That is, if HD sells its product for $148, it will realize a 30% return on its initial investment of $10 million.

In these pricing calculations, unit cost is a function of the expected sales, which were estimated to be 1 million units. But what if actual sales were lower? Then the unit cost would be higher because the fixed costs would be spread over fewer units, and the realized percentage markup on sales or ROI would be lower. Alternatively, if sales are higher than the estimated 1 million units, unit cost would be lower than $145, so a lower price would produce the desired markup on sales or ROI. It's important to note that these cost-based pricing methods are *internally* focused and do not consider demand, competitors' prices, or reseller requirements. Because HD will be selling this product to consumers through wholesalers and retailers offering competing brands, the company must consider markup pricing from this perspective.

Setting Price Based on External Factors

Whereas costs determine the price floor, HD also must consider external factors when setting price. HD does not have the final say concerning the final price of its product to consumers—retailers do. So it must start with its suggested retail price and work back. In doing so, HD must consider the markups required by resellers that sell the product to consumers.

Markup
The difference between a company's selling price for a product and its cost to manufacture or purchase it.

In general, a dollar **markup** is the difference between a company's selling price for a product and its cost to manufacture or purchase it. For a retailer, then, the markup is the difference between the price it charges consumers and the cost the retailer must pay for the product. Thus, for any level of reseller:

$$\text{Dollar markup} = \text{selling price} - \text{cost}$$

Markups are usually expressed as a percentage, and there are two different ways to compute markups—on *cost* or on *selling price*:

$$\text{Markup percentage on cost} = \frac{\text{dollar markup}}{\text{cost}}$$

$$\text{Markup percentage on selling price} = \frac{\text{dollar markup}}{\text{selling price}}$$

To apply reseller margin analysis, HD must first set the suggested retail price and then work back to the price at which it must sell the product to a wholesaler. Suppose retailers expect a 30% margin and wholesalers want a 20% margin based on their respective selling prices. And suppose that HD sets a manufacturer's suggested retail price (MSRP) of $299.99 for its product.

HD selected the $299.99 MSRP because it is lower than most competitors' prices but is not so low that consumers might perceive it to be of poor quality. And the company's research shows that it is below the threshold at which more consumers are willing to purchase the product. By using buyers' perceptions of value and not the seller's cost to determine the MSRP, HD is using **value-based pricing**. For simplicity, we will use an MSRP of $300 in further analyses.

Value-based pricing
Offering just the right combination of quality and good service at a fair price.

Markup chain
The sequence of markups used by firms at each level in a channel.

To determine the price HD will charge wholesalers, we must first subtract the retailer's margin from the retail price to determine the retailer's cost ($300 – ($300 × 0.30) = $210). The retailer's cost is the wholesaler's price, so HD next subtracts the wholesaler's margin ($210 – ($210 × 0.20) = $168). Thus, the **markup chain** representing the sequence of markups used by firms at each level in a channel for HD's new product is:

Suggested retail price:	$300
minus retail margin (30%):	–$ 90
Retailer's cost/wholesaler's price:	$210
minus wholesaler's margin (20%):	–$ 42
Wholesaler's cost/HD's price:	$168

By deducting the markups for each level in the markup chain, HD arrives at a price for the product to wholesalers of $168.

Break-Even and Margin Analysis

The previous analyses derived a value-based price of $168 for HD's product. Although this price is higher than the break-even price of $145 and covers costs, that price assumed a demand of 1 million units. But how many units and what level of dollar sales must HD achieve to break even at the $168 price? And what level of sales must be achieved to realize various profit goals? These questions can be answered through break-even and margin analysis.

Determining Break-Even Unit Volume and Dollar Sales

Based on an understanding of costs, consumer value, the competitive environment, and reseller requirements, HD has decided to set its price to wholesalers at $168. At that price, what sales level will be needed for HD to break even or make a profit on its product? **Break-even analysis** determines the unit volume and dollar sales needed to be profitable given a particular price and cost structure. At the break-even point, total revenue equals total costs and profit is zero. Above this point, the company will make a profit; below it, the company will lose money. HD can calculate break-even volume using the following formula:

Break-even analysis
Analysis to determine the unit volume and dollar sales needed to be profitable given a particular price and cost structure.

$$\text{Break-even volume} = \frac{\text{fixed costs}}{\text{price} - \text{unit variable cost}}$$

Unit contribution
The amount that each unit contributes to covering fixed costs—the difference between price and variable costs.

The denominator (price – unit variable cost) is called **unit contribution** (sometimes called contribution margin). It represents the amount that each unit contributes to covering fixed costs. Break-even volume represents the level of output at which all (variable and fixed) costs are covered. In HD's case, break-even unit volume is:

$$\text{Break-even volume} = \frac{\text{fixed cost}}{\text{price} - \text{variable cost}} = \frac{\$20{,}000{,}000}{\$168 - \$125} = 465{,}116.2 \text{ units}$$

Thus, at the given cost and pricing structure, HD will break even at 465,117 units.

To determine the break-even dollar sales, simply multiply unit break-even volume by the selling price:

$$\text{BE sales} = \text{BE}_{\text{vol}} \times \text{price} = 465{,}117 \times \$168 = \$78{,}139{,}656$$

Another way to calculate dollar break-even sales is to use the percentage contribution margin (hereafter referred to as **contribution margin**), which is the unit contribution divided by the selling price:

Contribution margin
The unit contribution divided by the selling price.

$$\text{Contribution margin} = \frac{\text{price} - \text{variable cost}}{\text{price}} = \frac{\$168 - \$125}{\$168} = 0.256 \text{ or } 25.6\%$$

Then,

$$\text{Break-even sales} = \frac{\text{fixed costs}}{\text{contribution margin}} = \frac{\$20{,}000{,}000}{0.256} = \$78{,}125{,}000$$

Note that the difference between the two break-even sales calculations is due to rounding.

Such break-even analysis helps HD by showing the unit volume needed to cover costs. If production capacity cannot attain this level of output, then the company should not launch this product. However, the unit break-even volume is well within HD's capacity. Of course, the bigger question concerns whether HD can sell this volume at the $168 price. We'll address that issue a little later.

Understanding contribution margin is useful in other types of analyses as well, particularly if unit prices and unit variable costs are unknown or if a company (say, a retailer) sells many products at different prices and knows the percentage of total sales variable costs represent. Whereas unit contribution is the difference between unit price and unit variable costs, total contribution is the difference between total sales and total variable costs. The overall contribution margin can be calculated by:

$$\text{Contribution margin} = \frac{\text{total sales} - \text{total variable costs}}{\text{total sales}}$$

Regardless of the actual level of sales, if the company knows what percentage of sales is represented by variable costs, it can calculate contribution margin. For example, HD's unit variable cost is \$125, or 74% of the selling price (\$125 ÷ \$168 = 0.74). That means for every \$1 of sales revenue for HD, \$0.74 represents variable costs, and the difference (\$0.26) represents contribution to fixed costs. But even if the company doesn't know its unit price and unit variable cost, it can calculate the contribution margin from total sales and total variable costs or from knowledge of the total cost structure. It can set total sales equal to 100% regardless of the actual absolute amount and determine the contribution margin:

$$\text{Contribution margin} = \frac{100\% - 74\%}{100\%} = \frac{1 - 0.74}{1} = 1 - 0.74 = 0.26 \text{ or } 26\%$$

Note that this matches the percentage calculated from the unit price and unit variable cost information. This alternative calculation will be very useful later when analyzing various marketing decisions.

Determining "Break-even" for Profit Goals

Although it is useful to know the break-even point, most companies are more interested in making a profit. Assume HD would like to realize a \$5 million profit in the first year. How many must it sell at the \$168 price to cover fixed costs and produce this profit? To determine this, HD can simply add the profit figure to fixed costs and again divide by the unit contribution to determine unit sales:

$$\text{Unit volume} = \frac{\text{fixed cost} + \text{profit goal}}{\text{price} - \text{variable cost}} = \frac{\$20{,}000{,}000 + \$5{,}000{,}000}{\$168 - \$125} = 581{,}395.3 \text{ units}$$

Thus, to earn a \$5 million profit, HD must sell 581,396 units. Multiply by price to determine dollar sales needed to achieve a \$5 million profit:

$$\text{Dollar sales} = 581{,}396 \text{ units} \times \$168 = \$97{,}674{,}528$$

Or use the contribution margin:

$$\text{Sales} = \frac{\text{fixed cost} + \text{profit goal}}{\text{contribution margin}} = \frac{\$20{,}000{,}000 + \$5{,}000{,}000}{0.256} = \$97{,}656{,}250$$

Again, note that the difference between the two break-even sales calculations is due to rounding.

As we saw previously, a profit goal can also be stated as a return on investment goal. For example, recall that HD wants a 30% return on its \$10 million investment. Thus, its absolute profit goal is \$3 million (\$10,000,000 × 0.30). This profit goal is treated the same way as in the previous example:[ii]

$$\text{Unit volume} = \frac{\text{fixed cost} + \text{profit goal}}{\text{price} - \text{variable cost}} = \frac{\$20{,}000{,}000 + \$3{,}000{,}000}{\$168 - \$125} = 534{,}884 \text{ units}$$

$$\text{Dollar sales} = 534{,}884 \text{ units} \times \$168 = \$89{,}860{,}512$$

Or

$$\text{Dollar sales} = \frac{\text{fixed cost} + \text{profit goal}}{\text{contribution margin}} = \frac{\$20{,}000{,}000 + \$3{,}000{,}000}{0.256} = \$89{,}843{,}750$$

Finally, HD can express its profit goal as a percentage of sales, which we also saw in previous pricing analyses. Assume HD desires a 25% return on sales. To determine the unit and sales volume necessary to achieve this goal, the calculation is a little different from the previous two examples. In this case, we incorporate the profit goal into the unit contribution as an additional variable cost. Look at it this way: If 25% of each sale must go toward profits, that leaves only 75% of the selling price to cover fixed costs. Thus, the equation becomes:

$$\text{Unit volume} = \frac{\text{fixed cost}}{\text{price} - \text{variable cost} - (0.25 \times \text{price})} \text{ or } \frac{\text{fixed cost}}{(0.75 \times \text{price}) - \text{variable cost}}$$

So,

$$\text{Unit volume} = \frac{\$20{,}000{,}000}{(0.75 \times \$168) - \$125} = 20{,}000{,}000 \text{ units}$$

$$\text{Dollar sales necessary} = 20{,}000{,}000 \text{ units} \times \$168 = \$3{,}360{,}000{,}000$$

Thus, HD would need more than $3 billion in sales to realize a 25% return on sales given its current price and cost structure! Could it possibly achieve this level of sales? The major point is this: Although break-even analysis can be useful in determining the level of sales needed to cover costs or to achieve a stated profit goal, it does not tell the company whether it is *possible* to achieve that level of sales at the specified price. To address this issue, HD needs to estimate demand for this product.

Before moving on, however, let's stop here and practice applying the concepts covered so far. Now that you have seen pricing and break-even concepts in action as they relate to HD's new product, here are several exercises for you to apply what you have learned in other contexts.

Marketing by the Numbers Exercise Set One

Now that you've studied pricing, break-even, and margin analysis as they relate to HD's new product launch, use the following exercises to apply these concepts in other contexts.

1.1 Elkins, a manufacturer of ice makers, realizes a cost of $250 for every unit it produces. Its total fixed costs equal $5 million. If the company manufactures 500,000 units, compute the following:

a. unit cost

b. markup price if the company desires a 10% return on sales

c. ROI price if the company desires a 25% return on an investment of $1 million

1.2 A gift shop owner purchases items to sell in her store. She purchases a chair for $125 and sells it for $275. Determine the following:

a. dollar markup

b. markup percentage on cost

c. markup percentage on selling price

1.3 A consumer purchases a coffee maker from a retailer for $90. The retailer's markup is 30%, and the wholesaler's markup is 10%, both based on selling price. For what price does the manufacturer sell the product to the wholesaler?

1.4 A lawn mower manufacturer has a unit cost of $140 and wishes to achieve a margin of 30% based on selling price. If the manufacturer sells directly to a retailer who then adds a set margin of 40% based on selling price, determine the retail price charged to consumers.

1.5 Advanced Electronics manufactures DVDs and sells them directly to retailers who typically sell them for $20. Retailers take a 40% margin based on the retail selling price. Advanced's cost information is as follows:

DVD package and disc	$2.50/DVD
Royalties	$2.25/DVD
Advertising and promotion	$500,000
Overhead	$200,000

Calculate the following:

a. contribution per unit and contribution margin
b. break-even volume in DVD units and dollars
c. volume in DVD units and dollar sales necessary if Advanced's profit goal is 20% profit on sales
d. net profit if 5 million DVDs are sold

Demand Estimates, the Marketing Budget, and Marketing Performance Measures

Market Potential and Sales Estimates

HD has now calculated the sales needed to break even and to attain various profit goals on its new product. However, the company needs more information regarding demand in order to assess the feasibility of attaining the needed sales levels. This information is also needed for production and other decisions. For example, production schedules need to be developed, and marketing tactics need to be planned.

Total market demand
The total volume that would be bought by a defined consumer group in a defined geographic area in a defined time period in a defined marketing environment under a defined level and mix of industry marketing effort.

The **total market demand** for a product or service is the total volume that would be bought by a defined consumer group in a defined geographic area in a defined time period in a defined marketing environment under a defined level and mix of industry marketing effort. Total market demand is not a fixed number but a function of the stated conditions. For example, next year's total market demand for this type of product will depend on how much other producers spend on marketing their brands. It also depends on many environmental factors, such as government regulations, economic conditions, and the level of consumer confidence in a given market. The upper limit of market demand is called **market potential**.

Market potential
The upper limit of market demand.

One general but practical method that HD might use for estimating total market demand uses three variables: (1) the number of prospective buyers, (2) the quantity purchased by an average buyer per year, and (3) the price of an average unit. Using these numbers, HD can estimate total market demand as follows:

$$Q = n \times q \times p$$

where

Q = total market demand
n = number of buyers in the market
q = quantity purchased by an average buyer per year
p = price of an average unit

Chain ratio method
Estimating market demand by multiplying a base number by a chain of adjusting percentages.

A variation of this approach is the **chain ratio method**. This method involves multiplying a base number by a chain of adjusting percentages. For example, HD's product is designed to stream high-definition video on high-definition televisions as well as play other video content streamed from the Internet to multiple devices in a home. Thus, consumers who do not own a high-definition television will not likely purchase this player. Additionally, only households with broadband Internet access will be able to use the product. Finally, not all HDTV-owning Internet households will be willing and able to purchase this product. HD can estimate U.S. demand using a chain of calculations like the following:

Total number of U.S. households
× The percentage of HDTV-owning U.S. households with broadband Internet access
× The percentage of these households willing and able to buy this device

The U.S. Census Bureau estimates that there are approximately 115 million households in the United States.[iii] HD's research indicates that 60 percent of U.S. households own at least one HDTV and have broadband Internet access. Finally, the company's research also reveals that 30 percent of households possess the discretionary income needed and are willing to buy a product such as this. Then the total number of households willing and able to purchase this product is:

$$115 \text{ million households} \times 0.60 \times 0.30 = 20.7 \text{ million households}$$

Households need to purchase only one device because it can stream content to other devices throughout the household. Assuming the average retail price across all brands is $350 for this product, the estimate of total market demand is as follows:

$$20.7 \text{ million households} \times 1 \text{ device per household} \times \$350 = \$7{,}245{,}000{,}000$$

This simple chain of calculations gives HD only a rough estimate of potential demand. However, more detailed chains involving additional segments and other qualifying factors would yield more accurate and refined estimates. Still, these are only *estimates* of market potential. They rely heavily on assumptions regarding adjusting percentages, average quantity, and average price. Thus, HD must make certain that its assumptions are reasonable and defendable. As can be seen, the overall market potential in dollar sales can vary widely given the average price used. For this reason, HD will use unit sales potential to determine its sales estimate for next year. Market potential in terms of units is 20.7 million (20.7 million households × 1 device per household).

Assuming that HD forecasts it will have a 3.6% market share in the first year after launching this product, then it can forecast unit sales at 20.7 million units × 0.036 = 745,200 units. At a selling price of $168 per unit, this translates into sales of $125,193,600 (745,200 units × $168 per unit). For simplicity, further analyses will use forecasted sales of $125 million.

This unit volume estimate is well within HD's production capacity and exceeds not only the break-even estimate (465,117 units) calculated earlier but also the volume necessary to realize a $5 million profit (581,396 units) or a 30% return on investment (534,884 units). However, this forecast falls well short of the volume necessary to realize a 25% return on sales (20 million units!) and may require that HD revise expectations.

To assess expected profits, we must now look at the budgeted expenses for launching this product. To do this, we will construct a pro forma profit-and-loss statement.

The Profit-and-Loss Statement and Marketing Budget

Pro forma (or projected) profit-and-loss statement (or income statement or operating statement)
A statement that shows projected revenues less budgeted expenses and estimates the projected net profit for an organization, product, or brand during a specific planning period, typically a year.

All marketing managers must account for the profit impact of their marketing strategies. A major tool for projecting such profit impact is a **pro forma** (or projected) **profit-and-loss statement** (also called an **income statement** or **operating statement**). A pro forma statement shows projected revenues less budgeted expenses and estimates the projected net profit for an organization, product, or brand during a specific planning period, typically a year. It includes direct product production costs, marketing expenses budgeted to attain a given sales forecast, and overhead expenses assigned to the organization or product. A profit-and-loss statement typically consists of several major components (see » **Table A3.1**):

- ***Net sales***—gross sales revenue minus returns and allowances (for example, trade, cash, quantity, and promotion allowances). HD's net sales for 2016 are estimated to be $125 million, as determined in the previous analysis.
- ***Cost of goods sold***—(sometimes called *cost of sales*)—the actual cost of the merchandise sold by a manufacturer or reseller. It includes the cost of inventory, purchases, and other costs associated with making the goods. HD's cost of goods sold is estimated to be 50% of net sales, or $62.5 million.
- ***Gross margin (or gross profit)***—the difference between net sales and cost of goods sold. HD's gross margin is estimated to be $62.5 million.
- ***Operating expenses***—the expenses incurred while doing business. These include all other expenses beyond the cost of goods sold that are necessary to conduct

» Table A3.1 Pro Forma Profit-and-Loss Statement for the 12-Month Period Ended December 31, 2016

			Percent of Sales
Net Sales		$125,000,000	100%
Cost of Goods Sold		62,500,000	50%
Gross Margin		$ 62,500,000	50%
Marketing Expenses			
Sales expenses	$17,500,000		
Promotion expenses	15,000,000		
Freight	12,500,000	45,000,000	36%
General and Administrative Expenses			
Managerial salaries and expenses	$2,000,000		
Indirect overhead	3,000,000	5,000,000	4%
Net Profit before Income Tax		$12,500,000	10%

business. Operating expenses can be presented in total or broken down in detail. Here, HD's estimated operating expenses include *marketing expenses* and *general and administrative expenses.*

Marketing expenses include sales expenses, promotion expenses, and distribution expenses. The new product will be sold through HD's sales force, so the company budgets $5 million for sales salaries. However, because sales representatives earn a 10% commission on sales, HD must also add a variable component to sales expenses of $12.5 million (10% of $125 million net sales), for a total budgeted sales expense of $17.5 million. HD sets its advertising and promotion to launch this product at $10 million. However, the company also budgets 4% of sales, or $5 million, for cooperative advertising allowances to retailers who promote HD's new product in their advertising. Thus, the total budgeted advertising and promotion expenses are $15 million ($10 million for advertising plus $5 million in co-op allowances). Finally, HD budgets 10% of net sales, or $12.5 million, for freight and delivery charges. In all, total marketing expenses are estimated to be $17.5 million + $15 million + $12.5 million = $45 million.

General and administrative expenses are estimated at $5 million, broken down into $2 million for managerial salaries and expenses for the marketing function and $3 million of indirect overhead allocated to this product by the corporate accountants (such as depreciation, interest, maintenance, and insurance). Total expenses for the year, then, are estimated to be $50 million ($45 million marketing expenses + $5 million in general and administrative expenses).

- ***Net profit before taxes***—profit earned after all costs are deducted. HD's estimated net profit before taxes is $12.5 million.

In all, as Table A3.1 shows, HD expects to earn a profit on its new product of $12.5 million in 2016. Also note that the percentage of sales that each component of the profit-and-loss statement represents is given in the right-hand column. These percentages are determined by dividing the cost figure by net sales (that is, marketing expenses represent 36% of net sales determined by $45 million ÷ $125 million). As can be seen, HD projects a net profit return on sales of 10% in the first year after launching this product.

Marketing Performance Measures

Profit-and-loss statement (or income statement or operating statement)
A statement that shows actual revenues less expenses and net profit for an organization, product, or brand during a specific planning period, typically a year.

Now let's fast-forward a year. HD's product has been on the market for one year, and management wants to assess its sales and profit performance. One way to assess this performance is to compute performance ratios derived from HD's **profit-and-loss statement** (or **income statement** or **operating statement**).

Whereas the pro forma profit-and-loss statement shows *projected* financial performance, the statement given in **»Table A3.2** shows HD's *actual* financial performance based on actual sales, cost of goods sold, and expenses during the past year. By comparing the profit-and-loss statement from one period to the next, HD can gauge performance against goals, spot favorable or unfavorable trends, and take appropriate corrective action.

The profit-and-loss statement shows that HD lost $1 million rather than making the $12.5 million profit projected in the pro forma statement. Why? One obvious reason is that net sales fell $25 million short of estimated sales. Lower sales translated into lower variable costs associated with marketing the product. However, both fixed costs and the cost of goods sold as a percentage of sales exceeded expectations. Hence, the product's contribution margin was 21% rather than the estimated 26%. That is, variable costs represented 79% of sales (55% for cost of goods sold, 10% for sales commissions, 10% for freight, and 4% for co-op allowances). Recall that contribution margin can be calculated by subtracting that fraction from one ($1 - 0.79 = 0.21$). Total fixed costs were $22 million, $2 million more than estimated. Thus, the sales that HD needed to break even given this cost structure can be calculated as:

$$\text{Break-even sales} = \frac{\text{fixed costs}}{\text{contribution margin}} = \frac{\$22{,}000{,}000}{0.21} = \$104{,}761{,}905$$

If HD had achieved another $5 million in sales, it would have earned a profit.

Market share
Company sales divided by market sales.

Although HD's sales fell short of the forecasted sales, so did overall industry sales for this product. Overall industry sales were only $2.5 billion. That means that HD's **market share** was 4% ($100 million ÷ $2.5 billion = 0.04 = 4%), which was higher than forecasted. Thus, HD attained a higher-than-expected market share, but the overall market sales were not as high as estimated.

» Table A3.2 Profit-and-Loss Statement for the 12-Month Period Ended December 31, 2016

			Percent of Sales
Net Sales		**$100,000,000**	**100%**
Cost of Goods Sold		**55,000,000**	**55%**
Gross Margin		**$ 45,000,000**	**45%**
Marketing Expenses			
Sales expenses	**$15,000,000**		
Promotion expenses	**14,000,000**		
Freight	**10,000,000**	**39,000,000**	**39%**
General and Administrative Expenses			
Managerial salaries and expenses	**$2,000,000**		
Indirect overhead	**5,000,000**	**7,000,000**	**7%**
Net Profit before Income Tax		**–$1,000,000**	**–1%**

Analytic Ratios

Operating ratios
The ratios of selected operating statement items to net sales.

The profit-and-loss statement provides the figures needed to compute some crucial **operating ratios**—the ratios of selected operating statement items to net sales. These ratios let marketers compare the firm's performance in one year to that in previous years (or with industry standards and competitors' performance in that year). The most commonly used operating ratios are the gross margin percentage, the net profit percentage, and the operating expense percentage. The inventory turnover rate and return on investment (ROI) are often used to measure managerial effectiveness and efficiency.

Gross margin percentage
The percentage of net sales remaining after cost of goods sold—calculated by dividing gross margin by net sales.

The **gross margin percentage** indicates the percentage of net sales remaining after cost of goods sold that can contribute to operating expenses and net profit before taxes. The higher this ratio, the more a firm has left to cover expenses and generate profit. HD's gross margin ratio was 45%:

$$\text{Gross margin percentage} = \frac{\text{gross margin}}{\text{net sales}} = \frac{\$45{,}000{,}000}{\$100{,}000{,}000} = 0.45 = 45\%$$

Note that this percentage is lower than estimated, and this ratio is seen easily in the percentage of sales column in Table A3.2. Stating items in the profit-and-loss statement as a percent of sales allows managers to quickly spot abnormal changes in costs over time. If there was previous history for this product and this ratio was declining, management should examine it more closely to determine why it has decreased (that is, because of a decrease in sales volume or price, an increase in costs, or a combination of these). In HD's case, net sales were $25 million lower than estimated, and cost of goods sold was higher than estimated (55% rather than the estimated 50%).

Net profit percentage
The percentage of each sales dollar going to profit—calculated by dividing net profits by net sales.

The **net profit percentage** shows the percentage of each sales dollar going to profit. It is calculated by dividing net profits by net sales:

$$\text{Net profit percentage} = \frac{\text{net profit}}{\text{net sales}} = \frac{-\$1{,}000{,}000}{\$100{,}000{,}000} = -0.01 = -1.0\%$$

This ratio is easily seen in the percent of sales column. HD's new product generated negative profits in the first year, not a good situation given that before the product launch net profits before taxes were estimated at more than $12 million. Later in this appendix, we will discuss further analyses the marketing manager should conduct to defend the product.

Operating expense percentage
The portion of net sales going to operating expenses—calculated by dividing total expenses by net sales.

The **operating expense percentage** indicates the portion of net sales going to operating expenses. Operating expenses include marketing and other expenses not directly related to marketing the product, such as indirect overhead assigned to this product. It is calculated by:

$$\text{Operating expense percentage} = \frac{\text{total expenses}}{\text{net sales}} = \frac{\$46{,}000{,}000}{\$100{,}000{,}000} = 0.46 = 46\%$$

This ratio can also be quickly determined from the percent of sales column in the profit-and-loss statement by adding the percentages for marketing expenses and general and administrative expenses (39% + 7%). Thus, 46 cents of every sales dollar went for operations. Although HD wants this ratio to be as low as possible, and 46% is not an alarming amount, it is of concern if it is increasing over time or if a loss is realized.

Inventory turnover rate (or stockturn rate)
The number of times an inventory turns over or is sold during a specified time period (often one year)—calculated based on costs, selling price, or units.

Another useful ratio is the **inventory turnover rate** (also called **stockturn rate** for resellers). The inventory turnover rate is the number of times an inventory turns over or is sold during a specified time period (often one year). This rate tells how quickly a business is moving inventory through the organization. Higher rates indicate that lower investments in inventory are made, thus freeing up funds for other investments. It may be computed on a cost, selling price, or unit basis. The formula based on cost is:

$$\text{Inventory turnover rate} = \frac{\text{cost of goods sold}}{\text{average inventory at cost}}$$

Assuming HD's beginning and ending inventories were \$30 million and \$20 million, respectively, the inventory turnover rate is:

$$\text{Inventory turnover rate} = \frac{\$55{,}000{,}000}{(\$30{,}000{,}000 + \$20{,}000{,}000)/2} = \frac{\$55{,}000{,}000}{\$25{,}000{,}000} = 2.2$$

That is, HD's inventory turned over 2.2 times in 2016. Normally, the higher the turnover rate, the higher the management efficiency and company profitability. However, this rate should be compared with industry averages, competitors' rates, and past performance to determine if HD is doing well. A competitor with similar sales but a higher inventory turnover rate will have fewer resources tied up in inventory, allowing it to invest in other areas of the business.

Return on investment (ROI)
A measure of managerial effectiveness and efficiency—net profit before taxes divided by total investment.

Companies frequently use **return on investment (ROI)** to measure managerial effectiveness and efficiency. For HD, ROI is the ratio of net profits to total investment required to manufacture the new product. This investment includes capital investments in land, buildings, and equipment (here, the initial \$10 million to refurbish the manufacturing facility) plus inventory costs (HD's average inventory totaled \$25 million), for a total of \$35 million. Thus, HD's ROI for this product is:

$$\text{Return on investment} = \frac{\text{net profit before taxes}}{\text{investment}} = \frac{-\$1{,}000{,}000}{\$35{,}000{,}000} = -.0286 = -2.86\%$$

ROI is often used to compare alternatives, and a positive ROI is desired. The alternative with the highest ROI is preferred to other alternatives. HD needs to be concerned with the ROI realized. One obvious way HD can increase ROI is to increase net profit by reducing expenses. Another way is to reduce its investment, perhaps by investing less in inventory and turning it over more frequently.

Marketing Profitability Metrics

Given the above financial results, you may be thinking that HD should drop this new product. But what arguments can marketers make for keeping or dropping this product? The obvious arguments for dropping the product are that first-year sales were well below expected levels and the product lost money, resulting in a negative return on investment.

So what would happen if HD did drop this product? Surprisingly, if the company drops the product, the profits for the total organization will decrease by \$4 million! How can that be? Marketing managers need to look closely at the numbers in the profit-and-loss statement to determine the *net marketing contribution* for this product. In HD's case, the net marketing contribution for the product is \$4 million, and if the company drops this product, that contribution will disappear as well. Let's look more closely at this concept to illustrate how marketing managers can better assess and defend their marketing strategies and programs.

Net Marketing Contribution

Net marketing contribution (NMC)
A measure of marketing profitability that includes only components of profitability controlled by marketing.

Net marketing contribution (NMC), along with other marketing metrics derived from it, measures *marketing* profitability. It includes only components of profitability that are controlled by marketing. Whereas the previous calculation of net profit before taxes from the profit-and-loss statement includes operating expenses not under marketing's control, NMC does not. Referring back to HD's profit-and-loss statement given in Table A3.2, we can calculate net marketing contribution for the product as:

$$\begin{aligned} \text{NMC} &= \text{net sales} - \text{cost of goods sold} - \text{marketing expenses} \\ &= \$100 \text{ million} - \$55 \text{ million} - \$41 \text{ million} = \$4 \text{ million} \end{aligned}$$

The marketing expenses include sales expenses (\$15 million), promotion expenses (\$14 million), freight expenses (\$10 million), and the managerial salaries and expenses of the marketing function (\$2 million), which total \$41 million.

Thus, the product actually contributed $4 million to HD's profits. It was the $5 million of indirect overhead allocated to this product that caused the negative profit. Further, the amount allocated was $2 million more than estimated in the pro forma profit-and-loss statement. Indeed, if only the estimated amount had been allocated, the product would have earned a *profit* of $1 million rather than losing $1 million. If HD drops the product, the $5 million in fixed overhead expense will not disappear—it will simply have to be allocated elsewhere. However, the $4 million in net marketing contribution *will* disappear.

Marketing Return on Sales and Investment

To get an even deeper understanding of the profit impact of marketing strategy, we'll now examine two measures of marketing efficiency—*marketing return on sales* (marketing ROS) and *marketing return on investment* (marketing ROI).[iv]

Marketing return on sales (or marketing ROS)
The percent of net sales attributable to the net marketing contribution—calculated by dividing net marketing contribution by net sales.

Marketing return on sales (or **marketing ROS**) shows the percent of net sales attributable to the net marketing contribution. For our product, ROS is:

$$\text{Marketing ROS} = \frac{\text{net marketing contribution}}{\text{net sales}} = \frac{\$4{,}000{,}000}{\$100{,}000{,}000} = 0.04 = 4\%$$

Thus, out of every $100 of sales, the product returns $4 to HD's bottom line. A high marketing ROS is desirable. But to assess whether this is a good level of performance, HD must compare this figure to previous marketing ROS levels for the product, the ROSs of other products in the company's portfolio, and the ROSs of competing products.

Marketing return on investment (or marketing ROI)
A measure of the marketing productivity of a marketing investment—calculated by dividing net marketing contribution by marketing expenses.

Marketing return on investment (or **marketing ROI**) measures the marketing productivity of a marketing investment. In HD's case, the marketing investment is represented by $41 million of the total expenses. Thus, marketing ROI is:

$$\text{Marketing ROI} = \frac{\text{net marketing contribution}}{\text{marketing expenses}} = \frac{\$4{,}000{,}000}{\$41{,}000{,}000} = 0.0976 = 9.76\%$$

As with marketing ROS, a high value is desirable, but this figure should be compared with previous levels for the given product and with the marketing ROIs of competitors' products. Note from this equation that marketing ROI could be greater than 100%. This can be achieved by attaining a higher net marketing contribution and/or a lower total marketing expense.

In this section, we estimated market potential and sales, developed profit-and-loss statements, and examined financial measures of performance. In the next section, we discuss methods for analyzing the impact of various marketing tactics. However, before moving on to those analyses, here's another set of quantitative exercises to help you apply what you've learned to other situations.

Marketing by the Numbers Exercise Set Two

2.1 Determine the market potential for a product that has 20 million prospective buyers who purchase an average of two per year and price averages $50. How many units must a company sell if it desires a 10% share of this market?

2.2 Develop a profit-and-loss statement for the Westgate division of North Industries. This division manufactures light fixtures sold to consumers through home-improvement and hardware stores. Cost of goods sold represents 40% of net sales. Marketing expenses include selling expenses, promotion expenses, and freight. Selling expenses include sales salaries totaling $3 million per year and sales commissions (5% of sales). The company spent $3 million on advertising last year, and freight costs were 10% of sales. Other costs include $2 million for managerial salaries and expenses for the marketing function and another $3 million for indirect overhead allocated to the division.

a. Develop the profit-and-loss statement if net sales were $20 million last year.
b. Develop the profit-and-loss statement if net sales were $40 million last year.
c. Calculate Westgate's break-even sales.

2.3 Using the profit-and-loss statement you developed in question 2.2b and assuming that Westgate's beginning inventory was \$11 million, ending inventory was \$7 million, and total investment was \$20 million including inventory, determine the following:

a. gross margin percentage
b. net profit percentage
c. operating expense percentage
d. inventory turnover rate
e. return on investment (ROI)
f. net marketing contribution
g. marketing return on sales (marketing ROS)
h. marketing return on investment (marketing ROI)
i. Is the Westgate division doing well? Explain your answer.

Financial Analysis of Marketing Tactics

Although the first-year profit performance for HD's new product was less than desired, management feels that this attractive market has excellent growth opportunities. Although the sales of HD's product were lower than initially projected, they were not unreasonable given the size of the current market. Thus, HD wants to explore new marketing tactics to help grow the market for this product and increase sales for the company.

For example, the company could increase advertising to promote more awareness of the new product and its category. It could add salespeople to secure greater product distribution. HD could decrease prices so that more consumers could afford its product. Finally, to expand the market, HD could introduce a lower-priced model in addition to the higher-priced original offering. Before pursuing any of these tactics, HD must analyze the financial implications of each.

Increase Advertising Expenditures

HD is considering boosting its advertising to make more people aware of the benefits of this device in general and of its own brand in particular. What if HD's marketers recommend increasing national advertising by 50% to \$15 million (assume no change in the variable cooperative component of promotional expenditures)? This represents an increase in fixed costs of \$5 million. What increase in sales will be needed to break even on this \$5 million increase in fixed costs?

A quick way to answer this question is to divide the increase in fixed cost by the contribution margin, which we found in a previous analysis to be 21%:

$$\text{Increase in sales} = \frac{\text{increase in fixed cost}}{\text{contribution margin}} = \frac{\$5{,}000{,}000}{0.21} = \$23{,}809{,}524$$

Thus, a 50% increase in advertising expenditures must produce a sales increase of almost \$24 million to just break even. That \$24 million sales increase translates into an almost 1 percentage point increase in market share (1% of the \$2.5 billion overall market equals \$25 million). That is, to break even on the increased advertising expenditure, HD would have to increase its market share from 4% to 4.95% (\$123,809,524 ÷ \$2.5 billion = 0.0495, or 4.95% market share). All of this assumes that the total market will not grow, which might or might not be a reasonable assumption.

Increase Distribution Coverage

HD also wants to consider hiring more salespeople in order to call on new retailer accounts and increase distribution through more outlets. Even though HD sells directly to wholesalers, its sales representatives call on retail accounts to perform other functions in addition to selling, such as training retail salespeople. Currently, HD employs 60 sales reps who earn an average of \$50,000 in salary plus 10% commission on sales. The product is currently sold to consumers through 1,875 retail outlets. Suppose HD wants to increase that number of outlets to 2,500, an increase of 625 retail outlets. How many additional salespeople will HD need, and what sales will be necessary to break even on the increased cost?

Workload method
An approach to determining sales force size based on the workload required and the time available for selling.

One method for determining what size sales force HD will need is the **workload method**. The workload method uses the following formula to determine the salesforce size:

$$NS = \frac{NC \times FC \times LC}{TA}$$

where

NS = number of salespeople
NC = number of customers
FC = average frequency of customer calls per customer
LC = average length of customer call
TA = time an average salesperson has available for selling per year

HD's sales reps typically call on accounts an average of 20 times per year for about two hours per call. Although sales reps work 2,000 hours per year (50 weeks per year × 40 hours per week), they spent about 15 hours per week on nonselling activities such as administrative duties and travel. Thus, the average annual available selling time per sales rep per year is 1,250 hours (50 weeks × 25 hours per week). We can now calculate how many sales reps HD will need to cover the anticipated 2,500 retail outlets:

$$NS = \frac{2{,}500 \times 20 \times 2}{1{,}250} = 80 \text{ salespeople}$$

Therefore, HD will need to hire 20 more salespeople. The cost to hire these reps will be \$1 million (20 salespeople × \$50,000 salary per salesperson).

What increase in sales will be required to break even on this increase in fixed costs? The 10% commission is already accounted for in the contribution margin, so the contribution margin remains unchanged at 21%. Thus, the increase in sales needed to cover this increase in fixed costs can be calculated by:

$$\text{Increase in sales} = \frac{\text{increase in fixed cost}}{\text{contribution margin}} = \frac{\$1{,}000{,}000}{0.21} = \$4{,}761{,}905$$

That is, HD's sales must increase almost \$5 million to break even on this tactic. So, how many new retail outlets will the company need to secure to achieve this sales increase? The average revenue generated per current outlet is \$53,333 (\$100 million in sales divided by 1,875 outlets). To achieve the nearly \$5 million sales increase needed to break even, HD would need about 90 new outlets (\$4,761,905 ÷ \$53,333 = 89.3 outlets), or about 4.5 outlets per new rep. Given that current reps cover about 31 outlets apiece (1,875 outlets ÷ 60 reps), this seems very reasonable.

Decrease Price

HD is also considering lowering its price to increase sales revenue through increased volume. The company's research has shown that demand for most types of consumer electronics products is elastic—that is, the percentage increase in the quantity demanded is greater than the percentage decrease in price.

What increase in sales would be necessary to break even on a 10% decrease in price? That is, what increase in sales will be needed to maintain the total contribution that HD realized at the higher price? The current total contribution can be determined by multiplying the contribution margin by total sales:[v]

$$\text{Current total contribution} = \text{contribution margin} \times \text{sales} = .21 \times \$100 \text{ million} = \$21 \text{ million}$$

Price changes result in changes in unit contribution and contribution margin. Recall that the contribution margin of 21% was based on variable costs representing 79% of sales.

Therefore, unit variable costs can be determined by multiplying the original price by this percentage: $168 × 0.79 = $132.72 per unit. If price is decreased by 10%, the new price is $151.20. However, variable costs do not change just because price decreased, so the contribution and contribution margin decrease as follows:

	Old	New (Reduced 10%)
Price	$168	$151.20
– Unit variable cost	$132.72	$132.72
= Unit contribution	$35.28	$18.48
Contribution margin	$35.28/$168 = 0.21 or 21%	$18.48/$151.20 = 0.12 or 12%

So a 10% reduction in price results in a decrease in the contribution margin from 21% to 12%.[vi] To determine the sales level needed to break even on this price reduction, we calculate the level of sales that must be attained at the new contribution margin to achieve the original total contribution of $21 million:

$$\text{New contribution margin} \times \text{new sales level} = \text{original total contribution}$$

So,

$$\text{New sales level} = \frac{\text{original contribution}}{\text{new contribution margin}} = \frac{\$21{,}000{,}000}{0.12} = \$175{,}000{,}000$$

Thus, sales must increase by $75 million ($175 million – $100 million) just to break even on a 10% price reduction. This means that HD must increase market share to 7% ($175 million ÷ $2.5 billion) to achieve the current level of profits (assuming no increase in the total market sales). The marketing manager must assess whether or not this is a reasonable goal.

Extend the Product Line

Cannibalization
The situation in which one product sold by a company takes a portion of its sales from other company products.

As a final option, HD is considering extending its product line by offering a lower-priced model. Of course, the new, lower-priced product would steal some sales from the higher-priced model. This is called **cannibalization**—the situation in which one product sold by a company takes a portion of its sales from other company products. If the new product has a lower contribution than the original product, the company's total contribution will decrease on the cannibalized sales. However, if the new product can generate enough new volume, it is worth considering.

To assess cannibalization, HD must look at the incremental contribution gained by having both products available. Recall that in the previous analysis we determined that unit variable costs were $132.72 and unit contribution was just over $35. Assuming costs remain the same next year, HD can expect to realize a contribution per unit of approximately $35 for every unit of the original product sold.

Assume that the first model offered by HD is called HD1 and the new, lower-priced model is called HD2. HD2 will retail for $250, and resellers will take the same markup percentages on price as they do with the higher-priced model. Therefore, HD2's price to wholesalers will be $140 as follows:

Retail price:	$250
minus retail margin (30%):	–$ 75
Retailer's cost/wholesaler's price:	$175
minus wholesaler's margin (20%):	–$ 35
Wholesaler's cost/HD's price	$140

If HD2's variable costs are estimated to be $120, then its contribution per unit will equal $20 ($140 – $120 = $20). That means for every unit that HD2 cannibalizes from HD1, HD will *lose* $15 in contribution toward fixed costs and profit (that is, $\text{contribution}_{HD2}$

− $\text{contribution}_{HD1}$ = \$20 − \$35 = −\$15). You might conclude that HD should not pursue this tactic because it appears as though the company will be worse off if it introduces the lower-priced model. However, if HD2 captures enough *additional* sales, HD will be better off even though some HD1 sales are cannibalized. The company must examine what will happen to *total* contribution, which requires estimates of unit volume for both products.

Originally, HD estimated that next year's sales of HD1 would be 600,000 units. However, with the introduction of HD2, it now estimates that 200,000 of those sales will be cannibalized by the new model. If HD sells only 200,000 units of the new HD2 model (all cannibalized from HD1), the company would lose \$3 million in total contribution (200,000 units × −\$15 per cannibalized unit = −\$3 million)—not a good outcome. However, HD estimates that HD2 will generate the 200,000 of cannibalized sales plus an *additional* 500,000 unit sales. Thus, the contribution on these additional HD2 units will be \$10 million (i.e., 500,000 units × \$20 per unit = \$10 million). The net effect is that HD will gain \$7 million in total contribution by introducing HD2.

The following table compares HD's total contribution with and without the introduction of HD2:

	HD1 only	HD1 and HD2
HD1 contribution	600,000 units × \$35 = \$21,000,000	400,000 units × \$35 = \$14,000,000
HD2 contribution	0	700,000 units × \$20 = \$14,000,000
Total contribution	\$21,000,000	\$28,000,000

The difference in the total contribution is a net gain of \$7 million (\$28 million − \$21 million). Based on this analysis, HD should introduce the HD2 model because it results in a positive incremental contribution. However, if fixed costs will increase by more than \$7 million as a result of adding this model, then the net effect will be negative and HD should not pursue this tactic.

Now that you have seen these marketing tactic analysis concepts in action as they relate to HD's new product, here are several exercises for you to apply what you have learned in this section in other contexts.

Marketing by the Numbers Exercise Set Three

3.1 Alliance, Inc. sells gas lamps to consumers through retail outlets. Total industry sales for Alliance's relevant market last year were \$100 million, with Alliance's sales representing 5% of that total. Contribution margin is 25%. Alliance's sales force calls on retail outlets and each sales rep earns \$50,000 per year plus 1% commission on all sales. Retailers receive a 40% margin on selling price and generate average revenue of \$10,000 per outlet for Alliance.

a. The marketing manager has suggested increasing consumer advertising by \$200,000. By how much would dollar sales need to increase to break even on this expenditure? What increase in overall market share does this represent?

b. Another suggestion is to hire two more sales representatives to gain new consumer retail accounts. How many new retail outlets would be necessary to break even on the increased cost of adding two sales reps?

c. A final suggestion is to make a 10% across-the-board price reduction. By how much would dollar sales need to increase to maintain Alliance's current contribution? (See endnote 6 to calculate the new contribution margin.)

d. Which suggestion do you think Alliance should implement? Explain your recommendation.

3.2 PepsiCo sells its soft drinks in approximately 400,000 retail establishments, such as supermarkets, discount stores, and convenience stores. Sales representatives call on each retail account weekly, which means each account is called on by a sales rep 52 times per year. The average length of a sales call is 75 minutes (or 1.25 hours).

An average salesperson works 2,000 hours per year (50 weeks per year × 40 hours per week), but each spends 10 hours a week on nonselling activities, such as administrative tasks and travel. How many salespeople does PepsiCo need?

3.3 Hair Zone manufactures a brand of hairstyling gel. It is considering adding a modified version of the product—a foam that provides stronger hold. Hair Zone's variable costs and prices to wholesalers are:

	Current Hair Gel	New Foam Product
Unit selling price	2.00	2.25
Unit variable costs	.85	1.25

Hair Zone expects to sell 1 million units of the new styling foam in the first year after introduction, but it expects that 60% of those sales will come from buyers who normally purchase Hair Zone's styling gel. Hair Zone estimates that it would sell 1.5 million units of the gel if it did not introduce the foam. If the fixed cost of launching the new foam will be $100,000 during the first year, should Hair Zone add the new product to its line? Why or why not?

Appendix 4 Careers in Marketing

You may have decided you want to pursue a marketing career because it offers constant challenge, stimulating problems, the opportunity to work with people, and excellent advancement opportunities. But you still may not know which part of marketing best suits you—marketing is a very broad field offering a wide variety of career options.

This appendix helps you discover what types of marketing jobs best match your special skills and interests, shows you how to conduct the kind of job search that will get you the position you want, describes marketing career paths open to you, and suggests other information resources.

Marketing Careers Today

The marketing field is booming, with nearly a third of all working Americans now employed in marketing-related positions. Marketing salaries may vary by company, position, and region, and salary figures change constantly. In general, entry-level marketing salaries usually are only slightly below those for engineering and chemistry but equal or exceed starting salaries in economics, finance, accounting, general business, and the liberal arts. Moreover, if you succeed in an entry-level marketing position, it's likely that you will be promoted quickly to higher levels of responsibility and salary. In addition, because of the consumer and product knowledge you will gain in these jobs, marketing positions provide excellent training for the highest levels in an organization.

Overall Marketing Facts and Trends

In conducting your job search, consider the following facts and trends that are changing the world of marketing:

Focus on customers. More and more, companies are realizing that they win in the marketplace only by creating superior value for customers. To capture value from customers, they must first find new and better ways to solve customer problems and improve customer brand experiences. This increasing focus on the customer puts marketers at the forefront in many of today's companies. As the primary customer-facing function, marketing's mission is to get all company departments to "think customer."

Technology. Technology is changing the way marketers work. For example, Internet, social media, mobile, and other digital technologies are rapidly changing the ways marketers interact with and service customers. They are also changing everything from the ways marketers create new products and advertise them to how marketers access information and recruit personnel. Whereas advertising firms have traditionally recruited "generalists" in account management, *generalist* has now taken on a whole new meaning—advertising account executives must now have both broad and specialized knowledge.

Diversity. The number of women and minorities in marketing continues to grow, and women and minorities also are advancing rapidly into marketing management. For example, women now outnumber men by nearly two to one as advertising account executives. As marketing becomes more global, the need for diversity in marketing positions will continue to increase, opening new opportunities.

Global. Companies such as Coca-Cola, McDonald's, Google, IBM, Walmart, and Procter & Gamble have become multinational, with manufacturing and marketing operations in hundreds of countries. Indeed, such companies often make more profit from sales outside the United States than from within. And it's not just the big companies that are involved in international marketing. Organizations of all sizes have moved into the global arena. Many new marketing opportunities and careers will be directly linked to the expanding global marketplace. The globalization of business also means that you will need more cultural, language, and people skills in the marketing world of the twenty-first century.

Not-for-profit organizations. Increasingly, colleges, arts organizations, libraries, hospitals, and other not-for-profit organizations are recognizing the need for effectively marketing their "products" and services to various publics. This awareness has led to new marketing positions—with these organizations hiring their own marketing directors and marketing vice presidents or using outside marketing specialists.

Looking for a Job in Today's Marketing World

To choose and find the right job, you will need to apply the marketing skills you've learned in this course, especially marketing analysis and planning. Follow these eight steps for marketing yourself: (1) conduct a self-assessment and seek career counseling; (2) examine job descriptions; (3) explore the job market, follow up, and assess opportunities; (4) develop search strategies; (5) prepare résumés; (6) write a cover letter and assemble supporting documents; (7) interview for jobs; and (8) take a follow-up interview.

Conduct a Self-Assessment and Seek Career Counseling

If you're having difficulty deciding what kind of marketing position is the best fit for you, start out by doing some self-testing or seeking career counseling. Self-assessments require that you honestly and thoroughly evaluate your interests, strengths, and weaknesses. What do you do well (your best and favorite skills) and not so well? What are your favorite interests? What are your career goals? What makes you stand out from other job seekers?

The answers to such questions may suggest which marketing careers you should seek or avoid. For help in completing an effective self-assessment, look for the following books in your local bookstore or online: Nicholas Lore, *The Pathfinder: How to Choose or Change Your Career for a Lifetime of Satisfaction and Success* (Touchstone, 2012), and Richard Bolles, *What Color Is Your Parachute? 2016* (Ten Speed Press, 2015; also see www.eparachute.com). Many online sites also offer self-assessment tools, such as the Keirsey Temperament Theory and the Temperament Sorter, a free but broad assessment available at Keirsey.com. For a more specific evaluation, CareerLeader.com offers a complete online business career self-assessment program designed by the Directors of MBA Career Development at Harvard Business School. You can use this for a fee.

For help in finding a career counselor to guide you in making a career assessment, Richard Bolles's *What Color Is Your Parachute? 2016* contains a useful state-by-state sampling. CareerLeader.com also offers personal career counseling. (Some counselors can help you in your actual job search, too.) You can also consult the career counseling, testing, and placement services at your college or university.

Examine Job Descriptions

After you have identified your skills, interests, and desires, you need to see which marketing positions are the best match for them. Two U.S. Labor Department publications available in your local library or online—the *Occupation Outlook Handbook* (www.bls.gov/ooh) and the *Dictionary of Occupational Titles* (www.occupationalinfo.org)—describe the duties involved in various occupations, the specific training and education needed, the availability of jobs in each field, possibilities for advancement, and probable earnings.

Your initial career shopping list should be broad and flexible. Look for different ways to achieve your objectives. For example, if you want a career in marketing management, consider the public as well as the private sector, and local and regional as well as national and international firms. Be open initially to exploring many options, then focus on specific industries and jobs, listing your basic goals as a way to guide your choices. Your list might include "a job in a start-up company, near a big city on the West Coast, doing new-product planning with a computer software firm."

Explore the Job Market, Follow Up, and Assess Opportunities

At this stage, you need to look at the market and see what positions are actually available. You do not have to do this alone. Any of the following may assist you.

Career Development Centers

Your college's career development center and its Web site are excellent places to start. For example, the Web sites of the undergraduate career services center provide lists of career links that can help to focus your job search. Most schools also provide career coaches and career education courses. Also check the National Association of Colleges and Employers Web site (www.naceweb.org). It publishes a national forecast of hiring intentions of employers as they relate to new college graduates (search "job outlook").

In addition, find out everything you can about the companies that interest you by consulting company Web sites, business magazine articles and online sites, annual reports, business reference books, faculty, career counselors, and others. Try to analyze the industry's and the company's future growth and profit potential, advancement opportunities, salary levels, entry positions, travel time, and other factors of significance to you.

Job Fairs

Career development centers often work with corporate recruiters to organize on-campus job fairs. You might also use the Internet to check on upcoming career fairs in your region. For example, visit National Career Fairs at www.nationalcareerfairs.com or Coast to Coast Career Fairs listings at www.coasttocoastcareerfairs.com.

Networking

Networking—asking for job leads from friends, family, people in your community, and career centers—is one of the best ways to find a marketing job. Studies estimate that 60 to 90 percent of jobs are found through networking. The idea is to spread your net wide, contacting anybody and everybody.

Internships

An internship is filled with many benefits, such as gaining experience in a specific field of interest and building up a network of contacts. The biggest benefit: the potential of being offered a job shortly before or soon after graduation. According to a recent survey by the National Association of Colleges and Employers, employers converted 51.2 percent of last year's interns into full-time hires. In addition, 63 percent of the seniors who had paid internship experience and applied for a job received at least one job offer. Conversely, only 35.2 percent of seniors without internship experience who applied for a job received an offer. In addition, survey results show that the median accepted salary offer for seniors with a paid internship was 40 percent higher than the median accepted salary offered to non-intern seniors.

Many company Internet sites have separate internship areas. For example, check out Internships.com, InternshipPrograms.com, MonsterCollege (college.monster.com/education), CampusCareerCenter.com, InternJobs.com, and GoAbroad.com (www.goabroad.com/intern-abroad). If you know of a company for which you wish to work, go to that company's corporate Web site, enter the human resources area, and check for internships. If none are listed, try emailing the human resources department, asking if internships are offered.

Job Hunting on the Internet

A constantly increasing number of sites on the Internet deals with job hunting. You can also use the Internet to make contacts with people who can help you gain information on and research companies that interest you. The Riley Guide offers a great introduction to what jobs are available (www.rileyguide.com). CareerBuilder.com and Monster.com are good general sites for seeking job listings. Other helpful sites are Disability.gov and Diversity.com, which contain information on opportunities for African Americans, Hispanic Americans, Asian Americans, and Native Americans.

Most companies have their own online sites on which they post job listings. This may be helpful if you have a specific and fairly limited number of companies that you are keeping your eye on for job opportunities. But if this is not the case, remember that to find out what interesting marketing jobs the companies themselves are posting, you may have to visit hundreds of corporate sites.

Professional Networking Sites

Many companies have now begun to take advantage of social networking sites to find talented applicants. From LinkedIn to Facebook to Google+, social networking has become professional networking. For example, companies ranging from P&G to BASF have career pages on LinkedIn (www.linkedin.com/company/procter-&-gamble/careers and www.linkedin.com/company/basf/careers) to find potential candidates for entry-level positions. And companies ranging from Walmart (www.facebook.com/walmartcareers) to Marriott (www.facebook.com/marriottjobsandcareers) have career listings pages on Facebook in addition to LinkedIn. For job seekers, online professional networking offers more efficient job targeting and reduces associated costs as compared with traditional interaction methods such as traveling to job fairs and interviews, printing résumés, and other expenses.

However, although the Internet offers a wealth of resources for searching for the perfect job, be aware that it's a two-way street. Just as job seekers can search the Internet to find job opportunities, employers can search for information on job candidates. Jobs searches can sometimes be derailed by information mined by potential employers from online social networking sites that reveals unintended or embarrassing anecdotes and photos. Internet searches can sometimes also reveal inconsistencies and résumé inflation. A recent study found that more than half of recruiters surveyed have reconsidered a candidate based on his or her social profile.

Develop Search Strategies

Once you've decided which companies you are interested in, you need to contact them. One of the best ways is through on-campus interviews. However, not every company you are interested in will visit your school. In such instances, you can write, email, or phone the company directly or ask marketing professors or school alumni for contacts.

Prepare Résumés

A résumé is a concise yet comprehensive written summary of your qualifications, including your academic, personal, and professional achievements, that showcases why you are the best candidate for the job. Because an employer will spend on average only 15 to 20 seconds reviewing your résumé, you want to be sure that you prepare a good one.

In preparing your résumé, remember that all information on it must be accurate and complete. Résumés typically begin with the applicant's full name, telephone number, and mail and email addresses. A simple and direct statement of career objectives generally appears next, followed by work history and academic data (including awards and internships), and then by personal activities and experiences applicable to the job sought.

The résumé sometimes ends with a list of references the employer may contact (at other times, references may be listed separately). If your work or internship experience is limited, nonexistent, or irrelevant, then it is a good idea to emphasize your academic and nonacademic achievements, showing skills related to those required for excellent job performance.

There are three main types of résumés. *Reverse chronological* résumés, which emphasize career growth, are organized in reverse chronological order, starting with your most recent job. They focus on job titles within organizations, describing the responsibilities and accomplishments for each job. *Functional* résumés focus less on job titles and work history and more on assets and achievements. This format works best if your job history is scanty or discontinuous. *Mixed,* or *combination,* résumés take from each of the other two formats. First, the skills used for a specific job are listed, then the job title is stated. This format works best for applicants whose past jobs are in other fields or seemingly unrelated to the position. For further explanation and examples of these types of résumés, see the Résumé Resource format page (www.resume-resource.com/format.html).

Many books can assist you in developing your résumé. A popular guide is Martin Yate, *Knock 'Em Dead: Secrets and Strategies for First-Time Job Seekers* (Adams Media: 2013). Software programs such as RésuméMaker (www.ResumeMaker.com) provide hundreds of sample résumés and ready-to-use phrases while guiding you through the résumé preparation process. CareerOneStop (www.careeronestop.org/resumeguide/introduction.aspx) offers a step-by-step résumé tutorial, and Monster (http://career-advice.monster.com) offers résumé advice and writing services. Finally, you can even create your own personalized online résumé at sites such as optimalresume.com.

Online Résumés

The Internet is now a widely used job-search environment, so it's a good idea to have your résumé ready for the online environment. You can forward it to networking contacts or recruiting professionals through email. You can also post it in online databases with the hope that employers and recruiters will find it.

Successful Internet-ready résumés require a different strategy than that for paper résumés. For instance, when companies search résumé banks, they search key words and industry buzz words that describe a skill or the core work required for each job, so nouns are much more important than verbs. Two good resources for preparing Internet-ready résumés are Susan Ireland's Résumé Site (www.gcflearnfree.org/resumewriting/9/print) and the Riley Guide (www.rileyguide.com/eresume.html).

After you have written your Internet-ready résumé, you need to post it. The following sites may be good locations to start: Monster (www.monster.com), LinkedIn (www.linkedin.com/job/home), and CareerBuilder.com (www.careerbuilder.com/jobseeker/postnewresume.aspx). However, use caution when posting your résumé on various sites. In this era of identity theft, you need to select sites with care so as to protect your privacy. Limit access to your personal contact information, and don't use sites that offer to "blast" your résumé into cyberspace.

Résumé Tips

- Communicate your worth to potential employers in a concrete manner, citing examples whenever possible.
- Be concise and direct.
- Use active verbs to show you are a doer.
- Do not skimp on quality or use gimmicks. Spare no expense in presenting a professional résumé.
- Have someone critique your work. A single typo can eliminate you from being considered.
- Customize your résumé for specific employers. Emphasize your strengths as they pertain to your targeted job.
- Keep your résumé compact, usually one page.
- Format the text to be attractive, professional, and readable. Times New Roman is often the font of choice. Avoid too much "design" or gimmicky flourishes.

Write a Cover Letter, Follow Up, and Assemble Supporting Documents

Cover Letter

You should include a cover letter informing the employer that a résumé is enclosed. But a cover letter does more than this. It also serves to summarize in one or two paragraphs the contents of the résumé and explains why you think you are the right person for the position. The goal is to persuade the employer to look at the more detailed résumé. A typical cover letter is organized as follows: (1) the name and position of the person you are contacting; (2) a statement identifying the position you are applying for, how you heard of the vacancy, and the reasons for your interest; (3) a summary of your qualifications for the job; (4) a description of what follow-ups you intend to make, such as phoning in two weeks to confirm that the résumé has been received; and (5) an expression of gratitude for the opportunity of being a candidate for the job. CareerOneStop (www.careeronestop.org/ResumeGuide/Writeeffectivecoverletters.aspx) offers a step-by-step tutorial on how to create a cover letter, and Susan Ireland's Web site contains more than 50 cover letter samples (susanireland.com/ letter/cover-letter-examples). Another popular guide is Jeremy Schifeling, *Get It Done: Write a Cover Letter* (Jeremy Schifeling, 2012).

Follow Up

Once you send your cover letter and résumé to prospective employers via the method they prefer—email, their Web site, or regular mail—it's often a good idea to follow up. In today's market, job seekers can't afford to wait for interviews to find them. A quality résumé and an attractive cover letter are crucial, but a proper follow-up may be the key to landing an interview. However, before you engage your potential employer, be sure to research the company. Knowing about the company and understanding its place in the industry will help you shine. When you place a call, send an email, or mail a letter to a company contact, be sure to restate your interest in the position, check on the status of your résumé, and ask employers about any questions they may have.

Letters of Recommendation

Letters of recommendation are written references by professors, former and current employers, and others that testify to your character, skills, and abilities. Some companies may request letters of recommendation, to be submitted either with the résumé or at the interview. Even if letters of recommendation aren't requested, it's a good idea to bring them with you to the interview. A good reference letter tells why you would be an excellent candidate for the position. In choosing someone to write a letter of recommendation, be confident that the person will give you a good reference. In addition, do not assume the person knows everything about you or the position you are seeking. Rather, provide the person with your résumé and other relevant data. As a courtesy, allow the reference writer at least a month to complete the letter and enclose a stamped, addressed envelope with your materials.

In the packet containing your résumé, cover letter, and letters of recommendation, you may also want to attach other relevant documents that support your candidacy, such as academic transcripts, graphics, portfolios, and samples of writing.

Interview for Jobs

As the old saying goes, "The résumé gets you the interview; the interview gets you the job." The job interview offers you an opportunity to gather more information about the organization while at the same time allowing the organization to gather more information about you. You'll want to present your best self. The interview process consists of three parts: before the interview, the interview itself, and after the interview. If you pass through these stages successfully, you will be called back for the follow-up interview.

Before the Interview

In preparing for your interview, do the following:

1. Understand that interviewers have diverse styles, including the "chitchat," let's-get-to-know-each-other style; the interrogation style of question after question; and the tough-probing "why, why, why" style, among others. So be ready for anything.
2. With a friend, practice being interviewed and then ask for a critique. Or make a video of yourself in a practice interview so that you can critique your own performance. Your college placement service may also offer "mock" interviews to help you.

3. Prepare at least five good questions whose answers are not easily found in the company literature, such as "What is the future direction of the firm?" "How does the firm differentiate itself from competitors?" or "Do you have a new-media division?"
4. Anticipate possible interview questions, such as "Why do you want to work for this company?" or "Why should we hire you?" Prepare solid answers before the interview. Have a clear idea of why you are interested in joining the company and the industry to which it belongs.
5. Avoid back-to-back interviews—they can be exhausting, and it is unpredictable how long each will last.
6. Prepare relevant documents that support your candidacy, such as academic transcripts, letters of recommendation, graphics, portfolios, and samples of writing. Bring multiple copies to the interview.
7. Dress conservatively and professionally. Be neat and clean.
8. Arrive 10 minutes early to collect your thoughts and review the major points you intend to cover. Check your name on the interview schedule, noting the name of the interviewer and the room number. Be courteous and polite to office staff.
9. Approach the interview enthusiastically. Let your personality shine through.

During the Interview

During the interview, do the following:

1. Shake hands firmly in greeting the interviewer. Introduce yourself, using the same form of address that the interviewer uses. Focus on creating a good initial impression.
2. Keep your poise. Relax, smile when appropriate, and be upbeat throughout.
3. Maintain eye contact and good posture, and speak distinctly. Don't clasp your hands or fiddle with jewelry, hair, or clothing. Sit comfortably in your chair.
4. Along with the copies of relevant documents that support your candidacy, carry extra copies of your résumé with you.
5. Have your story down pat. Present your selling points. Answer questions directly. Avoid both one-word and too-wordy answers.
6. Let the interviewer take the initiative, but don't be passive. Find an opportunity to direct the conversation to things about yourself that you want the interviewer to hear.
7. To end on a high note, make your most important point or ask your most pertinent question during the last part of the interview.
8. Don't hesitate to "close." You might say, "I'm very interested in the position, and I have enjoyed this interview."
9. Obtain the interviewer's business card or address and phone number so that you can follow up later.

A tip for acing the interview: Before you open your mouth, find out *what it's like* to be a brand manager, sales representative, market researcher, advertising account executive, or other position for which you're interviewing. See if you can find a "mentor"—someone in a position similar to the one you're seeking, perhaps with another company. Talk with this mentor about the ins and outs of the job and industry.

After the Interview

After the interview, do the following:

1. Record the key points that arose. Be sure to note who is to follow up and when a decision can be expected.
2. Analyze the interview objectively, including the questions asked, the answers to them, your overall interview presentation, and the interviewer's responses to specific points.
3. Immediately send a thank-you letter or email, mentioning any additional items and your willingness to supply further information.
4. If you do not hear from the employer within the specified time, call, email, or write the interviewer to determine your status.

Follow-Up Interview

If your first interview takes place off-site, such as at your college or at a job fair, and if you are successful with that initial interview, you will be invited to visit the organization. The in-company interview will probably run from several hours to an entire day. The organization will examine your interest, maturity, enthusiasm, assertiveness, logic, and company and functional knowledge. You should ask questions about issues of importance to you. Find out about the working environment, job role, responsibilities, opportunities for advancement, current industrial issues, and the company's personality. The company wants to discover if you are the right person for the job, whereas you want to find out if it is the right job for you. The key is to determine if the right *fit* exists between you and the company.

Marketing Jobs

This section describes some of the key marketing positions.

Advertising

Advertising is one of the most exciting fields in marketing, offering a wide range of career opportunities.

Job Descriptions

Key advertising positions include copywriter, art director, production manager, account executive, account planner, and media planner/buyer.

- *Copywriters* write advertising copy and help find the concepts behind the written words and visual images of advertisements.
- *Art directors,* the other part of the creative team, help translate the copywriters' ideas into dramatic visuals called "layouts." Agency artists develop print layouts, package designs, television and video layouts (called "storyboards"), corporate logotypes, trademarks, and symbols.
- *Production managers* are responsible for physically creating ads, either in-house or by contracting through outside production houses.
- *Account development executives* research and understand clients' markets and customers and help develop marketing and advertising strategies to affect them.
- *Account executives* serve as liaisons between clients and agencies. They coordinate the planning, creation, production, and implementation of an advertising campaign for the account.
- *Account planners* serve as the voice of the consumer in the agency. They research consumers to understand their needs and motivations as a basis for developing effective ad campaigns.
- *Media planners (or buyers)* determine the best mix of television, radio, newspaper, magazine, digital, and other media for the advertising campaign.

Skills Needed, Career Paths, and Typical Salaries

Work in advertising requires strong people skills in order to interact closely with an often-difficult and demanding client base. In addition, advertising attracts people with strong skills in planning, problem solving, creativity, communication, initiative, leadership, and presentation. Advertising involves working under high levels of stress and pressure created by unrelenting deadlines. Advertisers frequently have to work long hours to meet deadlines for a presentation. But work achievements are very apparent, with the results of creative strategies observed by thousands or even millions of people.

Positions in advertising sometimes require an MBA. But most jobs only require a business, graphic arts, or liberal arts degree. Advertising positions often serve as gateways to higher-level management. Moreover, with large advertising agencies opening offices all over the world, there is the possibility of eventually working on global campaigns.

Starting advertising salaries are relatively low compared with those of some other marketing jobs because of strong competition for entry-level advertising jobs. Compensation will increase quickly as you move into account executive or other management positions. For more facts and figures, see the online pages of *Advertising Age,* a key ad industry publication (www.adage.com, click on the Jobs link), and the American Association of Advertising Agencies (www.aaaa.org).

Brand and Product Management

Brand and product managers plan, direct, and control business and marketing efforts for their products. They are involved with research and development, packaging, manufacturing, sales and distribution, advertising, promotion, market research, and business analysis and forecasting.

Job Descriptions

A company's brand management team consists of people in several positions:

- *Brand managers* guide the development of marketing strategies for a specific brand.
- *Assistant brand managers* are responsible for certain strategic components of the brand.
- *Product managers* oversee several brands within a product line or product group.
- *Product category managers* direct multiple product lines in the product category.
- *Market analysts* research the market and provide important strategic information to the project managers.
- *Project directors* are responsible for collecting market information on a marketing or product project.
- *Research directors* oversee the planning, gathering, and analyzing of all organizational research.

Skills Needed, Career Paths, and Typical Salaries

Brand and product management requires high problem-solving, analytical, presentation, communication, and leadership skills as well as the ability to work well in a team. Product management requires long hours and involves the high pressure of running large projects. In consumer goods companies, the newcomer—who usually needs an MBA—joins a brand team as an assistant and learns the ropes by doing numerical analyses and assisting senior brand people. This person eventually heads the team and later moves on to manage a larger brand, then several brands.

Many industrial goods companies also have product managers. Product management is one of the best training grounds for future corporate officers. Product management also offers good opportunities to move into international marketing. Product managers command relatively high salaries. Because this job category encourages or requires a master's degree, starting pay tends to be higher than in other marketing categories such as advertising or retailing.

Sales and Sales Management

Sales and sales management opportunities exist in a wide range of profit and not-for-profit organizations and in product and service organizations, including financial, insurance, consulting, and government organizations.

Job Descriptions

Key jobs include consumer sales, industrial sales, national account managers, service support, sales trainers, and sales management

- *Consumer sales* involves selling consumer products and services through retailers.
- *Industrial sales* involves selling products and services to other businesses.
- *National account managers (NAMs)* oversee a few very large accounts.
- *Service support* personnel support salespeople during and after the sale of a product.

- *Sales trainers* train new hires and provide refresher training for all sales personnel.
- *Sales management* includes a sequence of positions ranging from district manager to vice president of sales.

Salespeople enjoy active professional lives, working outside the office and interacting with others. They manage their own time and activities. And successful salespeople can be very well paid. Competition for top jobs can be intense. Every sales job is different, but some positions involve extensive travel, long workdays, and working under pressure. You can also expect to be transferred more than once between company headquarters and regional offices. However, most companies are now working to bring good work–life balance to their salespeople and sales managers.

Skills Needed, Career Paths, and Typical Salaries

Selling is a people profession in which you will work with people every day, all day long. In addition to people skills, sales professionals need sales and communication skills. Most sales positions also require strong problem-solving, analytical, presentation, and leadership abilities as well as creativity and initiative. Teamwork skills are increasingly important.

Career paths lead from salesperson to district, regional, and higher levels of sales management and, in many cases, to the top management of the firm. Today, most entry-level sales management positions require a college degree. Increasingly, people seeking selling jobs are acquiring sales experience in an internship capacity or from a part-time job before graduating. Sales positions are great springboards to leadership positions, with more CEOs starting in sales than in any other entry-level position. This might explain why competition for top sales jobs is intense.

Starting base salaries in sales may be moderate, but compensation is often supplemented by significant commission, bonus, or other incentive plans. In addition, many sales jobs include a company car or car allowance. Successful salespeople are among most companies' highest paid employees.

Other Marketing Jobs

Retailing

Retailing provides an early opportunity to assume marketing responsibilities. Key jobs include store manager, regional manager, buyer, department manager, and salesperson. *Store managers* direct the management and operation of an individual store. *Regional managers* manage groups of stores across several states and report performance to headquarters. *Buyers* select and buy the merchandise that the store carries. The *department manager* acts as store manager of a department, such as clothing, but on the department level. The *salesperson* sells merchandise to retail customers. Retailing can involve relocation, but generally there is little travel, unless you are a buyer. Retailing requires high people and sales skills because retailers are constantly in contact with customers. Enthusiasm, willingness, and communication skills are very helpful for retailers, too.

Retailers work long hours, but their daily activities are often more structured than in some types of marketing positions. Starting salaries in retailing tend to be low, but pay increases as you move into management or a retailing specialty job.

Marketing Research

Marketing researchers interact with managers to define problems and identify the information needed to resolve them. They design research projects, prepare questionnaires and samples, analyze data, prepare reports, and present their findings and recommendations to management. They must understand statistics, consumer behavior, psychology, and sociology. As more and more marketing research goes digital, they must also understand the ins and outs of obtaining and managing online information. A master's degree helps. Career opportunities exist with manufacturers, retailers, some wholesalers, trade and industry associations, marketing research firms, advertising agencies, and governmental and private nonprofit agencies.

New Product Planning

People interested in new product planning can find opportunities in many types of organizations. They usually need a good background in marketing, marketing research, and sales forecasting; they need organizational skills to motivate and coordinate others; and they may need a technical background. Usually, these people work first in other marketing positions before joining the new product department.

Marketing Logistics (Physical Distribution)

Marketing logistics, or physical distribution, is a large and dynamic field, with many career opportunities. Major transportation carriers, manufacturers, wholesalers, and retailers all employ logistics specialists. Increasingly, marketing teams include logistics specialists, and marketing managers' career paths include marketing logistics assignments. Coursework in quantitative methods, finance, accounting, and marketing will provide you with the necessary skills for entering the field.

Public Relations

Most organizations have a public relations staff to anticipate problems with various publics, handle complaints, deal with media, and build the corporate image. People interested in public relations should be able to speak and write clearly and persuasively, and they should have a background in journalism, communications, or the liberal arts. The challenges in this job are highly varied and very people-oriented.

Not-for-Profit Services

The key jobs in not-for-profits include marketing director, director of development, event coordinator, publication specialist, and intern/volunteer. The *marketing director* is in charge of all marketing activities for the organization. The *director of development* organizes, manages, and directs the fundraising campaigns that keep a not-for-profit in existence. An *event coordinator* directs all aspects of fundraising events, from initial planning through implementation. The *publication specialist* oversees publications designed to promote awareness of the organization.

Although typically an unpaid position, the *intern/volunteer* performs various marketing functions, and this work can be an important step to gaining a full-time position. The not-for-profit sector is typically not for someone who is money-driven. Rather, most not-for-profits look for people with a strong sense of community spirit and the desire to help others. Therefore, starting pay is usually lower than in other marketing fields. However, the bigger the not-for-profit, the better your chance of rapidly increasing your income when moving into upper management.

Other Resources

Professional marketing associations and organizations are another source of information about careers. Marketers belong to many such societies. You may want to contact some of the following in your job search:

Advertising Women of New York, 28 West 44th Street, Suite 912, New York, NY 10036. (212) 221-7969 (www.awny.org)

American Advertising Federation, 1101 Vermont Avenue, NW, Washington, DC 20005. (202) 898-0089 (www.aaf.org)

American Marketing Association, 311 South Wacker Drive, Suite 5800, Chicago, IL 60606. (800) AMA-1150 (www.marketingpower.com)

The Association of Women in Communications, 3337 Duke Street, Alexandria, VA 22314. (703) 370-7436 (www.womcom.org)

Market Research Association, 1156 15th Street NW, Suite 302, Washington, DC 20005. (202) 800-2545 (www.marketingresearch.org)

National Association of Sales Professionals, 555 Friendly Street, Bloomfield Hills, MI 48341. (866) 365-1520 (www.nasp.com)

National Management Association, 2210 Arbor Boulevard, Dayton, OH 45439. (937) 294-0421 (www.nma1.org)

National Retail Federation, 1101 New York Ave NW, Washington, DC 20005. (800) 673-4692 (www.nrf.com)

Product Development and Management Association, 330 Wabash Avenue, Suite 2000, Chicago, IL 60611. (312) 321-5145 (www.pdma.org)

Public Relations Society of America, 33 Maiden Lane, Eleventh Floor, New York, NY 10038. (212) 460-1400 (www.prsa.org)

Sales and Marketing Executives International, PO Box 1390, Sumas, WA, 98295. (312) 893-0751 (www.smei.org)

Glossary

Adapted global marketing A global marketing approach that adjusts the marketing strategy and mix elements to each international target market, which creates more costs but hopefully produces a larger market share and return.

Administered VMS A vertical marketing system that coordinates successive stages of production and distribution through the size and power of one of the parties.

Adoption process The mental process through which an individual passes from first hearing about an innovation to final adoption.

Advertising Any paid form of nonpersonal presentation and promotion of ideas, goods, or services by an identified sponsor.

Advertising agency A marketing services firm that assists companies in planning, preparing, implementing, and evaluating all or portions of their advertising programs.

Advertising budget The dollars and other resources allocated to a product or a company advertising program.

Advertising media The vehicles through which advertising messages are delivered to their intended audiences.

Advertising objective A specific communication task to be accomplished with a specific target audience during a specific period of time.

Advertising strategy The strategy by which a company accomplishes its advertising objectives. It consists of two major elements: creating advertising messages and selecting advertising media.

Affordable method Setting the promotion budget at the level management thinks the company can afford.

Age and life-cycle segmentation Dividing a market into different age and life-cycle groups.

Agent A wholesaler who represents buyers or sellers on a relatively permanent basis, performs only a few functions, and does not take title to goods.

Allowance Promotional money paid by manufacturers to retailers in return for an agreement to feature the manufacturer's products in some way.

Approach The sales step in which a salesperson meets the customer for the first time.

Attitude A person's relatively consistent favorable or unfavorable evaluations, feelings, and tendencies toward an object or idea.

Baby boomers The 78 million people born during the years following World War II and lasting until 1964.

Behavioral segmentation Dividing a market into segments based on consumer knowledge, attitudes, uses of a product, or responses to a product.

Behavioral targeting Using online consumer tracking data to target advertisements and marketing offers to specific consumers.

Belief A descriptive thought that a person holds about something.

Benefit segmentation Dividing a market into segments according to the different benefits that consumers seek from the product.

Big data The huge and complex data sets generated by today's sophisticated information generation, collection, storage, and analysis technologies.

Blogs Online forums where people and companies post their thoughts and other content, usually related to narrowly defined topics.

Brand A name, term, sign, symbol, design, or a combination of these that identifies the products or services of one seller or group of sellers and differentiates them from those of competitors.

Brand equity The differential effect that knowing the brand name has on customer response to the product and its marketing.

Brand extension Extending an existing brand name to new product categories.

Brand value The total financial value of a brand.

Branded community Web site A Web site that presents brand content that engages consumers and creates customer community around a brand.

Break-even analysis Analysis to determine the unit volume and dollar sales needed to be profitable given a particular price and cost structure.

Break-even pricing (target return pricing) Setting price to break even on the costs of making and marketing a product or setting price to make a target return.

Broker A wholesaler who does not take title to goods and whose function is to bring buyers and sellers together and assist in negotiation.

Business analysis A review of the sales, costs, and profit projections for a new product to find out whether these factors satisfy the company's objectives.

Business buyer behavior The buying behavior of organizations that buy goods and services for use in the production of other products and services that are sold, rented, or supplied to others.

Business buying process The process by which business buyers determine which products and services their organizations need to purchase and then find, evaluate, and choose among alternative suppliers and brands.

Business portfolio The collection of businesses and products that make up the company.

Business promotions Sales promotion tools used to generate business leads, stimulate purchases, reward customers, and motivate salespeople.

Buying center All the individuals and units that play a role in the purchase decision-making process.

By-product pricing Setting a price for by-products in order to make the main product's price more competitive.

Cannibalization The situation in which one product sold by a company takes a portion of its sales from other company products.

Captive-product pricing Setting a price for products that must be used along with a main product, such as blades for a razor and games for a video-game console.

Catalog marketing Direct marketing through print, video, or digital catalogs that are mailed to select customers, made available in stores, or presented online.

Category killer A giant specialty store that carries a very deep assortment of a particular line.

Causal research Marketing research to test hypotheses about cause-and-effect relationships.

Chain ratio method Estimating market demand by multiplying a base number by a chain of adjusting percentages.

Channel conflict Disagreements—among marketing channel members on goals, roles, and rewards—who should do what and for what rewards.

Channel level A layer of intermediaries that performs some work in bringing the product and its ownership closer to the final buyer.

Closing The sales step in which a salesperson asks the customer for an order.

Co-branding The practice of using the established brand names of two different companies on the same product.

Cognitive dissonance Buyer discomfort caused by postpurchase conflict.

Commercialization Introducing a new product into the market.

Communication adaptation A global communication strategy of fully adapting advertising messages to local markets.

Competition-based pricing Setting prices based on competitors' strategies, prices, costs, and market offerings.

Competitive advantage An advantage over competitors gained by offering greater customer value, either by having lower prices or providing more benefits that justify higher prices.

Competitive marketing intelligence The systematic monitoring, collection, and analysis of publicly available information about consumers, competitors, and developments in the marketplace.

Competitive-parity method Setting the promotion budget to match competitors' outlays.

Concentrated (niche) marketing A market-coverage strategy in which a firm goes after a large share of one or a few segments or niches.

Concept testing Testing new product concepts with a group of target consumers to find out if the concepts have strong consumer appeal.

Consumer buyer behavior The buying behavior of final consumers—individuals and households that buy goods and services for personal consumption.

Consumer market All the individuals and households that buy or acquire goods and services for personal consumption.

Consumer product A product bought by final consumers for personal consumption.

Consumer promotions Sales promotion tools used to boost short-term customer buying and engagement or enhance long-term customer relationships.

Consumer-generated marketing Brand exchanges created by consumers themselves-both invited and uninvited-by which consumers are playing an increasing role in shaping their own brand experiences and those of other consumers.

Consumer-oriented marketing A company should view and organize its marketing activities from the consumer's point of view.

Consumerism An organized movement of citizens and government agencies to improve the rights and power of buyers in relation to sellers.

Content marketing Creating, inspiring, and sharing brand messages and conversations with and among consumers across a fluid mix of paid, owned, earned, and shared channels.

Contract manufacturing A joint venture in which a company contracts with manufacturers in a foreign market to produce its product or provide its service.

Contractual VMS A vertical marketing system in which independent firms at different levels of production and distribution join together through contracts.

Contribution margin The unit contribution divided by the selling price.

Convenience product A consumer product that customers usually buy frequently, immediately, and with minimal comparison and buying effort.

Convenience store A small store, located near a residential area, that is open long hours seven days a week and carries a limited line of high-turnover convenience goods.

Conventional distribution channel A channel consisting of one or more independent producers, wholesalers, and retailers, each a separate business seeking to maximize its own profits, perhaps even at the expense of profits for the system as a whole.

Corporate chains Two or more outlets that are commonly owned and controlled.

Corporate VMS A vertical marketing system that combines successive stages of production and distribution under single ownership—channel leadership is established through common ownership.

Cost-based pricing Setting prices based on the costs of producing, distributing, and selling the product plus a fair rate of return for effort and risk.

Cost-plus pricing (markup pricing) Adding a standard markup to the cost of the product.

Creative concept The compelling "big idea" that will bring an advertising message strategy to life in a distinctive and memorable way.

Crowdsourcing Inviting broad communities of people-customers, employees, independent scientists and researchers, and even the public at large-into the new product innovation process.

Cultural environment Institutions and other forces that affect a society's basic values, perceptions, preferences, and behaviors.

Culture The set of basic values, perceptions, wants, and behaviors learned by a member of society from family and other important institutions.

Customer-perceived value The customer's evaluation of the difference between all the benefits and all the costs of a marketing offer relative to those of competing offers.

Customer (or market) sales force structure A sales force organization in which salespeople specialize in selling only to certain customers or industries.

Customer equity The total combined customer lifetime values of all of the company's current and potential customers.

Customer insights Fresh marketing information-based understandings of customers and the marketplace that become the basis for creating customer value, engagement, and relationships.

Customer lifetime value The value of the entire stream of purchases a customer makes over a lifetime of patronage.

Customer relationship management The overall process of building and maintaining profitable customer relationships by delivering superior customer value and satisfaction.

Customer relationship management (CRM) Managing detailed information about individual customers and carefully managing customer touch points to maximize customer loyalty.

Customer satisfaction The extent to which a product's perceived performance matches a buyer's expectations.

Customer value marketing A company should put most of its resources into customer value-building marketing investments.

Customer value-based pricing Setting price based on buyers' perceptions of value rather than on the seller's cost.

Customer-centered new product development New product development that focuses on finding new ways to solve customer problems and create more customer-satisfying experiences.

Customer-engagement marketing Making the brand a meaningful part of consumers' conversations and lives by fostering direct and continuous customer involvement in shaping brand conversations, experiences, and community.

Customer-perceived value The customer's evaluation of the difference between all the benefits and all the costs of a market offering relative to those of competing offers.

Decline stage The PLC stage in which a product's sales fade away.

Deficient products Products that have neither immediate appeal nor long-run benefits.

Demand curve A curve that shows the number of units the market will buy in a given time period at different prices that might be charged.

Demands Human wants that are backed by buying power.

Demographic segmentation Dividing the market into segments based on variables such as age, life-cycle stage, gender, income, occupation, education, religion, ethnicity, and generation.

Demography The study of human populations in terms of size, density, location, age, gender, race, occupation, and other statistics.

Department store A retail store that carries a wide variety of product lines, each operated as a separate department managed by specialist buyers or merchandisers.

Derived demand Business demand that ultimately comes from (derives from) the demand for consumer goods.

Descriptive research Marketing research to better describe marketing problems, situations, or markets, such as the market potential for a product or the demographics and attitudes of consumers.

Desirable products Products that give both high immediate satisfaction and high long-run benefits.

Differentiated (segmented) marketing A market-coverage strategy in which a firm decides to target several market segments and designs separate offers for each.

Differentiation Actually differentiating the market offering to create superior customer value.

Digital and social media marketing Using digital marketing tools such as Web sites, social media, mobile apps and ads, online video, email, and blogs to engage consumers anywhere, at any time, via their digital devices.

Direct and digital marketing Engaging directly with carefully targeted individual consumers and customer communities to both obtain an immediate response and build lasting customer relationships.

Direct investment Entering a foreign market by developing foreign-based assembly or manufacturing facilities.

Direct marketing channel A marketing channel that has no intermediary levels.

Direct-mail marketing Marketing that occurs by sending an offer, announcement, reminder, or other item directly to a person at a particular address.

Direct-response television (DRTV) marketing Direct marketing via television, including direct-response television advertising (or infomercials) and interactive television (iTV) advertising.

Discount A straight reduction in price on purchases during a stated period of time or of larger quantities.

Discount store A retail operation that sells standard merchandise at lower prices by accepting lower margins and selling at higher volume.

Disintermediation The cutting out of marketing channel intermediaries by product or service producers or the displacement of traditional resellers by radical new types of intermediaries.

Distribution center A large, highly automated warehouse designed to receive goods from various plants and suppliers, take orders, fill them efficiently, and deliver goods to customers as quickly as possible.

Diversification Company growth through starting up or acquiring businesses outside the company's current products and markets.

Dynamic pricing Adjusting prices continually to meet the characteristics and needs of individual customers and situations.

E-procurement Purchasing through electronic connections between buyers and sellers-usually online.

Economic community A group of nations organized to work toward common goals in the regulation of international trade.

Economic environment Economic factors that affect consumer purchasing power and spending patterns.

Email marketing Sending highly targeted, tightly personalized, relationship-building marketing messages via email.

Environmental sustainability Developing strategies and practices that create a world economy that the planet can support indefinitely.

Environmental sustainability A management approach that involves developing strategies that both sustain the environment and produce profits for the company.

Environmentalism An organized movement of concerned citizens, businesses, and government agencies designed to protect and improve people's current and future living environment.

Ethnographic research A form of observational research that involves sending trained observers to watch and interact with consumers in their "natural environments."

Event marketing (or event sponsorships) Creating a brand-marketing event or serving as a sole or participating sponsor of events created by others.

Exchange The act of obtaining a desired object from someone by offering something in return.

Exclusive distribution Giving a limited number of dealers the exclusive right to distribute the company's products in their territories.

Execution style The approach, style, tone, words, and format used for presenting an advertising message.

Experimental research Gathering primary data by selecting matched groups of subjects, giving them different treatments, controlling related factors, and checking for differences in group responses.

Exploratory research Marketing research to gather preliminary information that will help define problems and suggest hypotheses.

Exporting Entering foreign markets by selling goods produced in the company's home country, often with little modification.

Factory outlet An off-price retailing operation that is owned and operated by a manufacturer and normally carries the manufacturer's surplus, discontinued, or irregular goods.

Fad A temporary period of unusually high sales driven by consumer enthusiasm and immediate product or brand popularity.

Fashion A currently accepted or popular style in a given field.

Fixed costs (overhead) Costs that do not vary with production or sales level.

Focus group interviewing Personal interviewing that involves inviting small groups of people to gather for a few hours with a trained interviewer to talk about a product, service, or organization. The interviewer "focuses" the group discussion on important issues.

Follow-up The sales step in which a salesperson follows up after the sale to ensure customer satisfaction and repeat business.

Franchise A contractual association between a manufacturer, wholesaler, or service organization (a franchisor) and independent businesspeople (franchisees) who buy the right to own and operate one or more units in the franchise system.

Franchise organization A contractual vertical marketing system in which a channel member, called a franchisor, links several stages in the production-distribution process.

Gender segmentation Dividing a market into different segments based on gender.

Generation X The 49 million people born between 1965 and 1976 in the "birth dearth" following the baby boom.

Generation Z People born after 2000 (although many analysts include people born after 1995) who make up the kids, tweens, and teens markets.

Geographic segmentation Dividing a market into different geographical units, such as nations, states, regions, counties, cities, or even neighborhoods.

Global firm A firm that, by operating in more than one country, gains R&D, production, marketing, and financial advantages in its costs and reputation that are not available to purely domestic competitors.

Good-value pricing Offering just the right combination of quality and good service at a fair price.

Gross margin percentage The percentage of net sales remaining after cost of goods sold—calculated by dividing gross margin by net sales.

Group Two or more people who interact to accomplish individual or mutual goals.

Growth stage The PLC stage in which a product's sales start climbing quickly.

Growth-share matrix A portfolio-planning method that evaluates a company's strategic business units (SBUs) in terms of market growth rate and relative market share.

Handling objections The sales step in which a salesperson seeks out, clarifies, and overcomes any customer objections to buying.

Horizontal marketing system A channel arrangement in which two or more companies at one level join together to follow a new marketing opportunity.

Idea generation The systematic search for new product ideas.

Idea screening Screening new product ideas to spot good ones and drop poor ones as soon as possible.

Income segmentation Dividing a market into different income segments.

Independent off-price retailer An off-price retailer that is independently owned and operated or a division of a larger retail corporation.

Indirect marketing channel A marketing channel containing one or more intermediary levels.

Individual marketing Tailoring products and marketing programs to the needs and preferences of individual customers.

Industrial product A product bought by individuals and organizations for further processing or for use in conducting a business.

Innovative marketing A company should seek real product and marketing improvements.

Inside sales force Salespeople who conduct business from their offices via telephone, online and social media interactions, or visits from buyers.

Integrated logistics management The logistics concept that emphasizes teamwork-both inside the company and among all the marketing channel organizations-to maximize the performance of the entire distribution system.

Integrated marketing communications (IMC) Carefully integrating and coordinating the company's many communications channels to deliver a clear, consistent, and compelling message about the organization and its brands.

Intensive distribution Stocking the product in as many outlets as possible.

Interactive marketing Training service employees in the fine art of interacting with customers to satisfy their needs.

Intermarket (cross-market) segmentation Forming segments of consumers who have similar needs and buying behaviors even though they are located in different countries.

Internal databases Collections of consumer and market information obtained from data sources within the company network.

Internal marketing Orienting and motivating customer-contact employees and supporting service employees to work as a team to provide customer satisfaction.

Introduction stage The PLC stage in which a new product is first distributed and made available for purchase.

Inventory turnover rate (or stockturn rate) The number of times an inventory turns over or is sold during a specified time period (often one year)—calculated based on costs, selling price, or units.

Joint ownership A cooperative venture in which a company creates a local business with investors in a foreign market who share ownership and control.

Joint venturing Entering foreign markets by joining with foreign companies to produce or market products or services.

Learning Changes in an individual's behavior arising from experience.

Licensing Entering foreign markets through developing an agreement with a licensee in the foreign market.

Lifestyle A person's pattern of living as expressed in his or her activities, interests, and opinions.

Line extension Extending an existing brand name to new forms, colors, sizes, ingredients, or flavors of an existing product category.

Local marketing Tailoring brands and marketing to the needs and wants of local customer segments-cities, neighborhoods, and even specific stores.

Macroenvironment The larger societal forces that affect the microenvironment-demographic, economic, natural, technological, political, and cultural forces.

Madison & Vine A term that has come to represent the merging of advertising and entertainment in an effort to break through the clutter and create new avenues for reaching customers with more engaging messages.

Management contracting A joint venture in which the domestic firm supplies the management know-how to a foreign company that supplies the capital; the domestic firm exports management services rather than products.

Manufacturers' and retailers' branches and offices Wholesaling by sellers or buyers themselves rather than through independent wholesalers.

Market The set of all actual and potential buyers of a product or service.

Market development Company growth by identifying and developing new market segments for current company products.

Market offerings Some combination of products, services, information, or experiences offered to a market to satisfy a need or want.

Market penetration Company growth by increasing sales of current products to current market segments without changing the product.

Market potential The upper limit of market demand.

Market segment A group of consumers who respond in a similar way to a given set of marketing efforts.

Market segmentation Dividing a market into distinct groups of buyers who have different needs, characteristics, or behaviors and who might require separate marketing strategies or mixes.

Market share Company sales divided by market sales.

Market targeting (targeting) Evaluating each market segment's attractiveness and selecting one or more segments to serve.

Market-penetration pricing Setting a low price for a new product in order to attract a large number of buyers and a large market share.

Market-skimming pricing (price skimming) Setting a high price for a new product to skim maximum revenues layer by layer from the segments willing to pay the high price; the company makes fewer but more profitable sales.

Marketing The process by which companies engage customers, build strong customer relationships, and create customer value in order to capture value from customers in return.

Marketing analytics The analysis tools, technologies, and processes by which marketers dig out meaningful patterns in big data to gain customer insights and gauge marketing performance.

Marketing channel (distribution channel) A set of interdependent organizations that help make a product or service available for use or consumption by the consumer or business user.

Marketing channel design Designing effective marketing channels by analyzing customer needs, setting channel objectives, identifying major channel alternatives, and evaluating those alternatives.

Marketing channel management Selecting, managing, and motivating individual channel members and evaluating their performance over time.

Marketing concept A philosophy in which achieving organizational goals depends on knowing the needs and wants of target markets and delivering the desired satisfactions better than competitors do.

Marketing control Measuring and evaluating the results of marketing strategies and plans and taking corrective action to ensure that the objectives are achieved.

Marketing environment The actors and forces outside marketing that affect marketing management's ability to build and maintain successful relationships with target customers.

Marketing implementation Turning marketing strategies and plans into marketing actions to accomplish strategic marketing objectives.

Marketing information system (MIS) People and procedures dedicated to assessing information needs, developing the needed information, and helping decision makers to use the information to generate and validate actionable customer and market insights.

Marketing intermediaries Firms that help the company to promote, sell, and distribute its products to final buyers.

Marketing logistics (physical distribution) Planning, implementing, and controlling the physical flow of goods, services, and related information from points of origin to points of consumption to meet customer requirements at a profit.

Marketing management The art and science of choosing target markets and building profitable relationships with them.

Marketing mix The set of tactical marketing tools-product, price, place, and promotion-that the firm blends to produce the response it wants in the target market.

Marketing myopia The mistake of paying more attention to the specific products a company offers than to the benefits and experiences produced by these products.

Marketing research The systematic design, collection, analysis, and reporting of data relevant to a specific marketing situation facing an organization.

Marketing return on investment (or marketing ROI) The net return from a marketing investment divided by the costs of the marketing investment.

Marketing return on sales (or marketing ROS) The percent of net sales attributable to the net marketing contribution—calculated by dividing net marketing contribution by net sales.

Marketing strategy The marketing logic by which the company hopes to create customer value and achieve profitable customer relationships.

Marketing strategy development Designing an initial marketing strategy for a new product based on the product concept.

Marketing Web site A Web site that engages consumers to move them closer to a direct purchase or other marketing outcome.

Maturity stage The PLC stage in which a product's sales growth slows or levels off.

Merchant wholesaler An independently owned wholesale business that takes title to the merchandise it handles.

Microenvironment The actors close to the company that affect its ability to engage and serve its customers-the company, suppliers, marketing intermediaries, customer markets, competitors, and publics.

Micromarketing Tailoring products and marketing programs to the needs and wants of specific individuals and local customer segments; it includes local marketing and individual marketing.

Millennials (or Generation Y) The 83 million children of the baby boomers born between 1977 and 2000.

Mission statement A statement of the organization's purpose-what it wants to accomplish in the larger environment.

Mobile marketing Marketing messages, promotions, and other marketing content delivered to on-the-go consumers through mobile phones, smartphones, tablets, and other mobile devices.

Modified rebuy A business buying situation in which the buyer wants to modify product specifications, prices, terms, or suppliers.

Motive (drive) A need that is sufficiently pressing to direct the person to seek satisfaction.

Multichannel distribution system A distribution system in which a single firm sets up two or more marketing channels to reach one or more customer segments.

Multimodal transportation Combining two or more modes of transportation.

Natural environment The physical environment and the natural resources that are needed as inputs by marketers or that are affected by marketing activities.

Needs States of felt deprivation.

Net marketing contribution (NMC) A measure of marketing profitability that includes only components of profitability controlled by marketing.

Net profit percentage The percentage of each sales dollar going to profit—calculated by dividing net profits by net sales.

New product A good, service, or idea that is perceived by some potential customers as new.

New product development The development of original products, product improvements, product modifications, and new brands through the firm's own product development efforts.

New task A business buying situation in which the buyer purchases a product or service for the first time.

Objective-and-task method Developing the promotion budget by (1) defining specific promotion objectives, (2) determining the tasks needed to achieve these objectives, and (3) estimating the costs of performing these tasks. The sum of these costs is the proposed promotion budget.

Observational research Gathering primary data by observing relevant people, actions, and situations.

Occasion segmentation Dividing a market into segments according to occasions when buyers get the idea to buy, actually make their purchase, or use the purchased item.

Off-price retailer A retailer that buys at less-than-regular wholesale prices and sells at less than retail.

Omni-channel retailing Creating a seamless cross-channel buying experience that integrates in-store, online, and mobile shopping.

Online advertising Advertising that appears while consumers are browsing online, including display ads and search-related ads.

Online focus groups Gathering a small group of people online with a trained moderator to chat about a product, service, or organization and gain qualitative insights about consumer attitudes and behavior.

Online marketing Marketing via the Internet using company Web sites, online ads and promotions, email, online video, and blogs.

Online marketing research Collecting primary data online through Internet surveys, online focus groups, Web-based experiments, or tracking of consumers' online behavior.

Online social networks Online communities-blogs, social networking Web sites, and other online communities-where people socialize or exchange information and opinions.

Operating expense percentage The portion of net sales going to operating expenses—calculated by dividing total expenses by net sales.

Operating ratios The ratios of selected operating statement items to net sales.

Opinion leader A person within a reference group who, because of special skills, knowledge, personality, or other characteristics, exerts social influence on others.

Optional-product pricing The pricing of optional or accessory products along with a main product.

Outside sales force (or field sales force) Salespeople who travel to call on customers in the field.

Packaging The activities of designing and producing the container or wrapper for a product.

Partner relationship management Working closely with partners in other company departments and outside the company to jointly bring greater value to customers.

Percentage-of-sales method Setting the promotion budget at a certain percentage of current or forecasted sales or as a percentage of the unit sales price.

Perception The process by which people select, organize, and interpret information to form a meaningful picture of the world.

Personal selling Personal customer interactions by the firm's sales force for the purpose of engaging customers, making sales, and building customer relationships.

Personality The unique psychological characteristics that distinguish a person or group.

Pleasing products Products that give high immediate satisfaction but may hurt consumers in the long run.

Political environment Laws, government agencies, and pressure groups that influence or limit various organizations and individuals in a given society.

Portfolio analysis The process by which management evaluates the products and businesses that make up the company.

Positioning Arranging for a market offering to occupy a clear, distinctive, and desirable place relative to competing products in the minds of target consumers.

Positioning statement A statement that summarizes company or brand positioning using this form: To (target segment and need) our (brand) is (concept) that (point of difference).

Preapproach The sales step in which a salesperson learns as much as possible about a prospective customer before making a sales call.

Presentation The sales step in which a salesperson tells the "value story" to the buyer, showing how the company's offer solves the customer's problems.

Price The amount of money charged for a product or service, or the sum of the values that customers exchange for the benefits of having or using the product or service.

Price elasticity A measure of the sensitivity of demand to changes in price.

Primary data Information collected for the specific purpose at hand.

Product Anything that can be offered to a market for attention, acquisition, use, or consumption that might satisfy a want or need.

Product adaptation Adapting a product to meet local conditions or wants in foreign markets.

Product bundle pricing Combining several products and offering the bundle at a reduced price.

Product concept The idea that consumers will favor products that offer the most quality, performance, and features; therefore, the organization should devote its energy to making continuous product improvements.

Product concept A detailed version of the new product idea stated in meaningful consumer terms.

Product development Company growth by offering modified or new products to current market segments.

Product development Developing the product concept into a physical product to ensure that the product idea can be turned into a workable market offering.

Product invention Creating new products or services for foreign markets.

Product life cycle (PLC) The course of a product's sales and profits over its lifetime.

Product line A group of products that are closely related because they function in a similar manner, are sold to the same customer groups, are marketed through the same types of outlets, or fall within given price ranges.

Product line pricing Setting the price steps between various products in a product line based on cost differences between the products, customer evaluations of different features, and competitors' prices.

Product/market expansion grid A portfolio-planning tool for identifying company growth opportunities through market penetration, market development, product development, or diversification.

Product mix (or product portfolio) The set of all product lines and items that a particular seller offers for sale.

Product position How a product is defined by consumers on important attributes—the place a product occupies in consumers' minds relative to competing products.

Product quality The characteristics of a product or service that bear on its ability to satisfy stated or implied customer needs.

Product sales force structure A sales force organization in which salespeople specialize in selling only a portion of the company's products or lines.

Production concept The idea that consumers will favor products that are available and highly affordable; therefore, the organization should focus on improving production and distribution efficiency.

Pro forma (or projected) profit-andloss statement (or income statement or operating statement) A statement that shows projected revenues less budgeted expenses and estimates the projected net profit for an organization, product, or brand during a specific planning period, typically a year.

Promotion mix (marketing communications mix) The specific blend of promotion tools that the company uses to engage customers, persuasively communicate customer value, and build customer relationships.

Promotional pricing Temporarily pricing products below the list price, and sometimes even below cost, to increase short-run sales.

Prospecting The sales step in which a salesperson or company identifies qualified potential customers.

Psychographic segmentation Dividing a market into different segments based on social class, lifestyle, or personality characteristics.

Psychological pricing Pricing that considers the psychology of prices and not simply the economics; the price is used to say something about the product.

Public Any group that has an actual or potential interest in or impact on an organization's ability to achieve its objectives.

Public relations (PR) Building good relations with the company's various publics by obtaining favorable publicity, building up a good corporate image, and handling or heading off unfavorable rumors, stories, and events.

Pull strategy A promotion strategy that calls for spending a lot on consumer advertising and promotion to induce final consumers to buy the product, creating a demand vacuum that "pulls" the product through the channel.

Push strategy A promotion strategy that calls for using the sales force and trade promotion to push the product through channels. The producer promotes the product to channel members who in turn promote it to final consumers.

Reference prices Prices that buyers carry in their minds and refer to when they look at a given product.

Relevant costs Costs that will occur in the future and that will vary across the alternatives being considered.

Retailer A business whose sales come primarily from retailing.

Retailing All the activities involved in selling products or services directly to final consumers for their personal, nonbusiness use.

Return on advertising investment The net return on advertising investment divided by the costs of the advertising investment.

Return on investment (ROI) A measure of managerial effectiveness and efficiency—net profit before taxes divided by total investment.

Return on investment (ROI) pricing (or target-return pricing) A cost-based pricing method that determines price based on a specified rate of return on investment.

Sales force management Analyzing, planning, implementing, and controlling sales force activities.

Sales promotion Short-term incentives to encourage the purchase or sale of a product or a service.

Sales promotion Short-term incentives to encourage the purchase or sale of a product or a service.

Sales quota A standard that states the amount a salesperson should sell and how sales should be divided among the company's products.

Salesperson An individual who represents a company to customers by performing one or more of the following activities: prospecting, communicating, selling, servicing, information gathering, and relationship building.

Salutary products Products that have low immediate appeal but may benefit consumers in the long run.

Sample A segment of the population selected for marketing research to represent the population as a whole.

Secondary data Information that already exists somewhere, having been collected for another purpose.

Segmented pricing Selling a product or service at two or more prices, where the difference in prices is not based on differences in costs.

Selective distribution The use of more than one but fewer than all of the intermediaries that are willing to carry the company's products.

Selling concept The idea that consumers will not buy enough of the firm's products unless the firm undertakes a large-scale selling and promotion effort.

Selling process The steps that salespeople follow when selling, which include prospecting and qualifying, preapproach, approach, presentation and demonstration, handling objections, closing, and follow-up.

Sense-of-mission marketing A company should define its mission in broad *social* terms rather than narrow *product* terms.

Service An activity, benefit, or satisfaction offered for sale that is essentially intangible and does not result in the ownership of anything.

Service inseparability Services are produced and consumed at the same time and cannot be separated from their providers.

Service intangibility Services cannot be seen, tasted, felt, heard, or smelled before they are bought.

Service perishability Services cannot be stored for later sale or use.

Service profit chain The chain that links service firm profits with employee and customer satisfaction.

Service retailer A retailer whose product line is actually a service; examples include hotels, airlines, banks, colleges, and many others.

Service variability The quality of services may vary greatly depending on who provides them and when, where, and how they are provided.

Share of customer The portion of the customer's purchasing that a company gets in its product categories.

Shopper marketing Focusing the entire marketing process on turning shoppers into buyers as they approach the point of sale, whether during in-store, online, or mobile shopping.

Shopping center A group of retail businesses built on a site that is planned, developed, owned, and managed as a unit.

Shopping product A consumer product that the customer, in the process of selecting and purchasing, usually compares on such attributes as suitability, quality, price, and style.

Showrooming The shopping practice of coming into retail store showrooms to check out merchandise and prices but instead buying from an online-only rival, sometimes while in the store.

Social class Relatively permanent and ordered divisions in a society whose members share similar values, interests, and behaviors.

Social marketing Using traditional business marketing concepts and tools to create behaviors that will create individual and societal well-being.

Social media Independent and commercial online social networks where people congregate to socialize and share messages, opinions, pictures, videos, and other content.

Social selling Using online, mobile, and social media to engage customers, build stronger customer relationships, and augment sales performance.

Societal marketing A company should make marketing decisions by considering consumers' wants, the company's requirements, consumers' long-run interests, and society's long-run interests.

Societal marketing concept The idea that a company's marketing decisions should consider consumers' wants, the company's requirements, consumers' long-run interests, and society's long-run interests.

Spam Unsolicited, unwanted commercial email messages.

Specialty product A consumer product with unique characteristics or brand identification for which a significant group of buyers is willing to make a special purchase effort.

Specialty store A retail store that carries a narrow product line with a deep assortment within that line.

Standardized global marketing A global marketing strategy that basically uses the same marketing strategy and mix in all of the company's international markets.

Store brand (or private brand) A brand created and owned by a reseller of a product or service.

Straight product extension Marketing a product in a foreign market without making significant changes to the product.

Straight rebuy A business buying situation in which the buyer routinely reorders something without any modifications.

Strategic planning The process of developing and maintaining a strategic fit between the organization's goals and capabilities and its changing marketing opportunities.

Style A basic and distinctive mode of expression.

Subculture A group of people with shared value systems based on common life experiences and situations.

Supermarket A large, low-cost, low-margin, high-volume, self-service store that carries a wide variety of grocery and household products.

Superstore A store much larger than a regular supermarket that offers a large assortment of routinely purchased food products, nonfood items, and services.

Supplier development Systematic development of networks of supplier-partners to ensure a dependable supply of products and materials for use in making products or reselling them to others.

Supply chain management Managing upstream and downstream value-added flows of materials, final goods, and related information among suppliers, the company, resellers, and final consumers.

Survey research Gathering primary data by asking people questions about their knowledge, attitudes, preferences, and buying behavior.

Sustainable marketing Socially and environmentally responsible marketing that meets the present needs of consumers and businesses while also preserving or enhancing the ability of future generations to meet their needs.

SWOT analysis An overall evaluation of the company's strengths (S), weaknesses (W), opportunities (O), and threats (T).

Systems selling (or solutions selling) Buying a complete solution to a problem from a single seller, thus avoiding all the separate decisions involved in a complex buying situation.

Target costing Pricing that starts with an ideal selling price, then targets costs that will ensure that the price is met.

Target market A set of buyers sharing common needs or characteristics that the company decides to serve.

Team selling Using teams of people from sales, marketing, engineering, finance, technical support, and even upper management to service large, complex accounts.

Team-based new product development New product development in which various company departments work closely together, overlapping the steps in the product development process to save time and increase effectiveness.

Technological environment Forces that create new technologies, creating new product and market opportunities.

Telemarketing Using the telephone to sell directly to customers.

Territorial sales force structure A sales force organization that assigns each salesperson to an exclusive geographic territory in which that salesperson sells the company's full line.

Test marketing The stage of new product development at which the product and its proposed marketing program are tested in realistic market settings.

Third-party logistics (3PL) provider An independent logistics provider that performs any or all of the functions required to get a client's product to market.

Total costs The sum of the fixed and variable costs for any given level of production.

Total market demand The total volume that would be bought by a defined consumer group in a defined geographic area in a defined time period in a defined marketing environment under a defined level and mix of industry marketing effort.

Total market strategy Integrating ethnic themes and cross-cultural perspectives within a brand's mainstream marketing, appealing to consumer similarities across subcultural segments rather than differences.

Trade promotions Sales promotion tools used to persuade resellers to carry a brand, give it shelf space, promote it in advertising, and push it to consumers.

Undifferentiated (mass) marketing A market-coverage strategy in which a firm decides to ignore market segment differences and go after the whole market with one offer.

Unit contribution The amount that each unit contributes to covering fixed costs—the difference between price and variable costs.

Unsought product A consumer product that the consumer either does not know about or knows about but does not normally consider buying.

Value-added pricing Attaching value-added features and services to differentiate a company's offers and charging higher prices.

Value-based pricing Offering just the right combination of quality and good service at a fair price.

Value chain The series of internal departments that carry out value-creating activities to design, produce, market, deliver, and support a firm's products.

Value delivery network A network composed of the company, suppliers, distributors, and, ultimately, customers who partner with each other to improve the performance of the entire system in delivering customer value.

Value proposition The full positioning of a brand-the full mix of benefits on which it is differentiated and positioned.

Value-added pricing Attaching value-added features and services to differentiate a company's offers and charging higher prices.

Variable costs Costs that vary directly with the level of production.

Vertical marketing system (VMS) A channel structure in which producers, wholesalers, and retailers act as a unified system. One channel member owns the others, has contracts with them, or has so much power that they all cooperate.

Viral marketing The digital version of word-of-mouth marketing: videos, ads, and other marketing content that is so infectious that customers will seek it out or pass it along to friends.

Wants The form human needs take as they are shaped by culture and individual personality.

Warehouse club An off-price retailer that sells a limited selection of brand name grocery items, appliances, clothing, and other goods at deep discounts to members who pay annual membership fees.

Whole-channel view Designing international channels that take into account the entire global supply chain and marketing channel, forging an effective global value delivery network.

Wholesaler A firm engaged primarily in wholesaling activities.

Wholesaling All the activities involved in selling goods and services to those buying for resale or business use.

Word-of-mouth influence The impact of the personal words and recommendations of trusted friends, family, associates, and other consumers on buying behavior.

Workload method An approach to determining sales force size based on the workload required and the time available for selling.

References

Chapter 1

1. Mark Fidelman, "Nike Is Dominating the World Cup—Here's Why," *Forbes*, July 1, 2014, www.forbes.com/sites/markfidelman/2014/07/01/nike-is-dominating-the-world-cup-heres-why/; Grace Chung, "Non-Sponsor Nike Trounces Adidas for World Cup Video Views," *Advertising Age*, July 14, 2014, http://adage.com/print/294114/; Scott Cendrowski, "Nike's New Marketing Mojo," *Fortune*, February 13, 2012, http://fortune.com/2012/02/13/nikes-new-marketing-mojo/; Mary Lisbeth D'Amico, "Report Sends Nike and Adidas to Head of Digital Marketing Class," *Clickz*, September 25, 2012, www.clickz.com/clickz/news/2208172/report-sends-nike-and-adidas-to-head-of-digital-marketing-class; Daniel Newman, "Risk Everything: Nike Does for World Cup 2014, and Wins!" *Forbes*, June 9, 2014, www.forbes.com/sites/danielnewman/2014/06/09/risk-everything-nike-does-for-world-cup-2014-and-wins/; "Top Ad Campaigns of the 21st Century: 2—Nike+," *Advertising Age*, http://adage.com/lp/top15/#nikeplus, accessed June 2015; and http://investors.nikeinc.com/Investors and https://secure-nikeplus.nike.com/plus/, accessed September 2015.
2. See "Leading Social Networks Worldwide," www.statista.com/statistics/272014/global-social-networks-ranked-by-number-of-users/, accessed June 2015; Justin Fox, "Still Sweet on Coke and Pepsi?" *Bloomberg View*, January 15, 2015, www.bloombergview.com/articles/2015-01-21/still-sweet-on-coke-and-pepsi; and "Top 250 Global Retailers, 2015," *National Retail Federation*, https://nrf.com/2015/global250-table.
3. See Philip Kotler and Kevin Lane Keller, *Marketing Management*, 15th ed. (Hoboken, NJ: Pearson Education, 2016), p. 5.
4. The American Marketing Association offers the following definition: "Marketing is the activity, set of institutions, and processes for creating, communicating, delivering, and exchanging offerings that have value for customers, clients, partners, and society at large." See www.marketingpower.com/_layouts/Dictionary.aspx?dLetter=M, accessed September 2015.
5. See Daniel P. Smith, "Keep in Touch," *QSR Magazine*, July 2013, www.qsrmagazine.com/executive-insights/keep-touch; and Phil Wahba, "Back on Target," *Fortune*, March 1, 2015, p. 86–94.
6. See Samantha Shankman, "The Simple Message behind San Diego's $9 Million Ad Campaign," *Skift*, February 5, 2015, http://skift.com/2015/02/05/the-simple-message-behind-san-diegos-9-million-ad-campaign/; and http://stoptextsstopwrecks.org/#home, accessed September 2015.
7. See Theodore Levitt's classic article, "Marketing Myopia," *Harvard Business Review*, July–August 1960, pp. 45–56. For more recent discussions, see Minette E. Drumright and Mary C. Gentile, "The New Marketing Myopia," *Journal of Public Policy & Marketing*, Spring 2010, pp. 4–11; Roberto Friedmann, "What Business Are You In?" *Marketing Management*, Summer 2011, pp. 18–23; and Al Ries, "'Marketing Myopia' Revisited: Perhaps a Narrow Vision Is Better Business," *Advertising Age*, December 4, 2013, http://adage.com/print/245511.
8. See www.americangirl.com/stores/, accessed September 2015.
9. See https://play.google.com/store/apps/details?id=co.vine.android, accessed September 2015.
10. "The Difference in Creating Companies and Categories," *happycustomer*, March 4, 2014, http://happycustomer.stellaservice.com/2014/03/04/column-the-difference-in-creating-companies-and-categories/.
11. See Michael E. Porter and Mark R. Kramer, "Creating Shared Value, "*Harvard Business Review*, January–February 2011, pp. 63–77; Marc Pfitzer, Valerie Bockstette, and Mike Stamp, "Innovating for Shared Value," *Harvard Business Review*, September 2013, pp. 100–107; "About Shared Value," *Shared Value Initiative*, http://sharedvalue.org/about-shared-value, accessed September 2015; and "Shared Value," www.fsg.org, accessed September 2015.
12. Michael Krauss, "Evolution of an Academic: Kotler on Marketing 3.0, "*Marketing News*, January 30, 2011, p. 12; and Simon Mainwaring, "Marketing 3.0 Will Be Won by Purpose-Driven, Social Brands," *Forbes*, July 16, 2013, www.forbes.com/sites/ simonmainwaring/2013/07/16/marketing-3-0-will-be-won-by-purpose-driven-social-brands-infographic/.
13. See Scott Campbell, "Lush Defies the Christmas Retail Slump," *The Telegraph*, January 6, 2014, www.telegraph.co.uk/finance/ newsbysector/retailandconsumer/10554068/Lush-defies-the-Christmas-retail-slump.html; and "Lush Life: We Believe," www.lushusa.com/on/demandware.store/Sites-Lush-Site/en_US/AboutUs-OurStoryShow?cid=we-believe, accessed September 2015.
14. Based on information from Keenan Mayo, "A Cooler Fit for the Apocalypse," *Bloomberg Businessweek*, October 28–November 3, 2013, p. 62, and http://store.yeticoolers.com/, accessed September 2015.
15. See Stuart Elliott, "Putting on the Ritz, Six Words at a Time," *New York Times*, May 29, 2015, p. B11; Michael Bush, "Why You Should Be Putting on the Ritz," *Advertising Age*, June 21, 2010, p. 1; http://corporate.ritzcarlton.com/en/About/Awards.htm, accessed June 2015; and "Stories That Stay with You," www.ritzcarlton.com/en/StoriesThatStay.htm, accessed September 2015.
16. "Delighting the Customer Doesn't Pay," *Sales & Marketing Management*, November 11, 2013, http://salesandmarketing.com/content/delighting-customers-doesnt-pay.
17. See www.walgreens.com/Balance, accessed September 2015.
18. For more information, see www.apple.com/usergroups/ and www.webernation.com, accessed September 2015.
19. See Gordon Wyner, "Getting Engaged," *Marketing Management*, Fall 2012, pp. 4–9; David Aponovich, "Powered by People, Fueled by Optimism," *Fast Company*, July 18, 2012, www.fastcompany.com/1842834/life-good-powered-people-fueled-optimism; Celia Brown, "Life is good Redefines Retailing through Joy," *Forbes*, January 17, 2014, www.forbes.com/sites/sap/2014/01/17/life-is-good-redefines-retail-through-joy/; and www.lifeisgood.com and www.lifeisgood.com/good-vibes/, accessed September 2015.
20. See http://mystarbucksidea.force.com, accessed September 2015.
21. "2014 USA Today Ad Meter," http://admeter.usatoday.com/, accessed February 2015; "How a $2,000 Doritos Super Bowl Ad Became a Million-Dollar Sensation," *Washington Post*, February 4, 2015, www.washingtonpost.com/news/grade-point/wp/2015/02/04/how-a-2000-doritos-super-bowl-ad-became-a-million-dollar-sensation/; and www.doritos.com/, accessed September 2015.
22. See "#Bashtag: Avoiding User Outcry in Social Media," *WordStream*, March 8, 2013, www.wordstream.com/blog/ws/2013/03/07/bashtag-avoiding-social-media-backlash; and "What Is Hashtag Hijacking?" *Small Business Trends*, August 18, 2013, http://smallbiztrends.com/2013/08/what-is-hashtag-hijacking-2.html.
23. See www.stewleonards.com/about-us/company-story, accessed September 2015.
24. See Mai Erne, "Calculating Customer Lifetime Value," HaraPartners, www.harapartners.com/blog/calculating-lifetime-value/, accessed September 2015.
25. See Timothy Stenovec, "Amazon Prime Members Spend an Astonishing $1,500 a Year, Survey Says," *Huffington Post*, January 27, 2015, www.huffingtonpost.com/2015/01/27/amazon-prime-spending_n_6556374.html; Brad Stone, "What's in the Box? Instant Gratification, *Bloomberg Businessweek*, November 29–December 5, 2010, pp. 39–40; and www.amazon.com/gp/prime/ref=footer_prime, accessed September 2015.
26. For more discussions on customer equity, see Roland T. Rust, Valerie A. Zeithaml, and Katherine N. Lemon, *Driving Customer Equity* (New York: Free Press, 2000); Roland T. Rust, Katherine N. Lemon, and Valerie A. Zeithaml, "Return on Marketing: Using Customer Equity to Focus Marketing Strategy," *Journal of Marketing*, January 2004, pp. 109–127; Christian Gronroos and Pekka Helle, "Return on Relationships: Conceptual Understanding and Measurement of Mutual Gains from Relational Business Engagements," *Journal of Business & Industrial Marketing*, Vol. 27, No. 5, 2012, pp. 344–359; and Peter C. Verhoef and Katherine N. Lemon, "Successful Customer Value Management: Key Lessons and Emerging Trends," *European Management Journal*, February 2013, p. 1.
27. This example is based on one found in Rust, Lemon, and Zeithaml, "Where Should the Next Marketing Dollar Go?" *Marketing Management*, September–October 2001, pp. 24–28; with information from Grant McCracken, "Provocative Cadillac, Rescuing the Brand from Bland," *Harvard Business Review*, March 4, 2014, http://blogs.hbr.org/2014/03/provocative-cadillac-rescuing-the-brand-from-bland/; Robert Klara. "Cadillac's Image Gets a Tune-Up," *Adweek*, February 23, 2015, p. 13; and www.dare-greatly.com, accessed September 2015.

28. Based on Werner Reinartz and V. Kumar, "The Mismanagement of Customer Loyalty," *Harvard Business Review*, July 2002, pp. 86–94. Also see Chris Lema, "Not All Customers Are Equal—Butterflies & Barnacles," April 18, 2013, http://chrislema.com/not-all-customers-are-equal-butterflies-barnacles/; Jill Avery, Susan Fournier, and John Wittenbraker, "Unlock the Mysteries of Your Customer Relationships," *Harvard Business Review*, July–August 2014, pp. 72–81, and "Telling Customers 'You're Fired,'" *Sales and Marketing.com*, September/October 2014, p. 8.
29. See "Internet Usage Statistics, *Inernet World Stats*, www.internetworldstats .com/stats.htm; accessed June 2015; and "Mobile Technology Fact Sheet," www.pewinternet.org/fact-sheets/mobile-technology-fact-sheet/, accessed September 2015.
30. "Digital Set to Surpass TV in Time Spent with US Media," *eMarketer*, August 1, 2013, www.emarketer.com/Article/Digital- Set-Surpass-TV-Time-Spent-with-US-Media/1010096; and Marla Schimke, "Mobile as Marketing's Savior," *Adweek*, December 15, 2014, p. 19.
31. Chris Gayomali, "Brands Are Wasting Their Time and Money on Facebook and Twitter, Report Says," *Fast Company*, November 19, 2014, www .fastcompany.com/3038801; "Greatness Awaits: Sony PlayStation PS4 Launch," *Empowered*, http://groundswelldiscussion.com/groundswell/awards/detail.php?id=1174, accessed June 2015; Roger Katz, "2015 Will Be the Year of the Brand Community—Here's Why," *ClickZ*, January 23, 2015, www.clickz.com/clickz/column/2391666/2015-will-be-the-year-of-the-brand-community-here-s-why; and https://community.petco.com/, http://community.sephora.com/, and http://greatnessawaits.playstation .com/en-us/, accessed September 2015.
32. See Stuart Feil, "How to Win Friends and Influence People," *Adweek*, September 12, 2013, pp. S1–S7; and Salesforce.com "Just Published: 2015 State of Marketing Report," January 13, 2015, http://blogs.salesforce.com/company/2015/01/2015-state-of-marketing.html.
33. See Calla Cofield, "Social Media: NASA's Not So Secret Weapon for the Orion Test Flight," *Space*, December 3, 2014, www.space.com/27912-nasa-orion-spacecraft-social-media-blitz.html; Laura Nichols, "NASA Soars on Social Media with Orion Spacecraft," *PRWeek*, December 18, 2015, www.prweek.com/article/1327011; "By the Letters EFT: Sesame Street Muppets Count Down to NASA Launch," *Collect Space*, November 24, 2014, www.collectspace.com/news/news-112514a-orion-eft1-muppets-countdown.html; and www.nasa.gov, accessed September 2015.
34. Michael Applebaum, "Mobile Magnetism," *Adweek*, June 25, 2012, pp. S1–S9; and Bill Briggs, "M-Commerce Is Saturating the Globe," *Internet Retailer*, February 20, 2014, www.internetretailer.com/2014/02/20/m-commerce-saturating-globe.
35. "Mobile Marketing: How Redbox Drove 1.5 Million Texts and Added 200,000 Mobile Participants in 10 Days," *Marketing Sherpa*, October 6, 2011, www.marketingsherpa.com/article/case-study/how-redbox-drove-15-million; www.youtube.com/watch?v=c1nLbQeXAXc and www .redbox.com/textclub, accessed September 2015.
36. See John Gerzema, "How U.S. Consumers Are Steering the Spend Shift," *Advertising Age*, October 11, 2010, p. 26; Gregg Fairbrothers and Catalina Gorla, "The Decline and Rise of Thrift," *Forbes*, April 23, 2012, www.forbes .com/sites/greggfairbrothers/2012/04/23/the-decline-and-rise-of-thrift/.
37. See "Our Mission," https://corporate.target.com/about/mission-values, accessed June 2015.
38. See Lisa Wirthman, "How a Lemonade Stand Sparked a Movement to Cure Pediatric Cancer," *Forbes*, January 15, 2014; Jennifer Aaker and Andy Smith, "The Dragonfly Effect," *Stanford Social Innovation Review*," Winter 2011, pp. 31–35; and www.alexslemonade.org, accessed September 2015.
39. "100 Leading National Advertisers," *Advertising Age*, July 13, 2015, p. 15.
40. www.aboutmcdonalds.com/mcd and www.nikeinc.com, accessed September 2015.
41. See www.benjerry.com/values, www.benandjerrysfoundation.org and www.unilever.com/brands-in-action/detail/ben-and-jerrys/291995, accessed September 2015.

Chapter 2

1. David Kaplan, "Starbucks: The Art of Endless Transformation," *Inc.*, June, 2014, pp. 82–86+; Laura Lorenzetti, "Fortune's World's Most Admired Companies: Starbucks, Where Innovation Is Always Brewing," *Fortune*, October 30, 2014, http://fortune.com/2014/10/30/starbucks-innovation-cafe-to-classroom/; "Starbucks Corporation: Fiscal 2007 Annual Report," http://media.corporate-ir.net/media_files/irol/99/99518/2007AR.pdf; Julia Hanna, "Starbucks, Reinvented: A Seven-Year Study on Schultz, Strategy, and Reinventing a Brilliant Brand," *Forbes*, August 25, 2014, www.forbes .com/sites/hbsworkingknowledge/2014/08/25/starbucks-reinvented/; http://roastery.starbucks.com, accessed March 2015; and Starbucks annual reports and other information accessed at www.starbucks.com, September 2015.
2. The NASA mission statement is from www.nasa.gov/about/highlights/what_does_nasa_do.html, accessed June 2015.
3. For more discussion of mission statements and examples, both good and bad, see Jack and Suzy Welch, "State Your Business; Too Many Mission Statements Are Loaded with Fatheaded Jargon. Play It Straight," *BusinessWeek*, January 14, 2008, p. 80; Setayesh Sattari et al., "How Readable Are Mission Statements? An Exploratory Study," *Corporate Communications*," 2011, p. 4; and www.missionstatements.com/fortune_500_mission_statements.html, accessed September 2015.
4. Based on information from Demitrios Kalogeropoulos, "3 Reasons Buffalo Wild Wings Can Keep Soaring in 2015," *The Motley Fool*, January 9, 2015, www.fool.com/investing/general/2015/01/09/3-reasons-why-buffalo-wild-wings-can-keep-soaring.aspx; "Buffalo Wild Wings," a 22SQUARED case study, www.22squared.com/work/project/buffalo-wild-wings, accessed June 2015; Brandon Southward, "The Crowd Goes Wild," *Fortune*, July 22, 2013, p. 18; Tanya Dua, "The Buffalo Wild Wings Recipe for the "Ultimate Sports Experience," *Digiday*, August 4, 2015, http://digiday.com/brands/buffalo-wild-wings-recipe-ultimate-sports-experience/; and www .buffalowildwings.com, accessed September 2015.
5. Information about CVS Health and its mission and activities from www.cvshealth.com/about-us, www.cvshealth.com/about-us/our-story-building-bridge-better-health, and www.cvshealth.com/our-businesses, accessed September 2015.
6. See "General Electric Co.," *Reuters*, www.reuters.com/finance/stocks/companyProfile?symbol=GE.N, accessed June 2015; and www.ge.com/ar2014/assets/pdf/GE_AR14.pdf and www.ge.com/products, accessed September 2015.
7. The following discussion is based in part on information found at www .bcg.com/documents/file13904.pdf, accessed September 2015.
8. See http://corporate.disney.go.com/investors/annual_reports.html, accessed September 2015.
9. H. Igor Ansoff, "Strategies for Diversification," *Harvard Business Review*, September–October 1957, pp. 113–124.
10. Information about Under Armour in this section is from Sarah Meehan, "Here's How Much Under Armour Spent on Marketing Last Year," *Business Journal*, February 24, 2015, www.bizjournals.com/baltimore/news/2015/02/24/heres-how-much-under-armour-spent-on-marketing .html?page=all; Bradley Seth McNew, "2 Ways Under Armour Inc Can Continue to Soar in 2015," *The Motley Fool*, December 15, 2014, www .fool.com/investing/general/2014/12/15/2-ways-under-armour-can-continue-soaring-in-2015.aspx; Nick Gardetto, "Under Armour: Growth at an Expensive Price," *Seeking Alpha*, July 31, 2014, http://seekingalpha .com/article/2364655; and various pages at www.underarmour.com and http://investor.underarmour.com, accessed September 2015.
11. See Michael E. Porter, *Competitive Advantage: Creating and Sustaining Superior Performance* (New York: Free Press, 1985); and Michael E. Porter, "What Is Strategy?" *Harvard Business Review*, November–December 1996, pp. 61–78. Also see "The Value Chain," www.quickmba.com/strategy/value-chain, accessed June 2015; and Philip Kotler and Kevin Lane Keller, *Marketing Management*, 15th ed. (Hoboken, NJ: Prentice Hall, 2016), Chapter 2.
12. Nirmalya Kumar, "The CEO's Marketing Manifesto," *Marketing Management*, November–December 2008, pp. 24–29; and Tom French and others, "We're All Marketers Now," *McKinsey Quarterly*, July 2011, www.mckinseyquarterly.com/Were_all_marketers_now_2834.
13. See www.gapinc.com/content/gapinc/html/aboutus/ourbrands/gap.html, accessed September 2015.
14. "100 Leading National Advertisers," *Advertising Age*, June 23, 2014, p. 16.
15. The four *P*s classification was first suggested by E. Jerome McCarthy, *Basic Marketing: A Managerial Approach* (Homewood, IL: Irwin, 1960). The four As are discussed in Jagdish Sheth and Rajendra Sisodia, *The 4 A's of Marketing: Creating Value for Customer, Company and Society* (New York: Routledge, 2012); and Kotler and Keller, *Marketing Management*, p. 26.
16. Tim Dunn, "Is the Era of CMO Over?" *Adweek*, March 2, 2015, p. 14.
17. "Study Finds Marketers Don't Practice ROI They Preach," *Advertising Age*, March 11, 2012, http://adage.com/article/233243/; "Accountability Remains Senior Marketers' Top Concern," *Marketing Charts*, March 7, 2013, www .marketingcharts.com/wp/topics/branding/accountability-remains-senior-marketers-top-concern-27565/; "Quantitative Proof of Marketing Spend's ROI Still Eludes CMOs," *Marketing Charts*, February 21, 2014, www .marketingcharts.com/wp/traditional/quantitative-proof-of-marketing-spends-impact-still-eludes-cmos-40005/; and Christine Moorman, "From Marketing Spend to Marketing Accountability," *Marketing News*, May 2014, pp. 24–25.

18. For more on marketing dashboards and financial measures of marketing performance, see Ofer Mintz and Imran S. Currim, "What Drives Managerial Use of Marketing Financial Metrics and Does Metric Use Affect Performance of Marketing-Mix Activities?" *Journal of Marketing,* March 2013, pp. 17–40; and http://marketingnpv.com/dashboard-platform, accessed September 2015.
19. For a full discussion of this model and details on customer-centered measures of marketing return on investment, see Roland T. Rust, Katherine N. Lemon, and Valerie A. Zeithaml, "Return on Marketing: Using Customer Equity to Focus Marketing Strategy," *Journal of Marketing*, January 2004, pp. 109–127; Roland T. Rust, Katherine N. Lemon, and Das Narayandas, *Customer Equity Management* (Upper Saddle River, NJ: Prentice Hall, 2005); Roland T. Rust, "Seeking Higher ROI? Base Strategy on Customer Equity," *Advertising Age,* September 10, 2007, pp. 26–27; Andreas Persson and Lynette Ryals, "Customer Assets and Customer Equity: Management and Measurement Issues," *Marketing Theory*, December 2010, pp. 417–436; and Kirsten Korosec, "'Toma- to, Tomäto'? Not Exactly," *Marketing News*, January 13, 2012, p. 8.

Chapter 3

1. Devin Leonard, "Bad News in Cereal City," *Bloomberg Businessweek*, March 2–8, 2015, pp. 42-47; John Kell, "Decline In Cereal Sales Bites Into Kellogg's Results," *Fortune*, October 30, 2014, http://fortune.com/2014/10/30/kellogg-breakfast-sales-drop/; Jack Lanshi, "These 2 Charts Show the Biggest Change in America's Breakfast," *Time*, February 12, 2015, http://time.com/3705987/skipping-breakfast-cereal-kellogg/; and http://investor.kelloggs.com/investor-relations/annual-reports/default.aspx and www.kellogg.com, accessed September 2015.
2. Ginger Christ, "Supplier Relationships Key to Honda's Healthy Profit Margins," *Industry Week*, May 23, 2012, www.industryweek.com/blog/supplier-relationships-key-hondas-healthy-profit-margins; "2014 Annual Automotive OEM-Supplier Relations Study Shows Toyota and Honda on Top," *PR Newswire*, May 12, 2014; and www.hondainamerica.com/parts-and-suppliers and http://world.honda.com/profile/philosophy/, accessed September 2015.
3. Information from Robert J. Benes, Abbie Jarman, and Ashley Williams, "2007 NRA Sets Records," www.chefmagazine.com, accessed September 2007; "Thought Leadership Begins with Experience," *fishbowl,* www.fishbowl.com/coca-cola-offers-restaurant-customers-new-digital-marketing-solutions-powered-by-fishbowl/, accessed September 2015; and www.cokesolutions.com, accessed September 2015.
4. See http://officedepotfoundation.org/, http://officedepotfoundation.org/?page_id=428, http://officedepotfoundation.org/?page_id=164, and http://officedepotfoundation.org/?page_id=196, accessed June 2015. Listen Learn Care® is a registered trademark of Office Depot, Inc.
5. World POPClock, U.S. Census Bureau, at www.census.gov/popclock/, accessed June 2015. This Web site provides continuously updated projections of the U.S. and world populations.
6. U.S. Census Bureau projections and POPClock Projection, at www.census.gov/main/www/popclock.html, accessed September 2015.
7. Charles Kenny, "The Reproductive Recession," *Bloomberg Businessweek,* February 11, 2014, pp. 4–5.
8. See Tracy Sestili, "5 Reasons Why You Should Market to Baby Boomers," *Social Media Today*, January 27, 2014, http://socialmediatoday.com/tracy-sestili/2115511/5-reasons-why-you-should-market-baby-boomers-45-65-year-olds; and "50+ Facts and Fiction: Size, Wealth and Spending of 50+ Consumers," *Immersion Active,* March 9, 2015, www.immersionactive.com/resources/size-wealth-spending-50-consumers/.
9. "50+ Facts and Fiction: Mature Consumers Online," *Immersive Action,* March 8, 2015, www.immersionactive.com/resources/50-consumers-online/.
10. See "50+ Active & Healthy Living," www.amazon.com/gp/browse.html/?node=5856180011, accessed June 2015; and http://www.boomnc.com/wp-content/uploads/BOOM-media-kit.pdf, accessed September 2015.
11. For more discussion, see Penney Fox, "Gen X and Social Media: Stuck in the Middle," *Business 2 Community,* July 9, 2014, www.business2community.com/social-media/gen-x-social-media-stuck-middle-0939476; and "Generations Divided on Device Preferences," February 6, 2015, www.millwardbrown.com/global-navigation/news/press-releases/full-release/2015/02/06/generations-divided-on-device-preferences;
12. See Joe Ruiz, "How Lowe's Is Sustaining Customer Relationships," *Maximize Social Business*, January 27, 2014, http://maximizesocial business.com/lowes-sustaining-customer-relationships-12506/; and www.lowes.com/mobile, www.lowes.com, www.youtube.com/watch?v=zbFX7p6ZGTk, and www.pinterest.com/lowes/, accessed September 2015.
13. See Greg Petro, "Millennial Engagement and Loyalty—Make Them Part of the Process," *Forbes,* March 21, 2013, www.forbes.com/sites/gregpetro/2013/03/21/millennial-engagement-and-loyalty-make-them-part-of-the-process/; and "AT&T's Catherine Borda Spills the Secrets to Millennial Marketing," *Adweek,* March 3, 2015, www.adweek.com/print/163219.
14. Ellen Byron, "Marketing Decoder: Kitchen Appliances for 20-somethings," *Wall Street Journal*, June 25, 2013; Alan Wolf, "GE Develops Kitchen Line for Millennials," *Twice*, July 8, 2013, p. 44; and www.geappliances.com/products/artistry/, accessed September 2015.
15. See "Moxy Milan Malpensa Set to Open in September Followed by a Further Five Hotels in Europe by End of 2015," *Marriott New Center,* March 3, 2014, http://news.marriott.com/moxy-hotels/; "Moxy Hotels Looks to the Future in Europe," Marriott News Center, March 3, 2015, http://news.marriott.com/2015/03/moxy-hotels-looks-to-the-future-in-europe-150-hotels-and-25000-rooms-expected-by-2020.html; and http://moxy-hotels.marriott.com/, accessed September 2015.
16. See Julia Glum, "Marketing to Generation Z," *International Business Times*, January 13, 2015, www.ibtimes.com/marketing-generation-z-millennials-move-aside-brands-shift-focus-under-18-customers-1782220; and Ruth Bernstein, "Move Over Millennials—Here Comes Gen Z," *Advertising Age*, January 21, 2015, www.adage.com/article/cmo-strategy/move-millennials-gen-z/296577/.
17. See "GenZ: Digital in Their DNA"; Shannon Bryant, "'Generation Z' Children More Tech-Savvy; Prefer Gadgets, Not Toys," *Marketing Forecast,* April 3, 2013, www.ad-ology.com/tag/tech-savvy-children/#.U5d9avldV8E; and Brett Relander, "How to Market to Gen Z," *Entrpreneuer*, November 4, 2014, www.entrepreneur.com/article/238998.
18. Robert Klara, "It's Not Easy Being Tween," *Adweek,* June 27, 2012, www.adweek.com/print/141378; Tim Feran, "Retailer Justice Shedding Brothers Brand," *The Columbus Dispatch,* February 19, 2015, www.dispatch.com/content/stories/business/2015/02/18/justice-shedding-brothers-brand.html; and www.shopjustice.com, accessed September 2015.
19. For statistics on family composition, see U.S. Census Bureau, "Family Households," Table F1, www.census.gov/hhes/families/data/cps2014F.html; and U.S. Census Bureau, "Households by Type, Age of Members, Region of Residence, and Age of Householder: 2014," Table H2, www.census.gov/hhes/families/data/cps2014F.html, accessed September 2015.
20. See U.S. Census Bureau, "America's Families and Living Arrangements: 2013," Table FG1, www.census.gov/hhes/families/data/cps2014F.html, accessed June 2015; Claire Cain Miller and Liz Alderman, "The Flexibility Gap," *New York Times,* December 14, 2015, p. BU1; Bruce Horovitz, "Diversity Reaches New Levels in Honey Maid Ads," *USA Today,* March 10, 2014, www.usatoday.com/story/money/business/2014/03/10/honey-maid-mondelez-coca-cola-cheerios-diversity-commercials/6131151/; and U.S. Census Bureau, "Parents and Children in Stay at Home Parent Family Groups: 1994 to Present," Table SHP-1, www.census.gov/hhes/families/files/shp1.xls, accessed September 2015.
21. Based on information from Bruce Horovitz, "Diversity Reaches New Levels in Honey Maid Ads," *USA Today,* March 10, 2014, www.usatoday.com/story/money/business/2014/03/10/honey-maid-mondelez-coca-cola-cheerios-diversity-commercials/6131151/; and www.youtube.com/watch?v=2xeanX6xnRU, accessed September 2015.
22. U.S. Census Bureau, "Geographical Mobility/Migration," www.census.gov/population/www/socdemo/migrate.html, accessed September 2015.
23. See U.S. Census Bureau, "Metropolitan and Micropolitan Statistical Areas," www.census.gov/population/metro/data/index.html/, accessed June 2015; U.S. Census Bureau, "Census Estimates Show New Patterns of Growth Nationwide," April 5, 2012, www.census.gov/newsroom/releases/archives/population/cb12-55.html; and "The 536 Micropolitan Statistical Areas of the United States of America," *Wikipedia,* http://en.wikipedia.org/wiki/List_of_Micropolitan_Statistical_Areas, accessed September 2015.
24. Mary C. Noonan and Jennifer L. Glass, "The Hard Truth about Telecommuting," *Monthly Labor Review*, June 2012, www.bls.gov/opub/mlr/2012/06/art3full.pdf; and "It's Unclearly Defined, but Telecommuting Is Fast on the Rise," *New York Times,* March 8, 2014, p. B5.
25. See "About WebEx," www.webex.com/why-webex/overview.html, accessed June 2015; www.gotomeeting.com, accessed June 2015; and "What Is Cloud Computing?" www.salesforce.com/cloudcomputing, accessed September 2015.
26. See http://nextspace.us/, http://grindspaces.com, and www.regus.com, accessed September 2015.
27. U.S. Census Bureau, "Educational Attainment," www.census.gov/hhes/socdemo/education/data/cps/2014/tables.html, accessed June 2015.

28. See U.S. Census Bureau, "The 2012 Statistical Abstract: Education," Tables 229 and 276, www.census.gov/compendia/statab/cats/education .html; and U.S. Department of Labor, "Employment Projections: 2012–2022 Summary," December 19, 2013, www.bls.gov/news.release/ecopro .nr0.htm.
29. See U.S. Census Bureau, "Projections of the Size and Composition of the U.S. Population: 2014 to 2060," March 2015, www.census.gov/content/dam/Census/library/publications/2015/demo/p25-1143.pdf; and "Multicultural Consumers by the Numbers," *Advertising Age,* April 6, 2015, p. 20.
30. See "Ads Targeting Asian Americans in the U.S., Multicultural Marketing Resources, http://multicultural.com/multicultural_markets/asian-american, accessed June 2015; Marilyn Much, "More Firms Reach Out To Asian Americans," *Investors.com,* September 29, 2003, http://news.investors .com; and www.chineseparade.com/, www.southwest.com/asianoutreach/, access September 2015.
31. Witeck Communications, "America's LGBT 2013 Buying Power Estimated at $830 Billion," November 18, 2013, www.witeck.com/pressreleases/lgbt-2013-buying-power.
32. For more discussion, see Stuart Elliott, "Commercials with a Gay Emphasis Are Moving to Mainstream Media," *New York Times,* June 26, 2013, p. B3; "Ad Campaigns Are Finally Reflecting Diversity of U.S.," *Advertising Age,* March 10, 2014, http://adage.com/print/292023; Kristina Monllos, "This Is Tiffany's First Engagement Ad to Feature a Same-Sex Couple," *Adweek,* January 12, 2015, www.adweek.com/print/162310; and www.aa.com/rainbow, www.facebook.com/AARainbowTeam, and http://toddallthetime.com/Allstate-LGBT, accessed September 2015.
33. Witeck-Combs Communications, "America's Disability Market at a Glance," www.witeck.com/wp/files/Americas-Disability-Market-at-a-Glance-FINAL-5-25-2006.pdf; U.S. Census Bureau, "Nearly 1 in 5 People Have a Disability in the U.S., Census Bureau Reports," press release, July 25, 2012, www.census.gov/newsroom/releases/archives/miscellaneous/cb12-134 .html; and Christina Ng, "Huge Demographic Virtually Invisible in Media Wants to Be Seen," *ABC News,* May 29, 2013, http://abcnews.go.com/Business/disabled-community-media-marketing/story?id=19143489.
34. "Ad of the Day: Paralympic Snowboarder Amy Purdy Perseveres in Toyota's Super Bowl Spot," *Adweek,* January 26, 2015, www.adweek.com/print/162542.
35. See Rob Walker, "Tiffany & Co: At What Point Does Affordable Luxury Prove Costly?" *Euromonitor International,* June 25, 2014, http://blog .euromonitor.com/2014/06/tiffany-co-at-what-point-does-affordable-luxury-prove-costly.html; and "Tiffany Moves Down Market and Makes a Mint," *Bloomberg Businessweek,* May 21, 2014, www.bloomberg.com/bw/articles/2014-05-21/tiffany-moves-down-market-and-makes-a-mint.
36. See U.S. Census Bureau, "Income and Poverty in the United States: 2013," Table 2, p. 17, September 2014, www.census.gov/content/dam/Census/library/publications/2014/demo/p60-249.pdf.
37. Drew Harwell, "Meet the Secret Army of Meteorologists Who Keep Your Holiday Deliveries on Time," *The Washington Post,"* December 8, 2014, www.washingtonpost.com/business/economy/meet-the-secret-army-of-meteorologists-who-keep-your-holiday-deliveries-on-time/2014/12/08/2d9d3c82-759d-11e4-9d9b-86d397daad27_story.html.
38. The 2030 Water Resources Group, www.2030wrg.org, accessed June 2015; and "The World's Water," *Pacific Institute,* www.worldwater.org/data.html, accessed September 2015.
39. Information from www.timberland.com, http://responsibility.timberland. com/, and http://community.timberland.com/earthkeeping/earthkeepers-collection, accessed June 2015.
40. See "Burberry Introduces Smart Personalization for Shoppers," *Integer,* March 25, 2013, http://shopperculture.integer.com/2013/03/burberry-introduces-smart-personalization-for-shoppers.html; and "Tracking Customers' Shopping Data: RFIDs, Barcodes or QR Codes?" April 6, 2015, www.bigdata-madesimple.com/tracking-customers-shopping-data-rfids-barcodes-or-qr-codes/.
41. See "A $1 Billion Project to Remake the Disney World Experience, Using RFID," www.fastcodesign.com/1671616/a-1-billion-project-to-remake-the-disney-world-experience-using-rfid#1; Brooks Barnes, "At Disney Parks, a Bracelet Meant to Build Loyalty (and Sales), *New York Times,* January 7, 2013, p. B1; and Claire Swedberg, "MagicBands Bring Convenience, New Services to Walt Disney World," *RFID Journal,* June 16, 2014, www.rfidjournal.com/articles/view?11877.
42. See www.shakeshack.com/tag/great-american-shake-sale/ and www .itcanwait.com, accessed September 2015.
43. See "Warby Parker: Do Good," www.warbyparker.com/do-good/#home, accessed June 2015.
44. John Biggs, "Three Things Warby Parker Did to Launch a Successful Lifestyle Brand," *TechCrunch,* May 7, 2013, http://techcrunch .com/2013/05/07/the-three-things-warby-parker-did-to-launch-a-successful-lifestyle-brand/.
45. See "Statistics Every Cause Marketer Should Know," www .causemarketingforum.com/site/c.bkLUKcOTLkK4E/b.6448131/k.262B/Statistics_Every_Cause_Marketer_Should_Know.htm, accessed September 2015.
46. See www.yogiproducts.com/ and www.yogiproducts.com/our-story/our-story/, accessed September 2015.
47. Sherry Turkle, "The Flight from Conversation," *New York Times,* April 22, 2012, p. SR1.
48. See Brent Snavely, "Chrysler Keeps 'Imported from Detroit' Tagline," *USA Today,* April 24, 2013; and "Apple Kicks Off 'Made in USA' Marketing Push with High-End Mac Pro," *Advertising Age,* December 19, 2013, http://adage.com/print/245765/.
49. See "Natural and Organic Foods and Beverages in the U.S., 4th Edition," *PR Newswire,* December 22, 2014, www.prnewswire.com/news-releases/natural-and-organic-foods-and-beverages-in-the-us-4th-edition-300013041.html.
50. Based on information from various pages at www.annies.com, accessed September 2015.
51. The Pew Forum on Religion & Public Life, "Nones on the Rise," www .pewforum.org/Unaffiliated/nones-on-the-rise.aspx, accessed October 9, 2012; and http://religions.pewforum.org/, accessed September 2015.
52. For more discussion, see Diana Butler Bass, "The End of Church," *Huffington Post,* February 18, 2012, www.huffingtonpost.com/diana-butler-bass/the-end-of-church_b_1284954.html.
53. See Brad Tuttle, "McDonald's Made the Right Move in Response to Gross 'Pink Slime,'" *Time,* February 5, 2014, http://time.com/4680/mcdonalds-made-the-right-move-in-response-to-gross-pink-slime/; www.youtube.com/watch?v=Ua5PaSqKD6k, accessed September 2015; Bruce Horovitz, "McDonald's to Customers: Ask about Food Quality," *USA Today,* October 13, 2014, www.usatoday.com/story/money/business/2014/10/13/mcdonalds-fast-food-food-quality-restauants/17213145/; and www.mcdonalds.com/us/en/your_questions/our_food.html, accessed September 2015.

Chapter 4

1. Jonathon Ringen, "When It Clicks, It Clicks," *Fast Company,* February 2015, pp. 72–78+; Jacob Davidson, "LEGO Is Now the Largest Toy Company in the World," *Money,* September 4, 2014, http://time.com/money/3268065/lego-largest-toy-company-mattel/; Katarina Gustafsson, "Rebuilding LEGOs for Today's Kids," *Businessweek,* November 7, 2013, www.businessweek.com/printer/articles/166234; Andrew Jack, "How LEGO Took to Anthropology," *Financial Times,* February 26, 2014, www.ft.com/cms/s/0/b071990c-9d4c-11e3-a599-00144feab7de .html#axzz3N8u6XIPH; Roar Rude Trangbaek, "LEGO Friends Doubled Expectations for Sales in 2012," February 21, 2013, www.lego .com/en-us/aboutus/news-room/2013/february/lego-friends-doubled-expectations-for-sales-in-2012; Christian Madsbjerg and Mikkel B. Rasmussen, "An Anthropologist Walks into a Bar...," *Harvard Business Review,* March, 2014, pp. 80–88; Nicole Lee, "Lego Fusion Lets You Build Virtual Playground with Real-World Bricks," *engadget,* June 19, 2014, www.engadget.com/2014/06/19/lego-fusion/; and www.lego.com, September 2015. LEGO, MINDSTORMS, NINJAGO, and LEGENDS OF CHIMA are Trademarks of the LEGO Group of Companies, used here by permission. © 2015 The LEGO Group. All rights reserved.
2. See Craig Smith, "By the Numbers: 175 Amazing Pinterest Statistics," *Digital Marketing Ramblings,* January 2, 2015, http://expandedramblings .com/index.php/pinterest-stats/; and Kerry Flynn, "Get Ready to See More Ads on Pinterest in 2015," *Huffington Post,* December 29, 2014, www .huffingtonpost.com/2014/12/29/pinterest-ads_n_6390662.html.
3. See "Big Data," *Wikipedia,* http://en.wikipedia.org/wiki/Big_data, accessed February 2015; and Michael Lev-Ram, "What's the Next Big Thing in Big Data? Bigger Data," *Fortune,* June 16, 2014, pp. 233–240.
4. See a detailed description at "Customer Insights Analyst," http://jobs .geico.com/geico/customer-insights-analyst, accessed September 2015.
5. See www.walmartstores.com/Suppliers/248.aspx, accessed February 2015; and "Retail Link 2.0," *8th & Walton,* http://blog.8thandwalton .com/2014/08/retail-link-2-0/, accessed September 2015.
6. Based on information from "Macy's: 150+ Years of Customer Centricity," *Slideshare,* February 22, 2013, www.slideshare.net/imediaconnection/2013-

2brandmacys; Allison Schiff, "Macy's CMO Shares Loyalty Insights at NRF Big Show," *Direct Marketing News*, January 16, 2012, www.dmnews.com/macys-cmo-shares-loyalty-insights-at-nrf-big-show/article/223344/; Emily Heitkamp, "Macy's Strategic Customer Focus: Love Your Loyals," *loyalty360,* September 19, 2013, http://loyalty360.org/resources/article/macys-strategic-customer-focus-love-your-loyals; and "Macy's Focuses on the Customer; Builds Comprehensive View Across Touch Points," Acxiom Case Study, www.acxiom.com/resources/macys-focuses-customer-builds-comprehensive-view-across-touch-points/, accessed September 2015.

7. Example based on information from Michal Lev-Ram, "Samsung's Road to Mobile Domination," *Fortune,* February 4, 2013, pp. 99–101; Jason Gilbert, "Samsung Mocks iPhone 5, Apple Fanboys Again in New Galaxy S3 Commercial," *Huffington Post,* September 1, 2012, www.huffingtonpost.com/2012/09/20/samsung-mocks-iphone-5-commercial_n_1898443.html; Suzanne Vranica, "Tweets Spawn Ad Campaigns," *Wall Street Journal,* October 22, 2012, p. B5; and Luke Villapaz, "Samsung Mocks Apple iPhone 6 and Apple Watch in New Series of Ads," *International Business Times*, September 11, 2014, www.ibtimes.com/samsung-mocks-apple-iphone-6-apple-watch-new-series-ads-video-1685 612.
8. George Chidi, "Confessions of a Corporate Spy," *Inc.,* February 2013, pp. 72–77.
9. For more on research firms that supply marketing information, see Laurence N. Gold, "The 2015 AMA Gold Global Top 50 Report," *Marketing News*, August 2015. Other information from www.nielsen.com/us/en/solutions/measurement/retail-measurement.html and http://thefuturescompany.com/what-we-do/us-yankelovich-monitor, accessed February 2015.
10. See www.iriworldwide.com/SolutionsandServices/Detail.aspx?ProductID=181, accessed September 2015.
11. See www.fisher-price.com/en_US/ourstory/research-at-the-heart/index.html, accessed September 2015.
12. E. J. Schultz, "Tapping into the Secret Town," *Advertising Age,* June 17, 2013, pp. 12–13. For other discussions and examples of ethnographic research in marketing, see Madsbjerg and Rasmussen, "An Anthopologist Walks into a Bar…"; and Christine Birkner, "C'est La Vie," *Marketing News,* June 2014, pp. 23-27.
13. See Birkner, "C'est La Vie"; and "Landor Families," http://landor.com/#!/talk/articles-publications/articles/landor-families/, accessed September 2015.
14. See Rebecca Greenfield, "How the Deepest, Darkest Secrets of Moms Shape the Products in Aisle 6," *Fast Company,* December 19, 2014, www.fastcompany.com/3039798/most-creative-people/how-the-deepest-darkest-secrets-of-moms-shape-the-products-in-aisle-6?utm_source; and www.momcomplex.com, accessed September 2015.
15. Molly Soat, "Everything in Moderation," *Marketing News,* April 2014, pp. 36–46, here p. 38.
16. See "Pew Research Internet Project," *Pew Internet,* February 27, 2014, www.pewinternet.org/2014/02/27/part-1-how-the-internet-has-woven-itself-into-american-life/; and "Internet World Stats," www.internetworldstats.com/stats.htm, accessed September 2015.
17. For more information, see www.focusvision.com and www.youtube.com/watch?v=PG8RZl2dvNY, accessed September 2015.
18. See www.lexusadvisoryboard.com and www.nascarfancouncil.com, accessed September 2015.
19. For more discussion, see "Do-Not-Track Online Act of 2013," www.congress.gov/bill/113th-congress/senate-bill/418; Fred B. Campbell, Jr., "The Slow Death of 'Do Not Track,'" *New York Times,* December 27, 2014, p. A17; and "Do Not Track Legislation," http://en.wikipedia.org/wiki/Do_Not_Track_legislation, accessed September 2015.
20. See Clint Boulton, "Snack Maker Modernizes the Impulse Buy," *Wall Street Journal*, October 17, 2013, p. B4; Aaron Taube, "The Maker of Oreos Has Invented a Store Shelf that Spies on You While You're Shopping," *Business Insider*, October 18, 2013, www.businessinsider.com/mondelez-smart-shelf-technology-2013-10; and "Mondelez Smart Shelf," http://vimeo.com/96148396, accessed September 2015.
21. Based on information from Amy Chozick, "These Lab Specimens Watch 3-D Television," *New York Times,* January 25, 2012, p. B3; Sam Thielman, "Time Warner's Media Lab Knows What You Like to Watch," *Adweek,* February 4, 2013, www.adweek.com/news/technology/time-warner-s-media-lab-knows-what-you-watch-147045; and www.timewarnermedialab.com, accessed September 2015.
22. See Adam L. Penenberg, "NeuroFocus Uses Neuromarketing to Hack Your Brain," *Fast Company,* August 8, 2011, www.fastcompany.com/magazine/158/neuromarketing-intel-paypal; and Carmen Nobel, "Neuromarketing: Tapping into the 'Pleasure Center' of Consumers," *Forbes,* February 2, 2013, www.forbes.com/sites/hbsworkingknowledge/2013/02/01/neuromarketing-tapping-into-the-pleasure-center-of-consumers/. For other examples and discussion, see Roger Dooley, "Is Starbucks Coffee Too Cheap?" *Forbes,* October 14, 2013, www.forbes.com/sites/rogerdooley/2013/10/14/is-starbucks-coffee-too-cheap/; and Thomas Zoega Ramsey, *Neuromarketing & Consumer Neuroscience* (Rorvig, Denmark: Neurons Inc, 2014).
23. See Jennifer Alsever, "Technology Is the Best Policy," *Fortune,* November 18, 2013; "Built in Record Time, the MetLife Wall Knocks Down Barriers to Great Customer Service," October 23, 2013, www.metlifegto.com/news/Built-in-record-time–the-MetL; and "5 Lessons Learned from the MetLife Wall," *Insurance Networking News,* www.insurancenetworking.com/gallery/5-lessons-learned-from-the-metlife-wall-34261-1.html, accessed September 2015.
24. Andrew Nusca, "Despite High Tech, the Future of Marketing Is Exactly the Same: Focus on Customers," *Fortune,* July 15, 2014, http://fortune.com/2014/07/15/big-data-future-marketing-customer-focus/; and Phani Nagarjuna, "Seven Steps to Understanding Your Business and Monetizing Analytics," *Sales & Marketing Management,* January 9, 2015, http://salesandmarketing.com/content/seven-steps-understanding-your-business-and-monetizing-analytics.
25. For more discussion, see Elizabeth A. Sullivan, "Analytics in Action," *Marketing News,* December 2014, pp. 24-33; and Jayson DeMers, "2014 Is the Year of Digital Marketing Analytics: What It Means for Your Company," *Forbes,* February 2, 2014, www.forbes.com/sites/jaysondemers/2014/02/10/2014-is-the-year-of-digital-marketing-analytics-what-it-means-for-your-company/.
26. Avi Dan, "How Data Nourishes Agile Marketing at Kraft," *Forbes,* October 26, 2014, www.forbes.com/sites/avidan/2014/10/26/how-data-nourishes-agile-marketing-at-kraft-foods/; and Jack Neff, "Kraft Says Content Delivers Four Times Better ROI than Ads," *Advertising Age,* September 15, 2014, p. 8.
27. "1-800-Flowers.com Customer Connection Blooms with SAS Business Analytics," www.sas.com/success/1800flowers.html, accessed September 2015.
28. See Daryl Travis, "The Best Omni-Channel Brands Look More Like a Cause than a Business," *The Hub,* August 2014, www.hubmagazine.com/the-hub-magazine/zappos-omnivalues-082014/; and https://zuul.zappos.com/zuul/login, accessed September 2015.
29. Based on information in Ann Zimmerman, "Small Business; Do the Research," *Wall Street Journal*, May 9, 2005, p. R3; with additional information and insights from John Tozzi, "Market Research on the Cheap," *BusinessWeek*, January 9, 2008, www.businessweek.com/smallbiz/content/jan2008/sb2008019_352779.htm; "Understanding the Basics of Small Business Market Research," *All Business,* www.allbusiness.com/marketing/market-research/2587-1.html#axzz2K8T92eOR, accessed February 2015; and www.bibbentuckers.com, accessed September 2015.
30. For some good advice on conducting market research in a small business, search "conducting market research" at www.sba.gov or see "Researching Your Market," *Entrepreneur*, www.entrepreneur.com/article/43024-1, accessed September 2015.
31. See "The 2015 AMA Gold Global Top 25 Report," *Marketing News*, August 2015, pp. 34+; and www.nielsen.com/us/en/about-us.html and www.nielsen.com/us/en.html?worldWideSelected=true, accessed August 2015.
32. For these and other examples, see "From Tactical to Personal: Synovate's Tips for Conducting Marketing Research in Emerging Markets," *Marketing News,* April 30, 2011, pp. 20–22. Internet stats are from http://data.worldbank.org/indicator/IT.NET.USER.P2, accessed September 2015.
33. Subhash C. Jain, *International Marketing Management*, 3rd ed. (Boston: PWS-Kent, 1990), p. 338. For more discussion on international marketing research issues and solutions, see Warren J. Keegan and Mark C. Green, *Global Marketing*, 8th ed. (Upper Saddle River, NJ: Prentice Hall, 2015), pp. 170–201.
34. Zach Miners, "Your Control of Your Personal Info Is All but Dead, Pew Respondents Fear," *PCWorld,* November 12, 2014, www.pcworld.com/article/2846855.
35. Based on information from Charles Duhigg, "Psst, You in Aisle 5," *New York Times,* February 19, 2012, p. MM30; and Kashmir Hill, "How Target Figured Out a Teen Girl Was Pregnant before Her Father Did," *Forbes,* February 16, 2012, www.forbes.com/sites/kashmirhill/2012/02/16/how-target-figured-out-a-teen-girl-was-pregnant-before-her-father-did/.
36. See Andrew Roberts, "In Some Stores, All Eyes Are on You," *Bloomberg Businessweek*, December 10, 2012, pp. 32–33; and "EyeSee Mannequin," www.almax-italy.com/en-US/ProgettiSpeciali/EyeSeeMannequin.aspx, accessed September 2014.
37. "ICC/ESOMAR International Code of Marketing and Social Research Practice," www.esomar.org/index.php/codes-guidelines.html, accessed

February 2015. Also see "Respondent Bill of Rights," www.mra-net.org/ga/billofrights.cfm, accessed September 2015.

38. "FTC Complaint Charges Deceptive Advertising by POM Wonderful," September 27, 2010, www.ftc.gov/opa/2010/09/pom.shtm; Ashley Post, "FTC Issues Final Ruling against POM Wonderful," *Inside Counsel. Break News*, January 17, 2013; and Brent Kendall, "Appeals Court Likely to Uphold FTC Ruling on Juice Maker Pom," *Wall Street Journal,* May 2, 2014, www.wsj.com/articles/SB10001424052702303678404579538123825242670.
39. Information at www.casro.org/?page=TheCASROCode&hhSearchTerms=%22code+and+standards%22, accessed September 2015.

Chapter 5

1. Quotes and other information from Ben Popkin, "How Harley-Davidson, Inc. Hopes to Gain Market Share," *The Motley Fool,* February 5, 2014, www.fool.com/investing/general/2014/02/05/how-harley-davidson-inc-hopes-to-gain-market-share.aspx; Susanna Hamner, "Harley, You're Not Getting Any Younger," *New York Times,* March 22, 2009, p. BU1; "Thousands of Thundering Motorcycles Rumble through Milwaukee for Harley-Davidson 110th Anniversary Parade," PRNewswire, August 31, 2013, www.prnewswire.com/news-releases/thousands-of-thundering-motorcycles-rumble-through-milwaukee-for-harley-davidson-110th-anniversary-parade-221946591.html; "Harley Owners Group," www.harley-davidson.com/content/h-d/en_US/home/owners/hog.html, accessed March 2014; and various pages at www.harley-davidson.com, accessed September 2015.
2. Consumer expenditure figures from www.cia.gov/library/publications/the-world-factbook/geos/us.html and "Household Final Consumption Expenditure," *The World Bank,* http://data.worldbank.org/indicator/NE.CON.PRVT.CD, accessed September 2015. Population figures from the World POPClock, U.S. Census Bureau, www.census.gov/main/www/popclock.html, accessed September 2015. This Web site provides continuously updated projections of U.S. and world populations.
3. See Danielle Britni, "African Americans Have $1.1 Trillion in Buying Power," *Clutch,* February 2014, www.clutchmagonline.com/2014/02/african-americans-1-1-trillion-dollars-buying-power-putting-good-use; U.S. Census Bureau, "U.S. Population Projections," www.census.gov/population/projections, accessed February 2015; and information from "Reaching Black Consumers," www.reachingblackconsumers.com, accessed September 2015.
4. "U.S. Forest Service and Ad Council Launch New Multimedia Public Service Advertising Effort to Encourage African American Families to Discover Nature," June 7, 2012, www.multivu.com/mnr/62047-us-forest-service-ad-council-psa-african-american-families-discover-nature; "US Forest Service Discover the Forest," National Environmental Justice Conference and Training Program, April 4, 2013, www.scribd.com/doc/134213528/US-Forest-Service-Discover-The-Forest#scribd; "Discovering Nature (African-American Market)," www.adcouncil.org/Our-Campaigns/Family-Community/Discovering-Nature-African-American-Market, accessed February 2015; and www.discovertheforest.org, accessed September 2015.
5. Advertising Age Hispanic Fact Pack, July 28, 2014, pp. 33–37; and "Population Projections," www.census.gov/population/projections/, accessed September 2015.
6. Lisa Gevelber, "Your Next Big Opportunity: The U.S. Hispanic Market," *thinkwithGoogle,* July 2014, www.thinkwithgoogle.com/articles/us-hispanic-market-digital.html; and Lee Vann, "5 Predictions for Hispanic Online Marketing in 2015," *MediaPost,* November 13, 2014, www.mediapost.com/publications/article/238136.
7. Based on information from Dale Buss, "Ram Redoubles Reach-Out to Hispanic Pickup-Truck Buyers," *Forbes,* October 23, 2012, www.forbes.com/sites/dalebuss/2012/10/23/ram-redoubles-reach-out-to-hispanic-pickup-truck-buyers/; Tanya Irwin, "Ram Truck Hispanic Effort 'Most Comprehensive,'" *Marketing Daily,* September 28, 2011, www.mediapost.com/publications/article/159482/?print; Michael D. Hernandez, "Big Brands Target Hispanic Consumers," *USA Today,* September 23, 2013, www.usatoday.com/story/money/business/2013/09/22/big-brands-target-hispanic-consumers/2845009/; and www.youtube.com/watch?v=-q3Ia1BXAg0 and www.ramtrucks-la.com/, accessed September 2015.
8. See Christine Birkner, "Asian-Americans in Focus," *Marketing News,* March 2013, p. 14; "Significant, Sophisticated and Savvy: The Asian American Consumer," December 3, 2013, www.nielsen.com/us/en/insights/reports/2013/significant-sophisticated-and-savvy-the-asian-american-consumer-report-2013.html; U.S. Census Bureau, "Facts for Features: Asian/Pacific American Heritage Month: May 2014," www.census.gov/newsroom/facts-for-features/2014/cb14-ff13.html; and U.S. Census Bureau, "U.S. Population Projections," www.census.gov/population/projections, accessed September 2015.
9. See Liang Guo, "Crowdsourcing—AT&T and Wong Fu Productions 'Away We Happened,'" *Voices,* November 4, 2013, http://liyangnewmedia.wordpress.com/2013/11/04/crowdsourcing-att-and-wong-fu-productions-away-we-happened/; "Multicultural Media: Rezonate Media, AT&T, Away We Happened," December 28, 2012, www.mediapost.com/publications/article/190095/multicultural-media-rezonate-media-att-away-we.html; and AT&T "Away We Happened," www.effie.org/case_studies/case/2237, accessed September 2015.
10. See Don Ricker, "Swiffer Makes Sweeping Statement about What Makes a Family," *Huffington Post,* January 1, 2014, www.huffingtonpost.com/2014/01/22/swiffer-interracial-amputee-ad-inclusive_n_4639794.html; Stuart Elliott, "New Ad Organization to Promote Cross-Cultural Marketing," *New York Times,* August 30, 2013, www.nytimes.com/2013/08/31/business/media/new-ad-organization-to-promote-cross-cultural-marketing.html?_r=2&; and www.youtube.com/watch?v=Z01qH-jqGBY and www.youtube.com/watch?v=LKuQrKeGe6g, accessed September 2015.
11. Kimberly A. Whitler, "Why Word of Mouth Marketing Is the Most Important Social Media," *Forbes,* July 12, 2014, www.forbes.com/sites/kimberlywhitler/2014/07/17/why-word-of-mouth-marketing-is-the-most-important-social-media.
12. "Mercedes-Benz: Take the Wheel," http://industry.shortyawards.com/nominee/6th_annual/It/mercedes-benz-take-the-wheel, accessed March 2015; and "Take the Wheel," www.wommapedia.org/#section8, accessed September 2015.
13. Kate Taylor, "For McRib Fans, Search for the Sandwich Is Worth the Effort," *Entrepreneur,* November 21, 2013, www.entrepreneur.com//article/230063#; and http://mcriblocator.com, accessed September 2015.
14. Chris Slocumb, "Women Outspend Men 3 to 2 on Technology Purchases," *ClarityQuest*, January 3, 2013, www.clarityqst.com/women-outspend-men-3-to-2-on-technology-purchases/; Bryce Covert, "More Men Go Shopping and Do the Cooking," October 24, 2013, http://thinkprogress.org/economy/2013/10/24/2830121; Sarwant Singh, "Women in Cars: Overtaking Men on the Fast Lane," *Forbes,* May 23, 2014, www.forbes.com/sites/sarwantsingh/2014/05/23/women-in-cars-overtaking-men-on-the-fast-lane/; and D'Vera Cohn and Andrea Caumont, "7 Key Findings about Stay-at-Home Moms," *Fact Tank,* April 8, 2014, www.pewresearch.org/fact-tank/2014/04/08/7-key-findings-about-stay-at-home-moms/.
15. See E. J. Schultz, "Tale of Two Ads: Cheerios 'How to Dad' Campaign Makes U.S. Debut," *Advertising Age,* December 29, 2014, www.adage.com/print/296429; Jack Neff, "Move Over Mom, It's Dad's Turn," *Advertising Age,* January 26, 2014, p. 6; and www.youtube.com/watch?v=6GYxH2-WeZY, accessed September 2015.
16. See Bill Goodwin, "The Undeniable Influence of Kids," *Packaging Design,* October 16, 2013, www.packagingdigest.com/packaging-design/undeniable-influence-kids; "Kids Spending and Influencing Power: $1.2 Trillion Says Leading Ad Firm," Center for Digital Democracy, November 1, 2012, www.democraticmedia.org/kids-spending-and-influencing-power-12-trillion-says-leading-ad-firm; and Michael R. Solomon, *Consumer Behavior,* 10th ed. (Upper Saddle River, NJ: Pearson Publishing, 2013), Chapter 10.
17. For more on the Nielsen PRIZM, visit www.mybestsegments.com, accessed February 2015.
18. See "Microsoft-Nokia Launches Cheap Lumia Phones for Price Sensitive Consumers," *Forbes,* January 15, 2015, www.forbes.com/sites/greatspeculations/2015/01/15/microsoft-nokia-launches-cheap-lumia-phones-for-price-sensitive-consumers/; and "Apple Expected to Increase Marketing Presence Abroad with Low-Cost iPhone," *Advertising Age,* September 10, 2013, www.adage.com/print/244072.
19. See Christopher Heine, "Appliance Brands Are Diving into Digital This Summer," *Adweek,* July 12, 2013, www.adweek.com/news/technology/appliance-brands-are-diving-digital-summer-150989; "KitchenAid 'So Much More' TV Commercial," www.youtube.com/watch?v=tr9KQQL5lgQ, accessed March 2015; and http://blog.kitchenaid.com/, www.pinterest.com/kitchenaidusa/, and www.kitchenaid.com/about-kitchenaid/, accessed September 2015.
20. See Jennifer Aaker, "Dimensions of Measuring Brand Personality," *Journal of Marketing Research*, August 1997, pp. 347–356; and Philip Kotler and Kevin Lane Keller, *Marketing Management*, 15th ed. (Upper Saddle River, New Jersey: Pearson Publishing, 2016), Chapter 6.
21. See "Air on the Side of Humanity," September 17, 2013, www.mullen.com/air-on-the-side-of-humanity/; Shubhodeep Pal, "Inspiration for 2015: The Best Airline Marketing Campaigns from Last Year, *SimpliFlying,* January 8, 2015, http://simpliflying.com/2015/inspiration-2015-best-airline-marketing-2014/; and www.jetblue.com/corporate-social-responsibility/, accessed September 2015.

22. See Abraham H. Maslow, "A Theory of Human Motivation," *Psychological Review, 50* (1943), pp. 370–396. Also see Maslow, *Motivation and Personality*, 3rd ed. (New York: HarperCollins Publishers, 1987); and Michael R. Solomon, *Consumer Behavior,* 11th ed. (Upper Saddle River, NJ: Prentice Hall, 2014), pp. 132–134.
23. See Ellen Moore, "Letter to My Colleague: We Can Do Better," *Adweek,* December 22, 2010, www.adweek.com/news/advertising-branding/letter-my-colleagues-we-can-do-better-104084; and Kelsey Libert and Kristin Tynski, "Research: The Emotions That Make Marketing Campaigns Go Viral," *Harvard Business Review,* October 24, 2013, http://blogs.hbr.org/2013/10/research-the-emotions-that-make-marketing-campaigns-go-viral/.
24. Example based on information found in John Berman, "Shrek Boosts Vidalia Onion Sales," June 29, 2010, http://abcnews.go.com/WN/shrek-boosts-vidalia-onion-sales/story?id=11047273; and "Vidalia Onion Committee Cinches Triple Crown of National Marketing Awards," October 20, 2011, www.vidaliaonion.org/news/vidalia_onion_committee_cinches_triple_crown_of_national_-marketing_awards. Vidalia® is a registered certification mark of Georgia Department of Agriculture.
25. The following discussion draws from the work of Everett M. Rogers. See his *Diffusion of Innovations*, 5th ed. (New York: Free Press, 2003).
26. Based on Rogers, *Diffusion of Innovation*, p. 281. For more discussion, see http://en.wikipedia.org/wiki/Everett_Rogers, accessed September 2015.
27. See "Electric Car Use by Country," *Wikipedia,* http://en.wikipedia.org/wiki/Electric_car_use_by_country, accessed March 2015; and "Plug-In Vehicle Tracker: What's Coming, When," www.pluginamerica.org/vehicles, accessed September 2015.
28. See Corning Gorilla Glass 3 Featured in Micromax Smartphones," *Yahoo! Finance,* August 13, 2014, http://finance.yahoo.com/news/corning-gorilla-glass-3-featured-123101319.html; David Matthews, "Coming in 2015: A Stronger Gorilla Glass for Smartphone Screens," *Fast Company,* November 20, 2014, www.fastcompany.com/3038850; and www.corning.com/AdvancedGlass/GorillaGlass.aspx, accessed September 2015.
29. See "CSX Transportation Takes Delivery of 300th Evolution Series Locomotive from GE," *Bloomberg*, July 19, 2007, www.bloomberg.com/apps/news?pid=newsarchive&sid=a79WICjr0_RI; and www.getransportation.com/locomotives, accessed September 2015.
30. This classic categorization was first introduced in Patrick J. Robinson, Charles W. Faris, and Yoram Wind, *Industrial Buying Behavior and Creative Marketing* (Boston: Allyn & Bacon, 1967). Also see Kotler and Keller, *Marketing Management*, Chapter 7.
31. Based on information from "Six Flags Entertainment Corporation: Improving Business Efficiency with Enterprise Asset Management," July 12, 2012, www-01.ibm.com/software/success/cssdb.nsf/CS/LWIS-8W5Q84?OpenDocument&Site=default&cty=en_us; and www-01.ibm.com/software/tivoli/products/maximo-asset-mgmt/, accessed September 2015.
32. See Kate Maddox, "Seven B-to-B Marketing Trends That Will Shape 2015," *Advertising Age,* January 13, 2015, www.adage.com/print/296518; and "USG 'It's Your World. Build it,'" www.pinterest.com/gyroideasshop/usg-its-your-world-build-it/, accessed September 2015.
33. Robinson, Faris, and Wind, *Industrial Buying Behavior*, p. 14. Also see Kotler and Keller, *Marketing Management*, pp. 198–204.
34. For more ads in this series, see www.accenture.com/us-en/company/overview/advertising/Pages/brand-print-advertising.aspx, accessed September 2015.
35. See www.makino.com, www.youtube.com/user/MakinoMachineTools, www.facebook.com/MakinoMachine, and https://twitter.com/MakinoMachine, accessed September 2015.

Chapter 6

1. Quotes and other information from Christine Champagne and Teressa Iezzi, "Dunkin' Donuts and Starbucks: A Tale of Two Coffee Marketing Giants," *Fast Company,* August 21, 2014, www.fastcocreate.com/3034572; Leslie Patton, "Dunkin' Donuts Adds Jazz to Get Less Pit and More Stop," *Bloomberg Businessweek,* June 7, 2013, www.bloomberg.com/news/2013-06-07/dunkin-donuts-adds-jazz-to-get-less-pit-and-more-stop.html; Janet Adamy, "Battle Brewing: Dunkin' Donuts Tries to Go Upscale, but Not Too Far," *Wall Street Journal*, April 8, 2006, p. A1; "Dunkin' Donuts' Great Eight: Brand Keys Ranks Dunkin' Donuts Number One in Coffee Customer Loyalty for Eighth Straight Year," Dunkin' Donuts Newsroom, February 4, 2014, http://news.dunkindonuts.com; Khushbu Shah, "Starbucks or Dunkin' Donuts? Where America's Coffee Loyalty Lies," *Eater,* January 15, 2015, www.eater.com/2015/1/15/7551497/starbucks-dunkin-donuts-peets-coffee-spending-percent; and www.dunkindonuts.com and www.dunkinbrands.com, accessed March 2015.
2. Susan Berfield, "Can Target Find Its Place in the Big City?" *Bloomberg Businessweek,* January 13, 2014, pp. 18–20; and Rebecca Cooper, "Target Aiming TargetExpress Format at Washington, D.C. Area," *Washington Business Journal,* January 21, 2015, www.bizjournals.com/twincities/news/2015/01/21/target-targetexpress-washington-dc-arlington.html.
3. See "Macy's—Set for Healthy Performance in 2015," *Seeking Alpha,* January 21, 2015, http://seekingalpha.com/article/2836036; Cotton Timberlake, "With Stores Nationwide, Macy's Goes Local," *Bloomberg BusinessWeek,* October 4–10, 2010, pp. 21–22; and Jim Tierney, "Macy's Confident in My Macy's, Magic Selling Customer Engagement Strategies," *Loyalty 360,* August 15, 2013, http://loyalty360.org/resources/article/macys-confident-in-my-macys-magic-selling-customer-engagement-strategies.
4. See www.amazon.com/gp/feature.html?ie=UTF8&docId=1000863021, accessed March 2015.
5. See www.dovemencare.com/, accessed September 2015.
6. See Oliver Wainwright, "Meet GoldieBlox: The Toy Designed to Get Girls Interested in Engineering," *The Guardian,* October 16, 2012, www.theguardian.com/artanddesign/architecture-design-blog/2012/oct/16/goldieblox-toy-girls-engineering-gender; Caroline Bologna, "GoldieBlox Video Tells Parents to Encourage Daughters to Take Risks, Not Fear Failure," *Huffington Post,* December 17, 2014, www.huffingtonpost.com/2014/12/17/goldieblox-music-video-_n_6340660.html; and www.goldieblox.com/, accessed September 2015.
7. "Inside a Department Store's Secret Shopping Service," *Wall Street Journal,* August 11, 2011, www.wsj.com/articles/SB10001424053111904140604576498733634049992; Alanna Greco, "A Day at Saks: Getting Personal with Their Personal Stylists," *Luxe Me Now,* March 12, 2014, http://lmnonline.com/saks-interview/; and www.saksfifthavenue.com/Saks-Stylist, accessed September 2015.
8. See www.vfc.com/brands, accessed September 2015.
9. For more on brand tribes, see Tina Sharkey, "What's Your Tribe?" *Forbes,* January 25, 2012, www.forbes.com/sites/tinasharkey/2012/01/25/whats-your-tribe-tap-into-your-core-consumers-aspirations-like-nike-gatorade-babycenter-and-rei-do/; Seth Godin, *Tribes: We Need You to Lead Us* (Portfolio, 2008); "Brand Tribalism," *Wikipedia,* http://en.wikipedia.org/wiki/Brand_tribalism, accessed September 2015.
10. Lisa Fleisher, "Pumpkin Spice Latte, the Drink That Almost Wasn't," *Wall Street Journal,* August 30, 2013, http://blogs.wsj.com/corporate-intelligence/2013/08/30/pumpkin-spice-latte-the-drink-that-almost-wasnt/; "Everything You Need to Know about the Return of Starbucks Pumpkin Spice Latte," August 20, 2014, http://news.starbucks.com/news/everything-you-need-to-know-about-the-return-of-starbucks-pumpkin-spice-lat; and www.starbucks.com/menu/drinks/espresso/pumpkin-spice-latte, accessed September 2015.
11. See Lisa Jennings, "CKE: Advertising, Turkey Burgers Drive Sales," *Restaurant News,* April 12, 2013, http://nrn.com/latest-headlines/cke-advertising-turkey-burgers-drive-sales; and "Introducing the New Big, Bold Texas BBQ Thickburger from Carl's Jr. and Hardee's," *Yahoo! Finance,* July 21, 2014, http://finance.yahoo.com/news/introducing-big-bold-texas-bbq-120000118.html.
12. See www.patagonia.com/us/ambassadors, accessed September 2015.
13. For this and other information on Experian's Mosaic USA system, see www.experian.com/marketing-services/consumer-segmentation.html and www.experian.com/assets/marketing-services/brochures/mosaic-brochure-october-2014.pdf, accessed September 2015.
14. See www.starbucksfs.com and http://starbucksocs.com/, accessed September 2015.
15. See Jay Moy, "Every Song Has a Place: Coca-Cola, Spotify Launch Groundbreaking Social Music App," June 11, 2013, www.coca-colacompany.com/coca-cola-music/every-song-has-a-place-coca-cola-spotify-launch-groundbreaking-social-music-app; "Coke Retools Teen Campaign in Second Year TV, Packaging Promotion Added to 'The Aah Effect,'" *Advertising Age,* March 26, 2014, www.adage.com/print/292314; and www.coca-cola.com/music, accessed September 2015.
16. See Michael Porter, *Competitive Advantage* (New York: Free Press, 1985), pp. 4–8, 234–236. For a more recent discussion, see Philip Kotler and Kevin Lane Keller, *Marketing Management*, 15th ed. (Upper Saddle River, NJ: Pearson, 2016), p. 221.
17. See Jack Neff, "Laundry Bounces Back by Playing Both Ends Against the Middle," *Advertising Age,* March 23, 2015, p. 28; Serena Ng, "New Tide Churns the Laundry Market," *Wall Street Journal,* September 26, 2013, http://online.wsj.com/news/articles/SB10001424052702304526204579099390487182058; Lauren Coleman-Lochner, "Laundry Detergent Maker Want More Suds," *Bloomberg Businessweek,* October 23, 2014, www.businessweek.com/articles/2014-10-23/laundry-detergent-sales-hurt-

by-water-saving-washing-machines; and www.pg.com/en_US/investors/financial_reporting/annual_reports.shtml and www.pg.com/en_US/brands/index.shtml, accessed September 2015.

18. Store information found at www.walmartstores.com, www.wholefoodsmarket.com, and www.kroger.com, accessed September 2015.
19. Sapna Maheshwari, "Stitch Fix and the New Science behind What Women Want to Wear," *BuzzFeed,* September 24, 2014, www.buzzfeed.com/sapna/stitch-fix-and-the-new-science-behind-what-women-want-to-wea#.jcA81lEoW; Bridget Brennan, "The Retailer Redefining Personal Service in Ecommerce," *Forbes,* December 4, 2014, www.forbes.com/sites/bridgetbrennan/2014/12/04/the-retailer-redefining-personal-service-in-ecommerce/; and www.stitchfix.com/referral/4097702 and www.stitchfix.com, accessed September 2015.
20. See Jay Moye, "The Next Big Thing: How Coke's Venturing & Emerging Brands Team Stays Ahead of Tomorrow's Thirsts," March 6, 2013, www.coca-colacompany.com/innovation/the-next-big-thing-how-cokes-venturing-emerging-brands-team-stays-a-step-ahead-of-tomorrows-thirsts.
21. See Joan Voight, "Marriott Chain Adds Some Local Flavor," *Adweek,* January 7, 2013, p. 9; "Renaissance Hotels Launches New Navigator Program to Help Guests Discover 'Hidden Gems' of Various Cities around the World," January 8, 2013, www.adweek.com/print/146321; and http://renaissance-hotels.marriott.com/r-navigator, accessed September 2015.
22. See www.shopkick.com/partners and www.shopkick.com/about, accessed September 2015.
23. See www.mymms.com, www.jhaudio.com, http://factory.puma.com/en, and www.harley-davidson.com/content/h-d/en_US/home/hd1-customization.html, accessed September 2015.
24. Mike Shields, "Nike and AKQA Turn People's Running Data into 100,000 Unique Videos," *Wall Street Journal,* January 7, 2015, http://blogs.wsj.com/cmo/2015/01/07/nike-and-akqa-turn-peoples-running-data-into-100000-unique-videos/.
25. See Carolyn Kellogg, "McDonald's Brings Back Happy Meals with Books," *Los Angeles Time*, January 8, 2015, www.latimes.com/books/jacketcopy/la-et-jc-mcdonalds-happy-meals-with-books-20150108-story.html.
26. Lucia Moses, "Kids and Ads," *Adweek,* March 18, 2014, p. 13.
27. Examples based on information from www.barbie.com/activities/fun_games/#whats-hot and www.nick.com/club/, accessed September 2015.
28. See "IC3 2013 Internet Crime Report Released," May 2014, www.ic3.gov/media/annualreports.aspx.
29. SUV sales data furnished by www.WardsAuto.com, accessed March 2015. Price data from www.edmunds.com, accessed September 2015.
30. See "Zappos Family Core Values," http://about.zappos.com/our-unique-culture/zappos-core-values; and http://about.zappos.com/, accessed September 2015.
31. David Rohde, "The Anti-Walmart: The Secret Sauce of Wegmans Is People," *The Atlantic,* March 23, 2012, www.theatlantic.com/business/archive/2012/03/the-anti-walmart-the-secret-sauce-of-wegmans-is-people/254994/; and www.wegmans.com, accessed September 2015.
32. See www.heartsonfire.com/Learn-About-Our-Diamonds.aspx, accessed September 2015.
33. See Bobby J. Calder and Steven J. Reagan, "Brand Design," in Dawn Iacobucci, ed., *Kellogg on Marketing* (New York: John Wiley & Sons, 2001), p. 61. For more discussion, see Kotler and Keller, *Marketing Management*, Chapter 10.

Chapter 7

1. Based on information found in Leo Sun, "Will GoPro Stock Pop or Flop in 2015?" *The Motley Fool,* January 5, 2015, www.fool.com/investing/general/2015/01/05/will-gopro-stock-pop-or-flop-in-2015.aspx; Marty Biancuzzo, "Why GoPro Is Set for a Strong Wall Street Debut," May 21, 2014, www.wallstreetdaily.com/2014/05/21/gopro-ipo/; Tom Foster, "The GoPro Army," *Inc.,* January 26, 2012, www.inc.com/magazine/201202/the-gopro-army.html; Ryan Mac, "The Mad Billionaire behind GoPro: The World's Hottest Camera Company," *Forbes,* March 3, 2013, www.forbes.com/sites/ryanmac/2013/03/04/the-mad-billionaire-behind-gopro-the-worlds-hottest-camera-company/; Gregory S. McNeal, "GoPro CEO Talks Drones, Innovation and the Future at CES," *Forbes*, January 8, 2015, www.forbes.com/sites/gregorymcneal/2015/01/08/gopro-ceo-talks-drones-innovation-and-the-future-at-ces/; and www.gopro.com and http://-gopro.com/about-us/, accessed September 2015.
2. Based on information from Joshua Brustein, "Verizon Has a Class for You," *Bloomberg Businessweek,* November 20, 2013, www.businessweek.com/articles/2013-11-20/verizon-has-a-class-for-you; Paul Macchia, "Verizon Wireless' Smart Stores—Enhancing the Customer Experience and Mobile Lifestyle through the Reinvention of Retail," September 8, 2014, www.verizonwireless.com/news/article/2014/09/verizon-wireless-smart-stores-enhancing-the-customer-experience-and-mobile-lifestyle-through-the-reinvention-of-retail.html; and Scott Charlston, "Seattle's U Village Showcases Verizon's Next-Gen Retail," January 27, 2015, www.verizonwireless.com/news/article/2015/01/seattles-u-village-showcases-verizons-next-gen-retail.html.
3. See "The B to B Best Awards 2015," *Advertising Age,* January 26, 2015, p. 28; and "Childlike Imagination—What My Mom Does at GE," www.ge.com/news/advertising, September 2015.
4. See www.neworleansonline.com and www.australia.com/campaigns/nothinglike/us/index.html, accessed September 2015.
5. For more on social marketing, see Philip Kotler and Nancy Lee, *Social Marketing: Influencing Behaviors for Good*, 4th ed. (Thousand Oaks, CA: Sage Publications, 2011); and www.adcouncil.org and www.i-socialmarketing.org, accessed March 2015.
6. Quotes and definitions from Philip Kotler, *Marketing Insights from A to Z* (Hoboken, NJ: Wiley, 2003), p. 148; and www.asq.org/glossary/q.html, accessed September 2015.
7. See "Thumbs Up for Chick-fil-A," http://press.chick-fil-a.com/Pressroom/Factsheets/Detail/thumbsup, accessed March 2015.
8. See Nathaniel Wice, "Sonos: The Best Wireless Speakers," *Barrons*, January 3, 2015, http://online.barrons.com/articles/sonos-the-best-wireless-speakers-1420260626; Tim Bradshaw, "Speaker Maker Sonos Raises $140m," *Financial Times,* December 3, 2014, www.ft.com/cms/s/0/bcf5add4-7ab0-11e4-8646-00144feabdc0.html#axzz3QhVK6ky0; and www.sonos.com, accessed March 2015.
9. Based on information from Gene Weingarten, "Pearls before Breakfast," *Washington Post,* April 8, 2007, www.washingtonpost.com/wp-dyn/content/article/2007/04/04/AR2007040401721.html; Jessica Contrera, "Joshua Bell's Metro Encore Draws a Crowd," *Washington Post,* September 30, 2014, www.washingtonpost.com/lifestyle/style/joshua-bells-metro-encore-draws-a-crowd/2014/09/30/c28b6c50-48d5-11e4-a046-120a8a855cca_story.html; and "Stop and Hear the Music," www.youtube.com/watch?v=hnOPu0_YWhw, accessed September 2015.
10. See http://cutieskids.com/what-is-a-cutie/, accessed March 2015.
11. See "3 in 4 Grocery Purchase Decisions Being Made In-Store," *MarketingCharts*, May 15, 2012, www.marketingcharts.com/direct/3-in-4-grocery-purchase-decisions-being-made-in-store-22094; "FMI—Supermarket Facts," www.fmi.org/research-resources/supermarket-facts, accessed April 2015; and "Our Retail Divisions," http://news.walmart.com/news-archive/2005/01/07/our-retail-divisions, accessed September 2015.
12. See Mary Mazzoni, "Amazon Continues Its Battle against 'Wrap Rage,'" *Triple Pundit,* December 9, 2013, www.triplepundit.com/2013/12/amazon-continues-battle-against-wrap-rage/; and www.amazon.com/b/?&node=5521637011, accessed September 2015.
13. See www.tiffany.com/WorldOfTiffany/TiffanyStory/Legacy/BlueBox.aspx, accessed March 2015.
14. Based on information from "Company Values," www.llbean.com/customerService/aboutLLBean/company_values.html; www.llbean.com/customerService/aboutLLBean/company_history.html?nav=s1-ln; and other pages at www.llbean.com, accessed September 2015.
15. See Anna Rose Welch, "Lowe's Leverages Mobile Initiatives to Improve Customer Experience," *Integrated Solutions for Retailers,* November 21, 2013, www.retailsolutionsonline.com/doc/lowe-s-leverages-mobile-initiatives-to-improve-customer-experience-0001; Vauhini Vara, "The Lowe's Robot and the Future of Service Work," *The New Yorker,* October 29, 2014, www.newyorker.com/business/currency/lowes-robot-future-service-work; and www.lowes.com/webapp/wcs/stores/servlet/ContactUsLandingPageView, www.lowes.com/how-to-library, and https://twitter.com/LowesCares, accessed March 2015.
16. Information on The Clorox Company's product mix from www.thecloroxcompany.com/products/our-brands/, accessed September 2015.
17. Devika Krishna Kumar, ""P&G to Sell Up to 100 Brands to Revive Sales, Cut Costs," *Reuters,* August 1, 2014, www.reuters.com/article/2014/08/01/procter-gamble-results-idUSL4N0Q745T20140801; and "All Eyes on P&G's Brand Consolidation Strategy as Currency Headwinds Weigh on Q2 Results," *Forbes,* January 26, 2015, www.forbes.com/sites/greatspeculations/2015/01/26/all-eyes-on-pgs-brand-consolidation-strategy-as-currency-headwinds-weigh-on-q2-results/; and Kevin Orland, "Coty Agrees to Buy P&G Beauty Brands for $12.5 Billion," *BloombergBusiness,* July 9, 2015, www.bloomberg.com/news/articles/2015-07-09/p-g-accepts-coty-s-12-5-billion-offer-for-43-beauty-brands.

18. See CIA World FactBook, www.cia.gov/library/publications/the-world-factbook, accessed March 2015; and "List of Countries by GDP Sector Composition," http://en.wikipedia.org/wiki/List_of_countries_by_GDP_sector_composition, accessed September 2015.
19. Based on information from Leonard Berry and Neeli-Bendapudi, "Clueing In Customers," *Harvard Business Review*, February 2003, pp. 100–106; Jeff Hansel, "Mayo Hits the Blogosphere," *McClatchy-Tribune Business News*, January 22, 2009; "Mayo Clinic Model of Care," www.mayo.edu/pmts/mc4200-mc4299/mc4270.pdf, accessed September 2014; and www.mayoclinic.org, accessed September 2015.
20. See James L. Heskett, W. Earl Sasser, Jr., and Leonard A. Schlesinger, *The Service Profit Chain: How Leading Companies Link Profit and Growth to Loyalty, Satisfaction, and Value* (New York: Free Press, 1997); and Heskett, Sasser, and Schlesinger, *The Value Profit Chain: Treat Employees Like Customers and Customers Like Employees* (New York: Free Press, 2003). Also see John Marshall and Dave Mayer, "Activate a Brand Internally," *Marketing Management,* Winter 2012, pp. 37–44.
21. David Rohde, "The Anti-Walmart: The Secret Sauce of Wegmans Is People," *The Atlantic,* March 23, 2012, www.theatlantic.com/business/archive/2012/03/the-anti-walmart-the-secret-sauce-of-wegmans-is-people/254994/. Also see Carmine Gallo, "How Wegmans, Apple Store, and Ritz-Carlton Win Loyal Customers," *Forbes,* December 11, 2012, www.forbes.com/sites/carminegallo/2012/12/11/how-wegmans-apple-store-and-the-ritz-carlton-wins-loyal-customers/; and www.wegmans.com/careers, accessed September 2015.
22. See "United States: Prescription Drugs," www.statehealthfacts.org/profileind.jsp?sub=66&rgn=1&cat=5, accessed March 2015; and "Postal Facts," http://about.usps.com/who-we-are/postal-facts/welcome.htm, accessed September 2015.
23. See Terry Maxon, "Horrible Flight? Airlines' Apology Experts Will Make It Up to You," *McClatchy-Tribune News Service*, August 24, 2010; Katie Morell, "Lessons from Southwest Airlines' Stellar Customer Service," *ehotelier.com,* August 29, 2012, http://ehotelier.com/hospitality-news/item.php?id=23931_0_11_0M_C; and Micah Solomon, "Customer Service: What Southwest Knows and You Don't (Hint: Being Nice Isn't Enough)," *Forbes,* September 22, 2013, www.forbes.com/sites/micahsolomon/2013/09/22/not-hiring-jerks-isnt-enough-your-systems-have-to-love-your-customers-too/.
24. See Micah Solomon, "5 Social Media Customer Service Best Practices to Handle (or Prevent) Customer Complaints," *Forbes,* January 28, 2015, www.forbes.com/sites/micahsolomon/2015/01/28/5-best-practices-for-social-media-customer-service-how-to-handle-and-avoid-customer-complaints/.
25. See "McAtlas Shrugged," *Foreign Policy*, May–June 2001, pp. 26–37; and Philip Kotler and Kevin Lane Keller, *Marketing Management*, 15th ed. (Upper Saddle River: Pearson Publishing, 2016), p. 316.
26. See "For Sale: Hessian, A Brand without a Product," *Fast Company,* February 12, 2013, www.fastcodesign.com/1671819/for-sale-hessian-a-brand-without-a-product.
27. Pete Pachal, "Love Your Vespa? Now You Can Do It Officially on Social Media," *Mashable*, August 21, 2012, http://mashable.com/2012/08/21/la-vespa-vita/; and www.lavespavita.com/, accessed September 2015.
28. For more on BrandAsset Valuator, see Kotler and Keller, *Marketing Management,* Chapter 11; and "BrandAsset Valuator," www.yr.com/BAV, accessed September 2015.
29. See Millward Brown Optimor, "BrandZ Top 100 Most Valuable Global Brands," www.millwardbrown.com/docs/default-source/global-brandz-downloads/global/2014_BrandZ_Top100_Chart.pdf, accessed September 2015. Also see "Best Global Brands," www.bestglobalbrands.com/2014/ranking/, accessed September 2015.
30. See Scott Davis, *Brand Asset Management*, 2nd ed. (San Francisco: Jossey-Bass, 2002). For more on brand positioning, see Kotler and Keller, *Marketing Management*, Chapter 10.
31. See "For P&G, Success Lies in More Than Merely a Dryer Diaper," *Advertising Age*, October 15, 2007, p. 20; Jack Neff, "Just How Well-Defined Is Your Brand's Ideal?" *Advertising Age,* January 16, 2012, p. 4; and www.pampers.com, accessed September 2015.
32. See Aaron Ahuvia Rajeev and Richard P. Bagozzi, "Brand Love," *Journal of Marketing,* March 2012, pp. 1–16; Doug Grisaffe, "Feeling the Brand Love," *Marketing News,* February 2014, pp. 26-27; and www.saatchi.com/the_lovemarks_company and www.lovemarks.com, accessed October 2015.
33. See "Bing," *Wikipedia,* http://en.wikipedia.org/wiki/Bing, accessed March 2015.
34. "New Pricing Study Highlights Savings for Store Brands while the Winter Drags On," *PR Newswire*, February 19, 2014.
35. See Evan Clark, "UBS Sees Private-Label Goods Diminishing," WWD, November 26, 2013, www.wwd.com/retail-news/trends-analysis/ubs-sees-private-label-goods-diminishing-7291838; "Private Label Foods & Beverages in the U.S., 8th Edition," *PR Newswire*, October 29, 2014; and http://plma.com/storeBrands/marketprofile14a.html, accessed September 2015.
36. See Bonnie S. Benwick, "Store Brands, the (Now) Welcome Option," *Washington Post,* February 25, 2014, www.washingtonpost.com/lifestyle/food/store-brands-the-now-welcome-option/2014/02/24/be4808c6-99b0-11e3-80ac-63a8ba7f7942_story.html; Alexander Coolidge, "Kroger Using House Brands to Power Growth," *Cincinnati.com*, September 20, 2014, www.cincinnati.com/story/money/2014/09/20/kroger-using-house-brands-power-growth/15955797/; and Thad Rueter, "Amazon Powers Ahead to 2015," *Internet Retailer,* December 31, 2014, www.internetretailer.com/2014/12/31/amazon-powers-ahead-2015.
37. Stephanie Strom, "Groceries Are Cleaning Up in Store-Brand Aisles," *New York Times,* October 2, 2013, p. B1; and Deloitte, *The 2014 American Pantry Study*, www2.deloitte.com/content/dam/Deloitte/us/Documents/consumer-business/us-cp-aps-brochure.pdf.
38. See "Private Labels Use Branding to Increase Sales," *FHC Marketing*, January 29, 2014, www.fhcmarketing.com/private-labels-use-branding-increase-sales.
39. Lauren Coleman-Lochner, "Laundry Detergent Maker Want More Suds," *Bloomberg Businesseeek,* October 23, 2014, www.businessweek.com/articles/2014-10-23/laundry-detergent-sales-hurt-by-water-saving-washing-machines.
40. Matthew Daneman, "Kodak Brand Is Returning to Store Shelves," *USA Today,* December 26, 2014, www.usatoday.com/story/tech/2014/12/26/kodak-branding/20910231/.
41. "Top 150 Global Licensors," *Global License*, May 1, 2014, www.licensemag.com/license-global/top-150-global-licensors-0; and Felix Gillette, "SpongeBob Muscles Up," *Bloomberg Businessweek,* January 20, 2015, pp. 63–65.
42. See Devin Liddell, "3 Reasons Why Co-Making Is the Future of Branding," *Fast Company*, March 7, 2014, www.fastcodesign.com/3027047/3-reasons-why-co-making-is-the-future-of-branding; and www.tacobell.com/food/menuitem/Doritos-Locos-Tacos-Supreme, accessed September 2015.
43. Haley Peterson, "McDonald's Is Reportedly Cutting These Items from the Menu," *Business Insider,* January 23, 2015, www.businessinsider.com/mcdonalds-menu-cuts-2015-1.
44. See "The Brand That Launched 1000 Chips," *Bloomberg Businessweek,* October 3–9, 2011, p. 30; and www.fritolay.com/our-snacks/doritos.html, accessed September 2015.
45. See Michael Brown, "'Works with Nest' Program Gains Traction with 15 New Smart Device Integrations," *TechHive,* January 5, 2015, www.techhive.com/article/2864067/works-with-nest-program-explodes-with-15-new-smart-device-integrations.html.
46. For interesting lists of good and bad brand extension candidates, see Christina Austin, "See the 10 Worst Brand Extensions Currently on the Market," *Business Insider,* February 9, 2013, www.businessinsider.com/the-10-worst-brand-extensions-2013-2?op=1; and Brad Tuttle, "Why Some Brand Extensions Are Brilliant and Others Are Just Awkward," *Time,* February 7, 2013, http://business.time.com/2013/02/07/why-some-brand-extensions-are-brilliant-and-others-are-just-awkward/.
47. "100 Largest Global Marketers," *Advertising Age*, December 8, 2014, p. 26.
48. Stephen Cole, "Value of the Brand," *CA Magazine*, May 2005, pp. 39–40. Also see "The Power of Customer Service," *Fortune,* December 3, 2012, www.timeincnewsgroupcustompub.com/sections/121203_Disney.pdf; and "Customer Engagement," http://thewaltdisneycompany.com/citizenship/community/consumer-engagement, accessed September 2015.

Chapter 8

1. Based on information found in Jon Gertner, "The X Factor," *Fast Company,* May 2014, pp. 67–72; Miguel Helft, "The Most Ambitious CEO in the Universe," *Fortune,* December 1, 2014, pp. 140–150; Brad Stone, "Inside the Moonshot Factory," *Bloomberg Businessweek*, May 22, 2013, pp. 56–61; Chuck Salter, "Google: The Faces and Voices of the World's Most Innovative Company," *Fast Company,* March 2008, pp. 74–88; "The World's 50 Most Innovative Companies," *Fast Company,* www.fastcompany.com/section/most-innovative-companies-2015, accessed October 2015; "Google's U.S. Search Ex-Mobiles Drops Below 75% as Yahoo Makes More Firefox Gains," *TechCrunch,* February 15, 2015, http://techcrunch.com/2015/02/02/googles-u-s-search-ex-mobiles-drops-below-75-as-yahoo-makes-more-firefox-gains/; Nathan Ingraham, "YouTube abd Mobile Ads Drove Strong

Revenue Growth for Google Last Quarter," *The Verge,* July 16, 2015, www.theverge.com/2015/7/16/8981461/google-q2-2015-earnings; and www.google.com and http://investor.google.com/financial/tables.html, accessed October 2015.

2. Andrew Cunningham, "Apple's Q1 2015: Ridiculously High iPhone Sales, 18% Drop in iPad Sales," *ars technica,* January 27, 2015, http://arstechnica.com/apple/2015/01/apples-q1-2015-ridiculously-high-iphone-sales-18-drop-in-ipad-sales/.
3. David Meer, Edward C. Landry, and Samrat Sharma, "Creating What Consumers Want," *Forbes,* January 26, 2015, www.forbes.com/sites/strategyand/2015/01/26/creating-what-consumers-want/.
4. See Michael Martinez, "Ford Opens Silicon Valley Innovation Center," *The Detroit News,* January 22, 2015, www.detroitnews.com/story/business/autos/ford/2015/01/22/ford-silicon-valley/22165837/; and "Chick-fil-A Innovation," Matchistic, http://matchstic.com/work/case-studies/chick-fil-a-innovation, accessed October 2015.
5. For these and other examples, see Dan Schawbel, "Why Companies Want You to Become an Intrapreneur," *Forbes,* September 9, 2013, www.forbes.com/sites/danschawbel/2013/09/09/why-companies-want-you-to-become-an-intrapreneur/; and "Time to Think," http://solutions.3m.com/innovation/en_US/stories/time-to-think, accessed October 2015.
6. Kevin Scott, "The LinkedIn [in]cubator," December 7, 2012, http://blog.linkedin.com/2012/12/07/linkedin-incubator/; and www.linkedin.com/static?key=what_is_linkedin, accessed October 2015.
7. See Jonathan Ringen, "How LEGO Became the Apple of Toys," *Fast Company,* January 8, 2015, www.fastcompany.com/3040223/when-it-clicks-it-clicks; and https://ideas.lego.com, accessed October 2015.
8. "Samsung Is Fueling Its Future with Open Innovation," *InnoCentive,* October 23, 2103, www.innocentive.com/blog/2013/10/23/samsung-is-fueling-its-future-with-open-innovation/; and www.samsung.com/global/business/semiconductor/aboutus/business/open-innovation/overview, accessed October 2015.
9. See "Victorinox Success!" September 2012, www.jovoto.com/blog/2012/09/success-story-victorinox/; Bastian Unterberg et al., *Crowdstorm: The Future of Ideas, Innovation, and Problem Solving Is Collaboration* (Somerset, NJ: Wiley, 2013), pp. 175–177; and http://victorinox.jovoto.com and www.jovoto.com/clients, accessed October 2015.
10. Guido Jouret, "Inside Cisco's Search for the Next Big Idea," *Harvard Business Review,* September 2009, pp. 43–45; Geoff Livingston, "Real Challenges to Crowdsourcing for Social Good," *Mashable,* October 12, 2010, http://mashable.com/2010/10/12/social-good-crowdsourcing; and "Creating Business Opportunities to the Tune of $1 Billion Plus," *Brightidea,* www.brightidea.com/Brightidea-Case-Studies-Cisco.bix, accessed October 2015.
11. See George S. Day, "Is It Real? Can We Win? Is It Worth Doing?" *Harvard Business Review,* December 2007, pp. 110–120.
12. This example is based on Tesla Motors and information obtained from www.teslamotors.com, accessed April 2015, and Daniel Cooper, "Tesla's Long-Delayed Model X SUV Is Testing in California," *engadget,* January 13, 2015, www.engadget.com/2015/01/30/tesla-model-x-footage/. Also see Ryan Bradley, "Full Charge Ahead," *Fortune,* February 4, 2013, pp. 10–13; Leah Hunter, "How Tesla Protects the Romance of Driving while Disrupting the Industry," *Co.Design,* November 7, 2013, www.fastcodesign.com/3021312; "The Future of EV," www.chevrolet.com/culture/article/bolt-ev-concept-car.html, accessed October 2015; and "Electric Car," *Wikipedia,* http://en.wikipedia.org/wiki/Electric_car, accessed October 2015.
13. See www.carharttgroundbreakers.com and www.carhartt.com/GroundBreakersSignUpView?storeId=10201&langId=-1&catalogId=10551, accessed October 2015.
14. See Maureen Morrison, "Marketer of the Year: Taco Bell," *Advertising Age,* September 2, 2013, pp. 15–16; Susan Berfield, "Baristas, Patrons Steaming over Starbucks VIA," *Bloomberg BusinessWeek,* November 13, 2009; and Tamara Walsh, "Starbucks Makes a Big Bet on New Product Mix in 2014," *The Motley Fool,* January 8, 2014, www.fool.com/investing/general/2014/01/08/starbucks-makes-a-big-bet-on-new-product-mix-in-20.aspx.
15. Austin Carr, "Starbucks Leap of Faith," *Fast Company,* June 2013, pp. 46–48; and John Heggestuen, "An Inside Look at the Starbucks App, the Most Successful Mobile Payments System in the US," *Business Insider,* October 17, 2014, www.businessinsider.com/starbucks-mobile-payments-app-2014-9.
16. For information on BehaviorScan Rx, see www.iriworldwide.com/default.aspx?TabId=159&productid=75, accessed October 2015.
17. See Jack Neff, "P&G Reinvents Laundry with $150 Million Tide Pods Launch," *Advertising Age,* April 26, 2011, www.adage.com/print/227208/; and Sheila Shayon, "Microsoft Unleashes Global Marketing Blitz for Windows 8, New Devices," *BrandChannel,* October 25, 2012, www.brandchannel.com/home/post/2012/10/25/Microsoft-Global-Windows-8-Launch-102512.aspx.
18. "iPhone 6 & iPhone 6 Plus Arrive in 36 More Countries and Territories This Month," Apple press information, October 13, 2014, www.apple.com/pr/library/2014/10/13iPhone-6-iPhone-6-Plus-Arrive-in-36-More-Countries-and-Territories-This-Month.html.
19. See Robert G. Cooper, "Formula for Success," *Marketing Management,* March–April 2006, pp. 19–23; Christoph Fuchs and Martin Schreier, "Customer Empowerment in New Product Development," *Product Innovation Management,* January 2011, pp. 17–32; and Robert Safien, "The Lessons of Innovation," *Fast Company,* March 2012, p. 18.
20. See Chris O'Brien, "How Intuit became a Pioneer of 'Delight,'" *Los Angeles Times,* May 10, 2013; Brad Smith, "Intuit's CEO on Building a Design-Driven Company," *Harvard Business Review,* January–February 2015, pp. 35–38; and http://investors.intuit.com/financial-information/annual-reports/default.aspx and intuitlabs.com/innovation.html, accessed October 2015.
21. Based in part on information from Min-Jeong Lee, "Samsung Chases 'Wow' Moment," *Wall Street Journal,* March 12, 2013, http://online.wsj.com/news/articles/SB10001424127887324096404578355781939805000; Max Chafkin, "Samsung: For Elevating Imitation to an Art Form," *Fast Company,* March 2013, p. 108; Adam Lashinski, "The Uncrowned King of Tech," *Fortune,* August 1, 2015, pp. 134-143; and information from www.sony.com, www.apple.com, and www.samsung.com, accessed October 2015.
22. This definition is based on one found in Bryan Lilly and Tammy R. Nelson, "Fads: Segmenting the Fad-Buyer Market," *Journal of Consumer Marketing,* Vol. 20, No. 3, 2003, pp. 252–265.
23. See Katya Kazakina and Robert Johnson, "A Fad's Father Seeks a Sequel," *New York Times,* May 30, 2004, www.nytimes.com; John Schwartz, "The Joy of Silly," *New York Times,* January 20, 2008, p. 5; "Drew Guarini, "11 Surprising Product Fads," *Huffington Post,* August 8, 2012, www.huffingtonpost.com/2012/08/22/product-fads_n_1819710.html#slide=1410262; and www.crazyfads.com, accessed October 2015.
24. Based on information from Stuart Elliott, "3M Says, 'Go Ahead, Make Something of It,'" *New York Times,* January 28, 2013, www.nytimes.com/2013/01/28/business/mutfund/3m-says-go-ahead-make-something-of-it.html?pagewanted=2&tntemail0=y&_r=3&emc=tnt; and "Post-it Brand. Go Ahead," www.youtube.com/watch?v=j_zUZb4EJTk, accessed October 2015.
25. See www.crayola.com/fashionshow/, accessed April 2015.
26. Tanzina Vega, "Quaker Oats Prepares to Court Younger, More Diverse Moms," *New York Times,* December 21, 2012, p. B3; E. J. Schultz, "The Quaker Man Is Growing a Milk Mustache," *Advertising Age,* September 8, 2014, www.adage.com/print/294857; and www.quakerup.com and www.quakeroats.com, accessed October2015.
27. See P&G Brand Divestitures Will Be Bigger Than Original Targets," *Advertising Age,* February 19, 2015, www.adage.com/print/297240.
28. For a more comprehensive discussion of marketing strategies over the course of the PLC, see Philip Kotler and Kevin Lane Keller, *Marketing Management,* 15th ed. (Upper Saddle River, NJ: Pearson Education, 2016), pp. 358+.
29. Jaclyn Trop, "Toyota Will Pay $1.6 Billion over Faulty Accelerator Suit," *New York Times,* July 20, 2013, p. 3B.
30. Based on information from "How PepsiCo Dreams Up New Products in China," *Advertising Age,* December 9, 2013, http://adage.com/print/245558; Louise Ho, "PepsiCo's Strategy Wins Market Share," *Global Times,* December 4, 2013, www.globaltimes.cn/content/829870.shtml#.Uu_5Q_ldV8F; Laurie Burkett, "PepsiCo Chips Away at China," *Wall Street Journal,* July 11, 2012, p. B3; and "PepsiCo's Greater China Region: Driving Growth and Innovation," *AmCahm China,* January 2014, www.amchamchina.org/article/12224.
31. Information from www.db.com, accessed October 2015.
32. Information from www.interpublic.com and www.mccann.com, accessed October 2015.
33. See "Global Powers of Retailing 2015," http://www2.deloitte.com/th/en/pages/consumer-business/articles/global-powers-retailing-2015.html; "Walmart Corporate International," http://corporate.walmart.com/our-story/locations, accessed October 2015; and information from www.walmart.com and www.carrefour.com, accessed October 2015.

Chapter 9

1. Based on information from Mike Shields, "Amazon Drives More Holiday Web Retail Traffic Than Biggest TV Ad Spender," *Wall Street Journal,* December 10, 2014, http://blogs.wsj.com/cmo/2014/12/10/amazon-drives-more-holiday-web-retail-traffic-than-biggest-tv-ad-spender/; Tom Gara, "When Elephants Fight: The Great Wal-Mart-Amazon War of 2013," *Wall Street Journal*, March 28, 2013, http://blogs.wsj.com/corporate-intelligence/2013/03/28/when-elephants-fight-the-great-wal-mart-amazon-war-of-2013; Shelly Banjo, "Walmart's E-Stumble with Amazon," *Wall Street Journal,* June 19, 2013, http://online.wsj.com/news/articles/SB10001424127887323566804578553301017702818; Sally Banjo, Suzanne Kapner, and Paul Ziobro, "Can Wal-Mart Clerks Ship as Fast as Amazon Robots?," *Wall Street Journal,* December 18, 2014, www.wsj.com/articles/can-wal-mart-clerks-ship-as-fast-as-amazon-robots-1418930087; "Walmart vs. Amazon Prime," *Advertising Age,* May 15, 2015, p. 6; and www.walmart.com and www.amazon.com, accessed October 2015.
2. For more on the importance of sound pricing strategy, see Thomas T. Nagle, John Hogan, and Joseph Zale, *The Strategy and Tactics of Pricing: A Guide to Growing More Profitably*, 5th ed. (Upper Saddle River, NJ: Prentice Hall, 2011), Chapter 1.
3. See Megan Willett, "How Swiss Watchmaker Patek Philippe Handcrafts Its Famous $500,000 Watches," *Business Insider,* July 12, 2013, www.businessinsider.com/how-a-patek-philippe-watch-is-made-2013-7; Stacy Perman, "Patek Philippe Crafts Its Future," *Fortune,* June 16, 2014, pp. 37–44; and www.patek.com/contents/default/en/values.html, accessed October 2015.
4. See Michael Johnsen, "Walmart Prepares to Expand Price First Launch," *Retailing Today,* August 21, 2014, www.retailingtoday.com/article/walmart-prepares-expand-price-first-nationwide; and www.mbusa.com/mercedes/vehicles/class/class-CLA/bodystyle-CPE, accessed October 2015.
5. See Maria Puente, "Theaters Turn Up the Luxury," *USA Today*, March 12, 2010, p. 1A; Dan Strack. "AMC Entertainment Set to Capitalize on a Strong 2015," *Seeking Alpha,* February 18, 2015, http://seekingalpha.com/article/2929046-amc-entertainment-set-to-capitalize-on-a-strong-2015; and information from http://dinein.amctheatres.com, accessed October 2015.
6. See www.traderjoes.com/our-story and www.traderjoes.com, accessed October 2015.
7. See Stan Schroeder, "Vertu's Luxury Android Smartphone Costs $10,000, *Mashable,* February 12, 2013, http://mashable.com/2013/02/12/vertu-ti/; Matt Vella, "The Ulter-Luxe Phone," *Fortune,* April 29, 2013, pp. 10–12; Lara O'Reilly, "Vertu Seeks to Broaden Appeal with Marketing," *Marketing Week,* October 13, 2013, www.marketingweek.co.uk/news/vertu-seeks-to-broaden-appeal-with-marketing/4008105.article; and www.vertu.com/us/en/discover-vertu/creating-extraordinary/ and www.vertu.com, accessed October 2015.
8. Based on information found in Joseph Weber, "Over a Buck for Dinner? Outrageous," *BusinessWeek,* March 9, 2009, p. 57; Tom Mulier and Matthew Boyle, "Dollar Dinners from ConAgra's Threatened by Costs," *Bloomberg Businessweek,* August 19, 2010, www.businessweek.com; and Barbara Soderlin, "ConAgra Tries to Change Consumers' Perceptions about Frozen Foods," *Omaha World-Herald,* May 20, 2013, www.omaha.com/money/conagra-tries-to-change-consumers-perceptions-about-frozen-foods/article_c9697b1b-e14a-5f31-a0a7-2675961eb70f.html.
9. For more information, see Annie Gasparro, "Whole Foods Aims to Alter 'Price Perception' as It Expands," *Wall Street Journal,* February 15, 2012; Julie Jargon, "Whole Foods' Battle for the Organic Shopper," *Wall Street Journal,* August 13, 2013, p. B1, http://online.wsj.com/news/articles/SB1000142412788732345510457901516213567613 6; and www.wholefoodsmarket.com/about-our-products/whole-deal, accessed October 2014.
10. See Stuart Elliott, "Whole Foods Asks Shoppers to Consider a Value Proposition," *New York Times,* October 20, 2014, p. B5; and Brad Stone, "Whole Foods, Half Off," *Bloomberg Businessweek,* January 25, 2015, pp. 45-49.
11. "Lower Cost Samsung GALAXY Unveiled in Kenya," *BiztechAfrica,* May 23, 2014, www.biztechafrica.com/article/lower-cost-samsung-samsung-galaxy-unveiled-kenya/2967/#.Uvo4bfldV8F; Bruce Einhorn and others, "Samsung's China Problems Come to India," *Bloomberg Businessweek,* October 23, 2104, pp. 44–45; and "Samsung Galaxy Pocket Neo," www.mysmartprice.com/mobile/samsung-galaxy-pocket-neo-msp2810, accessed October 2015.
12. Karis Hustad, "Kindle Fire HDX Keeps Amazon's Low Price, Adds Extra Features," *Christian Science Monitor,* September 26, 2013, www.csmonitor.com/Innovation/2013/0926/Kindle-Fire-HDX-keeps-Amazon-s-low-price-adds-extra-features.
13. See information found at http://investor.keuriggreenmountain.com/annuals-proxies.cfm, accessed October 2015.
14. See Oliver Strand, "With Coffee, the Price of Individualism Can Be High," *New York Times,* February 8, 2012, p. D6; and "$51 per Pound: The Deceptive Cost of Single-Serve Coffee," *New York Times,* www.thekitchn.com/51-per-pound-the-deceptive-cost-of-single-serve-coffee-the-new-york-times-165712, accessed October 2015.
15. See Bill Campbell, "Cheese to the Rescue: Surprising Spray Melts Road Ice," NPR, January 21, 2014, www.npr.org/blogs/thetwo-way/2014/01/21/264562529/cheese-to-the-rescue-surprising-spray-melts-road-ice; and "Four Foods That Help Prevent Slippery Roads," *AccuWeater.com,* January 22, 2015, www.accuweather.com/en/weather-news/beet-cheese-and-potatoes-roads/22447484.
16. For this and other examples, see Peter Coy, "Why the Price Is Rarely Right," *Bloomberg Businessweek,* February 1 & 8, 2010, pp. 77–78.
17. See Anthony Allred, E. K. Valentin, and Goutam Chakraborty, "Pricing Risky Services: Preference and Quality Considerations," *Journal of Product and Brand Management*, Vol. 19, No. 1, 2010, p. 54; Kenneth C. Manning and David E. Sprott, "Price Endings, Left-Digit Effects, and Choice," *Journal of Consumer Research*, August 2009, pp. 328–336; Travis Nichols, "A Penny Saved: Psychological Pricing," *Gumroad,* October 18, 2013, http://blog.gumroad.com/post/64417917582/a-penny-saved-psychological-pricing; and Bouree Lam, "The Psychological Difference between $12.00 and $11.67," *The Atlantic,* January 30, 2015, www.theatlantic.com/business/archive/2015/01/the-psychological-difference-between-1200-and-1167/384993/.
18. See John Kell, "JCPenney to Close 33 Stores, Cut 2,000 Jobs," *Wall Street Journal*, January 14, 2014, p. B2; Kyle Stock, "Is JC Penney Giving Away the Store?," *Bloomberg Businessweek,* December 4, 2013, www.businessweek.com/articles/2013-12-04/is-jc-penney-giving-away-the-store; Brad Tuttle, "JCPenney Reintroduces Fake Prices," *Time*, May 2, 2013, http://business.time.com/2013/05/02/jc-penney-reintroduces-fake-prices-and-lots-of-coupons-too-of-course/; Natalie Zmuda, "JC Penney Reinvention Is Bold Bet, but Hardly Fail-Safe," *Advertising Age*, January 30, 2012, pp. 1, 22; Steve Denning, "JCPenney: Was Ron Johnson's Strategy Wrong?," *Forbes,* April 9, 2013, www.forbes.com/sites/stevedenning/2013/04/09/j-c-penney-was-ron-johnsons-strategy-wrong/; and http://ir.jcpenney.com/phoenix.zhtml?c=70528&p=irol-irHome, accessed October 2015.
19. See Justin D. Martin, "Dynamic Pricing: Internet Retailers Are Treating Us Like Foreign Tourists in Egypt," *Christian Science Monitor*, January 7, 2011; Patrick Rishe, "Dynamic Pricing: The Future of Ticket Pricing in Sports," *Forbes,* January 6, 2012, www.forbes.com/sites/prishe/2012/01/06/dynamic-pricing-the-future-of-ticket-pricing-in-sports/; and Mike Southon, "Time to Ensure the Price Is Right," *Financial Times,* January 21, 2012, p. 30.
20. See Natalie Zmuda, "Best Buy Tries to Co-Opt 'Showrooming' This Holiday Season," *Advertising Age,* October 29, 2013, http://adage.com/print/244993/; and Meredith Derby Berg, "Is Best Buy's 'Showrooming' Campaign Working?" *Advertising Age,* December 26, 2013, http://adage.com/print/245831/.
21. Liza Lin, "Shhh…Luxury Goods Are Discounted in China," *Bloomberg Businessweek,* August 21, 2014, pp. 28–29.
22. Matthew Boyle, "Unilever: Taking on the World, One Stall at a Time," *Bloomberg Businessweek,* January 7, 2013, pp. 18–20; and Martinne Geller, "Unilever Sticks with Emerging Markets as Sales Rebound," *Reuters,* January 21, 2014, http://uk.reuters.com/article/2014/01/21/uk-unilever-results-idUKBREA0K09A20140121.
23. See Serena Ng, "Toilet-Tissue 'Desheeting' Shrinks Rolls, Plumps Margins," *Wall Street Journal,* July 24, 2013, http://online.wsj.com/news/articles/SB10001424127887323971204578626223494483866; and Serena Ng, "At P&G, New Tide Comes In, Old Price Goes Up," *Wall Street Journal,* February 10, 2014, http://online.wsj.com/news/articles/SB10001424052702304450904579368852980301572.
24. For discussions of these issues, see Dhruv Grewel and Larry D. Compeau, "Pricing and Public Policy: A Research Agenda and Overview of the Special Issue," *Journal of Public Policy and Marketing*, Spring 1999, pp. 3–10; Walter L. Baker, Michael V. Marn, and Craig C. Zawada, *The Price Advantage* (Hoboken, NJ: John Wiley & Sons, 2010), Appendix 2; and Nagle, Hogan, and Zale, *The Strategy and Tactics of Pricing*.
25. See Tim Worstall, "Apple Fined $670,000 in Taiwan for Price Fixing," *Forbes,* December 25, 2013, www.forbes.com/sites/

timworstall/2013/12/25/apple-fined-670000-in-taiwan-for-price-fixing; and Lina Chan, "The Age of Amazon Is Upon Us," *Salon,* January 16, 2015, www.salon.com/2015/01/16/the_age_of_amazon_is_upon_us_how_one_court_battle_reveals_the_growing_threat_of_monopoly/.

26. Based on information found in Lynn Leary, "Publishers and Booksellers See a 'Predatory' Amazon," *NPR Books,* January 23, 2012, www.npr.org/2012/01/23/145468105; and Andrew Albanese, "At Apple Hearing, Amazon Called a 'Monopolist'" *Publishers Weekly,* December 15, 2014, www.publishersweekly.com/pw/by-topic/digital/content-and-e-books/article/65063-at-hearing-second-circuit-questions-e-book-case-against-apple.html.
27. "FTC Guides against Deceptive Pricing," www.ecfr.gov/cgi-bin/text-idx?c=ecfr&sid=dfafb89837c306cf5b010b5bde15f041&rgn=div5&view=text&node=16:1.0.1.2.16&idno=16, accessed October 2015.

Chapter 10

1. Jim Edwards, "Uber Has Changed My Life and as God Is My Witness I Will Never Take a Taxi Again" *Business Insider,* January 22, 2014, www.businessinsider.com/uber-has-changed-my-life-and-as-god-is-my-witness-i-will-never-take-a-taxi-again-where-available-2014-1#ixzz3TYF7ZY29; Brad Stone, "Invasion of the Taxi Snatchers: Uber Leads an Industry's Disruption," *Businessweek,* February 20, 2014, pp. 38–42; Om Malik, "Uber Is the New Google," *Fast Company,* June 2014, p. 50; Rebecca Borison, "Report: Uber Generates 12X More Revenue Than Lyft, Despite Charging More per Ride," *Business Insider,* September 11, 2014, www.businessinsider.com/uber-12x-revenue-over-lyft-2014-9; Douglas MacMillan, "How Sharp-Elbowed Uber Is Trying to Make Nice," *Wall Street Journal,* January 29, 2015, www.wsj.com/articles/hard-driving-uber-gives-compromise-a-try-1422588782; Alan Murray, "Uber-nomics," *Fortune,* January 2015, p. 6.
2. Based on information from Joe Cahill, "Mind Your Franchisees, Mayor McCheese," *Crain's Chicago Business,* April 26, 2013, www.chicagobusiness.com/article/20130426/BLOGS10/130429841; "McDonald's Customer Service Push Irritates Some Franchisees," *Chicago Business Journal,* April 17, 2014, www.bizjournals.com/chicago/news/2013/04/17/mcdonalds-riding-fine-line-franchisees.html; and "Is McDonald's Broken? Franchisees Are Furious," *Yahoo! Finance,* April 15, 2015, http://finance.yahoo.com/news/mcdonalds-broken-franchisees-furious-133644537.html.
3. See http://investors.sherwin-williams.com/; and "The Kroger Co. Fact Book," http://ir.kroger.com/CorporateProfile.aspx?iid=4004136, accessed October 2015.
4. See the Inditex Press Dossier, www.inditex.com/en/media/press_dossier, accessed April 2015.
5. Franchising facts from "The State of the Franchise Economy in 2013," http://franchiseeconomy.com/wp-content/uploads/2013/09/The-State-Of-The-Franchise-Economy-In-2013-9-17-13.pdf; www.azfranchises.com/franchisefacts.htm, accessed May 2013; and company sources, accessed June 2015. Also see "Franchise Business Economic Outlook for 2015," January 2015, http://emarket.franchise.org/FranchiseBizOutlook2015.pdf.
6. See "Two Men and a Truck Wraps Up Successful 2014, Fuels Future Expansion in 2015," January 29, 2015, www.twomenandatruck.com/details.aspx?p=1EC0C69A41A54054&ppid=59896&naid=C0CACB36C71828B8; and www.twomenandatruck.com/history-of-two-men-and-a-truck, accessed October 2015.
7. See Eric Platt, "22 Companies That Are Addicted to Walmart," June 13, 2012, *Business Insider,* www.businessinsider.com/22-companies-who-are-completely-addicted-to-walmart-2012-6#; and Dan Mitchell, "Say Goodbye to Your Supermarket," *Fortune,* March 14, 2014, http://fortune.com/2014/03/14/say-goodbye-to-your-supermarket/.
8. See "General Mills: Joint Ventures," www.generalmills.com/en/Company/Businesses/International/Joint_ventures.aspx, accessed October 2015.
9. "Barnes & Noble Abandons Plan to Spin Off Nook Business," *New York Post,* February 24, 2015, http://nypost.com/2015/02/26/barnes-noble-abandons-plan-to-spin-off-nook-business/.
10. Lawrence Frost, "Volvo to Launch Online Car Sales in Marketing Shift," *Reuters,* December 15, 2014, www.reuters.com/article/2014/12/15/us-volvo-internet-idUSKBN0JT0D020141215; and Diana Kuryiko, "Volvo Dealers Are Hungry for the Redesigned XC90," *Automotive News,* January 25, 2015, www.autonews.com/article/20150123/RETAIL06/301249995/volvo-dealers-are-hungry-for-the-redesigned-xc90.
11. See "Ace Town & Country Hardware: Recommended Reviews," *Yelp,* www.yelp.com/biz/ace-town-and-country-hardware-chapel-hill-2, accessed April 2015; and www.acehardware.com/corp/index.jsp?page=about, accessed October 2015.
12. See http://new.pamperedchef.com/company-facts and www.stelladot.com/trunkshow, accessed October 2015.
13. See Grace Lavigne, "China Unveils Six-Year Plan to Cut Logistics," *Journal of Commerce,* October 7, 2014, www.joc.com/international-logistics/global-sourcing/china-unveils-six-year-plan-cut-logistics-costs_20141007.html; and Steven Butler, "Walmart China: Hitting Headwinds," *CNNMoney,* January 22, 2015, http://money.cnn.com/2015/01/22/news/economy/ozy-china-walmart/.
14. Based on information from Julie Jargon, "Asia Delivers for McDonald's," *Wall Street Journal,* December 13, 2011, http://online.wsj.com/article/SB10001424052970204397704577074982151549316.html; "Feel Like a Burger? Dial M for McDonald's Japan," *Asia Pulse,* January 23, 2012; and McDonald's annual reports, www.aboutmcdonalds.com/mcd/investors/annual_reports.html, accessed October 2015.
15. See Stephanie Strom, "CVS Vows to Quit Selling Tobacco Products," *New York Times,* February 5, 2014, p. B1; Bruce Japson, "CVS Health Kicks Smoking Habit and Still Has Record Sales," *Forbes,* February 20, 2015, www.forbes.com/sites/brucejapsen/2015/02/10/even-without-tobacco-revenue-cvs-reports-sales/; and http://info.cvscaremark.com/cvs-insights/cvs-quits, accessed October 2015.
16. See Rosalyn Wilson, "25th Annual State of Logistics Report: It's Complicated," July 1, 2014, www.logisticsmgmt.com/article/25th_annual_state_of_logistics_its_complicated.
17. William B. Cassidy, "Walmart Squeezes Costs from Supply Chain," *Journal of Commerce,* January 5, 2010; "Walmart to Save $150 Million Thanks to Sustainability Programs," *Triple Pundit,* October 16, 2012, www.triplepundit.com/2012/10/walmart-save-150-million-sustainability-programs/; and Phalguni Soni, "Walmart's Supply Chain and Distribution Model," *Market Realist,* February 18, 2015, http://marketrealist.com/2015/02/managing-walmarts-supply-chain-cross-docking-tools/.
18. Andy Brack, "Piggly Wiggly Center Offers Info-Packed Field Trip," *Charleston Currents,* January 4, 2010, www.charlestoncurrents.com/issue/10_issues/10.0104.htm; and information from http://en.wikipedia.org/wiki/Piggly_wiggly and http://news.walmart.com/news-archive/2005/01/07/our-retail-divisions, accessed October 2015.
19. Jessica Stillman, "Green Cred: Sustainability a Cost-Cutting Move for Suppliers," *Forbes,* December 11, 2012, www.forbes.com/sites/ups/2012/12/11/green-cred-sustainability-a-cost-cutting-move-for-suppliers/; and www.apparelcoalition.org/higgindex/, www.nikeresponsibility.com/, and www.nikeresponsibility.com/report/content/chapter/manufacturing, accessed October 2015.
20. Andrew S. Ross, "Forget the Elves; Amazon Turns to Robots This Holiday Season," SFGATE, December 21, 2014, www.sfgate.com/business/bottomline/article/Forget-the-elves-Amazon-turns-to-robots-this-5928294.php; and "Working at Amazon," January 2015, www.amazon.com/gp/help/customer/display.html?nodeId=200787540&view-type=stand-alone.
21. See Ross, "Forget the Elves"; Scott Kirsner, "Amazon Acquisition Puts Amazon Rivals in Awkward Spot," *Boston Globe,* December 1, 2013, www.bostonglobe.com/business/2013/12/01/will-amazon-owned-robot-maker-sell-tailer-rivals/FON7bVNKvfzS2sHnBHzfLM/story.html; Donna Tam, "Meet Amazon's Busiest Employee—the Kiva Robot," CNET, November 30, 2014, www.cnet.com/news/meet-amazons-busiest-employee-the-kiva-robot/; and www.kivasystems.com, accessed October 2015.
22. Bureau of Transportation Statistics, "Pocket Guide to Transportation 2015," January 2015, www.rita.dot.gov/bts/sites/rita.dot.gov.bts/files/publications/pocket_guide_to_transportation/2015; and American Trucking Association, www.trucking.org/News_and_Information_Reports_Industry_Data.aspx, accessed October 2015.
23. See Walmart's supplier requirements at http://corporate.walmart.com/suppliers, accessed April 2015.
24. For this and other UPS examples and information, see "Toshiba Laptop Repair," accessed at http://pressroom.ups.com/Video/Toshiba+Laptop+Repair, May 2013; and www.thenewlogistics.com and www.ups.com/content/us/en/about/facts/worldwide.html, accessed October 2015.
25. "3PL Customers Report Identifies Service Trends, 3PL Market Segment Sizes and Growth Rates," Armstrong & Associates, Inc., July 11, 2013, www.3plogistics.com/PR_3PL_Customers-2013.htm. Also see Robert C. Lieb, "25 Years of Third-Party Logistics Research & Studies," *Supply Chain 247,* December 31, 2014, http://www.supplychain247.com/article/25_years_of_third-party_logistics_research.
26. See John Langley Jr., "2014 Third-Party Logistics Study: The State of Logistics Outsourcing," Capgemini Consulting, www.capgemini.com/resource-file-access/resource/pdf/3pl_study_report_web_version.pdf., accessed May 2015.

Chapter 11

1. Based on information from "Fortune Global 500," *Fortune,* August 1, 2015, pp. F1-F6; Ashley Lutz and Mike Nudelman, "14 Facts about Wal-Mart That Will Blow Your Mind," *Business Insider*, October 17, 2013, www.businessinsider.com/facts-about-wal-mart-to-blow-your-mind-2013-10; John Huey, "Wal-Mart: Will It Take over the World?" *Fortune*, January 30, 1998, pp. 52–61; Michael Barbano and Stuart Elliott, "Clinging to Its Roots, Wal-Mart Steps Back from an Edgy, New Image," *New York Times,* December 10, 2006, www.nytimes.com/2006/12/10/business/worldbusiness/10iht-walmart.3845671.html; "Top 250 Global Retailers, 2015," *National Retail Federation,* https://nrf.com/2015/global250-table; and annual reports and other information found at http://corporate.walmart.com/our-story/heritage/sam-walton, http://news.walmart.com/walmart-facts/corporate-financial-fact-sheet, and www.walmartstores.com, accessed October 2015.
2. See "Monthly and Annual Retail Trade," U.S. Census Bureau, www.census.gov/retail/, accessed October 2015.
3. See "Just Released: P&G 2014 Annual Report," P&G Corporate Newsroom, August 20, 2014, http://news.pg.com/blog/company-strategy/just-released-pg-2014-annual-report; and "Procter & Gamble," *Growth Champions,* March 2015, http://growthchampions.org/growth-champions/procter-gamble/.
4. For more on digital aspects of shopper marketing and omni-channel retailing, see Tim Simmons, "The Keys to Unlocking the Retail Omni-Channel Advantage," *Forbes,* January 1, 2015, www.forbes.com/sites/teradata/2015/01/02/the-keys-to-unlocking-the-retail-omni-channel-advantage/print/; Lisa R. Melsted, "Retailers Turn to Omnichannel Strategies to Remain Competitive," *Forbes,* February 9, 2015, www.forbes.com/sites/samsungbusiness/2015/02/09/retailers-turn-to-omnichannel-strategies-to-remain-competitive/print/; and www.shoppermarketingmag.com/home/, accessed May 2015; and "ZMOT," *Google Digital Services*, www.zeromomentoftruth.com/, accessed October 2015.
5. John Russell, "Grocery Wars Certain to Flair Up on North Side," *IndyStar,* January 27, 2015, www.indystar.com/story/news/2015/01/25/grocery-wars-certain-flare-north-side/22125353/.
6. Jon Springer, "Pricing: WinCo Keeps Costs Down and Velocity High," *Supermarket News,* April 29, 2013, http://supermarketnews.com/retail-amp-financial/pricing-winco-keeps-costs-down-and-velocity-high#ixzz2uLcJzlvN; Brad Tuttle, "Meet the Low-Key, Low-Cost Grocery Chain Being Called 'Walmart's Worst Nightmare,'" *Time,* August 7, 2013, http://business.time.com/2013/08/07/meet-the-low-key-low-cost-grocery-chain-being-called-wal-marts-worst-nightmare/; Justin Corr, "Learning about Retirement from WinCo's Millionaire Checkers," *KTVB.com,* February 3, 2015, www.ktvb.com/story/news/local/2015/02/03/winco-checkers-retirement/22793933/; and www.wincofoods.com, accessed October 2015.
7. See Jonathon Berr, "7-Eleven Goes on a Healthy Kick," *MSN Money,* September 13, 2013, http://money.msn.com/now/post-7-eleven-goes-on-a-health-kick; and http://corp.7-eleven.com, accessed October 2015.
8. http://corporate.walmart.com/our-story/our-business/locations/#/united-states, accessed June 2015; and "Supermarket Facts," www.fmi.org/research-resources/supermarket-facts, accessed October 2015.
9. See "Dollar General Reports Record Fourth Quarter and Full Year 2014 Financial Results," March 12, 2015, http://newscenter.dollargeneral.com/news/dollar-general-reports-record-fourth-quarter-and-full-year-2014-financial-results.htm; Christopher Matthews, "Will Dollar Stores Rule the Retail World?" *Time,* April 1, 2013, http://business.time.com/2013/04/01/will-dollar-stores-rule-the-retail-world/; and http://investor.shareholder.com/dollar/financials.cfm, accessed October 2015.
10. Beth Kowitt, "Is T.J. Maxx the Best Retail Sore in the Land," *Fortune,* August 11, 2014, pp. 93-96; and "How We Do It," http://tjmaxx.tjx.com/store/jump/topic/how-we-do-it/2400087, accessed October 2015.
11. Phil Wahba, "Macy's Mull Taking on T.J. Maxx, Nordstrom Rack in "Off-Price" Wars," *Fortune,* January 8, 2015, http://fortune.com/2015/01/08/macys-outlet-off-price/.
12. Based on information from "Top 250 Global Retailers, 2015," *National Retail Federation,* https://nrf.com/2015/global250-table; Stan Laegreid, "The Choreography of Design, Treasure Hunts, and Hot Dogs That Have Made Costco So Successful," *Fast Company*, January 24, 2014, www.fastcompany.com/3025312; Susanna Kim, "7 Reasons Why People Can't Get Enough of Costco," *ABC News,* January 6, 2015, http://abcnews.go.com/Business/reasons-people-costco/story?id=26046572; and www.costco.com and http://www.costco.com/insider-guide-amazing-facts.html, accessed October 2015.
13. Company and franchising information from "2014 Franchise Times Top 200 Franchise Systems," *Franchise Times*, October 2014, www.franchisetimes.com/pdf/2014/Top200-2014.pdf, www.score.org/resources/should-i-buy-franchise; and http://www.aboutmcdonalds.com/mcd/our_company.html and www.subway.com/subwayroot/About_Us/default.aspx, accessed October 2015.
14. Numbers from "Top 200 Franchise Systems," *Franchise Times*, October 2014, www.franchisetimes.com/pdf/2014/Top200-2014.pdf. See also www.whichwich.com and www.whichwich.com/about_us, accessed October 2015.
15. Based on information from "How Do You See This Experiential Retailing Trend Working Its Way across Retail?" *Integrated Retailing,* www.integratedretailing.com/?p=131, accessed September 2014; and www.llbean.com, www.llbean.com/llb/shop/1000001692?nav=ftlink, and www.llbean.com/llb/shop/1000001704?page=campus-lander#, accessed October 2015.
16. See Justine Sharrock, "How Manufactured Smells Are Making People Shop Longer and Kill Better," *BuzzFeed,* March 15, 2013, www.buzzfeed.com/justinesharrock/how-manufactured-smells-are-making-people-shop-longer-and-ki; Alexandra Sifferlin, "My Nose Made Me Buy It," *Time,* December 16, 2013, http://healthland.time.com/2013/12/16/my-nose-made-me-buy-it-how-retailers-use-smell-and-other-tricks-to-get-you-to-spend-spend-spend/; Sarah Nassauer, "Using Scent as a Marketing Tool, Stores Hope It—and Shoppers—Will Linger," *Wall Street Journal,* May 20, 2014, www.wsj.com/articles/SB10001424052702303468704579573953132979382; and www.scentair.com/why-scentair-scent-studies/, accessed October 2015.
17. See various social media sites for Walmart and Fairway, accessed October 2015.
18. "CVS/pharmacy Revolutionizes the Way Customers Experience the Sales Circular with Launch of myWeekly Ad," October 17, 2013, http://info.cvscaremark.com/newsroom/press-releases/cvspharmacy-revolutionizes-way-customers-experience-sales-circular-launch; Stuart Elliott, "For CVS Regulars, Ads Tailored Just to Them," *New York Times,* October 10, 2013, www.nytimes.com/2013/10/11/business/media/for-cvs-regulars-ads-tailored-just-to-them.html?_r=0; and www.cvs.com, accessed June 2015.
19. For definitions of these and other types of shopping centers, see "Dictionary," *American Marketing Association*, www.marketingpower.com/_layouts/Dictionary.aspx, accessed October 2015.
20. See "Brick by Brick: The State of the Shopping Center," Nielsen, May 17, 2013, http://nielsen.com/us/en/reports/2013/brick-by-brick-the-state-of-the-shopping-center.html; "It's the End of the Mall as We Know It," *Real Estate Weekly*, February 22, 2013, www.rew-online.com/2013/02/22/its-the-end-of-the-mall-as-we-know-it/; Judy Keen, "As Enclosed Malls Decline, 'Lifestyle Centers' Proliferate," MINNPOST, August 30, 2013, www.minnpost.com/cityscape/2013/08/enclosed-malls-decline-lifestyle-centers-proliferate; www.cvs.com/weeklyad/browse/browse-home.jsp#Browse; Jennifer Duell Popovec, "Existing Lifestyle Centers Thrive, but Developers Prefer Mixed-Use for New Projects," December 11, 2014, *National Real Estate Investor,* http://nreionline.com/retail/existing-lifestyle-centers-thrive-developers-prefer-mixed-use-new-projects.
21. Nelson D. Schwartz, "The Economics (and Naiostalgia) of Dead Malls," *New York Times,* January 3, 2015, www.nytimes.com/2015/01/04/business/the-economics-and-nostalgia-of-dead-malls.html.
22. Jennifer Reingold and Phil Wahba, "Where Have All the Shopper Gone?" *Fortune,* September 3, 2014, http://fortune.com/2014/09/03/where-have-all-the-shoppers-gone/.
23. See Rick Brockmann, "Nike to Open Pop-Up Shop Near Barclays for NBA's All-Star Weekend," *The Real Deal*, February 9, 2015.
24. See www.gilt.com and www.zulily.com, accessed October 2015.
25. See www.rpminc.com/leading-brands/consumer-brands, accessed October 2015.
26. Thad Rueter, "The Web's Influence on U.S. Retail Grows," *Internet Retailer*, July 25, 2014, www.internetretailer.com/2014/07/25/webs-influence-us-retail-grows; and U.S. Census Bureau News, "Quarterly Retail E-Commerce Sales, 4rd Quarter 2014," February 17, 2015, www.census.gov/retail/mrts/www/data/pdf/ec_current.pdf.
27. See Greg Sterling, "Mobile Devices: 30 Percent of Traffic, 15 Percent of Sales," *Marketing Land*, February 28, 2014, http://marketingland.com/mobile-devices-generate-30-pct-traffic-15-pct-e-sales-75498; and Thad Rueter, "The Web's Influence on U.S. Retail Grows," *Internet Retailer*, July 25, 2014, www.internetretailer.com/2014/07/25/webs-influence-us-retail-grows.
28. Lauren Johnson, "Target Turns Its Stores into One Big Mobile Game for the Holidays," *Adweek,* December 2, 2014, www.adweek.com/print/161727.

29. "Store-Based Retailers Take the Early Lead among Top 500 Retailers in Online Sales Growth," *Internet Retailer,* February 18, 2014, www.internetretailer.com/2014/02/18/store-based-retailers-take-early-lead-among-top-500; and "Top 500 Guide," *Internet Retailer*, www.internetretailer.com/top500/top10/, accessed October 2015.
30. Paul Demery, "E-Commerce Becomes More Dominant at Williams-Sonoma," *Internet Retailer*, August 20, 2013, www.internetretailer.com/2013/08/30/e-commerce-becomes-more-dominant-williams-sonoma; Adam Blair, "Williams-Sonoma Invests $75M in Fast-Growing, Profitable E-Commerce," RIS, March 22, 2011, http://risnews.edgl.com/retail-best-practices/Williams-Sonoma-Invests-$75M-in-Fast-Growing,-Profitable-E-Commerce71523; and Laura Alber, "The CEO of Williams-Sonoma on Blending Instinct with Analysis," *Harvard Business Review,* September 2014, https://hbr.org/2014/09/the-ceo-of-williams-sonoma-on-blending-instinct-with-analysis.
31. Brad Tuttle, "The Creepy New Way Macy's Tempts You to Make Impulse Purchases," *Time,* September 26, 2015, http://time.com/money/3432693/macys-shopkick-ibeacon/.
32. See Lauren Johnson, "This $473 Billion Retailer Wants to Be the Next Ad-Tech Star," *Adweek,* November 18, 2014, www.adweek.com/print/161471; "Our Strategy: Winning in Global E-Commerce," *Walmart 2012 Annual Report*, www.walmartstores.com/sites/annual-report/2012/WalMart_AR.pdf, March 2013, pp. 12–13; and www.walmartlabs.com, accessed October 2015.
33. "Green MashUP: 7 Trends Transforming Retail Sustainability," *The Fifth Estate*, February 17, 2015, www.thefifthestate.com.au/business/trends/green-mashup-7-trends-transforming-retail-sustainability/71455; and "The IKEA Group Sustainability Report," www.ikea.com/ms/en_US/pdf/sustainability_report/sustainability_report_2014.pdf accessed October 2015.
34. See www.staples.com/sbd/cre/marketing/easy-on-the-planet/recycling-and-eco-services.html, accessed October 2015.
35. See http://news.walmart.com/walmart-facts/corporate-financial-fact-sheet, accessed October 2015.
36. See "Global Powers of Retailing 2015," Deloitte, January 2015, accessed at http://www2.deloitte.com/content/dam/Deloitte/global/Documents/Consumer-Business/gx-cb-global-powers-of-retailing.pdf.
37. Grainger facts and other information are from the "Grainger: Beyond the Box Fact Book," accessed at http://invest.grainger.com/phoenix.zhtml?c=76754&p=irol-irFactBook and www.grainger.com, accessed October 2015.
38. "Top 500 Guide," Internet Retailer, www.top500guide.com/top-500/the-top-500-list, accessed March 2014; and www.grainger.com, accessed October 2014.
39. Information from "About Us," www.mckesson.com; and "Supply Management Online," http://mckessonbop.com/solutions-services/mckesson-connect/, accessed October 2015.
40. Facts from "2014 Power 50," http://supermarketnews.com/2014-power-50-clickable-list, accessed June 2015; and www.supervalu.com, accessed October 2015.

Chapter 12

1. Quotes and other information from Dominique Mosbergen, "GEICO Creates 'Unskippable' Preroll YouTube Ads That You'll Want to Watch till the End," *Huffington Post,* March 2, 2015, www.huffingtonpost.com/2015/03/02/geico-unskippable-ad-youtube-preroll_n_6788894.html; E. J. Schultz, "Muscling Past Mayhem: GEICO Rides Giant Ad Budget Past Allstate," *Advertising Age,* July 8, 2013, www.adage.com/print/242980; "10 Most-Advertised Brands," *Advertising Age Marketing Fact Pack 2015,* December 29, 2014, pp. 7, 10; Michele Miller, "'Hump Day' GEICO Commercial: Creators Dish on Ad's Success, Its Development," *CBS News,* September 18, 2013, www.cbsnews.com/news/hump-day-geico-commercial-creators-dish-on-ads-success-its-development/; Andrea Paton-Ash, "Camels Return to the Spotlight in GEICO's Latest 'It's What You Do' Commercial," December 23, 2014, http://blog.geico.com/2014/12/23/camels-return-to-the-spotlight-in-geicos-latest-its-what-you-do-commercial/; and www.geico.com and www.youtube.com/user/GEICO, accessed October 2015.
2. For other definitions, see www.ama.org/resources/Pages/Dictionary.aspx, accessed October 2015.
3. "Ad Spending by Medium," *Advertising Age Marketing Fact Pack 2015,* December 29, 2014, p. 16; "Digital to Overtake TV Ad Spending in Two Years," *Advertising Age,* November 4, 2014, www.adage.com/print/295694; Natalie Tadena, "Magna Global: TV Will Remain Soft in 2015," *Wall Street Journal,* February 25, 2015, http://blogs.wsj.com/cmo/2015/02/25/magna-global-tv-ad-spending-will-remain-soft-in-2015; "P&G's Pritchard on Where Marketing, Media, and Metrics Are Going," *Advertising Age,* March 16, 2015, www.adage.com/print/297592; and Jack Neff and E. J. Schultz, "Overdose?," *Advertising Age,* February 9, 2015, pp. 14–15.
4. See Andrew Adam Newman, "With a French Accent, a Soap Brand Tells a Tale of Well-Scrubbed Lovers," *New York Times,* March 21, 2014, p. B4; Stuart Elliott, "Ad for Method Celebrates the Madness," *New York Times,* March 12, 2012, p. B1; and www.methodhome.com/cleanhappy/ and www.youtube.com/user/peopleagainstdirty, accessed October 2015.
5. See "Advertisers Blend Digital and TV for Well-Rounded Campaigns," *eMarketer,* March 12, 2014, www.emarketer.com/Article/Advertisers-Blend-Digital-TV-Well-Rounded-Campaigns/1010670.
6. See Troy Dreier, "How Lowe's and Vine Build Social Video Success," *Streaming Media,* May 2014, www.streamingmedia.com/Articles/Editorial/Featured-Articles/How-Lowes-and-Vine-Build-Social-Video-Success-96585.aspx; Alexxis Letozoa, "Lowe's Fix in Six," *–Ation,* December 1, 2014, http://ation.digitalmediauconn.org/lowes-fix-in-six/; https://vine.co/Lowes, www.youtube.com/user/Lowes, https://instagram.com/loweshomeimprovement/, www.pinterest.com/lowes/, and other Lowe's social media sites, accessed October 2015.
7. See Scott Collins, "Super Bowl 2015: Sunday's Game a Ratings Winner for NBC," *LA Times*, February 3, 2015; www.latimes.com/entertainment/tv/la-et-st-super-bowl-2015-ratings-20150203-story.html; Rick Kissell, "'NCIS' Has Become the World's Most-Watched TV Drama," *Variety,* June 11, 2014, http://variety.com/2014/tv/news/ncis-most-popular-drama-in-worldwatched-tv-drama-1201218492/; and www.youtube.com/watch?v=qaOvHKG0Tio, accessed October 2015.
8. See discussions at Mike Ishmael, "The Cost of a Sales Call," October 22, 2012, http://4dsales.com/the-cost-of-a-sales-call/; Jeff Green, "The New Willy Loman Survives by Staying Home," *Bloomberg Businessweek,* January 14–20, 2013, pp. 16–17; and "What Is the Real Cost of a B2B Sales Call?" www.marketing-playbook.com/sales-marketing-strategy/what-is-the-real-cost-of-a-b2b-sales-call, accessed October 2015.
9. "100 Largest Global Marketers," *Advertising Age*, December 8, 2014, p. 26.
10. For these and other advertising spending facts, see *Advertising Age Marketing Fact Pack 2015,* December 29, 2014, and "200 Leading National Advertisers," *Advertising Age,* July 13, 2015, pp. 14-23.
11. See "200 Leading National Advertisers," *Advertising Age,* July 13, 2015, p. 16; and "The CDC's Anti-Smoking Ads Now Include E-Cigarettes," *Bloomberg Businessweek*, March 26, 2015, www.bloomberg.com/news/articles/2015-03-26/the-cdc-s-anti-smoking-ads-now-include-e-cigarettes.
12. Bruce Horovitz, "Taco Bell Still Giving Ronald McDonald Grief," *USA Today,* April 3, 2014.
13. See "Microsoft Flips Famed PC vs. Mac Ads to Pitch Smartphones, Tablets," *Advertising Age,* August 12, 2014, www.adage.com/print/294551; and www.youtube.com/watch?v=yYC5dkQlQLA, accessed October 2015.
14. See Jean Halliday, "Thinking Big Takes Audi from Obscure to Awesome," *Advertising Age,* February 2, 2009, http://adage.com/print?article_id=134234; and "Audi U.S. Sales in February 2015 Rise to Record Level for 50th Consecutive Month," *Yahoo! Finance,* April 17, 2015, http://finance.yahoo.com/news/audi-u-sales-february-2015-170012501.html.
15. "Number of Magazines in the United States from 2002 to 2013," *Statistica,* www.statista.com/statistics/238589/number-of-magazines-in-the-united-states/, accessed June 2015; and Andrew Burger, "Nielsen: Despite Hundreds of Choices, Average Number of TV Channels Watched Is 17," *Telecompetitor,* May 9, 2014, www.telecompetitor.com/nielsen-average-number-of-tv-channels-watched-is-17/.
16. Kelsey Libert and Kristen Tynski, "Research: The Emotions That Make Marketing Campaigns Go Viral," HBR Blog Network, October 24, 2013, http://blogs.hbr.org/2013/10/research-the-emotions-that-make-marketing-campaigns-go-viral/; and data from YouTube, Facebook, Instagram, and Twitter from October 2015.
17. Steve McClellan, "4As Scraps Annual Ad Production Cost Survey," *Media Post,* February 11, 2014, www.mediapost.com/publications/article/219371/4as-scraps-annual-ad-production-cost-survey.html; Sam Thielman, "The New Hour Is 43 Minutes Long," *Adweek,* June 24, 2013, p. 12; Jeanine Poggi, "Football and 'Big Bang' Are Broadcast TV's Most Expensive Ad Buys," *AdAge,* September 25, 2014, http://adage.com/print/295130; and "What It Costs," *Advertising Age,* April 6, 2014, pp. 14–18.
18. See Anthony Grupi, "Are Nets Beating Back the Devil in the DVR?" *Advertising Age,* September 29, 2014, pp. 16–17; and Jeff Baumgartner, "76% of Homes Have DVR, Netflix or Use VOD: Study," *Multichannel News,* January 2, 2015, www.multichannel.com/news/technology/76-homes-have-dvr-netflix-or-use-vod-study/386584.
19. See Michael Sebastian, "Madison & Vine at 10," *Advertising Age,* May 12, 2014, pp. 18–19.

20. "Real Beauty Shines Through: Dove Wins Titanium Grand Prix, 163 Million Views on YouTube," *Google: Think Insights,* June2013, www .thinkwithgoogle.com/case-studies/dove-real-beauty-sketches.html; Nina Bahadur, "Dove 'Real Beauty' Campaign Turns 10: How a Brand Tried to Change the Conversation about Female Beauty," *Huffington Post,* February 6, 2014, www.huffingtonpost.com/2014/01/21/dove-real-beauty-campaign-turns-10_n_4575940.tml; "Powerful Dove Experiment Shows How Women Can Choose to Feel Beautiful," *Mashable,* April 7, 2015, http://mashable.com/2015/04/07/dove-video-doors-beautiful-average/; and www.youtube.com/watch?v=XpaOjMXyJGk, accessed October 2014.
21. See Seth Fiegerman, "The New Way Brands Like Hostess Use Social Media: Playing Dumb," *Mashable,* April 6, 2015, http://mashable.com/2015/04/06/brands-play-dumb/.
22. See Danny Sullivan, "Product Placement: The TV Ads Consumers Can't Skip or Hop," *Marketing Land,* May 28, 2013, http://marketingland .com/product-placement-tv-ads-45729; Jonathan Welsh, "Can 'Captain America' Help Harley-Davidson Sell Motorcycles?" *Wall Street Journal,* April 1, 2014, http://blogs.wsj.com/speakeasy/2014/04/01/can-captain-america-help-harley-davidson-sell-motorcycles/; and Jason Lynch, "'Modern Family's' Apple-centric Integration Is Product Integration at Its Best," *Quartz,* February 25, 2015, http://qz.com/350518/modern-familys-apple-centric-episode-is-product-placement-at-its-best-and-great-tv/.
23. Abe Sauer, "Announcing the 2015 Brandcameo Product Placement Awards," *BrandChannel,* February 20, 2015, www.brandchannel.com/home/post/150220-2015-Brandcameo-Product-Placement-Awards.aspx.
24. "Why *The Lego Movie* Is the Perfect Piece of Product Placement," *A.V. Club,* February 11, 2014, http://www.avclub.com/article/why-the lego-movie-is-the-perfect-piece-of-product-201102; and Abe Sauer, "Announcing the 2015 Brandcameo Product Placement Awards," *BrandChannel,* February 20, 2015, http://brandchannel.com/2015/02/20/announcing-the-2015-brandcameo-product-placement-awards/.
25. Michael Sebastionm "Nearly Two-Thirds of Marketers Plan to Increase Native-Ad Spending in 2015," January 29, 2015, *Advertising Age,* www .adage.com/print/296887.
26. For these and other examples, see David Gianatasio, "Ad of the Day: Cute, Quirky Chevy Commercial on the Oscars Was Made for $4,000," *Adweek,* March 3, 2014, www.adweek.com/print/156071; "Purina Pro Plan Debuts New Consumer-Generated Ad during Westminster Kennel Club Dog Show," *PRNewswire,* February 11, 2013; "Taco Bell Commissions User-Generated YouTube Ads to Promote New Fiery Doritos Locos Taco," *Viral Gains,* www.viralgains.com/2013/08/taco-bell-commissions-user-generated-youtube-ads-promote-fiery-doritos-locos-taco/; and www.youtube.com/watch?v=g9EU1Fw-D2s and www .youtube.com/watch?v=swFZ3QJmqu8#t=20, accessed October 2015.
27. Quotes and other information from Lauren Drell, "User Generated Content: Lessons from 4 Killer Ad Campaigns," *American Express Open Forum,* January 28, 2013, www.openforum.com/articles/lessons-from-4-killer-ugc-campaigns/; and http://thesweatlife.lululemon.com/, accessed October 2015.
28. Lauren Johnson, "How Social and Email Helped Mazda's Limited-Edition Preorders Sell Out Crazy Fast," *Adweek,* May 28, 2014, www .adweek.com/print/157985.
29. See Anna Rudenko, "Coca-Cola USA Prompting Youngsters to Contribute Their 'Ahh' Moments," POPSOP, March 24, 2014, http://popsop.com/2014/03/coca-cola-usa-prompting-youngsters-to-contribute-their-ahh-coke-moments/; and "Coca-Cola: The AHH Efect," *All Things Digital,* March 11, 2015, https://digitalcasestudies.wordpress .com/2015/03/11/coca-cola-the-ahh-effect/.
30. See Wayne Friedman, "Most Second-Screeners Don't Follow Ads," *Media Post,* December 16, 2014, www.mediapost.com/publications/article/240250/.
31. *Forbes* and *Bloomberg Businessweek* cost and circulation data found online at www.bloombergmedia.com/magazine/businessweek/rates/ and www.forbesmedia.com/forbes-magazine-rates/, accessed October 2015.
32. Natalie Tadena, "With the New Year Approaching, Weight Loss Ad Barrage Has Commenced," *Wall Street Journal,* December 30, 2014, http://blogs.wsj.com/cmo/2014/12/30/with-the-new-year-approaching-weight-loss-ad-barrage-has-commenced/.
33. For these and other examples, see Christopher Heine, "Lexus Nabs 100K Video Views on Facebook—in 10 Minutes," *Adweek,* January 23, 2013, www.adweek.com/news/technology/print/146726; Matt McGee, "Oreo, Audi, and Walgreens Newsjack Super Bowl 'Blackout Bowl,'" *Marketing Land,* February 3, 2013, http://marketingland.com/oreo-audi-walgreens-market-quickly-during-super-bowl-blackout-32407; and "Arby's Slayed the Grammys with This Tweet about Pharrell Williams' Hat," *Adweek,* January 27, 2014, www.adweek.com/print/155237.
34. Information on advertising agency revenues from "Agency Report," *Advertising Age,* April 28, 2014, pp. 8+; and *Advertising Age Marketing Fact Pack 2015,"* December 29, 2014, p. 26–29.
35. Stuart Elliott, "Visa Trims Slogan to Expand Meaning," *New York Times,* January 13, 2014, p. B6.
36. See E. J. Schultz, "Behind the Snickers Campaign That Launched a Global Comeback," *Advertising Age,* October 4, 2013, http://adage.com/print/244593; and http://adsoftheworld.com/media/outdoor/snickers_running and http://cargocollective.com/mirceaandronescu/SNICKERS-OOH, accessed September 2014.
37. Based on Glen Broom and Bey-Ling Sha, *Cutlip & Center's Effective Public Relations,* 11th ed. (Upper Saddle River, NJ: Prentice Hall, 2013), Chapter 1.
38. See Mark Fidelman, "8 of the Best Influencer Marketing Campaigns from 8 Hot Agencies," *Forbes,* August 6, 2013, www.forbes.com/sites/markfidelman/2013/08/06/8-of-the-best-influencer-marketing-campaigns-from-the-8-hottest-agencies; Melissa Malcolm, "Success Is Built with Chocolate Milk," *Dairy Foods,* February 2014, pp. 15–17; Polly Elmore, "Promoting Chocolate Milk as an Energy Drink," *PR Works,* February 3, 2014, http://prwrks.com/promoting-chocolate-milk-as-an-energy-drink; and http://gotchocolatemilk.com and http://gotmilksales.org/milk-sales-strategies/built-with-chocolate-milk/, accessed October 2015.
39. See Geoffrey Fowler and Ben Worthen, "Buzz Powers iPad Launch," *Wall Street Journal,* April 2, 2010; "Apple iPad Sales Top 2 Million since Launch," *Tribune-Review* (Pittsburgh), June 2, 2010; "PR Pros Must Be Apple's iPad as a True Game-Changer," *PRweek,* May 2010, p. 23; and "Apple Launches New iPad," March 7, 2012, www.apple.com/pr/library/2012/03/07Apple-Launches-New-iPad.html.
40. Quotes from Sarah Skerik, "An Emerging PR Trend: Content PR Strategy and Tactics," *PR Newswire,* January 15, 2013, http://blog .prnewswire.com/2013/01/15/an-emerging-pr-trend-content-pr-strategy-tactics/; and Mary Teresa Bitti, "The New Mad Men: How Publics Relations Firms Have Emerged from the Shadows," *Financial Post,* December 28, 2014, http://business.financialpost.com/entrepreneur/the-changing-role-of-public-relations-firms.

Chapter 13

1. Based on information from David Whitford, "Salesforce.com: The Software and the Story," *Inc.,* September 2014, pp. 113–117; Whitford, "Selling, the Story: Four Strategies Salesforce.com Uses to Stay on Top," *Inc.,* September 2014, p. 116; Heather Clancy, "Best Buyer for Salesforce?" *Fortune,* April 29, 2015, http://fortune.com/2015/04/29/best-buyer-for-salesforce/; "The World's Most Innovative Companies," *Forbes,* www.forbes.com/innovative-companies/list/, accessed June 2015; and www.salesforce.com and www.salesforce.com/company/, accessed September 2015.
2. See Chanin Ballance, "End Your Sales and Marketing Tug-of-War," *Sales & Marketing Management,* September 26, 2014, http://salesandmarketing .com/content/end-your-sales-and-marketing-tug-war; and Philip Kotler and Kevin Lane Keller, *Marketing Management,* 15th ed. (Hoboken, NJ: Prentice Hall, 2016), p. 644.
3. "Selling Power 500 Largest Sales Forces (2014)," *Selling Power,* www .sellingpower.com/content/article/index.php?a=10430/selling-power-500/largest-sales-forces/2014.
4. See discussions in Mike Ishmael, "The Cost of a Sales Call," October 22, 2012, http://4dsales.com/the-cost-of-a-sales-call/; Jeff Green, "The New Willy Loman Survives by Staying Home," *Bloomberg Businessweek,* January 14–20, 2013, pp. 16–17; and "What Is the Real Cost of a B2B Sales Call?" www.marketing-playbook.com/sales-marketing-strategy/what-is-the-real-cost-of-a-b2b-sales-call, accessed September 2015.
5. Green, "The New Willy Loman Survives by Staying Home"; Dave Stein, "The Evolution of Social Selling," *Sales & Marketing Management,* May/June 2013, p. 14; and Andris A. Zoltners, PK Sinha, and Sally E. Lorimer, "The Growing Power of Inside Sales." *Harvard Business Review,* July 29, 2013, https://hbr.org/2013/07/the-growing-power-of-inside-sa/.
6. Quote and facts from Jim Domanski, "Special Report: The 2012 B@B Tele-Sales Trend Report," www.salesopedia.com/downloads/2012%20B2B%20Tele-Sales%20Trend%20Special%20Reportl.pdf, accessed July 2013; and Kurt Shaver, "Why Inside Salespeople Make Great Social Sellers," November 12, 2014, http://blog.sellingpower.com/gg/2014/11/why-inside-salespeople-make-great-social-sellers.html.
7. See "Case Study: Climax Portable Machine Tools," www.selltis.com/productCaseStudiesClimaxPortableMachineTools.aspx, accessed June 2014; and www.climaxportable.com, accessed September 2015.

8. "Customer Business Development," http://we.experiencepg.com/home/customer_business_development_cbd_sales.html, accessed September 2015.
9. Scott Fuhr, "Good Hiring Makes Good Cents," *Selling Power,* July/August/September 2012, pp. 20–21; and "How Sales Rep Turnover Costs Your Company More Than You Think," *Insight Squared,* July 15, 2014, www.insightsquared.com/2014/07/how-sales-rep-turnover-costs-your-company-more-than-you-think/.
10. For this and more information and discussion, see www.gallupaustralia.com.au/consulting/118729/sales-force-effectiveness.aspx, accessed July 2012; Lynette Ryals and Iain Davies, "Do You Really Know Who Your Best Salespeople Are?" *Harvard Business Review*, December 2010, pp. 34–35; and Donal Daly, "6 Things Successful Salespeople Do," *Salesforce.com,* April 17, 2015, www.salesforce.com/blog/2015/04/6-things-successful-sellers-do-cso-gp.html.
11. See Steve Denning, "The One Thing the Greatest Salespeople All Have," *Forbes,* November 29, 2012, www.forbes.com/sites/stevedenning/2012/11/29/the-one-thing-the-greatest-salespeople-all-have/.
12. "Strengths Based Selling," www.gallup.com/press/176651/strengths-based-selling.aspx, accessed September 2015.
13. Corporate Visions, Inc., "ADP Case Study," http://corporatevisions.com/v5/documents/secure_downloads/CVI_caseStudy_ADP.pdf, accessed June 2015; and V. Kumar, Sarang Sundder, and Robert P. Leone, "Who's Your Most Valuable Salesperson?" *Harvard Business Review*, April 2015, pp. 62–66.
14. Based on information found in Sara Donnelly, "Staying in the Game," *Pharmaceutical Executive*, May 2008, pp. 158–159; Bayer Healthcare Pharmaceuticals, Inc., "Improving Sales Force Effectiveness: Bayer's Experiment with New Technology," 2008, www.icmrindia.org/casestudies/catalogue/Marketing/MKTG200.htm; Tanya Lewis, "Concentric," *Medical Marketing and Media*, July 2008, p. 59, www.hydraframe.com/mobile/project_reprace.htm, accessed July 2012; Andrew Tolve, "Pharma Sales: How Simulation Can Help Reps Sell," *Eye for Pharma,* March 28, 2012, http://social.eyeforpharma.com/sales/pharma-sales-how-simulation-can-help-reps-sell; and Krishna Depura, "Online Sales Training for Busy Sales Representatives," *MindTickle,* www.mindtickle.com/blog/online-sales-training-for-busy-sales-representative/#more-1474, accessed September 2015.
15. For more discussion, see Mark Roberge, "The Right Way to Use Compensation," *Harvard Business Review,* April 2015, pp. 70–75; and "Getting Beyond 'Show Me the Money,'" *Harvard Business Review,* April 2015, pp. 77–81.
16. See Louis Columbus, "Top-Five Focus Areas for Improving Sales Effectiveness Initiatives," *Accenture,* 2013, www.accenture.com/SiteCollectionDocuments/PDF/Accenture-Top-Five-Improvements-Sales-Effectiveness.pdf; and "2014 Sales Performance Optimization Study," CSO Insights, www.csoinsights.com/Publications/.
17. Lain Chroust Ehmann, "Sales Up!" *Selling Power,* January/February 2011, p. 40. Also see Pisello, "Death of a Salesman?"; Tony J. Hughes, "Back to the Future of Sales in 2015," *LinkedIn,* December 27, 2014, www.linkedin.com/pulse/back-future-sales-2015-tony-j-hughes; and "Getting Beyond 'Show Me the Money."
18. See Scott Gillum, "The Disappearing Sales Process," *Forbes,* January 7, 2013, www.forbes.com/sites/gyro/2013/01/07/the-disappearing-sales-process/; and Paul Nolan, "Mapping the Buyer's Journey," *Sales & Marketing Management,* March/April 2015, pp. 32–34.
19. NeilDavey, "UsingSocialMediaMarketinginB2BMarkets," *SmartInsights,* February 16, 2015, www.smartinsights.com/b2b-digital-marketing/b2b-social-media-marketing/b2bsocialmediamarketing/.
20. See "GE's Social Story," www.salesforcemarketingcloud.com/resources/videos/ges-social-story/, accessed June 2014; David Moth, "How General Electric Uses Facebook, Twitter, Pinterest and Google+," *Velocify,* May 2013, https://econsultancy.com/blog/62684-how-general-electric-uses-facebook-twitter-pinterest-and-google; and "GE Social Media," www.ge.com/news/social, accessed September 2015.
21. Example based on information from James C. Anderson, Nirmalya Kumar, and James A. Narus, "Become a Value Merchant," *Sales & Marketing Management*, May 6, 2008, pp. 20–23; and "Business Market Value Merchants," *Marketing Management*, March/April 2008, pp. 31+. For more discussion and examples, see Heather Baldwin, "Deeper Value Delivery," *Selling Power*, September/October 2010, p. 16; Thomas P. Reilly, "Value-Added Selling Is Smart," *Selling Power,* June 27, 2012, www.sellingpower.com/content/article.php?a=8917; and Ron Shapiro, "Selling While Holding Your Price," *Sales & Marketing Management,* January 5, 2015, www.salesandmarketing.com/content/selling-while-holding-your-price.
22. Kantar Retail, *Making Connections: Trade Promotion Integration across the Marketing Landscape* (Wilton, CT: Kantar Retail, July 2012), p. 5.
23. Ibid., p. 6.
24. See "Top 10 Retail Loyalty Programs," *BigDoor,* http://bigdoor.com/blog/2013/12/11/top-10-retail-loyalty-programs/, accessed June 2015; and www.bloomingdales.com/loyallist?cm_sp=FOOTER-_-BOTTOM_NAV-_-LOYALLIST, accessed September 2015.
25. Laura Petrecca, "Food Marketers Offer Super Samples before Super Bowl," *USA Today,* January 25, 2014, www.usatoday.com/story/money/business/2014/01/25/super-bowl-food-samples/4808625/.
26. NCH Marketing Services, "NCH Annual Topline U.S. CPG Coupon Facts Report for Year-End 2014," February 2015, www2.nchmarketing.com/ResourceCenter/assets/0/22/28/76/226/457/4bfe051da14f4f8f9e8bc7e48d9e510a.pdf.
27. See NCH Marketing Services, "NCH Annual Topline View: CPG Coupon Facts Report for Year-End 2014, https://www2.nchmarketing.com/resourcecenter/," accessed September 2015; and "One-Click Savings: A Quick Look at 2015 Mobile Coupon Statistics," *TrueShip,* March 24, 2015, www.trueship.com/blog/2015/03/24/one-click-savings-a-quick-look-at-2015-mobile-coupon-statistics/#.VS8RL2a-h5A.
28. Hilary Milnes, "Walgreens Uses Mobile Apps to Solve In-Store Headaches," *Digiday,* May 4, 2015, https://digiday.com/brands/walgreens-uses-mobile-apps-solve-store-headaches/; "Entering the New Era of Digital Coupons," *Adweek,* June 16, 2014, p. S7; and www.walgreens.com/topic/apps/learn_about_mobile_browser_app.jsp and www.walgreens.com/coupons, accessed September 2015.
29. See www.happymeal.com/en_US/, accessed September 2015.
30. See "The 2013 Estimate of Promotion Products Distributor Sales," *PPAI,* www.ppai.org/inside-ppai/research/Documents/2013%20SalesVolume%20Sheet.pdf; and "PPAI Distributor Quarterly Sales Barometer," www.ppai.org/inside-ppai/research/Documents/14SalesBarometerD-Q4.pdf, accessed September 2015.
31. Based on information found in Patrick Hanlon, "Face Slams: Event Marketing Takes Off," *Forbes,* May 9, 2012, www.forbes.com/sites/patrickhanlon/2012/05/09/face-slams-event-marketing-takes-off/; and www.redbull.com/us/en/events and www.redbull.com/cs/Satellite/en_INT/RedBull/HolyShit/011242745950125, accessed September 2015. The referenced wing suit flying video can be found at http://player.vimeo.com/video/31481531?autoplay=1.
32. Kantar Retail, *Making Connections*, p. 10.
33. See "CES Attendee Audit Summary Results," www.cesweb.org/Why-CES/2014-Attendee-Audit, accessed June 2015; "New Logo for Bauma Ahead of 2016 Trade Fair," *World Cement,* July 5, 2015, www.worldcement.com/europe-cis/07052014/Bauma_new_look_ahead_of_2016_show_145/.

Chapter 14

1. See Michael Ausien, "Cyber Monday Is Amazon's Busiest Day of the Year," *Indianapolis Star,* December 1, 2015, www.indystar.com/story/money/2014/12/01/cyber-monday-amazons-busiest-day-year/19749775/; Morten T. Hansen, Herminia Ibarra, and Urs Peyer, "The Best-Performing CEOs in the World," *Harvard Business Review,* January–February 2013, pp. 81–86; George Anders, "Jeff Bezos's Top 10 Leadership Lessons," *Forbes,* April 4, 2012, www.forbes.com/sites/georgeanders/2012/04/04/bezos-tips/; "Walmart vs. Amazon Prime," *Advertising Age,* May 15, 2015, p. 6; "Benchmarks by Company: Amazon," ACSI, www.theacsi.org/?option=com_content&view=article&id=149&catid=&Itemid=214&c=Amazon, accessed June 2015; "Number of Worldwide Active Amazon Customer Accounts from 1997 to 2014 (in Millions)," *Statistica,* www.statista.com/statistics/237810/number-of-active-amazon-customer-accounts-worldwide/, accessed June 2015; and annual reports and other information found at www.amazon.com, accessed September 2015.
2. Stan Phelps, "Three Lessons from Mountain Dew on Leveraging Events to Create an Authentic Brand Experience," *Forbes,* October 18, 2014, www.forbes.com/sites/stanphelps/2014/10/18/three-lessons-from-mountain-dew-on-leveraging-events-to-create-an-authentic-brand-experience/; Natalie Tadena, "Mountain Dew Ads Go Global with Return of 'Do the Dew,'" *Wall Street Journal,* March 29, 2015, http://blogs.wsj.com/cmo/2015/03/29/mountain-dew-ads-go-global-with-return-of-do-the-dew/; and www.mountaindew.com, accessed September 2015.
3. See "Priceline Profit Tops Estimates as Bookings Rise," *Reuters,* February 20, 2014, www.reuters.com/article/2014/02/21/us-priceline-results-idUSBREA1J26X20140221; and http://ir.pricelinegroup.com/financials.cfm, accessed September 2015.

4. For these and other direct marketing statistics in this section, see Direct Marketing Association, *The DMA Statistical Fact Book 2015*, 37th ed., May 2015; Dave Erlandson, "Direct Mail Ad Spending Forecast to Grow 1.1% in 2014," *PODi Insights*, January 23, 2014, http://blog.podi.org/direct-mail-ad-spending-forecast-to-grow-1-1-in-2014; Ginger Conlin, "Where Will Marketing Grow in 2015?" *Direct Marketing News*, January 9, 2015, www.dmnews.com/where-will-marketing-grow-in-2015/printarticle/391699/; and other information at www.thedma.org, accessed September 2015.
5. See "Worldwide Ad Spending," *eMarketer*, www.emarketer.com/adspendtool, accessed June 2015; "Total US Ad Spending to See Largest Increase Since 2004," *eMarketer*, July 2, 2014, www.emarketer.com/Article/Total-US-Ad-Spending-See-Largest-Increase-Since-2004/1010982; Erlandson, "Direct Mail Ad Spending Forecast to Grow 1.1% in 2014"; and Ginger Conlin, "Where Will Marketing Grow in 2015?" *Direct Marketing News*, January 9, 2015, .dmnews.com/where-will-marketing-grow-in-2015/printarticle/391699/.
6. See Pew Research Center's Internet & American Life Project, "Internet User Demographics," www.pewinternet.org/data-trend/internet-use/latest-stats/, accessed April 2015; "Mobile Continues to Steal Share of US Adults' Day Time Spent with Media," *eMarketer*, April 22, 2014, www.emarketer.com/Article/Mobile-Continues-Steal-Share-of-US-Adults-Daily-Time-Spent-with-Media/1010782; Aaron Smith, "U.S. Smartphone Use in 2015," Pew Research Center, April 1, 2015, www.pewinternet.org/2015/04/01/us-smartphone-use-in-2015/; "ITU Releases Annual Global ICT Data and ICT Development Index Country Rankings," November 24, 2014, www.itu.int/net/pressoffice/press_releases/2014/68.aspx#.VTRtbUthveI; "2 Billion Consumers Worldwide to Get Smartphones by 2016," *eMarketer*, December 11, 2014, www.emarketer.com/Article/2-Billion-Consumers-Worldwide-Smartphones-by-2016/1011694.
7. See "Retail Sales Worldwide Will Top $22 Trillion This Year," *eMarketer*, December 23, 2014, www.emarketer.com/Article/Retail-Sales-Worldwide-Will-Top-22-Trillion-This-Year/1011765; and "60% of U.S. Retail Sales Will Involve the Web by 2017," *Internet Retailer*, October 30, 2013, www.internetretailer.com/2013/10/30/60-us-retail-sales-will-involve-web-2017.
8. See "Internet Retailer: Top 500 Guide," www.top500guide.com/top-500/the-top-500-list, accessed June 2015; and "Amazon's Online Sales Dwarf the Competition," *Statista*, May 7, 2014, www.statista.com/chart/2214/10-largest-online-retailers/.
9. See "Staples Aims to Change Image with New Slogan," *Boston Globe*, January 3, 2014; Matt Linder, "Online Sales at Staples Grow 4.8% in Fiscal 2014, *Internet Retailer*, March 6, 2015, www.internetretailer.com/2015/03/06/online-sales-staples-grow-48-fiscal-2014; and annual reports and other information found at www.staples.com, accessed September 2015.
10. See Roger Katz. "2015 Will Be the Year of the Brand Community—Here's Why," *ClickZ*, January 23, 2015, www.clickz.com/clickz/column/2391666/2015-will-be-the-year-of-the-brand-community-heres-why; ComBlu, "The State of Online Branded Communities," http://comblu.com/downloads/ComBlu_StateOfOnlineCommunities_2012.pdf, November 2012, p. 19; and www.espn.com, accessed September 2015.
11. For these and other examples of rich media ads, see "Rising Starts: Display," *Jivox*, www.jivox.com/ad-gallery.php, accessed June 2015; and "Best Rich Media Online Ad," www.iacaward.org/iac/winners_detail.asp?yr=all&award_level=best&medium=Rich%20media%20Online%20Ad, accessed September 2015.
12. Conlin, "Where Will Marketing Grow in 2015"; and Google annual reports, http://investor.google.com/proxy.html, accessed September 2015.
13. "Social Media Is the Hot New Thing, but Email Is Still the King," *Advertising Age*, September 30, 2013, p. 18.
14. See Greg Sterling, "Report: 66 Percent of Email Opens on Mobile, Mostly iOS Devices," *Marketing Land*, November 19, 2014, http://marketingland.com/report-66-percent-email-opens-mobile-devices-108420; Nora Aufreiter et al., "Why Marketers Should Keep Sending You Emails," McKinsey & Company, January 2014, www.mckinsey.com/insights/marketing_sales/why_marketers_should_keep_sending_you_emails; Suzanne Vranica, "You've Got Mail and More Is Coming," *Wall Street Journal*, November 14, 2014, http://blogs.wsj.com/cmo/2014/11/14/youve-got-mail-and-more-is-coming/, and "5 Ways to Optimize Email Marketing ROI," *CMO Essentials*, March 10, 2015, www.cmoessentials.com/5-ways-optimize-email-marketing-roi/#sthash.OjGWLbE0.dpbs.
15. Carol Stott, "2014 Estimated Global Email Spam Rate Is 64%," *Business2Community*, May 7, 2014, www.business2community.com/email-marketing/2014-estimated-global-email-spam-rate-64-thats-almost-2-3-emails-0875585; and "Email: Unloved, Unbreakable," *Fortune*, May 1, 2015, pp. 54–55.
16. Linda Moses, "Online Video Ads Have Higher Impact Than TV Ads," *Adweek*, May 1, 2013, www.adweek.com/print/148982; and "comScore Releases December 2013 U.S. Online Video Rankings," January 10, 2014, www.comscore.com/Insights/Press_Releases/2014/1/comScore_Releases_December_2013_US_Online_Video_Rankings.
17. For these and other examples, see "Samsung, Wieden & Kennedy Rule Ad Age's 2013 Viral Video Awards," *Advertising Age*, April 16, 2013, http://adage.com/article/240900/; and Alexandra Jardine, "Always Viral Ad 'Like a Girl' Cleans Up at Webby Awards," *Advertising Age*, April 27, 2015, http://adage.com/print/298258.
18. See "Top 10 Branded Videos: Adidas Racks Up 21 Million YouTube Views in One Week," *Adweek*, February 25, 2015, www.adweek.com/print/163145; and www.youtube.com/watch?v=uiQVkoDlBbQ, accessed September 2015.
19. Troy Dreier, "The Force Was Strong with This One," *Streaming Media Magazine*, April/May 2011, pp. 66–68; also see Thales Teixeira, "The New Science of Viral Ads," *Harvard Business Review*, March 2012, pp. 25–28; and Hilary Masell Oswald, "The Biology of a Marketplace Sensation," *Marketing News*, September 2013, pp. 31–35.
20. Based on information found in Keith O'Brien, "How McDonald's Came Back Bigger Than Ever," *New York Times*, May 6, 2012, p. MM44. Also see Jayson DeMers, "How to Get Mommy Bloggers to Bring Customers to Your Brand," *Huffington Post*, November 6, 2014, www.huffingtonpost.com/jayson-demers/how-to-get-mommy-bloggers_b_6109064.html.
21. Jason DeMers, "The Top 10 Benefits of Social Media Marketing," *Forbes*, August 11, 2014, www.forbes.com/sites/jaysondemers/2014/08/11/the-top-10-benefits-of-social-media-marketing.
22. See http://newsroom.fb.com/company-info; www.youtube.com/yt/press/statistics.html and www.statisticbrain.com/twitter-statistics/, accessed September 2015.
23. For these and other examples, see www.kaboodle.com, www.farmersonly.com, www.birdpost.com, and www.cafemom.com, all accessed September 2015.
24. See http://nikeinc.com/news/nike-coach-feature-motivates-runners-with-customized-training-plans and www.nikeplus.com, accessed September 2015.
25. "3 Brands That Are Doing Live Chat on Twitter Right," *Adly.com*, January 28, 2014, http://adly.com/blog/3-brands-doing-live-chat-right/; and https://twitter.com/hashtag/wfmdish, accessed September 2015.
26. See www.instagram.com/etsy/, www.pinterest.com/etsy/, and www.etsy.com/about, accessed September 2015.
27. Example and quotes from "Meme Watch: Lay's 'Do Us a Flavor' Crowdsourcing Hilariously Backfires," *Uproxx*, February 5, 2014, http://uproxx.com/gammasquad/2014/02/best-of-lays-do-us-a-flavor-parodies/?showall=true; Michael Bourne, "Sailing of 14 Social Cs," *Mullen Advertising*, February, 13, 2012, www.mullen.com/sailing-the-14-social-cs/; and Jenna Mullins, "The Submissions for New Lay's Chip Flavors Are Getting Out of Control (but We Love It)," *EOnline*, February 6, 2014, www.eonline.com/news/508137/the-submissions-for-new-lays-chip-flavors-are-getting-out-of-control-but-we-love-it; and www.dousaflavor.com/, accessed June 2015.
28. Melissa Allison, "Re-Creating the Coffee Klatch Online," *Raleigh News & Observer*," May 6, 2013, p. 1D; Todd Wassermann, *Mashable*, December 13, 2013, http://mashable.com/2013/12/05/starbuckss-tweet-a-coffee-180000/; and www.facebook.com/Starbucks and https://twitter.com/Starbucks, accessed June 2015.
29. Facts in this paragraph are from "Wireless Quick Facts," www.ctia.org/your-wireless-life/how-wireless-works/wireless-quick-facts, accessed June 2015; "Smartphones: So Many Apps, So Much Time," Nielsen, July 1, 2014, www.nielsen.com/us/en/insights/news/2014/smartphones-so-many-apps–so-much-time.html; and Pew Research Center's Internet & American Life Project, "Mobile Technology Fact Sheet," www.pewinternet.org/fact-sheets/mobile-technology-fact-sheet/, accessed September 2015.
30. Jonathan Nelson, "Voice: One Screen to Rule Them All," *Adweek*, February 13, 2013, p. 15; Stephen Willard, "Study: People Check Their Cell Phones Every Six Minutes, 150 Times a Day," *Elite Daily*, February 11, 2013, http://elitedaily.com/news/world/study-people-check-cell-phones-minutes-150-times-day/; and "Mobile Continues to Steal Share of US Adults' Daily Time Spent with Media," *eMarketer.com*, April 22, 2014, www.emarketer.com/Article/Mobile-Continues-Steal-Share-of-US-Adults-Daily-Time-Spent-with-Media/1010782.
31. Lauren Johnson, "Target Turns Its Stores into One Big Mobile Game for the Holidays," *Adweek*, December 2, 2014, www.adweek.com/print/161727.
32. "IAB Internet Advertising Revenue Report," September 2015, www.iab.net/research/industry_data_and_landscape/adrevenuereport; "The Mobile

Movement," accessed at www.thinkwithgoogle.com/insights/emea/library/studies/the-mobile-movement, May 2013; and "Mobile Advertising Fast Facts," *Advertising Age,* April 04, 2014, pp. 20+.

33. See Lauren Johnson, "McDonald's Beefs Up Advertising Strategy with Mobile Game," *Mobile Marketer,* March 28, 2013, www.mobilemarketer.com/cms/news/advertising/12447.html; and Rimma Kats, "McDonald's Beefs Up Mobile Efforts via Targeted Campaign," *Mobile Marketing,* August 16, 2013, www.mobilemarketer.com/cms/news/advertising/13553.html.
34. See Judith Acquino, "JetBlue Voice-Activated Ad Teaches People to Speak 'Pigeon,'" *Ad Exchanger,"* September 26, 2013, www.adexchanger.com/online-advertising/jetblue-voice-activated-ads-teach-people-to-speak-pigeon/; and Lauren Johnson, "Top 10 Mobile Advertising Campaigns of 2013," December 24, 2013, www.mobilemarketer.com/cms/news/advertising/16847.html.
35. See "Direct Mail Marketing Essentials Guide 2014," *DMNews*, March 2014, http://media.dmnews.com/documents/64/eg_directmail_15763.pdf; Winterberry Group, "2015 Annual Outlook: What to Expect in Direct and Digital Marketing," January 2015, www.winterberrygroup.com/system/files/Winterberry%20Group–2015%20Annual%20Outlook–DMCNY%20Luncheon_1.8.14.pdf; Paul Vogel, "Marketers Are Rediscovering the Value of Mail," Postal Customer Council of Providence, June 27, 2014, http://providencepcc.org/marketers-are-rediscovering-the-value-of-mail/; and "Stats & Facts: Direct Marketing," *CMO Council,* www.cmocouncil.org/facts-stats-categories.php?view=all&category=direct-marketing, access September 2015.
36. Julie Liesse, "When Times Are Hard, Mail Works," *Advertising Age*, March 30, 2009, p. 14; and Lois Geller, "If Direct Mail Is Dying, It's Sure Taking Its Time about It," *Forbes,* December 4, 2013, www.forbes.com/sites/loisgeller/2013/12/04/if-direct-mail-is-dying-its-sure-taking-its-time-about-it/; and Craig Simpson, "4 Reasons to Use Direct Mail Marketing Instead of Email," *Entrepreneur,* February 17, 2015, www.entrepreneur.com/article/242731.
37. Bruce Britt, "Marketing Leaders Discuss the Resurgence of Direct Mail," *Deliver Magazine,* January 18, 2011, www.delivermagazine.com/2011/01/marketing-leaders-discuss-resurgence-of-direct-mail/. Also see Alex Palmer, "Insurance Marketers Leverage Targeted Marketing," *Direct Marketing,* February 1, 2012, www.dmnews.com/insurance-marketers-leverage-targeted-marketing/article/225127/; and Michele B. Peel, "4 Reasons Direct Mail Should Be Part of Your Plan to Acquire New Customers," *Insurance Journal,* March 9, 2015, www.insurancejournal.com/magazines/features/2015/03/09/359395.htm.
38. Rebecca R. Ruiz, "Catalogs, after Years of Decline, Are Revamped for Changing Times," *New York Times,* January 26, 2015, p. B1.
39. Kurt Solomon, "Is the Catalog Dead?" November 5, 2013, www.kurtsalmon.com/US/vertical-insight/Is-the-Catalog-Dead-?vertical=Retail&id=936&language=en-us#.UzTUVV5dCcC.
40. Ruiz, "Catalogs, after Years of Decline, Are Revamped for Changing Times."
41. Winterberry Group, "2015 Annual Outlook: What to Expect in Direct and Digital Marketing," January 2015, www.winterberrygroup.com/system/files/Winterberry%20Group–2015%20Annual%20Outlook–DMCNY%20Luncheon_1.8.14.pdf.
42. See Federal Trade Comission "FTC Issues FY 2014 National Do Not Call Registry Data," November 19, 2014, www.ftc.gov/news-events/press-releases/2014/11/ftc-issues-fy-2014-national-do-not-call-registry-data-book; and www.donotcall.gov, accessed September 2015.
43. See Rachel Brown, "Perry, Fischer, Lavigne Tapped for Proactiv," *WWD*, January 13, 2010, p. 3; Rahul Parikh, "Proactiv's Celebrity Shell Game," Salon.com, February 28, 2011, www.salon.com/2011/02/28/proactiv_celebrity_sham; "Guthy-Renker Honored with Nine Era Moxie Awards for Year's Best Direct Marketing Campaigns," *Marketing Weekly News*, October 19, 2013, p. 145; and www.proactiv.com, accessed September 2015.
44. Jeanine Poggi, "H&M Super Bowl Ad Lets You Buy Beckham Bodywear by Remote Control," *Advertising Age,* January 6, 2014, www.adage.com/print/290915.
45. "Best Buy: Consumer Electronics Retailing on the Go," www.zoomsystems.com/our-partners/partner-portfolio/; and www.zoomsystems.com/about-us, accessed September 2015.
46. See Internet Crime Complaint Center, www.ic3.gov, accessed September 2015.
47. See "Fear and Worry in America? Identity Theft and Cybercrime," *Huffington Post,* November 5, 2014, www.huffingtonpost.com/creditsesamecom/fear-and-worry-in-america_b_6102910.html.
48. See Susan Dominus, "Underage on Facebook," *MSN Living*, March 15, 2012, http://living.msn.com/family-parenting/underage-on-facebook-5; Josh Wolford, "Facebook Still Has a Big Problem with Underage Users, and They Know It," *WebProNews*, January 24, 2013, www.webpronews.com/facebook-still-has-a-big-problem-with-underage-users-and-they-know-it-2013-01; and Samuel Gibbs, "Facebook Patent Reveals Plan for Children to Join the Social Network," *Guardian*, June 3, 2014, www.theguardian.com/technology/2014/jun/03/facebook-children-join-social-network.
49. See Zach Miners, "Your Control of Your Personal Info Is All but Dead, Pew Respondents Fear," *PCWorld,* November 12, 2014, www.pcworld.com/article/2846855; Hadley Malcolm, "Millennials Don't Worry about Online Privacy," *USA Today,* April 21, 2013; and "2015 TRUSTe US Consumer Confidence Index," *TRUSTe,* www.truste.com/resources/privacy-research/us-consumer-confidence-index-2015/.
50. Based on information from Michael Bush, "My Life, Seen through the Eyes of Marketers," *Advertising Age,* April 26, 2010, http://adage.com/print/143479.
51. See "Facebook to Make Targeted Ads More Transparent for Users," *Advertising Age,* February 4, 2013, http://adage.com/article/239564/; and www.aboutads.info/, accessed September 2015.
52. See Richard Byrne Reilly, "Feds to Mobile Marketers: Stop Targeting Kids, or Else," *Venture Beat,* March 27, 2014, http://venturebeat.com/2014/03/27/feds-to-mobile-marketers-stop-targeting-kids-or-else-exclusive/; and www.business.ftc.gov/privacy-and-security/childrens-privacy, accessed September 2015.
53. Information on TRUSTe at www.truste.com, accessed September 2015.
54. Information on the DMA Privacy Promise at www.the-dma.org/cgi/dispissue?article=129 and www.dmachoice.org/static/privacy_policy.php, accessed September 2015.

Chapter 15

1. Based on information from "Our Mission Is 'Beauty for All,' Says L'Oréal Global CEO Jean-Paul," *The Economic Times,"* January 30, 2015, http://articles.economictimes.indiatimes.com/2015-01-30/news/58625572_1_l-oreal-loreal-jean-paul-agon; Hae-Jung Hong and Yves Doz, "L'Oréal Masters Multiculturalism," *Harvard Business Review*, June, 2013, pp. 114–119; Liza Lin, "L'Oréal Puts on a Happy Face in China," *Bloomberg Businessweek*, April 1–7, 2013, pp. 25–26; "A Worldwide Approach to Beauty Rituals," www.loreal.com/research-innovation/when-the-diversity-of-types-of-beauty-inspires-science/a-world-wide-approach-to-beauty-rituals.aspx, accessed September2015; and www.lorealusa.com/Article.aspx?topcode=CorpTopic_RI_CustomerInnovation, www.lorealusa.com/research-innovation/when-the-diversity-of-types-of-beauty-inspires-science/stories-of-multicultural-innovations.aspx, and www.loreal-finance.com/eng/annual-report, accessed September, 2015.
2. Data from "*Fortune* 500," *Fortune*, June 2015, http://money.cnn.com/magazines/fortune/fortune500/; Douglas B. Fay, "Multinational Customers: Are Their Needs Really Being Met?" www.globexintl.com/corporate/?p=82, accessed May 2015; and "List of Countries by GDP: List by the CIA World Factbook," *Wikipedia,* http://en.wikipedia.org/wiki/List_of_countries_by_GDP_(nominal), accessed September 2015.
3. "Modest Trade Recovery to Continue in 2015 and 2016 Following Three Years of Weak Expansion," WTO Press Release, April 14, 2015, www.wto.org/english/news_e/pres15_e/pr739_e.htm
4. Information from www.michelin.com/eng/finance/individual-shareholders/publications, www.jnj.com, and www.caterpillar.com, accessed September 2015.
5. See www.otisworldwide.com/d1-about.html; and UTC Annual Report, http://2014ar.utc.com/, accessed September 2015.
6. Rob Schmitz, "Trade Spat between China and EU Threatens Exports of Solar Panels, Wine," *Marketplace,* June 6, 2013, www.marketplace.org/topics/world/trade-spat-between-china-and-eu-threatens-exports-solar-panels-wine; Ben Blanchard and Francesco Guarascio, "EU, China End Wine Dispute Ahead of Xi's European Tour," *Reuters*, March 21, 2014, www.reuters.com/article/idUSBREA2K0QE20140321; and "EU to Benefit from China's 'New Normal' Economy: Ambassador," April 15, 2015, www.ecns.cn/voices/2015/04-15/161743.shtml.
7. Gardiner Harris, "Wal-Mart Drops Ambitious Expansion Plan for India," *New York Times*, October 10, 2013, p. B3; Paul Ausick, "Walmart Still Struggles in India," *247wallst,* April 8, 2014, http://247wallst.com/retail/2014/04/08/walmart-still-struggles-in-india/; Rhitu Chatterjee, "Indian Shopkeepers Greet Wal-Mart's Expansion Plans with Protests," *NPR*, November 20, 2014, www.npr.org/blogs/goatsandsoda/2014/11/20/365480337/; and "Budget 2015: Walmart See Increase in Domestic Consumption, Retail Growth in India," *The Economic Times,* March

15, 2015, http://economictimes.indiatimes.com/industry/services/retail/budget-2015-walmart-sees-increase-in-domestic-consumption-retail-growth-in-india/articleshow/46418646.cms.

8. "What Is the WTO?" www.wto.org/english/thewto_e/whatis_e/whatis_e.htm, accessed September 2015.
9. See "The Doha Round," www.wto.org/english/tratop_e/dda_e/dda_e.htm, accessed September 2015.
10. "The EU at a Glance," http://europa.eu/about-eu/index_en.htm; "EU Statistics and Opinion Polls," http://europa.eu/documentation/statistics-polls/index_en.htm; and "EU Position in World Trade, http://ec.europa.eu/trade/policy/eu-position-in-world-trade/, all accessed September 2015.
11. Jack Ewing, "European Banks Feel Heat in Crimea Crisis, with Austria Bearing Brunt," *New York Times*, March 28, 2014, p. B6; "France's Sapin: Euro's Weakening Phase Has Run Its Course," *Wall Street Journal*, April 17, 2015, www.wsj.com/articles/frances-sapin-euros-weakening-phase-has-run-its-course-1429300555; and "European Union: The Euro," http://europa.eu/about-eu/basic-information/money/euro/, accessed September 2015.
12. CIA, *The World Factbook*, https://www.cia.gov/library/publications/the-world-factbook, accessed September 2015.
13. Statistics and other information from CIA, *The World Factbook;* and NAFTANow.org, accessed May 2015.
14. See "Explainer: What Is UNASUR?" www.as-coa.org/articles/explainer-what-unasur and http://en.wikipedia.org/wiki/Union_of_South_American_Nations, accessed September 2015.
15. See Zeenat Moorad, "The Coca-Cola Company: Tapping Africa's Fizz," *Financial Mail,* May 4, 2015, www.financialmail.co.za/coverstory/2015/04/30/the-coca-cola-company-tapping-africas-fizz; Annaleigh Vallie, "Coke Turns 125 and Has Much Life Ahead," *Business Day,* May 16, 2011, www.businessday.co.za/articles/Content.aspx?id_142848; Andrew Cave, "Glaxo and Unilever Take Note: How General Electric and Coca-Cola Are Winning in Africa," *Forbes,* April 2, 2014, www.forbes.com/sites/andrewcave/2014/04/02/glaxo-and-unilever-take-note-how-general-electric-and-coca-cola-are-winning-in-africa/; and Coca-Cola annual reports and other information from www.thecoca-colacompany.com, accessed September 2015.
16. See "2014 Investment Climate Statement—Russia," U.S. Bureau of Economic and Business Affairs, June 2014, www.state.gov/e/eb/rls/othr/ics/2014/227933.htm; and "Welcome to the U.S. Commercial Service in Russia," http://export.gov/russia/, accessed September 2015.
17. Laurent Belsie, "What Will Venezuela Do with Its Oil?" *Christian Science Monitor,* March 6, 2013, www.csmonitor.com/Environment/2013/0307/What-will-Venezuela-do-with-its-oil-Top-five-energy-challenges-after-Chavez/Oil-bartering; John Paul Rathbone, "Venezuela: In Search of a Solution," *Financial Times,* March 2, 2014, www.ft.com/intl/cms/s/2/45c3cae4-a049-11e3-8557-00144feab7de.html#axzz2xgjEix7Y; and International Reciprocal Trade Association, www.irta.com/index.php/about/modern-trade-barter, accessed September 2015.
18. For these and other examples, see Emma Hall, "Do You Know Your Rites? BBDO Does," *Advertising Age*, May 21, 2007, p. 22.
19. Jamie Bryan, "The Mintz Dynasty," *Fast Company*, April 2006, pp. 56–61; Viji Sundaram, "Offensive Durga Display Dropped," *India-West*, February 2006, p. A1; and Emily Bryson York and Rupal Parekh, "Burger King's MO: Offend, Earn Media, Apologize, Repeat," *Advertising Age*, July 8, 2009, http://adage.com/print?article_id=137801. For other examples, see Chris Isidore, "Chevy Pulls Ad Offensive to Chinese," *CNNMoney,* May 1, 2013, www.money.cnn.com/2013/05/01/news/companies/offensive-chevy-ad/; Julia Lynn Rubin, "4 Offensive Ads You Won't Believe Are Real," *Contently,* September 5, 2014, http://contently.com/strategist/2014/09/05/4-of-the-most-offensive-ads-of-the-last-decade/; and "Misinterpretation or Culturally Insensitive," *IMC Hawk,* April 30, 2015, http://imcclass.com/.
20. For these and other examples, see Bill Chappell, "Bill Gates' Handshake with South Korea's Park Sparks Debate," *NPR,* April 23, 2013, www.npr.org/blogs/thetwo-way/2013/04/23/178650537/bill-gates-handshake-with-south-koreas-park-sparks-debate; "Managing Quality across the (Global) Organization, Its Stakeholders, Suppliers, and Customers," Chartered Quality Institute, www.thecqi.org/Knowledge-Hub/Knowledge-portal/Corporate-strategy/Managing-quality-globally, accessed September 2015.
21. Quotes and other information found in David Pierson, "Beijing Loves IKEA—but Not for Shopping," *Los Angeles Times,* August 25, 2009, http://articles.latimes.com/2009/aug/25/business/fi-china-ikea25; Michael Wei, "In IKEA's China Stores, Loitering Is Encouraged," *Bloomberg Businessweek,* November 1, 2010, pp. 22–23; Pan Kwan Yuk, "IKEA in China: Turning Gawkers into Customers," *BeyondBrics*, April 4, 2013, http://blogs.ft.com/beyond-brics/2013/04/04/ikea-in-china-turning-gawkers-into-consumers/?#axzz2SobYFh98; Emily Raulhala, "No, IKEA Hasn't Banned Customers from Sleeping in Its Chinese Stores," *Time*, April 10. 2015, http://time.com/3814935/ikea-china-customers-sleeping/; and "IKEA Group Yearly Summary FY2014," www.ikea.com/ms/en_US/pdf/yearly_summary/ikea-group-yearly-summary-fy14.pdf, accessed September 2015.
22. Andres Martinez, "The Next American Century," *Time*, March 22, 2010, p. 1.
23. Thomas L. Friedman, *The Lexus and the Olive Tree: Understanding Globalization* (New York: Anchor Books, 2000); and Michael Wei and Margaret Conley, "Global Brands: Some Chinese Kids' First Word: Mickey," *Bloomberg Businessweek,* June 19, 2011, pp. 24–25.
24. Adam Chandler, "How McDonald's Became a Target for Protest," *The Atlantic,* April 16, 2015, www.theatlantic.com/business/archive/2015/04/setting-the-symbolic-golden-arches-aflame/390708/.
25. "2015 BrandZ Top 100 Global Brands," Millward Brown, www.millwardbrown.com/mb-global/brand-strategy/brand-equity/brandz/top-global-brands/2015.
26. See Rachael Tepper, "Yum! Brands' International Product Strategy: How the Double Down Went Global," *Huffington Post*, March 11, 2013, www.huffingtonpost.com/2013/03/11/yum-brands-international-product-strategy_n_2814360.html; Molly Osberg, "How Colonel Sanders Became Father Christmas in Japan," *TPM,* December 23, 2014, http://talkingpointsmemo.com/theslice/kfc-christmas-in-japan-colonel-sanders-history-12-23-2014; and Jason Johnson, "KFC Christmas Tradition in Japan," *Brain Skewer,* May 2015, http://brainskewer.com/bs/20150506/kfc-christmas-tradition-japan.
27. See annual reports and other financial and review data from www.coca-colacompany.com/our-company/, accessed September 2015.
28. This Netflix example is based on information found in Sam Schechner, "Europe's Media Giants Prep for Netflix Landing," *Wall Street Journal,* January 29, 2014, http://online.wsj.com/news/articles/SB20001424052702303277704579348774128548520; and Joan E. Solsman, "Netflix Invades Europe: Why Expansion beyond the US Is So Critical," *CNET,* September 19, 2014, www.cnet.com/news/netflix-invades-europe-why-international-expansion-is-so-critical/.
29. See www.olc.co.jp/en/ and www.coca-colahellenic.com/aboutus/, accessed September 2015.
30. See "Škoda and Volkswagen Group Russia: One Year of Successful Production in Nizhny Novgorod," December 11, 2013, www.volkswagenag.com/content/vwcorp/info_center/en/news/2013/12/Nizhny_Novgorod.html; and www.pg.com/en_IN/company/pg-india.shtml, accessed September 2015.
31. See http://en.wikipedia.org/wiki/Doubletree, accessed September 2015.
32. Christina Larson, "Intel Buys Its Way Deeper into China," *Bloomberg Businessweek,* March 8, 2015, pp. 33–34.
33. "Intel in China," *iLook China,* May 28, 2010, http://ilookchina.net/2010/05/page/2/; and Christina Larson, "Intel Buys Its Way Deeper into China," *Bloomberg Businessweek,* March 8, 2015, pp. 33–34.
34. "A Tale of Two Countries: Starbucks in India and China," *Starbucks Newsroom,* March 27, 2014, http://news.starbucks.com/news/a-tale-of-two-countries-starbucks-growth-in-india-and-china; Anita Chong Beattie, "Can Starbucks Make China Love Joe?" *Advertising Age,* November 5, 2012, pp. 20–21; Bruce Horovitz, "China to Become No. 2 Marketing for Starbucks," *USA Today,* September 16, 2013, www.usatoday.com/story/money/business/2013/09/16/starbucks-china-flagship-stores/2820885/; and Rachael Lerman, "All the Tea in China: Starbucks' Biggest Market Isn't Where You Think," *Puget Sound Business Journal,* March 20, 2015, www.bizjournals.com/seattle/blog/2015/03/all-the-tea-in-china-starbucks-biggest-market-isnt.html?page=all.
35. See Warren J. Keegan and Mark C. Green, *Global Marketing*, 7th ed. (Upper Saddle River, NJ: Prentice Hall, 2013), pp. 303–308.
36. Toshiro Wakayama, Junjiro Shintaku, and Tomofumi Amano, "What Panasonic Learned in China," *Harvard Business Review,* December 2012, pp. 109–113.
37. Information on McDonald's menus and operations found in Lucy Fancourt, Bredesen Lewis, and Nicholas Majka, "Born in the USA, Made in France: How McDonald's Succeeds in the Land of Michelin Stars," Knowledge@Wharton, January 3, 2012, http://knowledge.wharton.upenn.edu/article.cfm?articleid=2906; Richard Vines and Caroline Connan, "McDonald's Wins Over French Chef with McBaguette Sandwich," *Bloomberg*, January 15, 2013, www.bloomberg.com/news/2013-01-15/mcdonald-s-wins-over-french-chef-with-mcbaguette-sandwich.html; Rob Wile, "The True Story of How McDonald's Conquered France," *Business Insider,* August 22, 2014, www.businessinsider.com/how-mcdonalds-conquered-

france-2014-8; and "McDonald's Food You Can't Get Here," *Chicago Tribune,* www.chicagotribune.com/business/ct-biz-mcdonalds-food-around-the-world,0,5168632.photogallery, accessed September 2015.

38. See Normandy Madden, "In China, Multinationals Forgo Adaptation for New-Brand Creation," *Advertising Age,* January 17, 2011, p. 10; Susan Adams, "The 10 Companies Considered 'Best for the World,'" *Forbes,* March 31, 2014, www.forbes.com/sites/susanadams/2014/03/31/10-companies-considered-best-for-the-world/; Meg Cichon, "Solar Making Big Strides to Power the Developing World," *Renewable Energy World,* May 7, 2014, www.renewableenergyworld.com/rea/news/article/2014/05/solar-making-big-strides-to-power-the-developing-world; and www.dlightdesign.com/, accessed September 2015.
39. Jeffrey N. Ross, "Chevrolet Will 'Find New Roads' as Brand Grows Globally: Aligns around the World behind Singular Vision," January 8, 2013, http://media.gm.com/media/us/en/gm/news.detail.html/content/Pages/news/us/en/2013/Jan/0107-find-new-roads.html; and Dale Buss, "Chevy Wins at Sochi by Giving Dimension to 'Find New Roads,'" *Forbes,* February 24, 2014, www.forbes.com/sites/dalebuss/2014/02/24/chevrolet-wins-at-sochi-as-find-new-roads-theme-gets-traction/.
40. "Nike Faces Ultimate Marketing Challenge in China: Make Running Cool," *Advertising Age,* October 31, 2011, pp. 1+; "Firms Help Spur a Running Craze in China," *China Sports News,* December 30, 2013, www.chinasportsbeat.com/2013/12/firms-help-spur-running-craze-in-china.html; and "Nike Faces Tough Competition in Europe and China," *Forbes,* March 4, 2014, www.forbes.com/sites/greatspeculations/2014/03/04/nike-faces-tough-competition-in-europe-and-china/.
41. See George E. Belch and Michael A. Belch, *Advertising and Promotion: An Integrated Marketing Communications Perspective,* 8th ed. (New York: McGraw Hill, 2011), Chapter 20; Shintero Okazaki and Charles R. Taylor, "What Is SMS Advertising and Why Do Multinationals Adopt It?" *Journal of Business Research,* January 2008, pp. 4–12; and Warren J. Keegan and Mark C. Green, *Global Marketing,* 7th ed. (Upper Saddle River, NJ: Prentice Hall, 2013), pp. 398–400.
42. See Brian X. Chen, "Motorola to Offer Moto G Smartphone Aimed at Emerging Markets," *New York Times,* November 14, 2013, p. B5; Nikhil Subramaniam, "Motorola Beats Nokia in India Smartphone Sales Thanks to Moto G, Moto E," *Tech 2,* August 4, 2014, http://tech.firstpost.com/news-analysis/motorola-beats-nokia-in-india-smartphone-sales-thanks-to-moto-g-moto-e-228420.html; and Luke Jones, "Motorola Moto G Brazil's Best-Selling Smartphone," *Mobile Burn,* March 29, 2015, www.mobileburn.com/24405/news/motorola-moto-g-brazils-best-selling-smartphone.
43. Anita Chang Beattie, "Catching the Eye of a Chinese Shopper," *Advertising Age,* December 10, 2013, pp. 20–21.
44. Drew Hinshaw, "Burgers Face a Tough Slog in Africa," *Wall Street Journal,* December 10, 2013, www.wsj.com/articles/SB10001424052702304607104579214133498585594.
45. See Claudia Penteado, "Brazil's Northeast Goes from 'Land of Laziness' to Next China," *Advertising Age,* June 13, 2011, http://adage.com/print/228070/; Richard Wallace, "Middle-Classes on the Up: Why Brazil Is Growing," *IGD,* September 15, 2011, www.igd.com/our-expertise/Retail/retail-outlook/4713/Middle-classes-on-the-up-why-Brazil-is-growing/; and www.nestle.com.br/portalnestle/nestleatevoce/abordo_sobre_projeto.aspx and http://nestleatevoce.com.br, accessed September 2015.

Appendix 3

i. This is derived by rearranging the following equation and solving for price: Percentage markup = (price − cost) ÷ price.
ii. Again, using the basic profit equation, we set profit equal to ROI × I: ROI × I = (P × Q) − TFC − (Q × UVC). Solving for Q gives Q = (TFC + (ROI × I)) ÷ (P − UVC).
iii. U.S. Census Bureau, available at http://quickfacts.census.gov/qfd/states/00000.html, June 13, 2014.
iv. See Roger J. Best, *Market-Based Management,* 4th ed. (Upper Saddle River, NJ: Prentice Hall, 2005).
v. Total contribution can also be determined from the unit contribution and unit volume: Total contribution = unit contribution × unit sales. Total units sold in 2016 were 595,238 units, which can be determined by dividing total sales by price per unit ($100 million ÷ $168). Total contribution = $35.28 contribution per unit × 595,238 units = $20,999,996.64 (difference due to rounding).
vi. Recall that the contribution margin of 21% was based on variable costs representing 79% of sales. Therefore, if we do not know price, we can set it equal to $1.00. If price equals $1.00, 79 cents represents variable costs and 21 cents represents unit contribution. If price is decreased by 10%, the new price is 90 cents. However, variable costs do not change just because price decreased, so the unit contribution and contribution margin decrease as follows:

	Old	New (Reduced 10%)
Price	$1.00	$0.90
− Unit variable cost	$0.79	$0.79
= Unit contribution	$0.21	$0.11
Contribution margin	$0.21/$1.00 = 0.21 or 21%	$0.11/$0.90 = 0.12 or 12%

Indexes

Brand, Name, and Organization Index

In this index *f* represents figures and *t* represents tables.

Subject Index

In this index *f* indicates figures, *p* indicates photos, and *t* indicates tables.

D

E

F

HEALTH NETWORK INNOVATIONS

HOW 20 COMMUNITIES ARE IMPROVING THEIR SYSTEMS THROUGH COLLABORATION

Richard Bogue, PhD
Claude H. Hall, Jr.
EDITORS

American Hospital Publishing, Inc.
An American Hospital Association Company
Chicago

This publication is designed to provide accurate and authoritative information in regard to the subject matter covered. It is sold with the understanding that neither the authors nor the publisher is engaged in rendering legal, accounting, or other professional service. If legal advice or other expert assistance is required, the services of a competent professional person should be sought.

The views expressed in this publication are strictly those of the authors and do not necessarily represent official positions of the American Hospital Association.

Library of Congress Cataloging-in-Publication Data

Health network innovations : how 20 communities are improving their
systems through collaboration / Richard Bogue and Claude H. Hall,
Jr., editors
p. cm.
Includes bibliographical references and index.
ISBN 1-55648-198-5
1. Community health services—United States—Case studies.
2. Medical cooperation—United States—Case studies. 3. Regional
medical programs—United States—Case studies. I. Bogue, Richard
J. II. Hall, Claude H.
RA445.H339 1997
362.1'2'0973—dc21 97-6224
CIP

Catalog no. 076100

Printed in the USA

AHA is a service mark of the American Hospital Association used under license by American Hospital Publishing, Inc.

Community Care Network, Inc., uses the name Community Care Network as its service mark and reserves all rights.

Text set in Garamond

Cover design by Lesiak/Crampton Design

Discounts on bulk quantities of books published by American Hospital Publishing, Inc. (AHPI), are available to professional associations, special marketers, educators, trainers, and others. For details and discount information contact:

American Hospital Publishing, Inc.
Books Division
737 North Michigan Avenue
Chicago, Illinois 60611-2615 FAX 312/951-8491

Contents

List of Figures and Tables

PREFACE

INTRODUCTION

PART I. METROPOLITAN NETWORKS

About the Editors

Richard Bogue is senior director of governance programs, division of trustee and community leadership, at the Center for Health Care Leadership. Following service in the Air Force and diverse work experiences, Bogue acquired a BA in English and an MA in Rhetoric and Communication Theory from the University of South Florida, and a PhD in Human Communication from the University of Texas. At the Hospital Research and Educational Trust, Bogue led a series of research and demonstration programs interconnected in their emphasis on how hospitals and health systems restructure to improve their value to communities.

Claude H. Hall, Jr., is director of the National Demonstration of the Community Care Network Vision, Hospital Research and Educational Trust. His experience prior to joining HRET includes service as director of the Model Standards Project with the American Public Health Association; health planning specialist with the Virginia Department of Health; and supervisor of the offices of local health systems and health facilities development in the Idaho Division of Health. He has served as adjunct faculty with the George Washington University Public Health Program. He acquired an MHA from Virginia Commonwealth University, an MA from the University of Virginia, and a BA from Baylor University.

Acknowledgments

Many people made this book possible, but we are grateful more for what the book means than for the book itself. Most important are those who make health network innovation happen, community by community, day by day, in the face of habits and traditions that encourage inertia.

Special thanks go to those who are committed to the 20 communities highlighted in this book. We are grateful to the many private philanthropies who have invested in community-responsive health system change. They help thousands of people help themselves make their communities better. We especially appreciate the W. K. Kellogg Foundation. The Duke Endowment, The Robert Wood Johnson Foundation, the United States Public Health Service, and the California Wellness Foundation also deserve special thanks here.

The American Hospital Association, and its Hospital Research and Educational Trust, has been a great home for this project. VHA Inc. and the Catholic Health Association of the United States have been reliable, generous, and trusting partners. The National Steering Committee for the demonstration program has been a rock upon which to build. As we celebrate the joy of working with this dedicated and wise group, we mourn the recent passage of Sister Pat Underhill.

When you commit to a course of action with others, and work hard on it together, you become dear to each other. Many staff people at AHA, HRET, VHA, and CHA have committed with us and worked hard with us. We are grateful to our many colleagues in these organizations and elsewhere.

To come full circle, back to the book itself, we have loved working with the staff of American Hospital Publishing.

Foreword

The British astronomer Sir Fred Hoyle once observed that space isn't remote at all. "It's only an hour's drive away if your car could go straight upwards."

The same could be said for the future of health care in America. We can get there if we have the right vehicles. *Health Network Innovations* is designed to take you to the places where the vehicles of the future are being built.

This book describes 20 evolving Community Care Networks[sm] around America—20 endeavors to link a variety of people, organizations, and resources and focus them on improving the health of communities. It's a concept that's still defining itself and which we, the undersigned, who represent the American Hospital Association, the Catholic Health Association of the United States, AHA's Hospital Research and Educational Trust, and VHA Inc., are committed to encouraging.

Each of these pioneering networks has past experiences and promise for the future that can be guidance and inspiration for everyone who has a stake in improving health care delivery at the community level. That means hospital and health system leaders and the people and communities they serve.

Health care in America is in a state of change and transformation. While hospitals, health systems, physicians, nurses, and others continue their historic role of curing and caring for the ill and injured they also are increasingly taking on the challenge of keeping people well and actually improving the health of the communities in which they live.

And this new challenge compels them to look beyond their traditional walls and reach out to others in their communities. Why? Because, quite simply, they know they cannot succeed alone.

This new challenge has planted the seed for community care networks. It is bringing together public health agencies, governments, schools, businesses, churches, civic organizations, and others. It is uniting diverse communities around a shared goal: a healthy, safe, productive community. It is generating dialogue where there was once silence. It is spurring action where there was once complacency. It is producing results where there once was a sense of helplessness in dealing with basic problems facing communities.

The cases depicted in *Health Network Innovations* show that reinventing health care happens community by community because every community is different. They make it clear that the work is long and hard, and that there always are more questions than answers.

Finally, these cases are not completed stories: They are chapters of stories that are still being written and may never be finished. The nation's hospitals and health systems are committed to the community care network vision. They are committed at the community level—to the tough task of making them a reality. And we're committed to them at the national level, through the American Hospital Association, the Catholic Health Association of the United States, VHA Inc., and the Hospital Research and Educational Trust.

We're determined to do all we can to promote the concept, clear the way for them in public policy and celebrate their success at improving the health of individuals and communities. Look at the communities and people whose efforts are described in *Health Network Innovations.* Then look around your community. Take stock of its health in the broadest sense of the word and begin your own voyage to the future.

Richard J. Davidson, president
American Hospital Association

C. Thomas Smith, president and CEO
VHA Inc.

John E. Curley, Jr., president and CEO
The Catholic Health Association of the United States

Mary A. Pittman, president, HRET

Preface

We have now entered an era in which the value and power of the conception of community care networks (CCNs) can be tested, improved, and perhaps validated in the daily experience of health and human service delivery systems across the nation. *Health Network Innovations* represents the first major step in that process of observing the CCN concept in practice.

Chapters 1 through 20 comprise case examples of emerging CCNs. Examples were selected from among the awardee and finalist partnerships in a three-step process.

1. We identified partnerships that scored especially high during the application review process in one or another of the four dimensions.
2. Editorial staff reviewed applications to determine which applications best told the stories of their partnerships, their prior experience in activities related to the CCN vision, and their future plans for making progress toward the vision.
3. We considered geographic dispersion and fit within the five major types of communities that make up the five parts of this book.

Each part (metropolitan, suburban, rural region, rural county, and special populations) opens with an analysis of the unique characteristics and issues of that type of community and a summary of the cases in that part. It will become apparent that within each part there is real variety and that the methods of one CCN in a part may depart completely from the methods of another CCN in the same part.

The cases are composed chiefly of edited versions of the applications originally submitted by the partnerships in the spring of 1995. Each case reflects the outline provided in the program's request for applications:

- The Community
- The Collaborative Partnership
- The Match Between the Community and the Makeup of the Partnership
- Prior Efforts That Represent Movement toward the Community Care Network Vision
    - Community Health Focus
    - Community Accountability
    - Seamless Continuum of Care
    - Managing within Fixed Resources

- Moving Toward the Community Care Network Vision
  —The Visioning Process
  —Plan for Future Progress toward the Community Care Network Vision

Accompanying each case is an executive summary written especially for *Health Network Innovations,* often by a public official who has worked closely with the CCN in their region. Each CCN has provided a summary of notable progress, describing what has happened since the application was submitted in the spring of 1995. In addition, each one has allowed us to print all or part of a tool that they used in developing their CCN. These tools include informational brochures, business plans, bylaws, special contracts, and statements of policy. It is hoped that a budding system can use these tools for reference or even as stencils.

Mainly, this book is designed to be used, rather than read cover to cover. As exemplars of a locally driven approach to the reform of health and human services delivery, the cases should serve as a sounding board, a reference point, and a source of encouragement for others. In these times of rapid and large-scale change, peers are seeking each other out, testing each other's ideas, and trying to learn from each other's successes and challenges. We designed this book with peer learning in mind. (See figure 1, "Questions for Health Network Innovators.")

We have adopted several measures to enable you to use the book for peer learning. We divided it into parts to help you more easily find the peer experience most pertinent to you. The part introductions and executive summaries help you to more quickly learn where you'd like to start to compare your experience with that of others who are on the voyage to improving health and human services. We organized each case using the same outline. We provide a tool or two from each case that you may find useful in your efforts to move toward the goals of the CCN vision. We prepared

FIGURE 1. Questions for Health Network Innovators

Here are some questions that this book might help you answer for yourself:

- Does the community care network vision offer a suitable framework for guiding the institution for which I am responsible?
- Can my institution become more effective by drawing on the experiences of others who have faced some of the experiences that now perplex my coworkers and me?
- How can today's business realities in health care delivery accommodate the goal of improving people's health?
- How can my organization better meet the intertwined challenges of competition and collaboration?
- How will my institution respond to the demands of capitated payments or other forms of financial risk sharing when these become features of our lives?
- How can patient care be improved by delivering lower-cost preventive services to people who do not yet realize that they are at high risk for becoming tragic, or at least costly, cases?
- What do public health agencies have to offer as partners in private-sector health care delivery?
- When does it make sense to engage schools, churches, or local governments in decision making about the health care system?
- How can businesses outside health care become proactive partners, rather than just another negotiator demanding price discounts?
- Are there elements of the community care network vision that do not fit my particular circumstances?

an index that is especially detailed and organized around many of the practical concerns you face.

Hunt down information specific to your interests. Perhaps you are more interested right now in only one of the dimensions of the CCN vision. Or perhaps you care most about the roles of certain kinds of partnering organizations, such as schools or public health agencies. Maybe you most want to learn how some of the emerging CCNs are attacking the health problems of a specific age group, say, teenage mothers or the elderly, or specific types of interventions, perhaps cancer prevention or substance abuse education. You could also want to read especially about the types of prior experience that the awardees and finalists brought to bear in applying for the CCN Demonstration Program; this inquiry could help you prepare for greater success in acquiring future grant support for your partnership's activities.

Health Network Innovations can be a valuable resource for policy makers, researchers, and others who require apprenticeship in the practical issues of the day in order to fulfill their obligations or identify new opportunities. This book can help community leaders in fields other than health care to imagine ways to motivate and lead their local health system toward the future. Mainly, *Health Network Innovations* speaks to leaders and change makers in health and human service delivery who recognize the real world experience of their peers as valuable knowledge for their own voyages toward the vision.

Introduction: Contexts for Health Network Innovations

There is a rich context for the health network innovations that are described in this book. That context includes:

- National politics during the period in which the community care network (CCN) vision—the set of principles guiding the innovations—emerged.
- The policy context for CCN, including those policies pertinent to the CCN vision that contribute to today's turbulent health care environment.
- Symptoms of change in health care, as well as the two most important underlying trends driving the future of health care.
- Recent history, as seen through projects and programs that contributed to the development of the CCN vision.

NATIONAL REFORM DEBATES AND THE COMMUNITY CARE NETWORK VISION

We are not permitted to choose the frame of our destiny.
But what we put into it is ours.

—Dag Hammarskjöld

From early 1993 until mid-1994, American politicians risked much on health care reform. On January 25, 1993, President Clinton announced the creation of a Task Force on National Health Care Reform.[1] In a Gallup poll in February, 1993, conducted for the Employee Benefit Research Institute, one-third of Americans said the Bush and Clinton positions on health care had affected their votes the prior November "a great deal," and another third said those positions had "some" effect.[2] The same poll showed that the debates awakened a dormant concern for citizens: 91 percent of Americans believed the U.S. health care system needed to be reformed, while 15 percent had believed so just three months earlier, and only 5 percent had believed so in October 1990. As the stakes grew, national health care reform seemed just beyond the horizon.

Back in January 1992, before the public debates had begun, the leadership of the nation's major hospital and health system associations had already adopted remarkable new positions on health care reform. While the American Hospital Association

WHAT'S DIFFERENT NOW?

It's the same each time with progress. First they ignore you, then they say you're mad, then dangerous, then there's a pause and then you can't find anyone who disagrees with you.

—Tony Benn, British politician

The political events surrounding national health care reform from the campaign trail of 1992 to the death knell of 1994 amounted to a portal, propped partly open. For a time, anyone could glimpse one of our nation's most profound problems. Major trends in health care delivery, and not the political trumpeting, had shaped the principles of health care reform developed by the hospital and health system leadership. The problems of the health care system that prompted public dispute in the early 1990s had been growing throughout the 1970s and the 1980s.

What does it matter that health care reform took center stage for a year and a half after the 1992 presidential election? Our nation's recent history is rich with health care crises, with pronouncements about the need for radical change.[10] For example, the attention paid to health care reform issues in the early 1970s was, at that time, unprecedented. The era produced an incredible flurry of private, political, legislative, and regulatory activity. But it did not produce comprehensive health care reform. What is different now?

We have not achieved comprehensive health care reform through legislation, and we now face ever-more-frightening versions of the same problems. Twenty-six million uninsured Americans in 1978 created access barriers, inefficient utilization, and human tragedy.[11] That number grew to 39.6 million in 1995 and is expected to reach 45.6 million by 2002.[12] Health care inflation continues to outpace general inflation. There are no signs that the trend is stopping or reversing, and it seems to have only temporarily slowed as the nation increased its reliance on managed care. Corporations face the challenge of providing increasingly expensive health insurance to their employees at a time when a great many other pressures—including global competition and infrastructure demands—are mounting. The government's ability to provide coverage depends on giving it priority over other concerns, including the environment, defense, and education. Indeed, for the first time in our nation's history, the percentage of jobs that offer health insurance benefits has begun to drop.[13] The costs of maintaining the Hospital Insurance Trust Fund rapidly outstrip investments in it, with the Medicare Trustees estimating in 1996 that the fund will be depleted early in 2001.[14]

So, the problems keep growing. But what is *different* now? Why should we expect reform of the health care system now?

Without legislated comprehensive reform, *health care is now undergoing virtually comprehensive reform.* Health care is now reforming in response to market forces, new ideologies, state legislation, increased waivers in federal programs, and new federal laws increasing the transportability of insurance. One astute scholar of health care has noted: "We have learned that reform is quite different from revolution. . . . Whereas revolutions usually represent a sharp break from the past, succesful reform almost always reflects acceleration of trends and developments that have been quietly underway for many years."[15] With or without comprehensive national legislation, the changes faced now are just the beginning.

In 1995 and 1996, momentum grew for an unprecedented level of reductions in Medicare and Medicaid payments to service providers. Access and coverage, the "right to health care," dropped off the national agenda. Policy discussions focused on how to use the marketplace to stimulate competition and to move more Medicare and Medicaid beneficiaries to private health plans, and especially to managed care options.

Meanwhile, Medicare restructuring proposals, all of which included options for provider-sponsored organizations (PSOs), were advanced as part of balanced budget proposals from the Republican leadership, the Democratic conservatives, and the White House. The ensuing controversies and debates, under the heading of balanced budget proposals, yielded the now famous string of government shutdowns and then collapsed into a presidential veto. Shortly thereafter, attention shifted to the 1996 election campaigns.

Another 2 years had passed since the last great push for reform, and still no national legislative action. But in the meantime, action at the state and local levels had been intense. Health care providers and their local and regional partners were furiously working to bring opportunity and responsibility back to their communities.

OUR NATIONAL ENVIRONMENT FROM 2000 TO 2030

It is curious to note the old sea-margins of human thought!
Each subsiding century reveals some new mystery; we build
where monsters used to hide themselves.

—Henry Wadsworth Longfellow

We may not have national health care programs on a par with other industrialized democracies. But prior efforts have produced changes that contribute to today's environment. This section acknowledges some of the symptoms of the current health care delivery environment and describes the two most important trends facing U.S. health care today.

The Blue Cross and Blue Shield movement has departed from its original form, provider cooperatives delivering services in exchange for community-rated, prospective payments. But it played a major role in swelling employment-related health insurance. Medicare, though perceived by some as an insensitive bureaucracy, is one of the most powerful symbols of citizens' rights in our national politics. While some people hold little faith in government's ability to act, the Prospective Payment System launched a generation of experimentation in payment and finance, as well as utilization control. Earlier efforts to encourage the formation of HMOs—while not quite meeting the hoped-for objective of locally controlled, community-rated health plans—kick-started today's managed care industry. Federal grant programs to increase the production of physicians bore an abundant crop and are among the reasons that independent, fee-based practice is giving way to group forms of practice and salaries. Many elements of today's health care environment are symptomatic of the times, and also products of prior partial reform efforts.

Much has changed over the past 50 years. Even a passing treatment of the significant contributors to today's health care delivery environment falls well outside the scope of this book. Two major environmental factors, however, will completely reshape health care in this nation during the next 30 years: overall resources and the baby boom.

After World War II, the United States was the one industrialized economy on the planet that had not been severely damaged. But now, the tide of global competition rises. For health care decision makers, as well as for citizens in general, a less dominant global economic position means slower overall growth or even periods of stagnation or recession. This climate should not frighten us. We are simply exiting an unusual phase of our national history. (See figure 2.)

Meanwhile, we have developed expectations about the proximity of our hospitals, about the quality of our schools, about the convenience of our road systems, and about the strength and reach of our national defenses. We expect to receive Social Security when we reach the right age, and we expect to benefit from a Medicare program. If we are poor or serve the poor, we expect a Medicaid program. These and many other expectations developed amidst postwar prosperity.

One response has been to increase debt. Taking a long look back in time, our federal government has been responsible about assuming new debt. Recently, as we struggled to maintain our rights, capabilities, and programs, we piled up a lot of debt. The past 15 years, and especially the 1980s, show an affinity to indebtedness by our federal government. (See figure 3.) Just the interest on our national debt consumes 15 percent of all federal spending. That's money we don't get to spend to meet our expectations, our hopes and needs. (See figure 4.)

Just when we don't need it, we are entering a unique demographic phase in our national history. The baby boom generation is more than a clever phrase for product selling points or consumer attitudes. It is a unique demographic bulge of huge proportions, and it's about to hit the health care system hard.

FIGURE 2. Average Annual Rate of Growth in Gross Domestic Product, Adjusted to 1987 Constant Dollars.

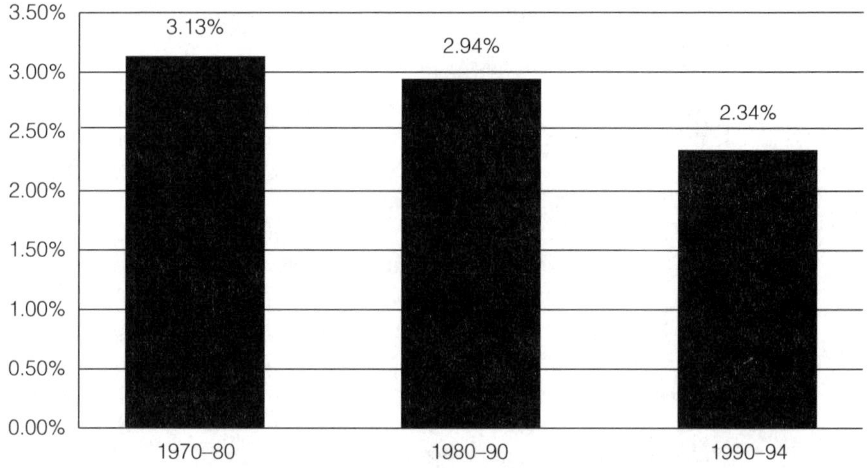

Source: Department of Commerce, Bureau of Economic Analysis. *Survey of Current Business* 74(2), Feb. 1995.

FIGURE 3. Gross Public Debt Per Capita

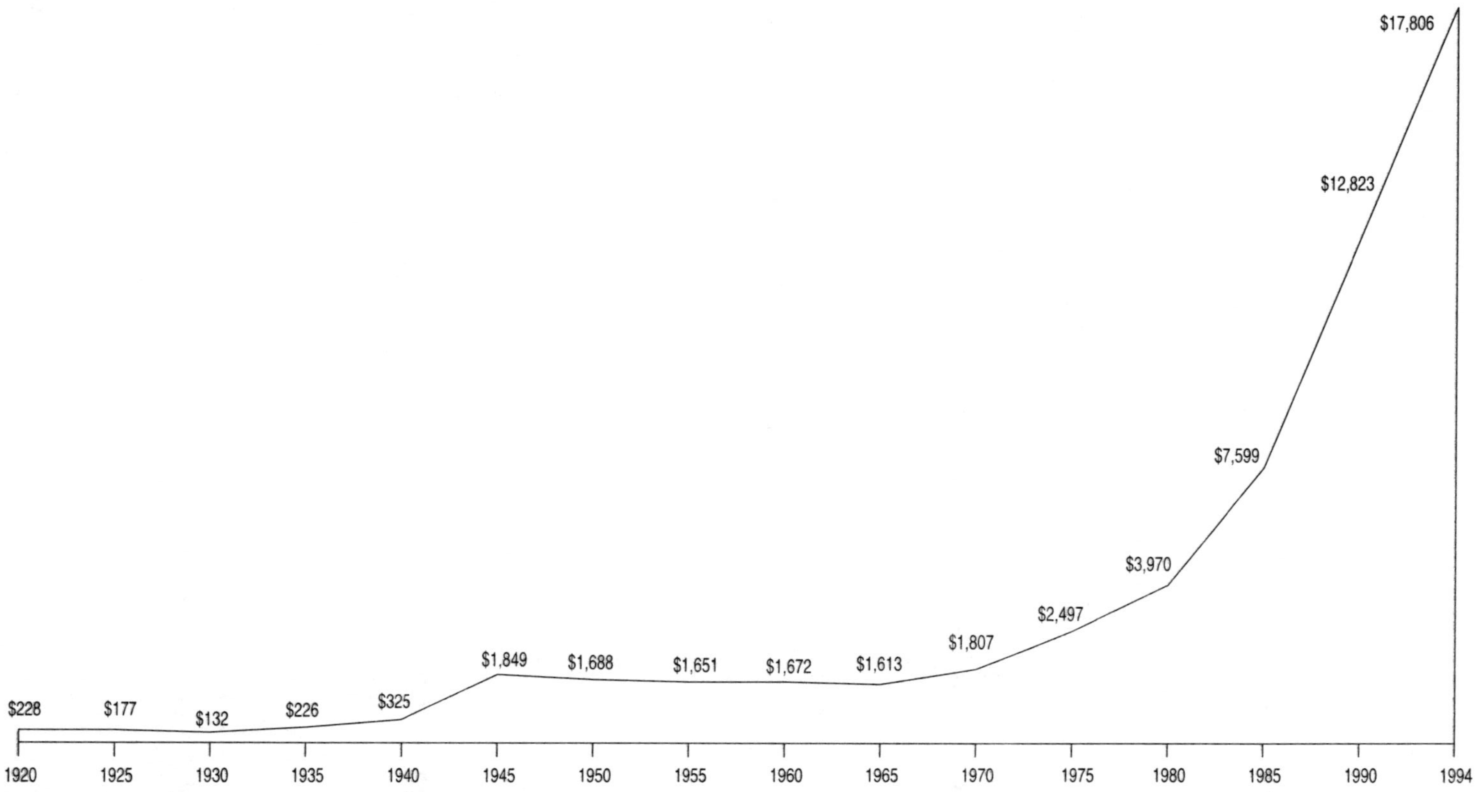

Source: Department of the Treasury, Financial Management Service.

FIGURE 4. **Debt Interest as a Percentage of Total Federal Outlays**

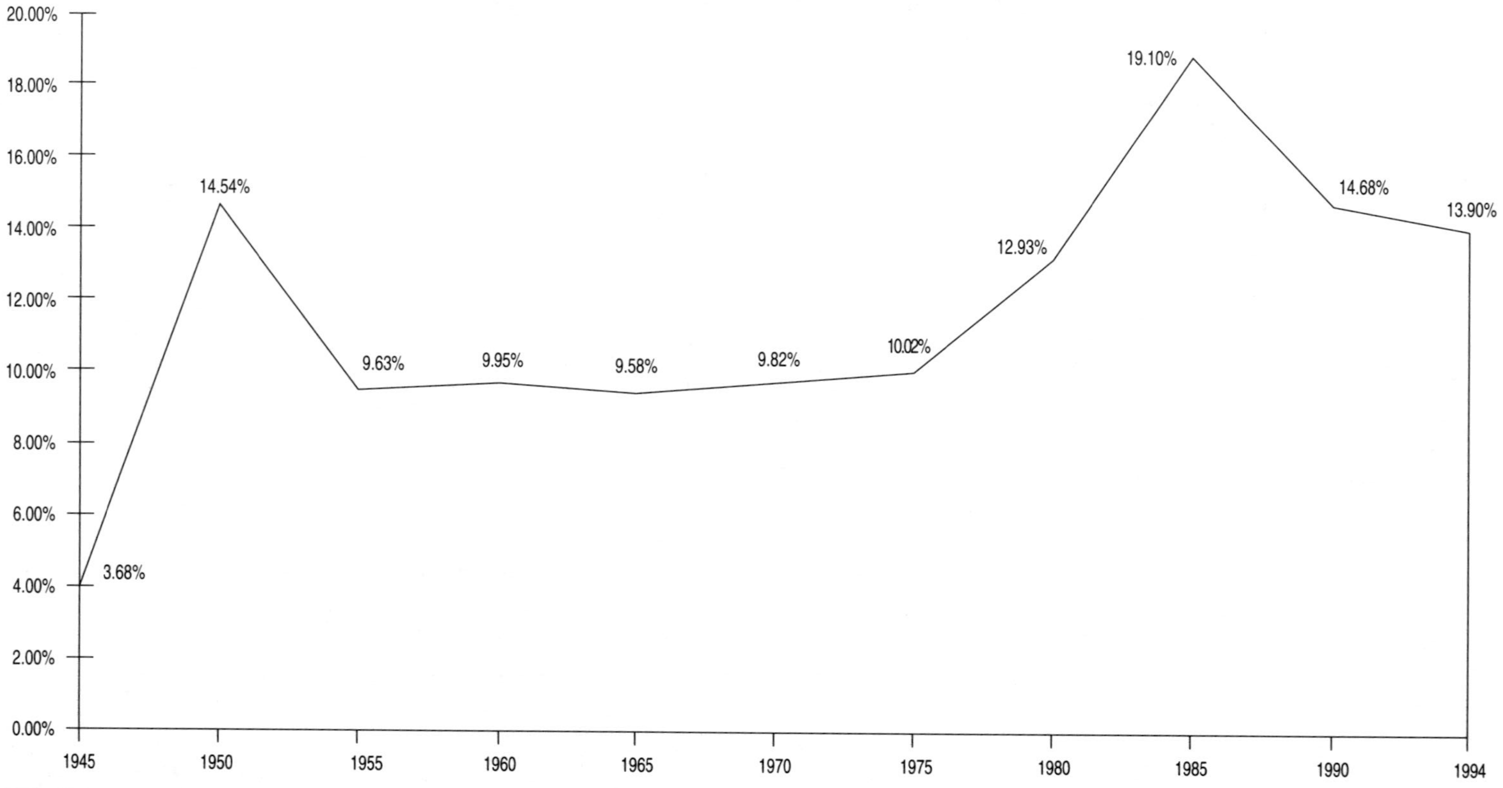

Source: Department of the Treasury, Financial Management Service.

So many babies were born from the late 1940s until the early 1960s that, for the only time in our nation's history, the median age dropped. (See figure 5.) That demographic bulge is about to enter its chronic care years, about to start drawing on Medicare and Social Security and private retirement funds and other benefits designed for the mature. As C. Holden wrote, citing a 1994 bipartisan congressional commission, "If unchecked, spending on these entitlement programs [for the elderly] plus interest on the national debt could consume the entire federal budget by 2012."[16]

Politicians and corporate leaders who say that we will adjust simply by reducing or delaying benefits for the elderly may not be paying close attention, or may be unwilling publicly to face the facts. The mature are today's most powerful voting bloc. How powerful will that voting bloc be when it makes up a much larger proportion of the population?

Pushing the problem a few years into the future by trimming social programs and payments to service providers lowers the near-term pressure a bit. But those reductions affect people's lives too, even though less directly. Limits will be reached, and reducing investment by trimming social programs will prove an inadequate strategy, as well as a source of pain and suffering for many Americans.

These pressures will be with us for some time. The people in the middle of the baby boom will reach their expected life terms about 2030. Shortly thereafter, of course, our underlying trends will rapidly shift toward a post–baby boom reality.

Comprehensive health care reform may be difficult for America for many reasons: our national character, political gridlock, powerful and entrenched interests, and a disinclination toward long-term planning. But some of these traits may prove beneficial over the long run, given the size of the underlying environmental shifts we will experience and an inescapable demand for change. The result may be more flexibility at the national and state level, with change designed and implemented locally.

FIGURE 5. Median Age in the United States

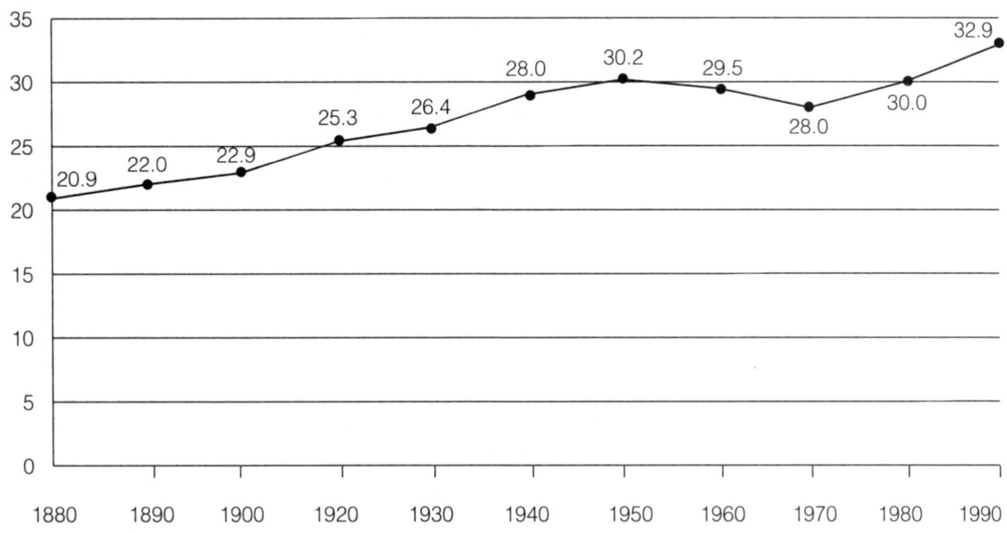

have also guided many communities through the phases of assessment and planning.[29] The Healthy Communities program of the National Civic League (NCL) has launched health community initiatives across the nation. The NCL's Civic Index is an especially useful assessment approach when local government is a partner.[30]

Thousands of specific initiatives have helped communities move forward. A few notable examples include Stanford University's valuable series of how-to guides on community health promotion, published in 1991 and 1992.[31] The *Community Collaboration Manual,* developed by The National Assembly of Voluntary Health and Social Organizations, has proven useful to many evolving partnerships through different stages of progress.[32] The United Way of America promoted the Healthy Communities–Healthy Cities concept, originally from the World Health Organization, in 1990.[33] Before 1991, Mountain States Health Corporation was giving hands-on assistance to rural hospital communities as they moved through a community decision-making model.[34] The Healthcare Forum produced its *Healthier Communities Action Kit* in 1993–94.[35] Numerous local and regional organizations, such as state hospital associations, have produced valuable guides, educational programs, and services.[36]

At the AHA, a most telling and influential sign of change was a change in the leadership. The AHA board's selection of Richard J. Davidson as the association's president in 1991 represented both a start in the process of consensus building among the leadership and an initiation of actions based on the strengthening consensus. The new AHA president consistently made the CCN vision the number one focus from the outset, shifting the association's resources to convert the board's symbolic act into the daily experience of the association, its members, and their local partners.

THE COMMUNITY CARE NETWORK VISION

In preparing for battle I have always found that plans are useless, but planning is indispensable.

—Dwight D. Eisenhower

The CCN vision is a clearly expressed framework for understanding, and then acting on, the interrelated web of changes occurring in health care delivery. As a vision, it illuminates long-range thinking. As a starting place, it enables leaders to imagine, design, and then act on their own local expressions of the vision. As a destination, it creates a healthier nation by providing affordable access to health services for all in a system reshaped to promote health and to manage within fixed resources.

The CCN vision stimulates health care organizations to *reform* health care delivery *locally* so patients, communities, and their resources, needs, and problems drive the reconfiguration of local health care. The reform of health care delivery toward the CCN vision accomplishes several objectives:

- Returning patients and communities to the center of health care delivery
- Working toward inclusion of those who are now outside the system of care (by virtue of poverty or cultural or other barriers) in the context of improving the health of the entire community
- Emphasizing prevention in order to reduce illness and disability
- Making the system more understandable and user-friendly for patients and enrollees

- Continually improving the continuity and quality of health care services
- Realigning the incentives to maximize the cost-effective use of health resources

Systemic thinking about improving the health system is not simple. While the CCN vision is as concise as staff could make it, it pushes one to simultaneously consider four intertwined goals. These goals are *community health focus, community accountability, a seamless continuum of care,* and *management within fixed resources.* (See the appendix to this introduction.)

Any local system of health care can work toward the CCN vision. Inspired by this vision, CCNs will employ many different methods and take numerous forms. In many cases, they will represent a collaboration of health care and human service organizations. They will manage a comprehensive array of health-related services for patients, for an enrolled population, and for the larger community. They will operate within a budget fixed by per capita payments or a set budget, thereby directly accepting at least some of the financial risk for the efficiency and effectiveness of their services. Most important, evolving CCNs will be continuously redesigned to best address the health problems of patients, enrollees, and the community at large. Indeed, a special characteristic of the CCN vision is its mix of an increased focus on accountability for the health of *communities* with improvement in the functions of health care organizations as *businesses.*

Groups of individuals and organizations under many names, such as coalitions, alliances, networks, and partnerships are engaging in collaborative efforts. Many of them are evolving toward the CCN vision in many different communities, from many different starting points. Any sector of a community, including government, public health, business, insurance, health care delivery, or citizens' groups, can initiate collaborative efforts and lead a community toward the CCN vision. Involvement by many sectors of a community is necessary to ensure that collaborative efforts focus on the ultimate goals of improving community health and maximizing the benefit derived from limited health care expenditures. Focusing on those ultimate goals necessitates the management of a full continuum of services as well, so hospitals, physicians, nurses, and other elements of the health and human services delivery system are essential and constant features of evolving CCNs.

THE NATIONAL DEMONSTRATION OF THE COMMUNITY CARE NETWORK VISION

A conception not reducible to the small change of daily experience is like a currency not exchangeable for articles of consumption; it is not a symbol, but a fraud.

—George Santayana

On July 18, 1994, the AHA, CHA, VHA, and HRET jointly announced a $6 million grant from the W. K. Kellogg Foundation. The time had come to convert the CCN concept into the currency of daily experience—a chance to begin testing how the CCN vision would work in practice. Commenting on one of the W. K. Kellogg Foundation's largest grants, AHA president Dick Davidson said, "These networks could help reinvent the American hospital so that they are not judged on the number of beds they have, but by the health of their communities."[37]

The National Demonstration of the CCN Vision soon received support from The Duke Endowment, the U.S. Public Health Service, and the Health Foundation of New York. On December 8, 1995, the W. K. Kellogg Foundation made a supplemental award of $722,000 to support a larger number of sites as well as to establish a CCN Fellowship Program. In November 1996, the W. K. Kellogg Foundation approved a second supplemental award for evaluation of and education on CCN sustainability and governance.

The Robert Wood Johnson Foundation has committed $800,000 to evaluation of the CCN sites' progress. Parke-Davis, Johnson & Johnson, the Health Alliance of Pennsylvania, the California Association of Hospitals and Health Systems, and others also have made financial contributions. By the end of 1996, over $8.5 million in philanthropic support had been invested in the CCN Demonstration Program and its evaluation, with participating sites committed to another $5.6 million in cash matches.

The National Demonstration of the CCN Vision has a straightforward goal: to learn how communities and their health care provider organizations together make progress toward the CCN vision, and to disseminate this experience widely. Achieving this goal requires a number of steps. Some of these are summarized below as a way of giving background on the demonstration program itself.

A national steering committee representing a variety of interests was established. Among the documents created to guide the identification of community partnerships for participation in the program was a steering committee policy statement on values to be emphasized in site selection. Notable among the values to be emphasized were both prior experience and future promise for making progress toward the CCN vision. The program was designed to recognize that many local systems of health and human service delivery had already been moving toward the CCN vision as a result of initiatives started under other names or for other reasons.

By the April 28, 1995, deadline, 283 applications had been received. Each of the applications represented a coalition of local organizations, totaling over 1,600 organizations nationwide. Each application sought to show how a local or regional coalition had past experience and future promise in initiatives that exhibit progress toward the CCN vision.

Applications were scored by at least three outside experts, and 163 outside reviewers volunteered to serve. They had been invited from research centers, public health organizations, community organizations, and hospitals and health networks. All reviewers signed statements attesting that they had no conflict of interest. They were also required not to use or make public any information about a specific partnership that they obtained from their review of applications.

The 49 applications that scored in the top 20 percent represented more than 20 rural and more than 20 low-income communities. Therefore, the objective was met of attaining high-quality applicants of suitable diversity for the steering committee for finalist workshop interviews. (See figure 6.)

Three-person teams from each of the 49 finalist partnerships went to Chicago for interviews with the program's steering committee. At the end of four grueling days (each day, committee members conducted and evaluated six hour-long interviews as teams), the steering committee, feeling that 49 worthwhile finalists had been interviewed, winnowed the group down to 25. Each of these 25 awardees is receiving support, from January 1996 through December 1998, in amounts up to $225,000. The 24 other finalists each have received $9,000 credits to assist them in continuing their efforts toward the CCN vision. The 20 cases in this book include both awardees and other finalists.

FIGURE 6. Community Care Network Demonstration: Applicants and Finalists.

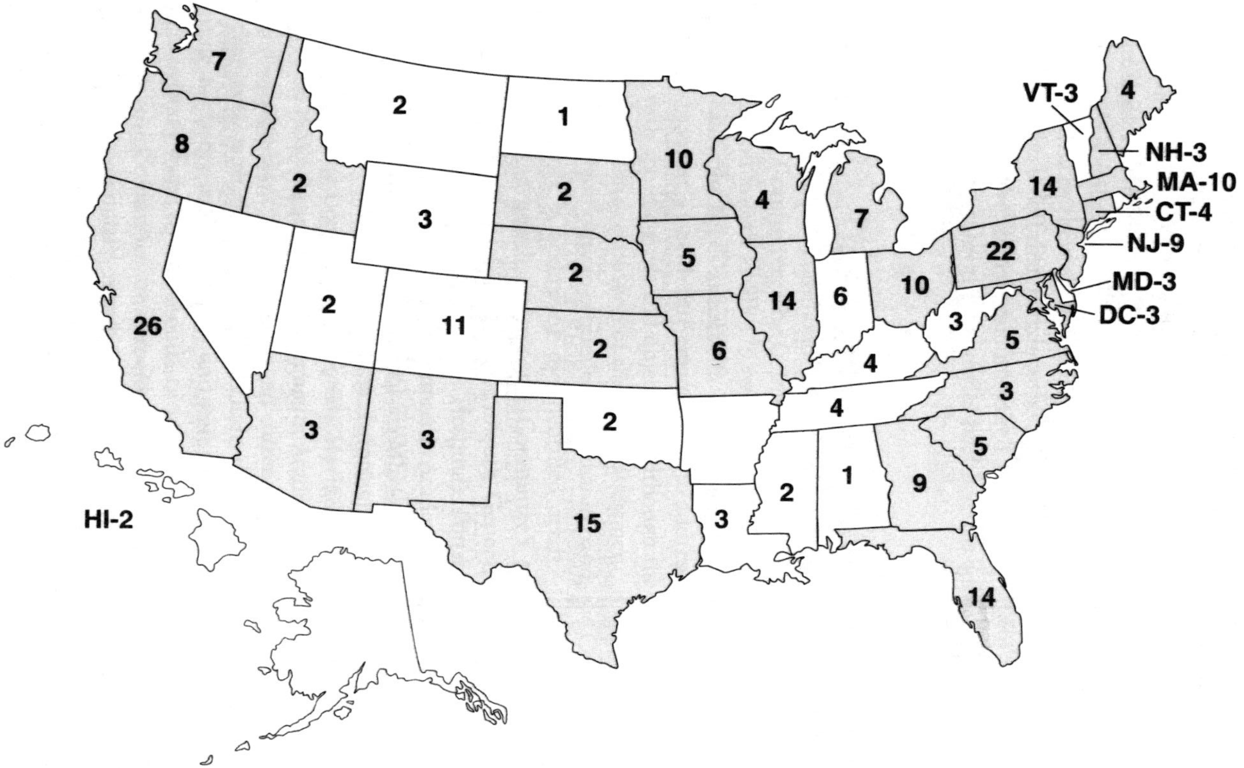

Source: National Demonstration of the CCN Vision.
Note: Shading indicates states that had finalists. Numbers indicate total number of applicants.

After their selection, awardees provided more specific operational definitions of the initiatives they would conduct in order to make and show progress toward the CCN vision. The initiatives had been part of their plans for moving toward the CCN vision as described in their applications. A simple matrix was developed so partnerships could describe their initiatives, measurement methods, baseline values, and expected future values over the 12 quarters of the program. (See figure 7.) Each of the awardees submits quarterly reports that include an update on its progress toward its initiatives, in addition to other information. (See figures 8 and 9.)

The program office provides assistance, financial support, and ongoing monitoring and evaluation to the awardees. These efforts include revisiting and improving both the participants' initiatives for moving toward the CCN vision and the methods for measuring performance in those initiatives, as well as annual site visits, annual CCN conferences, and the diffusion of the sites' expert knowledge to other communities. The national partners are also developing and disseminating new tools to help other community partnerships move toward the CCN vision.

A BRIEF STATISTICAL DESCRIPTION OF COMMUNITY CARE NETWORK PARTNERSHIPS

The ordinary [person] is involved in action, the hero acts. An immense difference.

—Henry Miller

Not every applicant could receive financial support through the program. But all 283 applications exhibited promise that meaningful, positive, and systematic innovation is happening in health care delivery all across the nation. This section gives some aggregate statistical information about the many different applicants to the program—the many unnamed heroes taking action in your community and ours.

You may find it interesting to compare your local efforts at building networks to the information found here. We do not expect the following to tell you what you should do. But this section can give some of the typical "design specifications" of the applicants' vehicles for moving into the future.

In the summer of 1995, 174 of the 283 applicants to the program completed a survey on organizational collaboration.[38] On the basis of that survey, three groups of evolving partnerships are compared here: awardees (those 25 sites selected for 3 years of support of up to $225,000), finalists (those 24 sites selected for partnership interviews and given $9,000 in credits), and other applicants.[39]

Moving toward the CCN vision can engage a broad range of organizations. No one should expect every organization in an evolving partnership to have the exact same role. In fact, one of the strengths of collaboration is that different individuals and organizations can bring different kinds of resources to mutual objectives.

The CCN demonstration program defines three general types of roles depending on the level of resource commitment each partner makes. A *full working partner* is an organization that has dedicated staff and/or financial resources that are used to plan and implement the initiatives of the collaborative partnership. Dedicated staff have all or some portion of their time devoted specifically to CCN initiatives. A *participating partner* has identified staff that work on the initiatives of the collaborative partnership as time permits. An organization is an *informing partner* if it has identified staff who act as liaison between collaborating partners and the organization.

FIGURE 7. Milestone Tracking Template

Partnership name ______________________

Key contact name ______________________

Initiative	Measurement method	Current value	New value /by qtr	New value /by qtr	New value /by qtr	New value /by qtr

Instructions

The purpose of the milestone tracking template is to describe in specific and measurable, but summary or shorthand form, the initiatives your partnership will engage in as you move toward the Community Care Network vision. Demonstration partnerships and national program staff will use your milestones as a guide for making and assessing progress throughout the course of the program. Narrative portions of quarterly reports will refer to the initiatives as established in the milestone tracking template to describe your steps, successes, barriers and techniques used to overcome barriers. Site visits will include sessions focusing on the initiatives, how they may be changing, and how progress can continue. Your milestones will be a key element of your contract.

Keep a blank copy of the template for your files. Using the following definitions, please complete one or more milestone tracking templates to specify, in simplified form, the initiatives your partnership described in your application to the program or modifications of the initiatives as described in your application if you have already had to modify them. If you have any questions, do not hesitate to call Richard J. Bogue at 312/422-2607.

Initiative

In your application to the Community Care Network Demonstration Program, your partnership proposed a series of initiatives that represented a plan for moving toward the Community Care Network vision. During the application review and selection processes, these initiatives played a very important role. For each initiative that it makes sense to your partnership to describe separately, a short name and brief description should be provided.

Measurement Method

Progress in each of your initiatives must be measurable. Generally, measurement methods may refer to changes in structures, processes, outcomes, or a combination of these. Changes in the measures, in the hoped for direction, should reflect meaningful progress in the corresponding initiative. Examples of measures could include the formation of new services or governing structures, counts of people being served or of organizations represented at meetings, health status measures for the community or number of inches of newsprint devoted to a topic. You must quantify, put a number on, your measurement method for each initiative. In this column of the template, please briefly describe each of the structures, processes, or outcomes that will be measured as evidence of progress on the initiative.

Current Value

Provide the current value, exact or very reliable estimate, of the measure.

New Value/By Qtr

Please give new values or quantities that represent your expected progress for each measurement method. And also write "BY" and the program quarter by which your partnership expects to reach that value. Program quarter 1 is Jan–Mar 1996, program quarter 2 is Apr–Jun 1996, program quarter 5 is Jan–Mar 1997, program quarter 12 (the last program quarter) is Oct–Dec 1998, et cetera. You do not have to give an expected value for each of the twelve program quarters. Each of the value BY quarter expectations that you give is one "milestone." You should make an entry in the NEW VALUE/BY QTR column only when you expect to reach a new milestone. For some initiatives, one measurement per year will be appropriate. For other initiatives, four measures over the course of only one year will make more sense. Any initiative, once initiated however, should have at least one milestone (NEW VALUE/BY QTR expectation) per year.

FIGURE 8. Quarterly Progress Report Instructions

The Quarterly Progress Report consists of three sections: a partnership progress report in which you must verify and update partnership information, a narrative progress report, which asks for more specific details regarding partnership activities in meeting your measurable objectives, and a copy of your milestone template, on which you can record modifications or additions. The focus of this exercise is the past quarter, unless otherwise noted. Please type all information. Save a copy of the completed progress report for your partnership's files, and mail the completed report back to the CCN program office. The quarterly progress report is always due at the end of the third week of the following quarter. (The fourth quarter ends on December 31. The report is due in the Program Office on Friday, January 24).

Partnership Progress Report

Please respond directly on this form, specifying the name of the person completing the partnership progress report. In the first column on the first page of the partnership progress report, please verify the names of all organizations that were described as participating in your partnership activities. The second column reports the role these organizations most often played in the collaboration, as taken from the Survey on Organizational Collaboration and completed by your partnership last summer.

Roles Of Collaborative Partners

If there has been a change in the information contained in the first two columns, please use columns three and four to record that change. Column three should be used to record a change in the role of the collaborative partner. (The definitions are provided below). Please circle the new role if there has been a change in status. Column four should be used to indicate if the organization has discontinued its involvement in the partnership. Please circle "yes" if the organization has discontinued, and "no" if the organization continues to be involved. If the organization has discontinued its involvement, please complete the "reason" column.

Full Working Partner (FWP): the organization has dedicated staff and/or financial resources that are used to plan and implement the initiatives of the collaborative partnership. Dedicated staff have all or some portion of their time (e.g., .25 full-time equivalent) devoted specifically to these initiatives.

Participating Partner (PP): the organization has identified staff that work on initiatives of the collaborative partnership as time permits given other staff responsibilities.

Informing Partner (IP): the organization has identified staff who act as a liaison so that collaborating partners know who to contact when communicating with the organization.

Use page two of the partnership progress report to note any additional organizations that have been added to your partnership. In the first column on the second page, please list the names of all the organizations that have been added to the partnership during the quarter. (If "none", please write "none" on the first line of the second page). If organizations have been added, specify the name in the first column, circle the role in the second column, and specify the type of organization in the third column, using the organizational codes on the next page.

Organizational Codes

Private Sector (non-Provider)

100 Citizen or citizen advocacy group
101 Religious organization
102 Insurer/HMO/health plan
103 Business or business group
104 Philanthropy or United Way
105 Economic development corps or planning commission
109 Other private sector

FIGURE 8. (Continued)

Educational Group

200 University/college
201 School (K–12)
202 Preschool/Head Start
203 School district, board, or superintendent's office(s)
209 Other education or youth development, non-sectarian

Public Sector (noneducation, nonmedical service provider)

309 Other public sector
310 Public health agency
320 Human service agency
321 Mental health/substance abuse focused agency
322 Aging or elderly focused agency
323 Children, youth, and/or family focused agency
330 Housing authority
340 Law or justice agency
350 Govt—executive office (municipal or county)
360 Department of health
370 Public sector health or human service coalition (including state coordinating agencies)

Medical Service Providers

400 Acute care hospital
420 Long-term care facility
443 Health system, medical service provider
449 Other health/medical service provider, private sector
450 Home & community based health service provider
460 Physician's practice
470 Private sector medical professional membership groups/health care interest group or coalitions

Narrative Progress Report

The narrative progress report contains twelve sections. Please read the twelve sections first, so that you can decide where to best fit the information on your partnership. Each section contains a description of the type of information required, as well as the *maximum* expected length of the response. Please respond directly on this form, specifying the name of the person completing the narrative progress report.

The information recorded here has a short-term use in allowing documentation of the progress on your initiatives, but it also has long-term purposes. In order for this information to be of use in the future to newly forming partnerships, we must stress the importance of chronicling challenges and/or barriers as well as the activities that went smoothly.

Milestone Template Update

A copy of your milestone template is appended for completing sections 1, 2, and 3. Please review and note on the template if any milestones or measurement methods have been either modified or abandoned. Provide details in sections 2 and 3 of the narrative progress report.

Thank you!

FIGURE 9. Narrative Report for 4th Quarter 1996

Partnership Name ____

Person Completing Report __________________________________

1. Using your milestone template as the base of reference, identify milestones achieved and highlight other important progress (1 page).
2. Specify which milestones or measurement methods have been modified (make appropriate notations in your attached milestone template). Identify and provide an explanation for milestones and measurement methods scheduled but not met during this quarter (½ page).
3. Specify which milestones or measurement methods have been abandoned (make appropriate notations in your attached milestone template). Identify and provide an explanation for milestones and measurement methods that will not continue to be pursued as previously planned (½ page).
4. Describe key external factors that have affected your progress and/or necessitated modifications to your plans (½ page).
5. Describe internal factors within your partnership that have affected your progress and/or necessitated modifications to your plans. For example, document staff changes or organizational changes that would affect the partnership (½ page).
6. Highlight key decisions made by your partnership during this quarter as the decisions affect future milestones and progress (e.g., addition or deletion of services, financial decisions, etc.) (½ page).
7. Document any special or unique learning experienced during the quarter that you think you can use to improve your partnership and your implementation of initiatives in the future. For example, a series of activities were designed and conducted according to plan, but looking back, there were some things that could have been improved if done differently (½ page).
8. At this point in time, describe the primary strengths of your partnership (½ page).
9. Document planned workshops, major events, or scheduled meetings for the next quarter that relate to your partnership's progress on any or all dimensions of the CCN vision (½ page).
10. Outline technical assistance needed that would aid in implementing initiatives, in further development of the community care network, or in the development of your collaborative partnership (½ page).
11. Document any benefits or disappointments of participating in the CCN Demo Program over the past quarter (½ page).
12. Please attach (if responding by diskette), or separately mail (if responding via E-mail), news clippings and other public reports about your CCN activities that were released during the quarter.

For different collaborative activities, one would expect organizations to commit different levels of resources. For example, an immunization effort might require public health agencies to serve as full working partners, while an effort to develop new managed care capacities might require a higher level of commitment from local businesses or health care providers. Since partners change in their interests and capacities over time as well, one would expect partnership composition to change over time and different organizations to lead at different times. For example, a partnering organization going through a change in leadership might need to commit to informing partner status, at least temporarily.

At the time of the survey, 49 percent of all partners listed were full working partners, 38 percent were participating partners, and 13 percent were informing partners. (See figure 10.) There is not likely to be a magical proportion that guarantees success for all evolving CCNs. In fact, these proportions probably change over time. The demonstration program office continues to track this information on a quarterly basis with the 25 partnerships that received awards.

Hospitals and health systems cannot make local health care delivery change happen all alone. Many different kinds of organizations have a stake in a community's health care delivery. Among the applicants to the CCN demonstration program, 39 percent of all organizations listed were health providers, 32 percent were public sector or government entities, 11 percent were educational groups, and 19 percent were private sector, nonprovider organizations. Each of the three groups (awardees, finalists, and other applicants) reported similar compositions. (See figure 11.)

In evolving CCNs, some capacities are best reflected in individual members, while other functions must be done collaboratively. In addition, some functions might be performed independently in some partnerships, while the same function is performed

FIGURE 10. Percent of Organizations According to their Collaborative Role

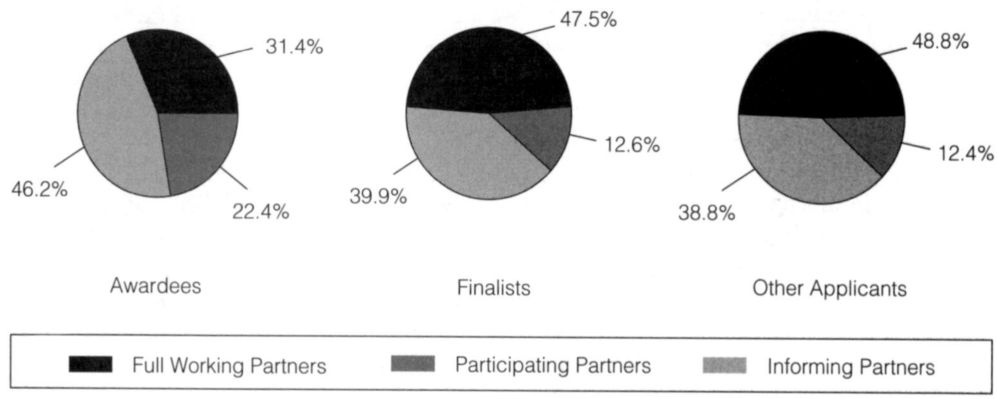

Source: Survey on Organization Collaboration, question 1a.

FIGURE 11. Organizational Structure of CCN Networks

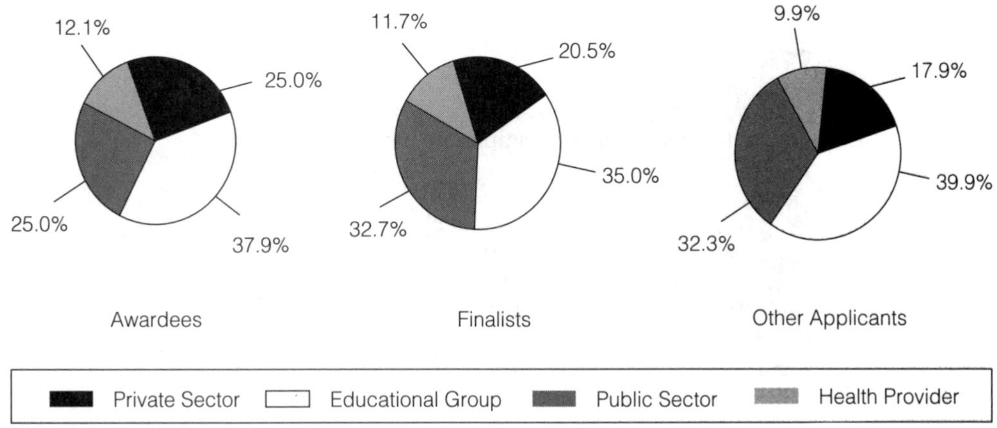

Source: Survey on Organizational Collaboration, question 1a.

collaboratively in other evolving CCNs. *Independent* can be defined as an organization making unilateral decisions about pertinent staffing, financial, and management issues. *Collaborative* can be defined as two or more organizations making joint decisions about pertinent staffing, financing, and/or management of services.

The degree of collaboration for awardees, finalists, and other applicants varied. (See figure 12.) A value of 1 indicates that half of all services are provided independently while the other half are provided collaboratively. A number above 1 signifies that more than half of all services provided are produced collaboratively. This ratio of the services provided collaboratively is highest among the awardees, lower among finalists, and lowest among other applicants. This ratio represents the role of collaboration within a partnership: It underscores not provision of services per se but the joint effort among partners to provide them. As a group, awardees seem to provide more services on a collaborative basis.

We also know something about the specific activities in which the applicant partnerships were involved. Example activities include community health needs assessment, the coordination of care, the reorganization of health care services, and accountability to the community. We organized the activities in four categories, one representing each of the four dimensions of the CCN vision: community accountability, community health focus, seamless continuum of care, and management within fixed resources. For each activity the partnerships were asked whether they are engaged in it, plan to do it, or have no plans to do it.

For each dimension of the CCN vision, we measured the percentage of activities in which each partnership has been involved collaboratively. Similarly, we measured the percentage of those activities for which the partnership was *planning* collaborative involvement. Once again we see differences in the collaborative involvement among the three groups (awardees, finalists, and other applicants). In each of the four dimensions, awardees appear to have been further along in their movement toward the CCN vision. The percentage of activities the organizations "have done" was highest among the awardees, lower among the finalists, and lowest among the other applicants. Although the survey data were not used to determine which applicants should receive grant funding, it is worth noting that CCN applicants were awarded 40 points

FIGURE 12. Collaborative vs. Independent Provision

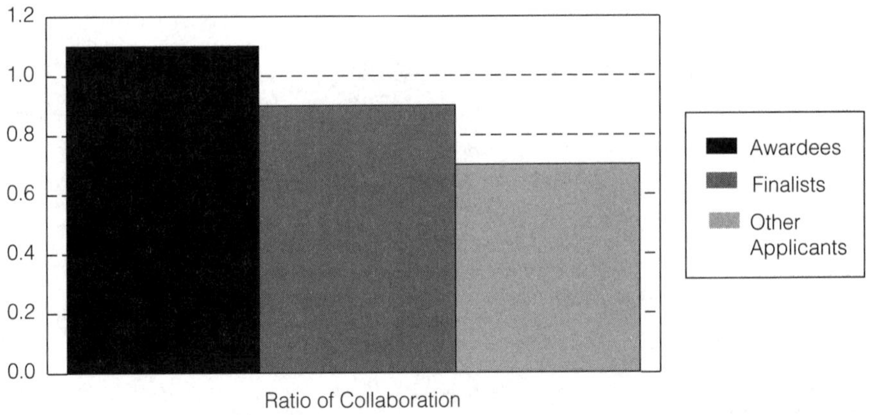

Source: Survey on Organizational Collaboration, question 2.

out of 100 for prior experience in collaboration. These survey results affirm that application reviewers were able to discern these differences.

In their outward appearances, the three categories of applicants look similar. They included a similar mix of partners with similar collaborative roles. Some differences did exist. Those evolving CCNs selected to participate in the program were more involved in the collaborative provision of health and human services and reported being further along in their progress toward the CCN vision.

HOW TO CONTACT US

Never doubt that a small group of thoughtful, committed citizens can change the world; it is the only thing that ever has.

—Margaret Mead, U.S. anthropologist

Call or write us if you want to learn more about moving toward the CCN vision. Call or write us if you have experience or expertise you want to share. Your experiences might be very helpful to others in their journeys. We will be happy to learn from your efforts and learn how to pass your innovations on to others.

Contact: Claude H. Hall, Jr.
National Demonstration of the Community Care Network Vision
One North Franklin, Suite 2900
Chicago, Illinois 60606
Phone: 312-422-2613
Fax: 312-422-4568
E-mail: 74327.107@compuserve.com

Meanwhile, we are going to keep learning about evolving CCNs. We will work directly with some, and learn by listening to others. We hope this book helps you do the same.

References and Notes

1. Remarks by the president during a meeting with the Health Care Working Group, Jan. 25, 1993.
2. Colburn, D. Health care, uninsured concern Americans. *The Washington Post* Health, Apr. 13, 1993.
3. In *A Responsive Society* (San Francisco: Jossey-Bass, 1991, pp. 127–52), Amitai Etzioni characterizes the communitarian perspective as seeking "to establish moral coherence within society, the moral foundations of a common good" on the basis of "the shared moral values, 'virtues,' and traditions of the community." Etzioni contrasts communitarianism to the contemporary liberal philosophy, which holds that "individual persons and their self-chosen ends are primary." In health care delivery, the natural tension between these two perspectives is often observed where collaboration, joint work on common purposes, meets competition, the idea that social ends are best met by encouraging each individual to assert her or his own interests.
4. Donald Light offers an excellent conceptual framework for comparing the communitarian perspective found in the CCN vision with medical professional and corporate conceptions

for characterizing change in health care delivery. See: Light, D. W. The rhetorics, and realities of community health care: the limits of countervailing powers to meet the health care needs of the 21st century. *The Journal of Health Politics, Policy and Law* 22(1):105–45, spring 1997. See also: Starr, P. *The Social Transformation of American Medicine.* New York: Basic Books, 1982.

5. Address of the president to the joint session of Congress, Sept. 22, 1993.
6. Remarks by the president and the first lady at Ambridge Area High School, Ambridge, PA, Nov. 3, 1993.
7. Morin, R. Americans in poll doubt health plan. *The Washington Post* Health, June 22, 1993: "Thirty-four percent of those questioned said they approved of the way Clinton was handling the health care system, down from 56 percent in April. . . . Still public displeasure with the current health care insurance system remains high. According to the poll, only 25 percent rated the system as either excellent or good, while 74 percent said it was not good or poor." Also, Brownstein, R., Clinton's job approval rating stands at 55%. *Los Angeles Times* Jan. 23, 1994: "47% said they generally approved of the plan, while 32% said they didn't like it. But those numbers have slipped since Clinton introduced the plan in September, when supporters exceeded critics by 30 percentage points."
8. Broder, J. M., and Tumulty, K. Clinton needs State of the Union to jolt a state of motion. *Los Angeles Times* Jan. 25, 1994.
9. Drinkard, J. $100 million fight for health reform. *San Francisco Chronicle* Apr. 25, 1994.
10. See, Starr, P., *The Social Transformation of American Medicine.* New York: Basic Books, 1982. The following tells of the sense of crisis in the early 1970s: "For the first time since the Committee on the Costs of Medical Care, the economic and political leadership of American society seemed ready to bring about changes in the organization of medical care over the opposition of the providers. The doctors, hospitals, and insurance companies were now completely on the defensive, trying to hold back a tide of dissatisfaction. So in a political sense, the medical system was very much in crisis, not because it was really about to break down, but because it had lost their confidence. Medicine had overdrawn its credit" (p. 383). See also: Anderson, O. W. *Health Services in the United States: A Growth Enterprise Since 1875.* Chicago: Health Administration Press, 1985.
11. Starr, p. 417.
12. Aston, G. Law solves only fraction of nation's access troubles, AHA president says. *AHA News* 32(37):1
13. Aston. Law solves only fraction of nation's access troubles.
14. Aston, G. Trustees warn: Medicare fund sinking fast. *AHA News* 32(23):1.
15. Sigmond, R. M. Back to the future: partnerships and coordination of community health. *Frontiers of Health Services Management* 11(4):8.
16. Roush, W. Live long and prosper? *Science* 273:42–46, July 5, 1996.
17. American Hospital Association. *Community Benefit and Tax-Exempt Status: A Self-Assessment Guide for Hospitals.* Chicago: AHA, 1988, p. 1.
18. Catholic Health Association. *Social Accountability Budget: Continuing the Community Service Tradition.* St. Louis: CHA, 1989.
19. Catholic Health Association. *Reporting Community Benefits: A Guide for Communicators.* St. Louis: CHA, 1989.
20. VHA Inc. *Voluntary Standards: A Framework for Meeting Community Needs.* Irving, TX: VHA, 1992. See also: VHA Inc. *Community Health Assessment: A Process for Positive Change.* Irving, TX: VHA, 1993; *Community Partnerships: Taking Charge of Change Through Partnership.* Irving, TX: VHA, 1993; *Sustaining Community Health Improvement Initiatives.* Irving, TX: VHA, 1996; and *Building Healthier Communities: A Guide for Assessing the Community's Health.* Irving, TX: VHA, 1996.

21. American Hospital Association. *Renewing the U.S. Health Care System: Report of Ad Hoc Meeting, Washington, D.C., Jan. 25–27, 1990.* Chicago: AHA Section for Health Care Systems, 1990.

22. Mannheim, L. M., Bazzoli, G. J., and Sohn, M. W. Local hospital competition in large metropolitan areas. *Journal of Economics and Management Strategy.* 3:143–67, 1994; Bogue, R. J., Shortell, S. M., Sohn, M. W., Manheim, L. M., and Bazzoli, G. Hospital reorganization following merger. *Medical Care.* 33(7):676–86, 1995.

23. Six monographs were developed with the leadership of the rural hospitals under the W. K. Kellogg Foundation–supported National Demonstration of Community Oriented Primary Care. The project was comanaged by the National Rural Health Association and the AHA's Hospital Research and Educational Trust. The monographs, published between 1989 and 1993, increasingly reflected a community health system orientation: *Rural Hospital Closure: Management and Community Implications* (1989); *Diversification and Conversion Strategies for Rural Hospitals* (1990); *A Prelude to Strategic Planning: Making Your Organization and Community Fit for Success* (1990) *Strategic Planning Workbook (1990) Increasing Rural Health Resources: Community-Based Strategies for Recruitment and Retention* (1992); and *Working from Within: Integrating Rural Health Care* (1993).

24. Hospital Research and Educational Trust. *Working Together to Improve Health Care Delivery: Observations on Collaboration By Rural Hospitals and Health Care Systems.* Chicago: HRET, Section for Health Care Systems, and Section for Small or Rural Hospitals of the American Hospital Association, 1992.

25. American Hospital Association. *Healthier Communities: Success Stories from Across America.* Chicago: AHA, 1995. See also: Hospital Research and Educational Trust. *Background and Resources for a Community Health Status Focus.* Chicago: AHA, 1996, rev. ed.

26. Seay, J. D., and Sigmond, R. M. Community benefit standards for hospitals: perception and performance. *Frontiers in Health Service Management.* 5(3):3–39, Spring 1989. See also: Kovner, A. R. Meeting hospital community benefit standards. *Healthcare Executive.* 6(5):30–31, Sept.–Oct., 1991.

27. U. S. Government Printing Office. *Healthy People 2000: National Disease Prevention and Health Promotion Objectives for the Nation,* stock no. 017-001-00474. Washington, D.C.: GPO, 1990.

28. National Association of County and City Health Officials. *APEXPH.* Washington, D.C.: NACCHO, 1991.

29. Centers for Disease Control. *PATCH (Planned Approach to Community Health).* Atlanta: CDC, 1996.

30. National Civic League. *The Healthier Communities Handbook* and *Civic Index.* Denver: NCL, 1993.

31. Stanford University. *How-To Guides on Community Health Promotion.* Palo Alto: Stanford University, 1991–92.

32. The National Assembly of Voluntary Health and Social Organizations. *The Community Collaboration Manual.* Washington, D.C.: NAVHSO, 1991.

33. United Way of America. *Building Healthier Communities—The United Way.* Alexandria, VA: UWA, 1990.

34. Mountain States Health Corporation. *Healthy Futures: A Development Kit for Rural Hospitals.* Boise: MSHC, 1991.

35. The Healthcare Forum. *Healthier Communities Action Kit.* San Francisco: Healthcare Forum, 1993–94.

36. See, for example: Missouri Hospital Association. *Community Health Improvement Manuals.* Jefferson City, MO: MHA, 1995; New Jersey Hospital Association. *Building Healthier Communities: A Guide for Assessing the Community's Health.* Princeton: NJHA, 1994; Hospital

and Health System Association of Pennsylvania. *A Guide for Assessing and Improving Health Status.* Harrisburg, PA: 1993.

37. *Health News Daily* July 19, 1994.
38. The National Demonstration of the Community Care Network Vision acknowledges Rebecca Stein, PhD, Economics Department, Northwestern University, for her role in analyzing and reporting on the survey.
39. The survey was not used in the evaluation of applications, and responses to this survey were tabulated and analyzed only after site selection took place. Surveys were returned from 25 awardees, 22 finalists, and 127 other applicants.

•••••••••••

APPENDIX. THE FOUR DI CARE NETWORK VISION

The community care network (delivery so that it works better for local health care work better require acting parts and the underlying values through four dimensions: community h less continuum of care, and managem

Community Health Focus

Community care networks, in addition to providing health ser committed to improving the health status of a given communit communities and work in concert with public health, social ser responsibility for measuring and improving the health status of

Community Health Foc

Existing Delivery Arrangements:	Independent Provider	Informal/Ad Hoc with Other Comm Services
Organizational Perspective:	Disease oriented → → → → → → →	
	Institutional focus → → → → → → →	
Description:	1. Focus on treating episodes of illness (secondary & tertiary prevention) 2. Health prevention initiatives/clinically based screenings 3. Minimal links with community organizations for purposes of improving health status	1. Provider-sponsored community health an prevention events with continued emphasis o treating episodes of medical care 2. Some linkages with community organizations, usually informal and event-specific 3. Explicit and ongoing commitment to collaborate with other community groups still not embraced

S OF THE COM

vision stimulates loca
ients, populations, and
a comprehensive, syste
. The CCN vision expre
ealth focus, communi
ent within fixed res

vices to enrolled p
y. Networks would
vices, and other
a community.

us

Linkages
unity

Co

The
migh
enrol
repre
migh d population
broa h drives
popul bodies

a process and an

Existin
Arrang

Organi viewed as a key
Perspe ool with formal
for enrollee and
feedback in place

is to ensure enrollee and
nity trust in network's
Descri itment to basing its activities on
essed community and patient needs

overnance and accrediting bodies and insurer oversight aligned with patient and community expectations and requirements

4. Standards are consumer focused and supported by regular monitoring and collection of data

APPENDIX. THE FOUR DIMENSIONS OF THE COMMUNITY CARE NETWORK VISION

The community care network (CCN) vision stimulates local reform of health care delivery so that it works better for patients, populations, and communities. To make local health care work better requires a comprehensive, systematic view of the interacting parts and the underlying values. The CCN vision expresses this systematic view through four dimensions: community health focus, community accountability, a seamless continuum of care, and management within fixed resources.

Community Health Focus

Community care networks, in addition to providing health services to enrolled populations would be committed to improving the health status of a given community. Networks would reach out into their communities and work in concert with public health, social services, and other organizations that also bear responsibility for measuring and improving the health status of a community.

Community Health Focus

Existing Delivery Arrangements:	Independent Provider	Informal/Ad Hoc Linkages with Other Community Services	Community Care Network
Organizational Perspective:	Disease oriented → → → → → → → → →		→ Health-oriented
	Institutional focus → → → → → → → → →		→ Part of a community of health and social agents
Description:	1. Focus on treating episodes of illness (secondary & tertiary prevention) 2. Health prevention initiatives/clinically based screenings 3. Minimal links with community organizations for purposes of improving health status	1. Provider-sponsored community health and prevention events with continued emphasis on treating episodes of medical care 2. Some linkages with community organizations, usually informal and event-specific 3. Explicit and ongoing commitment to collaborate with other community groups still not embraced	1. Focus on changing behavior to prevent disease and treat ill health as early in the disease process as possible 2. Ongoing community-wide efforts to assess and monitor progress in meeting explicitly stated health objectives 3. Work in concert with other organizations that also bear some responsibility for improving health status

Community Accountability

The goal is for networks to strengthen accountability to patients and the public. Community accountability might be demonstrated in various ways. Networks might provide greater information to the public and its enrolled population on the network services and performance or establish mechanisms for public representation in the network's governing structure. More advanced community accountability mechanisms might include activities designed to stimulate other organizations and individuals to join in carrying out a broad health agenda in a specific community, or projects to address the needs of the underserved populations or to contain the growth of health care costs.

Community Accountability

Existing Delivery Arrangements:	Private Sector/ Traditional Provider	Community Care Network
Organizational Perspective:	Explicit accountability → → → → → to governing body, Implicit accountability to patients/community	Explicit accountability to enrolled population and broader community, which drives accountability to governing bodies
	Accountability viewed as → → → → an "event" and as regulation	Accountability viewed as a process and an opportunity
Description:	1. Governed by an autonomous board or private owners 2. Accreditation and insurer oversight are primary mechanisms to ensure quality; tone is primarily punitive and regulatory 3. Sense of shared responsibility with patients and community not well developed 4. Disclosure to the community often takes the form of marketing	1. Accountability is viewed as a key management tool with formal mechanisms for enrollee and community feedback in place 2. The goal is to ensure enrollee and community trust in network's commitment to basing its activities on assessed community and patient needs 3. Governance and accrediting bodies and insurer oversight aligned with patient and community expectations and requirements 4. Standards are consumer focused and supported by regular monitoring and collection of data

Seamless Continuum of Care

Networks would make the system more user-friendly by truly managing care and by providing consistent and coordinated access to services across care settings. The community care network would provide: 1) a full continuum of health and related social services, 2) care coordination among provider organizations, 3) interorganizational planning, and 4) integrated systems (informational, financial, clinical, administrative) that track the patient and assist caregivers to manage care.

Seamless Continuum of Care

Existing Delivery Arrangements:	Single-Purpose Providers	Multipurpose Providers	Vertically Integrated Organizations	Community Care Network
Organizational Perspective:	Fragmentation → → → → → → → → → → → →			Integration
Description:	1. Generally focus on a specific segment of services within the continuum of care 2. Minimal linkages with other providers/insurers 3. Separate information systems for each entity	1. Provides a wider range of health services 2. Informal linkages among providers 3. Limited formal linkages with payers 4. Separate information system for each participating entity	1. Full continuum of services provided by one entity or via formal contractual arrangements among entities 2. Preliminary stages of coordination and integration among providers 3. In most cases delivery and payment organizations are independent	1. Full continuum of health and related social services 2. Care coordination including consistent access regardless of the care setting through which the patient first enters the network 3. Interorganizational planning 4. Integrated systems (financial, clinical, administrative)

Management within Fixed Resources

Community care networks provide the key to restructuring financial incentives. Risk-adjusted capitated payments or global budgets to networks would encourage providers within the network to avoid unnecessary duplication of facilities and services and conserve health care resources by providing care to patients at the most appropriate point in the continuum of care. Working within a fixed budget, networks would match local health care resources and strategies to the needs and circumstances of the enrolled population and the larger community.

Management within Fixed Resources

Existing Delivery Arrangements:	Provider Paid via Indemnity Plan	Provider Paid via Managed Care Contracts	Fully Capitated Health Organizations	Community Care Network
Organizational Perspective:	Subject to limited financial risk →	→ → → → →	→ → → → →	Assumes broad financial risk
Description:	1. Paid on a fee-for-service basis 2. Optional utilization review 3. Incentive to increase revenue via over treatment	1. Prospective or discounted pricing; some capitation 2. Mandatory utilization review for contracted services 3. Incentive to increase revenue in non-managed care segment	1. Risk-sharing financial arrangements via capitation 2. Mandatory utilization review 3. Limited capacity management 4. Capitated payments form budget for the health services for enrolled populations	1. Risk-sharing financial arrangements (capitation) linking insurer and provider 2. Incentive to avoid unnecessary duplication 3. Capacity as well as utilization management 4. Capitated payment forms budget within which networks would match resources to community need

Source: American Hospital Association. *Transforming Health Care Delivery: Toward Community Care Networks.* Chicago: AHA, 1993.

PART I

Metropolitan Networks

Two prisoners whose cells adjoin communicate with each other by knocking on the wall. The wall is the thing which separates them but is also their means of communication. . . . Every separation is a link.

—Simone Weil (1909–43), French philosopher, mystic

Something there is that doesn't love a wall,
And wants it down.

—Robert Frost (1874–1963), U.S. poet

INTRODUCTION

Accomplishing a specific goal often requires getting through to the right contact. In a city, one or a few from among hundreds of thousands or millions of people might be the right contact, and it is difficult to know how to find them. Complexity emerges in metropolitan communities from facing many choices and from the ambiguity that accompanies not knowing how to select from among all those choices.

The best approach to determining who to contact to move toward a specific goal in a metropolitan community may be by learning which organization best serves functions relevant to your goal. Which brings an additional layer of complexity. If and when the right person is found, the person is likely to be seen, not so much as a person, but as an institutional representative. Few people living in metropolitan communities, for example, can name any of the doctors or nurses that would attend to their child in the emergency room.

Metropolitan communities, and collaborative efforts within them, are more complex. Because the people who need to connect to get things done are, usually, institutional representatives, they serve for each other, at least at first, a *single function.* In other words, except for meeting that one specific goal, one may have no other reasons to work with them, make promises to them, or hold them accountable.

Dealing with institutional representatives to achieve single functions has its positive aspects. A single transaction is likely to be simpler. For instance, city shoppers rarely stop and talk with the retail clerk about the latest scandal in the mayor's office. It is also easier to maintain your privacy. Most important, bonds between institutions, ongoing operational reasons for organizations to collaborate with each other, can be much more sustainable and powerful than personal bonds. Indeed, many community action practitioners and theorists hold institutionalization of new objectives to be the ultimate objective of making change happen.

But to develop a common sense of purpose or to work on a variety of tasks together over time, encountering each other as institutional representatives pits potential partners against some special structural barriers to collaboration. Because there are more resources, competition among businesses is more acute. Because there are also more problems, the community organizations designed to fix them, such as development corporations, are also likely to be more competitive with each other. Institutional boundaries are less permeable, more aggressively defended. The turf is tougher.

These same principles can make ethnic and cultural barriers more significant in metropolitan communities. First, our cities tend to be more diverse than our nonmetropolitan communities. In addition, over time people of one group or another often have clustered in certain neighborhoods. In entrenched neighborhoods, it can become easy for people to spot others who don't "belong" there. In other neighborhoods, ethnic groups shift. A whole new set of challenges test our search for mutual objectives. Both in entrenched and transitional neighborhoods, ethnic, religious, and linguistic diversity affect the sense of community, the ability to coalesce political will, and the availability and use of health and human services.

Such factors as a complex, institutionalized communication network, stiff interorganizational competition, and barriers between groups and between groups and service providers affect the ability of any emerging network to achieve and sustain a coherent vision. Governance and management structures and mechanisms may be particularly sticky wickets. Generating and maintaining personal satisfaction through partnership may be both hard to do, yet especially rewarding.

You may want to attend to these features of the metropolitan cases in this book. Can institutional representatives form a strong basis for collaborative efforts in health system change? Is personal satisfaction important for partnership development and for success in system change? What kinds of mechanisms help evolving partnerships build meaningful bridges between groups and organizations? What historical experiences lay the foundation for more meaningful collaboration? Are certain kinds of collaborative efforts easier or harder in metropolitan communities?

This section highlights four metropolitan community care networks. The boundaries of each fall entirely within a metropolitan statistical area and circumscribe specific neighborhoods or census tracts that are part of the high-density population center around which the metropolitan area has grown.

Look to the Central Area Health Care Center of Seattle to learn how that partnership addresses access and continuity of care issues. They conducted a general assessment of current operations, created one-stop Family Support Centers and are improving disease management among vulnerable populations through specialized clinics such as adult dental services. In the Columbia-Presbyterian Community Health System of New York City, geographic and cultural access barriers are being overcome through the creation of six off-site practices. The partnership established clinics in four intermediate schools and a high school and developed a new 300-bed hospital. The partnership concentrates on management of chronic illnesses such as asthma, diabetes, and hypertension. Their physician service organization, composed of 60 mostly Latino physicians, evaluates managed care and practice management for members. Bridging the communities of Somerville and Cambridge, MA, the Somerbridge Community Health Partnership has a keen sense of how to design change for key population groups, with a special focus on chronic preventable diseases. The partnership emphasizes immigrant health, geriatric care, and the prevention and reduction of alcohol and substance abuse. The Portsmouth Mayor's Health Services Advisory Panel, Portsmouth, VA, seeks to improve access and continuity of care. They developed the Sunshine School/Community Health Center, which provides routine health services to people who are otherwise outside the health system. Using a task force approach to solve problems, the Mayor's Advisory Panel has tackled access to obstetric care for single mothers and HIV/AIDS. They are creating a computerized database of the medically indigent, and a process for obtaining specialist care for indigents.

1

The Central Area Health Care Center

Executive Summary

In the Central Area of Seattle, 21 percent of the households—the highest percentage in urban King County—are below the federal poverty level. This diverse community's racial demographics are quite different from Seattle as a whole. The Central Area is 49 percent African-American, while Seattle is only 11 percent African-American; Caucasians make up 39 percent of the Central Area, but 75 percent of the city as a whole. On the other hand, the percentages of Asian-Americans, Native Americans, and Hispanics are similar in both the Central Area and the city. Central Area residents experience significantly higher hospitalization rates for virtually all causes (including heart disease, cancer, low birth weight, lack of prenatal care, teenage parenthood, pneumonia, and influenza) and a disproportionate amount of violence, drug abuse, gang activity, and mental health problems within their community.

To respond to these clear and compelling needs, three health care providers within this community collaborated to colocate and create the Central Area Health Care Center, which opened in spring 1995, with capital funding from the city, county, state, and numerous local foundations. The founding partners were Odessa Brown Children's Clinic, a satellite of Children's Hospital and Medical Center; Carolyn Downs Family Medical Center, operated by Country Doctor Community Health Centers; and the Seattle–King County Department of Public Health. The fourth partner in this collaboration is Garfield High School, a large (1,730 students) urban public school that includes an on-site teen health center (Garfield/Nova Teen Health Center), operated by Odessa Brown Children's Clinic.

The Central Area Health Care Center community care network (CCN) project has six initiatives:

1. Sustain and increase adolescent services at the Garfield/Nova Teen Health Center to meet demand and explore ways to address the health care needs of other adolescents in the community.

2. Assess the Central Area Health Care Center's current operation and develop ways to improve customer services in a cost-effective collaborative manner.
3. Provide services to the Family Support Center, sponsored by the YWCA and located at the Garfield Community Center. The vision is a centralized and collaborative approach to improving family support services, including parenting education.
4. Fully coordinate critical services added to meet specific health needs of the community, including adult dental care, high-risk obstetrics, and mental health and substance abuse counseling.
5. Improve disease management by demonstrating a more effective and efficient model for managing childhood asthma and adult sickle cell anemia.
6. Expand the center's steering committee to enhance customer participation.

The paradigm shift from "colocation" to "collaboration" requires a renewal of commitment to the center's mission, the process by which partners make decisions that impact each other, and the mutually agreed-upon goals of the collaboration. Promoting the collaboration requires trust that individual organization identity will benefit from group identification.

On a personal note, I have supported the development of the Central Area Health Care Center from the beginning, and continue to do so. The organizations involved have started a genuine community partnership that is unique and can serve as a model for others. However, the true measure of the Central Area Health Care Center's success will be the improved health status of the community. We have made progress toward this goal and must continue working together to make better health a reality for all.

Norman B. Rice, Mayor
City of Seattle

THE COMMUNITY

The Central Area of Seattle, also known as the Central District, is home to more than 28,000 people. The wedge-shaped physical area, which consists of 2,111 acres, is generally bounded by Lake Washington on the east, Roy Street and Madison on the north, Irving Street on the south, and Broadway on the west. The Central Area is primarily residential in character, with a few commercial areas.

It is an older neighborhood with a long and interesting history, and community identification and pride are strong. In addition, socio-demographic information and health statistics are tracked by the Seattle–King County Department of Public Health (SKCDPH) and other agencies using this definition of the Central Area.

- *Demographics:* Of the Central Area population, 18 percent are 15 years old or younger (compared with 15 percent citywide), and 14 percent are 65 years old or older (compared with 15 percent citywide). Racial diversity is one of the most distinctive features of the Central Area:
  - —Forty percent of the population are Caucasian, compared with 75 percent citywide.
  - —Forty-seven percent of the population are African-American, compared with just 10 percent citywide.
  - —Twenty-six percent of Seattle's total African-American population live in the Central Area.

Central Area residents are less likely to have completed high school than the city as a whole. Households are larger. There are fewer married couples with no children, and more female-headed households with children. Also, the number of Southeast Asian immigrants in the Central Area is increasing.

- *Housing:* There is more multifamily housing, residential densities are slightly higher, and the housing stock is older than in other neighborhoods. More residents live in rental units, and the median rent paid is lower. The median value of owner-occupied housing units is $116,417, compared with $137,884 citywide.
- *Employment/income:* Unemployment is higher than in the rest of the city, and both median household income and per capita income are lower. Employment is primarily related to government and finance, insurance, and real estate. Between 1980 and 1988, the proportion of low-income households grew from 38 percent to an estimated 42 percent. The poverty rate among children is quite high—26 percent of the children under 18 are living in poverty, compared with 15.7 percent citywide. During the 1980s, population increased slightly. Although there were declines in the number of people of color, the population of both the young and the elderly increased. Forecasts for the next 20 years indicate that the Central Area will experience growth at rates comparable with those expected for the city as a whole—a 6.4 percent increase in population and a 15 percent increase in the number of households.
- *Critical social and health care problems: The Health of King County—1990* reported that the Central Area continued to have the highest rates in the county for infant mortality, low-birth-weight and very-low-birth-weight babies, babies born preterm, school-age fertility rates, deaths from heart disease and cancer, and hospitalization for asthma, chronic liver disease, diabetic ketoacidosis, pneumonia, influenza, and dental conditions. During 1990–92, adolescents in the Central Area had a birth rate of 81 per 1,000, an increase of 35 percent over the rate of 60.1 during 1980–82.

  This community also has the highest rates of gonorrhea, chlamydia, syphilis, TB, hepatitis A and B, and the highest incidence rate in the county of confirmed AIDS cases, a rate almost four times greater than the Seattle average and eight times greater than the county average.

  Too Many, Too Young: Violence in Seattle and King County, March 1994 identified the Central Area as having one of the highest rates of violence in the county. Homicides were concentrated in southeast and central Seattle. Central Seattle's robbery rate was nine times higher than the county average, and between 1988 and 1992, the aggravated assault rate was more than three times the county average.

  Central Area residents are more likely to die of suicide, poisoning, drowning, and fires and burns than other county residents, and have the lowest life expectancy in the county by fully 6.8 years. The critical need for health care is documented in three SKCDPH publications: a 1988 *Demographic Update,* the 1988 *Vital Statistics Report,* and the 1988 *Master Plan for Seattle–King County Public Health Facilities.* Planning studies conducted by the SKCDPH in March 1989 also indicated that 28 percent of the children in Central Area families with incomes below 200 percent of the poverty level were not receiving adequate preventive primary health care, and 58 percent of women were not being served. Nonrandom surveys of low-income county residents conducted by the SKCDPH revealed significant financial and nonfinancial barriers. As a result of this significant unmet need, the SKCDPH designated the improvement of primary health services in the Central Area as its highest priority.

Paradoxically, the neediest community in Seattle has a wealth of health and human services resources. However, those services are scattered over multiple sites, creating a physical barrier to care, particularly for low-income people. There is an increasing unmet need for comprehensive health care because a substantial percentage of patients require not only medical assistance but also dental care, mental health counseling, and social and/or substance abuse services.

THE COLLABORATIVE PARTNERSHIP

These and other findings prompted the following recommendations in the Master Plan for Seattle–King County Public Health Facilities:

- In collaboration with health care providers in the Central Area, the SKCDPH should focus on developing comprehensive services. Colocation of primary care and public health services should help eliminate duplication of services.
- The SKCDPH should initiate studies and negotiations with other health care providers to serve the Central Area and, over the long term, work to establish a comprehensive service delivery site.

The increasing city and community concern about the continuing deterioration of the Central Area population's health status and the renewed sense of urgency brought about by the SKCDPH's strategic plan coincided with the plans of two other well-established health care facilities to renew their efforts in the Central Area. As described in more detail later, these three agencies came together to support the creation of a comprehensive CCN.

Odessa Brown Children's Clinic

The Odessa Brown Children's Clinic (OBCC) was planned and developed as a collaborative effort of the Central Area community residents, Children's Hospital and Medical Center (CHMC), and the city of Seattle through the federal Model Cities program. Since 1970, the OBCC has operated as a not-for-profit satellite of CHMC, providing comprehensive medical, dental, and mental health care to community residents from birth to 21 years of age. Maintaining a partnership with this traditionally underserved community continues to be a major factor in the clinic's success. The development of a strategic plan for OBCC in 1989 and the willingness of CHMC to consider the clinic as the site for a comprehensive center made OBCC a natural partner.

Seattle–King County Department of Public Health

The SKCDPH is a public agency run by the city of Seattle and King County and supported by the incorporated cities, patient fees, and grants. Its mission is to protect and promote the health of the community and environment. This includes monitoring and assessing the community's health, advocating solutions to public health problems, and providing direct services aimed at meeting the health care needs of the communities within its jurisdiction.

The Carolyn Downs Family Medical Center

The Carolyn Downs Family Medical Center (Carolyn Downs) is owned and operated by Country Doctor Community Health Centers (Country Doctor), one of eight not-for-profit 501(c)(3) community-based health centers in King County funded in part with federal Public Health Service funds. As a community health center, Carolyn Downs must provide a basic set of services, be governed by a board of directors comprising the majority of users of the specific health center, and provide services on a sliding-fee discount schedule.

Originally part of a broad spectrum of community services overseen and developed by the Seattle Black Panther party, Carolyn Downs became a freestanding community health clinic in 1975, operating from a storefront in the Madrona neighborhood and serving primarily the Central Area. In 1988, Country Doctor, another community clinic founded by community activists and operating in the adjacent Capital Hill neighborhood, merged with Carolyn Downs. The two organizations maintained their independent sites.

By the late 1980s, the storefront was an inadequate, hard-to-maintain facility at a far-from-central location, and Country Doctor had launched an effort to relocate Carolyn Downs to a more accessible site. In 1990, block grant funds were awarded to Country Doctor to facilitate planning, site selection, and design for a new Carolyn Downs facility.

As a result of the visioning process described later in this chapter, these three organizations decided to colocate and collaborate to create the Central Area Health Care Center (CAHCC), a significant step toward realizing the vision of a comprehensive, community-supported health care network aimed at tackling the many health problems of the community yet remaining responsive to changing needs. As this facility was being planned, financed, and constructed, there was an opportunity to extend this partnership to the public high school located in the Central Area.

Garfield High School

Along with the Nova program (an alternative high school almost immediately adjacent to it), Garfield High School serves approximately 1,730 students in grades 9 through 12. Until desegregation goals and busing were adopted in the mid-1970s, many generations of Central Area families received their high school education at Garfield. Today approximately half of Garfield's students live in central Seattle and half are of an ethnic composition other than Caucasian.

The community, students, teachers, and parents were central to the effort to acquire a school health facility. In December 1991, at a community meeting that featured Seattle's mayor as the guest speaker, the health center was the first issue on everyone's agenda. Subsequently, a steering committee representing the Garfield community prepared a proposal for the development of an on-site teen health center as the first step in overcoming the serious challenges threatening the health of the community's adolescents.

The CAHCC's founding members, in partnership with Garfield High School, were instrumental in providing the leadership to secure funding. A space within the school was renovated, and OBCC opened the Garfield/Nova Teen Health Center (GTHC) in fall 1992.

This partnership has increased the health care resources for teens in the Central Area and will continue to be important in meeting the needs of adolescents. Improving a community's health requires promoting healthy behaviors in youth, and our schools are the most logical partners for accomplishing this outcome.

EVOLUTION OF THE PARTNERSHIP

The current public–private partnership includes the primary independent health care providers serving the Central Area, has established formal collaborative relationships, and is moving toward a common vision. However, each partner also has relationships with a wide variety of social and health service organizations to secure needed services. As the partners move forward, goals include increasing coordination and integration among these service providers and broadening the CCN.

PRIOR EFFORTS—MOVING TOWARD THE COMMUNITY CARE NETWORK VISION

Community Accountability

The SKCDPH's Epidemiology Planning and Evaluation Unit regularly tracks the health status of King County's communities and provides reports on specific health care problems. Recent reports have included *Too Many, Too Young: Violence in Seattle and King County* and *Lost Youth: Teen Pregnancy and Birth in King County.*

Because of this effort, the health status and specific health problems of the Central Area are highly visible. Reports and findings are made available to the community and its health organizations. Also, the two daily papers serving King County and the two publications that target the Central Area community routinely report health information.

A thorough review of reported statistics provides ample evidence of the Central Area's serious health care needs. Interorganizational planning efforts to improve health care service delivery have been made since 1985. In June of that year, the SKCDPH convened meetings of central Seattle providers to explore opportunities for working together to improve services for Central Area residents.

In 1988, the SKCPHD commissioned a strategic planning study to address its role in improving services and providing a common vision for the future, and to set its direction for the next several years. The planning process included interviews, group meetings, and retreats with a broad community representation. The *Master Plan for Seattle–King County Public Health Facilities,* published in October 1988, determined that the health care needs of the low-income Central Area could best be met by colocating three significant providers.

The *Patient Origin Study,* completed in 1989, concluded that children and young women in the Central Area appeared to be underserved and added further evidence that a change was desperately needed. In April 1989, a parent satisfaction survey conducted at OBCC found that the current users were very satisfied with clinic services. However, a community survey in February 1989 had revealed that many families in the community were in need of a reliable source of primary health care for their children, and the community needed more information about OBCC's services and their availability.

At the same time, updated health care statistics made the community—and all its health care providers—aware that health care needs were not being met.

Maternity care for high-risk pregnancies, substance abuse treatment, adolescent health care, and psychosocial problems were identified as underserved areas.

The SKCDPH convened discussions to determine the best course of action. Those discussions resulted in the vision of a community health care network (described later in this chapter). The first order of business was colocation. A community outreach and education campaign was initiated in January 1991 to survey the existing and future programmatic needs of the community and secure its full participation in the Central Area Health Campus Project, as the program was first known. During the planning and construction stages, Country Doctor targeted both large and small constituencies—schools, churches, clubs and fraternal organizations, community service centers, and government service agencies—to ensure high visibility and community ownership of the new health care campus.

The OBCC Advisory Board was instrumental in supporting colocation and collaboration activities. Community leaders were effective in lobbying the government and major employers to secure the financial backing needed for this project—$3.25 million. Funding for remodeling OBCC and constructing a new wing and a second floor came from four levels of government—the city of Seattle, the state of Washington, King County, and the federal government—and numerous local foundations, corporations, and other fund-raising efforts.

Opening ceremonies for the CAHCC were held on March 24, 1995. The dream of a comprehensive health clinic for the Central Area was realized. The community beginnings of the OBCC and Carolyn Downs were celebrated. Community leaders described the project as "a dream come true" but were quick to point out that this was only a beginning, not a culmination. There is much to be done. The partnership must lead to a new model for the delivery of health care that includes a comprehensive and preventive approach. The community has made a substantial investment, and the health care providers have made a commitment to provide high-quality medical care focused on the community's health problems. Continued input from the community on partnership activities and progress in moving toward the CCN vision will undoubtedly continue.

Community Health Focus

Prior efforts to provide early diagnosis and intervention programs with the goal of changing behavior to prevent disease and aimed at the specific health problems of the Central Area have been impressive.

Reducing Infant Mortality In 1990, newspapers announced that the country's "most livable city" had the second highest infant mortality rate in the nation for African-Americans during 1989. Community leaders called for action. In summer 1991, representatives of the CHMC, the SKCDPH, Region X of the U.S. Public Health Service, and many community organizations began working together to address the problem. A conference titled "Urban Infant Mortality: The Northwest Challenge" was organized to address the problem, bring together the disparate groups and individuals working on the issue, renew the larger community's interest, and create a comprehensive community action plan for reducing infant mortality during the 1990s.

The SKCDPH's work in documenting the health status of communities had identified the ethnic groups and neighborhoods most at risk and the factors that contribute most heavily to infant death. Targeted solutions outlined in the action plan included continued diligence in tracking infant health, the addition of outreach workers in central Seattle to concentrate on women at high risk of giving birth to low-birth-weight babies, work with the media to reach high-risk women with information about how to obtain prenatal care, identification of key community organizations and individuals who could be enlisted to further plans for intervention, and pursuit of funding for the CAHCC. The lack of comprehensive community health services in the Central Area was considered a key factor that limited access to prenatal care in the community that had the highest infant mortality rates.

Infant mortality outreach workers were placed at OBCC, and all three partners were involved in implementing many of the key recommendations of the action plan. Successes include an increase in the percentage of women seeking timely prenatal care and a decline in the percentage of women who smoke during pregnancy.

Garfield/Nova Teen Health Center As discussed earlier, the plan to create a teen health center called for a collaborative effort among several groups: OBCC, as the lead agency; Carolyn Downs; a provider of a wide range of counseling and family support services to Central Area residents; and six other agencies that agreed to play supporting roles.

To build an effective coalition, a broad-based steering committee was assembled. The partners were involved in the early planning, and reports were made regularly to the community through newsletters, open meetings, and phone banks that reached more than 400 parents. Students initiated class discussions, surveyed their fellow students, and circulated petitions. Their vision was funded through the city of Seattle. Contracting with the SKCDPH, OBCC opened the GTHC.

The GTHC is designed to be the focal point for all health-related activity within the school. Goals include increasing access to high-quality health services, building an active partnership to develop and support adolescent health services, and developing and implementing effective health promotion and disease prevention strategies relevant to the adolescent health issues in the community. Explicitly stated community health objectives include lowering the dropout rate and school absenteeism resulting from health problems; reducing teen pregnancies, infant mortality, alcohol and drug use, and risk-taking behaviors; and increasing adolescent access to affordable health care and health-promoting behaviors. Steps have been taken to ensure that the rich racial and cultural diversity of the student body is valued and reflected in the GTHC. All the agencies involved have long-established traditions of honoring diversity and designing programs to overcome cultural, linguistic, and economic barriers to health care.

Other Early Diagnosis and Intervention Programs Other programs designed to diagnose and intervene early with the goal of changing behavior to prevent disease include the following:

- The outreach programs of Carolyn Downs—which include health education, assessments, and preventive screening—increase awareness of community health problems and promote prevention. Activities include smoking cessation support for patients; workshops on self-esteem, sexuality, and communication for adolescents; glaucoma and blood pressure screening; and health maintenance and foot care services to the elderly. From time to time, community prevention and outreach activities are conducted at community events and at other community sites, including senior centers, food banks, and local stores.

- The SKCDPH and Carolyn Downs participate in the Hypertension Project, which is designed to study the effectiveness of additional supportive and counseling services in assisting diagnosed lower-income African-Americans and Caucasians to have better control of their hypertension. Funded by a federal grant, the project helps the intervention group attain healthier lifestyles and learn to manage their disease.
- Carolyn Downs provides primary care prevention services such as immunizations, family planning and sexually transmitted disease (STD) counseling and education, diabetes detection and education, HIV/AIDS risk reduction education, HIV antibody counseling and testing, an obstetrical program that includes prenatal care as well as maternity support services, and a community nursing program that provides, for example, home safety assessments to the elderly. Currently, a breast and cervical health program provides early detection and screening exams for women over age 40. Supported by a media campaign financed by the SAFECO Insurance Company, this program offers free Pap smears, breast exams, and mammograms.
- OBCC prevention services include immunizations (outreach and on-site), hearing and vision screening, safety counseling, and health education for adolescents that emphasizes such topics as sexuality, relationships, STDs, smoking, and substance abuse. The dental clinic emphasizes prevention and home care techniques. A licensed mental health facility, OBCC offers counseling and assists families in identifying resources to deal with home and school behavior concerns and strategies to effect change.
- Preventive programs offered by the SKCDPH include developing plans and obtaining medical care for children with a disability; dental disease prevention and screening, as well as referrals at schools and community sites; Buckle Baby First, an infant car seat loan and education program; community education for schools, community groups, and agencies on a wide range of sexuality education topics; health screening and interpretation for refugees; and public health nurse home visits to pregnant women, mothers with new babies, and young families with health or parenting concerns.
- All three organizations offer nutrition counseling and food vouchers without charge for eligible pregnant and breast-feeding women, as well as children under age five, through the on-site Women, Infants and Children supplemental food program.

Prior Efforts to Address Cultural and Other Barriers Prior efforts to address cultural and other barriers include the following:

- OBCC offers a course designed to assist African-American parents in raising competent and healthy children. Created with the guidance of nationally recognized African-American parenting experts, it represents one of the few parenting programs in America created specifically for African-American families. These in-depth classes are taught by a staff member trained and experienced as a Systematic Training for Effective Parenting (STEP) instructor. Demand for this course is high, court referrals are occasionally made, and participants have consistently praised the impact of this program on their family life.
- All three agencies have a significant number of minority health care professionals. From inception, the agencies have been very successful in providing services in a fashion that addresses cultural and other barriers to health care. This long history has earned them community trust and is a key to their effectiveness in taking action to address community concerns. Also, OBCC and Carolyn Downs have participated

in the Center for Cross-Cultural Care. Coordinated by the Pacific Medical Center, its purpose is to train providers in cross-cultural care, to enhance the training of medical interpreters, and to secure funding for other access services.

- In addition to the colocation itself, which is aimed at increasing access, the services at the CAHCC are available regardless of a patient's ability to pay.
- Access services at Carolyn Downs include eligibility screening and enrollment assistance for available state programs (that is, Medicaid and the Basic Health Plan [the state's vehicle for providing insurance to low-income people who are not eligible for Medicaid]).

Seamless Continuum of Care

Prior arrangements to ensure that all the community's needs are addressed have included the following:

- Carolyn Downs works closely with a variety of community mental health providers (Therapeutic Health Services, Seattle Mental Health Institute); substance abuse specialists (Stonewall Recovery Services); home nursing providers (Community Home Health Care); social service providers (Catholic Community Services); and others such as the Chicken Soup Brigade, People of Color Against AIDS Network, and the Northwest AIDS Foundation. OBCC offers First Time Parenting Classes for teens in collaboration with Harborview Medical Center and Columbia Children and Youth Clinic.
- Both Carolyn Downs and OBCC refer pediatric patients to the specialty clinics and inpatient care at CHMC. Adult patients of Carolyn Downs are referred to the specialty providers of Pacific Medical Center and Providence Medical Center; they are also admitted to Providence Medical Center where Carolyn Downs physicians have attending and obstetric privileges.
- The SKCDPH develops contractual and informal working arrangements with community organizations for targeted health services.

The colocation, which has just been completed, created an arrangement that will provide the full spectrum of services required to meet the needs of the community, improve service coordination among the major service providers, and reduce administrative and service delivery costs. Colocation makes it easier for patients and their families to access and navigate services—a one-stop health care center. The breadth of combined skills gives the CAHCC the capacity to respond rapidly to changing health care needs and provides a continuum of health services designed from a preventive perspective.

Formal contractual relationships and an organizational structure have been established to share power and control among the partners. The steering committee maintains and communicates a vision for meeting the Central Area's health care needs, ensures that strategic planning and program planning/development efforts are carried out, provides continuous and effective communication between the parent organizations and the clinics on campus, develops and uses community input for ongoing support and participation, and serves as a constant promoter of cost-effective services, seeking ways to avoid duplication at the CAHCC. The joint operating committee communicates and coordinates for maximum integration, operates the patient care systems, ensures access, coordinates interagency staff development, develops programs to meet patient/community needs, and reports to and provides staff support to the steering committee. The condominium board of directors governs the condominium property, develops a common expense budget, and makes assessments.

To date, the partners have been engaged with planning, financing, and constructing the facility. The facility is now built, the agencies have moved on-site, the governing structure is in place, and the partners have several years' experience collaborating. The time is right to move forward with fuller integration of services among providers and interorganizational planning to fulfill the vision of a full continuum of health and related services.

The new facility positions these successful health care providers to have a major impact on the health care needs in the Central Area. They will be at the forefront of developing new programs focused on the needs of the community, coordinating services, and moving toward the CCN vision.

Managing within Fixed Resources

Motivation for colocation included reduced service delivery costs. In addition to savings related to facility expenses (construction and maintenance), there is the opportunity to minimize duplication of services and reduce operating expenses. The cost of maintaining separate facilities and separate services, such as the pharmacy and lab, is avoided with a single complex. The base of shared knowledge and skills also reduces outside training costs and the costs associated with all partners attempting to develop internal staff expertise in all areas.

The state of Washington is rapidly moving in a new direction in health care. This movement has already changed forever the health care environment. Physicians, payers, and hospitals have responded rapidly and in an unprecedented manner to reduce health care costs. Locally, the health care priorities have shifted in the following four broad areas:

1. Maintaining wellness rather than just treating illness
2. Placing less emphasis on inpatient hospital care and more on outpatient treatment
3. Managing the health status of the community rather than treating and caring for one person
4. Paying for health care by capitation, or a fixed fee, rather than fee-for-service

Our strategy is to manage health from wellness to illness through partnerships with other providers, from preventive care to outpatient care, inpatient acute care—both secondary and tertiary care—and home care, in a seamless system. The goal is to serve all managed health plans as they evolve under state health care reform in a way that reduces cost by coordinating care and emphasizing primary, preventive, and outreach services. The emphasis will be on maintaining good health.

The state of Washington created Healthy Options in February 1992 to promote mandatory enrollment in managed care as the primary health care delivery model for Medical Assistance (Medicaid) clients. These include all clients who are eligible to receive Aid to Families with Dependent Children, pregnant women who become eligible in the third trimester of pregnancy, and low-income children. Two managed care delivery models are being used—full capitation and primary care case management. With full capitation, a health maintenance organization or prepaid health plan receives a monthly payment for each client to cover a wide range of services.

With primary care case management, services are paid fee-for-service, but the primary care provider is also paid a small monthly case management fee for each client. The financial incentive is to provide appropriate and efficient services and improve the health status of clients. Healthy Options is rapidly moving to full capitation in accordance with the state's health reform statute, the Health Service Act of 1993.

The CAHCC participates to the degree possible in capitated plans. At this point, OBCC's medical payer mix is 62 percent Healthy Options; 24 percent Nonplan Medicaid (those special-needs children who are exempt from Health Options and remain fee-for-service because of chronic conditions or social factors such as foster care—this is expected to change); 7 percent private insurance; and 7 percent self-pay or free care. Healthy Options patients are currently enrolled in one of four programs—58 percent Care Net (capitated), 22 percent Providence Health Care, 11 percent Community Health Plan of Washington, and 9 percent PacifiCare. The latter three are managed care plans that are expected to become full capitation plans in the next few years. Carolyn Downs is also a capitated Healthy Options provider through the Community Health Plan of Washington and participates in the Basic Health Plan through the Community Health Plan of Washington and PacifiCare.

MOVING TOWARD THE COMMUNITY CARE NETWORK VISION: VISION AND VISIONING PROCESS

In fall 1989, city and SKCDPH staff convened a Central Area planning group, with representatives from Country Doctor/Carolyn Downs, CHMC/OBCC, and the downtown Health Service Center. The goal of this group was to explore the architectural, financial, and programmatic feasibility of developing a full-service primary care health program in the Central Area by expanding the clinic on the Odessa Brown site to accommodate the relocation of Carolyn Downs and the inclusion of public health services.

The Central Area planning group drafted the following vision statement:

> To create a primary health care campus on the Odessa Brown site by building on the unique expertise of the colocated programs of the OBCC, Carolyn Downs, and the SKCDPH; and to provide culturally sensitive health care services to those who use the facility, regardless of their ability to pay, recognizing the individual dignity and value of each person served. The goals of this collaborative effort include the following:
>
> - To plan, develop, and provide comprehensive and high-quality health care services targeted to meet the health care needs of the Central Area community residents in a cost-effective manner
> - To ensure that the organizational structure and leadership is responsive to changing demands in the community in which the facility is located
> - To ensure that the organizational structure and leadership of colocated facilities is responsive to the changing demands in the health care environment
> - To increase the opportunities for new program development, thereby enhancing the mix of services provided
> - To maintain linkages with affiliated hospitals and specialists to provide a coordinated network of services for all patients

- To recruit and retain highly qualified professionals and staff to meet the needs of the patient population
- To operate in facilities that are modern, well maintained, and designed to adapt to changing patient needs

A three-step process was used to develop a proposed program outline, methods for communicating with the community, and evaluation criteria. First, a retreat was held in January 1990 with key management and provider staff from participating organizations including, at that time, Harborview Medical Center and the city of Seattle. During the day-long retreat, staff from the three collaborating agencies presented information about the services provided by their organizations and their overall missions.

Next, data were presented about the health status of the Central Area population. Time was spent identifying high-priority health care needs and ways in which participating organizations might collaborate to meet these needs.

Nine small program teams, comprising staff from all three organizations who provide services, convened to discuss program elements, space and staff implications, and potential obstacles to providing services. From this discussion came a list of programs needed in the Central Area. Some programs were already being provided by one or more potential partners, and some represented new initiatives that required start-up time and new funding both for capital and ongoing operations. Specific colocation issues related to each program were noted.

In summer 1990, this work culminated in a preliminary report that outlined the architectural, zoning, financial, programmatic, and organizational issues related to the project. The proposed CAHCC was discussed with community leaders and users of the health services offered by the three partners. The boards of the organizations, and OBCC's advisory board, confirmed their commitment to the community and this shared vision of a CCN. The hard work of making this vision a reality was under way. As the CAHCC opened, the vision was reframed and the strategic plans of the three organizations were reviewed to ensure their support of common goals.

Community Accountability

By undertaking this project, the partners acknowledged their joint accountability to not only their individual patients but also the broader community. This commitment would not be "over" when the CAHCC was constructed and opened, but would be an ongoing commitment to provide interventions that affect the health of the community. By analyzing encounters and users, the CAHCC would monitor, on an ongoing basis, the level of service provided to the Central Area.

The attendant demographic study of those users would identify the extent to which the community was affected. On a broader basis, and over a longer period of time, the effectiveness of the new health center would be evaluated by examining the SKCDPH's annual Vital Statistics Report. Health status indicators (trends) charted over 3 to 5 years would also indicate the CAHCC's effectiveness in impacting the health care needs of the Central Area.

Community Health Focus

In envisioning a set of health services, a major objective was the development of a preventive approach to community health care. The project would improve the health status of individuals and the community by teaching residents how to care for themselves and encouraging lifestyle changes. Results will be achieved by raising the profile of health care in the Central Area and reaching out to the community.

Seamless Continuum of Care

With Carolyn Downs located in the same building as OBCC, the combined clinics would offer care to anyone regardless of age. From the client perspective, the campus would provide one-stop "shopping" for health care. Not only would the community's access to care be increased, but also the project would increase the scope of services.

Future flexibility in responding to changes in the health care status and problems of the community by changing the mix of services is a key component of the vision. This vision of user-friendly, patient-focused care will require not only a full continuum of care but also care coordination among the partners, interorganizational planning, and integrated systems.

Managing within Fixed Resources

Cost savings would be shared directly by the partners and indirectly by the community at large. Community awareness of the available health care and broad-based community health education and outreach programs are expected to lead to decreased health care costs. This cost-effective venture best uses limited financial resources in site development and construction and creates a model health care campus that will promote the sharing of professional experience and expertise among community health care providers. As managed care and capitated payments become the norm, the partners will be in a position to evaluate more effective and efficient ways to provide services.

Through collaboration, the partners will create a comprehensive array of services while eliminating duplication of effort. Combining two not-for-profit health clinics with services of the SKCDPH will create a model health center that will be the focus of community health care services and related health education programs. The new health center will be the only one of its kind in the state of Washington.

INITIATIVES FOR MOVING TOWARD THE COMMUNITY CARE NETWORK VISION

The following six initiatives have been proposed to move the CAHCC toward the CCN vision:

1. Expand the CAHCC Steering Committee.
2. Maintain and increase services to adolescents.
3. Assess the CAHCC's current operation and move forward with integration, interorganizational planning, cost savings, and improved service delivery.
4. Create a Family Support Center.
5. Add critical services to meet the specific needs of the community.
6. Improve disease management.

Those initiatives, along with their proposed goals/milestones and target dates, measurable objectives/expected outcomes, baseline measures, the role of each partner, and technical assistance/funding are discussed in the following subsections.

Expand the CAHCC Steering Committee (Community Accountability/Seamless Continuum of Care)

Activity: Expand the current steering committee to include consumer participation and create a CAHCC Steering Committee. The purpose of this committee is threefold:

- Provide a formal mechanism for communication between consumers and the CAHCC.
- Assess/monitor progress in improving the community health measures.
- Identify all the agencies within the community that are addressing community health and social concerns and identify collaborations/referral arrangements that will result in creative solutions that make the most out of the communities' resources.

Proposed goals/milestones and target dates:

- Determine the specific composition of the committee and convene—4/96
- Draft a mission statement and discuss future accomplishments—7/96
- Prepare and adopt a three-year plan of action—1/97

Measurable objectives/expected outcomes: Create a formal mechanism for discussing community health care concerns, collaborative efforts, community expectations, and receiving consumer feedback.

Baseline measures: The CAHCC, as a whole, does not have a formal accountability mechanism or forum for discussing collaborations. The focus has been the movement toward integration of the partners' services, and an assessment of other possible collaboration represents work yet to be undertaken.

Technical assistance/funding: No further funding is anticipated.

Maintain and Increase Services to Adolescents (Seamless Continuum of Care/Community Health Focus)

Activity: Maintain and increase services to Central Area adolescents by:

- Creating a separate Adolescent Clinic at the CAHCC staffed by experts in providing the full continuum of care required by inner-city adolescents. Two exam rooms and a conference room have been designated and equipped for this clinic. The Adolescent Clinic will target:
  - —Adolescents who live in the surrounding community, are not in school, and do not now receive health services. Aggressive outreach will identify organizations that serve these youth, particularly the nearby Youth Detention Center and programs for dropouts.
  - —Adolescents who attend the two large middle schools in the area and Zion Preparatory Academy.
  - —Students from the GTHC whose health issues are difficult diagnostically or present unusual management problems. The clinic will also serve as a primary source of medical care during nonschool hours—evenings, vacations, and summer months.

- Identifying ways to expand the physical space of the GTHC. The demand for services currently exceeds the services available. Add one exam room and augment providers with health care professionals in training.
- Evaluating more stable sources of funding for the GTHC by piloting/testing ways to tap into third-party systems of reimbursement, including Medicaid.
- Exploring with Washington Middle School and the Zion Preparatory Academy the health care needs of their students. Develop collaborative efforts that are possible within the financial resources of both organizations. Explore funding possibilities for more costly interventions (for example, on-site services).

Proposed goals/milestones and target dates:

- Adolescent Clinic:
  - —Work out reimbursement/operational issues between partners—11/95
  - —Implement the clinic—3/96
  - —Advertise and identify referral sources; work out referrals with the GTHC—5/96
- Expand services at the GTHC:
  - —Review potential ideas for space expansion—10/95
  - —If space is identified, secure agreements between partners—1/96
  - —Hire a professional to develop renovation plans/secure funding—5/96
  - —Remodel/make arrangements for additional providers—8/96
- Stable source of funding for the GTHC:
  - —Develop and make operational agreements with payers—5/97
  - —Identify resources required and implement—7/97
  - —Evaluate the effectiveness in terms of ability to secure funding—8/98
- Explore collaboration opportunities with Washington Middle School/Zion Preparatory Academy:
  - —Identify health care needs—12/95
  - —Identify referral arrangements/low- or no-cost collaborative efforts—5/96
  - —Implement collaborative plans—8/96
  - —Identify and design the more costly approaches—5/97
  - —Explore funding possibilities and implement—8/97

Baseline measures: The CAHCC currently serves 1,501 adolescents in a decentralized fashion. There is little effort to draw in adolescents from the surrounding community who are not attending school, no formalized way to publicize the availability of adolescent health services to other agencies that deal with the teens on a daily basis, and no institutionalized effort to encourage use of the CAHCC when the GTHC is closed.

The GTHC serves approximately 300 adolescents annually and provides 1,100 visits, but many more could be enrolled. The GTHC currently depends on a funding source that expires in 1997. The adolescents attending Washington Middle School and Zion Preparatory Academy have unmet health care needs and are looking to the CAHCC to assist them in addressing those needs. No current collaborative efforts currently exist with these schools that serve a significant segment of the community's adolescent population.

Measurable objectives/expected improvements: Improve health care to adolescents in the community by increasing the number of adolescents who receive ongoing preventive health care. Process improvements include creation of an attractive adolescent clinic at the CAHCC, expanded space at the GTHC, and a financially viable plan to continue the GTHC beyond 1997. Because prevention is a prominent goal in providing health care services to this population, increased services are expected to eventually affect the measures used to track the health of adolescents in the community.

Role of each partner: The medical director at Carolyn Downs, fellow-trained in adolescent medicine, will implement the Adolescent Clinic, expand services at the GTHC, and provide ongoing guidance in developing effective new approaches and programs for adolescent health. That individual will also train staff in adolescent health issues, identify gaps in services, evaluate the possible referral relationships, and review plans for outreach activities.

OBCC will provide the physical space for the clinic and will work with the Carolyn Downs medical director to make it age-appropriate. Both Carolyn Downs and OBCC will advertise the availability of this clinic to adolescents currently receiving care and will establish a simple financial agreement between partners that will support this clinic. The SKCDPH will undertake aggressive outreach and lead groups.

Garfield High School and OBCC will explore options for increasing the on-site space available to the GTHC. OBCC will identify goals for the remodeling, hire and supervise an architect, prepare plans, and seek grant funding to accomplish the required work. The SKCDPH has developed guidelines for securing third-party reimbursement. OBCC will design ways to make operational those agreements at the GTHC.

OBCC, representing the CAHCC, will initiate discussions and identify potential collaborations with Zion Preparatory Academy and Washington Middle School. Partners will identify ways, within current resources, to address those needs.

Technical assistance/funding: OBCC will need architectural assistance in preparing plans to expand the GTHC. The SKCDPH and the state health department will provide assistance in exploring ways to address student health needs at the middle-school level. Grant support will be used to work out obstacles to implementing an Adolescent Clinic at the CAHCC, plan and implement outreach efforts and referral and reimbursement arrangements, prepare a plan to expand services at the GTHC, and design and implement/test the reimbursement plans developed for the GTHC. Reimbursement for services will sustain the Adolescent Clinic once it has been implemented. Grant support will not be used for capital improvements.

Assess the CAHCC's Current Operation and Move Forward with Integration, Interorganizational Planning, Cost Savings, and Improved Service Delivery (Seamless Continuum of Care/ Managing within Fixed Resources)

Activity: Now that the three organizations are physically colocated, rethink how the CAHCC is organized, identifying ways to better deliver customer-focused services at a reduced cost. This will require integration of service delivery systems and administrative processes as much as possible. A reengineering process will be used to accomplish these objectives.

Proposed goals/milestones and target dates:

- Provide all CAHCC employees with a solid understanding of each other's services and organizations, discuss the reengineering process, and air employee concerns—9/95
- Identify areas to be assessed at OBCC and across agency boundaries, including the lab, the pharmacy, and the Medicaid enrollment counseling service—11/95
- Organize work groups and design teams to evaluate areas and make recommendations for change/provide training—11/95
- Identify information needs and initiate data collection—1/96
- Work groups prepare recommendations; design teams review, refine, and approve recommendations—4/96
- Steering Committee approval—6/96
- Prepare an implementation plan; implement the new designs—9/96

Baseline measures: Employees at the CAHCC are not aware of the services each of the partners brings to the center. Carolyn Downs and OBCC both operate small labs. Although Carolyn Downs operates a pharmacy, only patients seen at its clinic can use the pharmacy; OBCC patients must go outside the CAHCC to have their prescriptions filled. Carolyn Downs has a Medicaid enrollment counselor who helps patients obtain health coverage, but this service is not available to families who use OBCC—they must travel to the local state Medicaid office to apply for health care benefits.

All the agencies are out in the community representing their individual agencies, and all have outreach services and patient education and are collaborating with various agencies in the community. No thought has been given yet to how best to present the CAHCC to the community and how to coordinate these efforts. Nor has creative thought been given to how to improve services from the customer's perspective.

Measurable objectives/expected improvements: The goals are to improve customer service by providing a seamless continuum of care, identify permanent cost reductions, foster a less bureaucratic environment, simplify systems, and involve employees in the decision-making process. At a minimum, we expect to reduce costs by 10 percent; make the pharmacy available to anyone and consolidate the labs; assist all patients with Medicaid eligibility; take advantage of opportunities for coordination, collaboration, and reducing duplication; and offer better service to enrollees and the community as measured by ease of accessing all services.

Role of each partner: CHMC will manage the redesign effort, provide financial and other analysis as needed, and address any needs for technical assistance. As a model, OBCC will redesign all areas of operation. All the partners will be involved in this process.

Technical assistance/funding: CHMC has just completed a 2-year effort to reengineer and redesign its operations and will provide technical assistance. The changes that result from the initial redesign will be completed by the end of 1998. Although we envision a continuous process of improving services and controlling costs, this will become institutionalized and will not need ongoing funding.

Create a Family Support Center (Seamless Continuum of Care/Community Health Focus)

Activity: Support and provide services to the Family Support Center being sponsored by the YWCA and physically located at the nearby Garfield Recreation Center, operated by the city of Seattle. The Family Support Center is envisioned as a centralized and collaborative approach to improving family support services, including parenting education. The partners will be involved in the development of the Family Support Center and will provide health-oriented information and services focused on changing behavior to prevent disease.

The Black Parenting Classes will be moved from the CAHCC to the Family Support Center and integrated into the curriculum. The CAHCC will refer patients to the Family Support Center as indicated.

Proposed goals/milestones and target dates:

- Participate in organizational meetings—8/95
- Determine how we can best provide health care information within current resources—12/95
- Move the STEP Program to the Family Support Center—2/96

Baseline measures: Currently there is a wide variety of community activities designed to support families. Frequently those activities are narrowly focused on a single objective, such as violence prevention or teenage parenting, and there is a fair amount of duplication.

Measurable objectives/expected improvements: With a centralized effort, the number of families taking parenting courses will increase, and the number of families on the waiting list for the Black Parenting Class should be reduced to zero. With a community-wide effort and convergence of resources, the amount and quality of information available from the parenting course should increase. A before/after comparison of the curriculum should be valuable. The full spectrum of services and information—violence prevention, self-esteem curriculum, Big Sister and Big Brother programs, and support for families headed by adolescents—will be provided.

Role of each partner: OBCC will act as the representative to this community-wide effort. All partners will potentially contribute to curriculum development and will be points of patient/student referral.

Technical assistance/funding: No technical assistance is required, and once organizational work and curriculum building is completed, no funding will be required.

Add Critical Services to Meet the Specific Needs of the Community (Seamless Continuum of Care/Community Health Focus)

Activity: Add adult dental care, high-risk obstetrics, and mental health and substance abuse counseling to the services available at the CAHCC.

Proposed goals/milestones and target dates:

- Identify obstacles/arrangements required to initiate services and work out solutions—6/95
- Phase in services:
  - —Adult dental—7/95
  - —Obstetrics and mental health—10/95
- Notify the community that this service is available—10/95
- Review service delivery and address problems—1/96
- Develop ways to continuously assess service delivery and contract compliance—12/95

Baseline measures: A SKCDPH survey in the early 1990s explored, among other things, the needs for adult dental services in the Central Area. Of the low-income adults who responded, 52 percent did not have a source of dental care, 58 percent had not been to a dentist in the past year, and 51 percent reported having a dental problem and being unable to obtain care. The need for high-risk obstetrics services at a convenient location within the community has been discussed for years. The SKCDPH operates these services at other locations, but referral out of the community is not effective. Again, the mental health and substance abuse problems in the community are extensive. Although these services are available elsewhere, the waiting lists are lengthy, and on-site services will increase access and allow for coordination with medical care.

Measurable objectives/expected improvements: A resource for adult dental care will exist within the community, the number of adults receiving dental care will increase, and the wait for adult dental care for low-income people should decline. With better access, the number of referrals and the number of women with high-risk pregnancies served will increase. Obviously, in the long run we hope to affect the community health statistics for infant mortality and low-birth-weight babies. With mental health/substance abuse services added, the number of patients treated for these problems will increase.

Role of each partner: Carolyn Downs will contract with experienced community providers for adult dental services and mental health and substance abuse services. OBCC and the SKCDPH will be referral points. The SKCDPH will convene involved agencies—the University of Washington Perinatal Group and the Carolyn Downs Family Practice OB Team—to work out the best method for providing high-risk obstetrical services. Carolyn Downs, OBCC, and the outreach workers, particularly the infant mortality workers, will refer women in need of this service.

Technical assistance/funding: No technical assistance is needed, and, once implemented, these services will be supported through payment for services.

Improve Disease Management (Community Health Focus/ Managing within Fixed Resources)

Activity: Capitation is clearly on the horizon, and there will be an increased demand for tested nontraditional models for effective management of chronic disease. The purpose of these projects is to demonstrate a more effective and efficient model for managing childhood asthma and adult sickle cell anemia. Carolyn Downs will develop a clinic for adults with sickle cell disease, and patients will be transferred from the Pediatric Sickle Cell Clinic. The Asthma Outreach Program was implemented at the CAHCC in February 1995. This project will be completed and results evaluated to determine future plans for managing childhood asthma in a cost-effective manner.

Baseline measures: These two chronic diseases are significant problems in this particular community. Also, if not managed well, they are costly as a result of substantial hospitalization and emergency room use.

Proposed goals/milestones and target dates:

- Identify the remaining funding to allow the asthma project to run one year—6/95
- Evaluate data collected; prepare recommendations for the future—8/96
- Convene all the players to identify/discuss obstacles and issues for an Adult Sickle Cell Clinic—1/96

- Prepare an implementation plan; identify needed funding—6/96
- Initiate the clinic—1/97

Measurable objectives/expected improvements: The goal is to treat these conditions early in the disease process. The Sickle Cell Transition Project will extend the success of the pediatric program to the adult setting, and we expect adults to need fewer crisis interventions and less hospitalization, and to be more employable. This transition program should replace a currently disorganized and distressing transition from pediatric to adult care with a seamless, continuous transition from one setting to the next. The Asthma Outreach Project's evaluation component will clearly identify the model's ability to reduce hospitalization rates and emergency room use.

Role of each partner: OBCC is managing the Asthma Outreach Project, and the SKCDPH is providing a public health nurse who delivers a standardized asthma curriculum and provides oversight and mentorship for the outreach workers. Carolyn Downs and the SKCDPH staff will refer to the asthma clinic. OBCC and Carolyn Downs will work together to develop the Adult Sickle Cell Clinic.

Technical assistance/funding: CHMC will provide technical support for the educational component and medical management for the Asthma Outreach Project. The Fred Hutchinson Cancer Center currently provides technical assistance to the Pediatric Sickle Cell Clinic and will extend its services to the adult clinic at Carolyn Downs. The Sickle Cell Task Force is also a source of technical assistance.

We are seeking funding from a private foundation to complete the support for this project. If these projects clearly demonstrate cost savings, we anticipate that managed care payments will be the source for continuing this method of managing these chronic diseases.

PERIODIC REVIEW OF MEASURABLE OBJECTIVES

The joint operating committee meets monthly and will track each initiative and identify the need to revise/refine the objectives or the milestones.

SUMMARY OF NOTABLE PROGRESS

The CAHCC has made substantial progress on its prime initiatives.

Expand the CAHCC Steering Committee

We have learned a great deal in our process to expand the CAHCC Steering Committee. This committee was established two years prior to the opening of the CAHCC facility. Its primary responsibility was to facilitate the colocation of Carolyn Downs, OBCC, and SKCDPH. The CAHCC is now ready to move from merely colocating to true collaboration. The steering committee acknowledges a need to review its mission, goals, and operating agreement to fully embrace this next level of working together. The steering committee also recognizes a need to augment its membership with CAHCC consumers and at-large community members. Committee members are particularly mindful of the process necessary to ensure the expansion addresses the CAHCC's need to be accountable to the Central Area community.

Maintain and Increase Services to Adolescents

The GTHC is located on the campus of Garfield High School, eight blocks from the CAHCC. OBCC is the lead agency for GTHC, which opened in spring 1992. Current providers include a family nurse practitioner, a mental health counselor and a substance abuse counselor on site, and an adolescent specialist one afternoon per week. Six hundred (38 percent) of Garfield's students are enrolled in the GTHC. There were 2,327 encounters for the 1995–96 school year. Encounters are limited because GTHC capacity has been exceeded. An additional provider is necessary to ensure that students have immediate access to services. The local medical school is interested in using the clinic as a training site; however, the center needs an additional examination room. CHMC has successfully raised 65 percent of the funds necessary to do a complete renovation, which was scheduled to begin in fall 1996.

The CAHCC began implementing Teen Mondays in January 1996. Adolescent clinic visits are scheduled every other Monday, alternating with adolescent discussion groups. Adolescents are seen by both OBCC and Carolyn Downs providers. Young adolescents make up the majority of the current clientele. OBCC and CHMC have successfully raised funds to expand the program to engage older adolescents, particularly young men.

Assess the CAHCC's Current Operation

Carolyn Downs and OBCC have identified pharmacy and lab services as opportunities to explore collaborative service delivery. Currently, Carolyn Downs operates an on-site pharmacy for its clients. OBCC clients have their prescriptions filled at local pharmacies. A large pharmacy just opened three blocks from the CAHCC. Cost-benefit analysis of the two models has begun. Lab services are outsourced to four different services. Contracts will be reviewed, and opportunities for sharing resources will be explored over the next six months.

Create a Family Support Center

The vision is a centralized and collaborative approach to improving family support services, including parenting education. The CAHCC offers the following parenting classes in the community:

- First Time Parenting Class
- Systematic Training for Effective Parenting (STEP)
- Effective Black Parenting
- Strengthening Multi-Ethnic Families and Communities (SMEC)

Classes are taught throughout the year by OBCC and SKCDPH staff. Locations vary, with over 75 percent of the classes taught at the Garfield Community Center. The SKCDPH public health nurses and outreach workers are at the community center every Wednesday afternoon, answering questions and providing referrals and health education to families served by the CAHCC.

Add Critical Services to Meet the Specific Needs of the Community

Adult dental care services were implemented in January 1996. Capacity was quickly exceeded. Two more dental chairs (for a total of eight) were added in spring 1996.

The adult dental provider, operating within a family practice model, and CHMC, provider of dental services for children, successfully negotiated the sharing of clientele. Dental services are now available at the CAHCC for clients and community residents from infancy through the senior years.

Adult mental health and substance abuse services were added by summer 1995. Referrals are primarily received from Carolyn Downs; however, both OBCC and the SKCDPH staff also make referrals. Because expected encounters have not been met, a more efficient internal referral system, as well as methods of promoting the availability of these services to the local community, are being developed.

Improve Disease Management

Asthma is one of the most common chronic conditions causing school absences and is among the leading causes of pediatric hospitalizations in the United States. In the past year, great progress has been made locally in developing a best-practices model for the management of inner-city pediatric asthma. The Asthma Outreach Project at OBCC has demonstrated success in reducing the hospitalizations, emergency room visits, and sick visits for asthma, and in increasing the number of scheduled follow-up visits for this problem. (See figures 1-1–1-3.) The Critical Elements of Care asthma management group, a project sponsored by the Washington State Department of Health, has just finished developing an asthma resource book. This book includes asthma management guidelines, management tools to help practices identify and organize care for their sickest asthmatic children; educational materials addressing the pathophysiology of asthma, asthma medications and environmental modification; and support information for the development of an outreach program or an asthma education program. OBCC is in the process of securing funding to expand on the success of these two projects with the Pediatric Asthma Management Support Center, a community-focused regional office that will facilitate dissemination of asthma resource materials by providing technical support to practices interested in developing an asthma management program.

OBCC and CHMC have also successfully run a comprehensive pediatric sickle cell anemia program since 1978. Carolyn Downs has agreed to pilot an adult sickle cell anemia continuity clinic at the CAHCC, recognizing that many young people are lost to follow-up once they graduate from the pediatric program. Carolyn Downs providers will provide primary care; specialty care will be provided on-site by local hematologists. Implementation was planned for September 1996, and we met this goal.

Contact: Paula M. Holmes
Program Manager, Community Care Network
Central Area Health Care Center
2101 E. Yesler Way
Seattle, WA 98122
Phone: (206) 461-8341
Fax: (206) 461-8342
E-mail: pholme@chmc.org

FIGURE 1-1. Establishing an Asthma Outreach Program in Your Clinic

Following are some suggestions for setting up an Asthma Outreach Program, based on a pilot project at Odessa Brown Children's Clinic, Seattle Washington. The approach to asthma management in your clinic will depend on available resources and the characteristics of your community.

I. *Define and identify your population of asthmatics.* Use automated data systems at your clinic and local hospital to identify patients having the most difficulty controlling their exacerbations, as evidenced by unscheduled clinic and emergency room (ER) visits, and hospital admissions for asthma.

A. Get a printout from your data system of *all patients* with an ICD-9 code for asthma (493 and any of its subcodes) over the preceding 12 months; match this list against the hospital's automated records for all ER visits and hospitalizations for asthma over the same time period. Alternatively, submit a complete *list of providers* to the local hospital to search for any patients under age 18 with a discharge diagnosis (ER or inpatient) of 439.xx (asthma and all of its subcodes) during the past 12 months.

B. To help identify the sickest asthmatics, the pilot project used a point system and assigned one point for an ER visit and three points for an admission; a patient needed a total of at least three points to be eligible for our program. Anyone with a significant co-morbid diagnosis was eliminated. Although this system is arbitrary, the pilot project found it to be a useful way to organize asthma patients according to their health service use.

II. *Establish a system of coordinated care, involving a minimum of an asthma outreach worker (AOW), a primary care provider, and a project coordinator.* In the pilot project's inner-city clinic, where approximately 30 children with severe asthma are managed, the outreach worker is full time, the physician is 20 percent full-time equivalent (FTE), and the project coordinator is 30 percent FTE.

A. The AOW functions as the "eyes and ears" of the physician, bringing relevant living circumstances to light that would be missed by the physician alone.

B. The physician provides the AOW with ready access to the health care system, as well as reinforcement and guidance for educational points.

C. The AOW has frequent contact with the public health nurse when issues regarding other family members, or those beyond the scope of the asthma project, are raised at home visits.

D. The project coordinator keeps the project running smoothly by organizing the clinic schedule, generating correspondence, coordinating meeting times, overseeing paper work, etc. The project coordinator also coordinates data collection.

E. Hire a community-based, indigenous, lay outreach worker (or nurse coordinator, or . . .) to build an open, trusting relationship with the families.

F. Train that individual in asthma management.

G. Ideally, establish a network of home visit mentoring for the outreach worker. In the pilot project, the outreach worker was hired through the local Health Department.

1. The AOW gathers information on a Home Assessment Tool, which addresses access issues (i.e., car, phone); indoor environment (i.e., pets, smoke), asthma management (i.e., mattress covers, presence of medications, equipment), and parental observations of the child's health (i.e., night awakenings, symptom recognition).

2. She re-emphasizes the asthma management plan and identifies and works with the family to resolve any barriers to compliance.

3. In addition to asthma issues, the AOW assists the family with a myriad of other issues, such as housing, clothing, and asthma management at school or day care.

FIGURE 1-1. (Continued)

H. Schedule a series of regular clinic visits for the patients. An initial program of three visits at six-week intervals was chosen for the pilot project.

1. Prior to each clinic, the AOW leads a discussion with the physician about the families to be seen that day and highlights any particular issues and concerns for each family.
2. The physician sees each child and family, focusing on asthma management and assessment, peak expiratory flow rate (PEFR) where appropriate, and medication delivery technique.
3. The physician, in conjunction with the family, develops or revises a home management plan. To insure consistent asthma management, distribute copies of current plan to child's medical record/file, family, outreach worker, school nurse, or day care provider.
4. The physician, project coordinator and AOW meet frequently between scheduled clinics to discuss episodic management issues.

I. Provide asthma management education sessions for parents and caregivers. (A health educator, nurse, or medical provider could lead this group.)

1. The pilot project used "Open Airways" for our inner-city population.
2. Content included basic information on asthma medications, controlling triggers in the home, helping children with asthma stay active, problem solving around lost school time, and renter's rights and insurance coverage.
3. The pilot project found classes to be most beneficial if half the time focused on basic asthma information and half allowed time for group discussion, so that parents and caregivers could learn from each other.
4. Schedule one or two 45 minute–1 hour group education sessions per clinic and organize the schedule to minimize wait time for families.
5. Provide day care during the education sessions.
6. Simultaneous class for school-aged kids can be offered.

J. Establish a maintenance schedule for clinic and outreach visits with each family, depending on social and medical stability. Establish criteria for "graduating" children from the program. For example, 12 months without an ER visit, 18 months without hospitalization, 6 months without symptoms. These same criteria could be used for discontinuing chronic medications.

FIGURE 1-2. Programs for Teaching Asthma Self-Management Skills to Children with Asthma and Their Families

Open Airways—Program developed by Columbia University Department of Pediatrics, 1984.

- Developed to meet the needs of inner-city families, including information about tenant's rights
- Designed for three different groups of participants: younger children (ages 4–7); older children (ages 8–14); and parents. Each group meets separately for seven 45–90-minute sessions. These sessions can be condensed and combined.
- Emphasizes group discussion and support
- Includes a series of stories about families with asthma-related problems that class participants try to solve
- Package includes teaching notes, reproducible posters, and handout sheets
- Supported by the Division of Lung Diseases, National Heart, Lung, and Blood Institute (NHLBI); U.S. Department of Health and Human Services, Public Health Service, NIH (NIH Publication No. 84-2365)

Air Power: Self-Management of Asthma through Group Education—Program developed by the American Institutes for Research and the Kaiser-Permanente Medical Groups (published in 1984) based on a "critical incident" study of children with asthma. This study reported things that children actually did or did not do that had an effect on the child's asthma, and thus defined what it means for a child (aged 9–13 years) to become competent in asthma *self*-management.

- Intended for use with children ages 9 to 13 and their parents. Program consists of four 1-hour sessions, to be conducted on a weekly basis with small groups of children (three to six per group); separate session for parents.
- Three components of each session: information giving, group problem-solving, and relaxation training
- General philosophy underlying the program: social learning theory, which holds that individuals are motivated to change behavior when they have a sense of personal efficacy, an incentive to perform the behavior, and the expectation that the behavior will have positive consequences.
- Supported by the Division of Lung Diseases, NHLBI; U.S. Department of Health and Human Services, Public Health Service, NIH (NIH Publication No. 85-2362)

Living with Asthma—Based on the program developed by Dr. Thomas L. Creer and associates at the National Asthma Center in Denver, Colorado. Published in 1987.

- Underlying philosophy: teach asthma self-management skills to children and give parents the knowledge and behavior modification skills to help their children take over responsibility for managing the condition.
- Two-part focus: (1) present basic information about asthma, its management, and medications; (2) methods for developing self-management behaviors.
- Designed for children ages 8 to 12 and their parents.
- Supported by the Division of Lung Diseases, NHLBI; U.S. Department of Health and Human Services, Public Health Service, NIH (NIH Publication No. 87-2364)

Teaching Your Patients about Asthma: A Clinician's Guide—Based on recommendations of the *Expert Panel Report: Guidelines for the Diagnosis and Management of Asthma,* developed by the National Asthma Education Program of the NHLBI and published in 1992.

- Fundamental premise of guide: patient education (for adults and children with asthma and parents of children with asthma) should emphasize the development of asthma management skills and stress the fact that asthma can be controlled.
- Emphasizes the need to go beyond providing information to developing a partnership with the family; involve the family in decision making about asthma management; demonstrate and have the patient demonstrate proper asthma management skills and techniques.
- Published by the National Asthma Education Program; Office of Prevention, Education and Control; NHLBI; NIH; U.S. Department of Health and Human Services, Public Health Service, NIH (Publication No. 92-2737)

FIGURE 1-2. (Continued)

Asthma Care Training for Kids (ACT)—Originally developed in 1993 at the UCLA School of Medicine.

- Developed for children ages 7–12 with asthma and their parents.
- Designed to encourage the parent, child and physician to work as a team to control the child's asthma.
- Primary objectives: to reduce the frequency and severity of asthma episodes; and to teach children and their parents asthma self-management skills.
- Key messages are conveyed using traffic analogies, with the central theme that children can learn to manage their asthma by getting in the "driver's seat" and taking charge.
- ACT is taught in three 1½–2-hour activity-oriented sessions; parents learn separately from their children, but they share what they learned at the end of each session; maximum of ten families.
- Comes with instruction manuals ($15), teaching materials ($37), and handouts ($85).
- Available through the Asthma and Allergy Foundation of America.

FIGURE 1-3. Parental Feedback Questionnaire

We would appreciate your feedback to help us give you the information you need. Don't worry about asking the same question more than once.

I have the following question(s) about my child's asthma medications:

- ☐ What does it do to improve my child's asthma?
- ☐ When should my child take it?
- ☐ How should he/she take it?
- ☐ What are the side effects?
- ☐ Are there any long-term side effects of this medication?
- ☐ How do I use the equipment (nebulizer, inhaler, spacer)?
- ☐ Other: ______________________________

I have the following question(s) about our home environment and what I can do to help with my child's asthma:

- ☐ What can I do about dust and dust mites?
- ☐ What can I do about pet allergens?
- ☐ What can I do to remove mold?
- ☐ What can I do about cigarette smoke?
- ☐ Can I get more information about how to quit smoking?
- ☐ Other: ______________________________

I have additional questions about the following issue(s):

- ☐ My child's night wakenings.
- ☐ Missing school or daycare because of asthma.
- ☐ Missing work to take care of my child with asthma.
- ☐ How I can help my child with her/his feelings about asthma.
- ☐ Other (please list any other concerns you have): ______________________________

____

____

____

2

The Columbia-Presbyterian Community Health System

Executive Summary

According to the 1990 census, 198,192 people officially reside in this community, more than 70 percent of whom are Latino. Most are poor, hard-working, recent immigrants from the Dominican Republic with little or no health insurance. More than 35 percent are Medicaid-eligible. Access to affordable health care has long been considered a critical, unmet need.

In response to that need, Presbyterian Hospital and many community-based organizations, with the support of local elected officials, have engaged in a process to develop a community care network (CCN). This collaboration has led to the development of many programs and services provided by Presbyterian Hospital as well as by several community groups. Our accomplishments have included six off-site practices throughout the community, clinics in four intermediate schools and the local high school, and a 300-bed community hospital.

One of the most exciting initiatives has been the establishment of the Physician Service Organization (PSO), comprising more than 60 local physicians, the majority of whom are Latin American–born and –educated. Many physicians, mostly operating solo practices, have provided health care to residents for decades but had no relationship with the hospital. We recognized that these physicians represent a valuable and, until recently, overlooked resource.

Forming a partnership with the community's only hospital—and overcoming the obstacles inherent in developing affiliations with a major academic health center—was not only necessary but vital to improve health care delivery overall. The PSO facilitates the medical staff application process for its members as well as evaluates managed care programs and practice management services for members. Together, the PSO and the hospital are working hard to adapt to this difficult cost-based health care environment while providing high-quality health care to our community. We strongly commend this innovative venture and hope that it can be replicated in similar, inner-city communities throughout the country.

Guillermo Linares and Stanley Michels
Members of the New York City Council

THE COMMUNITY

The Washington Heights–Inwood (WHI) neighborhood of Manhattan is the core of the hospital's service area and is a unique environment in which to deliver health care. A variety of factors, including cultural, ethnic, and linguistic, must be taken into consideration in the planning of any health care initiative. Unless the unique needs—health, cultural, or other—of this community are recognized and understood, any program of care will have little success. The following information provides detailed insight into areas of focus that the partnership has deemed most important.

Demographics

The WHI area is one of the most densely populated in the city, with approximately seven square miles supporting a population of more than 250,000 individuals. The census figures for Community District 12 indicated a population of 198,192 in 1990. However, it is widely acknowledged that many local residents were not counted in the 1990 census. U.S. Immigration and Naturalization Service data reveal that more than 100,000 legal Dominicans, the largest group of recent immigrants, live in Washington Heights. Urban demographic experts estimate that there is at least one undocumented Dominican resident in Washington Heights for every two registered immigrants. In 1960, only eight percent of all Dominican permanent residents who entered the United States became naturalized. Since 1977, that rate has risen to 18 percent—half the national average.

Poverty

Poverty is a serious issue in WHI. Per capita income is just over one-third the average for Manhattan, and a large percentage of households are on public assistance. The most frequently used indicator of poverty in New York City is the number of income support recipients as reported by the New York City Human Resources Administration (NYCHRA). That agency indicates that in 1993 there were more than 68,000 income support recipients in district 12—more than in any other community district in Manhattan. In fact, district 12, which comprises only 13 percent of Manhattan's population, contains over 35 percent of the borough's income support population. In the past 5 years, the public assistance rolls citywide have remained constant while the poverty population in WHI has increased by approximately 25 percent. With per capita income at $11,000 per year, there is little money available to stimulate the local economy and maintain acceptable standards of living.

The Family and Children

In WHI, the average occupancy rate is 2.8 residents per household. However, because newly arriving immigrants tend to rely on extended families, Dominican households in WHI average 3.9 occupants. Among WHI children, poverty rose 27 percent in 1990, while it declined 11 percent in New York City overall; the high rate is a result of increases in immigration and the widening gap between the rich and the poor that was seen during the 1980s. In 1990, 28 percent of WHI families were found to be living below the poverty line. Of those families, 45 percent were raising children under the age of five, and 62 percent were headed by a single female.

The latest census reveals that 52,000 children and adolescents under the age of 18 live in WHI. Of those, it is believed that only about 5,000 were registered with New York City Public Child Health Clinics (NYCPCHCs). Although that number appears average when compared with that of the city, it is actually well below average considering the large number of children in the WHI community.

Birth Rate and Maternal/Prenatal Care

One out of four women in this community were women of childbearing age in 1990. With 4,538 births in WHI, the 1991 birth rate (91.2 births per 1,000 women age 15–44 years) was about 30 percent greater than in New York City overall. WHI has an extremely high birth rate, yet a large percentage of residents do not receive prenatal care. In fact, 13 percent of pregnant women reported having no prenatal care as compared with 7 percent in New York City; 12 percent reported getting late prenatal care.

Education

Of WHI residents over 25 years of age, 26 percent have less than a ninth-grade education, and only 38 percent of this age group are high school graduates. In 1993, over 85 percent of the pupils in three local elementary public schools in the area were excused from the New York City testing program because of limited English proficiency. Two of the three schools in the area ranked in the bottom 5 percent of all 630 elementary schools citywide. School District 6 as a whole had one of the lowest reading score rankings in the entire city. That same school district is also one of the most overcrowded in the city, with most of its schools at more than 100 percent of the designed occupancy. As a result, the board of education has constructed three new elementary and intermediate schools; however, despite this new construction, the schools continue to be extremely overcrowded.

Language

Presently, over 70 percent of the WHI population is Spanish speaking, with a vast majority of individuals from the Dominican Republic—50 percent higher than the citywide average. In 1990, over 67 percent of the population came from Spanish-speaking countries, and today the remainder of the population speak nearly 50 different languages and come from places as varied as Bengal, Formosa, Vietnam, and Serbia. Of the WHI population, 70 percent "speak a language other than English at home," 65 percent speak Spanish at home, and 45 percent do not speak English "very well."

THE PARTNERSHIP

WHI Ambulatory Care Network Corporation (ACNC) is the ambulatory arm of Columbia-Presbyterian Medical Center (CPMC). The ACNC is responsible for more than 360,000 visits from approximately 80,000 WHI residents.

Primary Partner

Northern Manhattan Collaborates! (NMC!) is the coordinating structure for all the major consortia and most of the organizations operating in Manhattan Community District 12.

Secondary Partners

Northern Manhattan Improvement Corporation (NMIC) and Alianza Dominicana are among the secondary partners. In the present environment of drastic change in policy toward the poor and underprivileged in New York City, the desire to pool resources and collaborate has grown. It is only natural that the community's largest employer and principal provider of health care join with some of the more developed community organizations to care for people as comprehensively and cost-effectively as possible. This was the belief when NMC! and the ACNC first came together in 1994. The combination of those two partners created a powerful entity that links Presbyterian Hospital, the sole health care institution in Washington Heights, with an extensive network of community organizations.

Prior to the late 1970s, there was little communication between the WHI community and the Presbyterian Hospital. As the middle class started moving out of WHI in the 1970s and 1980s, so did the hospitals and physicians: several municipal and voluntary hospitals closed over a 15-year period. CPMC, a premier teaching facility and tertiary care center, was thrust into the difficult position of sole provider, responsible for primary care to a largely indigent population. In 1985, CPMC established the ACNC to be particularly responsive to the neighborhoods of Washington Heights and Inwood. Since then, the ACNC, with its network of neighborhood and school-based clinics, has made tremendous progress toward understanding the community's health care needs and developing programs and services to fulfill those needs.

Similarly and independently, NMC! was established in 1989 by more than a dozen community-based organizations. Functioning through approximately 14 issue-specific committees and guided by a critical needs assessment, NMC! has identified local priorities, advocated with government officials, created a large network of information sharing, and become heavily involved in program development and service coordination. One of those 14 groups is the health committee, of which the ACNC is a participating member. Membership is open to individual neighborhood residents, members of the business sector, clergy, schools, government agencies, and elected officials. In short, NMC! and the ACNC truly represent the people who live and work in the WHI community.

PRIOR EFFORTS THAT REPRESENT MOVEMENT TOWARD THE COMMUNITY CARE NETWORK VISION

Community Health Focus

Perhaps the best example of early diagnostic and intervention programs with a focus on changing behavior to prevent disease in the WHI community is the development of the program called Best Beginnings. The growing collaboration between CPMC and Alianza Dominicana led to the common concern that vulnerable children and their families were not being identified and helped. The leadership of the Presbyterian Hospital's Pediatric Service brought that fact to the attention of the New York Society for the Prevention of Cruelty to Children (NYSPCC). Together they raised government and private support to develop Best Beginnings, an innovative program that is a collaborative effort of five partners: The Hospital's ACNC; NYSPCC; Alianza Dominicana; Columbia University; and the NYC Early Intervention Program. By combining NYSPCC's extensive experience in family assessment and child protection with ACNC's expertise in delivering health care, along with Alianza Dominicana's history of providing services to the community, Best Beginnings has created a unique opportunity to forestall the destructive consequences which beset children of families with insufficient educational, health, and social services. Pediatricians, public health nurses, social workers, and paraprofessionals collaborate to produce this model of universal and continuous preventive health care and social services support. It is a home-based primary prevention program to prevent child abuse and neglect, support young families, prepare children for school, and ensure healthy productive citizens.

Best Beginnings is not the first effort to intervene early in the lives of particularly vulnerable community residents. The School-Based Clinics and Family Planning programs, sponsored by Columbia University and the ACNC, focus on the prevention of teen pregnancy and engage the parents of youth in these efforts. These projects bring together aspects of both public health and personal health; are of special interest to the partners in the CCN and progress in meeting certain health objectives, such as reduced teen pregnancy; and are continually assessed and monitored. Young men's clinic night is an exciting and very successful part of the Family Planning program, which has the enthusiastic support of many neighborhood leaders.

In the academic setting of Columbia University, the College of Physicians and Surgeons, the School of Public Health, and the School of Nursing are involved in numerous activities that monitor the health status of the population. As the only hospital in the area, the Presbyterian Hospital has created a large central database of patient information. With this database, it is possible to capture any individual who enters into the system of care, regardless of whether the point of entry is the emergency room or an ACNC site. By combining its expertise with independent community reports on health needs and information from community organizations, the Columbia-Presbyterian Community Health System can accurately assess and monitor the health status of the population in its service area.

As a result of their interaction with community-focused organizations, The Presbyterian Hospital and the ACNC have also been able to identify and address cultural and other barriers to health care in their primary service area. In a community with a large immigrant population such as WHI, it is difficult to address these needs when the cultural composition evolves in new directions. The medical center's target community serves as a destination for immigrants from more than 50 different countries. As they arrive, a variety of barriers to health care occur, including linguistic, social, cultural, and monetary, to name a few. These barriers are complex and require great understanding and hard work to overcome. Even Spanish, which is the language most often encountered, is often a barrier because of dialectic differences. CPMC has made tremendous efforts to bridge gaps in communication and overcome other obstacles. Much progress has been made, particularly with the large population of Spanish speakers.

In an effort to overcome barriers in communication, the ACNC has included community-based physicians in its network expansion. Called the Presbyterian Hospital Physician Service Organization, it is a group deeply committed to serving the community. The organization's ability to continue to provide high-quality care is greatly enhanced by help from the ACNC in negotiating managed care contracts, purchasing computers to establish formal linkages, and maintaining a 24-hour, shared coverage program. The provider network is significantly improved by the integration of these largely Spanish-speaking doctors.

Another effort focuses on the Spanish-speaking elderly, who often have the most difficult problems to address. To alleviate this dilemma, the Presbyterian Hospital hired a bilingual, bicultural health educator who is well versed in geriatric issues. That individual visits each of 10 senior citizen centers throughout the community every week to conduct classes in health promotion and disease prevention.

It is also noteworthy that many of the doctors and other personnel working in the community speak Spanish. Those who are not Spanish speaking have access to language classes, and many members of the staff have chosen to learn the language. A large proportion of the support staff are from the local community and speak Spanish as well as English.

Numerous sources of information regarding community health problems and assets are available to the community and the ACNC. These include data from the New York State Department of Health, New York City Department of Health, New York City Health Systems Agency (NYCHSA), and federal census reports. The most recent source of information is the Presbyterian Hospital market analysis, prepared by the Health Systems Agency in March 1995. It contains analyses of sociodemographics, health status, health program utilization, and hospital utilization. The United Way of New York City has also prepared a neighborhood profile for Community District 12, which specifically covers population characteristics, economic trends, and family life and health.

Complementary to the United Way publication is a community-based assessment called the Strategic Neighborhood Action Plan (SNAP). This plan, put together by NMC!, is a comprehensive needs assessment that sets priorities for state funding and local coordination efforts. Each of the assessment's 14 chapters addresses a specific concern. There is a health chapter put together by the health committee, as well as chapters on aging, immigration, mental health, the environment, education, economic development, alcoholism, and drug abuse. Much more is available, and it is all readily accessible to those who need information for planning and/or grant writing as well as market surveys.

Community Accountability

The ACNC itself does not collect data but takes advantage of the numerous information resources available from CPMC, New York City, New York State, and the community. All the information is shared among the groups with which the ACNC interacts. This information is then used to respond most appropriately to identify health and social needs. For instance, if a greater demand for pediatrics and family planning is demonstrated, appropriate staff are hired to adjust to changing needs.

Each year, CPMC updates a community service plan that summarizes present and future efforts to deliver health care to the community. It is a comprehensive survey of all the medical center's community activities. Included in this survey is a large section that focuses on the ACNC's efforts to meet explicitly stated needs of the community. The format is designed to clearly explain the CPMC's response to community and staff recommendations, thereby making it difficult to dodge sensitive issues. The plan is then sent to New York state and city officials and is made available to any organization or community member via the library or directly from CPMC. Developing this information helps facilitate the communication of community health-related problems and CPMC's response to those problems so that local, city, and state representatives can lead informed discussions with their constituents.

Seamless Continuum of Care

CPMC has begun a practice of engaging community groups and leaders in discussions of how it can begin to more comprehensively address community needs. In this way there is no duplication or fragmentation, and the care is continuously delivered. Excess cost is avoided and, with proper implementation, people are healthier and acute illnesses are prevented. By engaging the community in an open dialogue, the medical center gains an awareness of the services the community believes to be important. Fortunately, CPMC has the advantage of being able to provide the entire range of health care services and is not limited to primary care alone.

To get the ACNC more involved in preventive health care efforts, not only for its patients but for the broader community as a whole, many plans have been implemented. An education program in health promotion and disease prevention is currently under way, located inside the main medical center lobby. On their way in or out of the medical center, community members will be educated on ways to prevent injury, illness, and potential complications. Also, staff will be on hand to help patients and visitors access computers set up for exploring basic health issues, hand out literature, conduct demonstrations in health promotion and prevention activities, and answer questions. In the new Urgicare center, nurse practitioners are educating patients and family members about disease prevention, health promotion, and whether they would like to be part of the ACNC network of care.

Arrangements with the New York Visiting Nurse Service (VNS) facilitate access to patients' homes. Home access enables nurse practitioners to address concerns related to nutrition, environment, and mental health—issues that may go undetected in a formal office visit. During home visits, it is possible to evaluate the home environment and create a tailored health package that meets the family's most severe needs in the most economical manner.

SNAP provides a comprehensive list of resources available to the community. Efforts in this area eliminate duplication of services and promote linkages among the providers of these services and between the consumers of health resources and their caretakers. This represents the preliminary stage of a comprehensive, community-wide referral and case management system that can be accessed by an organization or provider in the community to direct any individual to the most appropriate health or social service.

Management within Fixed Resources

Evaluation of cost of services is primarily accomplished through the Presbyterian Hospital's computer network, which records all encounters at the ACNC sites. The analyses are performed by the Department of Finance; thus it is possible to review quarterly and monthly the number of visits, expenses, and the resulting revenue. Through this data collection, statistical analysis and monitoring are performed.

The ACNC is still in a growth mode, and evaluation systems are continually being upgraded. Currently there are determined efforts to speed up the appointment system to save time and effort for the patient representatives who follow up on patient care.

The ACNC has developed a provider base that has a mix of allied health professionals. Nurse practitioners and certified nurse midwives are key players in the delivery of primary care services. These professionals cost less than physicians and provide the regular continuity of care necessary to serve an indigent population. The combination of a doctor and nurse practitioner enhances the delivery of low-cost quality care. The situation is similar in the Presbyterian Hospital's dental program, where dental hygienists work in concert with the dentist to facilitate the delivery of care.

The allied health professionals are able to provide all necessary primary care services under the direction and supervision of the attending physician. The net result is the ability to see a larger number of patients in a set amount of time, thereby increasing efficiency and productivity without threatening the delivery of high-quality care.

The attitude toward serving needy areas has dramatically changed with the advent of managed Medicaid plans. In an effort to cut costs, a state-appointed Medicaid Task Force recommended for the executive budget proposal that all Medicaid beneficiaries be enrolled in managed care plans by March 31, 1996, but no mandatory date has as yet been set. In addition, it was recommended that capitated rates be reduced to 90 percent of regional per capita fee-for-service spending. Since then, managed care plans have been competing with one another to sign up Medicaid-eligible participants. The underlying fear is that local health care will be dispensed according to set formulas with strict treatment allowances and limited patient choice of providers.

In an effort to allay those fears, the Presbyterian Hospital and the ACNC have initiated the development of a managed care plan. In the interim, Medicaid recipients will enroll in the Bronx Health Plan, with which the ACNC has signed a contract. In this capitated setting, the financial risk is transferred to the provider, and the ACNC must provide all necessary services for a set amount per enrollee per month. Current assumptions of an average number of visits per member per year have been written into the contract; using this system, the revenue side of the accounting equation becomes more predictable. It is hoped that providing comprehensive, coordinated care will reduce expenses in the long run, but in the short run it is likely that utilization will increase as a result of growing awareness of the CPMC program.

MOVING TOWARD THE COMMUNITY CARE NETWORK VISION

The CCN vision provides a framework for the partnership's efforts to create a comprehensive continuum of care. Progress has been made in establishing a common set of initiatives to enhance the delivery of care. The CCN vision has provided guidance for the planning process and has served as an invaluable tool for generating discussion and inspiring creativity and leadership. As a result of the partnership meetings and increased communication that this project has demanded, potential barriers to collaboration have been overcome. A sense of trust and mutual understanding has begun to develop between the community and the hospital—a rare commodity at one time. The free and uninhibited exchange of information that the CCN vision promotes has facilitated and inspired the partnership. This vision has become an invisible mediator, and the sense of trust and enthusiasm that is evolving from the shared sense of a common goal has created a bond that carries the collaboration beyond previously expected boundaries. This bond will continue long after the completion of the proposed initiative as changing community needs continue to be evaluated. The successful completion of the proposed initiative will lay the groundwork for a variety of additional initiatives that must be undertaken.

To achieve the vision's goal of a truly comprehensive health care system for the entire population, it is essential to integrate promotional and preventive measures into the primary care service centers. In addition to health issues, social concerns that often precede the development of health problems must be addressed. Through the use of an information and communications network, proper referrals to the many social service agencies may be made promptly and accurately. Enhanced approaches to the collection and distribution of comprehensive health care and utilization data will help ensure that an individual will no longer be lost in the large network of providers. Monitoring of individuals will occur on a much broader scale that will enable tracking of diseases and/or social problems as well. The result will be a complete and confidential profile of the members of the community who require a full range of services. Regardless of the point of entry, be it social service or emergency service, community members will be captured by the system of care.

Without the community component of this partnership, access to social services would be greatly reduced. Therefore, regular input and the exchange of information is not only necessary but vital. The more information and data that are made available, the better the position in which providers will be to assume a greater financial risk. Working in a capitated setting, they must carefully measure the cost and risk of caring for a population. With a medically needy population such as that of WHI, it is difficult but necessary to implement new financing mechanisms that include managed care and global budgeting.

The partnership has determined that one of the ways to achieve its long-term goal of a healthy community is to focus first on children, its most valued treasure. Measurable objectives that will improve the life chances of children will be developed with community support. The first objective will be to immunize hard-to-reach children under the age of 2. It will also include efforts to bring these at-risk children into a medical home that will provide ongoing primary care. This initiative will also be used to advance the development of the CCN's information system infrastructure to track the immunization of children in the community by the different providers. As children become part of the primary care system, other health objectives will be developed and measured.

The partnership has also identified pediatric asthma as a longer-range focus of its efforts in engaging broad segments of the community striving to achieve the system of care outlined in the CCN vision. Most members of the community have had some experience with this potentially lethal illness, and have spent a large amount of time in the emergency room obtaining specialty and emergency services. Asthmatic children require careful surveillance; without this monitoring, medical services and medication are used inappropriately. Poor disease management results in school absence, over-restricting activities, isolation, and consequent psychological problems.

Ten percent of school-age children have asthma, and that figure is rising steadily. Although many factors, such as environment and stress, can contribute to the widespread occurrence of childhood asthma in urban centers, experts believe the principal causes are the unavailability of primary care as well as misinformation regarding effective treatments. Counseling on the avoidance of actions and contacts that produce symptoms or on the use of established and recently available medications can produce major improvements in a child's quality of life. However, to be effective, this type of program requires access to continuing care and education so that the treatment can be monitored and modified over time.

The pediatric asthma initiative plans to follow a case management approach, in which the child is assigned to a team of health care professionals, including a bilingual health educator/case manager, to facilitate the delivery of comprehensive treatment. To coordinate a child's total health care needs, a management plan will be developed that can be re-evaluated at each visit. The health educator will maintain close contact with the children and their parents to ensure program adherence, attendance at appointments, and so on. The health educator will not only recruit and counsel patients and their families, but will also conduct extensive outreach in the WHI area. When needed, the health educator will act as liaison between families and schools. Thus, the placement of a bilingual health educator in the community is crucial to ensure that vital information is shared in a culturally sensitive manner. As children and families gain knowledge and awareness of disease symptoms and available services, they are expected to take a more active role in maintaining wellness. The emphasis on prevention and education is expected to be particularly effective.

The pediatric asthma initiative is seen as an innovative solution to the vitally important issue of limited access to care. It can easily be replicated by other institutions focusing on childhood asthma. In addition, it will serve as a model of comprehensive, community-based health care provision for a wide range of illnesses and age groups. By serving as a model for forging vital ties to the community to ensure improved, cost-efficient health care for all, this initiative will have a wide range of positive implications and benefits for the medical establishment and the communities that require greater access to affordable, managed, comprehensive medical care.

The partnership hopes that by utilizing an illness that is most prevalent in the community, efforts to mobilize the community and establish linkages within a network of care will be greatly facilitated and enhanced. The partnership is certain that if resources can be devoted to engage a coordinator, this initiative can clearly be used to advance the vision of a CCN.

The wide array of health care resources offered by CPMC and the enthusiasm of partnership members provide the opportunity to create a seamless continuum of care for the WHI community. It is already evident that the ACNC and the community's independent physicians can come together to meet the primary care needs of the WHI population. Similarly, specialty care can be made more accessible. The VNA has expressed an interest in enhancing the provision of care, along with a large nursing home in the community. CPMC will provide all medical services for the program and will hire the appropriate resources, provide vital in-kind support, and ensure funding. The ACNC will expedite implementation. The wide range of additional resources provided by CPMC will be a major asset for the program. NMC! will help provide access to the community, promote the program, and disseminate information.

Alianza Dominicana has worked on similar projects with the hospital in the past to promote wellness, immunizations, and school programs, and will ensure the community's greater acceptance and endorsement of the program.

SUMMARY OF NOTABLE PROGRESS

The Columbia-Presbyterian CCN has made major progress during the past year in developing a greater focus on community health and expanding its continuum of care. Both the high rate of adolescent pregnancy and the lack of services for pregnant teens were initially identified as one of the community's most serious health issues. The Columbia University School of Public Health, a network partner, provided the leadership necessary to involve the administrators of George Washington High School in developing a school-based clinic program, which attracted financing by the State Department of Health. Last fall, this comprehensive primary care clinic, serving a student body of 3,700, began operations staffed by a complement of physicians, nurse practitioners, social workers, and others. The staff is experienced in responding to the medical and psychosocial needs of low-income immigrant youth, who make up the majority of the students. There is a special focus on education regarding family planning and HIV counseling by health educators as well as a midwife who sees pregnant students on a regular basis. The midwife is part of a larger group of midwives who deliver at CPMC.

ACNC, the Presbyterian Hospital's ambulatory health care network, adjusted the service focus of its new community-based primary care facility and initiated a midwifery practice especially sensitive to the needs of younger women. Although each patient is assigned to one midwife who closely follows her pregnancy, every patient meets all the members of the midwifery team, knowing that one of them will perform the delivery. Fridays are devoted to educational activities conducted by the midwifery team, which include: Lamaze method, exercise, nutrition, parenting, breast-feeding, and early child care.

In addition to the issue of teen pregnancy, the focus on community needs in Washington Heights led to identification of the lack of mental health services for the almost 100,000 Spanish-speaking immigrants as a major priority. Alianza Dominicana sought to respond to that need but lacked the experience and certification required to provide psychiatric intervention. Through the newly developed collaboration of service providers, a memorandum of understanding was signed between the Department of Psychiatry of The Presbyterian Hospital and Alianza Dominicana that will result in a program with the full range of mental health and alcoholism treatment services. (See figure 2-1.) The expertise in group, family, and individual counseling of this nationally recognized psychiatry department was joined with the social services experience and cultural competence of the Dominican organization to create a specialized project that was enthusiastically funded by the New York City Department of Mental Health.

As one can see, the Columbia-Presbyterian CCN is being driven by the vision of a healthy community and the role that can be played by the different partners in achieving it. The parties have proven extremely agile in aligning their programs to respond more directly to the health care needs identified by the CCN. The Presbyterian Hospital, a network partner, has established a new not-for-profit Medicaid managed care insurance company in association with two other hospitals serving northern Manhattan. The next step in advancing the CCN vision will include managing and improving the health of the community within fixed resources set by the state's Medicaid program.

Contact: Cesar Perales
Columbia-Presbyterian Medical Center
161 Fort Washington Ave.
14th floor
New York, NY 10032
Phone: (212) 305-8041
Fax: (212) 305-3637

FIGURE 2-1. Memorandum of Understanding (revised 2/20/96)

Alianza Dominicana, Inc. [establishes a subcontract for services from]
The Presbyterian Hospital in the City of New York

Subcontract:

Alianza Dominicana, Inc., and Presbyterian Hospital agree to enter into a subcontracting agreement to provide services according to the following outlines:

Scope of Work:

Mental Health Treatment
1. Individual/Group
2. Family
3. Psycho-social Evaluation
4. Medication Monitoring

Alcoholism Treatment
1. Urine Monitoring
2. AA Groups Monitoring
3. X-Rays/TS Screening
4. Group Treatment
5. Individual Sessions

Referral/Intake Process:

Subcontractor must identify key intake staff who will be directly responsible for processing all Alianza's referrals. Alianza identifies Ms. Sandra Harris as the Director of the Family Center program, or her designee, as the contract person for clarification and trouble-shooting around referral/intake procedures.

All Alianza-generated referrals, and other clients seen in fulfillment of this subcontract, must be clearly identifiable in whatever intake instrument is utilized. The intake form for Alianza's referring source's name, phone number, the Alianza program the source is calling from, and the date of the referral. All other outside referrals and/or walk-ins must also follow the above process with the exception that the referral source will be identified accordingly. The parties shall agree on protocol around record keeping.

Referral Response Protocol:

All Alianza-generated referrals are deemed to have priority. The time response for the average referral should not exceed the 2-week period between the referral date and the first face-to-face contact with the participant. Between the time of the referral and the initial visit, Alianza will process all entitlement applications the patient is eligible for. Alianza reserves the right to identify some cases as warranting an expedited or immediate response priority. Such cases will be kept to a minimum to the degree possible.

Documentation:

All participants' involvement in treatment—whether in groups, individual, or family, must be duly documented in participant-specific charts that must include:

- Referral/Intake form
- Initial Assessment
- Clearly Delineated Service Plan that includes a projected termination date.
- Evidence of worker's contract for work with the participant
- Ongoing process and/or Group notes
- Where applicable, the TB/X-ray results
- Where applicable, the urine toxicology
- Where applicable, Psycho-social evaluation

FIGURE 2-1. (Continued)

Service Coordination and Confidentiality:

All Alianza-generated referrals, and other clients seen in fulfillment of the subcontract, are deemed to be Alianza's primary clients who are receiving ancillary services from the subcontractor. It is important that all participants are made aware of the fact that all casework information will be shared and the work will be coordinated with the referring Alianza staff and/or the identified coordinator. The Subcontractor shall under no circumstance withhold participants' information from the primary provider. The Alianza referring source will have each participant sign a release of information prior to making the referral. The Alianza staff will explain the subcontractual relationship between the agency and the subcontracted entity. The staff will also explain the rationale behind subcontracting this service and the need to openly share the client's information in the coordinated service effort.

Coordinated services implies a direct open line of communication between the subcontracted service provider at the Alianza referring staff. The subcontractor must be available for a minimum of one face-to-face conference once per quarter per case. Alianza referring staff must have access to participants' progress both in the verbal and written form as needed.

Service Levels:

The mental health component shall have an average of 124.75 monthly contact units for a total of 1,497 contacts annually. This is inclusive of group contacts which are counted on a unit basis in accordance with the number of individuals present for the groups. The Alcoholism component shall have an average of 50 monthly contact units for a total of 600 annually. These service levels may be reviewed and considered for adjustment at any time during the contract.

However, since the first year of the subcontract will start April 1, 1996 and end June 30, 1996 the total contacts will be 524 for the abbreviated period.

Budget:

The budget shall not exceed $115,000, prorated to $28,764 for the abbreviated first year. Thereafter, the budget will be amended, based upon the normal cost of living increase awarded to Presbyterian Hospital staff. A detailed budget shall be submitted as part of the subcontract. Payments shall be made according to the standard agency policy. However, in the first year of the contract Alianza will make two payments to Presbyterian Hospital at the beginning of the subcontract at one-third of the prorated amount and will be reconciled after June 30, 1996 for the final payment.

Compliance:

All activities under the terms of this subcontract are subject to compliance under standard NYCDMH contracting procedures and specific compliance under the terms of Alianza Dominicana, Inc.'s services to Immigrant Populations contract with the NYCDMH.

Contracting Period:

Services under this subcontract shall be provided April 1, 1996, through June 30, 1996. Alianza Dominicana, Inc., retains the right to subsequent renewals.

Name Title Date

---

for Association of Alianza Dominicana, Inc.

Name Title Date

---

for the Presbyterian Hospital in the City of New York

3

The Portsmouth Mayor's Health Services Advisory Committee

Executive Summary

Portsmouth is a community that cares for and about its people. Although we are but a part of the Hampton Roads area of Virginia, our city is composed of neighborhoods that have roots into the 1700s, and we contribute daily to the life and vitality of the larger area. With a population of somewhat more than 100,000 citizens, we are big enough to make a difference and yet small enough to be a family. Our health problems are many, but our potential to solve these problems and work together is great. Because we work together, we have been successful in expanding health care initiatives and educating more of our citizens in the importance of preventing and reducing risks.

The Mayor's Health Services Advisory Committee (the Committee) is an initiative begun in 1990 when the Commonwealth of Virginia required all jurisdictions to conduct a health care needs assessment. We saw in the Committee a golden opportunity to plan for our community's health and not just react to its illnesses. By combining into a single forum the representatives of the health profession and the representatives of the community, we have been able to address issues as diverse as the need for a community health center and the role our rivers and environment play in keeping us all healthy. As Mayor, I rely on the Committee's advice and direction. By doing so, the Portsmouth family can develop the health care services most needed, prevent duplication, capitalize on successful programs, and afford every citizen a voice in determining their health care destiny. A representative body is a powerful force in dealing with government and the private sector.

Through initiatives such as the Community Health Center and the Sunshine School/Community Health Center, many citizens are now receiving regular and routine health services, which were not available in the past. Of equal importance, citizens are volunteering their time, energy, and skills to programs and projects initiated either directly or indirectly by the Committee. We have learned the importance of working together, sharing critical information, and encouraging involvement of the whole Portsmouth family. I believe that what we are doing is bringing to life the community care network (CCN) vision. Thanks for allowing us to share that with you.

Dr. James W. Holley III, Mayor
City of Portsmouth

THE COMMUNITY

Portsmouth is an independent city located in the Hampton Roads area of Virginia. The 28th largest Metropolitan Statistical Area (MSA) in the nation, the Hampton Roads area includes Norfolk, Chesapeake, Virginia Beach, Suffolk, Newport News, Hampton, Williamsburg, Poquoson, and the counties of York, James City, and Gloucester. The population of the MSA is 1.4 million. Bordered by some of these independent cities and the Elizabeth River, Portsmouth therefore has no land to acquire for growth. As a result of the high concentration of state, federal, and tax-exempt property within the city limits, Portsmouth has a higher percentage of nontaxable property than Washington, D.C.

Portsmouth demonstrates all the characteristics that plague every U.S. inner city. For example, it has the second highest homicide rate in Virginia, an above-average unemployment rate, and a small land area that provides a poor tax base. The school system is losing students, which is reflected in below-average standardized test scores. Because of poverty, 56 percent of public school students receive free or reduced-rate lunches. Adjacent bedroom communities are attractive to middle-income citizens, which contributes to the loss of retail business to the surrounding suburbs. Most recently, there have been major job layoffs (1,100) as a result of military base closings, fewer ships to repair, and the downsizing of the U.S. Department of Defense. With these problems comes loss of health care benefits and a bleak picture for future employment. The number of citizens who will not be able to afford health care will certainly grow as a result. These worsening conditions have exacerbated the health problems linked to the poverty rate in Portsmouth.

According to the 1990 census, the population of Portsmouth is 103,800—almost evenly divided among Caucasians and non-Caucasians. Females constitute 52 percent of the population. Overall, the population declined by 1 percent during the 1980s. This decline was not evenly distributed: The population aged 0–4, 15–24, and 50–59 declined, while the population aged 30–44 and over 65 increased. The February 1995 unemployment rate was 6.2 percent, compared with an MSA rate of 4.8 percent, a state rate of 4.5 percent, and a national rate of 5.9 percent for the same period.

The poverty population in Portsmouth includes 22,660 residents, amounting to 22 percent of the total population. The poverty rate among Caucasians is 9 percent, compared with 35 percent among non-Caucasians. Three groups account for over half of the poverty population: children under the age of 14, females between the ages of 15 and 44, and adults over the age of 65. Those groups account for virtually all residents who receive public assistance. Another 2,000 to 4,000 residents are eligible for public medical assistance but either have not attempted or have not completed the application process. If the definition of poverty is expanded to include persons with income less than 200 percent of the federal poverty level, the poverty population increases to 41,000 residents, representing 40 percent of the total population. This broader definition more closely approximates the number of medically indigent residents in Portsmouth.

Portsmouth has a 5-year average infant mortality rate of 17.0, 60 percent higher than the 11.1 state rate. Portsmouth's morbidity/mortality rates for conditions such as cancer, heart disease, and stroke are also higher overall than the state rates. Additionally, communicable disease rates for Portsmouth are much higher overall than the regional and state rates. The cumulative effects of these rates of disease, combined with the rates of poverty, aged population, and unemployment, rank Portsmouth as a medically underserved area (MUA) by the state health department. Among the 136 localities in Virginia, 104 were better off than Portsmouth. On a scale of severity ranging from 4 (least severe) to 20 (most severe), Portsmouth scored 16. As poor as this overall status is, it most likely still understates the severity of health status among the poor.

THE PARTNERSHIP

The driving partnership in Portsmouth's efforts to develop a CCN is the Mayor's Health Services Advisory Committee. The Committee was formed in 1990 as a direct result of state legislation known as SJR-179, which required that all Virginia jurisdictions conduct a health care needs assessment. As a result of that assessment, the Committee decided to create a health care environment to address the needs through a strategic plan, with specific goals and objectives. Although the Committee could easily have disbanded at the conclusion of the needs assessment, it approached the mayor and requested the authority to continue. With that in hand, the Committee immediately began its work of addressing the identified needs.

Chaired by the health director, the Committee's representative membership includes Maryview Medical Center, Portsmouth General Hospital, Naval Medical Center Portsmouth (Portsmouth Naval Hospital), Portsmouth Public Schools, the Portsmouth Health Department, Portsmouth Academy of Medicine (local medical society), Eastern Virginia Medical School (EVMS) (local medical school), Portsmouth General Hospital Foundation (the Foundation), Portsmouth Community Health Center, Elm Avenue Center for Health (EACH) (indigent care clinic), the Ministerial Forum (local clergy organization), Portsmouth Academy of Medical Alliance, the Portsmouth Department of Social Services, and citizens from the community. Other agencies that work with the Committee include the Portsmouth Redevelopment and Housing Authority, agencies of city and state government, and many not-for-profit social service agencies in Portsmouth.

Beyond the Committee are numerous coalitions and alliances composed wholly or partially of Committee members. For example, the Portsmouth Community Development Group (PCDG) and volunteer physicians and nurses from an evening acute care clinic are kept informed of the Committee's activities and take part in many of them. Another example is the Portsmouth Area Resource Coalition (PARC), a not-for-profit agency comprising many of the city's churches, which provides homeless shelters and transitional housing services. It is important to note that these agencies work in concert with each other for already scarce resources.

The partnership's membership is representative of the city's health needs. Problems are generally addressed by task forces, so that once the initial problem is resolved, the task force disbands but the Committee remains intact. Examples of topics addressed by the task force include the following:

- Obstetrical services for single mothers who lack health care services
- The development of a community health center
- HIV/AIDS in the community

PRIOR EFFORTS THAT REPRESENT MOVEMENT TOWARD THE COMMUNITY CARE NETWORK VISION

Prior to 1990, although there was a general belief that many of Portsmouth's citizens lacked health care, that was difficult to prove. In an effort to quantify needs and identify the complexity of the problem, the Foundation commissioned a report to study indigent health care in Portsmouth. The report was prepared by EVMS, Old Dominion University, and Norfolk State University. All three are located in Norfolk, only five minutes from downtown Portsmouth. The results were startling: Portsmouth physicians reported that 83 percent of Portsmouth's indigent population is at least sometimes unable to receive services, and 40 percent of the city's total population was at 200 percent or less of the poverty line.

The report did not go unheeded. The Foundation, which had just provided seed money for a clinic staffed by a nurse practitioner, renewed that grant and encouraged similar projects. A chronology of initiatives and projects follows, demonstrating how Portsmouth has taken a systematic approach to providing health care to those in the community most in need of it:

- *1989:* The Foundation provided full first-year funding for the EACH. This project was critical for two reasons. First, it was the first indigent care clinic to open in the city, besides the chronic care clinic at the Portsmouth Health Department, which eventually closed as a result of cuts in state funding. Second, it was the anchor for reclaiming an entire neighborhood. The PCDG began work in Prentis Place 2 years later and has facilitated a dramatic turnaround in a dying neighborhood. The work in that neighborhood continues and has been successful, and the concept has expanded to two other Portsmouth neighborhoods. The establishment of EACH also resulted in a better working relationship between the two hospitals in Portsmouth, with each contributing surplus equipment, services, and so forth. Finally, EACH has generated a corps of physician volunteers, which was previously nonexistent,
- *1990:* The indigent care study was funded, with two local universities and a medical school taking part. This provided the baseline data and helped to establish a game plan for creating a continuum of medical care for the poor. It also identified major and minor players.
- *1990:* SJR-179 created the Mayor's Health Services Advisory Committee. The Committee created a single body of key players who could both plan and implement the continuum of care, which is in fact the vision. Although not every agency that has a hand in providing health care and social services is on the Committee, key Committee members represent all those interests and share information. For example, the Director of Social Services represents and shares with those agencies and churches dealing with housing, spousal abuse, the homeless, meal programs, and so forth.

- *1990–91:* Through its family practice program, EVMS identified a major problem with service patients being released from the hospitals and then returning in worse condition than the first time because they had received no follow-up care. The faculty and residents, on a voluntary basis, established a small clinic at Portsmouth General Hospital to try to resolve the problem, which far exceeded available resources. It is important to remember that Portsmouth has a significant elderly population, a large population in the danger zone (drug users, alcoholics, and so forth), and a very poor population. All these risk factors add up to poor follow-up care, inability to buy prescriptions, and misunderstanding of or inattention to discharge orders. In 1992, EVMS received a grant from the Foundation to establish a postdischarge clinic two evenings per week. The clinic was a combined effort of EVMS, the two hospitals, the Portsmouth Health Department, and a local pharmacy. The health department provided space pro bono. EVMS provided medical students, initially on a volunteer basis, also pro bono. Board-certified physicians as well as support staff were paid through a grant. The clinic not only reduced the number of postdischarge visits and admissions to the hospitals, but also allowed the medical students to do a thorough social history of each patient, which is a critical piece in terms of securing additional health and social services. Serving at the clinic proved so popular with medical students that it was incorporated into the curriculum. The clinic was incorporated into the Community Health Center in 1995. EVMS will still provide students at that site.
- *1992:* The Committee began tackling the problem of obstetrical and gynecological coverage for service patients on nights and weekends. Through a joint venture with the hospitals, city government, and a private practice firm of obstetricians and gynecologists, the coverage issue was resolved and funding is now included in the city budget.
- *1992:* The Committee began exploring initiatives to obtain a federal grant to plan for and open a community health center (CHC). The first grant application was denied. The following year, a planning grant was received, and in 1994, funding was provided. This huge community project was orchestrated by the Committee until the CHC board was formed. The Foundation funded team-building seminars and retreats for the new board, which allowed them to work cohesively. Because Portsmouth is only 30 square miles, locating the CHC in the middle of the MUA brings it within fairly easy reach of most citizens who will use it. A host of agencies and organizations became involved in its development, from board selection to site selection, from equipping it to staffing it. The CHC serves as the medical home for many programs, allowing us to draw closer to the vision. Some older programs, such as EACH and the postdischarge clinic, were incorporated into the CHC with no loss of service.
- *1992:* While the EVMS postdischarge clinic was being born, the Portsmouth Academy of Medicine began planning for an evening indigent acute care clinic. The clinic is staffed completely by volunteers, from physicians to nurses to health educators. Once again, the Portsmouth Health Department became a willing partner, providing pro bono space, and once again the hospitals became involved as well. In 1993, the Portsmouth Academy of Medicine Acute Care Clinic opened. It developed a close working relationship with the other clinics, and academy members who are specialists agreed to see clinic patients in their offices on referral. The clinic will remain open but will relocate to the CHC site. It is noteworthy

that the physician community recognizes that although the CHC will provide a valuable service, it is not a panacea, and other systems must remain in place. Another piece of the vision falls into place.

- *1992:* One of the primary health care issues identified in Portsmouth is the number of teen pregnancies. The Foundation funded a community study to determine intervention strategies and used that study to help make decisions about its future grant-making efforts in that area. One of the most prominent and recurring recommendations from citizens attending the focus groups was the need for a pregnancy prevention "czar" to coordinate programs and services. With that foremost in mind, the Foundation responded by funding a pregnancy prevention coordinator through the Better Beginnings Coalition (BBC). This was followed by additional programs such as Resource Mothers and the Teen Pregnancy Prevention Initiative. By using the BBC as an advisory board to all these projects, time was saved and services were well coordinated, preventing duplication and waste. All these projects are ongoing, and the Portsmouth BBC was recognized with a national award in 1994.
- *1993:* The public school system had long recognized the need for health care that went beyond the school nurse. With the support of the Committee, the school system applied for and received a planning grant to develop a community/school center. Following a year of planning, the system then received a grant to open and staff the center with a part-time physician, full-time nurse practitioner, and support staff. Maryview Medical Center, Portsmouth General Hospital, and the city government all provided surplus equipment. The Foundation provided matching funds, and Portsmouth Naval Hospital is working with the center to provide volunteer health educators and other volunteer personnel for after-school hours. The center has opened in a middle school adjacent to Maryview Medical Center, and is available to all students in the community. It is another piece in the continuum of care in our community.
- *1993:* Recognizing the need for pediatric case management, a grant application was submitted to implement a comprehensive health investment project (CHIP), a community-based partnership between the Portsmouth Health Department, the STOP organization (a local antipoverty program), and private physicians and dentists. CHIP families are assigned to a care coordination team that consists of a public health nurse, case worker, physician, and dentist. The CHIP team's goal is to provide comprehensive preventive and acute care for children and to improve their general health and well-being. In 1994, first-year funding of $180,000 was approved, with additional funding anticipated over the coming years.
- *1994:* Because of the high number of teen pregnancies, coupled with all the risk factors associated with them, many children are not receiving any or all of their immunizations until age five, when they are required to attend school. The Portsmouth Health Department established a small manual tracking system, which demonstrated that constant tracking, coupled with frequent and consistent reminders, does make a difference within the target population. Based on that small success story, a not-for-profit organization, Hands Across Portsmouth for Preschool Immunizations, came into being. Composed of hospital, public health, foundation, community, and physician representatives, it applied for and received a grant in 1995 to purchase a computerized immunization tracking system modeled after the Boston program. Critical to making this successful was the involvement of every pediatric practice in the city. As a result, every clinic, hospital, primary

care physician, and emergency care center in the Portsmouth area will have access to a data bank of pediatric immunization records, allowing for prompt immunization whenever a pediatric patient is presented.

- *1994:* After several years of providing small grants to several not-for-profit health and social service agencies for prescription drugs, the Foundation met with these agencies as a group and asked them to merge their activities, data collection, and service delivery relative to prescription drugs. In 1995, the Foundation funded a proposal for $30,000 from the Portsmouth Medical Assistance Program. This program will be administered by the Portsmouth Department of Social Services, and is actively pursuing other funding to achieve a goal of $100,000.
- *1995:* It was announced that Medicaid funding in the Hampton Roads area, including Portsmouth, will be administered by four HMOs. This will have an impact on most providers.

All these efforts have come in an age of less funding, not more. To control costs, we have relied on several different strategies. First, we have created systems that are not redundant. A good example is the pharmaceutical program. Second, we are reducing the opportunity for patients to be seen in more than one location for the same illness or injury. An example is the computerized immunization records system for children. Third, we have asked the entire medical community to provide pro bono care to the extent to which they feel comfortable. This has been demonstrated through the EACH and the Portsmouth Academy of Medicine Acute Care Clinic. Fourth, the Committee has undertaken the task of seeking funding from alternative revenue sources (foundation and government grants) in an orderly, planned manner. Finally, we recognize the importance of collaborative efforts and plan and provide services accordingly.

MOVING TOWARD THE CCN VISION: VISION AND VISIONING PROCESS

The CCN vision reemphasizes, and lends substance to, the journey on which the Committee embarked in 1990. We understood the need all along; what we needed to do was improve on the process, the logic, and ultimately the provision of health care services. In Portsmouth, that means a grassroots effort to involve both the medical community and the community at large in planning resolutions to the problems and then implementing those plans. (See figure 3-1.) Sometimes this has been incremental, sometimes systematic. What the vision allows—in fact, demands—is that we stick to the systematic approach. Portsmouth is not going to become a wealthy city; we are not going to gain many new businesses or clean industries simply because the Hampton Roads urban environment does not need Portsmouth to be involved in that. What we do see happening is decreasing inpatient use of our hospitals, a growing use of home health care professionals, more preventive medicine, much more health care education, and a requirement for all our citizens, indigent or not, to make choices about their personal health care. The vision allows us to begin to use these forecasts in a formula that allows for the best health care available under these circumstances. Today we do not have that, although we have come a long way in the past few years. In reality, the vision today is much better defined than a simple "light at the end of the tunnel."

FIGURE 3-1. Mayor's Health Services Advisory Committee

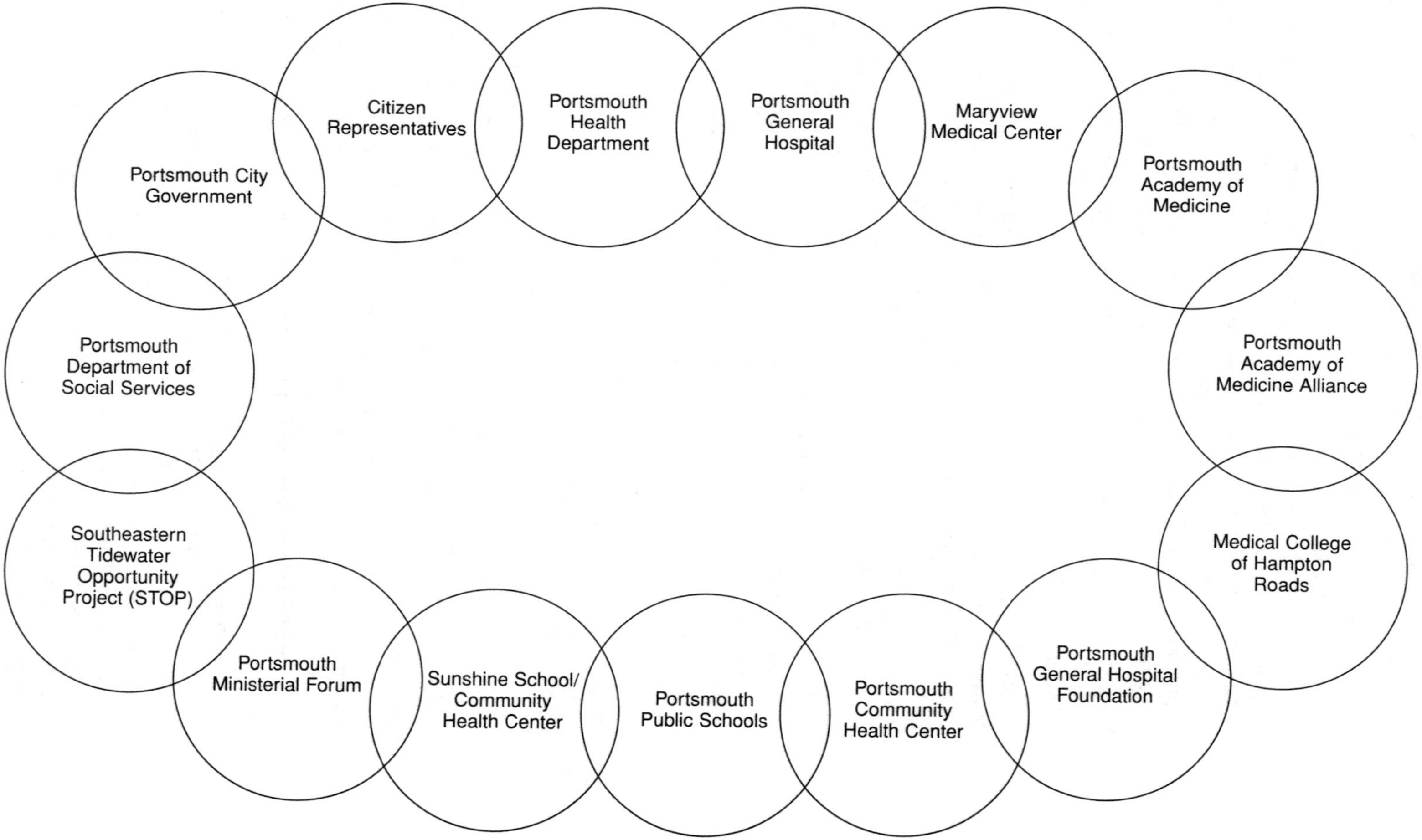

In 1990, the Committee had a single mission and goal: to conduct a community health needs assessment within the time frame prescribed by the state law and present it to the appropriate agencies. In 1995, that changed to an action plan and implementation schedule, with continuous revision of both the plan and the schedule. The vision is a more conscientious revision of both. On February 16, 1995, the Committee unanimously approved the following vision statement, goals, and objectives:

Vision Statement

The Portsmouth Mayor's Health Services Advisory Committee will strive to ensure the availability and accessibility of health services to Portsmouth residents, and the funding necessary to support those services. (See figure 3-2.)

Vision Goals and Objectives

- *Goal 1:* Develop a system of health care in Portsmouth that promotes the provision of high-quality, accessible, affordable primary care services for Portsmouth residents in a comprehensive and coordinated manner.
  - *Objective 1:* Make available to the public a list of transportation alternatives and assist in the development of alternatives where they are lacking.
  - *Objective 2:* Develop two grant applications annually to increase the availability and accessibility of health care.
  - *Objective 3:* Support the implementation by 1995 of the Portsmouth Community Health Center and the School/Community Health Center.

FIGURE 3-2. Tools for Success

One of the most critical tools is valid baseline data. When we began the CCN process and proceeded to craft a full proposal, we had to know what our needs were. Because the Committee was formed in 1990 to conduct a state-mandated health care needs assessment, we had a significant amount of data available. This was combined with other community data resources, such as the following:

- 1990 census data, provided through the Portsmouth Planning Department
- 1991 indigent health care survey, conducted by a consortium of local universities and funded by a local foundation
- Local community data, provided through various local government agencies and not-for-profit service providers

All such data are considered nonproprietary and should be shared with other agencies in your community who are seeking funding from a multitude of sources. By its very nature, baseline data have little value if they are dramatically out of date and therefore inaccurate. Be willing to commit some resources to keep them current.

Keep meetings on time and on track. Delegate. Use a total quality management process to guarantee that the meetings are not too lengthy or overloaded with topics to be covered. Recognize your limitations in this regard. The CCN vision is a hefty project that cannot be achieved in a short time frame.

Completion of the planning process was estimated to be September 1996, with implementation beginning immediately thereafter.

- Plan for and develop a transportation network that will guarantee a variety of ways to keep medical appointments. The goal is to advise patients of transportation options currently available and develop new ones. The primary objectives are as follows:

  —Advise patients through a variety of ways on what transportation is available to them.

  —Develop both a voluntary transportation service, coordinated though the Ministerial Forum or similar organization, and new routes, stops, and services by Tidewater Regional Transit.

  The first objective was scheduled to be accomplished by September 1996; the second objective, by September 1997.

- Develop a marketing strategy for health education and preventive health services. The goal is to develop both ordinary and novel ways of telling our citizens what health care is available and why they need it. The primary objectives are as follows:

  —Develop a marketing plan, including print, radio, television, and billboards.

  —Decide on what we are marketing and what results we expect.

  —Market it.

  This project was scheduled to be implemented by September 1997.

- Make the public schools full partners in this entire project and develop methods to use the schools in health education and disease prevention efforts. At the same time, capitalize more fully on the Sunshine School/Community Health Center. The goal is to have healthy, nonpregnant students. The primary objectives are as follows:

  —Develop an aggressive health care curriculum at all grade levels.

  —Encourage students who do not have a medical home to use the Sunshine School/Community Health Center.

  —Provide both treatment and preventive health education at the Sunshine School/Community Health Center.

  —Study the need for expanding the school/community health center system.

  Because of the political nature of the school board, we cannot predict a date for achieving these objectives. Some may involve windows of opportunity that simply cannot be defined.

- Reassess the community's health, including all members of the community and not just those who are medically indigent. The goal is to define the state of Portsmouth's health in current terms and to continuously do so as needed. Primary objectives are as follows:

  —Develop a plan, with the technical assistance necessary, to conduct the assessment.

  —Conduct the assessment.

  —Utilize the assessment data as needed.

  —Conduct additional assessments, either full or partial, as needed.

  Planning, conducting the assessment, and analyzing the data were scheduled to be completed by December 1996.

- Create a system of follow-up care, particularly in the area of medications/pharmaceuticals. Patients who do not follow up because they lack medications ultimately present themselves at a later date in a far more serious condition than when initially treated. The goal is compliance with physician directives to solve the medical problem, with the ultimate goal of becoming a healthier person. Primary objectives are as follows:

  —Enhance the current pharmaceutical assistance program so that no patient is noncompliant as a result of lack of pharmaceuticals.

  —Provide patient education as follow-up care.

  Both of these objectives are ongoing. Initial achievement for the pharmaceutical objective was scheduled for December 1995; for the education objective, September 1996.

- Identify and utilize all community resources that may have any bearing on improved health care in Portsmouth. Create a system of service delivery. Explore ways to have the Portsmouth Naval Hospital become more involved. The goal is to not miss any community opportunities to improve its own health. Primary objectives are as follows:

  —Create a community medical resource directory.

  —Remove barriers to the system concept by changing the paradigm to a barrier-free collaborative model.

  —Meet with the Commanding Officer, Portsmouth Naval Hospital, to explore areas of mutual concern and areas where the Navy's medical staff and expertise can be shared with the Portsmouth community.

  We are already exploring the medical resources directory, with possible grant funding in the near future. The barrier-free delivery system is a long-term project, with finalization in September 1998.

- Make it dramatically clear to city government that the community's health is of major importance in making the city whole and more functional. Use city resources already in place to share this importance with all citizens, individually and collectively. The goal is to make city officials, elected and appointed, aware of our city's health needs. Primary objectives are as follows:

  —Include good health in the city's goals and objectives.

  —Provide city services that enhance health.

  By December 1995, the city's goals were to include the importance of our citizens' health, singularly and collectively. The dates for providing specific city services vary depending on cost, scheduling, staffing, complexity, and other issues.

Technical assistance will be needed in the following areas:

- *Marketing:* We need to develop new ways to not only sell good health to the public but also guarantee compliance with our product. This is a tough market to crack; obviously, we have not been doing it well. Marketing staffs at local health care institutions, as well as major local marketing firms, will be approached for assistance.

- *Computerization:* From both a cost as well as technical perspective, we need to know whether developing and using patient data systems are feasible, and then how to do it and how much it will cost. We need to be very specific in defining our needs and then seeking assistance. Local hospitals, physician group practices, and city government may all be able to provide technical assistance.

- *Community health assessment and analysis:* If we are going to determine the state of the city's health and health care delivery systems, then methodology, survey instruments, population, types of analysis, and so forth all need to be determined. One of the local universities or the EVMS can provide this type of assistance.

SUMMARY OF NOTABLE PROGRESS

The basis for fulfilling the CCN vision is knowing the health care needs of one's community. Because it had been several years since Portsmouth conducted a health care needs assessment, we believed it was important to conduct a new one. With funding from the Foundation, a consortium of Old Dominion University, Norfolk State University, and Eastern Virginia Medical School (EVMS) has embarked on a health care needs assessment that will also factor in a multitude of economic and social indicators. This project, begun in July 1996, is scheduled for completion by March 1997. Full text will be provided to all not-for-profit organizations in Portsmouth to use as background information in any grant proposals they generate. In addition, copies will be available in public places such as libraries and government offices. Executive summaries will be given to all physicians. Because the Committee coordinates and initiates most new health-related programs in Portsmouth, the assessment data will also help us develop strategies and refine our goals and objectives.

The Portsmouth CHC, planned and developed by the Committee, has grown and also provides services to other not-for-profit health care organizations. A real sign of progress is the addition of a second full-time physician (pediatrician) and continued growth of community outreach initiatives. A second nurse practitioner and a gynecologist are also volunteering their services on a part-time basis. Additional initiatives, such as a podiatry clinic, are being discussed. Other health care agencies, such as the BBC, are now located at the CHC, providing the convenience of "one-stop health shopping." Since opening in May 1995, the Portsmouth CHC has become the primary care provider for 3,400 new patients.

The Committee is developing a marketing strategy using both government and private resources. Important health information, as well as information about the Committee itself, will soon be disseminated in a variety of ways, including the following:

- Coverage on our local government cable channel
- Informational flyers included in public utility bills
- Possible coverage on the local cable affiliate channel
- More inclusion in the local newspaper

The Portsmouth marketing and communications director and his staff will provide assistance. This is an ongoing project.

EVMS, which is represented on the Committee, is vitally involved in providing indigent care by supplying faculty and students to the Portsmouth community. The free evening clinic that EVMS provided for 3 years served as the basis for the CHC. Today, as part of their clinical training, medical students at the CHC improve their skills in diagnosing diseases and illnesses, learn how to take social and medical histories, and begin to recognize the problems of the medically indigent in receiving episodic care.

The four examples cited represent a broad picture of actions being taken and goals being achieved. Frequently, an approach to one goal will lead to initiatives that help fulfill another. As goals are ranked and reviewed and resources become available, the continuum of care begins to take shape and becomes fluid, not static.

Contact: Alan E. Gollihue
Executive Director
Portsmouth General Hospital Foundation
P.O. Box 1053
Portsmouth, VA 23705
Phone: (757) 398-4661
Fax: (757) 398-4353

4

The Somerbridge Communtity Health Partnership

Executive Summary

In the aftermath of the failed national health care reform debate, the attention of those committed to health care access has again focused closer to home. For many years, using slightly different methods, health and human service providers and community activists in Somerville and Cambridge have worked on local solutions to the health problems confronted by our communities.

Somerville and Cambridge have a combined population of 170,000. This population is extremely diverse from a socioeconomic, demographic, and cultural perspective. Both cities have experienced significant growth in immigrant populations, with dozens of languages spoken in the homes of these newly arrived residents. Both communities also have extensive health and human service networks and a high level of community activism.

Both Cambridge Hospital and Somerville Hospital have worked for years in collaboration with their respective communities. Separately, both cities conducted community needs assessments in partnership with their community hospitals. This work served to strengthen the connection between the hospitals and residents of each city. It also influenced programs and services provided by the hospitals. However, this work was not coordinated between the two cities until the opportunity for closer collaboration was presented through the community care network (CCN) program.

Through the CCN vision, the Somerbridge Community Health Partnership will facilitate this ongoing community health effort across both cities. The three issue initiatives of Somerbridge—substance abuse, geriatric health, and immigrant health—were identified as top priorities through the community needs assessment. It is our dream, as chief executives, that this new collaboration will result in greater opportunities for the residents of our cities as cooperation and improvement guide this project. We truly believe that the Somerbridge partnership will serve as a model of collaboration for other communities to replicate.

Michael E. Capuano, Mayor, City of Somerville
Robert W. Healy, City Manager, City of Cambridge

THE COMMUNITY

The cities of Cambridge and Somerville, MA, are adjacent urban communities that share a four-mile border across the Charles River from Boston. Both cities have large working-class and minority populations, with 26 percent of residents living below 200 percent federal poverty levels and a significant (15 percent) proportion of all children under 18 living under 100 percent of the poverty level.

Cambridge is well known for its progressive politics, prestigious academic universities, and innovative biotechnological industries. It is less well known as home to 95,802 residents of diverse socioeconomic and cultural backgrounds, living together in roughly six square miles. Twenty-eight percent of Cambridge residents are from minority racial or ethnic groups, reflecting a 50 percent increase in immigration in the past decade. The public schools report 50 different primary languages spoken in the home.

Somerville is a densely populated city of 76,210 people with a diverse socio-ethnic population. Over the past 20 years, Portuguese, Brazilian, Latino, and Haitian immigrants have formed communities that overlap the two cities. The growth of the minority population in both cities has been fueled by their status as sanctuary cities. In Somerville, the minority population grew from 4 percent in 1980 to 11 percent in 1990, a 190 percent increase. Twenty-six percent of Somerville residents speak a language other than English at home.

Both Cambridge and Somerville face problems typical of larger urban areas, such as substance abuse, violence, homelessness, teenage pregnancy, and AIDS. In both cities, infant mortality and low birth-weight rates, AIDS case rates, deaths from cancer, and alcohol and drug use are all higher than the statewide rates for these health problems. The incidence of tuberculosis and hepatitis B significantly exceed statewide averages. Substance abuse indicators suggest a large intravenous drug–using population and a significant number of residents admitted to inpatient as well as outpatient substance abuse treatment programs.

The definition of our community as "Somerbridge" (Cambridge and Somerville) represents an understanding by the key health care and human service providers in the two cities that collaboration will enhance everyone's efforts to build healthier individuals, families, and communities. The two cities share similar populations and many of the same service providers. Key agencies providing substance abuse, mental health, legal, social, and home care services, as well as transitional housing, pediatric care, and advanced life support consider Cambridge and Somerville to be their service area.

Both Cambridge and Somerville hospitals serve similar and often overlapping populations and have very similar missions. The two hospitals' governing boards have made a commitment to collaborate with all the other health care and human service providers in the community to ensure that a community-based system of health care services in the two cities can remain competitive in a rapidly changing health care environment. During the past several years, both hospitals have independently initiated community-wide forums for comprehensive health assessment and planning. These efforts, conducted separately in Somerville and Cambridge, have identified many of the same health problems.

THE PARTNERSHIP

The Cambridge and Somerville hospitals have long demonstrated their commitment to improving the health of their respective communities and have developed meaningful partnerships with other city and human service agencies for community health planning and program initiatives. Both hospitals have received national recognition for their community service efforts.

Both were among the first hospitals in the United States to have been awarded "Distinguished Recognition" by the Kellogg Foundation's Hospital Community Benefit Standards Program in 1992. Cambridge Hospital's commitment to community service also resulted in its selection by the American Hospital Association in June 1993 as the winner of the Foster G. McGaw Award for Excellence in Community Service. Somerville Hospital was a finalist for the Healthcare Forum Healthier Communities Award in 1993.

The positive experiences of the two hospitals in community health assessment and planning led to initial discussions of how the CCN vision could allow for the expansion of the community definition to include both cities. Representatives of the two hospitals began to discuss the opportunities that could be created through a partnership to address both cities' health problems. A broader planning group was then formed to explore how best to build upon the prior successful experiences of each city's health planning groups and to identify opportunities that would result from bringing both cities together.

The initial planning group included the key leaders involved in each city's community health assessment and planning efforts. It was carefully put together to create a parallel structure with equal representation from each city.

As the group began the visioning process, common interests in underserved populations, root causes of illness (violence, substance abuse, poverty), and populations at risk emerged, which helped cement the partnership. This new partnership has begun to develop a health agenda appropriate to the size and scope of the two communities that define it. We will add membership to represent all the health care institutions serving Cambridge and Somerville, as well as key human service agencies, school and government officials, and private-sector leaders. A structured set of committees and task forces will be established to accomplish the goals described in the section of this chapter titled "Moving toward the Community Care Network Vision."

PRIOR EFFORTS THAT REPRESENT MOVEMENT TOWARD THE COMMUNITY CARE NETWORK VISION

Over the past 5 years, the Somerville and Cambridge hospitals have provided the leadership for community-wide efforts to improve the health status of their communities. In each city, broad-based community coalitions were organized to establish explicit community health priorities and objectives, develop action plans to meet those objectives, and monitor progress.

The Community Health Agenda for Somerville, a formal community health assessment process initiated jointly by the city health department and Somerville

Hospital in 1990, used Assessment Protocol for Excellence in Public Health (APEX-PH) to identify the following priorities: HIV/AIDS, access to health care among immigrants and the uninsured, violence, tobacco, and substance abuse/mental illness. Work groups were established to address each of these issues. A variety of individuals and agencies representing a broad spectrum of the community have been involved in the work groups since they were first established. Results thus far include the following:

- Participation by a wide variety of individuals and organizations in the Community Health Agenda has grown, with 57 organizations and 102 individuals actively participating in the process in 1994.
- The number of community practitioners providing primary care services to HIV-positive patients has increased 266 percent, from 3 in 1992 to 11 in 1993.
- The number of bilingual staff and interpreters at Somerville Hospital more than doubled from 1991 to 1994.
- The local Visiting Nurse Association (VNA), in collaboration with the hospital, sought and received grant funding to expand outreach and services to newcomer families to reduce infant mortality in this population.
- The Somerville Health Department instituted comprehensive tobacco control regulations and developed an extensive new prevention-oriented Tobacco Control Program with $350,000 in new funding.
- Somerville Hospital developed a variety of new services to assist smokers, including "patch clinics" and behavior medicine services.
- A community-wide domestic violence conference was held, which led to the formation of a domestic violence task force for Somerville, coordinated by the district attorney's office. A "Safe Homes" network was established by local religious organizations.

The Cambridge Health Policy Board, responsible for establishing health policy and priorities for the city of Cambridge, is made up of consumers, health care providers, and other professionals. In 1992, the board implemented the APEX-PH community health assessment process and identified 15 health priorities. The top five were violence, immunization of preschoolers under the age of two years, HIV/AIDS, prenatal care, and substance abuse. Community health plans for each of those five problems were developed. Citywide task forces on violence, women's health, HIV/AIDS, and substance abuse became the principal work groups for developing action plans for each of the identified health priorities.

At the same time, the Health of the City consortium was established in 1990 with seed money from the Pew Charitable Trust and the Rockefeller Foundation. The Health of the City brought Harvard Medical School, the business sector, and other health care provider institutions to the table with health policy board members, Cambridge Hospital staff, and city government to improve the health status of the people of Cambridge. The consortium conducted extensive research on the health needs and perceptions of Cambridge citizens and created two citywide task forces, the Men of Color Task Force and the Healthy Children Task Force, to address the needs of its two principal populations of focus. Results thus far include the following:

- An antiviolence coordinator was jointly hired by the Cambridge Department of Health and Hospitals, the Cambridge Department of Human Services, the Cambridge School Department, and the Cambridge Police Department to develop a community-wide approach to preventing gender-based violence.

- The Immunization Action Project was initiated by Cambridge Hospital to provide targeted outreach efforts toward underserved minority populations and to measure progress toward specific immunization rate goals.
- HIV/AIDS prevention and early intervention services increased, including anonymous test site expansion, a new Haitian HIV Outreach and Education Project, and the development of a needle exchange program.
- The first midwife-staffed birthing center in the Boston area was scheduled to open on the grounds of Cambridge Hospital in 1995.
- The Cambridge Substance Abuse Task Force was developed to promote prevention and early intervention, particularly among youth.
- The Men of Color Task Force of the Health of the City hired a coordinator/health promoter who has developed a new men's clinic and targeted outreach programs that have led to increases in utilization of primary care services by men of color.

Each of these activities demonstrates the long-standing commitment of the two hospitals and health departments to improve the health of their communities through prevention of illness or the root causes of illness. The organized community health assessment and planning processes in each city have involved the sustained collaborative efforts of a broad spectrum of health providers, community organizations, and individuals over the past five years. The planning has included the identification of explicit community health objectives, the development of strategies that were expected to lead to improvement, and an organized effort to monitor progress in an ongoing way.

COMMUNITY ACCOUNTABILITY

The structures developed in each of the two cities—the Community Health Agenda for Somerville and the combined Health Policy Board/Health of the City approach in Cambridge—were designed to systematically involve community leaders in a meaningful assessment of the community's health and in the development of health priorities for the future. In each case, the local hospital governing boards agreed to use those priorities as a guide for program development and for resource allocation. In reviewing the programs developed in each city to address the needs identified by the assessment process, it is clear that this kind of systematic and inclusive approach to community health planning has had a remarkable influence on the development of targeted programs and services.

Many different tools have been used to develop and share data on the needs of Cambridge and Somerville residents. The Community Health Agenda for Somerville, the Somerville Collaborative Planning Group, the Cambridge Health Policy Board, and Health of the City developed working groups or task forces that included community organizations providing services to, and serving as advocates for, specific populations such as newcomer groups, men of color, adolescents, or substance abusers. The dialogue in those groups has resulted in increased awareness of and reduced fragmentation and duplication of services, and a significant increase in collaborative efforts. Another approach used by all these groups has been to seek input from community members directly, through town meetings and focus groups.

Focus groups have been conducted with residents of a local housing project regarding the need for primary care services, men of color regarding utilization of a neighborhood health center, and women who have given birth at the hospital regarding development of the birthing center in Cambridge. Knowledge of the community's health needs has also been accumulated through the use of formal surveys. A survey of high school students was administered by the Teen Health Center at the Cambridge Rindge and Latin High School in 1992 and 1994, which yielded valuable information about health concerns, problems, and utilization of services. The information that condom availability at the school-based neighborhood health center had not led to increased sexual activity in the high school in Cambridge, for example, was significant in the school committee debate about whether to allow students to obtain birth control at the Teen Health Center. A survey of residents at a Somerville public housing survey led to the establishment of on-site health screening and Women, Infants and Children (WIC) supplemental food program services. There has been significant progress in both communities toward the development of benchmark data for measuring and holding health care providers accountable to the community for progress toward the following identified goals:

- In both cities there has been a concerted effort to identify statistics on the incidence of gender-based violence and institutional responsiveness.
- The Immunization Action Project, serving both cities, has developed a system for auditing and disseminating immunization rates.
- Anonymous test sites have developed aggregate data sets on utilization of HIV/AIDS testing and rates of seropositivity.
- Both hospitals have developed the capacity to review data on the numbers of people enrolled in primary care and managed care programs.
- Both hospitals are developing the capacity to track utilization within their own populations identified as at-risk or vulnerable by the community assessment processes.

To date, planning efforts in the two cities have clearly demonstrated that for community health assessment and planning to be relevant and sustainable, it must directly and actively involve people in the community with a stake in improving health status—consumers, local government, and business.

SEAMLESS CONTINUUM OF CARE

The Cambridge and Somerville hospitals have a long history of collaboration within their cities in addressing health problems as well as the social and economic factors that affect the health of the entire community. Both hospitals established a network of neighborhood health centers in their communities in the late 1960s and early 1970s to ensure access to basic primary care for families in underserved neighborhoods. Both networks pioneered in the use of nurse practitioners to provide an economical, preventive, and comprehensive style of primary care services.

Somerville Hospital, in collaboration with the city and community activists, developed two neighborhood health centers in 1970, one in the Mystic Housing Project and one in East Somerville, a geographically isolated low-income neighborhood. In the late 1980s, the hospital developed one of the first school-based primary care clinics in Massachusetts at Somerville High School. It also provided support and hospital affiliation for the 60+ Health Center, then being established at the city's new senior community center.

Cambridge Hospital established a network of neighborhood health centers in the late 1960s to provide the city's most underserved neighborhoods with access to care. The six health centers have been extraordinarily successful in recruiting bilingual and bicultural providers that are representative of the multiracial and multicultural composition of the city. Haitian, Portuguese, and Latino mental health teams are also based in the neighborhood health centers.

In 1988, Cambridge Hospital, in collaboration with the school department and a network of community agencies serving adolescents, opened the Teen Health Center on-site at the Cambridge Rindge and Latin High School. The hospital also opened a new senior health center in 1995, developed in collaboration with the City Council on Aging, at the new community center for seniors.

The neighborhood health centers in each city have played a significant role in promoting community-oriented primary care as a way to improve service coordination across the continuum. The neighborhood health centers have been important vehicles for coordination of health and other human services, particularly for children, adolescents, pregnant women, the elderly, and ethnic minorities.

The Elder Service Plan (ESP), a new capitated service designed to prevent institutionalization of the low-income frail elderly population, serves Cambridge and Somerville. Opened in March 1995, the ESP provides an integrated system of primary care services, adult day health, other medical and long-term care services, assisted living, human services, transportation, nutrition, personal hygiene, and any other services that might be required to keep an enrolled high-risk population healthy.

The recent reorganization of the Cambridge Department of Health and Hospitals into a community health network is an effort to restructure the way health activities were organized to develop a seamless continuum of care for Cambridge. The network includes acute inpatient and outpatient services, nursing homes, neighborhood health centers, school health centers, and public health functions. The new system is led by an executive leadership council that includes the director of public health, hospital CEO, Health of the City project director, and clinical staff leadership. This council provides strategic planning and resource allocation, thereby improving coordination of efforts toward healthier communities. The previous hospital operating structure, with hierarchical nursing, ambulatory, and professional services divisions, has been replaced by interdisciplinary teams for health promotion and patient care throughout the continuum. Physicians and nurses play key roles in decision making and are developing systems to use community health status outcomes and customer feedback as measures of success.

The strong focus on community-oriented primary care, improvement of community health status, and community accountability has contributed to the development of the vision of a seamless continuum of care for Cambridge and Somerville. There has been a history of noncollaboration between Cambridge Hospital and Mt. Auburn Hospital. Although Mt. Auburn Hospital has traditionally served a more suburban population than either Cambridge Hospital or Somerville Hospital, recently there has been a renewed interest in collaboration and possible affiliation among the three hospitals. It is expected that the joint planning for a CCN will enhance the development of an integrated health care system for the two communities.

MANAGEMENT WITHIN FIXED RESOURCES

Cambridge and Somerville hospitals have developed a variety of initiatives to coordinate health services, avoid unnecessary duplication, and conserve resources. The development of innovative lower-cost models of care, including neighborhood health centers, the use of midlevel providers, and the birthing center have helped to provide care to patients at the most appropriate point in the continuum of care.

The development of capitation models will provide the most significant impetus toward the CCN vision. Although enrollment in managed care plans among Cambridge and Somerville residents has increased dramatically in the past year or two, most managed care arrangements with the hospitals do not yet involve full risk capitation.

The ESP is the first full risk-sharing arrangement undertaken by Cambridge Hospital. It is expected to be an important vehicle for utilization management for the population currently using the most costly services in the health care system.

Cambridge Hospital also planned to begin enrolling its Medicaid and uninsured patients in the new Metropolitan Health Plan in fall 1995, to serve as the managed care organization for capitation of the uninsured population currently financed through the Massachusetts Uncompensated Care Pool. The Metropolitan Health Plan was developed jointly by Cambridge Hospital, Boston City Hospital, and the Massachusetts Department of Medicaid as part of the recent Massachusetts application for a section 1115 Medicaid waiver. Somerville Hospital is exploring the feasibility of full participation in this effort.

Cambridge and Somerville hospitals have developed an excellent foundation in community health focus, community accountability, the development of a seamless continuum of care, and management within fixed resources in their own communities. Movement toward a capitation payment system will create enormous pressures for financial restructuring of the health care system. The Somerbridge Community Health Partnership (SCHP) recognizes that these environmental pressures will make the CCN vision more important than ever. The SCHP members are committed to using community-wide health planning and accountability for measurable health improvement goals to ensure that the new financial incentives will contribute positively to improving the health of the people of Somerville and Cambridge.

MOVING TOWARD THE COMMUNITY CARE NETWORK VISION

Key health leaders in Cambridge and Somerville met during September through December 1994 to begin substantive discussions about joint service delivery. A small planning group met in January and February 1995. A 14-member steering committee was convened in March, and met three times to develop a vision to jointly address health status issues in the two cities. This steering committee included the two hospital CEOs, members of senior management at the two hospitals and city health and human service departments, physicians, and executive directors of the two local Community Action Program (CAP) agencies.

Following is a list of this project's full working partners responsible for program development and implementation:

Somerville

- Somerville Hospital
- City of Somerville: Health Department, Mayor's Office of Human Services
- Community Action Agency of Somerville

Cambridge

- City of Cambridge: Health and Hospitals, Human Services
- Cambridge Economic Opportunity Committee

The vision statement developed by this group is as follows:

Cambridge and Somerville share the vision of healthy individuals, families, and communities.

Our partnership will provide a community-accountable, prevention-focused, cost-effective, seamless health and human service delivery system.

What Does Each of Our Organizations' Missions Call Us to Be and Do?

All the organizations that have agreed to join the SCHP have a strong record of service to the underserved, poor, and vulnerable populations of the two cities. Each organization has made a commitment to serve the special needs of linguistic minorities and communities of color. Each organization has a well-defined mission that highlights serving the needs of the community in partnership with their clients, patients, or citizens. All are committed to empowering their consumers to take responsibility for their health and well-being.

How Will the Future Health Care Delivery System Work?

The partners are committed to developing a health care system in Somerville and Cambridge that retains local access and identity while maintaining a preventive and public health focus through a seamless continuum of care. It will be driven by the needs of residents and accountable to an empowered community. Any consumer will have easy access to the full range of health and human services available in the two cities from any point of service in a well-integrated and coordinated delivery system. The SCHP will have the capacity to continually improve its performance with respect to access, community accountability, efficiency, and identified measurable health outcomes.

Whom Shall We Serve?

This system will serve the entire community while ensuring appropriate care for the underserved. It will focus on the root causes of illness such as violence, substance abuse, and poverty, while developing appropriate, accessible services for populations at risk, such as the young, elderly, ethnic, and linguistic communities and communities of color.

How Could Our Community Be a Healthier Place?

The education and empowerment of individuals to foster individual responsibility will ultimately improve health status. Attacking root causes of illness in a community, such as poverty, violence, substance abuse, environmental effects, and a lack of educational opportunities will increase human dignity and ultimately enhance the quality of life. Using prevention and early intervention approaches are crucial to achieving these necessary goals.

What Should Be Our Individual Roles in Achieving Our Vision?

All partners are committed to creating an integrated and coordinated service delivery system. Human service agencies, CAP agencies, city leaders, and health care provider organizations all have different and valuable skills, connections, knowledge, and perspectives on the broadly defined health care needs of the community. All the working partners are committed to participating actively in collaborative planning efforts and making necessary system changes to improve their collective capacity to serve the needs of the community.

The partners are committed to the goal of greater efficiency in the use of existing resources and the elimination of unnecessary duplication. Individual institutions should be prepared to sacrifice for the greater good, although this remains a challenge when the reimbursement system still rewards high-intensity service models over preventive ones.

What Characteristics Should Our Partners Have?

Key roles of all SCHP members will include promoting innovation and systems change. The full working partners will recruit a larger coalition that will have balanced representation from a wide variety of public and private sectors, including community and neighborhood activists, mental health providers, business, schools, city and other government officials, other acute and specialty hospitals (Mt. Auburn, Youville, and Heritage), health maintenance organizations (Harvard Community Health Plan), skilled nursing facilities, home health agencies, foundations, local media, faith communities, and human service agencies, especially those serving youth, the elderly, substance abusers, and ethnic minorities. They will be asked to buy into the shared vision and be committed to moving beyond turf issues when it makes sense while leaving room for civic diversity. A sense of humor and fun are also considered desirable characteristics for SCHP members.

INITIATIVES FOR MOVING TOWARD THE COMMUNITY CARE NETWORK VISION

The collaborative partnership for this CCN model program has chosen to focus on the following three challenging program areas:

- Substance abuse
- Geriatrics
- Health care for linguistic minorities and communities of color

The SCHP has chosen them for the following reasons:

- They provide a significant opportunity to restructure the health and human service delivery systems to achieve measurable improvements in health outcomes and reduce cost.

- They encompass the health care needs of the most at-risk vulnerable populations.
- Managed care and capitation are likely to be dominant funding mechanisms for these three program areas in the future. The SCHP's planning process will ensure that optimal service delivery systems will be in place during a time of significant change in the health care system.
- They encompass all four dimensions of the CCN vision.
- Focusing on them will build on the Somerville and Cambridge successes in providing basic primary care while addressing some of the more difficult issues our society faces in improving health status.

COMMUNITY HEALTH FOCUS

- Substance abuse, geriatrics, and health care for linguistic minorities and communities of color are high-priority health problems identified in broad-based community health assessments done in both Somerville and Cambridge.
- Ongoing collection and analysis of pertinent health status indicators will be a crucial component of all three initiatives.

SEAMLESS CONTINUUM OF CARE

- Substance abuse and geriatric services are often fragmented and uncoordinated as a result of the reimbursement system and its emphasis on institutionalized care. There is a significant, although challenging, opportunity to improve care through designing an integrated, continuous service system.
- Immigrant linguistic minorities and communities of color face barriers to continuous care as a result of a lack of adequate insurance and other access issues. Immigrants come from cultures that rely on hospitals and emergency room care; there are no primary care systems in their countries of origin.

COMMUNITY ACCOUNTABILITY

- Both cities have established a formal process for discussing community health status issues. The community health assessment and planning groups are ready to hold providers accountable for improving health outcomes.
- Substance abuse and health care problems of the elderly and linguistic minorities and communities of color all are served by publicly funded human service agencies that identify both Somerville and Cambridge as their primary service area. These community-based not-for-profit agencies act as advocates for their constituents and are important players in holding the health care system accountable.

MANAGEMENT WITHIN FIXED RESOURCES

- Substance abuse and geriatric services are currently high-cost and institutional-based. A significant opportunity exists to lower costs through new models of primary prevention, early intervention, and development of lower-cost community services.

- Immigrant linguistic minority populations are often uninsured or underinsured. This leads to their seeking health care late in an illness, requiring care in more expensive settings. Ensuring access to linguistic and culturally appropriate primary care and other preventive services for these populations will result in lower cost to the system.

IMPLEMENTATION PLAN FOR THE THREE INITIATIVES

1. *Substance Abuse:* The key goals are to (1) reduce substance abuse in the community by increasing primary prevention and early intervention and (2) restructure the delivery system for substance abusers and their families to improve treatment access and outcomes at less cost.

   A new, expanded coalition addressing substance abuse and related problems will be developed to accomplish the following:

   - Develop a community-wide service delivery plan with an increased emphasis on outpatient services, alternative therapies, prevention, and early intervention services. Involve managed care health substance abuse providers and insurers in developing a plan to reallocate resources from high-cost, intensive inpatient detoxification to lower-cost community-based sites.
   - Decrease hospitalization rates for substance abuse diagnoses per 100,000 population. The baseline rates during 1990–92 were 894 in Somerville, 1,142 in Cambridge.
   - Increase geographic, linguistic, and cultural access to ambulatory care services and alternative substance abuse therapies.
   - Link all local primary health care and human service providers to specific substance abuse providers to ensure continuous, coordinated, and cost-effective care for substance abusers in all stages of the disease.
   - Train all human service and primary health care providers in early intervention and prevention techniques and strategies, and develop a mechanism to track the number of providers using them.
   - Maintain and expand other community prevention work that includes public policy, media, and education initiatives. Affirm and strengthen local youth-oriented prevention activities such as recreation, mentoring, peer leadership programs, school and community-based education, and parent education by monitoring number and types of participants.

2. *Geriatrics:* The key goal is to improve health status and promote the highest level of independent functioning for Somerville and Cambridge residents over 65 years of age by (1) expanding managed care to the elderly population to improve primary care, reduce duplicative specialty care, and increase preventive services, and (2) developing additional lower-cost, noninstitutional alternative treatment and care sites. A new, expanded coalition in the two cities will be developed to accomplish the following:

   - Develop a community-wide plan for service delivery that will reallocate resources from high-cost, intensive inpatient care to lower-cost community-based services.
   - Increase the number and percent of Somerville and Cambridge elderly residents who have an identified primary care provider.

- Increase the number and percent of Somerville and Cambridge elderly residents enrolled in managed care programs.
- Develop a community-wide plan that will integrate a broad range of health and human services areas, including recreation, transportation, housing, and nutrition programming.
- Decrease the number of emergency department admissions for Somerville and Cambridge elderly residents over 64 with preventable diagnoses better managed in primary care programs (falls, urinary tract infections, bronchitis/chronic obstructive pulmonary disease, and dehydration).
- Develop a comprehensive plan for injury prevention education for target populations and health and human service providers.
- Reduce hospitalizations of elderly patients resulting from angina and bacterial pneumonia.

3. *Health Care for Linguistic Minorities and Communities of Color:* The key goal is to improve the health status of the linguistic minorities and communities of color in Somerville and Cambridge. This includes ensuring access to culturally appropriate preventive and primary health care while addressing underlying causes of poor health outcomes. A new, expanded coalition in the two cities will accomplish the following:
    - Develop a community-wide plan to identify and eliminate barriers to health care and human service access in the delivery system in Somerville and Cambridge.
    - Increase the number and percent of target populations who can identify a regular source of primary care. Develop a baseline by assessing emergency department use and determining barriers to local care by group, age, sex, and so on, using focus groups and survey methodology.
    - Identify trends in each population group for key health status indicators, including infant/neonatal mortality, teen births, adequacy of prenatal care, heart disease, cancer, and HIV/AIDS.
    - Assess preventive and early treatment access for appropriate health status indicators, develop preventive strategies for each disease in each population group, and identify and eliminate barriers to accessing appropriate care as indicated.
    - Develop appropriate preventive health education programs to encourage appropriate self-care and primary care usage and decrease emergency department usage. Some examples include the following:
        - —Increase the number of the target population diagnosed with asthma who have been trained in the use of a peak-flow meter and have a written care plan.
        - —Develop an audiovisual program to teach parents how to deal with fevers in young children.
    - Increase the number of health care, social service, and government agencies in Somerville and Cambridge with a policy and plan for (1) recruiting bilingual providers and other staff, (2) training for staff in interpretation services and cultural aspects of health care, (3) collecting data on client demographics, and (4) evaluating interpreter services.

PARTNERSHIP RESPONSIBILITIES

The full working partners will work collaboratively with a broad coalition of community organizations for each of the three initiatives. All three will involve consumers, other health care providers and hospitals, human service agencies, civic and church leaders, the schools, youth service programs, service organizations, mental health providers, health insurers, and state and federal health and social service agencies. The substance abuse initiative will also work with community- and hospital-based substance abuse providers, local federally funded Center for Substance Abuse community partnerships, and state and federal substance abuse agencies.

The geriatric initiative will involve chronic disease hospitals; home health care providers; elderly housing tenants and staff; skilled nursing facilities; geriatric day treatment programs; and local, state, and federal aging agencies. State and federal immigration agencies and local advocacy agencies for immigrant communities will be crucial members of the initiative for linguistic minorities and communities of color.

Most of these agencies have long been involved in ongoing local health planning efforts. Many have already indicated their willingness to join this coalition. One working partner organization from each of the two cities (one health care and one non–health care provider) will provide joint leadership for each of the three initiatives.

DATA COLLECTION SYSTEMS

Specific baseline measurements of process and health status outcomes are scheduled to be identified by 1996, when goals will be set for 1997 and 1998 and beyond. A baseline measurement will be either a known health status or process indicator, or will be developed via data collection in the first year.

For all three initiatives, the SCHP will do the following:

- Perform an assessment of utilization patterns to identify needed data collection systems and work with appropriate agencies to collect and organize uniform data for Somerville and Cambridge residents. Uniform data reporting for ambulatory diagnoses will be particularly useful.
- Identify appropriate baseline measurements and set numeric and process goals, including long-range health status outcomes.

School and community surveys to measure attitudes and behavior will also be used in developing baselines and measuring progress. This area will require more sophisticated technical assistance in epidemiology and information systems than is now available for this purpose.

SUMMARY OF NOTABLE PROGRESS

Major changes have taken place in the Somerville and Cambridge communities since early 1995. When they learned of the CCN demonstration program, Cambridge Hospital (a public hospital) and Somerville Hospital (a private, not-for-profit institution) began meeting to discuss the advantages of collaboration across the two cities. The hospitals each played a key role in organizing the committee that designed the Somerbridge proposal.

Little did those participating in this effort know that it would lead to changes in the way health care had been delivered in each city for nearly a century. Through the SCHP visioning process, both hospitals realized that they had much in common and would benefit from closer collaboration. After much discussion and work, the hospitals decided that a merger of the two institutions would benefit the residents of both communities.

This merger of a municipal hospital and a private, not-for-profit institution is historic among community hospitals in Massachusetts. For it to take place, Cambridge Hospital needed legislative approval allowing it to function independently of city government. A bill creating the Cambridge Public Health Commission (CPHC), a public authority governing both hospitals, had to be passed by the Cambridge City Council and the Massachusetts legislature. By reorganizing into the CPHC, Cambridge Hospital was free to enter into an affiliation with Somerville. With passage of this legislation, the 19-member CPHC began operating on July 1, 1996.

This successful merger will enable the new hospital network to meet the needs of the underserved by focusing on community health, preventive care, and continued collaboration with city departments and community agencies. It is an important step in creating a seamless continuum of care across the Somerville and Cambridge communities.

Background

Since the creation of the SCHP, progress has been made in the three issue initiative areas of substance abuse, elderly health, and immigrant health. Somerbridge is well on its way to addressing health problems across the two cities.

In summer 1995, the SCHP steering committee stated its commitment to a community-wide health effort. Since hiring staff in January 1996, the SCHP has been developing a community process and encouraging input from a highly diverse population of both cities. Building on the community needs assessment work, the SCHP has continued to go directly to those in need of services to learn what can be done to better meet their needs. In doing this, the concept of the SCHP had to be developed and presented to community members.

Problems

Individual communities feel a strong sense of pride toward their institutions and identities. In some ways, the SCHP goes against this grain by encouraging collaboration instead of competition. Early in the process of interviewing community leaders, many stated their skepticism toward a project that attempted to bring together communities as different as Somerville and Cambridge.

Many felt it would not be possible to focus across each community's boundary. However, these were the same people who were feeling the pains of a changing health care system. What the SCHP could offer was a perspective on the changing system and how it could influence the health of the community. Again, the SCHP vision speaks of shared responsibility across the two cities. Although the SCHP effort is still in the process of proving itself, many residents and health care providers find this approach sensible.

Another problem faced early on by the SCHP related to the fact that it began at nearly the same time that the merger of Cambridge and Somerville hospitals was in the public eye. Consequently, many community residents felt that the SCHP was a hospital-based effort specifically related to the merger. By welcoming individuals and community organizations to participate in initiative working groups, the SCHP was able to demonstrate its commitment to a process that involved more than just the large community providers.

Progress

Substance Abuse The SCHP has been working to define the substance abuse services currently provided across both cities. A small working group has been meeting to inventory the substance abuse services, collect and analyze data, and research new methods of treatment. Once this work is completed, an initial report will be issued and forums will be sponsored to solicit feedback and input from the community. The SCHP is also assisting in coordinating substance abuse prevention work in both cities. This effort involves designing an outreach and education campaign targeting youth and their parents.

Elderly Health The SCHP has created an Elderly Working Group comprised of geriatric providers, elderly service agencies, senior advocates, and activists. This group has identified public education as a top priority and is in the process of developing a guide specifically for the Somerville and Cambridge area. This guide will assist the elderly in making an informed decision when choosing a Medicare HMO. For geriatric health and human service providers, the SCHP designed training sessions to help them better meet the needs of their elderly clients. The first training, with strong participation from both communities, provided information on both state and federal laws designed to protect the elderly in the area of health care.

Immigrant Health The SCHP has been working closely with immigrant advocacy organizations and members of newly arrived immigrant groups to identify ways to improve the health of these populations. This work is illustrative of the SCHP vision of creating a true community health effort. Medical care is not necessarily the central focus of this program.

For many in the immigrant community, there is a desire to better understand the system. In response, the SCHP has convened an Immigrant Working Group to further identify pertinent issues and design a community outreach campaign.

However, a community health issue of great concern to many newly arrived immigrants is the opportunity to be gainfully employed. In this area, the SCHP is bringing together diverse interests. In conjunction with immigrant advocacy organizations, immigrant activists, and the staffs of health and human service organizations serving immigrants, the SCHP has identified the need to support immigrants as they enter the job market. In addition, it is researching a community training program that would provide training for multilingual, multicultural individuals interested in becoming medical interpreters or other medical professionals. (See figure 4-1.) Discussions are also taking place on the creation of a community forum through which to discuss diversity and multiculturalism.

The Future

It is the hope of all involved in the SCHP that our efforts will lead to the development of new models of care integrating the community into the decision-making process. By collaborating with the community, health networks will become closer to their customers and will better understand how to effectively meet their needs. We look forward to providing updates on the progress of our partnership as we endeavor to create a true CCN.

Contact: Mark Rukavina
Somerville Hospital
230 Highland Ave.
Somerville, MA 02143
Phone: (617) 666-4400, x179
Fax: (617) 666-0031

FIGURE 4-1. Medical Interpreters Training Proposal

Background

Somerville and Cambridge are cities with significant immigrant populations. Over the last decade the number of immigrant residents in each of the cities has grown dramatically. Consequently, the number of non–English speaking individuals accessing health care services in Somerville and Cambridge has also increased.

A survey of patients using services through The Cambridge Hospital's community health centers and primary care sites conducted in early 1996 found that nearly 50 percent of the patients were foreign born and that 56 percent did not speak English as their first language. Statistics such as these have implications for the large institutions providing health care in Somerville and Cambridge.

Effective communication is a crucial component in building a physician–patient relationship. Language may be a barrier to receiving care for patients with limited English-language skills. The use of trained medical interpreters provides a solution which enables patients with limited English skills to access the health care they need and minimizes possible errors which could result in serious consequences for providers.

Training & Program Certificate

In Massachusetts there is no required certification for medical interpreters at the present time. The Massachusetts Medical Interpreters Association (MMIA) has provided leadership in this area by designing standards of practice and a training curriculum for medical interpreters.

Somerbridge is interested in working in conjunction with the large health care institutions in Somerville and Cambridge and the MMIA to design a community training program for medical interpreters. This certificate training program would accomplish two goals. First, it would guarantee non–English speaking patients access to quality, consistent interpreter services throughout the two cities. It would also provide interested members of the immigrant community with a career development opportunity.

Proposal

Somerbridge proposes the establishment of a community-sponsored, college-level, certification program for medical interpreters. Those participating in the program would complete a series of college courses designed in cooperation with the MMIA. The classes would be taught in a community location in Somerville or Cambridge. Participants completing the curriculum would receive a certificate verifying the training received and skills developed through the program.

Curriculum

Human Biology 3 credit course 45 hours

Multiculturalism Perspectives I & II 3 credit courses 45 hours each

Medical Terminology I & II 1 credit courses 15 hours each

Interpreting Skills 3 credit course 45 hours

Practicum and System Orientation

PART II

Suburban Networks

The great challenge which faces us is to assure that, in our society of big-ness, we do not strangle the voice of creativity, that the rules of the game do not come to overshadow its purpose, that the grand orchestration of society leaves ample room for the [person] who marches to the music of another drummer.

—Hubert H. Humphrey (1911–78), U.S. politician
vice president 1965–1969

Perhaps the best definition of progress would be the continuing efforts of men and women to narrow the gap between the convenience of the powers that be and the unwritten charter.

—Nadine Gordimer (b. 1923), South African author

INTRODUCTION

Suburban communities are widely believed to experience smooth sailing in their voyages in community care. It is true that they generally have more resources per capita than other types of communities. They tend to possess few or no huge pockets of poverty. Health issues may more often reflect personal choices than social, economic, and environmental threats to health.

Being predominantly middle class, however, political and business interests may have particular difficulty recognizing abiding problems, such as domestic violence or substance abuse, that are "not supposed to happen here." In other words, suburban communities may enjoy relatively richer resource pools, but the business-as-usual interests of many residents and leaders may reduce or diffuse the attention given to community problems. Political will may be hard to coalesce, especially for problems that are not supposed to be there. Suburban communities may have a particularly difficult time representing the interests of the people who live in smaller pockets of ethnic minorities or poverty.

While community collaborative efforts and partnerships may have greater institutional resources per person than other environments, suburban citizens may often be more detached from a sense of community. As a result, the success and sustainability of collaborative efforts can be inhibited or heavily dependent on a small set of personally committed individuals. Moreover, the special appeal of large proportions of people with jobs, health insurance, and other sources of financial strength, makes suburban communities particularly susceptible to competitive impulses. The development of collaborative activities may be complicated by the competition for market share between providers and other businesses, and management may be diverted from strategic thinking about community-responsive, health system change by a comfortable focus on the bottom line.

Here are some questions you might want to consider when reading about evolving CCNs in suburban communities: How can relative wealth be a barrier to progress? Or is relative wealth always a net positive no matter how you slice it? If having a population that is relatively well-off financially can reduce people's collaborative impulses, how did the suburban partnerships become experts in collaboration? What techniques were enacted by the partnerships described here to overcome competitive tendencies? What techniques do they use to recognize "hidden" problems or the problems of groups that have relatively little political power?

Four suburban community care networks are highlighted. Each of these communities falls entirely or chiefly within a metropolitan statistical area but is defined by towns that are not the chief population centers of the area. Building a Healthier Ocean County, in New Jersey, addresses community problems through better communication across agencies and better information to the leaders of political institutions. This evolving CCN serves as a clearinghouse for all quality-of-life issues and has established task forces to address access and transportation issues, the coordination of resources, costs, ethical choices, education, prevention, technology, and universal care. In the near west suburbs of Chicago, the Metropolitan Chicago Community Care Alliance addresses access and continuity challenges through public–private partnership in the Genesis Center, a primary care clinic in a largely Latino pocket. This network also operates a state-of-the-art chronic care network. Through its Healthy Communities Partnerships, eight local communities are organizing to enact solutions on a larger geographic scale. The Solano Coalition for Better Health, at the northern end of the Bay Area in California, focuses on integration and coordination of social services and economic development initiatives. While a relatively well-off area, a shutdown of massive military installations has focused attention on community-responsive programs. Community capacity building is proceeding hand-in-hand with the integration of health and human services at the community level. A core group for this partnership is an interesting medical managed care plan that operates on the basis of collaboration among commercial health plans. In Wisconsin, the South Madison Health and Family Center also represents a public–private partnership, with a cornerstone of Medicaid managed care. Through centralization of efforts in the Center, economies of scale and effectiveness are being sought to enable expansion of Medicaid services and improved coordination with the tertiary facilities in the area. Such efforts also enable innovations in medical education. Access for Hispanics in the community has already improved.

5

Building a Healthier Ocean County

Executive Summary

Since its inception in 1993, Building a Healthier Ocean County has become an initiative encompassing the broadest variety of community groups as one coalition charged with the responsibility of improving health status. The three original sponsors of the initiative have taken a seat as Planning/Steering Committee members, and the coalition is driven by members of the community at large.

Historically a community of agencies working in isolation, Ocean County has gained tremendously through the efforts of the Building a Healthier Ocean County initiative. Communication among providers is probably the most notable immediate result.

Individuals who have participated in the Building a Healthier Ocean County initiative have commented that they are more knowledgeable about the community in which they live and they have a better understanding of the needs of the community from the residents' perspective. In addition, they also have a greater understanding of the difficulties experienced by other providers in effectuating behavior change, and have a familiarity with agencies and individuals throughout the county. Building a Healthier Ocean County has become a clearinghouse for all quality-of-life issues, and members now bring individual initiatives to the table, which results in the opportunity for feedback and keeps members abreast of countywide happenings.

One of the key lessons that has been learned throughout the process is that the Building a Healthier Ocean County initiative cannot be perceived as being owned by one institution or serving one particular agenda. It does not work unless it is a community-owned project. Maintaining this status as a true coalition requires effort on the part of all who are involved, but its reward is an initiative that has, as a natural outgrowth, a far-reaching effect on the community. In recognizing this, the area hospitals who were driving the initiative in the early stages have taken a backseat and encourage active participation by other agencies.

Another lesson learned was that of the importance of keeping work plans realistic and within the capabilities of all involved. A good example of a redefinition of objectives is found in the Women's Health Committee, a subgroup of the Prevention/Education Committee. This committee originally developed six extensive objectives that, when looked at more closely, began to overwhelm the group. With the assistance of members of the Planning/Steering Committee, the members selected two objectives that they felt could have the greatest impact on health status and were achievable, and proceeded to develop work plans associated with those objectives. In fact, one of the objectives, which began with the goal of reducing domestic violence, soon turned into a quest for finding out how many Ocean County women actually were victims of domestic violence, so that a baseline could be established for future measurement.

John F. Marcy, senior vice president for development
Community and Kimball Medical Center Foundations

THE COLLABORATIVE PARTNERSHIP

The partnership continues to evolve. Originally, the collaborative partnership was formed among Community Medical Center (CMC), the Ocean County Board of Health, and the Jersey Coast Health Planning Council (Local Advisory Board VI). These organizations came together in 1993 to sponsor a county health needs assessment. The partnership then grew into a planning committee for a Future Search Conference to introduce other county leaders and planners to the results of the study.

The original planning committee included approximately 30 representatives from eight identified stakeholder groups: health care, education, social services, community issues (environment, transportation, minorities, aging), religion, government and politics, business and industry, and safety and justice. Specific representatives came from Pine Beach Elementary School, CMC, Atlantic Computer Systems, the Police Department of Manchester Township, Medical Center of Ocean County, the Church of Grace and Peace, the Ocean County Board of Social Services, Jersey Coast Health Planning Council, Ocean County Health Department, Ocean County Human Services Department, Southern Ocean County Hospital, GPU Nuclear, Ocean County Office on Aging, Kimball Medical Center, Family Planning Center of Ocean County, Local Advisory Committee on Alcohol & Drug Abuse, local and state government, local physicians, Good Friend Electric, Asbury Park Press, and Toms River Regional Schools.

The actual participants in the first Future Search Conference were from the planning committee plus the League of Women Voters, Long Beach Health Department, Garden State Rehabilitation Hospital, Regional Perinatal Consortium, Southern Regional School District, The Arc (formerly Association of Retarded Citizens), the American Cancer Society, County of Ocean Prosecutor's Office, Township of Dover Police Department, New Jersey Coalition on Women with Disabilities, Manchester Township High School, the New Jersey Coalition on Women, the Ocean County Sheriff's Department, the Ocean County Planning Department, the Lacey Township Police Department, Jewish Family and Children Services, Ocean County Handicapped & Elderly Transportation System, Shoreline Behavioral Health Facility, and other businesses and citizens.

Today, these organizations are still active among the work groups. The original planning committee is completing a process of reaffirming its purpose and composition.

This process is described subsequently in this chapter; however, the collaborative partnership now consists of the reconstituted membership of the Planning/Steering Committee with Community and Kimball Medical Centers, Medical Center of Ocean County, Southern Ocean County Hospital, Ocean County Board of Health, Jersey Coast Health Planning Council, Ocean County Board of Social Services, Family Planning Center of Ocean County, and local business and industry representatives taking leadership roles. In fact, most recently, an administrator from the Ocean County Board of Social Services has agreed to serve as chairperson for the Planning/Steering Committee, and the public health coordinator of the Ocean County Health Department has agreed to be vice-chair.

PRIOR EFFORTS THAT REPRESENT MOVEMENT TOWARD THE COMMUNITY CARE NETWORK VISION

APEX-PH Study Brings First Partners Together

Building a Healthier Ocean County (BHOC) was initiated almost 3 years ago as an extension of the community benefits program of CMC of Toms River, NJ. At that time, CMC was one of 49 hospitals designated as a community benefit hospital by the Carnegie NYU National Demonstration Project funded by the W. K. Kellogg Foundation. CMC assembled a community benefit advisory board composed of community leaders and residents, and elicited feedback based on roundtable breakfasts and focus groups of community leaders, hospital board members, at-risk groups, physicians, and senior adults. Four key populations felt their needs were not being met in terms of physical, social, emotional, and psychological health. These were senior adults; women and young families; local businesses struggling with rising health care costs; and individuals at high risk for heart disease, cancer, and stroke. CMC developed three wellness-focused centers and began to seek collaborative partnerships with other organizations. In addition, CMC's board of trustees responded to this feedback by adopting a broadened definition of a healthier community:

> Healthier communities actively work to improve the health and quality of life of all the residents. Therefore, the definition of health goes beyond the absence of disease and the traditional medical concept and address factors in the quality of life such as environment, crime, literacy, et al.

(In fact, Community and Kimball Medical Centers [which is the consolidation of CMC in Toms River and Kimball Medical Center in Lakewood, Ocean County] recently received the American Hospital Association's NOVA Award for its community benefits efforts both alone and in the context of BHOC.)

At the same time, at least two other collaborating county organizations, the Ocean County Board of Health and the Jersey Coast Health Planning Council (Local Advisory Board VI) had reached similar conclusions about their missions and definitions of community health. These two organizations joined with CMC to cosponsor a health needs assessment using the Assessment Protocol for Excellence in Public Health (APEX-PH). The process took several months because it was the first time such a study had been conducted in the state.

Briefly characterized, Ocean County is located on the east central coast of New Jersey with a population of approximately 450,000. Over 22 percent of the population is over the age of 65, and 25 percent is under the age of 19. African-Americans and Latinos total 2.8 percent and 3.2 percent, respectively. There is a concentration of this minority population in Lakewood, which is in the northern part of the county.

The unemployment rate for Ocean County is slightly higher than the state average. Much of Ocean County's work force is employed in trade and service jobs. That factor, combined with the large number of retirees in the area, contributes to a per capita income of $15,598, which is less than the statewide average. The poverty rate of 6 percent includes 10.7 percent of all Ocean County children living in poverty. The number of eligible people for the Women, Infants and Children (WIC) supplemental food program is double the state average, and 20,224 residents receive Medicaid.

APEX-PH results indicated that, in most cases, the health status of Ocean County was better than the state average, but in almost all cases, the county was below the national Healthy People 2000 benchmarks. The two age groups that had the poorest health status were teens and young adults (ages 15 to 24) and middle-aged adults (ages 45 to 64). The APEX-PH study also prioritized health status indicators, which account for years of potential life lost before age 65.

Future Search Conference Expands Collaboration and Awareness

After reviewing this information, it was determined that a collaborative planning effort must be developed to be most effective. The three sponsoring agencies formed a planning committee to develop a forum for collaboration. The committee decided that a Future Search Conference, using the visioning process referenced in a book entitled *Establishing Common Ground,* written by Marvin Weisbord, would be most appropriate. The planning committee developed the purpose of the conference, as follows:

> The purpose of the Future Search Conference is to provide a forum to explore ways to maintain and improve the health status of Ocean County residents. The conference will bring together the community at large (consumers, providers) and key community leaders who have a stake in making Ocean County a healthier community. Participants will work collaboratively to develop and champion shared goals for ways of addressing multiple community needs.

In designing the conference, the planning committee nominated more than 350 leaders from Ocean County. Through a multi-voting technique, it then selected 80 individuals from the eight identified stakeholder groups—health care, education, social services, community issues, religion, government and politics, business and industry, and safety and justice—and invited them to the conference.

Three briefing sessions were held to inform the invitees about the Future Search process and the APEX-PH health assessment findings. The response was gratifying; 74 of the 80 invitees attended the three-day conference, held in early November 1993.

How to build a healthier Ocean County was the challenge presented at the three-day conference. This represented the first time in New Jersey that a countywide group had met to develop a common plan to improve its community's health status. The Future Search process was designed to engender an understanding among its participants of "whole systems." It allowed attendees to form their own process of understanding the overlapping and interrelated intricacy of whole system components. A picture of the community's values, history, and hope began to emerge, as common themes and trends were identified along with individual differences. Participants in self-managed teams were encouraged to honor rather than reconcile these differences and establish common ground. It was observed that Ocean County had a melting pot of different ages, lengths of residency, and life experience participating in the conference. Most notable were the references to the growth of the population and lack of infrastructure in roads, housing, health care, transportation services, and education over the past 40 years to meet the ever-growing demand.

The attendees listed their key important points from the APEX-PH study and then brainstormed the global trends affecting their future right now. Through multivoting techniques, the group then prioritized the health care issues affecting Ocean County today. The trends identified were the following:

- Growing dysfunctionality of family
- Need for health education
- Runaway health care costs
- Teen issues
- Increased incidence of disease
- Increased use of tobacco and alcohol
- Need for preventive care
- Access to health care
- Increased number of children in poverty
- Increase in child abuse

In stakeholder groups, the conference attendees then listed what is going on right now in Ocean County of which they are most proud and most sorry in relationship to a healthier community.

In the next exercise, attendees in mixed stakeholder groups prepared skits on desired futures. There were seven recurring themes:

- Ensure universal access to all residents
- Increase communication among agencies through information technology
- Coordinate resources to prevent duplication of effort
- Improve access and transportation within the county
- Reduce costs
- Improve family values
- Increase health prevention and education efforts

On the final day of the conference, seven task forces were formed consistent with the themes identified, and the attendees began working in the areas in which they were most interested.

The conference ended with the sponsors making a commitment to holding a reunion in one year. The task forces selected group leaders and an initial meeting date. Conference evaluations reflected a 95 percent satisfaction rate, with attendees' believing the conference had met or exceeded their expectations.

Task Forces Identify Missions

One of the first steps taken by each task force was to identify a mission. The seven missions are as follows:

- *Access/Transportation:* It is imperative that an accessible health care transportation system be in place by the year 2000. Consumers should be ensured universal access to all providers.
- *Coordination of Resources:* The mission of this task force is to coordinate all resources to include the identification and integration of all existing resources having an impact on the quality of life of Ocean County residents. The final product will include integrated and comprehensive information and referral, coordination of resources, and an efficient communication network among providers and users of resources.
- *Cost:* The mission of this task force is to reduce the cost of the Ocean County health system and provide affordable and accessible health care for all, while maintaining and improving quality and effectiveness, especially in those areas prioritized by the Future Search Conference.
- *Ethical Choices:* The mission of this task force is to help Ocean County residents make healthy life choices. We will cooperate with the BHOC stakeholders to eliminate the forces in our community that may fragment families. By creating a model, we will help people understand the process and the measures in making choices.
- *Education/Prevention:* The mission of this task force is to identify existing prevention and education programs, coordinate dissemination of information related to health status and prevention programs, and champion the development of programs designed to fill identified needs or newly identified health issues for all segments of the Ocean County population.
- *Technology:* The mission of this task force is to build a comprehensive database of information on community services and resources accessible to all Ocean County residents.
- *Universal Care:* The mission of this task force is to sponsor a series of community forums under the BHOC program dealing with access to and universality of health care for the residents of Ocean County.

Each task force then developed individual work plans and spent a year carrying out its plan to varying degrees. The Future Search Reunion was held in November 1994, during which each task force reported on its progress. Among the noteworthy results of the reunion was that two task forces, Coordination of Resources and Technology, were merged.

Although the task forces continued to meet and make progress in refining and fulfilling their plans, it became apparent to members of the original planning committee that further refinement of the overall process was needed. The committee, which had been formed originally to plan and organize the first Future Search Conference, also believed that a redefining of its own mission and description was in order.

The concern was that there was no overall authority monitoring the activity of the task forces. There was no group or body to whom the task forces reported or to whom they answered. At the same time, the members of the original planning committee recognized that there were interest groups in the county whom they were unable to involve during the first manifestation and that an attempt should be made to broaden the composition of the planning committee to include these groups.

As a result, the members of the original planning committee, which included the team leaders of the task forces, began defining both the composition and purpose of a planning/steering committee. The committee has refined its goal to accomplish the following:

- Provide a central focus point—to help coordinate efforts between task forces.
- Take responsibility for developing and implementing the plan and evaluating and directing the work of all involved with BHOC.
- Mediate conflicting points between the task forces and other groups.
- Motivate the common ground among the task forces—we want to have a healthier Ocean County.
- Assess and evaluate the goals and objectives of the task forces.
- Prevent duplication of efforts between the task forces and other groups.
- Help task forces establish their specific monitors/indicators to evaluate the change in the community's health status. Monitor activities and results.
- Ensure that all segments of our community have a voice in the process and have an opportunity to participate.
- Report activities and findings to the community and publicize the project throughout the community.
- Review results of any surveys, disseminate recommendations for improvement, and determine ways to fill service delivery gaps.
- Establish a mechanism for generating and allocating financial and other resources.
- Provide facilitation services, as requested, for the task forces. Use management/performance enhancement techniques to support the task forces' efforts.

In addition, the composition of the Planning/Steering Committee has become more inclusive. Members believed that an all-inclusive committee—even though it may number 35 or more representatives—was preferable to omitting any identifiable interest group. As a result, representatives from the following areas were recruited, with a "re-orientation" session scheduled for May 1995:

- Jersey Coast Health Planning Council (Local Advisory Board VI)
- Ocean County Health Department
- Hospitals (two representatives each):
  - —Children's Specialized Hospital
  - —CMC
  - —Health South Rehabilitation Hospital
  - —Kimball Medical Center
  - —Medical Center of Ocean County
  - —Shoreline Behavioral Health
  - —Southern Ocean County Hospital
- Team leaders from each task force and alternate representative
- Stakeholder group representation:
  - —Business/industries
  - —Community issues
  - —Education

 - Environment
 - Health care/health promotion
 - Politics/government
 - Religion
 - Safety/justice
 - Social services
 - Transportation
- Liaisons from other Ocean County health improvement efforts
- Constituency representatives, such as consumers, minorities, geographic representatives, physicians, underserved population

MOVING TOWARD THE COMMUNITY CARE NETWORK VISION

The six task forces have been successful in a number of ways. The Access/Transportation Task Force is compiling a transportation services inventory of the county. Once this baseline of current activity is determined, the task force will make plans to address the specific needs of various geographic areas and populations. The task force's composition is diverse, including government officials, hospital representatives, senior adult advocates, and representatives of people with disabilities.

In addition, the Access/Transportation Task Force is working to join with a Monmouth County, NJ, community benefits group to conduct a survey that will include a focus on behavioral patterns of identified areas of Ocean County. The belief is that prevention and education activities would be enhanced if certain detrimental lifestyles and behavior patterns became known. The survey is scheduled to be completed by the end of summer 1995.

After a few meetings, the Cost Task Force narrowed its focus to issues that could have an immediate and material effect on the cost of health care in the county. The group has compiled information and is devising plans to deal with two issues: misuse of emergency rooms by people with nonemergent conditions, and identifying "waste" created by state regulations that cause unnecessary duplication.

To collect the emergency room data, each of the four acute care hospitals in the county sent data to the chairperson of the Cost Task Force, who compiled the data with the assistance of an administrator from Medical Center of Ocean County. These data are now being studied by a subcommittee on emergency room misuse; that group comprises emergency room professionals from each hospital. The intention is to devise a communication plan and an emergency room process to provide an alternative to the inappropriate use of the emergency room, with the baseline established for both the in-season and off-season population. (As a local resort area, Ocean County has an influx of more than 100,000 summer residents.) These data will be examined annually to determine whether BHOC efforts are working.

The Technology/Coordination of Resources Task Force has spent a great deal of time examining fully integrated information systems that would link a significant number of, if not all, areas of the county. The group is formulating plans to carry out the implementation, which would include the countywide adoption of a management information system. The linkage of health care, social service, and other providers will ensure a comprehensive and updated delivery system to meet the needs of county residents.

The Ethical Choices Task Force has identified the fragmentation of the family as the cause of many symptoms, such as substance abuse, domestic violence, and child abuse. These symptoms are often addressed as isolated problems. This task force is committed to encouraging the treatment of the symptoms by promoting community-wide standards and values that will ultimately lead to healthier thinking and behaviors and an improved state of well-being.

In observance of Mother's Day and Father's Day 1995, the task force developed a self-evaluative survey to be printed in a local newspaper that is distributed county-wide. The questions are designed to help parents look at and improve the quality of time spent as a family unit. This self-evaluation tool was planned to help identify some causes of problems in a nonthreatening manner. The survey scoring process is planned to be printed in the same edition of the newspaper, alongside appropriate telephone numbers for local hospital parenting and family programs. This initiative is the result of more than a year's worth of work to identify the forces, both internal and external, that have led to the fragmentation of the family.

One of the objectives of the Universal Care Task Force is to sponsor educational forums to address health care reform issues facing consumers, providers, and employers. The first of three forums was held in October 1994. Entitled "Managed Care—At What Cost?" the forum explained the potential impact of managed care on Ocean County employers. A panel of speakers, including state health department officials and representatives of health insurance companies, answered questions raised by members of the business community and medical professions.

The second forum, entitled "Medicaid Managed Care: Where We're Headed in Ocean County" was held in December 1994. The forum was geared toward informing Ocean County health service providers about the options available to them as the Medicaid system undergoes changes.

The third forum, scheduled for May 1995, is entitled "Preparing for Community Placement of Persons with Developmental Disabilities and/or Mental Illness." The focus of the forum is to educate Ocean County providers about the impact of the transition of persons with mental illness and/or developmental disabilities.

The Universal Care Task Force will assess the participation and attendance at the three forums and determine how many more sessions should be held and/or in what form these methods of communication should take.

The Prevention/Education Task Force comprises representatives from various disciplines and agencies, including hospitals, public health departments, social service agencies, the Family Planning Center, school systems, law enforcement, local units of the American Cancer Society and the American Heart Association, the Regional Perinatal Consortium, The Arc, the Coalition on Women and Disabilities, and the Ocean County Women's Commission. This task force looked closely at APEX-PH community health assessment data by disease category to develop work plans that focused on the leading causes of years of potential life lost in Ocean County.

Using the APEX-PH data, the task force identified key strategy areas in which it would concentrate its work efforts. These strategy areas ranged from advocacy and support for activities, such as limiting youth access to tobacco and increasing Housing and Urban Development housing for seniors, to the development of new prevention and educational activities designed to make preventive care a routine practice for Ocean County residents spanning the socioeconomic stratum.

After completing its work plan, the task force prioritized the plan into the following five initiatives that would have the greatest impact on improving the community's health status:

- *Cardiovascular Disease:* To increase the number of Ocean County residents who modify lifestyle behaviors and understand early warning signs of heart disease and stroke, it is necessary to increase residents' exposure to risk reduction and risk avoidance educational programs. The results of the behavioral survey planned by the Access/Transportation Task Force will help this understanding. New sites in the general community will be identified to disseminate educational materials and plan interactive programs. These sites will have a liaison from the task force who will work closely with them to tailor programs that meet the needs of their particular clients and employees.

  Children were also identified as a target group for early and routine education that will be woven into their regular school curriculum. The goal of this activity is to work toward a community that will take responsibility for its own health status through the practice of healthier lifestyle behaviors. School-site nutrition will be promoted through the modification of home economics course curricula as well as the improvement of the school lunch menu throughout all Ocean County schools.
- *Cancer:* APEX-PH data clearly point to malignant neoplasms as a leading cause of death that is higher in Ocean County than in other areas of New Jersey. A countywide symposium for physicians and allied health professionals was identified as a method of laying the groundwork for a concerted effort to battle cancer in Ocean County. Because the support of physicians and health professionals is critical to the process, this symposium would encourage them to embrace the work of the task force.

  Early diagnosis and treatment of cancers of the medically indigent will be increased by expanding low-cost breast and prostate screening opportunities as well as ensuring clinic or physician access for the indigents identified through these screenings. In addition, lifeguards and other residents having outdoor occupations will be targeted for screenings and intensive skin cancer educational programs.

  Tobacco use among young people in Ocean County continues to grow even though it is the single most preventable cause of death. Efforts to prevent premature disease and death resulting from tobacco use will include an increase in smoking cessation programs offered throughout Ocean County. Concentrated efforts will be made to reach schoolchildren and pregnant women. A program to combine nicotine patch usage with formal smoking cessation classes at little or no cost to the participant will be instituted to study the benefits of using these two methods in tandem. The committee will also recognize and publicize smoke-free restaurants and organizations in the community and support all legislative and other measures restricting youth access to tobacco.
- *Adolescent Health:* At the Future Search Conference held in November 1993, dysfunctional and fragmented families were identified as factors contributing to the deterioration of the health of individuals as well as the community. Recognizing the multitude of factors that influence the behaviors of teenagers, and acknowledging the importance of addressing these factors from the perspective of teenagers themselves, a Teen Future Search Conference was planned for May 1995. The conference will assist the Prevention/Education Task Force in continuing to address addictions, physical and mental abuse, and suicide within the context of the entire family and community.

  A violence prevention, education, and intervention program has been instituted to focus on positive reinforcement of nonviolent behavior in children rather than negative reinforcement for children exhibiting violent behavior. An ethical choices program will be modeled after one that is currently successful and expanded to be used in all school districts.

- *Accidents:* Because Ocean County has a large percentage of senior citizens and lacks an adequate mass transportation system, many residents who should not be operating motor vehicles continue to do so for reasons of necessity as well as to maintain their independence. To prevent potential death and disability from automobile accidents, the task force will implement programs that assess driver capability and also expand programs that improve driving ability. Vision aerobics, a program sponsored by the Lighthouse at CMC, will be adapted by other agencies serving seniors throughout Ocean County.

  Ascertaining the number of children from low-income families who need bicycle helmets will prompt the organization of a campaign to provide helmets through donations made by civic organizations. The various committee member agencies will reinforce messages of bicycle safety and advocate measures requiring helmets to be worn also by children who Rollerblade. Boating accidents will be addressed by researching current boat license requirements and supporting change where necessary. A water safety curriculum will be adopted for schools to use at the end of each school year to decrease other water-related injuries.

- *Women's Health:* APEX-PH data showed a need for improvement in access to prenatal care during the first trimester of pregnancy as well as in reducing the numbers of low-birth-weight babies born to Ocean County women. The task force also identified a need to evaluate family planning curricula in all school districts to ensure that instructors are comfortable and familiar with the resources they are using. Family planning information will be added to all the parenting programs offered by hospitals and school systems to assist apprehensive parents in talking to their children about contraception. Intensive educational programs will be developed to reduce the increasing rates of sexually transmitted diseases and address clients (especially repeat clients) enrolled in STD clinics.

  Efforts will be increased to provide fetal alcohol syndrome and smoking cessation information to women enrolled in prenatal clinics. Services for battered pregnant women will be increased, and women enrolled in prenatal clinics will receive information about where they can access services if they are victims of abuse. Additionally, an infertility education series and support group will be maintained cooperatively by the local hospitals.

  Recognizing that lifestyle behavior change necessitates more than episodic contacts with educators and providers, the Prevention/Education Task Force has designed its action plans to be carried out by the diverse group of representatives who will use individual opportunities to reach the community but work jointly to carry out the stated objectives. It is the broad-based representation of consumers and providers who will serve to weave the concept of healthier individuals and a healthier community in their daily activities. Just as individuals will be encouraged to be accountable for their own health status through the educational empowering efforts of this movement, the agencies who are now participating—and those who may join—will be accountable to the community through their commitment to maintain the partnership. The BHOC project is designed to be a living process that can and will take different shape depending on results of future measurements of success, health assessments, and community input. The only constant in the project is the commitment and partnership of agencies and individuals who have a stake in the health of their community.

Community Care Network Vision Is Helpful

The CCN's vision, with its description of the four dimensions, has helped the BHOC leaders better identify their overall mission and focus. In terms of community accountability, it should be clear that from the earliest efforts, through the activity of the work forces, sensitivity to community needs and responsiveness to community feedback have been factors in decisions and activities. It is the expressed intention of the Planning/Steering Committee to report periodically to the public on its activity and success.

All the activity and involvement of the many groups and interests speaks to the desire for a seamless continuum of care. The efforts of the Technology Task Force are specifically oriented toward such a goal. Part of the challenge facing all members of the collaboration is that New Jersey's regulatory and health care environment sometimes makes it more difficult to act in concert with all groups. By involving representatives of government and political interests, it is believed that processes can alter themselves to the point that a greater good is achieved through the efforts of the collective body.

Driven by the feedback from the at-risk focus groups and the APEX-PH results, there has been an obvious community health focus as well as the adoption of an expanded definition of health to include prevention, wellness, and overall quality of life. The behavioral study should give the participants a clearer understanding of the kinds of behavior adjustments needed to effect a healthier lifestyle.

Management within fixed resources is the challenge that looms above all this. The BHOC philosophy is to create enough of a cooperative environment among all groups involved that management of limited resources should become a natural outgrowth of the process. The Cost Task Force is working on some issues in this regard, but it is believed that real progress will be made simply by the relationships developed through the BHOC initiatives. Because of increased communication, immunization programs are already being developed through the partnership of organizations of the Planning/Steering Committee. Thus, this cost-effective means of preventive activity has been enhanced through the BHOC process. Additionally, the Universal Care Task Force has taken on the task of educating county interests in the positive, cost-effective aspects of managed care. This concept has been experienced in New Jersey only during the past year or so. It is through increased cooperation and communication promoted by the BHOC initiative that more progress can be made in managing resources more effectively as a whole community.

The members of the recently organized Planning/Steering Committee believe this entire initiative is a "bud about to blossom." As mentioned previously, it became clear to these leaders that there was a great deal of task force activity that needed a more centralized level of coordination and focus. Clearly, the community benefits initiatives, which began almost eight years ago in singular efforts by local organizations, have progressed to the degree of collaboration that has been described. BHOC is an initiative that is ready to move to the next level of accomplishment. The strengthened Planning/Steering Committee intends to mentor the process of having each task force set more detailed, measurable objectives, as well as budgets commensurate with those objectives. This plan is expected to be in place by the end of August 1995.

Additionally, the Planning/Steering Committee will be forming a development committee to encourage greater financial support for the undertaking. Currently, most projects are funded through one of the hospitals and one or two of the agencies. In addition to requiring members of the Planning/Steering Committee to take greater responsibility for identifying financial support of the activity, a development committee will add to the potential for increasing such support. The intention at this point is to accept all financial support into a special fund located at the county board of health.

Finally, the leaders of the BHOC initiative take a great deal of pride in what has been accomplished. It is very clear, however, that there is a long way to go. Once the initiative truly became a countywide collaboration, it became that much more difficult to remain centrally focused with clear lines of authority and accountability. The leaders of the reaffirmed Planning/Steering Committee are confident, however, that enough of a structure of accountability and objective setting and monitoring has been established to begin to harness each group's enthusiasm and activity into a more coherent and deliberate effort.

At least two Planning/Steering Committee members have attended the Health Care Forum's Healthier Community Summit in California precisely to benchmark ideas and processes for our effort in Ocean County. Clearly, the leaders of BHOC are serious about succeeding.

SUMMARY OF NOTABLE PROGRESS

After the APEX-PH process was conducted in 1993, one of the first things that became apparent was the lack of, and fragmentation of, readily available Ocean County health status data. Recognizing that the community health needs assessment resulted in information that was valuable but not as extensive as we would have liked, the Planning/Steering Committee initiated a second process to gather data. This second attempt involved the collection of information about the health and behaviors of residents via a telephone survey of 1,200 randomly selected individuals. This behavioral survey was conducted by a consultant company and paid for by various members of the BHOC collaborative. Those survey results, coupled with the data from the original APEX-PH survey, will result in a more complete snapshot of the community and more focused work plans for the BHOC initiative. Since the Planning/Steering Committee made the behavioral health survey data available to the BHOC membership, the task forces are in the process of incorporating this information into their work plans, which is resulting in more measurable and defined objectives.

In addition to the behavioral health survey, the Prevention/Education Task Force's adolescent health subgroup conducted a three-day Future Search Conference for Ocean County teenagers. Jointly sponsored by BHOC member agencies, this Teen Future Search Conference enabled teenagers to voice their concerns and participate in the overall BHOC initiative. The conference also resulted in the formation of additional work groups within the adolescent health subgroup. The membership of these work groups includes teenagers, and the work groups are devoted to the specific problems/issues identified at the teen conference. Teen work groups include substance abuse, recreational activities, education, and violence.

The two above-mentioned activities are significant events in the progress of the BHOC initiative in that they expanded and further cemented the community partnership first formed as a result of the original Future Search Conference. Both the behavioral health survey and the Teen Future Search Conference provided a sense of ownership in that they involved current members from planning to implementation, were supported financially by member agencies, and provided an opportunity for community-wide exposure through media attention

In approximately 3 years, BHOC has evolved into a true community-owned project, involving more than 80 organizations and 170 individuals. It is recognized as a vehicle for collaboration and cooperation among community providers. An example of this type of cooperation is evident in a recently established centralized cancer screening information clearinghouse. Given the large older adult population, certain types of cancer are more common in Ocean County; as a result, various agencies have historically offered preventive screenings that were often duplicative. In looking for a way to maximize the current resources available to prevent cancer, the prevention/education cancer subcommittee now provides details of each agency's specific services to the American Cancer Society Ocean County unit, which serves as a clearinghouse for information to the public. This collection of information has also resulted in neighboring agencies' changing the intended dates of certain screenings so as to offer them throughout the year, rather than at the same time in nearby locations. The American Cancer Society is also collecting demographic information about those requesting information; the cancer subcommittee will use this information to refine its plans for educational and preventive activities that reach all segments of the population.

The Planning/Steering Committee has met with each task force and provided assistance in developing realistic and measurable plans and objectives. (See figure 5-1.) A recognized clearinghouse for all quality-of-life issues, the committee has strengthened its role in managing the process during the past year. Since the 1994 reunion, the task forces have undergone further consolidation and currently include the following: Access and Transportation; Technology/Coordination of Resources; Adolescent Health; Education and Prevention; and Behavioral Health Issues. The organizational chart (figure 5-2) shows the structure of the present BHOC initiative.

Contact: John F. Marcy
Senior Vice President for Development
Community and Kimball Medical Center Foundations
99 Highway 37 West
Toms River, NJ 08755
Phone: (908) 240-8131
Fax: (908) 886-4157

FIGURE 5-1. Establishing Measurable Objectives for Building a Healthier Ocean County

- Revisit the mission of the work group. Limit the number of priorities to something that is manageable (preferably one, two, or three priorities).
- Examine why items are a priority in the first place. What is the reason this is a priority?
- Break the priority/objective into its components.
- Trace back to the Health Needs Assessment to see if there is a cause and effect involved with the priority that you set.
- Is the objective reasonable? Is it something that can be accomplished in the context in which we are now working?
- Set an amount that is measurable, something that can be counted, added, tracked. Set a time limit on when it is hoped these objectives can be accomplished.
- S.M.A.R.T.: Specific, Measurable, Achievable, Realistic, Time-based.

FIGURE 5-2. Organizational Chart

Planning/Steering Committee
Executive Committee
Access and Trans.
Adolescent Health
Activities and Recreation
Education
Violence
Substance Abuse
Behavioral Health Issues
Healthy Family Choices
Education/Prevention
Cardiovascular
Cancer
Accidents
Women's Health

Technology/Coordination of Resources
Auxiliary Workgroups
Membership
Data
Marketing/PR
Universal Care
Cost
Hospital Initiatives
Community/Kimball Health System
Medical Center of Ocean County
Southern Ocean County Hospital
Other Initiatives
Childhood Immunizations
HIV/AIDS

6

The Metropolitan Chicago Community Care Alliance

Executive Summary

After 2 years of working with the Hispanic community and with more than 20 organizations, the Genesis Center for Health and Empowerment opened in 1995 in Des Plaines, IL. Its mission is to improve the health status of the underserved by collaborating with the community to identify its strengths, needs, and priorities, and to develop solutions. Sponsored by Lutheran General Hospital (LGH), Advocate Medical Group, and the Cook County Department of Public Health (CCDPH), the Genesis Center for Health and Empowerment is one way we are striving to make the community care network (CCN) vision real.

Des Plaines is home to one of the largest and fastest-growing Hispanic populations in the northern suburbs of Chicago. Like many of their urban counterparts, this population is confronted with the health problems often associated with poverty, yet is left without access to needed services. Of those who visited the Genesis Center during its first year, approximately one-third were covered by private insurance, one-third received public aid, and the remaining third were uninsured. Half of the patients reported that they visited the Genesis Center because they experienced financial and language barriers elsewhere. Community members also reported that when they have visited providers who do not speak Spanish, they often experience a loss of confidence and are made to feel incompetent. The consequences of these dynamics are readily apparent. Of the new patients visiting the center, 30 percent reported they had needed to see a doctor during the previous year but were unable to do so. More than half of those visiting the Genesis Center never had a routine physical, even though most had been residing in the United States for 10 years or more. Fewer than 25 percent of the children had gone without a physical exam.

From the beginning, the development of this program has had extensive community involvement, beginning with 60 members of the community who divided themselves into six task forces that met monthly. The community was involved in selecting a 6,000-square-foot site, determining its name, designing a resource area to house health education materials that the committee members selected, and, when necessary, translated into Spanish. Volunteers from the community conducted door-to-door interviews to assess the perceived strengths, needs, and priorities of the community.

Community members themselves also developed a sliding fee schedule. This began with becoming familiar with billing systems, insurance policies, medical costs, and other models of sliding scales already in use. The committee also considered the need to develop a payment system that fosters community responsibility for the success of the center. The sliding fee program was submitted to and approved by the board for all services offered by the LGH and Advocate Medical Group, which provide the full range of specialty services.

In addition to offering comprehensive primary care services, the center emphasizes community empowerment. Overall health depends on factors that reach far beyond the scope of medicine, and building a healthier community means creating an environment where community members work to achieve goals that they themselves define. In this model, community participation is an end rather than simply a means. The CCDPH plays a central role in providing services in the center, offering patient education, on-site Women, Infants and Children (WIC) services, special individual nutrition counseling, on-site case management services, and lead screening. This collaboration represents the type of public- and private-sector partnerships that will become increasingly important in providing health care to the underserved.

Within the first year, more than 1,600 patients visited the center. More than 1,200 people attended more than 65 educational classes on topics chosen by community members. These included classes on working within the community, folklore dancing, filing income tax returns, preventing child abuse, and building self-esteem. These also included more "traditional" health education topics, such as healthy diets, depression, and prenatal classes.

The Genesis Center is an outstanding example of the creativity and partnerships that will become more important as health care resources become more limited. It offers a unique opportunity to learn what it takes to improve the health of the underserved and what it will take to manage an effective partnership. We have learned that community involvement in establishing the priorities of the center and in the day-to-day operation is critical if we are to achieve our goals. We have also learned that keeping the partners working together in spite of differences of opinion, external challenges, and competing priorities requires ongoing management, commitment to a shared goal, and staying focused on the community. Each of the partner's activities link to and build on what is central to the identity of each, complement the activities of the other partners, and attempt to solve real problems existing in the community.

Karen Scott, MD, MPH
Director, Cook County Department of Public Health

INTRODUCTION AND BACKGROUND

The CCN Coalition has been formed to implement the CCN vision in communities surrounding Advocate Health Care's eight hospitals. Advocate Health Care (AHC) is the result of a full asset merger between Lutheran General HealthSystem (LGHS) and EHS Health Care.* This stage of AHC's evolution represents a unique opportunity for demonstrating the CCN vision. Launched in January 1995, AHC was developed largely because two faith-based health systems recognized that effectively achieving the CCN vision in the metropolitan Chicago area required the capacity to: organize health care resources across a wide geographic area; develop and maintain interrelationships among public and private organizations that can provide multiple levels and sites of care; and work effectively with diverse and complex communities to ensure that their health care needs are being served.

This new organization is one of the largest health care providers in metropolitan Chicago, with 20,400 employees providing care at 180 diverse sites (including hospitals, nursing homes, physicians' offices, older adult housing units, home care, and hospice) throughout Chicagoland. Both systems have embraced the CCN vision and have developed strong partnerships with their communities. In 1994, the two systems invested $115 million in social accountability progress and services. AHC and its partners believe that the best approach to furthering the CCN agenda requires collaboration at a local level where individuals who use and/or need health-related resources can interact with those who control access to community resources. The overall goal of the partnership efforts described in this chapter is to establish throughout Chicagoland a customer-oriented seamless system composed of services and integrating mechanisms, which guides and tracks individuals over time through a comprehensive network of health, medical, and social services, across all levels and sites of care for improving the health status of target populations.

Comprehensive in its scope and ambitious in its intent, this goal is being achieved in a phased approach. The initial focus for continued implementation of the four elements of the CCN vision is to build on the experience of LGH and its partners in the geographic area surrounding it. Based on this experience and the lessons learned working closely with the community and populations described below, those efforts will then be expanded into communities surrounding additional AHC hospitals and/or for targeted populations throughout Chicagoland.

THE COLLABORATIVE PARTNERSHIP

The Community

The community definition governing the development of the CCN vision is largely pragmatic. First, the community includes those persons that surround, use, and support local health care organizations and whose lives are influenced by them. Second, the community is defined according to the fact that individuals and organizations interact, share common interests, and possess the means to join forces to identify and achieve common goals. Both those attributes suggest that persons and institutions would form and participate in multiple, interlocking communities; however, for the purpose of developing the CCN, the initial community targeted

*This application was submitted at about the same time that LGHS and EHS Health Care merged to form Advocate, which acts as one of the collaborative partners in the coalition. Many of the experiences described in this chapter were carried out by one or another of the predecessor organizations. Throughout, we refer to the organization by the name it was known at the time the activities were initiated. Lutheran General Medical Group is now known as Advocate Medical Group; Lutheran General Health-System is now a part of Advocate Health Care; and Lutheran General Health Plan is now known as Advocate Health Plan.

by the CCN Coalition is the geographic area made up of Park Ridge, Niles, and Des Plaines.

Located in the northwest suburbs of Cook County and surrounding LGH, these communities had a population of 151,671 in 1994, including 37,908 individuals from Des Plaines, 30,260 from Niles, and 83,503 from Des Plaines. The community is relatively prosperous and ethnically homogenous; the largest non-Caucasian population is Hispanic, which makes up 10 percent of the population in Des Plaines. A high percentage of the population is over 55 years of age, with this age group making up 31.3 percent of the population in Park Ridge, 38.6 percent in Niles, and 24.3 percent in Des Plaines. Des Plaines has the highest number of women of childbearing age, with 23.3 percent of women between the ages of 14 and 44. Des Plaines also has the largest number of businesses (123 with 100–500 employees), followed by Niles (56 businesses), and Park Ridge (15). The unemployment rate is low in all communities, with the average being 2 percent.

In general, health-related statistics for the communities of Park Ridge, Niles, and Des Plaines suggest, at least from the most global perspective, that these three communities are relatively homogenous in terms of their main health care problems, their ability to access care, and their self-reported health status. These average characteristics, however, do not indicate the specific problems faced by subgroups within these communities. For example, although it has one of the largest Hispanic populations in the northwest suburbs, Des Plaines has the least access to medical care because of language and cultural barriers and lack of insurance. In essence, most of the adults in this population are the working poor. It is estimated that 8,600 Hispanics lived in Des Plaines in 1993, a growth of 4,934 individuals since 1990. In a 1992–93 North District study of prenatal care, the CCDPH found that the largest number of patients with inadequate prenatal visits were Hispanic.

In addition to meeting the special needs of the Hispanic population, other opportunities for improving health are in reducing risks for coronary heart disease, depression, stroke, and back injury, which are the most common causes of hospital admissions for diseases that could be reduced by risk reduction interventions. During 1993 and 1994, the CCDPH undertook the Illinois Project for the Local Assessment of Needs. This process identified resources and service gaps for the North District, of which Park Ridge, Niles, and Des Plaines are a part. These service gaps include services for senior citizens, services addressing multicultural community, transportation, and low-cost dental care.

Partnership Organizations

The primary activities that are the focus of this chapter involve numerous organizations that have had extensive experience jointly cooperating on one or more aspects of LGH's CCN vision. The selection of the partners and the partnership activities were based on several guiding factors, including: a philosophy of care that emphasizes concern for the whole person—body, mind, emotions, and spirit; a commitment by LGH and now AHC to work with its neighbors to enhance the quality of life of individuals living and/or working there; the belief that health care providers must take a leadership (but not dominant) role in improving health and attaining goals such as universal access and efficient allocation of resources; and the notion that individuals are most likely to adopt and continue to practice those risk-reducing and health-promoting behaviors when they have ongoing access to information and support through varied social institutions and community organizations. That is, an effective strategy to improve community health must involve mechanisms to reach individuals in the setting where their lives are lived and when they want information, support, or services.

AHC, therefore, has established partnerships with organizations whose mission and resources span much of Chicagoland as well as with organizations that primarily work in specific communities or with specific target populations. Those CCN organizations spanning Chicagoland make up the CCN Coalition and include: the CCDPH; the Metropolitan Chicago Synod, Evangelical Lutheran Church in America (ELCA); the Chicago Metropolitan Association, Illinois Conference, United Church of Christ; and Northeastern University's Center for Cardiovascular Research. All these organizations are currently partnering with LGH on programs in Des Plaines, Park Ridge, and/or Niles. As part of the CCN visioning process, representatives of these organizations have begun meeting to explore ways to work together to enhance already established partnership programs in these communities and, in the future, other Chicagoland communities. These Chicagoland partners and their roles are described below.

Cook County Department of Public Health The mission of the CCDPH, the recognized and certified public health department for suburban Cook County, is to promote health, prevent disease, and improve access to care for the entire population in its jurisdiction. The CCDPH has several prevention and outreach services as well as well-baby and immunization clinics. CCDPH staff identified as a major problem the availability of appropriate local referral services once their screening efforts identify a medical problem. LGH agreed to address this issue with them in the northwest suburbs. Their first long-term partnership with LGH is the Des Plaines Health and Empowerment Program.

Chicago Synod of the ELCA and the Chicago Metropolitan Association, Illinois Conference, United Church of Christ Until their merger, the 110 United Church of Christ churches in Chicagoland were corporate members of EHS Health Care, and the ELCA was a corporate member of LGHS; they are now cosponsors of AHC. After the merger, AHC's board established as one of its standing committees the Religion and Health Committee. Supported by a newly configured department of religion and health, an approved role of the committee is to "develop an Advocate Mission Partner capability to anchor AHC within the regional faith communions and to promote collaboration in ministry with other community organizations and businesses who seek to enhance the health status of the communities within the region." Prior to their merger, both health systems had a long-standing interest in and history of working with congregations of all faiths both in their immediate service areas and beyond. Both have parish nursing programs and both have established congregation-based programming in Des Plaines, Park Ridge, or Niles.

Northeastern University To address the concerns of local businesses, Lutheran General Medical Group (LGMG) partnered with Northeastern University's Center for Cardiovascular Research and established the Corporate Risk Reduction Group (CRRG). The CRRG is a direct outgrowth of concerns articulated by business leaders involved in LGH's board, namely concerns about the effect of health care costs on businesses. Recognizing that rising health care costs affect the continued viability of business and the overall health of the community and its employees, and that business leaders, particularly those who have family-owned companies, are very involved in decisions being made about managed care options, the partnership was designed to find bold new solutions for meeting long-standing employer needs by reducing costs and improving quality. The CRRG can call upon the expertise of the 252 LGMG physicians and more than 50 Northeastern researchers, specialists, and health educators. As described in more detail below, the CRRG is targeting businesses with 100 to 500 employees and cooperatively developing risk reduction strategies.

Lutheran General HealthSystem In 1990, the precursors to AHC made a commitment to develop and implement a CCN. Recognizing that achieving such a goal is a complex, costly, and time-consuming endeavor, it began moving toward this vision in stages through the implementation of numerous partnership activities. Internally, the system conducted an innovative process to plan and implement a comprehensive, fully integrated continuum of care; implemented continuous quality improvement (CQI) as its central operating philosophy; began a 5-year process to implement a wide-area, open-system computer network to link CCN components; developed incentives for physicians to increase their alignment with LGHS, including growing the salaried medical group with its emphasis on primary care; and further developed managed care products. Three key elements of LGHS and the CCN partnership are described below.

Lutheran General Hospital The fifth largest hospital in the Chicago metropolitan area, LGH is a tertiary-care teaching hospital with 742 licensed beds and a medical staff numbering over 800. The hospital annually serves more than 26,000 inpatients and 123,000 outpatients. LGH has a children's hospital, a comprehensive psychiatric program, a large obstetrical program, state-of-the-art cancer care and cardiac services, and level I and neonatal trauma centers. Many of its medical staff practice in the communities of Park Ridge, Des Plaines, and Niles, which surround the hospital. As one of the founding partners of this CCN, LGH has continually sought ways to work with the surrounding communities and has played an active role in maintaining and improving the overall health of the population living within its service area as well as within the broader metropolitan Chicago area.

Lutheran General Medical Group With its 252 physicians providing care at 35 locations, LGMG constitutes the largest nonuniversity medical group in metropolitan Chicago. In addition to their patient care responsibilities, LGMG physicians provide leadership resources to LGHS's continuum of care, CQI, and case management efforts; perform substantial medical administrative services for LGH; teach more than 250 resident fellows and an equal number of medical students; and actively engage in applied clinical research. LGMG is unique in that approximately 42 percent of its physicians are primary care practitioners.

Lutheran General Health Plan Established in 1984, Lutheran General Health Plan (LGHP), the first physician–hospital organization in the nation, is owned equally by LGH and Lutheran General Independent Practice Associates, Inc. LGHP arranges for the medical and hospital services for 48,000 members through contracts with 7 HMOs and 14 preferred provider organizations (PPOs) and offers point-of-service insurance products. LGHP is one of the few Chicagoland providers with a sophisticated enough managed care structure and health system–physician economic integration to enter into complex managed care arrangements. IPA members number 600 physicians (235 LGMG and 365 community-based). In 1994, LGHP began enrolling Medicare HMO clients on a full-risk capitated basis and currently has three such contracts.

Local Partnerships

In addition to these overall, Chicagowide partnerships, numerous other partnerships have been established at the citywide and target population level. The participating organizations are described under the names of the specific programs.

Healthy Community Partnerships LGH is working with the mayors' offices of Park Ridge and Niles to establish and maintain Healthy Community Partnerships. These partnerships were established for two main reasons. First, local government officials, through their policies and legislation, influence many of the environmental, social, and economic factors that impact the health of their respective communities. Second, because of their relationship with the public and business community, they are key to establishing community-wide health initiatives. This initiative is at varying stages within each community. Park Ridge, for example, has already established a Healthy Community task force, which is planning and implementing programs.

The Des Plaines Health and Empowerment Program The Des Plaines Care Coalition has been involved in planning and implementing the Des Plaines Health and Empowerment Program from its inception. It is made up of many Des Plaines agencies, including the city of Des Plaines, Maine Township, Maine Township high schools, District 62 primary schools, the park district, and police departments. The CCDPH and the LGMG are also important partners for this activity.

Congregation-Based Services LGH's pastoral counseling, parish nursing, and congregational health services partner with 36 interdenominational congregations on an ongoing basis. The Pastoral Counseling Center began in 1971 and provides counseling services on the LGH campus and in six churches throughout Chicagoland. LGH pioneered parish nursing in 1985 with 6 churches and has expanded to 18 parish nurses working in 22 diverse congregations. Congregational Health Services, a primary prevention screening and health promotion program, began in 1991. Since that time, the program has been implemented at 23 congregations, with a total of 2,087 adults, 19 adolescents, and 9 children being served. Parish nurses are in the Christ Church in Des Plaines and the First United Methodist Church in Park Ridge. First United Methodist and St. Isaac Jogues in Niles have implemented the Congregational Health Services Program. LGH also sponsors the National Parish Nurse Resource Center, which provides educational programming and materials to the ever-growing parish nurse population in 48 states.

Chronic Care Network for Older Adults In 1991, LGH joined the National Chronic Care Consortium. The 24 members of the consortium share a common commitment to develop networks that are person-centered, systems-oriented alliances between acute and long-term care providers who serve a common older constituency. To develop a local chronic care network, LGH brought together 10 sites of care (hospital units, older adult community services, a home care agency, a nursing home, and two physician offices) that used CQI to develop the processes and tools needed to manage and link chronic care services across their multiple settings. Through a project funded by the Retirement Research Foundation, 17 sites of care currently are linked in a network (described in the following section).

PRIOR EFFORTS THAT REPRESENT MOVEMENT TOWARD THE COMMUNITY CARE NETWORK VISION

LGH and its partners have achieved significant progress in moving toward the CCN vision over the past few years. To date, the progress has mainly occurred through a number of interrelated programs organized to achieve particular goals. Each program demonstrates commitment to one or more aspects of the CCN vision; together, they indicate the capacity to collaborate effectively around each of the four dimensions (community health focus, community accountability, seamless continuum of care, and managing within fixed resources).

Healthy Community Partnerships

As mentioned above, LGH has established Healthy Community Partnerships, based on a model developed by the Healthcare Forum, with the cities of Park Ridge and Niles. The Park Ridge Healthy Community Partnership, the oldest of these partnerships, was created in June 1993. Its mission, developed during the first 4 months of its operation, is to encourage the citizens of Park Ridge to play an active role in improving their health, to identify and prioritize community health-related needs, to work collaboratively with new and existing organizations, and to create programs and services to enhance the quality of life for all the citizens of Park Ridge.

Community health focus and community accountability have been central to the vision of this partnership. During 1994, the partnership conducted a comprehensive health assessment of a random sample of Park Ridge residents. The objectives of this telephone survey were to assess the overall health status and social well-being of Park Ridge residents, identify health risk behaviors among residents, identify community health and social service gaps, and identify at-risk individuals. The outcomes of this assessment are being used to help direct the partnership's efforts in developing community-based programs to promote a healthy community; they will also be used as benchmarks against which the impact of health promotion programs and services will be evaluated.

In addition to completing the needs assessment, the partnership has mounted three prevention-oriented programs for the citizens of Park Ridge: a pneumonia vaccination program, a stress-reduction program, and a family bike fest. The accomplishments of these activities are discussed below. Through the collaboration of LGMG, the Park Ridge Senior Center, and the CCDPH, the partnership vaccinated 1,106 high-risk older adults to prevent pneumococcal pneumonia. A free stress-reduction seminar, conducted by a biofeedback therapist from LGH, was held at the Park Ridge Community Center and was attended by approximately 50 Park Ridge residents. The program that involved the greatest number and variety of organizations was Bike Fest T94, the primary goal of which was to promote bike safety and bike helmet use. The members of the partnership, Park Ridge Police Department, local bike shop owners, LGH physicians and nurses, the Cook County Forest Preserve canine and equestrian units, and Maine South High School combined efforts to make the day a success. To continue to encourage bicycle safety, Park Ridge police officers have been awarding McDonald's food certificates to children who are seen wearing helmets while riding their bikes.

The Niles Healthy Community Partnership was established in spring 1994. Drawing on the experience of the Park Ridge partnership, the Niles Healthy Community Partnership also began with a community needs assessment. In addition to the goals outlined above, and as a means of gathering additional community input into the goals of the partnership, the survey was designed to ask Niles residents about the specific types of programs/activities they would like to see offered. A representative sample of 400 adult residents were surveyed in February 1995. During May, the mayor of Niles planned to complete appointments to a partnership task force charged with reviewing the results of the survey and developing an action plan. The top four overall problems identified by the citizens of Niles are crime (64 percent), air pollution (60 percent), drugs and alcohol (59 percent), and youth gangs (56 percent).

Des Plaines Health and Empowerment Program

In 1991, LGHS established the Chicagoland Health Initiative. Its goal is to work with government, churches, neighborhood groups, and social service agencies to improve the health of underserved populations—particularly to help increase primary care access and stimulate the development of networks of services for all populations. In 1993, LGMG, in cooperation with the Chicagoland Health Initiative, Des Plaines Care Coalition, and the CCDPH, formed the Des Plaines Health and Empowerment Program. The goals of the program are as follows:

- Establish a health center responsive to the needs of Hispanics living and/or working in Des Plaines
- Actively involve the target community in identifying their strengths, needs, priorities, and solutions as they relate to health
- Foster collaboration among community leaders, organizations, and the community to improve the health status of the underserved with an initial focus on the Hispanic population
- Provide education and training to health care providers related to community-based primary care for the underserved

From the beginning, the development of this program has had extensive community involvement. On December 4, 1993, members of the Des Plaines Care Coalition helped with a kickoff luncheon for Hispanics living and/or working in Des Plaines. As a result of that meeting, 60 community members divided themselves into six task forces that met monthly. They were involved in selecting the community outreach coordinator, made the final selection of a 6,000-square-foot site, and determined the name of the site—"Genesis Centro de Salud y Desarrollo/Genesis Center for Health and Empowerment." One of the most labor-intensive projects involving the community was the development of a system of fees for uninsured and underinsured patients. The expressed intent of the program is to serve anyone regardless of his or her ability to pay for services. The community members themselves researched existing programs, reflected on their own needs and resources, and developed a program of qualification and payment for services. Committee members are selecting health education materials, translating them into Spanish, and designing a resource area to give the community access to those materials.

In March 1995, community members conducted 210 door-to-door interviews to assess perceived strengths, needs, and priorities. As appropriate, the interviews were conducted in Spanish. The process, guided by researchers from Loyola University, began with three focus groups that identified a list of beliefs, issues, and strengths in the Hispanic community. From the focus groups' responses, a questionnaire was developed. (See figure 6-1.) The results of the survey have been presented at three community meetings to approximately 200 people, including members of the Des Plaines Care Coalition. Based on the survey results, new community task forces have been developed to address the following issues: access to friends and families, prenatal and postnatal care, pediatric care, dentists who speak Spanish, programs to help new immigrants, affordable housing, issues for adolescents, and parenting education. The CCDPH is playing a central role in providing services at the center.

Scheduled to open in June 1995, the new center's roles and responsibilities include the following:

- Assisting community task forces in the planning of services at the center, including written patient education materials
- Providing on-site Women, Infants and Children (WIC) services by stationing bilingual nutrition staff at the center
- Providing the necessary computer equipment to manage and implement WIC services
- Providing on-site case management services
- Providing group and/or individual health education as requested by primary care physicians or community, or as needed, based on health assessments
- Providing special individual nutrition counseling when requested by the primary care physician
- Providing adequate amounts of routine childhood and adult vaccine preparations
- Coordinating any appropriate Illinois Department of Public Health (IDPH) state laboratory assistance for the center
- Providing Medical Presumptive Eligibility training to staff
- Referring potential clients from CCDPH outreach or public health preventive clinics
- Working cooperatively with LGH to develop a joint information system for the center

To ensure that the center can effectively achieve its mission, the partners have agreed that, if possible, all center staff will be at least bilingual. The center's director is a bilingual, family practice physician; its on-site physician, social worker, community coordination, nursing, and administrative staff are also bilingual.

To date, three parenting groups have been formed at Plainfield and Apollo schools and Maine Township High School. Also, parents were concerned about youth not being occupied during the summer. In response, the Illinois Crossroads Girl Scouts awarded 85 scholarships for summer scouting, the Salvation Army awarded scholarships for a summer program in Wisconsin, and Maine Township also awarded six scholarships for a summer program. In addition, two Hispanic youths were employed by local agencies.

FIGURE 6-1. Community Concerns Survey

HISPANIC COMMUNITY OF DES PLAINES
COMMUNITY CONCERNS SURVEY

Instructions: I am going to read some statements to you. I would like you to tell me two things about each statement: how important it is to you and how satisfied you are that the topic is being addressed in Des Plaines.

LI = less important
SI = somewhat important
VI = very important
VD = very dissatisfied
D = dissatisfied
SS = somewhat satisfied
VS = very satisfied

	How important is this to you personally			How satisfied are you with how this is being addressed in Des Plaines			
1. Hispanics/Latinos get paid fairly according to the type of job they perform in comparison to other workers	LI	SI	VI	VD	D	SS	VS
2. There are prevention and treatment programs for alcohol and drug abuse	LI	SI	VI	VD	D	SS	VS
3. Activities and job opportunities are available for adolescents	LI	SI	VI	VD	D	SS	VS
4. Hispanic/Latino adolescents are not involved in drugs and alcohol	LI	SI	VI	VD	D	SS	VS
5. There are training and job placement programs for Hispanics/Latinos	LI	SI	VI	VD	D	SS	VS
6. City officials and the community respond appropriately to crime	LI	SI	VI	VD	D	SS	VS
7. Affordable housing is available for everyone	LI	SI	VI	VD	D	SS	VS
8. Hispanic/Latino people are respected and valued	LI	SI	VI	VD	D	SS	VS
9. Legal assistance is available	LI	SI	VI	VD	D	SS	VS
10. Services are available for people experiencing depression and anxiety	LI	SI	VI	VD	D	SS	VS
11. There is affordable and convenient day care for preschool children	LI	SI	VI	VD	D	SS	VS
12. Recreational/sports activities for Hispanic/Latino children are available and affordable	LI	SI	VI	VD	D	SS	VS
13. Services are available to prevent and treat child and spousal abuse	LI	SI	VI	VD	D	SS	VS
14. Neighbors of different nationalities help each other	LI	SI	VI	VD	D	SS	VS
15. Hispanics/Latinos are treated by landlords the same as any other tenant	LI	SI	VI	VD	D	SS	VS

(Continued on next page)

FIGURE 6-1. (Continued)

LI = less important
SI = somewhat important
VI = very important
VD = very dissatisfied
D = dissatisfied
SS = somewhat satisfied
VS = very satisfied

	How important is this to you personally			How satisfied are you with how this is being addressed in Des Plaines			
16. There are affordable doctors who give good care	LI	SI	VI	VD	D	SS	VS
17. Hispanics/Latinos have access to friends and family to socialize and get support when needed	LI	SI	VI	VD	D	SS	VS
18. Hispanic/Latinos avoid cigarettes and tobacco use	LI	SI	VI	VD	D	SS	VS
19. Transportation services are available for everyone	LI	SI	VI	VD	D	SS	VS
20. Adjustment programs for new immigrants are available	LI	SI	VI	VD	D	SS	VS
21. Dentists who speak Spanish provide services at a reasonable cost	LI	SI	VI	VD	D	SS	VS
22. Information for financial assistance is available	LI	SI	VI	VD	D	SS	VS
23. Hispanic/Latino or Spanish speaking doctors are available	LI	SI	VI	VD	D	SS	VS
24. Hispanic/Latino children are treated as well as other children at school	LI	SI	VI	VD	D	SS	VS
25. Youth are not involved in gangs	LI	SI	VI	VD	D	SS	VS
26. Families can preserve the Hispanic/Latino culture and customs when children are growing up	LI	SI	VI	VD	D	SS	VS
27. Family planning programs are available for Hispanics/Latinos	LI	SI	VI	VD	D	SS	VS
28. Hispanics/Latinos have opportunities to acquire more education	LI	SI	VI	VD	D	SS	VS
29. There are training and job placement programs for Hispanics/Latinos	LI	SI	VI	VD	D	SS	VS
30. Hispanics/Latinos have opportunities to work together to improve their community	LI	SI	VI	VD	D	SS	VS
31. AIDS/HIV and Sexually transmitted diseases prevention education is available	LI	SI	VI	VD	D	SS	VS
32. There are programs to help you stay healthy	LI	SI	VI	VD	D	SS	VS
33. Teenagers are taught how to prevent pregnancy	LI	SI	VI	VD	D	SS	VS
34. Hispanic/Latino women use pre-natal, post-natal and well child care	LI	SI	VI	VD	D	SS	VS

FIGURE 6-1. (Continued)

DEMOGRAPHIC QUESTIONS

Now I'd like to finish by asking you a few questions about yourself.

[1. Check gender ____ M ____ F]

2. What is your marital status? (read options)
   - ____ Single, never married
   - ____ Married
   - ____ Widowed
   - ____ Divorced/separated
   - ____ Living together

3. What is your age? ____

4. In what language do you read? (read options)
   - ____ Only Spanish
   - ____ Mostly Spanish
   - ____ Equally in Spanish and English
   - ____ Mostly in English
   - ____ Only in English

5. In what language do you think? (read options)
   - ____ Only Spanish
   - ____ Mostly Spanish
   - ____ Equally in Spanish and English
   - ____ Mostly in English
   - ____ Only in English

6. How many years of education have you completed? ____

7. Where were you born? ____________________________

8. Where was your mother born? ____________________________

9. Where was your father born? ____________________________

10. How long have you lived in US? ____ months or ____ years

11. How long have you lived in Des Plaines? ____ months or ____ years

12. What is your household income? (Check only one)
    - ____ less than $5,000
    - ____ $5,000 - $9,999
    - ____ $10,000 - $14,999
    - ____ $15,000 - $24,999
    - ____ $25,000 - $34,999
    - ____ $35,000 - $49,999
    - ____ greater than $50,000

    OR Monthly $________ OR Weekly $________ OR Hourly $________

13. How many people does this income support? ____

14. How do you pay for your health care?
    - ____ Self Pay
    - ____ Medicaid
    - ____ Medicare
    - ____ Private or Employer Insurance
    - ____ Other

15. Including yourself, how many people currently live in your household? ____ Adults ____ Children

16. Are there any other issues, needs or strengths we haven't discussed that are very important to you?

Thank you for completing this interview.

Lutheran General Congregational Partnerships

Congregations are logical places to facilitate education and reflection on the practical as well as moral dimensions of health and healing, and the following beliefs have guided the development of partnerships with them. First, congregations are places where many people seek information, discuss questions, and find meaning for important life events. Second, congregations draw upon enduring traditions of religious reflection and practice related to health, healing, and illness. Third, congregations are peopled with a diverse population—usually intergenerational, and almost always a mix of the healthy, the ill, and those who care for both. Fourth, congregations are one of the few forms of community that remain in an increasingly individualized society. Congregations can model the truly communal nature of health and healing, and activities that foster health and healing can revitalize a community.

In the early 1980s, as LGH searched for ways to enable individuals to have access to information and to mechanisms that support health, it also explored the role parishes might play in community health. As a result, the Congregational Health Partnership (CHP) was formed in 1986. The partners consisted of seven Chicago area Lutheran congregations, representatives from the Division for Life and Mission in the Congregation of the American Lutheran Church, and representatives from LGH. In 1987, the position of director of parish relations was established with the responsibility of enhancing relationships between the LGH and those parishes that reside in its geographic area. One result is a congregational council that meets monthly and develops programs that will assist professional leaders in congregations to minister to their members, especially when they are hospitalized at LGH.

Several programs have been established to work with congregations, including: Parish Nursing Services, Pastoral Counseling, Congregational Health Services, and the Park Ridge Center for the Study of Health, Faith and Ethics. Staff from these areas began to meet in 1993. Through these meetings, it became evident that, together, these areas, along with their congregational partners, have the skills, experience, and many of the processes and tools that would enable congregations to realize their potential as health and healing communities. To realize that potential, congregations can implement activities in four important areas and become places involved in (as outlined by the Christian Medical Commission of the World Council of Churches in its 1990 report summarizing its 12-year, 10-county study of congregations' role in health): primary health care (that is, cooperating with other agencies such as health care providers and the promotion of health, primary care, and disease prevention); health teaching (that is, providing health education and facilitating personal responsibility for health and self-discovery of causes of ill health); healing (that is, celebrating creative healing liturgies and supporting those in healing ministries); and caring community (that is, offering fellowship for those longing for mutual caring and solidarity; the sick, lonely, handicapped, oppressed, marginalized, and those with social problems such as divorce, unemployment, and unplanned pregnancies).

Parish Nursing Services and Pastoral Counseling have worked with congregations to address all four elements; Congregational Health Services has primarily addressed primary health care and health teaching. Congregational Health Services and Parish Nursing have both received outside funding to help them reach CCN goals. In 1993, Congregational Health Services received a 3-year Retirement Research Foundation grant to work with congregations with parish nurses to implement health promotion programs for older adults. In 1994, Parish Nursing Services and Congregational Health

Services were awarded a W. K. Kellogg grant with the overall goals of helping individuals and families who use congregations as a resource for health, more effectively and efficiently linking to evolving community health networks, and developing health promotion programming for individuals ranging from school-age children to older adults. Under development is a documentation system that will capture individual and group data that can be linked to information systems of health and/or social service providers.

Corporate Risk Reduction Group

After working with more than 100 companies to define and address their health care concerns, the CRRG has developed a data- and physician-driven process that will help employers control and manage their costs. This process involves analyzing health care and insurance costs to identify major cost drivers for health claims (less than 10 percent of the average company's employees generate 65 percent of that company's claims); involving CRRG physicians in utilization review, treatment planning, and improving compliance; and using health education as a tool to work with employees to manage their use of services and their health risks.

With ongoing data collection, the CRRG integrates information related to the company's insurance costs, employees' health behavior, and medical costs. Activities are constantly refined based on the data and from working with corporate officers and employees. The information collected is also useful to businesses when they negotiate insurance contracts. Health care costs of companies have been reduced by 15 percent to 30 percent in 1 to 2 years of working with the CRRG.

Chronic Care Network for Older Adults

From October 1, 1993, to October 31, 1994, the Retirement Research Foundation funded the first year of a multiple-year project to establish and test the effectiveness of a chronic care management system for older adults. This system allows for care coordination and clinician communication among sites providing services for individuals with chronic diseases. Project staff, along with clinicians from involved sites, developed and used tools, including intake, assessment, and continuing care pathways, to guide care management.

Chosen for tool development were chronic conditions that can result in long-term impairments and involve major costs: stroke, dementia, depression, hip or knee replacement, and hip fracture. In this first year, 203 older adults were enrolled with one or more of those chronic conditions. By year's end, 17 sites were involved in the project, including hospital units, a home care agency, older adult community services, physician offices, nursing homes, a comprehensive outpatient rehabilitation facility, and preadmission testing office. These sites include both LGHS-owned and nonowned sites. A major guiding principle upon which this project is based is that care management and coordination should be the responsibility of all sites serving the same individual and that tools are needed to expedite care management, coordination, and communication among sites.

The Chronic Care Network has begun collaborating with the LGHP to develop effective mechanisms to identify and manage the care of elderly patients within fixed resources. Together, they have established a task force that is working on care management tools for patients with congestive heart failure. The task force has also developed a screening tool that is being used with all Medicare HMO clients to identify those members with existing health care problems and who are at high risk for experiencing debilitating illness. All new members are sent a comprehensive health assessment questionnaire 2 weeks prior to their effective enrollment date (if they do not return the questionnaire by mail, a phone interview is conducted). Results from the questionnaire are used to assign individuals to one of three categories defined on the basis of the extent to which care management is required. All new members also have their medications screened; when necessary, they are reviewed by a pharmacist and recommendations are written for the primary care physician. The goal of the effort is to identify that segment of the population at increased risk of hospitalization and whose care can be proactively managed; this is premised on the belief that managing the care of populations within fixed resources requires targeting the right resources to the right persons at the right time.

Improving LGHS Systems and Structures

As discussed above, LGH has been committed to developing a CCN since 1990. In addition to establishing the various partnerships and programs described above, LGHS recognized that the success of a CCN critically depended on enhancing the integration, efficiency, and coordination of care within and across its own 76 sites of care, and developing a culture that supports innovation to solve operational problems and improve quality. Thus, LGHS launched initiatives related to CQI, information systems, and development of managed care products. Each of these is discussed below.

Continuous Quality Improvement To provide LGHS associates with the knowledge and methods to accomplish organizational redesign, the board, senior management, and physician leaders formally adopted a management theory of CQI. LGHS was an early adopter of CQI and derived much of its knowledge from the Harvard Community Health Plan. To this day, LGHS is one of approximately 30 health providers cooperating in a resulting national benchmarking and information-sharing group. CQI efforts are run out of the Offices of System Quality and Clinical Practice Improvement. They provide statistical consultation and support for ongoing measurement/monitoring systems and conduct all CQI-related education and training functions. Clinical practice improvement initiatives involving the hospital, the health plan, and the medical group are prioritized and coordinated through the center. The accomplishments of the CQI efforts are many and diverse. The board introduced a systemwide approach to its oversight of quality. LGHS leadership and physicians have completed extensive training in CQI: of 703 managers, 59 percent have completed two courses for managers; 89 physicians have completed the first course of the CQI curriculum, and 61 have completed the second course, resulting in 82 physicians participating in process improvement teams, 11 of whom are CQI team leaders. Team activities range from clinical improvement activities to improvement of physical access. Teams have developed and implemented more than 20 clinical guidelines. In July 1993, a multidisciplinary clinical process improvement team was chartered to reevaluate methods used for rapid diagnosis and treatment of patients with chest pain. The team developed, refined, and ultimately adopted a conceptual model to approach clinical management of a broad array of chest pain patients. After the pathway was introduced, the average length of stay declined from 36 hours of inpatient care to 20.6 hours of observation.

In another project, LGHP primary care physicians identified an opportunity to improve outcomes in patients taking the anticoagulant warfarin (Coumadin). Suboptimal monitoring of warfarin and potentially preventable hospitalizations for treatment complications were identified through a chart review. A physician team developed clinical guidelines for warfarin use and designed an algorithm for managing therapy; a multidisciplinary team developed care pathways for ongoing management of the ambulatory patient on anticoagulation therapy; and, another multidisciplinary team designed and opened a special warfarin treatment clinic. The aims of this clinic are to improve outcomes, increase patient and physician satisfaction, and conduct research. Results achieved to date show good laboratory control of therapy, excellent clinical outcomes, and a high degree of customer satisfaction.

As teams engaged in improvement/redesign of clinical processes, the need to address the related issue of physical access to sites of care came into sharp focus. Campus sprawl, lack of patient parking adjacent to sites of care, and confusing signs were cited as causes of delays in surgery schedules, failure to donate sufficient units of autologous blood prior to joint surgery, and delayed or canceled outpatient appointments. In January 1994, a cross-functional CQI team was appointed to address both short-term parking issues and long-term environmental impact. Using CQI tools and methods, the team collected and analyzed data describing peak times of patient demand and scheduling patterns of staffing. As a result, available campus parking space has been redesigned to provide both pay and free parking for patients adjacent to sites of care, and signage compliant with Americans with Disabilities Act standards has been installed.

Information Systems Managing diverse information resources, increasing access to uniform and clinically useful data to support decision making, and developing mechanisms for facilitating ongoing data analysis and reporting are critical to effectively managing the proposed CCN. In 1991, a 5-year strategic development, information systems plan was adopted to operationalize a wide-area computer network to link LGHS sites of care, community partners, and physicians. Costing nearly $60 million, the network structure is nearly 75 percent implemented. The eventual goal is for the network's database to include protocols for care, outcome measurements, and costs of care. To meet this goal, LGHS is working toward an "electronic medical record." Several interrelated efforts have been under way to support this development. LGHS has already established the Physician Information Network (PIN), which provides physicians and physician practices with on-line access to patient information. The following information can be obtained directly from the system: physician census; orders; results (lab, radiology, nuclear medicine, and heart station); demographic data; financial data; medical records data; pharmacy orders; consultant processing; guidelines; and electronic mail. Approximately 690 attending and resident physicians and 80 physician practices are currently using the PIN.

A clinical data system using the Ameritech Health Connections' Knowledge Keystone product is under development. This product allows data to be summarized and will initially include patient demographics, financial information, lab results, radiology results, and transcribed reports such as history and physicals. This product will be available to physicians from their homes and offices enabling them to get up-to-date information wherever they are. In addition to providing information that supports direct patient care, the Knowledge Keystone clinical repository will be used by clinical researchers in their studies to improve clinical outcomes.

Another important element of the evolving information strategy is the development of a Senior Information System (SIS). When the Chronic Care Network for Older Adults was first implemented, a courier system and/or project managers were used to transfer continuing care pathways and other information from site to site.

Since then it has begun to establish the SIS as part of its care management system. Its first step was to research the availability of computer software that will allow information transfer among community-based providers. Only one system was found—a computer system that was developed to link community-based senior service agencies in Battle Creek, MI, made possible through the support of the W. K. Kellogg Foundation. LGHS has contracted with the consultant for that project to implement the "Battle Creek" system as the first stage of its SIS. All sites have personal computers, and LGHS supplied them with modems. The SIS allows referrals to be sent over the system; stores and tracks service utilization for individual clients; provides reporting on average services utilization by client type; allows messages to be sent from site to site, thereby increasing communication; and provides a directory of care services, allowing the clinician to find the most appropriate service at the nearest location for the client. LGHS installed the SIS into its new open-architecture system to integrate it with the other LGHS information systems. Currently, the SIS has relatively limited assessment data on line; project staff have applied for grant funding to further develop the SIS to enable the transfer of medical assessments and care plans.

Managed Care Products To aggressively pursue the goal of managing care within fixed resources, LGH developed the LGHP in 1984. Before the merger, this organization negotiated all managed care contracts for the hospital and participating physicians. LGHP provides a forum for primary care physicians, specialty physicians, and the hospital to better understand how their futures are interrelated by reducing costs and utilization and by improving quality. LGH benefits from this partnership because it is able to compete for a growing percentage of the health care market and obtain financially beneficial rates. The inpatient hospital utilization rate for both capitated and noncapitated members is 233 inpatient days per 1,000 covered lives, which compares favorably with the Illinois averages of around 350 days per 1,000 covered lives. Currently, managed care contracts produce 25 percent of LGH revenues. One goal of the system is to increase the number of managed care contracts and primary care physician participation in the health plan. To help increase contracts, it developed a Medicare HMO product and is in the process of developing one for Medicaid patients with both the University of Illinois Medical Center and the state of Illinois. This level of performance has earned LGHP a reputation for managing high-quality, cost-effective care throughout Chicagoland. The LGHP expects to launch its third full-risk capitated Medicare HMO contract in June, 1995. It is expected that new enrollment in these plans will grow from 150 to 250 seniors per month.

To continue its aggressive approach to managed care, AHC has established a physician–hospital organization (PHO) at each of its hospitals as well as a "super" PHO that will assist in contract negotiations for each hospital PHO and for negotiations involving all PHOs. Physicians from LGHP have been appointed to leadership positions of the "super" PHO. Prior to the merger, LGH and EHS Health Care collaborated to increase the managed care products of Health Direct. Initially, Health Direct was a wholly owned subsidiary of LGHS devoted primarily to conducting utilization review and building a PPO. Recognizing the potential to develop an even stronger presence in Chicagoland, LGHS agreed to form a partnership with EHS by selling one-half of Health Direct to EHS. The partnership with EHS resulted in new vitality for the organization. With access to more capital and an enhanced market position, Health Direct established an HMO and point-of-service network in spring 1993. AHC currently covers 100,000 capitated lives. Through these efforts, AHC has gained extensive knowledge, experience, and insights into managed care and managing within fixed resources.

Miscellaneous Initiatives Designed to Improve the Experience of Patients Using LGHS In addition to the comprehensive activities described immediately above, LGHS has conducted a number of efforts to facilitate patient use of the system. These are briefly described below.

In early 1995, LGH opened the first comprehensive, multidisciplinary cancer care center to offer state-of-the-art technology in the Chicago/Northern Illinois region. The center's comprehensive, multidisciplinary approach to cancer care offers convenience and ease of access to patients. With capabilities spanning the full range of services from preventive diagnosis to the care and treatment of patients in the most critical condition, the center has been designed with the patient in mind. In addition to all services being housed in a single site, patient registration is done by phone, parking is immediately adjacent to the center, chemotherapy facilities feature private cubicles, and all patients have access to on-site counseling, nutrition counseling, pastoral care, and other supportive service.

In 1994, LGH opened its Patient Resource Center, a centralized, comprehensive pre-admission testing clinic. The center was initially established to better manage the process of performing same-day surgery. Prior to its opening, less than 30 percent of those patients were admitted for same-day surgery with all the necessary laboratory tests and examinations completed. This created numerous delays and difficulties for both patients and providers. Since its opening, more than 80 percent of these patients are now admitted with complete information. Delays and dissatisfaction have been greatly reduced because the needed information is available in a timely fashion. Patients admitted to inpatient units now also use the Patient Resource Center to complete necessary pre-admission testing.

To track patient and employee satisfaction, LGHS uses Parkside Associates, Inc. (PAI), a wholly-owned subsidiary of LGHS. PAI routinely conducts quality-of-care monitor surveys of LGHS patients, physicians, and employees with two goals in mind: (1) to identify key quality characteristics as perceived by patients, and (2) to measure the impact of quality improvement efforts on these key quality characteristics. Reports prepared quarterly include overall analysis, analysis of key subgroups (that is, nursing units, emergency room shifts, outpatient departments), trends over the previous four quarters, and comparisons with a national database of similar facilities. These reports are distributed to LGHS management.

Summary of Prior Efforts

The above-described activities—Healthy Community Partnerships, Des Plaines Health and Empowerment Program, Lutheran General Congregational Partnerships, CRRG,

Chronic Care Network for Older Adults, and improving LGHS systems and structures—provide abundant evidence of the commitment to the CCN vision and progress toward achieving it. Each of the partnership activities embody or are beginning to embody one or more aspects of the CCN vision. Taken together, they provide a solid base of experience on which to continue building.

MOVING TOWARD THE COMMUNITY CARE NETWORK VISION

Vision and Visioning Process

Beginning in 1990, LGHS began its formal process to develop its CCN vision. It established several partnership activities (Chronic Care Network for Older Adults, Healthy Community Partnerships, Congregational Health Services, Chicagoland Health Initiative, Des Plaines Health and Empowerment Program), all of which developed their own network-related visions based on their missions, goals, and target populations. In January 1995, LGHS merged with EHS Health Care largely because the two systems recognized that effectively achieving the CCN vision in the metropolitan Chicago area required the capacity to provide access to a range of medical and social services throughout Chicagoland. AHC is working with its various partners to take advantage of the resources and potential the new organization offers.

The visioning process initiated by LGH began with the establishment of a task force, chaired by the president and chief executive officer of LGHS, whose charge was to initiate the process of defining a Chicagoland continuum of care. The task force soon decided that it was enmeshed in so many day-to-day management activities that it was not able to devote sufficient time to designing a new delivery system. In 1992, the task force commissioned 15 LGHS associates (4 physicians and 11 health professionals) to design the continuum of care. The 15 associates spent their full time on this project for nearly 18 months, focusing their efforts on: (1) defining a continuum of care, 11 "critical success factors" and 55 "design characteristics," or those outcomes the organization would have to achieve to function as an effective continuum, and (2) developing a long-range plan in which all strategic business activities would be reorganized to achieve these outcomes. The continuum vision is to implement a "customer-oriented seamless system, composed of services and integrating mechanisms, that guides and tracks individuals over time through a comprehensive network of health, medical and social services, spanning all levels and sites of care, improving the health status of target populations."

Eleven teams with 110 members, including business and community partner representatives, were assigned to develop the concrete work plans that would move the organization to a continuum model. These teams and the issues they addressed are as follows:

- Strategy and Sponsorship—to provide strategic leadership for the overall effort
- Target Populations—to identify, develop, and maintain relationships with continuum target populations
- Providers and Facilities—to determine the adequate number and appropriate mix of providers, facilities, and sites and then achieve that mix
- Service Linkages—to establish and maintain a network of internal and external services linked by integrating mechanisms

- Promotion and Prevention—to implement a plan for target populations that assesses needs and baseline health status and employs promotion/prevention strategies
- Care Management—to establish and use a system of care management over time and across appropriate levels, sites, and providers
- Internal Incentives—to develop and use internal incentives that encourage alignment and optimize system performance
- Physician Alignment—to link physicians into the success of the continuum
- Information Systems—to implement an aligned and coordinated information system
- Risk/Capitation—to organize to manage health care services under systems of capitation
- LGHS Performance—to develop and use measures of LGHS performance

Initiatives for Moving toward the Community Care Network Vision

The specific initiatives that are being proposed are designed to further the development of the Metropolitan Chicago Community Care Alliance simultaneously on a number of fronts. The description of how the CCN vision will continue to be implemented over the next 3 years will focus on each of these three approaches, namely: facilitation of the development of the coalition; specific programmatic initiatives in the geographic area surrounding LGH, designed to advance the four dimensions; and dissemination of the model throughout AHC. Also, both EHS and LGHS brought significant strengths and resources together in the formation of AHC. To date, the principles underlying the CCN vision have been critical in shaping this system and will play a key role as it continues to evolve.

Coalition Development A critical function of the Metropolitan Chicago Community Care Alliance is to encourage program planning and linkages among partnership organizations. Specifically, during 1995–96, it will identify means to link congregation-based services with both the Health and Empowerment Program and the Chronic Care Network for Older Adults. Information from Parish Nursing supports that older adults make up a significant proportion of the members of congregations; religious activities also play a big part in the lives of the Hispanic population (as indicated by the community survey). A second focus of the coalition will be to enhance the function of the Healthy Community Partnerships. These efforts are still relatively immature; it is anticipated that the focus of activities and the commitments of the participant organizations will grow as work proceeds. The coalition will function as a resource to promote this development. Also, it will facilitate the use of CRRG data and risk reduction expertise with the Healthy Community Partnerships and the Chronic Care Network for Older Adults. The coalition will serve as a liaison between each of the parent organizations to ensure that its strategic directions are integrated with those of the partnership and, as necessary, bring to bear resources to promote effective responses to defined needs and refine the CCN direction.

Program Initiatives The overall process for moving toward the CCN vision in Park Ridge, Niles, and Des Plaines involves community assessment, program planning and implementation, evaluation, and communication of results. Community assessment will happen on an ongoing basis at the community-wide and program-specific levels.

Health indicators will be monitored by the coalition and Healthy Community committees and will include: public health data provided by CCDPH; inpatient, outpatient, and emergency room data provided by LGH and the LGMG; and evaluation data from each specific program. This information will be used for program planning and refinement and to determine parameters for determining success. Program initiatives will focus on the Chronic Care Network, Des Plaines Health and Empowerment Program, Corporate Risk Reduction, and the Information System.

Chronic Care Network for Older Adults The Chronic Care Network will adopt a comprehensive approach to furthering the four elements of the CCN vision. First, the network will enroll a minimum of 400 new clients during 1995–96 and 1996–97 (in addition to the 200 already enrolled). At all participating sites, the project will continue to enroll older adults (age 55 and above) with the diagnosis of stroke, depression, dementia, hip or knee replacement, or hip fracture. As described above, these problems were initially selected because they can result in long-term impairments of the elderly—a growing population—and have major costs allocated to them. In total, chronic diseases account for approximately 80 percent of all deaths and 90 percent of all morbidity in the elderly population. Rational approaches to managing care that cuts across a variety of sites is critical to improving the quality of care provided, the functional health of chronically ill persons, and, ultimately, in managing care within fixed resources.

In addition to focusing on the care of patients with the above-mentioned conditions, chronic care management tools, which are under development, will enable the network to enroll clients with the diagnosis of congestive heart failure as well as those considered to be generally at high risk for needing care management. This effort will draw extensively on the experience of quality improvement efforts developed by the former EHS Health Care and efforts under way in the LGHP (as described above). More specifically, generic care management tools will be developed for those clients that have a diagnosis not covered by existing pathways, or have multiple problems and experience more than one of the following: need assistance with three or more activities of daily living; have moderate to severe cognitive impairments; use six or more medications; have minimal social supports; and have a recent history of one or more hospitalizations. Once the above clients have been enrolled, project staff will determine what additional pathways should be developed and proceed with their development.

A major focus of the efforts here will be to collect, analyze, and describe the frequency, type, and cost of services used by the total pool of 600 clients; such information is critical to effectively managing the care of this population within fixed resources. For each enrolled client, data to be collected include the frequency and type of project sites used—particularly the frequency and cost of home occupational therapy, physical therapy, speech therapy, skilled home care, adult day care services, outpatient visits, emergency room, hospital admissions, length of hospital stay(s), and nursing homes. These data will be described by age group (55–65, 66–75, 76 and above) and by diagnosis. They will also be analyzed by the length of time clients have been enrolled in the project (6 months or less, 6–12 months, 12–24 months, and 24–36 months).

To enhance its focus on community health and accountability, the Chronic Care Network will survey client/caregivers and project providers (care coordinators and physicians) to ascertain their satisfaction with care and to determine ways to improve it (survey scheduled for summer 1995). The Chronic Care Network has already surveyed clinicians and has used these results to modify the program. Interviews with clients will also collect data on functional health status, which will then be used for ongoing monitoring of the effects of the program and, as appropriate, for treatment planning. Care coordinators and physicians will be surveyed before and after their involvement in the chronic care management system. If care management problems are identified, appropriate solutions will be designed and implemented. For example, last year it was found that nursing home staff needed to receive physician orders faster after a client is transferred to them from a hospital unit. To address this problem, appropriate standing physician orders were defined, piloted, and implemented.

In addition to accomplishing the above-described concrete activities, the Chronic Care Network is involved in extensive planning activities with the LGHP and the evolving managed care activities across the entire AHC system. This involvement stems from the commitment of the LGHP to increase the number of elderly enrolled in managed care and on the need to identify those patients whose care may need more extensive management. Plans are being formulated to: assist in integrating senior case management into physician offices systemwide; continue to evaluate and develop new contract arrangements for senior managed care; work with rehabilitation services to develop a plan to provide a capitated continuum of rehabilitation services; develop programs to provide and/or assist seniors to access education and wellness programs; and continue to refine and develop an integrated database to assist with the management of seniors across multiple sites. As these plans are formulated, they too will be implemented in the context of this effort. Of particular interest is the use of client surveys, interviews, and other data to guide the development of risk reduction and wellness programs. The resources of the CRRG could help focus and facilitate this process.

Des Plaines Health and Empowerment Program With its comprehensive approach to improving the health status of the Hispanic population living in Des Plaines, the Health and Empowerment Program has ambitious goals relevant to each of the four dimensions of the CCN. During the first year of this effort, the program will: open the Genesis Center of Health and Development (slated for June 1995); recruit additional family physicians; enroll the help of volunteer physicians to meet the full range of the population's needs; grow the patient population of the center; open the Health Resource Center; continue parenting groups; initiate prenatal classes; and refine the collaborative efforts with the CCDPH (for example, coordinating the scheduling of primary care visits with WIC visits). As in any new venture of this nature, a great deal of effort in the first year will be expended on making center operations client-oriented and efficient. An important focus of the next 3 years will be on community-initiated activities. The committees formed based on the outcomes of the assessment interviews will develop action plans to address their areas of responsibility.

Plans are to initiate a comprehensive approach to evaluating the Health and Empowerment Program during 1995–96. Measures will be collected related to each of the program's goals, including: empowerment (for example, number of projects defined and developed by community members), collaboration (for example, number of Hispanic community members involved in community programs and type of involvement), medical care (for example, improved health functioning as measured by health status questionnaire—based on the Rand Medical Outcomes Study), and professional education (for example, number of medical students involved). As with all other aspects of this initiative, the results of these evaluations will be reported in an ongoing fashion to the Des Plaines Care Coalition, the advisory committee of the Chicagoland Health Initiative, the LGH board, and the community itself. Moreover, the results will be used to refine the direction of the program, enhance the involvement of the community, improve services to meet the needs of the Hispanic population, and improve health status. Consistent with the planning efforts to date, the goals for 1996–97 and 1997–98 will be developed in collaboration with the Hispanic population and the coalition.

Corporate Risk Reduction Group The main goal of the CRRG in relation to this proposal is to launch a pilot project to demonstrate how a risk-sharing demand management partnership can work between the CRRG and Des Plaines employers. Specifically, the CRRG will work with a Des Plaines employer who has many Hispanic employees; the employer will be identified in collaboration with the Health and Empowerment Program and the Des Plaines Care Coalition.

The purposes of this effort are to train and educate employers, employees, and staff in developing a coordinated focus to achieve effective delivery of care; continue refining the methodology used to analyze utilization data and identify savings opportunities; improve the approach used to developing long-term solutions specific to employers' needs; build capabilities to monitor the effectiveness of coordinating medical and behavioral aspects of risk reduction services; assess the approach with a culturally diverse group of employees; and develop and implement outcome measures to evaluate the success of the program. While the demonstration project is being conducted, the CRRG will continue to work with other businesses. Its goal is to work with a minimum of three additional businesses per year in either Des Plaines or Niles. It will also work with other partnership programs to define and effectively use available data to help set priorities and guide program planning.

Information System A major focus of information system development will be on establishing an "electronic medical record," which will allow patient information to be accessed from LGH and medical staff sites. The Ameritech Knowledge Keystone product allows all data to be deposited in a central repository. Then systems must be developed to allow the data in the repository to be called up from a variety of sites and for all data related to an individual client to be obtained from throughout the network. Currently data from hospital units and departments are being connected to the repository. At the same time, LGMG and the LGHP are working with their vendor, IDX, to develop the physician information elements of the electronic medical record. Data from LGMG and the LGHP will be deposited in the repository in July. To make the system user-friendly and refine its usability, a pilot will be conducted using 15 physicians and two hospital units. The pilot is scheduled to last until December and then the system will be expanded to all hospital units, departments, and physician sites throughout 1996. Because the SIS is linked into the repository, when physicians are able to access information in the repository, they will also be able to access information from the sites in the Chronic Care Network for Older Adults.

Broadening the Community Care Network Vision throughout Advocate Health Care: A Multidimensional Approach

During the first year of the project, the necessary groundwork will be laid to continue to expand the CCN vision throughout AHC; this will primarily occur through educating the appropriate managers and clinicians about the effort through regular reports about CCN activities. During 1996–97, concrete planning efforts will be launched in the communities surrounding two inner-city hospitals (Bethany and Trinity, where a core of relevant community outreach activity is already under way). The process to be implemented in these hospitals will mirror the processes used in developing the approach at LGH, namely, reviewing and assessing demographic profiles, identifying and collaborating with local government authorities to address community health problems, defining and building on existing partnerships and establishing new partnerships to address the full range of health-related issues, and working with charitable foundations to fund start-up programs. As a result of these planning activities, the year 1997–98 will be devoted to implementing the CCN vision in the communities of the two designated hospitals. To facilitate these goals, Advocate Health Care Foundation has established the Office of Community Benefit Programs, whose main responsibility is to support community partnership programs in their development and in obtaining financial support for partnership activities.

It is expected that a number of planning activities under way at the newly formed AHC will soon result in the development of organizational systems and structures that will enhance the realization of the CCN vision. For example, the new system board has expressed a strong interest in and plans to enhance its strategic planning functions particularly as they pertain to community accountability and community benefits. Discussions are also under way about the responsibility of each hospital's governing council and the mix of expertise they would need to enable the assessment of hospital activities from a community health perspective (for example, public health, organizational expertise, community involvement, and so on). Once these systemwide plans are finalized, additional opportunities to further advance the continuum vision will be identified and aggressively pursued.

SUMMARY OF NOTABLE PROGRESS

Advocate Health Care and its partners in the Metropolitan Chicago Community Care Alliance (MCCCA) have been pleased to participate in the CCN Demonstration Program; it has given us a unique opportunity to reconceptualize and redesign the relationship between health care providers and their communities. Recognizing the importance of and building on partnerships—with the local community, other providers, and purchasers—the MCCCA is committed to improving the health of the communities of which it is a part.

As discussed in the Executive Summary, the Genesis Center for Health and Empowerment opened in 1995 and, in its first year of operation, saw over 1,600 clients. At the request of community members, it regularly offers educational programs in collaboration with other community groups. Notably, a comprehensive approach to monitoring the Genesis Center and the health of the community have been implemented. In addition to collecting health status data from new patients, the Center is compiling data on: empowerment (for example, number of volunteers involved in Center, number of classes offered, number attending classes) collaboration (number and names of organizations involved in health center activities, number of community members involved in other community organizations), access to medical care (for example, emergency room use, number of new patients per month, patient satisfaction) and professional education (for example, number of students involved in the Center). This comprehensive approach will ensure that Genesis remains committed and accountable to the community.

At its 1-year anniversary celebration, the Advisory Board of the Genesis Center identified the shortage of instruction on English as a Second Language as one of the major barriers to continued empowerment. Linguistic differences present the single most imposing barrier to fully participating in the community. It affects nearly every aspect of life. It affects the ability of parents to participate in their children's education, including helping with homework, meeting with teachers, and participating in school governance. It influences the relationship between parents and their children. For example, adolescents are sometimes embarrassed by parents who not only do not speak English but are often less educated than they are. The Advisory Board will begin exploring options to enhance the local capacity to provide the needed instruction.

The goals for the Chronic Care Network for Older Adults are also being met. The number of clients enrolled in 1996 will exceed the number anticipated. New pathways have been developed to better serve the elderly population, and current pathways have been revised to meet the needs of the clients and the clinicians. Staff are participating in redesigning the documentation system, improving care management in physician offices, and disseminating the approach throughout other AHC facilities. For example, staff at Bethany Hospital and Good Samaritan Hospital have recently worked with their local provider communities to implement the pathways and the information system.

The Healthy Community partnerships in Park Ridge and Niles continue to thrive. In Park Ridge a Bikefest was held, and free pneumonia vaccines have been offered to local citizens. Because of the success of the partnership, the Cook County Department of Public Health now sponsors these inoculations. In 1996 the Park Ridge Partnership held its first citywide Holistic Health Fair. Involving over 33 organizations, the fair provided medical screens and also information to help individuals enhance their overall quality of life. In Niles, the partnership conducted educational activities in conjunction with the 4th of July parade, addressing childhood, bike, car, and home electrical safety. The Niles Partnership recently adopted a project to decrease the use of alcohol and drugs among junior high and high school students.

Based on these experiences in Park Ridge and Niles, Healthy Communities has since been implemented in communities around all eight Advocate hospitals. A Coordinating Council has also been established to provide an opportunity for sharing information among partnerships under way in the communities surrounding the eight Advocate hospitals. The driving force behind some of these efforts has been other community organizations. This past spring, AHC sponsored a 1-day Healthy Communities Summit which was attended by over 200 representatives from diverse communities throughout metropolitan Chicago. Participants had the opportunity to learn about local and national initiatives and network with others engaged in these efforts.

Plans are being formulated to realize the CCN vision on Chicago's south and west sides. AHC, in conjunction with the Chicago Department of Health, Claretian Medical Center, Elmhurst College, and other community groups are looking at ways to expand access to primary care and more efficiently use community resources for underserved, inner-city communities. A somewhat different partnership in the same community has begun to explore how to address the issue of domestic violence, its relationship to infant mortality and morbidity, and coordinating/developing services to provide an integrated continuum of care for victims of abuse.

The CCN vision with its four elements—Community Health Focus, Community Accountability, Seamless Continuum of Care, and Managing within Fixed Resources—continues to guide the planning and implementation of programs and activities which are responsive to the identified needs of the community. We fully expect this vision to play an increasingly important role in shaping reform efforts and how health care is provided well into the 21st century.

Contact: James O'Brien
Advocate Charitable Foundation
8765 West Higgins Road, Suite 430
Chicago, IL 60631
Phone: (847) 723-7646
Fax: (847) 723-7485
E-mail: james.o'brien@advocatehealth.com

7

The Solano Coalition for Better Health

Executive Summary

In a time of crisis, it is relatively easy to bring individuals and agencies from different perspectives together to deal with that crisis. It is much more difficult to stay together over the long haul, to work toward a "common good" that is often gray and seems inherently to include conflict. It requires patience to articulate the common good, transcending personal or corporate interests. The Solano Coalition for Better Health is a model of what it takes to move from crisis to sustained collaborative action.

The planned closing of a primary care clinic serving many of Solano County's uninsured and underinsured created the crisis. The new "partners" found they had much in common. At a very pragmatic level, they realized they all bore the cost of poor prevention, late medical interventions, and—most critical—overutilization of hospital emergency room services. At a higher level, they also realized that "the system" was not meeting the medical, let alone the wellness, needs of many residents.

Thoughtfully, patiently, and through many negotiations, the coalition gave birth to the Solano Partnership Healthplan, a system of managed care for Solano's 45,000 Medi-Cal enrollees. As a board member of the HealthPlan and as a city councilman working with the coalition in developing the partnership, I witnessed firsthand what it takes to develop true partnerships. Each perspective, from provider to elected official to consumer, was critical in creating a workable system. Perhaps more important, each perspective was valued and respected. Medical service is not enough. The coalition, in its evolution, has focused more on the role of the community in promoting wellness and continues to explore ways to support local efforts to create healthier communities.

In 1992, with the support of the coalition and Kaiser Permanente, we initiated the Healthy Vacaville Task Force. This community group, which I have had the pleasure of chairing, has made a difference. Among its accomplishments, the task force has facilitated the creation of a community dental clinic, assisted in rerouting the city bus system to more efficiently access medical and social services, translated informational brochures into Spanish, conducted extensive immunization programs, and initiated a dialogue on teen risk-taking behaviors. Based on this model, the coalition has initiated the Healthier Solano Communities Project to help create "Healthy City Task Forces" in each of Solano County's seven cities.

We are, and will become, an even healthier community because of the Solano Coalition for Better Health. Partnership has its rewards.

Ernest Kimme
Councilman, City of Vacaville

THE BEGINNING

Eight years ago, a small group of local physicians, government officials, and hospital administrators met to stave off the closure of a San Francisco Bay Area county primary care clinic. The clinic was vital to a county that sprawled 898 square miles yet contained only three other primary care sites for its low-income and indigent residents. From that initial success of preserving an underfunded primary care system, the Solano Coalition for Better Health (SCBH) emerged and began to address the confluence of economic, social, and historical events that continue to impact the health of its community.

That Solano's new coalition would pioneer major reforms in health care financing, capacity building, access, and partnership was inevitable. Its membership included dynamic public officials, committed business leaders, community visionaries, and the largest HMO in the United States. Its vision greatly exceeded the provision of medical care and extended to the inextricably linked—yet seldom jointly provided—systems of social services, health promotion, public protection, employment, and education. Equally auspicious, progress toward one of the coalition's primary objectives—the creation of an integrated, full-service managed care system for the Medi-Cal population in Solano County—benefited from national and statewide political climates promoting with financial and other incentives the development of locally controlled, risk/surplus sharing and cost-effective health care systems.

THE COMMUNITY

Of Solano County's nearly 400,000 people, 97 percent reside within seven incorporated cities lying along the corridor between the Carquinez Straits in the north part of San Francisco Bay and the University of California at Davis, just south of Sacramento. Solano is the 13th most ethnically diverse county in the country. The largest city is Vallejo (116,000), which was mostly settled during World War II with the development of Mare Island Naval Shipyard and which became a major nuclear submarine base for the U.S. Navy and which completed a 6-year closure process affecting 10,000 civilian employees, more than any base closure in the country. Approximately half of the city's population are ethnic minorities, including African-American (21 percent), Hispanic (11 percent), and Asian/Pacific Islanders (23 percent). Vallejo presents significant urban problems, with illegal drugs and gang activity linked to the urban centers of Richmond, Oakland, and San Francisco. As is true of most of Solano County, Vallejo serves as a bedroom community for families seeking affordable housing and able to commute to employment centers in the more immediate Bay Area. Kaiser

Permanente is the largest health care provider in the county, insuring over 50 percent of Solano's population, and is Vallejo's second largest employer after Mare Island.

Benicia is a small (28,700) community adjacent to Vallejo and also close to major oil refineries and a sugar processing plant in neighboring Contra Costa County.

Fairfield (95,000) is the county seat of Solano and shares with neighboring Suisun (27,200) the proximity of Travis Air Force Base and David Grant Hospital, the largest U.S. Air Force hospital in the world. Plans are under way to relocate the U.S. Veteran's Hospital from Marunez to the Fairfield area to take advantage of David Grant Hospital. Fairfield is also a bedroom community, working aggressively through its redevelopment agency to attract employers to the area. Approximately 30 percent of the community are ethnic minorities with a mix of 13 percent of Hispanic origin, 13 percent African-American, and 10 percent Asian/Pacific Islanders.

The city of Vacaville (85,700) is a growing community that has recently been attracting biogenetic employers in addition to a significant number of factory outlet retail stores. It also sustains a large retirement community and two state prisons. Vacaville's population is 16 percent Hispanic.

Rio Vista (4,200) and Dixon (13,000) are small, somewhat isolated rural communities in the east and north part of the county. Dixon has a large farm worker population (28 percent Hispanic), a significant percentage of lower-income families, and links socially and commercially to Yolo County in the north. More affluent Rio Vista is in the Delta region close to San Joaquin County.

RECOGNITION OF LOCAL RESPONSIBILITY

Winning one of the Healthcare Forum's first Healthier Community Awards in 1993 was a significant boost to the SCBH as a fledgling collaboration. Initially, the community care network (CCN) development focused on addressing the issue of access to care as expressed in the organization's 1992 manifesto, "Toward a Local Healthcare Partnership: To Avoid Being Further Victimized by the National Health Care Crisis." That document served as a blueprint for addressing the needs of the uninsured and underinsured, physicians, hospitals, community clinics, the business community, and the public in general.

Through the shared commitment of the hospitals, the county, and city government, each of whom pledged one-third of the funding, consultants were hired to work with community leaders and elected officials to develop a network of health care that would serve as a local health care partnership. Solano County was the first of three counties to seek designation from the California Medical Assistance Commission as a "County Organized Health System," Governor Pete Wilson's AB336 "Alternatives to Medi-Cal Managed Care." The work of constructing what was to become the Solano Partnership Healthplan then began.

The Solano Partnership Healthplan

By undertaking research, financial analysis, and formal planning processes, the SCBH achieved the momentous task of moving the county-organized health system from concept to reality. Through the collaborative efforts of a diverse health and human services community and local government officials, a system of managed care—named the Solano Partnership Healthplan (SPH)—has been devised to serve the 42,000 Medi-

Cal (Medicaid) beneficiaries in Solano County. (See figure 7-1.) Fully operational since May 1, 1994, the SPH managed care system has replaced fee-for-service reimbursement between Medi-Cal providers and the state and has resulted in expanded health care access coupled with increased service capacity. In early 1994, after several years of hard work and collaboration, virtually all the county's primary care providers had agreed to participate in the SPH, resulting in commitments for 68,000 beneficiaries when there were only 42,000 to enroll.

Additionally, the SPH fostered the expansion of the county's primary care clinics (including the one the county was about to close in 1988), and three new community clinics were born, including a brand new Redwood Community Clinic in Vallejo and two family practice clinics created as a pilot by Planned Parenthood, expanding from reproductive to primary health care. The SPH also continues to foster coordination and build networks within Solano's health care infrastructure, including the following:

- The four hospitals' emergency departments have developed systems of cooperation that redirect patients requiring routine care to their primary care providers and stabilize and refer those with acute conditions.
- As a national model, Solano County and Kaiser Permanente have joined to provide an integrated system of mental health services to Kaiser's 10,000 Medi-Cal members that also retains management by members' primary care physicians.
- Even though it was not included in the capitation, Kaiser has made available its new alcohol and chemical dependency day-treatment services to its Medi-Cal members and is slated to receive an award from the Robert Wood Johnson Foundation's national Fighting Back program.
- Sutter Solano Medical Center has strengthened its birthing center, "Great Beginnings," to better serve higher-risk perinatal patients and has invested in expanding the capacity of Redwood Community Clinic to meet after-hours urgent-care needs of its Medi-Cal members in the Vallejo area.

The policy-making body of the SPH, the Commission, was appointed by the Solano County Board of Supervisors and serves as an independent political jurisdiction contracting directly with the state Department of Health Services. The Commission's membership reflects that of the SCBH's board of directors—two hospital organizations, Kaiser Permanente, the medical society (three seats), community clinics, county officials (two seats), a city councilman, and representatives of business, nursing, consumers, and consumer advocates. At its first annual planning retreat, in fall 1994, the Commission decided to work with the SCBH in developing health care access opportunities for uninsured Solano residents (60,000 and growing; mostly, working families and their children). Special legislation passed in Congress in 1996 and was signed by the president that allowed SPH to expand to neighboring counties and to include Medi-Cal beneficiaries in its Medi-Cal managed care network. Napa County will begin operation in July 1997. The SPH agreed to use some of its savings to work with the SCBH and its new relationship with Solano's transit systems to address the access problems of many Medi-Cal beneficiaries (particularly women with children) and has committed $500,000 each year for the next 2 years in "enhancement funding" for community-based prevention services to improve the health status of Medi-Cal beneficiaries in Solano County.

FIGURE 7-1. Solano Partnership Healthplan: Referral Physician Medical Service Agreement (sections 4–6)

SECTION 4
SERVICES TO BE PROVIDED

4.1 Management of Care

With the exception of Emergency Services and Limited Services, the Primary Care Physician shall determine what care is necessary and appropriate, prescribe any Covered Services, (either directly or through referral) and manage the care provided and authorized for Members in accord with sound professional principles and with proper attention to the need for containment of costs. Referral Physician shall abide by Case Management Protocols, incorporated into the Medical Services Agreement as Attachment A.

4.2 Consultation with Medical Director

Referral Physician or any other provider may at any time seek consultation with Medical Director on any matter concerning the treatment of the Member.

4.3 Covered Services

For each Member who has chosen or has been assigned to a Primary Care Physician, that Primary Care Physician shall provide or authorize the provision of all available services covered under the California Medi-Cal program when they are necessary and appropriate for the care of that Member, with the exception of Limited Services and Emergency Services. Covered Services include but are not limited to:

4.3.1 Timely access to Primary Care Physician, Referral Physician (upon referral from Primary Care Physician) or Attending Physician for medical advice when requested by the Member or some person legitimately acting on the member's behalf.

4.3.2 Consultation and treatment services by Referral Physicians including referrals for a second professional opinion as these may become necessary for (1) the prevention of anticipated illness, or (2) for treatment called for due to exposure to illness, or (3) for detection, treatment or diagnosis of illness or injury or the health effects of illness or injury, or (4) for care of mother and unborn or newborn child during and following pregnancy.

4.3.3 Admission to Hospital, Skilled Nursing Facility, Intermediate Care Facility, or other institutional care setting.

4.3.4 Audiology, physical therapy, occupational therapy, speech therapy, family planning services, and/or other therapeutic and diagnostic measures prescribed by the Primary Care Physician, Referral Physician or Attending Physician, which are held to be necessary and appropriate to the process of prevention, diagnosis, the management or treatment of diagnosed health impairment, or rehabilitation of the member.

4.3.5 Ambulance Services when necessary.

4.3.6 Other necessary durable medical equipment rental, medical supplies, and medical transportation. "Medical transportation services" means the transportation of the sick, injured, invalid, convalescent, infirm or otherwise incapacitated persons by ambulances, litter vans or wheelchair vans licensed, operated, and equipped in accordance with applicable state or

(Continued on next page)

FIGURE 7-1. (Continued)

local statutes, ordinances or regulations. Medical transportation services do not include transportation of beneficiaries by passenger car, taxicabs or other forms of public or private conveyances.

All services and goods required or provided hereunder shall be of quality consistent with community standards of care.

4.4 Direct Access

If a Member contacts the Referral Physician and requests medical advice, diagnosis, treatment, or relief, the Member's Primary Care Physician shall first authorize the rendering of any services by the Referral Physician, unless excepted in section 5.4 of this agreement. No payment shall be made by the PLAN unless evidence of such Primary Care Physician authorization exists.

4.5 Physician Authority

Nothing expressed or implied herein shall require the Referral Physician to provide to the Member, or order on behalf of the Member, Covered Services which, in the professional opinion of the Referral Physician, are not required.

4.6 Place of Service

All services are to be provided at a place which the Primary Care Physician or Referral Physician determines is appropriate for the proper rendition thereof, within the constraints of the State Medi-Cal program regulations.

4.7 Payment Made on Unapproved Services

Except in the case of Limited Services, Emergency Services and services obtained while traveling distant from Solano County and authorized by the Medical Director, PLAN shall not pay any charges from any Provider unless such services have been authorized by the Members Primary Care Physician or the Medical Director. PLAN shall seek recovery of any payments made in error.

4.8 Imposition of Additional Controls if Necessary

Referral Physician recognizes the possibility that Partnership through utilization management and quality assurance process may be required to take action requiring consultation with its Medical Director or with other physicians prior to authorization of services or supplies or to terminate this agreement. In the interest of program integrity or the welfare of Members, Partnership may introduce additional utilization controls as may be necessary at any time and without advance notice to Referral Physician. In the event of such change, the change may take effect immediately upon receipt by Referral Physician of notice from the Medical Director but Referral Physician shall be entitled to appeal such action to the Grievance Review Committee, the Physician Advisory Group and then to the Partnership.

4.9 Discrimination Prohibited

Referral Physician shall not differentiate or discriminate in the treatment of Medi-Cal Beneficiaries, nor discriminate on the basis of race, religion, sex, age, marital status, sexual orientation, or mental or physical handicap and except as limited by the scope of services he or she is qualified to provide. Referral Physician shall render health services to Beneficiaries in the same manner, in accordance with the same standards and within the same time availability as offered other patients, except as limited by existing Medi-Cal restrictions.

FIGURE 7-1. (Continued)

4.10 Hospital Privileges

Referral Physician shall secure and maintain staff privileges with at least one (1) Primary Hospital contracting with Partnership, unless specifically excepted from this section by the Medical Director.

4.11 Compliance with Committee Decisions
Referral Physician shall cooperate and participate in Quality Assurance and Utilization Review programs and grievance procedures, and comply with all final determinations rendered by the Quality Assurance, Utilization Review and Grievance Committees, unless decision is reversed by the Partnership upon appeal.

SECTION 5
EXCLUSIONS FROM AND LIMITATIONS ON COVERED SERVICES

5.1 Exclusions

In addition to those services not covered under the California Medi-Cal program as specified in Division 3, Subdivision 1, Chapter 3, Article 4, Title 22, California Code of Regulations, the Partnership shall not make payment for the following services if they are provided to Members:

5.1.1 Dental Services

5.1.2 Services which in the judgment of Primary Care Physicians (for services requiring referral) and/or Medical Director (for those services requiring prior authorization), are not necessary, appropriate, or cost-effective for the control of health-related illness, disease, or disability.

5.1.3 Services for chronic renal diagnosis and major organ transplants.

5.1.4 Any skilled nursing or intermediate care facilities (but not services provided in such facilities by physicians or other providers), long term in-home waiver service, -Purpose Senior Services, Adult Day Health Service and Short-Doyle Mental Health Services.

5.1.5 Other services as may be determined by the Partnership, and as noticed to the participating physicians.

5.2 Medi-Cal Restrictions

5.2.1 Services provided shall be subject to the limitations and procedures listed in the Medi-Cal Provider Manual unless Referral Physician is notified of modification to that policy. However, prior authorization shall be provided only through the Primary Care Physician. his/her on-call designee or the Medical Director of Partnership. The State Medi-Cal consultant shall not prior authorize services under this PLAN.

5.2.2 The Medi-Cal Provider Manual specifies certain restrictions and limitations with respect to abortion and sterilization. These services shall be subject to the limitations specified therein.

5.3 Formulary

Prescriptions payable by Partnership shall be subject to the restrictions on the State's Medi-Cal Formulary except where Formulary changes are authorized by the Partnership in accord with its contract with the State of California.

(Continued on next page)

FIGURE 7-1. (Continued)

5.4 Exceptions to Case Management Control

5.4.1 Primary Care Physician authorization is not required for Partnership payment to providers of Limited Services. The provision of such services shall, however, be subject to the same utilization controls and payment limitations which are applied to these services under the Statewide Medi-Cal Program. Prior authorization where required may be granted by the PCP or the Medical Director.

5.4.2 Certain Family Planning Services may be obtained on direct patient self referral to certain contracting providers in accord with Federal requirements at 42 CFR 441.20.

5.4.3 Primary Care Physician authorization is not required for beneficiaries designated as Special Case Managed Members.

5.4.4 Members eligible for California Children's Services (CCS) shall have CCS services authorized by the CCS Program.

SECTION 6
PAYMENTS

6.1 Payments

Referral Physician shall be compensated for services provided to eligible Members when those services are authorized by the Member's Primary Care Physician (Case Managed Members) or by the Medical Director, or Member's Temporary Primary Care Physician (Special Case Managed Members) at the prevailing Medi-Cal rates.

6.2 Fee-For-Service

The Referral Physician shall obtain and complete claim forms (as are currently in use in the Medi-Cal program as issued by the State Fiscal Intermediary) for all services rendered to Members and authorized by the Member's Primary Care Physician and/or the Medical Director, and send all claims, along with evidence of authorization, to the PLAN within six (6) months from the end of the month that service was provided. Upon submission of a complete and uncontested clean claim payment shall be made to the physician within thirty (30) days. An uncontested clean claim shall include all information needed to process the claim.

6.3 Member Liability

Unless Member has other health insurance coverage under Medicare, CHAMPUS, Kaiser, Blue Cross/Blue Shield, or a known insurance carrier or health plan, Referral Physician shall look only to Partnership for compensation for covered services and, with the exception of authorized share of cost payments, shall at no time seek compensation from Members or the State.

6.4 No Reimbursement from State

6.4.1 The Referral Physician agrees to indemnify, defend, and save harmless the State of California, and the Partnership and their respective officers, agents, and employees from any claims or losses for materials and/or services rendered by any subcontractor, person, or firm performing or supplying services, materials, or supplies in connection with the performance of this Agreement.

6.4.2 The Referral Physician shall hold harmless the State of California, and Members in the event the Partnership cannot or will not pay for services performed by the Referral Physician pursuant to the forms of the contract.

The Community Health Outreach System

Cost reduction's role as the major driving force behind the continuing efforts of health care reform in the public arena and in the marketplace is undisputed. In virtually all models under examination, some degree of managed care—with an emphasis on effective utilization of services and prevention of disease—prevails, in most cases coupled with nontraditional financing mechanisms such as prepaid capitation or other forms of provider risk sharing. In the realm of privately financed health care, HMOs and health insuring organizations have proven to be cost-effective models for delivery of health care services.

Whether managed care principles will directly benefit low-income and indigent people remains unclear, however. For example, although preliminary data from the growing literature on Medicaid managed care suggest that cost reductions and decreases in both emergency room use and inpatient hospital care can be realized, a number of critical and interrelated issues remain unresolved even as impending conversion to mandatory capitated managed care rapidly advances in California and elsewhere in the country. Chief among these significant concerns are the degree to which Medicaid managed care will result in improved health outcomes, the relationship between availability and actual use of prevention services in Medicaid care, the integration of managed care with existing public health, and community support resources available to this population.

It was to address these questions that the SCBH developed the 3-year Community Health Outreach System (CHOS) research and demonstration project, slated to begin in January 1996. Based on a model developed by Kaiser Permanente in Hawaii, the CHOS will field teams of four community health outreach workers headed by a public health nurse in each of three pilot neighborhoods in the county. The teams will make home visits to enrollees; conduct assessments; and assist families in accessing needed community services, understanding how to use managed health care, and overcoming barriers of transportation, culture, and language. Emphasis is placed on strengthening client/family self-sufficiency, with education in prevention and self-care. The nurses will provide primary care providers with information about the family's health status and assist clients/families in carrying out treatment plans. A community health training center was organized at the local community college to both prepare the teams and train members of the neighborhood health councils being organized for the project. An independent evaluation will determine the value of the project and to what degree it should continue.

The CHOS research and demonstration project is being supported with major investments by SCBH partners (Kaiser Permanente and Solano County), a state Medi-Cal case management program (SB910), and several private foundations (James Irvine, The California Wellness, Robert Wood Johnson). In addition to determining whether the CHOS should be expanded to serve all the county's Medi-Cal population, the evaluation will help (1) the county to determine how the CHOS helps re-create neighborhood-based public health and social services, and (2) Kaiser Permanente to determine how the CHOS will serve as a community extension of the primary care team in its managed care delivery system.

The Community Services Task Force

Initially organized 3 years ago to assist the SCBH in developing the CHOS, the Community Services Task Force (CSTF) began as an interagency coordinating group with a concentration of county health and social service providers. The CSTF soon expanded to include more community-based, not-for-profit providers, city and school district service providers, and eventually, representatives of neighborhood associations and organizational advocates of ethnic and special populations. Early on, the CSTF expanded its purpose to addressing difficulties in accessing care and services and organized special task forces dealing with information and referral, transportation, culture/language, and services to special-needs populations. Emerging on the local scene as a strong advocate for access to services and care, the CSTF acquired three seats on the SCBH's board of directors where it could interact directly with leadership of the Solano's health and social services system. The CSTF held a major planning retreat in the fall, using the same consultant used by the SCBH for its retreat, and has further formalized its relationship with the SCBH with a practical outcome of a joint task force to address the difficult issues of language and cultural diversity.

Healthy Vacaville

The SCBH's pilot city/neighborhood community health initiative has happened in Vacaville, where a cross section of community stakeholders, informed by local health risk information including a Healthy Start parents' survey, developed a community dental clinic and an immunization outreach program and is currently working on access to mental health services. Healthy Vacaville has been an important source of intelligence as the coalition plans the development of healthy city task forces in all seven cities in the county.

Mare Island Base Closure: Community Response Planning

In 1993, the federal government announced a series of military base closures, including Mare Island Naval Shipyard. The mayor of Vallejo, the local political leader of the Mare Island Futures Committee, asked the chairman of the SCBH to chair the Human Service Resources Group (HSRG), a committee to examine the impacts of the closure on the community's health and social services systems. Unique in the country, this committee completed an assessment of the impacts of the closure on Mare Island employees, their families, and families whose workers were at risk of losing their jobs in the community as a result of the overall economic impact on the region of a loss of a $600 million payroll.

The HSRG held hearings in the community and on the base and began to learn the magnitude of the closure's impact. The most pervasive response was denial that jobs, often secure for decades, were at risk. Such denial began to take its toll on families in the form of high levels of stress, alcohol and chemical dependency, domestic violence, and family disintegration. These family struggles were not confined to the employees and their spouses but were also manifested in the behavior of their children, as acting out in school and in the neighborhood escalated. Grandparents dependent on adult children for their care were no longer secure, and grandparents living independently became responsible for child care as parents took multiple jobs to make ends meet.

The coalition's partnership with the shipyard moved into action when Kaiser Permanente and the county helped Mare Island Employee Assistance organize the Peer Support Program. Seventy-five employee volunteers were trained to facilitate work-site support groups that helped many employees deal with the emotional and practical challenges to this major life transition. In late 1994, public and private funding was received to support a parallel program in the community, where 100 adults and 100 youth from economically impacted neighborhoods are being trained to facilitate peer support groups in the community. Although a study of the impact of the closure on employment and economic activity in the community has been completed, a drive through downtown Vallejo, with so many retail stores out of business, tells the story well. Congressman George Miller, whose district includes the base, successfully included funding in the 1994–95 Department of Defense appropriation to help communities highly impacted by base closures meet related human service needs. A small portion of those funds were used to meet immediate urgent needs within the city of Vallejo; the balance will support longer-term system changes and creative approaches that build the capacity of the community to achieve self-sufficiency and wellness.

The assessment completed by the HSRG recognized that the impact of the base closure on the community was to be long term and required restructuring of the community's response systems. While the majority of base employees either took early retirement or accepted transfer to federal employment in other states, the community suffered the loss from the region's workforce of some of its most competent employees, and from its churches, social institutions, and informal support systems much of its long-term leadership. With one year before the base is completely closed, approximately 2,000 employees remained, including approximately 800 who were physically and/or emotionally disabled and many who are functionally illiterate. U.S. Department of Labor funds have supported a job retraining and placement program, but it was not prepared for the complexities of these remaining workers. Given the needed cleanup of toxins and explosives and the protracted process of public action, prospects for reuse of the base seemed years away.

Realizing that the HSRG had more work to do, the mayor of Vallejo expanded the group's scope to include economic impacts on the community. Launched by a local conference featuring Grantland Johnson, regional director of Health and Human Services, the group convened three action groups of leaders from all sectors of the region who were charged with completing plans to address long-term impacts of the closure on the community. The groups finalized action plans for presentation at a conference in summer 1995. Also at that time, the mayor appointed a public/private policy steering committee of 12 leaders from the region, including a top person at Kaiser Permanente (after the base closures, the region's largest employer), a key business leader from each of Napa and Solano counties, and a community leader from each of the region's cities as recommended by each mayor. The Human Services Leadership Council, that new steering committee, has been charged with overseeing the implementation of the following four initiatives:

1. Fundamental changes that optimize coordination in the decision-making processes of economic development, job training, education, and human services to attract employers to the region who will provide decent jobs to local residents who have received the skill training, education, and supportive services needed to step into those jobs when they are available
2. The development of models from community capacity building that capitalize on assets within neighborhood-level informal support systems to effectively respond to families at the earliest possible point of crisis, facilitate access to the formal support system when required, and strengthen the social fabric of the community

3. The integration of appropriate health and human services at the neighborhood level that are designed to achieve desired outcomes, afford easy access to residents and their families, and mitigate the barriers caused by categorical funding, lack of coordination among providers, inadequate transportation, insufficient competence in culture and language, and other barriers
4. The development of a regional community support center that will maintain up-to-date information about community assets and needs, mobilize appropriate public and private resources from outside the region, facilitate coordination and system building among health and human service providers and informal support at the neighborhood level, provide community leadership training, and maintain a community foundation to support these and other initiatives

SOLANO AND THE COMMUNITY CARE NETWORK CONCEPT

Community Accountability

The SPH, the SCBH's major initiative to date, brings together the following fundamental elements of community accountability:

1. *Shared Local Responsibility:* The coalition's basic principle in organizing the SPH was embodied in its initial manifesto—to assume responsibility locally for securing access to health care for the county's uninsured and underinsured, and not be dependent (or "victimized") by federal and state inability to act.
2. *Shared Authority:* The SPH commission was structured so that all major stakeholders would share responsibility for its performance and outcomes. In addition to county and city officials and health care providers, the business community, nursing, consumers, and consumer advocates were given seats on the policy-making body overseeing SPH.
3. *Network of Interdependence:* The SPH's structure as a health insuring organization brought nearly all the county's private and public health care providers into a formal network of care based on managed care principles and risk and surplus-sharing incentives. This structure was the essential strategy for implementing shared community accountability.
4. *Accountability for Outcomes:* In February 1995, the SPH commission directed its CEO to develop a "report card" that would measure the performance of its contracted providers in categories of utilization and quality. That report card, geared to the Medi-Cal population, was to be in use by June 1995.
5. *Beyond Access:* In developing the CHOS research and demonstration project, the SCBH recognized that quality and utilization measures should be improved through this intervention by addressing the risks of poverty. The independent evaluation of the CHOS should provide important results. The coalition is committed to the completion of a countywide assessment that will establish benchmarks for the community's health status using Healthy People 2000 indicators.

Seamless Continuum of Care

1. The SPH has been designed as a managed care system with members (patients) selecting a primary care provider that "manages" the utilization of the full system

of capitated benefits in a way that minimizes utilization and maximizes health status.

2. The CHOS recognizes that access to medical care is insufficient for the low-income, multicultural Medi-Cal population and builds bridges to community services and strengthens individual, family, and neighborhood informal support systems.
3. The CSTF focuses on coordination of access to community services with emphasis on information, referral, and mitigation of barriers of transportation, language, and culture. Facilitating access of primary care providers to the coordinated services to special-needs populations is another example.
4. The Mare Island Action Plan has emphasized systems change and prevention/early intervention needed to collapse bureaucratic barriers to service and to foster easy access to integrated neighborhood services.

Community Health Focus

The story of the SCBH shows evolution from a narrow to a broad focus of community health. The coalition's first partners, hospital administrators, were centrally concerned with the imbalance of uncompensated care. As the underlying sense of the public's interest emerged, the focus shifted to access to health care. With the development of the SPH, the emphasis has expanded to the health status of the community. The CHOS recognizes that health status is directly related to individual, family, and neighborhood economic and social well-being, and develops access to services beyond health care. The Mare Island Action Plan moves to a recognition that jobs are at the core of family and community health and that system changes are required to secure and sustain this basic element for family/community self-sufficiency.

Management within Fixed Resources

Advancing from the fixed resources of individual hospitals, the SCBH has fostered the development of systems that collectively manage shared resources. The SPH and its system of capitation and shared risks and surpluses is the key example. The CHOS serves to extend the cost-effectiveness of managed care to the early identification and mitigation of barriers to optimal utilization and care. At the culmination of the demonstration period will be a cost-effectiveness evaluation.

The closure of Mare Island Naval Shipyard has made it clear that the community cannot afford systems of economic development and employment training that operate independently and keep a growing number of families in poverty. The SCBH's Healthier Solano Communities initiative strategically capitalizes on the assets within communities themselves and the importance of these assets to community capacity building and self-sufficiency.

NEXT STEP: THE COMMUNITY

The Retreat

In fall 1994, the SCBH board of directors and work group (principal support staff from major partners) completed a planning retreat. Concurrently, the CSTF had its own planning retreat and used the same consultant to pursue integration into the

SCBH's structure. The SPH commission also held its first planning retreat, resulting in objectives in concert with those adopted by the coalition. The coalition's retreat resulted in strengthening its vision and mission and developing a value statement and goals for the next two to three years. Most important, the SCBH determined to take new directions of actively involving the community itself as partners in pursuit of a "Healthy Solano." In this regard, the coalition determined to do the following:

- Open its membership to individuals and organizations in the community
- Convene quarterly forums to address issues of importance to the community's health
- Implement the CHOS and its neighborhood health councils
- Complete a countywide assessment and establish benchmarks (to be correlated with Healthy People 2000)
- Foster the development of healthy community entities in each city to shape the SCBH's assessment and plan and implement initiatives that address local health priorities and serve to strengthen the capacity of informal neighborhood support systems
- Continue to support the region's response to the closure of Mare Island by fostering the development of models of community capacity building, systems change, neighborhood services integration, and a coordinated approach to economic and job development decisions

As the SCBH's sole task force, the CSTF maintains three seats on the board of directors. With the coalition and the SPH commission, it will jointly plan and implement initiatives to address issues of language and cultural diversity in the county.

Extending the Community Care Network to the Community Itself

The SCBH is proposing that the national CCN become a partner as we creatively, productively, and effectively engage the community itself in securing a "Healthy Solano." This involves the following elements:

1. *Healthier Solano Communities:* The SCBH has organized and trained "city seed teams" composed of coalition leadership, major partner support staff, and CSTF representatives. These teams were charged with determining the readiness of each of the seven cities in Solano County to organize in a way that will engage residents in a collaborative process for improving the health and quality of life in their community and neighborhoods. As training and team building were accomplished, the teams met with city government officials to obtain their support and participation. The teams then spoke with a wide range and diversity of formal and informal leadership to identify efforts currently under way and discuss how best to build upon them. The SCBH employed a coordinator to support the work of the seed teams and take appropriate steps in each city to convene that city's Healthier Community effort.

   The SCBH completed a countywide health assessment that will help establish benchmarks for the future of Healthy Solano. The assessment will also generate data for each city that can be integrated into the healthier community process described above and be strengthened by input and perceptions from local leadership participating in that process. The SCBH will make available a modest amount of funds to match those city/neighborhood-level initiatives that first commit local resources and promise to build ongoing community capacity to improve health.

2. *Community Health Outreach System:* After 3 years in development, this project was scheduled to begin full implementation in January 1996. In many ways the CHOS represents the SCBH's recognition of the key role that family, neighborhood, and informal support systems play in securing individual and community health. Twelve community health outreach workers will be recruited from the three pilot neighborhoods from among those residents who have natural helping skills and reflect the language, culture, and life experiences of the families living in those neighborhoods. The outreach workers (along with the outreach nurses and each team's clerical support staff) received training and orientation to the CHOS intervention at the Community Health Training Center developed at Solano Community College. This training included techniques in assessment of family assets and issues, strategies for developing action plan/service contracts that build on family capacity for self-help, and skills in fostering family self-health care.

   Neighborhood health councils are being organized in each CHOS pilot neighborhood and are composed of significant numbers of Medi-Cal beneficiaries and other health consumers and their advocates. These neighborhood health councils will be linked with the Healthier Solano Communities initiatives being developed by the SCBH in each city. The neighborhood health councils will be supported in identifying local issues and priorities and organizing neighborhood-based initiatives to address them. They will provide support to the work of the CHOS teams and particularly advocate those system changes needed to address the difficulties that local families participating in the CHOS share with one another. Each neighborhood health council will have representation on the coalition's CHOS steering committee to support improvements in the project and to address those issues of access and service system responsiveness that surface in a number of the CHOS pilot neighborhoods.

3. *Community Health Leadership Training:* Although considerable work has been done to develop the curriculum for training the CHOS teams, the SCBH (through its CHOS Development Committee) has just begun to develop leadership training for the members of the neighborhood health councils. A model has been discovered that appears to be ideal for this purpose, "The Community Leadership Project Curriculum" developed by the Topsfield Foundation of Pomfret, CT. Leadership training will be incorporated into the training of the CHOS teams, but will be used particularly to strengthen the skills of members of the neighborhood health councils. (Commitments have been made to members of councils already organized that such training will be made available, thus leading to the discovery of this rich model.)

   Based on the experience of training for neighborhood health council members, appropriate adjustments will be made and community health leadership training will be made available to the various cities as they develop their Healthier Solano Communities entities. The SCBH will also borrow elements from the successful training curriculum for peer support group facilitator (see Mare Island below) and the Master Training program of Vallejo's Fighting Back (Robert Wood Johnson Foundation–funded drug prevention initiative).

4. *Base Closure Community Response Action Plan:* As reported above, the SCBH has provided leadership to the completion of action plans for mitigating the impact on the community of the closure of Mare Island Naval Shipyard. Among the action plans is included one that is central to the coalition's effort to extend the CCN concept to the community itself. That action plan proposes to "develop models

for community capacity building that capitalize on assets within neighborhood-level informal support systems in order to effectively respond to residents and families at the earliest possible point of crisis, facilitate access to the formal support system when required, and strengthen the social fabric of the community."

In addition to the community peer support-group facilitator training (patterned after its successful counterpart for Mare Island employees on the base itself), this action plan will encourage communities throughout the region (Solano and Napa counties) to create such models appropriate to each community. Operating costs to test these models should, in part, be funded by the new community foundation under the sponsorship of United Way. The coalition proposes to involve community member/trainees in tailoring the community health leadership training described above to help strengthen their skills to actively serve within these various models.

SUMMARY OF NOTABLE PROGRESS

Parents of children in three elementary schools serving low-income neighborhoods were increasingly concerned with the pain they saw resulting from poor dental health. School nurses were equally concerned. Children could not concentrate. Infections spread. Pro bono service, provided by dentists whom the nurses knew personally, helped, but not enough. Transportation, language, low reimbursement rates, and cultural insensitivities severely restricted service to Medi-Cal children.

Fortunately, under the leadership of the vice-mayor, a broadly based community task force of 25 was meeting regularly to identify and address community issues impacting health. Through the informal systems developed in creating the task force, nurses from these schools were able to place dental needs on the agenda. The rest of the story exemplifies community health. The task force partnerships not only created a community dental clinic but also addressed underlying issues: transportation, language, cultural diversity, and dental health.

Background

"The Community Itself: The Next Step in the Community Care Network" is the bold and optimistic title of the proposal submitted by the SCBH to the national CCN demonstration project. The proposal was bold to suggest that an initiative with limited resources could affect the health status of a county with 400,000 residents. It was optimistic because experience—particularly the experience of the task force described above as a pilot project of the coalition—has shown that community action can and does improve community health.

The SCBH, a countywide partnership of health and social service providers, educators, local government representatives, and business and community members, devoted its first years to developing a cost-effective managed care program that has greatly improved access to medical services for Solano County's 45,000 Medi-Cal beneficiaries. In that process, the SCBH fashioned a shared vision for a healthier community and its role in promoting that vision. The emphasis has shifted to "the community itself." The CCN project is a partner in strengthening the community through three initiatives.

Healthier Solano Communities

Of Solano's 400,000 residents, 95 percent live in one of its seven cities, whose populations range from less than 4,000 to more than 114,000. History and geography have resulted in unique, strong, and sometimes competitive city identities. The community, for most, is "my city."

Healthier Solano Communities, a community organizing project that respects the uniqueness of Solano's cities, envisions healthier individuals through healthier communities. Healthier Solano has two basic goals: (1) the creation of some type of formalized "team" in each city to promote improved community health, and (2) the implementation of city-specific initiatives to address one or more issues that impact wellness in that city.

Currently, the emphasis is on creating and/or supporting appropriate city teams. The SCBH is committed to processes that listen to, learn from, and partner with community members, and to initiatives that strengthen informal systems. This community-organizing effort has assessed the readiness and builds on the community's past experiences. A video, depicting community wellness and highlighting local partnerships promoting wellness, has been effective in initiating dialogue about city involvement in this project. Early learning from these seven different situations may provide insights for other initiatives:

- A small, semi-rural community was rocked by accusations of widespread sexual molestation by a long-time teacher. This crisis galvanized the community and prompted the formation of a group whose view and mission broadened to include advocacy for children's issues generally. Linkages with existing school, government, social service clinic, fraternal, and religious groups provide a resource network that is prepared to respond as this group defines its focus and action plan.
- Buoyed by the success of the dental clinic and an immunization initiative, the pilot community has designed and begun a process to work in a specific neighborhood to identify assets and barriers to wellness. The resources at the task force table and the credibility gained through the earlier initiatives have strengthened the task force's ability to respond to the outcomes of this grass-roots community assessment process.
- One city's plan for the creation of an alliance of providers and resource brokers to respond to issues from community input sessions was the vision of, and driven by, one powerful person. When the holder of the vision left the city, there was concern about ownership and continuation of the process. It was necessary to re-educate many to gain their support and participation. This broader base of support helps to ensure the success of the initiative and lessens the chance of extensive personal identification.
- The smallest city is replete with informal connections and is suspicious of outside interests. It has taken considerable effort to identify and begin to work with these informal connectors. Most organizations here are small, lacking extra time and resources to commit to new initiatives from either the inside or the outside. The challenge is to integrate this project with current activities.
- Getting elected leadership on board was an issue in one city. The informal relationship between a community leader and an elected official became the strategy to begin discussion of the appropriate role for city government. The video, which included a segment on a local neighborhood group, was particularly effective.

- Major changes in elected leadership, a sense of loss (and major economic loss) from the closure of a naval shipyard, and unresolved issues among several community groups were factors in Solano's largest city. "Go slowly" became the password. Planned conversations on many fronts about a "healthier community" have prepared informal and formal leaders to come together to begin to discuss an appropriate strategy to take another step toward this still undefined vision.
- Incorporation of a "Healthy City" chapter in the city's general plan became the goal of one small group. Having achieved that, the challenge has been to broaden this small group of insiders to better reflect the larger community and then develop a plan for extensive community input.

A basic structure is now (or nearly) in place in each city. The next phase is to engage the community in identifying its hopes, concerns, and strengths. From these will come priorities, action items, and partnerships to create healthier communities.

Community Health Outreach System

The CHOS is a 3-year demonstration project designed to enhance access, service, and prevention among the medically underserved in two targeted neighborhoods. A team consisting of a public nurse and four culturally appropriate outreach specialists has been assigned to each neighborhood. The teams have completed a rigorous semester of special training delivered through the county community college. Specialists have begun to develop relationships with the informal and formal leaders in each neighborhood pursuant to the development of neighborhood health councils. These councils also will receive community leadership training.

Solano Health Improvement Initiative

The SCBH has recently been awarded one of five one-year grants by the California Wellness Foundation's Health Improvement Initiative. This will allow the coalition to focus on the following:

- Coordinating disease management efforts of Solano's major health care providers with the addition of appropriate population health systems
- Working with local elected officials to ensure that public policy and budget decisions reflect the principles of community health improvement
- Strengthening the role of informal, natural helping systems within families and neighborhoods and effectively linking them with formal systems of care and service
- Engaging the media as more proactive partners in community health improvement
- Setting benchmarks to measure the progress in health improvement

Contact: Steve Graham
Kaiser Permanente
975 Sereno Dr.
Vallejo, CA 94589-2485
Phone: (707) 648-7688
Fax: (707) 648-6459

8

The South Madison Health and Family Center

Executive Summary

Over the past year, many of our important start-up goals have been achieved for the South Madison Health and Family Center. We have been in operation as a center since October 1995. Through a unique public–private partnership with the city of Madison, the University of Wisconsin, and several not-for-profit agencies, a new community resource has been created to meet a variety of health and social support needs. It is a vital example of the community care network (CCN) vision in a new community institution directed by a community-wide board.

At the heart of the South Madison Health and Family Center is a primary care medical clinic enhanced by important public health and prevention programs. Medical care is available every day of the week to anyone in the community. A financial cornerstone upon which regular medical staffing is based is the managed care initiative of the Wisconsin Medical Assistance Program, which has assigned 1,200 participants to our clinic for primary care. Their monthly capitation allows us to pay a core of medical triage and support staff. At the same time, we serve the uninsured residents of the community, who make up over 50 percent of our patient activity. Our ability to serve all depends heavily on the professional contribution of many university faculty physicians who see our patients at the South Madison Health and Family Center without reimbursement. At the same time, the community's contribution to the education of the university medical trainees is invaluable to them. Our efforts at cultural and racial diversity in staffing, service, and accountability provide important lessons for those trainees.

As a new center, we have focused on collaboration. Over the past year there has been a regular effort at cross-agency communication. Staff from all agencies are encouraged to meet weekly at either of two regularly scheduled team meetings. The managers from each partner agency meet monthly to cover operational and program concerns. The center's community-wide board of directors also meets monthly to review issues and plan for the future.

Warren Kmiec, Executive Director
Madison Community Health Center

THE COLLABORATIVE PARTNERSHIP

The community of South Madison has been one of unique growth and diversification, especially over the past 10 years. In the past, it was a community of small homes and small-town concerns; its distance from the University of Wisconsin campus and the state capital allowed it to carry on a community life relatively detached from those influences. For decades, the African-American residents of Madison have recognized this as a special neighborhood that gave them a focus and a home base in a predominantly Caucasian community. The area has been built up with a greater amount of rental housing stock than other areas of Madison. It is easy to see how a number of African-Americans and other new arrivals of working-class people have been attracted to the South Madison area over the past 10 years.

However, some of the characteristics of this new population growth indicate social problems connected with poverty, racism, single-parent households, minority students who are not achieving well in public schools, increased crime, and illegal drug activity. Some of the health indicators demonstrate the same level of health care system "neglect" of minority, poor, and uninsured people as in much larger urban settings. These indicators show a below-average level of prenatal care; a higher number of nonimmunized children; a higher number of late-diagnosed cancers, especially among women; a higher level of domestic violence and addictive misuse of alcohol and drugs; an unacceptable level of untreated chronic disease such as diabetes and hypertension; and a significant lack of any routine dental or mental health care availability.

The social and health problems alone are challenges enough to address. In addition, we often meet the barriers of no transportation, no phone, no child care, no financial support, and no ability to interact successfully with systems set up to assist the poor. Many times this is because such systems have been established with an internal logic that has everything but the client's success as a priority. Traditional institutions of caring and guidance, such as community groups and churches, try to alter the ugly outcomes facing community residents, but without substantial resources. Within this context of a quickly growing new urban setting, the South Madison Health and Family Center (SMHFC) partners have tried to map out a vision of meeting the health and educational needs of young children and the families they live in. We have created a public–private partnership of agencies that have missions, track records, and resources to make a difference through collaboration. The goals of the collaboration have been developed steadily since 1988. We feel that this collaboration, the SMHFC, will demonstrate the qualities of a CCN.

The history of the collaboration goes back to 1988. At that time, the city government was responding to the media stories about social problems in the South Madison area. The Madison Department of Public Health (MDPH) had taken an early role in locating a site for the delivery of health care and early childhood support programs. To obtain the funding necessary for such a venture, many public hearings were held, and the mayor appointed a special task force to make recommendations. The city council was convinced to buy a 5,000-square-foot Knights of Columbus meeting hall for $350,000. This was the beginning of the SMHFC on Hughes Place. What has arisen since then is a common vision for a new center of 35,000 square feet and many partners. This is covered in greater detail in the next section.

The original core of partners in 1990 comprised the MDPH, the Madison Community Health Center (MCHC), Planned Parenthood of Wisconsin-Madison, and Family Enhancement. Let us consider the unique differences of each of these agencies and the way they complement one another. The MDPH is a nurse-staffed system of routine health screening services and preventive health programs. It is in charge of the local Women, Infants and Children (WIC) supplemental food program, regularly conducts immunization clinics, and is involved in well-child examinations. Its staff is also known for field case management of difficult cases referred by communicable disease sanitarians, and it conducts a variety of public education programs about population-based health issues.

The MCHC is a not-for-profit, private agency supported completely by local funds. It has a 25-year history of providing health care to underserved members of the community. Its staff is a group of doctors and physician assistants who provide primary care. The MCHC has developed a strong component of allied health staff who provide everything from social work services to childbirth instruction. It operates on a sliding-fee basis and has a high percentage of uninsured clients.

Planned Parenthood of Wisconsin-Madison has a nurse- and nurse practitioner–based staff. It has long specialized its services in the area of reproductive health care. It offers instruction about birth control as well as maintenance of good gynecological health, provides routine gynecological physicals, treats sexually transmitted diseases of both men and women, and has begun to do colposcopy for abnormal Pap test results.

Family Enhancement is a not-for-profit agency active in parent education and support. It has developed a wide variety of discussion topics that it continually revises to meet the interests of its participants. It has been a community leader in empowering parents of all backgrounds to share the common concerns involved in raising happy and healthy children. Its activities at the SMHFC have been focused on the Early Childhood Family Resource Center. Activities are varied and include support groups for parents, social activities, general equivalency diploma (GED) training, a toy-lending library, and a continuous dialogue with drop-in neighborhood residents.

The initial collaboration of these four agencies provided a significant range of preventive and primary health care, with a specialty in women's reproductive health as well as a solid core of support activities for the parents of young children. As the vision of a larger center grew, other agencies were sought that could complement this same family and health focus. The local branch of the Madison Public Library, the Head Start Program, and the Department of Family Medicine of the University of Wisconsin (UW) were added to this initial partnership core in 1992. Let us now consider what each of these partners brings to the collaboration.

Located near the SMHFC on Hughes Place, the Madison Public Library serves a wide variety of the public from all over South Madison. It has been concerned about reaching new users from the immediate community for some time. The staff is very flexible and creative about promoting library use through story hours and other special services to children. It found that being included in a mix of health and social service agencies allowed it to be even more imaginative in complementing the activities of these partners, thus meeting its goal of greater immediate community access. Plans were for the library to be a resident partner in the new location when it opened.

The Head Start Program of Dane County has served children in South Madison for a long time and is funded chiefly by federal grants. Although it operates an early education program for 3–5-year-olds, its mandate goes far beyond education to include a strong health assessment and family support focus. The involvement of parents in running the program, as well as the staff's daily contact with the children's homes, brings a vital component into the partnership. This agency also does a great deal of daily busing of students to their learning centers. In the future, Head Start will be part of a health and family center that can use both its transportation as well as its programmatic ties to families at risk.

The UW Department of Family Medicine has provided medical services in an outpatient clinic in the South Madison area for many years. Its mission is to educate physician residents in the specialty of family medicine. Its commitment to the collaboration brought the SMHFC's primary care service to a more comprehensive level. The Department of Family Medicine will be able to not only support the primary care staffing of the health and family center but also prepare and deliver women in childbirth.

The initial partnership of four agencies has been delivering services at the SMHFC since 1990. With the additional three agencies, they worked out a common vision that has led to the inclusion of more partners. The UW Department of Family Medicine has been joined by every other primary care physician residency training program at the UW in signing on to the CCN mission. Those other partners include the pediatric, internal medicine, and obstetrics/gynecology departments, as well as the school of nursing. All will function as one community clinic under the management of the MCHC's core staff.

It is obvious that the medical staffing for our community clinic is broad and readily available to meet a high level of demand. The challenge and opportunity in this vision is to provide a health and human service delivery model that is based on collaborative staffing and focused on client satisfaction. We will be able to provide a full spectrum of preventive and primary health care for every age group. The objective will be to utilize a common administrative staffing that will provide a seamless service effect. Our services will be unified whenever possible and diversified where necessary for improved quality or choice for the client.

The use of community volunteer advocates, social work staff, and health educators in the delivery of health care will help make the access to service more client centered. The potential in CCN for various levels of health care professionals to work more as an interdisciplinary team is both a strength and a challenge. It is one reason why the different UW health training programs are very excited about having partnership in this collaboration. A major goal is to understand how prevention and health education can enhance primary care delivery.

As these collaborative partners worked at a common vision, the issues of governance and accountability presented a major challenge. However, we knew that once common ground was defined, future success would depend on defining our relationships and responsibilities. Key to our vision was the creation of a viable community institution that could direct and adapt the vision of the collaboration to the changing needs of the community. To this end we defined a board of directors to properly represent multiple levels of interest. The community and participants, the people who work in the center, and the stakeholders who provide major resources to create a space for this collaboration to happen all have representation.

The SMHFC board of directors is now a reality. We have come a long way to reach this point and have been working on this collaboration for more than 5 years. Although the collaboration began as a response to social conditions that need improvement, we also believe in the potential and positive assets present in this same community.

Our vision means to enhance and develop those potentials. In this spirit, the SMHFC is for all residents of the community, not just for those "at risk." All people can come, all can give, all can learn, all can benefit. This is the foundation of a successful CCN.

PRIOR MOVEMENT TOWARD THE COMMUNITY CARE NETWORK VISION

> A doctor's office right in the neighborhood is just a faded memory for most people today. But on the South Side, this convenient relic has been revived. On Wednesday, city officials and others dedicated the new South Madison Health and Family Center at 825 Hughes Place. The niche that it fills is offering neighborhood health care services—to make sure residents of South Madison have easy access to health care, said Gay Gross, a representative of the city's Public Health Department.
>
> (South Side gets dose of health care. *Wisconsin State Journal,* April 18, 1991.)

The above newspaper article speaks of a major step forward after 3 years of various meetings and reports about what the South Madison community needed in the way of health care access. The first location of the SMHFC was a tan metal building, formerly a Knights of Columbus meeting hall. The four original partners described in the previous section of this chapter were beginning a new venture. They did not have many answers; they were there to learn. Each agency provided its own unique services at its own regularly scheduled time—all in the same space. Collaboration began as several partners' using the same space to provide different services throughout the week.

It was the intention of the first partners to learn how to refer to each others' programs. As time went on, the sharing of space lead to an interstaff familiarity that helped interactions increase. Obviously, the need to meet frequently to discuss housekeeping issues was a necessity. But each agency learned through personal contact how to use their partners' resources for their own participants' needs.

It did not take long, however, before the Hughes Place site's space limitations began to hamper the growth of this vision. The SMHFC staff put together a list of examples, titled "Why South Madison Needs a New Health and Family Center," that clearly illustrate the problem of lack of space:

- The WIC program has been doing blood-lead screening at the SMHFC. To make space for this screening, the weighing and measuring of babies was moved out of a small room to the reception desk. Lead screening will be discontinued in the cold months, so the weighing and measuring can be done in the warm room.
- Severely limited space creates a very confusing health services schedule. People often come to the SMHFC during WIC hours wanting treatment for health problems. They come to Planned Parenthood wanting WIC services. This problem creates frustration in people seeking services and disrupts the services that are there. Each agency's staff spends a considerable amount of time telling people about the schedule and directing them to health services. This problem prevents people from thinking of the SMHFC as a place to seek ongoing health care.
- Family Enhancement's Early Childhood Program is no longer able to hold parenting classes at the SMHFC because of inadequate space. Parents are taken to other

locations for this activity. Head Start has South Madison children placed in scattered sites outside the community rather than in one neighborhood facility.

- One woman who was in Family Enhancement's GED class was preparing to take the exam. She was unable to study at the SMHFC because of the noise and transferred to a class elsewhere. Planned Parenthood finds that confidentiality is difficult to maintain because conversations can be heard in the waiting room through the closed exam room doors.
- The MDPH immunization clinics are held in the conference room. Two immunizers must share this undivided space. While one public health nurse is talking to a parent about immunizations, another nurse in the same room may be immunizing another child. The child awaiting immunizations is able to watch the other child getting a shot and gets more frightened and agitated.
- Family Enhancement needs a private space to meet with parents. Because there is no available space at the current SMHFC, it is located in an apartment building half a block away.
- The MCHC has social work staff who could work at their SMHFC clinics, but there is no available private space. WIC is unable to hold breast-feeding classes during WIC clinics because there is not enough space.
- Public health nurses with the MDPH would like to use the SMHFC to do health teaching, counseling, and breast-feeding counseling of their clients, but there is no private space available.
- Agencies now at the SMHFC are trying to establish a collaborative model; however, without more space, this is impossible. The present arrangement is like a family trying to live in a one-room cabin.

In response to the need for more space, architectural funds were included in the 1992 capital budget of the MDPH. An architect was hired to design the ideal space, with the input of the participating partners. This task was a defining moment (a moment that took about 2 years) because it caused the agencies to begin conceptualizing a unified model—a "one-stop shop" of health and human services. New questions of interaction among the group arose. As space needed to be designed and defined, so did our future partnership.

The potential of a new space caused us to consider what other partners should be included to meet the needs of the families to be served. The numbers of young children caused us to speak with the local Head Start Program, which was interested. The SMHFC's Family Enhancement program had already done positive things with the local public library branch that was just a block away. The partners thought inviting the library into the group would be a plus on several levels: Not only would it bring families into contact with the library, but, because many different types of people already use the public library, it would also make clear to the community that the SMHFC is for everyone.

This expanded group of partners began to plan how the newly designed space for the SMHFC could become a reality. We began formalizing our goals and objectives. At the start of 1993, two teams—the Finance Team and the Planning and Program Team—were formed to plan the new project. They included members from the collaborating agencies, the city council, city staff members, and the Wisconsin Division of Health. The Finance Team's task was to figure out how the capital could be raised to build a new SMHFC. The Planning and Program Team's job was to further refine the spatial design with input from SMHFC participants and other community groups. In this way, we attempted to anticipate the priorities of community residents in regard to our ability to provide service.

The MDPH took a lead role in developing links with the private health sector and the university in regard to planning the SMHFC. Its health planner and a consultant hired by the MDPH did a nationwide search for other operational models. Although no exact model was found, many "one-stop shop" collaborations of health and social services were surveyed. A report on the research provided the group with some key observations.

After several contacts and meetings, representatives from all private-sector health care organizations and educational institutions endorsed the concept of the SMHFC. Private health care organizations provided funding for further consulting, staff donated time to work on planning, legal services were donated to assist in incorporating and filing for IRS recognition of tax-exempt 501(c)(3) status, and help was given in creating a campaign for private capital fund raising.

On one hand, the help of the MDPH was very important at this stage; on the other, it was time to take another step toward collaboration and define what commitment to the project meant. A decision was made to request the governing boards of all interested partners for a formal commitment to making the project happen. Each partner agency was asked to invest $1,000 to fund the staffing of one planner who would continue to coordinate efforts with the partner agencies.

This official commitment of the participating agencies was made in November 1993. A seventh partner, the UW Department of Family Medicine, joined the group at this time. Its students had been providing a free health clinic at SMHFC on Saturday mornings with the support of their faculty physicians. The department wanted to pursue the potential for this type of community-based learning experience for its residency program. The other partners of the collaboration saw the Department of Family Medicine's involvement as a means to enhance the eventual comprehensive nature of the SMHFC services.

Thus it was that one representative of each of the following agencies became the first incorporating SMHFC board: Family Enhancement, Inc.; Planned Parenthood of Wisconsin; the MPHD; MCHC, Inc.; the Madison Public Library; Parent Council of Dane County—Head Start; and the UW Department of Family Medicine.

A federal grant provided an important resource in 1993. The MDPH had submitted the SMHFC project as a model for a block grant program, entitled Community Integrated Service Systems (CISS), conducted by the Maternal and Child Welfare Department. The SMHFC project, as it existed in Hughes Place, qualified and was funded for 4 years. The money from this grant is used to provide a center coordinator with clerical support, two outreach workers, and a benefits counselor. This staff is currently bringing existing partner agencies at the Hughes Place SMHFC together in a coordinated fashion. It also is doing a community outreach function with the area residents on behalf of the entire existing SMHFC. Although the current building's limitations required the SMHFC's coordinator to set up quarters in a nearby building (837 Hughes Place), the coordinator is present and active with the programs at 825 Hughes Place, the current SMHFC. The outreach workers are local residents hired by the grant through the partner agency Family Enhancement. They are out in the community contacting individual families as well as other organizations and agencies with which SMHFC should be coordinating efforts. The benefits counselor is a contracted position with still another partner agency, the MCHC. Although this staff person works with any community resident seeking help about social services or medical entitlements, she concentrates on assisting SMHFC participants referred by active partner agencies.

During 1994, the SMHFC project required continual development with the committed agencies. It also needed to respond to outside community concerns. The new SMHFC project sought approval from local government bodies and funding organizations. The Madison City Council had to consider the new construction request on several levels of its bureaucracy. This project was in direct competition with other requests for community centers and social service program budgets. The estimated cost of the proposed building was $3.4 million.

Events unexpectedly turned when a local developer suggested to the city real estate department that using long-underutilized commercial space in a neighborhood shopping center would be more cost efficient than erecting a $3.4 million building on city property. Upon review, the city department approved the recommendation. Thus, the SMHFC group now had a new scenario to consider: the original two-floor plan had to be redesigned for one floor. This resulted in the health care component's becoming a central hub of the new floor plan.

Concurrent with the new real estate situation came the request by a larger portion of the UW Health Professions Program to be included as partners in the SMHFC. This interest arose out of a desire both to be a supporter of community health improvement and to have increased community-based clinical teaching experience. This desire concurs with the recognized national need for a greater number of health care professionals to work in primary care settings.

The integration of the larger UW presence in the project was a major challenge in the collaborative process. One loves the strength a giant can bring, but the giant must be careful where it steps. The question of whether each new player needed to be recognized as a partner in the collaboration immediately arose. The acting board decided that new entrants need to (1) relate to the project as an adjunct to an already existing partner, and (2) function with the collaborative blessing of all. Thus, it was decided that the many UW health profession players would be resources to the community primary care clinic managed by the MCHC. When the UW department heads met in October 1994, they addressed this issue themselves: "During a meeting of all our department chairs," wrote Dr. Murray Katcher, MD, PhD, Director of Community Health Programs, in a letter dated Oct. 20, 1994, "there was also some discussion about whether the university would participate separately from MCHC. That suggestion was dismissed in favor of a partnership arrangement. (See figure 8-1.) The university has no desire to take over or diminish the prominence of MCHC in the community; rather, we feel this is a strong opportunity to strengthen it."

In March 1994, staff members from the medical services part of SMHFC met to discuss common values. The focus of service at the SMHFC was defined as family-centered preventive and primary care for families in South Madison.

The list of values included the following:

- Respect for individual client needs and differences
- Client-centered systems with customer feedback
- Affordable, high-quality care
- Seamless service delivery: unified when possible and diversified when necessary for improved quality or choice

FIGURE 8-1. Partnership Commitment

The agencies involved in this project have committed themselves to working in a public–private partnership so that services meet the needs and build on the strengths of the community and individual customers and families. The participating agencies and programs support the mission of the center and the governance structure set by the South Madison Health and Family Center board of directors. All participating groups support the mission and values that have been developed by the SMHFC board.

All partners commit to the integrity, spirit, and shared work of project goals and to the financing and maintenance of the facility. This includes the following:

1. Partners continuously improve their services by developing plans and methods that assure a customer-focused approach to conducting business. Improvement strategies are based on feedback, data and evaluation results.

2. Partners serve the community by pro-actively encouraging community and neighborhood partnerships while maintaining their individual missions, services and program integrity.

   Services are provided in a culturally respectful manner. When needed, partners actively pursue strategies to provide culturally specific services and programs.

   Programs and services build on individual and community strengths and promote independence and interdependence.

   Partners facilitate full access to all Center services and programs. They work to overcome barriers imposed by language, literacy, transportation, economic, and child care needs.

3. Partners collaborate and support other Center services and programs.

   Partners work in coordination with the Center Coordinator. (The initial coordinator is the CISS coordinator who is employed by the City of Madison Department of Public Health.) Partners will share nonconfidential data and other information to assist in the coordination of efforts and the demonstration of program effectiveness.

   Partners will provide information and seek approval from the SMHFC Board of Directors for any changes in scope of activity or populations served at the Center.

   Partners will enter into "Memorandums of Understanding" that identify interagency relationships including collaboration, referral, and the sharing of information, resources, expertise, and cooperative programming.

   Partners create opportunities and participate in efforts to share information and inform all staff of Center services.

   Partner agencies and groups provide time for program staff to coordinate programs and ensure nonduplication of services.

   Partners provide opportunities for Center staff to build relationships with each other.

- Cultural competence and sensitivity
- Linkage with outside services and partner agencies
- Accessible services that are welcoming and supportive
- A mutual learning environment
- Interdisciplinary teams
- Diversity of funding sources
- Focus on prevention
- Consumer choice

Throughout 1994, the health care provider agencies tried to come to some consensus on how a unified clinic structure could enable all participating providers: Creating interactive record keeping, as well as scheduling and coordinating provider service options, presented larger problems than could be sorted out in the abstract. Nevertheless, some decisions were made: to have a core staff that would give an assurance of continuity to patient services, to establish a single medical records system that all providers would access, and to organize ourselves to answer the more detailed questions.

As the year came to an end, important commitments were made. The city of Madison signed a 10-year lease for the use of newly designed space at the Village Shopping Center. Each of the principal partner agencies signed a letter of intent to lease from the city the space needed for their specific services when the building became ready for occupancy in 1995. The original SMHFC board of directors, which comprised the principal service agencies, turned the governance of the project over to a community-wide board made up of city and university seats, community and consumer seats, and service provider seats.

The community-wide board of directors has been active since January 1995. It has taken steps to make the SMHFC project better known throughout the South Madison area and is also helping plan the opening of the center, which was scheduled for fall 1995. The community-wide board brings the knowledge of the project to many different levels of social and business networks.

MOVING TOWARD THE COMMUNITY CARE NETWORK VISION

The South Madison community is a richly diversified one. However, this growing diversification results in increasing social service and health care needs. Many of the South Madison residents are "urban refugees" from central city neighborhoods in Chicago and Milwaukee who have come to Madison to seek a safer and more stable life. Local social service and health care agencies are understaffed and overburdened, and many community residents are unable to link with health and family services that would ease the transition to Madison.

Community Accountability

From its inception, the South Madison project has sought input from community members. The community currently uses the South Madison center on Hughes Place; however, the community's needs and wants are much greater than can be met at that site, in terms of space as well as human resources. Serving on the board of directors are three elected community members who ensure a continuous link between the center and the neighborhood it serves. In addition, there is a small work group charged with interfacing with employees hired by the CISS grant to work with users of the current site and future users of the proposed site. Concerns have long been expressed that projects of this type do not include input from those who stand to benefit from it. This project's vision is one of a partnership between the community and the agencies providing services to it. We seek to ensure that there is continuous, open communication between the neighborhood, the board of directors, and the service providers.

Seamless Continuum of Care

The SMHFC combines health and social service agencies under one roof in an effort to improve health care availability to community members who may lack access to services because of such barriers as a lack of transportation and/or telephones, language differences, and so forth. The intent is to provide a "seamless" menu of services. The project attempts to use many health care and other providers in an interdisciplinary mode. The traditional health care model has used physicians working in concert with a nurse or medical assistant to provide care to patients and has then referred those patients to outside agencies for unmet psycho-social needs. The South Madison model will integrate a wide variety of providers: physicians, nurse practitioners, physician assistants, nurse midwives, social workers, teachers of parenting, early childhood teachers, and an on-site branch of the Madison Public Library. This model will supersede the model of providers practicing in an isolated and fragmented fashion. Teams of diverse providers at the South Madison site will work side by side to provide comprehensive services where necessary. Physicians will learn to integrate midlevel providers in their practice for purposes such as general health education, dietary counseling, smoking cessation, individual and family counseling, and family planning, as well as for traditional patient care services.

In planning this project, the individual health care and social service provider groups have not only developed a better understanding of unmet needs in the community but also have come to better understand the services that each agency provides as well as the problems they each face—issues involving funding, equipment and resources, dealing with bureaucracy, and so forth. Sharing information enables the agencies to find ways of working together to fill in the gaps of the current system while striving to ensure that services are not duplicated.

Community Health Focus

Although the diversity of the South Madison community provides a richness of culture, it also presents a host of unmet medical and social needs. There is a high rate of rental housing in the area, and many of the "urban refugees" mentioned earlier relocate to this area of Madison. It is difficult, under the best of circumstances, for a newly relocated family to find health care and social service providers who are accessible to meet a wide variety of needs. The current South Madison population is susceptible to teenage pregnancy and low-birth-weight babies, and prenatal care is an extremely important issue. Domestic violence and drug and alcohol abuse have also increased in the community as families in crisis have moved into the area. The SMHFC will provide health education services, family planning, prenatal and delivery care, on-site counseling, assistance with parenting, early childhood education for at-risk children, a WIC program, early health screening exams, and a variety of other programs to address these unmet needs.

Management within Fixed Resources

Providers have actively pursued relationships with the two Madison-area HMOs that have contracts with the Wisconsin Department of Health and Social Services (DHSS) to provide managed care for the Medicaid population. The managed care model will provide a stable revenue base and well-coordinated care for the center. We anticipate that up to 50 percent of the population served at the center will be covered by a Medicaid managed care contract.

Other

One of the unique aspects of this project is that it will be used as a training site for nurses and resident physicians. The collaborators involved in the project strongly believe that health care and other service providers should develop a relationship with their clients that enables all participants to learn from each other and build on each others' strengths. Participating agencies are aware of the needs of individuals and families that go beyond health care, and realize the importance of understanding family background and home life factors in attempting to proactively meet those needs. Participants are also aware of many of the community, family, and individual strengths that can be built upon to enhance the larger community. This project seeks to train students and residents in this "new" model that goes beyond the individual and encompasses the family and the neighborhood. As the project progresses, we envision not only that the needs of the South Madison community will be better served, and its strengths enhanced in a more proactive fashion, but also that this model can and will be replicated across the country as nurses and physicians relocate after completing their training. Graduates will teach their colleagues, new teachers will teach new learners in training programs, and the model will grow and expand beyond the borders of Madison.

The Visioning Process We Followed in Arriving at Our Local Statement of CCN Vision

As the project has evolved over the past several years, and as new agencies have offered to provide service at the center, meetings have been focused on arriving at a common vision statement. The providers have agreed that any group that is unable or unwilling to "buy in" to the vision statement should not be a part of the project, and will use this as one of the screening mechanisms as new providers ask to become a part of the center. The project's vision is to provide community-based, culturally sensitive, comprehensive, and coordinated health and educational services to serve, promote, and support healthy independent families at one South Madison location.

After the vision or mission statement was developed, the participants created a "partnership commitment" that states: "The agencies involved in this project have committed themselves to working in a public–private partnership so that services meet the needs and build on the strengths of the community and individual customers and families. The participating agencies and programs support the mission of the center and the governance structure set by the South Madison Health and Family Center board of directors. All participating groups support the mission and values that have been developed by the SMHFC board."

The provider groups chose individuals who would be responsible as the initial contacts for the project and would then compose the original "temporary" SMHFC board of directors for the center. Board members worked on the above partnership commitment at biweekly meetings beginning in 1992; they also held several morning retreats, including one with an outside facilitator to assist in developing the vision. This was a fairly tedious process, as agencies around the planning table differed greatly in services provided, funding sources, and perceived "political power." One difficulty was that the UW was seen as too powerful and not community-oriented enough to really understand how this center would differ from a traditional university-based "clinic," and there was strong concern expressed by some smaller agencies that the university should not be allowed to participate in any but a very limited manner. However, with the facilitation of the MCHC's executive director, agencies began to develop working relationships that moved beyond the political fears evident early in the project. The UW medical providers have been willing to take a less visible role. Although university departments have been actively involved in the planning and work of the project, they understand that the model is different from a university health clinic and that they will be providers in a community clinic model rather than a university clinic model.

At present, smaller agencies still have concerns about maintaining their identity and independence, but we feel we have moved beyond the point where those concerns are among the largest issues confronting us. We anticipate that these concerns will be allayed over time, particularly after the center opens and participants begin working side by side to provide services. However, we are aware that we must continue to work to address those concerns.

The temporary board of directors has been successfully transitioned to a permanent board consisting of stakeholders, community members, and agency providers. In addition, a health service providers' group meets biweekly to discuss and plan the following four major components of the center's future:

1. Community relations
2. Health clinic operations
3. After-hours care of center clients
4. Duplication and overlap of services

Besides the biweekly large-group meetings, these groups also meet to plan provider schedules, staffing, and clinic systems, and to work with community members to ensure that the center focuses on the areas the community has identified, rather than on what the providers would like to do.

Initiatives That Move Us toward the Community Care Network Vision

Although we are still in the active planning stages for the CCN, the center is scheduled to open on November 1, 1995. We anticipate that long after the center has opened its doors, the concept of the center will continue to evolve. Representatives from all agencies will continue to meet at least biweekly to discuss problems they are encountering, and community representatives will be involved at all stages to

PART III

Rural Region Networks

Transport of the mails, transport of the human voice, transport of flickering pictures—in this century as in others our highest accomplishments still have the single aim of bringing [people] together.

—Antoine de Saint-Exupéry (1900–1944), French aviator, writer

I have found out that there ain't no surer way to find out whether you like people or hate them than to travel with them.

—Mark Twain (1835–1910), U.S. author

INTRODUCTION

Rural regions are, first and foremost, geographically big. Barriers to access due to weaknesses in transportation systems may be especially acute. This is not usually a consequence of arbitrarily defining a large rural area in a way that just does not fit the transportation systems. Transportation systems tend to reflect historical trade patterns, not just in health care but in all business. The match between economic strength and transportation can be seen easiest in rural regions. When people define their community as a rural region for the purposes of developing a community care network, decades of experiences in a variety of arenas, from emergency medical services to retail trade, shaped their choice.

While large geographic tracts exacerbate the impacts of transportation systems on health care, and everything else, the pressure to establish or maintain less efficient, decentralized service delivery systems may be high. Many rural hospitals, for example, were developed with a high degree of community awareness, and sometimes much local investment. Moreover, the births, illnesses, recoveries, and deaths of most people in a rural community are connected to specific places and people. Many rural health care providers enjoy an emotional investment by area citizens that those in metropolitan or suburban communities can rarely claim, even if it is most notable during crises.

The balance between maintaining or enhancing access, while decreasing redundancies in capacity, pulls geographically big communities in multiple directions. In rural region communities, how geopolitical boundaries get spanned, in order to hold the region together, can be particularly instructive. Since rural regions span political boundaries by definition, and since many rural institutions are public, local governments and larger businesses often play important roles.

Metropolitan communities have developed large tracts of poverty and despair, and these huge problems in large media markets tend to receive much attention. As a result, many Americans think that all of our more profound social problems occur in the big cities. It might surprise some readers to know that unemployment, underemployment, poverty, and lack of health insurance are all more likely to befall rural Americans.

Here are some questions that you might find interesting as you read the cases in part III on rural regional communities. Who is willing to give up what for the greater good? By what means can local government participation help or hinder community-responsive health care delivery change in rural regions? Does government participation, as we sometimes read in the popular press, slow down innovation? What mechanisms other than government can serve to cross the multiple geopolitical boundaries that are the hallmark of rural regions? What do the evolving CCNs showcased here do to achieve coordination over large geographic areas?

This book highlights five evolving rural regional community care networks. These communities are composed of multiple counties that are primarily or exclusively rural. Maine's Franklin Community Partnership has distributed a health card to almost all the members of its regional community. The health card gives holders access to discounts from many area businesses and thereby binds economic development and local health system change throughout the region. As more and more physicians' offices use the health card, the partnership gains in its ability to bind the interests of physicians in regional collaboration as well as to gather information for health education and promotion efforts aimed at the health card users. In addition to the health card, the partnership established and expanded mobile health units and built a regional network of rural health educators. The North Iowa Mercy Health Network focuses on preventable illness and death by improving rural access to health education for both professionals and citizens. Areawide networks and successful first steps in linking computer systems facilitate county level assessments and foster interorganizational planning. The North Iowa Mercy Health Network expects these efforts to enable the creation of a capitated insurance product. The Northwest Georgia Healthcare Partnership has drawn on the resources of an already integrated delivery system to emphasize prevention and wellness. Working intimately with a cluster of large businesses, all in the carpet industry and all of which self-insure, this partnership has achieved notable progress in obtaining the resources and support from the educational community for enhanced health education in the school system and from the business and government communities for work-site health promotion and education. Creation of a medical access clinic in collaboration with the health department improves continuity of care and leads to better cost management. In the Southcentral Health Network of Idaho, a fascinating experiment in replication of community care network development can be observed. Success in one county and updating regional assessments serve as the basis for seeding all of the counties' efforts throughout the region. Collaboration with a state transportation agency enables enhanced training activities as well as inclusion of transportation issues within their regional CCN model. Targeted improvements for mortality and morbidity in youth have produced initiatives to reduce motor vehicle mortality, teen pregnancy, and alcohol, tobacco, and other drug use. The West Texas Community Care Consortium emerged from a breast and cervical cancer screening program that serves 18 big west Texas counties. The Consortium currently links providers for a comprehensive array of cancer-related services and plans to grow the high level of coordination it has achieved into a full-blown set of women's health services for the region, across virtually all providers. A fascinating challenge for the Consortium is how to coordinate an ever-widening array of services, so community health becomes the objective, without shattering the highly effective coordination mechanisms they have developed for cancer services.

9

The Franklin Community Partnership

Executive Summary

The Franklin Community Partnership operates in an area of Maine that is primarily rural, where there are numerous barriers to the delivery of high-quality health care: widespread poverty, lack of education, lack of public transportation, and a population that is widely dispersed across a large area that extends all the way to the Canadian border. The Franklin Community Health Network (FCHN), Western Mountains Alliance (WMA), and the Healthy Community Coalition (HCC) are working together as the Franklin Community Partnership to make a difference.

The five projects they have undertaken are very much grass roots grounded and community driven, and although they could be somewhat freestanding, they are working synergistically to improve conditions for the delivery of health care in this area:

- FCHN has initiated the use of a computer-scannable identification card to promote health and to speed registration in the health care system for more than 30,000 people in the area. (See figure 9-1.)
- HCC's programs for the mobile health unit have been taking health education, prevention information, and health care needs assessments to many outlying parts of the service area by means of a specially equipped van. In addition, it has completed a needs assessment for rural health educators, and plans to place personnel in the field as soon as funding is available.
- WMA is progressing nicely with a project to develop a public access television station that will not only enhance the delivery of programming that deals with health issues but also improve the economic sustainability, environmental integrity, and quality of life in this somewhat geographically isolated area.

- Finally, WMA and HCC have collaborated to provide leadership training and mentoring to eighth graders in a yearlong program called the Youth Rural Leaders Forum. This year's class of 23 youngsters "graduating" from the program radiate a real feeling of hope for the area and its people, which is what our community care network is all about.

Scott Planting
Director, Mission at the Eastward, Presbyterian Church, USA
Pastor, Fairbanks Union Church, Farmington, Maine, and New Portland and North New Portland Community Churches, New Portland, Maine
Chair, Western Mountains Alliance
Co-Chair, Sustain Western Maine
Trustee, Franklin Memorial Hospital and Franklin Community Health Network

THE COLLABORATIVE PARTNERSHIP

The area served by the collaborative partners is in west central Maine. It includes all of Franklin County and parts of Kennebec, Androscoggin, Somerset, and Oxford counties. Its northern tier reaches to the Canadian border. Within this large geographical area are several small towns, plantations, and unincorporated townships, all served by five school administrative districts. The total population is approximately 40,000. The largest town (6,000 people) is Farmington, in the southern tier of the service area, where a majority of the population is in fact located.

A large portion of the service area is rural in character and retains much of its original economic base in agricultural and wood products. This economic base is expanded by manufacturing, retail trade, education, and the health care industry. The relatively few large employers include the University of Maine and Franklin Memorial Hospital (both in Farmington), Forster Manufacturing and G. H. Bass (both in Wilton), International Paper in Jay, the five school administrative districts, and Sugarloaf USA (a major ski resort in the northern tier).

Rural poverty is a crushing reality throughout the region. In Franklin County alone, the unemployment rate is over 8 percent. Per capita income is $10,830. According to the 1990 census, 12.9 percent of all Franklin County and Livermore Falls families with children under 18, nearly 40 percent of families headed by women, and 26.2 percent of households headed by men with children under 18, live in poverty. In Franklin County proper, over 60 percent of the population have no formal education beyond high school.

The combination of poverty, lack of education, and a population that is very widespread across a large and largely rural service area acts in a number of ways as a barrier to the delivery of high-quality health care and health education. National studies have shown that among other things, low-income people often lack a regular source of medical care, are less likely to receive appropriate preventive screenings, and are more likely to be hospitalized for conditions that could be treated in primary care settings.

Although there are five primary care clinics operated by HealthReach Network and one operated by Pine Tree Medical Associates in the service area, the absence of public transportation makes getting to the clinics difficult. The majority of primary care physicians (as well as Franklin Memorial Hospital itself) are based in the southern tier, and transportation to these locations is even more problematic for outlying patients. In fact, it is a 2-hour drive from the farthest point of the service area to Franklin Memorial Hospital.

By Maine standards, the region is relatively rich in social and health agencies and resources, and has a long history of innovation in community-based health initiatives. (During the 1970s and early 1980s, Rural Health Associates included the state's first HMO.) The University of Maine at Farmington offers a major in health education. Franklin Memorial Hospital's education department offers health education to the community, and the HCC promotes health and healthy lifestyles through education, prevention, outreach, and intervention. A number of other providers also offer education and outreach. However, at present, there is no overarching, coordinating program of health education and health outreach in this rural setting, and certainly not one using state-of-the-art technology that would bring education into homes, schools, and workplaces. As a result, FCHN is currently proposing the formation of a coalition to sponsor a rural health information center.

The changing paradigm in health care from an acute care hospital-centered model to a community care network (CCN) model is vastly changing the tenor of health care delivery in the region. The principal health concerns in the service area include access to primary care, mental health services, coordinated and ongoing health education, and dental care. The community itself identified these concerns in a community-wide Health Visioning Conference held in January 1994. As will be explained later in this chapter, an extraordinary number of initiatives have arisen as a direct result of that conference, leading to the development and growth of a richly textured CCN. The collaborative partnership of the FCHN, HCC, and WMA (Sustain Western Maine Project) is uniquely qualified to address a number of outstanding health and health-related issues in the community. The collaborative partners have been active participants in and drivers of these changes.

FCHN is a parent company to a diverse set of subsidiaries: Franklin Memorial Hospital (a 70-bed acute care hospital), Pine Tree Medical Associates (a primary care physician group of nine physicians and one physician assistant), HCC (a community-based health education, prevention, and outreach organization), and Evergreen Behavioral Services (a collaborative mental health outpatient services venture with the Sisters of Charity Health System in Lewiston, which is in turn the "parent" of St. Mary's Regional Medical Center). Over the past 2 years, FCHN has initiated a number of new affiliations or joint ventures to improve the health and welfare of the community. Some of the initiatives are: acquisition of HCC; expansion of Pine Tree Medical Associates to improve access to primary care; formation of Evergreen Behavioral Services with the Sisters of Charity Health System; affiliation with Central Maine Medical Center in Lewiston to develop an oncology clinic at Franklin Memorial Hospital; collaboration with Redington Fairview General Hospital in Skowhegan to purchase a laser for surgery; affiliation with Maine Medical Center in Portland to develop a pediatric cardiology clinic at Franklin Memorial Hospital; affiliation with HealthReach Network (which runs five primary care clinics in the service area) to recruit physicians (an initiative being funded in part by a Rural Transition Grant) and to develop a physician-hospital organization (PHO) (an initiative presently being funded by an Agency for Health Care Policy and Research [AHCPR] grant). Franklin Memorial Hospital and HealthReach Network also cosponsored the seminal Health Visioning Conference in January 1994, which resulted in a phenomenal wave of community interest in and support for a seamless health network in western Maine.

HCC is the preeminent outreach, education, and prevention organization in the community. The community-based coalition has taken its programs to schools, worksites, and the general public. With its acquisition later this year of a mobile health unit, the coalition will take its services to the outlying points of the service area.

In early 1995, the coalition published a long-awaited comprehensive community health assessment report, *A First Look: A Profile of Community Health in West Central Maine.* By using a number of health indicators such as occupational and other injuries, causes of death, use of available health services, rates of infant mortality, key environmental factors, and others, a "snapshot" of the community's present health was developed. This baseline information will be updated each year. In this way, health trends as well as the success or failure of health initiatives can be measured.

The WMA's Sustain Western Maine Project is funded by the Ford Foundation. Its mission is "to help the region to utilize its natural, human, and technological resources to ensure that all members of present and future generations can attain a high degree of health and well-being, economic security, and a say in shaping their future while maintaining the integrity of the ecological systems on which all life and production depends." The Sustain Western Maine Project represents one of two Maine sites chosen by the Ford Foundation to help with and study community sustainability. The project's various committees (education, economic development, environment, family development partnerships, and infrastructure and health) actively pursue sustainability through a number of economic, developmental, and educational projects.

PRIOR EFFORTS THAT REPRESENT MOVEMENT TOWARD THE COMMUNITY CARE NETWORK VISION

In late 1991, based on a new paradigm of health care delivery and recognizing that affiliation, collaboration, and the development of a diversified health care delivery system under a managed care scenario would soon be a very real part of Franklin County's world, Franklin Memorial Hospital made a change. Its corporators formed a not-for-profit corporation, Franklin Community Health Network. The new corporation would be the "parent" of subsidiaries to be developed in response to the rapidly changing needs and conditions.

Franklin Memorial Hospital became the first subsidiary. In response to the movement to have physicians directly employed by health organizations (and as a prelude to studying and/or developing a PHO), Pine Tree Medical Associates was then added. In 1992, the HCC became the health education, prevention, and outreach subsidiary. In late 1994, in response to direct community concern, a mental health services subsidiary, Evergreen Behavioral Services, was added. All the subsidiaries have separate boards, whose members are drawn from the health care field and from the community. In addition, board committees include non–board members, a strategy that allows even greater community participation.

Affiliation talks, then agreements, then actual collaboration happened under the FCHN umbrella (with Maine Medical Center, the Sisters of Charity Health System, Redington Fairview Regional Hospital, HealthReach Network, and Central Maine Medical Center, among others). Although FCHN is the largest health organization in the service area, a unique aspect of the movement toward the formation of a CCN here is that the effort has been exceptionally and increasingly community driven.

THE HEALTH VISIONING CONFERENCE

In January 1994, Franklin Memorial Hospital and HealthReach Network cosponsored a daylong health care visioning conference in Farmington. More than 160 participants were drawn from health care, government, education, the media, the clergy, and the community at large. They were charged with a twofold task: to identify important health care goals for the community, and to identify ways in which those goals could be reached. To ensure that all the goals identified would be researched and implemented, participants recommended the formation of a steering committee. This committee, Health Quest 2000, was charged with further clarifying and overseeing the implementation of the ideas generated that day. Membership of Health Quest 2000 was drawn from across the community, and meetings began in February 1994, a month after the conference. Task forces formed soon after the conference around specific issues and immediately began their work. A year later, in January 1995, a 13-page update, "Developing a Vision for Health Care Delivery in Western Maine," was sent to all the original conference participants.

The following is a summary of the issues identified that day, as well as the actions that have resulted a year later. Participants wanted a "shared vision" with community ownership and support, and Health Quest 2000 developed such a vision. Components of the vision statement are that: cooperation will be emphasized over competition; individual medical and preventive provider services will be connected for availability; the health care delivery system will be a shared responsibility of all participants; it will be locally controlled and will remain accountable to the public; high-quality care will be delivered; efforts will be focused on restoring, maintaining, and improving overall health (this will include mind, body, and spirit); care will be affordable (that is, costs will be realistic and sustainable by individuals, employers, insurance providers, and the government); and the success of these efforts will be tracked and measured over time against predetermined objectives and goals.

Participants wanted increased emphasis placed on wellness, the promotion of healthy lifestyles, and preventive services. The HCC hired a health educator to work on increasing health promotion activities in the region; she has worked closely with the school districts to act as a resource for health education in the schools. The coalition also raised funds to purchase a mobile health unit to bring education and services to the outlying regions of the service area. Populations at risk for health problems will be the primary focus of the unit. The HCC is also promoting and performing health risk appraisals in an effort to educate people on the risks associated with unhealthy lifestyles (smoking, being overweight, and so forth). And in January 1995, *A First Look: A Profile of Community Health in West Central Maine* was published, providing essential baseline data on the health status of the service area. The information will be updated yearly.

Participants also wanted improved access to primary care. In August 1994, Franklin Memorial Hospital hired a full-time recruiter to focus on the recruitment and retention of primary care and other needed physicians to the service area. Recruitment is a joint venture with HealthReach Network, which also has a full-time recruiter. During the past year, two internists have been recruited to the region. A primary care task force has also been established, with the charge of making recommendations on improving access to primary care, on developing a system for collaborative planning between primary care providers, and on the need for an urgent care system in the region. This committee (as are all committees arising from the conference) is composed of health care providers and members of the community. Participants also suggested the formation of an open clinic (offering "quick care," or "walk-in" care) with a sliding fee scale, which would serve anyone who needs care. The task force will study and address this item.

Participants wanted attention given to financing the current system and the degree to which the present system affects affordability. In fall 1994, Franklin County was chosen as one of two demonstration sites in Maine for a large grant from the AHCPR, a grant written by the Edmund Muskie Institute of Public Affairs at the University of Southern Maine. The other Maine site is in Washington County. Only five demonstration grants were awarded across the country. The grant, awarded jointly to FCHN and HealthReach Network, is funding the development of a managed care delivery system in the service area. A physician-hospital integration (PHI) committee, which was formed earlier in 1994 to research various PHI and PHO models, has moved this project forward very quickly. Community input has been crucial. The PHI committee is chaired by a community member, and the group's membership is a community/physician/administration mix. The current project will establish a PHO and link it to Franklin Memorial Hospital. The linking of primary care physicians to the hospital will create efficiencies in the health system and will allow the organization to take care of the enrolled population at a lower cost. The PHO is expected to be formed by July 1995. A key element in the success of the PHO, the Health Card project, will be discussed later in this chapter. Also recognizing that the burgeoning CCN would need funding from outside sources for the many projects being proposed, FCHN created a grant writer position. Although employed by FCHN, the grant writer is available to all health-related organizations in the area to help them in their search for project or program funding.

Participants wanted the system of care to have expanded, open access to people from all parts of the region. The efforts of the HCC (that is, the mobile health unit, services provided as part of the coalition's mission, and so forth) appear earlier in this chapter. Additionally, a dental task force has been established to consider ways to increase access to dental services for the financially disadvantaged in the region. The group has developed a proposal to open a dental clinic in the southern tier of the service area and is now seeking outside funding for the program. Health Visioning Conference participants identified the importance of collecting and sharing data among health care providers as a way to increase efficiencies and quality throughout the system, and to make it truly "seamless." A health information and data task force was established to evaluate the methods of sharing clinical information while maintaining patient confidentiality. The group is specifically looking to establish a community health information network (CHIN) in the service area. The Maine Health Information Center is working on a project to develop two CHINs in Maine, one rural and one urban. This region has been accepted as the rural site.

Participants expressed the need for expanded mental health and substance abuse services and for educating providers in the region on how to deal with substance abuse problems. In late September 1994, FCHN and the Sisters of Charity Health System collaborated to form Evergreen Behavioral Services. Based in Farmington, Evergreen has substantially increased the availability of mental health and substance abuse services to the area. The organization recently made its services available in the northern tier by offering them in Kingfield and Rangely. Tri-County Mental Health Services, also based in Farmington, has also expanded, opening a new office in Wilton (a neighboring town to Farmington). FCHN and the Sisters of Charity Health System also are working to create a network for all providers of mental health services (to include: Franklin Memorial Hospital, St. Mary's Regional Medical Center, Tri-County Mental Health Services, HealthReach Network, private providers, and school counselors).

Participants wanted home care services expanded and strengthened. In December 1994, FCHN's board of trustees approved a list of corporate priorities for 1995. Among them were the following:

- Determine improvements that FCHN or Franklin Memorial Hospital should seek in home health care.
- Evaluate the community need for assisted-living retirement housing.
- Determine whether FCHN should take a leading role in developing expanded capacity for assisted living by July 1, 1995.

A task force has been established and is now in the process of studying assisted-living options for the area. Also, Franklin Memorial Hospital has entered into discussions with Androscoggin Home Health Agency, the largest home health agency in the region, about the possibility of establishing a collaborative effort to expand home health care in the service area.

Participants wanted health education teams that could reach out to special populations and geographies. Special emphasis was placed on the elderly, though education and outreach across all ages was a concern in this large rural service area. The HCC's mobile health unit, scheduled for purchase and implementation in 1995, will bring outreach services and education directly to those who need them. The coalition will also weave women's health and wellness issues into its education programs. The WMA's Sustain Western Maine Project explores and develops ways in which the region can sustain its infrastructure, health, economy, and education. One of its projects is the development of a public access television station that would offer (among other things) programs on health and wellness topics for direct home viewing. In addition, as mentioned earlier in this chapter, FCHN has proposed and is in the preliminary stages of forming a coalition to sponsor a rural health information center, to be based in Farmington. The HCC is requesting funding to study the need for a community health educators program.

Participants felt that the school systems should be viewed as a resource for providing health services, information, and education. They also mentioned that school-based clinics would be a helpful early intervention tool. The health educator hired by the HCC focused on the development of a comprehensive resource for the school systems to use in their health curriculum. This program was implemented in September 1994 and has been used by health educators in many of the region's school systems. The coalition is also the lead organization in developing and implementing school-based health clinics.

Participants wanted more communication with government. They noted that elected and public officials should be kept aware of the region's health initiatives and efforts and that regulatory barriers to change should be identified and removed. In early 1995, the Health Quest 2000 steering committee, in collaboration with the WMA, held a legislative breakfast in Farmington to discuss current health care issues and to update the legislators on the status of the service area's initiatives since the Health Visioning Conference a year ago.

cardholders would be arranged with merchants throughout the service area for health-related items or services. Second, the back of the card would be imprinted with a series of telephone numbers for area health organizations. Third, each card would be accompanied by a mail-in sheet on which the cardholder could indicate interest in receiving various health newsletters or health-related information (such as the existence of a support group dedicated to a particular health issue).

Most important, the card's development would approximately follow the time line for the development of the PHO that is presently under way in Franklin County. The Health Card would build an identifiable enrollment list, which would allow negotiations of managed care contracts from a position of strength. It would empower the cardholder by making him or her a member of a community-wide health network that will negotiate future managed care contracts.

In addition, the Health Card project would establish a central database that could be used for marketing and research, conducting health-related surveys, and disseminating information throughout the service area. The Health Card will build customer loyalty to FCHN.

The Health Card has now been developed. Implementation is planned in phases, with an initial "test run" of approximately 1,500 cards (Franklin Memorial Hospital employees and their families) scheduled for mid- to late summer 1995. During phase 1, which will follow, approximately 22,000 people in the service area will be issued the card (those presently enrolled in the Franklin Memorial Hospital Meditech-based patient record system and residing in the service area's ZIP codes), and use of the card for registration purposes will begin exclusively at the hospital. Phase 2 will extend use of the card to the remaining FCHN subsidiaries (HCC, Pine Tree Medical Associates, Evergreen Behavioral Services) and to the hospital's medical staff. Phase 3 will extend use of the card to other health organizations and providers in the service area. Open registration will be a continuous option. By the time phase 3 has been implemented and use of the Health Card has become more universal across the spectrum of area providers, the cardholder will feel less connected to a hospital-based health model and more a part of a seamless community care delivery network.

The Mobile Health Unit

The goal of the mobile health unit project is to develop and implement programs for the mobile health unit. Those programs will extend education, prevention, primary care outreach, and health care needs assessment into the outlying parts of the service area. Milestones in the project include purchase of the mobile unit, development of programs, and making the unit operational. Measurable objectives for the project include actual use of the mobile unit, programs developed and implemented, health care trends and needs identified and met, and improvement of the community's health (as measured by indicators in *A First Look: A Profile of Community Health in West Central Maine*).

The HCC extends the CCN vision by bringing its numerous education and prevention programs to schools, worksites, and the general public. A subsidiary of FCHN, the coalition for the past 3 years has been largely funded by a grant from the Bingham Program. During 1994, the coalition proposed and raised funds to purchase a mobile health unit in mid-1955 and is now seeking developmental and evaluation funding for the first 3 years.

The importance of the unit to the outlying population in the service area is inestimable. There are 18 people per square mile in this defined service area. About half of these residents are located in four populated areas: Farmington, Wilton, Jay, and Livermore. The remaining population is spread thinly over small towns, unincorporated townships, and plantations. Some residents live 50 or more miles from Farmington. The population of some of the smaller municipalities swells considerably during the summer vacation months. The mobile health unit will allow existing education, prevention, and outreach services to be expanded into geographically isolated parts of this service area. The van will also provide new education and screening programs that are currently unavailable.

The coalition will work with groups within the service area to identify their specific needs. A possible core of services has been defined, including well-child clinics and immunizations, blood pressure and cholesterol screening, teen pregnancy prevention, nutrition counseling, parenting education classes, cancer risk assessment and screening, CPR training, breast and testicular self-examination training, glaucoma awareness, child safety and accident reduction education, substance abuse counseling, diabetes education, first aid follow-up training, and hearing testing. The mobile unit will also provide physical space for school-based clinic services to schools that do not have available clinic space. The mobile unit will extend the availability of primary care by providing these services and by referring customers to area primary care providers when necessary.

Everyone who comes through the unit will complete a health risk appraisal. Those results, as well as data from mobile unit usage, will be used to determine priorities when developing services and educational programs.

As an entity that will truly be "out in the community," the mobile unit will be a source of information on the status of and trends in the area's health care. The unit will play an important and unique role in identifying new or emerging health-related needs.

The HCC is seeking funding for program development, program evaluation, and implementation of the mobile health unit. The coalition has already raised funds for the purchase of the unit, and Franklin Memorial Hospital has pledged partial operational funding through its Annual Appeal campaign. In addition, a medical student will work in the van this year, on a stipend provided by the Maine Ambulatory Care Coalition.

Public Access Television Station

The goal of this project is to develop a public access television station to promote the mission of the WMA (Sustain Western Maine Project). Project milestones include program and community support development, purchase and location of equipment, and eventual enhancement to include the creation of an electronic "town commons." Among the project's measurable objectives are the richness and variety of programming and program development.

The WMA's mission is to promote economic prosperity, wise use of natural resources, and educational excellence in western Maine. The WMA Sustain Western Maine's Infrastructure Committee has chosen information and telecommunications technology as a means of enhancing and supporting economic security, environmental integrity, and quality of life. The committee proposes developing a public access television station as a vehicle for community service announcements, job service listings, from government or foundation sources. As a broad-based community health care group with an established mission and record of success in the areas of prevention, education, and wellness, the HCC is very interested in establishing and taking responsibility for this project.

As these proposed initiatives indicate, the collaborative partnership of FCHN, HCC, and WMA (Sustain Western Maine Project) is one whose goals are of outreach, education, and bringing together the community in ways that will improve and maintain its overall health and well-being.

SUMMARY OF NOTABLE PROGRESS

The Franklin Community Partnership in rural Maine is very much project driven. The partners came together in a community climate that was well along in the process of effecting a CCN at a time when the five projects proposed by the partners could make a significant difference in that process. In view of the unique examples set by this CCN demonstration site, the American Hospital Association hosted a Case Example On-Site at Franklin Memorial Hospital during July 1996. From around this country and Canada, 19 registrants came together to hear about the five projects, the FCHN, and the partnership, and all took away information they could apply to their own efforts.

The Health Card

At this writing, more than 31,000 Health Cards have been issued to the approximately 40,000 people who live in the FCHN service area. (See figure 9-1.) Cards continue to be issued at the rate of 15–20 a day through patient registration at Franklin Memorial Hospital. Additionally, card application forms are distributed at area health fairs, wellness seminars, and through the HCC's mobile health unit.

The cards have proved valuable in many ways. Not only do they speed registration into the health care system and make the holders aware of their "membership" in a wellness continuum, but also, for the CCN, they represent a segmentable database that includes nearly 80 percent of the people in the service area. Mailings of health-related information can be sent to the entire service area, and additionally to specially segmented populations—for example, information about breast and cervical cancer to women over the age of 50 years.

The database has also been used to inform the residents of seven communities about town meetings and focus groups conducted to measure their level of interest in a medical clinic being considered for their area that would improve access to health care. In addition, the database is used for specialized surveys, including one to measure the outcomes of community-based cardiovascular health interventions. Optically scannable surveys will be mailed to a large random sample of the database at the beginning and end of a three-year initiative that aims to raise awareness and change attitudes and behaviors that can affect cardiovascular health. Other surveys have been mailed to segments of the database to assess awareness of family violence, dental health, and breast and cervical cancer.

Health Card holders not only feel connected to the health network in their service area, but they also receive discounts at 39 cooperating businesses who support the community wellness concept. In the months to come, optical scanners will be installed in physicians' offices, further simplifying the health care registration process for cardholders and introducing them firsthand to the seamless continuum of care that characterizes the developing new delivery system.

The Mobile Health Unit

The HCC's mobile health unit has become a positive and viable force in the community, particularly in taking education and prevention interventions to outlying regions of this large, rural service area. A driver/coordinator has been hired, who has set up and carries out a monthly schedule of visits to 20 rural communities. Programs offered to date include bicycle safety instruction and helmet distribution, women's health education, dental health education, delivery of health risk appraisals, blood pressure screening, medication review and counseling, and instruction in recognizing early signs of chest pain. The mobile unit will also be delivering the services of dental professionals who will apply dental sealant to the molars of all second graders in the five school districts in the service area.

The unit has also provided a health care presence and wellness message in the communities it visits, and data gathered through the health risk appraisals will be used to determine priorities when developing future services and educational programs.

Youth Rural Leaders Forum

The HCC and WMA recently completed their first Youth Rural Leaders Forum, resulting in the publication of insightful essays on leadership written by the 23 Kingfield, ME, eighth graders who participated in the yearlong program. One youngster observed, "I feel it is an important thing to be an active part in the community, and to be the leader in one way or another is better than simply joining a group to give people the impression that you are the active type." He went on to note that he would like to lead a group of people in his neighborhood, collecting bottles and cans for recycling. "I would be good in this role because I have been studying and reading about the environment for quite some time," he said.

At an event culminating their participation, the youngsters presented to members of the town's board of selectmen, school board, and chamber of commerce their assessment of Kingfield's strengths and weaknesses and their vision for the town's future. During the school year, the students had completed training in listening skills, conflict resolution, and an introduction to peer mediation. They also attended workshops on Meyers Briggs Type Indicators (with an emphasis on learning styles), diversity training, decision making, and problem solving.

The Youth Rural Leaders Forum program has been enthusiastically accepted for another eighth grade in the same school district for next academic year. An informational meeting will be held in September, and the program will begin in October.

Health Educators

As a result of this funded study, the HCC's community-based Health Educators Task Force now meets monthly, with 10–12 regular members and a mailing list of more than 25. Unmet needs for community health care have been identified, as have numerous community resources for addressing them. A preliminary proposal as a start-up for this project has been written in response to a state request for proposals.

Community Access Television Station

WMA is in the process of developing a community access television station to carry community bulletin boards and news, including local health information, which will further strengthen the CCN. Progress to date has been steady but slow, in that the group has purchased the necessary computer equipment but has encountered difficulty in locating a site for the station that is served by cable. In recent hopeful breakthroughs, however, the University of Maine at Farmington has expressed a strong interest in collaborating on the project, and housing for the station has been found in the Community Center—moves that bode well for the accomplishment and sustainability of the project.

Contact: Betsy Kimball
Grant Writer
Franklin Community Health Network
P.O. Box 430
Farmington, ME 04938
Telephone: (207) 778-9465
E-mail: bkimball@fchn.org

10

The North Iowa Mercy Health Network

Executive Summary

The Regional Health Education Center was formed between North Iowa Area Community College and North Iowa Mercy Health Center (NIMHC) 10 years ago. The Regional Health Education Center is responsible for offering programs to meet the health education needs of patients, former patients, professional health care personnel, businesses, industries, consumers, and other groups. The purpose of the center is to provide accessible, high-quality education to the health care professionals and general public of northern Iowa, consisting of 15 rural counties. The extensive networks of the two organizations provide a means by which the center can meet the goals and objectives to fulfill its purpose.

Activities Programs offered for health care professionals are designed to improve skills, increase knowledge, and obtain and/or maintain licensure or certification. Specific categories of offerings for health care professionals are as follows:

- Continuing education programs are offered for health care professionals, that is, physicians, nurses, dietitians, physical therapists, occupational therapists, social workers, funeral directors, paramedics, radiology technicians, and pharmacists.
- Staff development programs are offered for NIMHC employees, long-term care personnel, home health agencies, and business and industry employees.
- Short-term career training programs are offered to certify geriatric aides, nursing assistants, residential attendants, emergency medical technicians/ambulance (EMT-A), emergency medical technicians/intermediate (EMT-I), paramedics, and limited practice radiographers.

In addition to education and training of health care professionals, the partnership provides for educational programs to help area residents live with, improve, or prevent various health conditions. They are categorized as either patient education or health promotion.

Challenges Top administration support minimized many problems. Financial support and technical expertise were available from both institutions. As new systems were created and actualized, the strengths of the individual institutions could be capitalized and the weaknesses could be minimized. This allowed the center to create a solid foundation from which to function.

Change tends to be difficult for most individuals, and this type of merger called for a new way of doing routine work. Daily operations (record-keeping systems, committee structures, policy and procedure manuals, computer systems, telephone systems, office space, and so on) were all merged from two distinct systems into one operation.

Promotion of the center and its programs, services, and activities presented a barrier in a variety of ways. Because of various sensitivities in the area, neither institution desired to make a news release to the media. Letters of announcement were mailed to health care professionals, various professional and volunteer groups/associations, and agencies served by both institutions. This was successful only to the degree to which those receiving the announcement read and understood their mail.

Although a new logo had been developed for the center, individuals did not identify the logo with the center. The hospital and college have been present in the area since 1916, making identification of a separate entity difficult. Promotion remained a problem for the first 2 to 3 years. However, currently the center has captured the identity as being the community resource to provide health education assistance.

Summary Education operations, services, and activities of the parent organizations have been unified and centralized except for the career health programs. In collaboration with regional hospitals, the center has expanded and improved health continuing education in the more rural sections of the region. The center's efforts complement the community health care system and the areawide networks established by the parent organizations.

Dr. David Buettner, President
North Iowa Area Community College

THE COLLABORATIVE PARTNERSHIP

The Community

The community served by the North Iowa Mercy Health Network encompasses 14 counties in north central Iowa with a combined population of approximately 225,000. This is a highly rural area with an elderly population that makes up nearly 20 percent of the total. The fastest-growing component of the population is those over age 85. The high proportion of elderly results in significant rates of heart disease, cerebrovascular disease, and cancer. In part because the emergency medical services have been well developed, many patients survive heart attack or stroke and become chronic patients whose care requires a combination of primary and specialty health services.

This collaborative partnership is a network of 9 small rural hospitals, 2 physician hospital organizations, 27 primary care clinics that provide primary care, and 1 referral hospital that provides specialty services. All these entities have a long history of working together, so the 14-county definition of community is logical for this partnership.

The Partnership

The partners in this collaborative relationship include the following:

- NIMHC (a network including a Medicare-designated rural referral center and 27 primary care clinics)
- Belmond Community Hospital, Eldora Regional Medical Center, Franklin General Hospital, Hancock County Memorial Hospital, Howard County Hospital, Kossuth County Hospital, Mitchell County Regional Health Center, Palo Alto County Hospital, and St. Joseph Community Hospital (primary care rural hospitals)
- Franklin Medical Center and Forest City Regional Medical Center (joint venture clinics)
- Elderbridge (Agency on Aging)
- University of Iowa Institute for Quality Healthcare

These partners have worked together to develop programs for people in north central Iowa for at least 5 years. The first management contract was signed between NIMHC and Eldora Regional Medical Center in 1978.

The initial participants were the 10 hospitals, banding together via a series of management contracts. The joint ventures—partnerships between NIMHC and local communities—have come into existence since July 1994. These joint ventures were created to ensure that primary care physicians would remain in the two communities, Hampton and Forest City. An additional joint venture was established at Mitchell County Regional Health Center, bringing the hospital and physicians together in a single entity. The management contracts with hospitals developed at the request of the small rural hospitals, which were finding it difficult to maintain necessary administrative expertise in the face of an increasingly complex health care environment.

Elderbridge is a not-for-profit organization serving the north central Iowa area. A relationship has evolved with this group as care management and aging services programs have developed out of NIMHC.

The University of Iowa has partnered with NIMHC on several major programs (development of heart surgery, family practice residency program, distance nursing education, and renal dialysis) in the past and is currently involved in a project to assess health needs of citizens in north central Iowa. The university's Institute for Quality Healthcare will assist in the evaluation and dissemination aspects of this project.

PRIOR EFFORTS REPRESENTING MOVEMENT TOWARD THE COMMUNITY CARE NETWORK VISION

Although the first management contract was signed in 1978, efforts in moving toward a community care network (CCN) vision began in a significant way in 1988. At that time, NIMHC first began to articulate the following three-step process to move toward this vision:

1. Assess the health status of people in the 14-county north central Iowa service area.
2. Develop a vision for providing services based on needs.

3. Develop strategies to work toward that vision. These strategies were:
   - Develop a modern, secondary referral center.
   - Develop relationships with components for an integrated delivery system.
   - Develop a system structure.

These efforts will be described in the sections of this chapter dealing with the four dimensions of the CCN vision.

Community Accountability/Community Health Focus

A number of approaches have been used to gain community input into the planning process for the North Iowa CCN. (See figure 10-1.)

FIGURE 10-1. Annual Planning Process

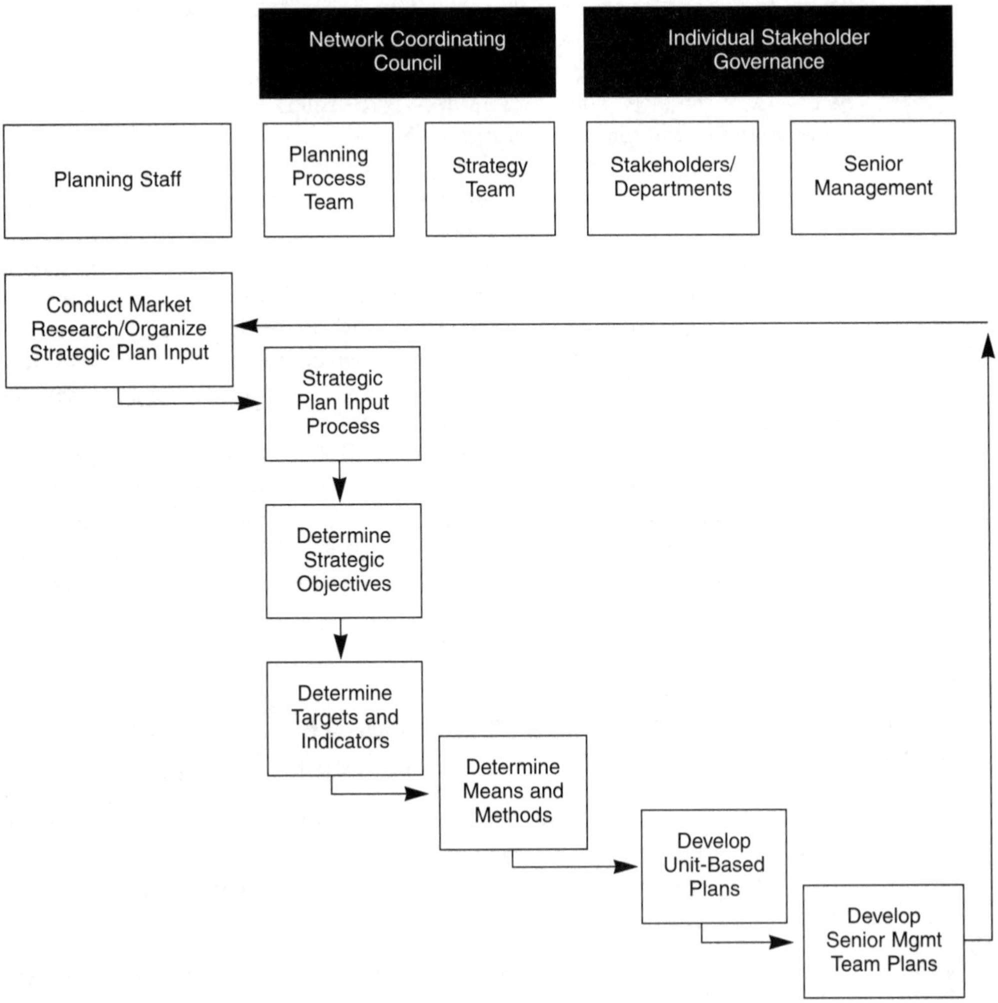

Community Assessment of Human Needs An extensive assessment of the needs of citizens, particularly of underserved populations, has been done regularly since 1987. NIMHC conducted the assessments until 1989, when it was determined that it would be more efficient to coordinate this effort with the United Way of North Central Iowa. Using a professional research firm, the United Way conducts an extensive survey every 2 years to assess needs throughout north central Iowa. Representatives from NIMHC serve on the board and committees of United Way and assist in overseeing the assessment process. The most recent assessment was completed in May 1994.

Town Meetings Town meetings were held in the nine communities with hospitals belonging to the North Iowa CCN in 1991. At these meetings, issues were identified relating to health care needs in the counties served by these community hospitals. Attendees at these meetings included individuals involved in social services, day care, adult day care, hospice care, mental health, schools, clinics, hospitals, and churches. Goals were set by each community. These goals were then reviewed for common themes that could apply to the north central Iowa region as a whole. These common themes were:

- Information dissemination
- Health education programs
- Ensuring access
- Transportation to care

Mortality/Morbidity Data Annual data on mortality and morbidity for the north central Iowa region are reviewed and used in setting health care goals for the area. These data have consistently shown heart disease, cancer, and cerebrovascular disorders to be the chief causes of death in north central Iowa. Incidence of disease in these categories exceeds state rates.

Health of the Public In 1994, the North Iowa CCN was chosen to work with the University of Iowa on a grant funded by Pew Charitable Trusts and the Robert Wood Johnson Foundation. The grant provides for a health needs assessment on a county-by-county basis for north central Iowa. The first two counties are in the process of being surveyed as pilots; the remaining counties will then be surveyed during the last year of the grant. Out of this assessment process, further recommendations will be provided to the North Iowa CCN for planning purposes.

Continuous Quality Improvement Initiative NIMHC and the North Iowa CCN are in the process of rolling out a significant initiative in continuous quality improvement (CQI). This initiative will train 3,000 individuals in hospitals and clinics throughout the CCN in the general concepts of CQI. Resources have been assigned throughout the CCN to carry this initiative forward.

Network Advisory Council A council comprising administrators and trustee representatives of all hospitals and clinic joint ventures in the CCN meets bimonthly for purposes of planning and education. An initiative to develop a shared information system throughout the CCN came from a recommendation made by this Network Advisory Council.

Rural Outreach Partnerships between NIMHC, Franklin General Hospital, Franklin Medical Center, St. Joseph Community Hospital, and physicians and dentists provide care to individuals who have no health insurance and do not qualify for programs such as Medicaid or Medicare. Although titled Rural Outreach, this program also covers those individuals living in towns in the north Iowa area.

Seamless Continuum of Care

The partners in the North Iowa CCN have been working toward a fully integrated, seamless continuum of care for the past five years. Several initiatives reflect progress in this dimension.

Information Systems The hospitals and clinics of the North Iowa CCN are in the process of linking all sites to a centralized data repository. A list of common data elements required has been compiled and prioritized. A hardware design has been completed by Daou Systems consultants. The first step in linking systems—creating local area networks in each community—was scheduled for completion by September 1995. The target date for initial connections to a common data repository was fall 1996. The design for this system was done in such a way as to allow social service agencies, public health, and other providers to access the system in the future at fairly minimal cost.

Telemedicine Three of the primary care hospitals (Franklin General Hospital, Kossuth County Hospital, and St. Joseph Community Hospital) are involved in a project with NIMHC to implement telemedicine services under a grant from the Healthcare Financing Administration. Telemedicine will provide additional access to specialist physician consultation in the smaller communities in the region. It will also allow quicker transmission of X rays and other medical data in emergency situations. This will enhance the emergency care available in primary care hospitals.

Emergency Medical Services An effort has been made by NIMHC to provide emergency services training and continuing education to the volunteer ambulance and First Responder groups throughout north Iowa. Other support services include purchase of defibrillators for several hospitals, provision of tissue plasminogen activator drugs to all area emergency rooms, biomedical support for emergency equipment, telecommunications, medical direction, hepatitis vaccinations for emergency medical services staff in the area, provision of standardized prehospital medical records, and quality monitoring support.

Care Management In January 1993, NIMHC established an aggressive community-based nursing care management program. Patients identified for care management had the following characteristics:

- High utilization of acute care
- Multiple system problems
- Chronically or terminally ill
- Frail
- Little social or family support
- Medicare/Medicaid

The intention of the program is to develop a long-term relationship with patients and families to help them manage their care more effectively. Nurses facilitate access to the continuum of health and social services, collaborate with physicians, monitor health status and functional ability, and enhance self-care. Results of this program indicate decreases in hospital admissions and emergency center visits, improved utilization of home care services, and improved health status and satisfaction of patients. As of March 1995, 158 patients were being monitored and an additional 80 patients were being actively managed under this program.

Management within Fixed Resources

The north central Iowa area has just come under a managed care contract for mental health services. This is the only significant managed care contract thus far in this area. Despite this fact, the North Iowa CCN has made efforts to move toward reduction in duplication of services and to provide care at the most appropriate point in the continuum of services. Planning efforts attempt to match resources and strategies to the needs identified in the region. Specific efforts made toward risk-sharing financial arrangements are described below.

Consolidation In 1993, years of discussion in Mason City culminated in the consolidation of North Iowa Medical Center and St. Joseph Mercy Hospital into the NIMHC. This consolidation resulted in a reduction in duplication of services in the community, reduced costs of care, improved integration of health services, improved ability to monitor/report quality, coordinated development of specialized services, and an improved ability to recruit physicians and other professional staff. It also encouraged the two large multispecialty physician practices in Mason City to come together into a single entity—the Mason City Clinic.

Mercy Health Plans Mercy Health Services has developed health insurance plans that are available throughout the north Iowa area. These PPO- and HMO-style plans include all the providers in the North Iowa CCN.

Integrated Health Delivery A statewide organized delivery system was implemented effective January 1, 1995, under the name of Integrated Health Delivery. This system includes the hospitals affiliated with Mercy Health Services, Blue Cross/Blue Shield of Iowa, University of Iowa Hospitals and Clinics, Iowa Health Systems hospitals and physicians, and Community Financial and Insurance Corporation. Integrated Health Delivery is offering an HMO-style product called UnityChoice Health Plan. The hospital and physician partners of the North Iowa CCN have all signed agreements with Integrated Health Delivery that allows this entity to negotiate managed care contracts as a whole network.

Clinic Joint Ventures NIMHC has partnered with organizations in three communities to maintain physician coverage in these communities. In all three cases, joint ventures were created with equal investments from all participating partners. These new clinics are all not-for-profit entities whose chief purpose is to maintain primary care in local communities where appropriate services can be provided as close to individuals' homes as possible.

Shared Equipment Equipment for specialized procedures has been jointly purchased by hospital partners in the CCN. This sharing allows for provision of services in many locations at a minimal capital investment.

Summary

The North Iowa CCN has made significant progress in developing an integrated, seamless continuum of care that is responsive to local needs and also to the changing environment of health care. Efforts have been made to prepare for capitation, although market forces have not yet brought managed care to the north Iowa area.

MOVING TOWARD THE COMMUNITY CARE NETWORK VISION

The CCN vision is evolving out of shared values and missions of the partners in the North Iowa CCN. Planning efforts over the past 5 years have focused the vision for health care in north central Iowa. This vision is to work toward improving the health status of area communities by improving access to appropriate services, creating a seamless continuum of care, improving quality continuously, reducing costs, and emphasizing preventive care. Goals will be based on assessments of health care needs throughout the region, making the CCN accountable to local communities. This vision has been articulated in many ways.

The process for developing the overall vision included many organizations and was spearheaded by NIMHC in 1991–92. Participants in this process included the following:

- 60 physicians
- 109 community leaders, NIMHC governance
- 5 competitor hospitals
- 57 staff in nine service line meetings
- 1,436 patient opinion surveys
- 495 staff members (from the organizational audit)
- 1 Amicare (home health) representative
- 1 Mercy Alternative representative
- 2 Aging Services representatives
- 48 department directors at NIMHC
- 6 vice presidents of NIMHC
- 9 managed hospital administrators

The visioning process involved a number of methodologies, as follows:

- Task force meetings
- Focus groups
- Input from staff surveys
- Patient surveys
- One-on-one interviews with community leaders and competitor hospitals
- Input from physicians in their hospital department meetings

Meetings were planned and conducted by the chief executive officer of NIMHC (at that time St. Joseph Mercy Hospital) and the hospital's director of planning. Focus groups were led by the director of planning. Vice presidents received input from physicians at physician department meetings. All input was summarized and provided to the planning task force to assist it in its charge to develop a vision for health care services for the area.

Although the process formally drew together many individuals from the north central Iowa area, it was not the end of the visioning process. This process continues on a daily basis as the partners in the North Iowa CCN meet to develop systems and programs and grow to understand the specific ramifications of creating a seamless continuum of cost-effective health care services. Partners are all beginning to include collaboration and health status as elements of their strategic plans.

INITIATIVES FOR MOVING TOWARD THE COMMUNITY CARE NETWORK VISION

A number of initiatives are already under way that will help move the North Iowa CCN toward its vision. These include the following:

- Development of a linked computer system throughout northern Iowa
- Assessment of health needs by county in the North Iowa CCN service area
- Enhanced interorganizational planning via a Network Advisory Council
- Working toward a capitation-style reimbursement system by learning methods to operate within Medicare payment constraints and by providing a capitated insurance product
- Reducing unnecessary use of service and enhancing overall quality of care by implementing care management throughout the North Iowa CCN

These efforts have been briefly described in earlier sections of this chapter. This section will describe the objectives and expected roles of the partners in each of these initiatives, as well as a plan for evaluation and improvement.

Development of a Linked Computer System

1. Develop local area networks linking physician offices to hospitals in each county. (Target: 9/95)
2. Create a shared central data repository housing data from all hospitals and physicians in north central Iowa. (Target: Fall 1996)
3. Provide patient data to providers throughout the region to enhance a seamless continuum of care. (Target: Fall 1997)
4. Provide regionwide scheduling of services. (Target: 1998)
5. Provide for single-bill generation for all health services rendered to an individual within the North Iowa CCN. (Target: 1999)

Roles of partners in this initiative are as follows:

- Hospitals/physicians: Develop initial local area networks and data repository.

- Social services and other health providers: Link to the network as resources and programming allow.
- NIMHC: Coordinate the development of the linked computer network.

Evaluation and plans for improvement are as follows: Evaluation will flow from successful completion of the networked system. This system will also be assessed using CQI principles that are being taught to individuals throughout the system.

Assessment of Health Needs

Objectives of this initiative are as follows:

1. Assess health needs of individuals in north central Iowa on a county-by-county basis through a direct-mail survey. (Target: 1996)
2. Review existing data sources for objective measures of health status in each county. (Target: 1995)
3. Develop recommendations for each county and for the region as a whole based on data and survey results. (Target: 1996)
4. Develop baseline data against which to compare for future health status improvement initiatives. (Target: 1995)

Roles of partners in this initiative are as follows:

- *University of Iowa:* Provide oversight and technical supervision to data collection and analysis; assist in making recommendations based on data collected.
- *NIMHC:* Coordinate development of the health assessment process through the managed hospitals in the region.
- *Managed hospitals:* Coordinate local (county) health assessments with other providers and social service agencies in each county; coordinate participation of social service and health providers in formulating recommendations.

Evaluation and plans for improvement are as follows:

- Goals will be set based on recommendations flowing from the assessment process.
- Achievement of these goals will be assessed by comparing with baseline data collected during the health needs assessment.
- CQI process teams will be used to plan, achieve, and continue to improve processes identified by recommendations.

Enhanced Interorganizational Planning

The objective of this initiative is to further develop the existing Network Advisory Council (which represents NIMHC and managed hospitals) into a governing structure for the North Iowa CCN as a whole.

Roles of the partners in this initiative are as follows:

- *NIMHC:* Reorganize its structure to reflect a system orientation. (Target: 7/1/95)
- *Managed hospitals/physicians:* Participate in the Network Advisory Council; empower the council to make networkwide decisions; work with local-level social services and health providers to integrate them into this council structure. (Target: 1996)

Evaluation and plan for improvement are as follows: Evaluation of changes in organizational and decision-making structures will flow from successful implementation of these structures. Improvement will arise out of continual evaluation of decision-making processes using CQI techniques.

Working toward Capitation Style Reimbursement

Objectives of this initiative are as follows:

1. Work with partners to develop the UnityChoice capitated insurance product throughout the state. (Target: 1995)
2. Achieve a break-even point on all Medicare reimbursed services. (Target: 1996)

Roles of the partners in this initiative are as follows:

- *Blue Cross/Blue Shield of Iowa/Mercy Health Services/University of Iowa Hospitals and Clinics/Iowa Health Systems hospitals and physicians:* Further develop the insurance product UnityChoice throughout the state; ensure provider coverage in all areas of the state.
- *NIMHC/managed hospitals:* Develop and share methods for reducing and eliminating deficits resulting from Medicare underpayments.

Evaluation and plans for improvement are as follows: Evaluation of the capitated insurance product will be based on enrollment numbers of entrusted lives and process and outcome measures of services rendered. Comparisons of mortality and morbidity data as well as health services usage will be made to baseline data collected prior to implementation of UnityChoice. Members will be surveyed to gain knowledge of their perceptions of services. Improvement will be based on data collected through these evaluation measures.

Implementing Care Management

Objectives of this initiative are as follows:

1. Extend care management in heart disease to rural counties in north central Iowa. (Target: Fall 1996)
2. Extend care management across the continuum of care, including prevention. (Target: Summer 1997)
3. Develop linkages between care management and community needs assessment. (Target: Fall 1996)
4. Develop education components to support care management (Target: Winter 1998)
5. Develop evaluation methodologies to assess the impact of care management. (Target: Fall 1996)

Roles of the partners are as follows:

- *NIMHC/Elderbridge Agency on Aging:* Coordinate expansion of care management into the rural areas of north central Iowa.
- *University of Iowa:* Provide guidance and expertise in developing linkages between care management and health needs assessment in each county.

- *Institute for Quality Healthcare:* Assist in developing the evaluation methodologies to assess the impact of care management in the North Iowa CCN.
- *Managed hospitals:* Coordinate local-level support and development of care management in counties.
- *Primary care clinics:* Assist in identifying clients who could benefit from care management.

Evaluation and plans for improvement are as follows: Evaluation will be developed with assistance from the Institute for Quality Healthcare at the University of Iowa. It will include consideration of mechanisms to collect baseline data, to structure appropriate experimental and control groups for care management, and to collect both process and outcome data relating to care management. Specific evaluation components will include the following:

- Patterns of health/social services usage
- Cost and comparative analysis of savings
- Perceived well-being of participants
- Care experience of participants prior to implementation of care management—cost and perception of service
- Number of admissions to acute care, emergency room use, costs of care
- Subjective perspectives of care management participants and their families

Data collected through the evaluation process will be used to improve care management as it is extended further.

Technical Assistance Needed

Technical assistance will be needed by the North Iowa CCN to achieve the initiatives discussed above. The partnership has already received funding and technical assistance through grants (enumerated in "Prior Efforts that Represent Movement toward the Community Care Network Vision"). In addition, partners have devoted resources from their operating and capital budgets toward linking computer systems, health care needs assessment, and developing care delivery systems that can work under capitation-style reimbursement.

SUMMARY OF NOTABLE PROGRESS

A number of initiatives have progressed significantly during the past year, including the following:

Management Information Systems

All cabling has been installed to connect the hospital and physician clinic portions of the North Iowa Mercy Health Network. Basic word processing and electronic mail functions are being implemented during July 1996. Further clinical, demographic, and billing applications are scheduled to be implemented during fall 1996.

Health Needs Assessment

The North Iowa Health Mercy Network is partnering with public health departments throughout north Iowa to perform health needs assessments on a county-by-county basis. This initiative is expected to be completed by 1997.

Interorganizational Planning

Progress continues to be made in joint planning and decision making by the boards of the hospitals and clinics involved in the North Iowa Health Network. (See figure 10-2.) There will be a joint strategic planning session involving all board members of all these organizations during fall 1996. In addition, a common planning framework has been adopted by all these groups to further integrate patient care in north Iowa. A common vision statement and objectives for the CCN have also been adopted. Some specific initiatives that have been successful include a joint advertising campaign sponsored by NIMHC, Mason City Clinic, local hospitals, and local primary care clinics throughout north Iowa.

The structure of NIMHC has been reorganized so that it mirrors the network model and thus supports it. As the largest health care organization in north Iowa, NIMHC's participation is critical to the success of the partnership of stakeholders. With a new organizational structure, this participation is ensured. The model for the network as a whole is provided in *North Iowa Mercy Health Center and Network Model: Vision, Stakeholders and Integrating Processes.* (See figure 10-3.)

Capitation-Style Reimbursement

The UnityChoice insurance product has been developed and marketed throughout Iowa. Preparations are under way to handle Medicare capitation should this be enacted by Congress.

Care Management

Care management is being implemented in a rural community during 1997. This will serve as a pilot for further implementation efforts throughout north Iowa during the succeeding 2 years.

Contact: Frances Hoffman
CQI Coordinator
North Iowa Mercy Health Center
84 Beaumont Dr.
Mason City, IA 50401
Phone: (515) 424-7963

FIGURE 10-2. Organization and Relationships

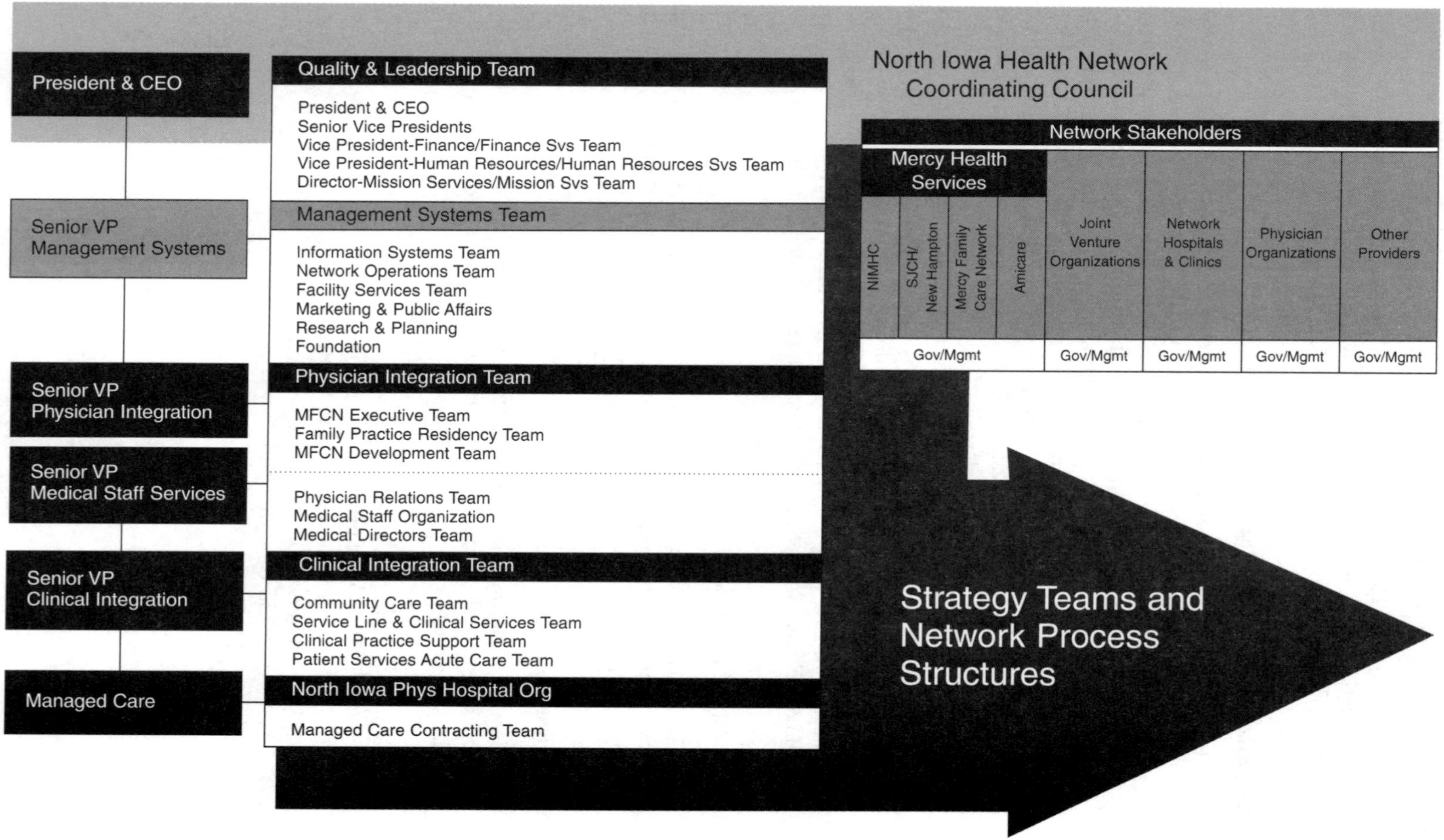

FIGURE 10-3. Vision, Stakeholders, and Integrating Processes

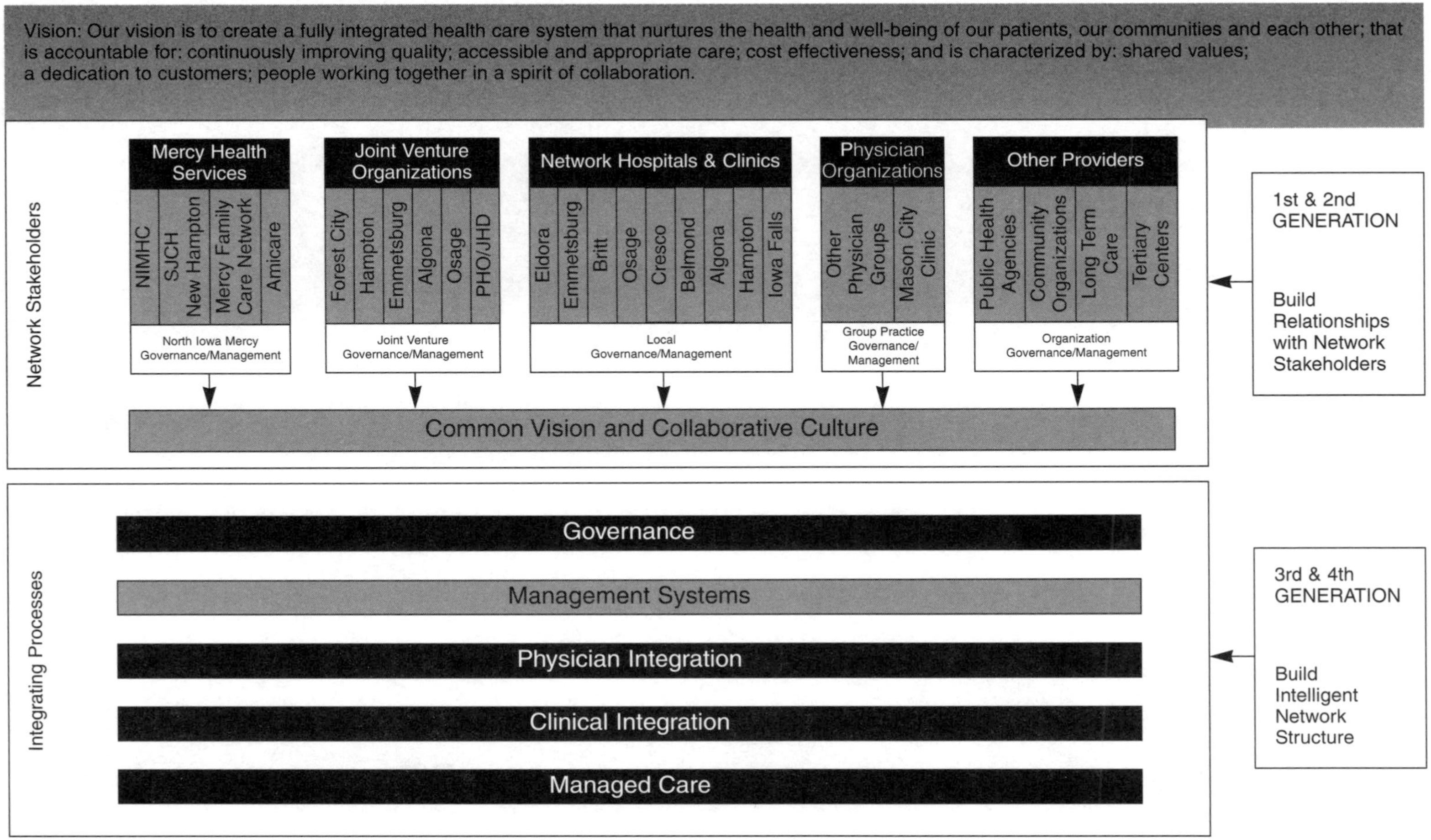

11

The Northwest Georgia Healthcare Partnership

Executive Summary

When asked to describe our community, the words that immediately come to mind are, "It's a 'can-do' community." It always has been and indications are that it will continue to be. It's a community whose leaders see obstacles as challenges and tackle them with vigor.

It was with this type of leadership that the Northwest Georgia Healthcare Partnership was founded. Ned Wilford, CEO of Hamilton Medical Center, had been in Dalton for a short time, but long enough to know that Murray and Whitfield counties not only should, but could and would rally together to form a collaborative partnership whose driving force would be to improve the health status of the community.

The Partnership's board of directors includes strong leaders in the community. It is imperative to include those whose position within their organizations makes them the key decision makers. These include the hospital CEOs, school superintendents, United Way president, director of public health, physicians, business/industry leaders, and city/county commissioners.

In the Partnership's 4-year existence, it has incorporated and become a 501(c)(3) organization, expanded its volunteer base to more than 100 individuals, and employed an executive director to administer, coordinate, and support its operations.

Two key programs have achieved major success in the past year. Growing Healthy, a comprehensive health education curriculum for grades K–6, will be expanded to reach more than 5,400 students this year. Working Well, our workplace wellness program, continues to grow and now reaches 6 percent of the workforce in Whitfield County.

In each phase of the Partnership's progress, key lessons have been learned. Ensuring that this endeavor would be a community-directed partnership was vital. The time spent in assessing and evaluating the community is essential, but going beyond that to put in place actual programs that affect the health status of our community is the true measurement of progress.

David E. Pennington III
President, Pruden Risk Management, Inc.
Co-Chair, Board of Directors, Northwest Georgia Healthcare Partnership
Chairman, Board of Directors, Dalton-Whitfield Chamber of Commerce

THE COLLABORATIVE PARTNERSHIP

The Community

Beginning in the 1950s, northwest Georgia shifted from a largely agricultural economy to a mostly industrial one. This shift was the result of the explosive growth of the local carpet industry. Currently, over 60 percent of the world's tufted carpet is produced in the northwest Georgia area, generating more than $6.5 billion in annual revenue. Although the emergence of a worldwide industry brought jobs to the region, it also created a large semiskilled workforce, many of whom frequently move from job to job.

Murray and Whitfield counties are classified as "rural" by the U.S. Office of Management and Budget. These counties have experienced rapid population growth in the past 30 years, averaging 29 percent in Murray County and 21 percent in Whitfield County. The combined total population of the two counties is approximately 101,700, with a racial composition as follows: 92 percent white, 3 percent African-American, and 5 percent Hispanic. Projections from the North Georgia Regional Development Commission estimate that the Hispanic population is increasing in our community at the rate of 50 individuals per month. The accelerated growth of the local Hispanic population significantly impacts the community's evolving needs for health care services. These needs must be met with new and creative strategies each year.

The elderly, 65 years of age and older, account for 10 percent of the area's total population. The largest age group is 25- to 44-year-olds, who account for 32 percent of the area's total population. The workforce is predominantly composed of this latter age group, many of whom are attracted to the community by the carpet industry. These individuals often bring children with them when they move into the community. Many of these children have special health care needs, chronic untreated health problems, and inadequate or unhealthy family support systems, and they cannot afford access to high-quality health care services.

Hamilton Medical Center (HMC), located in Dalton, GA, has the seventh busiest emergency department in the state. This emergency department treats a large population of medically indigent people who have neither a primary care physician nor any type of health insurance. Likewise, Murray Medical Center (MMC), located in neighboring Chatsworth, GA, has one of the busiest smaller rural hospital emergency departments in the state. As the carpet industry has become increasingly competitive and profit margins have continued to shrink, employers are concerned about the rising cost of providing health care insurance benefits.

Through the years, HMC and MMC have worked more and more closely with the business community to contain costs and develop health programs that meet the special needs of industry, but they have also worked apart. Meanwhile, social service agencies in the area took the pulse of the community and launched efforts to improve the quality of life. Unfortunately, in most cases these organizations worked separately, resulting in a lack of cooperation and collaboration that hampered their efforts.

Community health care resources include the two hospitals described above, with 282 beds at HMC and 42 at MMC. Serving Murray and Whitfield counties are approximately 120 physicians who are in family practice, internal medicine, pediatrics, obstetrics/gynecology, cardiology, general surgery, and other specialties. Additional resources include home health care and hospice services, a wellness center, and an array of services provided by the county health departments. There are four nursing homes, which have a total of 450 beds and operate at an occupancy rate of 99 percent.

Of the households in Murray and Whitfield counties, 23 percent earn less than $15,000 per year. Table 11-1 indicates the percentage of households at various income levels throughout Murray and Whitfield counties. Income is certainly one of the most important factors in determining health care needs for the community. As a group, those individuals with lower income assess themselves as having poorer health than those with higher incomes. Lack of access to affordable primary medical care often causes this same group to delay seeking medical treatment, which consequently often results in longer, more severe, and significantly costlier episodes of illness.

Heart disease is the leading cause of death in both counties. The most prevalent health conditions include heart disease, cancer, circulatory disorders, teen pregnancies, and pregnancy-related disorders. According to Emory University's School of Public Health, Murray and Whitfield counties rank consistently among the worst third of the state's 159 counties when it comes to juveniles committed to state custody, births to teens, students failing to complete high school, children retained in kindergarten, and number of arrests for driving under the influence of alcohol. These data strongly suggest that a problem related to substance abuse exists. Public health and mental health professionals in the state Department of Human Resources concur with the observation that these counties in northwest Georgia are communities with a high incidence of alcohol and drug use.

The Partnership

In 1992, the Georgia Hospital Association (GHA) responded to the state's many unmet health care needs by championing the idea of implementing a pilot community health partnership program. This idea was enthusiastically embraced by HMC's new CEO. The previous CEO had cultivated a strong relationship between the hospital and various groups and organizations in the community. The community health partnership concept provided an opportunity to bring all these groups together for a common purpose: to improve the health status of local community citizens through the promotion of efficient, effective, and caring use of resources. With this purpose in mind, the GHA and HMC jointly initiated the process of community planning that would lead to the formation of the Northwest Georgia Healthcare Partnership (the Partnership).

MMC was invited to participate in the initial planning and organizational efforts, thereby expanding the Partnership into a second hospital and county. Interest in the fledgling Partnership began to mount. Soon other key organizations and agencies such as the public health department and United Way expressed the desire

TABLE 11-1. Percentage of Whitfield County and Murray County Households at Particular Income Levels

	Annual Income in 1,000s of Dollars						
	0–9	*10–14*	*15–24*	*25–34*	*35–49*	*50–99*	*100+*
Murray	14	9	21	22	20	13	2
Whitfield	14	9	19	17	19	18	4

to participate. The concept did not call for any provider or agency to abandon its mission or autonomy; rather, it provided these groups the opportunity to integrate their resources and capabilities collaboratively.

In 1992, the Partnership hired a group of consultants to conduct extensive interviews of more than 50 local community leaders to determine their collective perception of community health needs. The interviewees ranged from CEOs of large corporations to family consumers of health care. Interviewees were asked to identify their perception of the strengths and weaknesses of the existing health delivery system and recommend ways health care delivery could be more effectively integrated with other social activities and services. Desirable goals and perceived barriers to the development of a restructured system were also reviewed in the study. Responses to the survey overwhelmingly indicated that Murray and Whitfield county residents believed the problems of accessibility, affordability, and availability of health care services could be improved and changed by action taken at the local level.

Consequently, the first community-focused health care delivery system in Georgia was officially launched in fall 1992. With the approval of its board of trustees, HMC provided the initial staff support and the majority of funding needed for the fledgling Partnership to get started. The GHA provided additional funding, legal advice, and a representative at Partnership meetings. MMC furnished the Partnership with an additional staff member to provide support on a full-time basis until it was fully organized.

From the beginning, the two hospitals and GHA all consciously recognized that their combined roles should be limited to that of serving as a catalyst for bringing together the many diverse elements of the community. Once empowered and charged with the responsibility for planning the future of health care for Murray and Whitfield counties, such a collaborative partnership could have the opportunity to become a powerful change agent for the community. With this in mind, a special committee was appointed to nominate members to serve on the Partnership's governing board. Specific selection criteria were identified. Each of the nominees was required to have demonstrated a strong history of community involvement and community leadership. Hospital representation on the board was limited to that of the hospital CEOs of the two local hospitals. Other constituencies and interest groups represented on the board included physicians, city and county government officials, the district health director, local school system superintendents, business and industry representatives, minorities, insurers, the United Way, and other community representatives.

The Partnership's membership composition has continued to evolve. Several other key community organizations and agencies that have since been identified as essential for the Partnership to be able to successfully achieve its goals of improving community health status, becoming more accountable to the community, facilitating the formation of a system that provides a seamless continuum of care, and managing care within the constraints of fixed resources have all enthusiastically agreed to participate as members of the Partnership.

PRIOR EFFORTS THAT REPRESENT MOVEMENT TOWARD THE COMMUNITY CARE NETWORK VISION

Community Health Focus

In addition to improving the quality and accessibility of health care services, the Partnership is also focusing on efforts to improve the community's overall health status by implementing programs designed to change health behaviors to prevent disease and treat ill health as early in the disease process as possible.

Community Assessments During the past 4 years, several local community health assessment surveys have been conducted. The most extensive needs assessment was completed by the United Way of Northwest Georgia. Randomly selected Murray and Whitfield county households, community leaders, and health care providers provided information about the nature and incidence of specific types of social and community health-related problems. As a result of this survey, specific community problems were identified, along with perceived barriers to receiving or providing needed services. Five key focus areas were identified:

- Affordable health care
- Alcohol and drug abuse
- Basic financial needs
- Education
- Information and referral

Simultaneously, United Way's subcommittee to address the number one issue of affordable health care, the Dalton-Whitfield Chamber of Commerce's Health Care Task Force was gathering momentum, and the Partnership was being formed. Rather than each working separately on very similar projects, United Way and the chamber of commerce believed they should work with the Partnership when called upon, rather than duplicate their efforts.

The Partnership's community survey was conducted by consultants. Approximately 50 individuals from Murray and Whitfield counties were interviewed, including physicians, hospital management, business leaders, clergy, and representatives from community organizations. This survey was conducted to assist in the development of a community-focused and -driven health care plan for northwest Georgia. The information gathered through the survey assisted in identifying the health care needs of the community, the strengths and weaknesses of the current system, and the issues that must be addressed. The top five health care issues identified according to importance were as follows:

- The high incidence of teenage pregnancy
- The need for better health education for children and adolescents
- The need for a better system of providing health insurance coverage
- The high cost of providing health care services
- The need for improving the overall affordability of health care services

The Community Decision Making (CDM) program was implemented in Murray County in December 1994. This grass roots type of community health care assessment and planning program is a service of the GHA in cooperation with the Georgia Department of Human Resources and Medical Assistance. Local sponsorship was provided by MMC, an actively participating member of the Partnership. The primary purpose of the CDM program is to help community members become directly involved in the process of completing a community-based health care needs assessment and plan to identify and address priority local health care issues and problems.

Currently, the Rollins School of Public Health of Emory University is conducting a needs assessment that specifically focuses on the area of the community's high incidence of alcohol and drug use. This type of focused assessment information will be critical to the Partnership as it continues its efforts to find realistic and cost-effective solutions to specific local health care issues and problems.

You Are Unique—God Made You Unique—Unique Parenting The Partnership's assessment survey clearly indicated that the high incidence of teenage pregnancy is the most important health care issue in our community. The following national statistics are from Sex and Family Education, Birmingham, AL, developers of the You Are Unique program:

- 72 percent of high school seniors and 40 percent of ninth graders have had sex.
- 3,000 teenage girls get pregnant daily.
- Sexually transmitted diseases (STDs) are epidemic.

Based on statistics such as these, as well as the community's high relative incidence of teenage pregnancy and its strong value system, the Partnership and the community are taking a serious approach to addressing the need for promoting sexual abstinence among teenagers. The purpose of the You Are Unique program is as follows:

- To educate teens about the physical and emotional consequences of premarital sex
- To motivate them to choose sexual abstinence until marriage
- To equip them with skills to control sexual desires and resist pressures

The three local boards of education have approved the You Are Unique program for implementation by teachers in the school systems to all middle school–aged children in Murray and Whitfield counties. The Partnership will be making follow-up efforts to have the corresponding God Made You Unique program accepted and available for presentation to teenagers at various churches throughout the community. In addition to character education and self-esteem building, this program module incorporates into the program Biblical references that teach God's plan for maintaining sexual purity. Fifteen churches were represented at the initial training workshop, including representatives from Baptist, Methodist, and Church of God denominations. Unique Parenting is another program module designed to help parents build solid relationships with their children; help them understand adolescent behavior, including family, peer, and social pressures; as well as provide a personal evaluation and goal-setting techniques.

Measurable outcomes from the implementation of these programs will include delayed or fewer teenage pregnancies and a reduction in the transmission rate of STDs in Murray and Whitfield counties. One local minister's thoughts on these programs were as follows: "If our young people hear similar messages at school, at home, at church, at scouts, etc., surely it will make a difference." The initial start-up cost for these programs as well as the facilitator training workshop has been directly financed by the Partnership.

Hamilton Healthmobile The Hamilton Healthmobile responds to several important issues and needs identified in the assessment process. The Healthmobile provides medical services for the indigent and the elderly, provides health education services, and addresses the issues of accessibility, affordability, and availability of health care services in our community. The Healthmobile is a 40-foot-long mobile health clinic that takes health care services directly to the people in the community. Services routinely administered are blood pressure readings, pregnancy testing and referral, cancer screening for women, diabetes screening, Head Start physicals, immunizations for children, HIV screening, vision testing and referral, and flu shots. This program provides a broad range of primary, preventive, acute, and chronic health care services in accordance with the CCN concept of seamless continuum of care. All services are provided on a sliding scale at either low or no cost, depending on each individual's ability to pay.

The Healthmobile clinic serves a population that for the most part would not receive any medical care if it were not for the services provided in accordance with the CCN concept of community accountability. Health care services are taken directly to those community members who reside in relatively remote areas of the county as well as to those who reside in public housing projects, trailer parks, and Hispanic neighborhoods.

Because approximately 30 percent of those served are Hispanic, identifying and addressing the language and cultural needs of the community's Hispanic population is an important consideration. In response to this need, both Healthmobile clinic registered nurses are proficient in Spanish. Additionally, videotapes about diseases such as diabetes are available in Spanish. In addition, brochures about a variety of subjects, including immunizations, other preventive measures, and specific types of diseases are available in Spanish.

Measurable outcomes are numerous, such as the percentage of local children who have received immunizations and the number of medical visits provided to the elderly. Approximately 60 percent of the elderly who use the Healthmobile's services do not understand the need for continuing preventive medical screenings for the chronic illnesses they might have. This setting provides an ideal climate for education.

The Healthmobile is an excellent example of the Partnership's continuing efforts to facilitate collaborative working relationships among providers, public and private agencies, and organizations. Because of the disproportionate share of residents without any type of health insurance, the state provides funds to enhance cost-effective health care services for this population. Some of these funds were used to purchase the Healthmobile. The staff members who operate this clinic are jointly provided by HMC, and the Whitfield County Health Department.

Community Accountability

To establish and continue to strengthen the Partnership's commitment to the CCN dimension of community accountability, the Partnership carefully reviewed and considered all the assessment data and priorities listed in this chapter's previous section, "Community Assessments." The results of key activities such as the United Way assessment have been reported back to the public in community-wide press conferences. The findings from the assessment process, the resulting priorities, and the future strategies planned to address each priority were presented, reviewed, and discussed. Follow-up newspaper articles and written reports were routinely made available to the public.

Leadership of Partnership Board The Partnership's board is fortunate to have among its members some of the community's most outstanding leaders and citizens. Each board member comes to the Partnership with a wealth of leadership experience and ability, and has a firm commitment to the Partnership's vision, mission, and goals.

Virtually all board members have supported either the Dalton–Whitfield or the Chatsworth–Murray County chambers of commerce at various levels, from president to founding members of the "Drugs Don't Work" or "Education Is Essential" programs. Almost 65 percent of those in Whitfield County are graduates of Leadership Dalton–Whitfield. The goal for this program is to build and strengthen a better community by training its leaders for tomorrow's challenges. This training program covers such topics as medical services, quality of life, local economics, education, state government, the judicial system, local government, volunteerism, and leadership skills.

In addition, virtually all Partnership board members have served the community by volunteering with the United Way of Northwest Georgia. Many are prior board members; others have actively worked toward raising funds for the annual campaign, allocating funds with the fund distribution panels, or studying community needs with the community problem-solving committee.

Monitoring Data Collection Through its Continual Improvement Principles and Tools, HMC's ongoing quality program monitors and collects data to ensure consumer focus. A prime example is in the way in which two partners, HMC and MMC, have provided information on Medicaid recipients' use of their emergency departments for nonemergency treatment. The Partnership has used this information in refining the Georgia Better Health Care program, discussed in this chapter's "Seamless Continuum of Care" section.

Collaborative Approach to Resource Effectiveness In response to ongoing monitoring and collection of data to ensure consumer focus, both acute care hospitals in the Partnership participate in the GHA Research and Education Foundation's Collaborative Approach to Resource Effectiveness (CARE) Program. The CARE Program began in 1992 with the mission of improving the quality and value of health care services through a collaborative approach to resource effectiveness by involving customers and interested parties in developing an objective and professionally accepted system to measure and monitor quality and value of services for continuous improvement and informed health care choices and decisions. The CARE Program uses the hospitals' patient level discharge data as its administrative database. Eleven performance indicators can be evaluated for 41 clinical services, in addition to diagnostic or procedure groups analyses.

Although data from the CARE Program are available mainly to supplement efforts to be accountable to the community, those data also identified two areas where improvements to the community health status could be made. The comparative data highlighted a problem with high numbers of patients with medical back conditions. A large number of people in the community work in the carpet mills and are subject to back injuries on the job. This information reinforced employer initiatives to prevent lower-back injuries. Employers were interested in these programs because back injuries are not only a high-cost, high-volume condition but also a major cause of permanent disability.

The second area for improvement identified in the analysis of the CARE data relates to both earlier diagnosis and intervention programs in the CCN dimensions of community health focus and seamless continuum of care. The high rate of patients admitted to the gastroenterology clinical service is hypothesized by some physicians to be related to a high level of chronic alcohol abuse as identified by the community assessment in the service area. Additional study is needed to gather the necessary data that will identify the root cause of the problem.

It is apparent that such data can be a critical component of moving toward the CCN vision. However, we have been unable to move forward with implementing programs based on the results of the performance data because of a lack of resources.

Reporting, Refining, and Improving Partnership Activities The Partnership is continuing to refine and improve its programs in direct response to the needs and priorities identified by the community itself. (See figure 11-1 for an overview of the Partnership's bylaws.) Each of the Partnership's working committees meets regularly to review both short-term and long-term goals and to strategize how these goals might be best accomplished. New members are frequently asked to serve on one of these committees. There are no limitations as to the number of individuals who can serve on each committee; it is important to involve those who are connected and interested. The Partnership's board of directors meets every other month, and the executive committee meets on alternating months. (See figure 11-2.) Every month, each committee's progress is reported, reviewed, and discussed by the Partnership's board members.

Seamless Continuum of Care

Murray and Whitfield counties are both well blessed with strong, visionary leadership and the relatively strong availability of local health care resources. However, what has been historically lacking are efforts to successfully integrate those available resources into a seamless continuum of care.

The Partnership has actively collaborated with Georgia Better Health Care, a pilot program operated through the Georgia Department of Medical Assistance that is aimed at providing medical care for Medicaid-eligible patients. The goals of this program include the following:

- Improving access to medical care
- Encouraging and enhancing continuity of care
- Reducing the unnecessary use of medical services, such as inappropriate use of the emergency room, to receive primary care medical services

Murray and Whitfield counties were selected as one of three pilot sites in Georgia for this program to be tested. Each Medicaid recipient either selects or is assigned to a primary care provider who is responsible for coordinating that recipient's health care. All 7,500 Medicaid recipients in the two-county area have been linked with a provider.

The Georgia Better Health Care program is an attempt to implement a managed care system for a fixed population of patients that promotes a seamless continuum of care and operates within fixed resources. The Partnership's responsibility was to monitor the program's effectiveness in its ability to provide health care for each enrolled Medicaid recipient under the direction and supervision of the recipient's assigned primary health care provider. Certainly a measurable outcome will be a decrease in Medicaid patients' going to the emergency departments for nonemergency treatment. This will require a significant change in behavior for many Medicaid recipients. Educational programs to inform them and encourage them to obtain health care services from their primary care provider will need to be implemented. Incentives, or perhaps even disincentives, will likely be required to successfully motivate them to adhere to the program's guidelines for receiving medical care.

FIGURE 11-1. Northwest Georgia Healthcare Partnership, Inc., Bylaws

Table of Contents

FIGURE 11-1. (Continued)

FIGURE 11-2. Articles 2 and 3 of Bylaws

ARTICLE TWO
Purposes

The corporation has been organized pursuant to the Georgia Nonprofit Corporation Code to operate exclusively for charitable, educational and scientific purposes, as set forth in the Articles of Incorporation. No director, trustee, officer, agent or employee shall at any time profit from the operation of the corporation or upon its liquidation or dissolution, except for reasonable compensation to such person(s) as shall be provided by these Bylaws for services actually rendered to the corporation in effecting one or more of its objectives or purposes.

ARTICLE THREE
The Board of Directors

3.1 Authority and Responsibility of the Board of Directors.

(a) The supreme authority of the corporation and the government and management of the affairs of the corporation shall be vested in the Board of Directors; and all the powers, duties, and functions of the corporation conferred by the articles of incorporation, these bylaws, state statutes, common law, court decisions, or otherwise, shall be exercised, performed, or controlled by the Board of Directors.

(b) The governing body of the corporation shall be the Board of Directors. The Board of Directors

(i) Shall have supervision, control, and direction of the management, affairs, and property of the corporation;

(ii) Subject to the provisions of subparagraph (d) below, shall approve an annual operating budget as well as short-term and long-term budgets, capital and operating, develop a long-term plan for capital expenditures as required by applicable laws and regulations, and monitor the implementation of such budgets and plan;

(iii) Shall be responsible for establishing policies or changes therein; and

(iv) Shall actively prosecute the corporation's purposes and objectives and supervise the disbursement of its funds.

(c) The Board of Directors may adopt, by majority vote, such rules and regulations for the conduct of its business and the business of the corporation as shall be deemed advisable, and may, in the execution of the powers granted, delegate certain of its authority and responsibility to an executive committee. Under no circumstances, however, shall any actions be taken which are inconsistent with the articles of incorporation or these bylaws.

(d) The Board of Directors shall not permit any part of the net earnings or capital of the corporation to inure to the benefit of any member, director, officer, trustee, or other private person or individual.

(e) The Board of Directors may, from time to time, appoint, as advisors, persons whose advice, assistance and support may be deemed helpful in determining policies, planning, and formulating programs for carrying out the purposes and functions of the corporation.

FIGURE 11-2. (Continued)

(f) The Board of Directors is authorized to employ such person or persons, including an executive director or officer, attorneys, trustees, agents, and assistants, as in its judgment are necessary or desirable for the administration and management of the corporation, and to pay reasonable compensation for the services performed and expenses incurred by any such person or persons.

3.2 Number, Election and Term of Office. The total number of directors shall vary between twenty (20) and thirty (30) and the exact number of directors shall be fixed by resolution of a majority of the Board of Directors from time to time. Each director and successor director shall serve for a three year staggered term of office. No later than five (5) days prior to the expiration of each of these three year staggered terms of office, a majority of the directors holding office shall elect successor directors, who shall each serve for a term of three years.

Notwithstanding, the members of the initial board shall serve staggered terms, with approximately one third (1/3) of the board members terms expiring in 1994, approximately one third (1/3) expiring in 1995 and the remaining third (1/3) expiring in 1996. Each director, except in case of death, resignation, retirement, disqualification, or removal, shall serve until the next applicable election of directors and thereafter until his/her successor shall have been elected and qualified.

No director shall be eligible to serve more than three consecutive full terms in office, which shall not include the unexpired portion of any term served by a director elected to fill a vacancy on the Board of Directors pursuant to Section 3.6 of the Bylaws. A director who has served three consecutive full terms in office may be re-elected to the Board of Directors after the expiration of one year following the end of his/her previous term and shall have the status of a newly elected director.

3.3 Qualifications. The Board of Directors shall be composed of individuals which represent a balance of community interest in regard to health issues whose members shall include, but not be limited to, representatives from local hospitals, physicians, government entities, educators, industry, public health agencies and insurance entities. Persons selected to serve as members of the Board shall be persons of distinction, honorable reputation and illustrious character within the Northwest Georgia area community, who shall evidence an interest in community health care and an awareness of the need for continued scientific research and development in the field of innovative methods of health care, as well as the need for educational programs in this field.

3.4 Conflict of Interest Policy. The Board of Directors shall from time to time adopt policies and procedures designed to disclose duality of interests and avoid potential conflicts of interest with respect to members of the Board of Directors as the Board shall from time to time deem appropriate.

3.5 Removal. Any director designated to serve as a member of the Board of Directors may be removed from office with or without cause by the affirmative vote of two thirds of the other directors holding office. Removal action may be taken at any directors' meeting, with respect to which notice of such purpose has been given, and a successor to any removed director may be elected at the same meeting to serve the unexpired term.

3.6 Vacancies. A vacancy occurring in the Board of Directors, arising at any time and for any cause, may be filled for the unexpired term by the affirmative vote of the majority of the directors present at a meeting at which a quorum is present.

(Continued on next page)

FIGURE 11-2. (Continued)

3.7 Compensation. Directors shall receive no compensation, directly or indirectly, for their services as directors unless authorized by the concurring vote of two-thirds (2/3) of all the directors. However, nothing contained herein shall be construed to prevent any director from serving the corporation in any other capacity and receiving reasonable compensation for services rendered in furtherance of the purposes and functions of the corporation.

3.8 Committees of the Board of Directors. The corporation shall have the following standing committees: (a) Executive Committee, (b) Finance Committee and (c) Nominating Committee. In addition, by resolution adopted by a majority of directors at a meeting at which a quorum is present, the Board of Directors may designate from among its members one or more other committees, each consisting of three (3) or more directors. Except as prohibited by law, each committee shall have the authority as set forth in the resolution establishing said committee.

Management within Fixed Resources

To control costs, early prevention and intervention are mandatory. The Partnership is focusing on preventing problems as well as solving them. Not only the indigent but the entire population is being affected by the Partnership's programs as it works to manage within a fixed budget.

The Partnership's Health Care Financing and Payment Committee has been charged with the responsibility for finding new and better ways to fund health care services for those employees of small businesses who are not currently covered by health insurance. Hundreds of small employers (250 or fewer full-time employees) in Murray and Whitfield counties have struggled with providing affordable yet high-quality health insurance coverage for their employees.

The development of a health care finance mechanism for small employers is becoming a reality with the introduction of a new health insurance plan specifically designed for their needs. Med Plan Select, planned for availability in May 1995, is the result of a joint business venture between HMC and local physicians called Health One Alliance L.L.C.

An example of seamless continuum of care, this integrated system uses an existing network of providers and health care facilities with HMC as the regional tertiary referral medical center. The underwriting and marketing will be completed locally. The financial risk for this program will be spread among an insurance company, a reinsurer (third largest in the world), and a second reinsurer developed by HMC. This new program will allow the health care system to begin operating under an element of risk and to learn how to manage in such an environment with further advancements in the market to HMOs and other capitation reimbursement. By working together collaboratively, the local providers will now be able to offer a highly competitive and cost-effective insurance product that meets the health care insurance needs of small employers and their employees.

MOVING TOWARD THE COMMUNITY CARE NETWORK VISION

Working toward the Optimum Local Health Care System

The Partnership is convinced that the key to its current success and its continued success is community collaboration. The CCN and the Partnership vision will keep the members focused on working collectively to improve the health status of the community. Overwhelmingly, the Partnership survey showed that the community believed that accessibility, availability, quality, and cost could be improved at the local level. This vote of confidence from the community has led the Partnership to tackle these difficult health care issues in a relentless effort. The prior efforts described earlier, as well as those identified in this segment, make sense for our community. Each relates to a health care need or issue identified in the Partnership survey. The Partnership will continue to monitor these results to ensure they are providing an optimal system focusing on community health.

Vision and Visioning Process

This community took a serious approach by commissioning a group of consultants to assist the community in developing a plan for a collaborative and cooperative community-focused health care delivery system. An all-day planning retreat was conducted in fall 1992 to review the current environment, create a community vision, and establish initial goals and objectives. This retreat was attended by those agreeing to serve on the board of directors, as well as several others. Discussion included the following steps:

1. Organize the community and empower.
2. Assess the environment for positive or negative trends.
3. Conduct an upside-down needs assessment.
4. Establish a process that will promote a team effort and build trust.
5. Create a vision.
6. Begin with projects that are noncontroversial and attainable.
7. Begin with a narrow focus.
8. Initiate the process with small steps and visible goals.
9. Establish measurable benefits.
10. Identify two or three physicians who will champion the project.
11. Don't wait for "enough" information.
12. Remember, there are no bad guys.

As the visioning process unfolded, it became apparent that those present were there because of a desire to serve the community and support this collaborative effort individually at each person's highest level of expertise. It was also clear that each partner possessed the unselfish desire to improve the health status of northwest Georgia.

This retreat provided the first opportunity for the board members to review the results of the Partnership community survey. The health care issues ranked by importance, and the service/program needs ranked according to need, were presented. Major strengths and weaknesses of health care services in our community were also outlined. This information gave the board the base needed to arrive at a consensus and to develop committees through which the short-term and long-term goals would be addressed.

It was then time to begin to reshape the health care delivery system. As a result of the retreat, the following vision statement for the Partnership was developed:

> We have a vision for the future which will create fundamental changes in the healthcare environment through cooperation and collaboration among providers,

business, government, educators, and the community in Northwest Georgia. Our responsibility is to create a healing environment that will maintain, restore, and improve the health of every man, woman, and child in the community. Working together, we strive to provide accessible, cost-effective, efficient and high quality health care in a community committed to the well being of every citizen.

Although this vision was developed over two years ago, it speaks to all four dimensions of the CCN vision on a community level. As the Partnership's strategic plan emerged from this vision, programs were envisioned and developed that would focus on community health, ensure accountability to the community, enhance the seamlessness of health and human service delivery, and work effectively within existing health care resources.

As a result of the visioning process, five committees were immediately identified by specific subject areas: indigent care and accessibility; data collection and medical information systems; health care financing and payment; legal and legislation; and education. To respond to the survey's concerns for health education and health promotion, the Workplace Committee was later established to develop and secure implementation of programs through the workplace. These programs would target changing behavior that will lower employers' health care costs and improve the health and welfare of employees and their families.

Community Health Focus

Working Well Milestones for planning and development have occurred with Working Well. The Workplace Committee studied 15 successful programs in various companies such as Johnson & Johnson, Coors, and Tenneco, and in communities including Birmingham, AL, and Ventura County, CA. After a group of seven committee members visited with officials from the city of Birmingham and consultants from the University of Alabama at Birmingham, they were convinced that the Birmingham workplace could be tailored to work in our community.

Early diagnosis and intervention programs with a focus on changing behavior are being addressed in a pilot program called Working Well. The city of Dalton, with 355 employees, has agreed to pilot this program for the community. Participation will be voluntary; therefore, marketing the program and information sharing with the employees prior to its beginning are key to its success. This milestone is currently being addressed by the city's appointment of a Wellness Council. This council includes employee leaders from all departments who will offer input to encourage participation, develop incentives, and make final decisions regarding intervention programs.

Working Well has the following three components:

- Screening/Awareness
- Data collection
- Interventions

The screening consists of a health risk appraisal, height, weight, blood pressure, full lipid profile, body composition, sit and reach, abdominal strength, vision/glaucoma, and a consultation. Employees are aware that they will not be tested for drugs or HIV. The database tracks the employee's progress. The employee's individual results of the screening process and health risk appraisal are not shared with the employer. A confidential report of each employee's screening, which includes their risk factors on such things as heart disease, cancer, or injury, is mailed to their home. The employer will receive an aggregate report. This combined employee information helps determine appropriate workplace interventions as well as track improvements from year to year.

Virtually all partners are involved with this committee. Progress in action will be exemplified in the Working Well workplace program. The intent of the Workplace Committee is to select three pilot employers, being very careful in committing to employers who not only want to improve the health status of their employees by managing health care within fixed resources, but also will agree to the long-term program of follow-up screenings, interventions, and providing appropriate incentives to encourage participation. Employer ownership of the program is key to its success.

Outcomes of Working Well will be measured individually as well as collectively. With the envisioned database, the individual employee's health status will be maintained from year to year; his or her personal progress will be evident by the results of the follow-up screenings. The employer will be able to measure in real dollars the success of the program by maintaining or reducing health care costs per employee, by increased productivity, and by decreased absenteeism. The employer's turnover and, consequently, training costs, will decrease, and there will be evidence of improved employee morale as measured by employee satisfaction surveys.

After the credibility of this program has been established with the community, it is the goal to expand participation to all employers. Bridging to the community accountability dimension, the health status of the entire community will be affected in that Working Well will not be associated with any one employer but rather will be in all workplaces. All employees will be exposed to the program even if they change jobs.

The participating employers are required to contribute to the expenses incurred in delivering Working Well. For the pilot organizations, the cost of $20 per employee will be achieved by a tremendous collaborative effort bridging to the dimension of community accountability. This will include industrial nurses assisting in the screening for employers other than their own, as well as by utilizing statistical and exercise physiologist majors from the University of Tennessee at Chattanooga to work on this project as their volunteer/community service/internship requirements. Additional employers are participating by investing $50 per employee for the screening and 1 year of tailored intervention programs.

School-Based Nurse Program Children who are unhealthy are children whose learning is impaired. Not only can education contribute to improving health, but a child's health status is a major determinant of educational achievement. To improve academic achievement, more attention must be devoted to health concerns by intervention programs. Toward that end, the Partnership has piloted the School-Based Nurse Program.

Currently, a registered nurse who has completed the Basic Skills Assessment Course is working 2 days a week at two elementary schools and 1 day a week at one elementary school. A wide range of services are provided, including physical exams and screenings; health education; referrals and assistance in making other health appointments; and diagnosis and treatment of illnesses that might include earaches, colds, sore throats, and head lice.

This pilot program evolved through the collaborative efforts of five Partnership organizations: Whitfield County Health Department, HMC, Dalton Public Schools, Murray County Schools, and Whitfield County Schools. This collective effort is providing a natural setting to teach children how to develop solid health care habits. A second nurse and a health service technician were added with grant money secured by Family Connection last year.

The goal of the Partnership is to place a school nurse in all elementary schools in the three school systems within the next three years. This can be accomplished by adding two nurses each year during the program period. When the nurses are integrated into all 21 schools, the annual cost to operate this program will be approximately $450,000. Business and industry in the community will be supporting this program along with Indigent Care Trust Funds, Medicaid reimbursement through the Targeted Case Management Program, the five partners mentioned above, and funds from Family Connection.

Measurable objectives will include dollars saved the community by decreased use of the hospital's emergency departments for treatment of minor illnesses. In addition, the parents (the workforce of our community) will continue to work as their children's illnesses are caught early and treated appropriately by the nurses. This will conserve health care resources by providing care to patients at the most appropriate point in the continuum of care, thus working within the CCN dimension of management within fixed resources.

Growing Healthy Growing Healthy is the nation's fastest-growing comprehensive school health education program. Its curriculum is designed to meet the health needs of children at the right time (early) and in the right place (school). From kindergarten through sixth grade, Growing Healthy teaches young students the knowledge and skills they need to make smart choices and grow up healthy. The physical as well as emotional and social dimensions of young people's health are addressed in the following 10 major content areas:

- Growth and development
- Mental/emotional health
- Personal health
- Family life and health
- Nutrition
- Disease prevention and control
- Safety and first aid
- Consumer health
- Substance use and abuse
- Community and environmental health management

All Growing Healthy teachers are required to attend a four-day workshop conducted by experienced trainers who have taught the curriculum themselves. This instruction gives the teachers the information, materials, and confidence they need to bring Growing Healthy to life in their classroom.

Each year the state Department of Education reviews new textbooks and allots funds to the local school systems for a specific curriculum. Currently, Growing Healthy is not on Georgia's approved list to qualify for state textbook funds; however, it will be reviewed and, it is hoped, approved for the 1996 school year. In addition, there is new flexibility with a state policy in that local school boards in Georgia can choose any classroom textbooks they approve and pay for them with state funds. Growing Healthy was piloted in 10 third-grade classes at Brookwood Elementary School.

Growing Healthy is proven and effective. It is validated by the National Diffusion Network of the U.S. Department of Education, which recognizes exemplary educational programs and promotes their adoption by the nation's schools. Since it was first developed, Growing Healthy has undergone several evaluations. The most extensive, the School Health Education Evaluation, studied 30,000 students exposed to one of four health curricula or to no health program at all. Measurable outcomes discovered by this study concluded that Growing Healthy students demonstrated the highest overall measures of health knowledge and attitudes among any of the groups. Growing Healthy also impacts students' behavior. For example, seventh graders enrolled in Growing Healthy were three times less likely to start smoking than those who had not received comprehensive health education.

The Partnership plans to implement the Growing Healthy curriculum in grades K–6 in three school systems at a cost of approximately $250,000. Partial funding will come from state textbook money; local staff development funds will assist in training expenses for the teachers.

Community Accountability

The Partnership's board members recognized early on that an infrastructure for a medical information network would be key to moving toward the CCN vision of community accountability. As a result, the Partnership spent time to establish a vision of a medical information network that will support the ongoing collection, quantification, analysis, and evaluation of the health status of the community. The network will also measure and monitor the value of health care services and provide information to develop benchmarks of excellence for continuously improving quality and resource effectiveness.

The Partnership sees the medical information network as part of the basic infrastructure necessary for delivering health care services across a seamless continuum of care. It plans to explore opportunities for creating a community health information network (CHIN) that links to existing databases such as the Georgia INPHO for data useful to community health planning such as the Centers for Disease Control and Prevention's (CDC's) behavioral risk factor (BRF) survey information. The ultimate intent will be to have all medical records for an individual in the network database so that a person's history can be easily accessed by a physician, the hospital, the health department, a pharmacist, or employer.

Eventually, the medical information network will serve as the basic architecture for the development of community pathways for improving health status along the entire continuum of care—from prevention and early detection of disease to patient education, primary care, acute inpatient care, subacute care, long-term care, rehabilitation, and mental health services. Initially, existing CARE data will be used to identify selected clinical conditions for focusing improvement efforts. Using CQI principles and the CARE Clinical Assessment Project model, pertinent community providers will be involved in developing and implementing a plan to improve outcomes for the specific condition(s). If appropriate, clinical pathways for conserving resources and improving outcomes will be developed. A consumer-focused effort to continuously monitor and collect data across the entire continuum of care will facilitate the seamless delivery of health care services to our community.

Components will be added to the medical information network as resources permit expansion based on identified needs in the community. The intent is to be resource effective by initially drawing on existing sources of data such as Georgia Information Network for Public Health Officials (INPHO) and data from the CARE Program. The medical information network will be expanded with additional data, such as linkage with the state Office of Vital Records for electronically registering birth certificates.

Although the CDC's BRF survey currently provides only state-level data, another potential addition to the medical information network is the results of locally conducted BRF surveys. The Partnership will explore ways these surveys could be administered to the community through a variety of possible voluntary activities with the United Way, School-Based Nurse Program, employers, and so forth. The results of the BRF surveys could then be used to plan community health screenings and educational programs targeted at specific population groups most at risk in the community.

The Partnership will continue its close working relationship with the GHA on developing the medical information network. Members of the GHA staff have worked with the Partnership's Data Collection and Medical Information Systems Committee, and a Partnership board member has been instrumental at the state level with GHA's CARE Program.

The role of the Partnership's board members is vital to the success of this project. The involvement of health care providers, insurance, the public health department, and employers in providing the data necessary for the network will be accomplished, as they will be eager to receive the output information. With the completion of the initial visioning and planning process, the Partnership is poised to move forward with the implementation of a medical information network that supports community accountability for health care services, helps improve the community health status, and promotes the delivery of a seamless continuum of health care services.

Technical staff/consultation from the American Hospital Association, as well as funding, will be required as plans are made to further enhance the integrated medical information system. The Partnership's goal is to have a fully functional medical information system that covers the entire continuum of care and focuses on improving community health status.

Seamless Continuum of Care

The needs of the underserved population in this community are being addressed with the Medical Access Clinic (MAC), operated by the public health department. A goal of the Partnership has been to expand the services of this clinic, and this has been partially accomplished. The actual space and staff have more than doubled over the past 18 months, and hours of operation have increased by 35 percent. Physician volunteer hours have also increased considerably. Nurse practitioners are used at the MAC, evidencing the dimension of management within fixed resources.

During the past year, there were 12,897 patient visits at the MAC, an increased caseload of approximately 212 percent over the average number of patient visits during 1983–89. For the first six months of fiscal year 1995, only 23 percent of all patient visits were covered by Medicare/Medicaid. The challenge remains to identify sources of revenue to support the current level of operation as well as to support further expansion. The need for further expansion is critical.

Traditionally, lack of space has been a problem; however, during the demonstration program's time frame, a new county health department will be constructed. The needed space will be available; however, to expand the services offered by the clinic, additional nurse practitioners will be required. Data show that many visits to the emergency departments are for nonemergencies. Certainly a measurable objective of the MAC would show a decrease in emergency department usage for nonemergency services if the clinic were open 24 hours per day, coupled with educational programs aimed at reducing inappropriate emergency department usage.

One recognized economic measure used to determine the approximate size of the medically indigent population in a community is the number of people with incomes below an amount equal to or less than two and a half times the federal poverty level. Almost 44 percent of the people in Whitfield County and about 45 percent of those in Murray County fall into this category. In numbers, this means that about 32,000 people in Whitfield County and almost 12,000 people in Murray County have incomes at levels that encourage them to forgo appropriate medical care, such as nonemergency health care and especially preventive health care, because they are unable to pay for all or part of the needed health care expenses. The MAC is designed to meet the health care needs of this population. A successful outcome of the clinic's availability to serve these people would certainly be an improvement in the health status of the community.

Two Partnership participants, HMC and the Whitfield County Health Department, have supported the MAC financially, along with money from the Indigent Care Trust Fund. Three Partnership board members are initiating action related to securing community scholarships for nurses to receive the training to become nurse practitioners. Two additional nurse practitioners would cost approximately $90,000 per year. It is acknowledged that this clinic will not be self-supporting because of the population it serves. Ongoing expenses will be offset by the county health department and funds generated by the Partnership from business and industry in support of its programs.

Management within Fixed Resources

Many citizens in Murray and Whitfield counties cannot afford to purchase their prescription drugs. Included in this population are the elderly, the unemployed, those working who cannot afford insurance coverage, and those whose insurance coverage does not cover the cost of prescription drugs. The primary focus of this committee is to address the prescription needs of MAC patients. The health department, physicians, and pharmacists will be working on this initiative. This initiative will assist in addressing the needs of those with chronic illnesses; however, it would not solve the problem of those with acute illnesses who need the drugs immediately.

The Partnership has been advised that Murray and Whitfield counties have been selected as one of four pilot communities for the Georgia Partnership for Caring Foundation program. This program will respond to the health care needs of more than one million persons in Georgia who at any given time do not have any type of health insurance. Medical professionals are being asked to donate their services; hospitals to donate space; pharmaceutical manufacturers to donate medications; state government to donate expertise and coordination; and the Georgia business community and private foundations to donate administrative funds. Certainly this program should affect the goal of obtaining drugs for the indigent as well as improve the overall health status of the community.

SUMMARY OF NOTABLE PROGRESS

A primary strength of the Partnership continues to be the people who serve on the board and committees. The Partnership had the foresight to target the leaders of our community to serve as board members. These leaders know the community, have the vision of a healthy community, are willing to collaborate, and are not concerned with "who gets the credit." They are not only dreamers but doers—people who recognize that time must be spent in identifying the needs of the community, and who are willing to go that extra step to do something tangible about it.

Working Well

Tangible results are now being realized with our workplace wellness program, Working Well. The city of Dalton's 355 employees have been participating in the intervention segment of the program for 9 months. Concrete results from this workplace include the following:

- Forty city employees attended the "Power to Stop Smoking" workshop.
- Six employees have stopped smoking.
- Thirty-two employees have joined the Bradley Wellness Center. The city subsidized the fee so that it would be more affordable.
- At the quarterly nurse/dietitian site visits, 93 employees had blood pressure checks and 13 did full blood lipid profiles at their expense.
- The Public Works Department has paved an area behind the "City Barn" to be designated as its walking track.
- Over 50 percent of all employees are participating in the monthly incentive program. They receive an incentive such as a stress ball, ball cap, ice scraper, T-shirt, and so on, for doing a variety of healthy activities on a daily basis.
- Commitment from the fire department is so great that it has designated 8:30 a.m. to 9:30 a.m. six days a week for group exercise led by staff from the Bradley Wellness Center.

We are beginning to see major changes in the lifestyles of Dalton employees. A fire department battalion chief has quit smoking after 20 years, lost 30 pounds, decreased his cholesterol by 30 points, attended the "Smart Eating" series and brought his wife, and started exercising five days a week; he says he feels wonderful!

Our first carpet-manufacturing Working Well site, Queen Carpet's Sample Facility, with 140 employees, has reported total weight loss exceeding 500 pounds. This is accomplished by attending the "Smart Eating" classes and increasing the level of exercise.

Textile Rubber & Chemical Co.'s 330 employees recently completed the screening process with 88 percent participation. The company has just completed construction of a ⅕ mile on-site walking track for its employees and will soon begin other intervention programs. Pruden & Brooks Insurance was our first workplace to have 100 percent participation in the screening process, and Hamilton Medical Center's 1,500 employees are currently being screened.

Our Workplace Committee is convinced that there are three key reasons for a highly successful Working Well program in any workplace:

- Commitment, enthusiasm, and support from top management
- Selecting the "right" people for the employee committee and allowing enough time to get their total buy-in of the program
- Ensuring as close to 100 percent participation as possible on a volunteer basis

Growing Healthy

Growing Healthy, a comprehensive health education curriculum, was piloted 3 years ago in 10 third-grade classrooms at Brookwood Elementary School. It has been a top priority of the Partnership and its Education Committee to implement this curriculum in grades K–6 in all three systems. The first quarter of 1996 was devoted to this task. Teachers from Dalton, Murray County, and Whitfield County participated in trips to Atlanta schools and to Brookwood to visit Growing Healthy classrooms, and presentations were made to many of the teachers in these systems.

As a result of this effort, Growing Healthy in all three school systems will be a reality this fall. It will be implemented as follows:

- Murray County Schools: Five third-grade classes at Chatsworth Elementary
- Dalton Public Schools: All third-, fourth-, fifth-, and sixth-grade classrooms
- Whitfield County Schools: All kindergarten, first-, second-, and third-grade classrooms

This means that more than 5,000 students began this curriculum in 1996.

Nurse Practitioner Scholarship Programs

A subcommittee of the Indigent Care and Accessibility Committee has planned, interviewed candidates, and has executed agreements for this scholarship program for three nurses. After completing the nurse practitioner program, the family nurse practitioner will work in Murray or Whitfield county at an approved not-for-profit entity, with the primary emphasis of adequately staffing the MAC. This will result in better access to care for the indigent and, it is hoped, reduce the nonemergency visits at the hospital emergency departments, thereby reducing costs.

Drug and Alcohol Project

This is an important project to which the Partnership has recently committed. The Rollins School of Public Health of Emory University was commissioned to conduct a community needs assessment of drug and alcohol use in our community. After examining the results of this study, some community residents believe the results are alarming; others say that, although alarming, they could have predicted the outcome. The CEO of HMC, a Partnership board member, asked the Partnership to consider taking the leadership role on this project. The board of directors accepted the challenge to review the study data, resolve the issues to be addressed, and develop an action plan of prevention/education for the schools and workplace.

The Partnership has benefited from a tremendous amount of favorable publicity from our local newspapers, television, and radio. The positive impact of our programs on the community is visible, and the creditability of the Partnership is increasing with each exposure to a civic group, new workplace, or the media. As the sole participant from Georgia in the CCN demonstration program, the Partnership is enthusiastic to not only learn from others but to share its experiences as well.

Contact: Nancy Kennedy
Executive Director
Northwest Georgia Healthcare Partnership
P.O. Box 182
Dalton, GA 30722
Phone: (706) 272-6013
Fax: (706) 278-5941

12

The Southcentral Health Network of Idaho

Executive Summary

The Southcentral Health Network is a community coalition representing 11 organizations in the eight counties of south central Idaho. Partnership organizations include six medical facilities, one chemical dependency treatment center, a community college, one local health district, a community and migrant health center, and the state regional department of health and welfare. We envision a system of community health care where collaboration with the community is the key concept. Our collective vision is of a Health Magic Valley 2012. This represents our ultimate goal of aligning the entire regional community toward improvement in health status so that children born in 1994 will live in a healthier community when they graduate from high school in 2012.

We completed a comprehensive community health assessment and ranked our top health priorities: (1) alcohol and other drug use, (2) tobacco use, (3) motor vehicle injuries, and (4) teen pregnancy. Strategies developed to address these priorities target prevention and youth through collaborative efforts.

The Southcentral Health Network will provide consultation, technical support, and facilitation of five local coalition implementation teams, each based in one of five geographic locations. These teams will begin by identifying one or more priority areas and respective strategies to implement in their community. The network steering committee will monitor and report progress toward improvements in specific health status indicators at the local level and across the district.

Two local coalitions—Blaine/Camas County and Gooding County—have selected their health priorities and begun work on implementing improvement strategies. They have both selected alcohol and other drug use, including tobacco. A third local coalition, Jerome County, is scheduled to begin in October 1996. Some key lessons we have already learned are the following:

- Allow plenty of time for community process. Our implementation timelines were probably too aggressive.

- New facilitators and coalitions need a great deal of support. We recommend role modeling by cofacilitating with technical assistance staff. Establish group norms early.
- Keep all coalition members involved and provide opportunities for all to feel of value to the work.
- Someone familiar with data should present and interpret them to community groups in a simple narrative format.
- Carefully coordinate local coalition efforts with any other similar coalitions that may be operating in the community.
- Plan for frequent formal and informal communication.
- Collaboration is hard work. Provide opportunities for celebration!

We have found the words of Paul Weisner to be true: "Reweaving the social fabric . . . requires the creative collaboration of poets, policy wonks, community activists, and thousands of ordinary citizens."

Cheryl Juntunen
Chair, Southcentral Health Network

THE COLLABORATIVE PARTNERSHIP

Vision: Healthy Magic Valley 2012

Our vision calls for long-term improvement in health status and reduction of health risks so our community will be healthier by the year 2012—the year that children born in 1994 will graduate from high school.

Mission: To Promote a Collaborative Effort of Communities to Improve the Health of Residents in South Central Idaho

The Community The Magic Valley community comprises all people who reside or work in south central Idaho. Spanning 11,000 square miles, Magic Valley includes eight counties, one of which is classified as frontier (fewer than 6 persons per square mile), six as rural, and one as urban (containing a city with population greater than 20,000). According to the 1990 census, the region's population is 136,831—a density of 12.2 persons per square mile, compared with a national average of 69.4 per mile. There are no metropolitan statistical areas (MSAs) in Magic Valley. Twin Falls, population 29,684, is the largest city in Magic Valley; the next largest is Burley, population 8,918. Although the region is expanding at a rate of 4.6 percent per year, Magic Valley will remain an intact community within a circumscribed geographic area, surrounded on all sides by either mountains or desert.

About half of the Magic Valley population is female (68,548). The median age is 32.4 years, and the ages are distributed as follows: 5 years or less (8 percent), age 5–14 (19 percent), age 15–24 (13 percent), age 25–44 (29 percent), age 45–64 (18 percent), and over 64 (16 percent). Hispanics compose the primary minority population (9 percent), African-Americans compose 0.1 percent, and other races (that is, Native American, Asian, and Pacific Islander) make up 6.4 percent of the population; thus, minorities make up 15.5 percent of the community. Per capita income is $16,413 (87.8 percent of the U.S. average). In 1992, unemployment was 7.2 percent. There are 6,878 recipients of Medicaid and 4,573 in the Women, Infants and Children (WIC) program (47 percent of potentially eligible). The proportion of uninsured is 12.3 percent, and 4.7 percent are partially insured. Under age 65, 1.5 percent of the population live under the designated poverty level; over age 64, 12.1 percent live in poverty. There are 11,832 migrant farm workers and 20,358 seasonal farm workers. Educational attainment is less than high school for 23.1 percent of the adult community; 15.1 percent have a college degree.

Magic Valley is primarily an agriculture-based community. Irrigation has transformed the valley into some of the most productive farmland in the country. Fish farming and dairy farming are important industries as well. Because of the trend toward fewer and larger farms, employment growth is shifting from agriculture to the trade, service, and recreation industries. Food processing companies, including Green Giant, Kraft, Ore-Ida Foods, Del Monte, Coors, Amalgamated Sugar, and Lamb-Weston Foods, are the largest employers in the region. The Sun Valley–Ketchum–Hailey area is a destination resort for skiing and snow sports in the winter, and white water rafting, golf, and hiking in the summer. The population during peak tourist times grows from 15,000 to 40,000.

There are seven medical centers in the region, with a total of 385 beds having served 14,389 hospitalizations in 1993. Twin Falls is home to two of the larger hospitals in Magic Valley. One of the hospitals, Twin Falls Clinic and Hospital, with a 44-bed capacity and clinic of 20 primary care and specialty physicians, is under private physician ownership. Magic Valley Regional Medical Center, a not-for-profit, county-owned hospital with a 165-bed capacity, serves as a secondary care institution for the region and is designated as the Medicare regional referral center. There are also smaller, rural hospitals (ranging from 14 to 53 beds) under private (two) and public (three) ownerships and funding; they are staffed primarily by family practitioners. There are 193 practicing physicians, of which 44 percent are in primary care. Idaho has the fewest physicians per capita of any of the 50 states (136 physicians per 100,000 population; national average is 184 per 100,000). Three of the eight Magic Valley counties are designated health and professional shortage areas and/or medically underserved areas. Within this environment, health care resources are geographically disjointed and sometimes difficult to access.

A recent epidemiological analysis of the Magic Valley community found that major causes of death before age 65 are unintentional injuries, cancer, and heart disease; for age 65 or older, heart disease, cancer, and stroke. Heart disease and cancer death rates in Magic Valley are higher than Idaho death rates but lower than U.S. rates. Annually, there are 1,000 myocardial infarctions in Magic Valley, 540 new cancer cases, and 2,000 active cancer cases. Magic Valley death rates (64.9 per 100,000 people) are higher than the U.S. (33.8) and Idaho (43.8) death rates for motor vehicle crashes, work-related injury, and other unintentional injuries, and higher than the U.S. death rate for suicides.

Preventable injuries result in 2,500 children requiring medical care and are the leading cause of lost productive years. The prevalence of low birth weight is 5.5 percent (5.3 percent Idaho, 7.1 percent United States), prenatal care is 63 percent (73 percent Idaho, 76 percent United States), and teenage pregnancy is 4.7 percent (3.9 percent Idaho, 7.4 percent United States). Among 2,291 deliveries in 1993, 45 percent were paid by Medicaid. The proportion of smokers in Magic Valley is 22 percent.

In a recent community survey, residents in Magic Valley identified alcohol abuse (67 percent), smoking (60 percent), drug abuse (57 percent), teen pregnancy (53 percent), chronic disease (51 percent), lack of exercise (43 percent), domestic violence (43 percent), and unintentional injury (38 percent) as the most important health problems in our community. Problems identified as having the least available services to address them include alcohol abuse, smoking, drug abuse, teen pregnancy, environmental protection, domestic violence, mental health, and poor nutrition. Of the residents in our area, 86 percent indicated they desire more programs focused on healthy living and disease prevention. Cost (20 percent), lack of education (19 percent), lack of concern (17 percent), no insurance (8 percent), and access (2 percent) were perceived as the primary barriers that prevent people from healthy living.

Resources In addition to multiple specialty and preventive health clinics in Twin Falls, the South Central District Health Department (SCDHD) has a number of outlying public health facilities throughout Magic Valley. The district office oversees a budget of $3.3 million and a staff of 85, and serves to prevent disease, disability, and premature death; to promote healthy lifestyles; and to protect and promote the health and quality of our environment.

Besides the seven medical centers, Magic Valley is served by additional health and social service agencies. Family Health Services Centers, a federally funded program for migrant community health, operates primary care clinics in three underserved areas to provide migrant workers and low-income residents with basic medical and prevention-oriented health care. Among 6,986 people receiving services in 1992, 64 percent were below poverty level. The Walker Center in Gooding County is a clinic and 22-bed facility for substance abuse. The Department of Health and Welfare provides social and mental health services, child protection and shelter care, nursing home licensing, and Medicaid.

Self-sufficiency, responsibility, quality of life, and commitment toward neighborly concern are Magic Valley's main community resources. The accomplishments of civic mobilization, described briefly in the next section, indicate the extent of personal commitment and financial contribution toward maintaining and enhancing our community. Participation by employers, corporations and small businesses, churches, schools and colleges, philanthropic foundations, civic groups, government agencies, and individual residents shows investment in the support of and involvement in a partnership for promotion of community health.

The Partnership Health care leaders in Magic Valley realized that solutions to community health issues require collaboration in seeking opportunities to work with providers across organizations and constituencies community-wide to improve the health status of the region. Southcentral Health Network (SCHN) was formed in 1990 to broaden the attention of the major health care providers from patient needs to the community. The founding members constitute the steering committee and include the SCDHD, six area hospitals, Family Health Services, the Walker Center, and the College of Southern Idaho. After a series of successful community health projects demonstrated that the group could overcome competitive concerns, the organizations formalized their commitment to SCHN as a community health coalition in fall 1993 by establishing the "Healthy Magic Valley 2012" vision and by providing funding to hire SCHN staff and support network activities. The Public Health District was identified as the appropriate agency to administer the SCHN, and a community health planner with a graduate degree in health and public administration was hired to coordinate it.

Recent SCHN activities have included assessment of the health status of our community and determination of community health priorities. Presently, SCHN is using the assessment to identify resources that could provide services and programs, and to develop a community health plan that involves the entire community in the planning process. New partners and collaborative relationships were solicited to form various working committees to accomplish these activities. Participants in the SCHN now include the Department of Health and Welfare, and individuals from across the community, including state senators and legislators, U.S. representatives, and county commissioners; clergy; educators from elementary and high schools, colleges and universities, and schools for deaf and blind; physicians, nurses, dentists, emergency medical services/ambulance providers, and hospice and residential care providers; representatives of Community Action, Chamber of Commerce, Office of Aging, La Gente Sana, Port of Hope, American Cancer Society, and American Heart Association; a Legal Aid attorney; state, county, and city law enforcement officers; representatives from Idaho Power and the banking and news establishments; and Magic Valley citizens and health care consumers.

We view SCHN as an evolving community coalition for bringing about a fully collaborative community health system for Magic Valley. SCHN has begun to advocate for community health and focus, but we must continue to engage representation from all constituencies of the community. Recently, the steering committee has created three membership slots allocated to community representatives who are not health care providers. SCHN has begun to build partnerships in select projects, but we must learn more about organizational issues of collaboration, particularly in a competitive environment that is undergoing rapid change to face new financial incentives. The opportunity to formulate a community care network (CCN) proposal has prompted us to discuss these issues and develop strategic plans. We accept the CCN mission wholeheartedly in our quest for a "Healthy Magic Valley."

PRIOR EFFORTS THAT REPRESENT MOVEMENT TOWARD THE COMMUNITY CARE NETWORK VISION

Community-Wide Continuous Quality Improvement

The "community as a system" view as a strategy for improving health is breaking new ground in the application of continuous quality improvement (CQI). Based on the specific needs of the community and guided by the objectives set out in Healthy People 2000, a topic is chosen for improvement and the community team departs on the mission to understand the chosen health status issue, develop measurement strategies, identify interventions, implement an intervention, and assess the effectiveness of the intervention. Our system for implementing CQI includes the following steps: (1) focus on a community-wide health status concern, (2) organize a community coalition, (3) understand the current health care status, (4) understand how health care may be improved, then (5) plan a community-wide intervention using plan-do-study-act (PDSA) cycles. The strength of the CQI paradigm is sequencing PDSA cycles whereby the scientific method is used to propose hypothetical improvements, implement changes for improvement, collect data to study whether there is improvement, and act on the results. In brief, the CQI paradigm provides answers to three critical questions: (1) What are we trying to accomplish? (2) How will we know that a change is an improvement? and (3) What changes can we make that will result in improvement?

John Bingham, administrator of the Magic Valley Regional Medical Center (MVRMC), began a CQI initiative in 1988 to make Magic Valley the healthiest place in America. MVRMC is now one of only 10 hospitals in the nation working with the Department of Commerce to adapt the Malcolm Baldrige Award criteria to the health care industry. MVRMC commenced implementation of CQI both in the hospital and community. The hospital was instrumental in having the Chamber of Commerce institute training for the business community and in persuading the College of Southern Idaho to offer courses on CQI to the community. The emphasis on systems thinking and customer relationships helped some area hospitals, businesses, and individuals in the community to become more appreciative of the interdependence among community, employers, and health care. Several years after beginning the CQI initiative, a large number of people in our community are now anchored into the concepts and language of CQI. Several churches have even begun using CQI methods, and surrounding industries jointly sponsor CQI seminars with health care. As a result, hospitals, city government, local businesses, and the community have begun to trust using CQI as a catalyst for bringing health care competitors and the community together to design community-focused solutions for health improvement.

Community Projects

The projects described below demonstrate our progress toward the CCN vision, illustrating shifts in health programs from an institutional focus to ad hoc linkages to a community focus.

Cancer Screening Project This project was a joint endeavor that included Twin Falls Clinic and Hospital, MVRMC, Minidoka Memorial Hospital, and Cassia Memorial Hospital. In 1992, local businesses donated $500,000 for hospitals to conduct free, community-wide prostate cancer screenings; 70 potential cancers were identified and referred for follow-up to the provider of their choice. This project commenced the effort toward building a cooperative health care community.

Pregnancy Program A community coalition consisting of six area hospitals, county agencies, and physicians organized to develop a coordinated, comprehensive prenatal care system and to improve access. To bring about changes in affordability of care, the group rallied the Idaho Medical Association and lobbied the state legislature to modify Medicaid eligibility from 43 percent of the federal poverty level to 133 percent and to increase Medicaid reimbursement for prenatal care and delivery from $400 to $1,200. The availability of physicians for deliveries was addressed by the county hospitals paying malpractice insurance, permitting family practitioners to see more pregnant women and perform deliveries. To improve access to care, the Public Health District and Family Health Services created four decentralized clinics providing comprehensive services, including pregnancy testing and education, Medicaid and WIC application, nutrition and smoking cessation counseling, dental assessment, social work intervention, and case management with referral to physicians and community resources.

From 1988 to 1991, all these changes were instituted. There were dramatic declines in the number of neonatal intensive care admissions (from 184 in 1988 to 137 in 1991) and low-birth-weight infants (from 6.6 percent in 1988 to 5.5 percent in 1991). The number of women receiving Medicaid increased by approximately 200 enrollees, each costing an average of $2,000 per pregnancy. This increase created an additional cost of $400,000, which was more than offset by savings of $564,000 for neonatal intensive care.

Safe Kids Coalition; Traffic Safety Coalition The Magic Valley Safe Kids Coalition in Twin Falls formed as a result of the national initiative that identified accident prevention as an area the community can affect. In 1988, the Safe Kids Coalition started tracking preventable children's injuries, providing accident prevention education to children in all grades, and conducting safety fairs and public awareness campaigns. The Safe Kids Head Smart program raised funding to purchase and distribute 1,200 bicycle helmets in Twin Falls. From 1990 to 1993, helmet usage increased from 1 percent to 32 percent, and bicycle-related injuries decreased from 120 to 51. The project was one of the initial CQI efforts at building collaboration between a hospital and community agencies in Magic Valley with a focus on community preventive care. In 1995, the project was boosted with an additional 3,000 donated helmets distributed. Jerome and Minidoka counties have also initiated Safe Kids and Traffic Safety coalitions to address preventable injuries.

Teenage Driver Learning Collaborative Motor vehicle crashes have ceased to be solely a traffic safety problem and have become a major focus of health reform in the United States. The community of Twin Falls has taken the initiative to improve community health by identifying one of the most prevalent health problems—teenage driver crashes. The most common causes of teen crashes are poor judgment and driving skills as a result of inexperience. Experience may be accelerated and judgment improved using a driving simulator, which has the flexibility to allow an instructor to program typical scenarios that have been identified as high risk for teen crashes. The desired outcomes of the simulator curriculum for improving teenage driving are reduction of vehicular crashes, improvement in survival, and prevention of injury and disability.

The preliminary groundwork for this project began in October 1993. At that time, Twin Falls was accepted by the Institute of Healthcare Improvement (IHI), Boston, MA, and GOAL/QPC as one of nine sites in the United States and Canada where projects to improve a particular aspect of community health could be developed using CQI principles. In this project, team members, including the SCHN project coordinator, Public Health District director, and Safe Kids director, have practiced and honed their CQI skills. Over the past 15 months, the project has completed crash data analysis, an information/marketing booklet, a videotape, community awareness and fund-raising plans, the simulator curriculum, and a detailed protocol for evaluation of the project. An instructor was hired using funds donated by the College of Southern Idaho and MVRMC foundations, one simulator was donated by Time-Warner Simulator Products, two simulators were purchased through a grant from the Idaho Department of Transportation ($150,000), and operating funds for curriculum development were granted by the Department of Transportation ($166,500). At this point we are estimating training costs at approximately $63.30 per student—$316,500 for 5,000 students over 5 years. Currently, the Office of Highway

Safety estimates the monetary value of one life saved at $500,000 and one injury prevented at $39,000. It is anticipated that this project will show a significant reduction in injuries resulting from crashes, which would more than offset the cost of the training and capital equipment. Once effectiveness of the simulator drivers education is demonstrated, the curriculum is portable to other communities in Idaho and throughout the nation.

Rural Health Connection Blaine County participates in a rural health outreach project called the Rural Connection funded by Robert Wood Johnson and Pew Charitable Trust. A consortium of six hospitals and Boise State University is developing a continuum of care model that includes prevention, early intervention, acute care, follow-up care, and aftercare. A collaborative community network in Blaine County has focused on persons experiencing chest pain with suspected cardiac origin. To date, protocols for continuum of care from early intervention to community follow-up and emergency medical technician (EMT) training have been implemented with successful process outcomes—provision of consistent EMT care and reduced time for initiation of thrombolytic therapy. The Rural Health Connection and the SCHN have established formal linkages to foster sharing of information, ideas, and resources as both collaborative community efforts move toward expanded areas focused on continuum of care.

Blaine County Interagency Health Council The concept of a local interagency council focusing on community health derived from the Rural Health Connection project. The Blaine County Interagency Health Council has representation from the school district, law enforcement, social services, environmental services, county commissioners, local businesses, and the local medical community. The council holds a retreat annually to assess community health goals, conducts quarterly meetings to monitor progress toward goals, and facilitates project-related task groups focused on specific health strategies on a monthly basis. Specific projects from the interagency council include establishment of a Drug Awareness, Resistance and Education (DARE) program in their schools, development of a school health nurse program, and establishment of a local alternative school.

Community Health Information Network We are planning a community health information network (CHIN) in Magic Valley that will integrate and automate the clinical information systems of six hospitals, 200 physicians in their offices, five public health offices, and other ancillary health care professionals. In planning the CHIN, we wish to facilitate improving the medical care and health status of Magic Valley residents through use of coordinated, integrated information and telecommunications network technology. We plan to use real-time clinical information systems to enable seamless patient care delivery provided across many care providers and through preventive care, primary care, hospitalization, and follow-up; extend wellness information services to residents' homes; integrate and interface the information systems of the various providers, payers, and employers in Magic Valley; provide systems integration to allow providers to measure clinical outcomes and health improvements, costs, and consumer satisfaction with health care; and facilitate analysis of health indicators to monitor community health initiatives. Because of health care reform and the need to drive costs out of the system, it is important to have an information system in place to be able to prove that what we do works.

Our focus is truly community oriented, tying not only county and private hospitals, clinics, and physicians together, but also mental health centers, psychiatric services, substance abuse agencies, nursing homes, and the entire public health effort as well, including its service to the most disadvantaged and underserved populations in our region. Such information services have never before been offered in such a large rural geographic area, nor have they been offered community-wide to serve a region's entire population.

The group formed to oversee the planning for this project is the Southern Idaho Medical Information Network (SIMIN), which received a $275,000 federal grant from the National Telecommunications and Information Administration to help plan the CHIN. Local matching funds were provided by area hospitals, the Public Health District, US West, and Blue Shield of Idaho. Community accountability is central to SIMIN and has been supported through a broad-based community steering committee, through the use of focus groups and town meetings to get input on the project from health care providers and the public, and through use of a SIMIN newsletter and ongoing educational presentations.

Network design for CHIN has been under way for a year. Extensive research has been conducted on eight software companies' abilities to provide such a system. SIMIN has established relationships with public and private common carriers in southern Idaho to provide scaleable telecommunications technologies to connect the disparate entities and to provide for remote access to the system from physician homes. SIMIN's mission is to coordinate the health care information infrastructure being developed in Idaho in a way that acknowledges the special needs of rural communities and the different interests of regions within Idaho.

Southcentral Health Network The formation of the SCHN represents our community's most dramatic shift away from individual institutions to a community focus. The foundation was laid for the development of the SCHN when our regional medical center incorporated its mission: "To make the Magic Valley the healthiest place in America." In accordance with the new mission, the external relations committee of the medical center board began to facilitate meetings focusing on community health that included representatives from other hospitals in the region. This regional group expanded to include community members and disconnected its close alignment with the regional medical center by adopting its own name (SCHN), vision, mission, goals, and objectives to become a true community health coalition.

To move toward its vision of a "Healthy Magic Valley 2012," SCHN's first goal was to assess current community health status. The thrust for community assessment quickly led to expansion of SCHN. Key regional agencies and community leaders were invited to collaborate with SCHN. Outreach and education was begun by informing all participating agency staff and boards, county commissioners, and legislators about SCHN and distributing a brochure describing SCHN and soliciting community involvement.

The framework adopted for community assessment was the Assessment Protocol for Excellence in Public Health (APEX-PH) of the National Association of County and City Health Officials. One adaptation of the APEX-PH model was to organize data, services, and policy advisory groups to review health status using the 20 categories of the Healthy People 2000 framework. The objective of the Services Advisory Group was to inventory health-related services. The Data Advisory Group reviewed secondary health status data and compared county, regional, state, and U.S. rates and

Healthy People 2000 goals. This group also designed a telephone survey for a random sample of 400 residents to assess community perceptions of area health needs and programs. Finally, the Policy Advisory Group reviewed area health policies.

All three advisory groups compiled their individual reports into a comprehensive "Review and Assessment of Health Status in South Central Idaho, Fall 1994." This summary information, along with the complementary background reports, was then reviewed by the full Community Health Assessment Task Force. The full task force consisted of 37 members with geographic representation from the eight counties, as well as representation among community disciplines such as government, health care, education, business, social services, legal, religious, ethnic, disabled, and retired. The task force systematically rated the 20 health categories according to three criteria: magnitude of the health problem, seriousness of the problem, and feasibility of correcting the problem. This first comprehensive community health needs assessment in south central Idaho was the basis for setting four community health priorities: alcohol and other drugs, cancer and heart disease, unintentional injuries, and maternal and infant health.

The next objective was to facilitate and encourage all area health officials to align with the community's health needs and expectations by setting priorities, goals, and programs around the four health priorities identified in the community assessment. One success we have already seen is that by providing our state Division of Health office with the needs assessment, the SCDHD has been able to obtain more noncategorical contracts that allow the flexibility to focus on local health priorities. Additionally, a local school district and a community development council have used the assessment information to write grants and do more tailored needs assessments.

SCHN's community outreach and reporting plan has been an integral management tool to keep the public informed. Our mailing list includes 350 community leaders in our eight-county area representing civic, religious, and social service organizations, government, health organizations, education providers, law enforcement officials, and many others. All task force final reports and a SCHN newsletter are sent to individuals on the mailing list. We are active in giving presentations to community groups about our various activities; we also disseminate press releases about our activities and milestones, which are followed up with personal contact with reporters or appearances on the evening news.

SCHN is also a participant in the state and national arena of health planning and assessment. We regularly preside at state conferences providing presentations and informational displays. Our documents are sent to health planning officials at the American Public Health Association (APHA) and the National Association of County and City Health Officials. As a member of the APHA Peer Assistance Network, we have received consultation and advice on implementing our community assessment.

Recently, the SCHN convened four health priority work groups comprising 45 different individuals with expertise concerning each health priority. Consistent with the SCHN's mission to collaborate, lead agencies were identified and represented with a facilitator for each health priority work group. The substance abuse coordinator at the regional Department of Health and Welfare led the Alcohol and Other Drugs work group; the director of the Safe Kids Coalition led the Unintentional Injuries work group; the pregnancy program coordinator at the District Health Department led the Maternal and Infant Health work group; and the health risk reduction coordinator at the District Health Department led the Cancer/Heart Disease work group. Each work group member conducted a more in-depth analysis of the health priority, reviewing data, using brainstorming techniques, and completing questionnaires on their community experience. Health priorities were analyzed for underlying risk and community factors. Community strategies were identified that addressed the underlying community factors of the health problem. Potential strategies were listed, including advocacy initiatives, direct services (including program enhancements or development), community activation projects, public education and awareness campaigns, and data and needs assessment activities. In addition, outcome, impact, and process objectives, sources of community expertise, and barriers for the strategies were identified. The analysis and strategies identified around the health priorities will serve as the first regional community health plan/strategy upon which the whole community will focus. The plan will serve as ideas for action for regional approaches as well as local community approaches to improving community health. Through these activities, the stage is set for SCHN's next milestone—implementing the community health plan/strategy with an operational community health network.

MOVING TOWARD THE COMMUNITY CARE NETWORK VISION

Visioning Process

The SCHN partnership recognizes that today's complex health problems require more than the services of one organization to address them. Success in improving the health of the community and providing high-quality health care will increasingly require focus on the community and continued development of mechanisms for access, coordination, and referral among agencies. The recognition of these concepts has prompted our partnership to envision a CCN that webs our large geographic area at the regional and local levels.

The SCHN visioning process emerged in 1990 as hospital administrators, other health directors, and leaders in health care delivery throughout the region began to meet monthly to share information and explore joint projects. Time, endless discussion, and successful projects built trust and respect. In spring 1993, SCHN was formalized when the boards and CEOs of the regional hospitals and the public health district passed resolutions and allocated money to support SCHN for achieving the vision of improved health in Magic Valley.

The founding SCHN members formed a steering committee and started their strategic process to create a road map for building collaboration, which included a consensus on the following vision, mission, goals, and short-term objectives:

- *Vision:* Healthy Magic Valley 2012—High school graduates of 2012 will live in a healthier community.
- *Mission:* To promote a cooperative effort of communities to improve the health of citizens in the Magic Valley.
- *Goals:*
  - —To serve as an organizing network for information and assessment of health services, including community, social, and educational
  - —To eliminate gaps, barriers, and duplication in services
  - —To motivate citizens to devote energy toward revitalizing the health of our communities

- —To develop and strengthen alliances while integrating services to implement our community health plan to achieve the vision
- *Objectives:*
  - —Community assessment of the current health status of our communities and the resources that could provide services and programs
  - —Community network to develop a community health strategy by involving the entire community in the planning process

Vision: Our Community Care Network Paradigm

Programs such as APEX-PH are available to guide successful implementation of community assessment. However, community initiatives on priorities identified from assessment are prone to falter because systematic methodologies for community intervention are evolving and have not yet identified the key ingredients for success. As a participant in the IHI and GOAL/QPC Community-wide Health Improvement Learning Collaborative, we have learned a system that promotes improvements in community health.

The system has two important features. First, the system uses CQI as a paradigm from which to approach community initiatives. It helps teams that are mobilized around specific community improvements to focus not only on processes by which health is improved, but also on the shared community vision and the needs of the residents of the community. CQI provides a methodology and tools to bring about change. With CQI techniques, we can translate big community aims into manageable smaller project aims by using short PDSA cycles, which apply the scientific method to understand and plan evidence-based interventions. The system helps teams keep their focus, plan solutions, collect only enough data to understand and monitor the process, use available resources, make community members partners in improvement, learn from failure, and celebrate small successes. Using this methodology, community teams, with input from others, are able to start on small "doable" projects, specify measures that will indicate that the intervention worked, collect and evaluate their data, and learn from experience. The focus on small changes builds momentum toward bigger changes and sustains movement toward the shared vision.

The second feature is structure. Community teams are part of a bigger collaborative that helps to shape the work of the coalitions. A central system of management serves to clarify priorities; administer communication processes and reporting mechanisms; lead, motivate, and monitor the coalitions; provide timely advice and expertise about continuous improvement, subject area, and team dynamics; and maintain support systems and resources for collaboration.

The SCHN collaborative is an alliance of local community coalitions. The leaders of each coalition will serve as liaisons and members of the collaborative. The collaborative will comprise the steering committee, the administration/operations branch, task force committees, and advisory panels. The primary functions of the collaborative are to develop cohesive strategic plans consistent with the mission and vision of SCHN, to provide linkages and resources for coordination and facilitation of the coalitions, and to track improvement in community health. The architecture of the Magic Valley SCHN is shown in figure 12-1.

The governing branch of the network, the SCHN steering committee comprises the administrators of organizations/agencies providing health care services, as well

FIGURE 12-1. Organization of the Southcentral Health Network of Idaho

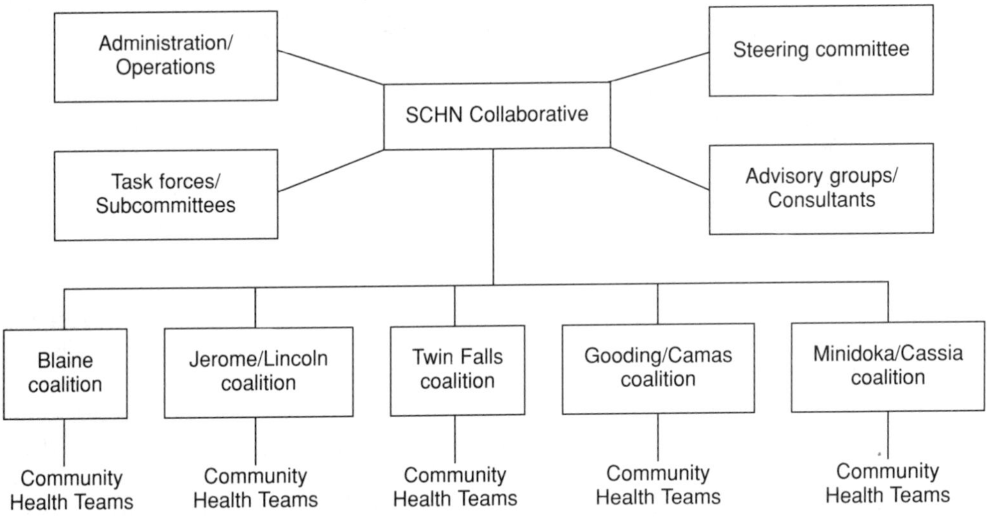

as a mix of regional community business and civic leaders, skilled professionals, and community representatives. The administrative arm, the Public Health District, and the steering committee will monitor the operations of the network to facilitate community collaboration and arrange for finding, providing, and planning resources for the coalitions. Such resources include local, state, and national consultants available to mentor the coalitions and advise the collaborative. The regional task forces and advisory panels are working groups of health professionals and community representatives who will keep focus on the community, rally its support, and keep it informed.

The county coalitions consist of the local community health leaders, representatives of local agencies and businesses, and concerned residents. The county coalition accepts the SCHN community health initiatives and adapts local intervention strategies to bring about health improvement. The coalition will identify a task force for each of the four community health initiatives. The task force will use CQI methodology and other health coalition models (for example, interagency council) and have consultation from the collaborative to enable sharing across the counties, acceleration of performing interventions, and provision of data measurement.

The mix between local (county) and central (regional) configuration has several advantages. Our SCHN allows for local resources to be fed back to the local area, provides opportunity for local individuals to become involved and buy into the process, allows flexibility to tailor solutions according to the resources and strengths of the local area, and keeps community involvement accessible to the local area. The central component of our SCHN integrates commitment across the whole Magic Valley region, permits buildup of trust and communication among competitors, and centralizes the common threads of project management, data analysis, facilitation, strategic planning, and funding.

Initiatives toward the CCN Vision

As mentioned, our SCHN has identified four primary community health initiatives. SCHN has begun developing a strategic plan for each of those four major health priorities. Each plan specifies a year 2012 goal and the type of indicator for measuring health outcome; it also lists factors within the community that contribute to the health problem and offers strategies for contending with the contributing factors. Indicators for process outcomes are suggested, as well as resources for and barriers against implementing interventions.

For example, the Maternal and Infant Health plan has a year 2012 goal of reducing pregnancies among girls age 17 and younger to no more than 40.0 per 1,000 adolescents. The regional rate is 46.8 and is the highest teen pregnancy rate in Idaho. Factors contributing to teen pregnancy included dysfunctional family environment, history of sexual abuse, limited access to community programs, and inadequate sexuality education. A strategy for contending with inadequate education is to promote consistent, comprehensive family life/sexuality education through the schools (grades K–12). Some possible process indicators include presence of a "male responsibility" component in sexuality education; development of partnerships with schools, churches, and parents; and efforts to advocate for mandated sexuality education programs. Resources include a listing of agencies (for example, SCDHD, Center for New Directions, Family Health Services, La Gente Sana) and institutions (for example, schools, churches, hospitals, parent-teacher associations) with an interest in reducing unwanted teenage pregnancy. The plan also draws attention to sensitivity with cultural, moral, and ethical issues.

The leaders and area liaisons to the collaborative will carry these four strategic plans to their local communities. Each of the local coalitions will develop operational intervention strategies tailored to the resources and interests of their locality. In each coalition, the community leaders in health care services, public health, interested partners in industry and business, and residents representing the community will form task forces and subcommittees for the health initiatives. Core members of the local coalitions are already established through their affiliation with SCHN. These core members have also been active in identifying individuals in the community with technical and/or communication skills who will serve on the coalition.

Some coalitions have more resources and are prepared to take on all four community health initiatives. The remaining coalitions may need to focus on one or two of the health initiatives and leverage the work done by the other coalitions at a later time. The SCHN collaborative will serve to monitor the progress of the local coalitions, facilitate sharing and linkages between coalitions, make expert consultations available, and assist in overcoming organizational or technical barriers and financial needs.

Four Dimensions of the CCN Vision

Community Accountability SCHN has valued community accountability since its inception. It has published the community assessment and planning reports and distributed them throughout Magic Valley. These comprehensive assessments will be annual reports. In addition, a SCHN newsletter summarizes the needs and health status of the community, presents easily grasped pictorial displays of the data, informs the community of planned actions, challenges residents to assume responsibility toward preventive care and participation in decision making, and invites the public to become actively involved or a financial supporter. Informing the public through SCHN newsletters, town meetings, and the media has provided a mechanism for communication and feedback.

As each local coalition begins its community mobilization and intervention, SCHN will incorporate area-specific reports. These may include community health team reports on intervention strategies or progress toward meeting goals in better health outcomes. One tool, for example, may be publication of CQI story boards for local projects and will become a convenient way of spreading to communities the activities and progress of their community health coalitions.

Because SCHN includes affiliation of administrators from health care organizations, it has requested and received resolutions from the boards that explicitly state their commitment to the SCHN vision and mission. Commitment is expressed in the form of financial support, collaboration, and incorporation of the SCHN goals into the organization's goals and annual reports. Another expression of this commitment is regional participation in SIMIN. SIMIN will provide a detailed CHIN database to generate regular monitoring reports, cost-effectiveness studies, and data support for local and regional initiatives.

The CHIN database will be a resource for SCHN to monitor process and health outcomes at both the regional and local levels. Data-driven decision making, use of data analysis (for example, run charts) to test whether our community and system interventions work, and our open-reporting process fit well with the CCN vision of accountability.

The commitment of our collaborative and local coalitions to the four community health initiatives demonstrates how our network has used principles of CQI and the APEX-PH health planning process to identify community health opportunities and base its activities on community needs and preferences. Another function of our collaborative will be to implement organizational assessment measures to provide its steering committee with a panel of information that both directs its progress and allows it to recognize where facilitation and support are needed. In summary, we view community accountability as one of our strengths. Our collaborative is a blend of community and health care providers, and the PDSA process is inherently accountable. Our rural makeup, public involvement, and newsletters are conducive to keeping the community informed and actively involved in the SCHN collaborative, area coalitions, and individual organizations. SCHN has planned a broad health agenda across the Magic Valley while tailoring the four health initiatives to its local areas.

Community Health Focus Another dimension of SCHN's strength is community health focus. The SCHN collaborative and local coalitions are guided by the focus of their community assessment and planning processes. The community health initiatives have a blend of disease and health orientation with emphasis on primary and secondary prevention.

Seamless Continuum of Care SCHN is working currently in an environment of multipurpose providers. Three factors contribute to our movement toward a seamless continuum of care. First, there is a movement toward managed care and physician-hospital organizations (PHOs) (this factor will be elaborated on in the next section). Second, the focus on community, the community health initiatives, and commitment to SCHN has provided a forum for health care providers to perceive the need and allocate resources for services in the community rather than the institution and realize the effect of barriers on health status (for example, the pregnancy program). Within their domains, many of the participating provider members of SCHN are changing to vertically integrated organizations for health care delivery.

The third factor is CHIN, a fully-integrated clinical and administration database system. Where the SIMIN collaborative is primarily concerned with technology issues, the SCHN collaborative will address the use of information and the concerns of the providers and community regarding use of information. SCHN will ensure coordination of the information system to assist in community accountability, facilitate the community health initiatives, and identify community issues in access and health care utilization. Sharing of data will move the community to compatible information systems and provide a gateway for coordinating access to services and recognizing unmet needs. A consistent consumer record will facilitate coordination and management of care. The CHIN data system will assist analysts in producing reports for strategic planning.

Management within Fixed Resources Providers in Magic Valley are on a fee-for-service basis. The scene, however, is rapidly changing. Managed care and PHOs are developing in all counties of south central Idaho. Twin Falls Clinic and Hospital, a physician-owned hospital since 1947, is a PHO. Four hospitals are restructuring to a PHO, and MVRMC is restructuring into an integrated health care system. Additionally, some hospitals have begun to contract with employers to provide services at discounted pricing. Furthermore, Magic Valley is the test-bed for Idaho's Medicaid managed care pilot program, in which a primary care physician serves as gatekeeper for medical services.

Within a relatively short time, we expect market forces to shape a capitated care environment of competing managed care systems. The SCHN will build trust and collaboration among competitors to keep focus on the community and reach for our shared vision. Legal (for example, antitrust laws) and cultural (for example, free trade and choice) precedents for competition will make a fully integrated health care system for Magic Valley unlikely during the next several years. However, reducing costs, duplication, and waste, as well as matching resources with community need, are important aspects of the SCHN agenda.

Initiatives for SCHN Operations

We propose an accelerated 3-year rollout for the implementation of our SCHN that involves infrastructure, community health initiatives, and project and program evaluation and dissemination.

Infrastructure Our first goal is to build the infrastructure for SCHN according to the schematic in figure 12-1. The steering committee will review and allocate grant resources to support the administrative operations at the regional and local levels. An immediate task is the development and organization of the local interagency-community health coalitions to understand and share in the vision, mission, and strategic plans of the regional SCHN collaborative. SCHN will encourage the local coalitions to form their community health teams to start addressing solutions to health problems and implementing community interventions. The time frame for these start-up activities is displayed in figure 12-2.

Throughout these activities, we envision the need for partnership development and technical assistance. Area coalitions will vary in their need for consultation in building coalitions, setting priorities, forming appropriate structure, identifying stakeholders and committed community leaders, and raising funds. SCHN will want to

FIGURE 12-2. Proposed Time Frames for Implementing the Southcentral Health Network of Idaho

```
                                                      Project Months
Goals                        0 1 2 3 4 5 6 7 8 9 10 11 12 13 14 15 16 17 18 19 20 21 22 23 24 25 26 27 28 29 30 31 32 33 34 35 36

Infrastructure
  Operations review          XXXXXXXX
  Coalitions                 XXXXXXXXXXXXXXXXXXXXXXXXXXXXXXXXXX
  Visioning                  XXXXXXXXXXXXXXXXXXXXXXXXXXXXXXXXXX
  Adopt initiatives          XXXXXXXXXXXXXXXXXXXXXXXXXXXXXXXXXXXXXXXXXXX
  Form teams                       XXXXXXXXXXXXXXXXXXXXXXXXXXXXXXXXXXXXXXXXXXXXXXXXXXXXXXXXXXXXXXXXXXXXXXXXXXXXXXXXXXXXXXXXXXX
  Partnership development     XXXXXXXXXXXXXXXXXXXXXXXXXXXXXXXXXXXXXXXXXXXXXXXXXXXXXXXXXXXXXXXXXXXXXXXXXXXXXXXXXXXXXXXXXXXXXXXXX
  Technical assistance       XXXXXXXXXXXXXXXXXXXXXXXXXXXXXXXXXXXXXXXXXXXXXXXXXXXXXXXXXXXXXXXXXXXXXXXXXXXXXXXXXXXXXXXXXXXXXXXXX

Community Health Initiatives
  Local priorities              XXXXXXXXXXXXXXXXXXXXXXXXXXXXXXXXXXXX
  Initiatives                   XXXXXXXXXXXXXXXXXXXXXXXXXXXXXXXXXXXX
  Implementation                       XXXXXXXXXXXXXXXXXXXXXXXXXXXXXXXXXXXXXXXXXXXXXXXXXXXXXXXXXXXXXXXXXXXXXXXXXXXXXXXXXXXXXXX

Evaluation
  Health initiatives         XXXXXXXXXXXXXXXXXXXXXXXXXXXXXXXXXXXXXXXXXXXXXXXXXXXXXXXXXXXXXXXXXXXXXXXXXXXXXXXXXXXXXXXXXXXXXXXXX
  SCHN                       XXXXXXXXXXXXXXXXXXXXXXXXXXXXXXXXXXXXXXXXXXXXXXXXXXXXXXXXXXXXXXXXXXXXXXXXXXXXXXXXXXXXXXXXXXXXXXXXX

Dissemination
  SCHN reports                  XXXXXXXXXXXXXXXXXXXXXXXXXXXXXXXXXXXXXXXXXXXXXXXXXXXXXXXXXXXXXXXXXXXXXXXXXXXXXXXXXXXXXXXXXXXXXX
  Grant reports                  XXXXXXXXXXXXXXXXXXXXXXXXXXXXXXXXXXXXXXXXXXXXXXXXXXXXXXXXXXXXXXXXXXXXXXXXXXXXXXXXXXXXXXXXXXXXX
  Community reports          XXXXXXXXXXXXXXXXXXXXXXXXXXXXXXXXXXXXXXXXXXXXXXXXXXXXXXXXXXXXXXXXXXXXXXXXXXXXXXXXXXXXXXXXXXXXXXXXX
  Marketing                    XXXXXXXXXXXXXXXXXXXXXXXXXXXXXXXXXXXXXXXXXXXXXXXXXXXXXXXXXXXXXXXXXXXXXXXXXXXXXXXXXXXXXXXXXXXXXXX
  Professional                      XXXXXXXXXXXXXXXXXXXXXXXXXXXXXXXXXXXXXXXXXXXXXXXXXXXXXXXXXXXXXXXXXXXXXXXXXXXXXXXXXXXXXXXXXX
```

Note: Not shown is the periodic return to these various activities for maintenance or new ventures.

benchmark what works in other communities and participate in facilitating exercises that move the health care system toward the true spirit of the CCN vision. A flow of technical assistance will be arranged for timely training in CQI and PDSA methods, needs assessment, indicator measurement and data collection, reporting mechanisms, media advocacy, health care delivery, cost analysis, leverage strategies, and expertise on selected topics.

Community Health Initiatives The driving force of our operation is the cooperative effort to improve health of the community expressed by the strategic plans that outline our community health initiatives. Each local coalition will need to review the SCHN strategic plan and select those problems and objectives of greatest importance to its community. The local resources on which the coalition can depend should bear on their decision making. Following selection of the community health initiatives, the community health teams will initially spend time understanding the health problem and refining measurements. We will encourage community health teams to consider potential interventions and conduct small-scale experiments to test whether the potential solutions produce change (that is, PDSA cycles). Effective implementation strategies are refined to improve their efficiency and may then be deployed countywide and perhaps community-wide. Time frames for these activities are shown in the Gannt chart for a 3-year period. (See figure 12-2.)

Evaluation There are two components to evaluation: one related to the community health initiatives and the other concerning evaluation of SCHN. The plan for community assessment, discussed previously, provides a yardstick for measuring change in community health status. In addition, each community health team and local coalition is expected to define and track process and health outcomes specific to their implementation plan. The SCHN collaborative will assist such data monitoring and require quarterly reports on activities and outcomes.

SCHN will also need to conduct program evaluation to determine the effectiveness and value of the network in meeting its goals. A suggested evaluation format includes indicators that would gauge SCHN's success according to the four dimensions of the CCN vision.

Dissemination SCHN must retool its reporting format from the short-term assessment and planning phase to the long-term implementation phase. The steering committee and local coalitions will need standardized reports that provide concise feedback on each community health team, community health initiative, and SCHN operations. Relevant information from these reports need extraction for the regular reporting to the funding foundation. Systematic procedures need development for the timely deployment of these reports while facing the rapid increase in activity and complexity of the network.

Although SCHN has done an excellent job at disseminating information, added effort will ensure Spanish editions for the Hispanic population and delivery to remote areas of Magic Valley. SCHN also needs to advocate and market the importance of its activities to community and state leaders who affect health care policy. In addition, SCHN will become more active in sharing its lessons and accomplishments through professional journals and meetings.

Opportunities and Future Directions

We believe our approach to community health will serve as a benchmark for many communities who are struggling to implement solutions for identified health priorities. Our architecture, coalition development, and implementation strategy and procedures will easily be portable. SCHN is very willing to help deploy what we have learned to other communities.

The first several years of our SCHN are focused on prevention and screening strategies. As coalitions work together, building trust and tearing down barriers, initiatives will spend additional years addressing issues related to treatment, rehabilitation, and follow-up services. The next logical step is for SCHN to address the full system of care.

SUMMARY OF NOTABLE PROGRESS

A Community Health Strategy for South Central Idaho

In spring 1996, the SCHN released the document titled *A Community Health Strategy for Southcentral Idaho,* which summarizes suggested health strategies focusing on youth and prevention. The strategies address our four health priorities: ***alcohol and other drugs, heart disease and cancer*** (focus: tobacco use), ***unintentional injuries*** (focus: motor vehicles), and ***maternal and infant health*** (focus: teen pregnancy). This document is the result of research and input of four work groups comprising 45 community representatives and youth from all eight counties of south central Idaho.

The strategy consists of the following:

- A plan for each health priority, which includes the definition of the health problem in our area
- Risk factors and proposed community factors that contribute to the problem
- A "menu of strategies" that serve as ideas for action for local and regional communities to identify prevention opportunities
- Measurable process, impact, and outcome objectives

Identified community factors that were similar across health priorities among our communities include the following:

- Lack of parental involvement and awareness
- Need for increased early prevention efforts
- Lack of an ongoing, reinforced message that is consistent across schools, communities, and counties
- Need for increased mechanisms for collaboration, coordination, and funding
- Need to use multiple preventive strategies
- Lack of recognition of attitude and feelings of youth regarding invincibility and peer pressure

Recommendations from teens participating in strategy development include the following:

- Target prevention programs to early age groups (before teen years).
- Emphasize positive messages.
- Involve youth who have experienced the health problems.
- Involve teens in peer prevention activities and teaching younger age groups.

Local Health Coalition Progress

To facilitate implementation of our community health strategy, SCHN is helping to form broad-based health coalitions in each of our local communities or service areas. These coalitions will serve as a local vehicle for reviewing and taking ownership of selected health strategies as well as directing their implementation at the community level. SCHN will offer technical assistance and other support to communities for coalition formation and plan development/implementation. Each of the five committees will have a lead agency that supports the local coalitions by hiring a facilitator and providing oversight, information, and operational resources. See figures 12-3 through 12-5.

Two coalitions are actively functioning at this time. The Blaine/Camas coalition began its work in January 1996, and the Gooding coalition in April. Following are some coalition highlights.

Blaine/Camas Coalition The health strategy developed by the Blaine/Camas coalition is focused on middle school and high school students. It involves a continuum of care that begins with prevention and includes early intervention, treatment, and follow-up of substance-abusing teens. Coalition members identified serious gaps in the current service delivery system, including lack of local access to outpatient treatment and ongoing aftercare to prevent substance abuse recurrence. The lead agency is Wood River Medical Center.

FIGURE 12-3. Application for Lead Agency

Agency(ies) name:

In what way is the mission of your organization(s) consistent with the mission of the Network? (15 pts)

Describe current community activities/partnerships/relationships that focus on improving the health of your community. (15 pts)

Is your Board supportive of your role in the Network and as the lead agency? (10 pts)

What support would you offer the lead facilitator for your community? (10 pts)

What is your interest in the outcome of the Community Care Network Demonstration project and what will you do to promote success in your local community? (20 pts)

Are there adequate resources available in your organization to serve as the lead agency? (10 pts)

How will you insure the involvement of other agencies, providers and groups in your area to make sure this is a collaborative process? (20 pts)

Other comments:

FIGURE 12-4. Services to Be Provided—Lead Agency Agreement

The responsibilities and services to be provided by ________________ as a lead agency in the Southcentral Health Network include, but may not be limited to the following:

- Recruit, hire and supervise a community facilitator in accordance to the job description. The facilitator will provide a minimum of ____ hours per week for the first ____ months and then ____ hours per week for the remainder of the contract. The lead agency will be reimbursed for the facilitator hours as specified above for the amount agreed to in the contract. All other expenses will be the responsibility of the lead agency.
- Provide two hours of clerical support to the facilitator per week for the duration of the contract. Hours to be reimbursed by the Network as specified in the contract.
- Provide necessary office support and materials necessary for the facilitator to fulfill job expectations. This could include telephone, copying, mileage and supplies, which would be tracked as in-kind expenses by the lead agency.
- Provide necessary data and documentation on a quarterly and as needed basis to evaluate outcomes, monitor progress and effectiveness and meet the requirements of the grant.
- Maintain a positive working relationship with the community as it relates to the work of the Network.
- Participate in Network activities as appropriate and the monthly steering committee meetings.
- Communicate work of the Network and local coalition to appropriate groups and individuals.

Gooding Coalition The 22-member Gooding coalition was organized in April 1996. Coalition representatives are from Hagerman, Gooding, Wendell, and Bliss, and include a judge, a sheriff, police chiefs, a physician, educators, school board members, counselors, clergy, a public health nurse, community advocates, probation and juvenile justice workers, parents, local business people, hospital administrators, and youth representatives.

The lead agency role for Gooding County is shared by the Walker Center and Gooding County Memorial Hospital. A local businesswoman and parent was selected as coalition facilitator; she is actively involved with the school and the Chamber of Commerce and has done an excellent job of recruiting members for the coalition.

The Gooding coalition selected prevention of tobacco and other substance use by youth as its health priority, based on available data and community perception. A tool with the following three measures was used to help them prioritize:

- Magnitude of the health concern in the community
- Seriousness of the health concern in the community
- Feasibility of improving the health concern in the community

The coalition has defined the problem and is currently developing specific strategies for its committees.

Future Coalitions The coalitions have received funding for this program from the local cities, the county, and the hospital and its foundation, and are currently working with individual communities. Jerome and Lincoln counties are scheduled to form the next coalition in November 1996. They have hired a local facilitator, and St. Benedict's Family Medical Center is the lead agency for the community. Twin Falls

FIGURE 12-5. Facilitators

Each lead agency will be responsible for hiring and supervising the facilitator for their community. It is recommended that staff from the Network participate in the interview and selection process.

FACILITATOR JOB DESCRIPTION

Role Purpose:
To facilitate a community coalition process to develop and implement local strategies that address the community health priorities.

Principal Responsibilities:

- Organize and facilitate a community coalition to develop and implement a health strategy which addresses at least one of the community health priorities.
- Function as the liaison between the community and the SCHN.
- Provide necessary information and reports to the community, coalition members and the SCHN.

Minimum Qualifications:

- High school diploma
- Some knowledge of:
  > psychology of human behavior
  > group process and dynamics
  > health service delivery
  > communication skills and techniques
  > principles of adult education
  > interpreting information related to health and socio-economic conditions
  > participating in collaborative community activities

- Experience
  > community education
  > participation in a collaborative community activity

- Demonstrates
  > ability to make oral presentations before groups
  > enthusiasm and ability to motivate others to do projects and fulfill agreed upon goals and time lines
  > good communication and interpersonal skills
  > good writing skills

County will organize its coalition in January 1997, and Cassia and Minidoka counties are scheduled to begin in September 1997. The staggered schedule is to ensure that each receives adequate support resources.

Contact: Cheryl Juntunen
South Central District Health Department
P.O. Box 547
Twin Falls, ID 83303
Phone: (208) 734-5900
Fax: (208) 734-9502

13

The West Texas Community Care Consortium

Executive Summary

As a native of west Texas, I have seen firsthand how cooperation, determination, and community spirit can unite the small towns scattered across this vast region. The same qualities have contributed to the success of the West Texas Community Care Consortium. The consortium has not only exceeded many of our preliminary expectations, but it has also improved the quality of life for an entire region of Texas.

Before the consortium was created, the distance between West Texas communities meant limited access to hospitals, primary care physicians or public clinics. Some Texans would have to travel 150 to 200 miles for routine cancer screening exams or medical treatment.

The lack of local accredited services could have been seen as an insurmountable problem, but in this case the challenge of providing high-quality health care for West Texans was a source of motivation, not consternation. It was an opportunity for four organizations to make a difference. The Cancer Consortium of El Paso, the Texas Cancer Council, Texas Tech University Health Sciences Center, and the West Texas Coalition for Cancer Control collaborated and formed the West Texas Community Care Consortium.

Rather than focus solely on providing health care for sick and terminally ill patients, the consortium broadened its scope to provide a full spectrum of services, including lifelong wellness programs and preventive health care. With the expertise of its members and the support of the people in each community, the consortium essentially turned a one-dimensional system into a three-dimensional cooperative effort.

Each community has been actively involved in developing a comprehensive network of health care services. West Texans now benefit from a wide range of programs, including education for lifelong wellness, regular exams and screenings, diagnosis, treatment, and follow-up care.

By its second quarter, the consortium had exceeded its own timetable. It had created steering committees, hired community service advocates, trained service providers, and planned initiatives with its partners. The consortium also had received matching funds from the Texas Cancer Council and had received funds from the Texas Department of Health for training and breast screening.

This alliance has evolved into a dynamic, flexible network that is fully capable of utilizing the resources of its communities. Three examples illustrate this point. First, when funding was reduced, the consortium decided to scale down its plan and provide full service to 12 counties rather than partial service to 36 counties. Second, when the Texas Department of Health rural clinic sites were closed, the communities created their own sites. County hospitals became local providers and contractors with the consortium. Third, when consortium members realized that the mobile mammography van would not be operating by the anticipated start-up date, members decided to provide more outreach community education. When the equipment was available, the communities were more thoroughly prepared for a smoother start-up.

The West Texas Community Care Consortium has filled a vital need in west Texas. The four organizations that collaborate on this successful enterprise have shown their commitment to doing something right the first time, much to the benefit of our entire state. The consortium is indeed a shining example of the true Texas spirit, and it is proof that, as the governor says, "What Texans can dream, Texans can do."

Laura W. Bush
State of Texas, Office of the First Lady

THE COLLABORATIVE PARTNERSHIP

The West Texas Community

The west Texas terrain encompasses dusty mountains, sun-scorched deserts, flatlands extending to the horizon in all directions, picturesque canyons, and rolling, grassy hills. The people of this vast, rugged rural region are as varied and colorful as their land: oil workers, cattle ranchers, cotton and peanut farmers, and migrant laborers. Geographically, the West Texas Community Care Consortium (WTCCC) covers 36 counties spread over 61,428 square miles (roughly one-quarter of Texas, the nation's second largest state). The region's southern boundary is a 300-mile international border shared with Mexico. Twenty-seven states, including New York and Illinois, are smaller than the 36 counties included in this network; 16 counties are large enough to hold Rhode Island.

To people residing outside west Texas, the size of this targeted area may seem overwhelming, unmanageable, and far beyond any traditional definition of "community." However, residents can attest that, despite the extensive land mass, the 36 counties share many characteristics, including geographic challenges, cultural heritages, economic forces, and service needs that are distinct from other areas of Texas. The WTCCC's boundaries conform to two state health and human services regions, which facilitates access to state programs.

Within the WTCCC area, towns are few and far apart. Odessa, the most centrally located town, is 280 miles from El Paso, 153 miles from Alpine, and about 140 miles from both Lubbock and San Angelo. The great distances and lack of urban centers create challenges for health care delivery. For example, women living in Alpine must currently travel 220 miles to El Paso, 153 miles to Odessa, or 362 miles to San Antonio for a simple screening mammogram. Problems caused by distance are magnified by inadequate transportation, illness, or being at high risk for chronic diseases.

The 1.1 million residents in west Texas are roughly 50 percent Hispanic, 40 percent non-Hispanic Caucasian, 5 percent African-American, and 5 percent of other ethnicity. About 125,000 residents are 65 and older, and more than 300,000 are age 40 to 64. Of the 36 counties, 69 percent have fewer than seven people per square mile, with a population density for the entire area at 18 people per square mile.

When comparing rural and urban Texans, rural Texans are generally older and slightly poorer, with less education, higher unemployment, and more dependence on public financing for health services. Following are some relevant socio-demographic characteristics of rural Texans:

- An average rural income is 21 percent lower than urban levels in 1992; 23 percent of rural incomes were at or below the federal poverty level in 1990.
- An average unemployment rate for minorities is 13 percent.
- Of adults, 26 percent have only a high school diploma/general equivalency diploma; 29 percent have some college or a degree (versus 21 percent and 42 percent, respectively, for urban).
- In 1993, 18 percent were without health insurance; more rural employees are without health insurance than in cities.
- In 1993, 13 percent were on Medicaid and 19 percent were on Medicare.

The lack of health facilities and primary care professionals plagues rural Texas—west Texas in particular. According to the Center for Rural Health Initiatives, rural Texans face shortages and maldistribution of health care professionals; a lack of health care services, which lowers the quality of care; a lack of coordination among rural communities, which restricts pooling of resources; and regulatory inflexibility. The center identifies six critical issues for rural areas: provider supply, facilities availability, system integration/coordination, fiscal stabilization, insurance reform, and opportunities for rural representation.

All these issues and problems affect the west Texas community in which the WTCCC operates. For example, one-fourth of the 36 counties have no primary care physicians, and eight have only one or two. Because they have few physicians, 47 percent of the area's counties are designated as health care shortage areas.

- Nine counties do not have a hospital.
- The few public clinics are part-time facilities that offer very limited primary care services.
- Accredited mammography facilities are not available in 30 counties.
- Fifteen counties lack a public transportation system. Two other counties do not serve outlying rural areas.
- The 36-county west Texas area has been divided into four subregions based on geographic considerations and service availability.

The West Texas Community Care Consortium

The WTCCC builds on prior efforts of several organizations that address the health care needs of west Texas. The national community care network (CCN) demonstration program has presented a model of community health and collaboration that inspired these organizations to unite their energies, imaginations, and efforts to reduce barriers to health care in west Texas.

The partnership began with 3 principal organizations and currently includes 11 partners. The WTCCC's partners will be involved in four types of activities: administration, prevention/education, screening/diagnostic services, and treatment/follow-up services. Involvement in community health care is a hallmark of the three primary partners in the WTCCC: the Cancer Consortium of El Paso, the Texas Cancer Council, and Texas Tech University Health Sciences Center and its West Texas Coalition for Cancer Control.

Cancer Consortium of El Paso The Cancer Consortium of El Paso (the Consortium), with its existing network of 34 service providers, 56 community-based health care members, and an executive committee chosen by members from the community, is a model of successful community collaboration. Originally established in 1990 with National Cancer Institute funding, its purpose has been to serve as a coordinating agency to improve the delivery of breast and cervical cancer screening services to low-income women in El Paso County. Today, the Consortium represents 85 percent of the El Paso health care community. (See figure 13-1.)

Prior to the Consortium's formation, El Paso health care providers were competitive and lacking in trust and cooperation, preventing equal access to cancer screening services. The providers lacked a unified system for delivering educational and prevention information to the county's underserved population. A major turning point for the Consortium occurred in 1991 when it was awarded funds from the national Breast and Cervical Cancer Control Program (an outreach education, screening, and diagnostic program currently funded by a grant through the Texas Department of Health and the Texas Cancer Council). As a result of this funding, the Consortium contracts with private physicians and with for-profit and not-for-profit health care providers to offer the highest-quality services with the fewest barriers to access.

In its first year, the Consortium provided Pap smears, mammograms, and diagnostic and follow-up services for 85 women, and developed a central database for tracking. Once an atmosphere of trust developed, dramatic changes occurred in patient service delivery. The number of women reached by the Consortium and its screening and outreach education programs exploded to about 500 in the second year, 4,000 in the third year, and should reach 10,000 in the fourth year. In economic terms, the cooperative effort by the public, private, and volunteer sectors through the Consortium allows the community's limited resources to serve more people and minimizes duplication of services. According to Allen Weikel, executive director of the El Paso Cancer Treatment Center, "Consortium members have found that by acting as a cooperative partnership, they have a much greater impact on the health care practices of El Paso women than if each agency acts independently."

Texas Cancer Council Strengthening cancer prevention and control efforts throughout Texas was the goal of the Texas legislature when it created the Texas Cancer Council (the Council) in 1985. The Council provides state funds to spearhead innovative responses to cancer prevention, screening, and diagnostic service needs. This state agency's unique strength is its ability to forge partnerships among public, private, and volunteer agencies in a multifaceted, collaborative attack on cancer. The Council's philosophy is to foster collaboration so that limited resources can serve more people, thereby minimizing duplication of efforts. The diverse programs funded by the Texas Cancer Council are organized into six categories: public education, professional education, early detection, information and referral, community cancer networks, and access to care/quality of life. During 1994, the Council provided cancer prevention

FIGURE 13-1. Breast and Cervical Cancer Screening Form

Contractor No.:	Clinic No.:	Visit Date:	Chart Number:	CD Number:

PATIENT INFORMATION

Last	First MI	Maiden	Race (please mark one or more) ☐ 1 White ☐ 4 Asian ☐ 2 Black ☐ 5 American Indian ☐ 3 Hispanic ☐ 6 Other/Unknown
Address		Social Security Number	______ (specify other)
City / State / Zip		Birth Date / Age	
Day Phone ( ) —	Night Phone ( ) —	Did the client graduate . . . ☐ High School ☐ College ☐ Neither	Referral Source ☐ Self ☐ Provider ☐ Other ☐ Unknown

BREAST CANCER HISTORY

1. Has the client ever had a mammogram before?
   ☐ 1 Yes → Approximate date: __/__/__
   ☐ 2 No (please estimate if not sure)
2. Did the breast symptoms (lump, discharge, abnormal test, etc.) lead to this visit? ☐ Yes ☐ No ☐ Unkn
3. Has the client ever had breast cancer? ☐ Yes ☐ No ☐ Unkn
4. Does the client have a breast implant? ☐ Yes ☐ No ☐ Unkn

CLINICAL BREAST EXAM (CBE)

5. Did the client receive a clinical breast exam this visit?
   ☐ 1 Yes ☐ 2 No, client refused ☐ 3 No, other
6. If yes, when was the CBE performed? __/__/__
7. What were the results of this CBE?
   ☐ 1 Normal
   ☐ 2 Abnormal (discrete palpable mass, nipple discharge, nipple or areolar scaliness, skin dimpling or retraction, etc.)
   ☐ 3 Other ______

SCREENING MAMMOGRAM

8. Did the client receive a screening mammogram?
   ☐ 1 Yes ☐ 2 No, client refused ☐ 3 No, other
9. When was the mammogram performed? __/__/__
10. When were the mammogram results received? __/__/__
11. What were the results of the screening mammogram?
    ☐ 1 Negative
    ☐ 2 Benign findings
    ☐ 3 Probably benign, short term follow-up recommended
    ☐ 4 Suspicious abnormality, biopsy should be considered
    ☐ 5 Highly suggestive of malignancy
    ☐ 6 Ascertainment incomplete, additional studies needed
    ☐ 7 Unsatisfactory, film could not be interpreted by radiologist
    ☐ 8 Results unknown (done elsewhere)
12. What was the funding source for the screening mammogram?
    ☐ 1 CDC ☐ 2 Other ______ (please specify)
13. Where was the mammogram performed?
    Agency: ______
    City: ______ Zip: ______

CERVICAL CANCER HISTORY

15. Has the client ever had a Pap smear before?
    ☐ 1 Yes → Approximate date: __/__/__
    ☐ 2 No (Please estimate if not sure)
16. Has the client ever had cervical dysplasia? ☐ Yes ☐ No ☐ Unkn
17. Has the client ever had cervical cancer? ☐ Yes ☐ No ☐ Unkn
18. Has the client had a hysterectomy? ☐ Yes ☐ No ☐ Unkn
19. If yes, was it for cancer? ☐ Yes ☐ No ☐ Unkn

PAP SMEAR

20. Did the client receive a comprehensive pelvic exam this visit?
    ☐ 1 Yes ☐ 2 No
21. Was the cervix present?
    ☐ 1 Yes (Cervical Pap) ☐ 2 No (Vaginal Pap)
22. Did the client receive a Pap smear?
    ☐ 1 Yes, this visit ☐ 3 No, client refused
    ☐ 2 Yes, but done elsewhere ☐ 4 No, other
23. When was the Pap smear performed? __/__/__
24. When were the Pap smear results received? __/__/__
25. What were the results of the Pap smear?
    ☐ 1 Negative (within normal limits)
    ☐ 2 Infection/Inflammation/Reactive Changes
    ☐ 3 Atypical squamous cells of undet. significance (ASCUS)
    ☐ 4 Low grade SIL (including HPV changes)
    ☐ 5 High grade SIL
    ☐ 6 Squamous cell cancer
    ☐ 7 Other ______
    ☐ 8 Unsatisfactory, results could not be interpreted
    ☐ 9 Results unknown (done elsewhere)
26. What was the funding source for the Pap smear?
    ☐ 1 CDC ☐ 2 Other ______ (please specify)
27. Where was the Pap smear performed?
    Agency: ______
    City: ______ Zip: ______

BREAST CANCER SCREENING FOLLOW-UP STATUS

14. Was the client referred for a diagnostic mammogram, ultrasound, breast biopsy, fine needle aspiration, or other diag. procedure?
    ☐ 1 Yes → Date referred for procedure(s): __/__/__
    ☐ 2 No → Date of next breast screening: __/__/__

CERVICAL CANCER SCREENING FOLLOW-UP STATUS

28. Was the client referred for a colposcopy, cervical biopsy, or other diagnostic procedure for possible cervical cancer?
    ☐ 1 Yes → Date referred for procedure(s): __/__/__
    ☐ 2 No → Date of next cervical screening: __/__/__

services to 540,000 Texans, furnished cancer prevention materials and training for 106,000 health care professionals, and received 71,000 hours of donated service for its prevention efforts.

The Council has supported community cancer networks across the state, ranging from sparse rural counties to major metropolitan areas. These networks use a grassroots coalition approach to create partnerships among health care providers, civic and community organizations, social service agencies, and community leaders to better educate local citizens about cancer prevention and control. Each project has a community-based infrastructure to address local cancer needs. The West Texas Coalition for Cancer Control is a community cancer network project funded by the Council and administered by Texas Tech University Health Sciences Center, which focuses on the west Texas region.

Texas Tech University Health Sciences Center and the West Texas Coalition for Cancer Control A shortage of comprehensive medical care in west Texas prompted the Texas legislature to create the Texas Tech University School of Medicine in 1969. Today this medical school and the Texas Tech University Health Sciences Center provide a regionalized system of medical education and support for health care services through four campuses in Lubbock, Amarillo, Odessa, and El Paso, with more than two dozen clinics and centers. The Texas Tech faculty provides medical consultation that enhances the primary care provided by family physicians and the secondary care offered in area hospitals.

The Texas Tech University Health Sciences Center is a primary referral center for west Texas cancer patients. In conjunction with the Texas Community Oncology Network, a statewide outreach program of the M. D. Anderson Cancer Center in Houston, Texas Tech provides regionalized access to clinical trials, cancer prevention trials, and the benefits of research, which would otherwise not be available outside Houston. In 1992, Texas Tech developed the West Texas Coalition for Cancer Control with the purpose of identifying existing cancer prevention, detection, and treatment services, and developing a regional cancer prevention and control plan for the area covered by the WTCCC.

The Match between This Network's Initiatives and the Community/Partnership

Various organizations have tried to meet the substantial health care needs of people scattered throughout this west Texas region. However, the obstacles are complex and formidable, including isolation of residents and a lack of transportation to services, facilities and health care personnel, financial resources, and education about prevention. The WTCCC believes the only way to make lasting service delivery improvements is through collaboration at local, regional, and state levels, and through flexible service designs that address local educational, economic, and health care resources and needs and account for local geographic and demographic characteristics.

Several of the initial partners have a long-standing history of working collaboratively. The Cancer Consortium of El Paso, Texas Tech University Health Sciences Center, M. D. Anderson Cancer Center, and the Texas Department of Health receive state funds for cancer prevention programs through the Texas Cancer Council and have collaborated on numerous community-based initiatives. Further, representatives of all the initial partners are American Cancer Society volunteers and are actively involved in cancer prevention programs within their local communities.

All the initial partners have strong ties to community health services and closely involve community residents in identifying local needs and implementing local programs. The strong, positive working relationships among the partners, their history of collaboration, and their emphasis on community-based programs facilitated formation of the WTCCC.

PRIOR EFFORTS

The WTCCC partners have many years' experience working in west Texas, particularly in the targeted 36-county area. As the following information will show, these partners were working toward the national CCN's four dimensions long before they were aware of them. In reading about programs of the WTCCC's partners, a history of collaboration will become apparent.

Cancer Consortium of El Paso

The Consortium's primary community health focus is on delivery of prevention/education, screening/diagnostic, and treatment/follow-up services to low-income women in El Paso County. The Consortium has 4 years of experience in conducting outreach to the fifth largest underserved minority population in the United States. With strong collaborative efforts from its 34 community-based health care organizations, the Consortium has developed an influential base of experience in community action and development. The Consortium's original membership of 25 has more than doubled to a current count of 56 members. The Consortium has secured more than $600,000 in funding over a 4-year period for programs to provide low-income women with breast and cervical cancer screening and education.

The "Luces de Salud" (Beacons of Health) project works with the Consortium as a community outreach program. The Luces de Salud office is responsible for volunteer education coordination and countywide scheduling of Pap smears and mammograms through the Consortium's service providers. No-cost cancer screenings are available for those who qualify. The volunteer health care role models and trained lay educators provide community education and distribute a quarterly newsletter, which has increased in circulation from 3,000 to 7,000 homes.

In its third year, the Cancer Consortium provided breast screening services to 1,378 women (63 percent of women 50 and older) and cervical exams to 2,718 (58 percent of women 40 and over). More than 8,000 women have received screening services since the program began in 1991.

This year, new cancer prevention outreach programs are available in senior citizen centers and the Roman Catholic church diocese. These programs will help the Consortium reach its goal of providing cancer screening services to at least 75 percent of El Paso women age 50 and older.

"Focus on Fifty" is a Consortium education module encouraging access to cancer screening services for Hispanic females over the age of 50. The outreach is being conducted by trained volunteer lay educators who themselves are more than 50 years of age. The National Cancer Institute awarded a grant to this program with matching funds from the Texas Cancer Council.

Feedback helps the Consortium to be accountable to the El Paso community. For example, a community cancer survey was conducted in 1989 to determine screening awareness, attitudes, and behaviors among Hispanic women in El Paso. The survey helped the Consortium determine its approach to education and service delivery and established a framework for accountability.

The Cancer Consortium of El Paso is accountable to its community in several other ways. For example, it holds quarterly meetings to address problems and barriers to service delivery, and meetings are held to determine prices for services whenever grant funds are received. These meetings help ensure that the community's scarce resources are used efficiently.

The Consortium considers the needs of its community residents when communicating with them. Before it distributes educational materials such as its newsletter, the readability of the bilingual materials is tested in focus groups so that the wording will be sensitive to shades of meaning used by local Spanish speakers. All materials, including videos, are tested in this manner before public use. The Consortium staff is also accountable to the El Paso community because it is governed by an executive committee whose members represent the county's health care providers.

The community's response to the Consortium's efforts is evident by the positive feedback it has received. The news media have given the Consortium's programs excellent coverage, and it has been approached by individuals and organizations within the community who want to collaborate. For example, physicians in private practice have offered their services, institutions have asked to be partners in applying for grants, and other groups want to coordinate community meetings with the Consortium. The Consortium's strong volunteer base, which has grown from 250 to 400 people, is another indication of the community's support for its programs.

The Consortium's ability to provide a seamless continuum of care has grown as its membership and respect have increased within the El Paso community. The Consortium's successful evolution into an organization that is both a representative of community organizations and a community service provider has helped it move closer to realizing a seamless continuum of cancer prevention and control services in El Paso.

In an effort to reduce barriers to care, such as those caused by financial or referral difficulties, the Consortium follows up its contracts for cancer screening and diagnostic services. Patients with abnormal findings are monitored and helped with referral to tertiary care providers when treatment is needed. The Consortium's computer database tracks patients through the system, ensures payment to providers, and provides any necessary follow-up so patients are not "lost" in a complex health care system. This database provides up-to-date information on screenings, stages at which tumors are discovered, and follow-up treatment with community service providers throughout El Paso. In addition to regularly following up on women using its services, the Consortium monitors the clinics, doctors, and hospitals delivering the service.

The Consortium also meets with migrant lay educators from the Migrant Stream Forum, a national program, to make certain that migrant women passing through the El Paso area obtain screening and learn how to get their test results. The Consortium also cooperates with the migrant program so that funds from the national Breast and Cervical Cancer Control Program are used for any follow-up diagnostic or treatment work that may be required, even if it is outside El Paso County. Lay educators from this national migrant program are currently taking resource management training with the Consortium's community workers so they can help migrant women avoid barriers to service.

The Consortium avoids duplication of materials and efforts to educate women about local programs by collaborating with the National Cancer Institute, the American Cancer Society, and various community groups. Examples of coordination with other agencies include the use of educational media, role models within the community, and production of a newsletter. Consortium members participate in numerous professional medical and health education networks and societies, such as the Texas Community Oncology Network, the Nurse Oncology Education Program, and the Society for Public Health Education.

To manage within fixed resources, the Consortium draws upon the cooperation of public, private, and volunteer sectors. This collaboration has reduced the expense of indigent patients on overburdened not-for-profit institutions and county facilities. For example, funds from the Breast and Cervical Cancer Control Program allow the Consortium to contract with various providers using a standardized cost for screening and diagnostic services. This funding source also is available to the WTCCC for use in the other targeted counties.

The Consortium's community networking efforts have resulted in donated services from the private medical community for treatment, anesthesiology, and hospital space. In addition, private physicians are now providing reduced-cost and free cancer diagnosis and treatment services for low-income Consortium clients. Collaboration is reducing the overall economic impact of cancer on the El Paso community through early diagnosis and education, which allows cancer to be detected at an earlier stage when treatment is less expensive. One significant sign of success in this program is a decrease in late-stage diagnoses made since 1992 as a result of earlier detection.

Texas Cancer Council

The Council's mission is to reduce the human and economic impact of cancer on Texans through the promotion and support of collaborative, innovative, and effective programs and policies for cancer prevention and control. The Council has developed statewide strategic plans and fostered collaborative partnerships among health care providers, community organizations, and cancer survivors to address cancer prevention and control needs at both state and local levels. The Council is an "initiatives" agency, one that provides state funds as seed money to stimulate critically needed cancer services. Council-initiated projects go on to become self-sustaining.

Since its creation in 1985, the Council has initiated a broad array of cancer prevention programs, such as statewide tobacco prevention and control, school health, and skin cancer prevention programs. The Council also has established strong collaborative partnerships to address cancer education needs of physicians, nurses, dentists, dietitians, social workers, and agricultural extension agents. Additionally, the Council has developed innovative grassroots approaches to local community needs through the formation of community cancer networks and culturally relevant prevention programs.

During 1992–93, the Council used a grassroots approach to solicit information and suggestions about breast and cervical cancer service problems through seven public hearings held around Texas. More than 400 participants, including health care providers and a wide variety of consumers, voiced opinions at these meetings, and more than 100 more submitted written testimony. These hearings helped identify needs and solutions pertaining to policy, geographic, economic, educational, cultural, and quality assurance barriers.

West Texas Coalition for Cancer Control

Community health has been the focus of the West Texas Coalition for Cancer Control (the Coalition) since 1992, when the Coalition was developed by the Texas Tech

University Health Sciences Center with Texas Cancer Council funding. Specifically, the Coalition has identified and is seeking to overcome barriers to health care in west Texas communities through analysis of local resources and extensive citizen input. In 1993 and 1994, the Coalition conducted a needs assessment throughout the 36 west Texas counties to determine the extent of the cancer problem and health care resources of this area. The needs assessment included a resource directory, phone surveys, questionnaires, and community focus group meetings.

The resource directory contains county-specific information about available health care services and demographic data. Directories were distributed at community focus group meetings and were mailed to hospitals, clinics, libraries, and various health and community-related groups.

Telephone surveys were conducted with county officials to gather information prior to conducting focus group meetings within local communities. Information collected included the following:

- Each county's current needs and projects in progress to address these needs
- Local opinion about the most serious health problems
- The status of the hospital, if one exists
- Active local community organizations

Approximately 8,000 questionnaires were mailed to rural households in the 36 counties to identify perceived rural population needs. Coalition staff conducted 25 community focus group meetings during 1994 to further determine priority problems in the counties. Notices were printed in local newspapers to invite the public. More than 300 local citizens participated in the meetings, including representatives from schools, churches, hospitals, businesses, and community organizations. Aided by information collected through the needs assessments, the communities developed county-specific action plans to address priority issues. In response to these plans, the Coalition staff members are focusing their efforts on the needs deemed highest priority by local citizens.

Since its formation, the Coalition has worked within west Texas communities to provide services that are responsive to the needs of local residents. It has been accountable to these communities not only by reporting the results of their needs assessments and involving citizens in identification of local solutions, but also by responding to priority issues identified by local citizens. For example, the Coalition has hired two part-time health coordinators to provide cancer education information and emphasize the importance of cancer screenings to rural residents.

In December 1994, the Coalition surveyed health care providers, county judges, school nurses, and other community leaders again to see if there was consensus of support for solutions to the lack of mammography services. This survey confirmed earlier findings and ultimately led to recent efforts to obtain mammography screening services for the west Texas community.

The Texas Cancer Council and Texas Tech University Health Sciences Center have been negotiating a long-term solution to the lack of mammography services in the 36-county area. At this writing, it appears that the Council will provide Texas Tech with funds to purchase a mobile mammography van and that Texas Tech will manage the provision of local breast cancer screening services. Plans are for the new services to be piloted in five counties near Odessa beginning in early 1996, and then expanded to other counties within the WTCCC's region as resources permit. The initiative actively involves local community hospitals and American Cancer Society volunteers. The mobile van will be stationed at community hospitals, and follow-up diagnostic and treatment services will be provided through local hospitals wherever feasible.

The Texas Department of Health and the American Cancer Society

Two other WTCCC partners, the Texas Department of Health and the American Cancer Society, have been actively involved in community health projects, including information gathering, for many years. For example, in 1987, the Texas division of the American Cancer Society analyzed the screening behavior of more than half of the 64,459 women served through the Texas Breast Screening Project. Since 1987, the Texas Department of Health has gathered information from Texas households through residential phone surveys under its Texas Behavioral Risk Factor Surveillance System. Additionally, both agencies deliver community-based services.

MOVING TOWARD THE VISION

The Visioning Process

A variety of state and local organizations have tried to address the unique health care problems of this vast rural west Texas area. The partners in the WTCCC have worked individually and in collaboration with other groups to overcome the formidable barriers to health care delivery that relate to rural isolation and poverty in west Texas. Unfortunately, these efforts fell short of expectations.

When the initial partners became aware of the vision, challenges, and opportunities presented by the national CCN demonstration program, they recognized new perspectives on how to broaden and attain the goals they had already been working toward. The WTCCC visioning process has provided a unifying force to consolidate these varied efforts so that available resources can be used more efficiently. In addition, the visioning process has actively involved local citizens and used a grassroots approach to creative problem solving.

The initial partners saw that the addition of coordinating personnel, a broad database for tracking patients, local steering committees to get in touch with the "grass roots" within local communities, and a unifying vision would permit them to use their existing expertise and materials to accomplish goals that had been elusive in the past.

Several important events led to the creation of the WTCCC in early 1995. In October 1994, the Texas Cancer Council expressed serious concern about the lack of mammography services in the 36-county region. The Council began exploring with Texas Tech University Health Sciences Center the possibility of these state agencies jointly responding to this need.

In January 1995, the Texas Cancer Council sponsored a grant-writing workshop for Council-funded projects, including the Cancer Consortium of El Paso and the West Texas Coalition for Cancer Control. These agencies discussed the lack of mammography services in west Texas and realized that they had complementary expertise and experience to address the problem.

In February 1995, representatives of these three organizations met with a representative of Ward Memorial Hospital who gave input from a new dimension—that of a rural hospital. The representative also offered to solicit participation from other community hospitals and county officials.

In early March, the Consortium, the Texas Cancer Council, and the American Cancer Society met to discuss the outcome of a network of telephone calls to community leaders in the region and to develop lists of current and potential partners. At a meeting in Odessa later that March, the subregions were reconfigured. The partners also clarified the WTCCC's structure and confirmed individual responsibilities and commitments.

The process of building the WTCCC was a direct result of the networking, collaboration, and communication that the Texas Cancer Council advocates among cancer service providers. The Council also encourages its projects to use resources wisely to reduce duplication and avoid waste of state funds.

The WTCCC has become a reality in a very short time because the partners were already working independently toward similar goals. The membership increased as more agencies with similar philosophies and complementary expertise were identified and signed on to support the WTCCC's objectives.

The Vision of the WTCCC

- *WTCCC Vision:* To achieve a west Texas in which residents are free of needless suffering from chronic disease and are active partners in a prevention-oriented health care system that is integrated, comprehensive, and nondiscriminatory
- *Subregions:* Rio Grande, Permian Basin, Pecos Valley, Concho Valley
- *Key Personnel:* Community service advocates, health education outreach coordinators, steering committees, facilitators for steering committees

The WTCCC envisions a west Texas in which residents are free of needless suffering from chronic disease and are active partners in a prevention-oriented health care system that is integrated, comprehensive, and nondiscriminatory. It is designed with the intention that high-quality health care should be easily available and accessible to all people living in west Texas regardless of gender, race, ethnicity, ability to pay, religion, sexual orientation, education, age, or place of residence. High-quality health care encompasses the following elements:

- Emphasis on the prevention and early detection of disease
- Individual responsibility for one's own health, including an awareness of personal risk, prevention behaviors, compliance with screening guidelines, and informed involvement in treatment and rehabilitation planning
- A process of collaborative planning and evaluation to create and sustain locally available programs tailored to the needs of local citizens and supported by local citizens, service providers, and dynamic community coalitions
- Up-to-date local chronic disease screening, diagnosis, and treatment services available at convenient times/locations in conjunction with other health, education, and human services
- Affordable services that meet state and national quality standards

Initial Partners' Roles Representatives from each organization and subregion will meet bimonthly to collaborate on administrative details. See table 13-1.

TABLE 13-1. Initial Partners' Roles

Initial Partners	*Administration*	*Prevention/Education*	*Screening/Diagnosis Services*	*Treatment Follow-up Services*
Cancer Consortium of El Paso, Inc.	• CCN Grant Administration • Facilitate Rio Grande steering committee • Supervise Rio Grande community service advocate • Community service advocate training • Media campaign • Technical assistance to all steering committees	• Public awareness campaign • Focus test education materials • Speakers • Training workshop	• Supervise Rio Grande community service advocate • BCCCP	• Database • Follow-up • Staging
Texas Cancer Council	• Matching funds	Projects: Tobacco, School Health, Agriculture Extension, Professional Education, Minority Health	• Money for breast cancer diagnostic services (if <200% poverty level)	
Texas Tech University Health Sciences Center	• Mobile mammography services • TCC grant administration • CCN grant evaluation • Community service advocate training • Supervise health education outreach coordinators • Technical assistance to all steering committees	• Health education outreach coordinators • Public awareness	• Mobile mammography services • Oncology consultation to local physicians	• Oncology consultation to local physicians
American Cancer Society	• Donate office space for two community service advocates and two health coordinators • Supervise Concho Valley and Permian Basin community service advocates	• Education materials • Speakers for all subregions		• Road to Recovery transportation (where available) • Patient support services
Ward Memorial	• Supervise Pecos Valley community service advocate • Facilitate Pecos Valley steering committee	• Community education in Ward County • Public awareness	• Screening site	• Treatment facility
Pecos Hospital	• Supervise Pecos Valley community service advocate • Facilitate Pecos Valley steering committee	• Community education in Pecos County	• Screening site	• Treatment facility
Texas Department of Health		• Put Prevention Into Practice sponsor	• Adult health/chronic disease services (where available) • Screening site • Federal breast and cervical cancer funds (<200% poverty level)	
M. D. Anderson			• Oncology consultation • Intensive physician/nurse professional training site	• Oncology consultation • Treatment facility

Network Service Delivery The WTCCC serves Texas Health and Human Services regions 9 and 10 by dividing the area into four subregions: Rio Grande, Pecos Valley, Permian Basin, and Concho Valley. As envisioned by the WTCCC, each subregion will have a community service advocate, a health education outreach coordinator, and a local steering committee and steering committee facilitators. The steering committees will be composed of community representatives who are knowledgeable about local health and human service needs, such as county judges, local business or law enforcement representatives, educators, and other local residents. Each steering committee will be guided by a team of facilitators who will solicit participation and initiate committee activities.

The WTCCC's service delivery approach focuses on wellness, addresses priority needs of west Texas residents, and builds on existing resources. Key elements are a continuum of care, referrals, data sharing, subregion and urban services, community service advocates, health education outreach coordinators, and public awareness and outreach.

The service priorities are divided into the following short-term objectives (for 1995 to 1997) and long-term objectives (for 1998 and beyond):

- *Short term:* Cancer prevention and control with priority to breast and cervical cancer for women without locally available services; and programs relating to skin cancer, tobacco use, and nutrition education for all residents
- *Long term:* Comprehensive chronic disease prevention services for all residents

To establish a continuum of care, the WTCCC will establish links between service providers, offer a full array of services from prevention through treatment, and reduce barriers to care. It will also improve the referral system by increasing awareness of available services (including the cost, hours, and appointment procedures) and facilitating the appointment process. By sharing patient data, the WTCCC will increase communication among health care providers about patients' medical histories and service needs. This will lead to an increased continuity of care and improved quality of service.

The WTCCC will seek to increase positive health practices; use of cancer screening, diagnostic, and treatment services, if available locally; and routine use of Put Prevention into Practice (PPIP) guidelines by local providers. Access to cancer diagnostic and treatment services in urban areas will be increased for citizens who do not have locally available services.

Community service advocates will act as advocates for citizens, facilitate transportation and access to services, and make referrals to existing services. Health education outreach coordinators, to be funded by a Texas Cancer Council grant to Texas Tech, will develop and implement health promotion programs. They also will assist the community service advocates in implementing public awareness campaigns, scheduling appointments, and facilitating transportation services. These personnel will be competent in Spanish as subregion needs dictate. The public awareness/outreach campaign will be designed to increase awareness of cancer, health promotion, and screening services and the use of PPIP personal health guides.

Put Prevention into Practice is a campaign developed by the U.S. Department of Health and Human Services to improve the use of prevention practices in primary health care. The Texas Department of Health and the Texas Academy for Family Physicians are providing PPIP materials and technical assistance to change harmful health habits, increase screening and immunizations, and increase the use of proper medications for preventive purposes.

There are specially designed PPIP materials for the physician, the patient, and the office staff, along with guidelines for their use. The physician's handbook gives the physician guidelines for delivering age- and gender-appropriate preventive services. Patients receive a personal health guide reminding them when to request preventive services, follow through with screening referrals, and return for appointments. The office staff's materials include patient flow sheets, chart stickers, and reminder postcards to help track preventive services for individual patients.

Network Goals and Organization The WTCCC will implement the following five goals of administration, prevention/education, screening/diagnostic services, treatment/follow-up, and planning/development. Roles of WTCCC partners in fostering achievement of the goals are described as follows.

Administration

Goal: Efficiently coordinate a network of wellness and prevention services for all residents of west Texas.

- *Program Management:* The Cancer Consortium of El Paso and Texas Tech will handle overall administration of the initiative and facilitate training of the community service advocates. Patients' appointments will be scheduled through the coordinated efforts of the community service advocates with the assistance of the local health education outreach coordinators.

  Statistics on services provided in each subregion will be collected by community service advocates in cooperation with the Cancer Consortium and Texas Tech. The media campaign will be the responsibility of the Consortium, and program evaluation is the responsibility of Texas Tech.

  The American Cancer Society will provide office space for two community service advocates and two community health coordinators. The community service advocate for the Rio Grande subregion will use office space at the Cancer Consortium of El Paso, and the remaining community service advocate will use office space provided by Pecos Valley steering committee members.

  Outcome evaluation will provide information about the degree to which the program is successful in building a seamless continuum of care and in helping to ultimately reduce morbidity and mortality in west Texas. Process evaluation will identify factors affecting collaboration, citizen involvement, and overall satisfaction with the WTCCC. Information on the number of people reached or served by the WTCCC will be generated quarterly through reports from its database.

  Following are some of the questions that will be addressed in the evaluation:

  – What percentage of the population's behavior changed to practice preventive health care?
  – What are the successful elements of prevention programs for high-risk rural populations?
  – What was the effectiveness of recruitment practice for community groups and individual participants?
  – What was the percentage of participation by WTCCC partners and community groups?

—What was the percentage of the population that was reached during the project?

- *Staff Supervision:* The community service advocates will be supervised by local steering committees in the subregions. The health education outreach coordinators will be supervised by Texas Tech University Health Sciences Center, with input from the local steering committees.
- *Fiscal Management:* Matching funds for the grants will be provided by the Texas Cancer Council. The administration of the Texas Cancer Council grant for salaries and benefits for the community health coordinators will be handled through Texas Tech. Participants in each region's county steering committees will assume partial support of the community service advocate, thereby creating ownership of this community effort by the participants:

  —Year 1 (1995–96): 100 percent grant supported

  —Year 2 (1996–97): 66 percent grant supported

  —Year 3 (1997–98): 33 percent grant supported

  Office space and administrative support will be provided by community groups on an in-kind basis.
- *Community Affiliations/Volunteer Coordination:* Technical assistance to all steering committees will be provided by the Cancer Consortium and Texas Tech. Staff support to steering committees in each subregion will be provided by community service advocates.

  Membership on the steering committees will be facilitated by the following:

  —*Rio Grande Subregion:* The Cancer Consortium, Big Bend Regional Medical Center, the Texas Department of Health, Presidio Family Health Center, and Texas Tech

  —*Pecos Valley Subregion:* Ward Memorial Hospital, Pecos Hospital, and Texas Tech

  —*Permian Basin Subregion:* The American Cancer Society and Texas Tech

  —*Concho Valley Subregion:* Kimble County Hospital, the American Cancer Society, and Texas Tech

  Transportation services will be provided by the American Cancer Society's Road to Recovery program (where available). Community service advocates and health education outreach coordinators will facilitate transportation services if not readily available.

Prevention/Education Services

Goal: Educate west Texas residents about the importance of lifelong wellness, emphasizing preventive care.

The Texas Cancer Council supports numerous statewide initiatives in the area of prevention education, among them the Office of Smoking and Health, the Comprehensive School Health Network, the Agricultural Extension Service, professional education networks, and minority health programs. The WTCCC will collaborate with all of these projects to expand health promotion services in the area.

The health education outreach coordinators, assisted by the community service advocates, will develop and implement breast cancer education outreach programs to prepare the community for mammography services and assist with local implementation of public awareness campaigns throughout the 36-county region. They will also conduct cancer prevention education programs in schools, workplaces, community gatherings, and business groups; expand cancer prevention information within established health fairs; and organize health fairs in counties without them. Education materials and speakers will be provided by the American Cancer Society. The PPIP program will be promoted among local physicians by the Texas Department of Health and the Texas Academy of Family Physicians.

Screening/Diagnosis Services

Goal: Provide screening and diagnostic services to residents throughout the 36-county west Texas region.

Community hospitals will serve as sites for screening and diagnostic services, as will Texas Department of Health clinics. Breast and cervical cancer services for women under the 200 percent poverty level will be financed through the Texas Cancer Council (state funds) and the Texas Department of Health (federal funds). The WTCCC will obtain free or reduced-cost services from local partners when residents do not have health insurance or do not qualify for government programs.

Oncology consultation will be available from M. D. Anderson Cancer Center and the Texas Tech University Health Sciences Center. Mobile mammography services will be facilitated by the Texas Cancer Council, and Texas Tech cancer prevention and detection training for health care professionals will be available through the Texas Cancer Council and M. D. Anderson Cancer Center.

Community service advocates will facilitate timely appointments for citizens, promote utilization of mammography services, facilitate transportation services, and track service delivery barriers and needs. The community service advocates and health education outreach coordinators will share office space, thereby increasing communication and coordination.

Treatment/Follow-Up Services

Goal: Provide basic treatment and follow-up services to residents throughout the 36-county west Texas region.

Patients requiring treatment or follow-up services after their screening and diagnosis will have oncology consultation available from M. D. Anderson Cancer Center and the Texas Tech University Health Sciences Center. Facilities that will be available for treatment include local hospitals, treatment centers, and M. D. Anderson Cancer Center.

The community service advocates will work to ensure continuity of care for patients requiring further medical treatment. They will assist with referrals for follow-up services; facilitate timely appointments; and track service delivery barriers and needs.

The health education outreach coordinators will assist the community service advocates in facilitating transportation to treatment services. In addition, the American Cancer Society provides patient support services and, in some communities, transportation services through its Road to Recovery program.

Planning and Development

Goal: Include local community members in developing a comprehensive network of health care services in west Texas, locate funding to extend services, and evaluate the effectiveness of the WTCCC's initiatives.

The Cancer Consortium of El Paso will have primary responsibility for facilitating achievement of this goal. Outcomes anticipated for each year are as follows:

- *First-Year Plan (9/95–8/96):* Service linkages and commitments are scheduled to be established along with the data collection and sharing system. Data collection and medical equipment are scheduled to be in place and accredited, and breast and cervical cancer services are scheduled to be expanded. Steering committees are planned to be formed and functioning. The design of the public awareness campaign and the evaluation are scheduled to be completed. The awareness campaign is scheduled to be implemented.

  By the end of the first year, the WTCCC plans to accomplish the following four major objectives:

  —Provide mammography screening services to 25 percent of the women aged 40 and older in the 36-county area—a population of 216,851, according to 1993 data from the Texas Cancer Data Center.

  —Increase service linkages within the area by 25 percent over the number in the initial partnership.

  —Through proper follow-up procedures, ensure that 90 percent of all patients receive necessary services.

  —Reduce barriers to service for 25 percent of the patients. The baseline population includes WTCCC patients identified with problems caused by lack of transportation, insurance, or culturally sensitive materials.

- *Second-Year Plan (9/96–8/97):* Cancer screening/diagnostic services are scheduled to be delivered while the public awareness campaign is in progress. Data collection/sharing of information and the evaluation is expected to take place. During this period, the WTCCC plans to begin broadening its focus to include diseases other than cancer.

  By the end of the second year, the WTCCC plans to reach 40 percent of its women with mammography services, increase service linkages 40 percent over the original level, ensure follow-up for 95 percent of patients needing additional services, and reduce barriers to service by 40 percent.

- *Third-Year Plan (9/97–8/98):* Services are scheduled to continue to be expanded to include chronic diseases other than cancer by implementing PPIP. Commitments for funding to continue the program will be explored, and the evaluation is expected to be completed.

  By the end of the third year, the WTCCC plans to reach 65 percent of its women with mammography services, increase service linkages 65 percent over the original level, ensure follow-up for 98 percent of patients needing additional services, and reduce barriers to service by 65 percent.

SUMMARY OF NOTABLE PROGRESS

During the WTCCC's first year of existence, a firm foundation has been laid for outreach efforts in the targeted communities. This accomplishment is remarkable for several reasons: the size of the service area, the area's prior lack of infrastructure, and the challenge of unifying the community around a common vision. The WTCCC's initiatives fall into four categories: (1) requesting and receiving matching/additional funding, (2) clarifying partners' roles and responsibilities, (3) organizing the communities, and (4) training medical professionals.

During the first quarter, the WTCCC acted on the first three of these initiatives. In addition to receiving the anticipated matching funds from the Texas Cancer Council, the WTCCC requested and received funds from the Texas Department of Health/Breast and Cervical Cancer Control Program. These supplementary funds support breast and cervical screening for indigent patients and provider training.

The major partners' meetings focused on scheduling of the mammography van, as well as on the roles and responsibilities of the partners. Meetings in the Pecos Valley and Rio Grande Valley subregions focused on development of steering committees, service delivery, and plans for hiring the community service advocates.

This careful early planning allowed the WTCCC to not only meet but exceed its projected timetable during successive quarters. As the WTCCC approached its first anniversary, it had gained experience in community networking, problem solving, and responding to unforeseen challenges. One challenge was how to overcome the closings of the Texas Department of Health's rural clinics in the subregions, because they were our intended service delivery sites. Approaching the local county hospitals who were frustrated by the state's actions, the CCN plan was surprisingly well received. We learned that although each county has its own political personality and focus, once again they all agreed on the central vision of providing a needed service to their community through cooperation and collaboration. The local steering committee is the force behind the vision. The community service advocate is the energy that keeps things going.

The steering committee members represent each county in this way:

- For a county population of 0 to 1,000, one member is appointed by county judge.
- For a county population of 1,000 to 5,000, one member is appointed by county judge, and one is a community member.
- For populations over 5,000, one member is appointed by county judge, and two are community members.

Within the local communities, the appointment of steering committee members proceeded smoothly. With their input, the community service advocate position evolved from one community service advocate per six-county subregion to three appointments in the Pecos Valley subregion and two appointments in the Rio Grande subregion, giving them much better networking capabilities and improved service delivery. We now have a web of five computers networked to communicate across hundreds of miles of west Texas and contacts at each site to see a patient through the barriers of an unfamiliar health care system.

The community service advocates are now less dependent on our salary dollars and are a permanent fixture in their community. The steering committee believed that they had someone in their community already in place and were willing to forfeit the 100 percent salary for one person, and split that salary three ways to supplement the additional work these individuals would be expected to do. This ensures that when the funding stops, we will not lose ground in the vision for community care.

Our first-year goal was to bring mobile mammography service to rural west Texas. The introduction of the mammography van became a media/community event. Laura W. Bush, the First Lady of Texas, was among the dignitaries who attended the van's ribbon-cutting ceremony in Odessa. Each of the county hospitals also had an open house to introduce the van to their community. The WTCCC stepped up training sessions on implementing screening services for the local communities, and training sessions for medical professionals were among the highlights of its efforts. The Nurse Oncology Education Program of the Texas Nurses Association coordinated a 2-day training workshop for regional registered nurses in May. Twenty nurses from the WTCCC contractors received training on clinical breast exams and Pap smears at this workshop. Prior to this training, a nurse practitioner from each subregion was sent by the WTCCC to attend cancer screening training at M. D. Anderson Cancer Center. In one subregion, an advanced nurse practitioner was sent to the community to cover the duties of the regional nurse practitioner who attended this training. These individuals provided a week of outreach education and adult health screenings for the Rio Grande subregion.

The WTCCC is also planning a physician's training workshop in breast and cervical cancer control in El Paso. Physicians from New Mexico, Arizona, and the 36 west Texas counties are being invited to this workshop, with continuing medical education credits provided.

Strong community support, an efficient project plan and timeline, and reliable partners are factors that helped the WTCCC build a strong working network that will enable it to carry out its ambitious plans for the second and third years of the CCN demonstration program.

This model is an attempt to duplicate the WTCCC process that has been ongoing in the El Paso community since its inception in 1987 and the evolution into a 501(c)(3) by 1993. The bylaws were developed by the Executive Steering Committee (board of directors) and a volunteer attorney. The membership is open to the community. The Executive Steering Committee is representative of the membership through nomination and vote, and the members hold staggered terms to ensure continuity. The administrative staff members are selected by the Executive Steering Committee and work solely for the community mission. They are allowed no vote to ensure no bias of provider or member. The administrative office is responsible for tracking all patients who receive services through the WTCCC provider group. The tracking system and provider liaison is the reason no patient has been lost to follow-up in 6 years. Although our case management program is only 2 years old, our reputation for service delivery has grown in the community, where we are receiving referrals from institutional and private-sector providers for those patients who have little or no resources as well as those who simply need advocacy support.

We know this can be duplicated in rural west Texas because the rural communities are already resourceful and understand the value of networking. They are able to see the benefit of having the ability to refer to one another to maintain their patient base, and refer outside their community only for extensive services unavailable in their community. However, the referral must ensure that those patients return to the community after the procedure has been delivered. This understanding aids in the development of relationships involving trust and cooperation. This is the seed to a successful consortium building we hope to nurture in rural west Texas.

Contact: Pat Graham-Casey
West Texas Community Care Consortium
6024 Gateway East, Suite 2A
El Paso, TX 79905
Phone: (915) 771-6305
Fax: (915) 771-0755

PART IV

Rural County Networks

The village had institutionalized all human functions in forms of low intensity. . . . Participation was high and organization was low. This is the formula for stability.

—Marshall McLuhan (1911–80), Canadian communications theorist

Change means movement. Movement means friction. Only in the frictionless vacuum of a nonexistent abstract world can movement or change occur without that abrasive friction of conflict.

—Saul Alinsky (1909–72), U.S. radical activist

INTRODUCTION

In smaller communities, people often already know the doctors or nurses who work in the emergency room. People are also more likely to have communicated with them in the past for reasons other than the fact that they work in the emergency room. The channels of communication people share in smaller communities often serve, in other words, *multiple functions.* They chat at church, plan at the PTA, and organize at the Rotary, in addition to providing services in the emergency room.

Having pre-existent, multifunction communication channels with others in the community offers a number of advantages. Finding the right person to work with on a specific goal is easier, since potential partners and their social roles are already known. Imagining, designing, and implementing new functions is easier, as these can simply overlay existing goals. Pushing through difficult moments in relationships can be facilitated by the fact that conflict over one set of goals is ameliorated by history and positive feelings about other goals. Since connections between individuals tend to rest on personal knowledge, institutional directives and boundaries represent less concrete barriers. As a result of these kinds of characteristics, there has been, in fact, substantial experimentation in community change processes in smaller communities, especially rural communities.

At the same time, however, these same qualities can present different kinds of problems. A long and storied historical knowledge about individuals or institutions can prejudice one against considering them as potential partners. If a set of beliefs and expectations about future possibilities is widely enough held, they can inhibit the development of new ideas or visions for the future. Accidentally or deliberately, excluding certain individuals or institutions from work toward specific goals is certain to catch their attention, and possibly lead to damaging backlash.

Perhaps the most significant characteristic of rural county communities is the weak resource base, especially with regard to institutional resources. There may be few or no institutions with the capacity to launch initiatives, even initiatives with low price tags. In many rural counties, there are no major locally based employers, no philanthropies, and few strong ties to regional or state level institutions. The institutions that do exist locally may not be able to draw on the variety and depth of expertise that many local health reform initiatives require. And rural America is disproportionately poor, underemployed, and underinsured.

But necessity often is the mother of invention. Experimentation to reconfigure health care delivery in the face of dwindling resources is old news in many rural communities. While much of this experimentation may occur on a small scale, it can represent major, sustainable change for the local area.

At first blush, these smaller scale efforts may make governance and management appear easier. But demands on the time and resources of both providers and other community organizations may be greater, as there is likely to be less "excess capacity" within a county system. Calling on the same leaders, over and over, for economic development, health care improvement, youth engagement, church functions, recreational activities, and so on, can lead to false starts and visible disappointments.

The following are some questions you may wish to consider when reading about rural county efforts. What do rural county efforts do to take advantage of the natural strengths of a small and multifunction communication network? What strategies help evolving community care networks with a rural county scope to overcome long-held biases and to avoid groupthink? How have the partnerships described here managed the pool of local leadership? How are difficult-to-find and expensive outside resources identified, and what does it take to manage them well? What practices help these partnerships balance their low level of resources with their high level of communication efficiency, without leaving unfulfilled hopes time and again?

Three rural county community care networks are highlighted. Each encompasses one entire rural county, and no more. The Community Health Partnership for Tioga County, PA, recognized the need to address broad community concerns comprehensively, nudging them to utilize many community strengths or face widespread social and economic deterioration. While initially integrating the delivery system, they are now embarking on a new phase with a broader scope, enabling recruitment of key community stakeholders. They will work to further reduce health delivery barriers, are developing clinical management protocols within a rural managed care system, and expect to coordinate the collection and use of patient care data throughout the community. The El Dorado Wellness Partnership of California represents a public–private partnership focusing on community mapping, assessment, and growing the base of local leadership. Seeking to improve access and continuity, the partnership has been planning a primary care center. The center will physically integrate medical care, as well as other health, health education, and social services. The care is integrated through comprehensive patient case management, using a system of assigned community advocates. Joint management of the center by the health department and the hospital takes advantage of the available community resources. The Community Health Plan of the Siskiyous is in an isolated area of northern California that has seen a substantial influx of early retirees from larger population centers. The partnership is developing a plan to reduce health insurance costs for employers. They are also expanding access to preventive services for low-income patients and creating a coordinated continuum of senior services. The Grundy County Health Commission in Iowa integrates health care services within a rural Iowa county in order to foster a total continuum of care. A partnership with two "urban hospitals" in nearby Waterloo, IA, provides cost-effective services to the community.

14

The Tioga County Partnership for Community Health

Executive Summary

Tioga County is located in north central Pennsylvania. Its northern boundary is adjacent to the southern boundary of New York State. The county is rural and sparsely populated. Its 40,000 people live in small communities whose populations range from a few hundred to 4,000. The economy of Tioga County is always struggling, and there are too many low-income families. Health and Human Services are uneven in terms of availability. The Tioga County Partnership for Community Health serves the entire county.

The Tioga County Partnership for Community Health consists of 125 citizens who represent themselves and the agencies/businesses/institutions of the county. The original partners were the Laurel Health System and the Tioga County Health and Human Services Agencies. The partnership has expanded to include other health care agencies, social service groups, economic development organizations, private businesses, and educational institutions. The structure of the partnership is straightforward: Six work groups, each with a mission statement and goals, carry out the initiatives of the partnership. The chairs of the work groups and the cochairs of the total partnership serve as an executive committee, which may be compared to a steering committee. Simply stated, the initiatives of the partnership relate to the following themes:

1. Youth
2. The elderly
3. Mental health
4. Community and family awareness
5. Health and human services
6. The creation of an ideal health care system

Key lessons learned by the partnership are the following:

1. The people of our county are seriously interested in health care services. The return rate of a 31-page survey instrument (see figure 14-1) was over 75 percent.
2. The major health problem identified by our citizens was employment.
3. There are gaps in services provided to the youth and the elderly.
4. Many health care services exist in the county. However, many people (including health care professionals) are unaware of some of them.
5. It is possible to create a cooperative environment within the health care service industry.
6. Even when services exist, the underserved population is difficult to penetrate.

The Tioga County Partnership for Community Health is now in the third phase of its operation.

Rod C. Kelchner, Chairman
President, Mansfield University

THE COLLABORATIVE PARTNERSHIP

The Community

Tioga County and its surrounding area is an extremely rural, ethnically homogenous region, with minimal population fluctuation. Its mountains are included in the Appalachians and are part of the Allegheny Plateau, with flat-topped hills and steep valleys. Agriculture is the main industry, with 33 percent of the land area dedicated to farming. Woodlands account for 64 percent of the land, and only 3 percent is designated as urbanized. Tourism is the next leading source of revenue. Minimal light industry exists within the area as a result of existing transportation inadequacies. There is no mass transportation system. Travel is chiefly by automobile on circuitous roads. Winters are often severe, and roads can be treacherous.

The geographic service area of the Tioga County Partnership for Community Health (TCPCH) and portions of several surrounding counties covers some 1,500 square miles. The area is dominated by large townships with small communities that are designated as health professional shortage areas and medically underserved areas. According to 1990 census figures, Tioga County's current population is 41,126 and has remained stable. The peripheral population within the service area is estimated to be an additional 8,000 individuals.

The lack of significant industrial employment opportunities in this rural area has resulted in a 1991 unemployment rate of 10.4 percent, which is higher than the Pennsylvania unemployment rate of 6.7 percent. During fiscal year 1988–89, the number of unduplicated persons eligible for medical assistance in Tioga County represented 10.4 percent of the population. The 1989 average annual wage for a family of four in Tioga County was $16,359. According to the 1980 census, 14.7 percent of the population is below 100 percent of the federal poverty guidelines; 20.9 are below 125 percent. During 1990, the user mix of the local community health center network, Laurel Health Center, showed that 53 percent of its patients were within 200 percent of the federal poverty level guidelines.

FIGURE 14-1. Excerpts from the Tioga County Health Survey

Your Health Care

The following questions ask about the health services you receive and the health plan covering these services.

31. Thinking about your own health care, how would you rate the following?

(circle one number on each line)

	Poor	Fair	Good	Very Good	Excellent
a. Convenience of location where you go for health care	1	2	3	4	5
b. Availability of transportation	1	2	3	4	5
c. Hours when the office is open	1	2	3	4	5
d. Access to the care of a specialist if you need it	1	2	3	4	5
e. Access to hospital care if you need it	1	2	3	4	5
f. Arrangements for making appointments for medical care by phone	1	2	3	4	5
g. Length of time spent waiting at an office to see the doctor or nurse	1	2	3	4	5
h. Length of time you wait between making an appointment for routine care and the day of your visit	1	2	3	4	5
i. Availability of medical information or advice by phone	1	2	3	4	5
j. Access to medical care whenever you need it	1	2	3	4	5
k. Getting prescriptions filled	1	2	3	4	5

(Continued on next page)

FIGURE 14-1. (Continued)

32. Thinking about your own health care, how would you rate the following?

(circle one number on each line)

	Poor	Fair	Good	Very Good	Excellent
a. Explanations of medical procedures and tests	1	2	3	4	5
b. Attention given to what you have to say	1	2	3	4	5
c. Advice you get about ways to avoid illness and stay healthy	1	2	3	4	5
d. Number of doctors you have to choose from	1	2	3	4	5
e. Ease of seeing the doctor of your choice	1	2	3	4	5
f. Friendliness and courtesy shown to you by doctors and staff	1	2	3	4	5
g. Personal interest in you and your medical problems	1	2	3	4	5
h. Reassurance and support offered to you by doctors and staff	1	2	3	4	5
i. Amount of time you have with doctors and staff during visit	1	2	3	4	5
j. Accuracy of bills	1	2	3	4	5

33a. What type of transportation do you use most often when going to visit your health care provider?

(circle one number)

Personal vehicle (car, truck, motorcycle)	1
Bus	2
Taxi	3
Walk	4
Bicycle	5
Other (please specify): ____________	6

FIGURE 14-1. (Continued)

33b. When you go to your health care provider, do you?

(circle one number)

Usually travel alone	1
Usually have someone go with you	2

34. Have any of the following been a problem for you or your doctor in arranging for your medical care? If so, how much of a problem?

(circle one number on each line)

	Yes, A Big Problem	Yes, A Small Problem	No, Not A Problem
a. Limited freedom to choose any treatment option you and your doctor believe is necessary	1	2	3
b. Limited access to certain doctors because of your insurance or lack of insurance	1	2	3
c. Lack of coordination or poor communication between doctors who treat you	1	2	3
d. Delays in your medical care while you wait for approval by your health insurance	1	2	3
e. Lack of services tailored specifically to meet your needs	1	2	3
f. Lack of educational programs to help you manage or prevent medical problems	1	2	3
g. Lack of reminders or encouragement to use timely preventive services (for example, screening for blood pressure or cancer and immunizations)	1	2	3

35. Thinking about your own health care (and <u>not</u> including dental care), generally how <u>satisfied</u> are you with . . .

(circle one number on each line)

	Very Satisfied	Satisfied	Not Satisfied or Dissatisfied	Dissatisfied	Very Dissatisfied
a. The results of your medical care?	1	2	3	4	5
b. The quality of your medical care?	1	2	3	4	5

(Continued on next page)

FIGURE 14-1. (Continued)

51. Is there one person or place in particular you usually go to when you are depressed, upset, or need emotional support and advice?

(circle one number)

Yes	1	→ continue with Question 52.
No	2	→ skip to Question 53.
Don't know	3	→ skip to Question 53.

52. If YES, Where do you go for emotional support and advice?

(circle all that apply)

a. Tioga County Human Services	1
b. Tioga County Mental Health Services	2
c. Laurel Counseling Services	3
d. A private psychiatrist, psychologist or counselor	4
e. A church or religious organization (minister, priest, rabbi, etc.)	5
f. College or University counseling service	6
g. Counseling service at my place of employment	7
h. Other, please specify: ____________	8

FIGURE 14-1. (Continued)

56. When you go for routine medical care, how often does your provider advise you about any of the following:

(circle one number on each line)

	Routinely	Occasionally	Never	Don't Know
a. Diet	1	2	3	4
b. Sleep cycles	1	2	3	4
c. Knowledge of poison prevention	1	2	3	4
d. Use of car safety seats or child vehicle restraints	1	2	3	4
e. Knowledge of how to prevent burns from hot water in the home	1	2	3	4
f. Risks for heart disease	1	2	3	4
g. Risks for stroke	1	2	3	4
h. Risks for high blood pressure	1	2	3	4
i. Mental health (stress management)	1	2	3	4
j. Level of exercise	1	2	3	4
k. Smoking habits and knowledge of the impact of smoking on your health	1	2	3	4
l. Regular preventive screening (mammogram, colon rectal cancer, etc.)	1	2	3	4
m. Alcohol	1	2	3	4
n. Non-prescription drug	1	2	3	4
o. Safer sex and the prevention of sexual transmitted diseases and HIV/AIDS	1	2	3	4
p. Smokeless (chewing) tobacco	1	2	3	4
q. Family planning	1	2	3	4

According to 1989 Pennsylvania Health Data Center statistics, the five leading causes of death in all age groups in Tioga County are (1) heart disease, (2) cancer, (3) stroke, (4) accidents, and (5) chronic obstructive pulmonary disease. These health indicators reflect national morbidity and mortality statistics, with cardiovascular disease, cancer, and stroke being the top three causes of death in the nation. Hypertensive cardiovascular disease and hypercholesterolemia are major health problems in this rural dairy farming area.

Review of the basic life cycle categories reflects some specific and noteworthy trends, as follows:

- *Perinatal:* Current data sources reveal that Tioga County has an exceptionally high rate of teenage pregnancy and neonatal mortality as compared with national averages. A total of 13.5 percent of these users represent teenage pregnancies. Infant and neonatal mortality rates for Tioga County are 10.4 percent. Of Tioga County pregnancies, 24 percent do not have prenatal care initiated in the first trimester. Twelve percent of Tioga County births are to mothers younger than 19 years of age. Teen pregnancies represent a Medicaid-eligible population at risk for poor pregnancy outcomes. Thirty-seven percent of all births are to unmarried mothers.
- *Pediatric—Infancy:* Although Tioga County does have an increased rate of teenage pregnancy, perinatal surveys reveal that the region has not had a problem with low-birth-weight infants. The local community health center network administers the well-child immunization program through a contract with the Pennsylvania State Department of Health. In combination with the sliding-fee program available through these health centers, immunizations are available to all Tioga County infants. However, despite this program, many children are not immunized or undergo a significant delay in their immunizations.
- *Pediatric—Childhood:* Preschool and school health are major concerns for our pediatric population. Head Start enrollment represents 4 percent of the 3- to 5-year-old population. Respiratory illness is the single most prevalent health problem of this age group, based on data obtained from Laurel Health Center's user profile. Trauma (minor accidents) represents a significant problem in this age group, also.
- *Adolescence:* As previously discussed, teenage pregnancy is a significant problem in our user group. Although regional prenatal care has been excellent for those using it, and their outcomes have been better than national averages for this group, 20 percent of 75 deliveries to local community health patients were to mothers aged 14 to 17 years. Sex education and contraceptive awareness are seriously lacking in the school districts throughout Tioga County. A hospital-sponsored interdisciplinary sexuality seminar was attended by fewer than 10 families in 1989 and had been canceled in 1988 because of lack of interest.

  Adolescents (age 13–21) constitute 15.8 percent of Tioga County's population and 19.2 percent of the community health center user population.
- *Adulthood:* Of Tioga County's user population, 44 percent is between the ages of 22 and 54; 34 percent of our user population is in this age bracket. The main health problems are minor episodic illnesses, routine health maintenance, and pregnancy. State health data reveal the major cause of death and morbidity to be cardiovascular disease, followed by cancer and stroke. Hypertension and hypercholesterolemia are major health problems stemming from dietary patterns in this agricultural area.

- *Geriatric:* The geriatric age group of Tioga County is a significant indigent population, with 5,531 individuals who make up 23 percent of the population. According to Department of Public Welfare profiles provided through the Area Agency on Aging, 40 percent of this population have incomes of less than $13,000.

  Tioga County's geriatric population (age 65 and over) makes up 13 percent of the area's population; 4.8 percent of this population resides in a long-term care facility. Chronic illnesses represent the major health problems of our geriatric user population. Cardiovascular and cerebrovascular diseases are the leading causes of mortality in the county.

The Partnership

As of April 1, 1995, more than 20 community health partners from within Tioga County and surrounding communities serve on this collaborative partnership. They include a comprehensive mix of health care providers, human service programs, educational facilities, business organizations, community development entities, and local governmental operations. Although the infrastructure for this community care network (CCN) is in place, the Community Health Partnership for Tioga County continues to recruit community partners and will submit names of additional participants as they become available.

In addition to community-wide organizational participation, individual memberships are permitted and encouraged. These include such nonorganizational ties as certified public accountants and other community-based specialists who are capable of bringing their technical skills and abilities to this comprehensive CCN. This CCN project is receiving endorsement from special national and state organizations and legislative representatives, including the American Hospital Association, Hospital Association of Pennsylvania, Rep. Matthew E. Baker (PA), Sen. Roger A. Madigan (PA), and Sen. Arlen Specter (PA). Each of the latter three individuals have significant expertise levels in one or more facets of our CCN project: Specter serves on the Aging and Appropriations committees; Madigan works diligently on the Rural Affairs, Local Government, Emergency Preparedness, and Labor and Industry committees; and Baker, through his active participation on the Aging and Youth Committee, has firsthand knowledge of the health care and human service needs of these special populations. He also serves on the Commonwealth's Local Tax Reform and Emergency Services Legal caucuses.

PRIOR EFFORTS REPRESENTING MOVEMENT TOWARD THE COMMUNITY CARE NETWORK VISION

Overview

Historical: Impetus for Community Care Network Development

Phase I The Tioga County region has had a long-established trend of community-based integrated service delivery. In 1973, North Penn Comprehensive Health Services (NPCHS), a not-for-profit multiservice provider, established its first community health center in Blossburg, PA. In the years that followed, a very deliberate planning initiative was implemented by the NPCHS board of directors to establish a comprehensive scope of integrated services within its not-for-profit corporate structure. Success to date includes nine specific integrated services: Sullivan Terrace (U.S. Housing and Urban Development-sponsored housing facility), Laurel Counseling, Northern Tier Youth Services, Home Health Agency, Home and Center Services, Bradford/Tioga County Head Start Program, Guideline (information and referral service), Regional Area Health Education Center (RAHEC) and, of course, the Laurel Health Centers (LHCs), which now number six and continue to serve many of the primary care needs of Tioga and parts of Potter counties.

Phase II In July 1989, the NPCHS board of directors took another bold leap to further integrate itself within the region by developing a formal affiliation with the Soldiers and Sailors Memorial Hospital and the Green Home (a long-term care provider). This vision led to the formation of the Laurel Health System (LHS) for the sole purpose of developing a seamless continuum of care and improving the health status of its communities. Each of the three member organizations that compose the LHS are separate legal entities that form a horizontally integrated service delivery mechanism for the provision of rural health care and human services.

One very significant highlight of the community-based integration activities that took place in both 1973 and 1989 service affiliations was the inclusion of a community health center network within the CCN vision. We believe that the involvement of these six U.S. Public Health Service–supported community health centers during phases I and II was truly innovative because this was the first time in Tioga County that community health centers became a part of an integrated system of care.

Phase III As previously described, phases I and II served as the key foundation for the CCN that is in place today in Tioga County. Because of the ability to unite various diverse human service providers as early as 1973 under the auspices of NPCHS as well as the formal development of the LHS, the mechanism was in place to implement phase III of the CCN philosophy and vision.

This third phase concerned the recruitment of key community stakeholders to work proactively with providers of health and human services to solve the many pressing health and human service needs of this rural region. Known as the Community Health Partnership for Tioga County, this infrastructure has brought together schools, businesses, churches, local government, human service providers, health care providers, and the citizenry of the region to improve access and quality of health care within a changing health care delivery system in the nation.

The TCPCH has proven to be one of the most successful rural CCNs in the nation, having captured the attention of health care professionals and policy makers at both the state and national levels. This is described in more detail in the following sections.

National Rural Health Care Policy The LHS was selected by the White House Health Care Reform Task Force to provide input on the impact of reform on rural health care organizations. In addition, in her August 8, 1993, address at the American Hospital Association's annual convention in Orlando, FL, Hillary Rodham Clinton cited the LHS as an example of a rural CCN to be emulated.

American Hospital Association The American Hospital Association and the Hospital Association of Pennsylvania, as well as state and federal officials, have recognized the LHS as a unique rural health care leader that has broken with tradition to strengthen and unify community-based health and human services under one umbrella. LHS medical staff leadership and executive management have been requested on many occasions to provide testimony before both state and federal legislative bodies. A complete copy of these sessions is available upon request.

Other Recognition The LHS, as well as the region's community health partnership, has been the focus of many national studies concerning rural health and human service integration activities. Robert Morris, who then served as president and CEO of the LHS, was featured in an early-1995 C-SPAN television segment on health care reform and its impact on the rural communities of our nation. In addition, the LHS was selected as the first rural site for an "Action Learning Lab" November 17–18, 1994, that was cosponsored by the LHS, the Hospital Association of Pennsylvania, and the American Hospital Association's Hospital Research and Educational Trust. The focus of this 2-day endeavor was to examine the role of successful rural community health care networks in building healthy communities.

Community Health Focus

During late winter and early spring 1994, a community health development firm was authorized by the TCPCH and the LHS to conduct a preliminary assessment of readiness for a community collaboration to improve the health status of citizens of the Tioga County region. Approximately 124 community individuals were interviewed for input into this study from diversified backgrounds and a wide geographic spectrum of the region. The results of this endeavor, combined with a recent Tioga County health profile conducted by the Hospital Association of Pennsylvania, produced a list of perceived key problem areas. (See table 14-1.)

This initial study, combined with the report provided by the Hospital Association of Pennsylvania, provided the basis for selecting what key areas should be undertaken for improvement areas within the region. Based on the key problem areas identified as a result of the in-depth interviews, a sequential action plan was developed to begin to address specific health and human service–related issues of the region. An implementation team was organized that included a diverse community representation. This team made recommendations to the TCPCH concerning policies and program development, opportunities for collaboration, and potential areas for integration of efforts to address the following topics:

1. The health status of the citizens of Tioga County and the availability of resources (policies, practices, institutions, facilities, services, and so on) to address needs and build on strengths and successes
2. The availability of primary health care and access to appropriate services (for example, preventive health services, primary care, tertiary care, and so on)
3. The involvement of young people of Tioga County in improving the health of its citizens
4. Continuity of care for the elderly population

To maximize all community and regional resources specific to this CCN, it was determined that the following four approaches would serve as the template for infrastructure activities:

1. Framing the partnership
2. Partnership building and community health status and resource assessment

3. Community health status intervention
4. Monitoring, evaluating, and supporting the partnership

Community Accountability

The TCPCH has developed a well-defined accountability mechanism for the active CCN. As mentioned in the previous section, an implementation team was established that represented a diverse number of community interests and professionals from inside as well as outside the community. Based on the in-depth community assessment, it was also determined that four specific work groups needed to be established to begin to address complex issues relating to rural health care service access and delivery. These work groups (primary care access, health status assessment and resource inventory, youth, and elderly services) have been established and maintain active meeting and project schedules.

Each work group is charged with the identification, investigation, and development of recommendations for submission to the implementation team. These include (1) the delineation of issues and concerns, (2) the identification of information needs for use by the Health Status Assessment and Resource Inventory Work Group, (3) the identification and consideration of existing models or successful programs that address the issues and concerns of Tioga County, (4) the description of state and local policies

TABLE 14-1. Perceived Health Problem Areas of Tioga County

Perceived Problem List	*Comments*
Increased Medicaid population	Perpetuated by state & family systems
Health issues among the poor	
Aging population within region	Will require broader thinking
Geographic isolation	Implications on managed care
No managed care	Clear state trend & potential national direction
Travel outside of region	Subspecialty & tertiary services
Lack of in-home services	Elderly population
Increased use of alcohol	Effects on family & alcohol-related crimes
National health care reform	Effects locally
Cost of health care	
Public transportation	Another potential access barrier
Low-income & working poor	Relationship to health & Social problems
Teen pregnancy	Improved prevention strategies & single parents
Tax base erosion	Aging population & impact on service delivery
Lack of insurance coverage	
Lack of community-wide service integration	Fragmented
Industrial health care needs	Unhealthy work practices

Source: Felix-Burdine, Inc. Preliminary Assessment for Community Collaboration to Improve Health Status of Citizens.

and programs that facilitate or hinder efforts to address the identified issues and concerns, and (5) the investigation and identification of areas of collaboration and integration of efforts. Chaired by members of the implementation team, the work groups comprise members of the implementation team as well as members of the CCN who are interested and informed in the topic area.

It is important to note that the comprehensive work and results of our CCN are communicated for input and feedback to the community on a routine basis through several mechanisms, including town meetings, news releases, and so on. Of equal importance to accountability features, the LHS has had a long-established policy of ongoing community advisory councils that provide critical input and feedback concerning many health and human service operational components.

Seamless Continuum of Care

The agencies and organizations that make up our local CCN represent the epitome of intra- and interorganizational integrated operations. At the LHS level, a full continuum of local services, such as primary care, inpatient, counseling, long-term care, and elder health care services, to name a few, are provided through central coordination. The presence of the Tioga County Medical Society, as well as the medical staff leadership of the Soldiers and Sailors Memorial Hospital, within the CCN infrastructure also adds a significant factor specific to continuum of care standards for subspecialty care within the region. Many of the region's patient services, such as outpatient testing, have been centralized to permit ease of access and reduction in duplication of services. Department and clinical managers cross beyond traditional operational lines by meeting on a routine basis to discuss improving continuum of care standards that affect patients as a whole.

The LHS has developed a formal continuous quality improvement (CQI) endeavor that includes a steering committee and CQI teams that address pertinent operational issues specific to consumer and patient issues. All employees of NPCHS, Soldiers and Sailors Memorial Hospital, and the Green Home have received training in CQI techniques and strategies.

Management within Fixed Resources

This CCN has demonstrable experience operating its previous and current services within fixed resources. For example, the success to date of the integrated initiatives of NPCHS, Soldiers and Sailors Memorial Hospital, and the Green Home operating under the LHS umbrella have produced significant savings in operational expenses. All these entities share centralized accounting and management information systems (MIS) functions, thus reducing expenditures of scarce resources and duplication of services. LHS maintains a corporate human resources department that is available to each entity for specific needs. Recognizing that many community health and human services are provided to this economically disadvantaged region at a reduced rate, LHS has established a formal fund development program that avails its services upon request to NPCHS, Soldiers and Sailors Memorial Hospital, and the Green Home. This is a tremendous shared resource that each LHS member entity would not be able to staff or operate independently. A centralized fund development program also allows for scarce (because of high regional poverty levels) private donations to be raised and targeted to meet the services in most need.

- *Module 3 (Cost Accounting Decision Support System):* A comprehensive assessment of managed care MIS needs has been accomplished. Changes in MIS staff reporting structures within LHS have been implemented. Meetings with software/hardware vendors have taken place. CCN participants have identified software needs to bridge the gap required for successful managed care participation. As soon as funding sources are identified, purchases will be made. In addition to the standard fundamental accounting functions, this module will equip our managed care efforts with powerful modeling, analysis, and reporting tools that will deliver timely, accurate information to support decision-making processes. By merging clinical and financial information, this module will foster an interdisciplinary approach that enhances both cost and quality outcomes. The CCN will be able to conduct detailed prospective analyses for potential contracts and evaluate the changes in reimbursement, product mix, and other key variables to help reduce the cost of service. Our CCN will have the ability to analyze the most effective treatment patterns to determine the appropriate resource allocations to facilitate the continual delivery of high-quality care.
- *Module 4 (Clinical Measures Decision Support System):* All physician providers have been introduced to the concepts of rural managed care clinical measures reporting via special town meetings. An analysis of clinical measures software requirements has been completed and the CCN has narrowed its search to either IAMETER or MEDES Groups. The ability to track clinical outcomes is crucial if rural managed care is to evolve beyond economically credentialed managed cost.

  The module will focus on an acuity index method of data analysis. Content required for ongoing managed care operations will include a severity-adjusted profile of length of stay, resource utilization, and mortality. Severity-adjusted outcomes for all diagnosis-related groups (DRGs) will be compared with the appropriate severity-adjusted normative database.

  Additional components will include a competitor profile, a clinical profile of selected DRGs, and individual outpatient practice assessment reports. Data derived from this module will be combined with the cost accounting module for overall analysis.

  All members of the entire local medical community, in addition to partnership administrative and governing boards of the CCN entities, will use these data. This includes members of the business community who, as purchasers of health care and human services, are extremely interested in providing high-quality and cost-efficient care for their employee bases.

SUMMARY OF NOTABLE PROGRESS

Following a restructuring, the initiatives of the TCPCH are now created and managed by six work groups. Each work group includes between 6 and 20 citizens who have volunteered to participate in the partnership. A summary of the work groups' activities follows:

Elderly Services Work Group

Twenty members of the Elderly Services Work Group represent Tioga County providers and users of services. This group meets once a month with a mission to continue to identify needs in service to the elderly and to develop and implement plans to address those needs. There are three subcommittees within the group: the Adult Day Care Committee, the Education Committee, and the Alzheimer's Committee.

The Adult Day Care Committee has studied adult day care in other counties, collected information, and is responsible for encouraging the providing of the service in Tioga County. In addition, two day care programs are scheduled to open in the next 3 months. One, sponsored by Community Alternative Resources for the Elderly, will be located in Covington; the other, sponsored by the Green Home, will be located in Wellsboro.

The Education Committee's mission is to provide education to the Elderly Services Work Group, service providers, and the general public, and to render that education continually inclusive and multimodel, using newspaper, radio, and public forum. A deliberate effort will be made to coordinate newspaper articles, radio programs, and public forums to provide information to the public regarding available services throughout the county from a multitude of agencies. Beginning in October, a 12-month schedule has been formulated around a weekly radio program. The Alzheimer's Committee is reviewing the need for nursing care and day care services for those with this disease.

Ideal Health and Human Services System Work Group

The Ideal Health and Human Services System Work Group was formed in spring 1996. The committee's mission is to develop an ideal plan to provide integrated health and behavioral health services that are fully responsive to the needs of Tioga County citizens. The committee's process is guided by the assumption that external financial pressures beyond our control at the local level are having a dramatic impact on the delivery of health and mental health services in our county. As a result, we are no longer able to continue with our past practices and provide services of reasonable quality. In many instances the very survival of our services seems at stake, and we are often confused about the best directions to take.

The Ideal Health and Human Services System Work Group is working toward a plan that will be comprehensive and ensure high-quality services. The group assumes that any plan must focus on keeping people healthy as well as diagnosing and treating their problems. The plan must also take into account the financial pressures we can envision for the foreseeable future. The group is committed to being proactive in developing a service system that addresses the unique needs of our rural setting. The goal is to submit recommendations to the partnership's executive committee this fall.

Health Status Assessment and Resource Inventory Work Group

The primary responsibility of the Health Status Assessment and Resource Inventory Work Group during phase I was to develop and implement a community-wide comprehensive survey to address the health assessment of our residents. Countless hours were spent in developing a survey instrument that addressed the needs of the TCPCH. The Tioga County survey (figure 14-1) went beyond the traditional medical health of a community and included the mental health and human service concerns set forth by the TCPCH. The Rural Services Institute of Mansfield University conducted the 31-page survey. Mailings of 2,500 surveys throughout Tioga County began on November 1, 1994.

The overwhelming response by nearly 76 percent of the citizens of Tioga County is commendable and certainly an indication of our residents' interest in health care. The survey, analysis, and cross-tabbing process provides the TCPCH with a comprehensive assessment of the medical, mental, and human services health of our citizens. Available to our community is a vast array of firsthand information and data that can be accessed to help us in developing a health care service delivery system at present unavailable to the rest of our state and country. In addition, we have access to several social concerns that we, as a community, will now be able to address.

Mental Health Work Group

The Mental Health Work Group addresses mental health issues. Its mission is to improve the quality and accessibility of mental health services that exist in Tioga County by identifying the gaps in services, and to develop and implement long- and short-term goals to overcome those gaps in the most cost-effective manner. This group has grown from 5 members to approximately 25. Gaps in service have been identified, and now the group members have identified three goals that they would like to implement. In October, on National Depression Screening Day, the group would like to provide free depression screenings throughout Tioga County. During school year 1996–97, this work group would like to develop a peer counseling program in at least one of the three school districts in Tioga County. The third project that the group would like to implement would deal with mental health needs of the elderly.

Health and Human Service Work Group

The Health and Human Service Work Group has been addressing the medical assistance access to dental care issues identified during the initial public survey. Meetings with Chemung County, NY, representatives shed light on financial issues as well as staffing and scheduling issues. Williamsport, PA, representatives discussed cooperative efforts with dental assistant education programs and issues related to age population difficulties. The group has information on reimbursement to Federally Qualified Health Centers for incentives for dentists to serve the medical assistance population. It will be the recommendation of the group to do a feasibility study for initiation of a community-supported dental clinic specifically to serve the medical assistance population and the uninsured. Meetings with the dental association must occur to determine their support for such a clinic in Tioga County.

Youth Work Group

The Youth Work Group struggled with its initial task of identifying all the services offered to the youth in Tioga County. In fact, our group struggled with how the word "youth" was to be interpreted. With the diversity of issues that surround young people from birth to 21 years of age, it seemed unlikely that our group could effectively evaluate all the needs of this group. With recommendations of focusing on youth between the ages of 12 and 21, we began our task with the blessing of the executive committee. Next, we attempted to review the volumes of programs offered to this age group and their intent of providing services.

Although the programs appeared to be meeting youth needs, it was difficult for our work group to determine their effectiveness. It was at that point that we decided to go directly to this population and ask their opinion of what it was like to live in their communities. This task was accomplished with the assistance of a survey tool put together by our task force with the help of our consultants.

The survey was reviewed by youth who sat on our committee and also by a health careers class comprising youth from most of the schools in our county. This input was extremely helpful in producing a document that was reflective of the information we wanted to gather. This survey was then distributed to each school in Tioga County, Galeton School District in Potter County, and two private religious schools. The total number of returned surveys was 3,040, which represents nearly every youth in our service area between the ages of 12 and 18.

The survey revealed that life in Tioga County as a young person is rather satisfying. Most youth reported that they felt safe in their communities and that access to information pertaining to health and nutrition was readily available. They also reported that although the area was lacking in employment opportunities, activities for sports and club events were easily obtainable. Few youth noted an interest in an area or activity where they could not participate. Despite these activities, most youth mentioned that the county needs to have more areas where youth can go to socialize and be with other youth. Although the youth believe that the communities are not representative of their interests, there was not much interest in becoming involved in local government to represent these needs to the governing authorities.

Without question, the development, distribution, and review of the survey has been our crowning accomplishment. The work involved a coordination of efforts with school districts, youth groups, and our work group. The results, though reassuring, also pose difficult tasks to pursue, such as how to engage the youth in community events that allow them to feel more connected to the community, assist them in finding places that they can meet for social events, and assist them in locating meaningful employment within our geographic area. Our work group is currently engaged with the Director of Guidelines, a telephone information service, to review a "Teen Guide" for distribution to this age group.

Contact: Rod C. Kelchner, Chair
Tioga County Health Partnership
North Hall, Room 203
Mansfield University
Mansfield, PA 16933
Phone: (717) 662-4046
Fax: (717) 724-1197

15

The El Dorado Wellness Partnership

Executive Summary

El Dorado County has continued to strengthen and expand upon its community wellness partnerships since participating in the community care network (CCN) process. More important, we have worked on strengthening the community participation and investment in the network.

The initial partnership of the Public Health Department and Marshall Hospital is still intact and prospering with the addition of new partners. Using lessons learned from our evaluation of the Divide Wellness Center in Georgetown, we have developed a strategy to develop a similar but unique approach in Pollock Pines. We continue to facilitate and identify the community leadership within Pollock Pines and are assisting them in mapping local resources and identifying areas of need. Key focuses during the past year include: community mapping and assessment, identification of local leadership, preliminary planning for a community health center, and assignment of a community advocate to the area.

Simultaneously, the partnership is working to ensure the Divide Wellness Center thrives and prospers. We are evaluating the project and have developed a business plan to help guide us in maintaining a sound fiscal foundation. (See figure 15-1.) In addition to the Pollock Pines area, the Community Wellness Partnership has also focused on strengthening the safety net for unserved and underserved populations. Work in this area has included a series of brainstorming meetings with key representatives from social, health, and medical services agencies to develop a vision of health and how to bring it about.

Gayle Erbe-Hamlin
El Dorado County Director of Public Health

participation, and the DCSN continued to grow. The DCSN consists of a wide representation of community members who come together each month to discuss community issues and institute community solutions. The DCSN was patterned after a similar community coalition in South Lake Tahoe, the Tahoe Prevention Network, which was created in 1990 and whose success serves as a model for community development initiatives nationwide.

In 1994, the El Dorado County Public Health Department (PHD) and Marshall Hospital joined to explore ways to improve the health of the Divide area. They developed the Divide Wellness Partnership in collaboration with the DCSN and the Black Oak Mine Unified School District to apply for a federal rural health outreach grant, which was successfully funded in September 1994. With funding from the grant and with significant in-kind contributions of staff, material, and cash, the Divide Wellness Partnership developed, outfitted, staffed, and opened the Divide Wellness Center.

In developing the rural health grant proposal, the Divide Wellness Partnership engaged in a process of involving the community in assessing their health needs and in developing components of the wellness center to meet those needs. Those involved in the Partnership believe that the success and vision that was experienced in the Divide area can be successfully replicated in other parts of El Dorado County. With the vision provided through the CCN, the Wellness Partnership intends to replicate this successful process in another rural area of the county, the Pollock Pines area. With the broadening of scope from the one community of the Divide to other communities, the name of the Partnership has changed from the *Divide* Wellness Partnership to the *Community* Wellness Partnership.

Community Assessment

The Community Wellness Partnership began the process of exploring the Divide community's needs by first studying the norms and culture of its residents: There is a large senior citizen population, many on fixed incomes. The middle class is composed largely of government and school personnel, small business owners, and skilled laborers. There are many unemployed, and there is a significant group of people who have "dropped out" of society for philosophical, financial, or legal reasons.

High school students talk of graduating and leaving the Divide. Those who are college bound see a means to accomplish this goal, but other students have a sense of hopelessness, of no options and no opportunities.

There are no official unemployment statistics for the Divide, but the general consensus is that the rate is high. The school district is the largest employer. The U.S. Forest Service and the El Dorado County Irrigation District are also significant employers. There are no large businesses or corporations, and most small businesses employ few workers.

Many residents are low income and qualify for health and social service aid programs. One indicator of poverty in this area is the enrollment of over 50 percent of students in the Black Oak Mine Unified School District in the free or reduced-fee lunch program. Another indicator is that 56 percent of the local physician assistant's patients are on Medi-Cal. It is reported by Divide school and medical professionals that many residents live in substandard housing, including rusted-out trailers on forestry property or borrowed land.

The Community Wellness Partnership obtained information about the health status of the Divide community in a number of ways. Interviews were conducted with key people in the Divide communities, schools, health and social service staff such as the physician's assistant, school district nurses, Women, Infants and Children (WIC) program director, and public health nurses. In addition, patients at the public health clinic in March 1994 were informally interviewed regarding their health needs. Hospital administrators provided data regarding emergency room utilization; other data were obtained via the vital statistics unit of the PHD, Department of Transportation, and the Employment Development Department. Most important, a community-planning meeting attended by 53 people, representing a wide variety of interests on the Divide, was held in February 1994. From these community assessment strategies, the most immediate problems experienced by residents of the Divide were determined to be: (1) inadequate access to health care services, and (2) a disproportionately high need for health and social services.

More about the Partnership

The four current entities that make up the Divide Wellness Partnership were selected based on the overall needs identified in the service area and the need for community participation. Each entity possesses a unique set of resources, which in turn are allocated to the specific goals of the project.

- *El Dorado County Public Health Department (lead agency):* The El Dorado County PHD is based in Placerville and provides health care services to low-income people throughout El Dorado County. Services provided by that department or through contracts with community-based organizations include: alcohol/drug treatment and prevention, emergency medical services, adolescent and child health screening, public health nursing, clinical preventive services, tobacco prevention, HIV/AIDS testing and prevention services, and epidemiology services.

  The PHD also provides advocacy on state and federal policy issues, and serves as a conduit for communication between the government entities and the community.
- *Marshall Hospital:* Marshall Hospital provides full-service inpatient and outpatient care in the western portion of El Dorado County. The hospital has consistently worked over the past 15 years to improve health care accessibility.
- *The Divide Community Services Network:* The DCSN was formed in 1993 to address and improve the health and social needs of Divide area residents. The network is composed of and represents parents, students, educators, health professionals, and residents from all walks of life on the Divide. The group is most interested in developing local solutions to local problems. In the past year, the DCSN has been successful in coordinating local health planning efforts, providing increased health outreach services, and addressing other community concerns.
- *The Black Oak Mine Unified School District:* The only school district located on the Divide, it is the most visible and functional public entity in the area. The schools serve as a focal point for education, meetings, recreation, and other social functions. Because the schools are highly visible and respected, they serve as a natural focal point for community activities.

As the vision of the Community Wellness Partnership is replicated in other communities, it is our intention that two current partners, the PHD and Marshall Hospital, will remain. The other two partners, the DCSN and the school district, will be replaced by appropriate entities in the new community. This structure will ensure both community accountability and decentralization while at the same time providing direction with a consistent vision.

Although the specific community partners in the Pollock Pines area have not yet been identified, the following criteria will be used to evaluate potential community organizations: involvement of a broad range of community representatives, strong leadership, a successful history in community work, a mandate that is compatible with health and wellness, and a willingness to join with the Community Wellness Partnership.

PRIOR EFFORTS THAT REPRESENT MOVEMENT TOWARD THE COMMUNITY CARE NETWORK VISION

Community Accountability

The guiding principle of the Community Wellness Partnership is to work within the community it serves to facilitate the health of its citizens. Critical to achieving this goal is to provide for accountability to the community. Several components of the Community Wellness Partnership ensure such accountability:

- Two of the four current Community Wellness Partnership members are representatives of community organizations: the DCSN and the Black Oak Mine Unified School District. The DCSN comprises representatives from a broad range of interests in the community—businesses, schools, parents, service providers, and so on. It is responsible for ensuring continued public communication with the Community Wellness Partnership and the project, including assessing the quality and quantity of services as perceived by the clients; ensuring that services meet the needs of the resident population; providing group feedback on any other services that need to be reconfigured, changed, or added; and facilitating local fundraising efforts. The DCSN is currently developing a patient satisfaction survey, which will provide valuable information that the Community Wellness Partnership can use to help modify the Community Wellness Center to better serve the community's needs. The Black Oak Mine Unified School District is responsible for managing school-aged children's services, including identifying and referring students and families in need of health care to the Community Wellness Center; ensuring, in conjunction with parents, that follow-up care prescribed is completed; and ensuring the integration of existing community school district services into the overall project.
- Working directly with the DCSN and other members of the community, the Community Wellness Partnership developed and successfully funded in September 1994 a federal rural health outreach grant. With the funding provided by that 3-year grant, the Community Wellness Partnership has developed and implemented the Divide Wellness Center.
- A subcommittee of the DCSN, working with the local evaluator for the rural health outreach grant, has developed and implemented a patient use survey to determine patient satisfaction with the Divide Wellness Center.
- The DCSN representative on the Community Wellness Partnership is a long-time Divide resident who provides regular and meaningful feedback and suggestions to and from the Wellness Partnership and the DCSN membership.

- The Black Oak Mine Unified School District representative on the Wellness Partnership is the principal of Georgetown Elementary School and a long-time Divide resident.
- Several community meetings and retreats have been conducted with members of the Divide community and participants in the Community Wellness Partnership. The purpose of these community events is to increase communication and understanding, explore community concerns, and foster a sense of teamwork.
- Members of the Community Wellness Partnership regularly make formal presentations to service and community groups and in other ways meet with community organizations (at lunches, breakfasts, association meetings, and community forums) to seek their input and to inform them of the Divide Wellness Center's activities and services.
- The Divide community has demonstrated its ownership of the Divide Wellness Center in many ways, including the following: the local art society has decorated the halls of the center with local artists' paintings, the local plant society has designed the center's landscaping, and the local Boy Scout and Girl Scout troops have adopted the center and participate in weekly upkeep work sessions.

Seamless Continuum of Care

The Divide Wellness Center is an integration of medical care, other health services, health education, community services, and social services. Its goal is to provide a continuum of care that facilitates the overall improvement of the health of the community. Intervention strategies were designed to improve the social and medical health of the area and reduce the amount of crisis care. A key component of the Divide Wellness Center is the array of site-based services that include dental screens, urgent care and stabilization, preventive health care, health education, referral and transportation to other area medical centers for intensive care, child health, domestic violence, health advocacy (outreach, home visiting, and follow-up), mental health, alcohol/drug services, and child abuse/neglect services. A patient advocacy team (PAT) coordinates these services at the center. The PAT is composed of representatives from service providers, including: the Women's Center, an alcohol and drug treatment program, an early childhood intervention and parenting program, and public health nursing. The PAT, along with representatives from the clinical aspect of the Divide Wellness Center, forms the patient case management team, which takes a holistic approach at looking at the needs of the client and provides medical, social, and community linkages that ensure a seamless continuum of care. These strategies reflect the goal of the Divide Wellness Center, which is to increase the overall health of the community.

The Divide Wellness Center's case management system is designed to ensure that patients get the health care they need. The system focuses on the clients' perception of health and illness and their ability to achieve optimal wellness. Linking clients with an individual family advocate provides the one-on-one relationship aimed at increasing the family's ability to access services for which they are eligible and to educate the family as to the value of healthy lifestyles. Two family advocate positions at the center perform many outreach functions, including: educating individuals and groups on the concepts of health prevention, advocating for patients, identifying areas that need to be improved, referring cases to appropriate services, and coordinating services among various providers.

The twice-a-month Community Wellness Partnership meetings are attended by staff from both the clinic and social service components of the Divide Wellness Center. In addition, all Divide Wellness Center staff attend weekly meetings. During these meetings, ways are explored to integrate the center's clinical and social service functions to most effectively serve the clients. These strategies have resulted in significant referrals of patients to other needed services.

Community Health Focus

The Divide Wellness Center was designed to meet the health and social services needs of an isolated population by providing the significant outreach and case management services necessary to change the perception of health and wellness in the community, and by augmenting currently available services with services from a wide variety of medical and nonmedical providers. Commitment to consistent and competent services is a critical strategy in attaining community trust and increasing access to health care. In addition to primary and urgent medical care and prevention services, the Divide Wellness Center also focuses on community and social services (mental health, domestic violence, alcohol/drug abuse, and child abuse/neglect problems) in recognition of the fact that these issues are often major factors contributing to health problems. The Community Wellness Partnership has demonstrated commitment to working within the community to facilitate improving the health of its citizens. Evidence of such commitment includes the following:

- The Divide Wellness Center's PAT includes representatives of community and social service providers in the community.
- The Divide Wellness Center sponsors four community health education training sessions each year. These sessions are developed by the DCSN, and each is sponsored by a local community service organization, such as Soroptimists or the Lion's Club.
- The Community Wellness Partnership is working with the DCSN to determine which hours and days of the week the Divide Wellness Center should be open to maximize community accessibility. Although the center encourages appointments, walk-in clients are always accepted. (Currently, walk-ins account for more than 60 percent of all clients served.)
- The Divide Wellness Center has at its disposal a van. Driven by community volunteers, the van provides transportation for clients to increase access to services.
- The DCSN is working with the Divide Health Auxiliary to conduct a health fair at the Divide Wellness Center this summer. The health fair will focus on preventive health issues.

The Community Wellness Partnership identified a number of barriers in the community that limit the accessibility of services for the population. The barriers include (1) lack of local services, (2) lack of knowledge regarding risks and consequences of health behaviors, (3) attitudes of the community that distrust government services, (4) lack of family and community support for seeking appropriate health and social services, (5) lack of transportation, (6) lack of continuity of care, (7) lack of insurance, and (8) lack of coordination/integration of community services. Virtually all the activities and components of the Divide Wellness Center were designed to help the community overcome these barriers.

Several programs at the Divide Wellness Center are aimed at early diagnosis and intervention. Examples include the Children's Health and Disability Program, public health nursing, the Department of Social Services Family Preservation Program, and the Family Advocate Program.

Management within Fixed Resources

The Divide Wellness Center is managed and administered jointly by the PHD and Marshall Hospital, and its staff comprises employees of both the PHD and the hospital. In general, the PHD is responsible for aspects of the center relative to preventive care, and the hospital is responsible for primary care. The integration of different budgets developed for prevention services, primary care, and public and private organizations has provided challenges for the Community Wellness Partnership. Specific issues that have arisen include equity of pay for employees across public and private not-for-profit organizations, reimbursement rates for preventive and primary care, outcome expectations for prevention and primary care, and use of a sliding fee scale. As the Wellness Center begins its second year of operation, the Wellness Partnership is devoting much time, effort, and discussion to exploring economical ways to express the integration of these functions and public versus private accounting principles.

An example of a creative way that is being examined with regard to the most effective utilization of funds is that the PAT has been given the authority to decide how to expend the funds that are budgeted as payment for services to the organizations it comprises. Originally, there was a set amount of money earmarked for each of the organizations to provide services. To better serve the interests of the community, however, the team is being asked to determine in conjunction with the community the most critical need for services and then direct the funds to provide the most appropriate service to meet those needs.

The Community Wellness Partnership is proactively seeking to collaborate on initiatives that will support its visions and efforts. In doing so, it will continue to explore innovative ways to increase community health and build on its successes so that it becomes more of a force and a systems change in the community.

Each Community Wellness Partner has contributed funding for the Divide Wellness Center. The amount of each partner's contribution was determined by their own resources. This strategy, which spreads financial responsibilities, ensures that partners share in the financial risks associated with the project as well as its successes. Community organizations also contributed in the form of services, gifts, or cash contributions.

MOVING TOWARD THE COMMUNITY CARE NETWORK VISION

Community Care Network Statement

The Community Wellness Partnership in El Dorado County shares the CCN's vision for a healthy community. Elements of the vision toward which the Community Wellness Partnership is working include a system of health care that possesses the following characteristics:

- *Decentralized:* Honoring and manifesting the nature of the community it serves. Services are delivered locally.

Phase Two: Program Development and Implementation Activities during this phase will include developing and implementing a Wellness Center in Pollock Pines that is consistent with the CCN vision and the needs and nature of the Pollock Pines community. With respect to the CCN vision, the goals of this second phase are to develop and implement a Wellness Center in the Pollock Pines area that has the following components: (1) provides for interorganizational planning, (2) provides a full spectrum of health and social services to meet the specific needs of the community that were identified in phase one, (3) provides structures that ensure coordination and integration of services within the Wellness Center and the community to ensure a seamless continuum of care, (4) provides for integration of financial, clinical, administrative, and staffing systems, and (5) establishes evaluation processes that provide for community monitoring of the Wellness Center.

Activities:

1. Conduct planning sessions for developing an approach for the Wellness Center that is consistent with the needs and resources of the community and that includes strategies for case management, community outreach, community health education, and medical, social, and nonmedical services.
   - Responsible entity: Community Wellness Partnership
   - Proposed completion date: 2/96
2. Establish structures for integrating financial, clinical, administrative, social service and staffing systems among all organizations involved.
   - Responsible entity: Community Wellness Partnership
   - Proposed completion date: 4/96
3. Develop pay for service, sliding-scale payment system.
   - Responsible entity: PHD, Marshall Hospital
   - Proposed completion date: 5/96
4. Select Wellness Center site.
   - Responsible entity: Marshall Hospital
   - Proposed completion date: 5/96
5. Develop public relations campaign for the Wellness Center.
   - Responsible entity: Community Wellness Partnership
   - Proposed completion date: 6/96
6. Develop memorandums of understanding with outside organizations (preferably organizations in the community) to deliver appropriate services at the Wellness Center.
   - Responsible entity: PHD
   - Proposed completion date: 7/96
7. Meaningfully involve the community in the preparing and opening of the Wellness Center.
   - Responsible entity: Community Wellness Partnership
   - Proposed completion date: 7/96

8. Conduct retreats for community and Wellness Center to develop vision for the center and to foster teamwork.
   - Responsible entity: Community Wellness Partnership
   - Proposed completion date: 8/96
9. Hire and train staff for the Wellness Center.
   - Responsible entity: PHD, Marshall Hospital
   - Proposed completion date: 8/96
10. Establish regular meetings of Wellness Center staff.
    - Responsible entity: Wellness Center
    - Proposed completion date: 8/96
11. Prepare Wellness Center site for opening.
    - Responsible entity: PHD, Marshall Hospital
    - Proposed completion date: 8/96
12. Begin Wellness Center services: medical, outreach, case management, social service, health education.
    - Responsible entity: Wellness Center
    - Proposed completion date: 9/96
13. Develop evaluation process for the Wellness Center that provides for community monitoring.
    - Responsible entity: PHD
    - Proposed completion date: 12/96
14. Conduct evaluation of the Wellness Center and issue a report to the community.
    - Responsible entity: PHD
    - Proposed completion date: 1/97

Phase Three: Project Continuation and Refinement During this phase, the services of the Wellness Center will be evaluated by input from the community, and services will be refined to best meet the needs. Also during this phase, continued funding will be acquired and the vision will be expanded.

With respect to the CCN vision, the goals of this third phase are to: (1) provide ongoing community-wide assessment and monitoring, (2) develop a capitated payment system, and (3) develop incentives for nonduplication of services.

Activities:

1. Revise Wellness Center strategies based on results of the evaluation.
   - Responsible entity: Wellness Center
   - Proposed completion date: 3/97
2. Develop and implement financial and other incentives that encourage nonduplication of services.
   - Responsible entity: Wellness Partnership
   - Proposed completion date: 4/97

3. Identify strategies for capitated payment systems.
    - Responsible entity: PHD, Marshall Hospital
    - Proposed completion date: 6/97
4. Identify potential funding sources of matching funds and gain commitment for years two and three.
    - Responsible entity: Community Wellness Partnership
    - Proposed completion date: 7/97
5. Help providers determine which clients they best serve and develop strategies to refer appropriate clients to them.
    - Responsible entity: PHD
    - Proposed completion date: 7/97
6. Identify strategies to appropriately link the various decentralized Community Wellness Partnership areas while maintaining local autonomy and working toward a balanced system of health care countywide.
    - Responsible entity: Community Wellness Partnership
    - Proposed completion date: 8/97
7. Develop and implement strategies to move toward global budgets.
    - Responsible entity: Community Wellness Partnership
    - Proposed completion date: 8/97
8. Identify strategies for ongoing funding beyond year three.
    - Responsible entity: Community Wellness Partnership
    - Proposed completion date: 5/98
9. Identify potential new communities within the county that would be appropriate to expand the Community Wellness Partnership to and develop strategies for doing so.
    - Responsible entity: Community Wellness Partnership
    - Proposed completion date: 6/98

SUMMARY OF NOTABLE PROGRESS

Our initiative continues to be committed to the vision of the CCN. Within those principles, we have achieved significant progress.

The focus of our original effort was to replicate our success in developing and implementing a rural health clinic, the Divide Wellness Center, in another area of our county. The focus of this summary is twofold: (1) to describe continued progress in the first successful program, the Divide Wellness Center; and (2) to describe our progress in using that model to replicate it in another area of our county, Pollock Pines.

Divide Wellness Center

The Divide Wellness Center has achieved notable success in many areas, particularly the following:

- A not-for-profit community-based agency specializing in perinatal parenting support (WEE CARE) obtained a family preservation/family support grant through the Department of Social Services to implement an intervention program for high-risk families in the Divide community through the Divide Wellness Center.
- The DCSN, which is the community representative on the Divide Wellness Center Coalition, partnered with seven other rural communities in California and Nevada to successfully achieve a Center for Substance Abuse Prevention community partnership grant through which was developed the Sierra Nevada Rural Health Coalition. The project aims to strengthen the individual community and coalition partnerships to more successfully garner resources for rural communities.
- An AmeriCorps intern developed and implemented an activity program for youth and families called "Saturday Night." One Saturday night a month, the local high school opens its gymnasium for youth, parent, and family activities.
- A subcommittee of the DCSN developed and implemented a domestic violence educational training program for local businesses.
- A subcommittee of the DCSN developed and implemented a mentoring program for youth and adults in the community.
- A telephone-calling program was implemented for seniors in the community. Volunteers telephone seniors at regular intervals to help them monitor their health and well-being.
- The Family Advocate Program has proven a valuable resource to the community and to the other agencies and organizations that provide services on the Divide. As trust of the community has grown, the caseload of the Family Advocate staff has greatly increased. As a testament to the value of the Family Advocate Program to other agencies and organizations, Family Advocate staff have been invited to regularly attend the staff meetings of other agencies and organizations (including Child Protective Services and Probation) to more effectively provide resources to those agencies/organizations.
- The Divide Wellness Center consortium developed a comprehensive business plan, which detailed the financial status of the rural health center and developed projections on its ability to be self-sustaining. If projections hold true, the Divide Wellness Center will be financially self-sustaining before initial grant funding from the Office of Rural Health Services expires.
- The evaluation of the Divide Wellness Center was developed and conducted by a subcommittee of the DCSN in conjunction with staff from the El Dorado County PHD. This community/public partnership represents a highly successful innovation to program evaluation.

Pollock Pines

The El Dorado County PHD successfully achieved a grant from the Sacramento Regional Foundation, which provides resources for developing strategies for increasing medical access for underserved populations. A portion of those funds is currently being used to coordinate the development of a Wellness Center in Pollock Pines. Following is a list of the achievements from that effort:

- Conducted a community-wide health assessment.
- Implemented a regular health column in the newsletter of a community-wide coalition.
- Brought together work groups of community members to discuss the health needs of the underserved populations.
- Conducted community-mapping and resource-mapping.
- Conducted preliminary planning for a community health center.
- Identified a list of community health indicators that broaden the definition of "health."

Contact: Gayle Erbe-Hamlin
El Dorado Public Health Department
931 Spring St.
Placerville, CA 95667
Phone: (916) 621-6191
Fax: (916) 642-8159

16

The Community Health Plan of the Siskiyous

Executive Summary

The Community Care Partnership of the Siskiyous is a partnership of several organizations in Siskiyou County, CA, a rural mountain region in the northernmost part of the state. The county has a land area of 6,281 square miles. Of the county's total population of 43,531, 14 percent are below poverty level. The median household income is $21,921. In families with a female head of household with related children under the age of 18, nearly 51 percent are below poverty level. Our partnership is working to address the health access issues that face our community. Our rural remote location, combined with a high level of unemployment and large numbers of uninsured or underinsured "working poor" in our area, creates significant barriers to health care for many in the community. In addition, south Siskiyou County has been federally designated as a health professional shortage area (HPSA). Tertiary medical centers are an hour's drive away from both small hospitals that serve the local communities. Winter snow conditions only exacerbate the difficulties residents experience in obtaining needed medical services.

Our partnership consists of the Community Health Plan of the Siskiyous, a collaborative effort of business leaders, health care providers, and consumers; the Health Services Council (HSC), a community-based health care planning group; the Mt. Shasta Medi-Cal Clinic; and Mercy Medical Center Mt. Shasta (MMCMS), a division of Catholic Healthcare West. Specific initiatives we are pursuing include the following:

1. Developing a local community health plan, designed to reduce or minimize the inflation of health insurance costs for local employers while maintaining and improving the quality and efficiency of our local health care system
2. Expanding access to health care for low-income residents, including an effort to purchase vital preventive health screens for the uninsured or underinsured in our community
3. Developing a continuum of care for the elderly in our community that would include assisted living, care coordination, adult day health, a geriatric clinic, and expanded home health services

was instrumental in the formation of the HSC and has demonstrated a commitment to incorporating the input from the community into its own strategic planning process. Many of the health promotion activities that MMCMS has developed are a direct response to the needs identified by the HSC in an effort to do the will of the community. As the only hospital in south Siskiyou County, MMCMS plays a critical role. MMCMS and Siskiyou General Hospital, in the north county, have put up initial funds of $4,500 to help in establishing the CHPS.

MMCMS and Siskiyou General Hospital have a long history of partnering in response to community needs. In 1985, when home health services for the county were in jeopardy, the two hospitals together created Siskiyou Home Health. Each hospital owns 50 percent of the equity interest in Siskiyou Home Health. They meet regularly to monitor the development of this community service, which has grown dramatically over the years, as evidenced in the increase in the number of annual home visits from 2,294 in 1986 to 26,714 in 1994.

The Mt. Shasta Medi-Cal Clinic has been extremely responsive to community needs wherever possible. By expanding its services to serve low-income residents who do not qualify for Medi-Cal, it has helped address access issues in our community. Northern Rural Health, another partnership effort, is a consortium of the five rural health clinics and the two hospitals in the county. This group came together to explore the feasibility of doing a pilot project for Medi-Cal managed care in a rural area. Although the program has not been implemented, the effort and ongoing dialogue of this group are of great value. In the future, we see the HSC coordinating community-based health care planning in the south county, the CHPS developing a local health insurance option for county employers, and the Mt. Shasta Medi-Cal Clinic working on access issues, with MMCMS supporting each of the efforts.

There is a commitment among all the members of our partnership to the value of collaboration and to the ideals expressed in the CCN vision. We will work with Siskiyou General Hospital, the County Health Department, the Family Interagency Services Council, the local community college, schools, and senior groups to further meet community health needs.

PRIOR EFFORTS THAT REPRESENT MOVEMENT TOWARD THE COMMUNITY CARE NETWORK VISION

Many activities and new projects have been established to respond to the health care needs identified in the HSC community survey. These activities reflect the values of the CCN vision.

Community Health Focus

In the area of access, education, and early intervention with a focus on changing behaviors to prevent disease, we have established the following:

1. *The Mercy-CHW Health Access Grant Program:* A $25,000 grant from the Catholic Healthcare West (CHW) Community Grants Program was matched by the MMCMS board, creating a $50,000 program designed to assist the working poor who have had difficulty accessing affordable health care. This program, administered by the Mt. Shasta Medi-Cal Clinic, offers important preventive health

screens to those uninsured or underinsured who do not qualify for Medi-Cal. Participants pay a nominal fee of $5 to $15 for mammograms, women's annual physicals including Pap smears, men's annual physicals, prostate screens, and a mini–blood panel to test for cholesterol and blood glucose.

The program also has a component for young pregnant women, which provides a free pregnancy test, prenatal vitamins, books on pregnancy and child development, referrals to physicians, bus tickets, and incentives for making all prenatal appointments, such as an infant car seat. In conjunction with the County Health Department, immunizations are also offered to low-income families. Since its June 1994 start-up, this program has completed more than 240 physicals, which have identified such problems as hematuria, undiagnosed hypertension, pelvic infections, and elevated cholesterol levels. Several suspicious mammograms have resulted in follow-up care, including two surgical candidates who were referred to the Early Breast Cancer Detection Program, which covers such procedures.

Seventy-five women have received prenatal care. Practitioners have noted a definite increase in women keeping their prenatal appointments through the incentive program. We would hope to see an improvement in low birth weights as a result of this effort. Teen pregnancy is a serious issue in our county. The conception age is lowering as more 14- and 15-year-olds are getting pregnant. These girls seem to have more tendency to smoke and often have low-birth-weight babies.

2. *Healthy Habits for Hospital Employees:* In this 12-week course that focuses on exercise, fitness, nutrition, weight management, and stress reduction, participants set goals for lifestyle changes with the assistance of coaches and team support. A new program, Healthy Habits for People with Diabetes, also has been offered to the community. This 12-week program focuses on offering experiences and group support in addition to education that promotes healthier living with diabetes. Future courses will target groups for cardiac risk management, arthritis, and senior fitness. Health education seminars for the community on such topics as depression, menopause, breast cancer, and cholesterol are sponsored by MMCMS and are free of charge.
3. *Healthwise for Life:* Working together, the Mt. Shasta Recreation and Parks District, the Senior Nutrition Program, and MMCMS obtained a grant to distribute books to seniors throughout Siskiyou County. *Healthwise for Life: Medical Self Care for Healthy Aging* and *Growing Wiser: The Older Person's Guide to Mental Wellness* are resource books to help seniors take a more active role in managing their health.
4. *Health Matters:* MMCMS has instituted a weekly newspaper column, "Health Matters," which provides valuable health information.
5. *Health fair:* The annual health fair brings together volunteers from throughout the health care community. Last year 680 people had their blood drawn for an enhanced chemistry panel that assesses cardiac risk and thyroid function.
6. *Sports physicals:* These are offered at the local high school by a large group of physicians, nurses, and family nurse practitioners.
7. *Fourth of July Fun Walk:* This very popular community event is cosponsored by Mt. Shasta Mountain Runners and MMCMS with the help of several local groups. This activity promotes health, fitness, and antismoking with flair. Last year nearly 5,000 people participated. In some instances four generations of families walk

or run in the 2-mile or 5-mile course. This is one of the biggest small-town races in the western United States, and was named one of the top 100 events by *Runner's World* magazine.

8. *The Nepenthe Trail:* MMCMS has begun to build a series of wheelchair-accessible trails throughout the hospital grounds to provide patients, families, and the community with another dimension of the healing process—the soothing calm of the outdoors. Nestled at the base of 14,000-foot Mt. Shasta, the hospital grounds offer spectacular vistas. This project has received extensive community support. The first loop of the trail was built entirely with community donations. With the active support of the Mt. Shasta Recreation and Parks District, the long-range plan for the Nepenthe project is to develop a trail system leading from the downtown area through the hospital grounds and on out to the city park, to provide a safe place for people of all ages to exercise.
9. *Senior Wheels:* In the developmental stage, this HSC project is designed as a volunteer program in which retired people would drive other seniors to medical appointments in an effort to respond to unmet transportation needs. Many of these projects work in concert with physicians, the hospital, physical therapists, the local college, and the County Health Department.

The enthusiastic participation of the community in the above-listed activities demonstrates the interest that exists for programs that promote health and disease prevention. We anticipate good community response for future activities. Giving the community a voice in planning programs enhances the likelihood they will be well received. To assess and monitor progress in meeting explicitly stated community health objectives, the HSC meets three to four times a year.

Community Accountability

After the extensive community participation in the initial assessment done by the HSC, members were asked to participate in MMCMS's strategic planning process. Community members on the strategic planning task force attended a hospital board–medical staff retreat. The recommendations from the HSC community assessment became an integral component of the visioning process for the hospital's upcoming 3-year plan. To complete the cycle of community involvement, MMCMS brings back to the HSC the final copy of the hospital's strategic plan and updates to the plan.

To maximize community participation in further health care planning, in 1993 the HSC sponsored a countywide forum on health care reform to educate the public. More than 80 community participants attended the 7-hour seminar. They represented schools, government, social service agencies, consumers, local businesses, and the health care community. The guiding principles of the forum were as follows:

1. Rural communities such as ours can affect their own health care future, and education is an essential first step in the process.
2. To do this, communities must collaborate, work together as a team. We can also gain much from efforts to regionalize, reaching out far enough to involve our neighboring communities, so as to avoid isolation.
3. If we work locally, we can control health care costs without damaging either the health care system or our access to that system.

Throughout the seminar, participants heard consultants discuss issues that affect health care from a national, state, and local perspective. Other communities' efforts also were presented. Break-out sessions were held in small groups to provide participants an opportunity to give input as to where we needed to head locally. The seminar closed with a visioning session. The resounding theme from the group was a desire to move forward in empowering the local community, and to establish a community health plan. The message was also very clear: The community wanted to be involved in the process rather than have it be driven by the provider community. The vision was a partnership. That evening a steering committee was formed to work toward the development of a community health plan. The steering committee and interim board have had active community representation, and the bylaws for the permanent board call for even greater community participation.

In yet another effort to solicit input and suggestions from the community, MMCMS has been conducting patient satisfaction surveys of all inpatient and emergency department patients. Processed by a marketing research firm, the patient experience surveys provide staff with an excellent source of information about how patients perceive the care they are receiving. The instrument is used throughout CHW divisions, providing an opportunity for benchmarking systemwide. We can compare performance and draw upon the expertise of other hospitals that demonstrate excellence in any given area. The survey process usually lasts for several months, and two surveys are done a year.

MMCMS has also recently completed a market demand survey to better understand what local people want in the area of health and fitness programs. The survey was conducted by telephone through a consultant. To identify individuals who would talk candidly about health issues, 100 people were randomly selected and screened. The data collected provide us with important information about consumer expectations and preferences for health and fitness activities.

The features most desired by local residents, in order of preference, include the following:

1. A personalized approach to assessing needs and help to achieve fitness goals
2. Weight loss and nutrition programs
3. Rehabilitation services for sports-related injuries
4. A lap pool for swimming and aqua-aerobics
5. Health and fitness programs specifically for adults over 60

The MMCMS board will use this study in its planning for future service priorities. The local media have reported the key activities of the HSC and the CHPS, as well as the health education activities of the hospital. MMCMS also has a newsletter that is distributed to nearly 7,000 residents, which explains these issues and developments.

Seamless Continuum of Care

One area of concern raised in the community assessment was the desire for a strengthening of the care partnership between the patient, the physician, and the family. In an effort to heighten the sensitivity of the provider community to these issues, Siskiyou Medical Group, a local primary care group, and MMCMS cosponsored training seminars in customer relations and patient satisfaction for all medical office staff, hospital employees, and physicians. The goal of these seminars was to improve service to patients and better coordinate the service delivery between physicians' offices and the hospital. Staff from the hospital and the doctors' offices continue to meet on a quarterly basis to facilitate service coordination and early problem resolution. The goal of these meetings is to make as smooth an experience as possible for patients and family members as they work their way through the local health care system.

The historical partnership of Siskiyou General Hospital and MMCMS that has sustained Siskiyou Home Health is looking at ways to facilitate enhanced service coordination for the future. A study is planned to make recommendations regarding the integration of home health care into patient care case management in order to bridge the continuum of care for patients. There is a growing awareness that the future of health care lies in our ability to create organized systems of care with physicians, hospitals, and ancillary and home health service providers.

In another effort to strengthen the continuum of care for the elderly in our community, Mercy Care Center, the skilled nursing facility that is part of MMCMS, has been working with the Robert Wood Johnson Foundation on the Coming Home Project. Funding and technical assistance were obtained to conduct a feasibility study of Mt. Shasta as a site for an assisted living housing project. Mercy Charities Housing would be the builder and owner of the facility. MMCMS would support it with case management services and programs designed to develop a continuum of care for the elderly. These programs would include: an information resource service; disease prevention education; geriatric fitness and conditioning; home health care; home delivered meals; homemaker chores; expanded patient and family education in the areas of pharmacology, caretaker training, and cancer support; and a desperately needed adult day care program. To date, the interaction and encouragement from the Robert Wood Johnson Foundation has been very positive. A decision on future funding from Robert Wood Johnson for the Coming Home Project is pending.

Management within Fixed Resources

In an effort to manage within fixed resources and to respond to the identified problem of access for the working poor, the Mt. Shasta Medi-Cal Clinic worked to expand its services. Starting in 1993, the clinic introduced a sliding fee scale for low-income residents who do not qualify for Medi-Cal. The fees for services provided are based on the individual's income level. The service area for south Siskiyou County recently received a federal designation as an HPSA. Because the Mt. Shasta Medi-Cal Clinic is located in the HPSA, it is now eligible to apply for one of two designations, the 95-210 or the federally qualified health clinic (FQHC). This will enable it to provide services to low-income working poor and the Medi-Cal population in a way that will give it a cost-based method of reimbursement.

Managing within fixed resources is at the heart of the CHPS efforts. We are working to develop a local health insurance plan, provide cost-effective high-quality care, and gather local data that will educate the community at large. Volunteers have worked tirelessly for these goals.

Several key concepts drive our work. CHPS is a group of stakeholders, each wearing more than one hat, with an interest in not only developing responsible health care alternatives but also the quality of life in our community. We are optimistic in our belief that we can work together to move past narrow self-interest to develop and then act out of commonly identified goals, concerns, and interests. To be truly innovative and creative in developing local options and cost-effective alternatives, we first need information about how people are consuming health care now. Data that are reliable, timely, and specific provide us a means of reality-based decision making.

Accurate information is critical to open communication, and is a means of avoiding "unmovable political" positions of any single group.

To date, we have obtained access to one year of baseline claims information from a 3,800-member group, a one-year baseline from a 100-member group (not-for-profit entity), and three months and ongoing claims information from an 800-member group. Analysis of these data is not complete, but the information will be instrumental in our planning strategies and will help us develop a comprehensive overview of medical care delivery in our county. With these data, we can then make informed decisions about where to put resources to realize cost-effective change. We will be looking to identify potential problem areas as indicated by poor quality or inappropriate utilization measures.

To find quantifiable evidence of factors impacting outcomes, we are interested in outcome measures. With accurate claims data, we can also educate employers about how their employees are consuming health care. The goal is to empower the employer to manage resources and maximize cost benefit. We will be working together to identify priority areas for prevention education and to create incentives necessary to encourage enrollees to make healthier lifestyle choices.

CHPS uses "Patterns of Treatment" computer software to analyze ambulatory claims patterns. We have access to the program on a service bureau basis, which makes it feasible to offer the program to small employers. (The cost of a license is normally cost prohibitive.) "Patterns of Treatment" standardizes case management and identifies abnormal utilization patterns. To provide the community with cost-effective, high-quality care or "value," we must establish efficient patterns of practice among local physicians. Physicians with exemplary case management efficiency and quality can then be chosen as case management consultants. CHPS provides a structure through which "Patterns" information can be used to identify and address provider education needs. Over 90 percent of practicing physicians countywide make fee discounts available to local employers through the CHPS PPO and agree to participate in peer review. Both hospitals offer discounts as well.

Although our county has had little involvement with managed care up to now, there is a growing belief that we must be proactive in planning for it. We are currently studying capitation and risk-sharing models. Our CHPS focus is to understand the forms risk is currently taking and develop means of managing it better as a whole community. Our tools in this endeavor are the following:

1. Data
2. Open communication among providers and purchasers of care
3. An understanding of current incentives and their related fiscal impact

Tracking our health care cost relative to populations (capitation indices) will allow us to measure the effect of incentive changes. "Patterns" and related quality-utilization review programs will help us look at the benefit-to-cost relationships, helping to identify areas where costs can be reduced without detriment to care.

MOVING TOWARD THE COMMUNITY CARE NETWORK VISION

The Vision

The CCN vision has served to crystallize the directions and philosophy inherent in the activities of our local partnerships for the past several years. With the help of the CCN vision language and our experiences in community-based health care planning, we have arrived at the following statement of our vision:

> We believe that rural communities can affect their own health care future. With education as an essential tool, we can empower the local community to be an active partner in identifying needs, shaping health care delivery to meet those needs, and managing the health care dollars to provide the most cost-effective care to the community. Where competition between providers has been a workable technique for reducing cost in metropolitan areas, we believe collaboration is the key to moving forward with our vision in a rural area where access is already a problem. We do not want to lose providers through competitive marketing campaigns. The development of a local health plan unites the two hospitals in the county, Mercy Medical Center Mt. Shasta and Siskiyou General Hospital, with physicians, alternative care providers, consumers, and business leaders in a common effort to improve the health status of the community. Reliable, timely, and specific data help us know who we are and how we can develop a vision that will work for us, rather than attempt to "graft" models from other environments. The health care delivery system we are creating will be integrated and provide a seamless continuum of care. It has a primary focus on wellness, prevention, and related cost savings, and emphasizes the individual's responsibility in making healthier lifestyle choices and consuming health care in the most cost-effective manner possible. By focusing on community health and being mindful of our accountability to the community, we are setting the direction for the future. We have created a partnership that is proactive, that seeks to improve access to health care, to manage within fixed resources while preserving the broadest appropriate range of local health services.

The Visioning Process

Our visioning process began in 1990, when MMCMS set in motion the development of the HSC. The extensive activities of the HSC in conducting and analyzing the community needs assessment played a major role in setting the future direction of community-based health care planning. MMCMS brought members of the community and the recommendations of the HSC into its own strategic planning process. Demonstrating its respect for, and the value of, the community process, the MMCMS board incorporated the input about community needs into the goals and targets articulated in its strategic plan. The 7-hour seminar on health care reform sponsored by the HSC in 1993 offered an effective opportunity for education and consensus building. The 80 people who worked together in the final session of the evening processed the information and mapped out a strategy for moving forward. The clear consensus of the participants was to actively work with community participation toward the development of a local community health plan that would create a structure for local decision making about health care delivery issues.

The steering committee for CHPS was formed that night. Acknowledging that effective management within fixed resources was critical for the health care system in our county, the community gave vision to the future work of CHPS as a key structure in addressing managed care issues. The CHPS steering committee and interim board have sought the input of many segments of the community in its planning efforts. Large employers in the area have been interviewed to ascertain what needs could be met with a local health plan. Representation of the business community, county government, and consumers has been invaluable in shaping our direction. When the information about the national CCN demonstration program became available, meetings were held to discuss the vision with both the HSC and the CHPS. Other interested community agencies were invited to join in the process to determine how we might most effectively participate in this demonstration program. There was clear agreement that the CCN vision was at the heart of the activities we had been pursuing for many years.

We have a strong foundation and a well-established coalition. We have experienced success in the actions we have taken to date. As a low-income rural community, we now need financial assistance to continue. Specifically, we need staff to expand initiatives already in progress, further develop the quality and utilization review functions, as well as oversee the updating of our database and information distribution to local employers and the community at large.

We see the national demonstration program as an opportunity to strengthen and expand our efforts. In fact, that is already happening. Our visioning sessions have been very stimulating, helping us to refocus our vision, to invite new participants to our partnership, and to take stock of which activities will prove most effective in making our community a healthier place in the months and years to come.

INITIATIVES FOR MOVING TOWARD THE COMMUNITY CARE NETWORK VISION

Community Health Focus

1. *Conduct a new community needs assessment and develop a responsive plan.*
   Responsibilities:
   a. HSC and MMCMS will develop an instrument and methodology for conducting the assessment.
   b. HSC will develop priorities for action and a response plan. The community needs assessment is scheduled to be conducted by January 1996. HSC will meet regularly throughout 1996 to develop the response plan.
2. *Develop a community benefit plan.* Create a formal plan for MMCMS community benefit activities and a mechanism for reporting back to the community.
   Responsibility: MMCMS for hospital activities
   Proposed Timeline: April 1996
3. *Expand access for low-income persons through the Medi-Cal Clinic.*
   Responsibilities Mt. Shasta Medi-Cal Clinic, HSC, and MMCMS
   Proposed Timeline: Develop new sources by June 1996
4. *Expand Healthy Habits program to serve target groups in the community.*
   Responsibility: MMCMS
   Proposed Timeline: Cardiac Risk—January 1996; Senior Fitness—April 1, 1996; Arthritis—October 1, 1996
   Baseline: Program structure already in place
5. *Stimulate government and private efforts to increase services for teenagers (counseling for pregnancy, substance abuse, behavioral problems).*
   Responsibility: HSC members

Proposed Timeline: Initiate in 1996; ongoing needs evaluation
Baseline: Dialogue with local high school ongoing

6. *Develop geriatric fitness and conditioning program; expand patient and family education in pharmacology, caretaker training, cancer support.*
Responsibility: Mercy Care Center—MMCMS
Proposed Timeline: December 1996
Baseline: In the planning stage

7. *Work with local employers on injury prevention programs.*
Responsibility: MMCMS Therapy Services Department
Proposed Timeline: Ongoing evaluation of employer needs
Baseline: Initiated contacts with six different companies

8. *Maintain current community health activities, that is, health fair, sports physicals, health education seminars, Fourth of July Fun Walk, smoking cessation clinic.*
Responsibilities: MMCMS, physicians, and other health care practitioners
Proposed Timeline: Annually
Baseline: All currently in place

9. *Develop the Nepenthe Trail from the downtown area to the city park for use by all residents for exercise and biking.*
Responsibilities: MMCMS, Mt. Shasta Recreation and Parks District
Proposed Timeline: To be completed by June 1998
Baseline: Initial loops of trail complete on hospital grounds, establishing contacts with property owners involved in full trail

10. *Implement Senior Wheels program to assist in transporting seniors to medical appointments, or identify other means of meeting senior transportation needs.*
Responsibility: HSC
Proposed Timeline: January 1996
Baseline: Volunteer coordinator recruited

Community Accountability

1. *Maintain HSC as the focus of community-based health care planning.*
Responsibility: HSC
Proposed Timeline: Meetings held quarterly
Baseline: Currently meeting three to four times a year

2. *Expand representation on HSC.*
Responsibility: HSC
Proposed Timeline: Ongoing

3. *Maintain patient satisfaction surveys to receive patient input.*
Responsibility: MMCMS
Proposed Timeline: Two surveys a year
Baseline: Currently two surveys a year

4. *Per bylaws, when appointing the permanent CHPS board, ensure extensive community representation.*
Responsibility: CHPS
Proposed Timeline: April 1996

5. *Commit to an ongoing evaluation of quality-utilization indicators and related priority-setting and action programs.*

Responsibility: CHPS
Proposed Timeline: Ongoing, with quarterly meetings

Seamless Continuum of Care

1. *Implement the continuum of care for the elderly as outlined in the Coming Home Project to include an assisted living housing complex, adult day care, patient care case management, home health care, and a full array of services.*
   Responsibility: MMCMS Mercy Care Center
   Proposed Timeline: Decision from Robert Wood Johnson, December 1995
   Baseline: Feasibility study complete
2. *Develop an information resource center.*
   Responsibility: MMCMS, HSC
   Proposed Timeline: April 1996
3. *Integrate home health services with patient case management.*
   Responsibility: Siskiyou General Hospital, MMCMS
   Proposed Timeline: December 1995
   Baseline: Feasibility study being planned
4. *Identify and implement other ways to extend outpatient services to outlying areas.*
   Responsibility: MMCMS
   Proposed Timeline: June 1996
5. *Recruit primary care physicians, especially OB-GYN.*
   Responsibilities: Physicians and MMCMS
   Proposed Timeline: Ongoing
6. *Identify through data evaluation, potential failures in care continuum, with related design of action responses.*
   Responsibilities: CHPS, HSC
   Proposed Timeline: Ongoing, with quarterly reporting

Managing within Fixed Resources

1. *Apply for the 95-210 or FQHC designation for the Mt. Shasta Medi-Cal Clinic to obtain cost-based reimbursement for contracted provider services.*
   Responsibility: Mt. Shasta Medi-Cal Clinic
   Proposed Timeline: January 1996
   Baseline: Obtained the prerequisite HPSA designation
2. *Continue the development of the CHPS and elect a permanent board of directors of 14 in accord with bylaws.*
   Responsibility: CHPS interim board
   Proposed Timeline: December 1995
   Baseline: Seven interim board members
3. *Expand the CHPS PPO to include not just physicians and hospitals but also dental, pharmacy, and alternative care providers.*
   Responsibility: CHPS
   Proposed Timeline: By December 1995, two additional provider groups on the panel. Add additional group every six months.
   Baseline: 90 percent of county active practicing physicians and 100 percent of hospitals.

4. *Build an exemplary data system and research capability that will support innovative quality and utilization review programs.*
   Responsibility: CHPS
   Proposed Timeline: December 1995 and ongoing
   Baseline: We have one quarter's worth of results from Patterns—automated ambulatory care screens from a large group. In addition to baseline data from other groups, we anticipate being able to complete an evaluation, identify priority goals, and set measurable objectives for the coming year.
5. *Establish the computer capability to manage data, including computers, software, printers, etc. Develop study library of research materials, periodicals, newsletters, and automated data, that is, census, birth statistics, morbidity, and mortality data.*
   Responsibility: CHPS
   Proposed Timeline: September 1995
   Baseline: We currently are acquiring a computer for the CHPS office.
6. *Explore feasibility of developing databases from other source files—immunizations, Medi-Cal clinics, hospital logs, court records, etc.*
   Responsibility: CHPS
   Proposed Timeline: June 1996
   Baseline: Early explorations
7. *Identify and utilize outcome measures to document program results.*
   Responsibility: CHPS
   Proposed Timeline: January 1996
   Baseline: Early Patterns data are under review.
8. *Support active physician peer review committees comprising PPO panel members. Provide staff support needed for collection of data, evaluation, reporting, and documentation of problem identification and resolution efforts.*
   Responsibility: CHPS
   Proposed Timeline: Ongoing
   Baseline: Peer review is being conducted by the medical director of CHPS with other volunteer physicians.
9. *Work with the large self-funded employer groups in the county, specifically the County of Siskiyou and the Siskiyou County Schools Joint Powers Agreement—establish a contractual agreement with each.*
   Responsibility: CHPS
   Proposed Timeline: December 1995
   Baseline: Currently the county is contracting with CHPS for the use of the physician panel. Negotiations are under way with the county schools.
10. *Develop a product specifically designed for small businesses and individuals.*
    Responsibility: CHPS
    Proposed Timeline: January 1997
    Baseline: Discussions are under way with potential insurance partners.
11. *Conduct feasibility study of capitation and risk-sharing structures.*
    Responsibilities: CHPS, MMCMS, physicians
    Proposed Timeline: January 1997

Baseline: Evaluation of current risk patterns and related cost measurements is under way.

SUMMARY OF NOTABLE PROGRESS

The community care partnership of the Siskiyous has been working diligently in key areas in the past year. A major focus has been the effort to get the CHPS established as a viable local community health plan. We have developed a business plan, hired a consultant, secured the participation of the vast majority of practicing physicians in Siskiyou County on our panel, and established contacts with several local employers and third-party vendors. (See figure 16-1.) A mechanism for analyzing patterns of treatment is in place. This computerized claims analysis program evaluates local care based on nationally accepted standards of care guidelines. It allows us to identify opportunities to improve cost-effective utilization of health care resources and initiate peer review.

We have continued our efforts to capitalize the project, soliciting support from both hospitals and the physicians participating in the plan. Discussions are under way with Blue Cross–Blue Shield and Wausau to negotiate a contract with a primary vendor to meet the needs of local employers. The process has been slow but steady. This collaborative work on the part of business leaders, physicians, and hospital staff holds the potential of creating in our rural area a health plan that will be responsive to both large and small employers. We will be able to provide employers with valuable information about how their employees are consuming health care. Our goal is to work with employers to design wellness education programs for their employees and to create incentives to encourage enrollees to make healthier lifestyle choices, thus creating savings in dollars spent locally on health care.

The effort to develop a continuum of care for the elderly in south Siskiyou County has involved ongoing collaboration. After working with a group of local community organizations, the Robert Wood Johnson Foundation selected our area as a national demonstration site for the Coming Home Project. The goal of this project is to design a continuum of care that includes care coordination, assisted living, adult day health care, a geriatric clinic, and expanded home health services. Robert Wood Johnson has supported this effort with $85,000 for planning activities. In the past year, we have secured the land for the assisted living complex, which will include the adult day health care and the geriatric clinic on site. Drawings for the complex are being finalized. The Mt. Shasta Medi-Cal Clinic received $150,000 for adult day health care start-up from the U.S. Department of Agriculture. These dollars were awarded for the potential jobs that will be created by this program.

Key players involved in this collaborative effort for elderly services include: MMCMS, the Mt. Shasta Medi-Cal Clinic, local physicians, home health, our senior housing facility, the Area Agency on Aging, Great Northern Corporation, Rural Community Assistance Corporation from Sacramento, Mercy Charities Housing in San Francisco, and the National Cooperative Bank.

MMCMS was instrumental in seeking and obtaining the HPSA federal designation for south Siskiyou County. That allowed the Mt. Shasta Medi-Cal Clinic to apply for the 95-210 designation as a rural health clinic. The clinic received that designation

FIGURE 16-1. Management Services Agreement

1. **Recitals**

Whereas Community Health Plan of the Siskiyous, Inc. ("Client"), a California corporation, requires the services of a professional management company, and

Whereas Trian, a California proprietorship, provides such services,

Therefore, Client and Trian enter into this agreement, effective September 1, 1996, pursuant to the following:

2. **Trian Responsibilities**

During the term of this agreement, Trian shall provide limited management services to Client, including:

- Administering Client's basic business functions, such as representing Client to other persons and organizations
- Formulating and proposing capital development plan options to Client's board of directors
- Implementing Client's business and capital development plans

3. **Compensation**

In consideration for Trian's services, Client shall pay Trian a Base Fee of two thousand five hundred dollars ($2,500.00) per month, plus a Capital Development Contingency Fee of fifteen percent (15%) of capital raised. Client shall pay Trian the Base Fee by the first day of the month to which it relates, and any Capital Development Contingency Fees earned within thirty (30) days of Client's receiving the capital. Client shall reimburse Trian for all direct expenses incurred by Trian on Client's behalf within thirty (30) days of receiving statements for such expenses.

4. **Term and Termination**

This agreement shall begin as of the above date, and shall continue until terminated by either party. Either party may terminate this agreement without cause on thirty (30) days' advance written notice.

5. **Limitation of Liability**

Client acknowledges that management cannot predict or control all of the factors which impact a company's performance. Therefore, except for gross negligence and willful misconduct on the part of Trian, Client hereby indemnifies and holds Trian harmless from and against any and all damages, liabilities, losses, claims and expenses of any type arising out of actions taken or not taken, or errors in judgment by Trian.

6. **Dispute Resolution**

In the event of a dispute regarding this agreement, Client and Trian shall submit to binding arbitration. Both parties shall designate legal counsel. The two counsel together shall select a member of the American Arbitration Association who shall confer with no more than two duly authorized representatives from each party and render a final and binding judgment.

7. **Miscellaneous**

California law shall govern this agreement. Trian and Client shall both comply with all relevant federal, state and local laws, and agree that such laws shall supersede this agreement. The unenforceability or invalidity of any term of this agreement shall not affect the enforceability or validity of any other term. Amendments to this agreement shall require written adoption by both client and Trian. Any communications between the parties shall be deemed delivered three (3) business days after being sent by certified mail, postage prepaid, to the parties' addresses of record.

In witness whereof, Client and Trian hereby execute this agreement as of the date first written above.

Client:	Trian:
____________________	____________________
James Hoss Chairman of the Board	David Vincent President

earlier this year, which means it can now receive cost-based reimbursement for services, which will allow it to expand services for the low-income people it serves. In particular, the clinic is currently exploring the possibility of offering dental care services. These designations acknowledge the difficulties that community members face in accessing health care and pave the way for enhanced funding opportunities aimed at addressing those issues.

Contact: Mona Johnston
Director of Planning and Community Development
Mercy Medical Center Mt. Shasta
P.O. Box 239
(914 Pine St.)
Mt. Shasta, CA 96067
Phone: (916) 926-9375
Fax: (916) 926-0517

17

The Grundy County Health Commission

Executive Summary

As chairman of the Grundy County Health Commission, I wish to provide my view and assessment of our project and its success to date. The creation of the Grundy County Health Commission is unique and the first of its kind in the state of Iowa. The purpose of creating a commission board was to integrate the various health care services of our local hospital with the health care services currently being offered through Grundy County. Working with two hospital partners in the Waterloo, IA, area, a continuum of health care services could be provided for our rural county population of 12,000.

Our focus was to bring together the services we currently offer with a larger health care network to be more cost effective and to ensure the availability of health care services to our county communities. The basic need for our community is the provision of good primary care, which can be enhanced with our integration project. We are also attempting a focus to create a healthier population with specific programs aimed at prevention, health education, and early detection of health care and medical needs. As one of the counties in Iowa with the highest percentage of elderly people, we have developed specific clinics with our public health nursing and hospital personnel to address the needs of our aging population.

At this point, we have learned that it takes far longer to integrate health care services than our initial time frame of three years. Legislative barriers have forced us to be more creative in handling governance and budgetary issues. Communication among a variety of boards related to our initiative as well as communication to the community has been a significant challenge but continues to improve. Grant support and political support from the state have been very helpful in allowing us the necessary human capital to make a transition from a loosely knit body of health services into what we hope will be a strongly integrated system of services meeting the specific health needs of the community.

Arnie Schultz
Chairman
Grundy County Health Commission

THE COLLABORATIVE PARTNERSHIP

The Community

The community consists of the 12,000 residents of Grundy County in the state of Iowa. Nearly 40 percent (4,709) live in the rural areas of Grundy County, while 60 percent live in the nine small towns, ranging from 113 in Morrison to 2,491 in Grundy Center. Twenty percent of Grundy County's residents are 65 years of age or older, which is the 14th highest percentage among the 99 counties in Iowa. This high percentage of elderly residents has resulted in a greater need to serve our people close to home and, at times, right in their own homes. A recent study conducted by the University of Iowa for its report, *Health Planning for Grundy County,* demonstrated there were 48 percent males and 52 percent females, which is the same as the state average. The percentage of white to other race/ethnic is greater (99.58 percent) than the state average (96.7 percent). Grundy County is a federally designated medically underserved area. Socioeconomic measures indicate fewer are on social assistance programs than the state average. Leading causes of mortality are cardiovascular disease, cancer, pneumonia, chronic pulmonary disease, and accidents. Town meetings indicated that the top priority of health concerns were health problems of the elderly, accidents, preventable and less severe health problems, health problems of children, healthy lifestyles, and heart disease.

Various community leaders and officials have identified a need to be proactive in addressing community health needs in Grundy County. As a rural, farming community, Grundy County is taking a proactive role in improving community health status. To do so, the county has created a new commission to oversee all health-related functions for Grundy County and its citizens. This integrated community care network (CCN) of health care services is the first of its kind to be developed in Iowa and possibly in the nation. It demonstrates cooperation of public, private, and governmental sectors and the collaborative efforts of many partners and constituents. We hope to build a model for the delivery of health services in rural communities. The goal of the project is to make a positive impact on the health of the citizens of Grundy County.

The Partnership

The partnership consists of the Grundy County Board of Supervisors, Grundy County Memorial Hospital, Grundy County Health Department, Allen Memorial Hospital, Covenant Medical Center, Rural Health Initiative, the regional Department of Human Services, and the newly formed Grundy County Health Commission (the Commission). In one or more ways, each partner can and will contribute to the evolving vision of a CCN. The following is a description of each of the partners:

1. *Grundy County Board of Supervisors:* As the elected leaders of county government, this five-member body forms the partnership's official and legal foundation, as well as its primary funding source other than patient-generated revenues and specific program allocations. Most notably, the board enacted an ordinance in January 1995 that created the Grundy County Health Commission, an umbrella health care body which reports directly to the board of supervisors. Four of the

partners sit on the Commission. It, in turn, provides the operational vehicle to move toward our vision.

2. *Grundy County Memorial Hospital:* Grundy County has one of only two chapter 37 "memorial hospitals" in Iowa. Chapter 37 represents many complex issues. The hospital board, made up of veterans, does not have property tax–levying authority; they must request their tax support through the board of supervisors as a part of the county's budget. Grundy County Memorial Hospital is the only hospital in the county and is located in Grundy Center, the county seat. It contains 33 acute care beds and a 55-bed, long-term care unit that serves many of our elderly residents. Although the traditional role of a rural hospital remains part of its mission, its future role likely will change to increasingly support primary care through diagnostic outpatient services and post-acute care through its swing-bed program. Grundy County Memorial Hospital is a member of the Commission and will be a large component of the seamless continuum of care.
3. *Grundy County Health Department:* The Grundy County Health Department is a policymaking board that oversees the Public Health Department. Under the direction of the County Board of Supervisors, it is also a member of the Commission. The Public Health Department will continue to perform traditional core functions of public health, but within the context of closer and collaborative relationships with other health care organizations. Preventive services and home care will be a primary focus in the seamless continuum of care.
4. *Allen Memorial Hospital:* Allen Memorial Hospital is a private, not-for-profit hospital located in Waterloo, IA, which is in Black Hawk County. Grundy County is one of 13 counties in the hospital's service area. Allen Memorial Hospital, a member of the Iowa Health System, provides primary care, comprehensive, secondary, specialty, and some tertiary services to Grundy County.
5. *Covenant Medical Center:* Covenant Medical Center is a private, not-for-profit hospital also located in Waterloo, IA, which is in Black Hawk County. Grundy County is located in the seven-county region in which it serves. Covenant Medical Center also offers primary care, comprehensive, secondary, and some tertiary services to Grundy County. Covenant Medical Center is a member of Volunteer Hospitals of America, Inc.
6. *Rural Health Initiative:* Rural Health Initiative is a partnership between Allen Memorial Hospital and Covenant Medical Center. Rural Health Initiative will fund the Commission for 3 years ($96,000 per year), act as a consultant to the partnership and, as requested, provide various services on a contractual basis. Combined, they offer a full continuum of care and can provide assistance for a community health focus, community assessment, and accountability. The Rural Health Initiative will be a partner in developing a mechanism to achieve fiscal responsibility.
7. *Department of Human Services:* The area office of the State Department of Human Services serves Bremer, Butler, Franklin, and Grundy counties. This office administers public assistance programs, title XIX, food stamps, and welfare services for children and adults. The Department of Human Services sees collaboration and "bridging" in several initiatives set forth, especially in the areas of children/elderly, periodic countywide health assessments, single information source for residents of Grundy County, and even integrated discharge planning. They look forward to being a part of working together to address community health needs.

8. *Grundy County Health Commission:* The Commission was established by a county ordinance on January 3, 1995. Its mission is to provide coordinated, cost-effective, and high-quality health services for the citizens of Grundy County. The vision of the Commission is to provide coordination and integration of the health care network. These services will improve access and referral mechanisms to achieve improved health for the rural, county-based community. The Commission plans to be responsive and meet the health care needs of Grundy County citizens. Members of the Commission, which is represented by all areas of the county, include two members of the Grundy County Memorial Hospital board, as well as representatives from Black Hawk–Grundy Mental Health, citizens on the Public Health Advisory Board, a county-based primary care physician, Emergency Medical Services, and the Grundy Center Chemical Dependency Center.

This integrated representation will help involve all communities of the county. The leadership abilities of Commission members, as well as the leadership abilities of the other partners, promise to add to the success of the project and fulfillment of the CCN vision.

PRIOR EFFORTS TOWARD THE COMMUNITY CARE NETWORK VISION

Movement toward a CCN vision was born out of crisis when Grundy County Memorial Hospital no longer had cash available to pay its debts. The County Board of Supervisors intervened through a $615,000 general obligation capital loan note to support hospital operations. Many county residents, as taxpayers and consumers, questioned the need to keep open a hospital that had experienced a cumulative 4-year loss of $715,696 and an increase in county tax of greater than 200 percent over 5 years ($160,000 to $502,963).

In response to the hospital crisis, the Grundy County Board of Supervisors engaged the Des Moines health care consulting firm of Cordes and Associates to prepare a study of hospital operations and to submit a report and recommendation by May 1, 1993. This report suggests the climate of the times in Grundy County and, as the consultants noted, "there is 'clear' impression that Grundy County Memorial Hospital should not remain open." The report suggested a number of alternative courses of action, including closing the hospital.

These alternatives were reviewed by the hospital board and the County Board of Supervisors. An Attorney General's Opinion was received that clarified some of the alternatives. A countywide planning task force also studied the alternatives and presented a strategic plan in July 1994. The hospital board and the County Board of Supervisors studied the plan and issued a challenge to Allen Memorial Hospital and Covenant Medical Center, two major hospitals in Waterloo, to participate in a joint venture.

The hospitals accepted the challenge and suggested initiating a countywide health planning process with the aim of redefining Grundy County Memorial Hospital's mission and vision to meet the county's current needs and priorities. It was the belief that the traditional role of a rural hospital needed to change, especially in its accountability to the community. This accountability would require both dialogue and education.

The Grundy County Memorial Hospital board of directors agreed, and initiated the process by forming a steering committee with representation from its board and the Grundy County Board of Supervisors. The steering committee, in turn, organized a 30-member task force consisting of a cross section of county residents, some of whom were providers, to advise the steering committee about the future role and services of the hospital.

James Rohrer, PhD, of the University of Iowa, assisted the task force by performing a county environmental health assessment using a modified APEX-PH protocol and met twice with the task force. At the first meeting, the University of Iowa team presented data describing the hospital, community health status, and medical utilization data. At the second meeting, the task force, through a nominal group process, identified the following needs, problems, priorities, and desired health services:

Problems

1. Health problems of the elderly
2. Accidents
3. Preventable health problems
4. Lifestyle
5. Less severe health problems
6. Heart disease
7. Health problems of children

Services

1. Ambulance
2. Emergency
3. Physical therapy (adult)
4. Physician offices
5. Pharmacy
6. Complete screening and advice on healthy lifestyle
7. Nursing home—intermediate
8. Immunization and prevention
9. Hospice

This stage of the planning process culminated with Dr. Rohrer's final report. The report included a summary of the environmental assessment, conclusions of the task force, and recommendations based on the vision of a community-oriented primary care (COPC) model. As Rohrer noted in his report, "COPC-focused community care health networks can serve as the building blocks for accountable health plans, since they can be both efficient and effective." It was further suggested that "with the decline of fee-for-service medicine, the emergence of inexpensive computer technology, and the acceptance of the need to address the root causes of illness through prevention, all combine to make possible the adoption of this model."

Based on general principles of health care organizations and Grundy County's special circumstances, Dr. Rohrer's report concluded that Grundy County should consider the following:

1. *Institutionalized Governance of the Local Health System:* A community-based group such as a permanent task force, the County Board of Supervisors, the hospital board, the Board of Health, or a newly elected system board should be empowered to manage the Grundy County health system.
2. *Coordination:* The governing body should seek to transform the current array of health providers into a coordinated community health network that is organized and managed to address the priority areas identified for Grundy County.
3. *Primary Care:* The network should change the mix of services offered by Grundy County Memorial Hospital along the lines recommended by the planning group. It should also monitor community health status; monitor performance of the network in regard to ensuring access, quality, and efficiency; and seek out resources for strengthening the capacity of the network.

On the basis of the report and needs and priorities identified by the task force, Grundy County Memorial Hospital shifted to an institutional strategic planning process as it revised its mission statement and developed new goals, strategies, and implementation plans. It soon became evident to the steering committee that, to be programmatically successful in implementing the hospital's plan, fundamental structural change was necessary. The hospital board responded by asking Allen Memorial Hospital and Covenant Medical Center to make either a joint proposal or separate proposals to establish some form of partnership/alignment with Grundy County Memorial Hospital. The two Waterloo hospitals made a joint proposal, which reflected the COPC model suggested by Dr. Rohrer.

Key elements of the proposal were as follows:

1. That Grundy County form a county health commission with representatives of the hospital board, Board of Public Health, emergency services, and other health services
2. That all health-related services, including the hospital, be managed by one administrator
3. That Covenant Medical Center and Allen Memorial Hospital form an alliance to be called Rural Health Initiative and financially support a new organization for 3 years ($96,000 per year)

Consensus among the various county health-related organizations and agencies built to the point that boards and management agreed to the concepts contained in the Rural Health Initiative proposal. The County Board of Supervisors passed an ordinance in January 1995 that legally created the Grundy County Health Commission.

The Commission is now active with representatives from the hospital board, Board of Health, Public Health and Home Care, Mental Health Services, Substance Abuse Services, and Emergency Services. The Commission reports to the Grundy County Board of Supervisors. By statute and regulations, both the hospital board and the Board of Health must continue, but the primary responsibility to create the CCN lies with the Commission. An administrator was recruited to serve both as hospital administrator and Commission administrator. Grundy County has also applied for a government service grant to integrate the financial management of all organizations.

In November 1994, prior to the finalization of the Commission, the planning task force held a daylong retreat to begin to develop a vision for the Commission (and by extension, the CCN). At the retreat, three questions were asked:

1. Why should the Grundy County Health Commission exist?
2. What should be its mission and vision?
3. What functions should it perform?

From a visionary perspective, the group identified and reflected upon the following words or phrases: healthy people, coordination, integration, planning, referral, cost-effective, identification of need, accessibility, evaluation, quality, prevention, marketing, and public education.

Experiences and lessons of the past 2 years leading to the formation of the Grundy County Health Commission have given the partners important insight into the possibilities of a CCN, although much more learning is required. Creating a legal network structure is the easy part; transforming network theory into a functional system will be the greater challenge. Nevertheless, the planning process has produced tangible accomplishments, and pieces of the puzzle are starting to fit together as our vision crystallizes and unfolds.

Forming the Commission and recruiting an administrator to manage all county health components were first steps toward integration of services. The formation of the Commission signals a shift from institution-centered accountability to community accountability. It also paves the way toward an integrated delivery network that is capable of managing fixed health resources using a capitated methodology.

The probability of forming a seamless continuum of services has improved through the collaboration of Allen Memorial Hospital and Covenant Medical Center in the Rural Health Initiative. Although competitors in Black Hawk and some other surrounding counties, they have found common ground in Grundy County. Both recognize the importance of maintaining Grundy County within their sphere of influence. There are four rural health clinics in the Grundy County network—one controlled by Allen and three by Covenant. Staffing these clinics are three family practice physicians and two midlevel professionals. The continued availability of these medical providers is critical to network formation and management.

The planning task force identified elder services as a countywide priority. In response, Grundy County Memorial Hospital created a position of director of elder services/case management. This role reaches beyond the walls of the hospital. Senior wellness and exercise programs now are being offered not only in Grundy Center, but at other rural community sites. Various types of senior health screenings, health education, and health management counseling are now offered at diverse sites with the assistance of the Public Health Department.

Working closely with the Cedar Valley Area Agency on Aging and the Home Care Services of the Public Health Department, the network is poised to begin a Medicaid managed care program aimed at supporting low-income senior citizens in their homes. The Cedar Valley Area Agency on Aging may request a waiver so that home services can be provided to these individuals, with funding up to $800 per month. Hospital and public health/homemaker staff would jointly manage and provide these services.

For the past 2 years, the Grundy County Memorial Hospital Foundation has sought to develop a 12–30-unit assisted living center on property adjacent to the hospital grounds. Professional support from an assisted living agency will manage the facility, while public health and hospital personnel will provide health-related support services.

Functional integration of county government, public health, and hospital operations has already begun, as illustrated by the following actions. Through the transfer of Grundy County Memorial Hospital's health insurance to the county's third-party administrator plan, the hospital will save approximately $30,000 annually. County and hospital employees as a single group are attending continuous quality improvement (CQI) education and orientation sessions. As cultural transformation, CQI is seen as a key common denominator across the network. A provider of home care services, the county public health nurses were hard-pressed to maintain a 24-hour, 7-day-per-week on-call schedule. Now the hospital switchboard acts as the home care answering resource, and hospital nursing staff are anticipated to back up the public health nurses in the near future. Two additional grants are being submitted collaboratively by the partnership, one to plan and implement an elder assessment protocol, the other to promote wellness and provide work-site screening services for businesses located in Grundy County.

As a response to the planning task force priorities, Grundy County Memorial Hospital has established phase 2 cardiac rehabilitation (with the assistance of Allen Memorial Hospital's cardiology department) and mammography screening (the Grundy County Memorial Hospital Foundation provided the funding for the purchase of new equipment). Finally, Grundy County Memorial Hospital, Allen Memorial Hospital, and the public health nurses are developing a case management system that includes common clinical pathways and an acute care referral mechanism that returns patients to Grundy County for care, either at Grundy County Memorial Hospital or at home, using the Grundy County home care service.

These concrete experiences have enabled the partners to refine their ideas about CCNs and, just as important, their leaders have developed working relationships with one another based on the recognition that self-interest is advanced best by vigorous pursuit of common interest.

MOVING TOWARD THE COMMUNITY CARE NETWORK VISION

Two years ago, when we began our search for new alternatives, we did not consider the possibility of seeking outside financial support. There seemed to be little basis to ask for support—financial distress of a small rural hospital was, and is, an all-too-familiar story. Since then, our experiences and resulting knowledge have engendered a growing confidence among Grundy County residents that the partnership is moving in the proper direction as its vision unfolds. Channels of communication among community providers, consumers, and government have expanded. Most significant, we are beginning to understand that health care issues are not solely provider or government issues, but are fundamentally community health focus issues that require broader community participation and new accountability relationships.

The Lessons of Crisis

Two years ago, conflict, competition, frustration, and public anger over the seeming lack of institutional accountability described the health care climate in Grundy County. There was little communication or collaboration among county providers. No community-based group existed to identify health care problems or unite county residents and providers around common goals. Instead, the question most commonly asked was, "Who is to blame for our problems?"—a revolving door of primary care providers, diminished accessibility to services within the county, or a rising tax burden on the community without perceived increase in value?

The work of the health care task force and the University of Iowa team, using a community health focus rather than institutional demand model, was the beginning. The task force's most important contribution was not necessarily its conclusions but the assumption that drove its process—namely, that *health care organizations are means and not ends.* Although most, if not all, health care organizations espouse some sort of community-directed service mission, all too often institutional success is measured by internally focused criteria: growth, financial stability, or survival. Bureaucratic insulation and isolation often follows, building a wall between the interests of those who serve and those to be served. Grundy County Memorial Hospital had fallen into this self-deceptive trap as it asked for more and more tax support without demonstrating accountability to county residents.

Traditional solutions, recruitment of physicians, the start-up of rural health clinics, and the resultant increase in hospital patient volume and revenue eased the crisis in 1993, thus providing some breathing room. Yet many believed that progress was only temporary. The hospital's position remained fragile and vulnerable to changes brought about by health care reform and other systemic forces. New ideas to bring about fundamental change were required.

One such idea is the notion that the health care problems Grundy County faced are not discretely hospital, physician, or health department problems; rather, health is a community matter. Health care organizations working in isolation can marginally improve health status if sufficient resources are available. But in a time of diminished resources, collaboration among organizations can leverage these resources to create significantly more value. (See figures 17-1 and 17-2.) In this light, collaboration becomes necessary for survival. Underlying this idea is the recognition that, while self-interest is a fundamental aspect of human and organizational behavior, our 2 years' experience suggests that self-interest can be served best through pursuit of common interest. Network synergy can add value to its components. Thus, this partnership is in one sense an expression of the partners' self-interest.

Action through Consensus

To understand and internalize an idea is a first step. To translate it into tangible form is perhaps the greater challenge, as individuals and organizations shift from low-risk theory to high-risk action. Rural Health Initiative's proposal, using the University of Iowa's suggested COPC model, provided the opportunity for this translation by clarifying the vision in a way that consensus among the various health care organizations and community could coalesce. It offered both a model and a funding source of $96,000 annually for 3 years to pursue its development.

In short, Allen Memorial Hospital and Covenant Medical Center mutually agreed to "assist Grundy County in developing a health delivery system," with a focus on the priorities identified by the health planning task force. This delivery system, by another name a CCN, would be organized around the following four principles:

1. To reinforce Grundy County Memorial Hospital as the hub of county-sponsored and/or -funded health services while recognizing that the role of the hospital will change in the future, consistent with health care and statutory reform
2. To optimize the use of increasingly scarce resources to improve the quality of targeted services—to increase the value of health services to county residents
3. To create a more efficient and effective health system in Grundy County through a reorganization and integration of governance, management, medical, and health services

FIGURE 17-1. Health Care Administrator Organizational Design—10/11/95

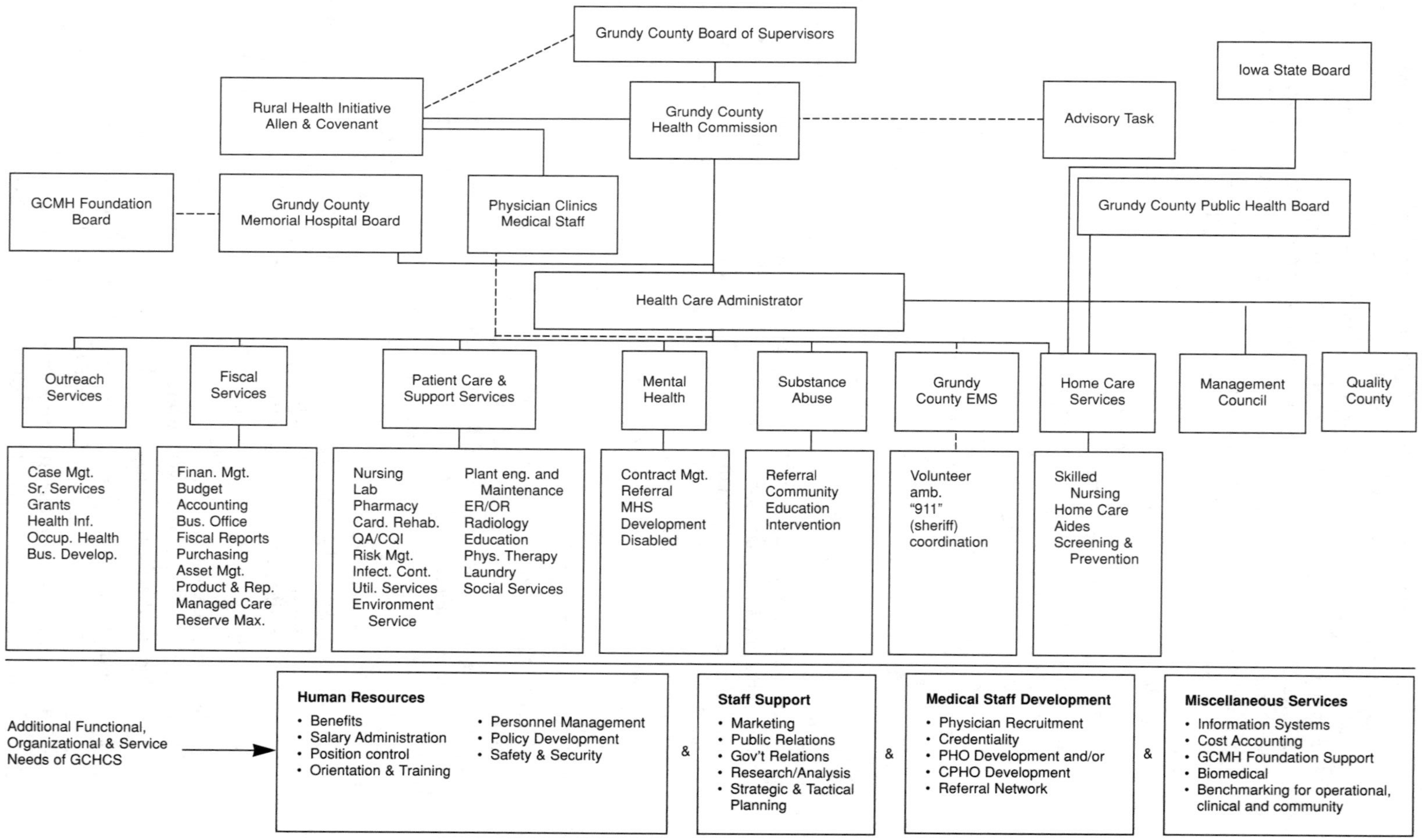

FIGURE 17-2. Existing Organizational Design—10/11/95

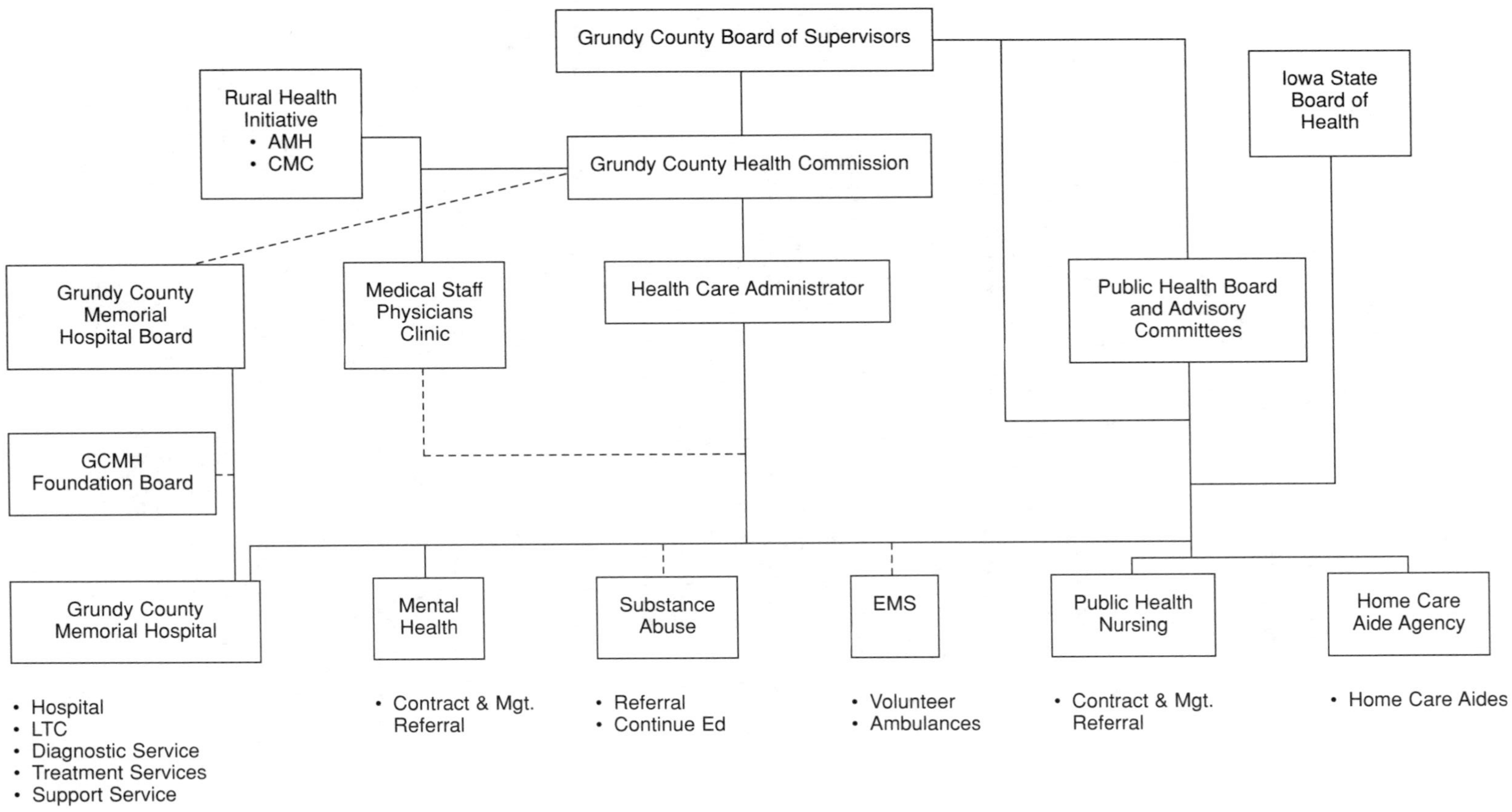

4. To establish a partnership between the Rural Health Initiative and Grundy County, in which the Rural Health Initiative:
   a. Assists the county in matters of policy formation and health planning.
   b. Participates ex-officio at the governance level in the decisions affecting hospital and other county services.
   c. Assumes limited risks in the financial operations of the "hospital."
   d. Acts as a vendor of services under contract with Grundy County Memorial Hospital when such contracts benefit the county. This does not mean, however, that contracts with other vendors could not exist, but rather that Allen Memorial Hospital and Covenant Medical Center would be given the opportunity to make proposals.
   e. Assists the county and its municipalities to retain and, as necessary, recruit primary care providers to meet the needs of the residents of Grundy County. The objective is to link such practices to Grundy County Memorial Hospital, Allen Memorial Hospital, and Covenant Medical Center, and to size and operate such clinics in order to eliminate or minimize subsidy for such practices.

Based on these principles, the Rural Health Initiative made the following proposals:

1. An umbrella Grundy County Health Commission reporting to the County Board of Supervisors would be created to direct and coordinate county health services. Possible membership could include the five hospital commissioners, all members of the County Board of Health, and ex-officio representation for existing county health services (mental health, emergency services, county nurses), other providers, Allen Memorial Hospital, and Covenant Medical Center. A county health administrator, employed by the county, would act as a part-time hospital administrator and would attend meetings of the Board of Health and the hospital board, and report to the Commission Board.
2. As an ex-officio member of the Commission, the Rural Health Initiative (one representative from Allen Memorial Hospital and one from Covenant Medical Center) would assist it by making policy and management recommendations as requested.
3. Grundy County, through the Commission, would subsidize hospital operations to an amount determined by the County Board of Supervisors.
4. Rural Health Initiative would contribute $8,000 per month, shared equally between Allen Memorial Hospital and Covenant Medical Center, to support the office of county health care administration. Contributions would be for three years or until the county is able to support the office through additional funds generated from health care operations, but in no case beyond three years.
5. Shared services such as financial services, electronic data processing, purchasing, laundry and linen, pharmacy, and laboratory may be provided to the hospital/county either by Allen Memorial Hospital or Covenant Medical Center. Grundy County Memorial Hospital would have the option to do one of the following:
   a. Accept a proposal from either Allen Memorial Hospital or Covenant Medical Center
   b. Provide all or part of the services in-house

   c. Select an alternative vendor
   d. Promote consultative services on a no-charge basis by members of the Allen Memorial Hospital or Covenant Medical Center staff
6. Rural Health Initiative believes the greatest opportunity for reduced or stabilized county health care funding exists by integrating all county services, rather than operating various services separately. Special attention should be given to determining which services should and can be provided locally by the health system to keep money in the county. If and when county services are placed under the hospital umbrella, county funding would be transferred to the hospital.

The formation of a commission was an idea that, on the surface, seemed to make sense. But an idea in itself is only one dimension of a vision. It needed to be nurtured to grow.

This growth began on November 18, 1994, with a full-day retreat for approximately 25 partnership leaders. Following is a composite of the ideas expressed in response to the question "why," categorized by the four dimensions of the CCN vision.

Community Accountability

1. Provide as many services within the county as possible.
2. Protect county resources; keep tax dollars within the county.
3. Develop a system to respond to the future needs of the community.
4. Tap into the leadership and expertise of the county.
5. Pull private and public sectors together; need to be accountable.
6. Enable the county to react more quickly to changes in the health care environment.
7. Focus on the number 1 priority—the aging population in Grundy County.
8. Focus attention on patient care and needs, not on individual structures that currently exist.
9. Act as a central point for knowing, coordinating, and monitoring health care options, needs, and prevention.
10. Make health care accessible to all citizens of Grundy County regardless of economic status, including those who fall through the cracks, have no insurance, etc.
11. Focus on quality assurance.
12. Spin off for economic development; link with housing, industry, and business.

Seamless Continuum of Care

1. Coordinate services to avoid duplication and reduce costs.
2. Maintain one central agency as a referral mechanism.
3. Increase administrative efficiency.
4. Improve existing services.
5. Provide 24-hour mental health services.
6. Evaluate and improve emergency services.
7. Use expanded home services as part of the network.

8. Evaluate/coordinate health clinics—physician clinics, physician assistants, as well as specialty clinics and nursing homes.
9. Pool resources for education and training of health care professionals.
10. Improve access to services not available within the county.

Community Health Focus

1. Coordinate among providers, so patient care is tracked and monitored.
2. Collectively address health problems of the community (data collection and analysis).
3. Increase public awareness of services available.
4. Plan and evaluate health care services collectively.
5. Help people promote healthier lifestyles.
6. Promote home care.
7. Emphasize prevention, health promotion/wellness, and staying healthier.
8. Provide for ongoing public health policy development.
9. Identify priorities for health care in the county.

Management within Fixed Resources

1. Have all agencies under one umbrella—potential cost savings.
2. Provide a common goal for all providers; integrate individual goals—move to managed care.

These elements are the raw substance of our vision. The CCN vision has been exceedingly helpful in extending and organizing our thoughts. The development of a network that integrates the mission of a rural hospital, public health, emergency services, mental health, substance abuse, and physician offices (including family practice physicians and midlevel professionals, human services, specialty clinics, and secondary referral sources) begins to define a future health care state for Grundy County affecting all its residents. Through operational integration, strategic planning, and budgeting, we will have an opportunity to better focus on community-identified needs, set priorities in a public forum, and husband scarce financial resources.

Our visionary process is the engine that drives change. On the one hand, these changes are manifest in contracts, agreements, ordinances, organizational charts, and diagrams—a road map for health care reform in Grundy County. On the other, underlying values and beliefs among the partners are changing. And the county itself is waking to fresh awareness of its own potential, the talents of the people within the county and their ability to solve problems. In this sense, Grundy County is experiencing a small cultural revolution.

Over the next 3 years, the Grundy County Health Commission and its partners will move forward with specific initiatives to redesign the county's health care system. Organizations, including those of the partnership and others (pharmacies, nursing homes, businesses), will form new relationships to redefine problems and seek value-added solutions to build a healthier community. We agree with LeAnne Kaiser Carlsen's comments appearing in her article "The Next Step" (*Health Care Forum,* May/June 1995), in which she suggests that health care transformation is like a journey up a mountain. It begins with a first step—a vision. To her and to us, this vision is of health, the ability to achieve one's potential and rediscover connectedness, community, well-being, and a supportive environment.

The second step is careful planning. Our resources are very limited and we do not have the luxury of making mistakes. Thus, we must do the right thing at the right time. This will require good advice and good information.

The Grundy County Health Commission, along with its collaborative partnership, has identified a set of initiatives that it will use over the next year to move further toward a CCN vision. The initiatives were identified after careful review of the Commission's purpose. Its mission, vision, and needs are identified in the strategic planning process and the Commission work plan.

Initiatives

The following initiatives will play a major role in moving the Commission and its partnership toward a CCN system. They are organized in terms of the four dimensions of the CCN vision. Several of the initiatives bridge dimensions of the CCN vision, while progress along the multiple dimensions will occur simultaneously.

1. Community Accountability

   a. *Develop a health advisory group and charter the Grundy County task force to become a permanent advisory council:* The purpose of this advisory council will be participation in further identification of priorities for services desired by the community, further planning for services to meet those priorities, and the identification of resources for strengthening the capacity of the network. The activities of the advisory council will ensure that the services to be provided in the future are aligned with patient and community expectations.

      In addition to the present members of the advisory council, the partnership would also like to include the USDA Extension Office in the group. The primary occupation of Grundy County is agriculture and related businesses, so the inclusion of the Extension Office will be an asset in meeting the needs of our community.

      The partnership will present an annual report card to the advisory council regarding the initiatives undertaken and their corresponding effects on the health of the community. This accountability is essential for establishing community trust in the partnership's commitment toward meeting its identified needs.

   b. *Establish a community health information system:* Establishment of such a system would provide a single information source for Grundy County citizens. One of the core functions of public health speaks to assessment of community health status and available resources and assurance that needy services are available. To assure does not always mean to provide. Rather, it is the responsibility of the CCN to see that services are available to people, whether they be private providers, not-for-profit agencies, community health centers, or government public health services. To be accountable, that information needs to be easily available.

      Providing information to people regarding health care and human services has a very fragmented past. There have been various attempts at developing resource directories. The most recent county resource booklet was edited in

February 1994 by a group called the Grundy County Human Resource Network. Despite collaborative efforts and careful research, the directory was outdated and omissions were cited before it even left the printer.

A single information source available and accessible to all residents to accomplish smooth access into service or care is a must to reduce fragmentation. Accessing the "information superhighway," a user-friendly computerized system of information, would also assist public and private providers to move people smoothly through the care continuum as well as meet their aftercare needs.

This initiative is one of the cornerstones of the project's vision, for without information enhancement and rapid information transfer, long-term innovation will be difficult. We recognize that this initiative is complex, and although much has been written about community health information networks (CHINs), few are in existence. Because of the expense in implementing a CHIN, it will be vital to do the right thing at the right time. We are not prepared to either benchmark or establish key indicators at this time. However, we are confident that our efforts will involve all partners and will affect all elements of the CCN vision. We have been in contact with Sierra Vista, AZ, to learn what that rural county is doing.

2. Seamless Continuum of Care

   a. *Integrate case management and discharge planning:* Case management, which includes discharge planning, is an integral part of the partnership's efforts to provide a seamless continuum of care within limited resources. It also provides accountability to those who receive the care. Grundy County Memorial Hospital recently established the position of director of case management, whose present tasks include the development of clinical pathways. Through the collaboration of the partnership, these pathways will expand from hospital-based to community-based pathways. Further mechanisms will be developed to provide an integrated, coordinated continuum of care to address the health care needs of our community in addition to the frail elderly.

   b. *Utilize data transmission, telecommunications, and telemedicine:* During the past decade, many significant changes have begun to reshape the way hospitals and similar organizations conduct their health care business. One of the most profound shifts is the emerging technology of telecommunications and telemedicine. This technology is the simultaneous exchange of voice, images, and data that empower staff members and community members in their clinical, educational, and administrative responsibilities at any distance. Telemedicine is the solution that can supply precise medical data with expediency and cost efficiency. Components of telemedicine are teleradiology, electronic film distribution, remote diagnosis and consultation, and professional education and training.

      In October 1991, the first fiber-optic cable for the Iowa Communications Network (ICN) was placed in Iowa soil. The ICN is a statewide fiber-optic network capable of transporting interactive two-way audio, video, voice, and data signals. The ICN reaches at least one end point in each of Iowa's 99 counties, providing all Iowans nearby access to geographically distant resources.

   c. *Integrate diagnostic services:* The Grundy County Memorial Hospital owns and operates its own laboratory within the hospital facility. However, it has found it necessary to contract with an outside source for reference laboratory purposes.

Currently, Grundy County Memorial Hospital uses the services of Allen Memorial Hospital as a reference laboratory. Both Grundy County Memorial Hospital and the community have benefited from the relationship with a larger facility as a reference library.

Allen Memorial Hospital currently offers services to Grundy County Memorial Hospital at a discounted rate; thus, health care expenditure regarding laboratory-related items has decreased. However, the most important benefit of the relationship is and will continue to be the focus on community wellness and a healthier community and access in Grundy County.

3. Community Health Focus

   a. *Implement new programs and initiatives for wellness/health promotion:* Risk reduction efforts would be aimed at the two leading causes of death in our county (heart disease and cancer), as well as special needs identified by the analysis of data at least annually. Health promotion, prevention, and protection programs in our county will be aimed at improving our overall health status as well as cutting health care expenditures.

      In addition, a task force is studying the feasibility of a wellness center for Grundy County. The nearest health facility for wellness is one-half hour to one hour of travel time from Grundy County.

   b. *Improve occupational health:* The partnership is committed to improving the health of our community. One additional focus for prevention and early screening is the arena of occupational health. Grundy County Memorial Hospital, the Grundy County Health Department, and several of the partners have collaborated in several screenings focused at work sites. This included blood pressure and cholesterol screenings at a number of Grundy County industries and a cholinesterase screening for members of the Farm Bureau. Collaboration with WorkSafe Iowa has also been initiated.

      The Grundy County Health Commission also proposes the formation of a task force of industries to survey the needs of Grundy County employers. This information will be used by the partnership to develop an occupational health program for our community.

   c. *Address the health care needs of the elderly:* During the planning process with the task force, the health care needs of the elderly were identified as a high priority. Grundy County has a rapidly growing elderly population requiring a seamless continuum of care.

      Grundy County Memorial Hospital and the Grundy County Health Department have begun collaborative efforts to expand services for the elderly in this community. These include well-elderly assessment clinics in one community; a senior life program, which provides educational and support services; a senior exercise group in two of the county communities; and a recently initiated frail elderly case management system, an interdisciplinary group of providers who meet regularly to plan care for homebound elderly who are very frail. This system includes a wide range of providers from energy assistance and social services to health care.

      In addition, the task force and steering committee identified several barriers to elderly receiving services. These barriers include transportation to medical specialists, inadequate number of primary care providers in the community, and the range of home care support services.

d. *Address the health care needs of children:* Our children are our greatest resource, the promise of our future as a community. It is necessary that we take action to protect their health and well-being to ensure a bright future for the community.

   It should be a focus of the community to see that every child receives adequate health care. This starts with good prenatal care and education. Public health entities, local hospitals and birthing centers, and private physicians that serve the county need to work together to produce healthy babies and prepared parents. With shortened hospital stays, the seamless continuum will flow into home intervention for physical assessment, education, and referral to appropriate infant care and support systems. Cooperation and contractual arrangements with the Department of Human Services will allow for case management activities to follow newly enrolled Medicaid families and ensure healthy development of their children. Special-needs children present a challenge to providers, and services to enhance their lives are essential.

   Grundy County has only two employed school nurses in the six-school system. Health screening and education are important to identify special needs to enhance learning and to create healthy lifestyle habits that will last a lifetime.

4. Management within Fixed Resources

   a. *Redefine management and financial structures and processes to support integrated governance.* How decisions are made will go a long way in forming the character of the network and drive the progress of our vision. The organization will be grounded on the principles of CQI, both as cultural transformation and process improvement. All partners will play an important role. This cycle will be repeated on an annual basis.

   b. *Develop a physician–hospital organization (PHO) or other integrated organization.* Develop a PHO that forms a new relationship between primary care physicians, Grundy County Memorial Hospital, and other partners in the network. The creation of a PHO redesigns the relation between primary care physicians (3) and physician assistants (2) with the hospital. This is an essential step in forming a seamless continuum of care, being accountable to the health priorities of the community, and moving toward managed care and global budgeting.

      It is believed that competition in a rural setting is counterproductive. So, as large organized delivery systems, controlled either by providers or insurance companies, develop in Iowa, the Grundy County network must be positioned to contract with these organizations in a capitated environment. In particular, Grundy County should form a strong relationship with Allen Primary Care Associates of Northeast Iowa and the Covenant Health System.

This initiative affects the four dimensions of the CCN. In the discussion of our initiatives, we have indicated some of the kinds of technical assistance needed by our partnership to carry out its plan in moving toward the CCN vision. We will collaborate and seek assistance from many sources.

We believe that within 3 years, sufficient resources will be saved through integrated management and other economies of scale to make the network more self-sustaining. The CCN vision will become a reality through the efforts of those who realize the importance of cost-effective, comprehensive health services delivered in the rural areas of America.

SUMMARY OF NOTABLE PROGRESS

Development of the Grundy County Health Commission served as a model to integrate health care services within a rural Iowa county to provide a continuum of health care services to improve the overall health of the community population. Given a population of 12,000 people and a demographic of having one of the oldest populations in Iowa, a partnership with two "urban hospitals" in nearby Waterloo, IA, was essential to providing cost-effective services to the community. As the creation of a health commission is the first of its kind in the state, a number of new and original organizational activities were required. Accomplishments of the Grundy County Health Care System since its inception in February 1995 include the following:

1. An administrator for the system was hired in August 1995.
2. Public health, public nursing, and home care aid agencies were relocated to an annex of the hospital to permit improved coordination between public health and the hospital.
3. Public health nurses use the materials management services of the hospital, which provides significant savings for this service.
4. A new materials management contract was obtained through our partnership with a Waterloo hospital that will save the system from $22,000 to $35,000 per year in supply and materials management costs.
5. Prevention and screening clinics for the elderly are being offered at three sites within the county through the coordinated efforts of nursing services from both public health and the hospital.
6. A senior wellness program is being offered at two sites, with a third possible site aimed at various forms of cardiovascular, stretching, and strengthening exercises for the elderly.
7. Case management has been developed to provide better coordination with people requiring services for seniors (including insurance coordination), mental health, home care, and subacute care within the hospital.
8. CQI training and education were provided at cost by a Waterloo hospital partner to the point where existing Grundy County personnel provide this training within our system for hospital, public health, home care, and mental health. The training is also available for the substance abuse and emergency medical services.
9. Clerical staff members are being shared between public health and the hospital business office to address personnel needs without adding staff to the overall system.
10. A table of organization was created to include all the boards, urban hospital partners, medical staff, and functional units of the Grundy County system that include both employees and volunteer groups.
11. A strategic plan for the system was developed by the boards, and the implementation plans are currently being developed.
12. A public relations plan for the system was developed, including an outline of the resources required to implement this plan. A logo, tag line, business cards,

new employee name tags, newspaper articles, and a "fact sheet/annual report" are either completed or ready for implementation.

13. A revised personnel manual, including updated policies and procedures, was developed for the entire system.
14. A budgetary plan was formulated to reduce overall costs by $118,000 to $125,000; approximately one-third of this goal has been met to date.
15. Managed care agreements are being negotiated with the assistance of the "urban hospitals" that would permit selected Grundy system services to be utilized within the community.
16. The hospital laundry is now outsourced to one of our Waterloo hospital partners, providing a savings of more than $15,000.
17. The pathology services of the hospital are being served by a Waterloo hospital partner, for a savings of $1,600 per year.
18. Quality improvement support has been brought to bear for our hospital pharmacy through the support of a Waterloo hospital partner.
19. Our fiscal, accounting, and information services and business office functions are being supported by one of our Waterloo hospital partners.
20. Some individuals have been cross-trained to permit a more efficient use of our total system's personnel. Clinical cross-training is being reviewed for selected nursing functions in home care and the hospital.
21. A community health care survey was completed, identifying the community's health needs and areas of concern for high-risk populations.
22. Because of legislative requirements within Iowa, a number of community boards must still exist by statute; however, some of the boards are now meeting at the same time, to better integrate and reduce duplication of effort.
23. A preliminary population database, focused on the health of the community population, has been created to serve as a tool to monitor our process in developing a healthier community.
24. Additional outpatient specialty clinics in podiatry and cardiology have been developed through the coordination of our Waterloo hospital partners.
25. Our cardiac rehabilitation program was developed through the assistance of our Waterloo hospital partners, representing new revenue for this community-based service.

Although many other things were accomplished over the past year, our organization is changing into a different type of service that will focus on the community services it can efficiently and cost-effectively offer to the county and to supplement these local services with the specialized and more advanced health care services found within an urban area. The integration of the local services with the services to be offered by our urban partners should provide a stronger health care delivery system and improve the health of our community.

Contact: Barbara Vos
Grundy County Memorial Hospital
201 East J. Ave.
Grundy Center, IA 50638
Phone: (319) 824-5421
Fax: (319) 824-3337

PART V

Networks for Special Populations

Wisdom lies neither in fixity nor in change, but in the dialectic between the two.

—Octavio Paz (b. 1914), Mexican poet

The foxes have holes, and the birds of the air have nests; but the Son of man hath not where to lay his head.

—Matthew 8:20

INTRODUCTION

The evolving community care networks in this part of the book focus on, or originated from a focus on, special populations. In these cases, the special populations were inner city teen mothers and infants, the homeless, and isolated rural elderly. Sometimes, population-specific gaps in the health system appear to be the best place to invest effort.

This higher level of focus enables a higher degree of certainty about customer or client needs. The mission, being tightly focused, may well proceed more quickly than more comprehensive efforts. Specialized expertise would likely be easier to identify and engage, as well as more efficiently developed by the partnership itself. An added benefit of a focus on a special population is that the tactics learned to develop and provide services and expertise should translate well to other communities where similarly focused efforts are launched. There are occasions in which the focus on a special population also benefits a partnership by creating a stronger draw on special interests, for example, when a local philanthropy identifies the same special population as a high priority. While these efforts do not start with community-wide, comprehensive problem analysis or solution design, they can lead there, as the Rural Health Outreach program shows.

While tactics such as intake and outreach methods and clinical protocol may translate well to other communities, a special population focus makes it likely that the problems and solutions will be idiosyncratic. Those working on special population efforts, therefore, may find it very difficult to learn strategic level lessons from each other, such as how to grow a sustainable base of financial support. Meanwhile, when efforts focused on special populations do arrive at a point at which a more comprehensive set of activities can be identified and launched, the awareness of the overall context will not likely be as rich as that emerging from more comprehensive efforts.

The fact that a special population focus draws on special interests sometimes carries more costs than benefits. Close ties to a narrow range of special interests may produce a more incrementalist, and less visionary, approach. Other potentially important partners may share only a narrow part of their agenda with the partners, resulting in less ground for identifying mutual objectives and generating joint action. Such efforts may be easier to marginalize or altogether ignore. A heavier reliance on categorical streams of funding, and the regulatory burdens that accompany them, may also make funds development and sustainability bigger challenges for special population partnerships. Both categorical and philanthropic streams of financial support can, from time to time, change focus, shifting support to activities that are not in the purview of the special population–focused partnership.

Three evolving community care networks that focused, at least at the outset, on special populations are highlighted in this book. What advantages and disadvantages accrue from a special population focus? What are the chances that these kinds of efforts can lead to comprehensive local health system change? What specialized techniques or tactics from these kinds of efforts can be translated for use in more comprehensive health system change efforts? When would it make sense for an emerging CCN to adopt a special population focus? How have these partnerships begun building sustainability in the face of sometimes fickle categorical funding streams?

In Connecticut, the Hartford Action Plan on Infant Health's "Breaking the Cycle" campaign targets teen pregnancy and infant health. Goals of this comprehensive community campaign include eliminating births to adolescents under 15, reducing them overall among adolescents, and providing adolescents access to basic opportunities for growth and personal development as alternatives to pregnancy. Their achievements include acknowledgment by the city and the schools of child health as a high priority, the implementation of a school-based health education curriculum, "best practices" for prevention, and funding sexuality training for adults. Health Care for the Homeless was created in Jacksonville, FL. The program ensures health care access for the 2,500 homeless living in the city. Building on the experience of one center, the partnership of the I. M. Sulzbacher Center for the Homeless and major Jacksonville medical centers has developed an additional comprehensive center, staffed with paid and volunteer professionals. In addition to basic medical services, they offer vision, dental, and mental health programs. The Rural Health Outreach program started as a program for the isolated elderly that live in this Appalachian area in central Virginia. The partnership's chief bridging mechanism from that special population program to a more comprehensive effort is found in their innovative Health Depots project. Health Depots are primary care clinics conducted at nontraditional locations, such as the fire station and the museum, throughout the county. The partnership seeks to develop a comprehensive program for the uninsured and underinsured through linkage of Nelson County primary care providers, and ultimately the development of a prepaid program.

TABLE 18-1. Teen Births in Hartford: From *Breaking the Cycle* Newsletter, November 1995

	Present Statistics					
Year	*Age <15*	*Age 15–17*	*Age 18–19*	*Total Births*	*Total Births to Teens*	%
1990	29	322	396	3,248	747	23.0
1991	23	323	393	3,131	739	23.6
1992	21	306	385	3,028	712	23.5
1993	23	293	334	2,793	650	23.3

Note: Teen pregnancy in Hartford has continued at epidemic levels in spite of several innovative activities to address it. Each year more than 20 young Hartford girls between 10 and 14 years of age bear children. Three hundred more 15 to 17 year olds also become mothers each year. Reprinted, with permission, from the Hartford Action Plan on Infant Health, Inc.

TABLE 18-2. Teen Birth Reduction Targets: From *Breaking the Cycle* Newsletter, November 1995

Year	*Age <15*	*Age 15–17*	*Age 18–19*	*Total Births to Teens*	*% Births to Teens*
		Based on 1993 population			
1996	23	293	334	650	23.3
1997	20	275	329	624	22.3
1998	15	250	320	585	20.9
1999	8	210	309	527	18.9
2000	0	150	294	444	15.8

Note: Reprinted, with permission, from the Hartford Action Plan on Infant Health, Inc.

TABLE 18-3. Budget Projections: From *Breaking the Cycle* Newsletter, November 1995

				PROSPECTIVE SOURCES				
Strategy	*1995*	*1996*	*1997–99*	*Identified Grants*	*Private Unidentified Grants*	*Medicaid*	*Other Public*	*In-kind*
Public Education Campaign	5,000	*60,000*	*200,000*		●		●	●
Provider/Community Enrollment	50,000	*50,000*	*150,000*	●	●			●
DIRECT SERVICES								
In-school program for all 2000 fifth grade girls and boys	10,000	*130,000*	*400,000*		●		●	●
Adult Advisor recruitment/training	15,000	*25,000*	*75,000*	●	●			
Intensive programs	150,000	*600,000*	*3,000,000*	●	●	●		
After-school programs	450,000	600,000	1,800,000	●				
Existing youth services	(not available)			●			●	
School curriculum re-enhancement	(not available)						●	
Monitoring/Evaluation	0	*45,000*	*150,000*		●		●	

Note: This table depicts preliminary sources and projections for the plan's cost elements. These represent anticipated ranges of costs borne by the partners and participating organizations. Numbers in italics represent unsecured funds. Estimated 5-year budget: $7.9 million. Reprinted, with permission, from the Hartford Action Plan on Infant Health, Inc.

"illness" to a "wellness" approach to youth services by providing a variety of growth opportunities. Called the "Passport to Success," these include access to health information and services, opportunities to develop special skills and hobbies, opportunities to participate in group activities, and opportunities to develop career choices.

Breaking the Cycle reflects the vision of a shared community responsibility for teen parenthood. To avoid assigning ownership to any one agency, this plan is governed jointly by the Superintendent of Schools, the city's Director of Human Services, and the Hartford Action Plan board president. Following initial drafting, more than 30 community organizations were enlisted to react to the plan's concepts and are helping to develop the public awareness campaign.

Key Successes to Date for "Breaking the Cycle" The campaign has an ambitious agenda and has drawn enthusiastic support. Staffing is collaborative, and the campaign has pledged community accountability through regular public reports on its progress. Initial achievements in the first 8 months include the following:

- Both the Hartford City Council and the Board of Education passed resolutions endorsing the campaign's goals and made funding and staffing commitments that included reinstatement of arts and music funding in the school budget. Teen pregnancy prevention is now defined as a priority on Hartford's federal funding needs lists.
- The cornerstone of early intervention is the school-based health education curriculum known as Postponing Sexual Involvement (PSI). PSI will be implemented for all fifth graders in Hartford. The model is one of few nationally tested teen prevention curricula that have been both evaluated and found to be effective. Through a cooperative effort of Hartford's hospitals (Hartford Hospital, Saint Francis Hospital and Medical Center, and the Connecticut Children's Medical Center), the Hartford Public Schools, and the Hartford Action Plan, this program will begin this fall. The Greater Hartford Jaycees Children's Fund has made a $100,000 grant to support this implementation, and each of the partners has committed financial and in-kind resources.
- More than 40 youth agencies have begun to develop "best practices" concepts on which all local prevention programs will be based. Eighteen "best practices" have been proposed for adoption.
- Kaiser Permanente has funded an Adult Advisor Academy to offer adolescent sexuality training to Greater Hartford volunteers who work with youth programs.

Mayor Michael Peters, City of Hartford

THE COLLABORATIVE PARTNERSHIP

The Community

The community defined in this community care network (CCN) vision is the 16,000 Hartford adolescents, aged 11 to 18, who face myriad health and social threats related to the city's poverty. A priority subgroup—fifth-grade girls and boys—has been targeted for a 3-year intervention. Although a substantial reduction in teen pregnancy levels within this community over several years is the prime objective of the intervention, the overall health and well-being of Hartford's adolescent population is the larger goal of this partnership, whose intervention has been designed to link integrally with the city's larger efforts in violence and gang prevention, youth employment, and educational excellence, and to collaborate in improving prospects for Hartford's young people.

Hartford, CT, is a poor urban area of 140,000 residents surrounded by affluent suburbs and served by three regional hospitals. The city's population is approximately one-third Latino (principally Puerto Rican), one-third African-American, and one-third non-Hispanic Caucasian. Ninety percent of Hartford's children are African-American and Latino.

The city's economy has been affected by considerable changes in the local corporate base (insurance, banking, and industry) over the past several years, as mergers have cut jobs and moved corporate headquarters out of state, and as waning defense contracts have reduced local employment. Nevertheless, the city has a strong philanthropic tradition, which has led to support for a number of strong public/private initiatives. This makes potential matching funding for initiatives such as the CCN program possible.

In 1992, the Children's Defense Fund called Hartford the sixth worst city in the nation for children. Nearly all the targeted children are estimated to be from moderate to very low-income families as defined by U.S. Department of Housing and Urban Development section 8 limitations. Over half of the city's children are known to be eligible for Medicaid; 12 percent of Hartford families lack health insurance. The city also is characterized by its youth: by the year 2000, nearly half the city's population will be under age 18.

Too-early parenthood is considered by many local leaders to be one of Hartford's most urgent health and demographic issues. Births to teens in Hartford led U.S. averages, at 23.3 percent of all local births. Two out of seven Hartford girls aged 15 to 17 were estimated to become pregnant in 1995, and one-fourth of Connecticut's births to mothers under 15 occur in Hartford. This group is nearly twice as likely to deliver prematurely than women in their 20s. In a statistic closer to home for Hartford residents, more Hartford teens will give birth this year than will graduate from high school.

This trend has shown no improvement over recent years; in fact, the average age of teen mothers has decreased. Along with the economic and social disadvantages too-early parenthood creates for young parents, an additional concern is the intergenerational cycle of poverty, abuse, developmental delays, and health problems it supports.

Through related causes, sexually transmitted diseases (STDs) strike nearly 2,000 Hartford teens, at a rate exceeding all older age groups. The occurrence of HIV/AIDS among residents in their 20s also exceeds both national levels and all other age groups, suggesting that many of these individuals acquired the disease during their adolescence. (All data provided by Connecticut Department of Public Health and Addiction Services.)

Target Population

The group of Hartford youths targeted for the intervention described in this CCN vision are 4,360 Hartford youths (equal numbers of girls and boys) who will attend fifth grade (approximate age 11) within the next three years. There are 2,000 youths in this age group in a given year; this intervention intends to reach one-fourth in the first year, and all in the second and third years of the intervention. For an abstinence-based, primary pregnancy prevention program to succeed, it has been shown that the intervention must begin before children are sexually active.

The Partnership

The collaborative partnership formed to address these pressing health issues through the CCN program includes a public/private partnership called the Hartford Action Plan on Infant Health (Action Plan), Hartford Hospital, Saint Francis Hospital and Medical Center/Mount Sinai Hospital, the Hartford Public Schools (HPS), and a resident/consumer advisory group called the Community Leadership Network (CLN).

These particular partners have all collaborated previously through the Hartford Action Plan, but not for the purposes of teen pregnancy prevention nor through this three-way configuration of school-community-hospital institutions.

Hartford Action Plan on Infant Health In 1985, a high-level group of corporate donors, health and social service providers, school and city government representatives, and community leaders convened to organize a joint approach to Hartford's staggering infant mortality and teen pregnancy levels. The Hartford Action Plan on Infant Health, Inc. (Action Plan), a not-for-profit organization, was formed with a unique purpose: not to duplicate but rather to connect existing services, innovate and improve on current models, and encourage collaboration.

The Action Plan has as its vision a city in which every young person is self-sufficient before becoming a parent, and every baby is born healthy and full term. Its mission and services are as follows:

- To prevent pregnancies among young teens in Hartford by developing programs that offer firmer emotional and practical ways to make informed choices about their futures. Current activities include the city's largest primary pregnancy prevention program (serving 500 youths since inception), and major organizing efforts to jointly reduce teen pregnancy citywide.
- To ensure the births of full-term, healthy babies to Hartford's women, establish an improved standard for prenatal and maternal care, ensure that all women receive early prenatal care, and ensure that women with high-risk pregnancies receive special services. The Action Plan created an innovative, citywide program operated by all seven maternal health providers focused on identifying and serving high-risk pregnant women to reduce preterm births and low birth weight.
- To change public and private institutional systems as necessary to ensure that all Hartford women, children, and youths receive preventive health care. The Action Plan is working closely with providers and the state's Medicaid agency to incorporate the preventive elements of its services as the state transitions to a managed care model.

In 1994, the Action Plan achieved a key long-term goal when it secured an agreement with its key partners, the city's hospitals and health department, under which these institutions assumed direct financial and operational responsibility for Action Plan maternal health programs that had been jointly operated. This effort at institutionalization resulted from a strong partnership developed over many years and leading to truly cooperative service delivery and resource sharing.

Funding for the Action Plan's $1 million annual budget has come from more than 40 local corporate and foundation grants and provider contracts and from national foundations such as the Annie E. Casey Foundation, the Public Welfare Foundation, and the W. K. Kellogg Foundation.

Saint Francis Hospital and Medical Center/Mount Sinai Hospital Saint Francis Hospital and Medical Center is a private, not-for-profit acute care hospital serving residents of the greater Hartford area. Saint Francis is affiliated with the University of Connecticut Schools of Medicine and Dentistry, and with Mount Sinai Hospital through a 1990 affiliation that resulted in the consolidation and expansion of child health activities within a single department of pediatrics. Together, the hospitals are licensed for 1,080 beds, and have 31,000 discharges, 78,000 emergency visits, and 89,000 outpatient visits annually. Saint Francis and Mount Sinai serve as a regional referral center with clinical concentrations in cardiology, oncology, women's and children's services, emergency/trauma care, and rehabilitation. Saint Francis conducts a school of nursing, and is a member of the Catholic Hospital Association and the American Hospital Association.

The adolescent medicine program is within the hospital's Center for Children's Health and Development. The center is committed to promoting access to primary and preventive pediatric care through innovative programs that address community needs and through public/private partnerships that further the well-being of the area's children. The director of the University of Connecticut School of Medicine's Section on Adolescent Medicine sits at Saint Francis, and will play an integral part in implementing the proposed project. Members of the hospital's pediatric department are active with community initiatives such as the Adolescent Health Council, Children's Health Including Life Development (CHILD) Council, primary care programs at Hartford Public and Weaver high schools, and a hospital/school partnership that provides an early intervention behavior and development program in three elementary schools known as Ready to Learn. Recently, Saint Francis/Mount Sinai offered several hospital executives to help manage the Hartford Health Department until a search was completed for a new city health director.

Hartford Hospital Founded in 1854 in response to a catastrophic industrial accident, Hartford Hospital has remained dedicated to its mission of serving the community. The hospital is a not-for-profit, 940-bed tertiary care institution employing more than 5,000 people. Hartford Hospital is one of New England's largest medical centers, with 56,000 discharges, 89,000 emergency visits, and 89,000 outpatient visits annually. The hospital is a full organ transplant center, and has medical specializations in cancer, heart, trauma, pediatrics, obstetrics, and, with the integration in 1994 of the internationally known Institute of Living, psychiatry. Hartford Hospital offers graduate programs in affiliation with the University of Connecticut Schools of Medicine and Dentistry. Hartford Hospital is a member of Voluntary Hospitals of America and the American Hospital Association.

The hospital sees itself as a community resource, serving as "physician to the neighborhood" through its many clinics (including cardiology, neurology, obstetrics/gynecology, surgery, dentistry, psychiatry, and pediatrics). Through membership in the Connecticut Health System, Hartford Hospital is affiliated with the Newington

Children's Hospital (the state's only children's hospital) and the Veterans Memorial Medical Center. It is expected that as of July 1995, Visiting Nurse Association Health Care would join Hartford Hospital to provide a seamless continuum of care that ranges from home-based to hospital-based services, and from preventive to acute tertiary to long-term care.

Among the community initiatives in which Hartford Hospital is involved is the Southside Institutions Neighborhood Alliance, which works with the neighboring community to improve economic, physical, and social conditions, offering a neighborhood mortgage program and other revitalization efforts. The hospital also operates a successful school-based cancer prevention program for Latino students; the Connecticut Children's Injury Prevention Center; and the Safe Kids program. In 1996, Hartford Hospital's pediatric merged with that of Newington Children's Hospital, which is constructing a children's hospital within the city (scheduled for completion in 1996).

Hartford Public Schools The Hartford Public School system includes three high schools and 30 elementary and middle schools serving 25,000 students. More than 90 percent of students are African-American and Latino. The Hartford Public School system made headlines in 1994 when it became the first school system to be managed by Education Alternatives Inc., a private, for-profit management firm.

Through an extensive school health services program, the Hartford school system is the largest provider of primary care services to Hartford school children. In addition, the system has the only school-based health sites statewide that have established Medicaid reimbursement. The schools operate three school-based health clinics (one each at a high school, a middle school, and an elementary school) and employ seven health educators.

School budgets have been severely constrained in recent years. At present, many extracurricular activities are unfunded; the high schools' Teen Parenting Program has been cut; arts and music programs have been virtually eliminated. To meet an element agreed upon by partners in the city's emerging teen pregnancy prevention strategic plan, the Superintendent of Schools asked, and the Board of Education agreed to replace arts and music funding in the 1995–96 fiscal year school budget.

Community Leadership Network The Community Leadership Network (CLN) is a consumer-led committee created in October 1994 and staffed by the Action Plan. The CLN was created to provide an independent consumer role in maternal and child health services of the city's hospitals and community health centers.

In creating this group, the Action Plan also sought to improve on current models of community participation, which often seek yet still limit consumer involvement. For example, initiatives that create minority slots on boards and committees for these individuals often limit the strength of the consumer "voice." And often, the consumer advocates chosen are not consumers themselves. Hartford, as with many other communities, has experienced programs that originated within institutions, sometimes with "community input," but that did not meet their objectives. In some cases, the resulting services were not culturally appropriate. In others, supporting needs such as transportation or child care were not adequately addressed.

The Action Plan partnership seeks to return to these models the elements of a more comprehensive community leadership model, where solutions initiate directly from the affected community. These elements include majority consumer membership, pregnancy prevention strategic plan. In addition, the Hartford Youth Commission and several parent coalitions are active in city programs and strategies.

Hartford providers have determined community needs through several studies and community assessments. Within the past 6 years, these include: the Municipal Health Services Assessment (city of Hartford, 1989), the Status of Hartford Adolescents (Adolescent Health Council, 1992), and the Youth Services Assessment Project Report (Hartford Department of Social Services, 1994). Principal limitations to date in meeting these reports' recommendations have been in three general areas: a less than "holistic" approach, so that essential ingredients such as transportation might be left out; lack of funding to finance more than small-scale models; and failure to meet the cultural/language needs of Hartford's diverse population (where many residents speak only Spanish).

In other areas, continued efforts are still required to meet community accountability standards. A 1995 report by Child Trends of Washington, DC, for the CHILD Council praised current initiatives but still cited an overall level of consumer dissatisfaction in the city. Child Trends' recommendations to the CHILD Council to obtain more active consumer participation included patient satisfaction surveys, parent medical advocates, and organization of hospital parent groups to give parents a role in the development of services.

Seamless Continuum of Care

The Action Plan is a public/private partnership that for 10 years has expanded and coordinated the city's prenatal/maternal health services through formal agreements with all three clinics and community health centers in the city, the three hospitals and city health department, the Hispanic Health Council, the Visiting Nurse Association, INFOLINE, the Adolescent Parenting and Development Program, several homeless shelters and shelters for battered women, and the Hartford Primary Care Consortium. The Action Plan partnership also spearheaded the identification and hiring of culturally appropriate prenatal nursing staff. Pregnant women who enter any of these sites for care, including hospital emergency rooms, are brought into this coordinated system of maternal health care.

Currently, following service institutionalization in 1994, the Greater Hartford Prenatal Care Continuum, as the partnership is known, continues to manage an integrated service delivery model to ensure that data collection and best practices, such as preterm birth risk assessment, occur.

The Reducing Infant Mortality (RIM) project is linked to Hartford's Prenatal Care Continuum. This project resulted from an innovative rate pass-through agreement with the state's hospital oversight commission. RIM financed maternal health outreach and preventive care, and was particularly useful in establishing stronger connections between hospitals and neighborhood outreach programs and in gathering outcome data. The project, originally funded for three years, continues to be financed by the city's hospitals.

Additional activities that share the CCN vision are the hospitals' development of a joint proposal, pending with a local foundation, to develop the Hartford Healthy Start Maternal Network, a system for electronically linking all the city's prenatal and maternal health clinics and sites. This network is essential to the city's ability to share and track patient data, and is expected to greatly enhance the efficiency of and access to prenatal intrapartum and postnatal care for Hartford's women and their newborns, and to support a seamless continuum of care for this population.

On a smaller but fully integrated scale, the Betances Health Partnership, a formal collaboration of Hartford Hospital, the HPS, and Travelers Corporation, operates a full-service health clinic at the Ramon E. Betances Elementary School. The "Creo en los Niños" Clinic provides a continuum of medical, dental, mental health, and developmental services, and has established a computer network between school and hospital to strengthen the continuum of care.

The Medical Home Project is a major collaboration of the city's hospitals, clinics, and health department that uses child health advocates to cut down on use of emergency room visits for children's health care by encouraging regular and consistent family use of a single medical provider. This intends to improve indicators such as immunization rates, and improve access to early and preventive well-child care in general.

In the arena of positive youth development services, the Hartford Youth Network and Hartford Department of Human Services (DHS) are in the midst of a tremendous innovation in service delivery, moving beyond cooperation to active institutional collaboration on a citywide scale. The DHS has divided the city into six geographic "clusters," within which community-based youth services will be coordinated and providers will be expected to cooperate to ensure a full menu of services and reduce duplication. The Hartford Youth Network's consortium members each have formally pledged to adhere to the goals of the "cluster" design.

Management within Fixed Resources

Hartford has had an interesting and, recently, fast-paced history of change in health financing, mirroring that of much of the nation. Because of the city's large Medicaid-eligible population, health reform has and will have a profound impact on Hartford. Formerly a fee-for-service system, the city's health system now uses a variety of financing mechanisms.

Because Connecticut is mandating Medicaid coverage for the Aid to Families with Dependent Children population (with Hartford as the first site), hospitals are moving toward a capitated, managed care system for this population. This will require unprecedented coordination of services among the city's health care providers. Patients will register with one of the city's available health plans and then be required to receive care through that plan unless referred to another provider. In such an instance, the primary care provider will be at financial risk for the services used elsewhere.

With the advent of Medicaid managed care, which will be phased in by the state over the forthcoming year, both providers and health plan members must respect the value of a consistent primary care provider and ensure that care is provided at the proper site for all beneficiaries. This should help ensure that services are not duplicated and that continuity exists within an identified medical home.

The state's new Medicaid system, under the Connecticut Department of Social Services, also will require providers to think differently about their role in providing preventive services and looking at different levels of partnership (for example, school/hospital partnerships).

Recently, the HPS entered into an agreement with the Action Plan to obtain fee-for-service reimbursements for the Weekdays at the Library teen pregnancy prevention youth programs, which the Action Plan operates at school sites. A part of the city's overall teen pregnancy prevention strategic plan is to further the Action Plan's work to integrate these services into Medicaid managed care through other health plans. Hartford's success in securing this partial financing is a very exciting development for all positive youth development programs that can meet criteria as "healthy life-style" services.

Because a large portion of health care for Hartford teens is provided through the HPS, all managed care providers will be required to contract with the schools for provision of services to school-aged children who seek care within school health facilities. If PSI can be shown to decrease teen pregnancy and the incidence of STDs and to provide an avenue for health education for adolescents, the city's hospitals would consider allocating some prevention dollars from capitation payments to the schools for funding of the program.

An additional, current example of managing within fixed resources is the Action Plan's organizational structure. At its creation, its board chose to use existing resources rather than create a new, freestanding agency. All services are contracted. Health staff have been hospital or clinic employees; program and administrative management has been provided by a consulting firm on an as-needed basis. This has given the Action Plan a great deal of flexibility and avoided many turf issues that might have surfaced with a new organizational entity.

Finally, the Hartford HealthTrack program was created by the state in 1993 to improve access to Medicaid's Early Periodic Screening Diagnosis and Treatment program for children. The $1.6 million program was an exciting reform for state Medicaid programs, and made use of the underutilized Federal Financial Participation matching regulation to leverage state money with a private grant. The combined funding flowed directly to several subcontracted community-based agencies to provide outreach and enrollment.

In terms of measuring financial risk sharing, cost/benefit studies have been limited. One small study helped lead to a program expansion by showing a substantially reduced medical cost for mothers and newborns who received preventive services through the Action Plan partnership.

MOVING TOWARD THE COMMUNITY CARE NETWORK VISION

What should our partnership work toward as an optimal system of health care? In Hartford, the CCN partnership envisions a system of adolescent health care with the following ingredients, outlined by the Hartford Vision Project of 1992:

> Each child and family in Hartford will have sustained good health. . . . Comprehensive, community-based preventive primary health care shall be the norm for all citizens. . . . The development of Hartford's children and families will be the city's highest priority. Government, nonprofit and private sectors will examine their policies and programs against the standard of how they contribute to this vision.
>
> Continuity of care means care will be comprehensive, ongoing, and will focus foremost on primary prevention and treat each person holistically and with respect.
>
> Specialized, preventive services for adolescents will be provided, recognizing their unique needs for services in appropriate settings, with assured con-

fidentiality. In particular, teen pregnancy will be eliminated by focusing community energy toward promoting behaviors that send messages to teens that adolescent pregnancy is unacceptable and detrimental to teens' reaching their full potential as adults.

The Visioning Process

These statements are part of a larger vision created in 1992 by more than 100 community members through the Hartford Vision Project. The 6-month process of the Hartford Vision Project, using work groups and focus groups that included parents, youths, providers, and community and civic leaders, was based on consensus decisions and on ethnically and culturally diverse participation. An overarching premise related to public health that resulted from the process was that consumers—the people of the city and region—must be active participants in making, implementing, and monitoring policies and programs that grow from the vision.

The Hartford CCN partnership believes it has a responsibility to work within the larger community of public health and adolescent service providers to advance this vision. Further planning in Hartford was indeed affected by the results of the vision process. In November 1994, a report was completed by 25 physicians and public health professionals at the request of Hartford's Mayor Peters to make recommendations on strengthening the role of the city's health department.

The "Report of the Mayor's Blue Ribbon Task Force on Public Health" made the following suggestions that are consistent with the CCN vision: The Hartford Health Department should "enhance family focused outreach and educational activities to increase the effectiveness of health promotion . . . encourage public/private partnerships to coordinate education and outreach efforts . . . develop linguistically and culturally appropriate educational programs and materials to provide practical and user-friendly information that consumers can incorporate into individual and family lifestyles and patterns of daily living . . . establish a formal mechanism to capture valuable consumer input . . . promote cultural awareness and sensitivity to assist staff of all private and public health agencies."

The recommendations for the health department are included here to show that the thinking in Hartford among both public and private providers has become increasingly focused both on common values within Hartford and on the values of the CCN vision. Moreover, these health professionals increasingly appear to consider themselves to be part of a community of social agents—as agents for change—with a common purpose and agenda.

This is not by any means a smooth process. Issues of ownership resurface, and misunderstandings occur between the institutions and their communities. Yet, in the case of one or two such recent events, these conflicts appear increasingly to be seen as part of a mutual learning process, and as opportunities to strengthen relationships and to address gaps in perception or services.

The plan described in this chapter is a strategic plan for teen pregnancy reduction in Hartford developed by school, corporate, community, and provider representatives under the auspices of the Action Plan. Initiated in fall 1994, the plan outlines a 5-year process for a substantial, citywide reduction in teen pregnancy levels—achieved through a two-pronged approach of service expansion and public mobilization. The plan is based on the following vision of what the successful principles of such an ambitious agenda would be:

- A message and public campaign of early intervention and high level leadership to end births to adolescents under age 15.
- Enrollment by all youth-serving agencies by enlisting agreement to expand/support best practices or key elements of successful prevention programs, rather than any agency's specific model or approach.
- Opportunities for all Hartford youths to obtain a variety of developmental and growth opportunities, called their "Passport to Success." These include: access to health information and services, opportunities to develop special skills and hobbies, opportunities to participate in group activities and teams, and opportunities to develop career choices.

The goals of the 5-year strategic plan are the following:

1. To eliminate births to adolescents younger than age 15 by the year 2000.
2. To reduce by 32 percent the percentage of births to adolescents by the year 2000, resulting in 15.8 percent overall.
3. To provide Hartford youths with access to basic opportunities that are essential and appropriate for their growth and development.

Although these are ambitious targets for Hartford, they are the reason the plan has generated such strong and enthusiastic support to date. One key member of the plan's leadership said he would not have signed on had the plan been a model program of limited scope and reach.

The strategic plan was designed to be consistent with the vision of a shared community responsibility for teen parenthood. To eliminate agency "ownership" or investment of responsibility in any one agency, this plan is governed jointly by the Superintendent of Schools, the city's Director of Social Services, and the Action Plan board of directors. Following initial drafting, its immediate task was to involve more than 30 coalitions and community organizations—the Hartford Violence Prevention Project, Girl Scouts, church leaders, the Hartford Youth Network, Catholic Family Services, philanthropies, the United Way, the city's hospitals, health department, and youth—in reviewing and completing the plan. Ongoing tasks are to continue to "enroll" key individuals and organizations in the goals of the plan. Focus groups of youths will be asked to react to the plan's concepts and, as the plan moves forward, will help lead development of the messages and approaches of the public campaign. The plan is scheduled to be completed in summer 1995.

When the partners involved in this CCN vision formed, each organization had already signed on in support of the goals of this citywide teen pregnancy prevention plan. The partners saw the CCN program as an ideal means for creating a specific role for the hospitals in the plan, while fulfilling the plan's potential as a truly integrated and community-oriented preventive health program.

Moving toward the Community Care Network Vision

This section describes the Postponing Sexual Involvement program, a specific component of the city's larger teen pregnancy reduction plan. The PSI program supports all four goals of that plan, but is targeted most specifically at the first goal, "to eliminate births to adolescents younger than 15 by the year 2000."

Hartford's CCN partnership has set the following objectives to reach that goal:

1. Over 3 years, provide 4,360 Hartford fifth graders with the PSI curriculum developed by Atlanta's Emory University/Grady Memorial Hospital collaboration.
2. Develop hospital/community linkages that can strengthen the health education, diagnostic, and medical referral activities of Hartford's community-based youth programs. This objective responds to a need expressed by many youth program staff for stronger institutional connections to meet health education or referral needs of children discovered through their participation in programs.
3. Expand the consumer-led CLN to take on adolescent health issues.
4. Based on evaluation results, integrate this model into managed care systems.

The following specific strategies and measures of success are proposed:

1a. Hartford and Saint Francis hospitals will hire/assign an adolescent health educator (AHE) to implement the PSI curriculum in coordination with the HPS at school sites citywide. In years two and three, the number of AHEs will be expanded from 1.0 to 1.5 full-time employees.
Target date and measures of success: Hiring scheduled to be done by October 1. Retention successful. AHE integrates smoothly into hospital and school cultures.

1b. Young men and women aged 15–16 will be enlisted and trained as peer educators to administer the PSI curriculum with the oversight and support of the AHEs and with school teachers. These peer educators will be paid a stipend by the sponsoring hospital and supervised by the AHE(s), and will receive at least 20 hours of initial education, ongoing support, and regular in-service training. (A job description will be developed for these positions.)
Measures of success: 20 teens hired and trained in year one; 40 trained in years two and three. Retention maintained at 50 percent or more.

1c. The HPS will provide the AHEs with school-based support through a half-time PSI coordinator to secure sites and coordinate student groups for the PSI curriculum.
Measures of success: Student groups at least 70 percent capacity on average; scheduling proceeds smoothly.

1d. Building on the existing health education curriculum in place, the HPS will be enlisted to deliver at least five initial sessions of reproductive health education that precede the five-session PSI curriculum. (Although this could be a role for the AHE, the HPS have a Pre-K through sixth-grade curriculum that can be used for this purpose.)
Measures of success: All students receive full 10 sessions of education; coordination is smooth.

1e. A total of 460 youths in the first year of implementation receive the PSI program; 1,900 youths receive PSI in year two and 2,000 in year three.
Target date and measure of success: Program scheduled to begin January 1996; target numbers are reached.

1f. The CCN partner group will contract an evaluator to administer a pretest/posttest evaluation, using the Emory/Grady model with additions or modifications as deemed appropriate to meet the overall evaluative needs of the strategic plan.
Measures of success: evaluation design meets needs, is administered smoothly, and secures appropriate number of students for control and intervention groups. Evaluation demonstrates positive behavior changes among participants.

regularly to plan and measure progress and will keep their own institutions apprised of progress and needs. Both this operational group and the overarching strategic plan partnership are intended to be the principal means by which objectives will be periodically reviewed and improved.

Technical Assistance

The CCN partnership may require two possible forms of technical assistance. The direct assistance of the Grady Memorial Hospital staff will be required to carry out PSI, so that Hartford may learn as much as possible from their experience. Additional assistance will be secured with current resources as needed. It should be noted that the director of adolescent medicine at Saint Francis Hospital has been trained in PSI; also, the city has a strong base of additional experience on which to draw.

In addition, the need may arise for specific expertise in areas such as training, cost evaluation, and insurance/managed care systems. To date, these resources have been secured locally.

Target Goals and Evaluation

Evaluation will be carried out in the following four ways:

1. Analysis of PSI's ability to change knowledge, attitudes, and behavior about sexual activity through the Emory/Grady model using a pretest/posttest survey and a control group. The control group most likely will be drawn from those youths not reached in the first year. The strategic plan partnership will supervise this activity, with assistance from the Action Plan's Evaluation Committee and other institutions as necessary.
2. Ongoing evaluation of the measures of success described under strategies and within the dimensions of the CCN vision. This will be a process-driven activity structured through the CCN partnership's regular operational meetings.
3. Development by the CCN hospital partners of a mechanism for measuring costs of the service delivered, and cost–benefits using available data on medical costs associated with births to teens. This will provide the means of determining how this program is "managed within fixed resources."
4. These evaluation activities will be closely coordinated with the larger evaluation planning effort of the strategic plan partnership. The partnership, for example, will be working with the Hartford Health Department's vital statistics staff to produce timely, neighborhood-based information on teen births. (State information currently is city-specific only, and at least one year old upon dissemination.) In addition, this partnership will be interested in creating a means of keeping a barometer on the related communities of parents, churches, teachers, providers, and neighborhood organizations, among others, to determine satisfaction with the plan (see "Measures of Success within the Four Dimensions of the Community Care Network Vision," below).

In these activities, the following premises will be followed (developed by a strategic plan work group charged with developing targets and outcome evaluation criteria for the plan):

- Services and opportunities provided to young people must be accounted for by individual and in the aggregate.
- Adolescents must be key sources of information regarding program satisfaction and adequacy.

Measures of Success within the Four Dimensions of the Community Care Network Vision

Community Accountability

- A means is established to measure youths' satisfaction with this program.
- A means is established to measure other communities' satisfaction with the program, and the PSI curriculum is accepted by parents, providers, churches, teachers, and other key supporting communities.
- The CLN provides an effective means of consumer input to providers on adolescent health service delivery.

Seamless Continuum of Care

- Resources are effectively shared; working relationships between hospitals and school are smooth.
- Youth service providers achieve stronger linkages and referral systems with health institutions.

Community Health Focus

- The PSI curriculum results in a delay in sexual activity and prevents too-early parenthood among 11–15-year-olds.

Management within Fixed Resources

- The cost and potential cost/benefits of the program are established.
- The program is integrated into the hospitals' managed care programs.

SUMMARY OF NOTABLE PROGRESS

Since the preparation of the original CCN proposal as described previously, two substantive changes have taken place in the Hartford environment. The Community Leadership Network now believes there is more need for advocacy on the part of consumers to prevent attrition of the gains made in reducing infant mortality; the CCN plans to collaborate with the CHILD council to create a stronger voice for consumers. One particular area of concern is the lack of Spanish-speaking nursing staff in prenatal care clinics and delivery rooms that are operated by the city's hospitals.

Second, the movement to Medicaid Managed Care in Connecticut canceled funding that had been received from fees for service tied to the school-based health clinics. The Action Plan is currently working with multidisciplinary committees that include the managed care providers to investigate cost–benefits and the types of health care components that could be supported by managed care plans as elements of prevention strategies.

Two particular areas of success stand out from the first 8 months of the campaign:

Implementation of the PSI Curriculum

PSI is a nationally recognized and proven health education curriculum developed in Atlanta and new to Hartford as a citywide project. This school-based curriculum is carried out over five sessions, preceded by basic health instruction from Hartford Public School staff. PSI works by using peers to deliver a positive, factual message about how to make the decision to begin sexual activity, encourages delay for young adolescents, and uses role play to practice refusal and other skills in real-life situations. The Breaking the Cycle campaign plans to have all 2,400 Hartford fifth graders receiving PSI within the 1996–97 school year.

In Hartford, PSI will use a team of three AHEs, up to 45 teenage peer educators, and a school-based coordinator to organize and deliver the curriculum. The AHEs will be hospital employees, to whom peer educators will report. Hartford Hospital, Saint Francis Hospital and Medical Center, and the Connecticut Children's Medical Center will be responsible for ensuring that PSI is delivered through each of Hartford's three high schools to their elementary feeder schools.

The project team is led by the director of elementary instruction for the HPS. Key staff include HPS health education staff, as well as staff from Hartford's three hospitals.

The peer educators are a central element of this project team. They will be hired and trained by the AHEs to deliver the curriculum to fifth graders. Aside from the value 11-year-olds will receive in hearing a positive abstinence message from an older peer role model, this project gives us an opportunity to strengthen the contributions Hartford's older youth can make through leadership and service and gives them the opportunity for paid employment from the hospitals. We believe this will significantly broaden their career horizons and give them valuable professional contacts in the health field.

PSI's elements include informational/training sessions for parents, evaluation and coordination by Action Plan and school staff, and technical assistance from PSI's originators in Georgia.

The Greater Hartford Jaycees Children's Fund has made a $100,000 grant to support PSI's implementation. The size of this grant required each partner to pledge additional support, and each partner has done so. We have not secured funding for future years for PSI.

Best Practices

Successful teen pregnancy prevention programs share many common elements. Nationwide, many different youth programs have proven these best practices to be effective. Examples of best practices include parent involvement, community acceptance, reproductive health information, and training for adults who work with teens. Through Breaking the Cycle, Hartford's youth programs are cooperating to define and adopt a comprehensive set of best practices for the city.

As the city manager's and mayor's representative on the Breaking the Cycle leadership group, the city's director of human services leads this campaign, along with the chair of the Hartford Youth Network. In April 1996, the director convened a group of more than 50 agency, neighborhood, and educational leaders, service providers, and council members at a planning meeting. After the meeting, a multi-agency work group formed to develop the initial ideas into one document.

The work group appointed by meeting participants has defined and drafted a list of 18 best practices for all youth agencies to adopt. Over the next few months, parent groups, agency leaders, and government agencies will all review these suggestions for their adoption. In 1997, youth agencies will begin using best practices in their programs for teens.

Contact: Flora Parisky
Chief Operating Officer
The Hartford Action Plan on Infant Health, Inc.
30 Arbor Street
Hartford, CT 06106
Phone: (860) 236-4872
Fax: (860) 232-8321
E-mail: Pariskygrp@aol.com

19

Health Care for the Homeless

Executive Summary

Health Care for the Homeless, a program of the I. M. Sulzbacher Center for the Homeless, Jacksonville, FL, is an excellent example of a private and public partnership that has joined forces to solve a pressing community need. Prior to the establishment of this program, the homeless were consistently falling through the cracks of our health care system. They had no access to health care outside hospital emergency rooms.

This lack of access to health care was particularly poignant for a city that is a nationally recognized health care center with a booming biomedical industry to complement our outstanding hospitals and health care facilities, including Baptist/St. Vincent's Health System, Mayo Clinic, University Medical Center, and others. High-quality health care is available, accessible, and affordable for low-, middle-, and upper-income citizens. But still each day, the estimated 2,500 homeless have struggled to have their health care needs addressed.

Jacksonville has the largest geographic area of any city in the United States. Our growing population surpassed one million this past year. Recognized as a financial, insurance, and medical center of the Southeast, our seaport town is also known for its port and military bases.

In spite of this strong economic base, homelessness continues to be a serious problem. The February 1996 census of the homeless showed an increase in their number, yet over 70 percent of the homeless call Jacksonville home, dispelling the myth that they are all transients. The survey also revealed longer periods of homelessness and a disproportionate number of African-Americans (58 percent). Health care continues to be one of the top three reasons why someone becomes homeless. More than 46 percent indicated they had health problems, 68 percent had dental problems, and 49 percent needed glasses. The census demonstrated that access to health care is an important factor that is impacting the number of homeless in our community

Health Care for the Homeless has made significant progress during the past year. Soon after the February homeless census, a comprehensive, on-site health center opened at the new I. M. Sulzbacher Center for the Homeless. A full-time medical staff headed by a nurse practitioner provides primary health care 6 days per week. Volunteer physicians and other health care workers also serve in the clinic, expanding its outreach.

Our community partnership has grown. We established a Health Center Advisory Committee that encompasses a broad cross-section of all the health disciplines. Our funding base increased with the addition of local funding partners who sponsored our health center's grant submission to the Robert Wood Johnson Foundation. We won the foundation's Local Initiatives grant and received a matching grant of $456,000. These funds will be used to further expand our health center staff, as well as establish vision and dental programs addressing the health concerns identified in the homeless census. With the addition of these programs and the new health center, I believe, next year's homeless census will show major progress in addressing the health concerns of our homeless population.

The key lessons we have learned to date involve the importance of the ultimate consumers' (that is, the homeless population's) input and the tremendous value derived through broad-based community partnerships. Throughout Jacksonville, we have a large number of individuals and organizations who have a stake in this health center. Together they create a synergy that is addressing this major unmet need for the homeless—access to health care.

A. Hugh Greene
Executive Vice President
Baptist/St. Vincent's Health System

THE COLLABORATIVE PARTNERSHIP

The Community

The Stewart B. McKinney Homeless Act of 1987 defines *homeless* as the following:

1. An individual who lacks a fixed, regular and adequate night-time residence.
2. An individual who has a primary night-time residence that is a . . . shelter designed to provide temporary living accommodations; an institution that provides a temporary residence to persons intended to be institutionalized; or a public place not designed for . . . regular sleeping accommodation for human beings.

The stereotype of homeless people as vagrants or transients is not an accurate portrayal of the homeless population in Jacksonville. This city's homeless citizens are a diverse population, their situation often related to economic/personal crises or mental/physical disabilities.

The Emergency Services and Homeless Coalition of Jacksonville has been conducting a homeless census annually for the past 4 years. The most recent census for which final results are available (1994) reveals that there are between 2,000 and 4,000 homeless in Jacksonville each day, or 8,000 to 16,000 annually, with an estimated average time on the streets of three months. Nearly three-quarters of our homeless are citizens of Jacksonville, rather than transient. Nearly 70 percent are "new" homeless, on the streets for months as opposed to years, and just as many have either full- or part-time employment.

Intact families with children account for 12 percent of these people. Children represent 14 percent of the homeless, senior citizens 6 percent. Almost 50 percent have completed high school; 22 percent have attended and graduated from college; 30 percent are honorably discharged military veterans. The median age of adult homeless people is 38; the overall median age in Jacksonville is 32. Although African-Americans account for only 26 percent of the overall Jacksonville population, they represent 54 percent of the homeless population.

Though homeless people can be found throughout the county, they congregate in the core downtown, in neighborhoods adjacent to the core downtown, and at the beaches. With the exception of the beaches, the majority of shelters and other services are located in these areas.

Snapshot of the Health Status of the Homeless

The health problems experienced by the homeless population in Jacksonville are multiple and continuous, often overlapping so that sporadic treatment of one or two problems does little to affect the overall health of the individual. The following health care statistics are derived from the National Coalition for the Homeless and the National Health Care for the Homeless Council:

- *Venereal disease:* 10–15 times more likely
- *Hypertension:* 2–4 times greater incidence
- *Gastrointestinal disorders:* 2–3 times greater incidence
- *Tuberculosis:*
  - —*Active disease:* 1.6 percent to 6.8 percent prevalence
  - —*Latent infection:* 18 percent to 50 percent
- *HIV positive:* 3.2 percent (2× national average)
- *Alcohol dependent:* 40 percent
- *Drug dependent:* 10 percent
- *Severe mental illness:* 33 percent
- *Other:* Poor nutrition/personal hygiene; frequent upper respiratory infection; trauma from beatings and rape; skin disorders, lice, scabies, and so on

The following statistics were extracted from the 1995 census of the homeless (to be published soon) and are in comparison to the general population of the city:

- 57 percent have immediate medical problems
- 27 percent reported being hospitalized last year
- 31 percent received no medical care in the past year
- 64 percent have immediate dental problems
- 76 percent reported receiving no dental care in the past year
- 32 percent have mental health problems

In Jacksonville as recently as 2 years ago, the indigent, the uninsured working class, the elderly, and all others in need could access health care services—all except the homeless.

- Although more than 50 agencies in Jacksonville provide some services to the homeless, not one of these agencies consistently offers primary and preventive health care to this population.
- Availability is complicated by the fact that all health care resources (except emergency rooms) available to the indigent routinely require a permanent residence address before health care services will be provided, effectively denying the homeless population access to these services.

It was to close this gap in the continuum of health services that our community care network (CCN), Health Care for the Homeless (HCH), was designed.

The Partnership

The partnership that has accepted responsibility for oversight, implementation, and resource development of the HCH program includes the following:

- The I. M. Sulzbacher Center for the Homeless
- We Care Jacksonville of the Duval County Medical Society
- Baptist Medical Center
- St. Vincent's Medical Center
- Duval County Public Health Unit
- Department of Health and Rehabilitative Services, State of Florida, District Four

HCH operates as a program of the I. M. Sulzbacher Center for the Homeless (Sulzbacher Center), a planned 24-hour facility providing emergency shelter and homeless case management. The goal of the center is self-sufficiency, and will include transitional living facilities, child care, and school facilities. It is anticipated that the center will serve 2,000 homeless adults and children in the first year of operation. The clinic operated by HCH and its administrative offices will be located in the Sulzbacher Center.

We Care Jacksonville is a program of the Duval County Medical Society and its Academy of Medicine. A consortium of physicians who volunteer medical services, We Care participates in a network of five clinics throughout the city that provide free medical care to the indigent and homeless. HCH operates the largest of these clinics; it is the only clinic providing primary health care services to the homeless. This clinic accounts for over 60 percent of all patients seen by We Care physicians.

Baptist Medical Center and St. Vincent's Medical Center are two of northeast Florida's largest not-for-profit medical centers, providing a wide range of medical services. Baptist Medical Center includes Wolfson Children's Hospital, Baptist Medical Center-Beaches, and Baptist Medical Center-Nassau County. St. Vincent's Medical Center is affiliated with the Daughters of Charity national health care network of medical centers and hospitals. A merger of these two medical centers is pending, awaiting state approval. Baptist Medical Center and St. Vincent's Medical Center provide no-charge hospitalization for homeless people seen through HCH, no-charge outpatient services, donation of supplies and equipment, and monetary support.

The Public Health Unit of Duval County is a section of the state's Department of Health and Rehabilitative Services (DHRS). The Public Health Unit contracts with HCH to provide HIV/AIDS testing and counseling, tuberculosis testing, case management and follow-up of those diagnosed, and a dental van staffed by volunteer dentists that tours two of the three HCH clinic sites. All homeless people diagnosed with HIV/AIDS receive health care services through the Public Health Unit's AIDS clinic.

The DHRS (district 4) provides sovereign immunity and workers' compensation for all physicians, dentists, nurses, allied health professionals, and clerical staff offering services on a voluntary basis to HCH. Additionally, DHRS provides screening of all volunteers and volunteer training for patient eligibility screening, and review of patient medical records for compliance with state and federal regulations.

PRIOR EFFORTS TO MOVE TOWARD THE COMMUNITY CARE NETWORK VISION

In 1989, the Emergency Services and Homeless Coalition of Jacksonville (the Coalition) was formed. Comprising more than 50 local human service, governmental, and religious not-for-profit agencies providing food, shelter, and emergency assistance to people in need, the Coalition encourages communication, coordination of activities, and provision of services without discrimination to individuals in need.

Originally, the Coalition was developed to address the issue of emergency services delivery to all individuals in need. Specific attention was not focused on the city's homeless population until revitalization of the downtown area became a priority of local government and business leaders. Downtown Jacksonville is where the great majority of homeless people are the most visible.

It was felt that, rather than relocate services for homeless people to other parts of the city—in effect relocating the homeless people themselves—energies should be focused on changing their circumstances and thereby improving their life conditions. To do this, it became necessary to know who the homeless were, why they were homeless, and what should be done to change their circumstances.

Census of the Homeless

The first census of homeless persons in Jacksonville was conducted by the Coalition in February 1992. The results of that first census dispelled the traditional understanding of homeless people as transient and vagrant. This first census also identified adequate health care as one of the most important needs of homeless people, along with affordable housing and jobs and job training.

This was the first clear indication that the health care needs of homeless people in the city were going unmet. The Coalition created a Health Care Committee, which conducted further investigation into the issue of health care provision to the homeless. The committee determined that there were no health care services available to the homeless, outside of medical center and hospital emergency rooms, even though such services did exist for people living in poverty.

Note: The distinguishing factor between homeless people and people living at or below the poverty level is the lack of a permanent residence address. Without an address, homeless people could not access health care services for themselves and their families.

Physician Involvement

For a number of years, physicians had been providing no-charge care to indigent people, but there was no effort to pool resources and address the issue of coordination of health care access for the indigent. In 1991, the Duval County Medical Society established an Indigent Care Committee to recommend changes to the current methods of practice. In 1992, the Coalition approached this committee to respond to the growing awareness of a need for health care access for the homeless by establishing a network of health care clinics to provide care that was immediate and continuous.

These two organizations solicited the cooperation of the DHRS (district 4), the Duval County Public Health Unit, area hospitals, churches, and government and business leaders to establish a network of primary health care clinics to serve people who have no funds or health insurance, do not qualify for Medicaid, or who are homeless.

Health Care Access for the Homeless

The first health care clinic site specifically for the homeless was opened in June 1993 in downtown Jacksonville. In January 1994, HCH opened a second clinic site at the Beaches Public Health Department. And in November 1994, a third HCH clinic site was established at Hubbard House, the city's shelter for women and children who are victims of domestic violence. We Care Jacksonville volunteer physicians, nurses, and allied health care professionals staff the clinics; medical centers provide inpatient and outpatient services, supplies, equipment, and laboratory services.

We Care Jacksonville

The Duval County Medical Society's Indigent Care Committee embraced the opportunity to become an integral part of a coordinated community-wide effort to provide primary health care services to the homeless and truly indigent, and reorganized in July 1993. The resulting not-for-profit organization, We Care Jacksonville, has as its mission to provide primary, secondary, and tertiary care to persons living at 150 percent of the poverty level or below in Jacksonville.

In addition to supporting the HCH clinic sites, We Care Jacksonville staffs four additional health care clinics dedicated to serving the indigent other than homeless. There are approximately 2,000 physicians in Jacksonville; currently more than 330 volunteer time to We Care Jacksonville.

I. M. Sulzbacher Center for the Homeless

Concurrent with the identification and development of health care service access to the homeless population of Jacksonville, a coalition of members of the religious community, spearheaded by the Bishop of the Episcopal Diocese, was developing strategies to better serve the spectrum of needs of the homeless. The resulting organization, the I. M. Sulzbacher Center for the Homeless, is a product of a collaborative effort by the interfaith council, city government, the human services community, and the city's civic leadership. Its mission is to provide (1) fully integrated case management, including a shared, interagency database of the homeless; and (2) services beyond those offered by the city's shelters that will assist people in reestablishing their independence, including transitional housing, job skills training, child care, and school facilities.

Because available health care is one of the three greatest needs of homeless people, along with jobs and job training and affordable housing, HCH has become a program of the Sulzbacher Center. This consolidation avoids potential duplication of services and ensures access to adequate health care by all the agencies offering services to the homeless under the coordination of the Sulzbacher Center.

Community Health Focus

The homeless population of Jacksonville has been the only segment of the city's population that had no access point to the community-wide network of health care services. Prior to the establishment of HCH, homeless men, women, and children had no access to health care through channels available to the indigent because they could not meet either residency requirements or eligibility requirements for Medicaid. Because of budget limitations, the Duval County Public Health Unit, the most logical provider, could not meet the health care needs of homeless people.

The only health care option available to homeless people was through medical center and hospital emergency rooms. Emergency room care focused only on the most urgent needs, paying minimal attention to other health care problems and often not addressing the core problem at all. There was almost certainly no follow-up care or patient compliance with treatment instructions because homeless people could not afford to purchase prescription medications. Preventive health care among the homeless population of Jacksonville was nonexistent.

Without readily available access to health care designed to meet their needs, homeless people tend to let treatable ailments deteriorate until they become serious health problems that affect others, both in the homeless community and the community in general. This combination of neglect of health problems until they become critical and no preventive care leads to reduced health status that affects the community at large in two ways: (1) excessively expensive medical care for this population, and (2) the spread of communicable and infectious diseases that go untreated or undertreated.

The community at large also feels the economic effects of poor health among homeless people. Without good health, homeless people are compromised in their ability to meet head-on the issues of employment and housing. Good health is a critical factor in a homeless person's ability to get a job, perform in a job, and keep a job. Potential employers reject homeless people whose poor health makes them liabilities in the workplace. Likewise, potential landlords refuse to provide housing opportunities to homeless people in poor health.

HCH is changing this pattern. By providing primary health care services, combined with referrals for specialty care and hospitalization when needed, through clinics designed to respond to the special needs of the homeless, HCH volunteer physicians and medical support staff are able to offer comprehensive care that addresses the full range of current and potential health problems. (See figure 19-1.) Effective case management ensures that symptoms are identified and managed, and medical histories are compiled and kept up to date.

Over a 21-month period (June 1993–March 1995), 1,520 homeless individuals, comprising 3,800 clinic visits, have been seen and treated by volunteer physicians, nurses, and support personnel through HCH. The number of patients seen at the downtown clinic, the first to be established, has increased 60 percent since it opened. Prescription medications are available for distribution through the clinics, thereby encouraging patients' involvement and interaction in their care.

FIGURE 19-1. Patient Satisfaction Survey

( ) Male ( ) Female

Age ______

Place of Residence ______________________________

1. Describe your use of the health clinic?
   ____ First Visit ____ 1 to 2 Visits ____ Over the past 6 months
   ____ 3 to 4 Visits ____ More than 4 Visits

2. How did you hear about this clinic? ______________________

3. What type of transportation did you use to get to the clinic today?
   ____ Walked ____ City bus ____ Car, own transportation
   ____ Taxi ____ Pavilion resident ____ Family Center resident

4. Where did you receive medical care before using the clinic? ______________

5. If health services were received from an emergency room:
   a. Which hospital did you use the most frequently? ______________
   b. How many times per month did you use the ER? ______________
   c. Have you visited the ER since becoming a clinic patient? ______________
   If so,
   Which hospital did you use? ______________
   How many times? ______________
   For what reason? ______________

6. Have you been hospitalized in the past year? ______
   If so,
   For what reasons? ______________
   How many times? ______________
   Which hospital? ______________

7. Do you receive health services from sources other than this clinic? ______________
   If so,
   Where? ______________
   Frequency? ______________

8. Have you had a TB test? ______
   When? __________ Result? ______________

9. Have you been tested for HIV? ______ When? __________

10. Describe your level of agreement with the following statements by checking the desired response.

    a. The clinic location is convenient.
       ____ strongly agree ____ neutral ____ somewhat disagree
       ____ agree ____ disagree
       ____ somewhat agree ____ strongly disagree

    b. The medical staff talk to me in a manner that I can understand.
       ____ strongly agree ____ neutral ____ somewhat disagree
       ____ agree ____ disagree
       ____ somewhat agree ____ strongly disagree

FIGURE 19-1. (Continued)

c. The staff treat me with respect during my clinic visits.

____ strongly agree ____ neutral ____ somewhat disagree
____ agree ____ disagree
____ somewhat agree ____ strongly disagree

d. The medical staff answer the questions that I have to my satisfaction.

____ strongly agree ____ neutral ____ somewhat disagree
____ agree ____ disagree
____ somewhat agree ____ strongly disagree

e. My medical condition has improved because of my clinic visits.

____ strongly agree ____ neutral ____ somewhat disagree
____ agree ____ disagree
____ somewhat agree ____ strongly disagree

f. My knowledge and understanding of my medical needs has increased because of my clinic visits.

____ strongly agree ____ neutral ____ somewhat disagree
____ agree ____ disagree
____ somewhat agree ____ strongly disagree

g. I am able to get an appointment at the clinic when I need to without a long delay.

____ strongly agree ____ neutral ____ somewhat disagree
____ agree ____ disagree
____ somewhat agree ____ strongly disagree

h. I am satisfied with the medical care I receive at the clinic.

____ strongly agree ____ neutral ____ somewhat disagree
____ agree ____ disagree
____ somewhat agree ____ strongly disagree

Community Accountability

To date, more than 100 not-for-profit health and human service, religious, governmental, civic, and grant-making organizations have been directly involved in the development of this program to provide health care services to the homeless of Jacksonville. Every one of these organizations has been represented in whole or in part by volunteers, and every one of them has acted on the approval and with the support of volunteer boards of directors comprising people from the community at large. In the case of governmental entities, they have been represented by elected officials who in turn are accountable to their constituents. Accountability by this program to the greater Jacksonville community is complete and continuous. Currently, as a program of the Sulzbacher Center, HCH is under the governance of that organization's board of directors. Because of the process by which the Sulzbacher Center was founded and is being developed and initially funded, this organization is under public scrutiny from the health and human services organizations with which it is affiliated, as well as city and state governmental entities.

Seamless Continuum of Care

Because the homeless population is unstable and unpredictable, very often those involved in providing health care services cannot feel any assurance that their efforts will be effective. HCH and its partner organizations are cognizant of the need to provide immediate, on-site response as much as possible. Significant progress has been made toward pulling together resources to meet social, psychological, mental health, and basic living needs of the homeless. Goals for the future emphasize continuing to strengthen the effort to create a seamless continuum of care.

Management within Fixed Resources

HCH was developed and, to date, has been primarily sustained through volunteers and donations of goods and services. The organizing partners brought little to the table in terms of initial monetary support, but came with a wealth of other resources, such as the following, that were more critical to the initiation of a program of this nature:

- Medical care is provided by volunteer physicians, nurses, allied health professionals and clerical staff.
- Clinic space is donated.
- Pharmaceuticals are partially donated.
- Supplies and equipment are partially donated.
- In-kind donations of time covered $111,700 (39 percent of all expenses).
- In-kind contributions of medical goods and equipment covered $24,000 (8 percent of all expenses).
- In-kind contributions of administrative goods and services covered $8,425 (3 percent of all expenses).

The majority of expenses to date have been directed to salaries for a director and a registered nurse case manager. Funding for these expenses has come from the private sector, primarily from United Way of Northeast Florida.

MOVING TOWARD THE COMMUNITY CARE NETWORK VISION

Statement of Purpose

It is envisioned that HCH will address the gap that prevents all citizens of Jacksonville from gaining equitable access to adequate health care services in a timely manner and in a way that is understandable and user-friendly. HCH envisions that it will accomplish this by applying the following:

- *Community health focus:* The health of a community relies on the health of its citizens. Because of their lifestyles and conditions, the homeless of a community are among the most vulnerable to disease, most likely to spread communicable and infectious diseases, and the least likely to actively seek treatment for disease in the early stages. This makes homeless people a health threat not only to themselves but also to the community in general.

  HCH is dedicating its efforts and resources to changing the patterns of behavior in homeless people with regard to the treatment of specific illnesses and the prevention of disease.

- *Community accountability:* The majority of services provided to the homeless of any community, Jacksonville included, have not traditionally been directed at improving lifestyles and life conditions. Feeding programs, clothes closets, and temporary shelters all offer services designed to keep the homeless population contained while maintaining a minimally acceptable lifestyle.

  With a more realistic understanding of who makes up the homeless population, however, communities are beginning to develop a better understanding of how to respond to their needs. Although in the past it was believed that, in terms of community image and appearance, the accountability for this segment of the population was to the community in general, it is increasingly recognized that a portion of the accountability must extend to the homeless themselves. Of the homeless in Jacksonville, 70 percent do not accept homelessness as a way of life. They are homeless because of economic or personal circumstances.

  With the establishment of HCH, Jacksonville is confronting the one necessity that is the key to changing the homeless person's life condition: good health. HCH provides the only comprehensive and continuous health care service to homeless people in the city, thereby closing the gap that has always kept all citizens from being able to access adequate health care.

- *Seamless continuum of care:* "When you are homeless and on the street, eating is hard enough. Affording medical care is impossible." These words, written by a patient of the downtown clinic, reflect the sense of utter defeat experienced by homeless people when poor health compromises their ability to practice basic survival skills.

  In offering health care services to homeless people, to record any progress at all, HCH must provide a full continuum of services, treating the whole person rather than taking a symptom-by-symptom approach to care that is fragmented and ineffective.

- *Management within fixed resources:* Because health care services for the homeless were not available in Jacksonville prior to the establishment of HCH, there were no funds to be accessed from governmental or third-party sources.

  When it was fully recognized how significantly the issue of health care for the homeless impacted the entire community, private-sector donors joined with the partnering organizations to facilitate the start-up of the homeless health services program. The partnership organizations are fully committed to continuing their participation and anticipate enlisting the financial support of a growing number of individuals, corporations, and organizations as the program expands its services.

Visioning Process

The evolution of HCH did not happen in a coordinated, carefully orchestrated manner. On the contrary, the concept of providing health care services to homeless people came into being when three separate and distinct community efforts were drawn together by the realization that they shared essentially the same vision. What is most striking about this process is that in each arena, regular people assumed responsibility for making decisions, taking action, solving problems, and recognizing that joining together to achieve the vision was more effective than trying to go it alone.

That which on the surface appears to be a fragmented, unorganized series of actions characterized by duplications of effort and potential gaps in service provision, in reality could not have evolved any other way. The best outcomes result from the interaction of people with diverse experiences, viewpoints, and interests, and the active, ongoing involvement of those who must ultimately implement the decisions they make.

The strength of HCH, and what will make it viable for the long term, is that the concept of providing high-quality, accessible health care to homeless people is built on a solid base of involvement and ownership from all parts of this community. There was nothing about the process that was contrived, controlled, or forced at any point along the way.

Evolution of the Vision of Health Care for the Homeless

- The Coalition evolved in 1989 from the board that was formed to distribute Federal Emergency Management Agency (FEMA) funds for emergency shelter and food. Membership in the Coalition includes more than 50 local not-for-profit human services organizations and governmental agencies that provide services to the indigent and homeless population in the city.

  Increased demand for FEMA funds at a time when the allocation was decreasing forced the Coalition to adopt a broader mission:

  > To improve the quality and quantity of services to individuals in need without discrimination, and to avoid duplication of benefits by the promotion of coordination of services and the collection and dissemination of services and needs.

  When downtown revitalization became a community priority, the issue of what to do with the homeless who congregated in large numbers in the downtown area came to the forefront. The Coalition interceded in an effort to relocate the homeless by offering a more lasting and practical solution: mobilize community resources to help them become self-sufficient.

  The Coalition initiated the first census of the homeless to gather information and, in the process, learned two things critical to the evolution of HCH:

  – Some 75 percent of the homeless in Jacksonville were residents of this community, rather than transients.

  – Adequate, accessible health care was among the top three concerns of homeless people.

  The Coalition served as the catalyst for the series of action steps that resulted in HCH. The Coalition is not a partner in this collaboration because its mission is to initiate and promote coordinated services by other organizations.

- We Care Jacksonville, a program of the Duval County Medical Society and its Academy of Medicine, is a physician volunteer program to provide primary health care services to the indigent and homeless. Concurrent with but not related to the expansion of the Coalition's mission, the Duval County Medical Society formed an Indigent Care Committee to organize the physician effort to volunteer medical services.

  Within months, the Florida legislature passed landmark legislation that provided sovereign immunity to physicians, nurses, and allied health professionals so that they could not be held liable for care they provided on a volunteer basis. With this release from liability, the physicians were in a position as a group to respond to the request by the Coalition to develop a means whereby health care could be provided at no charge to the homeless and those at risk of homelessness.

Together these two organizations created a network of clinic sites staffed by volunteer physicians, nurses, and allied health professionals, tapping the resources of the Duval County Public Health Unit and the DHRS (district 4). The second clinic, which opened in June 1993 at the downtown location, specifically served the homeless. Within 18 months, two more clinic sites for the homeless were established. The physician volunteer program evolved into We Care Jacksonville, whose mission is:

> To provide quality medical care at no charge to persons at 150 percent of the poverty level or below, who have no health insurance, do not qualify for Medicaid or who are homeless.

- The Sulzbacher Center grew out of an increasingly apparent need for coordination of services to the homeless population in Jacksonville. In 1988, an interfaith coalition, spearheaded by the bishop of the Episcopal diocese, began to develop strategies to better serve Jacksonville's homeless population. Many churches, particularly those in the downtown area, were already sponsoring feeding programs and clothes closets. The original coalition quickly grew beyond the faith community to include members from all segments of Jacksonville.

  First attempts were directed toward establishing a day center. But as the community's thinking about the homeless and their needs began to evolve, this coalition's plans were altered to better reflect the needs being expressed by other coalitions in the community.

  In November 1993, the concept of a homeless center coalesced, and the Sulzbacher Center received its tax exemption from the Internal Revenue Service. In a continuing effort to coordinate services to avoid duplications and gaps, HCH became a program of the Sulzbacher Center in September 1994. When the Sulzbacher Center opens, HCH will relocate the downtown clinic site while continuing to operate a clinic site at the Beaches and Hubbard House.

MICHAEL'S STORY

Michael, a homeless 61-year-old white male, accessed the downtown clinic of HCH in October 1993. He complained of a lingering sore throat. A volunteer physician examined Michael and diagnosed a "suspicious" throat lesion.

Michael was referred to an otolaryngologist through the We Care Jacksonville program. The physician performed a biopsy of several sites and determined that Michael had cancer of the throat, mouth, and tongue. Subsequently, Michael was admitted to Memorial Medical Center and underwent a tonsillectomy, hemimandibulectomy, and hemiglossectomy. His hospital course progressed well and he was discharged for follow-up by the physician and HCH.

Michael then underwent a 7-week course of radiation therapy, totaling 35 treatments. Under normal circumstances, Michael's medical care would have cost more than $100,000 for physician fees, hospitalization, medication, and therapy. HCH provided case management for Michael by arranging all health-related services and medical resources to assist Michael in his recovery. He was guided through the process of applying for and obtaining disability, housing, a resource for liquid nourishment, transportation, furniture, and clothing. HCH continues to provide Michael with health care at no charge.

Michael is typical of homeless patients seen by HCH. When Michael first came to the clinic, even though he was homeless, he had just completed a nursing assistant course through Florida Community College at Jacksonville and was looking for employment. For the past few months, Michael has volunteered clerical support for HCH at the Saturday morning clinic.

SUMMARY OF NOTABLE PROGRESS

1. *A Permanent Health Center Established:* On March 15, 1996, HCH permanently established an on-site medical clinic at the Sulzbacher Center, Jacksonville's largest homeless shelter and one of the original CCN partners. Our original walk-in clinic, which began in an oversize closet in a downtown church, has expanded. Today we are a health center with three examination rooms, a treatment room, a small pharmacy, and a vision-screening examination room.

   Open 6 days a week, the HCH clinic has a full-time medical staff, including a nurse practitioner, medical assistant, intake coordinator, and medical social worker. The staff continues to be supported by a large contingency of volunteer physicians, nurses, health aides, dentists, and clerical assistants who are members of the We Care Jacksonville program sponsored by the Duval County Medical Society. Our staff is also augmented by proposed academic rotations of health educators, social workers, and nursing students from the University of Florida, Jacksonville University, and University of North Florida. This has enabled the clinic to provide the full spectrum of medical care needed by our patients.

   The goal of HCH is to offer comprehensive care that addresses the full range of health problems experienced by the homeless people in Jacksonville. From the program's inception in June 1993 through August 1996, more than 4,000 unduplicated homeless individuals have been seen and treated at the clinic. This program offers health care to all the homeless in Jacksonville, not just to the residents of the Sulzbacher Center.

2. *Health Center Advisory Committee:* HCH is a living example of the value of partnerships. It has been critical to the success of the program that viable partnerships and collaborations were formed with all aspects of the medical community, health professional programs, academia, civic organizations, and the corporate and religious community to accomplish its mission. This past year, we formalized this partnership with the establishment of a Health Center Advisory Committee. Led by one of the key executives of the Baptist/St. Vincent's Health System, another of our original community partners, we draw on the varied resources of our advisory committee for guidance and strategic direction.

3. *Mental Health Program Incorporated:* Because of the high incidence of mental illness among the homeless, an important aspect of primary care service is working with the mentally ill homeless and the dually diagnosed. HCH has access to an on-site program with the Mental Health Resource Center's LINK Program, which serves the chronic, mentally ill, homeless population.

   Three full-time mental health counselors work with the clinic staff to provide case management to the mentally ill. Our mental health care is expanded with on-site drug and alcohol rehabilitation programs, support groups, and referrals to permanent housing and group facilities. Additionally, HCH's social worker works closely with the LINK staff to coordinate case management and provides some counseling.

4. *Robert Wood Johnson (RWJ) Foundation Local Initiative Grant:* In August 1996, HCH was chosen as a finalist for an RWJ Foundation Local Initiatives Funding Partners grant. It was awarded $456,000 to expand its primary health care services and establish vision and dental programs for the medically indigent homeless population of Jacksonville. This grant is part of the foundation's Local Initiative Funding Partners' Program, a cooperative funding program with local philanthropies. The Jacksonville funding partners who have matched each dollar awarded by the Johnson Foundation are: the Edna Sproull Williams Foundation; Genesis Health Foundation, Inc.; the Ida M. Stevens Foundation; the Riverside Foundation, Inc.; Herman and Mary Virginia Terry; and the United Way of Northeast Florida. These local funding partners were instrumental to the Sulzbacher Center's being awarded this national grant. The combined total funding from the RWJ Foundation and the local funding partners over a 3-year period is $912,000.
5. *New Vision Program:* The RWJ Foundation grant has enabled the Sulzbacher Center to establish a vision clinic to provide eye exams and glasses for the homeless. (See figure 19-2.) The eye program was needed because so few of the homeless had glasses. Poor vision not only impacted their quality of life but also diminished chances for employment.

   In cooperation with Vision is Priceless, the Eye Research Foundation, the Duval County Society of Ophthalmology, and the Ida M. Stevens Foundation, HCH designed a full vision program. Marco Ophthalmic was provided the equipment for a new eye lab with full refraction and diagnostic capability as well as vision and glaucoma screening, and 27 volunteer optometrists take turns staffing the weekly eye clinics. Eye surgery and treatment for eye disease is referred to volunteer ophthalmologists through the We Care Jacksonville network of physicians.

   The Morr-Sight System of Instant Eye Glasses was identified as a low-cost approach for supplying glasses to our patients. Morr-Sight has a patented system for making modular glasses that can be assembled in two minutes or less and sell for $12 per pair. These precision lenses correct every common vision problem: nearsightedness, farsightedness, and astigmatism. Safe-Lite Optical, a local optical laboratory, agreed to donate five bifocal prescriptions each month and supply any additional bifocals at $15 per pair. The Pilot Club of Jacksonville underwrote the initial set-up of 100 pairs of glasses, and concerned individuals have joined this effort with private donations to help offset the cost of the glasses. By charging our patients the nominal fee of $10 per pair, our cost of providing the glasses is partially covered and our patients' investment promotes better care and pride of ownership.

   The most rewarding part of this endeavor has been the response by the patients. Grateful to see once again, their response of joy and gratitude is a heartwarming experience for the team who made it happen. Our first patient was employed by the United Way as a result of her improved eyesight.
6. *New Dental Clinic:* The RWJ Foundation grant also addresses one of the greatest unmet needs of the homeless—dental care. Currently, access to dental care is impossible for the homeless. Other than a monthly visit by the pubic health dental van, all other dental care is either beyond their reach economically or they are not eligible. But this will soon change.

   HCH is establishing a full-service dental program that will include diagnostic and preventive services (X rays, examinations, and cleanings); complete dentistry, including restorations, extractions, root canals, periodontal care, dentures, and partial dentures; and emergency services. At this point we are planning to provide all services free of charge.

The grant underwrites the salaries of a dentist, dental hygienist, and dental assistant, as well as all the dental supplies. Area Health Education Centers and the dental programs of the Florida Community College of Jacksonville will expand our services through rotations by their dental assistant and dental hygiene students. The Northeast Florida Dental District is also sponsoring our efforts. Volunteer dentists, hygienists, and dental assistants will extend our services through their participation.

FIGURE 19-2. Vision Care Policy

To: All Patients

We want you to know that our only objective is to provide you with corrected vision. It is our desire to help you see, as we feel this will help you to be successful in all that you want to accomplish.

In an effort to accomplish this objective for you, we have many volunteers giving their time at no charge to the Clinic. First, the volunteer Optometrist will determine what correction you need. Depending on your spectacle correction, you will receive a new frame and lenses for a reduced cost of $10. You will receive your glasses the day of your exam unless we must obtain a special order. In this case you should receive your glasses in 1–2 weeks. Please note—if you lose or damage your glasses, you will be required to pay a $12 replacement charge.

Please keep in mind these spectacles are to help you see better. The lenses are basic single-vision lenses or flat-top 28mm bifocals only.

We do not provide any of the following:

Contact lenses
Special frames of any kind
Tints to lenses
UV coating (unless cataract problems)
Scratch coating
High index or Polycarbonate lenses
Progressive/No-line bifocals
Blended bifocals
Photo-gray lenses
Transition lenses
Polaroid or other sunglass lenses
Edge polish to lenses
Faceting to lenses
Etc.

I, ______________________________, have read and understand the above information, and I would like to be provided with these services.

____ ________________
Signature Date

Amount paid -------------- Date -------------- Initials --------------

This new program has captured the spirit of the whole community. A private contractor is leading the effort to build the dental clinic with donated services, similar to Habitat for Humanity. Local building tradesmen and dental supply companies have come forth to donate their services and goods to build a state-of-the-art dental clinic. The clinic is anticipated to open in November 1996.

7. *Expanded services and new directions:* With the addition of these two new programs and the on-site medical clinic at the Sulzbacher Center, HCH's small medical clinic has become a health center serving the comprehensive health needs of the homeless in our community. Barriers to health care have been removed; increased cost-effectiveness has been achieved by circumventing the emergency rooms. Additionally there has been the promotion of prevention, wellness, and positive mental health.

   We have made great strides toward improving access to health care for the homeless, but tremendous challenges remain. There are still homeless who do not know about HCH. We need to market to our customers. For the program to grow in quality as well as services, we must measure our efforts and evaluate our care. Mental health, outreach, prevention, and building positive health practices are but a few of the critical steps we must take as our program grows.

HCH has been recognized as a national model by both the Kellogg and RWJ foundations. We are enthusiastic about the lessons we have learned through our collaborative partnerships. We see great value in community-based initiatives and believe they are one of the important keys to shaping the future of our health care delivery system.

Contact: Julia B. Reid
Associate Director
I. M. Sulzbacher Center for the Homeless
611 E. Adams St.
Jacksonville, FL 32202
Phone: (904) 359-0657, ext. 265
Fax: (904) 359-0926

20

The Rural Health Outreach Program

Executive Summary

Nelson County is a rural county in central Virginia extending 475 square miles between the Blue Ridge Mountains to the west and the James River to the east. Its pristine beauty is unhampered by fast-food restaurants or stoplights. Lovingston, county seat and largest population center, boasts 600 residents. The total population numbers about 12,800. Forty percent of the population are under 200 percent of the poverty level, and 17 percent of the population are uninsured in this medically underserved area. About 40 percent of the adults over 25 did not complete high school. An estimated one-half of the work force is employed outside the county. Wintergreen Resort, the school system, and the county government are the major employers for those who do work in Nelson County.

In 1991, the Rural Health Outreach Program was founded to increase access to health care by providing community-based health services, case management, transportation, and health education. Oversight of the program was a collaborative effort of area health and community service providers in the form of the Nelson County Interagency Council (NCIC). Regular meetings facilitated a well-organized referral network for community outreach and enabled a seamless continuum of care for people served by these agencies. Since the establishment of the RHOP, great value has been placed on providing services that address priorities identified by people in the community. Outreach team members (including a program manager, nurse practitioner, nurse's aide, and community care worker) have spent much time listening to individual and group voices as decisions are made about what services to provide through outreach. As a result of that process, the following five initiatives are being implemented to support a vision of the future that includes health care that is "comprehensive, accessible, affordable, and known" to all citizens in Nelson County.

1. All Nelson County primary health care providers are linked in a cooperative effort to ensure that people can receive appropriate care when they need it. They are working together to provide varied hours, a common pamphlet listing all health services, efficient and appropriate cooperation regarding patient care, and joint projects such as sports physicals for student athletes.

2. A community care worker is a point of contact for access to all health and human services in the community.
3. Primary and preventive health care is offered at each of at least nine regularly scheduled Health Depots, which are community-based mini-clinics located in such sites as community centers, old stores, fire departments, schools, and a low-income housing complex.
4. A prepaid program is being developed for uninsured and underinsured people in Nelson County, which will cover a protocol of prevention services and limited primary care.
5. A Community Health Council provides a governance structure for the RHOP and our local community care network (CCN).

The most important lesson we have learned in Nelson County as outreach services have been developed and fine-tuned is that our most successful efforts have been based on what we have learned through attentive listening and observation. Our nurse practitioner spends time visiting with people in their own familiar environments. She listens to life stories, what people enjoy, what causes stress, what barriers exist, and what her patients want and need. Her observations provide her with an understanding of what treatment plans are most likely to produce positive results. She calls it an "anthropological approach" to health care. By whatever name, treatment based on this kind of understanding builds trust, is more likely to work the first time, and is very cost-effective.

Tommy Harvey
North District Supervisor
County of Nelson

THE COLLABORATIVE PARTNERSHIP

The Community

Nelson County is a rural county in central Virginia extending 475 square miles between the Blue Ridge Mountains to the west and the James River to the east. There is no major population center and no stoplight in the one village of 600 that is the county seat, Lovingston. The 1990 census reported a population of 12,800 and a population density of 27 persons per square mile. Because the county is a large territory, its citizens identify with their local area more than with the county as a whole. They gravitate to four cities for their commercial and employment needs: Charlottesville to the north, Waynesboro to the northwest, Lynchburg to the south, and Appomattox to the southeast.

As shown by the following demographic and health indicators, Nelson County is a medically underserved area:

- Of the Nelson County population, 80 percent are Caucasian, 19 percent are African-American, and 1 percent comprise other races.
- Fifteen percent of the population are under 100 percent of the federal poverty level; 25 percent are within the 100 to 200 percent poverty level.
- Regarding insurance coverage, 17 percent are uninsured, 16 percent are on Medicare, and 9 percent are on Medicaid.
- The physician-to-population ratio is 1:2,840.

The poverty level in the county is in part reflective of the fact that there are no major businesses or industries in the county except for Wintergreen Resort. The resort is the largest employer, with approximately 400 employees; that figure swells to 700 during the ski season. Otherwise, county government and the school system are the largest employers.

Needs assessments were conducted in 1991–92 by the Blue Ridge Medical Center (a community health center), the District Health Department, the Planning District Commission, and the University of Virginia. Highlights of these assessments show that poverty, illiteracy, and rural isolation are barriers to routine health care. The major causes of death in 1992 were cardiovascular disease and cancer.

Encouraging health status indicators are those related to maternal and child health. The 5-year (1988–92) average infant mortality rate for the county is 3.9, compared with 10 for the state. Low birth weight is at 6 percent, compared with 7.3 percent for the state. The teen pregnancy rate was 31.6 (11.1 percent) in 1992, compared with 42 (11.6 percent) in the state.

Another encouraging trend in the county is the increase in the number of primary care providers. Ten years ago there were two physicians with active practices in the entire county. This year, both single-physician practices in the northwest part of the county added a second physician. The community health center in the southern end has two physicians, one clinical nurse practitioner, and one outreach nurse practitioner.

In addition to the three small primary care practices and the health department clinics, the other health resources include a local home health agency in Lovingston, a 60-bed intermediate care nursing home in Lovingston, one optometrist, and 2.4 dentists. There are two pharmacies, one in the north at the physician's office and one in Lovingston. The mental health agency, Region Ten Community Services, has a branch office in Lovingston. The hospitals that serve the area are the University of Virginia Medical Center and the Martha Jefferson Hospital, both in Charlottesville; Centra Health in Lynchburg; and Augusta Medical Center west of Waynesboro.

Following several meetings of the NCIC in March 1995 to discuss current perception of needs, the following issues emerged: (1) barriers to access that stem from fear, lack of trust, and misunderstanding; (2) uninsured (estimated at 17 percent) or underinsured; (3) physician switching; (4) lack of funds for medications; (5) medication noncompliance; (6) no after-hours care available except at a distant emergency room; (7) lack of utilities and plumbing for many homes; and (8) inadequate access to dental care for the low-income population. It was believed that, to a large degree, resources are available, but county residents do not know how to access them. The importance of a person who can bridge this gap through outreach and acceptance cannot be overemphasized.

The Partnership

The partnership consists of two hospitals in Charlottesville (the University of Virginia Medical Center and the Martha Jefferson Hospital), the NCIC (a consortium of six health and human service agencies serving as the core group), and QualChoice of Virginia, a managed care company located in Charlottesville.

The NCIC was founded in 1991 as the sponsoring consortium to apply for a Rural Health Outreach grant from the U.S. Office of Rural Health. The original council members were Blue Ridge Medical Center, Nelson County Health Department, Nelson County Department of Social Services, Region Ten Community Services, Monticello Area Community Action Agency (MACAA), and Jefferson Area Board for the Aging

(JABA). They agreed to meet regularly to oversee grant activities, identify problems, make recommendations, and provide a forum for communication, learning, and discussion.

The NCIC expanded during the three years of the outreach grant. Limiting itself to not-for-profit organizations, it brought in the Cooperative Extension Service, JAUNT (the regional transportation agency), the Rural Elder Outreach Program, Project Care (volunteer training to assist the homebound), and a rescue squad representative.

At the end of the Rural Health Outreach grant in fall 1994, the NCIC decided that it would continue to meet and work together. The work of the Rural Health Outreach grant evolved into a program called Health Depots, which received 70 percent of its funding from a grant through the Virginia Health Care Foundation, a public–private partnership that supports innovative primary care projects. The other 30 percent was contributed by the Virginia Fibre Corporation in neighboring Amherst County, the University of Virginia Medical Center, Martha Jefferson Hospital, and Blue Ridge Medical Center (the administering agency). The NCIC adopted the CCN vision as a project in December 1994 (after the Health Depots program began in October 1994). The two hospitals in Charlottesville became involved both through their financial support of the Health Depots and their interest in the CCN vision.

The University of Virginia Medical Center, a part of the Health Sciences Center, is a tertiary care hospital with 579 licensed beds. Its mission is "to enrich the quality of human life by improvement of health, by advancement of medical and scientific knowledge, and by creation of an environment for professional preparation of individuals dedicated to health care services." The Health Sciences Center sponsored a community health promotion task force, which reported in 1992 the following recommendations for our planning district:

> The Health Sciences Center should recognize the need for taking a leadership role in developing and supporting a central, accessible resource for information relating to health promotion (including services and consumer health information). . . . Information should include health care sources available in the community . . . and general consumer health information. . . . This resource could potentially provide: . . . support for health care professionals and community groups including grant-writing assistance, program evaluation assistance, etc.
>
> The Health Sciences Center should participate in convening a group of community leaders to initiate the process of becoming a "Healthy Region" using the guidelines of the "Healthy Cities" initiative. . . .

These recommendations and the mission of the hospital provide a basis for the hospital's involvement in the CCN vision.

The Martha Jefferson Hospital is a not-for-profit community hospital with 221 licensed beds. The hospital has adopted a community health partnership program, which states:

> Martha Jefferson has an important role in improving the health status of the community it serves. The model for healthier communities is an integration of "systems" and services (for example, medical care, education, social services, and so on) in partnership organizations to improve community health status.

The hospital has further outlined "improved access to primary care" as a program in which it wishes to be involved. The hospital is ready to be engaged in Nelson County with the CCN vision.

Another partner in this project is QualChoice of Virginia, a new managed care company established in central Virginia. QualChoice will help this project move into the managed care framework through the design of a program that will introduce managed care principles to the underserved and uninsured populations of the county. Central Virginia is still frontier territory to health maintenance organization (HMO) activity; patients and providers are only beginning to see HMOs come into the area. The biggest impact of managed care came 2 years ago, when state employees were enrolled in a Blue Cross plan that required them to select a primary care physician for gatekeeper/referral services.

This partnership is especially timely in our community and to the CCN because the two hospitals now own the physician practices in the northwest part of the county, called Rockfish Valley. Combined with the community health center in the south, all three primary care practices are within the network. The partnership is effective for the network of health and social services that complement the primary care physician's practice. The University of Virginia Medical Center is the tertiary care center and provides most of the indigent specialty and hospital care. The involvement of the two hospitals broadens the scope from the county level. A 4-year history of working together as the NCIC and subduing turf issues will enable the group to continue to work together to meet the needs of clients while seeking to eliminate duplicative services.

PRIOR EFFORTS THAT REPRESENT MOVEMENT TOWARD THE COMMUNITY CARE NETWORK VISION

Community Health Focus

A focus of community health has been and continues to be the unifying characteristic of the NCIC, which is now joined with the two hospitals and a managed care company. In bringing six human service agencies together to form a consortium in 1991, the council agreed on the following basic community needs and developed a program to address those issues:

- People do not seek needed medical care because of financial barriers.
- Many people are unable to make or keep health and social service appointments or to obtain necessary supplies because of inadequate transportation and distance from health care facilities.
- People allow illnesses to develop into crises instead of addressing problems in early stages by seeking medical intervention.
- Health education programs have low attendance.
- Patients who are homebound are not receiving medical care.
- County agencies are fragmented in their approaches to client services.

The Rural Health Outreach grant established a solid program of community health screenings in small communities all over the county. At churches, local markets, schools, community and senior centers, rescue squad halls, businesses, and local events, the outreach team measured cholesterol, blood pressures, and blood sugars; educated people regarding health resources and proper diets; and took requests for home visits and other assistance. This team, consisting of a nurse practitioner, nurse's aide, and promotion coordinator, also worked closely with other agency personnel to coordinate the care that clients were receiving or needed to receive. Making home visits and managing care for clients became an important aspect of the program, along with providing transportation, medication assistance, weight-loss classes, and support groups for diabetics and Alzheimer's caregivers. The elderly became a target population for the work of the outreach team, which was especially appropriate because this population represents a greater percentage of the total population than the national average (16 percent in Nelson versus 12 percent nationally).

From this 3-year outreach program emerged a refinement known as the Health Depot program. Community screening clinics are now routinely scheduled in eight established locations, including three senior center sites and four community sites, plus migrant camps in season and, more recently, the high school. Services were expanded to include the Put Prevention into Practice (PPIP) program of the U.S. Public Health Service. Using booklets for adults and children, this program is a guideline for the nurse practitioner to use with patients to ensure that recommended preventive health services are provided. Some services are provided and minor acute care problems treated at the Health Depot; others must be referred to the local physician's practice. Screening clinics can also be scheduled at local industry and businesses. A community health focus has definitely been established through the outreach team and the newly evolved Health Depot team.

The community health focus has been targeted to the medically underserved, low-income, low-literacy, hard-to-reach population who have not used primary health care services routinely and who have had very little preventive care. The outreach efforts have been based on the concept of taking health care to the people in their homes, in their community gathering places, in their workplace, and through transportation. In Nelson County, health education is less likely to occur in a lecture session than in a one-on-one conversation with a health care provider in an informal setting within the community or even in the client's home. The NCIC staff members and the outreach/Health Depot team work according to this philosophy of taking the service to the people. Each wants more of the community to take advantage of available resources.

Community health focus also applies to the hospital partners. Because both hospitals have a practice in Nelson County, they are interested in the outreach and preventive health orientation of the Health Depot. By assisting in the funding, they recognize the need for follow-up with noncompliant or complex patients and those whose living situations may interfere with the doctor's orders. Martha Jefferson Hospital now brings its mammography and home health care services to its practice in Nelson. The dollar spent on preventive care and medication compliance is considered an excellent investment by both hospitals.

Nelson County schools have been another area of community health focus. Over the years, the health department has had nurses in the schools; however, funding was cut by the school board recently. One nurse who teaches in the occupational program at the high school rotates to the different schools. Also, Region Ten Community Services had brought a substance abuse curriculum to the schools, but funding was eliminated. The Health Depot then gained the approval of the school board to conduct a pilot site at the high school, with free services for the last 2 months of the 1994–95 school year. This is an area that could be greatly developed.

Community Accountability

Community accountability is built into the structure of the NCIC. Not only does each sponsoring member have a board of directors representing the geographic area it serves, but also the clients themselves give feedback to the outreach workers about needs, problems in service delivery, and health care providers. NCIC members are outspoken advocates for their clients in meetings. Organizing community health coalitions was a feature of the the Rural Health Outreach Program (RHOP); as a result, two communities formed active groups—one in Gladstone, in the far southeast corner, and one in Schuyler, in the northeast corner. Although these groups were invited to send representatives to the NCIC, they mostly stay in touch through the Health Depots staff. The Gladstone group took the initiative to get a senior center designated by JABA in cooperation with the county. The MACAA staffs a program that works with African-American churches in the county. This group has mobilized to teach blood pressure monitoring to its members and to start an exercise program. In this way, people are taking responsibility for their own health maintenance.

As a community health center, the Blue Ridge Medical Center has direct accountability to the community through its board of directors, all of whom are consumers. Patient feedback, obtained through patient satisfaction questionnaires upon discharge, is regularly provided to board members and is also reported to staff. The National Association of Community Health Centers recently conducted personal interviews of 40 patients in each of 50 sites to determine satisfaction with care. The satisfaction level at Blue Ridge Medical Center, one of those sites, was at 95 percent. The Health Depots also have designed patient satisfaction questionnaires and are tallying results. The participating partner hospitals also have excellent programs that monitor patient satisfaction among all groups.

Seamless Continuum of Care

Weaving a seamless continuum of care has been a goal of the NCIC for the past 4 years. Taking health care to the community and coordinating and communicating available resources are the foundations of the RHOP and the Health Depots. Specifically, services provided by the Health Depots include minor acute care; chronic care monitoring; wellness checks using PPIP booklets; pregnancy testing and reproductive health counseling; immunizations; blood pressure, blood sugar, and cholesterol testing; and flu and hepatitis shots. These services are also available at any of the three primary care practices in the county, and many are also available through the health department. Referrals are made from service providers to the Health Depots, but more frequently from the Health Depots to the health and social service providers. (See figure 20-1.) The key to linking people with services is usually an individual, such as a friend or staff person. The outreach work of the Health Depot staffs and the NCIC brings a personal touch to service. Home visits are a vital communication link in a rural county where third world conditions exist. Estimates from the Community Development Foundation, which targets housing needs, show that 25 to 35 percent of Nelson County homes lack complete plumbing. Literacy levels are low, as indicated by the fact that 23 percent of the population over 25 years old have less than a ninth-grade education and only 57 percent have a high school education (according to a 1990 Planning District report). Because Nelson County presents a

MOVING TOWARD THE COMMUNITY CARE NETWORK VISION

The Vision Statement

The community care vision of the NCIC is that primary care in Nelson County be comprehensive, affordable, accessible, and known to all its residents. The target population includes those who are underserved, uninsured, and underinsured. The services include clinical, educational, financial eligibility, care coordination and case management, communication, and referral. The strategy is to link the three primary care practices and the health department with all health and social services through communication, coordination, and the Health Depots. The link from primary to secondary, tertiary, and managed care is through the two hospitals in Charlottesville and QualChoice of Virginia. The broader link to the community is through an expansion of the NCIC. To be called the Community Council, this expansion will include business, government, and other interested parties. It will designate a steering committee to oversee the implementation of the goals and objectives as outlined in this section of the chapter.

The Process of Visioning

This vision is a natural outgrowth and expansion of the original mission of the Blue Ridge Medical Center; its formation of the outreach team and organizing of the consortium that became the NCIC; the success of the NCIC; its adoption of the Health Depot concept; and its progression to the CCN vision through partnering with hospitals and their practices, and the resources of QualChoice. The Health Depots are being embraced by all the providers in the interest of serving the patient.

The NCIC is being expanded toward a broader vision of what it means to be accountable to the community. It will be more than the not-for-profit health service providers; more than the hospitals; more than the social service providers. It will include the local government, the board of supervisors, and the school board; the business community (the Chamber of Commerce, corporations, and commercial health enterprises); and the consumers who come from the local health coalitions and community Health Depots. These groups will constitute the new Community Health Council, which will receive reports about the CCN and give feedback and direction. It will appoint a steering committee much like the NCIC, to provide closer oversight and make recommendations as the CCN activities are carried out.

The vision for this network has been hammered out in weekly meetings of the NCIC and the hospitals over the past two months. Although the concepts of cooperation and coordination are not new, shaping such cooperation and coordination more formally and with more partners is a challenge. From defining needs to setting goals and objectives, this has truly been a group process. The support of the two hospitals has been encouraging, and their ability to bring their local practices into the program ensures a basis for cooperation and communication.

The Set of Initiatives

The goal of providing countywide comprehensive, affordable, accessible health promotion and primary care in Nelson County has the following five major objectives:

1. Link the existing three primary care practices and the Nelson County Health Department to facilitate communication and share resources for the benefit of

patient access. This will be done through regular meetings, a common pamphlet stating policies and services, and tracking after-hours care of patients. The need for affordable, accessible services will be emphasized.

2. A care coordinator will assist the public in accessing health and social services. This person will be available at the Health Depots, by phone through a well-publicized number, and at civic meetings to provide a personal connection between those who need care and the professional who can provide it. The care coordinator will assume a proactive role in making known the community's health resources.
3. The Health Depot program will demonstrate that patients are active participants in their health maintenance and know how to access health services. Led by the nurse practitioner, its staff will work with patients and their health care provider to ensure compliance with medical orders and involvement in personal health maintenance through the PPIP program.
4. A prepaid primary care program will be developed that is targeted to the uninsured and underinsured as a means to continue the health maintenance program on a sustaining basis.
5. Community accountability will be vested in a Community Health Council and its steering committee, which will provide oversight of the above activities and track health outcomes within the county based on national models.

These initiatives are built on existing services and seek to coordinate, expand, and publicize what is already available and the potential that is ready to be developed.

SUMMARY OF NOTABLE PROGRESS

Community-Based Governance: The Community Health Council Initiative

The NCIC members decided that citizen involvement in RHOP governance could be accomplished with the establishment of a Community Health Council. This group would include representatives from communities, schools, churches, civic organizations, business, and government, as well as members of the NCIC and local CCN partners. Recruitment for council participation began in the fall, and the first meeting was held in January, 1996. Approximately 50 people attended and immediately provided input regarding the most pressing health needs of Nelson County citizens. The list was long, but the group unanimously agreed that the most pressing problem was the cost of medication for low-income, underinsured people.

In March, 1996, during the second of four scheduled annual meetings, the council prioritized health needs, established a mission for itself, and elected eight citizen representatives from the group to serve on a steering committee for the RHOP. These eight then joined the nine CCN partners in close oversight for RHOP activities. (The NCIC relinquished this function, but has continued to meet for coordination of community services for Nelson County citizens.) The first steering committee meeting was held in May 1996. Officers were elected, committees were established, and ideas flowed. Citizen members have already provided many hours of volunteer time in coordinating a school and community health fair in August 1996, a 5K run fundraiser in October, and a campaign to solicit donations from area businesses. Partner members of the steering committee have also provided many hours of consultation, "products" such as a brochure for RHOP (figure 20-2) and a kick-off event for the CCN program, and matches for CCN dollars.

FIGURE 20-2. Rural Health Outreach Program Brochure

(Outside)

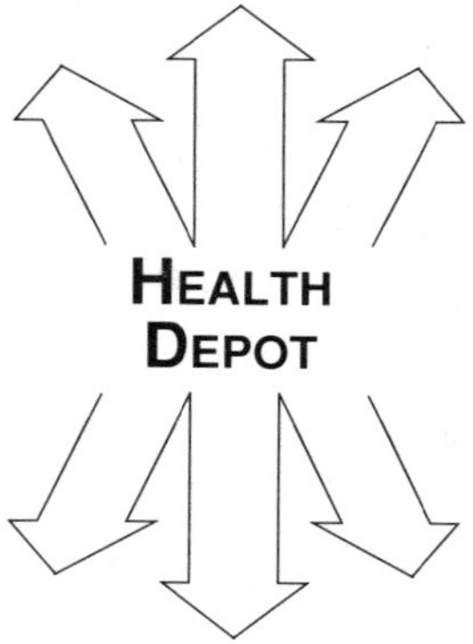

Sometimes it's hard to get to the doctor's office.
Things get in the way—the distance, not having a ride, your work hours, the cost, not having insurance.

There are lots of reasons.

The Rural Health Outreach Program makes it a little easier. We offer some choices that can help you get the healthcare you need when and where you need it. Look over our list. Call us—or come by and see us when we are in your community! We can usually find a solution.

Nelson County
Rural Health Outreach Program
4038 Thomas Nelson Highway
Arrington, Virginia 22922

Nelson County
Rural Health
Outreach Program

A Community Care Network

logo here

Health
Depots

Working to make healthcare available to all area residents

(804) 263-4858

(Inside)

photo here

photo here

photo here

photo here

Health Depots are community clinics where our nurse practitioner and assisting staff can:

- Treat your minor illness or injury
- Update your immunizations (call us ahead so we'll have the shots you need)
- Provide between-visit checkups if you are a diabetic, have hypertension, asthma or some other on-going health problem
- Check your blood pressure, blood sugar level and cholesterol level
- Screen for possible hearing and vision problems
- Review your medications and provide counseling about how to manage your prescriptions
- Provide assistance if your doctor prescribes a medicine you cannot afford to buy
- Provide follow-up care that has been recommended by your doctor
- Help you find assistance through other community services
- Refer you to your doctor for further care if necessary

Transportation

If you have an appointment with your healthcare provider or at a community service agency, but you do not have a way to get there, give us a call at least 24 hours ahead. We can help.

Health Calls

If you or a family member is home-bound, we will be glad to provide any of our depot services for you at home. Please call us if you would like us to visit.

For more information call
(804) 263-4858

The Provider Link Initiative

Health care is provided by nurse practitioners and physicians at four establishments in Nelson County:

- Blue Ridge Medical Center
- Stoney Creek Family Practice—operated by University of Virginia Medical Center
- Martha Jefferson Medical Services of Afton—operated by Martha Jefferson Hospital
- Nelson County Health Department

Since the establishment of the local CCN partnership, three "provider link" meetings have been held. Discussions have focused on the establishment of a referral system for patients and clients from all practices who could benefit from outreach services through RHOP, the development of a common brochure detailing information about health services available through all the practices, coordination of hours and activities to better serve Nelson County citizens, and a common in-service training to update providers on community service resources for their patients. The providers also detailed procedures for joint volunteer provision of sports physicals for Nelson County student athletes at the school and community health fair in August 1996.

The Community Care Worker Initiative

A community care worker was hired in March 1996 to become a point of contact for health care patients and clients who need community services, such as help with housing problems, aging services, counseling, financial assistance, or shelter in emergency situations. The worker, who is fluent in Spanish, has developed a system for access to services for Latinos experiencing language and cultural barriers, and for obtaining assistance with the cost of medication. She also promotes rural outreach services and provides extensive health education for target populations (that is, Nelson County residents who are experiencing barriers to health care).

The Health Depot Initiative

Health Depots are "mini-clinics" in at least nine regularly scheduled community locations in Nelson County. Preventive and primary care services are provided by the nurse practitioner and a nurse's aide. Health Depot services are also provided through home visits by the clinical staff. The provision of health care in environments familiar to the people served by the nurse practitioner has led to increased levels of trust, reductions in the cost of care, increased compliance with health care instructions, and at least anecdotal evidence of improved outcomes for many of the people served. CCN funding allowed for the purchase of both hardware and software to implement the nationally tested SF-36 health status questionnaire for patients and clients receiving Health Depot services. Extensive use of the questionnaire will help to establish baseline information for outcomes measurement. The SF-36 is a reliable tool; however, the reading level required to complete it without assistance is too high for many RHOP patients and clients. Personal interviews are therefore being conducted to complete each questionnaire—a process that is requiring more time than originally estimated. Help from health professions students and volunteers will be solicited for more efficient progress.

Beginning in 1994–95, Health Depot services were offered to students and teachers at Nelson County High School. This Health Depot, which continued during the following school year, was a pilot project for a comprehensive school-based health care program for students in all five Nelson County schools. That program is scheduled to be implemented in fall 1996. The RHOP is expanding to include an additional nurse practitioner and two registered nurses to provide school health through grant funding from the state of Virginia. School health services will provide an excellent opportunity to improve access to care for many youth and an avenue for increased community health in Nelson County.

The QualChoice Initiative

QualChoice of Virginia, a managed care provider and a partner in the Nelson County CCN, is providing in-kind consulting in the development of a prepaid program for underinsured residents of Nelson County. The program will provide a protocol of age- and gender-appropriate prevention services as well as limited primary care for people who are uninsured or underinsured in Nelson County. Currently QualChoice is gathering statistical data, which are needed to develop a program that is marketable, provides good services, and is not too burdensome for health care providers in Nelson County.

RHOP team members, CCN partners, and citizens are working together in Nelson County to achieve a vision of comprehensive, affordable, accessible, and known health care for all citizens in Nelson County. The mission also includes continual improvements in community health status as the vision is achieved. Exceptional cooperation among partners and enthusiastic participation by citizens are the keys to success in the Nelson County CCN. They are what make Nelson County a "community of solutions."

Contact: Peggy Swan
Blue Ridge Medical Center
Route 1, Box 340
Arrington, VA 22922
Phone: (804) 263-4000
Fax: (804) 263-4160

Epilogue

This book, *Health Network Innovations,* introduces 20 examples of progress. People in cities, suburbs, small towns, and large rural regions are building the right vehicles for getting to the future of health care. None of the 20 examples looks just like another. Health care is local. Leadership, improvement processes, decision making, reform—these, too, must be local. At first glance, one might wonder what can be learned here, if real health care reform seems idiosyncratic to each community.

I have served as CEO and chairman of a firm that has received praise as a quality service provider and a solid financial performer. During my service, I have learned a few things from others about innovation and success. To me, the partnerships described in this book resonate with those lessons.

Three themes run throughout this book. These themes tie 20 diverse cases together and teach the core knowledge needed for innovation: purpose, leadership, and people. One sentence can summarize: Clarity and constancy of purpose, motivated by servant leadership, can guide ordinary people like you and me to extraordinary achievements.

PURPOSE

What is the purpose, or mission, of your work with respect to health? Are you a health care worker? An elected official charged with running local government? A citizen, volunteering your effort to help other people? Are you the executive of a business outside health care who wants to make sure your firm gets top value from its health care expenses? A public health officer, ensuring appropriate and quality services? Perhaps your concern about the health care system is based on your experience as a patient or family of a patient.

When put this way—what is your purpose in health care—there may be as many answers as there are people. But if there are so many possible answers then where are the guiding principles? How can health care be improved if there is no larger purpose that we can move toward together? The answer is simple—it can't and won't be improved as long as each individual sees the system only in terms of personal interests.

The American system of health care is not just about *my* or *your* purpose as individuals. It is about a common purpose—*our* purpose. The mission of the health care system reaches beyond a particular task, or a specific individual's position, role, or title. It should serve a higher calling—one that dignifies us by showing us to care for the needs of others.

The community care network (CCN) vision teaches a set of goals that clarify the larger purpose of the system of health care. Forged in reality and in hope, the CCN vision both works in the marketplace and dignifies the work of the people who make it happen. It makes good common sense and good business sense to embrace these goals.

Why does the system of health and human services exist? To reduce suffering and to enhance the quality of life. People live and work in communities, and the system should be oriented toward a community health focus. Guided by the CCN goal of a community health focus, the 20 local systems highlighted in this book are guided by an emphasis on creating health, rather than only treating disease. As examples, they are improving the management of chronic illness, increasing the effectiveness of health education and health outreach, and developing community-wide collaborations around immunizations and other preventive measures.

How does a local system of health and human services do the right thing, and not just talk about it or continue business as usual? It is not that the bosses are happier or that more money is made. The final test for any organization or partnership must be the customer—the person being served. If customers are better served, if they receive and perceive better value—that is, better health outcomes relative to the overall costs—the partnership is doing the right thing. A successful firm or partnership has a covenant with its customers, an accountability that puts the customers' interests first.

Who are the customers of the health and human services system? It must be more than patients. It also includes those who pay or contract for health services on behalf of patients.

The total of all the people who are or someday could be patients, plus all the people who do or someday will pay for health services, equals the customer base for health care. It is the total of all the people who live in a community. To be direct, a local health and human service system serves, first, its community. It is, or should be, accountable to its community—all the people and organizations living and operating within a geographic area whose boundaries make sense to—engender a sense of belonging among—the people living there.

We learn some special things about what "community" means in this book. Communities, the cases show us, come in many shapes and sizes. In urban and suburban areas, communities are often, but not always, a part of political boundaries. A community may be a neighborhood or a subset of towns in a metropolitan area. The sheer size of some cities makes it impossible to act as though they are one community. Just ask the people who live in the Bronx or on Chicago's near west side how they would define their community. Meanwhile, historic trade and transportation patterns and the level of available resources are important parts of why people in rural areas tend to think of larger geographic areas as their community.

The system of health and human services is accountable to the community as understood by the people living there. There is no magical definition of community that produces areas of the same size or shape, or defined by the same geopolitical boundaries, for all communities. But it must not exclude certain people living in the area. A key to success for firms and partnerships alike is to harness the power of diversity—to recognize prejudice when it occurs and to deal courageously with it.

In addition to the goals of a community health focus and community accountability, the CCN vision guides health system improvement toward the goal of a more seamless, coordinated continuum of services, as well as the goal of managing within fixed resources. Working toward these goals emphasizes the relationship between the individual and the institution, the family and the firm, the self and the system.

People's usual experience, whether as individuals or business managers, with the delivery system is fragmented, sometimes disconcerting and confusing. This is one of those issues that raises two related questions. First, how can each person's experience with the services be made more seamless so she or he knows how to use the system correctly? Second, how can the services become better managed so duplication and waste are reduced?

The cases in this book are responding to both of these questions through innovative local action. A few examples will illustrate. Building a Healthier Ocean County has developed a sophisticated network of interorganizational communication, as well as coordinated capacity for delivering information about the system and consumer health issues to the people of Ocean County. A number of the cases are making better coordinated local systems through collaboration between health providers and the schools. Examples include the Columbia-Presbyterian Community Health System in New York City, the Portsmouth Mayor's Health Services Advisory Panel in Virginia, the Solano Coalition for Better Health in Solano and Napa Counties of California, the Northwest Georgia Healthcare Partnership, and the Hartford Action Plan on Infant Health. These and other evolving partnerships are discovering that schools can be natural and effective partners for increasing access to children and families who face access barriers to health care due to poverty, culture or language. Each in ways that make sense to local people, the partnerships in this book are striving to make people's experience with the health care system more user-friendly and accessible.

A well-coordinated system of care can also benefit the organizations that make it happen. The Central Area Health Care Center of Seattle seeks better cost-effectiveness of the overall system through one-stop "family support centers" and improved disease management for people who are vulnerable to health risks and access barriers. These steps can reduce unnecessary emergency room visits, as well as hospital admissions, and enable health risk avoidance. Improved chronic disease management is a feature of a number of the cases, including the Columbia-Presbyterian Community Health System, Somerbridge Community Health Partnership, and the Metropolitan Chicago Community Care Alliance. Many of the 20 partnerships include advanced community health outreach or low-cost case management systems. Reducing preventable admissions, discovering cost savings through reduction of duplicative functions, and increasing the health awareness of people who are not yet patients, can save money. Especially as partnerships learn to provide evidence of cost savings, the member organizations become attractive partners for payers of all stripes, in addition to better partners with each other.

It is important to acknowledge that the CCN vision is about business realities in health and human services delivery. No firm, no partnership, no community health improvement project makes sense if it can't deliver value in excess of its costs. In an era of increasing pressures on the bottom line of the health care delivery system, the CCN vision calls attention to the need to manage within fixed resources. This goal most directly refers to learning how to survive and thrive in an environment defined by capitated or fixed global budgets.

Forging stronger, more sustainable partnerships with payers can be an important element of managing within fixed resources. Many of the partnerships have strong relationships with public sources of financing. The Somerbridge Community Health

Partnership, under the Massachusetts Free Care Pool, can become a national model for managed care for the uninsured. Though much of this progress occurred too recently to be included in this book, you might find it interesting to revisit that chapter, searching for the seeds of their innovative program, and then, to contact the partnership directly to get an update. The Portsmouth Mayor's Health Services Advisory Panel focuses on care to the medically indigent as well. Medicaid and Medicare are important sources of sustainability and opportunities for innovation for many of the cases, with much experimentation in care management and managed care.

Commercial health insurers are key partners in the Solano Coalition for Better Health. The North Iowa Mercy Health Network is creating a capitated insurance product. The Rural Health Outreach Program in central Virginia is working toward prepaid primary care contracts with area health plans, and the Franklin Community Partnership in Maine is mixing social marketing for community health education with the development of increased capacity for health plan participation. The Northwest Georgia Healthcare Partnership has unusually strong participation by self-insured employers and the Community Health Plan of the Siskiyous seeks to show employers, directly, how they can reduce health insurance costs.

The four goals of the CCN vision give common purpose to people who are working together, from their various personal and organizational perspectives, in evolving partnerships across the nation. The cases in this book, along with their many differences, show this commonality of purpose. Reforming health and human services locally so that they work better for people and communities may sound trite to some, but the challenges are huge. Clear, common purposes are requisite. Leaders in communities all across the nation are accepting the challenges.

LEADERSHIP

Focus and clarity of purpose come from leadership. For many, focus is what leaders compel their counterparts or subordinates to develop. In my view, believing that leadership is exerted from above reflects a poor understanding of how leadership works.

Two principles of leadership that are often overlooked are legitimacy and subsidiarity. *Legitimacy* comes from earning the right to have power. For power to be legitimate, those who are subject to it must have the right to participate in setting the standard or framework within which the power is to be exercised. In other words, there must be effective checks and balances on power, even within a single organization.

Legitimacy is even more important in interorganizational partnerships such as the partnerships described in this book. The people making up each partner organization have a personal, historical, and financial stake in their own organization: They understand it better than they do the other partner organizations; they have connections with it; it pays their salary. Yet early efforts to move toward the CCN vision point clearly toward opportunities, and often the need, for the reallocation of resources. Sooner or later, true reform of the local or regional health and human service delivery system will implicate the pathways followed by the funds in the system. There must be effective checks and balances on the power of partnering organizations for these reallocations to remain focused on customer and community.

Often, public commitment to the common purposes is sufficient, at least at first. But it is notable in the cases found in this book that more formal mechanisms for balancing power, such as memoranda of understanding, bylaws or new governing bodies, often emerge early in partnership development. Leaders earn legitimacy through their commitment to others and through their service to the common purposes of the group.

Subsidiarity means the delegation of decision-making authority as close as possible to the point where the customer is served. It is essential for a customer focus—community accountability—and it is a chief source of legitimacy for leadership. It is a means by which people performing roles of all kinds in the partnership can see how their work is dignified by its meaningful connection to the larger purpose.

Leadership is not invested only, or even chiefly, in the powerful. Leadership is not a function of title or salary. Leadership is exercised through role modeling, risk taking, service to others, listening, and the promotion of others. Leaders exist for and strive for the benefit of their organizations, and for the benefit of their partnerships and their communities, not vice versa. The people behind the stories told in this book give me great faith that leadership is in ample supply across America.

PEOPLE

Tools and technologies are a chief feature of our environment. In health care delivery, tools and technologies become better on a daily basis. The cases in this book include tools that helped the CCN partnerships to meet special challenges in their innovative works. It has been my experience in the business of health care that getting and using the right tools is crucial to success. A tool's effectiveness depends less on its design and more on how people use it.

People are the key to progress. They must be given a chance to share a clear purpose that is tied to something bigger than their own self-interests, or yours. They must be given the opportunity to commit themselves to that larger purpose, to serve others in and through that larger purpose, and to take risks for that larger purpose. They must, in other words, be permitted to become the leaders that it is in their potential to become. Each of the evolving CCNs that you read about in this book unlocks the potential of ordinary people to make extraordinary achievements.

I advise you to build around ordinary people. They possess talents and skills that are less tapped than those of superstars. There are many more regular people to call to your cause. There is more opportunity for developing commitment and loyalty to the common purposes of the partnership.

Of course, it helps to have superstars, too. They bring special, hard-to-find talents. My point is neither to overlook the special importance of superstars nor to avoid recognizing their performance in special ways. My point is that people make better leaders and produce outstanding performance when they can feel committed to a purpose larger than themselves—a purpose that gives their work dignity.

The evolving CCNs highlighted in *Health Network Innovations* really illustrate the importance of people. With a strong focus on customers—communities—and an imperative to link the purposes of different organizations from various sectors of community life, people committed to the common purposes of the CCN vision can reshape health care delivery, community by community.

The stories in this book are rich in the history and development of the partnerships. What kinds of committees or boards first launched activities that led to the CCN work? What sorts of people gave of themselves to those initiating collaboration? How did they determine what kinds of decision-making methods to use? When did they discover they needed new, different or additional partners? How have the partnerships' decision-making structures evolved? What will they become next?

Perhaps most important of all, how is their leadership toward the common purposes of the CCN vision connected to their lives? Their families? Their values? How does your life gain dignity from the joys of labor toward a larger purpose that you can work toward in service to others? If you are already engaged in a local community change effort, you know that it is a challenging but rewarding endeavor. If you are contemplating an initiative in the direction of community care, find the other people in your community with whom you can learn to accept those challenges and reap those rewards.

C. William Pollard
Chairman of the Board, Hospital Research and Educational Trust
Chairman of The ServiceMaster Company

Index

(continued)